40⁰⁰

K

MUSIC IN WESTERN CIVILIZATION

Greek Vase with Cithara Player (Metropolitan Museum of Art)

MUSIC
IN WESTERN
CIVILIZATION

by Paul Henry Lang

W · W · NORTON & COMPANY

New York · London

W. W. Norton & Company, Inc., 500 Fifth Avenue, New York, N.Y. 10110

ISBN 0 393 09428 6

PRINTED IN THE UNITED STATES OF AMERICA
FOR THE PUBLISHERS BY THE VAIL-BALLOU PRESS
0

TO ANNE

Who Watched, Guided, Waited, and Understood

CONTENTS

꧁ ꧂

The *Cantus Romanus* in the Carolingian Empire
The Celtic Influence
The Offshoots of Gregorian Music
The Decline of Gregorian Art
Gregorian Chant in the Universal Sacred Art of the Romanesque Period
Secular Music in the Carolingian Period
Theoretical, Artistic, and Philosophical Conceptions of Music

LIST OF ILLUSTRATIONS AND MAPS

——》》 《《——

xv

MAPS

ACKNOWLEDGMENTS

GRATEFUL acknowledgment is hereby made to my colleagues in the Department of Music, Columbia University, for their friendly interest in this work and for the patience they exercised toward its author. I am particularly indebted to Drs. Eric Hertzmann and Myron Schaeffer and to Mr. Richard S. Angell, Music Librarian of the University, who were always ready and willing to help; to M. D. Herter Norton and Professor Moses Hadas for their excellent translations in verse; to Professors Austin P. Evans, William B. Dinsmoor, Meyer Schapiro, and Everard Upjohn for kind advice; to Miss Gertrude Norman and Dr. Walter Rubsamen for various favors; to the *Musical Quarterly* (G. Schirmer, Inc.) and the *Columbia Quarterly* (Columbia University Press) for permission to quote from my articles published in those journals; to the Metropolitan Museum of Art, New York City, and Durand-Ruel, New York City, for permitting the use and reproduction of material from their collections; to Mrs. Howard Cunningham, Miss Barbara Lewis, and Miss Justine Pecheux for helping with the preparation of the manuscript; and to the entire staff of W. W. Norton and Company for their imperturbable good will and ceaseless co-operation.

P. H. L.

*Singing Angels from the Ghent Altar,
Hubert (1366–1426) and Jan van Eyck
(1380–1440)*

INTRODUCTION

—》》 《《—

EVERY civilization is a synthesis of man's conquest of life. Art is the
ultimate symbol of this conquest, the utmost unity man can achieve.
Yet the spirit of an epoch is reflected not in the arts alone, but in
every field of human endeavor, from theology to engineering. Nor
must we take it for granted that there is a uniform spirit of the age which
is invariably expressed in every phase of art, and which transmits to us
the same content and meaning in each. Rather, we find what we are seeking in the sum of the meanings of the various arts, which taken thus in
conjunction form the essence of the artistic spirit of the age.

Artistic conception and forms of expression depend on time, place, and
the temperament of the artist. It is the historian's duty to master these
elements which separate us from a work of art. In the past, writers on
music believed it possible to explain a musician's contribution in terms of
the forms he perfected, maintaining with some art critics that in artistic
value "there is no difference between a well painted vegetable and a well
painted Madonna." When the pendulum swung in the other direction everything was considered from the biographical-psychological angle, and anecdotes and "interpretations" served as the medium of evaluation to the
exclusion of aesthetic criteria. But for a just appraisal, the two methods
must be held in constant balance.

Every great artist is part of his times, but he also helps to create them.
We speak of the "times," but time in itself is empty and meaningless unless
made conceivable by phenomena. Time is expressed through life, and life
is conflict, motion within the times. Thus time can never evoke one style
only; an individual may dominate his generation, but if we attach ourselves to the one outstanding personality we may miss the significance of
the whole era. By examining the individuals and following their development without regard for a larger aim we jeopardize a true understanding
of the development of an art. Wagner was almost twenty years old when
Goethe died; J. S. Bach was working on the last will and testament of
polyphony when Pergolesi's comic opera opened new vistas for music;
Beethoven soared to the pinnacle of classic symphonic architecture when

xix

Weber was inaugurating the romanticism of the German forest and the eerie atmosphere of nocturnal fairy tale. Beethoven, Schubert, and Weber lived together in the first quarter of the nineteenth century. We conveniently group Beethoven with Haydn and Mozart and call this trio of vastly different artistic personalities the "Viennese school." With Beethoven thus disposed of, we can then consider the two remaining "romanticists," one of whom died one year before Beethoven, the other one year after.

Every period of time has three elements: the dying past, the flourishing present, and the promising future. If we single out and emphasize one of the three, we miss our aim. Although we may point out the line of development in technical terms, we shall not be able to gain a complete picture, for we are neglecting the idea. It is a great mistake, indeed, to consider the second half of the eighteenth century—to take another example—as reflected only in the moral decadence of the rococo. The intellectual peaks of this great period were the creation of aesthetics and natural sciences as independent branches of learning, and the political philosophy of the Enlightenment; there were, furthermore, men like Klopstock, Lessing, and Herder, the French Encyclopedists, Burke, Kant, and Goethe, and, what interests us most of all, the galaxy of great musicians, the Bach sons and Hasse, Grétry and Monsigny, Jommelli and Piccini, Gluck, Haydn, and Mozart, to mention a handful from among the host of composers. Again, we cannot lift some of these composers from their environment and discuss their sonata forms or their orchestration, for no amount of technical analysis will explain the operatic conceptions and the symphonic thought of the classic school unless the whole broad expanse of the Enlightenment and the *Sturm und Drang* is traversed. Then we may find the starting point of classicism, and discover how and why the miniature and mosaiclike sensitive fabric of the *style galant* turned into the architectural logic and dramaturgy of classicism.

If we are so ill prepared to grasp the music of the eighteenth and nineteenth centuries, what will we face when approaching more remote periods? Those who cherish and admire the canvases of old masters, who look with awe at the soaring stone mazes of medieval cathedrals, who read with devotion the plays of Aristophanes and Shakespeare, experiencing the thrill of emotion which only great art can impart, are yet content to call these very same centuries a preparatory era for the coming art of music. For it is a deeply ingrained fallacy that music was slow in coming of age, that it trailed the other arts by centuries. Music of the centuries prior to the eighteenth, called "old" or "pre-Bach" music, is still shrouded in mystery. It was not until the nineteenth century that this music was "rediscovered," because in reality the music of the Middle Ages, the Renaissance, and the baroque era had ceased to be a living art; its traditions had vanished and all that was known were specimens. This is perhaps best illustrated by the fact that Mendelssohn's performance of Bach's *St. Matthew Passion* in 1829 had the effect of a revelation and started a veritable Bach renaissance. The old master died only seventy-nine years before the memorable Berlin revival; how, then, can we expect music from the times of Bede, of Dante, or of Michelangelo to be alive and enjoyed? Our immediate musical heritage is that of nineteenth-century romanticism. Romanticism discovered old music because the antiquarian tendency was one of its basic traits. But while the poetry and painting of the Middle Ages and of the Renaissance were soon giving out light of their own, besides reflecting the glow of the romantic enthusiasm that brought them to life, the nineteenth century stood impressed but strangely remote before its musical discovery.

The music of primitive tribes or of faraway Oriental nations strikes us by the unfamiliar nature of its melodies and rhythms. We acknowledge this strangeness by calling the music "exotic," and the term seems to qualify and justify such music. The majority of people—indeed, even trained musicians —gain a similar impression from medieval music; but since the term "exotic" cannot properly be applied to an art which grew with the great cathedrals, it is called primitive and undeveloped. Our ears are not so well educated as our eyes, and our musical knowledge and taste are so limited that we are at a loss when we try to reconcile music with the other arts of the centuries "before Bach." Opposed to this hazy and distant conception of ours stands the very real enjoyment of music expressed in the writings of men of letters contemporary with this "primitive" music, and the innumerable musical scenes that seem to have been the favorite subjects of painters and sculptors. If we read the inspired words addressed to music by Dante, Shakespeare, Milton, or Molière, we will realize that we have failed to acclimatize ourselves with this great music of the past, that we have carelessly deprived ourselves of a tremendous source of art and enjoyment.

At this point modern musicology comes to the rescue, unearthing, deciphering, and explaining the music of the past centuries and making it available in modern editions to the public of today. The research work of the past two or three generations, carried out by a legion of scholars, is a monument of human ingenuity and erudition. Our duty is to utilize the fruits of all this labor, performed with almost monastic devotion, and derive spiritual nourishment from them.

In writing this history of music, I have addressed myself to those lovers of music who combine enjoyment of their art with a curiosity as to all that goes to form a part of their intellectual estate. The reader must not expect a technical or biographical essay, for this is a chronicle of the participation of music in the making of Western civilization. To write about art, and especially about music, is a most difficult task, since the scholar's and the artist's views must be balanced. I have endeavored to prevent the many-sided shimmering wealth of art from becoming mere abstraction by searching always for the overtones that accompany facts and accomplishments, trying to see behind every detail the whole of the creative soul struggling for articulation and expression. The living man who attempts to penetrate into the mind of a strange human being, remote from him in time and space, finds in himself the deciding lines along which he reconstructs the picture of the past. This is why real historical understanding always exerts a fertile influence on the present. However far the object of our research is removed from us, we must somehow assimilate it within us, and when the hidden identity of this strange mind generates sparks in our mind, then, and only then, will the mind of the past become active again, because it carries with it something of our own.

Humboldt, the great representative of new humanism, once said that "the study of classical archaeology, philology, and history should lead to the understanding of the ancient man and his culture." This is the formula for all historical studies, for all humanism. The difference between our modern humanism and the older ones is only in the vastness of our researches, and the ability of the modern man to train his searchlight onto depths which once seemed bottomless. We are seeking the human being in the plenitude of his always new and yet typically related creations, because we find that every tone from the past raises an echo in us today.

Chapter 1

ANCIENT GREECE

※》》 《《

Music in the Cult of the Beautiful

THE close affinity of the "beautiful" and the "good" was most keenly felt and understood of all civilized nations by ancient Greece.[1] The concept of the union of beauty and virtue found literary expression in the term kalokagathia, *kalos* meaning "beautiful," *agathos,* "good." The mere order of these two ideas indicates that the emphasis is on the beautiful, and, indeed, moral precepts often followed and paid tribute to aesthetic principles. The eminent position of the arts, on the other hand, called for universal admiration and the fostering of their practice.

Of this exalted cult of the beautiful we can form a clear idea as far as it concerns literature and the fine arts. The admiration which the ancients professed for their Homer and Sophocles can readily be shared by the modern individual, who has many good translations at his disposal. The reverence expressed by the Hellenes for the sculpture of a Phidias or a Praxiteles has not diminished throughout the ages. Yet even those whose appreciation of the genius of Greece is boundless seldom stop to consider music, the art which occupies such a prominent place in our modern life. To most of us the Greeks represent a gifted nation of poets, philosophers, historians, sculptors, and architects; about their musicians we do not even speculate.

Curiously enough, the Greeks themselves paid much less attention to their plastic genius than to their musical achievements. Classical literature is almost barren of reference to sculpture and architecture, while music is mentioned frequently. There were no muses of the plastic arts, and looking around in the gallery of gods, if we wish to provide Apollo Musagetes with a companion of similar standing in the fine arts, we must be satisfied with the lame Hephaestus, the god of fire and of metalwork and other arts in which fire was used, who was in reality but the armorer of the Olympians and a constant target for their jokes. The Greek state, with its reverence and high appreciation for music, dealt with all questions pertaining to it with the utmost self-assurance, and the regulation of musical ideas and principles was considered an affair of the state. The role of music in the artistic aspects of life was so great that in general an educated and distinguished man was called a musical man (ἀνὴρ μουσικός), whereas an inferior and uncouth person was simply "unmusical" or a man without music (ἀνὴρ ἄμουσος). The pipe virtuoso, Midas of Agrigentum, was praised by Pindar as a conquering hero, and the trumpet player, Herodorus of Megara, won the Olympic prize ten times. Plato, who ordinarily professed little love for the arts,[2] gives a considerable treatment of music in his *Republic*.

Being a responsive southern people, the Greeks answered to the sensuous qualities of music. They had two souls in their breasts, one striving for clarity, temperance, and moderation (σωφροσύνη), the other driving them toward the fantastic and orgiastic, the cult of Dionysus. For this very reason they preached the idea of σωφροσύνη with great fervor: they were aware of their susceptibility to the other extreme. The opposition between Apollonian and Dionysiac is reflected in the domain of music. This same contradiction between calm and serene, stormy and sensuous music, which rocks and agitates the listener, reappeared when the war cry was sounded around Richard Wagner. Nietzsche himself was torn between the two extremes, and his experiences were responsible for *The Birth of Tragedy from the Spirit of Music,* in which Apollonian and Dionysiac music are opposed to each other in sharp contrast.

Music in Mythology and the Homeric Period

IN its two great periods, Greek genius created two independent, individually complete bodies of music. These it cultivated for centuries and imparted to posterity with characteristic expansive and propagative power. These two great periods are usually designated by the terms "ancient Greek music," which we shall call simply Greek music, and "medieval" or "Byzantine music." The unique achievement of Greek genius in the history of music can be realized only if we consider the remarkably enduring influence of both periods.

In the field of arts and letters we do not distinguish between a Christian and a pagan Greece, since we know that the former absorbed the latter's cultural wealth. Such a conception is not unjustified, for centuries-old prac- tices of everyday life do not immediately change with the advent of a new philosophy of life. Ancient Greek Christendom used the same music which was practiced by their earlier pagan brethren. A papyrus discovered in Oxyrhynchus in 1922 affords an excellent illustration of this point. It con- tains a Christian hymn of the third century, but its musical notation, meter, and melody follow strictly classical pre-Christian precepts. We shall see that Byzantine music exhibits characteristics which compel us to consider it an independent art, yet both phases of Greek music have principles in common which unite them when considered from the remote perspective of the twentieth century. Both are based on poetry; they cannot be separated from the prosody of the words. Therefore the history of Greek musical forms is for the most part identical with the history of Greek literature, because the two were bound together in an indissoluble unity, which persisted not only throughout classical antiquity but far into the Middle Ages. The sovereignty of melody in both Greek and Byzantine music and the absence of polyphony are thus not merely accidental phenomena. Lastly, we must not forget that throughout their history the two domains of Greek music are both, in the last analysis, based on the civilization of the Orient.

The first great period of Greek music embraced prehistoric and historic antiquity and lasted until the fourth century A. D. The twelve centuries which comprise this period present almost insurmountable difficulties to the historian. It was not until the eighteenth century of our era that historians of music advanced beyond it; so engrossed were the scholars with the baffling maze of facts and hypotheses that they could not reach even the Middle Ages. All attempts at writing musical history ended up as long and weighty dissertations on the music of the ancients. Yet these historians had very little actual *music* at their disposal. Even in our day, diligent archaeological research has given us only about a dozen pieces of music in Greek notation, most of them fragmentary and all of a comparatively late date. Our literary, plastic, and graphic monuments, however, are numerous and permit an approximate restoration and estimate of Greek musical life.

Like the other Greek arts, music had a solid theoretical foundation. Because of its importance in Greek intellectual life, philosophers assigned it a prominent place in the domain of ethics. The theory of music as we know it today was definitely formulated in the fourth century B. C., in the great century which created Greek science. In the works of Aristoxenus of Tarentum we have a theoretical system of remarkable unity and logic which exerted its influence far into the modern Western world. If we envisage the richness and wide distribution of monuments of the plastic arts, of literature, and of philosophy, we can see the embarrassment of the scholar who must try to extract from the retrospective parts of the work of such a "modern" writer as Aristoxenus a picture of the many centuries which passed before the culmination of Greek civilization in the fifth and fourth centuries. Greek musical theory never surpassed the constructive logic of Aristoxenus; those who came after him, even centuries later, always dealt with him as if he were a contemporary. Nor does the practice of music—composition, playing, singing, and teaching—seem to have gone beyond its great theoretician; it did not change materially after his time. The Hellenistic period with its "modern" music furnishes us the only historically complete segment of Greek music, but it demands an approach free from considerations based on the biological principles of evolution as historical criteria. Greek music neither developed nor declined after the Hellenistic period; it only followed established artistic trends which are also discernible in sculpture and literature.

In our modern Western civilization we are accustomed to speaking of musical art in a dual sense; we deal with popular or folk music and with "art" music. There is not enough material at our disposal to enable us to make this distinction in Greek music. Our sources mention various songs that were sung at rural festivals or which facilitated rhythmical work of all sorts, like threshing or rowing; there are even some texts which indicate by their rhythmic quality that they were originally sung, though the melodies are unknown. We have no records, either, concerning the utilization of folkloristic elements in art music, a procedure which has refreshed and regenerated our music from the time of the troubadours to Stravinsky. There is no doubt that such music existed, just as a popular poetry existed before the highly developed hexameter of Homer; but this whole phase of the antique world resembles a gigantic field of ruins, beautiful even in its decay, but of necessity incomplete. For this reason we must limit our study to art music.[3]

The Greeks were constantly engaged in the intensification and improvement of their art. Music was no exception to this rule. They were keenly interested in its technical and theoretical possibilities and accorded recognition to the inventors and perpetuators in this domain. Their historians and philosophers give an account of the origins of Greek music according to their own conceptions. These conceptions are often similar to our own, with the difference that with our strong sense for the historical we are apt to center our attention around facts, whereas they are interested in persons and personalities. The long list of mythical musicians mentioned in their writings carries the beginning of Greek music back into mythological times. Thus the first historians with whom we must deal were gods. While the sober modern historian will simply state that the whole nature of ancient Greek music is based on the lyre, and will consider this the indigenous national instrument, the Greek chroniclers present the same thing in one of the most engaging stories in the history of literature. The infant Hermes, having killed a turtle, fastened on its shell gut strings from the entrails of oxen stolen from his brother Apollo; then to appease his brother's anger the crafty little fellow permitted him the use of his invention—which last part of the story the modern historian interprets as evidence that lyre playing was an integral part of the Apollo cult.

Music is in all languages acknowledged, by its very name, to be a muse-inspired, muse-descended art. The Greek muses, later the guardians of all branches of art, were at first only three in number. Two of them embodied ideas characteristic of every art, study and memory; the third bore the name Song (ἀοιδή). Their first dwelling place was the Pierian plains at the foot of

Mount Olympus, whence they moved to Mount Helicon. The seat of the Apollo cult was the island of Delos and subsequently Delphi, in the shadow of Mount Parnassus. The myths suggest the contours of the primeval musical life of the Greek mainland, untouched by alien influences. They relate the marvelous deeds of heroes and of men endowed with divine musical gifts. Amphion and Orpheus conquer life and death by the power of their art; Musaeus, the son of Orpheus, carries his greatness in his very name, as does Eumolpos, "the one who sings well." These names are connected with the most ancient northern tribes which hail from Thrace, Thessaly, and down to Boeotia, and are closely connected with lyre music. The central parts of the Greek mainland are also represented in this mythical art world by Philammon, Thamyris, and Linus.

The Greek tribes moving south about a thousand years before the beginning of our era carried with them their ancient art, which can be traced in the migration of the various names. The Dorian migration was a movement from the north to as far south as Crete, where they displaced the two-thousand-year-old Aegean civilization that had flourished there. The Aeolians, also from the north, settled in the eastern islands of the Aegean. An equally important movement, the so-called Ionian migration, from west to east, carried Greek tribes to the central eastern mainland and to Asia Minor. This migration exerted immense influence on Greek art, especially on poetry, and, in connection with it, music, because this eastern group of Greeks was, in the eyes of history, the founder of poetry and music. The western Greeks brought with them their music and their national instruments but came under the decisive influence of Oriental elements. The myth tells this story poetically, relating how Orpheus dropped his lyre, which drifted in the sea until it reached the island of Lesbos. From the maze of beautiful legends the modern historian extracts the important fact that Asia Minor produced the other national instrument, the reed pipe or aulos (αὐλός). Hyagnis and Marsyas were supposed to be the inventors, masters, and propagators of the art connected with the new instrument; they came from Phrygia in Asia Minor. We further learn from the myths that there was a conflict between the cult of the two instruments, and it appears that the cause of the lyre did not stand well in the East. According to the myths, there was a certain repatriation or exchange between the mainland and the coast of Asia Minor. The Lycian Olen, championing lyre music, and the Phrygian Olympos, partisan of the aulos, were the two masters whose presence on the peninsula is mentioned. This information indicates that a movement leading to the integration of musical practice of East and West started in most ancient times. It is not impossible that Olen and Olympos represent historical figures, but we are still far from having tangible historical evidence that this is the case.

Music is present in the picture of the chivalric world of the nobility of Asia Minor, the world of the Homeric epics. The earliest musicians we encounter are the blind singers whose affliction is accounted for by a host of stories. While Demodocus, Homer's blind singer who plucks the strings to sing of the love of Ares for Aphrodite,[4] does not seem to have incurred the ire of the gods, old Thamyris[5] owed his blindness to boasting which offended the muses. The blind singer Tiresias paid the same penalty for revealing to men things which they should not have known.[6] There were many other singers who, possessed of a mood of insolence and haughtiness, challenged the gods and met with a miserable end. The Phrygian Marsyas, finding Athena's flute, was so inspired by the goddess's instrument that he challenged the lyre-playing god Apollo to a contest. Apollo won and Marsyas was flayed for his presumption. Misenus challenged the gods of the seas to a competition on the trumpet, but lost and was drowned by Triton. Among these hotheaded artists there was one laudable exception, Phemius,[7] who, upon leaving the court of Odysseus, went to Smyrna, where he taught music to young people and thus became the first propagator of musical culture.

Poetry, Song, and Instrumental Music

THE literary monuments of this period furnish us with the first references to actual musical practices in the ninth to seventh centuries, but we must proceed warily in appraising these evidences. The epics speak only of lyre music in connection with the Greeks, the aulos being mentioned only in the hands of the Trojans and their Asiatic allies. This is in reality a sort of stylized national conservatism, if not a deliberate reaction against contemporary aulos music. We read that the heroes themselves sang songs, that at weddings and funeral processions they sang to the accompaniment of the lyre. But we read also that for festivities and feasts they engaged professional recitalists (ἀοιδός), who recited or sang poetry to the accompaniment of the lyre. Unfortunately, the fact that Homer does not say anything about either music or accompaniment makes it impossible to reach conclusions about the performance of Homeric poetry. This constitutes the first great problem of musical archaeology. We know that the instrument employed in the accompaniment of epic and lyric poetry was the lyre, whereas the elegy and dramatic chorus used the aulos. Other genres of literature, such as the nome and the dithyramb, used the two instruments interchangeably; but we know nothing whatever about the melodies which were composed to accompany the hexameters.

Greek musical practice centers around the lyre in its two main forms, the lyre proper (λύρα), and its larger variety, the cithara (κιθάρα). The lyre[8] consisted of a hollow body, or sound chest, from which protruded two arms curved both outward and forward. These arms were connected near the top by a crossbar or yoke. Another crossbar, on the sound chest, formed a bridge to convey the vibrations of the strings to it. The cithara was similarly constructed, but was larger and more sonorous. As a rule the smaller lyre served the amateurs and was used for more intimate occasions, while the cithara was reserved for artists and virtuosi. The chief wind instrument was the aulos. This instrument used to be erroneously defined as a flute, and consequently was associated with soft and mellow sounds. In reality it was a reed instrument, not unlike an oboe or more precisely a pair of oboes, and emitted a shrill, penetrating sound. The offices of the two species of instruments were strictly separated. The lyre was the instrument of the Apollonian cult, while the aulos belonged to the followers of Dionysus.[9]

A third art, the dance, was so closely linked with music and poetry that no picture of Greek music would be complete without a consideration of its role. Originally probably a form of witchcraft, demon enchantment, and sex symbolism, the dance rose from the domain of magic to the position of an art of rhythmical expression, in a way that parallels the development of incantation into song. The dance has retained, however, something of its ritual character up to our times.[10] Thus it should not surprise us to find this art mainly in the drama, the highest expression of the cult of Dionysus. The chorus, while singing its strophes, executed dances which were not mere rhythmical gestures but an elaborate mimetic expression of the ideas in the poem. There were a few marchlike dances such as the processional of the chorus, the parodos, and the final recessional, the exodos. That we know little about the choreography of Greek dances is only to be expected. Even in our own day we learn the elements of poetry and music in the schools from suitable textbooks, but the art of the dance still lacks a satisfactory graphical notation, and is transmitted by the dancing teacher, who has no theories, only practical ideas.

A consideration of the combination of the various arts makes it appear that the text to which the music was sung had the leading role. The instruments are always designated as participants. Thus *citharodia* meant singing with the accompaniment of the cithara, and *aulodia* meant singing with the accompaniment of the pipe.

However, as we have said before, the relationship between the music and the poetical composition is by no means elucidated as yet. We are unable to restore the performance of the Homeric epics. It is doubtful that music and song would follow the repetitions of the hexameter lines; this would be unbearably monotonous. Furthermore, we do not know whether this music was continuous or whether it alternated with recitation. It is significant, however, that the rhapsodists, who first recited epic poetry, seem later to have chanted it.

In the hierarchy of literary types the *nome* (νόμος) is the one species which seems to have occupied the same important position in music as was held by the *epos* in literature. The meaning of the word is "law," but as a musical type "nome" designated a composition, a song or an instrumental piece, strictly following the laws of classical aesthetics. The idea and the whole nature of the nome are difficult to comprehend. The best way to an understanding of it is through comparison with architecture. A Doric or Ionian temple is a sort of architectural nome. Every architect was bound and pledged to a basic scheme and to basic ornaments; he asserted his individuality by a different organization of these same elements. The nome was probably a melody originally, or perhaps a whole composition, but it later developed into types.[11] It was usually associated with the name of some one master, but it was further developed, with certain restrictions, by other musicians without losing its basic melodic profile or rhythmic skeleton. The difference in the Apollonian and Dionysiac tendency which we observed with reference to the instruments is fully reflected in the nome. While the musical ramifications of the epos are lost in the haze of the mythological past, with the nome we are on somewhat firmer ground, and its chief exponents—Olympos for the aulos nome and Terpander for the cithara nome—are frequently mentioned in literature.

The nomes showed all the requirements and factors which call for music. Their prosody was rich in rhythmical variety, which was enhanced by the absence of strophes. The nome persisted for centuries, preserved its independence, and exerted a strong influence on the music of all the other literary genres.

We must add to the first two figures of Greek musical history a third man of genius whose importance and influence was boundless: Archilochus (fl. c. 660 B.C.). The fast "tempo" of his trochee and iambus gave to ancient Greek music its great mobility. Archilochus instituted technical reforms of far-reaching effect. Before his advent each note of the music was closely allied with the words (Πρός-χορδος), while after him there were all sorts of short embellishments (κρούσις) improvised between songs (ὑπὸ τὴν ᾠδήν).[12] This carries our knowledge a little further and we may assume that the musical accompaniment of the nomes followed the text, while instrumental solo playing came between the strophes or sections. Archilochus had the accompaniment play occasionally "dissenting" notes, that is, notes that were not in unison with the melody. This has led to an erroneous conception concerning the nature of Greek music, which was not harmonic or contrapuntal, nor written for several voices or parts. The Greeks, in common with the whole of antiquity and the early Middle Ages, did not know the principle of many-voiced music or polyphony. The proper term for these dissenting tones of Archilochus would be *heterophony*.[13]

The first evidence of Greek musical genius, the union of song and poetry, was soon joined by two other manifestations. One, pure instrumental music, exerted considerable influence on the nome and melic poetry; the other, choric dance and choric singing (χόρος), by placing several persons in the role of the nome narrator, relieved the monotony of recitation.

The known historical facts seem to cast doubt on the importance of instrumental music in the first historical phase of Greek civilization. The piper first appeared in a competition about 606, and the first lyre contestant is said to have played in 586. These dates are relatively late, considering the wide dissemination and practice of vocal music in the preceding periods. There are, however, definite signs which indicate the existence and great influence of instrumental music upon the development of lyric poetry, especially that variety which is based on strophic construction. The masters of strophic poetry, active in the seventh century, based their simplest strophic constructions, the distichs and the short melic strophes, on the principles of pure instrumental music. Phenomena like the two pauses in the pentameter, and feet of varying value placed in one line of the melic strophe, can be explained only by the possibility inherent in instrumental music of filling out a certain rhythmical unit by lengthened or shortened notes and pauses. These ideas are borne out by the fact that the profuse theoretical literature of classical antiquity does not deal with the laws of lyric poetry.

There were numerous treatises called "Poetics." We have fragments of an Aristotelian book called Περι Ποιητικῆς, and we have the *Ars Poetica* of Horace; but we should be wrong in concluding that the ancients treated, in their works on poetics, the organic laws of meter. These works contain certain counsels and advice which the poet should follow, and instructions about the nature of the various types of poetry, epic, dramatic, and lyric. But a study of the writings of Aristoxenus, Aristides Quintilianus (*De Musica*), Dionysus of Halicarnassus (*De Compositione Verborum*), and Plutarch (*De Musica*) will convince us that in ancient times prosody and metrics did not belong to the domain of linguistics and poetry, but formed part of the musical sciences and were practiced by musician-poets. Those, however, who took it upon themselves to continue the classical traditions were neither musicians nor poets, but the philologists of antiquity known as the Alexandrian Grammarians. They were not concerned with musical principles, and their activity centered around "the measuring of syllables," an activity which was later renewed by the timorous disciples of Boileau.

The musical origin of Greek lyric poetry appears to be an established fact, but full recognition and appreciation of pure instrumental music was delayed until later. From this early period, dominated by lyric poetry, there remains only one famous "bravura" piece which for centuries has often been mentioned with admiration. It is the *Pythic nome* (586 B.C.) of the aulete Sakadas and it is considered to be the first important product of the aulos art, the oldest example of program music.

The Pythic nome, which was played on the aulos, had five parts. Pollux, grammarian of the second century A. D., whose account seems to be the most reliable, calls this "five-movement sonata" a "demonstration (δήλωμα) of Apollo's fight with the dragon." The individual "movements" have the following titles: 1. Preparation, 2. Challenge, 3. Iambic part (the fight), 4. Song of praise, 5. Victory dance. We can readily see that the aulete's problem was very much akin to those faced by a Richard Strauss; that is, he was supposed to render action and plot in music.

The modern listener is naturally puzzled when he is asked to believe that such simple means of expression as are at the disposal of a single aulete or citharist could evoke the same profound impression that is created by the many-colored and powerful modern symphony orchestra. We must not forget, however, that we are dealing with a period of history which did not know harmony or polyphony. The listeners of antiquity followed a nonpolyphonic musical melody with an intensity unknown to us, and their composers carried the expressive faculties of such melodies to a high point of artistic development. The Greeks were capable of enjoying the slight and delicate inflections of a melodic line; their ears were keen enough to appre-- hend subtleties of intonation and color which we, with our harmonically and polyphonically trained ears, cannot perceive. Therefore it seems perfectly justifiable to assume that ancient classical music strove to attain aims just as high and complex as ours but, naturally, through different means and by different ways.

We must assume that the "program" of this music was known to the audi- ence in all its details and that the task of the aulete was not so much to cause a certain impression as to fortify and illustrate the action. Had the aulete neglected the prescribed order of the nome the public probably would have expressed its disapproval. There is consequently a fundamental differ- ence between ancient and modern program music. The ancient soloist fol- lowed a program sanctioned by tradition. His audience, perfectly aware of what *should* happen, was anxious to see in what way and by what virtuoso tricks he would solve the given task. The modern musician expects us to follow him into his own imaginary world and divine communications which are of his most personal invention.

The importance of the two national instruments was emphasized by the strict hierarchy which they followed, the aulos always preceding the cithara. Considering the ancient national origin and standing of the cithara and its role in the nome poetry, we are justified in suspecting that it must have been some outside influence which displaced Apollo's instrument from its original popularity. This influence may in fact be attributed to the dithyramb, one of the poetic genres most important from the musical point of view. The dithyramb represents the highest individual development in the field of choric poetry; it was a great vehicle of the cult of Dionysus. Performed by a large circularly grouped chorus, it was composed of the repetitions of voluminous strophic constructions (strophe, antistrophe, epodos). The first great masters of the dithyramb, Arion and Lasus, were active in Athens, the latter being one of Plato's teachers. The importance of the dithyramb in the literary ramifications of ancient Greek music is comparable only to that of the nome. The great choric songs, such as those by Pindar, were based on the composition principles of the dithyramb. Greek dramatic theory attributes to the dithyramb the origin of the drama.

"The Birth of Tragedy from the Spirit of Music"

MUSIC played an important role in the drama, but we must admit that this role is not very clear. We know that the chorus had vocal functions; it prefaced scenes and accompanied them. In the tragedy its original number, twelve, was later increased to fifteen, while in the comedy its number rose to twenty-four. We also know that the individual actors broke into song and that the aulos played during the action, thereby lending to the play a melodramatic touch (in the ancient, not the modern, sense). The aulos was the only and exclusive instrument of the theater; it was never employed except singly, and it was never exchanged for the lyre.[14]

However short some of the choruses might be, they formed a considerable portion of the drama, and being sung, they took much more time in the performance than spoken dialogues. In view of all these facts, it is not too bold to say that the artistic impression imparted to the audience in the Greek tragedy was, to a considerable degree, a musical one. To a twentieth-century individual this is difficult to understand, because we have no form of art which corresponds to the ancient tragedy with music. The opera, with its occasional spoken dialogues, has nothing in common with it, and the Wagnerian music drama is even more remote. And yet Christian civilization produced in the Middle Ages a drama, the *mysterium,* which by its very nature was not unlike Greek tragedy. The mystery play grew out of a religious cult and out of music, that is, from the same sources as Greek drama.[15] A study of these medieval plays may bring us closer to the understanding of the artistic nature and effect of ancient tragedy; for we must admit that to us this tragedy, with its choric songs, spoken dialogues, solo songs, and aulos playing, does not seem to have aesthetic unity.

Many a person who enjoys reading Sophocles and Euripides hastens over the chorus because in his mind the choric passages destroy the continuity of the drama and lessen the tension. This neglect and disregard for the choric passages started very early. Dion Chrysostom reports it toward the end of classical antiquity, maintaining that the tragedies were often performed without the choral parts. Why then are they there? Aesthetic speculations will not help us in this case; only historical considerations can lead to a realization of the nature of the drama.

It is in the nature of the simplest and oldest form of drama that, at the height of intensity of feeling and excitement, it turns into music, because music is able to continue to express emotions when the deeply stirred soul of man can utter only inarticulate cries. Sophocles was a dramatist; his strength lies in the conduct of a plot, an action. But Aeschylus, a musician, a choral lyricist, creates works prompted by a mood of profound inner excitement, the mood of a composer, one which precedes articulate poetic ideas.[16] To communicate this mood successfully he must appeal to the emotional responsiveness of the public, and the means he uses to this end are of a lyrico-musical nature. In the days of Aeschylus, music and lyricism still formed an indivisible entity, and word and tone, poem and melody were created simultaneously.

The *Agamemnon* of Aeschylus is the most consummate example of tragedy because the two elements which brought forth tragedy, choral song and narrative speech, are here combined and reborn in perfect artistic unity. The Cassandra scene is the most poignant picture ever painted by a poet. We see the hideous murder before it happens; more than that, we experience it with the seer. Our souls are captivated by the suggestive power of this prophetic madness to such an extent that the terrible events perpetrated in the palace seem to us a nightmare, until Agamemnon's death cry calls us back to the reality of the play. Only a lyricist, a musician, could attain such effects. We still shudder when we listen to this scene and admire its irresistible power, even without the music which once was associated with it. But we must not forget that almost all these scenes were sung, not merely declaimed, and it is beyond our ability to realize at this date the psychological effects created by Aeschylean music.

Before *Agamemnon* the tragedy had been a lyrico-musical genre; afterwards it became a drama with music. It was created when the aged Aeschylus saw the advent of the new art of the young Sophocles. The old master could not forget the lifelong career of a poet-musician, but he tried to assimilate the new with the old. *Agamemnon* convinces us that tragedy was indeed born from the spirit of music.

The Sociological Aspects of Music

WITH the beginning of the organization and political development of the Greek states, music, which exerted such an influence on the mood and spirit of the Hellenes, could not be left to the discretion of performing artists; it had to follow the rules laid down by statesmanship. In this trend Sparta was the leader. The lawmaker Lycurgus ordered that among the other sorts of youthful and popular education there should be instituted regular and supervised education in music. He justified his orders by experiences gained in Crete, where the practice of music, recommended by Minos, caused a remarkable devotion to the gods and made the Cretans into law-abiding people. No Spartan, of whatever sex, age, or rank, was to be excluded from these exercises; and each individual was to be required to do his part to further the moral, social, and political well-being of the state. The songs to be sung must not offend the spirit of the commonwealth; on the contrary, they should extol the fatherland and should lead to a sense of order, lawfulness, dignity, and a capacity for quick decision and fiery inspiration. The melodies of these songs should preferably follow the Dorian key, which evokes manly poise, temperance, and simplicity.

In Athens the champion of music was Solon. He hoped to promote moral sturdiness and responsible citizenship, which he considered the basis for the well-being, power, and fame of the state, by musical instruction imparted to the youth. The practice of music was prohibited to slaves, as music was considered a distinctive mark of nobility and of the education reserved for free Athenians.

The most intensive aesthetic and ethical discussion of music is to be found in Plato, who was, next to Aristoxenus, the greatest writer on music in antiquity. Among his works which abound in musical references the most important are *Timaeus* and the *Laws,* as well as the *Republic, Gorgias,* and *Philebus.* In Plato's system, as in Greek philosophy in general, music occupies the leading position among the arts. The philosopher sees an analogy between the movements of the soul and the musical progressions (φοράι); therefore the aim of music cannot be mere amusement but a harmonic education and perfection of the soul and the quieting of passions (*Timaeus*). Consequently music is, to a certain degree, the most immediate expression of *eros,* a bridge between ideas and phenomena. The primary role of music is a pedagogical one, which, in the meaning of the antique world, implied the building up of character and morals; therefore its practice is not a "private matter," but eminently a "public" affair. Every melody, every rhythm, and every instrument has its own peculiar effect on the moral nature of man and of the state. Good music promotes the well-being of the *res publica* while bad music destroys it; therefore good and useful music is closely bound to and determined by the norms of moral conduct. This is emphasized by the use of the same word, *nomos,* for correct musical "harmony" and logic, and for the moral, social, and political laws of the state.

The correspondence which was believed to exist between sounds—tone combinations—and cosmic phenomena—seasons of the year and parts of the day, sun and moon cycles, growth and weather, man and woman, birth and death, healing, reincarnation, etc.—is brought into relationship with human temperament. This conversion of magic into music, which started in the Orient, reached its culmination in the Greek conception of the "doctrine of ethos," which brings order into the domain of music, segregates its components, and poses the important question: What influence has music on character? This conception explains the extraordinary interest manifested by the Greeks in their music; it explains the dominant role they assigned to it in their education and in their political system. It is doubtful whether the art of music will ever again occupy such a high position in the mental and spiritual life of a nation.

The doctrine of ethos eludes definition in English, but we shall understand it better if we note the emphasis which the Greeks placed on the effect and influence of music on the will. According to their writers the will can be decisively influenced by music in three ways. It can spur to action; it can lead to the strengthening of the whole being, just as it can undermine mental balance; and finally, it is capable of suspending entirely the normal will power, so as to render the doer unconscious of his acts.

The doctrine of ethos, which found its greatest exponent in Plato, reflects the spirit of the classic polis ideal—the city as a moral, social, and political commonwealth—in its strictest and most profound sense, and in it belief in the primeval magic and healing qualities of music is preserved. This mystic-religious quality of music remains undiminished in Plato and in the developed polis ideal of the Greeks, but its moral side takes the upper hand and the ritualistic side is relegated to the background. Such a doctrine may seem to represent an arbitrary opposition to progress in that its element of compulsion apparently disregards the artistic freedom of deducing final consequences from the *laws*. Yet it is not opposition to progress; it is rather a harking back to ancient sources. In Plato's strictness we see a reappearance of the spirit of the great ancient heroes, opposed to the new hedonistic-formalistic musical doctrines. We see again the liberty of those ancient heroes, a liberty which knew no bounds but the infinite space of the universe. For this ultimate liberty every ephemeral liberty had to be sacrificed.

In the *Republic* Plato recognizes the general conception which considers gymnastics and music the basic elements in education. He deviates at two points, however, from the accepted theories. According to him, music should not follow gymnastics, but should precede and dominate it, because the body does not ennoble the soul; on the contrary, the soul should build up the body. Gymnastics is conducive to coarseness and rowdiness if not tempered by music. On the other hand, music without gymnastics leads to a sagging of energy and a lethargy of the soul. To ensure a lasting influence of the good in music Plato recommends the practice of art by all generations. The whole population should be divided into large choruses, the first of which would contain boys, the second young men up to the age of thirty, and the third all men from thirty to sixty years of age.

The Arcadians had state laws and regulations which called for compulsory musical education for every citizen up to his thirtieth year. In Sparta, Thebes, and Athens, everyone was supposed to learn to play the aulos, and participation in the chorus was one of the most important duties of Greek youth. The study of choral singing followed strictly chronological and historical lines, starting with the oldest hymns in praise of gods and heroes and ending with contemporary music. Not every sort of music was acceptable for educational purposes. The foremost place was assigned to melodies in the Dorian mode because their austerity was greatly valued as a character-building force.[17]

The fact that the two principal instruments displayed such different characteristics, the cithara being soft-voiced and the aulos possessing a penetrating tone, induced the Greeks to attribute ethical powers to each of them. In the same way, they attached an ethos to the individual scales; some of them were considered soothing and conducive to noble sentiments, whereas others seemed to incite people to violence and cause moral decay. Since the names given to various keys bear the names of different tribes, it is plausible that the different ethos or characteristic trait assigned to each is simply a reflection of the tribal temperament. To the northern immigrant, the austere and moral Dorian, the southern Asiatic people seemed weak, effeminate, and immoral; he was inclined to impute to the Dorian scale heartening and virtuous effects, while he considered the Phrygian scale orgiastic and maenadic. Thus there developed an ethical doctrine of the state-building properties of national music and the demoralizing effects of foreign music.[18]

While the actual musical activity of poets and dramatists may seem somewhat schematic, the importance of music in life was constantly rising and becoming more and more universal, and its practice was linked with the great events of national importance. Like accomplishments in athletics, the accomplishments in music were presented in the true competitive spirit of the Greeks on the occasion of the agones. The agones were contests in athletics, chariot or horse racing, music, or literature, presented amid the greatest splendor. The oldest agones were the gymnic agones which later developed into the Olympic games. In the sixth century B.C. appeared the Dionysiac agones, which preceded the drama proper. The rhapsodic agones, the recitations of epic poetry, seem to have originated with the Ionians, but were accepted later by the Spartans; the musical and orchestic agones, that is, the music and dance festivals, came from the Cretan Dorians and later spread over to the mainland. Beginning with the fourth century the musical agones show two main types: the scenic agones, which were theater or ensemble plays, and the thymelic agones—named after the small altar of Dionysus standing in the middle of a theater—which embraced all imaginable varieties of song and music. The popularity of the musical agones created, in the Hellenistic period, veritable concert societies and artists' "unions," such as the federation of "Dionysiac artists." The expenses for the festivals were defrayed by states, communities, rulers, or even public-spirited citizens. The programs featured, as in our day, old and new compositions.[19] The victor in a musical agone was, like his colleague, the athlete, a national hero.

The use of music in military operations, which is as old as warfare itself, played its role in the battles of the ancient Greeks. Of all the instruments the aulos occupied the chief place. Herodotus, Plutarch, Thucydides, and Gellius furnish us with ample data concerning this military music. We read about the Lydian king, Alyattes, who invaded the territory of the Milesians to the sound of auloi and other instruments. The Cretans and Lacedaemonians entered the battlefield to the accompaniment of the aulos. The Lacedaemonians are especially mentioned by Plutarch (*Mus.*, 26), who remarked that before the attack they blew the "Castor-song." Plutarch also tells us in his biography of Lycurgus (21–22) that the statesman, on his trip to Crete, observed a number of interesting new customs and habits, which, upon his return to Sparta, he introduced into his own country. While his person is enshrouded in the deepest mystery and we do not know for certain that he was a historical figure, this statement is corroborated by Xenophon (*Lac. Repl.*, 13, 8), who mentions the use of the aulos as a "military bugle" by the Lacedaemonians, and notes its introduction by Lycurgus into the Spartan armies. The use of the aulos was by no means left to the spur of the moment; in typical Greek fashion it had its well-defined role. The soldiers marched to battle to the sound of the aulos to retain an orderly grouping of ranks. The aulos players were distributed among them at strategic points. Before the battle the aulete played a "prelude" which was supposed to put the soldiers in the proper mood for fighting, while the so-called Castor-song gave the signal for the attack.

The Science of Music

CORRESPONDENCES and proportions, which play so important a role in music, can be expressed in numbers. To the Greek mind music was part of a mathematical philosophy which the Pythagoreans, the precursors of Russell, Eddington, and Einstein, held to represent the whole of philosophy. Or to put it differently, we may say that the mathematical theory of harmony was part of a general theory of the harmony of the cosmos. The disciples of Pythagoras, as well as the non-Pythagorean authors, agree in attributing the discovery of the numeric laws of harmony to the great philosopher, and they are unanimous in their praise of the importance of this discovery.

The general theory of proportions found a grateful meeting ground in the subtle eurhythmical correspondences of surfaces, volumes, and proportions in architecture. The Greeks added to these correlations explicitly musical ones and carried to its highest point of development a metaphysical conception of the theory of numbers and of phenomena that are the issue of numbers: proportion, rhythm, form. One wonders whether the Greek architects, who were not intimidated by the most subtle numeric combinations, did not attempt to incorporate in their designs, in addition to purely spatial symmetry and eurhythmy, the mathematical maxims deduced from the harmonic correlations between architecture and music. Vitruvius, our best source and authority on the architecture of antiquity, casually displays his knowledge of the mathematical theory of the diatonic scale and quotes Aristoxenus of Tarentum. A modern Greek scholar, Athanasius Georgiades, has studied the dimensions and proportions of the temples of Hellas from precisely this point of view. His work on *Harmony in Architectural Composition* [20] reveals a close connection between the disposition of columns and the elements of the Pythagorean scale.

While the Pythagoreans often drifted into what amounts to number-mysticism, their musical theory followed scholarly precepts of observation, and their conclusions based on the length of strings and number of oscillations form the basis of the modern science of acoustics. The greatest and most lasting impetus experienced by Greek musical science came from Aristotle. His approach to music was not so much that of an artist, as was the case with his teacher, Plato, as that of a scientist-scholar. Aristotle's writing on music comes much nearer to an independent system of aesthetics which no longer relies on extramusical elements. A thinker of universal orientation, in his system purely scientific-empirical investigations stand side by side with the doctrine of musical catharsis. The followers of Aristotle, the Peripatetics, brought the science of music to its apogee. While our information concerning some of the outstanding disciples is scant, we know that Theophrastus (372–287) was opposed to the idea of attributing medical powers to music, and we are also familiar with the historical work on music of Heracleides, preserved in an abridged form by Plutarch. We are much more fortunate in our knowledge of the most celebrated musical scholar of antiquity, Aristoxenus of Tarentum (fourth century), whom Horace called *musicum idemque philosophus,* and whose reputation was still great enough in the early nineteenth century to prompt Böckh, the great classical scholar, to name him *summus auctor.*

As a man he was not attractive, and his fellow citizens considered him a quarrelsome, envious, malignant individual, but as a scholar and scientific investigator he represents the peak of classical musical science. As a Greek philosopher, he considers music from the point of view of pedagogy and politics and accordingly pays much attention to the ethos doctrine; but in his writings we recognize the conception of a true natural scientist, because, contrary to the mathematical-numerical speculations of the Pythagoreans, he placed the study of musical sounds on a physical-acoustical basis. More than a physicist, he can be considered the first music-psychologist and aesthetician because he goes beyond the question of the *origin* of sound and investigates the problems of perception of sound by the human ear.

The Last Phase of Classical Music

THE rules which affected the development of Greek arts and letters in the following period apply fully to music. This epoch, which interested itself alike in idyllic trifles and in monumental creations, was a great epoch because it strove consciously to enact reforms, to rejuvenate art. It heralded new aims, new tasks, and new solutions. "I do not sing of the superannuated," said Timotheus, "the new is much more preferable. It is the young Zeus who reigns today; Cronus is the master of the past. To Hades with the old Muse!" The music of this period offers more positive marks of identification than does that of the previous era.

The important musico-poetical types were the *new* nome and the *new* dithyramb, represented by the musician-poets Phrynis, Timotheus, Philoxenus, and Polyeidus (fifth to fourth century). The different evaluation of the place and importance of music is symbolized by the change in the hierarchy of the instruments. The cithara definitely cedes the front rank to the aulos, and the aulete is not only mentioned in the *didascalia* (the catalogue of the dramas with names and dates), but, finally, his name is set ahead of that of the poet. This means the recognition of music as an independent art. There is a surprising analogy between the virtuoso era of the twentieth century and this sudden popularity of instrumental dexterity in the fifth and fourth centuries B.C. The serene and simple melodies disappear. Contemporary critics found the melodies overloaded with embellishments, tonalities too frequently changed, and the instrumental accomplishments noisy and thick. It is true that attempts at the emancipation of music were made remarkably early; Euripides himself was interested in it, but the philosophers and writers did not look on the innovations with favorable eyes, and Aristoxenus considered them outright decadence. While in previous times there had been uniformity in the employment of instruments, there now appeared a complex sort of music not unlike our modern instrumental ensemble: flutes, reeds, lyres, cymbals, and all sorts of other instruments were used together in the performance. The conservatives saw in this wild confusion, as they called it, a decline of the noble old art.

We should discuss first of all the celebrated Timotheus of Miletus (c. 446–357). His dithyrambs and nomes were redundant and prolix; his light and pleasant melodies were designed to thaw out the frozen majesty of the older art. He succeeded in creating, in his nomes, a richness of color previously unknown, which caused universal astonishment even among the critics. The dazzled public feted him exuberantly, but the cautious theorists declared their disapproval. Plato and Aristotle saw in this music a mischievous offense, an uncalled-for infringement of the laws laid down by the state. The literary world rewarded the new art with both scorn and cheers. The comedy under Aristophanes carried on a stinging crusade against the new tendency in music, because it adorned with flourishes the grave, majestic line of the old music.[21] Pherecrates, the writer of comedies, publicly scourged this "music of the future" by presenting the Muse as a violated virgin. Yet Timotheus, the futurist, created a new school, and Melanippides, Crexus, and Phrynis joined him to exploit further the possibilities offered by the new current.

The historian's experience warns him not to accept the picture painted by the conservatives. It is evident that the reforms brought things that were entirely new, and new things are always opposed by the majority. Furthermore, we cannot fail to appreciate the evident emancipation of music, and we must consider this the result of a progressive current.

At this point we can no longer truly speak of development. What had taken place was not an isolated phenomenon, valid only in the realm of music. It rested on causes universal in Greek intellectual life. The century which preceded the birth of Christ broke the independent tendency of Hellenistic Greece. Having lost its impetus, Greek genius turned to archaistic and classicistic tendencies, which prevailed, with occasional "reactionary" rallies, until the end of the antique world. One of the more intensive rallies —in literature and sculpture—occurred in the second and third centuries A. D. Among the few actual musical monuments of antiquity preserved for posterity there are two hymns by Mesomedes which originated in this late period. Significantly enough, their affected simplicity is in contrast with the general conservative trend in arts and letters, for their strong archaic character is not in keeping with the musical practice of the period. The most complete change in the position and importance of music may be seen in the last great dramatic genre of antiquity, the pantomime. Here the poetic conception becomes distinctly secondary, while the importance is shifted to the dance and to the music.

With the first actual musical examples at hand we can reach definite conclusions concerning principles of melodic and rhythmic construction. It appears that, preceding the Christian era, the accent of the Greek language influenced considerably the pitch of the musical sound associated with it. More precisely, the pitch of the musical sound on one syllable of a word did not exceed the pitch of the accented syllable, and a light accent placed on the last syllable of a word was given a musical sound of lower pitch than the accented syllable of the following word. The musical monuments dating from the second century A. D. no longer follow these principles, a circumstance indicative of the fact that the musical accent had been transformed into our present dynamic accent.

If we examine the above-mentioned Oxyrhynchus papyrus,[22] which contains the fragment of a Christian hymn dating from the third century A. D., we come to other important conclusions. This fragment is a purely vocal piece. Although very short, it is a unique document, our only actual musical source for the illustration of the transition period from the music of antique Greece to that of Christian Greece. The piece still shows the characteristics of classical music intact. Its rhythm is likewise based on the length of syllables. This furnishes us with valuable indications concerning the complicated state of the music of the early Christians. While other literary sources indicate a merging of elements, this papyrus confirms the hypothesis that the original Hebrew songs as sung by the early Christians were displaced by examples of the highest type of antique musical practice soon after early Christendom came into contact with Greek civilization.[23]

Chapter 2

BYZANTIUM

⇶

Music in Eastern Christendom

THE logical continuation of the history of music in Western civilization should lead us into the Roman Empire and to the beginning of Christendom. It is advisable first, however, to discuss the music of the Eastern Roman Empire, Byzantium, even though this necessitates a considerable excursion into late medieval times.

The harmonious association of Neoplatonism and Neo-Pythagoreanism, uniting with new tenets emanating from Palestine, formed a new philosophical system. Strange metaphysical ideas emerged from this system, particularly in the regions of conflict between Syrian and Egyptian cultures, and their dissemination in some cases gave rise to new religious sects.

In this atmosphere the oldest chants of Christian poetry originated, finding their way into the circle of civilization in Syria and Palestine, which was soon dominated by Greek culture. The new Christian poetry and music was later transplanted to the West, where, having undergone considerable alteration and having absorbed elements of Occidental origin, it produced, in the central Middle Ages, an Occidental theology, liturgy, and music.

We shall not attempt to examine the initial functions of this Syrian-Egyptian-Byzantine music, for they are lost in the contourless mystery of magic and incantation. Suffice it to say that the original role of music in prehistoric times—incantation, purification, conjuration, and exorcism—survived for a long time, and that certain aspects of it became, in a stylized form, standard elements of Christian liturgy. In the Catholic Church today the priest, intoning a Psalm, sprinkles holy water around the altar and the congregation before he begins the celebration of the Mass. To us this is merely a liturgical ritual, but the Antiochean priests employed the same procedure because they believed that the devil dreaded church music especially, while Basil spoke of the evil spirits which could be effectively chased away by music.

The focal point of Eastern Christendom was Byzantium—renamed New Rome and later universally known as Konstantinopolis—and this capital of the Byzantine Empire was for a millennium the site of a remarkable flourishing of arts and letters. On account of the almost uninterrupted warfare in which parts of the empire were involved until the final capture of Constantinople by the Turks in 1453, we have been prone to assume that Byzantine culture underwent a continuous decline. Upon examination of the history of the Eastern Roman Empire, however, we see that the main provinces, and especially the capital itself, suffered relatively little from the ravages of continuous warfare, and that, on the contrary, they developed a spiritual and artistic life of the highest order.

As long as Byzantine art was considered a decadent continuation of classical Greek art, it was impossible to reach a real understanding of its nature. Constantinople, after its establishment as capital of the Roman Empire, became the center of a composite civilization, based upon both classical and purely Oriental traditions; but by the sixth century A. D. Byzantine culture and art had crystallized into something definitely divergent from the antique. In the centuries after the fall of centralized Western government, the arts remained alive in Byzantium, destined later to transmit to the West both their classical inheritance and their own distinctive character.

To give a general and comprehensive summary of Byzantine music is as impossible an undertaking as a similar task in classical Greek music.[1] Some phases of Byzantine music are well known to us because we are dealing with a living art, but others are as legendary as the musical practice of the Homeric age. As in the music of antiquity, we must omit a discussion of popular music because of the complete lack of material; but more than this, we must forgo the discussion of any secular, worldly music. It is reasonable to suppose that there was some kind of secular music practiced in the Byzantine world, but there is no evidence of it. This is not the result of mere accident, but rather the logical outcome of the new role played by music in the intellectual life of Christian Greeks; for their conception differed fundamentally from the ideas of their pagan ancestors. Music ceased to be the indispensable factor of the highest intellectual wealth of the individual; it ceased to be one of the cherished symbols of the commonwealth; it ceased to inspire statesmen, rulers, philosophers, and artists to devote their care and attention to its practice. Spiritual and mental leadership in this new world of Christian Greeks was assumed by the Church, and the worldly part of ancient classical music fell victim to her transcendental principles. Secular music plays such a modest role in this new cast that it is not even mentioned among the *dramatis personae*. The Church recognized, however, the importance and adaptability of music to her own aims and purposes. She appropriated it and made it great in her own peculiar way.

Byzantine music was church music. As such it became an institution closely associated with the destiny of the Church, an institution in itself not subject to temporal changes. It became timeless, and we are therefore not surprised to find the "period" of Byzantine music still flourishing. As a matter of fact, the roof of its edifice was not completed until the nineteenth century. At the beginning of this era, lasting sixteen hundred years, we see —the Oxyrhynchus papyrus is our witness—that Byzantine music was based on the music of antiquity. In modern times, it has relied on contemporary European music. But in the intervening millennium and a half—from the fourth to the nineteenth centuries—it created within the severe limitations of Byzantine life [2] a musical practice of distinctive style and principles. The peculiar character of the medieval mind is responsible for an artificial archaic current which from time to time has crossed the sturdy, continuous, artistic development of this music. Fortunately, this studied archaic tendency is confined chiefly to theoretical writings. The representatives of Byzantine musicography—Suidas (tenth century), Michael Psellus (eleventh century), Bryennius (twelfth century), and Pachymeres (thirteenth century) —do cast some furtive glances toward the music of their own time, but their main activity is reserved for the rediscovery of ancient musical doctrine. This explains why Byzantine music did not produce an independent musical science comparable to that of antiquity, a fact which is responsible for the endless and complicated task that confronts the musicologist and the archaeologist interested in Byzantine art.

The few words and notes of the Oxyrhynchus fragment furnish an invaluable document with which to demonstrate the uninterrupted continuity that existed between ancient and Christian Greek civilization. It testifies to the fact that the educated Christian Greeks accepted and transplanted the musical system of their ancestors. However, this is our sole document, and taking it for a model, we can only imagine how the hymns sung in the Christian communities of the great Egyptian cities sounded. Our conception is borne out by analogies apparent in early Byzantine fine arts, which show distinct Hellenistic elements. We must not forget, however, that the origin and heritage of Christianity is an Oriental one, or, more precisely, Hebrew; consequently the first Christian hymns and songs were taken from the Jewish liturgy or were direct imitations of it. This practice was acknowledged by St. Paul and Pliny the Younger. Unfortunately, we must be satisfied with such literary allusions, since we have no actual documents extant which would elucidate the exact nature of this Oriental heritage.[3]

As to the classical heritage, concerning which we have only one actual musical document, we know from our literary sources that besides the serene music of the Oxyrhynchus papyrus, early Byzantine civilization absorbed a good deal of lighter, even frivolous, secular music. It was said of Arius, the head of the most powerful heretical sect, that he smuggled his doctrines into people's souls through songs whose melodies came from the theater, the tavern, and ships. It is small wonder, then, that the more zealous members of the Orthodox Church, such as the monks and the hermits of the desert, were opposed to music altogether.

Following the archaistic tendency in literature and the general interest in theological problems which eliminated worldly and everyday subjects, secular music disappears completely from our records. Church music remains and is joined by a newly born art. When Constantinople became the seat and symbol of the empire, the court of the emperors produced this new art, a semisacral, solemn, and dignified music which we may call "court" music. The churches of the great Eastern intellectual centers, Jerusalem, Alexandria, Antioch, and later the capital itself, accepted music, or rather, song, as an integral element of the liturgy. The primitive congregational singing they replaced by choirs (usually boys' choirs, but occasionally mixed choirs of boys and men which sang antiphonally) and soloists, and thus elevated church music to the status of an art.

The Psalms of the transition period were rather simple. Following the Biblical text the choir sang a troparion or "round," but this soon developed into a piece independent of the Psalm, with original text and music. This was, however, not a Greek invention, but the adaptation of a practice originating in the Orient, that is, Syria. The Christian Greeks in this case were the recipients of Oriental cultural elements, a fact that characterizes the later development of Byzantine civilization. Oriental influences now assumed a dominant position in the realm of music. Hellenistic musical traditions disappeared from the liturgy of the Church and the ceremonies of the court. The older liturgy of the Mass was displaced by the two main types of the Mass created by St. Basil the Great and St. John Chrysostom (both fourth century). The first type covered the liturgy of the new year and certain other holidays, while the second type governed the Masses to be sung on ordinary Sundays and holidays. These two types of liturgy continued unaltered for centuries, not only among the Greeks, but among all the west Asiatic, north African, and east European (especially Slavic) peoples who accepted the Greek rites. Many centuries later some minor alterations came about in the liturgy—as, beginning with the sixteenth century, a slight Turkish influence, and during the last two centuries some traces left by western European music—but the foundation of this ancient music has remained intact.

Comparison of the Music of Ancient Greece and Byzantium

COMPARISONS of the music of ancient Greece with that of medieval Byzantium are interesting. First of all, both were predominantly vocal in nature; but while ancient Greek music developed an instrumental genre

from its very inception and evolved a special system of notation for its recording, Byzantine music never encouraged the growth of instrumental music.
Both these great branches of Greek music entrusted their instrumental music
to a few basic instruments. The Greeks had—as we have seen—two main
types, the aulos and the lyre, while the Byzantines allotted the limited use
they had for instruments to only one, the organ, which figured not in their
church music, but only in what we have called court music. Cithara and
aulos, which accompanied the entire musical production of Hellenistic
Greece, disappeared with the annihilation by the Laodicean Council of the
theater, pantomime, and virtuoso music. Like the aulos, the organ is of
Oriental extraction. Plastic monuments, especially bas-reliefs, testify to the
fact that it was well known in the Occident before Constantine Copronymus,
the Byzantine emperor, presented one to Pepin, King of the Franks, in the
eighth century. The organ accompanied the melodies which were sung in
court ceremonies, but its importance was not comparable to that of the
aulos.

Byzantine music was more exclusively vocal than Greek music and was
more closely bound by and subordinated to the text. Here again we note
a remarkable similarity between ancient and Byzantine music; yet, paradoxical as it may seem, this very similarity also accounts for their distinctive
traits. The characteristics of ancient Greek music were the musical accent of
the language and the rhythmical system of the poetry. Byzantine music
differs from Greek music because the nature of these two basic characteristics was changed. In the first centuries following the birth of Christ the
musical accent of the Greek language gave way before a system—familiar
to us—consisting of emphases and dynamic accents; a system which recognizes as "long" the accented syllables only, and which classifies all other
syllables of various lengths as "short." This procedure put to an end the
rhythmical system based on the length of syllables. There was no longer
any *metron,* or measuring of the length of syllables; their number had to
be counted. The formulae of Byzantine rhythm were not the symbols ⌣ —,
— ⌣, ⌣ ⌣ — ⌣, etc., but ! . . . , ! . . , etc. This new artistic principle, based
on accents and numbers of syllables, the Byzantines took from their teachers, the Syrians.

Some of the most important summaries of classical Greek music were
written in Byzantine times, if not on Byzantine soil (Alypius, fourth century; Boethius, fifth to sixth century). Nevertheless, the musical system of
ancient Greece disappeared under the pressure of an Oriental tendency,
and with it disappeared also its system of notation. New principles of music
and notation, pointing, as we should expect, to Eastern sources, came into
being.

There exists a similarity between the great social value attributed to music

by ancient Greece and the universal, majestic, and solemn character of
Byzantine music, performed on the occasion of church services and court
ceremonies. The musical part of these functions is fairly well known. The
ceremonial book of the Emperor Constantine Porphyrogenetus (tenth century), and the descriptions of travelers furnish material for a reconstruction
of the court music. The double choir appears here, representing the two main
political parties, the "Blues" and the "Greens," who present their songs
alternately.[4] Another unmistakably Oriental trait is the marshaling of the
choirs behind curtains. This music, like all Oriental music, was in unison
and not polyphonic. The organ was the only instrument used for accompaniment. Travelers speak of silver and gold organs, but our knowledge
concerning the nature of their accompaniment is just as limited as that about
the cithara accompaniment of the Greeks. Festivals, family reunions, receptions, and nuptials all had their appropriate share of music, and the Byzantines were especially eager to present elaborate musical settings when barbarians were present. Byzantine instrument makers developed a highly
respected art. The imperial throne room boasted musical automatons which
stirred profound admiration in barbarian guests and ambassadors. Statues
of lions situated near the throne had ingenious instruments placed in their
bodies which imitated realistically the great beast's roar. It is interesting to
note that the organ, which in Byzantium was distinctly a secular instrument, changed its status when introduced into the Occident, where it became an instrument of the Church.

There were many varieties of songs performed in the imperial palace, but
the chief form was the so-called "acclamation" or praise-song for the emperor. The ruler of the empire was at the same time God's representative
on earth; he carried the double title of King (*Basileus*) and Apostolic Prince
(*Isapostolos*); his exalted position required a ceremonial and ritual in which
formulae of chanted greetings were of considerable importance. These acclamations were short pieces of poetry sung at all public ceremonies in the
presence of the emperor. Other forms were the *polychronismos* or "wishing-
many-years" song and the *euphemesis,* which conveyed good wishes. The
last-named was a sacred variety of the *polychronismos* and was sung in
honor of patriarchs. One such acclamation and *euphemesis* is extant, dating
from a late period, the fourteenth century. It was sung in praise of the
Emperor John Paleologus and the Patriarch Joseph.

The real soil from which Byzantine musical theory and practice arose was
church music. While we have access to a rich theoretical and historical literature concerning the music of ancient Greece and merely a few fragments
of actual music, the state of affairs is exactly the opposite as regards Byzantine music. It is true that the earliest period (fourth to eighth centuries) is
as barren of monuments as the Homeric era, but the period between the

ninth and twelfth centuries gives us some valuable material, and from the thirteenth century on, our sources are abundant. Theoretical and historical tracts, however, are scarce; they consist mostly of encyclopedic entries, literary allusions, and short introductory remarks which prefaced the compositions. Still, these data enable us to draw a picture of early Byzantine music, although its contours are vague and do not give us a sufficiently precise outline of the relationship between Byzantine music and the Western music of its own time and the more recent music of the Orthodox Church.

Byzantine Church Music and Spiritual Poetry

THE basis of Byzantine church music is a religious poetry of exceptional wealth. This poetry also forms the elements of the main types of the Mass mentioned above. The Eastern Church still possesses a great number of liturgical works which contain monuments of poetry and music fifteen hundred years old. Among these the important types are the following: the *Evangeliar*, containing the Evangelical passages read at services; the *Psalterion*, with the Psalms of the Old Testament divided into twenty groups; the *Octoechus*, which arranges the liturgy according to the eight "church keys" or scales; the *Euchologion*, containing the liturgies and rites of the sacraments; the *Apostolos*, with the Epistles for the whole church year; the *Triodion*, containing the office before Easter; and the *Pentecostarion*, containing the office from Easter to Pentecost. Besides these accepted and sanctioned works, countless manuscripts have preserved a great number of hymns, some of which are used officially, and some of which are simply of literary value. The attention of Byzantine historians is now directed especially toward these manuscripts.

The *Evangeliars* are of limited importance to us, because these prose texts, which have not changed materially since the first centuries of our era, were chanted in a simple, monotonous way. Consequently, they disclose neither poetical rhythm nor music as such. They offer, nevertheless, one great advantage to the historian because of the remarkably clear and intelligible system of signs of performance. This system, whose signs appear above or underneath the prose text, is called *ecphonesis*, "reading aloud," and goes back to prehistoric antiquity. The Byzantines took it probably from Semitic sources. Ignoring proper musical indications, ecphonetic notation had the purpose of elucidating the meaning of words by judicious divisions with the aid of nine basic signs. It suffices to mention two of these signs, which have been accepted and used by all modern languages: the apostrophe and the hyphen.

Of great interest to the student of music and poetry is the song and hymn poetry which followed the new rhythmical principles based on numbers of syllables and dynamic accents. The first centuries of the Christian era knew simple strophes composed of an even number of syllables, such as the famous Cherub-hymns of the Mass. The simple troparions were succeeded— beginning with the third century—by hymns of monumental proportions. Among the important creators of these figures we should mention the Syrian Bardesanes, and his later compatriot, St. Ephrem. This new hymn poetry consisted of lyrico-epic-dramatic elaboration of Biblical scenes and the stories of saints, and it evolved a particular artistic form of its own. Following an introductory strophe (κουκούλιον) came a great row of generally long strophes of identical rhythm (οἶκος) which had an identical refrain. The strophes manifested subtlety and considerable pathos, to be surpassed only by the grandiose closing sections of the refrain. The rhythm was given by a "model strophe" (εἱρμός) which the author either borrowed or invented himself. It would be misleading to compare these hymns to our Occidental hymns for they are purely Oriental, resembling the *sugithas* of the Syrians. We should rather consider them as a sort of lyrical preaching, performed by a soloist while the refrain was sung by the choir. Both the simpler and older hymns, and the larger and later ones, the *canons,* became completely settled classical norms which did not change materially after the eighth century. They completed and enhanced the scintillating pomp of the Byzantine liturgy. The older poet-authors of hymns, like their ancient Greek precursors, composed their own music, and hence were called poets of melodies; but the younger ones had to be satisfied with the title of hymn writer, hymnographos. Three great poet-composers molded this musico-poetic type: St. Romanus, St. John of Damascus, and the Patriarch Sergius. The *Acathistus*-hymn of the last-named, composed as a thanksgiving to the Mother of God for her defense of Constantinople against the Avars, is as mighty and eternal a possession of the Eastern Church as "Ein' Feste Burg" is of the Lutheran.

A change, largely connected with the Iconoclastic controversy, was wrought in the Greek service books during the seventh, eighth, and ninth centuries. The names of the defenders of the sacred icons fill a large space in the calendar; and their elaborate doctrinal hymns replaced the more animated and poetical poems of Romanus. The new form which rises into view and continues henceforth to be the highest mode of poetical expression is the canon. The canon was of colossal dimensions, consisting of eight or nine long odes, every ode having its special melody, repeated in each strophe. We may gauge the proportions of these gigantic compositions by the famous "great canon" of Andrew of Crete which had two hundred and fifty strophes. After the eighth century the great creative period of Byzantine music was over, and up to the fifteenth century only imitations appeared.

The first great era of poetry used a musical accompaniment which consisted of simple "concise melodies" (σύντονιον μέλος), while the later period developed a coloratura song (ἀργὸν μέλος), no doubt under renewed Oriental influences. This later period almost defies analysis because of the marked archaistic tendencies manifest in Byzantine art. The theoretical writers show a stubborn adherence to the musical science and doctrines of ancient Greece, although this science was practically extinct. Classical musical theory was taught to a certain extent in the schools of the Byzantine Empire, but that musical practice and its theoretical literature were certainly new and different from the classical, even before the end of the great creative period (fourth to eighth centuries), may be ascertained from a work entitled *Hagiopolites,* which dates from the end of that period. St. John of Damascus is credited with the compilation of the *Octoechus,* "the book of the eight keys"; but this may in fact antedate him, as the principle of eight keys is certainly found earlier.[5]

A characteristic feature of Byzantine singing is the prolongation of the last note of a phrase. Since the auxiliary signs of Western notation were unknown to the writers of this music, the use of bar lines in modern transcriptions can be only arbitrary. The melodies are divided into phrases which follow the units of comprehension of the text. We mentioned in the previous chapter the monodic character of ancient Greek music, whether solo or choric. Byzantine music, in its unadulterated form, is mainly monodic, except that the choir occasionally holds what may be termed an accompanying tone. This method of singing prevails up to this day in those domains of the Eastern Church untouched by Western music.

Byzantine music notation evolved independently of the notation of classical Greece, and should be considered one of the great and truly original achievements of Byzantine civilization. It is a purely vocal notation, but within this domain it shows two subspecies: one of which was used for the musical recitation of the Gospels, while the other served for singing proper. By means of this notation we gain admittance to an entirely new world. Instead of a letter notation with its unequivocal symbols, the Byzantine used signs that attempted to give a graphic indication of the design and progress of the melody, without, however, giving the exact pitch. These signs, the neumes (νεῦμα = sign), are known to us in three chief medieval varieties (though there were many subvariants in the Middle Ages) and one modern variety. The oldest system, fully developed by the eleventh or twelfth century, shows signs similar to the ecphonetic signs; their interpretation is still uncertain. In the twelfth to fourteenth centuries Byzantine notation changed abruptly, for reasons unknown to us, but the new system added a great number of new signs to the existing ones, and made it possible to express and record all the subtleties of which this music was capable. The third reform enriched the chironomic signs, manual gestures made by the precentor, and reveals a new style, the melismatic, which is almost unbearable to Western ears on account of its strange mannerisms.

While Byzantine music is not so universal an art as was the music of classical Greece, it is the foundation of the music of Eastern Christendom. It may rightly be considered a parallel to Gregorian music, but beyond the comparison thus established there is a more intimate relationship between these two great branches of monodic song; for the origins of our Western church are to be traced back not to Rome but to the Eastern part of the empire. Greek was the liturgical language of the new faith until the end of the third century, and the first part of the Catholic Mass still begins with a Greek invocation, *Kyrie eleison!* The influence which emanated from the East and was transmitted to the West by Byzantium continued to be active with varying force. Especially noticeable during the reigns of popes of Syrian and Greek origin (eighth century), it did not altogether cease until the final division of the Church in 1050.

Chapter 3

ROME

→》》 《《←

WE cannot speak of a Roman in the same way that we can
speak of a Greek musical art. While the Romans must
have had simple folk songs of their own, these songs were
lost in the influx of a foreign musical culture, which, when
transplanted to Roman soil, took root and flourished. When we speak of
Roman music, therefore, we mean Greek music developed and practiced
in Rome.

The word "development" needs qualification, for in transplanted arts development does not necessarily mean progress. The practice of music, not
unlike that of the other arts which were introduced from Greece to Rome,
consisted of a strengthening, or rather, coarsening, of its means of expression through the addition of heterogeneous elements to suit the rather uncouth and vulgar taste of the Romans. By Augustus's time the aulos had
been developed into a mighty instrument which could compete with the
tuba, and Ammianus Marcellinus mentions lyres "as big as chariots." Besides
increasing the tonal volume of the individual instruments, the Romans
united considerable numbers of instruments into fantastic ensembles. True
enough, the tendency for mass ensembles was evident in Egypt, and the
Romans had some gigantic examples to follow. Ptolemy Philadelphus (d.
246 B.C.) describes a procession at the court in Alexandria in which the
participants numbered six hundred men, three hundred of them playing on
golden lyres.

The music of other nations found its way into Rome at an early period.
At the beginning of imperial times, the influence of Egyptian-Alexandrian
music was marked, as Alexandria retained, even under Roman rule, a rich
and varied musical life, and its musicians and singers enjoyed a high reputation in the empire. Thus the changes experienced by Greek music in Rome
were largely of an Oriental nature. The greatest difference between Greek
and Roman music is displayed by the large "symphonic" ensembles, so popular in Rome, which were unknown in ancient Greece. Performances of vocal
music were characterized by the same display of colossal assemblies. Seneca
says that on such occasions there were more singers assembled on the stage

31

than there had been spectators in the old days, and the overflowing number of musicians filled all the seats not occupied by the public.[1] He adds that the accompaniment consisted of a multitude of brass instruments distributed in the auditorium, and auloi and organs of all sorts placed on the stage. If we recall that the Roman theaters accommodated from seven to twelve thousand spectators, we may safely assume that these performances exceeded the dimensions of modern American and English choral festivals.

With the increase of the grandiose element, Roman music gradually abandoned the last vestiges of the lofty ideals which had once dominated it in its original Hellenic home. The simple dignity of Greek melodies gave way to complicated rhythmical tunes which went through veritable contortions of modulation. This emancipation from ancient simplicity led to a quick artistic downfall, promoted especially by the dominant popularity of the pantomime, the music of which was characterized by contemporary writers as weak, void of dignity, lascivious, and full of frills and fanfares.

If with the Romans the art of music degenerated to a means for the mere gratification of the senses, it must be admitted that they saw to it that all its possibilities were exploited. As in all other arts, their objective was to enhance the enjoyment of life. They had in slavery an institution which permitted the training of musicians and professional entertainers on a large scale. Among the hordes of slaves there were always numerous gifted individuals, and it was not difficult to single them out from the hundreds and often thousands of slaves belonging to an aristocratic household. Chrysogonus, Sulla's rich freedman, had among his own slaves such a number of musicians that the vicinity of his residence reverberated day and night with the sound of instruments and voices. Musicians accompanied their masters on journeys, and fashionable resorts echoed with music of all varieties. Maecenas cured his insomnia by listening to soft, distant music, and Caligula enjoyed the music of choruses and instruments while his galley rode the waves in the Gulf of Naples. Music could not be missing from the repasts which, in true Roman fashion, endeavored to satisfy many pleasures simultaneously. At great feasts there were choruses accompanied by the castanets of beautiful Andalusian dancers, but even modest tête-à-tête dinners were not considered complete without music. Pliny the Younger offered one of his dinner guests the choice between a lecture, a comedy scene, or lyre playing; and Martial, promising an exceedingly frugal meal to one of his friends, offered him—in compensation—some aulos music.

It is apparent that there was no public event of any sort, whether religious or theatrical, that did not call for music. Nor was there any difference made between sacred and secular music. Such a distinction was, in fact, unknown to the whole of antiquity, as theatrical performances formed a part of the religious service. Because of the almost unlimited freedom in admission to theatrical spectacles, melodies and "hits" found a much quicker and more universal popularity than in the nineteenth century, or in the twentieth century before the advent of radio. In Cicero's time there were connoisseurs who were able to identify a composition after the "first flute tone," and Cicero was duly impressed by such ability. He also testifies to the fact that the public exercised critical scrutiny over artists and gave vent to its disapproval if the singer or player made mistakes.[2]

In 170–160 B. C., the Roman public was still so vulgar and uneducated that the foremost Greek musicians could not interest them unless their musical performance was associated with some scrimmage or wrestling. But one century later it was not uncommon for musical virtuosi, accompanying their songs on the cithara, to win the plaudits of the populace. Besides the cithara players, there were also dramatic singers who performed their songs in costume and mask, and lyrical singers who sang hymns and short songs. The Emperor Nero reintroduced the periodical musical agones of classical Greece, as he wished to exhibit his prowess as a citharoedus. In A. D. 60 he founded periodic "holy festivals" in which music occupied the most important place.

On a much higher plane stood the Capitoline games, founded by Domitian toward the end of the first century. Poets, musicians, and singers competed in these games, which were held in the odeum (or odeon) on the Campus Martius. The building had been reconstructed especially with a view to musical performances. The games occurred every fourth year, and the winners received the laurels from the emperor's own hands. Owing to the presence of the emperor and the select audience of nobles, these games lent considerable dignity and fame to the competing artists, and a winner was considered the foremost artist in his domain, his fame spreading even beyond the limits of the empire. Artists came from far countries, from Asia and Africa, solely to participate in the games. They were for the most part composers themselves and, as in ancient Greece, they usually wrote their own poems. The most famous virtuosi, such as the singer Tigellius, in the service of Augustus, and Menecrates and Mesomedes, who lived in Nero's and Hadrian's courts, performed their own compositions.[3]

The musical virtuosi of the Roman Empire lived in an atmosphere much like that familiar to their present-day followers. They studied with renowned singing teachers, whose names are often mentioned on inscriptions. The ancient singers went through the same meticulous and tedious solfeggio exercises as their modern confreres and sang their scales up and down daily.[4] They were supposed to lead well-regulated, sane lives in order to develop and preserve their voices. Quintilian relates how they protected their throats by holding handkerchiefs before their mouths when speaking, and how they avoided the sun, fog, and wind. On the other hand, Martial reports that some of the singers overexerted themselves to such a degree that they suf-

fered ruptured blood vessels. This was due, no doubt, to the large propor
tions of the theaters and rooms, which demanded loud singing. Famous
singers undertook regular concert tours, and communities which were the
scenes of their triumphs erected statues in their honor and gave them honorary citizenship. The earnings of these artists were princely. Even the
avaricious Vespasian paid hundreds of thousands of sesterces to the artists
who participated at the inauguration of the reconstructed Marcellus theater.
Private music teaching was a no less lucrative undertaking, and caused an-
noyance and jealousy among the men of letters and the scientists. Nineteenth-
century adulation of rotund operatic heroes and thunderous pianists, and
twentieth-century admiration of virtuoso orchestra conductors are hardly
comparable to the often scandalous worship enjoyed by the artists of ancient
Rome. Rich and noble women risked their whole existence for the love of
an aulete or citharoedus. The wife of the Emperor Pertinax, for example,
carried on an ill-concealed love affair with a citharoedus. According to
Juvenal, these gentlemen sold their affections for sizable sums. The inevitable result of such adulation was a supercilious and temperamental virtuoso. As a typical example Horace mentions the famous singer Tigellius,
who refused the request of Augustus, although the emperor could have
forced him to perform had he so desired; yet if this favorite of the whole
empire felt like singing, no one could keep him from singing throughout
a whole supper.

The jealousy of musical artists was fed by the agonistic competitions. They
watched one another's performance, and professed the greatest reverence
and loyalty toward the judges and the public, but if they could not surpass
a competitor by sheer artistry, they resorted to bribery. Nero observed
elaborately the accepted and time-honored etiquette of the citharoedus, and
addressed the crowd with "gentlemen, kindly pay me your benevolent attention." At the end of his song, he spoke more courtesies honoring the
audience, and then waited with simulated anxiety to hear the verdict of the
populace. Even the most famous virtuosi took pains to assure applause by
subsidizing a claque, and from some remarks of Martial we may conclude
that professional clapping was a flourishing industry.

Such a vivid musical life must have had its repercussions in nonprofessional quarters, and, indeed, the number of dilettanti was considerable and
ever growing. It must be remarked that the original distrust of free Romans
for what they considered an effeminate pastime, or an occupation for slaves,
at first stood in the way of the practice of music among men of standing;
but the increasing influence of Greek culture and customs overcame this
early repugnance, and by the time of the Gracchi there were numerous
music and dance schools in Rome where patrician families sent their chil-

dren for instruction. Cicero was not ashamed to state that a very distinguished friend of his, Numerius Furius, indulged in the art of singing.[5]

In the earlier years of their history the Romans, unlike the Greeks at a similar period in their development, were not interested in musical theory and science; but by the time of Marcus Terentius Varro (116 B. C.–27? B. C.) the science of music figured among the elements of education. Varro's book *De Musica* was the seventh volume of his *Disciplinarum libri IX,* which we know only from citations by Censorinus, Martianus Capella, Boethius, Cassiodorus, and Isidore of Seville. It was the chief source for other theoreticians for centuries to come. By imperial times the theoretical study of music had become fairly common. Suetonius and Seneca repeatedly mention the excellent musical training of Nero and Britannicus. In fact, another great historian, Tacitus, insists that the shameful murder of Britannicus was hastened more because the boy's excellent musical abilities annoyed Nero than for any other reason. Marcus Aurelius especially mentions his master's proficiency in geometry and music, thus calling attention to the association of these subjects, which remained a standard scientific discipline throughout the Middle Ages and the Renaissance.

The practice of music was not limited to men. Its vogue among women is seen in the writings of Lucian, who lavishes praise on the singing and cithara playing both of women of the aristocracy and of courtesans. Amateur musicians flourished during the empire, and the erstwhile opposition gave way to such universal acceptance of music as a social asset that we see a number of the emperors devoted to it. Hadrian, Caracalla, Antoninus Pius, Heliogabalus, Alexander Severus were experienced singers and players on the cithara, the tuba, and the water organ. In Nero's zeal for musical recognition we may see another phase of social development, for the emperor did not insist on his ability as a royal dilettante: he wanted to be counted among the real artists, the professionals. In his dying hour, according to the legend, the foremost thought in his mind was *qualis artifex pereo!* (What an artist is lost in me!) [6]

In the domain of the theater we re-encounter the Greek drama, but the Latin version differed from its Hellenic ancestor in many particulars. The chorus was missing entirely; the Romans had only spoken "solo" parts or songs, accompanied by the tibia, the Latin equivalent of the Greek aulos. Enough of the Greek spirit was left in this changed drama, however, to influence the music to a certain degree. The same is true with regard to the comedy. The dramatic poets did not compose music as had their Greek precursors, but entrusted professional musicians with the task. The tragedy soon disappeared from the Roman stage and disintegrated into its elements: the individual "bravura" scenes were taken separately and performed in "concert" form. Such dramatic scenes were the Emperor Nero's favorite pieces. The most popular form of music in imperial Rome, the *pantomimus,* was, as we have seen, of a low order, as the attention was centered around the choreography—usually liberally filled with fights or other athletic spectacles—and the music was mere patchwork.

Toward the end of antiquity, when new religions and philosophies made it increasingly difficult for people to orient themselves, when, weary of searching for enlightenment, they longed for redemption and revelation, the old musical aesthetics of Greece came into their own once more. But this musical science lacked driving power and lost itself in fruitless speculation. While attempting to continue the acoustic-mathematical researches of their predecessors, the Neo-Pythagoreans, by insisting on the mystical-occult significance of numbers and tones, really ended in the old field of magic. But even in this period of decline they and the Jewish-Alexandrian and Neoplatonic philosophers produced a handful of brilliant authors on musical aesthetics, among whom should be especially mentioned Plotinus, the last great philosopher of antiquity. Plotinus built, from Platonic and Aristotelian elements, a doctrine of the beautiful; but this doctrine was interwoven with ethical, metaphysical, and theological ideas which prevented its conversion into actual artistic practice. The Neoplatonists continued this philosophic current, and with them it found its way into the aesthetics of the Middle Ages. But once the creative power vanished from music, aesthetics also faded away, and the age-old primitive conception of musical magic regained its popularity. The doctrine of ethos did not vanish, however, but, going through various metamorphoses, continued to live into the Christian era.

The few extant fragments of ancient classical music show convincingly how difficult it is for us to penetrate into the inner world of antique music. Its expressive means and power seem to speak an entirely unfamiliar language. The Middle Ages and subsequent centuries were not acquainted with these fragments, which were deciphered only later; but the exalted descriptions of their philosophers aroused in men of later periods a boundless and at times almost religious admiration for the music of classical antiquity, for the wonderful theoretical edifice of Greek musical science, the high social and ethical role played by music. And this admiration has borne fruit in periods of musical reform. The ideas of Richard Wagner were just as much influenced by the unattainable ideal of Greek music as were the reformatory activities of the Camerata in Florence or as have been the neoclassical oratorios of Stravinsky today.

Chapter 4

THE PATRISTIC PERIOD

➤➤ ⫷⫷

"Middle Ages" *versus* "Renaissance"

THE Middle Ages fascinate the modern man not only because of their civilization, which to many people seems as distant and strange as the civilization of India or China, nor because these centuries form one of the periods which lead to our present era. We are fascinated because we are still bound with invisible ties to the times of St. Augustine, Boethius, Abélard, St. Thomas Aquinas, Wolfram, St. Francis, Dante, and the multitude of nameless authors and artists. Most of our social and economic institutions go back to medieval times; feudalism has lived until our own day; our bourgeoisie developed from the ranks of the medieval city burghers; even the proletariat, no new product of modern industrialism, manifested its burning problems during the Middle Ages.

The understanding of the nature of the Middle Ages—a world which seems to us an independent and original link between antiquity and modern times—requires a penetrating study of the driving forces and spiritual tendencies which created its new conception of life and new forms of art. Only such a study will reveal to us the tragic greatness of the decline of the antique world and the meaning and importance of the civilization of the Occident, which, with the triumph of Christianity over the spiritual life of mankind, led to such a wonderful rise of arts and letters. The internal destruction of the mighty and scintillating Roman Empire was awe-inspiring. The monumental building of Roman world power, outwardly magnificent and politically strong, collapsed upon itself owing to the lack of internal greatness and spiritual substance.

Redemption came from the East, and a new conception and ideal of life appeared. This supplemented the old ideal, which had placed an abstract, religious-transcendental philosophy of life above the material enjoyment of sheer existence. But the clinging of Occidental humanity to the cultural ideals of antiquity, not only at the beginning of the Christian era but throughout the Middle Ages, influenced definitely the spiritual and intellectual make-up of Europeans. And if we wish to attribute a special character to this period, which even recently has been most inappropriately called "The Dark Ages," it should be based upon the era's relationship to antiquity.

Following the conquering wars of Alexander the Great, Hellenism established a spiritual tie among the nations of the antique world. The Jewry of Jerusalem, especially later in the Diaspora, was strongly attracted by Hellenistic ideas and entered upon a new phase of intellectual development. The spiritual and intellectual intercourse between the Hebrew and the Hellenic civilizations, which resulted, among other things, in the translation of the Old Testament by Hellenistic Jews into Alexandrian Greek (Septuagint), constituted the great prelude to the establishment of the Christian Church. The final stage of this merger of civilizations was reached with the appearance of Paul at the Apostolic Council in the year 49. The "pagan Christians" stood henceforth on an equal footing with the "Hebrew Christians." Beginning with this event and continuing through the period of the Apologists of the second century, the Catholic Gnosticism of Clement of Alexandria, and the exegetical writings of Origen, there is an uninterrupted, ever-deepening Hellenistic influence which penetrates Christian theological speculations and leads to a union of Christianity and Hellenism.

In some of their phases, such as the times of the crusades, of the Catharists, of the Councils of Constance, Basel, and Ferrara, the Middle Ages were possessed of a spiritual and intellectual agitation which stood without parallel until our post-World War era after 1918. The period was subjected to political, economic, scientific, and artistic changes of considerable proportions, but the medieval mind remained convinced that the welfare of humanity is based not on fundamentally new things nor on steady progress, but on the release and development of the powers and values preserved in its inheritance from antiquity. The "true," the "good," and the "beautiful" did not have to be invented and shaped into form again and again, because the "ancients" had created these elements once for all; the problem was to acquire the knowledge of these elements and to practice and propagate them. This conservative conception, which did not prevent people from unwittingly striking out on unbeaten paths, explains many a baffling phenomenon which has puzzled historians.

Enthusiasm for the cultural wealth of antiquity did not have to be awakened by the Renaissance, for the Renaissance could not surpass the Middle Ages in admiration for the ancient world. However, while the Middle Ages accepted this wealth as a self-evident mandate and in its unconcerned continuation and development of that inheritance deviated from the spirit and forms of antiquity and grew beyond it, the Renaissance, in a reflective mood, deliberately reached back to antiquity. Both epochs acknowledged the completeness and perfection of ancient civilization, but the Renaissance realized that this ideal had in reality been abandoned. This realization caused a new and critical orientation in two directions, the first concerned with the present, and examining the extent and nature of the abandonment of classical ideals, the second concerned with antiquity itself, as Renaissance thinkers tried to determine what should be considered as pertaining essentially to antiquity.

While it is not our purpose here to trace the philosophical background of the movement of the Renaissance, it seems advisable to insist on the common fundamental idea which underlies both historical periods. The Renaissance must not and cannot be separated from the Middle Ages as sharply as nineteenth-century historical writers were wont to separate it, either at its beginning or even at its height.

The Problem of Christian Church Music

So often as I call to mind the tears I shed at the hearing of Thy church songs, in the beginning of my recovered faith, yea, and at this very time, whenas I am moved not with the singing, but with the thing sung (when namely they are set off with a clear voice and suitable modulation), I then acknowledge the great good use of this institution. Thus float I between peril and pleasure, and an approved profitable custom: inclined the more (though herein I pronounce no irrevocable opinion) to allow of the old usage of singing in the Church; that so by the delight taken in at the ears, the weaker minds be roused up into some feeling of devotion. And yet again, so oft as it befalls me to be moved with the voice rather than with the ditty, I confess myself to have grievously offended: at which time I wish rather not to have heard the music.[1]

THESE words of an illustrious Father of the Church, well versed in the philosophical ideas of antiquity, afford the best illustration of the ethical and moral problems faced by the new faith. But more than that, they represent the very problem of church music, which, in the early Middle Ages, stood out in sharp contrast to ancient ideologies, but which reappeared repeatedly during the many centuries that followed.[2]

The beginnings of Christianity take us to Palestinian territories where the native Aramaean civilization of the open country mixed with the Hellenism of the cities, and where Roman garrisons and colonial governmental officers introduced the Latin language. At its inception, Christianity was not well disposed toward arts and letters because it saw in them the continuation of pagan civilization. We must remember that the Greek philosophers professed great admiration for music, not for music's own sake or for its beauty, but on account of its ethical and pedagogical value; therefore we cannot expect the young Christian Church to have started with a purely artistic conception. If the ancient classical philosophy of life, with its purely earthly aims, recognized the sensual power of music and tried to justify it by utilizing its ethical properties, what shall we expect of Christendom, which considers life merely a preliminary stage to a heavenly abode? It could accept and admit art only if it helped man toward his ultimate destiny.

But music was living all around the organizers of the Church. They had to take cognizance of it, and the more they recognized the influence of music on man's soul, the more evident became the dualism expressed in these lines quoted from St. Augustine. On the one hand, this powerful influence must be harnessed and utilized for worthy purposes; on the other hand, its sensual, carnal influence must be combated. The Greeks of the classical period considered it the state's duty to watch over the destinies of music, to mold its nature so as to avoid harmful influences; now it was the Church which assumed this task. The consequences of this change will be important; music will not have much value as an art for its own sake, its only raison d'être will be as a servant of the Church. It will contribute to the edification of the faithful, it will help to fortify their faith, to fire their zeal. But to attain this aim the melodies must yield first place to the words.

The task of the young Church was made more difficult by the hostile atmosphere in which it lived, an atmosphere opposed to Christian conceptions of the purpose of life and the vocation of man, and one in which music had sunk to the lowest regions of lascivious amusement. Indeed, it is surprising that music found entrance into the severe young Church at all. But the Holy Scriptures spoke of it as saintly, and in this point both the Old and the New Testaments agree. Divining the great events which will descend upon her, Mary praises God in jubilant songs even before the birth of the Lord. His nativity is heralded by angelic song to men of good will. Music sounds at the end of Christ's earthly course of life, as at the Last Supper the Lord intones a praise-song with His disciples before going out to the Mount of Olives (Matthew 26, 30). Also the apostles remind the faithful to sing Psalms when they rejoice (James 5, 13) and to praise the Lord with music (St. Paul to the Colossians and to the Ephesians).

Thus the admission of music to Christian worship was assured in principle, but the extent of its use and its character and nature gave rise to grave problems. We read that even in the early fifth century Bishop Chrysostom of Constantinople exhorted his congregation, telling them that while very few of them knew a Psalm or a section of the Holy Books by heart, they were perfectly familiar with all the lascivious songs and "hits" of the times. Ammianus Marcellinus, a keen and reliable observer of social trends, relates how Christian and pagan society of the fourth century shunned serious education, indulging in an idleness in which singing and cithara playing dominated; singers displaced philosophers, and music supplanted rhetoric; libraries were closed, but, says the historian with indignation, the musical-instrument industry flourished.[3]

It is regrettable indeed that we do not have a more abundant supply of documents to reconstruct the musical life of postclassical times. We possess no music from this period, but we are fairly familiar with the role of music and with the struggle for and against it. The real musical scholars do not give us much information; first, because the earliest Church was not interested in musical theory and science; second, because the musical science of the whole first millennium of the Christian era had no organic connection with actual musical practice. The protagonists of church life, however, the Church Fathers, were very much concerned with music. That they made so many utterances about music should convince us of the problematic character of music in the Church of the time. Even those among them who were lovers of music, and others, like Ambrose and Basil, who not only loved it but knew a great deal about music and musical theory, remain always men of the Church when discussing it. They are concerned only with the good of the Church and mention nonreligious music only when they exhort their flocks. Taking into consideration the great authority of these men, we must conclude that what they required or forbade must have had the force of a canon. Music could be considered by the Church only if it served the purposes of the Church, and therefore the subject and aim of Christian cult music was and remained the *gloria Dei* and the *aedificatio hominum,* the glorification of God and the edification of man. From the very beginning the liturgy created an *ars sacra* which became an organic part of its solemn ritual.

Thus it happens that in spite of the great number of medieval musical tracts we do not have descriptions of secular music until well into the late Middle Ages. This was evidently due to the fact that, unlike literature, which made possible the expression of "dangerous" tenets or ideas in a learned style or in a foreign language not accessible to the average person, music had only one language, understood by all. The only alternative was complete ignorance. Medieval musical writers act as if they were not aware of the existence of music outside the Church. Music suffered, no doubt, by this attitude; on the other hand, it had the immense advantage of being admitted to the official worship and celebrations of the Church, a role denied to the other arts. This one-sidedness seems much more acute when viewed from the perspective of our day; but as a most intimate art, a language coming from the very bottom of the soul, music was always nearest to religion and could very well develop and expand within the walls of the Church. The Middle Ages saw the ever-increasing triumph of the ideals of the Church, saw a unified outlook on life; and the more this intense Christian-Church spirit penetrated everyday life, the less are we conscious of a specific church style in music. Finally we reach a stage where there is no longer any difference between sacred and secular art.

The Origins and Elements of Christian Ritual Music

FOLLOWING the theories of nineteenth-century archaeologists and historians, musical scholars of the romantic era attempted to trace Christian music to Rome as an organic continuation of Roman art. Such theories, as represented by Gevaert [4] and other authors, are now definitely refuted in the light of recent research in the history and civilization of the Near East, and we must start out with a conception based not on conjecture but on actual historical evidence. The cardinal point of this conception is that the first important era of Christian music originated in the period which began with the cessation of the persecution of Christians and ended with the reign of Pope Gregory the Great. Politically and artistically this period was dominated by the Eastern half of the Roman Empire, and, indeed, the earliest products of Christian music came from the same territory which formulated the earliest Christian theologies, the Syrian-Egyptian circle of civilization. The Christian Church began its existence in the shadow of the synagogue; Christianity was, in the eyes of the Gentiles, a Jewish sect. Why should we then search for the origin of this music among the proud Roman patricians, reared and nourished on ancient classical doctrines? The older theories concerning the origin of Christian music were due to the fact that the oldest preserved readable records of this music date from the Carolingian period, that is, from a time posterior to the main organization of Gregorian music. Investigation of the preceding period has had to rely on circumstantial evidence, gained from literary and liturgical sources, and stylistic analysis. If we add to these difficulties the fact that the voluminous melodic treasure of early Christian music survived until the end of the first millennium mostly through oral tradition, which precludes exact preservation, we can imagine the difficult situation faced by the scholar who attempts to penetrate this labyrinth. Admiring the remarkable, compact integrity of Catholic liturgy and the profundity and beauty of the organization of its music throughout the church year, one is tempted to consider it the creation of an artist of immense genius. Scientific research has proved, however, that this magnificent structure was erected by countless hands. More than that, it has proved that while this edifice seems to express the essence of Catholicism, which it represents uniformly all over the world, its stones and bricks were brought together from far-flung corners of this same world.

Rites and music influenced each other to such an extent, in the liturgy of Christian antiquity, that a history of music cannot be written separately from a history of religion. The oldest part of Christian church music is the psalmody, left as a legacy to Christianity by the Hebrew world after the collapse of its political and religious power. Psalm singing was practiced by all strata of society, clergy, people, and children. St. Ambrose profusely praises

Psalm singing. Although recalling the dictum of the apostles that women should remain silent in the congregation, he amends it by saying that "they too sing their Psalms well, as Psalms are sweet for every age, and are becoming to each sex . . . they create a great bond of unity when the whole people raise their voices in one choir." Almost all the Church Fathers speak of Psalm singing with the same enthusiasm, but while the participation of the congregation in Psalm singing was further encouraged, the women's prerogatives were soon revoked. The universal popularity of Psalm singing caused the church authorities to urge the clergy to learn the Psalms by heart. Pachomius, author of the first monastic rules and regulations, required this of his monks, and the second Council of Nicaea decreed that such an ability was indispensable for the incumbent of a bishopric. The widespread use of Psalms was due not only to the surviving Jewish traditions and their wonderful poetic content, which reflected every aspect of human hopes and desires, but to the fact that by association with melodies they could be remembered and sung even by people whose mental capacity did not rise to the high poetic conceptions of King David.

Early Christian worship centered around the Psalms, but there was another variety of simple song, also taken from the lyrical parts of the Old and New Testaments, called *cantica* or canticles. These simple songs did not aspire to artistic or aesthetic recognition; they were of a strictly devotional character. There was also an antiphonal form of song, the so-called *cantus responsorius,* which represents a more advanced stage of church music.

The rite of the Lord's Supper was originally held in the evening and was linked with an agape or love feast, a common meal interspersed with prayers and songs. This represents the beginnings of Christian hymnody. The agape became distinct from the Lord's Supper as early as the second century; but the Lord's Supper was also held in connection with the "watches" or "vigils" (*vigilae*), especially in connection with the vigil on Easter Eve. People gathered together for the services and then waited until dawn for the liturgy.[5] Later it was generally held in the morning in conformity with the synagogical service of the Sabbath morning. This had been the custom before the ritual division from the synagogue. After these community services were Christianized, the vigils occupied, for a time, a position of equal importance with the Eucharist.

The vigils are the oldest parts of the prayers which make up the canonical hours. During their persecution it was difficult for the Christians to gather in daylight and their nightly vigils resulted in these prayers. Pliny the Younger mentioned, in his famous letter on the Christians, written to the Emperor Trajan, that "on certain days they get together before sunrise and sing songs to Christ as if he were God." At first the vigil was limited to Sundays; that is, the Saturday meetings were prolonged until daybreak, when the Eucharist took place. Soon Sunday became associated with the Eucharist and displaced the Sabbath, that is, Saturday, as weekly holy day. Later again the meetings started at dusk, when the lamps were lighted, from which circumstance this prayer hour took the name *hora incensi*. This is, in reality, the oldest form of the vespers. In the Syrian churches there was a third vigil, a morning office, later called *laudes*. Thus the ground stock of the hourly offices consisted of vespers, nocturns (later called matins), and lauds.

Vigils were held even on days when the Eucharist was not celebrated, and they constituted the starting point in the formation of an extensive system of daily hours of divine office (*Officium divinum, Cursus, Horae canonicae*). How early these offices were established we gather from Tertullian, who speaks of vigils, lauds, and vespers as being practiced in the Carthaginian Church around 200. Clement of Alexandria mentions similar practices in his city.

Further development of the offices was carried out by the ascetic communities which sprang up in the Orient in the fourth century. The monks kept vigils every night and added to the three existing vigils (evening, midnight, and morning) others at the third, sixth, and ninth hours. The Egyptian monastic communities, started by Pachomius shortly after 300, instituted daily vigils at an early period. The service of worship in Jerusalem consisted, according to the description of the Aquitanian pilgrim Etheria (385), of vigils, lauds, tierce, sext, nones, and vespers; the offices consisted of Psalms, antiphons, hymns, lections, responds, and collects. The church year, although still in a formative state, seems to have been already observed. At the same period the first hour, the prime, appeared in Bethlehem, followed by the *completorium*, or compline, in Chalcedon. Thus the canonical hours were organized and practiced within a remarkably short period.

The formation of the *officium* took place almost exclusively in the Orient, but on account of the expansion of the monastic communities in the West, modeled as they were on Eastern examples, the offices were almost identical in all church provinces as early as about 400. Cassian's monastic manuals furnish the documentary proofs. While preserving old common elements, the various liturgy types continued to develop the offices according to their own rites.

The vigils were soon recognized and accepted by the Church and their private character changed into an official rite toward the very end of the fourth century. The Church Fathers were enthusiastic about these nightly congregations. St. Basil used to go around and visit several churches on one night to hear the faithful sing Psalms, and Gregory Nazianzen departed from Constantinople with regret at leaving behind the Psalm singing of the congregation.[6]

The oldest order of the vigils, the offices, is contained in the Rule of St. Benedict; and the Benedictines, who had established communities in Rome in the sixth century, became the acknowledged experts in these matters, a standing which they retained throughout the Middle Ages.

Beginning with the late second century, the Lord's Supper assumes the character of sacrificial worship and, because of the central position of the thanksgiving prayer, is called the Eucharist. By the time of St. Ambrose it is called *Missa*. The vigil becomes now a preparatory service, the so-called "catechumenical Mass." A catechumen was a person who was receiving rudimentary instruction in the doctrines of Christianity, preliminary to admission among the faithful. The catechumenical Mass preceded the Eucharist proper, which was reserved for the faithful. Justin, the widely traveled Christian philosopher (c. 150), described the order of this early Mass: readings from the Old and New Testaments were followed by a sermon by the "leader," offering of bread and wine, prayer of the faithful, the "kiss of peace," eucharistic (thanksgiving) prayer, and, last of all, communion.[7] Justin's description gives us the standard setting of Christian liturgy in the second century. A somewhat later type of the liturgy of the Mass is to be found in the *Apostolic Constitutions,* VIII, 5-15. These books probably originated in the fourth century.

Beginning with the third century of our era, the Christians, who in the first two centuries had been compelled to take refuge in secret, subterranean places, were able to congregate for worship in public places. The chroniclers report the erection of churches of considerable dimensions. This was made possible by the conversion of wealthy people. When Marcion, the future leader of a heretical sect, was received into the Church, he presented the community with two hundred thousand sesterces. Toward the end of the third century, Porphyry, the Greek Neoplatonic philosopher, mentions Christian churches "which rival in size the temples of the heathen." By the time of the pontificate of Melchiades (311-314), Rome could already count some forty Christian basilicas. It is natural that in these edifices the ritual was amplified, and in it music played an increasingly important role.

After the Constantinian edict which gave Christendom its liberty and raised the new faith to the position of "licensed religion," the Christian Church entered upon a public life. The development of its liturgy was greatly promoted, especially in the direction of the establishment of the church year. Monastic communities, organized under rules set up by the various orders, exerted a penetrating influence on the spiritual, economic, and musical life of the Church. Among the Syrian monasteries there arose a new musical practice, antiphonal singing, probably modeled on ancient Hebrew temple rites. The verses were sung responsively before and after the Psalms and other liturgical songs. The monks and those of their disciples who rose to bishoprics carried antiphonal psalmody into the Church, where it found wide dissemination among the secular clergy. The main propagators of this form were two Antiochian monks, Flavian and Diodorus (c. 350), who were active in Syria; Basilius, active in Nicaea and Palestine; and St. John Chrysostom, active in Byzantium.

St. Ambrose introduced antiphonal singing to the Occident. From Milan (owing to the favorable geographical position of the city and the high reputation of its bishop) it spread rapidly into other domains of the Latin Church. The use of responsorial singing had already become general during the life of Ambrose, as can be ascertained from the writings of his friend and secretary, Paulinus. Rome followed suit, and antiphonal singing was probably introduced officially into the Roman liturgy by act of the Roman Council of 382, which was presided over by Pope Damasus. We come to this conclusion because a number of Greek and Syrian bishops—naturally familiar with this aspect of church music—were present; and because St. Jerome, liturgical adviser to Pope Damasus, having spent many years in the Orient, was well acquainted with Oriental liturgical practices. At any rate, a generation later Pope Celestine I incorporated this practice into the Roman Mass.

Pope Damasus is responsible for the introduction of another typical Oriental practice of singing, the ornate exultations which are exemplified in the alleluia or hallelujah (praise ye the Lord). This highly important form of ornate song was originally connected with the Psalms, and the so-called alleluiatic Psalms are still so marked in modern editions of the Bible. According to St. Jerome, the alleluia was widely practiced in Bethlehem in the fourth century. It was the people's *refrain* to the psalmody sung by the precentor. Alleluia singing was very popular in the Oriental churches, and the Greeks had special books containing alleluia melodies. Priests in the Egyptian Coptic churches still sing them in the ancient manner. The duration of these highly ornamented songs often exceeds a quarter of an hour.

The melismatic exultation, which occurred on the last syllable, "a," of the alleluia, was called the jubilus (from *jubilatio*). It led, as we shall see in the following chapter, to important developments in the history of Gregorian music. Suffice it to say here, that while melismatic singing was a matter of course to the Orientals, whose writers do not indulge in explanations concerning its nature, the Western Church Fathers tried repeatedly to explain and justify the use of the jubilus. St. Augustine says that the jubilus is a praise of the Lord: it expresses things which cannot be expressed by words or letters.

The main use of the alleluia was, of course, in the liturgy, but it became exceedingly popular among the people as an exclamation of Christian joy. Mariners shouted it from ship to ship, and Christian soldiers used it as a war cry. Bede relates how St. Germanus led the Britons to war in Wales, where they defeated an Irish and Pictish marauding party. As it was Easter, the war cry was alleluia and the battle became known as the "Alleluia Victory."

If we wish to examine the origins of the other large body of early church music, the hymns, we must leave the domain of the Psalms. These hymns were songs of praise, devotion, and thanksgiving. They reflect the favorite theme of Stoic-Platonic philosophy, which flourished in the time of the early Church—namely, the beauty of the cosmos. For this reason we are not surprised to find their origin in the Alexandrian catechetical schools. These schools, headed by Clement of Alexandria (d. c. 215), were engaged in the teaching of the rudimentary doctrines of Christianity, and considered it their duty to bring about an assimilation between Hellenistic and Christian culture and civilization. Our main document relative to this tendency is the oft-mentioned Oxyrhynchus hymn,[8] a musical composition of great nobility. It was written at the close of the third century, and is evidently modeled on Hellenistic odes from the time of Hadrian.[9] There are two more examples of this sort of hymnody in the *Apostolic Constitutions*, but only the texts have been preserved. The secular origins were manifest for a considerable time, and in their presentation by certain heretical sects the hymns approached the folk song. From the exhortations of various church writers it appears that before the regulation of the order of the vigils, hymn singing was accompanied by hand clapping and dance movements. Such heterodox, popular, and distinctly secular hymnody invited reforms, and indeed, about the middle of the third century the Church reacted by initiating a movement called Biblicism. This movement retained the Biblical hymns and the few others already sanctioned by the liturgy, but banished everything else. Biblicism, which maintained itself for a time, at last caused its own downfall by its exclusiveness and its ignorance of popular psychology; but it had lived long enough to cripple and almost to annihilate the creative spirit of an artistic period of the greatest importance. Heterodox, folk-songlike hymnody managed to survive, however; it again became popular, and soon exerted its influence on the hymns of the Church. It found great favor with the heretics, especially with Arius. To stem this abuse, the Laodicean Council (380–381) renewed the Biblicistic prohibitions in its fifty-ninth canon. Much literature, valuable despite the term *psalmi idiotici* applied to it by the Council, must have been lost in this fluctuating warfare. We shall see that this rigid attitude was later changed and that, after mitigating the abuses, extra-Biblical hymnody flourished in the Middle Ages.

The growth of these hymns started in the fourth century. They began to shed the last vestiges of antique metric poetry, and with the activity of the literary school which flourished in Edessa under the leadership of St. Ephrem, rhythmical hymnody assumed the upper hand. The prevailing character of this poetry was not Hellenistic, but Jewish-apocalyptic. It was also influenced by Mazdaism, that religion of the ancient Persians which was so popular in the first Christian centuries. St. Gregory Nazianzen carried this tendency into Greek poetry, while St. Augustine, Bishop of Hippo, and Hilary of Poitiers made the Latin Church acquainted with it.

Hilary of Poitiers (d. 366) became familiar with Syrian hymnody while in exile in the Orient. Upon his return he translated several Oriental hymns into Latin and added to them some from his own pen. Isidore of Seville names him explicitly as the first Latin poet of hymns. To his disgust, Hilary could not arouse his compatriots to a love of these new hymns. He made no secret of his opinion of the musico-poetic talents of the Gauls, whom he called *in hymnorum carmine indociles,* and so the task of acclimatizing hymnody in the West fell to St. Ambrose.

The first hymns were sung when St. Ambrose, followed by his faithful, fled from the Arians.

At this time was it here first instituted after the manner of the Eastern Churches, that hymns and Psalms should be sung, lest the people should wax faint through the tediousness of sorrow: which custom being retained from that day to this, is still imitated by divers, yea, almost by all Thy congregations throughout other parts of the world.[10]

St. Augustine describes the overpowering impression created by these hymns:

How abundantly did I weep to hear those hymns and canticles of Thine, being touched to the very quick by the voices of Thy sweet church songs! Those voices flowed into mine ears, and Thy truth pleasingly distilled into my heart, which caused the affections of my devotion to overflow, and my tears to run over, and happy did I find myself therein.[11]

The Ambrosian hymns are more finished works of art than Hilary's creations. They represent Christian ideas shaped into magnificent antique classical forms. All his hymns are composed of eight strophes, each of four lines in iambic dimeters; since they were widely imitated, this formula came to be known as the Ambrosian hymn. Were the melodies composed by Ambrose? It is impossible to answer in the affirmative, but it is probable that they originated in his time. While the authorship of many of these hymns is disputed, there are at least four whose authenticity is attested by St. Augustine: *Aeterne Rerum Conditor, Deus Creator Omnium, Jam Surgit Hora Tertia, Veni Redemptor Gentium.* The artistic value and vitality of these hymns is best illustrated by the fact that after so many centuries they have retained their original freshness and are still sung and enjoyed by everyone. Luther used the last-named for his sturdy song "Now Come, the Heathens' Saviour."

Among hymn poets who followed in the wake of Ambrose the most illustrious were Paulinus, Bishop of Nola, and especially the Spanish-Latin poet Prudentius (d. after 405), who was also completely under the influence of classical poetry. With him Latin hymnody of the first Christian centuries comes to a close.

Our knowledge of these hymns is restricted to their texts, but all indications point to the fact that the oft-praised pleasing melodies to which they were sung must have had the character of folk songs; the evenly built strophes indicate this plainly. As we have remarked before, whether the melodies were composed by the poets themselves cannot be ascertained, but some of the melodies associated with these hymns are of exceedingly great age and may be contemporary with the poetry.

Ambrose's hymns were intended for public worship. They were composed to be sung by the entire congregation, and this is the reason for their simplicity. The hymns of Prudentius were much more brilliant, but they were intended for private edification, although the Church later adopted some of them. In general the hymns were considered superior to the Psalms. While the Psalms had many uses, the hymns were reserved for purely divine purposes. *Hymnus specialiter Deo dicitur,* says St. Ambrose, and St. John Chrysostom maintained that there is nothing human about them: they are essentially divine. This is the more surprising since, as we have seen, popular elements predominated in a number of these songs.

The hymns became popular in other countries, although several synods were still opposed to them and preferred Biblical texts. Rome, in the ninth century, was the last to accept and introduce them into the liturgy. Iberia and Gallia, on the other hand, took up hymn composition with enthusiasm.

Another important element of liturgical song owes its name to a circumstance of the early method of delivery of the liturgy. When delivering his songs, the psalmist stood in an elevated place, on the steps of the ambo, a large pulpit or reading desk. The singing from the ambo, or more precisely from the steps (*gradus*) leading to the altar, was considered so characteristic (the lector read his parts standing at the foot of the altar) that these "step-songs" were soon called graduals, and became the most important body of church music.

When at the end of the third century the Romans abandoned the Greek liturgical language in favor of their own Latin, the Occident started on a historical path which led to the establishment of an independent Western liturgy. Beginning with this time, the Mass and the offices continued their development increasingly independent of each other, both in the East and in the West. The recognition of the Christian Church by Constantine (313) gave new impetus to this development, and the numerous variants and species which had sprung up, especially in the Orient, caused a certain reaction toward simplification. Attacks and abuses by the heretics necessitated a dogmatic fixation of the texts. We cannot speak, in these early centuries, of organized, uniform ritual; there were only local liturgies built on a common foundation. Gradually regions were grouped together in provinces, and then in nations, until finally the authority of the Church was sufficiently centralized in the individual countries to co-ordinate the liturgy of all churches of the same language.

In the countries around the Mediterranean, from Egypt through Asia Minor up to Byzantium, there was a fairly homogeneous liturgical practice, which, in the beginning, used the Greek language for ritual purposes. Within this circle there were several subspecies of liturgies such as the Western-Syriac, with its important center in Jerusalem; the Egyptian, with its center in Alexandria; the Byzantine, with Constantinople as its main center. The East-Syriac liturgy, popular in the extensive outlying territories, retained the Syriac language. In the Latin West there was the same grouping of subspecies. The first large territory was the Roman, but Roman liturgy was also employed in North Africa, with Carthage as its center. Large parts of lower Italy (Magna Graecia), which, being early colonized by the Greeks, belonged to the Hellenic circle of tradition and civilization, retained the Greek liturgy in its original form as it was taken from Jerusalem. Out of regard for the Italo-Greeks even Rome made some use of the Greek liturgy, but it played, naturally, an insignificant part in the Roman world.

The next large group was the Gallican, with four subdivisions: the Gallic proper in Gaul; the Hispano-Gallican or Mozarabic in Spain; the Milanese or Ambrosian in the province of Milan, which is still in use but largely assimilated with the Roman; and finally, the Celtic, used in Great Britain and Ireland, and perhaps in Brittany, until supplanted by the Roman in the seventh century. The Mozarabs (would-be Arabs) were the Christians of Moslem Spain; and the term "Mozarabic" means only the liturgy used by them, and not that it contained Arabic elements. The Mozarabic rite was the national liturgy of Spain until superseded by the Roman rite in the twelfth century. It is now observed on a few days in the year in the Cathedral of Toledo and in a chapel in Salamanca.

The number of liturgies in the beginning of the Christian era was, as we have seen, considerable, but as Christianity became a general and public religion the tendency to stabilize the liturgy became ever stronger. Hence there is today a comparatively small number of liturgies. One should not overlook the fact that while the power of the Bishop of Rome was limited in these centuries, the history of the Eternal City and the remembrance of the foundation of the Church by St. Peter lent him a prestige which foreign bishops could not disregard.

The Organization of the Service of Worship
Secular Music—Ecclesiastical Opposition

EARLY church music had an improvisatory character. The legendary origin of the *Te Deum,* said to have been composed in the solemn ecstasies which overwhelmed St. Augustine and St. Ambrose on the occasion of St. Augustine's baptism, is another indication of the ecstatic-improvisatory character of this music.[12] The Christian writers repeatedly mention the prevalence of ecstasy; Tertullian knows of songs which were the products of such a mental state and holds up these improvisations as characteristic of Christian prayer and music.

The leaders of worship were recruited at first from the ranks of educated laymen. They did not occupy an official position in the Church and were not ordained; they were respected people whose position would be called an honorary one today. Their erstwhile status may be explained by the fact that with the office of the cantor the Christian Church took over an old synagogal institution, and also in many cases probably employed musicians who had received their education in Jewish musical practice and who introduced their art into the new Christian liturgy. Idelsohn, in his various publications of the songs of Oriental Jews, has given us examples of the astounding virtuosity of these Jewish cantors. Beginning about 150 in the West and some seventy-five years later in the East, the leader's function was raised to an office with the title of lector or anagnost. The office did not carry with it, at first, a clerical status, but a century later its holder took the first of the minor orders. Owing to the number of lessons that had to be read, there were several lectors attached to a church, and the larger churches often had a considerable staff. Under the Emperor Justinian the choir of the Cathedral of Constantinople numbered one hundred and eleven lectors and twenty-five cantors.[13] It is significant that the earliest architectural arrangements for the accommodation of a choir date from this period. The Roman Basilica S. Paolo Fuori le Mura, which was built in the early fifth century, had a large space around the altar surrounded by choir rails for the singers, an arrangement which is still popular in Italy. When the monastic orders secured a dominating position in the Church in the early Middle Ages, they exalted the importance of the ritual and insisted on increased space for choir and clergy. The offices of lector and cantor were, in the first centuries, strictly separated, but as the reading became more and more a sort of chanting, this difference vanished.

Since the demand for ritualistic leaders must have been considerable, there arose, undoubtedly under the influence of the Jewish synagogical schools, a *schola lectorum* with a *primicerius* as its head. This school enrolled men as well as boys. While the lector was vested with ecclesiastical honors, the cantor or *psalmista* seems to have remained a layman, although he is sometimes mentioned among the *minores ordines*. Roman inscriptions from the second half of the fourth century often displayed laudatory remarks concerning the musical ability of the psalmists. Boy lectors and singers were very popular in the post-Constantinian period, both in the East and in the West. To become good psalmists they lived in the *schola* and studied under the supervision of ecclesiastic tutors. Their activity was not restricted to study; on the contrary, they took an active part in the services. Most of the church dignitaries passed through these lector schools, which represented the first step in clerical education. The age of the boys was sometimes astonishingly tender for such a responsible function as that of lector; some of them were known to have sung the Psalms at the age of five and six. The second Council of Toledo (531) and the second Council of Orange (529) decreed important rules concerning the boy lectors. The Council of Orange was presided over by St. Cesarius of Arles, who was most anxious to improve the spirit of his only recently converted diocese; accordingly, under his guidance, the Council decreed important rules concerning the administration of the Church. Among these was an order to the parochial priests requiring them to employ "junior lectors," following the Italian custom. The founder of Western monasticism, St. Benedict, was also interested in the musical education and usefulness of boys, and in his Rule devoted several chapters to them. In chapter forty-five, he even advocates corporal punishment for those who do not sing in tune.

Since the reading of the Epistles or excerpts from the Old Testament alternated with songs, the singer's role grew in importance. The Laodicean Council saw itself obliged, about 350, to defend the rightful singers against the encroachment of undesirable people. Some forty years later the fourth Council of Carthage formulated rules concerning the singers' office. Following the example of the *schola lectorum,* a *schola cantorum* was called into existence. Simple congregational singing must have become incompatible with the soaring development of the other arts in the service of the Church, and the councils saw to it that music joined in this development. The order of the Laodicean Council, which prescribed that only specifically designated singers might sing in the services, meant the first step toward the ultimate elimination of active participation in singing by the congregation. This act was often misinterpreted, although its purpose was a logical and artistic one. The Byzantine and Roman branches of the Christian Church have always endeavored to place the arts in the service of worship. The sound of the choir, coming from outside the congregation, completes the atmosphere created by the wall paintings and the moving poetry of the ritualistic texts.

While the reported existence of a papal school for singers under Pope Sylvester (314–336) cannot be proved historically, the existence of such an institution in the second half of the same century is highly probable, and the liturgical measures undertaken by Pope Celestine presuppose a choir of trained singers. Pope Sixtus (432–440) established a monastery for the daily practice of psalmody, and his successor, Leo the Great (440–461), founded another one, dedicated to St. John and St. Paul. The religious of this monastery were required to furnish the liturgical prayers and songs for the services in the papal church. The *scholae* developed a vocal technique and culture which found appreciation among the widest circles of Christianity.

At the time when the future pope, Gregory I, was named archdeacon in Rome (585), the appreciation of good singing and the love of a beautiful voice produced a custom which illustrates a high regard for musical ability. People who possessed good voices were often made deacons, even though they might be otherwise simple individuals. (Curiously enough, these singers also wore the rich mane of which nineteenth-century musicians were so fond.) One of the first acts of Pope Gregory was to abolish this practice. Papal objection, however, was not directed against the vocal qualities of the singers, because all patristic writers insist on good singing. We have already mentioned the Rule of St. Benedict, but the Rules of St. Paul and St. Stephen also contain numerous passages concerning the music of the Church. They require that the psalmody be executed by the choir "as if it were one voice; none of the singers should sing faster or louder than the others."

Pope Gregory assured the final establishment of the *schola cantorum* by setting aside two buildings near the Lateran. In one of them singers and clergy of the papal church lived together; the other building was an orphanage which undertook the task of educating future members of the choir.[14]

All our sources deal amply with the vocal music of the Church, but they are chary with mention of any other manifestation of musical art. That there existed a considerable vogue of profane music and entertainment may be guessed from such passages as the following, taken from St. Basil's *Hexaemeron* (IV, I): "There are towns where one can enjoy all sorts of histrionic spectacles from morning to night. And, we must admit, the more people hear lascivious and pernicious songs, which raise in their souls impure and voluptuous desires, the more they want to hear." Many of the Church Fathers were aware of the sensual attraction of a good voice and tried to keep people away from professional singers. They were especially disturbed by the great number of people who went to the theater to listen to women singers, and went so far as to declare that "those who delight their eyes and ears on such spectacles commit adultery."

Musical instruments were just as much feared as the pleasing tunes which the heretics used with such astonishing success in their propaganda. Many a writer characterized the aulos as intoxicating and warned the faithful to leave these instruments "to the superstitious and to those who are inclined to idolatry." Almost every one of the earlier churchmen exhorted his congregation on this subject. They had ample reason for doing so. The feasts of the martyrs—to mention one of the excesses known to us—were usually celebrated in a noisy fashion, to the accompaniment of all sorts of instruments. This was understandable inasmuch as they were usually connected with what we may call a fair. St. Ephrem exhorted his congregation to celebrate such feasts like Christians and not like heathens. The same noisy ceremonies must have prevailed at funerals, because we find that the Nestorian Synod (576) forbade the use of tambourines and castanets during those services.

The development of Western music was decisively influenced by the exclusion of musical instruments from the early Christian Church. "We do not need the psalterium, the tuba, drum, and flute, which are liked by those who prepare themselves for war," said Clement of Alexandria. There was no objection, however, to the use of "noble" instruments in the home. The tolerated instrument was the lyre, and we are, no doubt, dealing here with a continuation of classical citharoedia; the tibia, however, was condemned on account of its connection with orgiastic rites. The Church always endeavored to keep liturgical singing within very definite boundaries, with the exclusion of harshness and noisiness. Nevertheless, some of the Oriental churches must have had rather noisy services, accompanied by hand clapping and dancing, a practice which offended Clement of Alexandria. The Coptic churches, especially in Ethiopia, still like dances, and accompany their ritual songs and dances with drums which they occasionally play with deafening furor.

The Oriental elements, which did not disappear for a long time, place extraordinary difficulties in the path of the historian. Even a superficial examination of such elements leads us into forbidding fields of magic and incantation; all we can do here, therefore, is to mention the vitality and tenacity of incantation and magic. In the fourth century all classes of society were profoundly superstitious, and the magicians were still omnipotent. The Christians themselves were wont to turn to them if they were taken ill or had some misgivings. "If we have a headache," says St. Augustine, "we run to the singer of incantations; I see this occur every day." How closely these songs of incantation and primitive worship affect our history of music is shown by the role of the exclamation *Kyrie eleison,* which begins the Mass. Widely used in the first Christian centuries, this exclamation originated in the Orient in pre-Christian times, and was used in pagan rites in honor of the Sun-god.

While the Oriental influence upon Western civilization was probably the more important, we must record a similar infiltration of Western elements into the East. The exchange became noticeable soon after the Constantinian edicts. The feast of the Epiphany, observed in the East for some time, was now introduced into the West, while Christmas, observed in Rome at least in 354, soon became popular in the Orient.

Theological, Philosophical, and Scientific Foundations of Christian Ritual Music

THE more music and liturgy developed in the post-Constantinian period, the more it was felt that this new cult music required a theological justification and a philosophical foundation and orientation. This led to renewed study of Hellenistic and Byzantine sources. Christian art had accepted the motif of the ram-carrying Hermes as the symbol of the Good Shepherd, and it painted Orpheus as Christ. Many of the poets, such as Prudentius, based their whole poetry on classical precepts. Music could not remain isolated in this general tendency, and, indeed, the doctrines and speculations of the Hellenistic philosophers of Alexandria attracted the attention of Western Christian writers and thinkers. Definite relationship between Christian music and the musical science and philosophy of antiquity was established in the fourth century. The simple religious music and psalmody practiced in the preceding centuries had been oblivious of classical civilization, but it contained the elements which, when amalgamated with classical musical doctrines, led to our Western music.

The fusion of two cultures placed intellectual leaders in a difficult position. The Orient did not have much difficulty in adjusting itself. It was Origen (c. 185–c. 254) especially who brought about a reconciliation between the old civilization of Hellas and the new Christian outlook on life. The same question became much more delicate in the Latin West, for many prominent ecclesiastics were opposed to the inclusion of secular knowledge in Christian thought and education. Even St. Augustine, who to some extent settled this question, hesitated to give unequivocal support to the idea, and so it should not surprise us to learn of renewed quarrels and disputes springing up around the arts and sciences in the early Christian world.

The early Middle Ages did not establish direct contact with classical musical science, although the last great writers produced their works during the Christian era. Boethius and Cassiodorus furnished the Occident with its foundation of musical thought, but before their advent we have to deal with the Neoplatonic and Neo-Pythagorean ideas which ranged music in the magical cosmos of their speculative symbolism. The legendary person of Pythagoras now reappears, to become one of the principal figures in the musical mythology of the Middle Ages—a mythology which created a conception of music preoccupied with the symbolism and theoretical speculation of numbers rather than with actual sounds and melodies.

St. Augustine intended to write a voluminous treatise on music but did not get beyond the sixth book. While these books contain a great deal of interesting material, they are mostly concerned with the *ars poetica*, which, in truly classical fashion, was inseparable from music. In the sixth book, however, we drift into the number-mysticism of the Neoplatonists. The opinions of Augustine the philosopher and those of Augustine the theologian and bishop are often in contradiction; but when it comes to music, the great churchman does not hesitate to assign to it an important place in the catalogue of sciences. The Hellenistic elements are evident when he attributes the order, measure, and beauty in the world to the formative power of numbers, or when he considers music a domain subject to sensory observations. A study of St. Augustine's six books on music (*De Musica*) will convince us that he considered music a matter of mathematical law and order, which presents a strict analogy to all other organized existence and follows the same fundamental rules. We are clearly on our way toward the Boethian precept which states categorically that "all music is reasoning and speculation." [15] But before we can discuss *ratio* we must take a quick glance at *speculatio*.

The Neo-Pythagorean number-symbolism of Nicomachus was continued by the Christian writers, and music played an important role in their allegorical explanations. We cannot discuss this involved subject fully, but it will be interesting to mention a few examples.

The number three is the first number with a beginning, a middle, and an end; besides this, it represents the sum of the values of the two preceding numbers. Its perfection is manifest in all domains. In morals it is the fundamental source of all good; furthermore, it is the master and the constitution of all music. We shall see what enormous importance was attached to the number three in the later Middle Ages. Number four is remarkable for various reasons. It represents the quadrivium; there are four elements, four general directions, four seasons, four virtues, four kinds of beings (angels, demons, animated creatures, plants). Number seven is the source of the various sorts of tones, that is, the harmony of the seven planets, of which the seven strings of the lyre are the earthly image. The number eight, which is the double of four, represents all the harmonies. The decade is the whole; it occupies the supreme position among the numbers.

To the existing allegories which the Christians took from the ancients the patristic writers added several new ones. In the group of four we find the four musical concordances (*symphoniae musicae*), and in the group of seven we find, together with the seven days of the week, the seven tones of the scale and the seven graces of the Holy Ghost.

Considering music from this point of view makes it apparent that with our Christian Neoplatonists and Neo-Pythagoreans, as exemplified by St.

Augustine, music belongs to the scientific disciplines and does not pre-eminently serve moral and pedagogical purposes as with Plato. A person cannot claim to be educated without mastering it in connection with the other branches of learning. Since a lack of knowledge and education prevents a person from reaching the ultimate aims of life, the liberal arts should be studied assiduously as a preparation to the comprehension of the truth.

But the other strain in St. Augustine, that of the theologian, evaluated the importance of the liberal arts in a different manner. The various disciplines did not appear to be only the road to God; they were also a means of warding off the insidious temptations offered by the learned heretics. The mental agility gained through a study of the liberal arts—and music especially—should show the road to salvation to those who, by indulging too much in worldly learning, erred on the wrong path, while the truly faithful will win their purification not through reason but through the fire of divine love.

This conception led to a temporary neglect of the study of the liberal arts, but the curious sociological conditions of the period did not permit real abandonment of erudition and learning. There was still an appreciable number of people with heretical tendencies who possessed a broad classical education. As long as they were present, the vestiges of ancient learning could not be abandoned, for they had to be met on their own grounds. Furthermore, most Christians considered the music practiced by heathens to be diabolic music. It had to be opposed, and people, especially young people, had to be protected from its effects. Here the cultivated classes encountered great difficulties, because in the fourth, fifth, and sixth centuries the Church did not yet have educational institutions meant for Christian families. Young men went to the rhetorical schools, which were still under the influence of classical civilization. Such a state of affairs called for solution, and in the course of the early Middle Ages two solutions were offered. One advocated complete ignorance of profane learning; the other admitted antique culture to Christian civilization. The second solution becomes understandable only somewhat later, in a period in which antique culture had ceased to be a tangible reality; it had become history and, as such, was not subject to theological objections. We shall see the practical working of these ideas in subsequent chapters.

While it is perfectly true that music was considered and taught from its scientific aspects, we must record a third conception of it, which is also represented in St. Augustine's writings; namely, music as the embodiment and expression of Christian devoutness, the intermediary between God and man. It is not clear how the Bishop of Hippo—whose exhortations to people to break into song when their hearts were filled with joy were mentioned above in describing the hymns—arrived at the point of recognizing emotion in music. This recognition is indeed far removed from the original Augustinian and Quintilianian conception of a strict mathematical discipline which does not recognize emotional qualities and rejects the musician, the mere practical exponent of a science. Music had been rediscovered and reinstated among the elements of education, but the late Augustinian ideals had to go through many a campaign and metamorphosis before they gained a foothold in Italy and Gaul. Negation of the world and abhorrence of still-prevalent heathen tenets led to a monasticism with strong leanings toward asceticism which became the ideal of Christian life. The idea of self-discipline and catharsis reigned. It was only later that this ideal was modified by the infiltration of ideas represented by Irish, Scottish, and Anglo-Saxon monks.

Music played an important role in the Christianization of heathens and in the subduing of occasional pagan uprisings—for paganism was still strong in the outlying districts. But the cities were also far from being entirely Christianized for many centuries to come. In Rome, for instance, the offices were not celebrated on Thursday, which was Jupiter's day. The clergy realized the captivating influence of music and ritual and endeavored to make the divine service resplendent but at the same time accessible to the simple people. It appears that participation in the services was often considered an excellent way to keep the somewhat unruly faithful occupied.

With the foundation of a monastery by Cassiodorus (540) in Vivarium, it seemed that the earlier Augustinian ideas—the turning away from all profane knowledge—would be continued and expanded. The great historian, statesman, and philosopher used his erudition, however, for different purposes. His aim was to provide for the transmission of divine and human knowledge to later ages, to secure it against the tide of barbarism which threatened to sweep it away. The duty which he enjoined upon the members of his monastery was the acquisition of knowledge, both sacred and profane, the latter, however, being subordinated to the former. The monks collected and copied manuscripts and translated Greek works into Latin. But this meant that the learned and intelligent monk was still in demand, even though his erudition had some secular sources. In fact, Cassiodorus encouraged the cultivation of the intellect, and did not follow the other founders of monasteries who, in deference to the Augustinian doctrines, re-stricted the activities of their monks to physical labor and prayer. Cassiodorus reached then the intermediary position taken by Augustine himself in his *De Doctrina Christiana,* which considers the practice of the liberal arts not an aim in itself but a means to the better understanding of the Scriptures. But while Augustine affirms that bliss may be attained by those who are ignorant of the liberal arts, Cassiodorus insists on learning, because when one "encounters profane things in the Holy Scriptures these passages will naturally be better understood if one has already a knowledge of the worldly."

The explanation of the meaning of the Scriptures occupied early medieval authors. Every passage was subjected by them to a quadruple examination, which consisted of *explanatio ad literam, ad sensum, ad allegoriam*, and *ad moralitatem*. The allegorical explanation often resorted to music because of the frequent mention of musical subjects in the Psalms, and the almost constant occurrence in the text of words like *cantare, jubilare, exultare, psallere*. etc.

In late Hellenistic pedagogy music belonged to the so-called seven liberal arts; the Latin Middle Ages accepted this system, which they took from Martianus Capella. It is a great mistake, however, to translate the meaning of *artes* as "arts," pure and simple, because the term meant not technical mastery and practice of an art but the philosophical examination and understanding of the nature of the various domains of knowledge. Considered from this angle, it will be clear why music became a member of the higher group of the seven arts—arithmetic, music, geometry, and astronomy—and why the early medieval scholars thought that "without music no scientific discipline can be perfect." [16] While the ranging of music among the sciences hampered its development as an art, we must not overlook the fact that the inclusion of music among the liberal arts represents a unique privilege enjoyed by it throughout the Middle Ages, and that the so-called fine arts did not figure in the systematic picture of the universe. We must now examine this picture, a task which leads us to the greatest early medieval figure in the world of music and scholarship, Boethius.

Boethius (d. c. 524–526) and Cassiodorus (d. c. 580) represent the end of antique musical science in the Occident. With them and with Isidore of Seville (d. 636) ends the important mediative function of the South, and the continuation falls to the young peoples of the North, which will develop a specifically Western literature of music in the ninth century. This date marks the beginning of what we may rightfully call the medieval theory and science of music. On the other hand, these same authors who stand at the end of classical musical learning furnished the material which the medieval scholars used for their dissertations. Both men held important positions at the court of Theodoric. Both incurred the king's displeasure, but while Boethius paid with his life, the more astute Cassiodorus lived to be a nonagenarian. Cassiodorus was a Christian, but Boethius was "the last of the Romans whom Cato or Tully could have acknowledged for his countryman" (Gibbon). The influence of Cassiodorus was felt for several centuries after his death; Boethius, however, had an uninterrupted reign until comparatively recent times. Yet it must be said that he did not give us in his *De Institutione Musica* anything of his own invention, but rather summarized everything that was known before his times. This almost anachronistic Roman gentleman and scholar, best known for his *Consolation of Philosophy,* was steeped in the classical disciplines. His father, his master, was Pythagoras. He uses Greek terminology and expounds Greek ideas as if he were a Greek himself. His point of view is never that of a real musician, but that of a speculative mathematician. All subsequent medieval historians leaned on the authority of Boethius when they defined music as a science and not as an art. He was called "the one who translated, corrected, and developed musical science itself." As late as the end of the fifteenth century Adam of Fulda, the most eminent German musical scholar of his period, when speaking of uninformed musicians exclaimed: "The unfortunates! they do not seem to know that Boethius said in the XXXIII chapter of the first book of his Institutione: *id musicus est, qui ratione perpensa"* (the musician is one who measures [examines] by reason). This should be our motto and point of departure for the understanding of the picture painted in the most influential work on music that the Middle Ages produced.

The opening chapter of Boethius's *De Institutione Musica* gives a succinct description of the effect of music on man, and defines its domain. *Musica mundana* is expressed in the motion of the spheres, the organization of the various elements, and the alternation of the seasons. The dependence here on classical precepts is immediately obvious, for it was Pythagoras and his school which originated the idea of ethereal music produced by planetary motion. Among later classical authors, Nicomachus, Cicero, and Macrobius made comments about the music of the spheres, and the general consensus of opinion was that we do not perceive it because it is constantly sounding and our ears are accustomed to it. The other two varieties of *musica mundana* are not sonorous phenomena: the emphasis is on numerical correspondences. *Musica humana* combines the incorporeal, eternal spirit with the body in a manner similar to the formation of consonances by high and low tones, and unites the parts of the soul with elements of the body in a certain numerical order. The third species of music, *quae in quibusdam constituta est in instrumentis,* is, finally, music proper in its sensuously perceptible form.

We must not forget, however, that Boethius, the philosopher and rational scientist, was not so much interested in the sensuous nature of musical tone, or in the enjoyment of its sound: his interest centered around the factors which cause its appearance, that is, he was still following the classical precepts, which considered numerical proportions the basis of all musical understanding. Since numerical proportions are discernible only through *ratio* and not through the sense of hearing, which often leads to mistakes, the analytical power of the mind is held to be superior to the faculty of discernment by the sense of hearing, which fact again makes the theorist superior to the mere musician. Taking all this into consideration, and adding to it the conspicuous absence of *musica vocalis,* one must come to the conclusion that the instruments mentioned in the third genus of music in Boethius's classification are used not for instrumental music, but as the tools which permit scientific observation.

The Boethian conception of music, which dominated the early and central Middle Ages, will explain, once more, the presence of music in the quadrivium, the "science" division of the liberal arts; and we must admit that even those who shared the Augustinian ideas, like Cassiodorus, refrained from a systematic exposition of practical music just as much as their formidable classical colleague, the *ampliator musicae.*

In the measure that Rome lost its prestige and became, after 552, a mere provincial capital of the Byzantine Empire, its intellectual and spiritual activities were also limited to the role of recipient of Eastern cultural movements. But the proud Eternal City retained, in its conservatism, something of the essence of old Rome. This stubborn clinging to her own traditions, with the careful introduction of new elements into the practice of the old, gives the Roman rite its particular traits.

The Gregorian reform made Rome the indisputable center of development of church music, and music in general. As in classical times, the Eternal City acquired this position not on the ground of its original creations but by its remarkable ability to collect things and then organize them. Once the Oriental elements were brought to the West, Rome examined them, carefully selecting what it thought to be best, and, by remodeling and polishing, crossing and mixing them with existing materials, created something new which, because it was not native to any country, was eminently suited to be a universal medium. It is noteworthy that this new, reorganized church music bears the name of the man who was first to represent with authority and might the idea of a universal papacy by the enforcement of papal supremacy and the establishment of the temporal position and power of the pope. Gregory I, called the Great, church statesman, organizer of genius, despised Greek philosophy and rhetoric; he was a real Roman, but in his devoutness, with his demons, spirits, and miracles, he is already the typical medieval man.

Chapter 5

GREGORIAN ART AND ITS SPHERE OF INFLUENCE

⇛ ⇚

Gregory the Great

MANY legends surround the figure of the great pontiff whose name was perpetuated, by the music of his Church, to outshine the fame of all other Vicars of Christ. Because these legends started early in the Middle Ages and were incorporated into serious scientific tracts, it is difficult to see clearly his role in the history of liturgy and music. The original misconception of Gregory's intentions and deeds started with the authors who, writing two or three centuries later, imputed to him the knowledge of ideas which were characteristic of their own period though there is no tangible evidence of their existence in the times of the great reformer.

While Gregory deserves the epithet of "the Great" as far as his work in the practical organization of all domains of the Church is concerned, his other activities cannot be regarded with the same admiration. Indeed, this great organizer is directly responsible for the decline of the artistic aspects of Christian literature. In his writings we see speculative imagination displaced by wildly subjective pictures. Mysticism, superstition, and the love of wonders take the place of logical demonstrations. He was also responsible for the neglect of Biblical research, which interested the Christians of the fifth and sixth centuries to such a great extent, substituting forced allegorical explanations, and attaching to the Biblical stories sweeping moral conclusions alternating with grotesque tales of wonders. On the other hand, his *Liber Regulae Pastoralis,* which gives instructions concerning the conduct of the life and office of a priest, is filled with profound and sincere moral convictions. All these writings are of exceptional importance because they belong to the works which shaped the mental attitude of the Middle Ages. One thing becomes certain from their examination, and that is Gregory's definite exclusion of the worldly sciences and arts from the domain of spiritual education. By the sixth century the educational system of antiquity was in full decline and the number of representatives of classical civilization had greatly diminished. This state of affairs made the study of the liberal arts "as a means of defense against learned heretics" superfluous, a fact that assumes paramount importance in any attempt to discover the motives which actuated Gregory's reforms. Gregory's ban on secular learning gave theological studies a preponderance and assured Rome of its dominant position in theological matters, which it kept for many centuries. The few passages in his writings in which he recommends the study of the *artes* have been proved conclusively to be interpolations by a certain Abbot Claudius, of which Gregory himself disapproved, as they modified and even falsified his intentions. In his own words, *inveni dictorum meorum sensum valde inutilius fuisse permutatum*.[1] It is clear that Gregory was opposed to the cultural ideal professed by Cassiodorus and his followers.

In view of these facts, it becomes evident that music, which formed an essential part of profane learning, must have come under the same ban that affected the other members of the quadrivium. How, then, can we reconcile this attitude with the old tradition that Gregory not only organized the liturgy but composed a part of the antiphonal? It is certain that he did not compose the liturgic songs, for the material included in this mysterious codex originated prior to his time. The original antiphonal was lost, but the concordance of the numerous manuscripts which appeared beginning with the ninth century banishes all doubt that there must have been an original collection of which they are the copies. Only one country outside of Italy became acquainted with the Roman chant in Gregory's lifetime and appears to have possessed the first copies of the Gregorian antiphonal, and this was England. In 596 Gregory dispatched the Benedictine monk Augustine with forty companions to the British Isles, entrusting them with a number of manuscripts and all the articles necessary for the divine cult. But even Gregory's role of organizer of liturgical music must come under scrutiny. The popes of the fourth, fifth, and sixth centuries, especially Damasus I, Leo I, Gelasius I, Symmachus, Boniface II, and John II, contributed much toward the organizing and systematizing of musical liturgy, but it is evident that a definite organization took place either in Gregory's time or within a century or so of his pontificate. Gevaert, the great Belgian musicologist, doubts that this definite organization took place during the reign of Gregory I and attributes it to later popes, Gregory II (715–731) and Gregory III (731–741).[2] The truth will perhaps be found in a compromise between the two extreme views, as we shall hardly be able to verify the contents of the original antiphonal and it seems plausible that these two popes finished the task begun by Gelasius and continued more vigorously by Gregory I.

Gregory is usually credited with the establishment of the *schola cantorum*, but there is little doubt that when he was elected to the pontificate in 590 this company of singers was already firmly established. In many of the ordinary churches, however, the regular singers had more or less disappeared, and the musical parts of the services were again being performed by the priests and the deacons in charge. Gregory, on the occasion of the Concilium Romanum held in 595, after censuring the ministers of the Church for spending too much time on the cultivation of their voices to the detriment of their other duties, such as administering the sacraments, preaching, visiting the sick, and distributing alms, issued a decree which directed that the deacons were to sing nothing in church except the Gospel and that the rest of the musical part of the service was to be performed by subdeacons, or by clerics in minor orders.

The decree shows the hand of a practical organizer, but it also indicates that the pope did not care much for music in general, only acknowledging its existence and necessity for worship. Accordingly, he took immediate steps to assure a supply of singers to relieve the priests of their burden. At this time there were in Rome two seminaries for youths who were studying for the priesthood. One had been in existence for a long time, and the other was conducted by the religious of the Benedictine monastery of Monte Cassino, who after the destruction of their monastery by the Lombards in 580 had come to Rome and placed themselves under the protection of Pelagius, the predecessor of Gregory. Owing to the scarcity of liturgical books, it was absolutely necessary that those intended for the priesthood should memorize at least the psalter along with its music, and it was to the aforementioned seminaries that Gregory first turned for a supply of efficient singers. He also established orphanages for the instruction of youths for the ministry and for the supply of singers to the papal choir (*schola cantorum*). The use of the word *schola* has confused the clerical seminary and the papal choir in the minds of later writers and has given the erroneous impression that the latter was instituted by Gregory himself, whereas it had been in existence for over a hundred years at the time of his election to the pontificate. To have been educated in this orphanage was of great assistance to ecclesiastic advancement, and not a few of the pupils reached the pontificate itself.

The great personal interest shown by Gregory in the work of the *schola* and the frequently emphasized importance of its influence throughout the world presuppose a curriculum that would reflect the views of the pontiff. A comparison of the official *Vitae* of Gregory's successors discloses that the popes who had been pupils in the *scholae* were all interested in a simple education, which included grammar, scriptural studies, and musical training in the rendition of the liturgy. They were just as remote from the Cassiodorian ideal as Gregory. We must therefore conclude that under Gregory's pontificate his strong restrictions on profane learning were observed in the *scholae*. Significantly enough, almost all the other popes, who were either of Oriental origin or were brought up in the Orient as were Leo II and Gregory III, while insisting on a practical education, were very much interested in a thorough study of the liberal arts. But these popes represented a civilization which differed from the Roman. They were, in reality, emissaries of the Greek spirit which gained a foothold toward the middle of the seventh century in southern Italy, without, however, influencing the *Curia Romana* to any perceptible degree. Gregory himself had never come under the influence of Greek thought, even though he spent several years in Byzantium as a legate of the Holy See; he came back from his mission without even having learned the Greek language.

Gregory's influence explains why Italy did not take a conspicuous part in the scientific and literary revival of the Carolingian period and why Italian scholarship was dormant until the late Middle Ages. The tendency to turn away from profane arts and learning which started with the last writings of St. Augustine, and was afterwards advocated by St. Benedict, reached its greatest intensity in Gregory, who implanted these doctrines in the Church and its schools. Penitence and discipline took the place of encyclopedic learning. All subsequent restrictions on monastic life hark back to the model set by this earnest, austere, and strong-handed occupant of St. Peter's throne.

In his reorganization of the liturgy and its music Gregory was motivated by practical requirements of the administration of the Church and could not have in mind anything but the immediate needs of Rome. The prestige of the papacy transformed this reform into a precious instrument which spread all over the Christian Occident.

The Cantus Romanus *in Britain*

ROMAN missionaries first appeared in England toward the end of the sixth century. Bede informs us that Gregory the Great organized, as we have said, a body of monks, placed them under the direction of Augustine, and sent them to England as missionaries. After passing through Gaul they crossed the Channel and landed on the shores of Kent in the spring of 597. Their task was not too difficult. The people of Kent naturally had more contact with the Continent than any of the more distant British nations. Furthermore, Ethelbert, King of Kent, had taken to wife the daughter of the Frankish King, Claribert. Ethelbert's wife was a Christian and had been accompanied to England by a Christian bishop. At the time of Augustine's arrival she was already using for private worship an old Roman church on the outskirts of Canterbury. In 598 Ethelbert himself embraced the Christian faith and Canterbury became the chief center of Roman influence in England. Missionaries continued to arrive from the Continent, and by 650 all of England, with the exception of Sussex, had become Christian. The South Saxons were converted later in the century.

After the Synod of Whitby (664) the Christian Church in England became a firmly established body, bringing with it a distinct advance in all phases of English civilization. Canterbury became an extremely important center; its archbishop, Theodore of Tarsus, and his companion, a monk named Hadrian, were instrumental in spreading the Greek language. Hadrian had been educated in the southern part of Italy, where there was a flourishing Greek colony. We shall see what influence the presence of Greek cultural elements in England and northern Germany was to have on the development of music and liturgy on the Continent. One of the outstanding disciples of the school at Canterbury, Aldhelm, founded the monastery of Malmesbury at Essex, one of the first seats of culture in England. Besides the schools in Canterbury and Malmesbury, the Northumbrian monasteries of Wearmouth and Jarrow, founded by Bishop Benedict, who made several journeys to Rome and brought back liturgical books and other manuscripts, attained great fame. Bede, who was educated at these monasteries, tells us that Benedict introduced the *Cantus Romanus* (Gregorian chant) into Northumbria and requested Pope Agatho to send the chief precentor of St. Peter's to teach at Wearmouth. The *archicantor* Johannes (c. 680) then became the first official teacher of the *Cantus Romanus* in England, although a few years before his appearance there is mention of several singers who traveled to Rome in order to study the art of singing. The fame of Johannes extended far beyond the monastery, and he is thought to have written some treatises on music. The Venerable Bede himself was one of his students, and Bede's commentary on the Psalms is proof of his acquaintance with music. The fact that he mentions verses not only in Latin but also in the vernacular shows how little England was dominated by Rome.

The Irish-Scottish circle of civilization had unusual power and a wide expansion in the sixth, seventh, and eighth centuries. The Irish Church assumed the nature of a missionary church and exerted considerable influence, in music as in other fields, on the Frankish, and even northern Italian countries. Almost nothing is known of the activities of the Irish and Scottish monks in their own country, but we shall see how, as the leaders of Frankish civilization, they effected a union of antique tradition with Christian spirit.

The Cantus Romanus *in the Carolingian Empire*
The Celtic Influence

IN spite of the importance of early British civilization, the first really distinct cultural period which followed antiquity was Charlemagne's epoch. It was a period of genuine culture because people's attention was turned now to a large variety of spiritual and artistic activities and because they began to appreciate the products of such activities. The circle of educated men was considerably widened by the increased number of schools, even though the introduction of compulsory school laws—attributed to Charlemagne—must have failed at such an early date. At any rate, the court school and the "Academy," a sort of literary society connected with it, together with various decrees of the emperor, raised arts and letters to a high standard. It goes without saying that the artistic ideal was that of the antique world, and scientific and literary efforts were directed toward the understanding of the intellectual legacy of antiquity and early Christendom. A noteworthy fact is the participation of the Germanic element of the Frankish Empire in the intellectual life of the country. They are still the pupils, but with the disciples of Alcuin they were to join the ranks of the teachers and leaders.

Despite their classical orientation, Carolingian arts and letters are almost completely dominated by the point of view of the Church. This is understandable, for after the collapse of the antique world Western humanity was compelled to go through a spiritual, monastic schooling to be receptive to a new free and progressive mental work. The Carolingian monks with their tireless copying of ancient and Christian authors contributed the most important stimulus for succeeding generations. Humanism could not have arisen without this industrious activity in copying and critical commenting of the eighth and ninth centuries, since the bulk of classical writings were preserved for posterity in Carolingian manuscript copies.

Beginning with the meeting of Pepin the Short and Pope Stephen II in 754, a great effort was made toward the organization of the Gallo-Frankish churches. This represents also the beginnings of a political idea of a united empire built on a uniform liturgy and ritualistic music. Crowned emperor by the pope in Rome (800), Charlemagne revived the office of Emperor in the West, his dream being to establish a united and uniform empire, and he was unwearying in his efforts to achieve this aim. His continuous interest in ecclesiastical affairs was shown at the Synod of Frankfort, over which he presided in 794. Charlemagne himself was an enthusiastic lover of church music. Like the stern pontiff who reformed the instruction of the Roman *schola,* he supervised the school instruction personally. According to Alcuin, vocal instruction was imparted by a certain Sulpicius. The emperor's zeal in establishing a true Gregorian practice caused the burning of all books of Ambrosian ritual to safeguard the unity of song and liturgy. As early as 774 he sent some monks to Rome for vocal instruction, and the learned monks were installed in various monasteries. Metz and Soissons became famous for their *scholae* in a short time. Metz enjoyed an especially high reputation, and the *cantores Mettenses* were known throughout the whole empire. In 790, acceding to the repeated requests of Charlemagne, Pope

Hadrian dispatched two well-trained singers to the north; they carried with them copies of the antiphonal. One of them, Petrus, reached his destination, Metz; the other, Romanus, fell ill while stopping at St. Gall, where, after having recovered, he remained as head of the school for ecclesiastical singers.

The centers of Carolingian-Ottonian musical culture, including secular music, were the monasteries. (We must, of course, remember the unique position held by the royal court.) Following the inspired leadership of Alcuin at the Abbey of Tours, the culture of the Middle Ages was concentrated in them. In this intellectual culture music occupied an important position. The reformatory activities of Charlemagne caused a sudden development of monastic schools and learning both in France and in Germany. The old Benedictine monasteries found a happy and harmonious middle way between the sacred and the secular, and from their seats emanated a spirit which has captured the imagination of modern historians, who, basing their judgment on the lively, enthusiastic, but not very accurate chronicles of the St. Gall monk Ekkehard IV (c. 980–1060), are inclined to overrate and even grant a monopoly of importance to the monastery of St. Gall in matters musical.

St. Gall, an Irish hermit who in 614 built his cell in the thick forest which then covered the site of the future monastery, lived there with a few companions until his death in 640. Many pilgrims later found their way to his cell and about the middle of the eighth century the collection of hermits' dwellings was transformed into a regularly organized Benedictine monastery. For the next three centuries this monastery played an important part in the cultural life of the West, but its real flourishing as a school of learning and education dates from the abbacy of Greinald (841–872), a monk educated in Reichenau. Numerous other monasteries deserve equally high if not higher admiration. Among them are the neighboring Reichenau, as well as St. Amand in Flanders, Fleury on the Loire, the two Provençal Abbeys of St. Pierre in Moissac and St. Martial in Limoges, and the renowned Abbey of Winchester across the Channel, but perhaps the most important scientific-literary training school for young monks was at St. Martin's at Tours, under the leadership of Alcuin. Charlemagne counted on him to accomplish the great work which was his dream—a united empire with a universally educated population.

Church music accompanied the life of the religious in St. Gall from the midnight invitatory Psalm *Venite* to the evening prayer of the next day. Many famous musicians were connected with this monastery, among them the famous teacher Marcellus (Moengal), an Irishman, and his three pupils: Tuotilo (d. 915), whose versatility as sculptor, painter, wood carver, architect, and musician suggests a man of the Renaissance; Ratpert (d. c.

884), a Swiss nobleman, whose Gallus-song became a folk song; and, the most important of them, Notker Balbulus (d. 912).

The century following Charlemagne's death (814) saw the gradual dissolution of the gigantic empire created by the great monarch, and the formation of the German and French "nations." While the political changes were considerable, cultural life did not materially change on either side of the Rhine. Poetry, arts, and the sciences evolved in the tracks created by Charlemagne and the men whom he invited to teach his people.

Besides the monastery schools the other important centers of education were the cathedral schools. While their activity was mainly restricted to practical and elementary teaching, with the decline of the monasteries they seem to have embraced the idea of encyclopedic learning as the aim of education and thus to have become the chief carriers of literary-scientific culture until the advent of the universities. Among the most important cathedral schools were those in Chartres and Rheims. Rheims owes its great fame to its learned teacher, Gerbert of Aurillac. During Gerbert's teaching career the *artes liberales* regained their important place in education. Among the other disciplines he took an active interest in the theory of music, but instead of following the precepts of his Gallic predecessors who spurned the scientific speculations of the Scottish monks, he made Boethius the center of studies and with this established a tendency which was to dominate musical thought and scholarship until the end of the sixteenth century. The movement, emanating from Rheims, with its emphasis on the mathematical sciences, influenced all other schools. Chartres followed suit and, under the guidance of its Bishop Fulbert, became as famous for its practical musical instruction as for the excellent training it imparted in the theory of music. Fulbert himself declared that the knowledge of the theory and science of music is imperative, because *sine cujus arte vera nulla valent cantica* (without that art the songs are worthless); a point of view which became a maxim of medieval conceptions about the art of music.

The cathedral schools in Liége, Laon, Utrecht, Freising, and Cologne all followed the example of Chartres and Rheims. The German cathedral schools of Halberstadt, Hildesheim, Magdeburg, and Ratisbon, while retaining something of their old fame, could not remotely match the splendid achievements of the Lotharingian and French schools. This excellence is in harmony with the leading position held by the French in the fields of architecture, sculpture, illumination of manuscripts, and poetry.

The dominant position of the French schools was due to the pronounced and prolonged Celtic influence experienced in all domains of spiritual life. The first migration of Celtic monks to the Continent occurred about 600; this was followed two hundred years later by a second ecclesiastic colonization. The Irish monasteries seem to have taken up the scientific and literary movement inaugurated at Vivarium by Cassiodorus, but it is impossible to ascertain in what way the Cassiodorian doctrines were carried into the British Isles. We hear, however, that the famous monasteries at Armagh, Bangor, and Lismore were the seats of considerable mathematical and musical activity, and Irish music teachers were sought after on the Continent. The Celtic monks who were instrumental in carrying out Charlemagne's plans for educational reforms brought with them, together with their superior learning, an extensive collection of books. Ninth- and tenth-century German and Swiss inventories and catalogues often mention *scottice scripti,* which referred probably to the books brought from Bangor or Armagh; the name Scottish was used to denote all people of Celtic origin, and the Irish were also simply called Scotti.

Ireland and Scotland had never experienced antique civilization as a reality. The Celts came into contact with Rome, the colonizer, much as the East Indians made the acquaintance of modern England. Consequently they did not face the grave conflict between ancient learning and Christian faith which caused a sharp reaction in the countries within the orbit of classical civilization. They were thus eminently suited to bring about a reconciliation of the two philosophies and outlooks on life, and communicated their ideas not only to their neighbors, the Anglo-Saxons, but, through their monastic settlements in the Frankish Empire and northern Italy, to the whole of Christian Europe. Important seats of Celtic civilization were in St. Gall, Luxeuil (Burgundy), Liége, Laon, and Bobbio in Lombardy. Carolingian musical literature written by Frankish and Romanic writers was not permeated by the inquisitive and speculative scientific spirit of the Irish writers; it was concerned chiefly with the improvement of liturgical practice. Jacques Handschin suggests that the famous tract, *Musica Enchiriadis,* the oldest important source for the history of many-voiced music, long considered a work of Hucbald of St. Amand, was known to Johannes Scotus and originated in Ireland toward the middle of the ninth century.[3] The work shows an intimate and penetrating knowledge of musical theory based on a careful study of antique sources.

The Offshoots of Gregorian Music

AT the time of the division of the empire in 843, the Roman-Frankish liturgical merger had been concluded in its basic principles. The new Occidental liturgical music, based on Gregorian art, penetrated with the missions to the Scandinavian, West-Slavic, and Hungarian territories, and displaced, in the time of Gregory VII, the Mozarabic ritual in Spain, leaving only the Ambrosian liturgy in Milan as an enclavement in an otherwise uniform liturgical practice. This explains the similarity of numerous musical manuscripts preserved from the beginning of the ninth century documenting the unity and purpose of Frankish culture and church politics. Nevertheless, the Roman emissaries found in Gaul a church music which differed so much from the older Ambrosian chant from which it originated that it was called *Cantus Gallicanus*. The ready musical understanding of the Gauls was praised by Gregory of Tours, but he noticed also their preference for new paths and ways and a tendency toward the secular. This tendency was responsible for the ultimate destiny of church music and the rise of secular art. Charlemagne was already obliged to reorganize the liturgy, offices and Mass, and his intentions, carried out by Paul the Deacon, the learned historian, and by Alcuin, resulted in the inclusion of certain Gallic liturgic elements. But the body of the musical part of the Gregorian antiphonal remained intact. During the reign of Louis the Pious (814–840) there was a lively exchange of emissaries between Rome and the empire and the liturgic songbooks were repeatedly corrected to bring them into conformity with the latest developments.

The original pre-Gregorian church song could not be entirely eradicated, and the curious fact remains that a large liturgical domain, comprising Gaul, western Germany, and parts of England, still showed elements of Byzantine origin sung in Greek. While the knowledge of Greek in southern Gaul must have been almost extinct, its use was repeatedly renewed by monks who brought it with them from the British Isles and from Magna Graecia. Johannes Scotus and his Irish confreres, as well as Paul the Deacon, were all learned Greek scholars, and the number of Celtic monasteries distributed all over the country continued to cultivate the study of Greek liturgical elements.

The fate of Gregorian art was not so well assured in Germany proper. John the Deacon, the biographer of Gregory, was of the opinion that the Germans were not able to learn the chants. "Their coarse voices, which roar like thunder, cannot execute soft modulations, because their throats, hoarse from too much drinking, could not emit the inflexions required by a tender melody." This is assuredly a devastating judgment, but we must qualify the criticism by remembering the difference in language. After this period the development of music in the Germanic countries showed remarkable steadiness. An interesting phenomenon made itself felt, in that the Germanic countries evolved a plain-song dialect of their own, manifested in melodic characteristics going through the whole range of Gregorian music. The Romanic nations continued to cultivate melodic curves which followed a consecutive, stepwise motion, while the Germanic plain-song dialect favored larger intervals, especially the third. Romanic and Germanic traditions seemed to adhere to ethnographic frontiers and influences. Thus when Fin-

land came under the influence of the Parisian Dominican missions in the
fourteenth century, the originally Germanic plain-song dialect turned toward
the Romanic type. The manner of notation reflects the same difference.
The forces which prompted such a distinction in musical dialect can be
explained only by the natural musical instinct of the Germanic races, which
was of a different nature. Whatever the cause may have been, this plain-
song dialect persisted in the northern Germanic countries until the Reformation, while the south clung to its version until the times of the Trent
Councils.

The songs making up the Ordinary of the Mass, the *Kyrie eleison, Gloria,
Credo, Sanctus,* and *Agnus Dei,* which later acquired such importance in the
musical settings of the Mass, were the least ornate among the chants in the
Gregorian antiphonal, because they were originally either simple folk songs
sung by the congregation (Credo, Sanctus) or were allotted to the minor
clergy. We shall not now discuss the question of the organization and musical significance of the Ordinary, as we shall deal with it in subsequent
chapters. Suffice it to say here that when in the tenth century the Kyrie and
other parts were assigned to the *schola* instead of being sung by the people
or the minor clergy, these simple songs went through a period of great
artistic development, being subsequently used as the basis for experiments in
the composition of many-voiced music.

Of capital importance were, however, the so-called *sequentiae,* or sequences. The sequence was the issue of the textless jubilations mentioned with such enthusiasm by St. Augustine. In the older Roman church
song the alleluia was sung "with the pneuma," that is, the melismatic
coloratura lasted as long as the breath (πνεῦμα) of the singer held out.
Durandus, the great French canon jurist of the Middle Ages and author
of *Rationale Divinorum Officium,* an important work on the symbolism of
the Mass which expresses the spirit that inspired much of medieval art,
remarked that "the *pneuma* or jubilus conveys the inexpressible joy in the
eternal, and occurs on the last syllable of the antiphon, to indicate that
God's praise is incomprehensible and inexpressible." As we have remarked
in the chapter on Byzantine music, such melismata were even more extended in Greek hymnody. Gregorian melodies were transmitted from
generation to generation by oral tradition, reinforced by the rather vague
indications of the neumatic notation, so that in a few centuries the meaning
of the larger group of neumes became hazy. The melodies which followed
a more or less syllabic construction, in which every syllable of the text had a
corresponding note, were easier for the memory to retain and withstood
the test of time. In order to avoid confusion, the method of furnishing texts
to the wordless melodies was adopted. In the ninth century in France such
adaptations of words to a jubilus were called "proses," because they followed

the lines of the music and not a system of meter. When these compositions had won a place for themselves, fresh ones came to be written in regular meter, and the older, no longer suitable appellation of prose gave way to the new name, sequence. Contrary to this definition of prose is the recent theory of its derivation from *pro sā*, a Latin abbreviation for *pro sequentia,* the interpretation of which would be "to be sung instead of the textless jubilation." [4] The sequence owes its name to its position in the Mass, because it appears there as the continuation of the gradual and the alleluia. The word may be a Latin translation of the Greek ἀκολουθία, meaning succession. [5]

Another manner of musical ornamentation of Byzantine origin was the custom, which in time spread through almost the whole range of liturgical music, of making interpolations in the church chant. Such interpolations had the generic name of trope. The interpolated words were either adapted to the already existing music, or words and music arose together. As a rule the melodies of the songs comprising the Mass were safeguarded, but the melismata were dissolved into individual notes following individual syllables. Among such interpolations were, for instance, *Kyrie* [*fons pietatis, a quo bona cuncta procedunt*] *eleison,* or *Kyrie* [*rex genitor ingenite*] *eleison.* The words within the brackets were adapted to the group of melismatic notes originally written over the single word *Kyrie.* As the development went on, the tropes invaded almost every domain of church music. Even the Epistles, matins, and other parts of the offices were "troped." Viewed from this angle, the sequence may be considered as a trope to the alleluia of the Mass. [6]

Beginning with the tenth century the artistic sense of the sequence composers in Swiss and French monasteries led them to depart from the mere adaptations of texts to long melodic lines, and they began to invent the music as well as the text. The resultant form was a piece of original poetry set to an original tune of a simple, hymnlike, syllabic nature. These sequences reflect the influence of folk song and also the individuality of their composers. It is remarkable that this personal note was observed by the composers' contemporaries. Ekkehard remarked about Tuotilo's melodies that "they are peculiar and very distinguishable . . . and have a certain sweetness of their own." Another period of sequence composition arose in the twelfth century, exhibiting a tendency toward hymnlike composition, owing to the increased use of rhyme. Adam de Saint-Victor, poet-composer of Paris, was the leader of this movement. In the wake of his simplified syllabic sequence poetry, literally thousands of sequences were composed, hastening the ecclesiastic doom which befell the movement at the Council of Trent.

Recent musicological research compels us to change our conception of the origin, age, and nature of this important form of medieval poetry and music.

We cannot help seeing in the sequence faint traces of descent from the ancient Greek nome, perhaps also from the age-old sacred lore of the druids. The influence of the Byzantine troparion is another important point of departure. The exclusive derivation from the alleluiatic jubilations, advocated by most historians, who also attribute the first organization and composition of sequences to Notker Balbulus, cannot be maintained in the light of recent historical and philological research. Blume and Handschin [7] unearthed several pre-Notkerian sequences coming from St. Martial in Limoges and other places, and this fact indicates that instead of originating with Notker, the sequence reached its first stage of classical completion with this renowned "Stammerer" of St. Gall. In fact, we must assume that the texts of these sequences, which were probably much older than Notker's time, originated, independently from the alleluia, somewhere in the Orient. When and where such works were created is impossible to determine, but one thing is certain, and that is their affinity with poetical forms of the Orient.[8]

In the beginning of the interpolating art, sequences and tropes were confined to the monasteries, but later they found wide dissemination in the secular church parishes; they were, however, never recognized as an official part of the liturgy. Following the liturgical and philological objections of the Council of Trent, Pope Pius V abolished them with the exception of the few which are still in use. These are: the Easter sequence *Victimae Paschali Laudes,* attributed to Wipo (c. 1024–1050), chaplain of Emperor Henry III; the sequence for Whitsunday, *Veni Sancte Spiritus;* the sequence for the festival of Corpus Christi, *Lauda Sion,* the author of which was St. Thomas Aquinas; the *Sequentia de Septem Doloribus Mariae Virginis,* better known as *Stabat Mater Dolorosa,* by Jacopone da Todi, the ardent Franciscan of the thirteenth century who went about the Italian hill towns singing hymns and exhorting the people to repentance; and the most celebrated of all, *Dies Irae,* written during the latter half of the twelfth century or the beginning of the thirteenth, by Thomas of Celano and sung in the Mass for the dead. In the triple stanzas of this wonderful poem the rhymed Latin of the Middle Ages attained its highest perfection. A special place among sequence composers should be saved for the profound poet and musician Heriman, called Hermannus Contractus, or "the Lame" (1013–1054), who belonged to the Suabian family of the counts of Vehringen. He studied at St. Gall and became a Benedictine monk in the monastery of Reichenau. Author of important chronicles and tracts on mathematics and music, he is chiefly remembered for the beautiful sequences *Ave Praeclara Maris Stella* and *Alma Redemptoris Mater.* In his most mature work, *Salve Regina,* Heriman unites sequence and antiphon into an organic, solemn, and independent musical composition. In these poignant compositions we are celebrating the coming of age of Occidental music. Here begins its history, and here begins

Twelfth-Century Sculpture from Chartres Cathedral Showing Carillon and Psaltery

Carolingian Ivory with Liturgic Scene

Allegorical Bas-Relief from the Campanile in Florence, by Giotto (c. 1266–1337), and Andrea Pisano (1290–1343)

Late Fourteenth-Century Wood-carving from Bamberg Cathedral

also the history of national music, because the difference between the French and German sequences (Italy still being inactive) is apparent.

A third flourishing of sequence poetry occurred at the beginning of the sixteenth century in St. Gall under the abbacy of Francis Geisberg, owing, no doubt, to the inspiration of Notker's canonization.

The sequences were the means through which sacred music found its way into the world, although the opposite procedure was equally important. The monks themselves endeavored to substitute new Christian songs for the heathen songs of the world. Otfried's *Evangelienbuch* (the book of Gospels in the vernacular) owes its existence to such intentions.

The Decline of Gregorian Art

WITH the introduction of new feasts the wealth of plain song grew considerably. The new compositions, which increased continually beginning with the ninth century, differed little in their musical style from the traditional songs, because a certain procedure was followed by which model melodies were equipped with new texts and developed into new antiphons. Some melodies had as many as seventy or eighty variants. Thus the old composition method and technique of Christian antiquity, as exemplified in the Byzantine *heirmos*,[9] found an exact parallel in the medieval West. While the style did not change materially, the musical language of the new compositions, especially the responds, was enriched.

With this period we arrive at a turning point in the history of music. The lack of guides, hasty copying of manuscripts, the incapacity of singers to present the delicate songs, weaken the laboriously built edifice. In the tenth century the theorists sound an alarm at the sight of the disintegration which takes places in the domain of Gregorian art, but their voices go unheeded. The monument of this great art crumbles under the inexperienced hands of the professional musicians of the tenth century, and at the opening of the eleventh the commentators and chroniclers of the art predict the passing even of that which remained from the great period. And the following generations, after the chroniclers disappeared, knowing only a disfigured monument, cannot imagine the splendor which characterized its mature state. Thus a *tradition* is established in the light of which the monument seems imposing merely on account of its vastness, its mass, and not because of the purity of its architectural lines. In the twelfth century, pure Gregorian art ceased to live, but on the ruins of the old art was to be built a new edifice, the so-called *musica mensurata,* or "measured" music.

What were the causes, direct and indirect, of the downfall of Gregorian art? The main one was perhaps its rapid expansion, carried on with great zeal by Rome and its emissaries. Northern Occidental singers, however, found it difficult to assimilate this music, Oriental in nature, with their natural musical instincts and traditions. If in the eleventh century the musical theorists, especially Guido and his commentator, Aribo (Scholasticus), considered it their duty to aid the preservation of the laws of music by a clear and unequivocal system of notation, they were motivated by the uncertain diffusion of Gregorian tradition and practice. The supervision and correction of liturgical music, imposed officially in all lands to carry out the desire of Rome for a uniform liturgic chant, was opposed by age-old local usages the guardians of which were reluctant to accept an alien musical idiom. The antiphonals carried the practice of Gregorian chant to the confines of the Christian world, but by receding farther and farther from its center of authority, the music, like a ray of light which becomes less and less distinct the farther it gets from its point of origin, gradually lost the certitude of its proper execution. An original manuscript was copied twenty, thirty times and a legion of mistakes crept into the copies. St. Bernard, concluding his treatise on ecclesiastic chant, voiced the truth when he remarked: "Take the antiphonal of Rheims and compare it with that of Soissons, Amiens, or Beauvais; if, beginning with the first page, you find any similarity, render homage unto God." Aribo expressed the same opinion: "Formerly the composers and singers exerted the greatest care in writing the manuscripts and executing the noted songs, but for some time these considerations have been dead letters and are interred."

The opposition of the musical instinct of faraway Franks and Gauls engendered another direct cause for the disintegration of Gregorian music, the tropes, which speedily affected all the music of the Ordinary of the Mass. In place of the simple original melodies grew songs of an elaborate character, and even the new melodies were further elaborated by tropes. As the development continued there was little left that had not suffered from these parasites. And before the definite organization of the material, requested by erudite theorists and theologians, could take place, the first timid experiments in polyphony opened a new vista, full of promise and of possibilities which soon occupied all speculative and eager minds.

The interpretation of the Gregorian melismata became more and more vague, and by the time of the Renaissance the tradition was almost obliterated. Sixteenth- and seventeenth-century editors mutilated the melodies and forced them into strict rhythmical frames in order to make easier an instrumental-chordal accompaniment by the organ. Gregorian chant became the rather monotonous plain chant with organ accompaniment which reigned until the Benedictines of the Congregation of France, led by Guéranger, Pothier, and Mocquereau, started a genuine revival of Gregorian traditions. These scholars collated all the available manuscripts and proved that the printed editions presented a corrupted version of the chants. The service books published by the Benedictine monks of Solesmes showed their superiority and their greater conformity to the true tradition, and the scientific handling of the questions at issue was carried on in the successive volumes of the monumental collection entitled *Paléographie Musicale* (since 1889). Through this patient work and ardent and devoted enthusiasm the Vatican itself has been conquered, and since the *Motu proprio* of Pope Pius X (1903) Gregorian music has been restored to its ancient eminence, while the *Editio Vaticana* makes it available to the smallest church. It is regrettable, however, that the wholly arbitrary practice of chordal accompaniment still persists in most Catholic churches. The work of the Benedictines of Solesmes is a magnificent example of scholarship, and we may consider as solved the melodic problems of the restored Gregorian song, but the rhythmical aspects remain obscure despite the activities of Dom Mocquereau and his brothers religious. One has only to compare the theories of the leading scholars of ecclesiastic music on rhythmic interpretation to discover the chasm that separates them.

Gregorian Chant in the Universal Sacred Art of the Romanesque Period

GREGORIAN chant is not merely a form of music, it represents an epoch; it occupied an enormously important position not only in the history of arts and letters, but in the history of civilization. For centuries it was the only kind of music officially known, taught, and practiced. Having originated in Rome, Gregorian chant spread, carried by the ambassadors of the Holy See, all over the Christian world and entered into conflict with the life, religious rites, and music of the people. It sought to suppress everything else, or at least to assimilate the indigenous. Sometimes it had to face a prolonged struggle, as in Spain; sometimes it was even unable to impose itself on local customs, as in Milan; but it ended by triumphing, and gradually plain chant absorbed all other music. The medieval man heard in the psalmody, in the numerous vocalizations and jubilations of the alleluia, in the finely wrought melodic line and the truly basilicalike solidity of the *cantus planus,* things that we cannot evoke today, for all this is a resurrected art. When listening to the restored Gregorian melodies we admire them, we are even able to experience religious fervor, but the very fact that we accompany them on the organ shows that the essence of this art has escaped the modern man.

The beauty of Gregorian chant requires study and familiarization. Just as the eighteenth and nineteenth centuries regarded Romanesque art as the curious expression of a barbaric age, so this noble music was always relegated to introductory chapters on primitive music. Romanesque architecture has regained an important position in the appreciation of medieval art, but most of us still fail to see that music constitutes one of the prime factors of the Romanesque period. The great difference between sacred and secular art that was typical in the last centuries of Christian antiquity disappeared, because the very existence of a secular art was ignored by the spirit of the period. Like architecture, music united and fused into its orbit secular elements in order to bring them into the service of divine worship, and with its beautiful melodies became the most powerful and effective member of universal Romanesque art. This great liturgic music represents a period in the life of peoples in which slowly evolving national traits were united in the light of the great unifying force of the papacy. The singers and composers collected and invented their melodies for the greater glory of the Church; they did not as yet know the lure of personal ambition.

The intimate connection between Gregorian music and Romanesque art becomes evident when we examine the stylistic phenomena in Romanesque architecture and compare them with the music of the period. Springing from Roman and Byzantine traditions, both architecture and music retained and developed the characteristic traits which had showed only tentative beginnings in late antiquity, such as the turning away from the plastic and a penchant for the ornamental. These elements remained more or less dominant, though blended with Eastern influences and with Celtic and Lombard elements which lent the barbaric vigor that so vitalize Romanesque art. The primitive Norman and Anglo-Saxon carving was surpassed by the more decorative Celtic expression, and this was paralleled by the influence of music in the Carolingian period. Early Christian style was continued in the unvaulted churches, bare of sculptural treatment and very much like the unadorned majestic melodies of the early plain chant. In the tenth and eleventh centuries, when Gregorian art showed a tendency to large and elaborate constructions exhibiting endless melismata of embellishment, the advanced and differentiated Lombard, Norman, Rhenish, and other local varieties of architecture displayed the round arch and vault, the decorative use of arcades and colonettes, and a profuse application of carved ornaments. The interiors of buildings did not yet offer a unity composed throughout: the flat, colorfully painted ceilings of the German cathedrals, and the cylindrical vaults of the southern French churches did not grow organically from the side walls; they merely solved the problem of a necessary completion of an enclosed space like the ever-evolving melos of the contourless chant. Plastic monuments as well as gigantic murals, easily accommodated in the large buildings, did not contribute to general unity and did not carry out the functions of representation determined by the laws of their respective arts. Sculpture fulfilled an almost purely ornamental role, while the few examples of painting that have been preserved show, despite the monumental effect they create, a distinct leaning toward the decorative.

Musicians and artists followed the scholars in restricting themselves to the elucidation of tradition which had been handed down to posterity.

Viewed from the perspective of many centuries, the Romanesque world shows that the spiritual and artistic life of an epoch, originating from dissimilar and independent conditions and exigencies, had united in a rhythm which embraced all of its components and which gave it a sharply defined profile. If the early Romanesque period did not know the richness and dramatic qualities which characterized subsequent periods, it now captivates by its evenness, steadiness, and symmetry. Wherever we look, whether at the *summae* of the scholars, the cathedrals of the architects, the hymns and songs of the musicians, or the philosophically serene chronicles of the historians, we behold that *gravitas* which, a legacy of Rome's most glorious times, lends to this period a truly aristocratic majesty. This majesty was equaled by an inner force which we used to see and appreciate only in the mighty edifices of Romanesque architecture, because the scientific tracts and the major part of literature retained only the interest of the scholar. But do we really appreciate the meaning and function of the great cathedrals if we exclude an essential element of Romanesque art and life which filled their naves with sounds and melodies?

Economic conditions were, according to available sources, simple. It appears that people acquired only things that were essential for the pursuit of a simple life. Yet there arose, in all places where the political situation reached some stability, cathedrals of such gigantic proportions that it seemed as if the towns and cities for which they were built harbored thousands and thousands of inhabitants instead of the relatively small number of souls who could fill the nave. Even the monasteries, which housed a few hundred religious, built spacious churches. The universal simplicity of life and the sparseness of the population did not justify such enormous edifices. They stand as monuments of the religious convictions of the man of the Romanesque era; they represent the humble Benedictine ideal of holiness and, at the same time, the ideology of the aristocracy which provided the means for the erection of the cathedrals. In the Benedictine-Gregorian conception of the Romanesque man, God stood infinitely closer to the center of life and worship than in the Franciscan-mystical conception of individual piety of the Gothic man. Divine service was still a purely courtly honoring of the highest Lord and Ruler, and it was befitting that this all-highest majesty be provided with a palace such as no king on earth could possess. Homage was rendered to him day and night, with Psalms and hymns, and it was this music which embodied the Romanesque religious ideal, without which the universal sacred art of these centuries presents mere samples of architecture, sculpture, or literature. What St. Augustine said hundreds of years ago is still the motto of universal Romanesque art:

Sing with your voices, and with your hearts,
and with all your moral convictions,
sing the new songs, not only with your tongue
but with your life.

Secular Music in the Carolingian Period

THE picture of secular and popular-spiritual music of the courtly art of the Carolingian and post-Carolingian period is much more colorful than that of the uniform liturgic art. In the Latin poetry of this art lived, clad in antique garments, the German and French narrative songs, alternating with the odes of Horace and other classical poetry newly set to music and accompanied by the fiddle or the harp. While we have no corresponding musical documents, the quality of this poetry is indisputably musical. A little later we encounter the first specimen of Old French poetry, a short song recorded in 882 celebrating the martyrdom of St. Eulalia. The music is unfortunately missing but the title of the original Latin sequence, *Cantica Virginis Eulalie Concine Suavissona Cithara,* which served as a model for the French version, indicates that a minstrel was required to play the accompaniment on an instrument. The tradition of the antique citharoedia did not disappear with the dissolution of the Western Roman Empire. The numerous decrees and canons issued by various councils prohibiting profane cithara playing attest its popularity. The cithara survived in western Europe far into the Middle Ages, partly because its construction was so similar to the traditional accompanying instrument of the Celtic bards. The ancient Celtic lyre, very popular in the early Middle Ages, became one of the chief musical instruments in the Carolingian period under the name of *rotta,* which was the Middle High German equivalent for the original old Irish *crot* or *cruit* and the Welsh *crwth.* The extreme old age of this instrument may be gauged by the fact that Diodorus of Sicily (first century B.C.) mentions it in the hands of the Celtic bards. Venantius Fortunatus (530–609), Bishop of Poitiers and the chief Latin poet of his time, already calls it *chrotta britanna.* Besides the *rotta* the Carolingian period favored especially the harp, which attained its greatest popularity in the British Isles. This old Asiatic instrument, equally favored in Byzantium and in Britain, became so closely associated with the British that around 1000 the Continentals called it *cithara anglica.* Dante mentions it as an instrument coming from Ireland, and it is still the symbol and emblem of that country.

Also of Asiatic origin were the bells which were brought to Europe at an early age by the Celts. The earliest bells had the shape of a sugar loaf and must have had a rather dull tone. The well-known contour of our church bells was introduced by the Gothic, and with it came the typical sonority of the bell. Besides being highly appreciated for their music throughout the Middle Ages, bells had the important function of regulating the daily lives of the people. In the France of the thirteenth century the day was divided into three parts: matins, *midi,* and vespers. Bells were rung at six in the morning (the *Ave Maria* bells), at noon, and in the evening (vespers). Somewhat later the bells rung in the morning, noon, and evening were called the *Angelus* bells. The institution of the Angelus is ascribed to Pope John XXII, and the bell is rung in the following way: thrice, thrice, thrice, and nine times. The *midi* bell is called *none* from the Latin, signifying the ninth hour after sunrise, and from which our word "noon" is derived.

There are many old customs connected with the use of church bells. The best known and perhaps the oldest of these is the curfew (*couvre-feu*), originally the bell-ringing signal to cover up the fire, extinguish all lights, and retire for the night. The custom was common throughout Europe in the Middle Ages, and applied to all classes of people. The "harvest bell" and "seeding bell" fixed the hours for beginning and leaving off gleaning, so that everyone might start fair and have an even chance. The "market bell" was a signal for selling to begin; the "passing bell," rung for the dying, is now generally rung after death. All this may be summed up in an inscription stamped in monkish Latin upon a bell:

> Funera plango, fulgura frango, Sabbata pango,
> Excito lentos, dissipo ventos, paco cruentos.

> ("I mourn for death, I break the lightning, I fix the
> Sabbath, I rouse the lazy, I scatter the winds,
> I appease the cruel.")

According to St. Augustine and Cassiodorus, the Occident knew the organ long before King Pepin received one from the Byzantine emperor in 757. Numerous miniatures and bas-reliefs confirm their statements, but the interesting fact remains that this instrument, expressly secular in nature and usage in the East, became a symbol of religious music in the West, and its players were recruited, until the Reformation, mostly from among the clergy. Shortly after the year 800 an organ constructed by an Arabian maker was sent to Charlemagne by the Caliph Haroun Alrashid, and was placed in a church in Aix. It was a wind organ of extraordinarily soft tone. Another organ was built at the order of Charlemagne and erected in the cathedral, and soon German, French, and English monks were busy constructing similar instruments. The native artisans in England even introduced the custom of pipe decoration. The little organs they built served mainly to improve the intonation in singing the plain chants and as an auxiliary instrument for vocal instruction. They had the compass of one diatonic octave. Instead of a regular keyboard and keys, these instruments had small wooden plaques in a vertical position, upon each of which a letter indicated the note it gave out. The player flapped up the plaque, whereupon the wind gained access to the pipe until the player relaxed his hold. This manner of playing, to be ascertained from several contemporary tracts, refutes the frequently expressed idea that organ playing was rough, slow, and heavy throughout the Middle Ages, for these small instruments were neither heavy nor slow.

Toward the middle of the tenth century we already encounter larger instruments which play an important role in the church services. A veritable giant among organs is reported at Winchester in 980; but while this instrument had some four hundred pipes, it did not yet have a regular keyboard, this having been introduced only in the twelfth century. In the twelfth and thirteenth centuries the addition of many stops complicated the mechanism of the instrument and the playing became more difficult, in spite of the introduction of the keyboard. The early keys are described as being from three to five inches wide, or even more, two inches thick, from a foot and a half to a yard or more in length, and with a fall sometimes as much as a foot in depth. The traction naturally became heavy, especially in damp weather when the wood swelled, and the players had to use their fists and elbows; hence the term, *organum pulsare* or *Orgelschlagen,* to hit or beat the organ. The great future church organ with several keyboards, a pedal board, and a variety of stops was a product of the Gothic period.

Among the other instruments, we should mention the psaltery, which came from Spain although it was of Arabic-Persian origin, and, the most important bowed instrument of the Middle Ages, the fiddle. Like most other instruments the fiddle attained its final Occidental form during the ensuing Gothic. The Orient also furnished the West with a number of wind and percussion instruments. Flutes, trumpets, and horns, as well as cymbals and snare drums, were all popular with the itinerant musicians. Early medieval miniatures testify to the great popularity of chimes, little pear-shaped or semispherical bronze bells hung up on a rod and manipulated by one or several players with small metallic hammers.

In addition to the sequence and its variants, the chief form of secular music everywhere known, we naturally find a rich literature of school songs, legends, and love songs, which will be discussed in the next chapters, although chronologically they belong here. First we must follow, however, the destinies of the Gregorian song and the musical types engendered by it, as such a procedure will help us to gain a complete picture of the role played by Gregorian art in the history of civilization.

The struggle inaugurated by the patristic writers against secular music was vigorously continued, and it was especially aimed at the introduction of profane music into the sanctuaries. Judging, however, from the various acts of church legislature, it is apparent that this much-feared profane music was far from having been eradicated. The Council of Cavaillon (650) expressed indignation over the obscene songs which could be heard at religious ceremonies, dedications of churches, and on feasts honoring the martyrs. Despite all efforts at curtailment, profane music continued to enjoy considerable vogue. The priests themselves were evidently attracted by it, and the Church felt obliged to remind them constantly not to poison their minds and endanger their dignity by listening to the performances of minstrels. The Council of Tours (813) ordered the priests to be on their guard against all things that tended to soften their souls, were it by hearing or by sight. It was especially the manner of singing that concerned ecclesiastic authorities, who reminded the clergy that they should respect the act of singing in a consecrated place and that their singing contributed to the glorification of God and the edification of the faithful. The Council of Glasgow (747) decreed that the priest should imitate neither the soft enunciation of worldly poets nor the tragic accents used by actors, because this would bring confusion in the sacred texts. All these acts indicate, indeed, that, while despised, profane music held its own.

In the movement associated with the name of Hildebrand, the future Pope Gregory VII, the influence of the Abbey of Cluny was thrown strongly on the side of religious and ecclesiastic reform. By the middle of the twelfth century Cluny had become the center of a great order embracing several hundred monasteries in all parts of Europe and even in the Holy Land. This movement left its stamp on all domains of life and renewed the strong opposition to secular art and learning. The ascetic ideal overshadowed the Carolingian ideal of universal learning, the individual traits making up its nature being discipline, obedience, taciturnity, humility, abstinence, hospitality, and fostering of the practice of psalmody. Indeed, the cultivation of psalmody was one of the most important tenets of the Cluniac reform, a fact often overlooked by historians. There was a tendency to prolong and multiply the church services far beyond the canonical office, so that they came to occupy nearly the whole day. According to the chroniclers the daily psalmody exceeded one hundred Psalms! Odo, the great abbot of the monastery of Cluny, whose work made the institution one of the greatest monastic centers in the Middle Ages, was himself an accomplished musician and was described as singing Psalms on his trips of inspection.[10] All his biographers praise him as a skilled teacher and composer. As in the period of Gregory the Great, who may be considered Odo's model, the practice of music became a means of discipline, and we can see that in this new austere world of devotion sciences and literature were not welcome; the Cluniac monasteries were true to the Gregorian spirit and allotted little time for study of the humanities. From the middle of the tenth century until the middle of the twelfth, Cluny was the chief seat of religious influence throughout western Europe, and its abbot, next to the pope, was the most important ecclesiastic in the Latin Church.

Theoretical, Artistic, and Philosophical Conceptions of Music

WHILE the Italian monasteries and schools did not contribute much to the advancement of arts and letters in the early Romanesque period, they produced at least one important figure, Guido d'Arezzo (c. 980–1050). Of his life little is known, although references to him in the works of contemporaries are by no means rare. The place of his birth is uncertain in spite of some evidence pointing to Arezzo (Tuscany). Dom Germain Morin [11] advocated the theory that Guido was born near Paris and received his early education in the monastery of St. Maur-des-Fosses. While this possibility was generally disregarded, in spite of the fact that some manuscripts indicate the authorship of a certain Guido de Sancto Mauro, it appears that the question is not yet closed. The fact that Italy did not take an active part in scientific and literary undertakings shows the prevalence of the Benedictine and Gregorian precepts. It is remarkable, then, to find among the Italians a man who was such an eminent scholar that he was called *Beatus Guido, inventor musicae*. Certain traits in his works show convincingly that he was an adherent of the Cluniac reforms. His aim was to educate the singer as rapidly as possible to the point where he would be able to sing unfamiliar melodies by merely looking at the written notation. To achieve this end he left out everything "that was irrelevant to good singing and which was contributed by the philosophers, as not worth mentioning." [12] Thus the scientific aim was discarded, according to Cluniac precepts.

At his first appearance in history Guido was a monk in the Benedictine monastery of Pomposa, and it was there that he taught singing and invented his educational method, by means of which, according to his own statement, a pupil might learn within five months what formerly would have taken him ten years to acquire. The jealousy of his fellow monks drove him to Arezzo, where he remained until his fame had spread to Rome. Pope John XIX invited him in 1027(?) to demonstrate his method. Guido handed over to the pope an antiphonal written in his new mode of notation and, "after explaining the rules to the pontiff, the latter, to his great astonishment, was able to sing a melody unknown to him, without the slightest mistake." [13] Guido's achievement, one of the most significant in the history of music, was the organization of previous timid attempts at concise notation into a system which still forms the basis of our modern notation.

In early medieval notation pitch relationship was only approximately conveyed. That this method of notation originated in the Orient, as we have seen to be the case, is evident from its name, neuma, from the Greek νεῦμα, meaning "sign"; consequently we are dealing with a chironomic system of direction. In the oldest times the signs, which resemble stenographic symbols and were put above the text, did not indicate pitch or intervals; they merely showed the direction in which the melody was moving, giving vague indications as to its rise and fall. If we recall the lucid and precise system of musical notation of ancient Greece, so primitive a method of musical writing seems almost unbelievable. We must assume, however, that the classical system was not transmitted, because as late as the beginning of the seventh century, Isidore of Seville, the great polyhistor, appears to be ignorant of any means by which music can be preserved for posterity. "For if music is not retained by man's memory, it is lost, since it cannot be written down." This is indisputable testimony to the fact that even if ancient notation had been known in the first centuries of the Christian era, it was completely forgotten by this time. Neumatic notation presupposed oral tradition; the singers sang by heart and watched the gestures of the precentor or leader, who took his bearings from the neumes. Only when the important innovation of the lines came into use did the neumes become more than "an auxiliary to aid the memory," as Hucbald still called them in the tenth century. The elements of notation which Guido used as a starting point were one or two lines (usually one) which, while clearing somewhat the ambiguity of the neumes, still afforded only a vague method of recording. Guido's introduction of a system of four lines and four spaces (*spatia*) between the lines, marked by clefs, put an end to all ambiguity. Besides his significant innovation in the field of graphical notation, Guido was the inventor of the use of a set of syllables to denote the individual tones of the scale. "Inventor" is again somewhat misleading, because such systems (later called solmization) were age-old and the earliest Chinese, Egyptian, and Greek records testify to their use. But Guido's invention had a decisive effect on the development of musical instruction in the Occident. He used the first syllables of six lines of an ancient Sapphic hymn addressed to St. John the Baptist.

> *Ut* queant laxis *Re*sonare fibris,
> *Mi*ra gestorum *Fa*muli tuorum,
> *Sol*ve polluti *La*bii reatum,
> Sancte Joannes.

The invervals between the individual notes resulting from this new nomenclature were a whole tone between *ut-re, re-mi, fa-sol, sol-la,* while that between *mi* and *fa* was a half tone. The system was applicable, through transposition, to any scale, provided the *mi-fa* interval and its position in the scale were observed. In France and Italy the syllables *ut, re,* etc. have become identified with the notes *c, d,* etc., but except in France, *do* has supplanted *ut* as being more sonorous. In addition to this Guido is credited with the invention of the so-called Guidonian hand, a figure representing the tones of the gamut on the left hand, used in teaching solmization. Each note of the scale was assigned to a joint of the hand, to which the singing master pointed. When the pupils memorized the meaning of the "hand" they had the intervals and scales literally at their finger tips.

Guido's memorable reformatory activity made it possible for every monastery and church to obtain an exact copy of the antiphonal, thereby minimizing the importance of the *schola cantorum* as the only place where oral tradition was faithfully observed, and indeed, the importance of the *schola* continued to decline until it became the champion of the great polyphonic art of the Renaissance.

Guido's writings and the tracts of the principal musical authors are united in the two important anthologies of Gerbert and Coussemaker. These collections give us works dealing with musical theory and philosophy from the eighth to the fifteenth century, that is, from the great period of Gregorian art to its decline. It is remarkable how Gregorian science and music were handed down in an uninterrupted line of masters and disciples, from the time of Charlemagne to the period of Guido, after which the tradition gradually faded away.

When reading these tracts one is surprised at the extraordinary flourishing of theories and doctrines which often drift into the fantastic, especially when speculating about the origin of music. Who was the inventor of music? This is a question which interested many authors. Jerome of Moravia [14] and "Pseudo-Aristotle," [15] a musical scholar of the twelfth and thirteenth centuries, were strongly in favor of Jubal, son of Cain. Their theory is frequently encountered even in more recent times. It appears in the *Musurgia* (Rome, 1650) of the learned German Jesuit archaeologist and scientist, Athanasius Kircher. Chaucer and his contemporaries made frequent references to the origin of music which they also connected with Jubal, or Tubal as it is written in Middle English texts, owing to the graphical similarity of Middle English *I* and *T*. Thus Chaucer in his *Court of Love* speaks of "Tuball himself, the first musician," and Wyclif says that "Tuball was the fadre of syngerys in harp and orgon." Other authors considered Pythagoras the father of music, while still others indulged in fantastic etymological explanations which would carry us into forbidding fields.

In the institutions dominated by the Cluniac doctrines musical instruction consisted of the teaching of singing. The function of music was to supplement and enhance prayer and was supposed to be the expression of spontaneous religious feeling and sentiment. On the other hand we observe the learned musicians among the clergy beginning to take the point of view of the artist. The following passage, taken from Hucbald's writings in the second volume of Gerbert's anthology, also indicates that the competition between secular music and official church music must have been lively: "The flute and lyre players and other secular musicians and singers exercise the utmost care to evoke pleasure by their artistic productions, melodies, and compositions. And we, who have the honor to utter the words of divine majesty, pronounce them without any art and with negligence. We should, perhaps, seek the beauty of art for the saintly things, the beauty which is abused by the histrions and musicians for their vanities."

Beauty and perfection of liturgical singing was evidently a thing close to the heart of the monk of St. Amand, but unlike his immediate predecessors, he did not try to find justification and remedy in the doctrines and customs of ancient times; he wished to keep pace with his own epoch. He did not hesitate to reproach his contemporaries for their lack of knowledge in the theoretical branches of music, by reminding them how the wandering minstrels and histrions, despised as they were, tried to satisfy the public by progress in their art. In the next century the writers already insist on the necessity of a thorough knowledge of music and its science for all church musicians because, in their opinion, this would distinguish them from the minstrels. Soon we read opinions which convince us that times have changed, in spite of the reign of Cluniac ideals. John Cotton, learned and much-traveled English musical scholar (fl. 1100), declared that a singer without theoretical training is a useless person. "I can compare him to a drunkard who, while he is able to find his home, is completely ignorant of the way that took him home." [16] The conception of medieval scholars may be summarized in a poem supposedly composed by Guido d'Arezzo, and mentioned by Jerome of Moravia at the very beginning of his treatise.

Musicorum et cantorum magna est distancia:
Isti dicunt, illi sciunt que componit musica,
Nam qui canit quod non sapit, diffinitur bestia
Bestia non cantor qui non canit arte, sed usu,
Non uerum facit ars cantorem, sed documentum.

Your musician and your singer dwell the poles apart,
These recite, those understand the true musician's art.
Who sings whereof he knoweth not, a mere brute is he;
A brute by rote and not by art produces melody.
But doctrine too, not skill alone, is musician's warranty.

All authors of the Romanesque period exhibit a curious mixture of conservatism and progressive views. They all respect the traditions and the writings of the Church Fathers, yet they keep pace with progress. Cotton has great regard for the maxims of the past, yet he is something of a modern liberal. Like most of his contemporaries he has vague notions about the origin of liturgic music and gives credence to the legend that it was St. Gregory who, with the aid of the Holy Ghost, composed the melodies and organized the music of the Roman Church. (This should again remind us how old the Gregorian legends are and how little people knew about the origin and history of this music even as early as the tenth and eleventh centuries.) But the pious Englishman also insists that he and his contemporaries have an equal right to contribute to the development of church music, and to set to music the words of worship. To counteract the evident popularity of secular music, most writers enlarged upon the legend of Gregory and the Holy Ghost and insisted upon the presence of angels during prayers and devotional music. It is surprising how widely this idea, which first appeared in the writings of St. John Chrysostom and St. Basil, was disseminated in the Middle Ages. Bede and Cotton in England and Bernard de Clairvaux in France were the chief exponents of this conviction among the older writers, but we can follow the idea up to the beginning of the fourteenth century, at which time we encounter the first musical scholar and chronicler who assumed an ironical attitude about celestial music. Johannes de Grocheo (fl. c. 1300) [17] speaks of authors who pretend that "music is particularly agreeable because it is practised by the angels"; "however," adds our skeptical historian, "it is not within the province of a musician to talk about the song of angels, unless he is a theologian or a prophet." With Grocheo we reach the first person who does not deal exclusively with the music of the church, and it becomes evident that his ironical attitude has something to do with the fact that for the first time in musical literature we are now entertained by the description of *musica civilis* and *musica vulgaris*. The sympathetic treatment accorded these subjects by Grocheo indicates that we are entering upon a new era.

Chapter 6

FURTHER DIFFUSION OF GREGORIAN ART

≫≫ ≪≪

Emergence of Drama from the Liturgy

MEN have always been fond of singing, and the Church permitted them to borrow her music for purposes not connected with religious worship. The medieval man sang the Psalms and canticles in church, adding to them songs of his own, and when he departed from service he carried with him the memory of the melodies, which he turned into love songs. The Church allowed him to sing profane songs modeled on those which were meant for the exaltation of divine love, and sanctioned the singing of songs in the midst of battle, because she knew that after the carnage he would come back and, tamed again, would return to his church, his saints and virgins, and the same lips which sang the songs of love, mockery, farce, and blood would repent and sing in honor of his submission to the Alma Mater. The Church showed herself indulgent in these matters because the supposedly crude realism of the Middle Ages hid an idealism which forgave man his weaknesses in order to lead him to the idea of his duty to God.

Every religion generates drama, and religious rites take on voluntarily and spontaneously a dramatic, theatrical aspect. But gestures and words are not sufficient to convey the ideas engendered, wherefore music and the dance came to complete the gamut of expressions. Thus the Catholic rites and their dramatic development were responsible for the formation of the medieval theater, both serious drama and comedy. Such also had been the course of evolution in classical times when Greek drama issued from the cult of Dionysus. One would think that with the gigantic creations of Greek tragedy and the highly developed Latin comedy of the Romans, the theatrical art of the Middle Ages already had a solid foundation to build on. The classical authors were not forgotten, it is true; they were not only read but imitated, and Terence and Plautus, especially, enjoyed great popularity. But they were known in the schools only, especially Orléans and Fleury-sur-Loire in France.

Gustave Cohen has published two remarkable volumes of Latin comedies written in France in the twelfth century.[1]

The attempt to bring home to the unlettered people the reality of the chief events connected with the Christian religion was the point of departure for the medieval stage. The shepherds who at Christmas time come into Rome from the mountains to pipe before the picture of the Virgin, or the German and Bohemian peasants who, down to the nineteenth century, used to go round their villages in the guise of the Three Kings, illustrate the way in which the efforts of the Church were seconded by the common people Not from imitations of Euripides and Terence, but from such simple cus toms as these did the medieval theater take its beginnings. We must not for get that in England the great cycles of mystery plays and moralities repre sented theatrical art almost to the time of Shakespeare, and that in France, as late as the seventeenth century, the principal theater of the country, the Hôtel de Bourgogne, belonged to the Confraternity of the Passion Players.

Dramatic art, in its cradle, was a religious art, and the theater emerged from the Church. The actors were, in the beginning, the ministers of the cult, and the plays they presented were episodes taken from the divine drama; there fore the pious artists who appeared at the beginning of Christian dramatic art found their emotional wealth in their faith. The liturgic drama developed throughout the Occident. Its presence is attested from Mont-Saint-Michel in France to Bari in Italy, from Silos in Spain to Vienna in Austria, and from Prague in Bohemia to York in England. There were two poles of the liturgy between which the liturgic drama evolved, the Resurrection and the Incarna tion. It is in the dialogued Gospels sung at the feasts of these two events that we must search for the origins of Christian drama. In the middle of the liturgic office, too short and too abstract for the multitude, the priest inserted dialogued representations of the evangelical scenes celebrated on those days: the Nativity and the Resurrection. The drama was short, reduced to its essentials, a simple paraphrase of the sacred text, carried out in a solemn and grave performance. Personal initiative soon claimed a larger place in the liturgic drama. The actors took liberties with the sacred texts, reserved the Latin for the versicles, the responds, and the lessons, and carried on the dialogues in the vernacular. Some of the plays are noteworthy in that their refrains in Old French are occasionally extended to short speeches. Similarly, German and Latin are mingled in German plays of the same period. These refrains and short speeches paved the way for the composition of whole plays in the vernacular, of which we find very early French specimens. The plays had been enacted in front of the altar by priests and clerks, but with the development of the vernacular element the presentation was transferred from the altar to the portal of the church, and the place of clergymen was taken by laymen who soon formed confraternities of actors.

Being an enlargement of the office, liturgic drama was, to a great extent, if not completely, executed in music. For a text borrowed from the liturgy, the music used was naturally the corresponding liturgical chant, but later, when the author of the drama wrote a dialogue for a special circumstance, he usually composed the melodies to be sung with the new text. It is only natural that these melodies followed, for some time, the general style and mood of Gregorian music, and were therefore sung in the liturgical manner. Yet in studying the music of such liturgic dramas as have been preserved, we may see that while the plain song-like melodies are faithful to the Gregorian tradition they show a very human quality and an intensity of expression which proves that Gregorian art is far from being a "purely objective and impersonal liturgic device."

The entirely musical character of the liturgic plays is demonstrated by the fact that a great number of the manuscripts contain the music in notation. Edmond de Coussemaker published a valuable collection of music taken from such plays.[2] Some of the miniatures found in the manuscripts disclose the use of a veritable orchestra. Besides the organ, prominently displayed, a variety of stringed and wind instruments and a whole battery of percussion instruments were employed. We shall see how later even cannon were used to enhance the spectacular splendor of the mystery plays.

A close examination of the liturgic drama, the semiliturgic drama, and the mystery plays will convince us of the fallacy of the sharply defined lines of demarcation between these types advocated by some literary historians. Conclusions such as theirs could have been reached only because the scholars in question neglected to examine the musical aspects of these dramatic creations. Even if the music were not available in perfectly legible plain-chant (chorale) notation, the utterances of the *dramatis personae* call for special music at every important point. The songs which were liberally inserted make the reading of the plays rather difficult, but if we place ourselves in the mental state of the medieval man, and attempt to listen to the music as the play unfolds, we shall gain an entirely different impression—one akin to that created by a Passion play or the musical setting of a Biblical story.

The first appearance of dramatic dialogue in the services of the Church may be traced back to the ninth century, when tropes and sequences flourished. The tropes were, as we have remarked before, phrases, sentences, or clauses with which the sung parts of the Mass were farsed, that is, amplified by interpolations. Especially widely known and admired was Tuotilo's trope to the Introit of the Christmas Mass: *Quis est iste puer quem tam magnis praeconiis dignum vociferatis?* This trope, which originated about 900, was sung by different singers who alternated in the presentation of the story, and thus belongs to the oldest monuments of that dramatization of the liturgy which gave rise to the various spiritual plays. The farsing was later done in the vernacular, the liturgic text remaining intact in Latin. It appears that the interpolations were very popular, no doubt because they conveyed the meaning of the celebration to the simple people ignorant of Latin. The rendition of such tropes was in dialogue form. The subdeacon mounted the ambo, where he read or sang the Epistles; opposite him stood two or three clerks robed in copes, who made the responses, and sang the paraphrase in the vernacular. The tropes and the farsed Epistles (*epistolae farcitae* or *épitres farcies*) acquired, a little later, meter and rhyme. This rhythmic invasion of the forms of liturgy spread and increased until there arose the so-called rhymed offices. As every church wished to pay homage to its local patron saint by an appropriate commemoration, a great number of specially composed offices called *historiae* were created, recounting the life of the saint. It is easy to see that this form of dramatic musical poetry was to lead to larger epico-dramatic types and, indeed, we shall have to fall back on these *historiae* when we come to discuss the origin of the oratorio. Owing to the great delight in poetry characteristic of the late Middle Ages, the rhymed offices enjoyed a lasting popularity. Their decline came with the general decline of hymns, which set in in the fifteenth century, and subsequent reforms of the breviary eliminated almost all of them.

The dramatic atmosphere was not restricted to the dialogue: an actual scenic setting furnished a truly theatrical background. The incidents which mark the birth of Christ, the adoration of the shepherds and of the Magi, the wrath of Herod, the massacre of the Innocents, provided the material for the Christmas cycle; the Resurrection that for the other important cycle of Easter. From the following simple dialogue sung at Eastertime developed the colossal literature of the Passion.

A monk representing an angel advances at dawn, palm in hand, and seats himself beside a veil, representing the grave-cloth, which has been spread out on the floor. Three *fratres* clad in dalmatics, representing the three Marys, enter as if seeking someone. They engage in the following dialogue with the first monk:

THE ANGEL: Whom seek ye in this sepulcher?
THE MARYS: We seek Jesus of Nazareth Who was crucified.
THE ANGEL (*lifting the veil*): He is not here, He is risen as He said. Go and announce His resurrection.
THE MARYS (*turning to the choir, sing*): The Lord is risen.

Many churches possessed, in the center of the nave or at the entrance to the choir, a crypt which enclosed the body of the saint to whom the church was consecrated, and which served for the scene of the Paschal drama.

The Christmas office goes back to equally humble origins. The manger scene which typifies this story even in our day existed at a very early date.

The *canonici* who played the shepherds, dressed in dalmatics, having received the announcement from the angels, arrive at the manger. Two priests of superior rank receive them. They are also dressed in dalmatics and represent the midwives. "Whom seek ye in this manger?" they ask the visitors. After the shepherds' answer the curtain is drawn and the Infant is shown to the people. This trope is evidently an adaptation of the Pascal trope.

Far from being a simple procession of figures, the liturgic drama showed all the elements of theatrical art which we associate with modern times. The facial expression, gestures, and accentuations of the players indicate that they tried to depict the mental state of the personages they were supposed to represent. This may be ascertained from the miniatures and other illustrations of the various mystery and liturgic plays, which display gesticulation and facial expression from tearful sorrow to ribald laughter. Judging from the requirements of these ancient libretti, particular emphasis was laid upon the vocal qualities of the actors, which is not surprising if we realize that the liturgic drama was in reality a music drama. The various manuscripts demanded explicitly that the lector of the Epistles, who usually took the role of Jesus, must have a soft voice, whereas the cleric who impersonated Judas must have a sharp and disagreeable voice. The voices of the angels were expected to be sweet, and the women's voices were to have a "humble" quality.

Some of the scenes were almost operatic in their lyrico-dramatic arrangement. The slaying of the Innocents was depicted in vivid drama, the children (whose parts were played by choirboys) being brutally slain by the soldiers, who did not heed the supplication of the mothers. Sprawled on the floor, the children sang antiphons with the angels, who were placed on a higher platform. Rachel was led in by two women who tried to comfort her. At the sight of the murdered children she expressed her grief in an extended lyrical scene, interrupted occasionally by her companions, until, when her sorrow became unbearable, she fainted.

The "lamento aria" of Mary Magdalen, which goes back to the fifth century, was connected with one of the most dramatic figures in the Easter play, a figure which provided an opportunity for poignant musical portrayals.[3] Her principal aspect is that of the penitent, hence the epithet "Magdalen." Artistic representations deal particularly with her repentance and with her meeting with Jesus after the Resurrection. While she is familiar to many from the paintings of Fra Angelico, Titian, and Correggio, little is known about her important place in the history of drama and music. The Mary Magdalen laments should be considered the very core of the musical drama. Little is known about the earlier forms of these laments, but beginning with Wipo (c. 1024–1050) they are numerous, and are always set to music with the greatest care and with tremendous dramatic inflection. Coussemaker [4] published a Mary Magdalen lament of the thirteenth century which contains not only music of highly dramatic quality, but precise stage directions.

A gradual increase in the number of dramatic personages necessitated the inclusion of lay actors, as the clergy were often not able to fill all the roles. The more lay people were admitted to the performance the less strictly was the use of Latin enforced. The participation of laymen apparently created a very profane atmosphere and elicited official censure. The Synod of Worms even prohibited lay participation and, in order to avoid regrettable incidents and vulgarities, decreed that the play of the Resurrection be acted, with due reverence, before the public was admitted to the church; consequently this became a sort of dress rehearsal without benefit of an audience other than "stage folk." This was, however, observed only locally. Many centuries of Christian education of the people of the Occident could not efface the age-old, pagan, and worldly enjoyment of life characteristic of peasants and burghers; and as soon as lay people were admitted to the active performance of liturgic plays, jollity and profanity appear within the sacred precincts of the church. The realism with which the truths of the Christian faith have been apprehended, and the underlying meaning of the irreverence and prurience with which the most sacred subjects were occasionally handled make us aware of that dualism of the medieval soul which prompted pious historians to call this dynamic period the "Dark Ages."

The organization of the liturgic dramas was entrusted to the clergy of the chapter, but the numerous pontifical directions and severe admonitions indicate that the secular influence became so strong that the dignity of their office was often disregarded, while the choirboys and minor clergy held veritable masquerades, on which occasions there were card playing and dice throwing right at the altar. The actors were recruited from all ranks of the clergy, together with laymen from all walks of life. Canons and monks, deacons and subdeacons, sextons and choirboys all participated and considered it a great privilege to do so. The feminine roles were given to clerics who donned tunics in semblance of feminine attire, and the part of angels was entrusted to choirboys. The most joyful and carefree among the actors were the students. Acting must have been very popular with them, because the scholastic plays have held their own uninterruptedly to our day. While the sincerity of the actors and their belief in the sanctity of their religious roles is not to be doubted, they were far from possessing the moral qualities of the personages they represented. A monk named Guibert gave an alarming description of the disorders and debauches which took place in conjunction with the solemn plays.[5]

Men and women, students and monks, rogues and noblemen, peasants and burghers were all eager spectators. Their interest in these religious dramas was twofold. They saw in the holy scenes a way to salvation, and their eagerness to contribute to the play was enhanced by the belief that they would receive their part of the grace emanating from the dramatized divine office; hence their desire to sing the response in their own tongue in which they could express themselves. But that they also enjoyed a large amount of curiosity and simple pleasure and fun in the spectacular cannot be denied. The predilection of the public for real and symbolical animal scenes has existed since classical times, and we can follow it up to the Wagnerian drama. In the medieval liturgic play it was the donkey which enjoyed the greatest popularity, and nothing was sung with more relish and deep-throated sonority than songs celebrating the Virgin's flight into Egypt. The Feast of the Ass, or the Feast of Fools, as it was often called, was the most celebrated feast in the Middle Ages, and was observed in many towns, especially in Sens and Beauvais. In spite of repeated remonstrances by the bishops and the powerful theological faculty of the University of Paris, the feast maintained for centuries its popularity in churches, monasteries, and schools. Such licentious plays and ceremonies must have originated in the disorder and confusion which followed Charlemagne's death. The people, only recently Christianized, did not entirely forget the memory of the ancient Lupercalia, the peculiar rites of the Roman feast to induce fertility, and the Saturnalia, celebrating the end of the year with a sort of carnival in which masters served their slaves and distributed gifts.

The story of the pretty girl riding an ass into the church has often been told and quoted in medieval and modern sources.[6] The famous "Prose of the Ass" known as *Orientis Partibus* was sung to different melodies of which the two principally known are the Sens and the Beauvais versions. There is a "modernized" edition in *Hymns Ancient and Modern* (London, 1909) which, unfortunately, disfigures the original melody to suit the musical taste of the people accustomed to "sweet" nineteenth-century hymns. From this collection it was transferred to the *American Episcopal Hymnal*. The "Song of the Ass" is now also sung to Wesley's words, "Christ the Lord Is Risen Today," and may be found in the *Harvard University Hymn Book*.

No restriction could curb the celebration of the Donkey Mass and other insolent audacities, especially in the drama of the shepherds, because no restriction could alter the temper of the medieval man, whose simple soul passed so rapidly from laughter to tears. Like children, these people laughed open-mouthed at the slightest provocation, and great was the joy of an audience when dignified clerics acted with the clownish gusto that would befit bedraggled actors of the *commedia dell' arte*. But when Herod finished his clowning and ordered the children put to death, the audience shed sincere tears in its commiseration with the poor mothers. This dualism of the medieval soul perplexes us even more if we leave the simple and credulous audiences of the liturgic plays and examine the works and philosophy of the men who continued the trope and song poetry and whose favored field was parody and persiflage.

Lyric Poetry, Parody, and Persiflage

AFTER the founding of the universities in the twelfth century many young theologians of all nations took to the road, eventually reaching one of these institutions. We know how much these students and clerics studied, but we also know that in the Parisian student homes (*bursae*) they led a merry life, sang wild songs, gambled, and drank freely. Going from university town to university town these students spent considerable time on the highways and in the taverns, and it is small wonder that after a few years of this carefree and worldly life many of the young *clerici* were reluctant to rejoin the strict monastery or take up the monotonous duties of a village priest. They strolled around on the highways as so-called *vagantes,* or vagrants, and earned their living by quackery and by entertaining the peasants and such other people as dared admit them into their company. The song-books of the *vagantes,* written in monkish Latin and neumatic notation, are interesting documents of the international lyric poetry of the twelfth to fourteenth centuries. A remarkable collection of them, found at the monastery at Benedictbeuren in Bavaria and published by Schmeller under the title *Carmina Burana,* was made toward the middle of the thirteenth century, but the origin of these songs is much more remote.

In England, France, and Germany these wandering clerks and students, the *vagantes,* were better known as "goliards." The term itself is a subject of philological discussion. It may come from the Latin *gula* (gluttony); from Golias, the legendary *archipoeta,* "ancestor of Pantagruel and Panurge alike"; or from Goliath, the giant being to medieval theologians the symbol of the enemies of Christ, or simply Satan himself. The *falsi fratres,* the goliards, were considered the creatures of Satan, who opposed everything that was sacred, true, and righteous. All the terms by which these fellows were known—*falsi fratres,* goliards, or *vagantes*—were rather vague and did not denote any specific person. But whatever the name meant, these student-polemists, practical jokers, and dice throwers were poets and musicians who, when they sang of love and the spring, were elegant and tenderly poetic, but when they turned to wine and gambling produced lines that represented the ultimate in obscenity. They did not restrict themselves to classical sources, and their urge for creative activity was not satisfied with original compositions of their own; they invaded the sacred fields of religion and applied those graceful verses to all sorts of profanities. Biblical passages were used for texts, and unbelievable as it may seem, no form of worship or ritual—hymns, litanies, even the Mass—was spared. The pious world must have suffered to hear these sung in sacred precincts in vestments; but on the other hand, the clergy themselves occasionally, in their effort to eradicate certain evil practices, used the parody Masses—a fact we must bear in mind when passing judgment on the nature of medieval parody.

Many of these drinking songs go back to the famous Marian sequence of the eleventh century which begins with

Verbum bonum et suave	A noble "Hail," word sweet and goodly
personemus illud Ave	We shall chant as is seemly;
per quod Christi fit conclave	Christ's is then our company
virgo, mater, filia . . .	Maid, mother, daughter.

Numerous variants from German, French, and Italian sources are known which usually start with *Vinum bonum et suave*. Other Marian songs were similarly parodized. *Ave virgo benedicta,* "Hail Blessed Virgin," was changed to *Alba limpha maledicta,* "Cursed clear drinking water," and the last amen was replaced by *stramen* (hay).

One must come to the conclusion that however secular and profane their intentions, Middle Latin poets could not sever themselves from the Church. The allusions indicate that most of them, even if they were not clerics, went through a theological education, and that their poems were meant for people who would understand the implications. The height of the tavern literature is represented by the parodistic versions of the Mass and the offices. Several manuscripts mention such works as *officium lusorum* (office of triflers), *Missa de potatoribus* (Mass of drinkers), or *officium ribaldorum,* etc. While the manuscripts are distributed throughout many countries, including England, Lehman is of the opinion that the first Mass parodies originated in France because French universities of the twelfth and thirteenth centuries excelled in this type of literary amusement.[7] The music of these Masses was not neglected; it followed the text faithfully, indicating that they were sung like regular celebrations.

All this sounds formidably cynical and depraved, but it would be manifestly unjust to see in these vagrant poets mere dissipated and besotted geniuses. Equally misleading is the tendency to consider all the authors of the *Carmina Burana* as lecherous priests. Many of the songs were composed by laymen who kept them in the *vagans* style for the sake of parody, and through the intermediary of the roaming students these songs reached the utmost popularity in the widest circles of the people. Nor must we be misled by the conception, still prevalent, of the historians of the romantic era, who were the first to consider the Middle Ages *the* Christian era—a conception based on the works and deeds of outstanding figures of the period. For even a cursory examination of the ecclesiastic literature of the multitude will disclose that, although the dignitaries of the Church enjoyed privileges in state and government equaled only by those of feudal lords and temporal rulers, the Cross had not yet conquered the world. Throughout the Middle Ages, but especially in the twelfth and thirteenth centuries, there were many people whose whole conception was antagonistic to the Church and often to the whole Christian religion. The materialistic and atheistic scoffers were not restricted to the ranks of the *falsi fratres* but were to be found among the learned *magistri* within the universities as well. Many of the goliards looked back on an excellent education; the great pleasure they found in imitation required a considerable dexterity and knowledge of theology and the liberal arts. The prime motive of their parodies was to create comical effects rather than to sneer at and soil the original texts. Medieval man readily turned to the profane for amusement, and amused himself vastly in doing so at the expense of the *representatives* of the Church, but his shafts were not aimed at the Church itself. In truth, the same spirit of secular enjoyment of life so widely disseminated even among the clergy emanated from these songs and parodies. This tendency was furthered by the influence of the scholars of the Sorbonne who claimed to be followers of the great Spanish-Arabian philosopher Averroës; they declared the mind free of all shackles of faith, and refused to recognize dogmas. The goliard poems are as truly "medieval" as the monastic life they despised; they are merely the voice of another section of humanity, and the goliard movement is indicative of the wide diversity of temperament among those who crowded the medieval universities, and who found in the privileges and advantages of the clerk some attraction to the student life. Their songs, which show an alert mind and a happy appreciation of nature, are very singable and are filled with manifestations of real fantasy which we cannot find in any other literature of their days.[8]

The Musical Origins of Medieval Lyric Poetry

> Les faibles d'Artur de Bretaigne
> E les chançons de Charlemaigne
> Plus sont cheries e meins viles
> Que ne soient les evangiles.
> Plus est escoutés li jugliere
> Que ne soit saint Pol ou saint Pierre . . .

FRENCH literature continued to dominate western Europe. England under the House of Anjou (Plantagenet) became one of the principal centers of French literary production, Flanders and the Rhine countries accepted and translated the French originals, the *chansons de geste* were sung by pilgrims going to Italy—as proved by Franco-Italian versions of the *Chanson de Roland*—and Italian poets wrote in Provençal. Dante himself, well acquainted with Provençal poetry, hesitated whether or not to write his great epic poem in the language of the troubadours. This wealth of lyric poetry has been the object of literary and historical research in many countries, but until recently scholars have concentrated their investigations on its purely poetical side and have failed to make it understood that the lyric poetry of the Middle Ages, since it was intended to be sung, must be considered as a combination of two arts, music and poetry, ceaselessly influencing each other. This incomplete conception is unfortunate, for it has resulted in erroneous views concerning both the music and the poetry of these centuries. The two cannot be separated because the accompanying music is in a large measure responsible for the disposition of the verses and strophes of the poems. Medieval lyric poets were themselves musicians and created melody and poetry simultaneously, fitting their lines to the musical cadences. In spite of many excellent monographs devoted to the subject,[9] the origin of this delicate and subtle poetry remains obscure; but one thing is certain, that it was accompanied by music in which we can see the astounding persistence and flowering of Gregorian art.

The art of the troubadours descended from the liturgic chant, preserving traditional church scales and even motives of liturgic origin. This is most clearly visible in the religious poetry which flourished in the southwest of France in the eleventh century. Here we are dealing with exact documents. In the chanson of *Sainte Foi d'Agen* it is stated that the song was "guided by the first tone" (*guidal primers tone*), which means that it evolved in the first Gregorian tone or scale. The carefree wandering minstrels—"no man wot from whence they come nor where they go"—soon appropriated these melodies for their use and, strolling through France, England, Germany, and Italy, sowed seeds for the development of European art music.

Feudalism and Its Art

FEUDALISM created the chivalric orders and classes, a phenomenon which occurred all over Europe and which was of prime importance in the history of civilization. The great feudal lords had their vassals, cavaliers, and footmen, and when these men acquired small fiefs of their own there arose a large group of small landowners who formed, together with the manor lords, a feudal-military society used to giving and executing orders, and spending its time in riding and hunting. This society evolved, according to its needs, a civilization of its own, opposed to the culture and educational system of the Church, laying great importance on the development of the body for war and for the tournament, exaggerated reverence of women, and the pursuit of material pleasure through the holding of feasts and other luxurious, spectacular, and exclusive gatherings. There is a certain analogy between medieval chivalry and the aristocratic-warlike life of the military of ancient Greece, but the medieval aristocracy assumed, as opposed to the independent city-state consciousness of the Greeks, a specific international character through the unifying force of Christianity. This consciousness of their international Christian solidarity may be clearly seen in the Crusades, in which the chivalric societies of the various Christian lands opposed to Islam appeared as a unit. Made possible through the existence of the knightly orders, the crusades strengthened and glorified the whole chivalric system.

With the French and German armies engaged in the Holy Land, and the Germans also in Italy and the south, the original purpose of armed forces, the defense of the home, became illusory and the semireligious atmosphere of the long struggle caused the iron-clad knight and his horse to assume a romantic character and to become a symbol of Christian fortitude and nobility. Love poetry and music and the courtly epic are the peculiar creations of the armored knights. It was thus the external organization of society which caused the rise of a culture and civilization of an original stamp.

In this international society there came into being first a new form of warlike heroism and respectful courtesy, and the rules of courtesy were not less binding to enemies than to friends. Observance of the rules was the sacred duty of the knights. Their heroism was now severed from the immediate military needs of the nation, and honor, fidelity, and dignity of demeanor became the new virtues of the military state. There was also a new orientation in the knight's relationship to women as the idealized woman came to occupy the center of chivalric poetry. From the holy wars, the feasts, the tournaments, the universal opposition to Islam, the unity of Christian thought, there arose now a new art in which the sober requirements of reality were relegated to the background. The combination of the fantastic elements communicated by the Orient with the rather contourless religious ideals of the Occident was eminently suited to an art which took its first flight in France.

The experiences of knightly society found immediate expression in lyricism. The nature of this expression was such that even epic poetry had lyrical foundations. With the poetry of the troubadours and trouvères we pass from the reign of the sword to that of love and tenderness, causing a change in the morals and customs of the people. The new literature introduced a certain delicacy and respect for integrity; the armed knight ceased to conquer his beloved by force, but stood instead under her window singing love songs.

The triumph of grace and beauty is one of the great achievements of the so-called Dark Ages. Indeed this whole period deserves the title of

"Renaissance" because, in addition to the change in the tenets of romance, we observe a rebirth of classical letters, which were understood and enjoyed in the late twelfth century as thoroughly as in the period which centuries later was to bear that proud epithet. Another distinctly Renaissance feature was the rediscovery of the joys and pleasures of life and love, so cherished by the ancients. This does not mean, of course, that human passions had been kept in a dark cellar before the advent of the knightly singers of love. Songs of love sounded in all their shades and varieties, from shy adoration and stammering admiration to ardent songs of impatient desire. The heroic, adventurous, and amorous epic appears beside the *vita* of the saint, and the knight who writes poetry and sings music offers competition to the learned and devout man of the Church. Courtly love dominates the whole era and imposes its rules both on the art and on the everyday life of the rising social order.

Both the strength and the weakness of the new lyrical art were conditioned by the movement from which it arose. Its strength lay in its sources, for the well-developed social life of the nobility possessed a homogeneous and widely disseminated culture. Its weakness was caused by the limitations set to its intrinsic profundity by the conventions of this society, typifying and generalizing every experience and idea. The symbol, the personification, the type, were the artistic means of this art, though in the representation of the typical it often reached a truly plastic force. The great emotional crises of man seldom found expression in the art of this age. Love itself was not experienced as a congenial passion, its subject was not yet the individual. The knightly poets of France and Germany placed love on the highest pedestal and praised the universal merits of beauty, comeliness, steadfastness, fidelity, and virtue in the beloved woman. Her perfection differed from that of any other woman only in its degree, not in its nature. There was a constant "measuring" of the universal ideal; perfection was considered quantitatively.

Originally the troubadour's concept of love included two independent spheres of emotion. One was the sensual, glowing passion which considered woman simply as the object of a burning desire which had to be satisfied; the other was the moral, chaste love ethic in which the woman was considered primarily as the unattainable lady. In the first troubadours both concepts were present, but the erotic strain, which came from the songs of the goliards and other roving poets, was later, through religious influence, displaced by the feeling of love as an ethical power. The letters of St. Boniface, the indefatigable and ardent purifier of Christianity, speak of *caritas* as love transcending the physical which pleases God and for the preservation of which one implores Him. From its religious beginnings the original idea went through various metamorphoses. On the one hand knightly poetry developed into disguised Marian songs, on the other the thirst for love became the motive power of the passion for honor. With the poet it was the honor of serving a great and virtuous lady, with the lady the honor of being praised by a great knight.

The art of "finding" songs was called a "gay science" (*gay saber* or *gaya ciencia*) by the Provençal troubadours. But a really profound and great art is not a gay science, and we must admit that the conception of life and the artistic creed of international knighthood did not measure up to the transcendental *Weltanschauung* which we, following nineteenth-century romantic historiography, attribute to them. As we have remarked before, a real expression of love is rare with both the troubadours-trouvères and the Minnesinger, and while the knightly poets of France and Germany exalted love and placed it above all other sentiments, the greatest love epic of the period, *Tristan and Isolde,* was written by men who were not true hereditary knights, the trouvère Thomas and the Minnesinger Gottfried of Strassburg. But even Tristan and Isolde seeem to be unable to express the feelings of passionate earthly love until the love potion excites them to an elemental passion quite out of keeping with aristocratic moderation. Viewed from this angle, one can understand why chivalric art and civilization, having given a great impetus toward the development of poetry and music, vanished, ceding its domain to the growing middle-class civilization. Its finely wrought verses and melodies did not fare well in the rough and inexperienced hands of the citizen poets, but their work, the awakening of poetry and art in the civilized Occident, was accomplished and it bore fruits long after the last troubadour had vanished.

Troubadours and Trouvères

TROUBADOUR art originated in radiant and sun-drenched Provence, where every castle seemed a miniature imperial court. The oldest known troubadour, the seventh Count of Poitiers, who became William IX, Duke of Aquitaine (1071–1127), seems to carry the origins back to Poitou; but the great efflorescence of troubadour poetry occurred in the neighboring province of Limousin—the Catalans used to call the whole troubadour literature *lemousi.* The names given to the poet-musicians, "troubadour" and "trouvère," may be derived from the verb "to find," thus referring to the poet's finest qualities, that is, inventiveness and imagination, although it is equally possible that the derivation may be from the trope, the Latin *tropus.* In practice the name was given only to individuals of noble birth who exercised their art for art's sake without expecting reward or remuneration; even the greatest of them reverted to the rank of minstrel or jongleur if he used his art to make a living.

The great period of the troubadours lasted from about 1150 to 1210, and this period lived and dreamed in the rosy light of poetry until the burning pyre of the Inquisition awoke it. The troubadours composed verses which were remarkable for their accomplished artistic craftsmanship. Originality and vigor were less in evidence, which fact convinces us that this was a real French art, rational and conscious, sometimes perhaps a little too highly refined. The ideas of love and service were the subjects which were in the forefront of this poetry, and these are the phenomena which should be investigated. Although one may not go so far as to assert that in the Latin poetry of the Middle Ages there already existed a form in which the troubadour song had its roots, we may state that the most important intrinsic elements which are found in the art of the troubadours—the theme of love and worship of love—had already been prepared by Latin medieval poetry. If we consider the fact that secular music, tropes, sequences, and other songs were universally liked and practiced, we can see that the apparently sudden rise of songs in the south and north of France did not come about without a long tradition of chanson composition in both Provençal and French.

Of particular importance was the goliard poetry, which had a notable center in the vicinity of Angers, which maintained connections with and was influenced by the regions lying to the north and south, Maine, Normandy, England, Poitou, and Aquitaine. In addition to metrical poetry of the Angevin variety and to the Odes of Horace contained in tenth-century manuscripts with the music recorded in neumatic notation, there was also a vigorously flourishing rhythmic poetry, some of which has been preserved with its music. The nature of the poetry clearly indicates that it was sung without exception. Who would not recognize the vein of the true lyric poet in such a song as this?

Jam dulcis amica, uenito,	Soon sweet darling shall you come
Quam sicut cor meum diligo,	Beloved as my very heart,
Intra in cubiculum meum	Within my chamber shall you come,
Ornamentis cunctis ornatum.	Comely, adorned with every art.

Or the following goliard song—does it not reflect, with its elegant effrontery, the spirit of modern poetry?

Meum est propositum in taberna mori,	In the tavern! Resolved am I there to meet my death;
Vinum sit appositum morientis ori,	Set a wine-cup to my lips to catch my dying breath.
Ut dicant cum uenerint angelorum chori:	May the choirs angelic say, looking on my face,
Deus sit propitius huic potatori.	To this toper, dear Lord, vouchsafe kindly grace.[10]

One may come to the conclusion that troubadour art came from two principal sources: from the music and thought of the Christian world, as expressed in sequences, tropes, hymns, and litanies, and from the secular songs of roving poets such as the goliards. Both sources were somewhat colored by Ovid and similar influences and one cannot often enough repeat that classical poetry was not dead in this misjudged dynamic age. To the two sources corresponded two conceptions of love: love as sensual desire, and love as ethical courage. The reconciliation of these two did not take place in troubadour poetry. The sensual direction is represented by William IX, Cercamon, and Bernart; in the transcendental movement, by far the more typical, were enrolled the majority of the knightly poets, notably Marcabru and Jauffre Rudel. The troubadours were never able to bind together these heterogeneous elements, the unification of which, in a modest way, remained for the Minnesinger.

Thus the troubadour sang principally of courtly love, a sentiment so abstract as to be barely intelligible to the plebeian. There is nothing more learned and involved than the art of these courtly musician-poets who practiced the genre which they called *trobar clus,* "closed" poetry, that is, a form of art not accessible to the uninitiated. And yet this savant treatment utilized material which retained the freshness of its popular origin. The highly artistic quality indicates that the subject of the love songs was really a fictitious person in whose beautiful body resided a proud and haughty soul which did not readily condescend to bestow her favor on the poet. The high admiration for the virtue of the ladies gave the tone to this poetry and indicates its final philosophical, Neoplatonic orientation. It became more and more abstract and turned toward the religious; the deification of woman was conducive to a feminization of the Divinity, and the Virgin became the source of all virtue.

The various students of this period have collected as many as some twenty-six hundred songs and over two hundred and fifty melodies by four hundred troubadours, among whom one should mention Jauffre Rudel, Peire Vidal, Raimbaut de Vaqueiras, Folquet de Marseilles, Bertran de Born, and Gaucelm Faidit. The outstanding poet of love songs, Bernard de Ventadour, and the most significant poet of "political" song, Bertran de Born, both gravitated around the powerful king of the Western Kingdom, Henry II Plantagenet, and around Eleanor of Aquitaine.

Southern France possessed lyric poetry in a fairly well-developed stage when the earliest trouvères first composed songs north of the Loire. The Crusade of 1147 brought together nobility of both the north and the south, and the numerous visitors who frequented the courts of the two daughters of Eleanor of Aquitaine afforded other points of contact between the various provinces. The two daughters, Marie and Aelis, married Henry I of

Champagne and Thibaut of Blois and played a prominent part in the cultural intercourse of the two spheres of artistic activity. Many a wandering jongleur found employment in northern castles, and his northern colleagues drifted into the south. The poet-composers of the north, the trouvères, seemed to be less influenced by religious elements than the southern troubadours, but from the point of view of music there is no fundamental difference between their art. One may safely affirm that it was only the language that separated them, the troubadours having used the *langue d'oc,* whereas the trouvères wrote in the *langue d'oïl.* Their poetry was even more courtly and sophisticated than that of the troubadours, and includes the great group of chansons de geste. The several manuscripts which preserve the poetry and music of the northern knightly poets contain some four thousand poems and fourteen hundred melodies. Chief among the trouvères were Quesnes de Béthune, Blondel de Nesle, Gace Brulé, Thibaut, King of Navarre, Gillebert de Berneville, Colin Muset, Gautier de Soignies, and Adam de la Hale, who will be the subject of more discussion. The last-named, also called the Hunchback of Arras, marks perhaps the highest point to which the delicate, frosty art of the trouvères attained.

Other Aspects of Knightly Lyricism

THE Middle Ages called the narrative songs *chansons d'histoire,* a term which denotes their epic character. However, as we have remarked before, lyricism was the basis of the whole art of the troubadours and trouvères, as can be seen from the fact that the primitive assonance of the chansons de geste was later displaced by rhyme. These "songs of deeds" (from the Latin *gesta*), composed by trouvères, were a group of epic song-poems varying from one to twenty thousand lines. They were grouped in cycles about some great central figure such as Charlemagne, and described historical events of national importance. Sung by wandering minstrels to the accompaniment of a little harp or a fiddle (*vièle*), they spread to Germany, Italy, Spain, and even as far north as Iceland, where traces have been found. The oldest, as well as the most significant, is the famous *Chanson de Roland,* the conjectural date of whose composition has been placed between the years 1066 and 1095. The most important cycle of chansons de geste was that which was collected around the name of Charlemagne, and was known as the *Geste du roi.* Another cycle was that of Duke William Shortnose, *La Geste de Guillaume,* while a third large group, *La Geste de Doon de Mayence,* formed the cycle of the rebellious northern family of Ganelon, hostile to the Carolingians. There is not much art and grace in these chansons, but in their straightforwardness there is a magnificent display of force and Gallic pride, and they breathe the spirit of the fighting aristocracy. The musical rendition of these chansons was monotonous, as a great number of verses, if not all, were sung to one melodic phrase, interspersed with little instrumental interludes to give the singer a breathing spell. While the texts of the various cycles of songs have been preserved in great number, there are, unfortunately, only a handful of fragments of the music which accompanied them, but we have some information concerning their performance.[11]

The short strophes had an appendix or closing formula (*laisse*) which was considerably more artistically conceived than the chansons de geste proper and found great popularity later in the *chansons de toile,* or weaving songs, the melody of which usually concluded with a short independent refrain. The nature of the *laisse strophique,* the closing formula, indicates that we are dealing here with a Gregorian derivation, as these refrains were probably modeled after the alleluia or the lesser doxology. The last two words of the lesser doxology, *saeculorum amen,* were contracted into a formula which used the last six vowels of the two words, E U O U A E. The formula used to designate the trope of the doxology was later corrupted into EVOVAE and appears repeatedly in medieval Norman songs as *Enne hauvoy,* or *Enne ovoi.*

Leaving the chansons de geste, we must consider a large variety of songs, for love was not the exclusive subject of knightly poetry. There were the *sirventes* (from *sirvent,* one who serves, as for instance a soldier), in which the troubadour addressed himself not to a lady but to a prince or a potentate. The *sirventes* were either songs of praise or ironical songs of reproach. To this category belong the various crusader songs and the *planh* (i. e., *plainte*), a complaint or lamentation over the death of a hero. The *lai* (English "lay" and German *Leich*) was a simple lyric song, originally sung by the Breton harpists; later it designated the long introductory narrative of chansons. On the other hand, the *Leich* of the Minnesinger, which originated from the French *lai,* stood nearer to the sequences, judging from the religious allegories which fill these long poems. The lays present a series of parts, each of them subdivided into a great number of unequal strophes. The whole was set to music integrally, except in the case of two semi-strophes of identical structure, in which the same melody served for both. The further development of the lays led to songs built on semi-strophes of varying meter, which carried with it a similar change in the melodies. The thirteenth century called these lays *descorts* (discord or disorder). The *chanson d'aube,* the tower watchman's song, which warned lovers that the approaching dawn menaced their security, was a particular favorite of the Minnesinger, who called them *Tagelieder.* The German collections contain some hundred chansons of dawn, but in French poetry much fewer examples are to be found. Another popular variety of chanson was the *pastourelle,* or *pastorita* as it was called in Provence. Their subject was the story of the repulsed knight who wanted to ravish a shepherdess. The original *pastourelles* of the knightly poets were tame and courtly, but with the gradual influence of middle-class poetry and minstrelsy they often end with rape followed by a good beating received from the hand of the husband or lover, or a group of enraged peasants.

The jongleurs carried the chansons everywhere, accompanying their songs on the *vièle;* but the chansons were also accompanied by dances in which the roles were distributed, and a lively dialogued mimic play arose from these chansons. The medieval dance probably possessed none of the infinitely expressive grace and studied pose of the ancient dance, nor does it appear to have approached the style or technical perfection of the modern dance. It was rather clumsy and monotonous, but its close connections with poetry and music are undeniable, and these connections were not less important than the associations in the *orchesis* of the ancient Greeks. The taste for dancing was generally diffused and deeply rooted among all classes throughout the Middle Ages and the Renaissance, and the original object of the songs in set form was to accompany dancing. The *ballades, estampies, rondeaux*—to mention a few of the dance-type songs and chansons—all show simple rhythmical phrases sung by a singer and followed by a refrain, sung and danced by the chorus.

These simple forms were greatly enriched and complicated by clever artists of the subsequent period. The *estampie* or *estampida* deserves special consideration as it is one of the oldest forms of pure instrumental music. The old Provençal form *estampida* is the participle of the verb *estamper* or *estampir,* to strike with the foot, or stamp; consequently the name itself indicates the dance character. These chansons, first mentioned by Grocheo, who in his learned makeshift Latin calls them *stantipes,* were meant to be played by a jongleur on his *vièle.*[12] A special group among all the chansons is that of the discussion songs and dialogues, which may be called argument or contest chansons. These conversations in music dispensed with amatory and rural topics and indulged in a free exchange of moral, philosophical, or political subjects. They are remote descendants of the Virgilian *alterna* now called *tensons* or *jeux partis,* and must have been the work of several poets, to judge from the allusions and the acrimony of some of the disputes. The *jeu parti* usually offers two conflicting solutions of a given topic of discussion, leaving the choice of one to the singer's adversary and undertaking the defense of the other. As Jeanroy says, "the type clearly belongs to a period which no longer takes a serious view of the idealistic conceptions that had charmed the close of the twelfth century, and presages the downfall of the poetry which these ideals had fostered." [13] While they presage the decline of courtly art, we shall see how much the rising art of the lyric theater owes to these dialogues.

In this connection we must mention the *Jeu de Robin et Marion* by Adam de la Hale. The Hunchback of Arras was not a knightly trouvère like his predecessors, but represented even at this early period the spirit of the rising middle class. Middle-class lyricism often turned toward the satirical, and this tendency has led to the comical theater, which is but the dramatic form of lyric poetry mixed with satire. This movement reached its apogee with Adam (c. 1240–c. 1288), who again, like most of the outstanding poets of the period, was an equally versatile musician. Author of much lyric poetry, chansons, and *jeux,* in which he imitated Provençal models, Adam turned, in his later years, to the writing of the graceful pieces which mark the beginning of "modern" theatrical art in the comic vein. *Robin et Marion* is the oldest preserved French play with music on a secular subject. It consists of dialogues varied by refrains already current in popular song. The melodies, some of which are simple folk songs, including the old popular chanson "Robin m'aime," are spontaneous and superior to the melodic products of contemporary art music, not excepting the other, more learned works of Adam himself. The designation "first comic opera" which is occasionally given to this little masterpiece is not so farfetched as some critics consider it, although, in view of the ambiguous meaning of "comic opera" in English, the term "musical play," in the sense of the German *Singspiel,* would be more appropriate. We are not dealing here with an isolated phenomenon, as there are several *jeux* extant from this period. The popularity of these musical plays was such that the chronicles mention performances of *Robin et Marion* a hundred years after Adam's death. [14]

The Minstrels

THE union of poetical and musical creative ability is not often accomplished in a perfect blend, and some of the troubadours and trouvères, even though experienced poets and gifted composers, nevertheless needed the assistance of someone whose daily bread and occupation it was to play and arrange music. Another reason for this resort was the ethical code of the knightly artists which forbade their being subjected to unnecessary contact with the populace. If the knight was an able composer but a poor vocalist he usually called on a *chanteor,* while if his ability to put together his music and play was defective he called in an *estrumenteor. Chanteors* and *estrumenteors* belonged to the great body of itinerant musicians which the late Middle Ages and modern times called minstrels but who answered in the times of the troubadours and trouvères to the name of jongleur.

The jongleurs look back on a past which antedates the appearance of the troubadours by a millennium. The origin of the itinerant entertainers goes back to Roman times, and their knowledge of literature and their musical ability were a remainder of the public theatrical performances and other festivities of antiquity. The *mimes* and *ioculatores* followed the conquering Roman legions and appeared everywhere with the expanding Roman civilization. They were just as active during the patristic period and the early Middle Ages, but their memories and traditions reflected the pagan past too vividly for the comfort of the Christian Church and so they were ignored by most chroniclers and pious writers. Our information concerning minstrelsy in the early Middle Ages is of a negative order, that is, we read about acts and decrees against it.

Jongleurs and minstrels were well-nigh indispensable throughout the Middle Ages. They appeared at court festivals and in the castles of the highest nobility; but they were also in evidence at the noisy feasts of the citizen class, at tournaments and warlike assemblies, and were not averse to furnishing the music for peasant weddings. They took the major part in the performance of religious plays, and their activities embraced, besides singing and fiddling, the recitation of legends, acrobatic stunts, and magic tricks. They went from town to town, saw many things, and always interested people with their stories, thus fulfilling the role of the modern newspaper. But however indispensable, they were held in great contempt throughout the Middle Ages. The picture we gain from this paradoxical situation is, no doubt, confusing, but it can be explained by the fact that the ban emanated from the Church. Ever since the time of the Church Fathers and later, during the Cluniac reform, the Church saw in the minstrel's instinctive and genuine love of life and its pleasures the gravest threat to the spiritual welfare of the people. The poor fiddlers came under the same ban from partaking in communion and the sacraments as was applied to epileptics, sleepwalkers, and sorcerers. Frowned upon and despised, they strove nevertheless, and even *jongleresses* were known to be admitted to public performances. Ecclesiastical dignitaries had them in their households, princes and nobles harbored them in their castles, and even the monasteries called occasionally on their services. Remarkable as it seems, there is ample evidence to prove that whenever a church council was held the jongleurs congregated there in great numbers. On the occasion of the Council of Constance some five hundred jongleurs were reported to have assembled in the town. We owe to these harassed musicians a great debt, for they salvaged for us a great deal of what remained of the popular epics and secular music and poetry of the early and central Middle Ages.

The jongleur was essentially an itinerant musician, and this was what distinguished him from the *ménestrel* or *ménétrier* (minstrel) who was permanently attached to the court of some nobleman or to some community. The term "minstrel" became, however, more and more inclusive and toward the end of the thirteenth century it was applied to both jongleur and minstrel alike. As time went on the minstrel occupied an intermediary position between trouvère and jongleur; he lived like a jongleur, but composed his chansons himself like a trouvère. Troubadour and minstrel often became real and devoted friends, as is shown in the beautiful legend about Richard Coeur de Lion and his favorite minstrel Blondel de Nesle. The legend relates that when the king was captured and imprisoned by Leopold, Duke of Austria, in 1193, Blondel, wandering through Germany, discovered the king's whereabouts and made himself known to Richard by singing a song they had composed together.

By the thirteenth century the minstrel became a powerful factor, loved and feared. In a single person he played the role of newspaper, theater, and music hall. He sowed pleasure wherever he appeared, and people flocked to hear him and loved him for his fantastic nature and dexterity. Yet they feared him because of his multiple abilities, which seemed sinister not only to the Church, which realized the power and enticing charm of entertainment, but to the people too, who suspected supernatural powers at play. Thus the jongleur usually obtained from nobles, burghers, and peasants what he wanted and lived in relative comfort and plenitude. His luxurious, carefree life fascinated many people and great was the desire to take up this marvelous métier. Their number grew constantly, and toward the end of the century and in the fourteenth century the chronicles deal with veritable armies of minstrels. Chambers [15] mentions the presence of a hundred and fifty jongleurs on one occasion, and Italian chronicles speak of more than a thousand minstrels assembled at festival gatherings. The days of the bedraggled, hunted beggar minstrels were over.

The minstrels were easily recognizable by their attire. Contemporary illustrations show them clad in red jackets, with a yellow hood, and in dresses of two colors, divided vertically, such as were later worn by court jesters. Among the German minstrels (*Spielleute*) we find many adorned with curious names: Regenbogen (Rainbow), Frauenlob (Ladies' Praiser), Hasensprung (Jumping Hare), Saitlein (Little String), etc. Some were named after their country or origin, others again gave themselves names which betray a sense of humor, but often also a complete negation and despising of life. A good jongleur was expected to play several instruments, and according to the *romans* and other narrative poems the number of instruments in general use was imposing; but their chief instrument was the fiddle, or, as it was called in France, the *vièle*. The arched bow of this instrument was eminently suited for playing drone basses, which held out long notes while the singer proceeded with his recitation.

The minstrels were not only the principal active secular musicians of the tenth to the thirteenth centuries, but also the most active poets of popular verse. These *chanteors* and *estrumenteors* were the musical virtuosi of the times. Their natural inclination to distinguish themselves when performing the songs entrusted to them by their masters led to an embellishment of the music which varied in degree but sometimes reached proportions in which the original melody was almost unrecognizable. Several of the troubadours warned their minstrels not to distort their songs. This strong musical initiative of the minstrels must be responsible for the fact that the melodic wealth of French aristocratic lyric poetry is richer than the music of the German Minnesinger, in whose art the union of poet and musician was the rule, limiting the independent minstrel's activity.

The Decline of Chivalric Art

TROUBADOUR art was, as we have said, a rather aristocratic genre of art, called *poésie courtoise*, yet it was not so exclusively aristocratic as commonly believed. In its last period courtly art began to decline, following the distribution of wealth which took place through the rise of a middle-class mercantile and industrial society. The large cities in Picardy and Artois, with their well-developed population, joined in the literary movement, thereby giving a truly national expansion to troubadour poetry. The citizens, organized in corporations, founded schools of poetry as in Arras, which produced an amazing number of poems, fables, moral and satiric *dits,* and chansons. The new bourgeois class with characteristic common sense began to imitate the manners of the feudal lords. Observing that it was the minstrels who, by singing the virtues and magnanimity of their masters, carried their fame far and wide, the burghers hired troubadours and minstrels of their own. The greatest of these poets, Rutebeuf (c. 1230–1280), a veritable François Villon of the thirteenth century, was the first real, subjective, individual, and independent French lyric poet of the Middle Ages.

The invasion of middle-class spirit becomes apparent in all domains of arts and letters, and is best illustrated in the two parts of the great epic poem called *Le Roman de la Rose.* The first part, a graceful courtly epopoeia written about 1230 by Guillaume de Lorris, was followed some forty years later by a second part from the pen of Jean de Meung. The monotonous verses of the latter can hardly be labeled courtly; the rose loses its petals in his heavy hands. A certain encyclopedic tendency indicates the presence of another influence, scholasticism, which emanated from the universities. While middle-class lyricism was steadily gaining, Provençal poetry was rapidly declining. This was due partly to the fact that, in its last stage, courtly poetry was characterized by more and more finish and ingenuity in rhythmical combinations and by complexities without end, and partly to the persecutions instituted by the Church. Pursued by the Church on account of its connections with heretical manifestations, troubadour art turned slowly from a sensuous secular world to moral and pious subjects. The cult of the *dame* or *domna* changed into the cult of *Notre Dame,* and even the Mother of God soon became a mere idea, an abstraction.[16] The establishment of the Inquisition at Toulouse and the foundation of the Order of Preachers by St. Dominic brought a wave of moral rigor which proved to be fatal to secular lyric poetry and music. Henceforth we must look toward Italy if we would follow the destiny of poetry and music.

The Awakening of Italian Lyricism by Provençal Art

THE awakening of Italian literature and music can legitimately be attributed to the troubadours and trouvères who migrated to Italy following the religious persecutions in France. The presence of French jongleurs in Italy is attested by various twelfth- and thirteenth-century manuscripts, and they were soon followed by their masters, who were the guests of the various princes. It was from these courts that Provençal poetry and its accompanying music were diffused.

The first half of the thirteenth century in Italy was dominated by the imposing figure of the Holy Roman Emperor Frederick II (1194–1250), who was also King of the two Sicilies. His love of poetry and his dislike of the Church created an ideal atmosphere at the court of Sicily for the émigrés from France, and a remarkable galaxy of men of letters gathered around the great emperor. The French troubadours were joined by Italian poets and the circle was later called the Sicilian school, the cradle of Italian literature. The title "Sicilian school" is not entirely justified. There were many at Frederick's court, who, like Guittone d'Arezzo, came from different parts of the country. Nor must we forget when considering the origin of Italian letters and music that a great number of troubadours found asylum in the friendly and equally art-loving courts of the Marquesses of Montferrat, where the most famous love songs of Raimbaut were composed, of the Estensi, of the Marquesses of Saluzzo, and of the Counts of Savoy. The influence of this lyric poetry on the Italians was powerful and lasting. Dante mentions seven troubadours in his *De Vulgari* and the *Divine Comedy,* and Petrarch recalls fifteen of them. Of the lives of the Italian troubadours, as of those of their French colleagues, we know little. Most famous were Odo delle Colonne, Ciullo dal Camo, and Rinaldo d'Aquino. Their poems were usually in dialogue form and resembled the troubadour songs in that the participants in the dialogue were man and woman, the man asking for love, the woman refusing. Contrary to the relatively rich musical legacy of the French poet-musicians, little is known of Italian music in the twelfth and thirteenth centuries, but the course of history and French influence can be followed in that part of their art which concerns poetry.

The principal role in the development of Italian poetry was played by St. Francis and his disciples, although the French influence remained evident. The young Giovanni Bernardone received the name Francesco (Frenchman) from his father, a frequent traveler in France. The young man was nourished on the chivalry of the French *romans* and dreamed of becoming one of his hero knights. But after a short military career occurred his well-known conversion, and henceforth the object of his admiration changed and he became the champion of the poor. Yet this consecration still has a Provençal touch about it; the *dame* was still to be served, although this service was transformed into humility and devotion. And the saint who goes about singing French songs soon bursts forth into a poetry of his own, in his own language.

Because the Church in the Italy of the Middle Ages and the Renaissance was a political power, sincere religious feeling often was not inculcated by its leaders. The people took it upon themselves to express their own pious sentiments and poured out their devotion in the most representative form of religious poetry, the *laude,* usually in the vernacular. The laude composers, most of them Franciscan monks, cultivated their own dialects, as the Florentine language was not yet elevated to the rank of a literary language. The greatest merit of the laude poetry consisted in its being the sole carrier of folk song and its spirit. Behind its feverish and hysterical exaggerations there emerges a sincere, warm humanity that has nothing of the stilted formality of courtly art. It is interesting to note that the laude singers were called *giullari di Dio,* jongleurs of God, a fact which indicates the far-flung popularity of the *mimes* and *ioculatores.* Among the followers of St. Francis we find the Franciscan Jacopone da Todi, the most noteworthy author of laudi and the head of the Umbrian school. First a doctor of law, then (after the sudden death of his wife) a hermit, next a Franciscan and a poet, Jacopone led as varied an existence as did the master of his order, but, unlike Francis, he was keenly interested in public affairs. Boniface VIII, whom he opposed violently, had him arrested, and it was only the sudden death of the pope which saved his life.

Like all strophic poems, the laudi were eminently musical in character. The first laudi were simple affirmations of faith, but in their later dialogued form they indicated the part that they were to play in the formation of the Italian mystery plays. Some of them, like the sensitive "Donna del Paradiso," were veritable sketches of dramas in the vernacular, evidently inspired by the liturgic dramas then performed in the Italian churches, as in all churches in the Occident. The Manuscript of Cividale used by Coussemaker proves that the liturgic drama was known and practiced in Italy. There was also the Compagnia del Gonfalone, an institution formed in 1260 to give annual dramatic performances of the Passion, which held its meetings in the Roman Colosseum.[17] However, the origins of the mystery play in Italy must not be sought exclusively in the liturgy, as in France and Germany; they were much more the outgrowth of the simple religious songs as represented in the laudi. Thus the religious spectacle in Italy was, from its very beginnings, something much more human, much less abstract than its northern counterpart, and we can see the powerful influence of simple songs in the molding of the spirit of a people. It is appropriate that this form of cult should have originated in Italy, for the inhabitants of the country "which has the fatal gift of beauty" believed in a beautiful world which can be loved and admired with spontaneity. This typically Italian trait is manifested in the peasants and in the saints. Through all his asceticism and all his tribulations St. Francis preserved a playful fancy, a delight in outdoor life, and a keen interest in his fellow creatures. The laude poetry of Jacopone da Todi often turned into the dramatic, and he lived to see some of his works performed in dramatized form by the brotherhood which had organized the singing of laudi, the Flagellants. The Italian texts often contain stage directions in Latin.

The organization of the people into religious groups to sing the laudi and other hymns of praise had been sporadic until the fanatical movement of the Flagellants (although condemned by the Church) succeeded, in the latter part of the thirteenth century, in winning the masses to discipline and regular song meetings. These *compagnie de' laudesi* grew to such numbers by the turn of the century that almost every important city in Italy had at least one, and Florence possessed no less than nine. This practice continued in Florence for centuries. The search for musical monuments of past centuries led the eminent musicologist Carl Proske to Florence in 1834. His diary for September 8 of that year includes the following entry: "A delicate and beautiful experience was granted me as I saw small Madonnas and altars on various street corners of Florence illuminated at night, in front of which religious groups would pray and sing. I also noticed various chapels and cloisters being used by pious companies dressed in white, which sang Psalms and hymns in praise of Mary."[18] While the music and poetry sung at these meetings changed constantly throughout the centuries, it retained almost invariably the simple song style for one voice, until the flowering of the many-voiced laudi in the fifteenth century.

Popular poetry and music continued in Italy along the lines started in the first half of the thirteenth century. In the secular field there were the *contrasti, ballate,* and *strambotti.* The contrasti were poetical dialogues in which a man tried to entice a young woman, usually a shepherdess or peasant girl, into a love affair of short duration. The savory popular style and the effort-less unrolling of the dialogue characterize these songs, which are evidently related to the French *pastourelles*. The ballate were dance songs, whereas the strambotti were short epigramlike folk songs. All these varieties were musical pieces either sung in their entirety or, as in the case of the ballate, recited with interspersed musical refrains. In the field of religious poetry there was the continued flourishing of the laudi.

In the meantime Tuscany was evolving a school of her own. The Uni-versity of Bologna had been growing in fame and had become a center for students from all parts of the peninsula. The influence of the Provençal-Sicilian school was manifest in this circle, and was characterized by erudition and the extensive use of symbolism. Poetry ceased to be the expression of every man's feelings and passions: it has become the art of the chosen few. The *trobar clus* of the Provençals found its counterpart in the Italian *maniera oscura*. These poets were most learned in philosophy, both ancient and Christian, and in the sciences and mathematics. They entertained rebel-lious ideas about the dogmas of the Church and expressed themselves freely with supreme conviction. Still, in spite of its remoteness, the learned poetry of the Sicilian and Tuscan schools with its finely balanced *canzoni* and son-nets was, perhaps, more important for the ultimate development of Italian art than the popular lyrics. Great art does not seem to arise and thrive without the professional skill and craftsmanship which these artists pos-sessed so abundantly; yet their philosophical idealization of love robbed their poetry of that certain vitality necessary for their art to be universal. The warmth of lyrical feeling could hardly penetrate through the maze of its allegorical mysticism.

The two tendencies continued side by side until there emerged a genius who, by uniting them in the *dolce stil nuovo*, "the sweet new style," infused real feeling, new art, and fresh thought and imagination into an art which having passed its prime had become the prey of conventions and stale re-productions. To the Sicilians and Tuscans Dante opposed his sweet new style, and the new poetry, graceful and suave in its harmoniousness, wanted to be as sincere as it was inspired. Dante acknowledged the learned poet Guido as his master, and called him "my father and the father of all my betters who ever wrote sweet rhymes of love," no doubt because he was so deeply interested in the art of versification and in the literary possibilities of the various languages. But for the poet of the *Vita Nuova*, beyond the perfection of the métier was the significance of the individual soul, free and self-sufficient, the exploration and expression of which is the poet's supreme task

As some Provençal troubadours took refuge in Italy and were welcomed in the courts of the nobles, others found an equally friendly asylum on the

Iberian peninsula. The *cantigas* which arose at the court of Castile bespeak the Provençal influence. Similarly we discover *seglers* and *joglars* in Portugal, a country which was entirely under the influence of Provençal poetry, as can be seen from its own *arte de trobar*. Lyrical song poetry must have been exceedingly popular in Portugal, for over a thousand poems have been preserved from the thirteenth and fourteenth centuries, and these represent only a small part of the popular poems and the *cántigas de amigos,* songs of young lovers. The *Cancioneiro de Ajuda* and another collection in the Vatican contain the chief remnants of the popular song literature, which was almost entirely absorbed by the more sophisticated poetry of succeeding centuries.

Troubadours and Minstrels in England

THE Norman Conquest (1066) introduced a tremendous French influence upon English civilization. French became the state language and French literature and art dominated English intellectual life. This was especially true after the Angevin line assumed the rule of England. In the first few years after the conquest, William and his followers were occupied chiefly with maintaining their supremacy, extinguishing revolts, and laying down the laws of the land. By the time of the reign of Henry II (1154–1189) the government was firmly established. The King of England was simultaneously Count of Maine and Duke of Normandy, through inheritance from his mother. From his father, Geoffrey of Anjou, he obtained Anjou and Touraine and later the overlordship of Brittany. By means of his marriage to Eleanor of Aquitaine he added to his dominions Poitou, Guienne, and Gascony. We have mentioned above the important role played by some of these provinces in the development of chivalric poetry and music; it will not be surprising to see the emergence of a similar literary movement on English soil, as the cultural intercourse between the British Isles and the continental provinces was lively.

About the middle of the twelfth century Bernard de Ventadour made his appearance in England. From this time onward there occur frequent allusions to the Plantagenet family in Provençal lyrics. The troubadours were intimately related to court life and participated in politics; a typical example of this was the life of Bertran de Born, Viscount of Hautefort, one of the most eminent love poets of the period. Richard Coeur de Lion appeared among them, and his popularity and that of his faithful minstrel, Blondel, gave rise to many songs and legends. During the reign of Henry III (1216–1272) the translation of French romances became extremely popular, and under Edward I and his son this branch of romantic poetry received considerable impetus.

In the days of Richard Coeur de Lion a great many French singers came to England, when, upon the king's request, his chancellor, William of Ely, invited them in the hope of stimulating native art. There were two chief types of minstrels: those in the service of a court and those who wandered about freely, not attached to any particular household. These two categories persisted even in the Elizabethan period; there were some musicians attached to a particular city, while others preferred to travel from town to town. Under Hugh, the first Lord of Chester and founder of the Abbey of St. Werburg, the traveling minstrels were assigned a free piece of land. Randle, third Lord of Chester, transferred the protectorate over these minstrels to the constable of the city, Roger de Lacy. At Tutsbury in Staffordshire John of Gaunt, brother of Edward the Black Prince and one of the most powerful nobles in England, set up a court of minstrels in 1380. At Beverley in Yorkshire the minstrels had formed a corporation as early as the end of the thirteenth century. During the reign of Henry VI (1422–1460) the corporation became so wealthy that it helped finance the construction of a church, upon which was inscribed "Thys pilor made the meynstrils." Five of them are depicted there, playing upon the flute, viol, lute, and drums. It is also likely that these minstrels even performed in the church. At the court of Edward III (1327–1377), who married Philippa of Hainault, there was a whole circle of French poets and musicians centering about the chronicler Jean Froissart, and foreign musicians were frequent visitors. While all this testifies to a fairly animated musical life, the continuous French influence did not produce a distinct art in Britain comparable to its Italian and Iberian offspring, and we must turn toward Germany if we want to follow the amazing dissemination and germinating power of Gallic genius.

The Minnesinger

THE German *Minnesang,* although in a strict sense concerned with the poems expressing the homage (*Minnedienst*) rendered by the knight to his lady, generally denotes the whole body of lyric poetry of the twelfth and thirteenth centuries, whether dealing with love, religion, or politics. The idea of courtly love, with its almost religious worship of woman, its elaborate code of etiquette, and its artificial sentiment, was introduced into German poetry from Provençal literature; but the German *Minnesang* was neither a slavish imitation of the poetry of the troubadours, nor was it derived solely from French sources.

The sources seem to be many and varied. It appears that the Gregorian element was the oldest among them. Another point of departure was from Latin letters and verses of rhythmic form. Even in the beginning of this art we have poetic personalities like Meinloh, Kürenberg, Dietmar von Aist, who joined their individualities, strong even though archaic, to the period of transition.[19] Dietmar was enabled, by his acquaintance with the poetry of the *vagantes,* to introduce new material and new artistic forms. Since the beginning of the eleventh century the erotic songs of the goliards had been known in the Rhineland, in northern Germany, and particularly in Bavaria. The songs were popular and found a number of German imitators, especially among the clergy. This Latin poetry was one of the important sources of the early German minnesong, and the early Minnesinger had to thank the clergy for their art.

The erotic world of thought which came to expression in Latin medieval poetry is in direct relation to the oldest German minnesong. With Friedrich von Husen (Hausen) begins the definite epoch of the minnesong, but while the French influence now becomes apparent we must mention once more the purely Christian components of this art. The minnesong was indebted to Christian spiritualism for its profound sadness, thoughts of death and tears. The ascetic self-denial of the period preceding the chivalric era covered an intense longing and desire, a dreamlike world which sought vainly for an emotional outlet until it satisfied itself in the religious song-poetry as exemplified in the Marian songs. This poetry touched the highest peaks of exaltation and the greatest depths of profundity but exhausted itself in its shadowy domain. Searching for the shores of reality, the spirit of asceticism is forced to touch the worldly and rapidly loses its exalted nature. German art was still unable to choose decisively between these two spheres, but in its dilemma it found help in the creative activity of the Provençal troubadours, and, by reconciling the Christian and the erotic-secular aspects of life, brought into being the minnesong. In the early period before Husen, the problem rarely occurs. At that time God is conceived solely as the guiding power of knighthood and is treated simply as the knightly poet, the confidant, the protector of the people. After Husen the minnesong separates into different channels: his Limburger neighbor, Heinrich von Veldecke, and Morungen clarify it and Reinmar carries it to a new point of development until the turning point is reached with Walther von der Vogelweide.

Gennrich has proved [20] that the melodies of seven minnesongs which were known as translations of French originals were also of trouvère origin, a fact which illustrates the extent to which French art influenced the German minnesong. In the original melodies of the Minnesinger that have been preserved, especially those by Walther von der Vogelweide, one can see the combination of Provençal art with an indigenous song tradition which goes back to Heriman and Wipo. The external organization of the art of the German knighthood was similar to that of the French, except that the relationship of composer and minstrel was often a necessity on account of the knight's ignorance of letters and notation. Wolfram von Eschenbach (c. 1170–c. 1220), one of the greatest of the Minnesinger, never mastered writing and dictated his *Parzival* to a scribe. Ulrich von Lichtenstein's (c. 1200–1276) skillful songs were also written down by a learned cleric. As to the melodies, their noting down was similar to the method used by our modern composers of popular song: they were sung or whistled to a trained musician, who set them into musical notation. On the other hand, when a knight wanted to learn a melody he had it repeated to him until he remembered it. While all this is true as far as the majority of the Minnesinger is concerned, many of them possessed a rounded literary and musical education.

The Minnesinger remained, in many ways, medieval men who could not sever themselves entirely from the scholastic tendencies of their period. Compared to the spirited, artistic, sensuous, and graceful love lyrics of the Romanic poets, the Germans seem heavy-footed and angular; on the other hand they exhibit a much more profound feeling for the emotion of love than is evident in the often detached attitude of the troubadours, and the German penchant for mysticism was far more religious in nature than the clever skepticism of their French colleagues. Thus the general mood of the minnesong with its close relation to mysticism was not an un-Christian attitude—as some scholars maintain—but one more akin to the position taken by the Protestants; considered from this angle the nature of their art will be more understandable.

Under the protective power of the Hohenstaufen dynasty people felt free to express themselves about the Church, the pope, and the clergy, and they began to make a distinction between papacy and Christianity. Only through such an attitude could the terrible contrasts of the period be suffered. Political passion, fed by the imperial idea, which often lost itself in the fantastic, spurred thinkers, historians, poets, and artists to an animated participation. The two poles, imperial aims and dreams and spiritual culture, challenged each other and yet complemented each other. In this world of love, song, religion, and politics there appeared a lyric genius whose importance in German art is comparable only to that of Goethe. Folk song, artistic minnesong, poetry, and polemic were all united in the sensitive soul of Walther von der Vogelweide (c. 1170–c. 1230), who gave words to everything that animated his time, wandering from court to court and singing in Bavarian dialect his poems set to music of his own composition. He stood removed from the learned spirit of the monasteries, the Latin poetry of the goliards, and the philosophy of the universities; he lived undisturbed and serene in the culture of his class.

Walther lived through a period of the Middle Ages which was extremely rich in ideals, and his nature, thirsting for beauty, found gratification in the pomp and fullness of life at the courts of the Hohenstaufen, and of the Thuringian and Austrian high nobility. The great lyric poet himself belonged to the nobility, but the place he occupied, lying between that of the wandering minstrel and the knightly poet-musician, was somewhat uncertain. On the other hand, his very position resulted in that mixture of the popular and aristocratically artistic which makes his art so enticing. While entirely steeped in the chivalric ideals, Walther does not show the international orientation which was so characteristic of the French nobility, and which was so strongly evident in Wolfram von Eschenbach and the poet of *Tristan,* Gottfried von Strassburg. In his maxims (*Sprüche*) we can see that the religiousness of the Minnesinger was divorced from institutions such as the papacy. If we assemble the maxims of Walther, the German *sirventes,* the paragraphs of the Saxon lawbook *Sachsenspiegel* (1220–1230), and the words and ideas which emanated from the court of Frederick II, we may see the astounding breadth and energy of the antipapal movement of the period. In the eyes of the German poets of the thirteenth century the pope became Antichrist, an attitude taken in the sixteenth century by Luther, and every reproach addressed to the pope by the latter is present in Walther's maxims. One cannot help being impressed by the logical development of events which led to the great art and literature of Schütz and Bach; it is manifestly a fallacy to attribute the rise of German church music to the immediate followers of Luther.

Walther's writings disclose that his keen eyes perceived also the political strife and intrigue of the princely courts and the Janus face of the courtiers, all looking for spoils and advantages. With approaching old age came the decline of the chivalric world, and it was Walther's lot to witness the increasing power of the papacy under the great Pope Innocent III, and the sinking of the German Empire. Poetry became too artificial or turned to the less exalted status of peasant life. The decline of courtly influence is evident in the appearance in poetry of sturdy peasant elements which show a certain kinship to the peasant scenes of a Breughel. Walther's last songs fight passionately for the great ideals of his youth. In the midst of this decline the great poet, disillusioned and wisely pondering about the past, found a new form of lyricism which rose high even above his own art. Majestic and solemn in his new style, he takes leave of "Frau Welt," whom he served with devotion and joy but whose real nature he now recognizes.

Es hat dein Kosen mich betrogen,	Thy caressing has deceived me
Es war so voller Süssigkeit,	It was so full of sweetness,
Gott geb euch Fraue gute Nacht,	God give thee, woman good night.
Zur Herberg' will ich nunmehr fahr'n.	To the inn I will henceforth go.

Secular lyric poetry of the Middle Ages reached its highest flowering in Walther, who does not yield his exalted place in German literature until the advent of Goethe. Romanic lyric poetry reached its apex in Petrarch, in whose universal nature we see a harmonious union of Christian intensity of emotion with the heroic mood and perfection of form of antiquity. His poems are detached from the hour which saw their birth, they express life itself and the illusions which it offers. In Walther there is no such universality of conception; the world impresses him and evokes melodies which express the diversity of life and embrace all themes, all poetic genres.

* * *

"A verse without music is a mill without water," said the troubadour Folquet of Marseilles; this dictum should preface all studies which deal with the history of lyric poetry in the Middle Ages. We saw how poetry and music lived together, inseparable and indivisible, in Greek antiquity; but the line of Occidental tradition is Ariadne's thread, which leads back to its beginning. The rough hands of the lance-carrying armored knights found this thread; their ears perceived through the noise of battle the secret sounds of faraway centuries. We must never forget that they were musicians, and that their eminently musical chansons with their instrumental accompaniments not only were at the bottom of the various polyphonic musical forms which arose toward 1300 to spread all over Europe, but were responsible also for the birth of Renaissance poetry.

Chapter 7

THE GOTHIC

>›» ‹«‹

The Rise of the Gothic

CENTURIES had elapsed since the language of Rome had been the language of a people. During these centuries the former Roman colonies had embarked on an existence of their own, still conditioned by the Latin language, indeed, but now this was the language of their new religion, their new Mother Church, as strange to them as had been the Latin of the Roman soldiers and public officials. The merger of the vulgar Latin of the legionnaires with the native idioms of the peoples of the southwestern quarter of Europe resulted in the formation of the various Romance languages. Although the French influence on English was considerable, the Germanic races, in general much less subjected to Roman domination, were evolving their own languages. As the centuries passed and people emerged from the profound conflict between their native heritage and a Christianity saturated with antique classical elements, their hearts became filled with new joys and sentiments which loosened their tongues. There set in that creative era of young nations which called to life the language of the troubadours, the Minnesinger, the epic poets, and Dante. The tragic mood of old German poetry disappeared. A happy young generation, sure of the present and confident of the future, yearned for a friendlier outlook on life. As tongues became free, hands became lighter. The broad and heavy mass of Romanesque art was separated and articulated; it turned toward the Gothic, which made flowers sprout from stone carried up to dizzy heights as if it had no weight.

This Gothic period is called the apex of the Middle Ages; but if we study with devotion its spirit and examine the great phenomena of its culture, we shall see that this era was not a final high development of the previous era, any more than we should consider the period that came after it as an inferior one. The Gothic was connected by innumerable threads to the past, yet it was something new; it possessed an atmosphere exclusively its own even though the results of its spiritual and artistic activity continued to influence coming ages. It is futile to place St. Thomas, St. Francis, and Dante at the culminating point of the Middle Ages and at the same time to consider them the first heroes of the Renaissance or modern times. It is equally fallacious to assume that certain thinkers and artists of this era should be considered as more properly belonging to some other period because of their theological, philosophical, or artistic doctrines. The pious and the unbelievers, the churchmen and the heretics, the emperors and the popes, the knights and the politically-minded citizens, the poets, the philosophers, and the artists were all imbued with that longing, passion, and conviction which is the expression of the *juventus,* the spirit of youth, which is the spirit of this time.

The eleventh century was an incubator from which emerged the civilization of the Occident. With the full development of Romanesque art there appeared scholastic philosophy, the *chanson de geste,* the liturgic drama, Provençal poetry, the poetry of the north of France and of Italy and Spain. The Scandinavians created their *Eddas,* the Anglo-Saxons their *Beowulf,* and the Germans their *Nibelungen.* At the same time Byzantine and Arab arts and letters flourished and exerted a certain influence on the intellectual evolution of the Occident. Finally, this was also the century which saw the definite orientation of the new art of polyphony, signifying the development of an Occidental musical art par excellence.

The twelfth century inherited all the wealth of the preceding century and brought its remarkable renaissance of arts and letters to full bloom; but it was the following century which was characterized by the renaissance of antique thought. Immense was the power of abstraction of the thirteenth century as manifested in the allegories of the *romans,* the mysticism of the legends of the Grail, the great expositions of St. Bonaventure, or the *summae* of philosophers such as St. Thomas Aquinas.

One of the most important factors guiding intellectual life in the thirteenth century was the development of the universities. While it is true that the beginnings of the universities go back to earlier times these institutions did not reach their definitive constitution before the advent of the thirteenth century.

The medieval university was not only a corporation for the conservation, dissemination, and advancement of learning; it played an important role in public affairs and harbored a veritable intellectual theocracy. However powerful the theological faculties which predominated in the universities, the great faculties of arts, law, and medicine represented developments which took place outside the sphere of the Church. The omnipotent faculty of theology was followed by the faculty of arts, with its curriculum based on the trivium and quadrivium; by the faculty of law, frowned upon by the Holy See on account of its predilection for studies in Roman law; and by the faculty of medicine, which developed somewhat later, although Montpellier boasted an excellent one in early times. The sciences, which usually form an independent faculty in our day, were incorporated in the philosophical disciplines—a system still followed, however, in many modern universities.

The rediscovery of Aristotle imposed the spiritual supremacy of Greek philosophy and pure science even on the highest spiritual power of the time, and triumphed, after half a century of hesitation, in the second half of the thirteenth century. This important step liberated medieval thought from futile dialecticism to turn it toward profound speculation upon the system of the world as conceived by reason. An intellectual fermentation took place the magnitude of which we cannot measure, since the growing menace of the Inquisition prevented the communication of many contemporary ideas and experiences. Architect, sculptor, and painter united with philosopher, poet, and musician in an effort to raise a monument to the genius of the time. The monument best known and appreciated today is the Gothic cathedral, but the *summae* of the philosophers, the *Divine Comedy,* and the great polyphonic motets are all "cathedrals" in their own way, and our picture of the Gothic is indeed incomplete if we exclude these other monuments. For there was music in the churches, in the homes, in the universities, and wherever arts and letters were practiced and appreciated. The same atmosphere created Gothic architecture and musical polyphony. Everything that Western music had produced up to the end of the twelfth century—the delicate art of the Provençal troubadours, the sturdy hymns of the Church, the first experiments in polyphony—awaited synthetic order and summary. This was accomplished by the Gothic, a period with which music enters upon a significant phase of its existence.

The spokelike radiation of Gregorian and Provençal art into national varieties now came to an end, and in the ensuing alternation in the importance of the individual varieties, the protagonist, usually a whole geographic if not national entity, succeeded in maintaining its leadership for generations. From the end of the twelfth century to the beginning of the fifteenth, artistic leadership in the domain of music fell to the territory which had its nucleus in the Ile de France, Picardy, and Champagne, and which exercised a dominant influence over the music of the rest of the Western World. This was the country which "originated" many-voiced music, and this most important step in the development of music as an art determined its future course; polyphony will be henceforth synonymous with the art of music.

The history of many-voiced music from the ninth to the fourteenth centuries constitutes a chapter unique in the whole history of Western civilization. Heterogeneous and often hostile factors and forces had to be reconciled and enrolled in the service of a universal cult. Here was an art entirely new, entirely pointing toward future development and yet its scientific and ideological background relied on ancient sources; its means of expression were new, yet they were defined by tenets and doctrines of the past. While modern research in the history of arts and letters has acknowledged the great importance and influence of intellectual life on medieval art and utilized the results of its labors in drawing up new formulations and conceptions of the arts and literature of the period, in the domain of music we are still at the beginning of such interpretations. It is true, however, that the reconstruction and understanding of medieval music hinges on obstacles which are often insurmountable and the magnitude of which is not even known to scholars and students in the allied fields.

The Origins of Polyphony

THE origins of European many-voiced music are still enshrouded in conjecture and hypothesis.[1] The publications of various anthropologists and students of comparative musicology [2] indicate that playing and singing together, whether in the form of parallel song or in the form of a drone-bass accompaniment provided by instruments like the bagpipe, is fairly widespread among aborigines untouched by civilization. Consequently modern musicology reverses the question and now inquires why it is that these apparently age-old practices did not come down to us in a continuous succession of stages. For it is evident that the first-known form of many-voiced music, the *organum* of Hucbald, well known and universally practiced in the tenth century, does not represent the beginning of polyphony; on the contrary, it should be considered as a closed and developed musical form. It seems significant that one of the most eminent medieval theorists, Walter Odington, called the two-part organum *genus antiquissimum,* and that Giraldus Cambrensis speaks of polyphonic song and instrumental music in terms that imply great antiquity. Both of these authors were Britons, living in a country remote from constant and immediate Gregorian-Christian influences, and it was in Britain that the oldest developed examples of many-voiced music known to us originated.

The young Christian Church based its music on monophony, on a single musical line. This entailed a conception of music which knows only a succession of tones. The recognition of the existence, beauty, and expressive quality of simultaneously sounding tones, introducing a vertical as well as a horizontal disposition, created a conception of music which was fundamentally different from everything in its previous history. The question arises whether polyphonic music derives by evolution from a previous stage attained by monophonic music, or whether we must consider the two varieties, monophony and polyphony, as juxtaposed phenomena. If we do not endeavor to approach and judge the music of this period by modern principles of musical construction, we shall see that the evolutionary conception, dear to the advocates of biological methods of historiography, is contradicted by tangible documents.

The fact that our present musical sense and equipment do not help us to explain the music of the Middle Ages, whereas this same equipment seems to obtain good results when applied to music beginning with the sixteenth century, should show us that the very notion of the musical, as we understand it today—consisting of a balanced union of melodic, rhythmic, and harmonic components, which we consider something innate and natural— did not exist in the Middle Ages. Closer examination, indeed, convinces us that we are dealing with a phenomenon exactly opposed to our notion; namely, instead of the balanced union of the various components, there is a predominance of one or the other which leads an entirely independent life. The mutual penetration of the individual components is not discernible before the end of the medieval period.

We have seen how foreign plain chant was to all but the lands of its origin. North of the Alps it remained foreign in spite of long practice, sometimes forced on the people, sometimes springing from a sincere desire to assimilate the rites of the Church. This universal opposition was not inspired by theological or philosophical reasons; it was the instinctive musical reaction of the northern people running counter to an unfamiliar idiom introduced to them from the East. The naïvely skeptical and culturally untouched transalpine and northwestern man was confronted with the great task of assimilating the new liturgic idiom with his undeveloped but original and independent musical taste in order to obtain a musical language which should better satisfy his new needs. Had the culture of these peoples been permitted to follow its natural course, the indigenous traits which we now perceive through their handling of Gregorian art would probably have manifested themselves much more clearly, as in the case of literature, which withstood foreign influences and restrictions more successfully. But the restraint put upon music by the Church was too powerful, involving as it did the very nature of the whole service and liturgy. The Church accepted music as a specifically devotional art, and any music outside the Church was banned. If in Italy, where Gregorianism was much closer to the spirit of the people, the Church was not able to ward off the intrusion of secular elements into its music, it faced a more serious struggle in the northern countries to which the whole organization of its ritual, and especially its music, was foreign.

The greater part of the Middle Ages, then, was occupied with this latent conflict of musical tastes, casting and recasting the existing musical material which, in its slow change from the conception of melody as the most significant musical element and toward the organization of rhythm, produced polyphony: a unique phenomenon and a unique treasure of Western civilization. The germs of polyphony were present in the West but because of the conflict of musical heritages could not find artistic expression. We must conclude, then, that the development of polyphony was due to psychological and ethnological forces manifested in the popular music of northern and northwestern cultures. Ultimately, medieval musical science and philosophy were to reconcile this indigenous musical culture with the musical doctrines of classical antiquity and with the practice of Gregorian art, since the opposition could not continue in the face of the insistence of the Church on the nature and quality of the music of its rite.

The modern scholar encounters polyphony at the moment when this reconciliation had been partly accomplished. It is doubtful that we shall ever be able to present more than circumstantial evidence of the origin of polyphony, since documents are missing because the music was not noted down. Indigenous music could not maintain itself in its original vein under the powerful influence of the music of the Church. The people who sang the Gregorian songs—and we must not forget that the early Mass was sung by the congregation—could not help molding their own melodies to the songs they sang in church. This will also explain the Gregorian character of the folk songs of many nations which otherwise have nothing in common. Finnish and Canadian, Hungarian and Scottish folk songs often show characteristic melodic turns which make them almost similar. Were it not for the characteristic rhythms created by the natural prosody, inflections, and accents of the various languages, one could hardly tell these songs apart.

The Church insisted on its own songs, the Gregorian melodies had to be preserved intact; any other music, if there was to be more than one voice, was permitted only in *addition* to the existing consecrated melodies. The original polyphonic incentive of the people slowly acquiesced and thus adapted itself to the musical art which was forced upon them. The improvised instrumental music of the minstrels, however, did not come under the close surveillance of the Church; therefore the jongleurs, minstrels, and *Spielleute* retained much more of the original character of their respective folk music. The oldest documents of popular instrumental music testify to the vogue of a major-minor conception of tonality among these simple musicians, a fact which is an exception with the art music of the period. Medieval musical science was contemptuously opposed to these tonalities, against which it cited the doctrines of the ancients. It took many centuries before the learned scholars and theoreticians bowed to the natural instinct of musicians and codified, in the sixteenth century, widespread practices which were as old as their civilization.

Forms and Devices of Early Polyphony

THE well-developed musical life of Wales and of northern England has persuaded many authors to declare that those provinces were the first to evolve polyphonic music. In this they have relied especially on the writings of Giraldus Cambrensis (1147–1220), notably on his *Descriptio Cambriae*,[3] where, in his discussion of Welsh music, he tells us that the inhabitants sang not in unison, as did other peoples, but in different parts, so that in Wales one would hear as many different voices as there were singers present. This remark should be interpreted to allude to the singing of canonic rounds, known to be ancient forms of popular music, in which a number of singers can join in at a given interval of time with the same melody. The fact that the famous Summer Canon was written barely half a century after Giraldus's treatise affords sufficient proof of this theory. Beyond the Humber and along the coast of Yorkshire a similar practice was employed, but here it was restricted to two voices. According to Giraldus this was not an artistic manifestation but the result of custom, the practice seeming so natural and familiar that even the children sang in the same fashion and it was quite unusual to hear a single melody sung by one voice. Giraldus advanced the belief that this practice originated with the Danes, an assumption that seems to gain credence by the discovery of very ancient popular polyphonic devices in Iceland. It is significant that the name and nature of the Icelandic *twiesöngvar,* described by von Hornbostel in the second volume of the *Deutsche Islandforschung,* are identical with the *gymel* or twinsong. The existence of polyphony in England is indicated by even older authors. The Anglo-Saxon Bishop Aldhelm, at the end of the seventh century, and Johannes Scotus Erigena (ninth century), seem to allude to "harmony" as the simultaneous sounding of tones. Finally, the first records of actual music for more than one voice also come from England.

The oldest documents of many-voiced music are the musical examples included in the text of a tract entitled *Musica Enchiriadis,* written in the second half of the ninth century and called *organum* (solemn song or musical work) or *diaphonia cantilena* (twinsong). The organum consists of a given liturgic melody with a melody underneath following the original note for note in the interval of a fourth. Another interpretation, also plausible, connects the name with the organ, supporting the idea that the nonliturgical second part was not sung but confided to the organ.

The oldest and most interesting manuscript of organa, the Winchester Troper, comes from England and dates from the first half of the eleventh century.[4] It contains, besides numerous sequences, tropes, and Mass songs, some hundred and fifty two-part organa. Since these early examples of many-voiced music consist mostly of liturgic songs which were usually performed by a solo singer, it must be assumed that many-voiced music had close connections with the tropes, an individual solo art. Thus the thread leads back again to Provençal territory, notably to the great Abbey of St. Martial in Limoges. While the earlier English organa show unmistakable derivation from Limoges, the later specimens of English polyphony relied on the musical practice of the Notre Dame school in Paris. These facts refute the claim for the British "invention" of polyphony, advanced on sentimental grounds by some authors. The cultural intercourse between the British Isles and the Continent was lively; the Norman feudal lords held possessions in both countries and English students were frequent visitors in Paris. Many Englishmen occupied important positions in France, among them several professors and high ecclesiastic dignitaries who cannot be separated from the intellectual history of France. The continental experiments were still slow and vague when England already possessed well-developed and universally practiced polyphonic church music, and Wooldridge and Handschin have shown how manifold and rich was this art in the later Middle Ages; [5] but English polyphony of the Middle Ages was always strongly influenced by French art and did not itself exert appreciable influence on continental art before the fifteenth century. The main seat of organal art was central France. The fact that English musicians adapted themselves so well to the new art of polyphony merely indicates the soundness of the theory which considers the growth of polyphony as an issue of the struggle between Gregorian art and indigenous music, for the British Isles were less subject to Gregorian influences than the adjacent countries on the Continent.

Owing to the absence of musical documents from the early history of the Nordic peoples, our knowledge of the earliest examples of specifically north European musical culture, the often ridiculed parallel organa, must necessarily be conjectural and retrospective. Hucbald did not "create" the organum by theoretical speculations; he rather codified systematically an age-old practice, a procedure which is paralleled in other arts. In this domain the Nordic penchant for motion struggled with the classical desire for space. The struggle was liveliest where the two spheres of culture met, in France; and when the great reconciliation between Nordic and classic ended in the advent of the Gothic, a style predominantly influenced by the conception of the North, there arose also a similar style in music which may be called early Gothic as it reflected the same spirit and the same characteristics as the other products of human ingenuity. It remained, however, to associate this popular polyphony with liturgic music before it could develop into an art form. This association took place in the tropes.

The customary definition of "organum" is simple: the original or given melody, the *cantus firmus* (fixed song or melody), usually a plain-chant tune, was accompanied by another melody, the latter paralleling the first at the interval of the fourth, or, after Guido, also in the fifth. But this definition does not give a satisfactory description and does not indicate the great significance of the procedure. By adding a second melody to the given song the free melodic flow of the latter is restricted; the single tones, unimportant in a melody of Oriental type, where they are only an infinitesimal part of the melos, now acquire a certain status. Having been detached and isolated from the succession of tones making up the melody, the individual tones receive a vertical force and become part of a sound-complex created by the simultaneous sounding of two tones. The sound-complex takes the foreground and relegates the melodic aspect of the music to the background. The cantus firmus is deprived of its purely melodic nature—a fact which is valid throughout the Middle Ages—and becomes exactly what its name implies: a fixed or rigid song. These Gregorian melodies which served as cantus firmi, considered by the Carolingian era as purely spiritual, transcendental expressions of art, become now the foundation upon which the genius of northwestern Europe was to build a new musical world, as typical for its civilization as was the one-dimensional melodic conception for the Orient.

The melodic-linear element, however, could not be kept out of the growing practice of polyphony. It was centuries old, and the Western mind, having struggled against it and reduced it to its own taste, began to explore its possibilities within the frame of the new musical art. Here we observe another remarkable metamorphosis of musical thought. In spite of its dependence on the cantus firmus, which retains its unalterable character, the organal part gradually assumes an increasingly independent melodic aspect. With this, the development of polyphony entered upon a new stage which was to have far-reaching consequences. The uniform progression by single notes, entailing a corresponding motion, note for note, in the so-called "organizing part," gave way to more differentiated motion-relationships between the two parts. Another important step was the shifting of the given melody from the upper position to the lower. The cantus firmus becomes more and more drawn out while the upper part begins to spin melodies over its sluggish line. In the late eleventh-century organa this contrast between the animated upper part and the slowly moving cantus firmus was carried out with the greatest logic. John Cotton wrote the following rule around 1100: "If the main voice is ascending, the accompanying part should descend, and vice versa." [6] This sentence, with its allusion to obligatory contrary motion, states for the first time the most important principle of musical construction, namely, independent voice leading or part writing. The developed two-part organum was henceforth known by the name of *discantus* (descant) or *déchant,* the rules of which were given in a tract called *Discantus Vulgaris Positio,* printed in the first volume of Coussemaker's collection. The author of this treatise written toward the middle of the twelfth century gives the rules for the composition of the independent part (which itself assumed the name of *discantus*) and adds, "Commit these rules to memory, and apply them in practice, and you will have mastered the whole art of *discantus*."

This means, of course, that polyphony was still an art of improvisation, but an improvisation following logical rules. In these two-voiced compositions we see two melodic lines united in most intimate combination. They appear in parallel motion, then cross each other, then again continue their motion in oblique direction. A similar description would be applicable to contemporary linear ornaments, such as webwork; but curiously enough, while we recognize and admire the rich and fantastic play of patterns created by the winding lines of Gothic ornamentation, we have been given to calling the corresponding musical phenomenon merely a "crude" attempt at musical composition. The evolution of the musical lines within the frame defined by tonal space, their crisscrossing, and their final stage of quiescence reached in the cadence, were all caused and conditioned by the same creative urge which animated the creator of the visual ornament. They represent the only musical taste possible to the period. It is irrelevant to accuse the composer of Gothic polyphony of a lack of sense for euphony and transparent setting, because these criteria did not figure in the aesthetic conception of the period.

The great monastery of St. Martial in Limoges was the most important center of organum composition, and this seems only natural when we remember that it was one of the most important centers of culture of the time. This phase of polyphonic art spread not only to England but to Spain, as is illustrated by the twenty organa in the famous *Codex Calixtinus* written for one of the most celebrated places of pilgrimage in the Christian West, Santiago de Compostela.

The Ars Antiqua

IN the second half of the twelfth century there was a distinct change of style in all branches of art. The verse-novel, or *roman,* with its short rhymed double lines running uninterruptedly, took the place of strophic verse, creating a new form. The new poetry, like contemporary Gothic art, emanated from France and the French-dominated British territory. An inexhaustible joy and pleasure in telling fables animated this literature and kept it in continuous motion, action following upon action in fast tempo. The narrative becomes more and more fluent and mobile, and the action seems to observe a linear evolution; it proceeds in lines for a time parallel, then divergent, then crisscrossing at seemingly accidental points. The events of the narrative follow in rapid succession like the pictures in a roll of film. The characteristic metamorphosis of style discernible in the artistic trend from Romanesque to Gothic, the change from heavy and massive forms to animated interplay of forces, is manifest in this literature, and as in the other arts, turns in the late Gothic into a playful virtuosity that becomes almost offensive in nature. The difference of conception is also evident in the style of presentation. Unlike antique epic poetry, which tended to present large portions of the narrative in individual heroic "scenes," the Gothic *roman* travels from fact to fact; the great allegorical-poetical *tableaux* of the classical poets are missing, we follow an almost matter-of-fact description of events in linear succession; instead of unity of place we have change of place in continuously unfolding action. A typical Gothic trait is the repeated indenting of the linear sequence by reopening a completed action and starting it again *in medias res*. All this was coupled with a great interest in the most minute detail. Wherever one looks one perceives a trend toward animated motion. The guiding principle of Gothic architecture was to attain the greatest possible richness in architectural motion; the static image of space played a subordinate role. The same principle is manifest in Gothic music and is expressed in the rhythmical motion of the independent parts.

In the second half of the twelfth century the composition of organa came to a standstill. Jacobus of Liége, author of *Speculum Musicae*, remarks in this important treatise that toward the end of the thirteenth century "the moderns use only *motets* and *cantilenae*." The appearance of the motet coincided with the emancipation of the cathedral churches from their monastic foundations, for this movement was followed by music, and the development of polyphony was associated now with the secular church.

The increasingly independent polyphony of the individual parts is manifest in the frequent extension of the individual sections, or *clausulae*, of the organa, whereby the upper part often received a completely new text. The old principle of the trope is revived here; while the tenor part holds the liturgic word (the *mot*) and music as a cantus firmus, the contrapuntal parts declaim a paraphrase. Soon the troped accompanying parts became so imposing that they forced changes in the Gregorian cantus firmus. The derivation and definition of "motet" presents some difficulties. Its contemporary name, *motetus*, designated in the beginning the upper contrapuntal voice, which was evolving above and against the lower part, which "held on" (tenor, from the Latin *teneo*) to the *mot;* the third voice was called *triplum*, whence is derived our modern treble. Later the name was applied to the whole composition. The motet, like the sequence, which had been equally influential in promoting musical art at an earlier date, was of liturgic origin, but soon found its way into the realm of secular art. There it associated itself with troubadour art and interpolated the popular melodies in its polyphonic structure. The result was an incomparably animated and expressive secular polyphonic art.

The first organization of contrapuntal polyphony was the work of the early Gothic church music school of northern France which centered about the cathedral of *Beatae Mariae Virginis* (later Notre Dame) in Paris. The flourishing of this school coincided with the building of the new cathedrals. An anonymous Englishman who appears to have studied in France toward the end of the thirteenth century and who received from his first modern editor the name of Anonymous IV, described the nature and practice of the polyphonic art in a treatise of great value.[7] It is to the writings of this scholar that we owe our knowledge of who the leaders of the Notre Dame school were. Magister Leoninus (Léonin) was, according to our English chronicler, the first. This old musician, active in the twelfth century, composed a whole cycle of organa in a work entitled *Magnus Liber Organi*. Anonymous IV calls the composer and choirmaster of the cathedral *optimus organista,* the greatest composer of organa. (This term is frequently misinterpreted to mean "great organist.") The next leader of the school, Magister Perotinus Magnus (Pérotin), active in the first decades of the thirteenth century, is, as his epithet implies, one of the great figures of musical history and the builder of musical "cathedrals" of the Gothic. The tendency was away from the improvised polyphony of the earlier organa toward a rhythmically organized polyphonic art. It was in this sense that the new master, called *optimus discantor,* undertook the revision of the work of the *optimus organista*. Perotinus went beyond the two-part *organum duplum* and added a third and fourth part to his compositions. His art reached its peak in the monumental *organa quadrupla* which exhibit a perfection of musical technique and a logic of construction found only in the works of the great masters.

The term "organum" for a while was used to denote all polyphonic music, but about the time of Perotinus its meaning became restricted to liturgic works, while the conductus and the motet acquired an independent status with marked stylistic characteristics. The conductus, a composition with a poetical text and with a basic melody not necessarily pre-existent but often invented by the composer, used the same text in all parts, the syllables being pronounced simultaneously as in the organa. This trait distinguishes the conductus from the motet, which used different texts in the individual parts, a procedure that becomes essentially an embroidering of a given theme of words and music by two or more further sets of words and music. The rise of the motet eclipsed the vogue of the conductus, as the conjunction of several texts constituted a step in advance of the conductus and of the liturgic organa in general, introducing new possibilities for the rendering of musical expression. The melodies, now furnished with individual texts, became more independent, and soon the motet emerged from the narrow circle of liturgical functions into general musical activity.

The motet developed further in three main directions. First, the old forms of the two- and three-voiced Latin motet continued to be practiced. But a significant phenomenon in the church music of the thirteenth century, a growing alienation from the spirit of Gregorian art, made itself felt in the art of polyphony. Plain chant became more and more a symbol of the past; while still revered, it ceased to be a living thing. The motet began to absorb secular elements, and we see the appearance of French texts in a form once exclusively Latin. This second type, the so-called French motet, did not differ from the Latin motet as regards musical form. It finally appeared as a two-voiced form with a simple syllabic melody in the upper voice and a liturgic tenor as accompaniment—a tenor, however, which had completely lost its significance as a section of a liturgic melody and which was no longer sung but was played by an instrument, its origin being still evident in the fragments of old liturgical texts which accompany it. A third variant of the oldest motet was achieved by adding two contrapuntal parts to the tenor, thereby enlarging the construction to three parts. The tenor, originating from a liturgical piece, served as foundation for the whole, while the other two parts were more or less related to each other. This three-part motet type soon became the most important genre of art music.

The music of the French motet may be considered, as we have remarked before, an imitation of the Latin, notwithstanding the fact that its textual content was markedly different. Most texts in the Latin motet were based on religious poems of a hymnlike or contemplative nature. The French texts, on the other hand, were purely secular, generally dance songs, love songs, and the like. The frequent use of refrains shows the close connection between the motet and secular solo lyrics. The French imitation of the Latin motet might appear in several ways. In some instances only the style of the Latin motet was imitated; in others, melodies set to French texts were introduced over the tenor of a Latin motet; and finally, a Latin motet might be translated in its entirety into French, only the music remaining the same. The Latin motet, too, was tremendously enriched by this process of transplantation, because French motets were often translated into Latin.

The great growth and development of independent part writing called for a new system of notation, as the old mnemotechnic system of the neumes could not render the intricacies of this music. The exact indication of pitch was immediately followed by a system that permitted the measurement of the duration of tones; thus arose *musica mensurata,* or measured (measurable) music. Simple and easily recognizable signs were selected from the existing material, and the ratio of the short note to the long was established. There appeared also a new system of rhythmical continuity and organization, which came into music presumably from the mathematical precision of the verse rhythm of French poetry. The typical melodic motion of the plain chant was now rationally organized in the so-called rhythmic modes, six in number, which supplied rhythmic patterns of various combinations of short and long values.[8] The prevalence of rhythmical principles was accentuated by the restriction to ternary rhythm. The scholastic spirit endeavored to suppress the sensual element believed to accompany binary rhythm, by emphasizing the perfection of the ternary division which symbolized the Holy Trinity; hence the name *tempus perfectum* for ternary time. The organization of measurable music reached a considerable perfection at the turn of the twelfth century, spreading with the victorious diffusion of the Gothic from France to other countries.

The application of the new rhythmic devices to independent melodies created a great variety of effects. The *modus* could differ in every voice, resulting in an interplay of independently organized rhythmical patterns of such incredible rhythmic-dynamic intensity as music has never known before or since. This rhythmical motion became so powerful that—especially after Perotinus—even the hitherto "immobile" and sluggish tenor part with its Gregorian cantus firmus could not withstand the general trend. Yet, characteristically enough, the tenor part in true Gothic tradition retained its unearthly spiritual nature, living its own life in the midst of the fantasy that reigned in the other parts. There were motets, like some in the famous manuscript preserved in the library of the medical faculty at the University of Montpellier, France, which show (in a modern transcription into measures) four syllables to one bar in the treble, three to a measure in the next lower part, the contratenor, and two to a measure in the lowest part, the tenor; to add to the complexity, the three texts are entirely different, exhibiting unequal verse length and dissimilar strophic construction. The result is a composition of unheard-of complexity in which the rhythmic points of division never occur together in the several parts. One should never think in this case of primitive form and technique; it is all highly rational polyphonic construction.

Such use of independent texts for the individual parts not only increased rhythmical intensity, but occasionally created singularly dramatic situations where the various parts expressed different sentiments and different principles. Friedrich Ludwig [9] mentions an example in which one part is devoted to the dutiful priest: "the pious priests' works shine like stars of the firmament" (*velut stelle fundamenti fulgent facta praelatorum*); opposed to this voice, held in the quiet first rhythmic mode, stands the upper part, the *triplum,* which with its vivid rhythms of the sixth mode, thunders against the "hypocritical, malicious, drunken and lecherous priests, tormenters of the Church" (*ypocrite pseudopontifices, ecclesie diri carnifices*); while the whole motet is supported by the broad melody of the tenor part, *et gaudebit,* the alleluia sung on the Sunday between Ascension and Pentecost to the parting words of Christ (John 14, 16 and 18), *non vos relinquam orphanos,* which allude to the miracle of Pentecost. This juxtaposition of artistically symbolized ideas gathered into a comprehensive symbol testifies to the idealistic conception of the Middle Ages, reflected in music as well as in the other arts. In a later period, heralding the coming of a new artistic era, the use of multiple texts led both to increasingly independent texts and to domination by the text of the uppermost part.

Romanesque and Gothic

ONLY a short time ago even learned musicians spoke of the Gothic motet in terms that early nineteenth-century historians of the fine arts were wont to apply to Romanesque sculpture or the "primitive" pictures of early Flemish masters. Recent historians, furthermore, saw nothing but confusion in Gothic music, being unable to reconcile the curious mixture of the sacred and the secular. Yet the motet, which to the modern man seems incomprehensible and barbaric, illustrates better than any other artistic phenomenon the temper and ideology of its times. Better than the *summae* of the philosophers, the motet could express simultaneously both the original text and commentaries upon it. The error in the approach of the nineteenth-century man to Gothic music, as to early Flemish paintings, lay in his attempt to apply the aesthetic doctrines of the nineteenth century to an art which obeyed entirely different conceptions. He tried to view the juxtaposed and superimposed scenes of the paintings as he tried to listen to the music: as one spatial unit. But the Gothic followed an entirely different conception of space, different means of expression, and a taste which preferred motion to rest.

Romanesque art created a homogeneous vault construction; the Gothic vault is a jointed structure, a labile system achieving balance by the reciprocal pressure of forces. The inexorable logic of the Gothic system of construction prevails even when there are no more organic ties evident between the individual members of the structure. Robert de Lasteyre describes the construction of the choir of St. Ouen in Rouen, the arches of which are supported by buttresses that lean against the extremity of a wall which serves both as an abutment to the arches and as a partition between the lateral chapels. But for the interplay of forces, the simultaneous attraction and repulsion, the central nave would collapse.[10] Such boldness of construction was unimaginable in the Romanesque era, which operated with quiet and stable masses. Gothic architecture is not static in nature, a mere mass at rest; it is the expression of the animated interplay of forces, an active process which takes hold of the entire building. Since the components of the building all take part in this movement, the walls also lose the quiet homogeneous mass they assumed in the Romanesque period, joining in the general trend to overcome weight, to expand and soar as if they would reach the very sky.

The metamorphosis of the massive homogeneous organum into an animated structural web of rhythms and melodies in the Gothic motet was in every way analogous to the stylistic changes that took place in the fine arts and literature. It required from the listener a new approach and a new conception of listening to music, for the Gothic motet did not establish an intimate relationship between listener and singer. Instead of concentrating on a group of singers, the listener had to follow three individual parts presenting three distinct moods: the tenor with its solemn cantus firmus, and the other parts taking turns in vivid and fast-moving or in slower, melancholy passages. The listener—and this applies to the modern musician as well—must make his choice, select a part and follow it, and then become a part of the polyphonic web. If he thus follows the individual melodies, he will be rewarded by a remarkable wealth of musical ingenuity, entirely lost to the conventional harmonic approach of a different era.

Medieval Musical Doctrines and Theories

THE acceptance of polyphony in the music of the Church resulted, as was to be expected, in theoretical discussions of its principles and practice. Far from being mere vague speculations, as historians have been wont to consider them, these first tracts represented the acknowledgment of an established musical practice. Brought up on the doctrines of Boethius, the theoreticians attempted to find a common denominator for polyphony and classical Greek musical science. Artificial as the attempt was, considering the ancients' complete ignorance of polyphony, it fitted very well into the Carolingian renaissance by its deliberate harking back to antiquity. The task of the musical *magistri* of the eleventh and twelfth centuries had been to consolidate and clarify the various doctrines and rules of the science of music; the main aim of those of the thirteenth, the century of the *juventus,* was to codify and organize the rules of mensural music. They did not neglect the philosophical side of their science, however, but continued eagerly their speculations about the nature of music and its classification among the arts and sciences. While most medieval musical tracts exhibit a similarity in subject matter traceable to their common sources—Boethius, Cassiodorus, and Isidore of Seville—beginning with the middle of the thirteenth century there is a marked enrichment of material, the importance of which has only recently been acknowledged.[11] This new influence emanated from Arabian literature, known and appreciated in Europe since Archbishop Raymond of Toledo instituted a college of translators in the twelfth century.

The chief figure in Arabian musical science was the philosopher Al-Farabi (d. 950), author of an encyclopedic work drawn largely from Aristotle. Al-Farabi was one of the earliest Moslem thinkers to develop a philosophical method reconciling Aristotle and Islam. His translator and propagator, Domenicus Gundissalinus (c. 1150), was responsible for the wide dissemination of his ideas. Al-Farabi divided music into *musica speculativa* and *musica activa,* a classification which harks back to classical times, but which appears for the first time in the Latin literature of the Middle Ages as a result of his work. He then contemplates this musical world from the point of view of the actual musician, who may be a theoretician, belonging to the first group, or a practicing musician, a partisan of *musica activa.* Al-Farabi revived another important classical conception in his division of the theoretical fields of music into *melos, metrum,* and *gestus,* a step which brings the dance once more into the domain of music, the old Greek conception of the unity of poetry, music, and the dance now taking its place beside the more abstract Boethian theories.

The Arabian doctrines, as transmitted by the translations of Avicenna, Averroës, and Gundissalinus, aroused a tremendous interest in Aristotle, but the Aristotelians did not come into their own without difficulties. Since the Aristotelian theories came from Islamic sources, the translations introduced the philosophy of Islam to Western Christendom, horrifying many devout Christians who foresaw a battle between faith and reason. It is interesting to see how the tendency to reason influenced the musical scholars who began to be interested in the practical side of music. The first signs of Arabic-Aristotelian interpretation appeared early in the thirteenth century in the works of a musical scholar, appropriately calling himself Aristotle but customarily referred to by modern historians as "Pseudo-Aristotle," [12] who had a remarkable philosophical schooling and was also thoroughly familiar with the musical practice of his day. The Arabian influence was carried further by Vincent of Beauvais, and especially by the great English scholar, scientist, and philosopher, Roger Bacon (1214?-1294), who, in his *Opus Majus* and *Opus Tertium,* both finished about 1267-1268, devoted many pages to music and insisted on its thorough mastery by theologians. Bacon's most remarkable achievement was his clear anticipation of the methods of modern science. His approach to music was mathematical yet, in spite of his strong leanings toward a purely mathematical conception, one can see the Arabian influence in his concern with the empirical nature of music and with its sonorous-aural qualities.

Beginning with Bacon, Jacobus of Liége, and Johannes de Grocheo, the last two writing about 1300, the Boethian *musica mundana* began to lose its importance. Besides the theological considerations which weakened the Boethian, purely scientific speculative conceptions, a new musical species, called *musica coelestis,* appeared in the general classification, no doubt as a result of the Aristotelian writings now available in Latin translations. Another new term was that of *musica artificialis,* comprising all music humanly conceived as opposed to the *mundana* and *coelestis.* A number of eminent English writers on music—Robert Kilwardy (d. 1279), Aluredus or Amerus Anglicus (1271), and Walter Odington (d. c. 1330), who was one of the most important musical scholars of the Middle Ages—testify to the high regard entertained for music by men of letters, but they also indicate the disinclination of English scholars to clutter up their writings with metaphysical speculations of this sort. Odington [13] doubts outright the empirical-sonorous existence of *musica mundana,* and his scientific treatment shows a thoroughly practical, modern conception of the nature of music. It is interesting to note that both Bacon and Odington include the art of acting in their discussion of music, a fact which is also due to the Arabian-Aristotelian influence.

Ecclesiastical Opposition to Polyphony

WITH the increasing popularity of the Aristotelian doctrines in the thirteenth century the tendency to restrict musical discussion to the practical side of music, vocal and instrumental, becomes noticeable. At the same time the opposition of many Christian thinkers to these doctrines created a situation comparable only to that which grew up from the critical attitude of the eighteenth-century literary world toward the opera. Musicians and public enthusiastically favored the new art of polyphony, while ecclesiastic leaders and learned scholars opposed it, giving frequent expression to their feelings in their writings, presaging the decay of musical art and deploring especially the intrusion of a secular spirit into the music of the Church. Among the earliest opponents of the musical practices which had their beginning in the Gothic period were the great scholastic philosopher John of Salisbury (c. 1115–1180), Bishop of Chartres, and Aelred, Abbot of Rievaulx (d. 1166). The tone of criticism became sharper and sharper until attacks were made upon the very principle of polyphony. Durandus [14] called the motet "disorganized music," and Roger Bacon deplored the vanishing of the solemn traditions of church song, blaming the "silly pleasure in manifold *cantilenae*" for this state of affairs. The second Council of Lyons (1274) created several canons to stem what the Church considered injurious practices; but a more energetic rebuke came in 1324–1325 from John XXII, a pope of French extraction who resided in Avignon. The papal decree was directed against the art of *discantus;* it deplored the substitution of the products of a new art for the "good old melodies" and scolded against the adulteration of church song. "They chop up the melodies by *ochete,* mollify them by *discantus* and *triplum* so that they [the melodies] rush around ceaselessly, intoxicating the ear without quieting it, falsify the expression, and disturb devotion instead of evoking it."

The ochete, better known as *hocket* or *hoquetus,* was a device of the early medieval contrapuntists by which the notes of a melody were interspersed with rests in a complementary manner. The result was akin to our modern staccato and, if not carried too far, was very effective and at times dramatic. The ecclesiastics were especially aroused by the use of the *hoquetus,* presumably because its very expressive and dramatic qualities were entirely opposed to the Gregorian spirit. Aelred's description of it is typical of the attitude of the more ascetic church leaders.

"Sometimes thou mayest see a man with an open mouth, not to sing, but as it were to breathe his last gasp, by shutting in his breath, and by a certain ridiculous interception of his voice to threaten silence, and now again to imitate the agonies of a dying man, or the ecstasies of such as suffer." [15]

John of Salisbury [16] expresses his disapproval in even stronger terms which remind us of the tone of the early Church Fathers:

"Music defiles the service of religion. For the admiring simple souls of the congregation are of necessity depraved—in the very presence of the Lord, in the sacred recesses of the sanctuary itself—by the riot of the wantoning voice, by its eager ostentation, and by its womanish affectations in the mincing of notes and sentences."

Such sharp opposition was not based on aesthetic grounds; it appears rather that social and church-political reasons prompted the leading churchmen and musical scholars to take sides against the motet. While only a short time ago organum, conductus, and the earliest two-part Latin motet had been generally considered purely liturgic music, the developed contrapuntal motet had gone out beyond the boundaries of liturgy and found a place in secular circles; in fact it had become the preferred and highest form of secular art. The Church began to realize that its monopoly on music was being seriously challenged as the development of polyphony went forward on a more universal basis than strictly liturgic aims could afford. Its opposition produced tangible results, however. It stimulated a marked increase in the practice of the older, simpler forms of organum. Furthermore, it brought the establishment of a specific church style, which accepted innovations in the realm of music but applied them to its own art only after a generous period had elapsed. This principle of "probation" remained a characteristic trait of the musical doctrines of the Church, and we shall see its application throughout the history of music.

Dissension and mistrust were not lasting. The generation of Albertus Magnus, St. Thomas Aquinas, and St. Bonaventure undertook the reconciliation of faith and reason in a magnificent synthesis, in which they saw nothing contrary to reason in faith. In order to clarify the division of the sciences, which included all realms of knowledge, they raised a distinction between theology and philosophy; the former was the divine science, the latter investigated everything else which had reference to humanity. In the field of musical scholarship a strong theological tinge was still noticeable, but all discussions now had connection with actual music and were not lost in symbolical speculation. The various trends were reconciled in the important treatise called *Speculum Musicae,* written by Jacobus of Liége. For centuries this work was ascribed to Johannes de Muris and was held in such admiration that students at the universities referred to the study of music as the "study of Muris." This ascription was doubtless owing to the great renown of the universally learned scholar Muris, but the authorship of Jacobus is now established beyond question.[17]

With all his remarkable erudition and scholarship, Jacobus of Liége was still a man who revered traditions, and for the point of view of a liberal of his day we must return once more to Jean de Grouchy, or, as he was known in this era of Latin dignity, Johannes de Grocheo, whom we have mentioned before as the first champion of secular, nonliturgic music. Grocheo's *Theoria* is a phenomenon unique in the history of musical writings. Its author had no predecessors and—apparently—no immediate successors. Instead of the universally accepted Boethian conception of the musical world, he created an original formula of his own, dividing music into *simplex, composita,* and *ecclesiastica*—a thoroughly practical conception which ushered in a new era.

The Impact of the French Gothic on Neighboring Civilizations

THE great musical art which arose in France and spread to the adjoining countries was not an isolated phenomenon: the changing structure of society was paralleled by changes in all fields that contribute to culture. The increasingly independent towns acquired importance not only in political but in economic life. The relative security and peace within their walls invited the practice of arts and letters. Exclusive rights and unchallenged authority over subordinates were the prerequisites of chivalric-aristocratic society, and as long as their foundations were intact they permitted the flourishing of aristocratic art. But the small artisans and merchants, escaping from serfdom, found their way into the towns and, beginning with the twelfth century, contributed to the rapidly growing mercantile character of these places, which soon became the seats of industry and finance. By opposing the autocracy of the nobility the towns became the chief supporters of the reigning princes in war and peace. The magnificence of the chivalric courts waned with the expiration of the class civilization of the knights. A new nobility of officeholders, with a spirit nearer to that of the middle classes was being organized around the rulers. In this atmosphere poetry became partly more sober, partly more religious. But the middle-class poets did not know the lyricism that thrives in the refreshing open spaces of nature; their texts are unctuous and their atmosphere is that of the closed room. The learned musicians and singers, on the other hand, who came from the middle classes, developed the dominant church music in the serious and thorough manner characteristic of their class. Although some of the troubadours, like Adam de la Hale, learned from them the art of polyphony, they did not produce important works in this field, which remained the domain of the ecclesiastic masters. The latter, in their turn, accepted secular elements as inevitable but endeavored to place them in the service of their religious art.

We have said before that instruments participated in the performance of motets. Instrumental music played an important part in the musical life of the Gothic middle classes. We possess only a few late thirteenth-century manuscripts containing pure instrumental music, among them instrumental motets, yet, judging from the numerous pictorial documents, instruments were widely used. It is not surprising, then, that this instrumental music was soon popular and important enough to appropriate the motet to its own uses. The influence of the parodistic spirit of the goliards is also discernible in the numerous imitations of motets that appeared. The upper parts of these pseudo motets were written with great virtuosity, and the principle of the cantus firmus remained intact, but the tenor part to which it was assigned was now definitely confined to instruments. The decline of the motet starts with the increase in these secular tendencies; gradually they eliminated the liturgic cantus firmi in favor of secular tenors, thus displacing the symbolic with the naturalistic and destroying the unique balance between the spiritual and the sensuous that had made the motet what it was. As a purely secular form the motet did not show enough vitality to maintain leadership and was forced to give way before the French songs, rondeaux and ballads, which succeeded it. As solemn church music, it continued to exist in the fourteenth century, but a leveling process eliminated the essential quality of contrast which had given the motet of the Gothic period its characteristic stamp.

We have seen how the great polyphonic art of the Gothic period in France found an echo in early English music. The scarcity of documents, unfortunately, does not permit us to follow the development of musical art in England as clearly as in France. The English manuscripts show, besides distinctly original compositions, a number of Notre Dame works, partly in their original form, partly in a specifically British adaptation. There are even a few conductus with English texts. But the most celebrated product of English polyphonic art of the thirteenth century, the well-known "Summer Canon," represents a species seemingly original with English art, a form which had barely traces on the Continent. The form of the composition is an endless canon—the first recorded in history—for four voices, accompanied by two ground basses singing interchangeable melodies. The ingenuity of construction of the six-part setting, the perfection of the writing, and the freshness of its mood make this piece a unique monument of medieval polyphony, and it is highly regrettable that it still remains an isolated example. The date of composition of "Sumer Is Icumen In" is now generally accepted as 1240, and its author is supposed to have been one John of Fornsete; the manuscript comes from Reading Abbey. The composition was equipped with a Latin text also (*Perspice Christocola*), presumably for ecclesiastic use.

Germany contributed to the musical culture of the Middle Ages the profound spiritual songs of the Minnesinger, but she was conspicuously backward in the field of polyphony. The products of this period hardly indicate that the country was one day to count among its musicians a John Sebastian Bach. The practice of Gothic polyphony spread from France to Spain, as may be seen in several manuscripts from Burgos and Toledo. A number of Catalan manuscripts now gradually being published by the great student of Spanish music, Higini Anglès,[18] begin to shed more light on this little known yet important phase of musical history.

The use of vernacular elements in the various lands indicates that the influence of popular art was on the increase, but genuinely national elements were assimilated only in the measure permitted by the growing national consciousness of the Middle Ages. This consciousness was, for the time being, far inferior to the traditional power of the Church, and this fact accounts for the overwhelming uniform practice of liturgy-born polyphony, which took the lead in the art of music as did church architecture in the realm of the fine arts.

Chapter 8

THE ARS NOVA

→→→ ←←←

The Collapse of the Medieval Order

HISTORICAL periods are established by historians who are forced by practical necessity to divide their material according to certain events and general characteristics. While such "periodizations" are feasible on paper, the periods themselves do not follow well-defined lines; the end of each is usually marked by a time of confusion from which humanity emerges with new force and new ideals. One of these periods of transition was the fourteenth century. The great harvest had been reaped, and the late harvest was scant, but it yielded the first signs of a new era.

The fourteenth century and the beginning of the fifteenth have been referred to as the "waning of the Middle Ages," no doubt because of the devastation the historian beholds. The fourteenth century was, indeed, visited by many catastrophes. The Franco-Flemish wars, six decades of the terrible Hundred Years' War, the peasant uprisings, and the Black Death devastated western Europe, while Italy was kept in a state of grave disorder by endless internal strife. The two great forces of Christendom, Church and Empire, had lost much of their importance. The papacy suffered the greatest crisis in its entire history by the half-enforced, half-voluntary exile to Avignon (1309–1376) and the subsequent schism of the West (1378–1417). No question of faith or practice was here involved, for the forty years' struggle was entirely a matter of persons and politics, to the dismay of the faithful and the pious; great uncertainty prevailed among theologians, but in general they agreed with the political authorities of their respective countries as to which of the two, pope or antipope, they should obey. But while the permanent effects of the schism were slight, in its own period it delayed the reforms admittedly needed in the Church.

The empire ceased to be a world empire: it became a German Empire dominated by Wittelsbachs or Habsburgs. Occidental-Christian universalism declined; the Christian West failed in every endeavor it undertook in its capacity of defender of the faith. In 1291 it gave up its last possessions in the

Holy Land, and 1453 saw the fall of Constantinople. Proud and glittering knighthood became an anachronism; wherever it took the field against hostile forces, whether Hussites, Swiss peasants, or Polish folk armies, it was defeated.

Peasants and burghers were terror-stricken by the Black Death, and when the plague was over, the picture of death indelibly impressed on their minds turned them as never before toward contemplation of the transitoriness of earthly life. Artists vied with each other in depicting death; the *danse macabre* was the theme of many literary and artistic works. The emphasis on death and the charnel house is characteristic, however, not so much of the Middle Ages, as some historians like to think, as of the times immediately following the collapse of the medieval order. The collapse was terrifying, especially in its moral aspects. Innumerable people danced, danced over death, and gave themselves freely to all vices, not shrinking from the most repulsive crimes. "The moral corruption was greater than the physical," says a chronicler. As soon as the plague receded to the worst slums of the towns and the imminent danger had passed, all the lowest passions of the horrified populace came to the fore and were given free rein. The threatening proximity of death seems to have enhanced the love of life and pleasure. Crime appeared unchallenged, as there was no one to enforce law. Even the obvious danger of death did not deter the people in their boundless greed, wrangling over the possessions of the already dead. Monks descended to the towns to dispose of their monasteries' revenues—now distributed among a handful of them, as their brethren were wiped out—and took part in the wildest celebrations. All these were unmistakable signs of a culture gravely ill and on the decline. Yet in this atmosphere of putrefaction there was a color and intensity of life which we can hardly reconstruct or understand today. A stimulus emanated from everyday life, a passionate suggestion, which, enhanced by continuous contrasts, made itself manifest in the wavering moods of vulgar exuberance, violent barbarism, and tender and profound emotion. Such play of contrasting colors hardly suggests decline and dusk; the sun which shines on the scene is warm and brilliant.

Medieval belief in eternity, in the inevitable triumph of the right, was shattered by the Mohammedan victories in the East, by the fall of the imperial idea, and by the descent of the papacy from the pedestal of a serious religious and moral power to the less noble position of the greatest financial and political power in the Occident. But the genius of young Europe was not consumed; it triumphed over the carnage by imposing *will* as the greatest power on earth. Intellect ceased to be the starting point for understanding and action; the will took its place. Voluntarism, the new philosophical system which conceived will to be the dominant factor in experience and in the constitution of the world, superseded the rationalism of the philosophers and

theologians of late scholasticism. It is true, of course, that as long as philosophical and ethical voluntarism remained in the domain of theology—until
after the Reformation—its critical faculties could not be fully utilized.
Changed conceptions also permeated Christian piety, especially in the renewed tendency toward practical Christianity coupled with a retreat from
public life to the quiet of pious contemplation. The *Imitation of Christ* of
Thomas à Kempis, breathing gentle piety and unworldliness, represents the
purest expression of this spirit. Voluntarism brought with it a strong accentuation of the individual with less reliance on the Church, but a renewed
interest in the Eucharist—we shall see the first polyphonic settings of the
Mass—and in the Passion of Christ shows that purely religious feeling was
always present. The religious movement affected the various sects. The
heretics, in preceding epochs preoccupied with Gnostic speculations so wild
as to make any cultural co-operation impossible, settled down to a much
more moderate state of existence commensurate with the general way of
living.

Humanity's realization that the hopes of the previous centuries had not
been fulfilled lent a certain air of resignation to the latter part of the Middle
Ages and to the period of transition to the full Renaissance. This fact, to
which we should add the attacks of the humanists and reformers, contributed
substantially to the widely professed belief that the late Middle Ages was a
period of complete decline in civilization and culture. But the passionate
voice which reverberated through the fourteenth and the early fifteenth centuries clamoring for a *reformatio in capite et membris,* "a reformation in
head and members," indicates that people were not quietly accepting an
autumnal twilight of civilization.

Between Middle Ages and Renaissance

WE have arrived at a point at which in literature—and soon it was to be so
in the other arts as well—"Middle Ages" and "Renaissance" cannot be differentiated from each other, another indication that the vital power of the
Middle Ages must not be underestimated even in this period of decline.
There was more of the medieval in the humanist and Renaissance man than
he was aware of; on the other hand, men and phenomena which we still
consider purely medieval, as a sort of epilogue to the Middle Ages, could not
escape the influence of early humanism and the Renaissance spirit. Even the
popular was not free from these new influences. The greatest poetical work
of the Middle Ages was created at the beginning of this era. The *Divine
Comedy* is still medieval in character; its excursions through heaven and
hell follow the well-known pattern of the visionary literature of earlier centuries, while its scientific coloring is another reminder of the thirteenth cen-

tury, recalling the second part of the *Roman de la Rose*. Boccaccio's literary atmosphere, again, often drifts back into that of the mystery plays, farces, and drolleries; and in the numerous fourteenth-century translations of the literary output of various nations, especially in the prose arrangements of the old chivalric epics, one can see the curious mixture of medieval and humanistic. Older historians of art considered Cimabue the "first" representative of modern painting, yet in majesty and magnificence his work is entirely medieval even though the figures show more life and movement and are more natural in expression than those of his contemporaries. The motet of the fourteenth century still shows a truly medieval spirit which reflects the belief in *musica mundana* as the harmonic synthesis of the world, the idea of the empire and the Universal Church, at a time when the medieval order was disintegrating.

Yet there were many new traits discernible in this late medieval world, traits which cannot be entirely reconciled with the past. The fifteenth century already considered Giotto as the artist who began the *Rinascimento,* the rebirth of art, and indeed, when he appeared, majesty was suddenly supplanted by loveliness. With his earliest works he turned from the rigidity of Italo-Byzantine painting to the study of nature. The iconographic pattern used by artists for a millennium did not satisfy him, for the psychological motives underlying this old art had ceased to have a meaning to the man of the *trecento*. Giotto's figures possess a massive grace, a dignity, a naturalness, and an individuality. Again and again we are reminded, however, of the medieval world, for the old Gothic pleasure of epic storytelling is still present in the subtle relationship linking figure to figure, which lends to these strangely actionless figures the intensity of life.

But the divorce from the literary, temporal, narrative-discursive style of the Gothic was definitely begun. The same change was to take place in architecture as the successive, temporal space of the Gothic was supplanted by the geometrically determined simultaneity of Renaissance construction. The Gothic building was not closed and finished, it did not represent something rigidly static; always in the making, it was continuously telling its stories. For this reason an unfinished cathedral never created the feeling of a fragment; on the contrary, an unfinished tower often enhanced the impression of greatness and importance. Fragments are not tolerated by the geometrical-spatial unity of the Renaissance. Objective space changed into subjective, a phenomenon closely paralleled in music. The counterpoint of the thirteenth century was typically Gothic, striving in surely constructed purposeful arches toward its destination, entirely disregarding harmonic principles, dissonances, between the starting point and the end of the arches. Renaissance counterpoint was conditioned by harmonic principles, which is but a change from objective space to subjective. The principles of smooth part writing demanded, of course, a linear style, but this linear counterpoint had a chordal basis, always bent on euphony.

The Middle Ages considered art a handicraft, whereas the early Renaissance recognized the mysterious force of inspiration from which emerges the artist's idea. It also recognized that the shaping of this idea into a work of art is possible only through the creative individuality of the artist. The artist cannot present us with anything which remains strange to his nature. Natural as this seems to us, it represents a new artistic requirement not found in the aesthetic doctrines of the Middle Ages. Boccaccio and Villani praised Giotto's figures, which they contended were so natural that "people thought they lived and breathed"; but it could not have escaped them that the great painter's trees and mountains were not to be seen in nature, that his buildings were not habitable, and that his human figures were characterized from the inside out. For what Giotto discovered was not so much nature in its external form—a discovery of the fifteenth century—but the nature of the soul. The intensity of his characterization of man's soul so fascinated his contemporaries that they did not notice the fantastic in his natural surroundings.

The medieval element maintained itself in arts and letters in the countries north of the Alps and also in France until the Reformation. In literature humanism is evident also, but its presentation still definitely leans toward the medieval; in the fine arts and architecture of France the Gothic still prevails, although the realism of the early Burgundian school, as exemplified in the admirably powerful figures of Claus Sluter (d. c. 1406), changed its conception and style; in music the renewed contrapuntal style of the Burgundian and Franco-Flemish schools maintained its Gothic elements, in spite of interruptions, until the sixteenth century. It was only in Italy that the Renaissance triumphed completely immediately after its Florentine beginnings.

Ars Nova and Ars Antiqua

MAGISTER Philippus de Vitriaco, *clericus, notarius regis,* whose real name was Philippe de Vitry (1291–1361), was the author of a treatise called *Ars Nova.* By this weighty title he meant the logical and consequential application of a reformed system of music and of musical notation. Besides triple time, the *Ars Nova* recognized duple or binary divisions, heretofore prohibited in the realm of "official" art music. Historians have until recently taken literally the name of this technical tract designating the musical art beginning with the second quarter of the fourteenth century, thus lending to the whole of this century the semblance of a closed and unified musical period. In reality, the fourteenth century does not present such a fixed period; while it shows unmistakable signs of the new, it seems, in music as in the sister arts, still attached to the Middle Ages. The practices against which the learned scholars directed their complaints and Pope John XXII his edict were but the final stages in a medieval art which had become overripe. Historians used to date the beginnings of the musical Renaissance from about 1600, with the appearance of the opera. This absurd idea, confounding baroque with Renaissance, was then carried to the other extreme by pushing the date back three hundred years. The "new art" of the fourteenth century should be considered transitional, showing once more that no sharp division of the medieval from the Renaissance can be made with any pretense to scholarly accuracy.

On February 15, 1350, Petrarch, then residing in Padua, wrote a long letter to Vitry, paying homage to the French "musician," whom he considered the "greatest, the only poet of his period," while Simon Tunsted, an important English writer of the time, called him "the flower of musicians of the whole world." One of his contemporaries and fellow officials in the king's retinue thought that the learned Bishop Vitry "knew [composed] motets better than any other man." [1] We are assuredly dealing with a man of great importance. It appears, however, that it was not on account of his motets—as only one authentic and several doubtful ones are known—or his high ecclesiastic and political status that Vitry survives in history, but on account of the impetus he gave to the ars nova. His chef-d'oeuvre was the theoretical tract *Ars Nova;* three other tracts commonly attributed to him were probably inspired by his doctrines and teachings and placed under his name by reason of his great prestige.

But in spite of the regard in which he was held, one should not attribute the "invention" of binary rhythms to Vitry. Marchettus of Padua also speaks of the *tempus imperfectum,* binary time, which is "new" as opposed to the theologically sanctioned *tempus perfectum,* triple time. This would indicate that the Italians knew and practiced direct rhythms together with their French colleagues, and one might say before, because Marchettus was a practicing musician who transmitted customs and not mere theories. We must conclude, then, that Vitry's role was to sanction and expound the musical "innovations" of the ars nova which he did with remarkable lucidity, indicating the measure by judiciously organized signs with a precision which disposed of the incertitudes of the past, and by the addition of colored red notes permitting graphic indication of complicated rhythms, triplets, syncopation, etc. But the fact still remains that the stimulus seems to have come from Italy, and this fact raises serious problems concerning the nature and origins of the ars nova.

Italy appeared relatively late on the scene of musical history. We have seen how Gregorian art became stationary there, while north of the Alps the anti-Gregorian musical feeling of the people caused a great musical activity.

We have seen also the influx of troubadour elements and the rise of the religious song poetry of the followers of St. Francis; how the laudi were the most important products of indigenous art; and how besides the laudi there appeared at the beginning of Italian music the Latin sequences and the instrumental pieces of the minstrels. But Italy did not go through the long and significant development from organum and *déchant* to the great polyphonic motet of the Gothic; her first examples of polyphonic music, the madrigals, appeared in the fourteenth century, when Gothic polyphony was at its height. The strangeness of Gothic art to the Italian mind closely parallels that of Gregorianism in the transalpine countries. Italy's curious application of Gothic architecture shows her instinctive rejection of it; the earthbound obviousness of her broadly spaced Gothic cathedrals, whose form is opposed to the soaring transcendentalism of the northern cathedrals which cast away everything that was sensual, shows that what she accepted was not the essence of the Gothic but its outward earmarks. The situation was not different in music; the spirit of Gothic polyphony was strange to the musical sense of the southerner.

The influence of French art is obvious, but significantly enough, it comes from sources which either antedate the real Gothic or represent one of its minor branches. The satirical and allegorical tone and the strophic structure of the madrigal recall the art of the Provençal-Italian troubadours of the early thirteenth century, while the technique of its two-part setting indicates dependence on the type of organum which emanated from Limoges. But even the earliest compositions of the Florentine school show an artistic breadth which goes beyond their Provençal models. In spite of its obvious derivation, the music of the trecento in Italy exhibits a conception of polyphony which was not only new, but fundamentally opposed to Gothic principles. From the madrigals, ballads, and *caccie* there emanates again the sensual-naturalistic feeling and spirit of a southern race. Melody occupies the foreground and rules the form. The earth-bound, natural, and innate musical sense of the Italian trecentists rejected the liturgic tenor melodies and set out to compose music without recourse to a *cantus prius factus*. Gothic polyphony aimed at individual parts of equal importance, each moving in a rhythmical world of its own; Italian trecento polyphony regarded the two parts as an entity, lavishing great care on the melody-carrying upper part, which now proceeds freely, being bound to no predetermined factor. This melody was a happy medium between Nordic rigidity and the contourlessness of Oriental melismatic flow, and, free from the shackles of modal meter, it obeyed a natural sense of free symmetry and articulation. The tenor part carried—for the first time in the history of music—the burden of *supporting* the music above it and thus assumed the functions of a bass part.

All these facts bespeak a remarkable musical culture, seemingly totally original and independent. They impressed historians sufficiently to cause them to declare categorically that the ars nova originated in Italy and represents an indigenous art which determined the further development of music. There are two facts, however, which should make the modern historian hesitate to accept their view. One is the late appearance of Italian polyphony; the other, its inability to withstand the influence of the French ars nova.

The inability of Italian trecento music to hold its own is surprising. Already the generation of Landini (d. 1397) was thoroughly influenced by French art, and Italian music soon gave up its own character to accept and continue the practice of northern forms of music. The *ballata,* which displaced the madrigal and *caccia,* was in fact an issue of the French *virelai* and displayed at the close of the century many characteristic traits of the French Gothic. Toward the middle of the century, when the two-part compositions were displaced by three-part works, one may observe the linear thinking of the north taking hold of the madrigal.

The late appearance of Italian polyphony is puzzling to explain. While it is evident that its well-developed features exclude its being considered a mere beginning, the total lack of earlier documents makes it impossible to draw conclusions of unquestionable validity. One thing seems certain, however: that if France was Italy's teacher in literature and social life, it probably assumed the same role in music, an art closely connected with literature during the Middle Ages. In the final analysis, the Italian ars nova was but an organic continuation of medieval French art. The culturally exhausted France of the fourteenth century could not keep pace with the fresh and forceful Italy of the rising Renaissance and gave up its leadership to its cisalpine neighbor—though only temporarily. Almost all the innovations that originated in Italy go back to French sources. The rejection of the cantus firmus, distinctive of the Italian ars nova, was but the finishing touch to a tendency manifest in French music toward favoring the three other parts of the four-part motet to the detriment of the given tenor. The merit of Italian genius was to discover these tendencies, accept them, and carry them out. The resulting reorganization of old music and its conversion into an early Renaissance art was the achievement of the Florentine trecentists. Italy gave the Gothic melody, held in bounds by rhythm, direction, and profile; she steered the new art toward sonority and introduced into the new musical world order, symmetry, and perspective.

In appraising the historic significance of the cultures of the two countries we must, then, divide the laurels between them. France represented the older type of art, Italy the newer. France attracted students and scholars from all over Europe, and in the fourteenth century Italy—even more than other countries—was profoundly influenced by French culture. We have seen that at an earlier time Italian poetry and literature was an imitation of French-Provençal art, but throughout the fourteenth century the intercourse between the two countries flowed in both directions and was continuously animated. While Paris was still the capital of the world of learning and art, the Italian cities began to gain in importance and to assert their independence in cultural matters. The first half of the ars nova, then, was dominated by French art, while the second half experienced a short-lived Italian supremacy. Let us now retrace the course of events and return to the discussion of the French ars nova as the rightful starting point.

The Ars Nova in France

BOTH countries in which the ars nova evolved still lived in the atmosphere of the late Middle Ages, but Italy stood nearer to the spirit of the approaching Renaissance, for it had always remained within the actual domain of its antique heritage. This accounts for the nature of Italian medieval culture, which did not reach the profundity and fervor of the medieval spirit in France and the northwestern countries. France could not detach itself with the ease of Italy from medieval culture and civilization to which it was more wedded than any other Romanic nation. The Italian influence, on the other hand, reached France but, very naturally, could not displace the Gothic heritage, which was to the transalpine what the classical heritage was to the cisalpine. It is noteworthy, however, that with Guillaume de Machaut, the chief representative of the French ars nova, dependence on external generating forces is on the wane, the anonymous composer disappears, and the late Gothic begins to acknowledge that artistic creation springs from creative man. As long as they were under the influence of scholastic musical doctrines, the French ars nova composers wrote melodies that were stunted and fettered, but when they followed their natural rhythmical instinct and abandoned Gothic ornaments, they wrote plastic, well-rounded melodies. The austere, impersonal, almost ascetic character of medieval creative will vanished and was replaced by a personal, individualistic genius. The ars nova motet abandoned the abstract linear continuity of the Gothic and with it the principle of independent polylingual texts. Its texts were now more closely related to each other in meaning, and usually employed the same language; the contents were varied, sometimes lyrical or religious, sometimes moral or political. Altogether the motet became an ultra-refined art, headed toward its decline. The Gothic still lived, but had lost its form-building vitality; it exhibited the tendency toward symmetry which became so typical in subsequent periods.

The great complexity of the motet inevitably caused its supreme position to be challenged; the public wanted to restore the always popular song to its old eminence. A temporary revival of the chivalric world favored this plan, and romantically colored medieval ideas reappeared in the short reign of Henry VII (1308–1313), who, a second Barbarossa, dreamed of reviving the Hohenstaufen domination. While his abortive Italian campaign only served to prove the futility of any attempt to revive the ancient imperial policy, his armies were greeted by many—among them Dante—as the heroes who were to end the seemingly endless strife of Guelphs and Ghibellines. His son, John of Luxemburg (1296–1346), King of Bohemia (1310–1346), a romantic figure who seemed to step out of the twelfth century, had his court filled with adventurous persons, who for a short period resuscitated the old glory of the chivalric world. It was in this court, in the service of King John, that Guillaume de Machaut, the greatest figure of the French ars nova and one of the great figures of musical history, found his inspiration. One of the last of those great learned ecclesiasts of the Middle Ages, poet, scholar, and mu- sician, he was the incarnation of the French ars nova as Perotinus was of the ars antiqua. But these two do not oppose each other; Machaut continued the work of the old master of Notre Dame.

As a new trouvère, Machaut undertook to conjure up with new means of expression the lost world of chivalric art; but he had before him the Gothic motet as practiced by Vitry and his school—a model which, being the chief contemporary musical form, could not be neglected. Thus the early ars nova motet became Machaut's starting point, but his usual substitution of French love lyrics for the customary Latin texts testifies to his attempt to infuse into this art a pseudochivalric song literature. The procedure did not prove suc- cessful; a re-creation of the aristocratic art of the twelfth century through the austere majesty of the Gothic motet was hardly feasible. Much more fitting models were provided by the old trouvère songs, rondeaux, and ballads. Machaut the poet endeavored to recall the spirit of the *amour courtois* in his lyric poetry, but this poetry proved to be mere imitation, a virtuoso word and rhyme-play on bygone models. But Machaut the musician gave us in his song melodies a deeply felt, expressive music which breathes a roman- tic spirit full of fantasy, raising the polyphonic ballad at the end of the Gothic period to a position equal to that of the motet. He transformed this ancient form of dance song into a complex genre which incorporated the qualities of both the motet and the rondeau, utilizing all the resources of polyphony with a sovereign ability surpassed only by his taste. These polyphonic ballads were, in reality, songs with the accompaniment of two or three instruments, as usually only one part was sung. They represent the last stylistic expression of the Gothic, for after Machaut's death the Gothic heritage became adulter- ated by foreign elements.

The song accompanied by instruments became the kernel of the secular musical repertory of the ars nova for a hundred years, in both France and

Italy. Its influence was soon apparent in church music. Unaccompanied solo songs disappeared entirely, while a leveling process worked to reconcile the motet and the ballad, already close neighbors. The resultant mixture was far more advantageous to the ballad than to the motet: the ballad gained in craftsmanship while the essential nature of the motet was weakened, leaving it with a musical physiognomy which, in reality, was removed from the Gothic and shows the influence of the early Italian Renaissance.

The ars nova was a secular art. The practice of spiritual, especially liturgic, music played a minor part in the creative activity of its composers. In this it offered a striking contrast to the ars antiqua, to the towering organa of Perotinus. Vitry and his circle definitely dropped the old organa and conductus. The decree of John XXII (1324–1325) admonishing "certain followers of a new tendency (or school)" indicates clearly that the vitality of Gothic church music was at a low ebb; even its traditions were half forgotten, as musicians shaped their works on secular models. The hostile attitude of Pope John had its influence, of course, but could not prevent the slow infiltration of new tendencies into the music of the Church. So the polyphonic motet-ballad style made its entrance into church music proper. As the old organal art disappeared composers turned to the polyphonic setting of the five unchangeable parts of the Ordinary of the Mass, namely, the Kyrie, Gloria, Credo, Sanctus, and Agnus Dei, which they set to music in the prevailing motet style. After the middle of the century the song style made itself felt in the church style, without, however, the vitality and expressive quality of the secular song, as the Church insisted on an archaic dignity in liturgic music. Two of these Masses have been preserved for posterity, the older, from the beginning of the fourteenth century, being still in the old conductus style,[2] while the other, composed by Machaut, already shows the influence of the ars nova. Italian Masses of the period are extant only in fragments and exhibit a ballad style. Interest centered around the Mass, but the ars nova had spent its energies and was not able to extend itself into the field of sacred music to create a new style commensurate with the importance of the new secular art. This style was to come from fresh sources in the fifteenth century, and with it began a new era.

In its decline the Gothic still showed a molding influence which insisted on architectural design despite all tendencies to the contrary. It clung to its rights far into the Renaissance by furnishing the technical foundations of musical construction. While these foundations retained their spiritual character, the communicative effect became sensual owing to the individual and naturalistic inclination of the artist, who reduced the rigidity of serene architectural principles of construction to such an extent that they are scarcely perceptible. The Gothic influence is responsible for his interest in such strict constructions as the canon. The origins of the canon are obscure, but it seems safe to assume that it was the result of the instrumental improvisation of minstrels, in which the alternating players "contracted" their dialogue to a point where one melody followed on the heels of the other. In the fourteenth century it gained artistic recognition in the shape of the *chace* (*chasse*), a two-part hunting song progressively composed or "through-composed," that is, not in strophic form, in which two identical parts or voices followed each other in strict canonic imitation. Machaut's canonically written rondeau "Ma fin est mon commencement et mon commencement ma fin" marks a step beyond the simple *chace* and leads to the intricate canonic art which was to appear in the following century. It is a composition of complicated construction, written so that all three voices are capable of double employment, that is, they may be sung either forward or backward.

The complete works of Machaut are now available in an edition which is a monument of scholarship.[3] In it we may find "Le Livre du Voir Dit" in which the sixty-year-old poet tells the story of his love for a young noblewoman in the purest chivalric manner recalling the *amour courtois* of the old trouvères, ballads of a tenderness which belies the period, and motets displaying all the skill of late Gothic counterpoint. Some of the great musicologists of the past decades—Abert, Ludwig, von Ficker—have been able to prove that the apparently freely composed late motets of Machaut still follow, in an infinitely subtle way, the strict principles of Gothic polyphony and that all the mysticism of Neo-Pythagorean and Arabic number-symbolism of bygone ages still lives veiled in the seemingly free upper parts of these motets. How subtle these medieval elements are may be gauged by the fact that so great a scholar as Hugo Riemann could not detect them although he sensed that the melodic element was—in truly Gothic fashion—the least important in the order of creative factors. It is difficult to appreciate these so-called "isorhythmic" motets: many will even declare them outright unmusical. But the conversion of the purely spiritual with its infinitely complicated and rigid architecture into the aesthetically sensual is accomplished with such consummate skill in these works that, if we study them with patient and unbiased scholarship, we must agree with the judgment of von Ficker, who counts them among the great creations of musical art of all times.

The Ars Nova in Italy

WITH the aid of what we have learned of the French ars nova, let us now turn back and continue our examination of trecento music in Italy. Italy, like the rest of Europe, reacted to the terror of the tortured world, but reacted with artistic freedom. Italians did not paint *danses macabres* as did the people of France, Germany, England, and Spain. Petrarch's poem on the Triumph of Death, and the mural in the Campo Santo in Pisa almost glorify the power of death; such were the artistic echoes of the catastrophic year 1348. A country which in encountering the destructive forces of the times can bring forth artistic creations that reflect tragedy not in its morbid aspects but at its idealistic height will also produce art which, in the midst of misery, will reflect peace and joy. *Rispetto, strambotto,* and madrigal were sung and recited everywhere, and their delicate mood does not seem overcast by the horrors that still hung about the people and their villages. It is not easy to understand this idyllic mood. It is not enough to call it a naïve abandonment which, in the brief moments of peace between political, social, and elemental storms, is ready to forget the past and enjoy the present. There must have been an unfathomable spiritual health which stemmed the destructive forces. The resistance of the trecento in Italy was not a conscious struggle, to be sure; the merriness expressed in arts and letters is spontaneous throughout, and it remained for the quattrocento to meet fate with serious deliberation.

We can readily understand that a period in which a youthful Italian poetry flourished must have been well adapted to promote musical art. It is nothing short of remarkable, however, that all that actually happened before the advent of the ars nova should have passed into oblivion. The composers of this new art wrote with such assurance and natural freshness that any suspicion of its origin in mere theory—advanced by some scholars —is impossible. It is unlikely, furthermore, that triple measure ever was exclusively employed in a country not dominated by scholasticism. The new art must have grown out of a great musical activity of a high order. At a period when the other Romance languages were still in a state of fermentation the Tuscan produced Dante, Petrarch, and Boccaccio, all of whom had sovereign command over a flexible and subtle language. The appearance of these poets and of Giotto and his fellow painters was not an isolated event; Florentine and other Italian composers joined them as artists of equal rank.

The trecento madrigal (*madriale* or *madrialle*) may be traced back to the Provençal *pastourelle,* but its character underwent a great change in the interval, for it now no longer treats of adventurers in love with rustic beauties. Its poetic form is strictly regulated and its object—especially in the older madrigals of Petrarch, Boccaccio, and Sacchetto—is the contemplation of nature. The most ancient madrigal composer whose name is known to us was Pietro Casella, Dante's friend, commemorated in the *Purgatorio.* None of Casella's compositions is extant, however. Another favored form of Italian art music was the ballad (*ballata*). At the opposite extreme from the Gothic motet, it represented the ideal of the new times, an animated nervously delicate miniature. These Italian ballads cannot be identical with the dance ballads often mentioned by the poets, because they are not dancelike in character. The original popular dance form lost its real character when taken over and stylized by art music. A similar phenomenon occurred in the eighteenth century when popular dances like the gavotte and minuet appeared in stylized form in the instrumental suite literature of the period. The French *chace* was admirably fitted to the new contrapuntal style, which, having eliminated the "tenor" part, created the accompanying bass part, which assumed a distinctly subordinate position, seconding the melody by furnishing it with a harmonic foundation. The Italian *caccia* soon became an autonomous form differing from the French model by a logical application of the principle of accompanying bass; thus the *caccia* had two canonic upper parts sustained and accompanied by a comfortable, ambling, independent bass. These Florentine canons are wholly different from the "Summer Canon," for instance, with its four measures of underlying fixed ground bass or *pes* and its constant harmonies. The vocal virtuosity of the madrigals and *caccie* and the dialogues which appear in them are singularly evocative of the duets of the first operas in the early seventeenth century.

The chief exponents of the Italian ars nova were the Florentine masters Francesco, Giovanni, Ghirardello, Lorenzo, Donato, Andrea, and Paolo, the Paduan Bartolino, and the Bolognese Jacopo. The outstanding artist, however, was Francesco Landini (or Landino, 1325-1397), son of the painter Jacopo Landini dal Casentino; though afflicted with blindness from his childhood, he became a universally admired organist, composer, poet, and philosopher.[4] As organist of San Lorenzo in Florence he became a virtuoso of almost legendary fame, but he was equally versatile on the flute and lute. His compositions, about two hundred secular pieces, preserved in various manuscripts in Florence, London, and Paris, now are available in a modern edition.[5] There is in the Laurentian Library in Florence an exceedingly beautifully executed fifteenth-century manuscript which belonged to Lorenzo the Magnificent's famous organist, Antonio Squarcialupi, and which contains very rich material relating to the Italian ars nova. Its 352 pieces, a number of which have been published by Johannes Wolf, represent the bulk of our musical documents of the period.

Glorious as was the blossoming of trecento music in Italy—it reminds one of the brief but beautiful flowering of the Elizabethan madrigal in England —Prosdocimus de Beldemandis, learned professor and philosopher at the University of Padua, found it necessary to undertake, in his *Tractatus Practice de Musica Mensurabili ad Modum Italicorum* (1408), a defense of the value and originality of Italian music, which had at the end of the century come under the domination of French art. The return of the papal see from Avignon to Rome had encouraged a general orientation toward French music. French singers and *magistri* came to Italy and brought with them Gothic traditions which had been strong enough to make even the Italian residents of Avignon set French ballad texts to music in an entirely French manner. Not only was the national music modified along French lines, but French musical notation was accepted as the most advanced form of musical writing. The influence was so overwhelming that even people ignorant of the language took it upon themselves to set to music French ballads. The most famous manuscript collection of French ballads, the Chantilly Codex, was evidently written in Italy by such a person. Yet, although the period of its flourishing was relatively short, the developed Italian ars nova blended the three musical factors, melody, rhythm, and harmony, into a new conception of the "musical," the basic features of which—despite many intermittent changes—have remained valid up to our day.

The Practice of Trecento Music

CONTEMPORARY paintings and miniatures testify to the extremely rich and varied musical life of the fourteenth century; literary sources mention dances, folk songs, and love songs which have been almost entirely lost. But even the manuscripts containing the music itself do not constitute satisfactory documents for a complete picture of the music of the period, because this period was an era of improvisation in which the written composition represented only the frame upon which the musical piece was built. Parts were added, the *hoquetus* applied, and all sorts of instruments joined the singers. Drone basses, supplied by the drone tubes of the bagpipe or the strings of the *vièle,* were exceedingly popular but, although their use changes the whole complexion of the composition, they were never noted down. A composition was executed according to its graphical aspect only if all the required factors happened to be on hand. But if a singer or an instrumentalist was missing, his part was simply omitted, or if there was a player too many another part was composed or improvised and added to the existing parts. Musical compositions were as readily altered as the lengthy *romans,* excerpts from which were arranged for recitation to suit the occasion.

Throughout the ars nova no distinction was made—save in dances—between vocal and instrumental music. All pictorial and literary sources oblige us to acknowledge the two varieties to be of equal significance. Every historical and stylistic document speaks against the romantically idealistic conception advocated by many historians that the music of the Renaissance was exclusively vocal. On the contrary, it is evident that the instrumental element must have not only played an important role in the performance of this music, but contributed materially to the formation of its style. We may go even further and assert that the vocal literature of the fourteenth and fifteenth centuries was often performed by instruments alone. That this was an acknowledged practice may be seen from the remarks of Machaut, who held that the playing of his ballads on the organ, bagpipe, and other instruments was entirely permissible and indicated that such a procedure constitutes a musician's *droit nature*.[6]

Contemporary paintings and literary documents, as well as the descriptions of great marriages and other religious solemnities, inform us about the surprisingly rich collection of instruments in general use in the fourteenth century. *Les Echecs Amoureux*,[7] a tract from the second half of the century written by a French dilettante, furnishes us with excellent information about music and musical instruments in general. Viols, harps, psalteries, lutes, hurdy-gurdies, trumpets, drums, chimes, cymbals, bagpipes, reeds, horns, and flutes are a few of the many instruments mentioned, some of them called *haulz*, others *bas*. These terms have been interpreted to mean "high" and "low" instruments, but from the text it becomes clear that they designated loud and soft instruments. This distinction is borne out by the pictorial documents and by instruments in a good state of preservation. The *instrumens bas* appear in intimate settings while the other group is used outdoors or at festive gatherings and dances. The tone of the latter was sharp and penetrating, although of a rather flat and dry quality. Even the "low" instruments, frequently called *doux*, were not very soft from a modern point of view because sharp sonority was much nearer to the spirit of the time. There was a certain Oriental touch about these instruments which also characterized music of the period in general. They were all of Oriental origin and were used in a rather monotonous way, excluding all dynamic changes. This same Oriental quality must have prevailed in the nasal falsetto singing which may be clearly identified from a great number of pictures where the physiognomy of the singers is rendered with great accuracy. The nasal performance of cult music, always sung with falsetto voice in Oriental countries, which has survived to our day in the intonations of Catholic priests, found its way into the secular art music of the Middle Ages. The universal use of the bagpipe and the shawm (*chalumeau*), both nasal reed instruments, indicates the general prevalence of a nasal tone color.

Judging from many pictures and descriptions, the viol must have been the favored instrument of amateurs, the fourteenth-century equivalent of the much-abused piano of today. The organ reached a highly developed state of playability. Besides the big church organ there were two smaller varieties, the so-called *positive* or stationary "chamber organ," and the *portative*, which, as its name implies, was a small instrument that could be carried about. Contemporary pictures show that the little instrument was omnipresent; people took it with them even to merry outings in the country. The organist was the most experienced of musicians, whose duties were to fill in missing parts, to hold together the ensemble of players and

singers, to enrich and embellish the music, and to relieve the singers by playing little interludes.

The pictorial sources indicate that ensembles of instruments and singers,
ranging from two to a dozen or more, were quite common. Another important inference we may draw from these sources is that the instruments
were not used in homogeneous groups, as in modern times when all the
members of the violin family form the string choir, with a resultant blending of sonority and color, but that, on the contrary, the greatest possible
contrast and individuality in color and sonority was sought. This fits in
very well with the Gothic tradition of individual contrapuntal parts and
texts.

New Trends in Musical Theory and Aesthetics

THROUGHOUT the scholastic Middle Ages, art had been considered the
servant of the Church. Most of the theoreticians of the ars nova still reflect
this conception, and while the authors take into consideration the progress
made in the practical application of the rules of measured music, their
philosophical and aesthetic utterances are mostly restricted to abbreviated
summaries from older tracts. Even the *Ars Nova* of Philippe de Vitry repeats
the old doctrines concerning the nature of music, and Marchettus of Padua
is still lost in nebulous speculations concerning the origin of music. The
musical scholars who taught at the universities continued to emphasize
their independence of singers and instrumentalists, and most of their tracts
uphold the old distinction between *musicus,* the scholar, and *cantor,* the
singer. The Middle Ages scarcely attempted the formulation of an aesthetic
doctrine; their main aesthetic ideas and motives were perfection, purpose,
proportion, splendor, and sweetness. The last-named, *suavitas,* usually
coupled with "loveliness," was a general term of late medieval aesthetics;
but we must not take these words in their literal modern sense because the
music of the period was not particularly "sweet" according to our notion of
sweetness, any more than the hard groups of consonances which characterize late medieval French represent to us what was then called *la doulce
langue françoise.* And yet there was an irreconcilable gap between the ars
nova and medieval universalism, for the strong individual imagination of
the later artists took refuge in aesthetic isolation, which they mistook for freedom.

Intellectual currents toward the beginning of the fourteenth century reflected the same new orientation that we have noticed in the arts. In philosophy and theology the system which endeavored to establish a concordance between profane knowledge and belief in revealed religion was
succeeded by a penetrating examination, based on remarkable erudition, of
philosophical and theological maxims. This tendency appeared with Duns

Scotus (d. 1308), who taught at Oxford and at Paris, and who was convinced that St. Thomas was wrong in holding possible a rational demonstration of God's existence and of the immortality of the soul. His disciples, the Scotists, were, then, opposed to the Thomists, the followers of St. Thomas. But if the *doctor subtilis*, as Duns Scotus was surnamed by his contemporaries, abandoned the path blazed by St. Thomas, this did not indicate a retrograde act. He was as religious and as erudite as the great Dominican, but believed, as did the "invincible doctor," William of Occam (d. 1349), that religious dogmas cannot be supported on rational grounds, and can be accepted only as a deliberate act of faith. A similar movement is noticeable in the theoretical expositions of musical scholars. Besides the large group of "official" theoreticians, there appears another smaller group of writers who, emancipated from scholasticism under the influence of the rising middle classes, go to battle with fresh energy and enthusiasm against antiquated musical science. Two tracts originating from this circle are known to us. One is the already-mentioned *Theoria* of Johannes de Grocheo, the other the *Echecs Amoureux*, quoted above as our best source of information concerning the musical instruments of the fourteenth century. These two authorities reject number-mysticism and theoretical implications and take a skeptical attitude toward the *musica mundana*, although the author of the *Echecs Amoureux*, unwilling to break with the past altogether, recommends music as a source of speculative thinking, as useful in the education of children, and as recreation after daily work. But the bold Grocheo admits no compromise; he throws the whole maze of Pythagorean-Boethian doctrines of *musica mundana* overboard.

The two great scholars whose personality dominated musical scholarship in the late Middle Ages—Jacobus of Liége and Johannes de Muris—came from the larger group of savants who represent the last peaks of medieval learning; both of them were, however, intimately connected with the rising art of the ars nova, either because they opposed it or because they supported the tenets of the early Renaissance. We have already mentioned the famous treatise of Jacobus of Liége called *Speculum Musicae*. The original purpose of this work was an attack on the "modern" *cantores, notatores*, and *scriptores*, the representatives of the ars nova; but Jacobus subsequently changed his plans to include, besides the critical section, chapters embracing all fields of musical knowledge. From his thoroughgoing treatment of the whole field it may be assumed that the great scholar realized that "the noble musical science, which remained far more perfect than the practice" was threatened with oblivion unless someone undertook to unite, in a final synthesis, all its past achievements. This synthesis, then, was his *Speculum*, the last great medieval treatise on music. Jacobus had no followers, as the rapidly growing art of musical notation occupied the minds of the theoreticians, who were now all concerned with purely practical problems.

Johannes de Muris, whose authority throughout the fourteenth and fifteenth centuries was comparable only to that of Boethius in the early Middle Ages, remains an enigmatic figure. Extravagant claims were formerly made for Muris as a pioneer and inventor. Some sixteenth-century authors stated in their writings that musical notes were his invention. Universally admired as a polyhistorian, especially eminent in mathematics, astronomy, and music, Muris showed his forward-looking spirit by espousing the cause of Vitry. This modern and liberal attitude excludes any possibility of his having been the author of the *Speculum,* a work which, as we have seen, is permeated by a thoroughly conservative attitude.

The medieval conception of the *musica mundana* appears in the philosophical system of Dante. The *Paradiso* is full of a cosmic conception which can only be identified with the medieval idea of *musica mundana* as expressed by the representative Italian theoretician of the trecento, Marchettus of Padua, who professed the doctrine that the greatness of music envelops all things, the living and the dead. Despite the criticism of realistic men, the symbolic aspects of a music of the universe still appealed to the great medieval minds. "Music is a science," says Machaut, and Johannes de Florentia, one of the "modern" composers of the Florentine ars nova, exclaims, *O tu cara scientia mia, musica!* This, recalling the tone of the Boethian scientist-philosophers, seems to contradict the course of events. But the meaning of "science" changed in the fourteenth century; it came to be used for dexterity, ability, and practice. Such a change in significance implies a change in the *raison d'être* of music; and indeed, the ethical and speculative conception changed into what one may call the utilitarian approach. In this spirit the second line of Machaut's poem will harmonize with the seemingly austere declaration of the first: "And music is a science, whose purpose is to make people laugh and sing and dance." [8]

In applied musical theory the development of polyphonic writing led to a more subtle control of the simultaneous sounding of the parts and found expression in the theory of "note set against note," or, as the symbol for a musical note was a dot (punctus), *punctus contra punctum,* or counterpoint. This term first appeared about 1300, but the tenets of the theory of counterpoint were more concisely expounded toward the end of the century, when the theoreticians declared that "the aim of counterpoint is to perform several melodies simultaneously and bind them together by good and well-regulated consonances." If we bear in mind the continuously changing meaning of consonance, this definition may be considered valid in all subsequent epochs of musical history.

The physical nature of sound was very well understood by learned men.

Chaucer's explanation may be singled out as an excellent practical demonstration, often used by teachers of elementary physics today.

> . . . Every word . . .
> That loude or privee spoken is
> Moweth first an air aboute
> And of this moving, out of doute
> Another air anoon is meved,
> As I have of the water preved,
> That every cercle causeth other.
> Right so of air, my leve brother.[9]

Chaucer obtained his information from Vincent of Beauvais's *Speculum Naturale* and from Boethius's *De Musica,* to which he expressly refers on several occasions. The further we advance in the fourteenth century the less we hear of that old animosity toward music which started with the incertitude of St. Augustine, who feared that its sensual qualities might impair the devotional nature of liturgic chant. But the Augustinian ideas continued to live, although the gentle persuasiveness of the saint changed into a stern denunciation which was to lead to the inexorable attitude of Calvin. A passage from the writings of Wyclif will give us a good idea of the echo of the Augustinian thoughts in the mouth of this most important forerunner of the Reformation:

First men performed songs of mourning when they were in prison, in order to teach the Gospel, to put away idleness, and to be occupied in a useful manner for the time. But those songs and ours do not agree, for ours encourage jollity and pride and theirs led to mourning and to dwelling longer on the words of God's law. A short time later vain tricks began to be employed—discant [deschaunt], many voices [contre notes], organum [orgon], and *hoquetus* [small brekynge], which stimulate vain men more to dancing than to mourning. . . . But these fools should dread the sharp words of Saint Augustine which say: "whenever the music [song] delights me more than does the sentence which is sung, than I confess that I sin grievously." . . . When there are forty or fifty in a choir, three or four proud and lecherous rascals perform the most devout service with flourishes so that no one can hear the words, and all the others are dumb and watch them like fools.[10]

The Universal Dissemination and Appreciation of Music in the Fourteenth Century

IN the period of the ars nova not only did cathedrals reverberate with the mystical solemnity of church music, not only did learned university professors speculate on abstruse theoretical problems, but a new secular musical art flourished everywhere, inspiring nobleman and bumpkin alike to a love of its freshness. Wherever we look, in paintings, bas-reliefs, poems and stories, we find abundant proof of the universal enjoyment of music. The atmosphere of Boccaccio's *Decameron* is literally saturated with music, as each day is terminated with music and most days begin with it. For instance, after dinner on the first day several members participate in a dance song, which could have been nothing else than the popular *ballata*. The dance described by Boccaccio was performed by a group of dancers led by a youth or girl; their song is often contrasted with *ritornelli* or interludes played by the others, who carry musical instruments. Knowledge of music was general among people of education. When Boccaccio describes Dante's familiarity with music he says that the poet found in his youth special joy in song and play, and whoever was a good singer or musician was his friend; he composed a great deal of poetry which he asked them to set to music. Wandering in Purgatory, Dante meets one of these musician friends of his youth, Casella, who, in response to the poet's call, answers with Dante's lovely *canzone,* "Amor che ne la Mente Mi Ragiona," and the party is enraptured with the sweetness of the music.[11] This is, unfortunately, the only mention we have of the musician who may have been the master of the great Florentine artists of the ars nova.

Music sounded not only on festive occasions but also in hours of leisure, during daily work, and especially on pilgrimages. That the pilgrims who wandered to the grave of Thomas à Becket crossed the towns singing and playing is proved by documents from many sources. The mystery plays were replete with music as we have shown in the chapter dealing with the expansion of Gregorian music. In English mystery plays there are many allusions to the use of music. Often one of the actors invites the others or the public to sing with him, as in the Digby Mysteries.[12]

The English were very fond of music, and it formed an important element in their education, their religion, and their amusements. Most schools in the fourteenth century were still connected with religious institutions, although some were independent. In the most elementary grades musical instruction was very simple, suitable for only very small children. Song schools were on a higher level, their main purpose being "to teach children for to learne to singe for ye mayntenance of God's divine service in ye Abbey." It is likely that reading and writing were also taught in them. In this connection the French choir schools were much more severe. The statutes regulating the conduct of the choirboys at Notre Dame in Paris (1408) required that the choirmaster should teach the boys "plain chant and counterpoint," to which he might add a few "decent déchants"; but the musical exercises "must not prevent the boys from learning their grammar." [13] It appears that in England writing was not considered so important as read-

ing or singing. Chaucer's Prioress, in her tale, gives a description of a small
school in which not a word is said about writing:

> Swich maner doctrine as men used there,
> This is to seyn, to singen and to rede . . .

Music was not neglected in the education of the nobility, either: they
were taught to harp, pipe, sing, and dance. Chaucer's description of the
Squire sums up the effects of knightly training:

> Singinge he was, or floytinge, al the day;
> Wel coude he sitte on hors, and faire ryde.
> He could songes make, and wel endyte,
> Iutse and eek daunce, and wel purtreye and wryte.

People of the higher nobility, especially reigning royalty, were not only
fond of music but endeavored to have the best musicians attached to their
court, often paying small fortunes for artists and prized instruments. The
account books of the Kings and Queens of France show many entries concerning the purchase and repair of instruments. Froissart in his *Chronicles*
relates that at the coronation of Charles VI (1380) there were "more than
thirty trumpet players whose play was marvelously clear." The music-loving
King of Aragon, John I (1350–1395), desired to engage in his service a
famous organist then residing at the Burgundian court and spared no expense to obtain his portable organs and his "book in which were written
the *estampies* and other pieces he played." [14] The list of musicians in the
service of Edward III of England (1327–1377) named five "trompettes," one
"citoler," five pipers, one "taberett" (small drum), two clarions, one "mak-
erer" (player of a small Arabian drum), two "fidelers," and three "waytes." [15]
The waytes, wayghtes, or waits were originally certain minstrels or musical
watchmen attached to the households of kings or great nobles, who walked
about in assigned districts sounding the hours at night. They used a sort of
double reed or hautboy. Musicians in the service of high dignitaries and
princes carried on their instruments the crest of their masters; on the
trumpets and bagpipes, for instance, hung small flags embroidered with the
coat of arms.

In those days there were never festivities without minstrels, who appeared on all occasions, whether solemn public ceremonies or private receptions in the manors. A person returning from foreign lands was greeted
with music; a visitor appearing at the gates was accompanied by music
to the interior. A bishop on his pastoral rounds was occasionally greeted
by minstrels, hired for the purpose of cheering him. At festivities the minstrels played both during the meals and for dancing afterwards. Tournaments opened with flourishes of trumpets, and at the end the winner was

acclaimed with music again. When the armies went to war musicians accompanied them and continued to play their instruments during battle, because "musicke moveth affections and exciteth the wits of divers dispositions." The richer nobles imitated the king and had their own companies, whom they allowed to play at times in various parts of the country (as was the case later with actors) and whom they supplied with testimonial letters vouching for them and their artistic ability.

Besides the minstrels serving with princes and nobles, there were many unattached musicians who earned their living by teaching the burghers and by playing as independent artists. The number of minstrels grew so large that both the authorities and the musicians themselves were forced to organize their ranks, and beginning with the thirteenth century municipal and other guilds were formed. The earliest of these was the Nicolaibruderschaft in Vienna (1288), followed by the Company of Trumpeters in Lucca, and by the great brotherhoods of pipers and fiddlers such as the Confrérie de St. Julien des Ménétriers in Paris (1331), which even had its own hospital. The presiding officers of these organizations—then called minstrel kings—held a position similar to that of the directors of our large musical institutions, but their disciplinary powers were extensive and severe. The organization of the confréries was as efficient as that of any modern trade union. Their members were not permitted to render any musical service without a fixed compensation, and minstrels belonging to other organizations were prevented from playing in their district. While the minstrels now enjoyed much more freedom than they had in the early Middle Ages, the authorities frowned upon them because they were able, under the guise of singing, to encourage social or political revolt. Their sympathy for ideas of emancipation, which had made such progress in the fourteenth century, often embroiled them not only with the authorities but with the people as well. In France the performance of chansons concerning the Schism were prohibited in 1395; songs mocking the Burgundians and the Parisians were so much resented in the respective countries that fatal knifings resulted from their performance; a minstrel was arrested and jailed in Melun near Paris because he dared sing the Burgundians' song.[16] At the beginning of the fifteenth century, the English House of Commons denounced the Welsh minstrels as instigators of rebellion: "No westours and rimers, minstrels or vagabonds, be maintained in Wales to make kymorthas or quyllages on the common people, who by their divinations, lies and exhortations, are partly cause of the insurrection and rebellion now in Wales." [17]

The municipal councils, supreme political powers, especially in the free cities of Germany, had many musical ordinances and created musical offices. Perhaps the first of these official positions was that of the town shepherd who received his horn from the council. The Strassburg city council ordained in 1322 that no one should play "after the third bell" trombones, trumpets, drums, horns, and cymbals, only shawms and soft pipes—an ordinance which in its wisdom puts the medieval city far ahead of our modern cities. On the other hand, it was customary in the same city to give a horn signal between eight and nine o'clock in the evening from the tower of the city hall, whereupon all Jews were supposed to leave town; but this ordinance could be evaded through the payment of a sum of money. Most of the musical ordinances concerned marriages and public dancing, and the number of musicians employed on such occasions was minutely regulated.

Another century, and we shall see rise from the organizations of these humble musicians a musical literature which leads directly to the great symphonies we admire so much today.[18]

Chapter 9

THE RENAISSANCE

⇛ ⇚

Renaissance and Humanism

TOWARD the middle of the past century the historians of the romantic school, animated by the rediscovery of medievalism, endeavored to draw a line between the Middle Ages and modern times. They established a buffer state between the two ages and called it the Renaissance. Michelet (1798–1874), by entitling the ninth volume of his great history of France (1855) *La Renaissance,* first used the term in its modern historic sense, but the most lasting impetus emanated from Jacob Burckhardt's memorable work, *The Culture of the Renaissance,* which appeared in 1860.

As most writing of history, conditioned by romantic, religious, or practical purposes, seeks to pick out obvious and momentous occurrences as recognizable landmarks, schoolteachers and writers tend still to determine the end of the Middle Ages by the fall of Constantinople, the flight of Byzantine scholars to Italy, the discovery of America, or Luther's secession. The fall of Constantinople, with the presence of Byzantine scholars in Italy, is interpreted as having given the decisive orientation to humanism; but the advocates of this theory forget that humanism was largely a Latin movement, while the conquest of Constantinople affected the political, religious, and economic domains but had little immediate influence on arts and letters. The discovery of America was again an event which had political and economic significance that was to appear later, but had no immediate repercussion on civilization. The date of Luther's rebellion, however, is of considerable importance, as this act really brought about an upheaval not only in religious life but in all domains of intellectual life, although by the time Luther's activity produced results the Renaissance movement was nearing its height and in its rising waves the stern religious warfare rode as a true renewal of medieval earnestness and self-denial.

The fiery Michelet's unbounded imagination often overrode his great erudition, but his poet's intuition sometimes helped him to remarkably clear conceptions which were not realized by his colleagues for decades. He considered *la découverte du monde, la découverte de l'homme* the essence of the Renaissance, and indeed, Renaissance and humanism did not appear because some learned minds rediscovered the monuments of antique arts and letters; they originated from a profound desire for and a glowing expectation of a new era, a longing for a second youth. The spirit of Rome had not died; on the contrary, it had never ceased to exert its influence. Roman poetry was known, liked, and recited not only in Italy but in other countries. Virgil, Ovid, Lucan, Juvenal, and Horace were ever popular, and Sallust cast his shadow over the whole of medieval history writing. While we associate the idea of "rebirth" with the fifteenth and sixteenth centuries, there occurred during the Middle Ages several veritable rebirths which came to be designated by the term Renaissance. Thus we speak of the Carolingian, the Norman, the Old English, or the Hohenstaufen Renaissance. The knowledge of Roman law, Greco-Roman philosophy and science was not negligible in medieval times. John of Salisbury had a more than respectable humanistic culture, and the School of Chartres revived Platonism as distinctly as did Petrarch and his school in the fourteenth century. "Renaissance ideas," such as the nobility of man, regardless of rank or birth, the God-given talent of the poet, which cannot be acquired by study, and the idea of literary immortality, were known and expressed in the Middle Ages although we attribute them to the so-called modern era. Humanism and Renaissance, viewed through the acts of their leading representatives, did not attempt a studied reconstruction of old ruins, but contributed toward the building of a new world according to original plans, utilizing experience gained in the past. They did not want to resuscitate a forgotten civilization: they searched for a new life of their own.

Burckhardt shared one fundamental misconception with Voltaire and Michelet; he treated the fourteenth century as an era preparatory to the Renaissance. To view Dante, Petrarch, Boccaccio, Giotto, Landini, simply as forerunners of the quattrocento is to consider the individuality of genius a mere flash of the coming age. Such a conception—carried to still more absurd extremes in the history of music—can spring only from insufficient knowledge of the culture of the Middle Ages. The further the Renaissance and its culture have been explored, the further back have its beginnings been relegated. Walter Pater was among the first to descend to periods that preceded Dante and Boccaccio, declaring all phenomena that seemed too advanced for the thirteenth century to be Renaissance phenomena. Modern history followed this trend of interpretation, and soon everything that seemed spontaneous and peculiar in the late Middle Ages was incorporated into the Renaissance; everything alive in those centuries was taken away, leaving them stripped and empty. But the Renaissance is not one mighty, sudden change in man's civilization. It is a lengthy process. Changes, turns, hesitations and transitions, mixtures and assimilations characterize the movement; thoughtful searchers who have liberated themselves from the romantic conception will not consider it a perfectly uniform expression of the spirit of the times condensed into a formula called "Renaissance," but will face the essential heterogeneity of the era and will meet patiently the conflicting components of old and new one by one. "Middle Ages" and "Renaissance" should not be opposed to each other, for many medieval elements continued to live throughout the Renaissance and even beyond it, an overlapping paralleled by the survival of Renaissance ideas far into the seventeenth century, when the baroque was already in full blossom.

The historian's dilemma was acute, however, on account of the vagueness of the terms "Renaissance" and "humanism," and on account of the varying conceptions held by the protagonists of the movement. A great desire for reform, rejuvenation, and rebirth was present in the Middle Ages and found magnificent expression in the works and deeds of St. Francis, and of St. Bonaventure, and in the prophetic utterances of Joachim of Floris (died 1202), the Cistercian Abbot of Corazzo who held that a new age was approaching, the "Age of the Spirit." While one cannot say that the Renaissance sprang directly from this atmosphere, the tremendous influence of these thirteenth-century reformers is undeniable, and the close connections of the Renaissance with their spiritual wealth is evident, for humanism converted their dreamy-religious world into a creative, life-saving, and life-giving world. The three great pioneers of humanism, Dante, Petrarch, and Rienzi, stood in close relationship to the reformatory ideas of the Franciscans; the great desire for a rebirth of culture was paralleled by that for a reform of the Church. The word *reformatio* was uttered frequently during the Middle Ages, and the reformation of the two great powers of medieval Christendom, empire and papacy, was repeatedly advocated in their period of decline. Humanism and Renaissance appeared when these great powers had spent their force, inheriting their aims and ideas. They retained the idea of universalism, but theirs was a nonpolitical empire of fantasy, virtue, art, and learning. Oddly enough, politically they were anti-universal, championing the newly born idea of nationalism. It is this national stamp, and the emphasis on Latin civilization, which mark the dividing line between the Middle Ages and the Renaissance. The birth of humanism is the awakening of Italian national consciousness to an independent leadership of European culture. This nationalism is, of course, not identical with our modern conception of the term, as Latin nationalism was still embedded in medieval universalism, which had been widened and deepened by the addition of classical elements. The idea of universal culture, the avowed aim of humanism, was again an old medieval thought, but what the Middle

Ages had sought to establish through the Church was now attempted out-side the Church, again signifying a distinct break with the past.

"Humanism" and "Renaissance" are almost interchangeable terms; they designate two closely related cultural currents, in continuous touch and often completely converging. Both strove for an ideal type of humanity and considered antiquity the model of civilization and culture upon which a new era could be built. The term "humanism" is often used to mean vir-tually the cultivation of the classics, while "Renaissance" designates the ar-tistic activity of the period or is meant to embrace the whole life of the times. But if considered from a true perspective, with the issues involved carefully weighed, humanism and Renaissance represent a unity; the difference in meaning is due mainly to a loose application of the two terms. The whole Italian trecento was already permeated by the spirit of humanism, though it was only toward the end of the century that a new style, based on the knowledge of classical precepts, appeared in Italian art. Even this new paint-ing, sculpture, and architecture of the quattrocento remained for a long time dependent on the counsel of erudite littérateurs, the humanists, who showed the artist his path. The literary dependence of the arts is but another indica-tion that humanism and Renaissance cannot readily be divorced from each other; the driving forces of the two were identical. If humanism enjoys precedence over Renaissance it is only because the motive common to both, the search for a new type of humanity, *la découverte de l'homme,* as Michelet puts it, appears in a developed form in literature before it is clearly per-ceptible in the arts.

The new national humanism of Italy, breaking the hegemony of French culture, which heretofore had led the way, established anew the old Roman attitude toward "barbarians," the revised epithet being applied to the French and Germanic nations, to whose invasion the temporary decline of Italian culture, now restored, was credited. Here we touch on the problem that perplexed the historians: the conception of rebirth and regeneration held and expressed by the men of the Renaissance themselves.

The first half of the sixteenth century, popularly considered as the Renais-sance period par excellence, was itself convinced that its sons had redis-covered the very sources of knowledge and beauty, and believed that their creations would henceforth stand as the eternal models and monuments of wisdom and art. In the "barbarian" countries this consciousness of rebirth was largely limited to the field of literature, which, under the name of *bonae litterae,* comprised the whole domain from poetry to philosophy. Thus Rabelais speaks of the *restitution des bonnes lettres* as if it were an estab-lished fact, and Erasmus was considered the first man "to study the new let-ters as they emerged from the ugly filth of age-old depravity." In Italy pride and joy in the revival of arts and letters had been expressed a century earlier, and there the Renaissance idea embraced arts and letters alike. Lorenzo Valla (1407–1457), author of a treatise on "Elegant Latin" (*Elegantiae Latini Sermonis*), dreamed of the re-establishment of the Roman language, which—as he envisaged it—would flourish more gloriously than ever and restore the luster of all sciences.

The first to consider the rebirth as a historic fact related to a definite period of time was Giorgio Vasari (1511–1574), the famed author of the *Lives*—*Vite de' più Eccellenti Architetti, Pittori, e Scultori Italiani* (1550) —and no mean artist himself. His collection of biographies may be regarded as the earliest prototype of modern art criticism. Vasari used the word "rebirth"—which he took from the Latin *renasci*—as a standard term for the period we have come to call the Renaissance. He carried the boundaries of the Renaissance much further back, however, than did the rank and file of Italians, considering that the rebirth occurred at the turn of the thirteenth century. He divided his work into three periods, which in our present classification would correspond to Early, Middle, and High Renaissance. While Vasari was the first to deal systematically with the question, however, we must not forget that, among others, Boccaccio and Leonardo da Vinci expressed their belief in the epoch-making importance of Giotto long before Vasari, and that north of the Alps Erasmus and Dürer considered the rejuvenation or rebirth of the arts as having taken place two or three hundred years before their time.

The feeling of rebirth and rejuvenation pervading the sixteenth century was too universal and too much dominated by aesthetic and ethical ideas to be considered a mere imitation of the classical world. If the ancients were revered and admired it was because they were thought to have found their wisdom and art at the same source of knowledge and beauty to which the Renaissance man had turned in his quest for a new life and new art. The leading artists were now busily engaged in a systematic examination of the remnants of classical civilization, measuring and weighing them for use in productive work. But this great activity and the change of forms and style were not caused by the mere rediscovery of antiquity; the appreciation and imagination of the era had reached a point where they seemed to come in actual contact with the culture of the ancients, constantly about them and within their reach. Artists now took possession of the classical heritage deliberately and with a clear idea in mind of what this legacy meant to them.

If we use the term "Renaissance" as a style designation, then we must dissociate it from the idea of rebirth and interpret it as indicating a style current which, following in the wake of the Gothic, achieved its creative ideal by a new feeling for nature, proportion, and tectonics, and by a utilization of stimuli from antique sources. This style is at the same time the real expression of the spirit of Renaissance culture. It brought the artistic longing of the first Renaissance and humanistic generations to fulfillment. The scientific and critical spirit of humanism led art to methods which resulted in the discovery of linear perspective, anatomic studies, the construction of the human body according to mathematical measurements, and, in music, to the modern principles of harmony. The harmful results of humanistic rationalism do not really appear before the sixteenth century, when they are manifested in the so-called "mannerism."

The Renaissance is so closely associated with Italy that in most people's minds the idea cannot be separated from that country. Burckhardt called Italy the first-born among modern Europe's children; other historians have considered the Italian Renaissance the final emancipation from the theological and chivalric world of France which dominated the Middle Ages. The question now arises whether this type of civilization and artistic style which we consider characteristic of the Italy of the fourteenth to sixteenth centuries also held across the Alps. Burckhardt himself would not hear of a non-Italian Renaissance: others, however, have considered the Renaissance a world style which, emanating from Italy, was ultimately accepted by other countries. It is only natural that the original regions of the Gothic, thoroughly saturated with the spirit of that great era, should have retained a good deal of their heritage; yet like humanism, which gave a new impetus to spiritual life in the northern countries, the Italian Renaissance wrought deep changes in the artistic and literary life of the transalpine world. The northern Renaissance acquired a southern cultural strain which it handled in a free and individual manner, developing distinct and forceful local characteristics. It was carried by the middle classes, whose life and manners differed greatly from that of the Italians; the manifestations of their artistic and spiritual activities would therefore, of necessity, be entirely different, though still retaining the kindling spark which came to them from the Mediterranean. While the spirit of Breughel's art is intimately bound to the art of his native country, to the spirit of Jan van Eyck, his treatment of space cannot be explained without Italian influence. He remained faithful to his Flemish landscapes and peasants, but his eyes looked at the world in a different manner. The songs and Masses of the Burgundian composers of the fifteenth century continue the great traditions of polyphonic construction but are permeated by a suavity which comes from the carefree folk songs of Lombardy, Sicily, or Tuscany. When the sixteenth century opened there was a veritable exodus of Italian artists and craftsmen, who were encouraged to settle in France and, to a lesser degree, in other countries. Handsome and livable châteaux replaced the grim feudal castles; Gothic traditions were losing their hold, and classic proportions and methods of composition were being assimilated in all branches of arts and letters.

Renaissance Music Vindicated by Modern Research

THE music of the Renaissance, though long misunderstood and neglected and still burdened with misconceptions and false aesthetic appraisals, is coming to occupy its proper place among the arts. The idea that in the centuries preceding the appearance of opera music remained untouched by the spirit of the Renaissance had been supported by the fact that specifically Renaissance phenomena, such as the revived interest in antiquity, did not manifest themselves in this field until the end of the sixteenth century. But we have seen in the foregoing pages that the revival of the classical, while an important factor of the movement of the Renaissance, cannot be considered the governing force of this great movement, for antique culture had not been dead and its current in arts and letters never ran dry though it often became shallow. We have noticed that interest in the culture of antiquity became from time to time more intense and took on greater proportions; preoccupation with the music of the ancients fluctuated little, however, as the extant musical wealth of ancient Greece was restricted to a few fragmentary pieces. The little there was to know was out of reach of the people of the Renaissance, because they could not decipher the musical notation of antiquity, the riddle of which was solved only centuries later. The great number of theoretical tracts and mathematical-philosophical dissertations which had been preserved did not give a picture of the real, living music of antiquity, and the conclusions and deductions arrived at through the study of these writings belonged in the realm of fantasy. Something happened, indeed, around 1600 that might be called a revival of antique music, when a group of exceptionally cultured gentlemen, members of a literary and artistic society in Florence, decided to reform music according to classical traditions. For their model they chose Greek tragedy, which they imagined to have been performed in song from beginning to end. Naturally what they created resembled anything but antique tragedy; in fact, instead of resurrecting the past, it looked forward. Nevertheless, this event became the source of a very regrettable error among musical historians. Misled by its purely superficial relations to classical Hellas, they considered the year 1600 as the beginning of the musical Renaissance, overlooking the fact that music was thus made to appear as trailing behind the other manifestations of human artistic ingenuity by two or three centuries. It is unthinkable that the person who knew Petrarch by heart, whose eyes were educated by Raphael's pictures, should become a medieval being when he sat down before his clavichord or took his viol in his hands, or that Leonardo da Vinci became medieval when he exchanged his brush for the lute, his favorite instrument.

Such erroneous conceptions of musical history may be partly explained by the fact that historians of culture and civilization displayed an almost complete ignorance of music in the history of civilization, in spite of the fact that every court, every church, every library, every museum, and every gallery they scrutinized for their purposes should have reminded them of the tremendous popularity and importance of music in the cultural history of mankind. If the historians were simply uninformed, the musical scholars were prevented from reaching a true understanding of the role of music in the movement of the Renaissance because they isolated music from the rest of the artistic world. On the one hand they examined its nature through the eyes of the nineteenth century and, restricting their appreciation to matters technical, set down as primitive everything that could not readily be assimilated with the musical dialect of recent times. Thus arose the most ridiculous of all stylistic and historical terms, the "pre-Bach" era, lumping together Romanesque, Gothic, Renaissance, and baroque in an inarticulate mass of "old music."

The gigantic work of musicologists, begun in the second half of the nineteenth century, has produced marked changes in our conception. The intricate note writing of the Middle Ages and the Renaissance was deciphered, and the technique and methods of competent scholarly research work became well established in the musicological institutes of European universities. In the wake of the researches of the pioneer scholars, extended work began all over the world, having for its aim the restoration of what was called "old music." This work can by no means be considered as conclusive, but one fact emerges with certainty—namely that the theory of the belatedness of the musical Renaissance is false. It is clear that music was a vital part of the culture of the Middle Ages and the Renaissance, both in quality and in quantity, that it was as conscious of a Renaissance in itself as the other arts, and that it was affected by the same intellectual tendency that animated the painting, literature, or philosophy of the time. The significance, construction, and development of this music are the same as those of the other manifestations of the Renaissance.

The Final Manifestations of Late Gothic Music

THE great musical productivity of the trecento, which rose so mysteriously from the school of the legendary Casella, passed away as suddenly as it had appeared. It exerted considerable influence during its existence, but having spent its energies it disappeared, leaving no followers; it became history. This historic, antiquarian tendency is unmistakable in the famous Squarcialupi Codex,[1] our chief source for the ars nova. Its compiler collected the monuments of a vanishing national art for posterity. The early Renaissance appeared in music, then, by the same route which Giotto and Boccaccio trod, but—and this constitutes one of the curious aspects of Renaissance history —it refused to follow the other arts further and marched on its own path. This path led through the French ars nova and Burgundian and English music, to the domination of Franco-Flemish vocal polyphony. It was in Burgundy that the forces of medieval culture converged to stage a final great manifestation of their heritage. Burgundy assumed unquestioned leadership in the domain of music and became the center of the musical world. This course of events seems to indicate that the medieval spirit was so strongly embedded in the art of music that it could not develop organically outside the Gothic territory where it first grew to adulthood. The Italian music that came after the beautiful adventure of the trecento was negligible, whereas the productivity of the old Gothic lands had never lagged and now, enriched by the stimulus of the fresh and joyful art that streamed from the Mediterranean, burst forth with prodigious vitality.

It is customary to label the fifteenth and sixteenth centuries as the period of the Netherlands schools. Our manuals of music history speak of a first, second, and even a third Netherlands school, giving the impression that French Gothic music passed, almost overnight, into Germanic lands and reached imposing heights within a few years. Considered from the cultural point of view, rather than from the usual political-geographical angle, the Netherlands do not represent a purely Germanic civilization, diametrically opposed by nature to Romanic genius. "Netherlands," in the fourteenth and fifteenth centuries, is a purely geographic term, the ethnographic connotation being of more recent origin. Thus the designation "Netherlands school" is, in reality, misleading. For, considered historically, Burgundy, the state that first organized some of the provinces in the Low Countries into a political unit—and as such was a forerunner of the Netherlands, or Holland— was a country dominated by French culture and civilization and large parts of it were purely French counties. The court of the Dukes of Burgundy in Dijon was entirely French and was, in fact, one of the great intellectual centers of France.[2] The duke was the first peer of the realm, and many high personages in his court possessed domains in portions of France belonging directly to the crown and held offices under the king. The duke himself exerted considerable influence on the internal politics of France. Not until the middle of the fifteenth century did the French begin to consider Burgundy as an alien political body in their land; even then, it still took several years before their enmity was reciprocated. Finally, after the Battle of Nancy (1477), the duchy was actually united with the crown.

After the reunion of Burgundy with the French crown the difference between the Latin and Germanic elements' became more and more pronounced. The difference in language, negligible before, now became marked, and the Germanic element gained rapidly in power and dignity. The situation had changed now; the four provinces of the Burgundian heredity— Brabant, Flanders, Holland, and Zeeland—were overwhelmingly Germanic, only Hainaut and Namur remaining Romanic. The country as a whole was now much more "Netherlandish" than French, and the name "Burgundy" became almost an anachronism, though the old Burgundian traditions did not disappear altogether in these war-torn years. It seems as if the Lowlands, having outgrown the French influence, were ready to form a political-cultural state of their own, but they were destined to pass through another period of transition and make the acquaintance of another Latin civilization; the seventeen provinces were annexed and incorporated into the Burgundian circle of the Holy Roman Empire and came under the political domination of Spain. In the measure that Charles VI succeeded in adding to his Burgundian heritage the northern and eastern Netherlands, the ethnographic complexion changed toward the Germanic. In the Netherland state which Philip II inherited from his father, the Low-German-speaking provinces outweighed the Walloon and Picard both in territory and population. But the French cultural influence, still unimpaired, remained a living force even after the establishment of the independent Netherlands following the insurrection against Spain. The country was now an entity distinctly separated from both her powerful neighbors, France and Germany, and the sharp difference between the provinces began to be less accentuated and soon became mere regionalism in a national culture.

The enormous influence of French civilization was, as we have said before, especially powerful in the neighboring Low Countries. Flanders and Brabant counted large Romanic colonies within their borders, and Hainaut was purely Romanic. Holland proper, farther removed, received most of its cultural impetus from the richer and older south, and took part—even though through an intermediary—in the cultural advancement experienced by the south through its contact with French civilization. The French influence was increased through the numerous French-speaking officials who came to reside in the Flemish lands, and thus the rising middle-Netherlandish literature was born under French auspices, without, however, losing its Germanic character. Similarly the Burgundians accepted and continued the French musical traditions, and in the beginning of the fifteenth century there can be no question of a specific "Netherlandish" music. We see the same colorful and independent tonal world of the Gothic, for the Burgundians still liked to oppose heterogeneous instruments, and even further emphasized the multicolored aspect of music, especially through the use of antiphonal choirs of voices and instruments.

The Stylistic Reconciliation of Gothic and Early Renaissance Elements
The English Influence

BEGINNING with the second quarter of the century the native character of the musicians coming from the provinces of Brabant-Limburg, Flanders, and Hainaut began to assert itself. They took over a highly developed Gothic musical culture and enriched and rejuvenated it with their fresh unspoiled energy. Thus the old Gothic art was instilled with new vigor. Changed it was, but the fundamental adherence to polyphonic sonority and instrumental accompaniment indicates that this art was a continuation of Machaut's work. Besides the similarity in the sonorous quality of their music, the early Burgundians also cultivated the same musical forms which were developed during the late Gothic. The instrumentally accompanied song and the polyphonic ballad as formulated by Machaut flourished, even the fantastic, romantically colored tone of the ballad being successfully recaptured. The period assimilated a great many of the minstrel elements that had already begun to assert themselves in Machaut's time. This meant simplicity as opposed to the complicated constructive principles of the Gothic. Simplicity was also the guiding principle in the construction of melodies, which became quiet and plastic, well shaped and singable. A great stylistic reconciliation now took place; French, English, and Italian elements were united and found new relationship to the Gregorian melodies, thereby opening a new chapter in the history of sacred music. The resulting spiritual art was of such profundity and sincerity as church music has seldom known. The artistic and liturgic power of this remarkably productive new art quickly displaced the conservative remnants of the old organa, a fact which may be credited to the newly thriving polyphonic settings of Gregorian tunes. In the secular field the gracefulness of the later Renaissance chanson is already evident in the Burgundian chansons, written on French texts, and the light and winged Gallic national traits are unmistakable in the simple yet cleverly composed songs of the musicians who gathered at the court at Dijon.

While the Gothic preference for sharply contrasted sonorities still prevailed, there appeared the beginnings of a tendency toward homogeneous sonority, partly attributable to English sources. At the turn of the century a strong wave of English musical influence reached the Continent, which commands the historian's attention. English music of the period exhibited the characteristic national traits of the British: a strong but not unmotivated conservatism which was productive and defensive at the same time, and a cautious weighing of the new for the purpose of possible adaptation. Their compositions show a musical conception based on natural and unsophisticated choral singing as opposed to the more instrumental tendency on the

Continent. Good choral singing has remained an eminently British art throughout the centuries, maintaining itself despite the arid and sentimental periods of the eighteenth and nineteenth centuries. The vigorous reassertion of English national musical style, which commenced in the fourth quarter of the nineteenth century and has led to a remarkable school in the twentieth, established direct connections with the music of the fifteenth and sixteenth centuries and brought the old virtues of English vocal music into their own once more. English singers were acclaimed at the Council of Constance in 1418, and about the same time the characteristic qualities of English musical style began to be appreciated in France and Burgundy. An exchange of stylistic elements was a natural sequel to the political situation. The Hundred Years' War was entering its final phase; the English allied with the Burgundians were taking a firm foothold on the Continent.

The most important stylistic element that came from England was the peculiarly euphonious quality of the English discantus, avidly taken up by the Burgundians. The meeting of the two varieties of the discantus, the chordal-euphonious English, and the coloristic Continental, produced the so-called fauxbourdon, or faburden, as Shakespeare called it. In a brilliant dissertation Manfred Bukofzer has convincingly proved that the origin and nature of fauxbourdon has long been misunderstood. It appears that, far from being a continuous succession of parallel thirds and sixths, fauxbourdon was one, and a late, phase of the general discantus doctrine and provided opportunity for contrapuntal motion alternating with parallel motion.[3] The cantus firmus in a fauxbourdon is ideally considered to lie in the lowest voice, and is so noted; it is, however, in reality performed by the topmost voice because the two upper voices, conceived in relationship to the written cantus firmus in its original position, are obtained through the application of the principle of "sights" or transposed readings, sounding a fifth and an octave above this cantus firmus. The latter, however, never appears in its original position, but takes the interval of a third above, except at the beginnings and endings of periods, when the cantus firmus notes are in their original position. This seemingly complicated system is in reality very simple. The medieval discantors always gauged their melody in terms of intervals above the given melody. Thus a cantus firmus, at least in an imaginary form, had to be provided for a starting point. Since the cantus firmus was really not executed in its noted position, it was called fauxbourdon or false bass. It is significant that Bukofzer could not find an English equivalent to this obviously French term, and that the earliest corruptions, such as faburden, appear considerably later than the Continental originals.

Some fifteenth-century theoreticians gave instructions for singing the fauxbourdon. The treatises, printed in the appendix of Bukofzer's essay, make it plain that we are dealing with an art of improvisation bearing out the contention that what takes place here is the introduction of a popular musical practice into art music. The artistic elaboration of the fauxbourdon was the work of the Burgundian school.

The importance of the English school is manifested in many documents, some of them in England, as the famous Old Hall manuscript in St. Edmund's College, containing some 138 compositions of English origin, but most of them in Bologna, Modena, Rome, Venice, Florence, Paris, Cambrai, Vienna, and Munich. This fact places the historian in a difficult position especially if we take into consideration the works of Dunstable, the leading master of English music, which are scattered over the Continent while only a few specimens are to be found in England itself. The most important collection of fifteenth-century music consists of a number of codices containing over fifteen hundred compositions from the first two-thirds of the century, discovered by the eminent musicologist Francis Xavier Haberl in the Cathedral library at Trent.[4] While the manuscripts contain mostly Burgundian and Franco-Flemish music, English compositions are included. Unfortunately, most of the latter are simply marked *Anglicus* or *Anglicanus,* which makes identification exceedingly precarious. But though actual musical examples may be scarce, the literary allusions to English music and to its guiding master, John Dunstable, are numerous and highly laudatory. "Thus in our time music took such a wonderful flight because it seems to be a new art which originated with the English under the leadership of Dunstable, whose contemporaries in Gallia were Dufay and Binchois. Their immediate successors were the modern [composers] Ockeghem, Busnois, Regis, and Caron; the most eminent masters of music that I have ever heard." These lines were written by Johannes Tinctoris (c. 1446–1511), celebrated Flemish theoretician and choirmaster at the court of Ferdinand of Aragon in Naples.[5] In his younger years Tinctoris could very well have observed the results of English musical influence on the earlier generations of his native land, and he speaks with authority backed by an encyclopedic knowledge of the art and science of music.

Little is known about Dunstable beyond the date of his death, 1453, and his interment in St. Stephen's in Walbrook. Famous as an astrologer and mathematician, he was the outstanding representative and acclaimed leader of the English school counting among its members Lionel Power, John Benet, Forest, and others. While earlier writers praised him as a great composer whose strong influence upon his contemporaries was unquestionable, later authors, among them recent historians, went beyond all sane precepts of history and criticism in affirming that he was the inventor of counterpoint. Dunstable's works rose above the strict and antiquated technique of the French motet and display melodic invention and free ornamentation of striking originality and simple, poised beauty. The ample sonority of his settings, the harmonic purity of his three-part construction, prove him to be that epoch-making master which he has been considered throughout the centuries.

If we continue reading Tinctoris's treatise we find interesting remarks to the effect that the "English" were compelled to abandon the leadership to the "moderns" (the Burgundians) because the latter's imagination was so lively that they invented songs in a *"novissime"* manner day after day while the former did not change their manner of composition. This statement confirms the theory that the English influence was due mainly to stylistic elements that had survived the Gothic and now found a fertile soil in the rising musical style of the fifteenth century. The greatness of the Burgundian school at once becomes imposing if we realize that neither the English nor the Italian schools were able to carry on the development in their own domain; the leadership passed to the Burgundians, who with their great heritage from the Gothic now united the healthy influence coming from England and the suavity radiating from Italy in a magnificent synthesis, and a musical style arose which was to conquer Europe and determine the evolution of music for generations. The Italian influence is unmistakable in the compositions of Dunstable, who is supposed to have spent some years in Italy, where most of his manuscripts were found.

The Burgundian School

THE leading master of the Burgundian school was Guillaume Dufay, born shortly before 1400, probably in Chimay (Hainaut), died in 1474 in Cambrai. He received his musical training in the cathedral choir at Cambrai and in his late twenties joined the papal choir, which already included a number of Burgundian singers. During his stay in Italy he accompanied the pontiff, Eugene IV, to Pisa and Florence; further visits to the court of Savoy and Paris carried him to other important musical centers, and he became well acquainted with the styles and tendencies of European music. At the height of his creative power he settled down in Cambrai and, as canon of the cathedral, took charge of the music there. Dufay's connections with the court of Burgundy were very close, but he must have entertained amiable relations with other courts also, judging from the many tokens of esteem presented to him by Louis XI, René of Anjou, and Lorenzo de Medici, found in his estate. Dufay's art rested partly on the traditions of the late Gothic and partly on Italian elements, and the reconciliation of these two musical cultures with each other and with that of Dunstable was largely his work.

The Burgundian school showed its indebtedness to the Gothic by the re-organization of music along stricter lines of construction, lessening the improvisatory character assumed by musical composition in the fourteenth century. The old veneration for polished artistic form following well-established conventions returns in the light, melancholy pathos of the incredibly gentle, intimate, and autumnal art of Dufay's school. The dreams of the trecento took shape and form in this music; what had been timid experiment in the former era found a perfect solution in the quattrocento. The first essays of the Florentines were transformed into an elegant and mature technique of musical composition. The times when consecutive fifths and octaves were in order are definitely over; passages in sixths and thirds dominate, making this music rather soft and mellow. In general, a hitherto unknown quality of healthy sensuality is noticeable. A rather plaintive and subdued tone emanates from the music of this age, an age which united the joy of life to religious fervor. As the revolutionary tendency of the trecento favored the epic form in the arts, this mystic era provided a good soil for the lyrical. The Dufay period cultivated the song (in the modern sense of the word), the song which gives a perfect picture of the poem and its content. The trecentists linked music and text somewhat superficially; the Burgundians view the poem as a whole, and their aim is to make the music correspond as a whole. It is true that their emotional scale is not very extensive. Heroic and passionate subjects are beyond their reach, and in comparison with the objective virility of the ars nova they seem somewhat effeminate and sentimental. Quiet, profound, transcendent feelings are their domain and self-restraint and tasteful expression is their ideal. They are never without a trace of melancholy.

While Burgundian secular music, especially the accompanied polyphonic song, continued its uninterrupted development of Machaut's legacy, church music showed a definitely Italian influence. Dufay's generation displayed a marked interest in the polyphonic settings of the unchanging parts of the Mass, and endeavored also to establish a continuity between the five parts and place the whole sacred art within the regular divine service of the Church. The earlier Masses were not unified compositions but consisted of individual settings of the five invariable parts (*Ordinarium Missae*), presumably selected and grouped together by the choirmaster, as may be seen from the manuscript collections which contain dozens of Credos, Agnus Deis, etc., in groups. The Trent manuscripts exhibit already a number of complete or "closed" Masses in which the composer attempted to treat the five parts as an integral and consecutive whole. The stylistic and liturgic unity of this new religious art was established by a renewed use of Gregorian melodies. At the same time, the polyphonic settings of the variable parts of the Mass (*Proprium Missae*) and of the offices brought new life to these liturgic forms, stationary since the time of the organa.

The cherished art form of the Gothic, the motet, was not ignored by early fifteenth-century composers, and the large number of motets composed in the old Gothic style by Dufay and other masters of the Burgundian school, as well as by Italian and English composers of the period, indicates that this Gothic tradition was an active force. The Italian and English influences softened the stern and strictly architectural qualities of the old motet, and the same melodiousness which appeared in the polyphonic song permeated the new versions. In the hands of the Burgundians the motet now became a form of solemn festival music performed at coronations, the concluding of peace treaties, the consecration of churches, and great marriages. There was a definite barrier between church music and courtly musical art. The motet belonged to neither but occupied a position between the two, playing the double role of spiritual "family music" sung at home for edification and contemplation, and of festival music presented at public functions. While the Italian and English influences are evident in Burgundian music, the Gothic desire for judiciously planned architecture was retained to a certain degree, resulting in a remarkably balanced form. The renewed interest in the use of the cantus firmus necessitated the development of a real fundamental bass part, which was assumed by the so-called contratenor, lying underneath the tenor part.

In the third quarter of the century the aging Dufay rallied around him a number of disciples at Cambrai, where the cathedral became the most notable musical center of polyphonic art music. Another center of importance that also attracted many students was the court at Dijon, where the leading master, whose name is usually mentioned together with the famous director of music at Cambrai, was Gilles Binchois (c. 1400–1460), regarded as one of the first composers of his day. As a composer of secular songs (chansons) Binchois was an artist of infinite subtlety. His melodies are pliable and fresh, and his three-part settings show a mastery of flowing ornamentation skillfully blended with the lightly swinging parts.

The Rise of a Neo-Gothic Style

THE younger generation of musicians which assembled around the leading masters was recruited chiefly from the Low Countries, and there began a definite ascendancy of the Netherlandish-Flemish elements of the north. The Romanic genius, tiring of its centuries-long efforts, began to yield to the Germanic element, still young, vigorous, and eager to take its place in the musical world. The young musicians were initiated by their teachers in the Burgundian style, a style based essentially on the accompanied polyphonic song. But this generation had lost contact with the spirit of the late French Gothic, a spirit which already had begun to vanish from the works of the later Dufay. The accompanied song ceased to be the vehicle for their musical thoughts and was succeeded by a polyphonic choral idiom which did not favor one part over another but distributed the flow of polyphony among the several parts with equal care and importance.

This represents a stylistic change of capital importance. Henceforth every voice becomes a part of a musical organism which relies on smooth functioning through mutual dependence and deference. This is not the absolute polyphonic independence of the Gothic nor the accompanied polyphony of the late Gothic; it is something new, a resuscitated, perfectly balanced, thoroughly organized, contourless, mystical Neo-Gothic. The profound and fervent religious feeling of the Germanic races, their world-despising asceticism, and a certain inclination to mysticism, were kept alive both in philosophy and the arts throughout the late Gothic and the era of the Burgundians. While Italy was unfolding the marvels of the quattrocento, majestically ugly figures with their faces deformed by religious ecstasy, skinny, emaciated old women, and crippled old men, appear in Rogier van der Weyden's pictures like the first tremors of a distant earthquake. Before long the same traits that characterized Flemish painting—minute realism, erudition, problem seeking, and intense religiosity—appear in music. Needless to say, the strict rhythmical structure of the old Gothic motet has vanished altogether, and in the works of Dufay's pupils we are dealing with an entirely new species. The rational order of the Gothic has given way to a polyphonic web of admirable sonority, contrasting with the quiet, lightly rhythmical nature of the music of the older Burgundian school; nevertheless, in the field of song composition, the courtly chanson art, the late Burgundian style had created a model of fragile beauty which continued to hold its own until the advent of the sixteenth century. The Flemish disciples of Dufay and Binchois reached back to early sources, their art growing out of the old improvised *déchant* and fauxbourdon. The very fact, however, that at the bottom of this art we find the fauxbourdon precludes a purely Gothic conception of polyphony with its individual strata each having two dimensions of its own. The fauxbourdon changed the rhythmical diversity of the individual parts into a more homogeneous system permitting the introduction of the cantus firmus—which formerly supported the whole musical structure—into the middle parts. This led to a great variety of possibilities, as the cantus firmus might either appear in the tenor or wander from one part to the other, and even the use of two cantus firmi was not rare. The interrelation and interdependence of parts permitted the unfolding of ideas; their passing from one part to the other, and their filling out of the boundaries of form, created a musical perspective not unlike the perspective with which quattrocento painting solved its problems.

It has been supposed that the intellectual atmosphere and tendencies of the quattrocento were expressed primarily in the fine arts and architecture;

in these, rather than in music and letters, historians have seen the new conception of the world reflected in its full proportions. The scientific-theoretical aspect of the art of the Renaissance was not merely an academic acknowledgment of principles and laws of artistic creation; it was the very essence of Renaissance art, expressed with especial clarity in the quattrocento. The subject and its representation now enter into a relationship which obeys strict laws. The visual image loses the uncertainty of a purely subjective interpretation and receives the certainty of mathematical definitions. Painters are all concerned with the scientific exploration and exploitation of perspective, and are measuring, planning, distorting, superimposing, in an eternal quest for true representation. They considered the invention of perspective painting a fact the importance of which could not be overestimated, and there were demands that perspective should be added to the quadrivium as a sister art. The Renaissance artists regarded themselves as obviously superior to the ancients, whose works were so "regrettably lacking" in the use of perspective. It is not quite correct to speak of the "invention" of perspective by the quattrocento, since the geometrical principles underlying linear perspective had been known in antiquity, and the Arabian writings, with which the Renaissance theoreticians were admittedly familiar, transmitted these theories, especially Euclid's optics, to the medieval West—though the curious fact remains that the Middle Ages made no effort to put these theories into practice. But now the northern attempts at linear perspective show a feeling different from that of the Italian Renaissance. The perspective skeleton of lines does not represent a geometrical stabilization, but remains, in the true Gothic spirit, the carrier of powerful dynamics, evolving, creating, and filling space. The difference between the earlier nonperspective representation of space and the perspective consists in the consummation of the technical means rather than in the invention of new means. How truly all this is reflected in the music of the time, heretofore considered outside the realm of the Renaissance! As the paintings of the quattrocento gained in depth through the application of perspective, the same extension of range toward the bass takes place in music. The exploitation of the lower ranges of musical sonority, aided by the natural good singing which came from England and which displaced the old falsetto singing, created a new tonal picture of a virile, sturdy nature which contrasted with the melancholy-esoteric world of the Burgundians.

The first great master of this new Flemish art, dominating the second half of the century, was Jan van Ockeghem (c. 1425–1430 in Flanders—1495 in Tours). His influence was tremendous, and practically the whole succeeding musical generation studied with him. Composers mentioned him in their motets, the great theoretical writers dedicated their works to him, and the title "Prince of Music" was affectionately conferred on him by admiring colleagues while he was still a relatively young man. At his death the artistic world mourned him deeply, the musicians composing motets in his honor, and the poets, joined by Erasmus of Rotterdam, writing "lamentations" and "deplorations." Ockeghem continued the art of the Burgundians although he spent most of his life outside the immediate Burgundian sphere of influence. He carried on the work of Dufay, but converted the simplified style of the Cambrai master into a freely unfolding polyphony which did not know set forms and which dissolved even the categorical cadences of the Burgundian style into a contourless, undulating, flowing music enveloping everything in its path. This mystical music, which once more resurrected all the fantastic richness of Gothic art, emanates from the works of Ockeghem's contemporaries and pupils, Jacob Obrecht (c. 1430–1505), Gaspar van Weerbecke (c. 1440–?), and Antoine Busnois (d. 1492), to mention only a few among many eminent composers.

Ockeghem's mature style displays a careful polyphonic balance and a judicious alternation of full and divided choir. Strict observance of the ecclesiastic tonalities, and a majestic and dignified musical language following the text with a true and pure musical feeling always in accordance with the liturgic requirements, combine to make him one of the outstanding church musicians of all time. Ockeghem and his circle restricted the new polyphonic style to church music, while in their secular chansons they followed the Burgundian models much more closely, thereby widening the difference between cult music and courtly art. The sacred musical style centered around the polyphonic settings of the Ordinary of the Mass, which now constituted the highest form of art music. One of the characteristic traits of the Burgundian-Flemish polyphonic art was the use of secular cantus firmi.

Some historians have seen the retention of the cantus firmus as a necessity, the Ariadne's thread which enabled the composer to find his way in the labyrinth of contrapuntal parts; but this was not the case. Burgundian-Netherlandish polyphony was rooted, as we have seen, in the old *discantus* or *déchant* the composers of which considered the given melody, the *cantus prius factus,* the essence of musical art, aiming merely to embellish the sacred melody. If we wish to understand the vogue of the cantus firmus in the fifteenth and sixteenth centuries we must not approach the question from the point of view of musical form, aesthetics, or ethics; for although the tradition of using given "tenors" lived uninterruptedly throughout the many centuries, the meaning and purpose of the cantus firmus changed as the Gregorian melodies lost their living force and significance, the given melody ceasing to be an essentially spiritual factor and becoming a vehicle enabling the other parts to display all their artistry. Since it no longer had a spiritual significance and served merely as a principle of artistic construction, the source of each particular cantus firmus became irrelevant; once a melody was selected, the whole Mass was based on it and named after its first words. Thus we have Masses called *Salve Regina, Ave Maris Stella, Da Pacem,* etc., in which the cantus firmus was obviously a sacred melody; but there were numerous Masses based on folk songs and chanson tunes such as "Adieu Mes Amours," "Malheur Me Bat," "Mio Marito Mi Ha Infamato," "Baisiez Moi," etc. Some of these secular melodies were exceedingly popular with fifteenth- and sixteenth-century composers and, like the tune about the armed man, "l'Homme Armé," were used as a cantus firmus by a host of composers. In the more unusual case when the composer did not borrow a cantus prius factus but made it up himself, his work was called *Missa sine nomine,* or the individual notes of the invented tenor melody were named by the respective solmization syllables, as in Josquin's Mass "La, sol, fa, re."

The use of secular melodies as the basis of most exalted religious works may seem to the uninitiated strange, if not frivolous, and many an author has called this practice outright profanization. But we accuse the Renaissance composer of a crime which was the furthest from his mind. The secular songs underlying these cantus firmi can be recognized by a trained expert only, and the accusations and complaints of those who condemned polyphony altogether on account of these secular elements were founded on religious, theoretical objections rather than on dissatisfaction with the actual effect of the music. These melodies were not used in their original form with their original text: they were incorporated in the tenor part and consequently were entirely covered by the other parts. They were, furthermore, changed and diluted rhythmically. But even if the secular melody was recognizable, the listeners, whose intellectual world was not so sharply divided as ours into religious and secular, would not think of profanization; they would, on the contrary, consider the secular melody to be ennobled, becoming spiritual through incorporation into a Mass. In general, the importance of the words was secondary, as the repeated setting of the unchanging Ordinary of the Mass lessened the significance of the individual words in the eyes of the musician, who was forced to treat them again and again. This explains the ascendancy, in the sixteenth century, of the new Latin motet with its use of a great variety of Biblical texts or of free Latin poetry. It is interesting to note that the repeated musical setting of the same texts was to create a similar situation in the early opera.

We have been given in the past to considering the highly complex polyphonic music of the quattrocento a peculiarly archaic phenomenon not really representative of the spirit of the times. But the music of the quattrocento is a closed, finished art resting on its own merits. To call this period archaic, or "Early Renaissance," is as much a misnomer as to call its painters "primitives." Or should the youthful searching spirit which characterizes this era be taken for primitiveness? Romanticism is responsible for the relegation of the fifteenth century to the background, considering it inferior to the sixteenth, the *cinquecento,* which became synonymous with "Renaissance." The case is different, it is true, with the more popular genres of secular music, but the people who sang their carefree street-songs, *villanelle* and *frottole,* liked and admired the great polyphonic art of the *magistri* and tried to imitate it in their own way, as witness the "learned" art of the Meistersinger. Leonardo da Vinci considered painting the noblest of all arts because it is a "science" while sculpture is an *arte meccanissima.* He meant, of course, that to give the impression of three dimensions while actually employing two is a superior art to a "mere copying and rendition of something that exists in nature in the same form." This scientific aspect of art, cherished throughout the Renaissance, was faithfully expressed in music; and, indeed, the contrapuntal technique of the Burgundian-Flemish and Franco-Flemish musicians defies description. All imaginable varieties of canon, such as inverted, mirror, or "crab" (backward-moving) canon, were employed with the greatest facility. To complicate matters, compositions often took the form of a riddle; their execution was impossible until the hidden meaning of the directions was correctly interpreted.

This complicated, erudite art reminds us that the real meaning of the verb *componere,* from which we take our term for musical composition, is merely "to put together"; and indeed this phase of musical history is usually prefaced by the reprobative epithet, "the canonic artifices of the Netherlanders." But besides enormous technical skill, these works show inspired imagination and taste; to overlook these qualities is tantamount to calling Bach's *Art of the Fugue* a collection of contrapuntal exercises. As in so many other branches of arts and letters, this is a case of unfamiliarity with a world of expression that is remote from us. The modern listener always forgets that the artistic manifestations of a bygone age should not and cannot be judged by the standards of present-day musical life.

More important than canonic virtuosity was the systematic development of a technical principle of composition known as "continuous imitation," in which a voice (or part) repeats a melodic figure previously presented in another voice. Such imitation does not entail literal copying of the first statement, as in strict imitation (canon); it is used rather freely, preserving approximately the rhythm and general outline of the original figure. This new device of thematic development affords, through its continuous interlacing of the various parts by means of imitation, a principle of coherence which ever since its inception has constituted one of the foundations of our musical architecture. The timid beginnings of imitation appeared with the early Burgundians, but it remained for Ockeghem and his school to develop the principle into a stylistic element of prime importance. Thus the opening words of every line, and significant words through the text, wander, accompanied by the same thematic material, through all parts. Repeated in this way and occurring here and there, these melodies attract attention and gain in importance and effectiveness. The result of these new principles of composition was a music which in its endless, inexorable flow came close to the contourless mysticism of Catholic liturgy. The same *devotio moderna* that emanates from the works of Thomas à Kempis fills this music; the same gentle piety and unworldliness breathes through the interlaced contrapuntal lines of Ockeghem's Masses that permeates the sturdy Latin of the *Imitatio Christi*. The current of artistic creation, though trained to rational principles of construction and proportion, had still its intuitive side which, fed by Gothic traditions, flowed on along with "scientific" art, influencing and animating the theory and mitigating its severity.

After the turn of the fourteenth century aesthetic realism became one of the foremost problems occupying the attention of artists and thinkers. The connection between realism and the Renaissance is clear. The Christian doctrine that life is only a preparation for eternity implies a contempt for the empiric world, and this attitude is reflected in the works of medieval artists. But the early Renaissance saw a lessening of the emphasis on the hereafter and a consequent quickened interest in the natural world. The contradiction between the flesh and the spirit became less apparent, and the existence of evil was not permitted to overshadow the beauty of the universe. In accordance with the new philosophy the sacred paintings were overspread with flowers, trees, animals, rocks, and clouds. This pleased the taste of the middle classes, who were little inclined toward asceticism. They were rather inquisitive, ingenuous people, to whom it was quite important to see such familiar things as people and landscapes, and who measured the artist's ability by the skill with which he was able to render reality. The abstract faces of medieval art were transformed into well-characterized personalities —and the portrait made its appearance in the art of painting. Indifferent and unimportant objects in the surroundings were depicted with loving care, until finally these elements almost supersede the main subject in importance. One can distinguish the glistening dew on every blade of grass, and every hair of a patriarch's beard is painted with photographic accuracy. This is the real art of the bourgeoisie.

Germanic thoroughness and ability, demonstrated in Nordic architecture and wood carving, presented a more favorable medium for realism than the more esoteric Latin genius. Flemish painters reached a height of realistic representation that has never been surpassed, but the Italians, wrestling with the solution of linear perspective, reflect the same tendency to render natural objects in their immediate and individual shape, a tendency which culminated in the quattrocento, the High Renaissance having little in common with it. But realism was not an end in itself; it was merely a transitional stage of stylistic development, and does not represent the essence of the culture of the period. Strict realism is especially evident in the secondary, accidental aspects of art, and usually maintains itself in these aspects. Art with a high destiny must rid itself of realism, but realism inevitably reappears when the guiding faith and idea of that art is on the wane. Realism appears at the beginning of the great rejuvenation of Western civilization and accompanies it part way, then falls back to a secondary position; this happened at the end of the Gothic period, and again at the end of the Renaissance.

Although realistic manifestations in the fine arts are easy for us to follow, the same cannot be said of music. Nevertheless, stylistic currents are invariably expressed in music, and in this case realism appeared in the form of musical illustration of the text. Ockeghem and his school applied it to the smallest details, observing human speech, noting where the natural accents lie, their quality and quantity, and how they are influenced by different moods. They copied all these and transferred them into music, trying to express in their melodies joy and sorrow, pity and hatred, quiescence and ribaldry. It is truly amazing to see with what patience they filed and polished little fragments of melody in their effort to interpret the meaning of the text. If there is anything in the words which gives an opportunity for picturesque imitation they make use of it. Motion, the opening of eyes, genuflection, etc., all find graphic expression in music. Many illustrations lead, however, into regions where we cannot follow. Whenever the text mentions night or darkness, for example, the composer uses black notes only, and the evocation of eternity elicits long-drawn-out notes. By such means anything can be set to music, and indeed, among the more unusual subjects we find a description of Christ's family tree faithfully executed. Canonic imitation was drawn into the service of text interpretation, but, like the canonic artifices themselves, realism went through a period of evolution, and, as in literature, the painstaking realism of the earlier period disappeared.

Migration of Flemish Musicians—Italian Music in the Quattrocento Emergence of Franco-Flemish Composers

WHILE the generation of the aged Dufay became inbred and its activity was generally confined to the Low Countries, toward the end of the fourteen seventies there began a new exodus of Flemish musicians to Italy. Flemish singers and musicians had been known and appreciated there ever since the popes had made their acquaintance at Avignon, but the individual visitors were now succeeded by a small legion of Flemish and Franco-Flemish musicians. Beginning at about 1430, Burgundian music, especially its songs, had rekindled Italian musical art. The Italians accepted the practice of the fauxbourdon (*falso bordone*) with avidity and soon the standard four-part construction of the Burgundians also. This is a fact of great importance, as four-part writing has ever since that time remained the foundation of musical construction. Rome now emerged as a center of church music. Singers and composers, attracted by the artistic policies and grandiose liturgic display of the Holy See, the warmth and natural flow of popular Italian music, and the splendor of Renaissance life, flocked to Italy, later returning to their respective countries imbued with the spirit of that seductive peninsula. With the great musical wave came a reorganization and readjustment of musical institutions. The most important changes were effected in the Holy See; the rebuilding of St. Peter's was begun and Pope Sixtus IV caused the Sistine Chapel to be built (1473), which, named after him and originally serving as auxiliary chapel for St. Peter's, was to become one of the glories of the Vatican. The papal chapel choir, which developed from the Gregorian *schola,* was moved there, receiving the title Capella Sixtina, and was henceforth warmly supported by the popes. Sixtus IV built another special choir chapel for St. Peter's, which obtained its final organization under Julius II in 1512; the Capella Julia, as it was called, fulfilled the role of the old *schola* as it prepared singers for the Sixtina, one reason for its existence being the training of Italian singers, since the papal choir had depended too much on foreign, mainly Flemish, singers.

While the Burgundian and English influence on Italian music had been manifest since the first quarter of the fifteenth century—we have only to recall the number of manuscripts of Dunstable, Dufay, and others found in upper Italy—the "learned" and "heavy" variety of art music was very slow in developing. After the passing of the brilliant era of the ars nova and the three great poets of the early Renaissance, Italian poetry, like music, lost its momentum and descended to a somewhat sterile Petrarchism. Sonnets, *canzoni,* and *terzine* were numerous, but the short lyric songs had disappeared. Lorenzo de' Medici (1449–1492), ranking with the better Italian Renaissance poets, and the group of eminent poets in his entourage were responsible for the rejuvenation of this overcultivated body of verse, and the rejuvenation came through the usual channels—popular art. Lorenzo's verse reflects that reverence for learning and classicism which is so characteristic of his period, but he was able to adapt these elements completely to Italian poetry. The new lyric poetry was greatly bolstered by the recent victory of the *lingua volgare,* emerging from its long struggle with the classical language to start a vigorous and fresh song poetry. The Medicean example was readily taken up, especially in the princely courts in upper Italy, and there arose a musical genre of a popular, captivating nature which was equally removed from Flemish polyphony and from the Franco-Burgundian chanson.

The term *frottola* (meaning a little amusing story in song), as the new genre was called, designated a number of popular songs, among them the *ballata* and the *barzelletta*. There were similarities between the ballata and the frottola, but there was one fundamental difference, namely, that in the frottola the characteristic uniform meter, an octosyllabic trochee, was scrupulously observed throughout the poem. The Italians' delicate sense for form created here a vehicle eminently suited to the strophic song. The same uniformity of meter and brevity of proportions which had proved so popular in the *laude* were employed in the frottola. The close connection between the frottola and the laude, indeed, may be seen from the fact that melodies could be interchanged between them without difficulty; many laudi carry the inscription "to be sung like the *canzone* [naming it]." The reigning voice in the frottola was the topmost, and was called, therefore, *soprano*. The other voices followed in simple harmonic blocks in a clearly defined vertical arrangement. The tremendous popularity of the frottola is attested by the numerous volumes published at the very beginning of music printing in the early years of the sixteenth century. But this great popularity had its adverse side, and the frottola was discredited through its veritable mass production. The fluent octosyllabic verse lent itself too readily to makeshift doggerel; thus a poetic-musical form which had originated and reached its artistic height in aristocratic court circles declined to a mere facile street-song when thousands of popular poets took up its cultivation. Its music did not suffer the same degradation, however, for the composers were of considerably higher caliber, and the printer Petrucci engaged excellent musicians to work for his publishing house. His collections represent the best of the genre.

The northern pilgrims discovered in this simple harmonic music something very attractive yet puzzling to them. Used to the intricacies of architectural polyphony and steeped in Germanic mysticism, they were startled by its radiant and unsophisticated nature. But they could not escape the infectious lilting rhythm and light melody of the frottola, and the Italian influence—already evident in Dunstable and Dufay, but temporarily eclipsed in the post-Dufay period—began to make considerable inroads into their art. On the other hand, the Flemish visitors' art impressed the Italians profoundly, although it took a few decades before this was reflected in their music. The northern musicians in Italy, with their typical international-mindedness, set out to cultivate the indigenous forms of music, but it was not a light task for them to forget their superb schooling in the art of counterpoint. Because of this the frottola, a popular form, became art music in their hands, and their superior knowledge of part writing invaded the simple harmonies of the Italians.

Their reaction to the Italian art was diversified and led to momentous consequences in their musical outlook. Henricus Isaac (c. 1450–1517), most versatile composer of his time, who came from his Flandrian home to succeed the famous Squarcialupi at the court of Lorenzo de' Medici about 1480, appropriated the Italian form and filled it with graceful music that would honor a native Italian for its true rendition of the national spirit. But Obrecht reacted differently; the pulsating rhythm, the effortless harmonies of the frottola awakened somnolent memories of the folk music of his own Netherlandish home, and this supreme master of the Flemish style, familiar with the most intimate secrets of polyphony, now broke radically with the pure linear polyphony of Ockeghem's school. He retained its profound religious mysticism but his Masses and motets emit a new sonority and show clear and balanced periodic construction based on well-founded harmonies, bringing music close to the fulfillment of the Renaissance ideal. Obrecht's whole art was rooted in folk music, which gave even his most mystical religious compositions an earthly, human touch. The combination of the colonnade-like harmonies of this new majestic art with the subtleties of Flemish polyphony indicates the advent of a new style period. The quattrocento was nearing its end, but before the cinquecento could fully take possession of the wealth of its predecessor, the dying century produced a genius who seems to crown the work of centuries, becoming the embodiment of the music of the Renaissance.

Josquin Després (or more correctly Desprez, as he himself signed it—though his name may have been Josse van der Weyden, as Rogier van der Weyden the painter was called Roger de la Pasture) was born about 1450 in the province of Hainaut, perhaps in Condé, where he died in 1521. He began his musical education in the cathedral choir at St. Quentin and continued it with Ockeghem. When the exodus of Flemish musicians to Italy started, Josquin—as he is always affectionately called, this being a diminutive for Josse—traveled in the company of Gaspar van Weerbecke and spent some years in various Italian courts and at the papal chapel. After leaving the papal chapel he appears to have entered the service of Louis XII of France, and after another Italian visit, in Ferrara and Rome, retired and became Provost of the Collegiate Church of Condé. The young composer's style reflects the characteristic traits of all of Ockeghem's disciples: a preponderance of polyphonic figuration carefully carried out to the smallest detail and a tendency to avoid any clogging of the polyphonic web. His works, instrumental in nature like most of the choral works of the fifteenth century, have commendable qualities and show considerable technical skill but do not single out the composer from his fellows. Many of them are somewhat archaic; we find even a polylingual motet, which was rare at this late period. The Netherlandish penchant for complicated canonic construction is also evident in some exceptionally clever virtuoso pieces. Then came Italy, and the sober northerner, already fascinated by the majestic art of Obrecht, forgot the mystical polyphonic flow of his forebears to apply all his great technical wealth to the sublime, clear, well-defined and articulated, emotionally profound, and varied music which became the quintessence of Renaissance musical art. Josquin was the creator of the new Mass, the new motet, and the new chanson, and it was in these works that we see the approach of the *a cappella* ideal.

Among the disciples of Ockeghem and Josquin there was a prodigious number of distinguished composers, many of whom were Frenchmen: Antoine de Févin, called *felix Jodoci* [Josquin's] *aemulator;* Eléazar Genet, called Carpentras, whose works were so popular that when, long after his death, Palestrina's works were substituted for them, the singers were reluctant to give them up although the order came from the high authorities; François de Layolle, Benvenuto Cellini's music master; Jean Mouton, whose works are second only to those of his teacher, Josquin; and many others. With them the Germanic-Netherlandish nature is again diluted by a French strain. Once more we must beware of the simple term "Netherlanders." The Netherlandish-Flemish monopoly which followed the Burgundian era is over; henceforth we shall be dealing with a Franco-Flemish school. The younger generation of Flemish and Franco-Flemish composers now faced grave problems. While not themselves imbued with the all-embracing mysticism of their great mentor, nevertheless the polyphonic style of their elders was their natural idiom, with which they were not willing to part; yet they could not ignore the song poetry, the well-shaped, rhythmical melodies that came streaming from Italy. They tried to stem the uncontrolled flow of music by rational means, such as articulation, symmetry, and motivic logic, and these innovations, together with a new relationship between text and music, were to determine the style of the generation that came on the scene with the birth of the new century.

The Problems of Cinquecento Music

THE problems of cinquecento music were the problems of the cinquecento itself. The whole aesthetics of the Renaissance were based on proportion, the relationship of different spaces to each other, in which symmetry is only one among other possibilities. But to compare various spaces one must see them together, simultaneously. Leonardo da Vinci, Josquin's great contemporary, an able musician himself, expressed this when he remarked that the simultaneous perception of the proportions of "all members" creates a harmony (*concento*) which for the eye is a sensation equivalent to that experienced by the ear upon hearing music. This conception of proportionality was not known in the Gothic period, which favored rhythm and motion-dynamics both in architecture and in music. The Gothic artist's conception was of successive space, whereas the Renaissance created the conception of simultaneous space. The Gothic era, although not uninterested in its actual extent, regarded space as a temporal succession of parts and members. Constant care to establish the most accurate and pleasing relationship of proportions does not mean a mere clever play with figures, but shows intense feeling for precise and clear representation of proportional circumstances expressed in form. The principle of harmony, considered by the Renaissance the essence of beauty, was eminently quantitative, concerned with measures and proportions; all qualitative requirements such as color, character, mood, status, etc., are, strictly speaking, requirements only of correctness and truth, resulting from the observation of nature. In the measure that the northern artists became acquainted with the spirit of Italian art their conception of beauty changed. The definite change in Dürer's studies in proportion, prompted by his Italian journey, illustrates the difference between Gothic construction and the minute scientific quest for proportions that sprang from the spirit of the Renaissance.

The predominantly optical, spatial imagination of the Renaissance could not invade the field of music and poetry with the rapidity with which it conquered the fine arts. A somewhat longer period of gestation was required before simultaneous representation could take a definite hold on the lyric arts. They show a certain hesitation, a certain avoidance of the main problems of the Renaissance as manifested in Italian art. In the measure that music avoided these problems it remained closer to the spirit and atmosphere of northern religious humanism whose child it was—a humanism largely imbued with medieval traditions and tending toward melancholy in its profound meditation. The northerners—even men like Erasmus—were in reality strangers to the spirit of the Renaissance which attempted the perfection of earthly life through art, an idea slow to gain ground in the north. Elemental joy over the mere existence of art was a sentiment unknown to them; it was natural, then, that music hesitated to embrace the conscious and proud joy in itself characteristic of the other arts. This explains why even the inspiration of Josquin's towering genius could not maintain the true Renaissance ideal in the works of his followers. The generation of composers born near the beginning of the sixteenth century professed a limitless admiration for him, but turned back to continue in the footsteps of Ockeghem. This should not surprise us. The Renaissance embraces not the whole culture of the sixteenth century, but only some of its most important aspects.

One cannot possibly consider Francis I and Luther, Thomas Münzer, the fiery Anabaptist, and Loyola, Calvin, and Julius II as all reflecting the spirit of the Renaissance. They all reflect the spirit of the sixteenth century but not that of the Renaissance. In reality the spirit of the Renaissance is much less modern than we are wont to concede. It did not regulate life and art as strictly as had the Middle Ages, but neither did it give free rein to the individual's own choice and outlook on life. The great admiration for antiquity and the constant search for the eternal laws of beauty and politics, virtue and truth, are but a voluntary subjection to the enforced universalism of the Middle Ages.

It was only beginning with the first years of the cinquecento, when the Venetian printer Aldus Manutius (1450–1515) began to print the first editions of many Greek and Latin classics, among them Aristotle's *Poetics,* that an interest in the laws and aesthetics of poetry, comparable to the theoretical interest in perspective, began to be evidenced. It took some time, however, before the literature on poetics and the advisory manuals for poets approached even remotely the proportions of the many writings on columns, and textbooks on perspective. This renewed interest in and better understanding of Latin and its prosody had far-reaching consequences in the development of polyphonic music and compels us to examine once more the physiognomy of Burgundian and Netherlandish music before the advent of Josquin.

Until recently the music of the Middle Ages and the Renaissance was considered a purely vocal art. Many of our manuals of music history still speak of the *"a cappella period,"* meaning the fourteenth, fifteenth, and sixteenth centuries. The instrumental nature of the "music of the Netherlanders" has been uncovered by modern musicology.[6] The vocal performance fortified with instruments which had flourished during the Gothic and the ars nova was continued in the French, Burgundian, and Netherlandish cathedrals and churches, as well as in the courts and princely estates. That the art of this era was considered purely vocal is owing to the fact that it originated in the Church and was nurtured on Gregorian chant. Since most writers had no firsthand knowledge of late medieval and early Renaissance music—the few things actually sung are usually restricted to late Tudor composers, the *Missa Papae Marcelli,* and a handful of other compositions by Palestrina and his immediate circle, that is, to works eminently vocal—they failed to notice the instrumental character of Flemish polyphony, although some of these works, or parts of them, could not be sung at all. A distinguished German scholar, Arnold Schering, has gone so far as to declare that even Josquin's Masses were played on the organ, the voice taking one part only.[7] Late in the fifteenth century, when the technique of voice leading began to take into consideration the specific requirements of the human voice, going beyond the most abstract "utilitarian" writing intended for whatever medium could be mustered for its execution, polyphony embarked on the road that led to the pure *a cappella* style, though there were still in the old polyphonic style infinite possibilities which could have been exploited without changing to an entirely new style. It is significant that this phase of development received its impetus from Italy and was carried out, to a great extent, in that country, although the protagonists for a long time remained the Flemish and Franco-Flemish musicians.

In the most natural combination of word and tone, the folk song, the relationship of the two elements stands on a healthy basis; hence the folk song has always been the fountain of youth from which music has gained new vitality whenever fatigue and overcultivation threatened it with sterility. Folk song flourished in the time of the Netherlanders in all countries which contributed to musical life, and art music appreciated its value by borrowing freely from its wealth. But this appreciation was accorded to the spirit of the popular, rather than to the music itself. In the general current of art music the influence of folk song was indirect, the borrowed popular melodies being inserted into a frame and elaborated by a technique totally opposed to the spirit of this essentially robust, simple art. This was especially true in sacred music. The use of popular musical material in secular music presented much simpler problems, and here composers learned to appreciate the importance of words and acquired a taste for their beauty and significance; yet they could not help neglecting all this in their religious compositions because the text of the Mass had become formal and almost meaningless to them through constant repetition. It was really the music that carried the words. The earnest devotees of liturgic music were aware of this danger and tried, without much success, to remedy the situation.

Humanism entered at this point as a saving agency for a better conception of the role and importance of the text in vocal compositions. The fact that humanism often appeared hostile to the Church should not mislead us, for wide ecclesiastic circles expressed themselves in sympathy with the humanistic ideals, and the admiration and veneration of the arts and letters of antiquity was in itself not objectionable from the point of view of the Church. The renewed interest in the Latin language and a better acquaintance with its laws was one of the factors that turned many churchmen against the faulty and neglected musical prosody of the sacred texts in current church music. As appreciation of the texts became impressed on the minds of the leaders, they came to call any neglect of a judicious prosody "barbarism." Beginning with the second quarter of the sixteenth century, following on the heels of the tracts on poetry and prosody, there appeared a number of textbooks and treatises dealing with musical declamation, and composers were expected to study the rules of accentuation and quantity. Knowledge of these matters was what distinguished them from the "old composers." Hermann Finck declared in his *Practica Musica* (1556) that "if the old composers were eminent in the treatment of difficult mensural procedures, the newer composers are superior to them in the matter of euphony and are especially eager to fit the notes to the words of the text in order to render their meaning and mood with the greatest clarity."

This is the Renaissance idea which agitated musical minds. They wished to resuscitate the music of antiquity, but as the monuments of this music were missing, theoretical speculations took their place. One thing was, however, firmly established at the very beginning of the century; that was the importance of the text in the music of the ancients, and that their music followed the meter and rhythm of the words. Therefore the zealous humanists reached back to the very sources and set to music classical poetry. As early as 1507 Petrus Tritonius (Peter Treybenreif) set to music the odes of Horace *secundum naturas et tempora syllabarum et pedum,* that is, according to the nature and time value of the syllables and feet. Other collections followed quickly. Besides the settings of Horatian and other poetry of Greece and Rome, newly composed Latin poetry attracted the attention of musicians. The choruses of school plays, dramas and tragedies, were set to music as early as 1494; and long before the birth of the opera, until recently regarded as the first application of humanism to music, a Strassburg musician composed music to the choruses of Scaliger's Latin translation of Sophocles's *Ajax.* In these works we are dealing with poetry that was sung, and not with music equipped with a text.

All this would not be of great importance if it were only the philological dilettantism of a handful of rabid humanists; but humanism was not yet philology, it was still a living force, and these musical compositions were not concerned solely with accent and quantity, enunciation and declamation; they were going much deeper, they were trying to find a more profound and subtle explanation for the existence of music. Truly enough, these music lovers wanted to abolish the "barbarism" of the older schools, but first and foremost, animated by the Renaissance ideal, they wanted to bring music back to the forgotten path which should lead again to the dreamed-of wonders of ancient civilization. The same conviction of superiority and the pride in the discovery of "real art" that filled the artists of the Renaissance from Alberti to Vasari are manifested in the works of the musical writers. Tinctoris speaks of the Flemish music of his time as if it were an entirely new art. "It is only during the last forty years," he writes in 1477, "that there have been compositions which according to the judgment of the experts are worth hearing." [8] It is the same self-confidence, the same firm negation of the past, the same intuitive divination of the great importance of the times that we have encountered in the theoreticians of the fine arts. Yet in spite of the remarkable analogy we discover that the various generations of musicians during the Renaissance were not so fully aware of their historic position as their confreres in the other arts. Vasari and Leonardo da Vinci considered Giotto's era the pioneer period of the Renaissance and paid great tribute to his art; Dürer professed that the art of painting "was rediscovered some two hundred years ago by the Italians"; but music lived in its own generation only. Tinctoris called Dunstable the oldest master; Glareanus, the great Swiss scholar, placed the very beginnings of musical art seventy years before his time (1547), which omits the whole Burgundian school and makes Ockeghem the Giotto of music; and to the generation of Palestrina Ockeghem was a meaningless name found in old treatises. It appears that our modern champions of "the birth of music from the spirit of Bach" have a more distinguished ancestry than they may be aware of.

The dissemination of music was greatly facilitated by the invention of music printing, which followed quickly upon that of ordinary typography. At first only the red staves were printed, and the notes were written in by hand, but already in 1476 Ulrich Hahn of Ingolstadt printed a complete missal at Rome, using his system of so-called double printing, that is, lines were printed first in red ink, and the notes, in black, were worked off at a second printing. The system was successful, and the first printed volume was soon followed by a missal by the Würzburg printer Jörg Reyser (1481) and one by the Venetian Octavus Scotus (in the same year). A number of other German and Italian printers followed suit, and the printing of liturgical music folios became a well-developed and profitable industry by the time Petrucci, the first printer of mensural music, obtained his letters patent at the turn of the century. "Ottaviano dei Petrucci (1466-1539) solved his problem with such brilliant éclat that for many years he was regarded as the actual inventor of the art of printing music with movable type. The comparatively recent study of the printed plain-song books has deprived him of that proud title, but the Italian's merits, even thus, are so noteworthy that he will probably remain the greatest figure in the history of music printing." [9] Petrucci's system was as expensive as it was beautiful and finished, a fact which prevented large-scale utilization of his invention. The double printing process had to be simplified, and this was accomplished by the French type cutter and printer, Pierre Haultin, about 1525.

Reformation and Renaissance—Humanism in Germany
The Meistersinger

THE secular origin of the Italian Renaissance was unfailingly present throughout its history. Theological influences did not hinder the development of the movement even where art served religious purposes, until the

Counter Reformation began to agitate Catholic circles; but by that time the Renaissance was practically over and the early baroque had begun to appear. Even the popes, generous patrons of art, were connoisseurs liberal enough not to force narrow restrictions upon creative artists. In Germany, on the other hand, the young humanistic movement was overwhelmed almost at its start by a religious upheaval which rocked the country and left profound impressions on prince and peasant alike. Formalistic history writing has erroneously considered Renaissance and Reformation as a joint phenomenon marking the advent of the modern era, independence of thought, freedom, and truth displacing the bigotry and coercion of the medieval spirit. But the two movements do not run parallel. The Reformation has a popular character; the Renaissance is courtly, aristocratic, learned, and at times snobbishly exclusive. The earnest and severe religiousness of the adherents of the Reformation is in contrast with the indifference of the humanists.

But although the Renaissance is generally adorned with the epithet "pagan," it did not represent a complete break with medievalism. The anticlerical and antireligious utterances of the humanists are always emphasized as representing the characteristic mental make-up of the period. There are the mocking, sarcastic, and often insolent remarks directed against clergy and religion in Boccaccio's *Decameron* and in the virulent satires of Poggio (*Facetiae,* 1474), and we may continue the list to include the keen humor of the broadest of humanists, Erasmus. But this was nothing new; the scholastics of the Middle Ages were not sparing in their criticism of Church and clergy, and the *Carmina Burana* cannot be surpassed in sacrilege and robust heathenism. As Huizinga has said, "the lecture rooms of the Sorbonne, and the towns and courts harbored many parlor heretics who boasted of their disbelief in immortality but were careful enough to keep peace with the authorities." In spite of its classical orientation and great secular freedom, the Renaissance was a civilization as Christian as that of the Middle Ages, and the seemingly unbridgeable chasm between Reformation, Renaissance, and Counter Reformation is due largely to a faulty knowledge of the Middle Ages and to a confusion of modern Protestantism with its erstwhile form. The Middle Ages were not so completely antagonistic to the pleasures of life that Renaissance worldliness represented an entirely new departure. A great many sentiments and desires ascribed to the Renaissance were really the achievements of the century of the Enlightenment. If the Middle Ages did not profess such ideas, the Renaissance saw only their none too certain beginnings.

The theological events of the sixteenth century had a strong repercussion on German art, which, toward the end of the previous century, had passed into secular hands although it retained its religious foundations. As the urban atmosphere demanded a different orientation, art no longer served exclusively religious purposes and assumed a middle-class, a guildlike character. Slowly and with difficulty began a new era which—with certain notable exceptions—did not yet depend on the artistic current flowing from Italy. The intensity of feeling, the fantasy, and the profundity of the German genius now emerges; its austerity, its brusqueness, its robust yet dreamy, blunt yet sincere nature comes to the fore. The Germans loved nature and life but lacked a refined sense for form, proportion, and organic articulation. The formal tasks of the artist were dwarfed by the ethical and philosophical content of his work. This lack of line and proportion, and of the realization of organic laws, is unmistakable and is often joined to a certain inflexibility. Instead of simplicity and clearness, German art shows an overabundance of detail without proper articulation. This world needed, indeed, the great formal art of the south, which taught it purpose and organization without destroying its original material and spirit. Dürer, Cranach, the Holbeins, and the composer Thomas Stoltzer (c. 1480–1526), were the outstanding products of this meeting of north and south. It is true, however, that in the case of Cranach, for instance, the classical touch seems at times almost comical when it shines through his unmistakably German figures.

The lack of a national literature in the vernacular has been ascribed to the philological inclination of the humanists, an inclination which has always strongly tempted the German intellectual up to our own day; but the humanists were only partly responsible for this lack, and theirs was not a decisive influence. Italy counted among her humanists a goodly number who regarded it a sacrilege to use other than Cicero's idiom; yet they could not impede the triumph of the *lingua volgare*. Luther was practically the only author to use a sturdy and remarkable German; its other influential champion, Hans Sachs, was—in spite of Goethe's praise—a man too limited in talent and horizon to lift the petty middle-class guild spirit to higher flights. Dürer, although loyal to the last, was freezing in his own country, craving the warm sun of Italy and the recognition of patrons. Holbein the Younger, hard-pressed materially and mentally, once he had tasted the sympathetic atmosphere of the English court, took up his residence in England.

The German artist of the fifteenth century still employed all his technical and formal means to illustrate feelings and moods. In contemporary Italy art was a source of joy for its own sake, but to the Germans it was merely a means of expression for a people still longing for that "reform in head and members." Every pulsation of the human heart had its counterpart in pictorial representation, but the human body interested the German artist only as the organ of feeling; he did not value it, as the Italians did, for its absolute beauty. It is not surprising, then, that his artistic conception was unacquainted with the beauties of form. But there was another aspect of the

German soul, expressed notably in the Passion plays of the period. Even the most intense creations of Italian art, the works of a Donatello or a Mantegna, appear serene in comparison with the violently emotional and terrifyingly dramatic German representations of the Passion. The ardent search for a truthful depiction of the sufferings of Christ is indicative of the whole want of temperance and measure in German art, while the Italians, carrying in themselves the classical spirit of moderation and equilibrium, sought the divine in the innermost secrets of art and beauty. The life and death of the Saviour was in the Germans' eyes a supreme negation of the world of phenomena, inexpressible in set forms, and their deep emotional exaltation, fed by religious fervor, led them to widespread aesthetic aberrations.

It was in this atmosphere that the Flemings crossed the path of German art, and the heavy soul of the Germans paused in its eternal sorrow. They lifted their eyes and discovered nature, and saw the peaceful faces of men; landscape and portrait appeared in their art. Then the introduction of woodcutting and etching provided the Germans, addicted to heavier mediums, with a means of expression which, by its nature and materials, invited a lighter and easier treatment. It was in Dürer's woodcuts and etchings that German genius and fantasy found, finally, its adequate expression. But this giant of German art, through his intercourse with the humanists of his native Nuremberg and through his Italian journeys, had become conscious of the laws underlying artistic creation. It is deeply moving to see the former painter's apprentice plunge headlong into the study of mathematics and geometry, and journey from Venice to Bologna (1506) "to be initiated in the secret art of perspective," as he wrote to his friend, the humanist Pirckheimer. But the Nuremberg master was one of a privileged few whose view took in the picture of nature and life in all its manifestations. The narrow guild spirit of German artistic life and the concentration of intellectual life on the religious problems raised by the Reformation prevented a final victory of the Renaissance spirit. In Germany the Renaissance remained an uncompleted movement.

Nothing more aptly illustrates the essentially small-bourgeois nature of German art than the widespread and popular art of the Meistersinger. It is difficult to view the honest and righteous craftsmen and artisans and dignified burghers who assembled Sunday afternoon at the town hall, the guild hall, or the church, as the successors of the knightly Minnesinger whose whole art seems to be illuminated by the light of a joyful romanticism. And yet the artistically inclined workingmen had a right to consider themselves the heirs of the *Minnesang*. They were indeed the heirs of a musical practice of long standing, but one which, while continuous from Walther von der Vogelweide to Oswald von Wolkenstein (1377–1445), the last great representative of the medieval lyric art of his class, by the end of the fourteenth century was no longer a living force. Wolkenstein himself, already fully acquainted with the principles of many-voiced art music, remained true to the vanished traditions of medieval romanticism and led an adventurous life which carried him from Spain to Persia, while the homebound German burghers developed their own variety of the *Minnesang,* which began to spoil with old age. Neglected and ignored for centuries, the artisan now pressed his claim for recognition, and the rising middle-class civilization recognized the merits of the small industries and their craftsmen and welcomed them into their guilds.

The Meistersinger regarded as their spiritual ancestors and the founders of their guild twelve poets of the Middle High German period, among whom was Heinrich Frauenlob (d. 1318), the poet-musician who is said to have established the earliest Meistersinger school at Mayence early in the fourteenth century, thereby becoming the mediator between aristocratic court art and the music of the artisans and tradespeople. While this is only a tradition, the institution of such schools undoubtedly originated in the upper Rhine country. At an early period Strassburg, Frankfort, Würzburg, and several other important cities established Meistersinger schools, and in the fifteenth and sixteenth centuries most of the German cities, from Vienna to the Baltic, boasted similar organizations. Toward the middle of the fifteenth century, the barber and Meistersinger, Hans Folz of Worms, came to Nuremberg, and with him starts the "historic" period of the *Meistergesang,* with which we are so familiar from Wagner's opera. The Nuremberg artisans and craftsmen—at that time still receptive to artistic impulses— were introduced by the newcomer to the rules and regulations of the Meistersinger's art. Each guild comprised various classes of members, ranging from apprentices and journeymen to masters, the latter earning their high status through their ability to invent new melodies. The rules of Meistersinger art were laid down in the so-called *Tabulatur* or lawbook of the guild. The old Minnesinger custom of calling their "tones" or melodies by poetic names was continued, but these sober tradespeople, practicing their art with the same thoroughness that characterized their craft, invented for their tones the most extraordinary and often ridiculous names. Among the simpler titles were the "Writing Paper Tone," the "Green Lily Tone," and the "Sad Bun Tone," but the student of their literature will also discover such poetic designations as the "Fat Badger Tone," the "Tailed-Ape Tone," and the "Little Half Jug Tone."

By the end of the fifteenth century the compositions of the Meistersinger took on a curiously "modern" aspect as the solid burghers endeavored to create new melodies *à tout prix,* which led to a system of embellishments of a tremendously laborious and involved nature. Their honorable art and craft reached its height with the appearance of the celebrated cobbler-poet-musician, Hans Sachs (1494–1576). Unlike his predecessors, this likeable hero of Wagner's opera received a formal education, and the Latin school of his native city and his years of wanderings as a journeyman brought him into contact with humanism. To him Nuremberg owes the leading position it acquired among the Meistersinger schools in Germany. Sachs mitigated somewhat the rigid rules of the guild and with his prodigious output of over four thousand songs and some two hundred plays spurred the song fraternities to a last flourishing. The period ended with the activity of Sachs's pupil Adam Puschman (1532–1600), whose *Songbook* and *A Thorough Description of the German Meistergesang* are our most valuable sources for the history of this curious phase of German national art.[10]

The literary value of the poetry of the Meistersinger and the quality of their music were in proportion neither to their great industry nor to the art of their predecessors, the Minnesinger. Poetry was to them mechanically achieved by a close observance of metrical rules. Theirs was not a happy fiction but the decoration of everyday existence backed by the ethics of the new middle classes. Their melodies were fitted to the words, or vice versa, with a supreme disregard for rhythm and sense. Thoughts and sentiments were the last things to which the Meistersinger gave heed. While their art seems rather desolate if dispossessed of the romantic Wagnerian halo that has endeared them to the modern public, a certain healthy aspect in the cultivation of the Meistergesang among the German middle classes reflects their earnest faith and honesty of purpose. In this respect it was an important factor in the rise of that middle-class literature which found expression in the period of the Reformation. The Meistergesang attached itself to the Reformation and took a conspicuous part in the dissemination of the new faith. Sachs himself was an ardent follower of Luther. The origin of a number of Protestant hymns goes back to the "tones" of some honorable baker, tailor, or bootmaker. Wagner, who was acquainted with the source material of the Meistergesang as well as with the critical literature concerning this art, appreciated the deep earnestness of the ambitious tradesmen and paid them a tribute in Sachs's last song, at the end of his opera, which sums up admirably their historic significance.

> Disdain not thus our masters, friend,
> And honor well their art. . . .
> This art our masters tended well,
> And gave it service true;
> And though not honored as of yore,
> When courts and kings her banner bore,
> Though evil days she's seen,
> German and true she's been;
> And though she won not due renown,

Save in the dense and busy town,
You see how she is honored still:
Have then the masters done so ill?

Burgundian and Franco-Flemish Influence in German Art
The Emancipation of German Composers

THE Burgundian and Flemish composers of the fifteenth century stood in
the center of an animated cultural movement between the north and the
south, which for a period seemed to attract and assimilate the artistic forces
of Europe, from the Low Countries to Italy and Portugal. This was the
time of the migration of singers and composers to the cathedrals and princely
courts of France, Burgundy, Italy, and Spain, whose extraordinary mobility
and international-mindedness continued unabated far into the sixteenth century. German musicians exhibited entirely different traits: they were much
less inclined to leave their country, and their whole activity seems to have
been closely defined by the habits and customs of their native land. But
Germany's geographical position and her political circumstances nevertheless subjected her to foreign cultural currents which were to awaken her
own national art, built on the structure of the adopted. Thus fifteenth-
century German art received its impetus from the Burgundian-Flemish circle. The music of the Germans came to be entirely dominated by the
stylistic principles of their neighbors, Burgundian-Flemish polyphony after
the middle of the fifteenth century being one of the most important style
contributions received by German music in its entire history, and constituting, moreover, an exact analogy to what happened in the field of
painting.

The generation of composers born in the third quarter of the fifteenth
century and represented by the eminent masters, Isaac, Finck, Stoltzer, and
Hofhaimer, was the generation of Josquin, Pierre de La Rue, Brumel, and
Mouton, and was entirely under the spell of these Franco-Flemish musicians.
But though these leading German masters—with the exception of Isaac, a
Germanized Fleming, who retained the characteristic peregrinating habits
of the Netherlanders—could not avoid being drawn into the great international network of music, their main theater of action remained Germany;
the minor composers belonged to a specifically German middle-class musical
sphere and adhered to their German folk songs, which they now used as
cantus firmi according to the principles of Flemish polyphony. The German
folk song—not to be confused with the artificial flourishes of the Meistersinger—had retained its popularity undiminished since the times of the
Minnesinger, and now began to infuse its warmth and expressive force
into the polyphonic art of Germany. We are fortunate in possessing a prized

monument which contains not only some of the oldest known German folk songs but also several of the first-known examples of the German secular polyphony which sprang from these songs. The so-called *Lochheimer Liederbuch,* or *Lochamer's Liederbuch,* originated in the years between 1455 and 1460.[11] The quality of the song texts indicates that we are dealing here with an urban middle-class art. The line of development which started in this collection of songs continues uninterrupted through the great German composers of the sixteenth century, to culminate in the works of the "last of the Netherlanders," Lassus. Several of the engaging melodies taken from the *Lochheimer Liederbuch* later became popular again in German homes and schools through the beautiful settings of Brahms.

The blind Nuremberg organist Conrad Paumann (1410–1473), whose fame rivaled that of Squarcialupi, was the leading figure of the ever-growing instrumental music of Germany. While his works are partly of a didactic, partly of an improvisatory nature (*Fundamentum Organisandi,* c. 1452), they show the interesting procedure of the time which, in default of an original instrumental literature, transcribed vocal works for instrumental use—a procedure promoted by the fact that the French texts of the popular Burgundian chansons were unintelligible to the Germans, who then resorted to instrumental arrangements and paraphrases. The same tendency, which ultimately produced an independent instrumental style, was apparent in Italy.

Printed publications of the beginning of the sixteenth century in Germany disclose how absolute was the reign of Flemish and Franco-Flemish composers of Josquin's generation, a situation closely paralleled in contemporary French and Italian printing. The first German compositions appear in songbooks; Emperor Maximilian's court printer, Erhard Oeglin, published his first collection in 1512, and this was soon followed by others. The first printed collection of Latin motets also to contain German works was the *Liber Selectarum Cantionum* (Augsburg, 1520), which included, besides eighteen motets by Josquin, Mouton, and other Franco-Flemish composers, compositions by Ludwig Senfl (c. 1492–1555), the greatest representative of German music of the time. In the following decade the Netherlanders shared the honors with an ever-growing number of German composers, until the printing establishment of George Rhau (or Rhaw) poured out an imposing number of German compositions, leaving the Netherlanders in the minority.

But Rhau's patronage of German musicians had reasons intimately connected with the historical tendencies of his time (we are entering the period of the Lutheran movement), as the sequence of Rhau's publications and Luther's plans for the execution of his musical reforms show a correspondence which cannot be accidental. A thoroughly trained musician, Rhau be-

came a lecturer in the University of Leipzig and cantor at St. Thomas's.
On the occasion of the memorable public discussion held in Leipzig (1519)
between Luther and the brilliant Catholic apologist Johann Maier von Eck,
when the latter forced Luther to declare his stand as at variance with some
of the doctrines of the Church, Rhau conducted the performance of a
greatly admired twelve-part Mass of his own composition. This learned
professor-composer's sympathies for the new religious movement led him
to give up his position in Leipzig; his convictions were strong enough to
cause him to be satisfied with the modest position of village schoolmaster.
In 1523, however, he moved to Wittenberg, stronghold of early Protestantism,
where he ultimately became a *Ratsherr,* or senator. Once settled, Rhau
opened in 1525 the most important musical printing establishment of the
new faith. His great twelve-part Mass has been lost, but it seems more than
plausible that he is the author of the anonymous compositions in a song-book
printed in 1544 for the use of Lutheran parochial schools. They disclose a
musician of great power, whose art was closely related to that of Thomas
Stoltzer. Rhau added a great deal to the fame and importance of Wittenberg
by materially furthering the growth of a new literature which bore the
marks of the religious movement. The whole atmosphere of the Lutherstadt,
as it is sometimes called for its close associations with the Protestant leader,
was that of a newly found national spirit which asserted itself in every domain of life. The translation of the Bible, popular poetry, the finè arts, community singing—all those activities were closely interrelated, tending to
diminish the seeming divergencies of the epoch and drawing them together
in an ideological unity.

Luther and German Protestant Music

IN the center of the new musical movement which accompanied the
Reformation stands the great figure of Martin Luther. He does not occupy
this position because of his generalship of the Protestant movement, and
nothing is more unjust than to consider him a sort of enthusiastic and
good-natured dilettante. The ultimate fate of German Protestant music depended on this man who, as a student in Eisenach singing all sorts of merry
student songs, and as a celebrant priest familiar with the gradual and the
polyphonic Masses and motets, lived with music ringing in his ears. The
places Luther frequented, Wittenberg, Erfurt, Torgau, and Leipzig, all had
respectable musical institutions, and his trip to Rome (1511) introduced him
to the art of Josquin and the other contemporary Franco-Flemish composers. He himself played musical instruments and had a well-schooled
tenor voice. Several contemporaries mention the intimate after-dinner musicales in the Reformer's home, at which the best sacred and secular works

of Isaac, Josquin, Senfl, Walter, and other notable composers were sung.

Luther's writings disclose a love of music and a remarkable understanding of its nature.

Is it not singular and admirable that one can sing a simple tune or tenor (as the *musici* call it) while three, four, or five other voices, singing along, envelop this simple tune with exultation, playing and leaping around and embellishing it wonderfully through craftsmanship as if they were leading a celestial dance, meeting and embracing each other amiably and cordially. Those who have a little understanding of this art and are moved by it, must express great admiration and come to the conclusion that there is hardly a more unusual thing than such a song adorned with several voices.

This statement is remarkable not only because of its profound understanding of the nature of polyphonic music but also for the absence of the typical classical comparisons and quotations usually displayed by Luther's contemporaries when praising music. He does not invoke Apollo and Orpheus; to him music is a living art, the art of the present. His favorite composer was Josquin Després, whom he characterized as "master of the notes; others are mastered by them." This observation betrays again a keen musical sense and a sure judgment of art; Luther recognized in Josquin the sovereign genius to whom the subtleties of counterpoint were only a means of expression, in contrast to the rank and file of *Gesangmeister* who were too preoccupied with the niceties of the mensural theory.

Yet the teacher and theologian in Luther could not always follow the instincts of the musician. As with all the arts and sciences, he considered music not for its intrinsic value only, but, like languages, as a means of education to make youth more receptive to God's gospel. It is commonly supposed that Luther's interest lay only in furthering active participation of the community as a whole in the divine service; hence his insistence upon the use of the German vernacular. But an examination of his writings will disclose that his was a much broader conception. Thus, although the fundamental idea in Luther's mind was to arrange his music for the sake of what he called the "common ordinary man," he endeavored to leave the door open for a possible artistic development. This remarkable man realized that a one-sided, popular, and earth-bound movement in art must inevitably decline. He avoided the straits of experimentation, but also the puritanic primitiveness of Calvin, who banished even the simple accompaniment of hymns. Plain community singing without accompaniment became inexorably severe with the Calvinists, who, not satisfied with mere musical "reform," set out systematically to destroy everything that might have reminded them of the abominable vanity of the music of popish sinners. The cathedral organist in Zürich watched, with tears streaming down

his cheeks, the destruction of his magnificent instrument; and the famous
Bern organist, Hans Kotter, made homeless by his unwavering faith in
Protestantism, saw himself reduced to the status of a schoolteacher when
the very champions of his faith destroyed his instrument. The violent
persecution of music in some parts of Germany and Switzerland lasted for
over a century, because the faithful saw in vocal polyphony and organ music
a popish conceit which violated the spirit of the Scriptures. We shall see the
same hostile attitude in the cold, unadorned, and uncomfortable churches
of the English Puritans. The more open-minded followers of Luther realized that the destruction of music would not promote the new faith and
turned their energy toward its reorganization rather than its extinction.

Knowing of Luther's excellent musical education, it is not surprising to
learn that he was an outstanding composer of popular melodies. His musical
authorship of the Lutheran chorales, or hymns, is doubted by some, but contemporary statements and authentic correspondence speak greatly in its
favor. Even Johann Walter, the eminent musician whom Luther invited to
help him organize the music of his new Church, explicitly stated that several
of the famous hymns, as well as the beginning of the German Mass, were
Luther's own compositions, and some of his disciples simply called him
unser Gesangmeister, "our music master." There are several authentic musical manuscripts in the Reformer's own handwriting, among them a setting of the Lord's Prayer and sketches for a musical liturgy. Luther's friendly
relationship with some of the leading musicians of sixteenth-century Germany is well known. His correspondence with Senfl, Walter, Agricola, and
others discloses that his knowledge of the technique of polyphonic composition was respectable, and, indeed, we possess a complete four-part
motetlike composition of his which appears in *Lazarus,* a play by Joachim
Greff, one of the poets in his circle.[12] Another composition by him, a
printed four-part setting of a well-known Gregorian tune, has been discovered recently.[13]

We must know Luther's musical background to appreciate the able,
liberal, and artistic manner in which he dealt with the tremendous task of
reorganizing the music of his church. It is significant that his endeavors to
establish community singing, a logical carrying out of the evangelical idea,
went back to the same source which had produced the whole hymn and
antiphon literature of fifteen centuries of the Christian world—the Psalter.
He himself led the way with examples that are unsurpassable for their
rugged strength: Psalm 46, "Ein' feste Burg ist unser Gott" ("A Mighty
Fortress is Our God"), Psalm 130, "Aus tiefer Not schrei ich zu Dir" ("Out
of the Depths I Cry unto Thee"), and others. Luther associated himself with
two excellent musicians, Conrad Rupff and Johann Walter, who proceeded
under his direction to select the best Latin chorales for use—in a Germanized

form—in the Evangelical church. Many well-known Gregorian hymns were translated or arranged for the German congregation. The number of these songs grew rapidly. While one Wittenberg edition of 1524 contained 38 German and 5 Latin songs, a 1551 edition of the song-book listed 78 German and 47 Latin songs.

An interesting phase of this transformation of Catholic church music into Evangelical-Lutheran was the so-called *contrafactum* (from the Latin *contrafacere*), consisting of a textual arrangement which changes the meaning of secular texts to sacred ones. Various German and Latin hymns to the Virgin and other Catholic church songs were paraphrased so as to fit the tenets of the new creed. Although Luther himself was not opposed to the cult of the Virgin and the saints, his successors were of the opinion that such songs must be improved upon in a "Christian sense." A few of the Meistersinger songs also found their way into the repertory of the new church, notably a few of Hans Sachs's compositions.

The musical services of the early German Protestant churches present an extraordinarily rich picture which differs markedly from the simplified form practiced today in most Protestant churches, with the possible exception of High churches in the Anglican and Episcopal communions. For about a century after Luther's activity began, many German churches continued to perform complete Masses, and a number of new Masses were written by Protestant composers, the only distinguishing feature of which was their German cantus firmus. This clinging to the Latin Mass—interrupted only by the sermon in German after the Credo—seems to contradict Luther's Germanization of the liturgy, but we must not forget that the Reformer was also a humanist who supported ardently the cultivation of the classics. Besides the Ordinary of the Mass, the *de tempore* of every Sunday was a faithful celebration of the proper event of the church year— which today is only alluded to in the selection of the hymns, and that frequently only on the principal holy days—while introits, responds, and sequences were sung in their appropriate orders.

Protestant church music did not assert its individual nature until close to the end of the sixteenth century. Where the strong pietistic opposition did not cut musical services to the minimum, the old Gregorian melodies generally continued to be used, although their Latin texts were translated into German. Even the introduction of German spiritual songs, long the cherished property of the people, did not change the situation for some time, but as their number grew they slowly displaced the Gregorian chorales and lent a characteristic trait to the music of the new church. It was only in the seventeenth century, when these songs and the Lutheran hymns invaded the larger musical forms such as cantatas, Christmas pieces, Passions, and oratorios, that a definite literature arose that rivaled the music of the Catholic Church. The well-arranged hymns of Luther's time were still under the influence of contemporaneous Catholic music. Thus the historian is faced by a profound paradox: stylistically he can hardly detect any difference between Catholic and Protestant music, yet a wide gulf between the two was manifest before Protestant church music reached its unequivocal stylistic integrity in the seventeenth century.

The prefaces to musical publications, as well as the various writings of Luther, Melanchthon, and others, reflect the essence of Protestant musical thought. The conceptions which Luther and his disciples entertained concerning the place of music in the universe were singularly archaic, having their roots in Luther's theological outlook and in the still cherished thoughts of St. Augustine. The Bible and St. Augustine occupied the central place in Luther's theology, and the prefaces in Rhau's publications echoed the same conception. The conservative and, in many aspects, strongly medieval character of early Protestant musical thought placed religious considerations decidedly before aesthetic ones. It was this spirit which gave a specifically Protestant character to this music founded on the traditions of the old church, and which made it possible to disregard the virtual stylistic identity of Catholic and Protestant church music: the two sounded the same, though they had different meanings in the two camps. Antique and medieval ideas about the divine origin of music are current in these Protestant writings, and the exhortation of the Church Fathers to employ music only in the praise of God is again held before composers. But specifically Protestant traits may be detected in the selection and arrangement of the hymnals. The hymns were published because they contained many edifying manifestations of faith on the part of the martyrs of Christendom; but as some of these men "erred," the songs and hymns which contained their errors had to be cleansed. This point of view is fully evident in Rhau's hymn collection of 1542. The sincere religious earnestness and profound conviction of the reawakening of evangelical truth which emanate from the antiphon and hymn collections of Sixtus Dietrich (between 1490–1495 and 1548), one of the most important liturgical composers of early Protestantism, are in sharp contrast with the language and spirit of similar works originating from humanistic and Renaissance sources. It is evident that these publications were written with a clear conception of what the nature of Protestant church music was to be.

At this time the slowly forming Protestant musical thought found a philosopher who lifted it to higher spheres. Philip Melanchthon, after Luther the chief figure of the Lutheran Reformation, rejected, in the preface to his *Officia de Nativitate,* the views of the fanatic partisans of the secession from Rome. The *cultus dei,* said Melanchthon, should permeate the whole life of man, because where church music ceases to sound, it is to be feared that it will be followed by a disintegration of the sacred doctrines. The learned Wittenberg professor's proposed application of religious music to active everyday life is a veritable sanctification of that life: the people in the church, the boys in the schools, the girls in their domestic work or in the garden, the farmers in the fields, and the soldiers on the battlefield all sing the words of the prophets and the apostles. The old doctrines of the *cultus dei,* as formulated by the Church Fathers, now appear again; music becomes again a servant of the Church whose only duty should be to give the holy words more significance. But Protestant musical thought is not essentially opposed to artistically polished church music, as may be seen from the fact that it deliberately made contemporary art music the basis of its own musical culture, endeavoring to infuse it with its own tenets and so turn it into a specifically Protestant sacred art. Opposed to the more universal-objective nature of the Gregorian conception, which elevates man to higher regions by grades of perfection through a long-continued process, the Protestant conception rests on a personal and immediate faith, experienced once for all, and prepared and continued through a personal religious process. It was this principle of spiritual religion as opposed to sacramental religion which dominated musical thought.

The German towns, with their powerful middle-class populations and independent municipal governments, constituted the most important factor in the Protestant movement; and the middle-class musical sphere, as illustrated in the creative activity of the minor masters, reacted most favorably to the religious tendencies. These musicians formed an integral part of the social structure, and as teachers, cantors, organists, or pastors, depended on municipal governments and churches. However varied their services and positions, they were fundamentally members of the citizen class and their activity was closely bound to church and school. Protestant schools arose, then, in this atmosphere of organized middle-class society, differing fundamentally from the clerical chapel choirs which produced the Catholic musicians who carried with them the unfailing traditions of centuries of medieval culture directed by the Church and the aristocracy. The creative activity of these middle-class musicians consisted essentially in making music available for church, school, and home, these three domains being closely associated in the musicians' field of action. In their work they utilized the current musical material of their time, Gregorian chorales, secular "tenors," and folk songs, arranging and rearranging them to suit the occasion. The dominant musical style of the Burgundian and Franco-Flemish composers passed into their sphere and was entirely absorbed, but by mixing with the local traditions of musical craftsmanship it prepared for the rise of a national art. These musicians, who were so proud of their métier, remained Germans in the midst of the international artistic orientation all around them, because the school and the church for which they worked provided them with ample occupation.

Musical instruction in the Protestant *Gymnasia* and parochial schools was exemplary and cannot even be approximated in our modern schools. The young boys had a carefully graded curriculum starting with solmization and the singing of simple songs and plain-chant melodies, and leading up to four- and eight-part choral works in their final years of study. The musical exercises were compulsory, and no exemptions were granted. To practical singing was added a thorough training in musical theory and conducting. The burden of instruction fell on the cantors, whose high position is indicated by their rank in the school hierarchy, usually immediately after the rector or principal. These cantors were highly educated persons who usually supplemented their musical duties by lectures on the classics, Hebrew, or history, or by discourses on mathematics or philosophy. These traditions, evidently of humanistic origin, were maintained for a long time. (Herman Schein [1586-1630], cantor of St. Thomas's in Leipzig and one of the great masters of the early German baroque, already objected to his "teaching load," which required him to give ten hours of academic and four hours of musical instruction, because he was eager to devote his time to composition; and even Johann Sebastian Bach had repeatedly to petition the authorities to unburden him of nonmusical duties.) This active and well-directed musical life furnished the background for the incomparable musical culture of the Saxon-Thuringian provinces, a culture which produced Schütz, Bach, and Handel.

The Classical "Netherlands" Style and Its Internationalization

THE radiant, free, and deeply emotional art of Josquin proved to be too powerful a reaction to the older Burgundian and Flemish schools. His art was too prophetic, too personal to find immediate followers. Indeed, while musicians continued to worship him, the scales turned back to the warm and uniformly expanding polyphonic ideal of Ockeghem, which the following generation continued to cultivate, enriching it with the superior technique of composition acquired after Josquin's time. The leader of the generation, the composer who formulated the final classical language and style of Franco-Flemish polyphony, was Nicholas Gombert. We know very little about him, and even the dates of his life are based on conjecture. In 1520 a singer in the chapel choir at Brussels, this Flemish musician went to Madrid in 1537, taking with him twenty singers, and probably became choirmaster to Charles V. In 1552 he was living in Tournai, but he must have died after this date. Unknown to most students of music in our day, this fervently religious composer, with a passion for magnificent, sensuous euphony which enhanced the deep mysticism of his incomparable choral works, is one of the greatest church composers of all times. His technical knowledge of musical composition was perhaps superior even to that of his master Josquin. While first and foremost a church composer, Gombert was also the author of a volume of French chansons composed with easy grace, fluent declamation, and fine voice leading. The ability to be equally at ease in both fields of music is typical of Gombert's generation.

The two other representative Franco-Flemish masters of the period, Thomas Crecquillon (d. 1557) and Jacques Clément (c. 1510–d. 1557), were both masters of pregnant declamation and light chanson settings, although their polyphonic thoroughness betrays the "Netherlander" and does not permit them to reach the ultimate gracefulness of the truly French chanson composers. But in the field of the motet and the Mass they were sovereign and, together with Gombert, unrivaled until the appearance of Lassus, their great compatriot. Crecquillon, more nervous and animated, stands nearer to the French, while Clément occasionally falls into the more sober style of the earlier Flemish composers; but both were consummate Renaissance artists whose works, crystalline and chiseled to the last detail, glorify the balance of proportion and the judicious application of technical means cherished by the Renaissance. Clément, better known as Jacobus Clemens non Papa—a name he assumed to prevent confusion with another celebrated Jacobus of his home town, the poet Jacobus Papa of Ypres—exhibits a definite penchant for modern harmonic construction, which often gives his works a certain popular tone. His predilection for folk songs led him to the musical setting of Flemish Psalms, and these *Souterliedekens* were frequently used in later editions of the Psalter.

Virtuoso contrapuntal technique became to this generation as natural a prerequisite as the technique of the *basso continuo* or thorough bass was to Bach's era. The strictly architectonic nature of their style was wonderfully maintained by the systematic and continuous imitation of the polyphonic web formed by the voices. Motives wandered from voice to voice with the greatest ease, never resting or merely idling or filling up space; everything had a purpose and everything was logically motivated. Realistic tone painting and illustration, together with canonic stunts, occupied but a minor position in this art. The great figure of Josquin had not appeared in vain; the immense impetus he gave to music was not lost but was used in the building up of the stylistic current started by Ockeghem. The Mass ceded the dominant position it had held in the previous century to the renewed motet, which remained the highest form of contrapuntal art up to the time of Palestrina and Lassus. Thus the polyphonic art of the Flemish and Franco-Flemish musicians of the post-Josquin generation adhered to the idea of a universal European musical culture which knew no national boundaries. The religious currents of the time, and also the position of great dignity and esteem held by Latin civilization in the humanistic era, supported this conception. With Gombert and Clemens non Papa the Franco-Flemish style reached its apex. Lassus and his contemporaries enriched the style of their predecessors with many new elements, mainly Italian and German, but did not create a new style, and we must consider the middle of the sixteenth century the point at which the true style of the "Netherlands" reached its classical constitution. This fact is acknowledged by the theoretical literature of the following decades, which considered the principles activating the works of Gombert's generation as producing the universal picture of musical art.

With the internationalization of Flemish musical culture the number of foreign composers joining the ranks of the Netherlandish masters constantly increased. Since the language of secular art was French, and most of the composers coming from Picardy and Hainaut grew up speaking French, the first important independent branch of their art was French, soon followed by several Italian offshoots. Because of the close relationship of the Low Countries with Spain and Germany, we find a number of Spaniards and some Germans within the Netherlands sphere of art, and it is no longer possible for us to follow a strictly chronological and national order. However great the Netherlanders were in their exclusive field of sacred polyphony, in the chanson they yield the crown to the French, who filled this literary-musical genre with truly Gallic wit, clever and brilliant turns, and a grace not native to the Germanic artist. There was one exception to this rule: the profound spiritual content, intense melancholy, and smiling contemplation of Josquin's chansons remained unique, and found no echo during the whole period of the French Renaissance chanson until the advent of that other great Netherlander, Lassus, in whose chansons the same qualities occasionally reappear. Thus before we start out to review the history of the French chanson in the period of the Renaissance we are confronted with the interesting situation of seeing a Flemish composer supreme at the opening and another at the close of the era of its flowering.

French Music of the Renaissance

BEAUMARCHAIS concludes his *Mariage de Figaro* with the words of Judge Bridoison, *tout finit par des chansons*. From the time of the Gallic bards up to that of the *café-concert* the chanson has always reflected the racial qualities of the French people: good humor, sensibility, gracefulness, mischievousness, and prudence. There were "sing-song" chansons sung by the populace in the street, and there were highly polished polyphonic art chansons sung by kings and their entourage in the Louvre. Perhaps the best illustration of the universality of the French chanson is the curious *Abrégé de l'Histoire de France* (1694), by the Duke of Nevers, a history of France written entirely in chansons; similarly, the educated valet in Molière's *Les Précieuses Ridicules* boasts of setting in madrigals "toute l'histoire romaine."

Already the chansons of the troubadours represented a national art in which musical rhythm was largely determined by the prosody and rhythm of the text. In the union of poetry and music, it was the former that dominated; the words commanded the notes. Thus from its earliest beginnings French music finds itself imbued with a verbal element, with an intellectualism following the word, the instrument of discursive language. This is a fundamental characteristic of French music, a characteristic which one meets in every manifestation of French art. Instrumental music, "not at all agreeable," said Ronsard, "without the accompaniment of the melody of a pleasant voice," never attained great popularity in France until the nineteenth century. Not that it was not practiced, of course, but it failed to please the French, who up to this day insist upon *du chant,* and always desire music whose sounds please the ear while its words engage the mind. In instrumental music, pure intelligibility loses ground, and the Frenchman is horrified at the thought of listening to something that he cannot follow and understand step by step. The French chansons of the Renaissance—unlike the English madrigals—are an entirely independent species and thoroughly intellectual in nature. It is true that their emotional range is limited; in this they resemble the English madrigals, which were more dainty than profound. But the wit, finesse, grace, and cleverness of these French chansons is limitless.[14]

At the beginning of the sixteenth century two interdependent tendencies appeared in French literature, the one known as Italianism, and the other as humanism. The former began to be apparent after the first French military expeditions into Italy, where the Renaissance movement had reached its height. The French were jealous of the supremacy of Italian culture at the time, and attempted to capture that supremacy for their own country. The upshot was the development of humanism, since from Italy came a revival of interest in the classics. The French literary Renaissance, extending, roughly, from 1515 (the accession of Francis I) to 1610 (the death of Henry IV), had three causes: the above-mentioned wars with Italy, the introduction of printing, and the Protestant movement. The tendency in literature was primarily humanistic, and it remained so throughout most of the sixteenth century; but withal there was a search for a new art and an original style, with an attendant predominance of lyricism and a genuine expression of personal feeling. Parallel to this ran the tendency among French composers in the beginning of the century to reject the *technique savante* of the Flemish and return to the genre that always interested them, the song or chanson.

The importance of the chanson becomes immediately apparent upon an investigation of the enormous number of publications given over to it in the sixteenth century, both in Italy and in France.

The first of these was made in Venice in 1501 by Petrucci, and was called *Harmonice Musices Odhecaton*. Franco-Flemish masters were most numerous in this collection, and four-fifths of the compositions were French chansons. The fact that the first publication of a newly established printing house paid this homage to the French chanson attests its widespread popularity, and, indeed, this Gallic art was to have a decided influence on the rising flower of Italian secular art of the Renaissance, the madrigal. The chansons which at this time appeared in Venice, however, belonged to an older school and, with all their grace, were not exempt from a certain weightiness which betrayed their Burgundian-Flemish origin. The haunting beauty of Josquin's chansons did not find an immediate echo, but it must have contributed to the almost revolutionary change that took place in the style of the chanson between the first publication of Petrucci and the first French printings of Attaingnant (1528–1529). The scant quarter of a century which separates these works is still shrouded in darkness, from the musicological point of view, and will have to be explored to close the gap in the remarkable history of the chanson. It is more than plausible that musicians returning from Italy brought with them a renewed appreciation for simple, popular art, as expressed in the frottola. But they substituted for the playful doggerel of the frottola the elegant and piquant poetry traditional with the French, and with their superior knowledge of musical setting, gained by long association with the artistic Burgundian-French chanson, they created almost at once a new literature of their own. In this connection one cannot fail to notice that one of the two protagonists of the new Renaissance chanson, Claudin de Sermisy, accompanied his king to Italy in 1515 and resided later in the court of the Duke of Ferrara, while the other, Clément Janequin, took part in the Italian campaigns of Francis I and witnessed the Battle of Marignano, which he later commemorated in an astounding musical composition.

In Italy the development of secular music did not parallel that of literature as it had in France, for Italian musicians in the sixteenth century were still attached to the poetry of the two preceding centuries and in trying to reproduce the spirit of a previous age often fell into artificiality. The French, on the other hand, used a literature in harmony with contemporary conditions. This situation was probably due to the fact that the Renaissance movement began in Italy considerably before it came to France, and its course there covered a much longer span of years. Consequently, when developments in France tended toward the Renaissance, they began more suddenly, almost with the advent of Francis I to power in 1515, and rose rapidly, since they were imitative of a culture already completely evolved in Italy. The king, conspicuous as a patron of the Renaissance, brought Leonardo da Vinci, Cellini, Andrea del Sarto, and numerous other artists to France, and was liberal in his purchases of Italian art, thereby giving added impetus to the rapidly developing French Renaissance.

In poetry, the first important representative of the period was Clément Marot (1496–1544). His grace and brilliance appeared in a style unique in a classical-humanistic era, and in his chansons his caustic wit was mingled with pious irony. Marot had many admirers, most notable among them being Ronsard, and his fame did not diminish throughout the years; he was especially admired by the romanticists of the mid-nineteenth century. Marot's translations of the Psalms were set to music by Calvinist composers, among them Goudimel. Contemporary with Marot, and an interesting example of the twofold intellectual currents of the time, was the school at Lyons, where arose the movement known as Petrarchism and Platonism. The members of the school undertook to create for French literature a new form based on the Petrarchian sonnet and having for its poetical content the Platonic ideal of love. Following similar intentions Joachim du Bellay (1522–1560), friend and disciple of Ronsard, published a manifesto entitled *Défense et Illustration de la Langue Française* (1549) in which he applied the vindication of the Tuscan language to the French, maintaining that since Latin was already perfected, it was the duty of men of letters to perfect their own language. He suggested the study of old ballads (and other forms popular in the provinces) with the idea of developing forms that would replace the ode and other classical models. This work was more than a manifesto it was a revolution; after it French became the language of humanism. A few more years, and French literature was to experience a veritable revival of lyric poetry with the group of poets rallying around Pierre Ronsard, the Victor Hugo of the sixteenth century.

But for once, music succeeded in conjuring up this lyrical Renaissance several decades before the corresponding movement in literature. A casual glance through Attaingnant's first volume of chansons (1528) reveals a freshness of invention, a true vocalism of setting, and a fine lyricism which defy comparison. Another striking feature is the superbly rounded form of the compositions included there. Unlike the Italian and English madrigals, especially the earlier ones, which consisted largely of series of short sentences, these chansons contain long, perfectly rounded statements of each idea. They are, almost without exception, clear two- or three-part forms, setting forth logically in the first part the purpose of the song, developing the material in the middle, and ending with a little recapitulation. The three-part form is especially clear in the long dramatic chansons of Janequin. We are fortunate enough to have in Henri Expert's *Maîtres Musiciens de la Renaissance Française* several volumes filled with this extraordinary music; among others there are several of Janequin's large descriptive choral works.

These chansons brought a new element to choral music and are veritable little "symphonic" tone poems. With his great choral frescoes, *Le Chant des Oiseaux, La Chasse, La Bataille,* Janequin added a heroic-epic touch to a lyrical genre which had not known the heroic since the times of Roland. The inventive genius which created a form and style entirely new and fresh conquered the astonished musical world. Gombert did not disdain to essay the composition of a *Chant des Oiseaux* and a *Chasse du Lièvre* of his own, and "battles" and "hunts" appeared everywhere. The Italian lute and harpsichord virtuosi transcribed Janequin's *Bataille de Marignan* (the master having produced several *Batailles* himself), and the later Venetian musicians orchestrated it for a larger ensemble.

In sheer musical grace the other leading composer, Claudin de Sermisy, outdoes Janequin, being less inclined to imitation in a realistic sense and more polished in both technique and musical idea. Like Janequin, he presents one long, beautifully sculptured sentence as an introduction to his compositions, but he does not extend them to anything approaching the length of Janequin's. In Sermisy's music we see the advent of the intimate lyric chanson of the period of Lassus. Although he died only three years after Janequin, he really belongs in the next period of the French Renaissance chanson. This next period saw, however, the reciprocation of the early French influence on Italian secular music. The new influence was largely responsible for the creation of the Renaissance madrigal and gave a decided madrigalesque touch to the chanson. In order to trace it let us examine the events that took place in Italy toward the middle of the century.

The Venetian School

THE colonization of the musical world by the peregrinating sons of Hainaut, Brabant, Picardy, and other northern provinces reached its height when the generation of Gombert entered the scene of musical history. Flemish musicians settled down in many of the important cities of Europe, and the appearance of highly organized musical knowledge and skilled craftsmanship among the musical "amateurs" of other countries wrought profound changes in the destiny of the whole art of music. Florence, Ferrara, Venice, and Rome; Constance, Vienna, Munich, and Prague; Madrid, Paris, and London, all greeted these newcomers with admiration and envy, but none offered them a more gratifying field of action than the Queen of the Adriatic.

The proud Venetian Republic, its glamorous city amply protected against any invasion, kept aloof from the intense party strife that dominated the rest of Italy. It concluded alliances, but usually for ephemeral purposes and at a high price. The fifteenth century had brought the city-state, nominally a republic but in reality a close-knit oligarchy, to the height of its success in world commerce, with a fleet of hundreds of ocean vessels and a powerful navy; but the end of the century saw the maritime power of Venice waning with the steady advance of the Turks, and the sixteenth century, with its conflicts with France and the Emperor Charles V, left her holding but a part of her possessions.

Orient and Occident met in Venice and created a remarkable culture which we admire highly, but which is difficult for us to penetrate because of the city's unique history; the men who made it are so different from other Italians, they seem to belong to another race with a philosophy and a world outlook of their own. The philosophers of Tuscany, animated by a desire to create an ideal state, lost themselves in profound thought and plans which they could never realize. The Venetians possessed a superbly organized state, but, while they took great care in promoting the affairs of their government, they took its existence as a matter of course. This is the reason for their internal peace and personal happiness, and for the brilliant, dazzling beauty of their art, to which their acquaintance with the Orient added an exotic touch. But for the same reason they did not know the struggle for the highest values of human intellectual life which their Tuscan brethren experienced. Tuscany gave humanity eternal works of art; Venice was not sufficiently serious often to reach those depths: instead it made the world happy. Before abdicating its empire, the old city still had enough power to create a second empire in the domain of art. Bellini, Giorgione, Titian, Veronese, and Tintoretto radiate glowing colors, and Willaert, de Rore, Vicentino, and Monteverdi move with their equally colorful music before this second empire sinks to make the gilded city the bacchanal of Europe, the city of princes, adventurers, and courtesans who hold there an eternal carnival.

St. Mark's, the chapel of the doges, was the center of the political and religious life of Venice; here also its musical life converged. The clergy of St. Mark's was directly responsible to the doge and not to an ecclesiastical authority; thus even the choirmasters and organists of the church were intimately bound to the cultural and political development of Venice. Although several of St. Mark's organists are known from as early as the fourteenth century, the oldest choirmaster mentioned in its archives was Pietro de Fossis, appointed in 1491 and remaining in service until 1526. Most historians think that this musician was a Fleming by the name of Des Fossés or Van der Gracht. While the Flemish influence was prominent during the incumbency of de Fossis, it became decisive with the arrival of Adriaan Willaert (born between 1480 and 1490, died in 1562). Appointed in 1527 to the position of choirmaster at St. Mark's, this pupil of Jean Mouton (and perhaps of Josquin himself) spent the rest of his life, affectionately called Messer Adriano, among the admiring Venetians. Through his enormous influence on his pupils—an influence comparable only to that of Ockeghem, but with more momentous consequences—he established the so-called Venetian school, which flourished for a century and a half, creating the language and forms of pure instrumental music and transmitting the technique of polyphonic composition to the seventeenth century. The notable achievement of Willaert's immediate school was the madrigal, the most characteristic musical genre of the late Renaissance. Whether it is Willaert himself, his compatriots Arcadelt and Verdelot, or the Italian Festa who may claim the "first" madrigal is impossible to ascertain; but the first madrigals, appearing in the early thirties, started a veritable deluge of such compositions. The madrigal was not, of course, the invention of an individual, yet, with slight exaggeration, one may say that when the first northern composer took an Italian lyric poem and set it to music, the main step toward the creation of the madrigal was accomplished. Thus the madrigal arose in various Italian cities almost at the same time, and its appearance coincided with the height of the influx of Flemish and Franco-Flemish musicians to Italy.

In the final analysis, the madrigal—at least musically—represents an artistically ennobled form of the colorful and flourishing frottola and villanella literature of the turn of the century, and this is one of the reasons for the eminence of Venetian madrigalists, for Venice seems to have been the chief seat of frottola composition. From 1504 to 1514 Petrucci published eleven books containing over six hundred pieces. The original frottole were little songs which were born and died like butterflies; they were lively, graceful, and attractive, but lived for only a short while. The Netherlanders, accustomed to the use of cantus firmi and to the skillful combination of several contrapuntal parts, were intrigued by such a free and unconstricted art. The earlier frottole were simple dancelike homophonic compositions, but in the later volumes of Petrucci one may already recognize the influence of the north. These later frottole exhibit a tendency toward more independent part writing in the upper parts; and the superb compositions of Michele Pesenti, Veronese composer active about 1500, and those of Josquin and some of the early Flemish visitors, lead directly to the madrigal. The merger of the two musical conceptions, to which we must add the influence of the French chanson, took place in a remarkably short time. The madrigal constitutes one of the most beautiful expressions of humanism, the carefully declaimed text of which was faithfully reflected in the accompanying music. Without relying too much on superficial realistic tone painting, this music reaches amazing perfection of text interpretation; subtle shadings translate the most delicate ranges of the emotional scale, leading to entirely new musical effects. The composers oppose and combine homophonic and polyphonic writing, whittle the rhyme to infinitely delicate points by ingenious use of the *chroma* (the sixteenth note or semiquaver)—whence the name "chromatic madrigal"—and carry the possibilities of diatonic melody and harmony to its limits, resulting toward the middle of the century in a complete reorientation and an audacious experimenting in the use of chromatic (this time meaning successive half-tone steps) melody and harmony.

The exact nature of the madrigal has never been closely defined, but one thing is certain, that the Renaissance madrigal had very little in common with the Florentine madrigal of the trecento. This new madrigal used texts which belonged to all varieties of lyric poetry, and the literary form expressly called madrigal constituted a very small part of the output. The madrigals of the mid-sixteenth century show a verse structure of great freedom. They are rather short irregular lyrics, in which neither the amatory nor the complimentary tone seems to be obligatory, although most definitions call the madrigal "a short lyrical poem of amatory character." The number of verses varies from six to sixteen, containing from seven to eleven syllables. After Gian Giorgio Trissino (1478–1550), author of the first Italian poetic drama written according to classical rules, included blank verse in his *Sophonisba* (1515), the new type of free poetry was taken up by his fellows and found fertile expression in madrigal texts, providing the capricious musical nature of the madrigal with a congenial poetic form. The matter of rhyme now depended entirely on the pleasure of the poet and composer; some lines in the middle of the composition might rhyme, while others were entirely free. It was customary to leave the first line outside of the rhythmic scheme. The first madrigals were exceedingly well received, and it was not long before a legion of composers was turning out hundreds of volumes of madrigals. Even the serious and severe church composers, among them Palestrina, could not escape their infectious popularity.

Besides the colorful madrigal, the Venetians composed not only grandiose motets for antiphonal choirs, which opened up new territories for sonority and euphony, but independent instrumental music as well. Willaert is supposed to have conceived the idea of using choirs placed opposite each other in the apses of the nave, after observing the two organs in St. Mark's; [15] but antiphonal choirs were by no means unknown in the earliest times, though Willaert and his pupils used them with especially felicitous skill and effect. Similarly, we cannot assign the invention of independent instrumental music to the Venetian masters, although they were the chief representatives of its rapidly growing literature. Emulating the vivid and graceful vocal style of the French chanson and the early French instrumental transcriptions, first published by Attaingnant in 1530, they developed the *canzone,* hereafter an instrumental piece, one of the chief ancestors of all our instrumental forms. These innovations and developments were the work of an international group of musicians, Flemish, French, and Italian, but they all stem from Willaert, whose works display a flair for color, a wonderful sense for modulation and euphony, and a consummately flexible technique of expressive musical setting.

Willaert's disciples were legion. Among them we find many Italians, but several Netherlanders should first be mentioned. There were Jachet Buus (d. 1565), second organist of St. Mark's and one of the most important composers of *ricercari*, instrumental counterparts of the motet which "searched and researched for the theme" and by exploring the polyphonic-thematic possibilities of pure instrumental writing led to fugal constructions; [16] Jachet van Berchem, a somewhat obscure Flemish organist of Ferrara whose fine madrigals belong to the best of the early period; and, most important of all, Cipriano de Rore (1516-1565), one of the most subtle and refined musicians of his time and an inspired leader of the madrigalists. His works crown the efforts of the earlier madrigal composers and are the model creations of the Italo-Flemish madrigal. De Rore, who was much admired and whose madrigals were even published in the form of a "study score" as early as 1577—a procedure unknown before—closes the ranks of the Netherlanders in Italy. With him ends the northern hegemony, giving way to the ascending, rejuvenated genius of Italy.

The Italo-Flemish Style

THE Franco-Flemish technique of composition still held sway, but the spirit of music began to be Italianized, and the last phase of Netherlandish musical history cannot be separated from that of Italy. The crosscurrents of musical development present a picture of extraordinary complexity. The prevailing ideas are still of Flemish origin, but they cannot be carried out in the north: they seem to need the Italian sun, and old and new are twisted in a seemingly inextricable maze. Although bound to the old traditions, the composers, reawakened to the importance of the text, were ready to sacrifice some of the riches of polyphonic voice leading for the sake of a true musical rendition of the words. Imitation and counterpoint lost some of their weight and value while the words rose to eminence. This was the era of *a cappella* art. The humanistic ideal was to limit the formal musical element in order to lend more expression to the words and their meaning, to create a more immediate and lively effect.

The composer was now confronted with different tasks. Formerly, employing all the contrapuntal skill at his command, he had constructed his parts by developing them over a suitable cantus firmus, which, with its coun-

terpoints, furnished the form and the support for the words, and which was
not changed even if the accompanying words changed. But now composers
began to insist that the role of music was to bring out and render musically
the ideas, passions, and effects inherent in the words, and henceforth vocal
music was supposed to derive the laws of its development more from the
words than from the cantus firmus. The new orientation, the truly Renais-
sancelike, perfectly balanced expressive style, unlike the earlier technical skill
of the Flemings and the emotional outbursts of an Obrecht, but faithfully
observing the time-honored laws of music and poetry, had once again come
from the north. It started with Josquin and his school, branched off with
Gombert to Spain, and reached Italy through Franco-Flemish and Spanish
composers. Adrien Petit Coclicus (c. 1500–1563), a pupil of Josquin, was the
first person to publish, in a work entitled *Musica Reservata* (1552), compositions in the new style, which he explicitly attributed to his master.

Josquin left no literary legacy; Coclicus tells us that "the master did not
teach from books." But all chroniclers attribute the "invention" of the *musica
reservata* to the great Fleming and call him the "painter" of music. Thus the
Nuremberg printer, Johannes Otto, in the preface to the second volume of
his *Novi Operis Musici* (1538), in speaking of the motet *Huc Me Sidero* remarks that no painter could express with the aid of pencil and colors the
suffering face of the Crucified more convincingly than Josquin with his
music. But the musical composition alone was not capable of transmitting
the reservata qualities; these had to be interpreted by the performance. Consequently the musica reservata was not only a new style of composition but
also a new style of performance, and the two factors were inseparable. All
the great composers from Josquin to the Gabrielis and Monteverdi were inspired by this double task, which grew to pervade every particle of their
music, and which finally passed over from the calm atmosphere of the
Renaissance into the unruly world of the baroque.

The reservata is a product of the Renaissance, the result of humanistic
impulses. Though started by a Fleming and first practiced by Franco-
Flemish composers, it received its final shape and elaboration in Italy. The
logical development of systematic continuous imitation—at first a purely
technical element—now turned to a close observance of the quality of the
text and soon went beyond the syntactic and musical logic, endeavoring to
interpret the ideas expressed in the words. The fuguelike imitations, the
question-answer game of the parts, established a close alliance with the words,
and in the disciples of Josquin this led to the pure *a cappella* art. The other
characteristic of the reservata, the emphasis on musical interpretation, on
expression, on the drawing out of the *affects*, was, as we have remarked, of
equal importance. In fact, the great prestige and popularity of the Flemish

singers, which reached its zenith toward the middle of the century, was due to their incomparable ability to perform in the reservata manner. This rich phase of musical history, to the understanding of which the reservata style evidently affords the key, still needs a great deal of research and elucidation.

We are not even sure of the meaning of the term "musica reservata." It seems to have a double meaning: partly a dignified reservation against the excesses of the older Flemish style, partly the observation of established rules; but it is not unlikely that this new style was "reserved" to those connoisseurs who were able to appreciate the subtle and manifold details not discernible in the notation itself but which were the result of skillful interpretation. The great importance of the interpretation will not surprise us if we remember that the improvisatory music making of the medieval *déchant* was still a living force in the fifteenth century. We see it in the so-called *cantus a mente* or *cantus super librum,* that is, "mental" or improvised song over a cantus firmus, as described by Tinctoris. In fact, with the rising instrumental litera- ture, especially organ transcriptions, there is a veritable wave of free instru- mental "coloration," by which term was meant the instrumental embellish- ment of simple melodies, not unlike the coloratura practice of the operatic aria, largely improvised in its first stage. At this point we become aware of the curious fact that the freely ornamented musical style, derived from in- strumental sources, gaining steadily, coincides with the rising *a cappella* style.

The musica reservata established, then, a definite system of musical aesthet- ics based on the interpretation of affects, or, as the Italians call it, the *affetti*. The term is not a familiar expression in modern English, but we cannot very well replace it; fortunately it has been accepted and adopted by psychologists as a term designating feeling, emotion, and desire, with an implication of the importance of these factors in determining thought and conduct. In more simple form we may say that the reservata demanded jolly music for a jolly text and sad music to accompany sad words. This truly Renaissance musical system discovered that music is a language which, like any other, follows certain rules: those that govern the parts of speech, in this particular case govern the parts of melody. The parts of melody included the so-called colo- ratura and embellishment elements as an integral part of speech, or melody; consequently their role was not that of mere embellishment. To the Renais- sance musician those little twists and turns had a profound meaning, although it is difficult for us to see or hear them otherwise than as intarsia, but here again we must remember the nature of Renaissance art, its loving care for the judicious elaboration of every detail. One more generation in musical style and the chromatic alterations, the dynamic outbursts of the double choirs, will be understood by all as deeply moving musical language. But with this music of the last few decades of the sixteenth century we enter into a new domain. For this music carries the affects toward the dramatic, the intensity of emotion becomes almost perceptible to the eye, and, indeed, the way for the music drama is opened.

The Final Synthesis of Polyphony
Catholic Reform and Counter Reformation

THE approach to this new period of musical history is defined with unusual clarity. The composers who belonged to Gombert's generation—including such leading masters as Willaert, Crecquillon, Clemens, Arcadelt, de Rore and their German, French, and Spanish contemporaries, Senfl, Sermisy, Janequin, Morales, Cabezón, and Luis Milan—all died in the sixth decade of the century which saw the culmination of internationalized Flemish art in the era of Roland de Lassus (c. 1532–1594). The final synthesis of polyphony, the final triumph and glory of centuries of Burgundian, Flemish, and Franco-Flemish music, now basking in the warm sunshine of Italian art, was the work of this great Netherlander and his countryman, Philippe de Monte (1521–1603).

De Monte, born in Malines, spent some time in Italy, perhaps served in the Chapel Royal in London, and thereafter returned to Naples and Rome, ending his career in the service of the Habsburgs in Vienna and Prague. Like his great Italian contemporary, Palestrina, he followed one central problem, worshiped one ideal of style, although, unlike Palestrina, he was active in both sacred and secular musical composition. It was the madrigal which fascinated him, and not only the twelve hundred odd madrigals that are extant among his works but some three hundred Masses and motets testify to this. While de Monte's madrigals are not inferior to the finest works of the Italian madrigalists, they represent an independent species, more polyphonic, more unified and close-knit than the Italian compositions. His Masses and motets are enriched with all the refinements that the madrigal literature had produced. His technical equipment is phenomenal, unsurpassed by that of either Palestrina or Lassus; but with all his contrapuntal mastery he is always able to adhere to a simple and artistic style which finds suitable expression for every word.

Both de Monte and Lassus visited Italy in their early youth and were captivated by the richly colored world of secular music. Their earlier works, madrigals, chansons, and popular songs, reflect the deep impressions this country made on them. But while the Italian influence was strong enough to make Lassus (*de là-dessus*) change his name into the Italian form, Orlando di Lasso, his art, like de Monte's, remained fundamentally "Netherlandish"; and it is in these masters, and not in Palestrina, that the great period which had begun with the Burgundian Dufay reached its apex. The pure Netherlandish style was carried on by a whole group of Franco-Flemish musicians living in Germanic lands who, by retaining the generations-old traditions of their art, constituted a last group of Netherlandish composers. Jacobus de Kerle (c. 1531–1591), Jacob Regnart (c. 1540–1590), Jean de Clève (1529–1582), François Sale (active in the last third of the century), all were eminent masters whose many publications display all the virtues of the great polyphonic school. In church music, however, the leadership was now definitely in the hands of Rome; the Holy See attracted the great creative artists of all Europe, uniting them in the spirit of the Catholic Reform. Thus it is that when discussing the life and works of these masters, especially Lassus and his Italian colleague, Palestrina, we must first of all realize that they lived and created their works under the strong influence of the Counter Reformation and the enormous pressure of the spiritual upheaval which plunged the Netherlands and France into religious civil wars and caused the convocation of the Council of Trent. This influence was faithfully reflected in their art as it was in all arts and letters of the second half of the century, and impressed a truly international stamp especially on church music. Frenchmen, Netherlanders, and Italians, as well as Spaniards and Poles, all were part of this universal European musical culture which had practically no geographical subdivisions.

The Catholic Reformation was of a different nature from the Protestant movement. The only similarity between the two lay in their attack upon the corruption prevalent among the clergy and their desire for piety and Christian fortitude. After 1521 compromise between Luther's adherents and the Catholic Church, although it was constantly attempted and desired, became impossible, henceforth the two faiths confronted each other with fire and steel until the end of the Thirty Years' War. It is popularly assumed that the Catholic Reform was an answer to the great moral uprising which produced Protestantism, and Protestants have sometimes taken credit to themselves for the reforms in the Catholic Church which by the end of the sixteenth century had done away with many of the abuses against which councils and diets had so long been protesting. But the movement had in reality started long before Luther's rebellion. Throughout the fifteenth century and earlier, a constantly increasing number of men had called for a restoration of Christian life, and the movement, which had many facets, resulted in a great revival of mysticism and of asceticism, although it had little effect on the secular clergy and the papal court. The reform party in the Church was steadily growing, and carried on a quiet but effective work, founding new religious orders for the spread of evangelical life among the people. Thus the incentive for reform was present when the expansion of Protestantism added to it new fuel and a militant hue.

In 1534 the Catholic Reform entered upon a new stage of development;

Paul III assumed the pontificate and Ignatius Loyola and six companions took their vows. It is sometimes said that the Jesuits were founded to combat the Reformation, but this is erroneous; all these were independent events resulting from the triumph of the reformers at the head of the Church and from the renewed mystical movement which had begun in the fifteenth century. In 1545, after long delays, the Council of Trent was convened by Paul III and codified the results of the Catholic Reform. The enunciations of the Council of Trent, which lasted with several interruptions from 1545 to 1563, were carried to all religious communities of the far-flung Catholic world and yielded tangible results. The worship and the law of the Church were standardized and the papal government and that of the religious orders entirely reorganized. The clergy came under close scrutiny and was infused with the austere and humble spirit which had characterized it in the early centuries of Christendom and again since post-Tridentine times. The Jesuits were now the chief aides of the Holy See in diffusing education and inculcating obedience to the papacy, and by the end of the century they, together with other missionaries, had done what arms had not been able to do: they regained the wavering states of Austria, Poland, Hungary, the southern Low Countries, and parts of Germany and Bohemia for the Catholic faith. This more than anything else gained them the enmity of the Protestant world.

The spirit of the Catholic Reform soon found expression in arts and letters. In literature we find among the first examples of a restored church thought the *Jerusalem Delivered* of Torquato Tasso (1544-1595), which, with its topic—the first crusade—and several reactionary traits in its presentation, recalled the tone of medieval art. In music, so closely attached to the liturgy of the Church, the new spirit was naturally strongly reflected. When Pope Pius IV ordered the continuation of the Council of Trent, originally called to deliberate over matters touching liturgy and music, grave complaints were aired about the state of church music. Humanists and churchmen alike complained of the neglect of the text, the bad enunciation and irreverent attitude of singers, the presence of a secular spirit in the music, and the overabundance of instruments in the services. The deliberations became animated when certain zealous adherents of the Catholic Reform wanted to eliminate polyphonic music altogether while others eagerly defended the great art built up by centuries of musical culture. The decision, reached in the twenty-second session, September 17, 1562, is not a clear document and does not contain such sweeping resolutions as the following generations attached to it. It merely recommended the avoidance of everything that was inconsistent with the dignity of the service. The nineteenth-century romantic revival created the story, still universally accepted, that Palestrina was responsible for the salvation of church music because, at the request of Cardinal Borromeo, who with seven other cardinals had been especially delegated to supervise the execution of the Tridentine decrees, he composed a Mass dedicated to Pope Marcellus, demonstrating so ably and clearly the virtues of pure church music that the commission decided in favor of polyphonic music in the Church. In the light of modern research this becomes a mere legend. If we must find a "savior of church music," we shall find him rather in the Flemish composer Jacobus de Kerle (c. 1531–1591).[17]

As in the case of the Catholic Reform, which antedated the Counter Reformation caused by the Protestant uprising, the reform movement in church music started before the Tridentine resolutions. The driving force in the committee of cardinals was the Bishop of Augsburg, Otto Cardinal Truchsess, who had resided in Rome for some time. It was through his initiative that Jacobus de Kerle, the cardinal's choirmaster, was commissioned to compose several works for the Council. These were written in a clear and moderate style, uniting homophony with polyphony, and were performed repeatedly during the services at the Council, winning great admiration and commendation from the assembled churchmen. The activities of Cardinal Truchsess, which were carried on with papal approval (his correspondence, furthermore, shows that his was not the only establishment working for a regeneration of church music) together with the universal acceptance of Kerle's *Preces Speciales* by the Council, indicate that the problems of church music had been clarified and practically settled before the final deliberations took place. This explains also the lack of details and the general admonitory tone of the resolutions of the twenty-second session. The twenty-fourth session, held on November 11, then emphasized the positive value of liturgic music, leaving specific regulations in the hands of the local hierarchy. The much-debated question concerning the use of chanson tunes for cantus firmi did not even enter the deliberations, and the practice was continued, except that Palestrina and some of his colleagues later refrained from naming the original tune, calling their Masses *sine nomine*.

If carried out according to older interpretations, the Tridentine reform would have affected adversely church music, which was not only a prodigious treasure of sacred art, but an art permeated by that humanistic spirit which characterized the liturgic reform. The freely flowing expressive polyphony, reacting to the most subtle rhythmical changes with a facility which our modern notation is not even capable of indicating, represented the ideal of church music. With the works of de Monte, Lassus, and Palestrina, vocal polyphony reached its greatest height, a perfect equilibrium between counterpoint and harmony, a style in which the individual parts move about in perfect freedom though always jealously observing the rights of harmony.

We have discussed the merits of Philippe de Monte, the first member of this illustrious trio; the remaining two masters require, however, even more attention, because Lassus was the most versatile and universal composer of the sixteenth century, while Palestrina's very name stands as the symbol of Catholic church music, and of "old" music in general.

Born in 1532 (1530?) in Mons, the territory which gave to music a host of great composers, among them Dufay and Josquin, Lassus started his career in the usual manner as a choirboy in his native town. Ferdinand Gonzaga, Viceroy of Sicily and general of the Netherlands armies of Charles V, took the boy with him to Sicily and Milan. When young Lassus lost his soprano voice, he left the service of the Gonzagas, changing masters frequently until, in 1553, he assumed the position of choirmaster of the Lateran. Here he remained only until December, 1554, resuming his journeys in the company of Cesare Brancaccio, a Neapolitan nobleman, traveling through France, the Low Countries, and perhaps England, and finally settling down in Antwerp in 1555, where he soon became the leader of musical life. It was not long before his fame spread to other countries and Duke Albrecht V of Bavaria invited him to come to Munich. Lassus accepted the position and remained in the service of the Bavarian dukes until his death, June 14, 1594.

Lassus became a child of the Italian Renaissance; during the first two-thirds of his life he was much more receptive to Latin, and particularly to Italian, influences than to anything else. Besides the Italian traits which carried him from artistic poetry to erotic stories and the *commedia dell' arte* as well as to macaronic verse, there is a strong French current, which is apparent both in the man himself and in his art. The combination of Germanic earnestness, profundity, and artistic traditions with the secular world of the Italian Renaissance created his style, to which was added a goodly share of Gallic wit. In his old age the spirit of the Counter Reformation made him abandon the Renaissance literature of which he was so fond, and he turned to poetry that voiced the sentiments of his Church.

The spiritual madrigal now took the place of the erotic secular song. The new church thought asserted itself more and more. In 1568 Gabriel Fiamma, canon at the Lateran (later Bishop of Chioggia), published his *Rime Spirituali,* the preface of which served as a manifesto: "In our language there is an almost infinite amount of poetry, almost all amorous, which fact seems to me quite insupportable and a great mistake. I have therefore redirected Tuscan poetry, in as lofty a manner as possible, towards virtue and towards God." Lassus set to music several of the *rime,* which are all permeated by a profound, submissive, and unearthly spirit. There is no trace of the former elegant and perfumed eroticism; these are penitential Psalms. The old Netherlander here denies his past, and damns the mistakes of youth and ignorance. We are dust, and death follows upon our heels: a welcome death because it will unite us with God, to seek whose mercy should be our main thought.

Beginning with 1576, Lassus abandoned the musical setting of madrigals and by 1585 we see a complete change in his attitude. The aging master still composed works that were entitled madrigals, but they were of the spiritual type. When casting about for texts, he now turned to Italian Psalm translations and to a new lyrical genre, the so-called *lagrime,* or "tears." It is said that one of Dürer's pictures in which the Madonna's tears were depicted with astounding realism inspired this new poetry. Tasso was among the first to contribute to the new literary genre with *Le Lagrime di Maria Vergine,* but the founder of the *lagrime* poetry seems to have been Luigi Tansillo (d. 1568), whose unfinished *Le Lagrime di San Pietro* was published in 1585 and attracted Lassus's attention. The twenty works that he composed on Tansillo's poems together with a Latin motet were his last creations. They were dedicated to the pope by a devout old artist who had made peace with the world, who was to such a degree concerned with the hereafter that a few years before his death his mind was clouded for a period and he spent his days in idleness, sunk in deep melancholy.

The works of Lassus, some two thousand compositions,[18] embrace every form of music of his period and show the composer equally at home in all of them. The lovesick complaint of the Italian madrigal, the subtle delicacy of the French chanson, the robust quality of the German part song are each expressed as from the heart of an Italian, a Frenchman, a German. Yet this Netherlander rose in his Psalms to majestic heights, conveyed in his Masses and other liturgic pieces the serene mood of the liturgy, and spoke in his motets with the voice of one deeply wrapped in awe-inspiring mysticism. Lassus displayed remarkable literary taste and a sense of humor given to few people. Within the wide range of his forms of composition variety abounds, and one can hardly speak of a "Lassus style," as no two of his works resemble each other. All of them have, however, one common characteristic: a consummate and miraculous mastery of the technique of musical composition, expressed with equal brilliance in the little vulgar villanelle and the most complicated cantus firmus Mass.

Withal, Lassus was not a revolutionary; on the contrary, he cherished the great traditions of his Flemish ancestors and liked to exhibit his great prowess in counterpoint. He was acquainted with all contemporary tendencies and made use of new styles and devices, but he did not follow any of them all the way, preferring a certain conservatism. While ranking among the best that the era produced, his madrigals did not quite reach the height marked by the great Italian madrigalists or by de Monte, but his chansons crown the development of the French Renaissance in that field; his Masses do not always match the grace and exquisite tenderness of those of Palestrina, although he can speak the great Roman's language with such fidelity that one cannot tell them apart; but in the motet he had no peers. His *oeuvre* is a synthesis of what two hundred years of musical culture had produced, a synthesis of such convincing strength and plastic beauty as the history of music has since experienced but once again in the art of Mozart.

Palestrina

GIOVANNI PIERLUIGI, called da Palestrina from the place of his birth (the old Roman Praeneste), born in 1525 (1526?), spent his apprenticeship in the choir of the Roman basilica Santa Maria Maggiore and then returned to his native town, where he occupied the position of choirmaster and organist for seven years. Soon after the titular Bishop of Palestrina, Cardinal Giulio del Monte, had been elected pope, assuming the name of Julius III, the choirmaster was made *magister puerorum* of the Capella Julia at St. Peter's. As a token of gratitude, Palestrina dedicated the first printed edition of his works, a volume of Masses, to the pope (1554). This volume was followed in a year by his first collection of madrigals. His august patron made him thereafter a member of the Sistine Chapel choir, although as a married man he was not eligible to this quasi-ecclesiastic position. Pope Paul IV, who succeeded Julius III (Marcellus II, the immediate follower of Julius, reigned for only twenty-one days), found this inadmissible and dismissed Palestrina together with two other married singers. Intrigue, privation, and sickness clouded his life for years, and although an appointment at St. John's afforded him a precarious existence, Palestrina resigned to return to the church of his childhood, Santa Maria Maggiore. Here he stayed until 1571, when he finally assumed the leadership of the Capella Julia, a position he held until his death. Pope Sixtus V intended to make him a member of the Sistine Chapel, but the clerical members were still opposed to the appointment of a married man. He received, however, the honorary title of *maestro compositore* to the papal chapel, a title awarded only once again in later years, to Felice Anerio. This honor was a recognition of the eminently liturgic quality of his music, which conformed admirably to the ideals promulgated by the Council of Trent. Besides his official position, in the last period of his life, Palestrina occupied several offices in Rome, but he declined invitations offering him good positions in Vienna and Mantua. The death of his wife (1580) plunged him into such despair that he was ready to give up the world and take orders. Things took a different turn, however, and, after marrying again (1581), he lived in relative security, his last years being devoted to producing an impressive number of masterpieces. His death in 1594 was mourned by all Rome; although the account of his last hours and his burial given by his biographer Baini is purely fictitious, it is certain that he was buried with great honor in one of the side chapels of the old Church of St. Peter's, the plate of his coffin bearing the inscription "Prince of Music."

With the exception of a few madrigals, Palestrina's whole output was sacred music, and even most of the madrigals were entirely spiritual compositions. Secular music had no place in this art. Palestrina's school grew out of the Church; it was the flowering of a new religiosity, and it created a sacred art based on the Catholic principles of universality. But universality excludes subjectivism and nationalism; it even bars any temporal demarcation. Such universality represents the final divorce from the earthly, and the essence of the medieval world outlook, the metacenter of which is not on earth but in the beyond, returns in this art. It is moved by the same spirit which prompted Dante—well acquainted with the vicissitudes of actual earthly existence—to present man in hell, in purgatory, and in paradise, but not on earth. In the eyes of many, church music ended with Palestrina and became history, and less than twenty years after his death the "Palestrina style" was codified in Pietro Cerone's *El Melopeo y Maestro* (Naples, 1613). At about the same time his figure began to be surrounded with awe and mystery and he became a legendary saint of music. The less people knew about him—and the Palestrina style had to be rediscovered in the nineteenth century—the more they exalted him. Then came the romantic revival of Palestrina, inaugurated by the great biography by Giuseppe Baini (1775-1844) which appeared in 1828. Baini's biography displays romantic attachment to a heroic past, and while it contains interesting material concerning sixteenth-century music and musical life, obviously compiled by a learned man, the biographical part proper is highly unreliable, and affectionately and romantically colored to a marked degree.

The German champion of the Palestrina revival was Justus Thibaut (1774-1840), a keen-minded Heidelberg jurist who sought rest from the fatigue of his profession in the cult of the *a cappella* art of the sixteenth century. Thibaut linked Palestrina's style with the Latin liturgic language, a language which was no longer the living tongue of any man but which for this very reason evoked a certain sense of eternity. "True spiritual music is neither too varied nor too passionate, because its subject is supernatural. It presupposes, then, a profound, calm, introspective, and pure mood and attitude, and a staunch moral power capable of carrying and upholding the sublime and of resisting earthly passions." [19] The further we advance into the nineteenth century the more obvious it is that Palestrina has become a mythical being, admired and venerated by musicians and music lovers, although familiarity with his works is usually restricted to an acquaintance with the Marcellus Mass and a handful of spurious works (*O Bone Jesu, Tenebrae Factae Sunt,* etc.) which have been definitely attributed to Marcantonio Ingegneri (c. 1545-1592), the bold and radical madrigalist who was Monteverdi's teacher. A few excerpts from the writings of musicians whom we consider typical representatives of their period will convince us that even they heard this music through the legend connected with it. (The italics are ours.)

The hearing of a work of Palestrina produces something analogous to the reading of one of the grand pages of Bossuet. *Nothing is noticed as you go along,* but at the end of the road you find yourself carried to prodigious heights. . . . *It is this absence of visible means,* of worldly artifices, of vain coquetry, that renders the highest works absolutely inimitable.[20]

These lines were written by Gounod, the famed composer of *Faust*. How illusory and unconvincing Gounod's remarks are is illustrated by his own liturgic works, abounding in "visible means." The creator of the modern musical version of the mystery of the Holy Grail, Richard Wagner, after due fulminations against the Jesuits and Italian opera, also declares that when listening to this music "we get a picture almost as timeless as it is spaceless; a spiritual revelation throughout, that rouses unspeakable emotions as it brings us nearer than aught else to a notion of the essential nature of Religion, *free from all fictional dogmatic conception.*" [21]

Palestrina's art betrays the spirit of the Counter Reformation; he served the new church current. In his exclusive attachment to church music he represented an attitude which the Renaissance had not known. Thus Palestrina became the creator of a church style par excellence; he was the "first Catholic church musician." His art did not originate in the atmosphere which saw the rise of the classical style of architecture, sculpture, and painting, nor did it grow out of the soil of humanism and Renaissance. On the contrary, it has much closer ties with the new idiom which the historians of art call "manneristic," a style which resulted from the spirit of the Counter Reformation. Mannerism was not a sterile eclecticism, but rather an excessive adherence to a newly found mood of meditation, awe, and elation; a new religious consciousness before which the world-conquering, optimistic will of the Renaissance was compelled to retire to the background. One might say that the new world outlook was nowhere so purely expressed as in the music of Palestrina, but the manneristic spirit did not lead to artificiality in his works as it did in the fine arts. His tonal language, in its devout, incense-diffusing softness, in its colorful plenitude, is that of manneristic spiritualism. The fact that Palestrina even carried his spiritualism to the point of one-sidedness seems to call for a fundamental re-examination of his classical position.

Palestrina's art does not represent the culmination of music in the age of the Renaissance. As early as 1834 Carl von Winterfeld (1784–1852), author of a work which is a model of scholarship and judicious and careful interpretation undimmed in importance by the passage of a hundred years, remarked that Andrea and Giovanni Gabrieli, Palestrina's Venetian contemporaries, should at least share the honors with him, if indeed they were not fully his equals.[22] With our present knowledge of musical history, it is clear that the great body of Burgundian, Flemish, and Franco-Flemish choral polyphony of the fifteenth and sixteenth centuries culminated in the work of de Monte and Lassus. Approached from whatever angle, Palestrina will prove to occupy a more or less peripheral position; he stands at the end of a period, but even this end is represented in him only partly. We have mentioned the far-reaching consequences that were attached to Palestrina's Marcellus Mass; a similar misunderstanding surrounds his participation in the reform of the Gradual. Pope Gregory XIII undertook the great task of the reformation of Gregorian music, and Palestrina, associating himself with the able choirmaster of the Lateran, Annibale Zoilo (d. 1592), set out to revise the melodies. Several reasons, among them objections from the Spanish hierarchy, made him abandon his plans. The revision, finally printed in 1614 as the famous *Editio Medicea,* was in reality the work of Felice Anerio and Francesco Suriano. The great interest in Palestrina which started with the appearance of Baini's biography soon enveloped everything with the master's glamour, and the Medici edition was considered the true Palestrinian revision of Gregorian chant although it represented a misconception of plain chant with maimed and disfigured melodies. Not until the Solesmes Benedictines presented the results of their gigantic research work were the older editions based on the *Medicea* discarded.

This revising of Palestrina's position in no way lessens his merits or his importance; he remains one of the greatest geniuses who have graced the arts and letters of all time. But in discussing the composer Palestrina apart from the "Prince of Music," it becomes evident that appreciation of his style—considered unique and isolated until the advent of modern musicological research—requires reorientation as did his historical role.

Palestrina had evidently a wide acquaintance with the works of his Flemish predecessors, and in his "l'Homme Armé Mass" (composed long *after* the supposed Tridentine prohibition of chanson Masses) demonstrated that there was no secret or problem in the intricate polyphonic art of his spiritual ancestors that he could not rival with consummate skill. In spite of contrapuntal complexity his setting is transparent and ethereally crystalline, his declamation fluent and pregnant. He was also fully acquainted with the achievements of the other camp, the dazzling art of the Venetians, and made use of their innovations. However, this musical priest of the Church restricted all the new material that came to him to such elements as could be safely used in a strictly diatonic, modal church style. Very few of his contemporaries, and they only occasionally, could rise to the plastic and monumental yet tender and seraphic beauty of his Masses. In the motet he must yield the crown to Lassus, and, while the great innovations of the times did not leave him untouched, the tone of his madrigals is too conservative; he does not achieve the vivacity and charm of Marenzio's melodies and rhythms, or the indescribable suavity of de Monte.

In the eyes of the musicians of modern times Palestrina's music seems to exclude human emotions; "nothing is noticed as you go along," Gounod remarks of it; and Wagner considers it "free from all dogmatic conceptional fiction." But these observations speak of the music of the legendary church musician and not of the music which fathoms human sentiments and emotions. If we listen to the cycle of motets drawn from the Song of Songs, we are overwhelmed by the glow of passionate feeling which emanates from them. The Mass *Assumpta Est Maria* stirs us by its mysterious mood; the unbridled jubilation of the motets *Viri Galilei* and *Surge Illuminare Jerusalem* disperse the clouds of doubt and worry, while the sad chords of *Peccantem Me Quotidie* plunge us into deep mourning. No, the mythical Roman was not the creator of anemic, expressionless and motionless church music; his works, glowing with dogmatic faith and passion, show a man of the coming baroque. No one said with more ardent conviction, *Credo in unam Sanctam Ecclesiam Catholicam*. So strong was his feeling that he signed his madrigals with the pseudonym Gianetto, for he thought that his calling as the high priest of sacred art did not permit him to lend his name to secular lyrics, however innocent, even though it was customary for the most distinguished church musicians—among them ordained priests—to set and publish love lyrics.

Thus whatever we behold in this strong-willed music, we not only "notice as we go along" the supposedly missing human feelings in abundance, but realize that Palestrina's church music, like that of de Monte and Lassus, could not have been created without the madrigal. What the slightly self-conscious Gianetto could not achieve in his madrigals the composer of the *Canticum Canticorum* brought to fruition. One glance at the first volume of Masses will bear out this contention; they are stiff and academic. But when Palestrina became acquainted with the "wordly artifices and vain coquetry" of the Italian madrigal and with the gloriously scintillating double choirs of the Venetians, life and vigor, color and élan appeared in his music. His motets became a transfiguration of the madrigal and his magnificent eight-part *Stabat Mater,* inspired by the Venetian *cori spezzati* (divided choirs), reflects the early baroque tonal splendor of the antiphonal and superimposed double choirs.

*
* *

VENICE became a center of this universal Catholic church art second only to Rome, but while the moving spirit which governed the two musical metropolises was the same, they represent two aspects of the Counter Reformation, differing from yet complementing each other. Rome stood for dogmatic conservatism, seeking order, measure, and tradition. The art of the Roman school was retrospective, embedded in the old Flemish tradi tions; not the classical style of Gombert's generation, but the older strict style of the canon composers lay at its foundation. The ecstatic passion, elemental power, and mystic fervor of the Venetians, led by the two Gabrielis, express the same renewal of faith in incomparably more colorful, bold, and progressive music. But the towering tone clusters of Gabrieli's double and multiple choirs, the scintillating orchestral accompaniments, the brilliant solo passages, and the sharp dynamic contrasts are already leading into the dramatic and monumental world of the baroque.

Changes in the Musico-Political Situation

THE musico-political situation had now changed completely. The Italian composers of madrigals, villanelle, and many other forms had acquired an undisputed supremacy. The Netherlanders, a few years ago the envied masters of musical composition, had begun to vanish from the chapels and princely courts, and Italians were taking their places in all fields of music. The rate of production took on such proportions as only the mass production of modern times can rival, but a certain reaction set in against the facility of madrigal composition. The reaction was twofold, directed partly against antiquated Petrarchism, partly against the stereotyped formulae of the music. Madrigal composers began to employ all available means of musical craftsmanship to lend some spice to their music. Soon a number of older musical and poetical genres were revived and some new ones invented; "dialogues," "echoes," *enigmi, capricci, balletti,* and *scherzi* appeared in increasing numbers. Together with this tendency there was a penchant for increasing the number of voices. The spirit of the new tendencies seems to have concentrated its efforts on the new madrigal; the chromatic alterations became bolder and bolder and many new elements found their way into its orbit. The *a cappella* nature of the madrigal began to be undermined by the gradually growing use of instruments; strict polyphony was more or less relegated to the background, as the treble was favored above all the other parts, which were often taken by instruments. The instrumentally accompanied solo madrigal became a rival form. This whole art was clearly approaching the domain of the theater. Not only did the individual madrigals stress the emotional to such an extent that the delicate frame seemed about to burst, but whole cycles of madrigal comedies appeared. These polyphonic comedies assigned dramatic characters to the chorus and conducted veritable dialogues. Such madrigalesque comedies were so popular that even the successful debuts of the first operas did not eliminate them for several years.

Orazio Vecchi (c. 1550–1605) was one of the greatest masters of the madrigal style; his bold and colorful dramatic tableaux, with their vivacious scenes, popular dance rhythms, and brilliant and illuminating humor, represent the last stage in the development of *a cappella* music. His virtuosity in handling the choral medium is unsurpassed; at the same time, his ability in dramatic musical portrayal indicates clearly that we have arrived at the limits of secular choral polyphony and are entering the world of the drama. Vecchi's celebrated madrigal comedy, *Il Amfiparnasso,* is, indeed, a musical translation of the *commedia dell' arte,* the largely extemporaneous comedy derived from ancient models and presented by groups of strolling players in Italy. The characters in the *Amfiparnasso* are the same fixed types which appear in the *commedia:* Pantaloon, Harlequin, Columbine, and the others who wielded such an important influence on literature and drama throughout the Continent and England. While it is evident that Vecchi's aim was still purely abstractly choral-musical (the title calls for a *commedia harmonica*), there was only one more step to be taken toward the real theater.

The number of excellent and resourceful madrigal composers was legion, but one musician rightly claims the title *primus inter pares:* Luca Marenzio (1553-1599), who carried the madrigal to its culmination. The intensity of expressive power, the highly personal accents, and the dramatic warmth of his compositions make this musician the first modern composer in the fullest sense of the word. Marenzio placed the whole infinitely flexible and polished technique of madrigal composition in the service of the poetical content of the text. With the free, at times highly complicated, at times simple homophonic, grouping of the parts he attained virtuoso sound and color effects. His rich imagination grasped every idea, every gesture, and transformed them into lyrico-dramatic pictures of extraordinary communicative power. These pictures follow each other like the acts of a play; they are dramatic visions. Finding the old choral idiom insufficient to paint such pictures, Marenzio abandoned it to enter into the field of modern tonality. But he did not stop there: we soon see him on the barricades; his restless, elemental, subjective art, struggling with feverish visions, opens a new revolutionary period in music. Not only were Gesualdo and the other bold harmonists, and the late madrigal school in England, entirely under his spell, but the universal genius of the following age, Claudio Monteverdi, received from Marenzio the great impetus that enabled him to realize the dreams and aspirations of his nation toward a new free and passionate art.

The original musica reservata has changed; the new artists of the *ars recte, et pure, et ornate, eleganter, suaviter canendi* compose their wonderfully "pure, ornate, elegant, and suave" lyrical pieces for aristocratic and accomplished singers, who perform their parts with mimic gestures. The road turns here, and the musical traveler must get his bearings by looking forward into the world of the baroque; he has definitely lost sight of the past, the Renaissance.

Instruments and Instrumental Music

AT the turn of the fifteenth century the instruments of the Gothic era underwent considerable changes, and some of them were discarded as instruments of art music. Psaltery, portative, bagpipe, and the old fiddle lost their eminent position, while the instruments capable of rendering polyphonic music gained such importance as warranted a specific literature designed for their use. Henceforth it was the great church organ, the other keyboard instruments, and the lute which commanded attention. The heavier wind orchestra composed of cornets, trombones, fipple flutes, and bombards, the latter a deeper variety of the bassoon, especially popular in Germany, was now diluted and relieved by the string ensemble, to which was added the pleasant sound of the plucked instruments. In this instrumental practice one can observe the reconciliation of opposite styles. Sacred and secular music are brought together; monumental church music, traditionally performed also on the occasion of secular events of great importance, had always used wind instruments but was now combined with intimate chamber music. The reservata preferred the string and keyboard instruments, as well as the lute and its varieties, because their technically more perfect and artistically more aesthetic tone offered infinitely greater possibilities than the rather raucous, unwieldy, not well-tuned wind instruments, many of which could not play chromatic tones.

Since the first important schools of lute and violin players and composers originated in Italy, one should expect to find the great luthiers, as the makers of stringed instruments were called, among the natives of that country. It is surprising to discover that the majority of early luthiers were Germans, a number of them originating in Füssen, a little village in the Tyrol at the foot of the Alps. Among the many Füssen lute makers to be found in Italian and French cities one family name stands out in importance—the Tieffenbrucker. Members of this family have been proved to have resided in Padua, Venice, and Lyons, to mention only the most famous. Thus, while the Italians owe the development of their music to the Netherlanders, they are indebted to the Germans for the art of building stringed instruments—an art which they later carried to a perfection that their masters never dreamed of achieving. The lutes of Padua became famous all over Europe after Wendelin Tieffenbrucker launched a school of lute makers in the Venetian colonial city. Venice also contributed a great deal to the development of musical instruments. The archives mention, toward the end of the fifteenth century, a "Sigismondo Maler Thedescho," that is, Sigismund Maler the German, who may have been an older brother, or perhaps the father, of Laux Maler, the Stradivari of the lute. The last-named master craftsman, whose history is entirely unknown, was active about 1523 in Bologna.

That the German lute and viol makers retained an important position in their craft in Italy until the first half of the seventeenth century was due mainly to the exquisite instruments turned out by Magnus Tieffen-brucker, who was active at about 1560; however, the greatest renown attached to the Tieffenbrucker name fell to Caspar (c. 1514–1571), who represented his family in Lyons beginning with 1533. The fact that his long and unfamiliar German name was Gallicized to Gaspard Duiffoprugcar led some authors to believe that the "inventor of the violin," the proud title assigned to him, was a Frenchman. The violin was, of course, not invented by any one person; it was the result of a slow metamorphosis from the older viol into its present form which took place approximately between 1480 and 1530. One little change followed another until eminent masters, of whom the famous Lyonese Tieffenbrucker was one, began to standardize the shape of the instrument. The oldest true violins came from the work-shops of Gasparo da Salò (1542–1609), of Brescia, and of his important pupil G. P. Maggini (1581–1632), and it was from this school that the founder of the great Cremona luthiers, Andrea Amati (1535–c. 1611), descended. The Tyrolean lute and viol makers can be traced to many French towns, and one of their members, Jacob Rayman, settled in London about 1620 to become "the father of violin making in England."

While the violin was slowly gaining the dominant position which it assumed in the following century, its predecessor was still widely used. The successor of the medieval fiddle, the viol, came into general use in the fifteenth century and continued to be used, especially in England, until the eighteenth. The viols were built in three principal sizes: the treble or discant viol, the tenor viol (*viola da braccio*), and the knee or bass viol (*viola da gamba*). The largest variety, belonging to the same family although not used in chamber music, was the double bass viol (*violone*), and there were numerous subsidiary types sometimes combining features found in other stringed instruments. The three principal types were kept in a so-called "chest of viols" and constituted the standard equipment of English chamber music in the late sixteenth and seventeenth centuries. The chest was a piece of furniture usually housing three pairs of treble, tenor, and bass instruments carefully matched as to size and tone.

Among the large number of stringed instruments whose tones were elicited by plucking the strings, it was the lute and its many varieties which were universally appreciated and played throughout the Renaissance and the baroque period. The origin of the instrument is obscure, but one must search for its primeval history in periods that antedate by thousands of years its introduction into medieval Spain by the Moors. It is not our purpose here to study the complicated history of this favorite instrument of the Renaissance; suffice it to say that in the fourteenth century the instrument is already frequently mentioned, and many illustrations testify to the fact that European varieties began to develop at an early date. The magnificent instrument of the Renaissance had a pear-shaped graceful body built of staves of wood or ivory, its belly pierced by several sound holes in a decorative "rose" pattern. Attached to the body was a neck of moderate length covered by a finger board divided by frets of brass or catgut into a measured scale, and ending in a pegbox turned back at right angles to the neck. In the sixteenth century, when the demand for sonority forced an enlargement of the delicate instruments, the larger archlute and *theorbo* were added to the smaller instruments. These were equipped with a second neck extending several feet, upon which were fixed the extra strings.

The universal popularity of the lute and its varieties all over Europe resulted in a thorough confusion in the use and nomenclature of the instruments. The Spaniards, creators of lute music of great originality used another instrument called *vihuela de mano* (hand viol) in contrast to *vihuela de arco* (bow viol), which was the tenor or bass (knee) viol. The fact that bowed and plucked instruments were frequently derived from the same primitive ancestor, and that they were often confused to the extent that plucked instruments were played with a bow and bowed instruments plucked with the fingers, raises an interesting question. The great difference between the musical instinct of the northern nations and that of the peoples bordering the Mediterranean, a difference we have detected in every phase of cultural history, is equally evident in the selection and use of instruments. Curt Sachs has established the fact that the advent of the two large groups of stringed instruments, representing two distinct types of playing, is not a chronological question, but one pertaining to ethnology.[23] The fluent, mystic polyphonic idiom of the northerners was much more adapted to the rather flat, solemn tone of the viols, while the clear chords of the lutes corresponded very well with the concise, chordal music of the frottole and other popular and semipopular musical forms. Advancing time gradually eliminated the sharp differences between the two types of technique, but their fundamental opposition remained a latent factor, although visible only in certain subtle manifestations. It is most interesting to see that the natural inclination of the southerner to pluck the strings was still strong enough in the early seventeenth century to produce the so-called *pizzicato,* the "pinching" or plucking of the strings of the violin, a device which became popular in orchestral and chamber music writing.

All the musical instruments that we have so far encountered were, without exception, of Oriental origin. The group of keyboard instruments from which evolved our modern pianoforte was, however, a development of the Occident, although their ancestors, the dulcimer, the monochord, and the psaltery were, of course, ancient Oriental instruments. The fundamental departure from Eastern instrument construction was the application of a keyboard. The origin of this device is unknown, but it was fairly well developed in Europe in the central Middle Ages, whereas it never took root in the Orient.

The clavichord, the smallest and most delicate of stringed keyboard instruments, is the oldest of the species. It originated somewhere in the twelfth century when a keyboard was attached to the monochord, the age-old experimental instrument of the Greeks. It is the only old keyboard instrument which permits a "singing" tone and a very expressive manner of playing. This quality of the instrument, well known and described by musical writers in the fifteenth and sixteenth centuries, caused its restoration to favor in the era known as "the period of sentimentality" (*Empfindsamkeit*). Johann Sebastian Bach himself wrote a number of his keyboard works for the clavichord.

The *clavicembalo,* or, as it is better known in its shortened form, the *cembalo* (English harpsichord, French *clavecin*), which appeared about 1400, became the chief keyboard instrument of the string variety in the sixteenth and seventeenth centuries. Unlike its delicate sister, the clavichord, the more robust harpsichord was incapable of dynamic modification of tone by difference of touch. Its strings were plucked by points of quill or hard leather, elevated on small wooden stilts called "jacks." The instruments made in the mid-sixteenth century were very serviceable and possessed a brilliant crisp tone. A second keyboard was added to the existing one, and several stops and couplers permitted a great variety of sound combinations, from the muffled "lute" stop to the brilliant "full" registration employing sub and super octaves. This instrument, together with the organ, became the representative musical solo instrument of the late Renaissance and the baroque; at the same time, because its tones, unlike those of the modern piano, blended very well with the sound of stringed and wind instruments, it became the fundament and backbone of the orchestra.

From the time of Henry VII almost to the close of the seventeenth century the most popular keyboard instrument in England was the virginal. The etymology of the name is still a matter of controversy. English lexicographers lean toward the explanation given in Blount's *Glossographia* (1656): ". . . called Virginals, because maids and virgins do most commonly play on them," but Curt Sachs's derivation from the medieval Latin *virga,* rod, or jack, seems more plausible. As a matter of fact the term seems to have been applied to all quilled keyboard instruments, the harpsichord, spinet, and the rectangular virginals mentioned by German writers in the sixteenth century. In Queen Anne's reign we hear no more of the virginals; the "spinnet" is the favorite domestic instrument.

All these instruments exhibit exquisite workmanship and are decorated with great care. Harpsichords made in the late sixteenth and early seventeenth centuries by Dutch and Italian masters were still in good playing condition in the late eighteenth century, and many of them have been successfully renovated and restored to active use in our day.

The organ, which we saw well developed in the time of Landini, was, when the great productivity of instrumental composition began in the sixteenth century, the lordly instrument which we know today. The pedal board appeared in the Low Countries and Germany in the early fourteenth century and was quickly accepted by the composers and players of these countries, and soon by those of Spain and France. The Italians were slower to accept the pedals, but began to employ them in the sixteenth century. Curiously enough the pedals seem not to have been introduced into England until 1772, when a pedal board was installed on the organ of the German Lutheran Chapel in London. At the beginning of the fifteenth century most notable churches on the Continent had good-sized organs, many of them two. The great organ served for independent organ playing, while a second smaller one aided the singers in their intonation and accompanied their singing In the sixteenth century, organs were equipped with two or even three keyboards, an independent pedal board, and a variety of stops and couplers.

The contents of lute, harpsichord, and organ books, as well as certain collections of music for bowed string instruments and wind instruments, remain, unfortunately, absolutely unintelligible to the present-day musician. They were written in a specific instrumental notation called tablature which indicated by letters, numerals, and other signs the string, fret, finger hole, organ key, etc., to be touched, instead of by the actual musical notes as in our modern notation. This method of musical writing, carrying with it a different application for each type of instrument, varied from country to country, and, to complete the picture, the individual composers added to their tablatures variants of their own personal design and use. Theoretically the translation of a tablature into modern notation seems fairly simple, but as soon as we get beyond the fundamental principles our task becomes more difficult as it becomes evident that our modern notation does not possess all the signs that are necessary to render the subtleties and details of execution that characterize this music.

Tablature notation gives us a succession of points without exact value, leaving us the task of establishing a reasonable musical text. Thus the tablature is the notation of a manual practice, whereas ours is the realization of auditive phenomena. The translation consists, then, of the transformation of a material execution into an idealized graphical picture. We address ourselves to intelligence instead of merely preparing the movement of the fingers. The best solution would be not to have recourse to translations, but to acquire a knowledge of the tablatures and then play the pieces from them; thus we should hear the pieces more nearly as they sounded in their own time.

Although tablatures did not come into general use before the fifteenth century, they were of great antiquity. The more instrumental solo playing became popular, the more it was necessary to provide the player with a "tabulated" ensemble of the parts he was supposed to play together. The organists and other instrumentalists, all versed in the regular vocal, mensural notation, had some difficulty in summarizing the contents of the part books, although Otto Kinkeldey in his important work on the keyboard music of the sixteenth century has proved that early sixteenth-century organists were able to play from several juxtaposed part books placed on the organ, an ability we could scarcely match today. The tablature simplified the procedure considerably by providing the player with piano and organ "reductions" of the several vocal parts. These organ books soon assumed the character of a modern two-stave score as mensural and tablature notation converged slowly into our modern notation.

Types and Forms of Instrumental Music

DEPRIVED of the powerful aid of words, instrumental music is compelled to offer an abstract and ideal musical substance, in an idiom and form created by itself. Being the art of pure fantasy, instrumental music must act without the intermediary of other elements. Such a course is not possible through the adoption of the means employed by vocal music, whose very nature is different and whose form and character are more or less dependent on the text. The intrinsic features of instrumental music will emerge, consequently, in the measure in which it eludes the influence of vocal music and pursues its own path. This emancipation took effect slowly, as musical thought and form had been associated for a long time with words. The excellent studies of Leichtentritt, Kinkeldey, and Schering [24] have proved the universal practice of instrumental music even in earlier centuries which did not leave behind musical documents of their instrumental art. The popularity of instrumental music was so great in the fifteenth century that Adam of Fulda complained indignantly against the "inordinate" influence exerted by the instrumentalists upon musical composition, and was appalled by the threatening possibility of the "buffoons and minstrels becoming the composers of the future." [25]

Improvisation, a natural ability of all good instrumentalists, exercised a formative influence on the technique of composition and explains the volatile, virtuoso quality of much of the lute music and the brilliant passage work of keyboard music. The independent handling of the instruments gave this music a freedom and vivacity full of imagination, which hastened its deliverance from the bonds of vocal music. Most choral compositions, secular or sacred, which attracted attention were transcribed in lute or keyboard tablature in order that a single person might be able to play them, much as in the case of modern piano transcriptions. We have seen that in the time of Paumann a great many transcriptions were made, but the method and purpose have now changed. The older composers of the fifteenth century utilized the melody of a chanson or Mass and paraphrased and "colored" it in their translations; the composers of the sixteenth century, well on their way toward an independent instrumental style, adapted whole choral works for instrumental use, displaying remarkable skill in condensing several contrapuntal parts for the lute, organ, or harpsichord without unduly jeopardizing the independence of part writing. In spite of the runs and coloratures inserted at points which permitted their use, and other licenses growing from the natural inclination of the instrumental virtuoso to adorn his own part, these transcriptions endeavored to be faithful to the original.

Lute players introduced dance music into the sphere of art music, and the dances, especially those of the Romanic peoples, became an important factor in the formation of an autochthonous instrumental style. The most important elements of this style, rhythm, and the division of phrases into periods, were all derived from dance music. Dances, even in the sixteenth century, were closely connected with vocal music. They could be accompanied by a chorus instead of by instruments, and in early sixteenth-century prints (Attaingnant's) one can often find, besides the dance music in lute tablature, the original song in mensural notation, called *subjectum*. This accounts for the strangeness of such dance titles as "La Magdalena," "Le Corps s'en Va," "Patience," etc. Although we may find the names of dances in vogue in the sixteenth century mentioned in the times of the troubadours, the date of the introduction of dance rhythms into art music cannot be set before the beginning of the sixteenth century.

The French dances of the sixteenth century occupied a particular place; they were popular everywhere, and the *pavane, gaillarde, allemande, courante, basse-danse,* and the various *branles* were known in England, Spain, Italy, and Germany. The names designated their character (*gaillarde, courante*) or made allusion to their geographic origin (*padoana, branle de Champagne,* etc). A very interesting and detailed description of these dances, and the influence of their choreography on musical composition, is given in the *Orchésographie* of Thoinot Arbeau (1519–1595), published in

1589. The author, whose real name was Jehan Tabourot (of which the pen name is an anagram), was a priest in Langres; nothing else is known of him, but his work remains one of the earliest and most valuable treatises on dance music.[26] A similar work by Fabritio Caroso (1535–c 1610), a dancing master of Sermoneta, entitled *Il Ballarino* (Venice, 1581), gives valuable and colorful information about the dance in Italy, its performance and the accompanying music, the latter in lute tablature. The work was so popular that a second, entirely rewritten and enlarged edition, was published in 1600 and 1605, entitled *La Nobiltà di Dame,* with numerous plates showing the various postures assumed by the dancers. Unfortunately, there are no such sources concerning dance and dance music in sixteenth-century England and Germany, although there are numerous allusions in English literature which, systematically assembled, might lead to interesting source material. The Italian dances, among which we should mention the *passamezzo, saltarello, canario, piva,* and the *ballo* and *balletto* (the *gagliarda, corrente,* etc., being Italian variants of the original French dances), seem to be more purely instrumental than the French, as there are few titles in the Italian tablatures which would suggest vocal derivation. But when we turn toward Germany the poetic origin of the dances is at once noticeable.

The great number of German dances can be reduced to two groups: the *Schreittanz,* a slow, "walking" dance in binary time, and the *Springtanz,* in a vivid ternary rhythm. In all these dances the musical construction is clearly periodic, something we have not before encountered in vocal music, with the exception of some types of semipopular Italian folk songs and the French Renaissance chansons. A period of eight measures, repeated with a different cadence at the end, constitutes a finished little musical form which became the basis of all instrumental and vocal forms of future centuries. The desire to avoid mere repetition of the short periods produced another principle of modern musical construction: the variation. The Italian lute composers of the mid-sixteenth century displayed an astounding technique and ingenuity in variations, and these short forms of musical composition grew rapidly to reach, in the works of the English virginal composers of the late Elizabethan period, a stylistic perfection.

Soon composers discovered another way to amplify their works—by linking several dances together. This principle was to acquire great importance in the history of instrumental music, as it led to the suite. The germ of the suite appeared in the German lute pieces in which a dance was followed by a "post-dance" (*Nachtanz*), which was a rhythmic variation of the first. This combination was already known in the fifteenth century, and is probably much older. Its origin is not difficult to establish. The people knew only two sorts of dances: the slow and measured dance in duple time and the animated variety in triple time. Dancing usually started slowly, then as the gaiety mounted the dancers turned around faster and faster, and the original dance was transformed, changing to triple time. The same liaison of simple dances took place in France, but for some reason neither the Germans nor the French went much beyond the simple coupling of two dances. It was in Italy that the dance suite developed to a remarkable degree, beginning with the very first instrumental publications of Petrucci. His fourth lute book (1508) already contained a respectable form consisting of three dances: *pavan, saltarello,* and *piva.* The order of these compositions is always the same, indicating a definitely established musical form. A quarter of a century later we find several well-developed suite forms consisting of from two to five dances. These were soon accepted by both the French and the Germans who added to them some of their own dances and also the popular Spanish *saraband,* which had acquired citizenship in their countries. The initial tuning of the lute—a delicate and important operation—evolved into a short introductory piece which with its simple chords gave an opportunity to the player to tune up his instrument. This short piece, which appears also in the "limbering up" runs of the organ pieces, called prelude or *preambulum,* later lost its utilitarian character and became the stylized opening movement of the suite.

Toward the end of the century the dance pieces were joined by a number of other musical forms, and a combination of the suite with the variation principle offered infinite possibilities for expansion. Thus when the seventeenth century dawned it found a wealth of instrumental forms attracting the attention of composers who heretofore had held themselves aloof from the "art of minstrels and buffoons." The simple dance suite led directly to the overture and symphony and to the various chamber music forms of the seventeenth and eighteenth centuries. The revival of the baroque in the mid-nineteenth century resuscitated the old dance suite, and many delightful piano compositions tried to recapture the fresh and dainty atmosphere of the lute and clavichord player's art.

The list of lute virtuosi opens with Francesco Spinaccino of Fossombrone, whose two lute books, published by Petrucci in 1507, belong to the oldest documents of this interesting branch of music. Among the great number of lute virtuosi and composers of the next decades we should single out Francesco da Milano (c. 1490–c. 1566), who was not only an incomparable player on his instrument, earning the epithet *il divino* from his contemporaries, but a composer of great originality. His "fantasies" inspired the succeeding generation of musicians throughout Europe. Where his predecessors were satisfied with pleasant runs and chords, this sensitive artist spun graceful counterpoints which, far from assuming the stereotyped technique of "coloration," seem to be different in every one of his compositions.

A host of great players and composers followed Francesco da Milano: the Paduan Antonio Rotta, the Bolognese Marc Antonio del Pifaro, the Milanese Pietro Paolo Borrono, the Apulian Giacomo Gorzanis, and the Florentine Vincenzo Galilei, father of the astronomer, to mention a few of the leaders who wrote and published innumerable dances, fantasies, transcriptions, and *ricercari,* furnishing the cinquecento with an intimate chamber music of great variety. Toward 1590 the lute reached its apogee. Two player-composers, Giovanni Antonio Terzi and Simone Molinaro, appear as leaders, and their tablature books, published in the last decade of the sixteenth century, celebrate the advent of a finished, graceful, and sovereign instrumental style, capable of all shades of expression and of a technique which we usually associate only with the vocal music of the period.

With the organists and clavichord and harpsichord players, instrumental art advanced still further. The Flemish organists Willaert and Buus are now rivaled and supplanted by great Italian musicians whose number is legion. Girolamo Cavazzoni published in 1542 in Venice his *Intavolature cioè Recercari, Canzoni, Himni, Magnificat,* etc., which started the great literature of Italian keyboard music. As in the case of the lute, which created for itself an independent instrumental style, the organists shook off the last shackles of vocal composition technique and endowed their instrument with a rich and brilliant literature. Among the leading masters—and almost every church had a good organist—there were three who occupied exceptional positions in the musical life of the sixteenth century. Claudio Merulo (1533–1604) composed *toccate, ricercari,* and *canzoni* filled with brilliant passages, marked by interesting and typically idiomatic instrumental turns and rhythms. His fluent command of virtuoso writing and the variety of style which characterized his output stamp him as one of the great masters of the sixteenth century. Andrea Gabrieli (c. 1520–1586), a pupil of Willaert and successor of Merulo, and his nephew and pupil Giovanni (1557–1612), both organists at St. Mark's, culminated the school of instrumental music that began with the simple transcriptions of vocal pieces. An independent instrumental style is already an accomplished fact in the works of these two composers. The improvisatory flourishes and figures added by the earlier composers to their pieces at the time of performance are now incorporated organically in the written score, and the ephemeral quality of older instrumental music has disappeared. The two Gabrielis set out to endow music with more color by extracting from each instrument the sounds that typify it and by mixing the specific colors judiciously with others. We are at the threshold of the modern orchestra, when instrumental color becomes a factor of composition; but the orchestral ensembles of these composers lead us to another era, to be dealt with in subsequent chapters.

*
* *

IT is difficult to understand why some of the most eminent historians of our modern era, who, unlike their predecessors, do not restrict their attention to wars, treaties, and royal dynasties, but consider the history of arts and letters, politics and religion, economics and science, an integral, and perhaps the most important, part of history writing, are still completely uninformed about the role of music in the history of civilization. No reputable historian of today would accuse the painters and architects, poets and philosophers of the cinquecento of laboring diligently within the limitations of a still undeveloped technique, yet this is exactly the phrase used in connection with music. "The men so greedy of all delicate sights and pleasant, would fain also stuff their ears with sweet sounds. And so they did, within the limitations of a still undeveloped technique. They had organs, lutes, viols, lyres, harps, citherns, horns, and a kind of primitive piano known as the clavichord or the clavicembalo." [27] These lines were written by a historian whose voluminous work is a masterpiece of research and who lavishes great care on all the other manifestations of human ingenuity, while he deems a scant page or so sufficient to deal with an art which graced the daily life of the people, adorned the festivities of the princely courts, and ennobled the mystic ritual of the ancient church and the sturdy liturgy of the new. The same chronicler who uses the most scrupulous care in consulting sources and possible sources is satisfied with the writings of inconsequential musical essayists and, for once, abandons the creed of the true historian, measuring the accomplishments of a bygone age by the yardstick of Victorian aesthetics. Yet a glance at contemporary writings will tell him that those supposedly primitive instruments excited people to the same manifestations of boundless admiration that are today the lot of the clever performer on the Steinway grand or the mammoth organ. When Merulo played, the church doors had to be closed to prevent people from crushing each other in their eagerness for admission. His playing fascinated musician and layman alike, and students, attracted by his fame, streamed to the great virtuoso from all countries. Composers and players of the "kind of primitive piano" reveled in a music that elicited from Shakespeare the greatest praise.

The forms of instrumental music stood, then, on an equality with the vivacious madrigal, the infinitely polished polyphonic motet, and the majestically mysterious Mass. The instrumental counterpart of the chanson and madrigal was the *canzone,* while the more strictly polyphonic form, molded after the vocal model of the motet, was the *ricercar.* All these musical forms utilize the modern principle of thematic treatment, and in the fantasies and *toccate* we have instrumental forms that lived uninterruptedly for centuries to come. The *toccata*, developed from the brass fanfares of the late Middle Ages, retained its introductory character. The name derived from the beating of the drums which accompanied the trumpet choirs (*toccare*, "to beat"), and the percussive-festive character of the medieval toccata was retained in the keyboard music of the late Renaissance and the baroque, extended and amplified by a virtuoso treatment. The great organ toccatas of J. S. Bach echo this, as do the overtures of the early operas. The fantasies, or fancies, as they were called in England, were in reality extended *ricercari*. While in modern times the term means "a piece of music unrestricted by any prearranged formal condition," in the sixteenth and seventeenth centuries the great liberty accorded to the composer was interpreted in a general sense, and the thematic unity of the work—a truly symphonic principle—was carefully observed. The great variety of technical means at the composer's disposal is best illustrated by the remarks of the eminent English composer Thomas Morley (1557-1603), author of *A Plaine and Easie Introduction to Practicall Musicke* (1597), when describing the fancy. "When a musician taketh a point at his pleasure, and wresteth and turneth it as he list, making either much or little of it according as shall seem best in his own conceit. In this may more art be shown than in any other music, because the composer is tied to nothing [i. e., to no text, or as Morley says, "without a ditty"], but he may add, diminish or alter at his pleasure." These words describe the principles of construction and aesthetics of music that have been cherished and followed for many centuries. Such principles were not the result of laudable dabbling in a primitive medium, but the distilled maxims of a great and flourishing art.

German Music in the Late Renaissance

LEAVING the main theater of music we shall see that while other countries cannot rival the prodigious wealth of Italo-Flemish art they had a goodly share in the flourishing music of the Renaissance.

We noticed the slow development of German music until the presence of the great Fleming, Henricus Isaac, gave it the necessary impetus that produced a Stoltzer and a Senfl. We also saw that the Lutheran movement was materially aided by several eminent musicians led by the Wittenberg theologian-composer himself. The second half of the sixteenth century saw the growth of the German song. Large collections appeared, beginning with the volume entitled *Guter, seltzamer und künstreicher teutscher Gesang* (1544), by Wolfgang Schmeltzl (c. 1500–c. 1561), which also contained some burlesque quodlibets ("what you please"), humorous compositions which were incongruous either in their musical character, using little bits and snatches of various compositions, or in the words with which they were

Luca della Robbia (1400–1482), Group of Singers from the Cantoria (Begun in 1431)

The Distribution
of
Flemish (and Franco-Flemish) Composers,
During the Height of
Their Dispersal
c.1470~1550

Political Boundaries: 1519

NORTH
Sea

BRITISH ISLES

Atlantic Ocean

London   The Hague   Ams
Utre
o's He
Boulogne   Bruges   Antwer
Lille   Ghent
Arras   Tournai   Brussels
Cambrai   Mons   Liège

oRouen
Paris(27)   oRheims
Str

FRANCE

oTours
Dijon   Veso
oLyon
Turi

oToulouse   oAvignon

Burgos
oValladolid
oSalamanca   oSaragossa
Lisbon   oMadrid(47)   oBarcelona
oToledo(10)

PORTUGAL

SPAIN   Mediterranean

SWEDEN

Baltic Sea

LIVONIA

RUSSIA

o Riga

KURLAND

DENMARK

o Copenhagen

PRUSSIA

o Hamburg

...osch

ogne

...E EMPIRE

Berlin (6)

o Braunschweig

o Wittenberg

POLAND

o Warsaw

o Weimar

Dresden (9)

o Frankfurt

o Bamberg

o Prague

o Cracow

Heidelberg

o Nuremberg

...sel

o Stuttgart

o Augsburg

Munich (10)

Vienna
(15) o

o Pressburg

o Salzburg

o Innsbruck

o Budapest

HUNGARY

VENICE

o Milan (24)

Verona
(5)

Padua

Mantua o (15)

Ferrara

Venice
(13)

Parma

o Modena
(5)

o Florence
(5)

Adriatic

PAPAL
STATES

o Perugia

o Rome (107)

Sea

NAP

Bari o

o Naples (17) LES

Sea

R. E. Falconer.

This map naturally
cannot lay claim to
completeness. Many more
Flemish composers could be
found scattered through Europe and
in the Spanish colonies in America.
Moreover, dozens of musicians are
listed in available sources merely as
residing in "Germany," or as being
members of the emperor's chapel
choir, which may be located anywhere
from Prague to Madrid. The figures
in parentheses indicate the number of
Flemish composers resident in the city
during the period under consideration.

Raphael (1483–1520),"Ecstasy of St. Cecilia"

Matthias Grünewald (first third of 16th Cent.), Section from Isenheim Altar

associated. There followed collections by the Germanized Netherlander, Matthew Le Maistre, court composer at Dresden (1563), and, most notable, the great collection of *Gute, alte, und neue teutsche Liedlein* in five fascicles, published between 1539 and 1556 by the humanistically-minded Nuremberg physician Georg Forster (c. 1514–1568). After Forster's last volume the foreign influence once more became powerful, and Netherlanders, Frenchmen, and Italians dominated German musical life. The frottola and the villanella found their way over the Alps, and their frank gaiety was soon echoed in the works of the Germans. Thus Leonhard Lechner spoke of his "New Gay German Songs" as composed "in the manner of the Italian canzoni" (*nach Art der welschen Canzonen*).

Although the outlanders counted among their number such composers of genius as Le Maistre, Scandello, Ivo de Vento, Lassus, Regnart, and many others whose very presence held German musicians in awe, the second half of the century produced a German master worthy of their company. Hans Leo Hasler (1564–1612) was among the first of the Germans to go to Italy (1584), where he studied in Venice with Andrea Gabrieli and formed a fast friendship with the latter's nephew, who was a fellow student. Like other foreign pilgrims this Bavarian was deeply impressed by Italian art and came home with seductive melodies ringing in his ears. While not the first German musician to visit Italy, Hasler was the first great German composer who assimilated his newly won Latin mastery with his fundamentally German nature. His canzonets and madrigals, fine-grained delicate compositions, rivaled the Italians' best, and the broad and colorful musical frescoes of his typically Venetian double choirs brought new life into the world of German music, which now entered on its ascendancy. Hasler's *Lustgarten neuer teutscher Gesäng* (1601) represents the first great milestone on this long road. Every one of the songs contained in this collection is a small masterpiece of a wonderfully balanced musical style in which harmony, counterpoint, and declamation are blended with superb artistry. One of the songs, "Mein G'müth ist mir verwirret," haunted German composers for centuries. It is the tune of the familiar Passion chorale "O Sacred Head now wounded" (*"O Haupt voll Blut und Wunden"*), well known from Bach's numerous settings. Two other sterling masters round out the century: Joachim à Burck (1546–1610) of Magdeburg and the Thuringian Johannes Eccard (1523–1611), both of them pillars of early Protestant music, and versatile and profound musicians.

The German lute and organ composers (the term meaning, according to the practice of the time, composer and performer) did not lag behind their choral colleagues. Hans Kotter (c. 1485–1541) of Strassburg, an early convert to Protestantism, the Suabian Leonhard Kleber (c. 1490–1556), and Hans Buchner (1483–1538), also of Württemberg, represent the southern wing of organists (the northerners lead us over into the seventeenth century); they were all skillful, if not very original, composers. The greatest organist of this period was Paul Hofhaimer, or Hofhaymer (1459–1537), teacher of most of the afore-mentioned Germans and of many other celebrated organists. This Austrian master, gifted with a melodic invention of rare beauty which was expressed in exquisite songs, was also the musician who transformed the awkward "coloration" of the Paumann period into a refined and elegant instrumental ornamentation.

Although lute composers were numerous in the fifteenth century, the voluminous literature of lute music started only with the *Tabulatur etlicher lobgesang und Liedlein uff die orgeln und Lauten* (1512) of the blind Heidelberg organist and lute player Arnold Schlick (d. after 1527). The number of lute players and compositions following Schlick is so vast that no attempt can be made here even to enumerate them. Hans Gerle (d. 1570), Hans Newsidler (1508–1563), Wolf Heckel, and Matthew Waisselius (second half of the century) were a few of the leading masters among the many whose activity continued through the following centuries. Bach himself was the author of several lute compositions.

The Second Period of the French Renaissance

THE tendencies in music and literature which were apparent in the first period of the French Renaissance, humanism and Italianism, are still evident in its more advanced stage. The French still imitated the Italians, but with an imitation that had a serious spirit of rivalry. The scholars and poets of the time had an implicit faith in antiquity, a faith which guided them even in practical matters.

Among the poets the whole field was dominated by the group called the Pléiade, led by Pierre de Ronsard, a student of art, seriously seeking for a new beauty of style. In his search he vehemently denounced his French predecessors and turned back to the ancients. With an avowed passion for glory, a keen sensitivity and imagination, coupled with consummate taste, Ronsard rapidly became recognized as *prince des poètes français*. A friend of Ronsard and a coleader of the Pléiade was Jean-Antoine de Baïf (1532–1589), an inventive genius, more learned than artistic. Among the other members of the group were Pontus de Tyard, an idealistic nobleman and a confirmed Platonist; Rémy Belleau, a courtier and graceful poet of pastorals; Etienne Jodelle, court poet to Charles IX and creator of modern French tragedy. Among the so-called disciples of Ronsard were four men whose life and works reflect the artistic creeds and tendencies of the time. Philippe Desportes was a typical popular lyricist; Théodore-Agrippa D'Aubigné, a militant Calvinist and vigorous poet, turned to the prophets of Israel for his literary models; Mathurin Régnier, brought up in Italy, represented Italianism and freedom of style; and François Malherbe, his opponent, one of the most influential poets and severest literary critics of the century, attempted to restrict lyricism by rigid rules, at the same time demanding simplicity and reasonableness.

The music of this period, which we may arbitrarily designate as the third period of the French Renaissance chanson (following the death of Janequin) exhibits the same tendencies as literature, likewise with humanism in the ascendancy. The importance of literature, especially poetry, during the sixteenth century rested upon its intimate connection with music. Seldom has music reflected so immediately the spirit and the development of its own age. Poets wrote with the object of making verses which were suited to music; thus they were the real humanists, interpreting music and poetry as an undivided lyric art recalling the world of Anacreon and Sappho. Ronsard and Baïf, in an attempt to discover a form which could be chanted after the manner of the Greeks, developed a chanson form based on Latin and Greek models. The result was a vague plan, and the attempt to imitate Greek art exactly was soon abandoned for a more inclusive purpose. Henceforth their aim was to create a new lyric art, a modern French lyricism conceived on classical lines. Thus humanism in France became more artistic and more creative than in Germany. In the latter country real musical art was subordinated to a pedagogical interest in the strict reproduction of the methods of classical antiquity. The French created a new style of their own, using the Latin and Greek forms as models only. In Germany the art was the product of highly specialized, formal schools, whereas in France it was produced spontaneously. The Germans composed relatively simple music for Latin verse; the French created a *musique savante,* setting to music French verse constructed on classical patterns. These were the *vers mesurés.*

The earliest attempts at measured verse were made in the late fifteenth century in France, but the first successful measured verse was produced in Italy as a result of Claudio Tolomei's *Versi e Regole de la Nuova Poesia Toscana* (1539). Under him was founded the *Accademia della Nuova Poesia,* in which only measured verse was permitted. The movement was carried to France, and after several earlier essays there appeared in 1562 a treatise by de La Taille, *Manière de Faire des Vers en françois, comme en grec et en Latin.* Thus, despite his claims, Baïf did not invent the measured verse, but it may justly be said that he was the first to use it systematically, and the first to point out the possibility of a liaison with music.

The originality of the vers mesuré as conceived by Baïf lay in the fact that it was not merely a copy of classical verse, but was constructed in the French language and spirit along lines designated by the principles of classical versification. The strict measure of this form, cultivated by many musicians connected with the subsequently formed "Academy," imposed its rhythm on music, even influencing polyphony in this respect. The vers mesuré, one of the most curious and forced instances of applied humanism, represents an important aspect of artistic doctrine in the age of the French Renaissance, but alert musicians were keenly aware of the fact that the ingenious Baïf really attempted to force the French language into arbitrarily chosen rhythms to which it was not suited. There was the further impossibility of restricting the language for the sake of the musical beat, since the ancient music he attempted to imitate was divided by phrases and not cut up in group rhythm, which suggests instrumental music. The leading chanson composers of the second half of the century rejected his theories, believing that to force music into pulsating group-rhythm (bar-rhythm) was to destroy its intrinsic expressiveness. They therefore refused to employ this device and in so doing actually approached the classical idea more nearly than did any fervent humanistic philologist.

As a literary form, independent of its musical setting, the vers mesuré was severely criticized by contemporaries, but it was accepted in certain literary circles where humanistic interests predominated. One of the institutions devoted to the cause of humanism was the Académie Françoise de Poésie et de Musique, the first Academy organized in France maintaining an artistic standard purely intellectual, never attempting to popularize its undertakings. We shall have an opportunity to discuss the Academy in a subsequent chapter.

Like Baïf, Ronsard was interested in reviving Greek art, but in quite another way. He believed that he could achieve a revival of the Greek spirit indirectly by imitating the Italians. The fact that Ronsard's poetry was always intended to be "merveilleusement propre pour la musique" cannot be repeated often enough.[28] This musical point of view on the part of the great Renaissance poet was largely responsible for the incomparable musical culture of sixteenth-century France, a culture which so admirably reflected Gallic genius. The sonnet had been considered an independent literary form until Ronsard realized the possibilities of a musical rapport. The result was the creation of the sonnet in its modern guise. The publications of 1552 contained four types, all suited to music and composed by the greatest chanson composers of the period, Janequin, Muret, Certon, and Goudimel. Another interesting aspect of Ronsard's activity was his condemnation of singsong and his insistence that polyphonic settings be made for his verse. From this there developed a conflict between him and some of his contemporaries, but actually much of his verse fell victim to popular monophony. With the accession of Henry IV and especially after his reign, musicians turned to the *ballet de cour* and the *air de cour*. Artistic polyphony vanished, and with it Ronsard, for Ronsard's name was synonymous with finely wrought polyphonic music.

In the last period of chanson composition the spontaneous expression incorporated in the typical Renaissance chanson style of the middle period changed to a more sophisticated and polished style, and the chanson became a less tangible medium. As a type it became more eclectic, already under the influence of the Italian madrigal of the late Renaissance. Among the many composers of the period we may select a few typical representatives. Guillaume Costeley (1531–1606), said to be of Celtic origin, lived, nevertheless, his whole life in France. His unusually fine and clear chansons show a remarkably closed form, consisting of distinct sections which occasionally produce the impression of a formal structure which can be described by the symbol A-B-A. Or, again, by the candid restatement of a section, the composer seems to use the form of a rondeau, despite the fact that the material is not identical. Claude Le Jeune (c. 1528–1600), court composer to the king, was perhaps the most eminent French composer of the second half of the century, and one of the adherents of Baïf's vers mesuré. His style is characterized by great vivacity and sparkling declamation, and his melodies are engaging in their freshness. But the changing spirit is already evident in many works of this exquisitely musical poet. In his music for Ronsard's *Le Printemps,* which is somewhat in the style of Vecchi, he exhibits a tendency to fall into the more solemn style of the motet. His counterpoint, although very fluent, often becomes monotonous, especially when he chooses to write for more than four parts—for he even undertook as many as eight, an unusual number for the chanson. In so doing he is inclined to fall back upon contrapuntal artifices of a conventional nature, increasing the formal element in his style. These tendencies in the work of a superbly gifted musician can be attributed to his affiliation with the Huguenots and to his espousing the doctrines of Baïf, which necessarily had the effects of a strait jacket on this naturally light and graceful composer. Pierre Certon (d. 1572), again, was a full-blooded chanson composer of the "old school" and not less important as a church composer.

There remain two important chanson composers, Jacques Mauduit (1557–1627), one of Baïf's ardent partisans and creator of many four-part *chansons mesurées* and Roland de Lassus, whose chansons properly consummate the evolution of this admirable musical form. Mauduit furnished numerous typical examples of the music composed on the vers mesurés. There is relatively little to be said of such music. What may be said of one piece applies rather well to the rest, since the nature of this verse form was stereotyped. Mauduit's examples consisted for the most part of short chansonnettes written in simple chords, not unlike the early Lutheran chorale. Lassus's versatility and wide experience with various forms provided him with a technique through which he could express himself in any style skillfully and artistically. He could assume the typical French style of a Janequin with all its mannerisms, or the straightforward Gallic pointedness of a Certon. Despite the limitless variety of accents displayed in his chansons, the music is invariably adapted to the text, though it is never descriptive in the Janequin sense. It would be difficult, if not impossible, to find fault with the chansons of Lassus, which will remain the crowning glory of the Renaissance chanson, yet one can occasionally detect a certain aloofness, a certain irony in these compositions, expressed in a most subtle manner. Here and there we see a miniature postlude added to the finished chanson, or a sudden turn toward a complicated polyphonic setting done with such ease that the prevalent style is not the least disturbed, yet the initiated may discover in it a sort of subtle mocking. This reminds one of the placid and undemonstrative Bach, who occasionally took a fugue subject or other theme by a less exalted composer and made a gigantic composition out of it, as if wanting to show its possibilities.

Comparing the products of the last Renaissance chanson period with those of the previous era, it may safely be said that the chanson became far too complicated, losing under the influence of the motet and madrigal (which it had helped to create) the freshness and spontaneity requisite to it as a unique art form. Interestingly enough, the madrigal had by this time far surpassed the chanson, and the French, from whom the Italians and the English had learned, were eclipsed by the expansion of the Italian and English forms. Despite the greater popularity of the latter, there still remains a rich and interesting field in French music which is largely unexplored.

The Huguenots and Their Music

PROTESTANTISM arose in France early in the sixteenth century and received a great impetus from Lutheran ideas. It was immediately persecuted, in spite of the comparative tolerance of Francis I, whose sister Margaret of Navarre was a leading protector of the Protestants. The persecutions increased as the Huguenots became more numerous, but by 1559 there were enough to hold a national synod, which set up a church with Calvinistic doctrine and presbyterian government. Its unity was one of the principal causes for the success of the Huguenots in fighting against overwhelming odds. The eventually ruthless persecution of the Huguenots was, no doubt, largely due to their efficient organization, which constituted a political menace to the crown. This seems to be confirmed by the fact that Pope Paul III remonstrated with Francis I on the severity with which the Protestants were treated.

The cause of the Reformation in France was advanced by the musical settings of Clément Marot's Psalm translations more than by anything else, as the vernacular prose translations of the Scriptures were in that country of little merit, and, true to the spirit of humanism, the form of poetry was still preferred to prose, even for the most incongruous subjects.

The music of French Protestantism was dominated by the spirit of its leader, a situation which recalls the role of Luther in the music of the German Reformed Church. John Calvin (1509–1564) was not well disposed toward music; like the Church Fathers, he recognized that "properly practiced it affords a recreation but it also leads to voluptuousness . . . and we should take good care that it does not furnish the occasion for dropping the reins to dissoluteness or for causing us to become effeminate in disorderly delights." The spirit of St. Augustine and St. Gregory speaks in these words, the same austere devotion and sincere conviction which, in its inexorable severity, held Italy spellbound for centuries; but it was this spirit which prevented Italy from partaking in the rich musical development of the Gothic world. The severity of Calvin's discipline has given rise to condemnation. The course of time has substantially modified many of his doctrines; even the churches which trace their descent from Calvin's work and faith no longer hold his views in their entirety. But his ardent sincerity cannot be doubted, and his system had an immense value in the history of Christian thought. It is noteworthy, however, that the countries which accepted the doctrines of Calvinism—Scotland, where John Knox implanted them, some parts of Holland and Switzerland, and the New England states—did not excel in music once these doctrines became an essential factor in their life. In France, where the Huguenots remained a small minority, and in England, where the Puritans had to relinquish their leadership, matters took a different course; but the great musical culture of the followers of Luther always stood in strange contrast to the sober and almost hostile attitude toward music of a part of England and Wales, Scotland, and certain parts of Switzerland and Germany. That the indestructible love of music in the people could not be stifled can be seen in the beautiful folk songs of all these countries, and even the most inarticulate Scots produced them in profusion. But their art music either fell behind that of the surrounding countries or failed altogether to develop.

After being expelled from Geneva, Calvin took up his residence in Strassburg (1538) and resolved to emulate the Lutheran example by compiling a Psalter for the use of his church. While the intentions of the Swiss divine were similar to those of Luther, the results of his activity were diametrically opposed to the German's musical policies. The turning away from the Lutheran conception of music in the Reformed Church had begun with Ulrich Zwingli (1484–1531), although this Swiss reformer was himself a poet and musician; the trend took a definitely hostile turn with Calvin, who purposely broke down the musical traditions so carefully preserved by Luther. While Calvin's deliberate action severed the ties of church music with art, exaggerated emphasis on the moral aspects of the movement threatened to extinguish the secular folk song, which had such wholesome influence on early Protestant music. The austere simplicity of Calvin's ritual and the strictness with which the ministers sought to enforce not only the laws of morality, but certain sumptuary regulations respecting the dress and mode of living of the citizens, were brought to bear on matters musical. Loys Bourgeois, the eminent, patient, and peaceful composer working for next to nothing for the parsimonious city council of Geneva, was thrown into prison for having, "without leave," altered the tunes of some of the Psalms.

The Calvinists were, under such conditions, faced with the problem of creating their own music along new lines. Calvin counseled Protestant musicians to set the Psalms to music, but he held that polyphonic settings of the Scriptures should be sung only in the home, in the family circle and with friends, for edification and the praise of the Lord. When it came to specifically devotional music in religious services of the church, he refused to admit anything beyond simple congregational singing. Laboring under these severe liturgic-aesthetic creeds, the musicians composed simple harmonizations of the Psalm tunes which were rather colorless, more utilitarian than artistic. The "home" variety of French Protestant music grew, however, and soon resulted in a dignified counterpart to the polyphonic motet, the contrapuntal apparatus of which was employed here with great skill and understanding. In fact, the more elaborate Psalm settings of Claude Goudimel, Jacques Mauduit, and Claude Le Jeune are great motets composed on French Psalm translations.

Clément Marot published in Geneva (1542) thirty Psalms, followed by another set of fifty with a preface by Calvin. The theologian admitted that when fitted with *mélodies modérées* the songs could be used "even in the church." After the death of Marot, the work was continued by Theodore Beza (Bèze) (1551–1562), the learned humanist and chief advocate of all Reformed congregations in France, and musical settings of the Psalms began to appear.[29] The chief composers engaged in this work were Loys Bourgeois (c. 1510 to after 1561), composer of many of the tunes of the Geneva Psalter, and Claude Goudimel (c. 1505–1572), tragically killed in the massacre of the Huguenots in Lyons, August 27, 1572. An able and well-schooled composer, Goudimel joined the ranks of the Huguenots after having composed a number of Masses and chansons, and was well equipped to undertake the musical organization of the Psalter. Goudimel's Psalter grew to eight books by 1566 and contained monumental settings in the motet style. There are two other Goudimel settings of the Marot-Bèze Psalter. In 1564 he published it in an abridged form, with musical settings in a moderate motet style, and in 1565 the complete Psalter in a very simple style, scarcely more then a mere chordal harmonization. These Psalms, purposely held in a simple vein, were destined for congregational singing.

The Huguenot Psalter became, in both its textual and its musical forms, an inalienable part of Protestant music and exerted a tremendous influence on all of Protestant Europe and the American colonies. In the sixteenth century alone there were over a hundred French editions, and soon the Lutheran world was to experience the powerful pressure of this religious thought, interpreting not only the spirit but the letter of the Scriptures, with its deliberate limitations and negation of the Lutheran type of music, and devoid of any artistic intention. The great importance of the Psalter lies not so much in the melodies which became the revered property of the various Protestant denominations, as in its convinced, authoritative opening of a new tendency, style, and manner of musical setting. Under its influence, the theologians insisted again with more weight on the use of the vernacular and, in association with musicians, began to drift away from Luther's aesthetic-artistic conception, which they deemed dangerous as it might divert sincere piety and devotion. The epoch-making stylistic consequence of this renewed Augustinian tendency was the abandonment of the so-called tenor melodies. The chorale tune was lifted from the relative obscurity of the tenor part and given to the treble or soprano part. Lucas Osiander (1534–1604), court preacher in Württemberg and a man of great culture and versatility, published the first hymnbook, *Fifty Spiritual Songs and Psalms,* etc. (1586), in which the new principle was carried out methodically. With this publication we reach a new phase of development in church music: artistic merit and value became opposed to religious expediency. The new hymnlike Protestant songs, in their austere simplicity, appeared as a sort of *Gebrauchsmusik,* conceived solely in the interest of congregational use and renouncing any help from artistic quarters. Forbidding and sterile as it may seem, this new orientation was to produce great art once its initial Calvinistic hostility to the world of art had faded away; but the ultimate development did not take place in the land of its origin.

Spain and Its Music During the Renaissance Era

FORMING a united nation relatively late—in the fifteenth century—Spain was the most medieval and most Catholic land in the Catholic world. The contrast of neighboring Islam acted as a constant reminder and kept the Church more alert and united than in any other country, and the crusade against Granada filled it anew with a glowing fervor. It was only after the expulsion of the Moors in 1492 that the Spanish Church, heretofore living in isolation, entered upon a European mission. The Spanish Church was national, but absolutely and elementally Catholic, very little affected by the Renaissance, and almost untouched by the Reformation. Its struggles with Islam, its pure morals and correct scholastic precepts, its model organization, its all-embracing mysticism, and its isolation preserved the great strength of the medieval Church. Then came the Habsburgs, knightly and imperialistic, who raised the Iberian peninsula to a world power; but its ambitions remained saturated with Catholic passion. This land and atmosphere presented the Holy See with a formidable arsenal of political power in the persons of Charles V and Philip II, and Ignatius Loyola, the motivating power of Catholic action. Spanish nationalism became dissolved in the universalism of Rome and produced the ideals of the Counter Reformation. It is for this reason that Spanish culture cannot be detached from the Church; the sole approach to the arts and letters of Spain leads through the doors of her churches.

The extreme diversity of Spain's racial mélange, including Iberians, Celts, Basques, Goths, Arabs, and Berbers, gave Spanish national culture a certain exotic quality which segregates it from the other Romanic nations. In the predominance of passion over will may be found an explanation of the cruelty of the Spanish character, which imposed the Inquisition and accepts the bullfight as a ritual. The Spaniard's asceticism, his strict and severe cult of tradition, his hypnotic perseverance in the service of the Church, and his soul, crushed by the centuries-long struggle with the African invaders and hardened under the extreme climate of rocky Castile, produced an indescribable culture.

Unswerving faith in tradition and the aristocratic pathos embedded in the nation by feudal chivalry gave rise to a proud pomp and aristocratic sense of form, a nobility of speech, poetic flight, and a remarkable ability for rhetoric, all of which are present in every manifestation of Spanish art. One must take into consideration the importance of the culture of the Moors, installed in Spain until 1492; but while the Oriental influence cannot be neglected, it is impossible to make it the fundamental basis of Spanish culture. Besides having the undeniably Oriental tendency for ornamentation, the Spaniards have always been partial to realism, which is the antipode of ornamentation. Stark, unadorned naturalism, devoid of any illusion, is fundamentally Spanish and is not to be found in the make-up of the other Romanic nations.

Spain was as remote from classical art, from a pure Renaissance, as Germany; Spanish art reached its maturity in the baroque, into which the late Gothic merged without an influential Renaissance period acting as intermediary. The Renaissance was, to repeat Michelet, the *découverte de l'homme,* but it was the habitat of man's spirit which was discovered rather than his spirit itself. The baroque found his soul, and discovered that it was a suffering soul. The Renaissance man smilingly said *vivamus,* but the man of the baroque said *memento mori.* No other nation has spoken these words with such ardent fervor as the Spanish. The eternal riddle of the beyond fascinated the Iberians, and they shuddered at the thought of fate. How different is the mood of the Italians. Even their saints are free and friendly, familiar with this world, knowing and appreciating earthly pleasures. These national characteristics explain why Italy was predestined to be the champion of the Renaissance, leaving Spain, where everything was enveloped in the cosmos of the Church, to the fantastic, emotional, and monumental world of the baroque.

Spanish music in the Middle Ages, the Renaissance, and the early baroque is as yet hardly explored; and church music, especially, of the earlier periods is almost entirely unknown, owing to a lack of publications.[30] Yet the musical life of Spain must have been extraordinarily rich, as musical intercourse between Castile, Catalonia, and Aragon, and with France, Flanders, and Italy was animated and frequent. In this connection music shows a much more appreciable Renaissance influence than the fine arts do. Alfonso the Magnanimous (c. 1396-1458), King of Aragon, conqueror of Naples, and enthusiastic patron of arts and letters, did much to advance the Renaissance influence. At his death he left Naples to his son Ferdinand, and Aragon to his brother John II, thereby continuing the relationship between the two countries. Many Spaniards were in the papal chapel choir, and a number of them were in the court of the Sforza in Milan. The connections between the Low Countries and Spain were close even before the time of the Regency.

The Spanish descendants of the chanson de geste (the *cantar de gesta*) were the romances sung by wandering minstrels and jongleurs (*juglares*) to simple tunes called *tonadas*. These romances occupy a position of even greater importance than the madrigal did in Italy. Spanish lute composers used the tonadas as subjects for variations, which served as accompaniments to the recitation of the romances. The Spanish theater received its wonderful fables, its noble pathos, its animated, lyrically colored, and epically panoramic tirades from these centuries-old romances, which reflected all shades of Spanish national and literary characteristics. As the tone of the romances conveyed the atmosphere of the future national theater, the *Libro de Buen Amor* ("Book of True Love") by the poet Juan Ruiz (1283-1350), one of the most engaging chronicles in world literature, illustrates the great realistic literature of coming centuries, the picaresque novel. Spanish humor and the Spanish art of characterization appear in these novels in their purest form. The aristocratic pathos and impeccable language of the derelict picaro and the often bawdy story afforded an inexhaustible source of the heroicomic.

Besides the original forms of Spanish poetry, especially the *cancioneros,* or collections of romances and other songs, we must henceforth count the growing court poetry, artificial and pretentious, as it developed under the influence of the Italian Renaissance. The Spanish Petrarchists did not fall behind their Italian colleagues; the sheer formal beauty, the intoxicating ring of the verses, the sensuous melody of the words of their poetry represent the utmost in beauty that any language can produce. The original romances still lived, but by the last third of the sixteenth century the triumph of the school *al itálico modo* was assured. A host of poets were engaged in recasting the old romances and in composing new ones. The stage took the place of the romances of the previous age; here, and in their novels, Spanish genius revealed itself with the greatest vigor and originality, with all the passions and aspirations of the Spanish people. But with the stage we are already in the most typical domain of the baroque.

This remarkable period of poetry produced music which reflected faithfully the spirit that animated the poets. The romances, sonnets, and *villancicos* published in the *Cancionero Musical de los Siglos XV y XVI* (1890) by Francisco Asenjo Barbieri give us an idea of the marvelous musical productivity of these centuries. Among the four hundred and fifty pieces in three and four parts included in the volume, sixty-eight are compositions by the great poet Juan del Encina (1469–1534). It is interesting to note that this poet, when discoursing on the condition of the poetic art in Spain, uses the term *arte de trobar;* thus the old troubadour principle of the union of poetry and music, and poet and musician, reappears, or, more probably, survives, in these ballads and songs remarkable for their intense sincerity and devout grace. The few songs with lute accompaniment by the great lutenist song composers of the first half of the sixteenth century—Don Luis Milan, Luis de Narvaez, Alonso de Mudarra, and Miguel de Fuenllana—that are now available in modern editions disclose a musical art of such grace and finish as elevates Spain among the leading musical nations of the Renaissance.

Secular vocal music was well developed and practiced throughout Spain, but instrumental music for the lute and keyboard instruments was of such excellence as we have seen only in the finest compositions of the great Renaissance composers. If the musical treasures of Spain are unearthed and published by scholars of the type of Pedrell and Anglès, the musical history of the Renaissance may be open for considerable revision.

We have already mentioned the peculiar guitarlike Spanish lute, the *vihuela*. By the sixteenth century the vihuela had become one of the chief instruments of art music and the favorite of the aristocratic court circles. During the early decades of the century the vihuelists transcribed for their aristocratic masters all types of complicated vocal polyphony. Later, in order to amuse their patrons, they collected popular songs, ballads, and dance music, which they arranged for their instrument. The author of the first printed tablature book in Spain was Don Luis Milan. His book, entitled *El Maestro,* appeared in 1535 and was probably written to facilitate instruction in an instrument which was a necessary adjunct to good breeding. Three years later

Luis de Narvaez published a volume of tablatures containing transcriptions of vocal works by Josquin, Gombert, and other celebrated composers, foreign and Spanish, as well as Spanish folk music.

Outstanding among these composers was Miguel de Fuenllana. His tablature book *Orphenica Lyra* (1554), indicates not only the remarkable technical progress made since the appearance of *El Maestro,* but a grasp of a truly instrumental style that was unique in his time. Fuenllana's fantasies are the utterances of a virtuoso instrumentalist who not only knows every technical secret of his vihuela but invents his expressive and bold music in a style that is the perfect medium for his instrument. There is no trace in these works of the *Gebrauchsmusik* character of contemporary compositions, and the usual subtitle applied to such composition, advising the players and singers that the work is "apt for singing or playing," is meaningless in the face of music written in so admirably instrumental a style.

The last work intended solely for the vihuela was that by Esteban Daza published in 1576, after which the aristocratic instrument began to be popularized, finally being replaced by the guitar.[31]

A generation ago little was known about the early history of keyboard music, and no one paid much attention to the Spanish composers of organ and harpsichord music. The universal literary praise and renown of keyboard music was accompanied by an almost total lack of information concerning its nature and products. It was the great accomplishment of Otto Kinkeldey to fill in this gap. In his *Orgel und Klavier in der Musik des XVI Jahrhunderts* (Leipzig, 1910) he opened a new chapter in our knowledge of the music of the Renaissance, and this book—the result of vast erudition and painstaking research—acquainted us with the eminence of Spanish keyboard music. Interest in organ and harpsichord music was so lively in Spain toward the middle of the sixteenth century that special instructive works were published to enable musicians to perfect themselves in the technique and manner of composition of their instrument. Among these works the *Declaración de Instrumentos Musicales* (1555), by Juan Bermudo, and the *Arte de Taner Fantasia,* etc. (1565, but finished ten years earlier), by Thomas de Sancta Maria, are our chief sources for the study of the keyboard music, and the instrumental music in general, of the period. These authors, especially Sancta Maria, did not limit themselves to the statement of rules and precepts, but illustrated their principles with a generous number of examples, thereby providing us with an excellent anthology of Spanish instrumental music of the sixteenth century. While most of their forms correspond to the Italian instrumental species, the Spanish variations (*diferencias*) excel in their ornate and brilliant style and clever modulations, and their ricercari (*tientos* and fugues) show an earnestness and depth, associated with a modern conception of tonality, which lifts them above the rank and file of their contemporaries.

The greatest representative of this art was Antonio de Cabezón (1510–1566), organist and harpsichordist to Charles V and Philip II, accompanying the latter to England and Flanders. Like so many famous organists, Cabezón was blind from infancy. This affliction did not deter him, however, from composing keyboard music of such stunning originality as was entirely unknown before or immediately after his time. His admirable variations, bold chromatic "fugues," and clever transcriptions display a nobility of melody and polyphony which we shall not meet again until the advent of the great organists, many years his juniors, who appeared at the close of the century.[32]

The epoch of Ferdinand and Isabella (1474–1516) marks both the beginning of Spain's colonial expansion and world power and the great flourishing of arts and letters. The brilliant Spanish court was well provided with musicians, organists, a distinguished chapel choir, instrumentalists, and minstrels. Contrary to the custom elsewhere on the Continent, these musicians were all native Spaniards, possessors of a thoroughly grounded local musical tradition; they remained so until, following the marriage of the Infanta Joanna to Archduke Philip the Fair of Austria (1496), who inherited from his mother the Burgundian lands, there started the influx of Flemish musicians. Although during the time when the rest of Continental Europe was overrun with Flemish musicians the Spanish seemingly relied on local talent, we must assume that they were acquainted with the music of the Burgundian and Flemish schools, because of the presence of Flemish manuscripts of the eighties and nineties in Spanish libraries. With the visits of Philip and his wife, whose entourage included the brillant choir headed by such composers of renown as Pierre de La Rue, Alexander Agricola, Antonius Divitis, and Marbriano de Orto, the Flemish visitors became numerous. The Spanish-Flemish influence was reciprocal, however: the various imperial choirs during the reign of Charles V alternated the best works of Flemish, French, and Spanish composers.

At the court of Ferdinand and Isabella music was a flourishing art. Among the many musicians at the court, we should mention Juan de Anchieta (c. 1450–1523), the choirmaster of Don Juan, only son of the reigning pair. Anchieta was almost exactly contemporaneous with Josquin Després, and was one of the outstanding Spanish composers of the period, leaving a number of Masses and motets as well as popular music to posterity. He stands at the end of the remarkable period of native music which musicologists are now studying with increasing interest. For although French, Burgundian, and Italian music found its way into the courts and was well received in Castile and Aragon, its popularity did not prevent the rise of a native art. The native music was entirely subordinated to the aims of its poetic text, a fact which distinguishes the Spanish song from the Franco-Flemish, and which indicates a remote Provençal-troubadour origin. It seems as though the

Spanish musicians did not relish the highly complicated polyphonic technique of the Flemish, for they endeavored to make their constructions simple, with a moderate use of polyphonic subtleties. It is the simple Castilian folk song which lies at the bottom of this art. As we approach the turn of the fifteenth century, the situation begins to change. The acceptance of the Burgundian and Franco-Flemish style of composition must have occurred in the fourth quarter of the fifteenth century, because musicians like Anchieta were already fully conversant with it. When we enter, finally, into the period of Spanish history which leads up to the Catholic Reform, we find musicians who appropriated the Franco-Flemish and Italo-Flemish style to such an extent and with such perfection that we must consider them together with other composers as members of the so-called "Roman school." The great fame of Spanish music rests on these composers, who were active in Rome, embracing, in the measure permitted by their racial characteristics, the Palestrinian ideals. Thus, if we wish to form an idea of a more specific Spanish style in the sixteenth century, we must turn to the works of the less famous masters active at the cathedrals in Málaga, Seville, and Barcelona.

The Choral Composers of the Hispano-Flemish School

WHETHER we are dealing with the Spanish composers who were active in the cathedrals of their native land or with the many famous musicians of Spanish origin who could be found in all the great artistic centers, Rome, Vienna, Brussels, Naples, etc., they all shared the same ecstatic mysticism, the same sobriety and austerity, the same emotional fantasy of Spanish Catholicism that characterizes Spanish painters of the period. The political situation, the structure of the empire, and the increasingly vigorous policy of the Vatican contributed a great deal to the expansion of Spanish music and musicians, much admired and sought after everywhere in Europe and America. Francisco Guerrero (1528–1599) is one of the great masters who spent most of his life in Spain as choirmaster in the cathedrals in Seville and Málaga, although his greatly admired works were published in France, Flanders, and Italy. In 1588, however, he finally realized his ardent desire to visit the Holy Land, for the reasons naïvely and piously expressed in his travel diary entitled *El Viaje de Jerusalem,* of which some ten editions were printed in the course of the seventeenth and eighteenth centuries. "One of the main obligations of my service was to compose annually new *chanzonetas* and *villancicos* for Christmas, and each time I encountered the word Bethlehem, I felt my desire grow to visit that sacred place and to perform my music there in the company of the angels and shepherds who attended the first ceremony." The Christmas compositions mentioned by Guerrero were composed to Spanish texts, in imitation of popular music. It was in these villancicos that the austere composers gave free rein to their imagination, because they were veritable dramatic pieces purporting to characterize the *dramatis personae* of the Christmas legend. The colorful mixture of characters giving honor to the birth of Our Lord included, besides the traditional shepherds, soldiers, students, and ordinary folk, Negroes and the Indians of America, who often spoke in their native dialect, giving the composer the opportunity to imitate the popular songs of the various Spanish districts and colonies. Another Spaniard of great stature who was active in his native country, never venturing abroad, was Juan Pujol (c. 1573-1626), Catalan composer and choirmaster in Tarragona, Saragossa, and Barcelona. Were it not for the scholarship of the eminent Catalan musicologist, Father Higini Anglès, who has published several volumes of a projected complete edition of Pujol's works, we should not know about this great musician; and he is, undoubtedly, only one of the self-effacing Spanish masters whose works, buried in cathedral and monastery libraries, are awaiting the searching eyes of scholars.

The Roman group of Spaniards included many notable musicians: Bartolomé Escobedo (d. 1563), Francisco Soto de Langa (1539-1619), Cristobal Morales (c. 1500–1553), and Tomás Luis de Victoria (1540-1611), the last two being considered the greatest masters of Spanish-Roman sacred polyphony.

Morales and his pupil Victoria wrote in the purest Franco-Flemish polyphonic style as represented in its Roman incarnation. The style was the universal polyphonic style of Catholicism, but the spirit was Spanish. Their music glows with the visionary power which emanates from the mystics; they discover in the text dramatic moments which they illustrate with poignant music, without dropping for an instant the perfect fluid polyphonic style of the Roman school. Morales studied in Seville and was trained in the pure Franco-Flemish traditions. The choir books of the cathedral in Seville contained many works by internationally known masters; some manuscript copies of Josquin's compositions are still preserved in the choir library. The fact that Morales's first works appeared in collections of motets published by Gombert (1541) supports the possibility of his having met the Flemish composer when the latter, accompanying the Emperor Charles V, visited Seville in 1526. In 1535 Morales was accepted as singer in the papal chapel choir, which counted among its members several Spaniards. The Spaniard did not stay long in the Eternal City, however, and soon we find him mentioned at various places in Spain. The rest of his life was spent in wandering from one place and position to another, until the Cathedral Chapter in Toledo disposed of "the house left vacant by the death of Morales" on October 7, 1553.

This unruly and restless man was one of the greatest composers of the century, representing more than any other Spaniard the noble austerity of

Spanish art. His stupendous contrapuntal technique never led him to exaggerations, and all his works—Masses, motets, and Magnificats, as well as some secular compositions—are models of clearness of thought and expression and display a rare sense for the lyrical and for choral beauty.

Victoria was born in Old Castile, in the diocese of Avila, at about 1540. Of his early years and education little is known, but a grant from Philip II enabled him to journey in 1565 to Rome, where he entered the Collegium Germanicum, a Jesuit college founded by Loyola. All indications point to the fact that he was ordained before leaving Spain, and he must have received a copious musical education along Franco-Flemish lines before he became, successively, choirmaster of his college and of St. Apollinare's. During his stay in Rome, cut short by his appointment as chaplain to the widowed Empress Maria, daughter of Charles V and sister of Philip II, Victoria formed an intimate friendship with Palestrina. Returning to his native country, he occupied the modest position of choirmaster and organist of the convent known as the home of the Descalzas Reales, the retreat of the empress and her daughter, the Infanta Margaret. In fulfilling the duties of chaplain he was several times on the verge of bidding farewell to music in order to dedicate himself entirely to the duties of the priesthood, but, happily, events took a different course. This was to be expected, as in the dedication of one of his works to Pope Gregory XIII Victoria described himself as driven by a sort of natural instinct to the cultivation of sacred music. Soon after becoming choirmaster in Rome, Victoria composed and dedicated a volume of motets to Cardinal Truchsess, the great connoisseur of church music and sponsor of Jacobus de Kerle. This volume contains the well-known motets *O Quam Gloriosum* and *O Vos Omnes* (the latter mistakenly attributed to Morales in some modern publications). These motets show the Spanish composer already in the full possession of his great expressive powers. Where some of his Roman colleagues write artistic and refined counterpoint, Victoria displays a greater warmth of feeling, at the same time ascetically abstaining from rhetoric. Publication of his works, continued, sometimes at long intervals, after his return to Spain. Among the Masses, motets, and Psalms there are many written for six, eight, nine, and even twelve voices, displaying the early baroque pomp and majesty of the Venetian double and triple choirs with which the Roman composers were familiar.

Victoria was the first musician to set to music all the hymns of the liturgic year. This work, published as *Hymni Totius Anni Secundum Sanctae Romanae Ecclesiae Consuetudinem,* appeared in Rome in 1581. In March, 1603, the Empress Maria died, and Victoria composed a Requiem Mass as a tribute to her memory. This composition, published in 1605, is the crowning glory of his art and one of the most magnificent choral compositions of the entire literature. Victoria himself called it his swan song and apparently did not compose anything afterwards. When death overtook him on August 27, 1611, he was acting as chaplain to the Infanta Margaret and as organist of the convent, having abandoned the post of choirmaster after the death of the empress. The reputation of this retiring priest was not confined to Europe: it extended to the Spanish colonies in America, as is shown by the record of a gift sent to him from one of his admirers in Lima, Peru.

Victoria's birthplace was also the birthplace of St. Theresa of Jesus (1515–1582), the most striking embodiment of the Spanish religious spirit. We do not know whether Victoria knew the saint personally, but the coincidence of birthplace is not merely symbolical: the musician proved to be one of the spiritual companions of St. Theresa, St. John of the Cross, and Loyola. This austere, inspired priest of the Church never composed one line of secular music. Palestrina wrote a volume or two of spiritual madrigals, which, while far from being secular in character, still were not employable for liturgic purposes. Victoria never even used a cantus firmus of secular origin. The general resemblance of his style to that of Palestrina is so striking that many of his works could not be distinguished from the great Roman's compositions. But if a Palestrinian influence is claimed for Victoria by some authors, such influence was at least reciprocal, for Palestrina's motets from the year 1584, with their ardently passionate style, show the unmistakable marks of that mystic glow which emanated from his Spanish friend and colleague. If we can forget the perfect lines of choral polyphony, the distilled and ethereal effect of Italo-Flemish composition technique which was the medium of expression of these two musicians, we shall perceive that they lived in different worlds: the Roman, transfixed in a dream of beatitude, piety, and tenderness, approaching the universal conception of spiritual beauty as expressed by Raphael, and the Spaniard, enduring the sufferings of the Crucified with a glowing fervor that becomes almost sensual in its dramatic passion. Victoria's settings of certain parts of the Passion according to St. Matthew, included in the publication entitled *Officium Hebdomadae Sanctae* (1585), testify to a dramatic expressiveness that is without parallel in purely choral literature. Compared with the intensity of his mystic emotion, aided by the freely unfolding polyphonic style made infinitely pliable through its union with the madrigal, the eighteenth-century Passions, including those of Bach, seem almost formalistic.

This art does not belong to the Renaissance. Like the Spanish theater and Spanish painting, Victoria's music carries us into the passionate world of the baroque. This is not the world of the serene Madonnas of Raphael, but that of the elongated figures of El Greco, distorted by the dramatic intensity of religious passion.

Music in Pre-Tudor England

IT is recognized that many of the dominant ideas of modern Europe had their roots in England. The freedom of the individual, a principle underlying modern society, was first acknowledged in England. English statecraft and social progressiveness have been universally admired. But all those who have united in praise of these qualities of the British have been equally unanimous in denying to them artistic inventiveness.

The theory of artistic sterility is not incompatible with the nature of the modern commercial cosmopolite, and—in the instance of music—it has, indeed, been well demonstrated in recent centuries. The necessity of shaping the vocations of men to serve the interests of Church and commonwealth created an economic creed that called for "a society composed of individuals who make work the handmaid of religion and morality, and who find in the earnest pursuit of honest vocations the greatest service that can be rendered to church and state. Such, indeed, was the ideal that the Protestant clergy tried to inculcate in the English public, and so well did they succeed that by the beginning of the seventeenth century there were few to gainsay their teachings." [33] Adventurous voyages in search of gold or new territories to be colonized, the growth of English industry, the phenomenal development of commerce following Antwerp's loss of its dominant position, the animated intercourse with the Mediterranean and Baltic countries, all contributed to the well-being of the commonwealth and filled the Englishman with pride, instilling in him the conviction that he was destined to lead the modern world. Out of utilitarian works on geography and the accounts of merchants and seamen grew a vast literature inspired by and appealing to the middle class. The reaction that followed this orientation was not slow to make itself felt in the realm of arts and letters and all that the Continental historians and musicians of the nineteenth century could discover were tirades against art and a tremendous decline of music and musical composition after the Tudor era. By failing to explore the great treasures of their own musical culture English musicians and musical scholars aided the world in forming an unjust picture of their music. They forgot that

> The old gentle Britons in her dayes
> Of divers aventures maden layes,
> Rymed first in her Mother tongue
> Whych layes with her Instruments they songe.

We must admit that the disastrous period of the War of the Roses almost exterminated native music, and Henry VIII was inclined to encourage foreign musicians to practice their art at his court. But national art was only dormant. We must, therefore, go back to the times of Dunstable to pick up the thread which will enable us to restore the picture of English music during the Renaissance.

It has been deemed necessary, for the sake of continuity, to deal with Dunstable in relation with music on the Continent, without considering his period in England. His influence upon the development of European music was of such proportions that it was imperative that we preface the rise of the Burgundian school by an appraisal of this eminent composer. In doing so we failed to emphasize sufficiently the importance and nature of the English school. Let us go back, then, to the musicians who carried over the old art into Dunstable's century.

On October 25, 1415, the miserable, starved little army of Henry V was facing a well-equipped enemy ten times its size. Not since the days of the Macedonian was a victory so astounding and incredible achieved as that at Agincourt. And music played a conspicuous part in it. The king's chaplain, Thomas Elmham, who was present at Agincourt, relates how the priests sang the Miserere "vociferously" to the attacking English soldiers. At the end of the battle the king intoned with his soldiers a thanksgiving song. The chroniclers are unequivocal in their statements concerning this song, and we can safely conclude that the famous *Deo Gracias Anglia* is the song that was improvised on the battlefield.

> Deo gracias Anglia redde pro victoria.
> Owre Kynge went forthe to Normandy
> With grace and might of chyvalry.
> Ther God for hym wrought mervelusly,
> Wherefore Englonde may calle and cry:
> Deo gracias!
>
> Chorus:
>
> Deo gracias Anglia redde pro victoria.

The eminent Dr. Burney called this composition "very incorrect" but forgot that such an improvised polyphonic song testifies to a remarkable musical culture. The composition is a sturdy piece of music and cannot, of course, be considered from the point of view of the eighteenth-century "thorough bass man" that was Burney. The Agincourt song recalls once more the latent musical power of Celts and Anglo-Saxons, somnolent since age-old heathen days, which in previous centuries had rebelled against the *cantus Romanus* and created polyphony, and which could not be eradicated "with all the holy water of the world." It reappeared again in these songs. One glance at the music of the Agincourt song [34] will convince us that while the prosody of the English text is natural and the music follows it with ease, the Latin prosody is entirely disregarded by the melody, visibly shaped to fit the rest of the song. The folk song, a legacy from heathenism, was victorious over kings and popes and triumphantly invaded every domain of music.

The sovereign who sang with his soldiers at Agincourt, Welch-born Henry V, was a musician of the first water. Historians endeavoring to establish the identity of the composer whose works in the Old Hall Manuscript are signed "Roy Henry" were long uncertain about awarding the palm and leaned toward Henry VI. There can be no question that the musician-king was Henry V, whom contemporary poets and chroniclers likened to King David. The literary testimonials are corroborated by the fact that in the second volume of the recent modern edition of the Old Hall Manuscript the date of its writing—which in the first volume was assumed to be about 1450—was placed some sixty years earlier. Henry V's great interest in music contributes to the impressive picture of musical England and explains the culmination of old English music in the school of Dunstable.

In 1416, in an attempt to heal the schism in the Church, King Sigismund (later Emperor) of Germany, Bohemia, and Hungary visited England. How deeply the visitor was impressed with what he saw and heard may be seen from his farewell message, mentioned in John Capgrave's *Chronicle of England*.[35]

> Farewel, with glorious victory,
> Blessed Inglond, *full of melody.*
> Thou may be cleped of Angel nature;
> Thou servist God so with bysy cure.
> We leve with the this praising;
> Whech we schul evir sey and sing.

Martin le Franc in his *Champion des Dames* [36] still praises the English musicians of the middle of the fifteenth century, and maintains that their playing at the court of Burgundy was of unsurpassed excellence. These testimonials bespeak a musical art of the highest order which contributed materially to the course of musical history, but the horrors of the war between 1455 and 1485 put an end to the flourishing musical culture of England. The chronicles and other literary sources, heretofore abounding in musical references, are no longer concerned with the muses; Chaucer's "gentle Britons" are no longer rhyming and singing, for fire and sword turned against brothers discourage lyricism.

Nevertheless, a national art of centuries cannot be wiped out entirely, and while the chronicles are chary of information, the great rise of Tudor art cannot be explained without a latent continuation of national art. In spite of the terrible fratricidal years, arts and letters were not wholly stamped out, and the reputation of the English musicians in foreign countries was great enough to prompt the Duke of Milan, Galeazzo Sforza, to send his chapel-

master to England in 1471 to choose some good English singers for his choir
in Milan. According to Wooldridge, "the censure passed by Tinctoris upon
the followers of Dunstable applies also, though with less force perhaps than
we should have been inclined to suppose, to the main body of the English
composers." [37] There can be little doubt that by the end of the fifteenth century the Continental branch of English music was extinct, hence the critical
comments of Tinctoris; but these comments do not apply to the home country, to "the main body of the English composers."

Early Tudor Composers

AFTER the accession of Henry VII there was a group of composers of
whose lives very little is known but whose achievements, extending into the
first quarter of the sixteenth century, can be estimated by their various manuscripts, scattered in English libraries. Like Chaucer and Wyclif, who, while
dependent on forms and influences from abroad, were nevertheless the products of the national genius rather than of universal Catholic thought, these
musicians could not entirely ignore the art of the neighboring Flemish countries, yet the mystical and speculative art of the Burgundian circle was foreign to these Englishmen accustomed to straightforward singing. Many of
them weathered the troubled years of internal strife to found the great body
of Tudor composers. Even the younger generation which appeared in the
first decade of Henry VIII's reign grew from this national school, the beginnings of which hark back to the days of Giraldus Cambrensis. The in-
sular spirit would not flourish under foreign influences, and at that time
there was no indication of the future power and role of England in world
history. But the world as a whole was undergoing profound changes as it
emerged from medieval civilization. Industry and commerce, expanding
rapidly, forced a new economic orientation which in its turn called for new
political and cultural tenets. England could not remain entirely isolated, and
with the advent of the Tudor dynasty there started her spectacular rise in the
world. With the coronation of Henry VII in 1485 begins the modern period
of English history. The accession of Henry, an astute political leader, brought
order from the chaos created by the War of the Roses, and his diplomatic
skill kept England at peace with all her enemies, within and without the
country.

Henry Abyngdon seems to have been the teacher of some of the earliest
composers of the late fifteenth-century group. He was succeeded by Gilbert
Banestre (d. 1487), who commemorated the union of the two roses of York
and Lancaster by a five-part motet, the manuscript of which is now in the
Eton College Library. Walter Lambe (second half of the fifteenth century)
was another of the earlier composers whose manuscript compositions are ex-

tant. William Newark, (c. 1450–1509) enjoyed a great reputation in his day but shares obscurity with several of his colleagues for want of modern publication. We are better informed about Richard Davy (last mentioned in 1515), who after some years spent in Magdalen College at Oxford became in 1501 chaplain to Sir William Boleyn, the grandfather of Anne, and remained in the services of that family until 1515. Among his compositions there is an incomplete four-part Passion for Palm Sunday written in an animated and dramatic style. This is not only the earliest example of passion music in England, but its dramatic conception antedates the first Continental attempts at setting the music of the "crowd" (*turbae*) for a chorus instead of a solo voice.[38] With Hugh Aston (c. 1480–1522) we reach a Tudor composer of great importance. This composer, a canon of St. Stephen's, Westminster, wrote in an elegant and fluent "pianistic" style at the very beginning of the sixteenth century when such typically instrumental setting (running scales, etc.) was entirely unknown elsewhere. Those who have naïvely claimed for Aston the "invention" of instrumental music did not realize the injustice they were doing to English music. For such a mature technique and style does not arise within one man's short lifetime. Most famous of Aston's compositions is a "Hornpipe" for virginals showing a remarkably developed conception of the variation form with a drone bass. William Cornyshe (c. 1468–1523), a great favorite of Henry VIII, was, besides being a musician, a dramatist and actor who presented interludes and pageants at the court. When the king met Francis I of France on that memorable occasion at the Field of the Cloth of Gold, Cornyshe accompanied him to take charge of the musical part of the sumptuous and unexampled splendor of the pageantry. Among his works now in the British Museum there are several part songs for two and three voices with humorous and satirical English texts, but there are also several which suggest Burgundian and French models. We reach, finally, Robert Fayrfax (d. 1521), in whose works the art of the early Tudor composers culminated. W. H. Grattan Flood in his biographical study of early Tudor composers [39] has proved that Fayrfax was a member of the Chapel Royal in the last quarter of the fifteenth century. In 1501–1502 he took the degree of Doctor of Music in Cambridge University and ten years later was the recipient of a similar degree from Oxford. His last public appearance was at the head of Henry VIII's musical delegation at the Field of the Cloth of Gold in 1520, one year before his death. Fayrfax was in his day, as Anthony à Wood, the painstaking English chronicler, said of him, "in great renowne and accounted the prime musitian of the nation." When Jeffrey Pulver [40] calls him "a reactionary composer who broke away from the traditions of the Low Countries" he is guilty again of neglecting the possibility of a living and original English school. A large choir book preserved in Eton College, dating, according to Wooldridge, from 1490 to 1504, shows that the native traditions persisted, because while there is a difference between the compositions contained in this collection and the works in the Old Hall Manuscript, the technique of setting and composition in both seems to be untouched by foreign influences. There was, consequently, no need to break away from any foreign tradition. The works of Fayrfax, whose austere and noble melodic settings recall the sonorous music of Dunstable, are still chiefly unpublished, and the few modern prints are disfigured by incompetent editing. We can, however, get a glimpse of his musicianship through the few excerpts published in the manuals of Burney and Hawkins.

It is indeed lamentable that the research work of W. H. Grattan Flood was not followed by competent editorial activity. When we consider that in the catalogue of the British Museum alone there are hundreds of names of Tudor composers it becomes apparent how musically prolific the period was, and how large is the number of manuscripts that remain to be published. The ten volumes of *Tudor Church Music* published by the Oxford University Press for the Carnegie Trust do not contain works by the older Tudor composers; the earliest master in the series is Taverner, a musician with whom a new style period opens. Publication in modern score of the music of these old masters is the more urgently needed because of the apparent confusion that reigns among students of this important period of national music in England. While Pulver calls Fayrfax a reactionary composer, other writers go to the opposite extreme. "One *Gloria* by Fayrfax can give more feeling of inspired spiritual exaltation than a dozen Masses by Josquin, Clemens, Willaert and Goudimel. . . ." [41] One wonders whether this is the most appropriate way to counteract the old legend of "the country without music."

The Reformation in England

FOR more than a century after Dunstable's death the major field of English musical composition was church music. Its forms—Masses, motets, Magnificats, etc.—remained unchanged until the Reformation forced a complete reorientation at the very moment when the Flemish style of polyphony came to be accepted by the rank and file of English musicians. But the English Reformation was not final; Henry's children and their counselors caused one upheaval after another with their respective acceptance and rejection of the religious reforms. English church music followed the vicissitudes of political and doctrinal warfare and emerged with wounds that never healed.

It would not be reasonable to assume that a lasting change in the religious and political life of England should be ascribed to such an ephemeral affair as the king's infatuation for Anne Boleyn, or, for that matter, to his desire for a male heir. The nationalization of the English church was rather the result than the cause of the secession from Rome. Its national traits, its dependence on the king, its use of the vernacular for worship were all established by Parliament after the separation and were not theses adopted and advocated by the Church before the schism. Nationalism had been victorious over the state, and now it was about to triumph over the Church, but not without assuming some of the distinguishing marks of its victims. How clear were the political aims of the anti-Roman movement, and how little the doctrinal elements counted in the Englishman's opposition before the late sixteenth century, can be surmised from Thomas Walsingham's *Chronicle,* which dates from the early fifteenth century.[42]

Henry VIII found it expedient to find a legal justification for his assumption of the leadership of his church following his differences with the papacy. One by one the ties binding England to the Holy See were broken, resulting finally in a complete severance and the establishment of the Church of England. In the Act of Supremacy he obtained acceptance of his declaration that according to divine law the pope had no authority over England, and recognition of his place as "only supreme head on earth of the Church of England." Two years later all officials in England were required to renounce the authority of the pope. This declaration was nothing but a codification of the old tendencies once advocated by Wyclif. The new church was not the Evangelical church of Luther but still an Anglo-Catholic church under the crown. Thus the Reformation in England under Henry VIII was at first a political and personal matter and, except in regard to the position of the papacy, not a doctrinal departure; the theology of the Church was largely untouched. Opposition to the king's acts met with stern suppression, and various religious institutions such as churches and monasteries were abolished and pre-empted. While the road traversed was different from that taken by the German movement, the English Reformation arrived finally at the same end: the elimination of centuries-old hieratic rule. The English church, founded directly by Rome and for a long time its privileged daughter, turned away from the alma mater to take up the fostering of an independent Church of England, begun by zealous Englishmen two centuries before. This movement, being purely political at the beginning, had little if anything in common with the doctrinal reforms of the Germans; but the king already realized the political import of the German situation and sought ways and means of establishing contact with the German Protestants and allied himself with the Schmalkaldic League.

Under Edward's advisers the progress of Protestantism was greatly accelerated. High church offices were filled with avowed Protestants, and Parliament issued a new Prayer Book and a standard of faith, which later became the Thirty-nine Articles. When the Catholic Mary came to the throne in 1553 she was determined to restore to the full the religion still held by most of her subjects. Mary's reign retarded for a short time the great national development. She caused all the measures that had separated the Church of England from Rome to be reversed, the old ritual was restored, and the nation was formally received again into the Catholic communion under the pope. Elizabeth restored, with some changes, the decrees of Henry VIII and Edward VI. The Act of Supremacy was enforced over the bishops, the saying of Mass prohibited under severe penalties, and the Anglican Church took on the general outlines of its modern form.

The religious differences now reached a greater intensity of feeling as the Counter Reformation spread over the western countries. France, the Netherlands, and England were in the throes of religious warfare such as had raked Germany in the first half of the century. Over them towered Spain, unrestricted, unified, and Catholic to the core, the leader of the Catholic world party. Then the flames of war lit up the map of the world. The Counter Reformation, led by Gregory XIII and Philip II, rose to inestimable power, France and the Netherlands lay prostrate, and there remained only one obstacle in the way of restoration: England. The role of the French fell to the British, who became the political, economical, and religious enemies of Spain. This enmity, deeply ingrained, did not stop at immediate hostilities, but was carried across the ocean and inherited by the American colonies. The persecution of the Catholics in England and the tremendous advance of the English merchant marine, which was preying heavily on foreign, especially Spanish, shipping, aroused Philip II to send his mighty Armada against England. Its defeat in 1588 made England into the world power she is today, and Elizabeth became the defender of Protestantism, warring on the Catholic enemies of the Protestant countries of the Continent.

The Conflict of Humanism, Renaissance, and Reformation
Its Effect on Music

DURING the reigns of Henry VII and Henry VIII, Edward VI, and Mary the final period of English Gothic architecture and decoration, the so-called "Perpendicular style," reached its culmination. The prevailing sturdy angularity of this style is very much akin to the rectilinear style of early Tudor music. The first infiltrations from the Continent of those Renaissance influences which were to become more decisive in the Elizabethan and Jacobean styles are traceable to this period. By the first years of the sixteenth century humanism began to make itself felt in England. John Colet (d. 1519), lecturer on exegetics at Oxford, became the leader of the movement. The group of humanists called the Oxford Reformers who gathered around Colet included such men as William Grocyn (d. 1519), one of the earliest scholars to teach Greek in Oxford, Thomas Linacre (c. 1460–1524), founder of the Royal

College of Physicians in London and one of the first modern physicians to study the medical works of ancient times, and Sir Thomas More (1478–1535), author of *Utopia,* a classic picture of an ideal state. Accompanying, if not preceding, these cultural and artistic currents was the introduction and acceptance of the Burgundian-Flemish polyphonic style of musical composition. It is difficult to establish the actual date of introduction of the new principles of composition, but it must have taken place in the last quarter of the fifteenth century; for at the beginning of the sixteenth, in the works of Taverner, the polished technique of motivic work and of systematic-continuous imitation appear in a remarkably advanced stage, henceforth influencing English choral style by adding to its stateliness and clear sonority the advantage of close-knit construction. One of the causes of the new influence was the exchange of manuscripts, while another may have been the cultural intercourse with Flanders, France, and Scotland. During the wars with France the Flemish fought on the side of the English, and there must have been a certain cultural intercourse between the two allies. There were also many mixed marriages between the nobility of the two nations. Musical life in Scotland was very active and benevolently supported by the reigning monarchs, nearly all rulers from James I to Mary being well disposed toward music. There were numerous *sang schoils* where youths were taught singing, the cathedrals had well-trained choirs, and a great number of minstrels were employed by the towns. Scottish literature abounds in references to the music of the common people.[43] Since political circumstances led to a close union between Scotland and France, there was a marked French influence noticeable in Scottish architecture and literature, and it is only to be expected that we find the same tendency in music. Flanders also was allied to Scotland by commercial ties, and Scottish court minstrels were sometimes sent to Flanders to learn their craft.

But the Flemish musicians themselves must have appeared in England toward the end of the fifteenth century, because in a collection dated 1516, containing music by Sampson, dean of the Chapel Royal, there are several anonymous motets entirely in the Flemish style, while one motet is signed Benedictus de Opicijs. This Benedictus was an organist at Notre Dame Cathedral in Antwerp. The cathedral archives explicitly state that he left for England in mid-February 1516, and the Chapel Royal archives state that a Benet de Opicijs was appointed court organist to Henry VIII in March, 1516. A glance at the roster of Henry VIII's musicians will convince us that Benedictus was not the sole experienced professional musician of the Flemish school at the court in the early years of the king's reign, for names like Guillaum Deventt or Peter Vanwilder obviously belong to immigrants from across the Channel. The various biographers of Charles V all agree that in 1520, when still an archduke, the future emperor visited England in the company of his music master, Henri Bredeniers (or Bredemers), a noted musician of his time. There were many other foreign musicians in the sovereign's service. The Venetian ambassador's dispatches mention a "Brescian musician to whom this king gives 300 ducats annually for playing the lute," and the Venetian organist Dionisio Memo met with such success in the court that Henry gave him a prebend in 1515. The whole course of English national music now received an entirely new orientation.

The rise to wealth of new trading families and the enrichment of many court favorites by the king with lands and wealth derived from his suppression of monasteries resulted in great artistic activity. Musical establishments similar to the Continental chapel choirs and *maîtrieses* flourished in the large churches, and the great lords also maintained excellent private choirs. While the choirs of Lincoln, Wells, and various other cathedrals were all excellent, the leading musical group was the Chapel Royal in London, the artistic supremacy of which caused, in the sixteenth century, a centralization of creative activity, since most of the important composers were attached to it as gentlemen of the Chapel.

Musical life—as in the times of Henry V—was greatly animated by a sovereign seriously enough interested in music to take up its study in a thoroughgoing manner. Edward Hall (c. 1498-1547), barrister and historian (and author of a great work entitled *The Union of the Noble and Illustre Famelies of Lancastre and York,* commonly called *Hall's Chronicle*),[44] having been an eyewitness to life in the king's court, states that Henry VIII "dyd set ii. goodly masses, euery one of them in fyve partes, whiche were songe oftentymes in hys chapel, and afterwardes in diuers other places."

During the first years of Henry's rule the assimilated Franco-Flemish polyphonic style found a master of the first magnitude in the person of John Taverner (c. 1495-1545 [1548?]), in 1526 musical leader of Cardinal Wolsey's college at Oxford. This composer of exceptional merit and ability, a worthy contemporary of the Josquinian circle, produced an imposing array of church music, published in the first and third volumes of the "Tudor Church Music" collection. After he left Oxford in 1530, Taverner went through a complete metamorphosis as a result of his embracing the Reformation. This brings us in contact again with the politico-religious events that took place in the time of Henry VIII and which affected the future of English music more profoundly than that of any other country.

The dissolution of the monasteries was a serious blow to the art of music, as every monastery had a well-established choir and one or several organists. In the six hundred monasteries and convents which were broken up there was a ruthless destruction of music. It is unfortunate that the more bigoted Reformers won the upper hand in many instances, for although Henry himself tried to preserve the Catholic ritual, they continued the havoc wrought on liturgical works. But more unfortunate was the attitude of some of the great composers themselves. We have mentioned the conversion of Taverner after he left Oxford in 1530. The musical poet in him was silenced, and he became possessed by a fanatical obsession that drove him to acts of violence. As a paid agent of Thomas Cromwell he spent his remaining years in persecuting monastic establishments in the fiercest manner. John Foxe (1516–1587), famed author of *Actes and Monuments,* giving the history of the persecution of Reformers, says that "this Taverner repented him very muche that he had made Songes to Popish Ditties in the time of his blindness." Another eminent musician, John Merbecke (d. c. 1585), whose conception of the nature of Protestant church music was of exceptional clarity, and whose gifts would have enabled him to change the whole course of Reformed music in England, also fell victim to his theological zeal. However, from the point of view of the musical historian other issues were far more weighty than the regrettable creative idleness of a few eminent composers. The whole future of English music was at stake.

The abolition of ritual and ceremony, religious pictures and sculptures, artistic polyphony in music, the negation of transubstantiation, all had the immediate effect of weakening the awe and reverence of the masses, for the people's mind revolves around symbols. Only those devoid of all aesthetic and artistic sense can deny the religious value of painting, sculpture, music, and poetry, and yet many of the leaders of the movement in England declared themselves opposed to the arts in religion. This they did partly because artistic impulses passed by them unnoticed, partly because their strong political desire for autonomy and freedom from intellectual bondage overshadowed their love of art, which was too closely associated in their mind with "popish vanity."

The Church has often been considered an institution of the clergy rather than of the people. As a clerical body it continually insisted on its prerogatives and its monopolies in spiritual and intellectual life. While its members were the sole custodians of learning, which they communicated to each other in the language of the Church, inaccessible to the people, the monopoly was maintained, but by the time of Henry VIII the situation had changed. The growing middle class had produced its own chroniclers and poets, who made the clerical scholar into a specialist, and now its musicians were called upon to assert themselves by providing the new church with new music. The German Reform movement had arrived at the same crossroads, but its leaders were fully aware of the importance of music and poetry in the worship of God. It is evident that while introducing a more popular element into the music of the Reformed Church Luther was anxious to retain the cultivation of artistic music, although he was perfectly well aware of the "popish" quality of such music. Thus he wrote in the "Exhortation to Prayer" (against the

Turks, 1541) the following lines, which reveal the great difference between
the English and German conceptions concerning the Reform and music, and
which explain why German Protestant music produced such marvelous
shoots whereas English church music—in spite of many admirable compositions—has never recovered from the effects of the Reformation:

I rejoice to let the 79th. Psalm, *O God, the heathen are come,* be sung as usual,
one choir after another. Accordingly, let one sweet-voiced boy step before the desk
in his choir and sing alone the antiphon or sentence *Domine, ne secundum,* and
after him let another boy sing the other sentence, *Domine, ne memineris;* and then
let the whole choir sing on their knees *Adjuva nos, Deus,* just as it was in the
Popish Feasts, for it sounds and looks very devotional.

How penetrating and psychologically indisputable the last remark is, and
how truly it is reflected in English Reformed music. The noblest and most
profoundly religious *Services* for the Church of England were written by
Byrd, not because he was a staunch Catholic, but because he was still imbued
with the sheer devotional grandeur of polyphonic church music.

The abolition of the daily celebration of the Mass in the English churches
was a great blow to the excellent musical establishments maintained by most
cathedrals and collegiate churches. A demand arose for some suitable substitution which, while conforming to the new religious doctrines, would continue the great choral traditions cherished by the British. At first, adaptations
of Latin Masses were used, but with the appearance of the Book of Common
Prayer English composers devoted themselves to its musical settings. These
settings, called services, can be grouped under three headings: the Office of
the Holy Communion, Morning Prayer, and Evening Prayer. The portions
of the Communion office that were set to music were the Kyrie, the Credo,
the Sanctus, and the Gloria. There are five canticles in the morning service
of the Prayer Book which may be set to music: Venite, Te Deum, and Benedictus with the alternative Benedicite and Jubilate. The canticles of the
Evening Prayer are the Magnificat and Nunc Dimittis with the alternatives
Cantate Domino and Deus Miseratur. With the increasing doctrinal controversy in later Elizabethan times, the Benedictus, Agnus Dei, and Gloria
were dropped from the Service.

The musical experience gained in the setting of Masses and motets provided the composers with a technique and style in setting the English
Communion service, but the canticles left the composers in a dilemma. Archbishop Cranmer in a letter to Henry VIII gave the directions which determined the simple style of the services called "short services." "The song
should not be full of notes, but, as near as may be, for every syllable a note so
that it may be sung distinctly and devoutly." These precepts seem familiar

and, indeed, resemble the musico-aesthetic dictates of Calvin; but as Calvin was unable to stifle the imagination of Goudimel and Le Jeune, the doctrinal requirements of Cranmer could not eradicate from the English composers' imagination the wonders of polyphony they had learned a generation or two ago from their Flemish colleagues. Contrapuntal technique, which in Elizabethan times was the natural equipment of English composers, demanded to be applied. Thus arose the so-called "great" services in which the motet technique was applied with great felicity. It is significant in this connection that the finest of all the existing great services was composed by Byrd, a musician thoroughly trained in the contrapuntal traditions.

Among the first printed works representing an endeavor to provide a style of church music in the English language complying with the new requirements were John Merbecke's *The Booke of Common Praier Noted* (1550) and John Day's *Certaine Notes Set Forth in Foure and Three Parts to Be Sung at the Morning Communion, and Evening Praier* (1560). Merbecke's work represents the first musical setting of the English liturgy as authorized by the Act of Uniformity of 1549. Among the militant English Reformers Merbecke's ideas seem to be isolated in their kinship with Luther's musical reforms. His desire to furnish "playne tunes" for congregational singing led him to select and adapt traditional melodies and to write original music on similar lines. But the second Prayer Book, issued under Queen Elizabeth, displaced the first and thereby Merbecke's music, because the new version contained numerous modifications in response to the growing opposition to the musical office. Far from following up his original intentions by composing music to the new Prayer Book, this gifted musician joined the opposition condemning church music as "vanity." Merbecke's procedure was remarkable, as he sought to retain the traditions of Gregorian music and at the same time to champion the cause of the English language. In this he succeeded to a marked degree, but the advantages and fine points of the music of the *Booke of Common Praier Noted* found no echo among his contemporaries, and as Merbecke himself gave up composition the choral setting of the service soon claimed the attention of all musicians.

Another musical product of the English Reformation was the anthem, which took the place of the motet of the Latin Church. The meaning of the word—undoubtedly deriving from the Greek *antiphona*—varies with different times. It was used even before Chaucer and is applied today to any type of solemn song, such as "national anthem," but essentially it means a specifically English "hymn or such like song in churches" to be sung at the conclusion of Morning and Evening Prayer. It was in its late Elizabethan form that the anthem acquired its definite status as a piece of church music with a definitely assigned place in the liturgy. The first anthems were again adaptations of Latin motets equipped with English texts. After the first waves of the new Italian style reached England, passages for solo voice with the accompaniment of the organ, or a chest of viols, were introduced into the anthem, notably by Byrd and Gibbons. Remarkable works were written in a compromise form, the nonliturgic Latin motet, which, while retaining the old majesty of the Latin motet style, evaded such controversial subjects as were ill received by the authorities of the new Church. These motets represent the most important phase of English church music of the period, aside from the superior works of Tallis and Byrd, but the latter wrote his best works for the services of the old faith.

Christopher Tye (c. 1500–1572/73) and Thomas Tallis (c. 1505–1585) were the most eminent of a group of musicians whose activity was henceforth devoted to the service of the new Church. Tye, in 1553, produced one of the first major creations of the spirit of the Reformation: *The Actes of the Apostles*. Fourteen chapters of the Acts were in this publication, which was not continued, presumably because the poetry of the good Doctor in Musyke was not commensurate with his music. Strangely enough, this earnest amateur theologian was the composer of a six-part Mass called *Euge Bone* which is among the finest examples of Tudor polyphony. Tallis, who also started his musical career as a composer of Latin church music, disclosing a mastery of the Franco-Flemish polyphonic style, was able, owing to his versatility and excellent training, to compose works not only in the simple style of the Reformation service but also in the most elaborate contrapuntal vein of his foreign colleagues. Next to Tye and Tallis, the most important composer of the mid-sixteenth century was Robert Whyte (c. 1530–1574); most of his works are, unfortunately, still in manuscript.

Like most of her house, Elizabeth was fond of music, and she exhibited skill in playing the lute and the virginal. She was on friendly terms with her chapelmasters, who brought together in the royal chapels the finest voices in the realm. The erstwhile austerity caused by Cranmer's ordinances gave way to an elaborate liturgy, for Elizabeth loved pomp and magnificence in religion as in everything else. This created a lively musical stimulus which imparted to English music a momentum strong enough to carry it over into James I's reign, although this first ruling member of the Stuart dynasty was not musically inclined. We have already mentioned the great fame of earlier English singers and choral organizations, but their reputation was eclipsed in Elizabethan times, when large choirs, numbering up to sixty or even more, were to be found in the cathedrals, singing in that fresh and euphonious English manner which has remained a typical attribute of English choral singing since the days of the old English conductus. While church music continued to flourish under Elizabeth, during the last third of her reign secular music took over the leadership and created new forms and new means of expression.

The Elizabethan and Jacobean School
Vocal Music

THERE has been no other case in which a people with a great musical position has allowed it to lapse entirely for three centuries, and during this time has contentedly borne the reproach of unproductiveness." These are the words of Sir William Henry Hadow in his preface to W. H. Grattan Flood's *Early Tudor Composers*. This is indeed the grave truth, except that what Hadow and the other defenders of Elizabethan musical art are extolling is—in spite of its great artistic value—in reality a form of Italian music transplanted into England: the madrigal. The first madrigal books appeared in 1588, that is, half a century after their appearance in Italy. Their success in England was instantaneous, and a host of eminent composers turned to the madrigal, which enjoyed a brief but exceedingly popular and flourishing period in Elizabethan and Jacobean England. The national song disappeared during the great period of the madrigal, and very little is known about the state of truly national music, as scholars and writers have concentrated their attention on the madrigal. English musical writers have considered this a natural state of affairs, because the cultivation of "true polyphonic music which was being composed at this time gives England its surest title to be considered a musical nation." Nevertheless, the same author states that the "vocal display of the Italians, and the inconsequent flippancy of many French *chansons*" are both opposed to the English temperament.[45] It is almost inconceivable that it should have taken half a century for the Italian madrigal and French chanson to reach England, but it is even more improbable that a country inherently musical and possessing excellent musical establishments would not have produced secular music of its own genius, and this very half century should be the subject of intensive research work on the part of English scholars. The preponderance of sacred music among the extant manuscripts of the period may be explained, in part, by their having been kept in cathedral and college libraries.

Wooldridge has called attention to the fact that a set of part books in the Fellows Library at Winchester College contains examples of the works of Willaert, Lassus, Arcadelt, and other celebrated composers of chansons and madrigals. The set is a quarter of a century older than the first English madrigal publication. But a quantity of foreign madrigals in manuscript collections and the visit of several Flemish and other musicians toward the middle of the century show that there must have been a decided cult of foreign secular choral music. Finally, we should mention the concrete case of madrigallike songs by an English composer who had traveled "in sundry forrein land," observing and studying music wherever he journeyed, "but chiefly the Italian, among the which is one that called is Napolitane (a pretty mery one)." Thomas Whythorne (1528–c. 1590) was the name of the musician so much attracted by the Neapolitan villanella, but he must have heard a good many madrigals too while in Italy. This composer has been simply dubbed an "amateur" by English musical historians who refused to see his great historical significance. Peter Warlock (Philip Heseltine), who edited twelve songs from Whythorne's collection,[46] rightfully claims that several of these songs are worthy to rank with the best of the "ayres" of the composers who flourished a generation later.

Carrying the search backward one can find still earlier connections with the Continental chanson and madrigal art. Adrien Le Roy's celebrated instruction book for the lute (1557?) was translated into English as early as 1568; since it included a number of chanson transcriptions, it could not have missed communicating the "flippancy" of the French Renaissance chanson to the English lute players, whose number was legion. In 1562 the presence in England of an eminent Italian madrigal composer is attested by the conferring of a pension, payable during the queen's pleasure, to Master Alfonso. Alfonso Ferrabosco (1543–1588) came from a musical family. His father, a Bolognese by birth, was a singer in the papal chapel and a fairly well-known madrigal composer. The recipient of the queen's pension must have arrived in the country earlier, possibly shortly after the middle of the century. Alfonso enjoyed a great reputation among English composers and was on friendly terms especially with Byrd. Many of his madrigals appeared in English collections, beginning with the *Musica Transalpina* in 1588. His family settled down in England and played an important role in the following century. All these facts led to the great popularity of the Italo-Flemish madrigal toward the end of the century. Continuing our retrogression, we discover that the foreign influence becomes less and less marked and we are actually in the presence of a native art, neglected and unexplored as yet. But the older historians were aware of the fact that the early Tudor era, often represented as having been devoted entirely to sacred music, produced much secular choral song. In fact, most of the composers were considered to be "merely secular composers." Commenting on the musicians around Cornyshe, Burney remarked that

most of these Musicians seem to have been merely secular Composers, as I have met with none of their names, except that of Fayrfax, among those for the Church. Cornyshe, indeed, seems more a secular Composer than the rest; and, if we may judge of his private character, by the choice of his poetry from Shelton's Ribaldry, he may be supposed a man of no very refined morals, or delicacy of sentiment. His compositions, however, though clumsy and inelegant, if selecting such words be forgiven, are not without variety or ingenuity, for so early a period of Counterpoint. . . .[47]

This statement is remarkable both for its real appraisal of the situation and for the typically supercilious moralizing tendency which characterizes the writings of most English musical historians endeavoring to drag the gloom and conventionalism of the arid periods of the nineteenth century into the wonderful era from Chaucer to Shakespeare. There was, to be sure, a crowd of worthless and forgotten versifiers and musicians, but as the old-fashioned romances declined, the lyric which sang of the outlaw and the forest, the joys and woes of love, and later of the wild border life, gradually took form. It is refreshing to find ourselves in the open air surrounded by persons who have human hearts and human emotions of which they are not ashamed, people who have a free vein of humor, mocking and dancing to their heart's content.

The timid beginning of this national art, a truly social art, appears at the opening of the sixteenth century with Aston's virginal pieces and the songs of Cornyshe, Tallis, and others. Wynkyn de Worde's *Song Book* of 1530 (unfortunately incomplete) is an important document of this little-known secular song art in England; however, there are many other songs that require attention, although at present most of them are still merely titles, as this art seems to be too lowly to merit the publishers' attention. But how suggestive they are of an age-old tradition! "Jhoone's Sike" (Richard Davy); "Who Shall Court My Fair Ladye?"; "I Love, Loved, and Loved Would I Be" (Fayrfax); "Blow Thy Horn Hunter"; "Trolly-lolly-loly-lo"; "Manerly-Margery-Mylk and Ale" (Cornyshe). All these songs must be a direct continuation of the remarkable secular song of the fifteenth century. The examples found in the publications of Stainer, Myers, and Fuller-Maitland [48] indicate the continuous influence of the old bards and minstrels. The violence of the change following the Reformation can be seen from the fact that many of the names heretofore familiar in musical collections have disappeared entirely, and, as Wooldridge has convincingly declared, "nothing but the wonderful inherent vitality of the English music could have supported it under so great a shock."

The flourishing of the great madrigal art started in earnest in 1588. Nicholas Yonge (d. 1619) edited the first printed collection of Italian madrigals equipped with English words. The collection, entitled *Musica Transalpina,* contained fifty-seven compositions by the most eminent madrigalists, including Marenzio, Palestrina, Ferrabosco, Lassus, de Monte, and others, and also two works by Byrd. The English translations do not make good poetry, but the prosody is well fitted to the note values of the music. A second book with a similar title followed in 1597. In the dedication of the first book, Yonge speaks of entertaining guests in his house by "furnishing them with Bookes of that kind yeerely sent me out of Italy and other places." This is another proof that the singing of Italian and Italo-Flemish madrigals was a fairly well-established custom by the time of the appearance of the *Musica Transalpina,* but the fact still remains that the final impetus was supplied by

Yonge's compilation, probably because of its use of the English language. A veritable avalanche of delightful and highly artistic music ensued. Thomas Watson edited in 1590 *The First Sett of Italian Madrigals Englished*. In the dedication there is an epistle addressed to Luca Marenzio, from whose works twenty-three of the twenty-eight madrigals published in the set were taken. The great Roman composer became the worshiped model of English madrigal composers. Another influential Italian was Giovanni Giacomo Gastoldi (c. 1556–1622). His five-part *balletti di cantare, sonare e ballare*, melodious and graceful dance songs with lilting refrains, were extraordinarily popular and affected English composers, especially Morley, who modeled on them his *Ballets* or *Fa-las*.

The Italian examples were followed not only in the style of composition but also in the manner of presentation. The Venetian printer Gardano in 1592 issued a collection of madrigals entitled *Il Trionfo di Dori*. The set contained twenty-nine madrigals by as many noted composers, most of them Italians, every one of the songs ending with *Viva la bella Dori*. Following this example twenty-nine English composers under the leadership of Morley assembled a collection of madrigals written in honor of Queen Elizabeth. The title, *The Triumphes of Oriana,* the number of contributing composers, and the refrain "Long live fair Oriana" all indicate that Gardano's original collection was here imitated in every detail.

This lively and aristocratic art produced a number of eminent composers. Thomas Morley (1557–1603?), William Byrd (1542/43–1623), Thomas Weelkes (d. 1623), and John Wilbye (1574–1638) are the most eminent of the earlier madrigalists, while of the later group we may mention Orlando Gibbons (1583–1625), John Ward (fl. first quarter of the seventeenth century), Thomas Tomkins (1573–1656), and Francis Pilkington (d. 1638), although there were many others second only to the leaders.

Besides his fine madrigals and canzonets, Morley was the author of one or two of the songs written to Shakespeare's plays, which have survived. His *Plaine and Easie Introduction* (1597), written in a pleasant dialogue form, following the current type of Italian *dialoghi* but in an unmistakably English vein, is our most valuable source dealing with Elizabethan musical life. He was the most popular composer of his day, and still holds the affection of the modern listener on account of the light, graceful, and merry tunefulness of his music.

William Byrd appears in the archives as organist of Lincoln Cathedral. After a few years in this position he was sworn in as a member of the Chapel Royal, where he met Tallis, with whom he formed an intimate friendship. After Shakespeare, Byrd is without doubt the most imposing figure of the English Renaissance, towering above all his contemporaries. When discussing him, comparison can be made only to the other "princes" of music, Palestrina and Lassus, and, indeed, he has been called the English Palestrina. If Byrd needs any godfather it would perhaps be more appropriate to call him the English Lassus, for, like the great Netherlander, he was equally at home in all fields of music, although his most congenial domain was church music. Byrd remained a steadfast Catholic throughout his life, and this explains the otherworldliness of his church music, whether written for the Latin or the English rite. While he was aware of the tastes of the public and the tendencies of his time, he did not yield to any passing vogue as did most of his colleagues. Conservative by nature, he liked to retain all the useful traits of the musical material at his disposal. Utilizing the same sources as his fellow musicians, his prodigious poetic power often transformed worthless pebbles into precious stones, and when the sources were precious stones themselves he made them shine still brighter. The somber grace of his Masses reflects the eternal mystery of classical Latin polyphony, while his English services sing the praise of the Lord in a noble and human tone that should have become the embodiment of Protestant church music, but which was not approached by any English Protestant musician of his time. It bespeaks Elizabeth's devotion to art that, apart from small annoyances, the great composer—politically absolutely loyal—was not seriously inconvenienced because of his faith. On the contrary, he was universally recognized by musicians and patrons alike as the greatest of their composers.

This versatile and profound composer, who continued the great traditions of English music, was much less influenced by Italian art than those of his contemporaries. In the year of the appearance of the *Musica Transalpina* but probably preceding it, Byrd published his *Psalmes, Sonets and Songs of Sadnes and Pietie*. Although these songs are written in the accepted contrapuntal manner for five voices, they betray their distant kinship to the accompanied solo song, the topmost part being much more melodious than the others, which were presumably intended for a quartet of viols. At this stage of research concerning the English song before the Elizabethan era, any opinion advanced is, of necessity, merely conjectural; but it seems more than plausible that here we are again face to face with the vestiges of an old and almost forgotten national art which cannot be judged by applying to it the standards of a different style.

Thomas Weelkes and John Wilbye were the composers of exquisite madrigals; both of them, but especially the latter, rank with the best composers of that genre on the Continent. It is a great misfortune that most of Weelkes's church music has perished, because the preserved fragments indicate great gifts in this line of composition. Orlando Gibbons's entire output of sacred music was for the English rite, a fact which singles him out from among all his contemporaries, because even the staunchest adherents of the Church of England cultivated the form we called the "compromise Latin motet."

Among his forty anthems, some fifteen are written in the great polyphonic style of the sixteenth century, disclosing a mastery possessed only by the leading musicians of the "golden age of polyphony." In the other anthems and services he joined Byrd in experimenting with instrumentally accompanied solo passages, embarking on the grandiose dramatic style which was to crown the English anthem in the works of Purcell. The fourth volume of *Tudor Church Music* contains all that is known of his church music. The remarkable contrapuntal technique and sense for vocal setting displayed by this admirable composer are most happily combined in his madrigals, which are written in the daring style of his Venetian colleagues.

However artistic, fresh, and impressive the Elizabethan and Jacobean madrigal art, it was an imitation of the original Italian genre and reflected English musical genius to a limited degree only. The melodic phrases and the wholesome sonority of choral writing had a certain English quality, but the construction and technique of composition was entirely Italian. (While the fact does not detract from his ability, Morley sometimes lifted whole phrases from the works of Gastoldi, and in his canzonets he resorted to similar borrowings from the works of Felice Anerio, Palestrina's successor as composer to the papal chapel and *maestro* at the English College in Rome.) The simpler songlike compositions, the lute songs of John Dowland, and the various instrumental pieces are much more typical of pure English art. Dowland's four-part "Songes or Ayres," especially in their arrangement for a solo voice with lute accompaniment, and similar works by Thomas Campion (1567–1619), Philip Rosseter (c. 1575–1623), and the already mentioned Francis Pilkington, turned the Italian models, the *balletti* and *arie* of Gastoldi, into a strikingly English form. Indeed, these works were so typically English in character that, although well known, they did not exert any perceptible influence on European vocal music, the means and forms of expression of which were already too well established along Italian lines.

John Dowland (1563–1626) was considered the unsurpassed lute virtuoso of his day, but as a composer, while very popular, he did not impress his contemporaries so much as he deserved, for this *wanderlustig* musician was one of the most original and progressive composers that England has ever produced. His *Songs or Ayres* are modern lyrico-dramatic songs in the fullest sense of the word. It is almost unbelievable that in the midst of the madrigal era such works could be composed, for Dowland's songs do not indulge in the more or less inconsequential, dainty, and graceful play of four or five merrily rolling contrapuntal parts; the solo voice concentrates in its part the essential musical material while the other parts act as accompaniment. The sculptured melody follows the words, rendering the poetry with the utmost faithfulness; but the accompaniment is by no means a mere chordal skeleton. It is astounding to see the most modern precepts of song writing employed in these accompaniments written for the lute or for viols. Certain important thematic elements are picked up and organically elaborated in the accompaniment, or sometimes the main musical interest is in the accompaniment itself while the voice holds long notes. Dowland's journeys and acquaintance with Continental music are not a satisfactory explanation for his original style, for the Continent did not know such a song style in his time. Bearing in mind the fine polyphonic songs of Byrd and the works of Dowland, as well as some of the lesser lutenist song writers,[49] we must come to the conclusion that here the genius of English music is again expressed, enriched but not altered by foreign influences.

Instrumental Music

EVEN the works of the English virginalists sprang from the native song, which was temporarily eclipsed during the era of the madrigal. The nucleus of this literature for the virginals was a variation art entirely independent of Franco-Flemish polyphony. This can be seen from the fact that its subjects were dance and song forms with a definite favoring of the treble voice as opposed to the tenor melody of the Netherlanders. The difference is equally marked in the nature of contrapuntal setting, for even when the composer used a cantus firmus he did not write linear counterpoint but displayed a characteristic instrumental figure-play bound together by long sequences. Thus, in the very midst of the polyphonic era which favored abstract part writing in disregard of the characteristic nature of the medium of expression, we here have an instrumental style derived entirely from the nature, spirit, and sonority of the keyboard instrument. Needless to say, an art so original and so independent of foreign impulses must have antecedents reaching far into the past of English music; and, indeed, in these variations and in other virginal pieces lives the heritage of the art of the English minstrels of the fourteenth and fifteenth centuries. Nothing or next to nothing is known, unfortunately, of the early history of this art, but that it was fully developed at the very beginning of the sixteenth century is illustrated by the fact that the oldest keyboard composition, Aston's "Hornpipe" mentioned above, does not show hesitation or incertitude. If we cease considering Aston's piece as the beginning of keyboard music, and consider it rather as a remarkable specimen from the closing period of the first great era of English instrumental music, we shall be much nearer the truth. This "first era" of instrumental music must have been of great richness and variety and the instruments many and well made. At the death of Henry VIII an inventory of his musical instruments was made at the order of Edward VI. This truly amazing document, listing literally hundreds of instruments, could not have been the result of a collector's whim; the king possessed, in a more generous degree, that which his less well-to-do fellow musicians possessed in their homes.[50]

The first printed volume of English virginal music, *Parthenia,* appeared in 1611. Other interesting collections are *My Ladye-Nevells Booke,* written in 1591, containing forty-two compositions by Byrd; William Foster's and Benjamin Cosyn's *Virginal Books,* both from the first quarter of the seventeenth century. But the most remarkable collection of English keyboard music is contained in the so-called *Fitzwilliam Virginal Book.* Written in the first quarter of the seventeenth century, and now preserved in the Fitzwilliam Museum in Cambridge, the book contains almost three hundred keyboard pieces by Bull, Byrd, Morley, Phillips, Tallis, and Dowland.[51]

It is not necessary to extol the merits of Byrd once more; his keyboard music was not only distinguished but fluent and idiomatic. Similarly, Gibbons, one of the most celebrated organists and virginal players of his time, has left us compositions which reflect his brilliant technique. John Bull (c. 1562–1628), however, the third author of the *Parthenia,* was a specialist on the clavier and as such commands our attention. Like his eminent contemporary, Dowland, he led an adventurous life, finishing his career as the highly appreciated organist of Notre Dame Cathedral in Antwerp. An accomplished virtuoso, he was famous for his mastery of the keyboard, as was Dowland for his lute playing, and his brilliancy of clavier technique contributed to the growing instrumental literature the stylistic features which Continental musicians, among them Sweelinck, the great Dutch organist, received with obvious pleasure and interest. We shall see how the genius of these unruly, capricious, and fantastic, but highly original and thoroughly English, musicians affected the development of the music of the coming baroque.

Another branch of instrumental music which enjoyed great popularity toward the end of the sixteenth century and throughout the seventeenth was ensemble music, for viols or other instruments, which can be rightfully called chamber music. From the time of Elizabeth the viols were the most popular instruments of amateurs; and viol ensembles (the so-called consorts), for three to six parts, were especially favored by aristocratic music lovers and played at their musical soirées. Both varieties, the "hand" and the "knee" viols, were used. The latter was probably introduced from Italy, as the designation "viola da gamba" seems to have been current; Shakespeare mentions the "viol de gamboys" in *Twelfth Night.* The term "consort" was equivalent to the modern designation "ensemble." A consort of instruments was any group playing together, but there existed a certain distinction between consorts made up of instruments belonging to the same family, called "whole" consorts, and mixed ensembles or "broken" consorts. The publications of Anthony Holborne (d. 1602) and Thomas Morley, both appearing in 1599, opened this phase of chamber music, and the two pioneers were soon joined by other notable vocal and keyboard composers, such as Byrd and Gibbons.

Originally these consorts were cantus firmus works, that is, polyphonic settings of so-called Miserere and *In Nomine* tenors, soon followed by free solmization themes, *solfainge songs,* and song melodies. The In Nomines, instrumental fantasies based on a plain-song cantus firmus, were especially popular with instrumental composers, almost every one of them trying his hand at them. They declined in favor after the Restoration but were still known toward the end of the century, as Purcell composed two In Nomines in 1680. While the nature of these compositions clearly indicates that they are an English variety of the ricercar, that is, polyphonic instrumental music stemming from the motet, the term "In Nomine" has created some confusion. Older historians believed that the compositions so designated were based on a cantus firmus beginning with these words, but it appears that the melody employed is the well-known Gregorian *Gloria Tibi Trinitas.*

The Continental practice of stringing together several dances in a so-called "suite" was adopted in England at the turn of the sixteenth century. "Suites of lessons" or "setts of lessons" became very popular a few decades later. A considerable number of Continental dances, together with some of English origin, are already mentioned in Morley's *Plaine and Easie Introduction,* but the simple dances were soon expanded into larger instrumental compositions of great artistic merit. Here again it was Dowland who contributed the most original and at the same time most finished work, in his *Lachrymae, or Seven Tears, Figured in Seven Pavans* (1605).

Beginning with the seventeenth century the chief form of instrumental ensemble music became the "fancy," occupying a place in English music similar to that of the Continental ricercar, to which it bears a certain resemblance. The fancy, obviously the English for the Italian *fantasia,* meaning an instrumental composition without a strictly set form, appeared in the keyboard music of the second half of the sixteenth century. Morley speaks of the fancies as "the chiefest kind of music made without ditties," alluding to their purely instrumental character. The fancies of Byrd and Gibbons, to mention the leaders again, are not only incomparable masterpieces neglected for no good reason, but, together with other works of the first half of the seventeenth century, they furnished the backbone for English baroque music, as did the instrumental fugues for the baroque style on the Continent. And, again, this music and its composers have received only scornful acknowledgment from the historians of their own land. Ernest Walker disposes of them in the following words: "They [the fancies] bustle along with plenty of serious-minded energy; but there is no trace of inventiveness of any kind worth mentioning, and though in a sense they may be called the precursors of English concerted chamber-music, yet the special type vanished, never to reappear. . . ." [52] These fancies were the rightful ancestors of English chamber music, and without them the wonderful fantasias of Purcell would have

never been written. The attitude of the modern historians is the more surprising because they cannot be ignorant of the admiration expressed by
seventeenth-century English musicians for their instrumental music. They
admitted the superiority of the Italians in the madrigal—a fact denied by the
modern historian—but insisted on the excellence and originality of their
consorts.

Looking back on the musical world of Elizabethan and Jacobean days,
the student is amazed both at the incomparable richness of the period and
at the incomparable neglect of its many branches for only one, its most pleasing aspect. "When the task [of resuscitating all this music] is complete
we shall realize, perhaps with some lingering surprise, that here is an achievement which may without exaggeration be set in comparison with that of the
Elizabethan drama." [53]

Aesthetic Doctrines of the Renaissance

THE last phase of Gothic music, overlapping into Renaissance times, passed
through the same profound conflicts which were experienced by the other
arts in the quattrocento, and like them underwent changes that determined
its entire future history. The development of successive-horizontal part writing went hand in hand with developments in literature and painting. The
elaborate contrapuntal style of the Flemish school, its mirror, crab, and riddle canons, are all characteristic of a style which in its maturity possessed a
wealth of technique that in reality outweighed the necessities. The descriptive "tone poems" of Janequin reflect the same spirit, that of the storytelling
pictorial art of the late Gothic, in which idyllic scenes alternate with chivalric
courtly life, aristocratic hunt and love songs with the robust dances of the
stalwart peasants of Breughel. All this does not represent the future: it belongs—the times notwithstanding—to the past. The new style based on continuous but not strict imitation, which appeared when the late Gothic reached
its climax, required an entirely new conception of voice leading; it had to
abandon the older principle of successive part writing and demanded a
simultaneous-vertical conception of the whole art of composition. The simultaneous setting of the individual parts acquired an entirely different significance. Simultaneity of seeing was the main conception and problem of
Western painting during the Renaissance, and music and the sister arts, including literature, joined painting in quest of an ideal settlement of this
basic problem.

At the bottom of this new style lies a new way of listening and hearing
comparable to the new way of viewing arrived at in painting. The composer
now hears primarily the simultaneous-chordal, and not the linear-melodic as
had the older composer of the late Gothic; he plans and drafts in a vertical

rather than in a horizontal manner, and consequently has to deal with the whole complex of parts rather than with consecutive single parts. Pietro Aron (c. 1490–1545) in his *Il Toscanello in Musica* (1523) declared that the music of the "moderns" is better than that of the older composers "because they consider all parts together and do not compose their voices one after the other." This clear statement parallels exactly Leonardo's statement on simultaneity in pictorial composition. Attempts at a theoretical comprehension of harmony (in the modern sense) were occasionally essayed in medieval musical theory, much as the theoretical comprehension of perspective, if in a rudimentary fashion, was attempted in early trecento painting. The important fact is that neither of the two succeeded in their time, as theirs was not a merely technical problem but a fundamental conception of art. For this very reason it is an anachronism and misnomer to call the perspective and harmonic conceptions of these artists "primitive." It was only in the second half of the fifteenth century that the great achievements of the Flemish composers compelled the theoreticians to take cognizance of the changed precepts of musical composition.

Bartolomeo Ramos de Pareja (c. 1440–c. 1495), a Spanish musical scholar active in Salamanca, Bologna, and Rome, was the first theoretician to sift the mathematical properties of the major and minor third and declare the triad a natural phenomenon, thereby laying the foundation for the modern doctrines of harmony. Pareja's immediate predecessors and colleagues, such as the Fleming Tinctoris, the Englishman John Hothby (d. 1487), and the Italians Giovanni Spataro (c. 1458–1541) and Franchino Gafori (or Gafurius) (1451–1522), were eminent scholars and musicians, although a certain pedantic dryness and remoteness from living art is undeniably present in their writings. But the Renaissance spirit impressed itself more and more strongly on musical scholars. While most of the theoreticians were still under the influence of the Boethian doctrines, the rising school of the sixteenth century turned away from the great mediator and started to explore the original sources of classical Greek musical theory. There followed a thoroughgoing revision of musical knowledge.

Renaissance musical theory laid the foundations for a new comprehensive musical system which, taken as a whole, is still the basis of our present-day music. It represents a complete break with the musical systems of the Middle Ages. Medieval musical theory was speculative and symbolic, filled with the ancient traditions of the Pythagorean doctrines as transmitted by Boethius. Suffice it to recall the complicated system of the *musica mundana*. A physically defined and mathematically documented system as propounded by the Renaissance was diametrically opposed to medieval conceptions. The philosophical and theoretical changes in the domain of music were but a corollary to the change from symbolic-speculative astrology to physical astronomy which occurred almost at the same time. The last vestiges of the medieval spirit which lived in the inherited Netherlandish musical traditions were so powerful, however, that the onslaught of the Italians, who wanted to dispose of their Nordic heritage, gained ground but slowly, and the advent of the modern era which started with Monteverdi was preceded by a struggle for autonomous music that lasted for decades. The struggle was the more serious because some of the defenders of the great traditions of the Franco-Flemish and Italo-Flemish schools were incomparable scholars and musicians. They were all permeated by the spirit of humanism, but they stood at the end of the great wave of the new humanistic trend which was most typically and eminently represented by Erasmus. The time of a revival full of hopes had passed away, and the belief in the advent of a golden age had diminished; men of letters, fearful of the passing of the great traditions, turned, as the aged Erasmus did, toward a glorification of the past. One of the most eminent among the scholars of this group was Heinrich Loris (1488–1563), or Glareanus, as he is better known, from his native Swiss canton of Glarus. Crowned poet laureate by Emperor Maximilian I, and a teacher of Latin, Greek, history, and literature in Basel, this savant of profound and extensive learning was especially outstanding in the field of musical scholarship. His chief work, the *Dodecachordon* (1547), is especially valuable for its exhaustive treatment of the complicated polyphonic method of composition of the Franco-Flemish school. To Glareanus it was Josquin Després who represented the fulfillment of a classical-humanistic spirit, the absolute embodiment of the ideals of a noble and sublime form, natural majesty, and the harmonious balance of parts and details. And when he declared that 'this is the perfect art, to which nothing can be added," he did not align himself with the opponents of the dawning baroque: he was simply convinced that any "addition" to the admirable style of choral polyphony, within whose domain every voice is confined within the boundaries of its natural range, would change the balance between the polyphonic-linear forces and harmonic-vertical forces. Truly enough, with Palestrina and his contemporaries linear polyphony came definitely under the laws of a chordal organization.

The theoretical discussions of the Renaissance were summarized and fully treated in the works of the Venetian composer and theoretician Gioseffo Zarlino (1517–1590), a pupil of Willaert and successor to de Rore as choirmaster at St. Mark's in Venice. Not only the spirit but the whole terminology of the literature and doctrines of the fine arts appear in his writings. His insistence on proportion and measure could figure in any dissertation on architecture or painting. The rigorously logical and systematic arrangement of Zarlino's chief works, the three treatises entitled *Istitutioni Harmoniche* (1558), *Dimostrationi Harmoniche* (1571), and *Sopplimenti Musicali*

(1588),[54] their definitive nature and clear understandability, and the philosophical force with which their author reshapes traditional ideas, distinguish the Venetian author-composer as the representative of the last peak of Flemish-Italian polyphonic art. In spite of the remarkably progressive attitude he displays in matters of tonality and his advocacy of the division of the octave into twelve equal semitones, a principle espoused much later as the only practical method of tuning, his most important concern was to safeguard the great art implanted in Venice by Willaert, his master. We shall have to turn to another master to get a picture of the vivid activity in musical theory and aesthetics characteristic of the late Renaissance. Don Nicola Vicentino (1511–1572), a fellow pupil of Zarlino's in Messer Adriano's school, is the most typical representative of the prevailing Renaissance ideal, which endeavored to save music from "the excesses of old-fashioned" contrapuntal polyphony by returning to the study of the ancients. While the Italo-Flemish traditions continued to live in Vicentino, his joy in harmonic subtleties, his leaning toward sonorous combinations of tone color, and his realization of the nature of instrumental music indicate that he was also fully aware of what lay ahead of him.

The title of Vicentino's important work, *L'Antica Musica Ridotta alla Moderna Prattica* (1555), exhibits the very problem of his period. As a true child of the Renaissance, the author ignores medieval ideas and tries to connect the musical practice of his time with the doctrines of antiquity. As a man and a musician he is possessed by the conviction of the importance and magnitude of his era, and radiates an optimism in regard to both the present and the future. He pays his respects to Guido d'Arezzo and to Muris, but when he has made his obeisance to those venerable but already legendary heroes of music, he proceeds to statements which are hardly reconcilable with his veneration for the old scholars of Gregorian art. The old diatonic music is relegated to the antiquarian, whereas the new chromatic-enharmonic art is declared to be for "discriminating and cultivated ears." It is interesting to observe how the ancient chromatic and enharmonic system of the Greeks, which was, of course, a purely monophonic melodic system, appears here as a radically modern system of harmony. The five books of Vicentino's work portray the musical atmosphere which surrounded him. Their content unites the traditional High Renaissance system of composition with the new Italian chromatic and enharmonic theories of the author; but a certain opposition on the part of Vicentino to the pure Renaissance theory of music is evident in the occasional changes in the traditional theories which he presents, in new interpretation, and in modern developments. The tradition is strong enough, however, to check the disintegrating influence of chromaticism and of enharmonic modulations which sprang from distinctly un-Renaissance principles.

In the first book our radical author admonishes those musicians who are opposed to the new because it usually is coupled with difficulties until properly understood. In insisting on the "good old music" these musicians fail to realize that art is in a continuous process of rejuvenation, development, and perfection.

Vicentino's aesthetic theories are not less interesting. He makes a distinction between "singing in church" and "singing in the chamber." Church music should have, besides the necessary liturgic text, a sonorous polyphonic construction, solemn beginning, and a serene, unhurried atmosphere. Animation should be restricted to words which express pious devotion, and the ecclesiastic scales should be strictly observed. These rules can be considered the first theoretical formulation of the *stilus gravis* of the coming baroque. While Vicentino still follows the fundamentals of Franco-Flemish polyphonic technique and lists all the rules for canonic construction and cantus firmus work, he warns the composer that the strictness of canonic writing may act as a hindrance to sonorous beauty of style.

The most notable part of Vicentino's aesthetic conceptions is his insistence on the value and importance of the words in a vocal composition. His ideal was a perfect alliance of words and music, dominated by the words, which are made more telling and animated by the music. He cites oration as the true model of music. This attitude and conception is practically identical with that shared by the first representatives of the early baroque, and many of Vicentino's sentences reappear in the writings of Monteverdi and other protagonists of the rising new era.

Zarlino and several other eminent musicians and scholars criticized Vicentino severely, accusing him of a complete misreading of the doctrines of the ancients. Their accusation may be just, but the misreading resulted in the most important stylistic development of the late Renaissance, leading directly to the recitative style of the baroque, while his bold experiments with the "misinterpreted" chromatic system of the ancients were avidly taken up by the "romanticists" of the late sixteenth century.

Music in Renaissance Life

EVER since Burckhardt and Nietzsche used the expression "man of the Renaissance," it has denoted a romantically conceived bohemian individual, a free, inspired personality impudently indulging in bold sinfulness, the embodiment of an aesthetic immorality, an imperious man of pleasures seeking power and fame, frivolously despising religion, yet keeping peace with the Church and its servants, considering them indispensable in the attainment of his objective of governing the masses by deception. Such a picture is a fitting portrait of some men who lived in the Renaissance period, but it does grave injustice to the multitude. It is sheer folly to condense the endless variety of individualities into a universal personality. The political and social conditions of the Italian states were such that the attitude and relationship of men to the state and to life were much more individualistic than in the rest of Europe. The thirst for power, the defiance and the licentiousness, the subjective attitude toward religion, sometimes tolerant, sometimes skeptical or mocking, perhaps fanatically devout or else devoid of any trace of faith, the classical superstition and modern freethinking of the so-called man of the Renaissance—all these have again and again been explored and presented in numberless essays and "historical" novels. The student of history is confronted here with a profound riddle. How can he reconcile a seemingly bottomless moral profligacy with the most sensitive aesthetic feeling and with a boundless enthusiasm for arts, letters, and sciences? That the tyrants who did not shrink from the most violent acts to uphold their power believed earnestly that political action derives its laws from the feasibility of its ultimate success and not from the moral precepts of ordinary life is evident from the admiration bestowed on a Marius, Sulla, or Julius Caesar, surrounded even today with the same venerable mantle of classical authority which the man of the Renaissance regarded as the irreproachable symbol of public life. It does not seem easy to ascertain how it was that such a moral conception guided many notable persons, but we must conclude that the philosophical formulation of the traits of character and the methods of procedure necessary to the successful ruler was prompted by honest intentions and not by diabolic cunning. Machiavelli's *The Prince* was the work of an independent, keen-minded, rational, and honest thinker, for Machiavelli represented the haughty princes of the Renaissance, who did not hide their acts behind vain hypocrisy; their conception of political expediency was as openly professed as was their genuine interest in arts and letters. When reading about the colorful world of kings, tyrants, *condottieri,* diplomatists, hetaerae, artists, churchmen, philosophers, and adventurers, the average man associates the image of the typical man of the Renaissance with Cesare Borgia or Pietro Aretino, the "scourge of princes," who wrote abusive works for hire. Yet there were in fair numbers similar men in the Middle Ages whose thirst for power did not know scruples; on the other hand, the Renaissance produced many noble princes, saintly clerics, and virtuous artists. We should, in justice, look into the virtue, courage, and loftiness of this man of the Renaissance. His period saw the creation of thousands upon thousands of religious pictures commissioned for churches, and great was the number of Masses and motets composed for the services celebrated in those churches. The majority of these pictures and musical compositions reflects a sincere and devout religious feeling seldom attained in subsequent periods and scarely known by our musicians and painters of today. Were all these works of art creations alien to their time or did the man of the Renaissance possess a double personality? The north-erner and the Anglo-Saxon will never entirely understand this animated era, because the Renaissance was the triumph of the Romanic spirit; nor can he reconcile its profound seriousness with gay lightheartedness, its firm as-sertion of will with naïve irresponsibility.

Music occupied a position in the life of the man of the Renaissance and contributed to his intellectual wealth and social grace in a manner and de-gree which has not yet been taken into account by the historians of Western civilization. The ideal of the times was the *uomo universale,* the universally educated man who, in the classical tradition, was a perfect physical specimen as well. To rear such a man a well-rounded musical education was considered indispensable. Baldassare Castiglione (1478–1529) in his *Libro del Cortegi-ano,* a treatise on etiquette, social problems, and intellectual accomplishments, regarded as one of the great books of its time, devotes considerable atten-tion to music in the education of well-bred people. It is, indeed, most inter-esting to notice the extraordinary vogue of music in the royal and princely courts during the Renaissance. Every monarch of note was interested in music, and many of them were capable players, singers, or even com-posers. We have mentioned the splendid musical establishment at the court of Burgundy and seen how Henry V of England, himself an excellent musician, sought to emulate the example set by his ally. The German em-peror, Maximilian, husband of Mary of Burgundy, also founded a court chapel on Burgundian models, entrusting its leadership to two eminent masters, Hofhaimer and Isaac. The emperor took his large household, in-cluding the chapel choir, on his numerous voyages to all parts of Germany, and the greatly admired choir inspired other princes to institute similar or-ganizations. The chapel choir and court musicians were considered an essential part of a king's retinue; as a rule they followed the monarch even in war—Charles VIII of France took them on his Italian campaign (1495)—and a victory was usually celebrated on the battlefield by a solemn *Te Deum* performed by the chapel choir. On certain occasions visiting royalty com-bined their choirs in especially solemn performances. At the meeting on the Field of the Cloth of Gold the royal choirs appeared in magnificent vest-ments and attended all ceremonies. At noon the Archbishop of York cele-brated Mass, the Introit being intoned by the singers of Henry VIII, and the other parts of the Mass sung by the French choir. It was agreed that when the English choir sang the organ accompaniment was to be rendered by the French organist, while the English organist was to accompany the singing of the French choir.

We have mentioned the musical proclivities of the Tudor kings, but the sovereigns of many other countries, even the smallest, could be considered to possess the education approved by Castiglione. When James IV of Scotland came to seek the hand of Princess Margaret "he began before her to play of the clavichord and after of the lute, which pleased her very much." At the court of King Matthias Corvinus of Hungary (1440–1490) we find one of the greatest musical centers of Europe. The Hungarian sovereign was in constant contact with the Italian nobility, engaging new talents as they appeared on the musical horizon. Matthias's choir was rated as equal in artistry to the papal choir, an organization composed entirely of musicians of international reputation. Francis I of France, upon concluding an alliance with Sultan Soliman II (an alliance which earned him the universal condemnation of the Christian world), sought to present the sultan with some royal gift and sent him a group of musicians. What the Oriental potentate did with these artists is, of course, another story. Louis XII requested Josquin to compose some polyphonic pieces in which he could take the tenor part, and then proudly sang the *vox regis,* skillfully arranged by the great composer to suit the king's rather limited musical abilities. The Emperor Charles V was known to have a keen musical ear and to have been a great patron of the art. A biographer describes Charles's delight in music especially after his abdication and retirement to a monastery. Many times the monks heard him behind the door of his rooms beating time and singing with the choir, which was within earshot.[55]

In the courts of the Medici, the Gonzaga, the Sforza, the Este, as well as in the exceedingly brilliant courts of such art-loving popes as Julius II and Leo X, music was an inalienable part of daily life; but the numerous contemporary paintings, cuts, and etchings demonstrate that not only royal and aristocratic circles were interested in music. In his *Journal du Voyage en Italie* Montaigne writes that he was "astounded to see these peasants [in Tuscany] with a lute in their hands, and at their side the shepherds reciting Ariosto by heart; but this is what one may see in all of Italy." Luis Milan, the famous Spanish lutenist, described Portugal as being "a sea of music," so much was the art understood and appreciated there. The poets of France endeavored to reform the French language in order to make it more adaptable for musical setting; and the German religious leaders of the new faith dreamed of a people singing in the homes, in the fields, in the churches, and in the barracks. The extraordinary love of music is manifested in the curious fact that at the time when satiric poetry was at its height, attacking with devastating vehemence anything that was vulnerable, no one seemed to find anything objectionable in music, although painters and poets were ridiculed in countless pamphlets. The polemical works were restricted to the scholars who waged the usual battle for the sanctity of old laws and customs, and to the adherents of Calvin who feared the seductive charm of music, attributed to it ever since the times of Orpheus.

The great love of music produced a legion of active amateur composers.

Landini had already complained that everyone seemed to be bent on writing music. The professional musicians found the competition most unfair, because the large number of accredited members of their craft made it hard enough for them to survive. Flourishing international commerce, the development of communications, especially maritime shipping, the advances in scientific knowledge, the beginnings of world politics, all gave more and more weight to the urban elements. Kings and aristocrats ceased to be the only patrons of art, and the rich merchant-princes of the rapidly growing cities had their share in artistic life. The guild spirit declined with the increasing freedom of work, and the privileged position of the wandering professional artist was gradually diminished with the help of the general spread of printed music. It was characteristic of the individualism of the Renaissance period that the decline of the guild spirit manifested itself especially in the centers of art. The seeking of beauty and enjoyment, long established in the fine arts, now permeated music; and the Renaissance witnessed the advent of a music-loving *public* whose musical interest was not consumed in going to church for Mass, or in listening to the accompaniment of solemn processions, or in table entertainment: they attended musical performances organized for the sole purpose of enjoying music, and often joined the ranks of the performers. Dilettantism was rapidly becoming an important factor in art, and, with the increasing freedom of religious life, the arts which are associated with the practice of religion also showed a tendency to cater to the layman. The remarkable development of amateur music in the sixteenth century was due, besides the numerous minor chapel choirs established on papal or royal models, to the religious movement. Luther was among the first to institute many choir schools which required the cooperation of the citizenry, and the amateurs appeared not only in the choral and instrumental ensembles but among the composers themselves, often displaying abilities fully equal to those of the learned *magistri*. The chroniclers of Italian cities never omit to praise the local amateurs, and even the learned musical theoreticians and historians mention the noble dilettanti of renown. Pietro Aron in his *Lucidario* (1545) gives a whole list of eminent lute singers and adds to the professionals a number of aristocrats, city magistrates, and clerics.

The vogue of intimate "social" music was chiefly responsible for the flourishing of the great madrigal art, and every person of culture was expected to be able to take part in an improvised musicale; otherwise he was considered uncouth and wanting in social grace. The Elizabethan tradesman who sang the madrigals was so fond of his music that he contributed to its fostering and dissemination with a liberality of spirit unknown to his twentieth-century descendants. Robert Dove, a merchant-tailor, bequeathed funds for the teaching of music at Christ's Hospital, although the chief function of this institution was in utilitarian learning.

The practice of instrumental "parlor" music was a veritable fad in all classes of society. Those who could not afford a spinet or clavichord could procure an inexpensive lute which could be had in English barbershops. A certain discrimination between instruments resulted in their grouping into "noble" and "plebeian" instruments. A nobleman was supposed to cultivate the more intimate instruments, while the bagpipes, reed pipes, trumpets, and the shrill variety of flutes were not considered suitable for educated and refined people. The most popular instrument of the Renaissance was the lute, comparable to that of the piano in our day.

Instrumental music in private homes became so widespread that the available original literature was not sufficient to satisfy the demand. The public, familiar with the great polyphonic choral works of the period, both sacred and secular, demanded to be able to enjoy these works at home; therefore the sixteenth century provided lute scores, organ scores, and spinet scores similar to our modern piano reductions of symphonies and operas. Such arrangements appeared with the first printed music books of Attaingnant.

The monkish theology of the early Middle Ages belittled women and considered them the most pliable tool in the hands of Satan. Knightly romanticism of the following era elevated womanhood to a sphere where it almost ceased to be a part of earthly life. It was left to the Renaissance to reinstate woman in human society and endow her with that ideal of beauty which the ancients saw in her. Already in the *Decameron* we see women often as the representatives of a practical philosophy of life, and soon they take part in the intellectual life of the Renaissance, admired and recognized by men. This does not mean, of course, that there were not many people left who opposed, sometimes successfully, the emancipation of women; on the other hand, most of the finest characters of the Renaissance ardently supported their cause. The feminine influence exerted on all phases of life contributed markedly to the aesthetic enjoyment of arts and letters. As could be expected, there was scarcely a single woman of name and standing whose accomplishments in the field of music were not worth praising. Musical prowess was expected of the noble ladies as well as of the courtesans, an attitude which reminds us again of classical times. The noble ladies were not behind the *uomo universale* in intellectual attainments and in many instances came perhaps nearer to the perfect specimen than the men of the Renaissance. The most accomplished figure, the perfect dilettante, the very *donna universale* of the Renaissance ideal was Isabella d'Este. Her sphere of interest was truly amazing. Besides carrying on a correspondence with

Perugino and Giovanni Bellini, she was a literary confidante of Ariosto. Among her art treasures there were pictures by Perugino, Bellini, Mantegna, and Correggio, but she also collected bronze and marble statues, gems and jewels, and her agents combed the country for fine musical instruments. Great was her interest in the fine arts and in letters, but she was passionately devoted to music. Trissino and Pietro Bembo dedicated ecstatic lines to her singing, recitation, and playing. She was equally fond of her chapel choir and was constantly on the lookout for new and well-trained singers, often securing them from abroad.

Musical organizations founded and conducted by women were numerous, especially in Italy, and the religious in almost every convent were devoted to music. They sang and played various instruments so well that the Venetian, Bolognese, Neapolitan, and Milanese public flocked to the evening services to hear their magnificent choral singing. The religious were not only engaged in the study and performance of sacred music but were skilled in all varieties of secular music.

While women took an active part in musical life, their chief merit and contribution to Renaissance art was their interest in the furthering of music. In their brilliant "salons," which antedated the famous literary drawing rooms of the French women of letters and royal mistresses, they were the centers of attention; poets, artists, and musicians owed them inspiration and encouragement. In the actual performance of music women seem to have been rather restricted to their own circle. Eminent soloists no doubt took part in madrigal singing and other intimate performances, but the preferred medium for alto and soprano parts was the boy's voice, and in many of the famous choirs such as the papal choir the treble part was taken by male falsetto singers, whose voice was stronger than that of the boys. A little after the middle of the sixteenth century a new type of treble singer appeared whose marvelous art was to astound the musical world for two centuries. The first of the *castrati,* emasculated male sopranos, entered the papal choir in 1562, and he was soon followed by others. The account books mentioned these singers as *eunuchi.* Their employment was not restricted to Italy, as is popularly supposed; the Bavarian court chapel, to mention one of the important musical centers, under Lassus numbered several castrati among its famous singers. Since castration took place at an early age, usually when a boy soprano showed extraordinary vocal and singing ability, these singers, when full grown, possessed not only a voice of high pitch much more powerful than a boy's voice, but looked back on many years of continuous vocal training uninterrupted by mutation of the voice. The castrati were held in high esteem both for their incomparable vocal technique and for their beautiful "sexless" voice.[56]

At the beginning of his third book on painting, Leone Battista Alberti, the distinguished artist and humanist, remarked that the ultimate aim of an artist should not be to amass a fortune but to earn artistic fame and the patronage, pleasure, and good will of his contemporaries. Such an aim presupposes an intimate contact between the artist and the receptive public, and indeed the social position of singers and composers, as well as the appreciation accorded to them, was not inferior to that of artists, poets, and philosophers. Lodovico Zacconi (1555–1627), eminent humanist, member of some of the outstanding chapel choirs in Italy and Germany, and author of one of the most excellent theoretical tracts of his time (*Musica Prattica*, 1592 and 1622), testifies that "the singer lives surrounded by great admiration and esteem and is everywhere received with open arms. He is always considered a gentleman and is favored and honored by everyone." Some of the outstanding singers and composers enjoyed privileges seldom given to other court or church functionaries. Isaac did not remain at the court in the service of which he was employed but was free to spend many years in his beloved Florence with the emperor's explicit permission and the command that the aged master should not be disturbed. Singers in the Sistine Chapel were often marked in the account books as *absentes;* their pay was, however, seldom withheld. Another reason for the regard shown to singers and composers was their almost universally high education and culture. Besides a musical training, the thoroughness of which can hardly be explained to the musician of today, these men were well grounded in the classics, philosophy, and literature. The Bavarian envoy in Brussels, in reporting to Duke Albrecht V about Philippe de Monte, remarked that the composer "knows his Italian as if he were a native of that country, and besides Italian masters Netherlandish, French, and Latin."

Repercussions of Humanism—Tendency Toward the Lyric Stage Various Aspects of Renaissance Musical Practice

AMONG the most interesting documents concerning the vogue of music during the Renaissance are the statutes of the Académie de Poésie et de Musique, founded by Jean-Antoine de Baïf with the aid of King Charles IX of France, the dowager queen, the Dukes of Anjou and Alençon (the king's brothers), and several other great lords whose powerful support overcame the stubborn opposition of the University of Paris, jealous of an institution that was evidently escaping its control. The historians of French literature have often alluded to this academy as an important landmark in the history of French letters, yet even a cursory reading of the statutes will prove that it was mainly concerned with music.[57] Through their intense interest and diligent work, the members of the Academy developed a large repertoire. Unfortunately, very little of their work remains: they were not allowed to copy manuscripts, and single copies were easily lost, many of them being destroyed by fire when Baïf's house burned.

The ultimate aim of the Academy was probably the revival of the "musical drama" of the Greeks. To this end Baïf composed his play *Brave,* which differed from ancient classical models as much as the similar essays of the Florentine Academy of Count Bardi, from whose circle were to emerge the first operas. It is significant that the Académie de Poésie et de Musique actually embarked on a literary-musical movement almost identical with the one started in Florence a quarter of a century later, though it remained to the Italians to crown the long-evident tendency toward the creation of the lyric stage by the "invention" of the opera. The typical Gallic traits of character finally asserted themselves, and music and poetry in the short-lived Academy were soon replaced by *"éloquence"* and *"philosophie."* The original Academy, disbanded six years after its foundations, was reorganized for a short time as l'Académie du Palais and was not revived again until it became the Académie Française under Richelieu.

The repercussions of humanistic thought were equally evident in Germany, where the newly born science of classical philology turned with great interest toward the problems of antique metrics. The tendency to form "academies" was not so manifest as in Italy, and there was no institution that could be compared to Baïf's elaborate literary-musical club, but there were some more informal centers, usually grouped around one eminent individual. In southern Germany there was such a cultural center in Augsburg, where humanism found a great champion in Conrad Peutinger (1465–1547), antiquarian, diplomatist, political scientist, and economist. In the social life of these circles music was a factor as essential as in the courts of the emperor and the nobles. Through the examination of the various rhythmic and metric properties of the choruses of classical tragedies and the odes of Horace, these classical scholars soon reached the same conclusion that seemed to prompt the French poets and scholars, namely, that these literary monuments were originally sung. There followed a movement which constitutes one of the most curious aspects of humanism in Germany. Conrad Celtes (1459–1508), German humanist and Latin poet, lecturing in Ingolstadt on classical letters, had his students sing the odes of Horace in newly composed four-part settings, thereby starting the vogue for such compositions. Unlike the French, who attempted to adapt their own language to classical precepts with a view to making it more appropriate to musical settings, the Germans set to music the Latin poets—better known than the Greeks—in their original text.[58] All these works had a distinctly pedagogic aspect and served to illustrate antique prosody. The humanistic traits appeared not only in the complicated metaphorical titles of musical publications and in the frequent citations from classical authors in the prefaces of even organ tablatures; the learned humanists translated everything under the sun, even rendering Luther's hymns in Latin and Greek. The forced application of classical metric principles to German texts and the frequent interpolation of Latin and Greek words threatened to ruin German prosody. Musicians exhibited a great interest in classical texts; and certain famous passages, like Dido's parting words in Vergil's *Aeneid* (IV, 651, *et seq.*), were set to music by a number of composers.

Literary men were so pleased with their resuscitated school dramas, whose choruses seemed to evoke the serene atmosphere of Greek tragedy, that they essayed the conquest of even the popular theater. The first attempts were, however, rather discouraging. When the humanistically-minded clerics of Metz substituted a Latin play by Terence for the customary mystery play, the audience stormed the scene and gave the actors a thrashing. In the later development of school and public theatrical performances a twofold tendency is discernible. Simple folk songs and Lutheran hymns were interpolated into the text, the public being invited to join in the singing, while at the same time the use of accompanying instruments became more and more popular. Thus we are dealing here with a play that has a decidedly "operatic" appearance, with its songs, choruses, and orchestra.

The careful observer of all these events cannot but be impressed by the almost universal tendency in all lands toward that combination of music and poetry which was to result in the creation of the lyric stage, the opera. We have seen the poets and scholars preoccupied with the reconstruction of the classical theater and with classical lyric poetry, which they considered to be intimately connected with music. This same tendency is noticeable in England, where among all forms of entertainment during the Renaissance period none flourished with greater vigor than the drama. The memory of the mystery plays produced by the trade guilds was still fresh even in Shakespeare's lifetime, and plays were an important part of all entertainments, receptions, and other festivities. Stage plays afforded enjoyment to all classes of society, and, although a differentiation of taste appeared in the seventeenth century, the taste of the court and that of the city were not far apart until almost the end of the sixteenth century. Robust drama, full of buffoonery, dancing, song, and an infinite variety of spectacular elements, beguiled a public which was developing the habit of playgoing so strongly that theatrical ventures became a profitable business.[59] The English stage exhibited, then, a decided leaning toward the "operatic" at a remarkably early period. Marlowe (*Edward II,* Act I, Sc. 1) testifies to the influence of the Italian *intermezzi* and *rappresentazioni:*

> Therefore I'll have Italian masks by night,
> Sweet speeches, comedies and pleasing shows.

The masque, which reached its height in the reigns of James I and Charles I, was originally introduced in the early sixteenth century. Derived from the Italian improvised comedy, it became a favorite form of private entertainment, and its use at court and elsewhere to entertain royalty led to its elaboration into a magnificent and expensive spectacle, with great emphasis on costumes, scenery, and music. We shall see in what measure this form, a dramatic favorite of Ben Jonson, contributed to the foundation of English opera.

Coronations, aristocratic weddings, municipal receptions, all called for solemn Masses; and no event of importance was celebrated without an adequate and highly artistic musical background. The predominantly intimate character of Renaissance music, and the unique position of the papal choir, led to the belief that this era knew only suave and gentle music. The legacy of the Gothic was, however, not extinct; it continued to infuse certain domains of music with a dazzling splendor which again found universal recognition in the approaching baroque spirit. Erasmus complained in 1526 that the churches reverberated with the sound of flutes, pipes, trumpets, and trombones. The aged humanist's complaint was directed not at some unwelcome innovation, but against the wonderfully developed "fanfare" playing of medieval times. At the elevation of the Host the spacious naves of cathedrals "resounded with many harmonious symphonies [chords] emitted by a great variety of instruments." Dufay, Ockeghem, Obrecht, Josquin, La Rue, Brumel, and their contemporaries were all fond of this splendor of instrumental sonority, the organ always being employed in the accompaniment of their choral works, and trumpets, trombones, and kettledrums often being included in the instrumental equipment. The brass instruments and the drums were especially prominent in the Sanctus of the Mass. (We shall see how the seventeenth century was to appreciate the festive character of these instrumentally accompanied Masses, enhancing their splendor to an almost unbelievable degree. It was quite customary, in the baroque period, to have batteries of cannon thunder away in the fortifications of the city during the Sanctus.) To perform these works strictly without accompaniment is to divest them of an essential stamp of their time. The pure *a cappella* conception is contradicted, furthermore, by numerous allusions on the title pages of compositions. Inscriptions such as *da sonare ò cantare, convenables tant à la voix comme aux instruments, tam instrumentis musicis quam vivae melodiae,* all indicate that the compositions can be performed by a chorus or by an ensemble of instruments. Significantly enough, similar directions are to be read even on such works as the motets of Lassus. Some of the Renaissance Masses display a tonal splendor that we associate only with modern times, because of our popular conception of the so-called "pure *a cappella* period."

Otto Kinkeldey has mentioned the great festivities that took place on the occasion of the marriage of Costanzo Sforza with Camilla di Aragona in Pesaro (1475), and this is a typical example of such events. After a spectacular performance of an allegorical play in the palace, the guests went to hear a triumphal Mass, "celebrated with organs, pipes, trumpets and untold number of drums, together with two choirs and many singers." [60] The Renaissance orchestra, taking the place of the heterogeneous conglomeration of instruments which characterized the Gothic ensemble, was a well-blended group of families of instruments, comparable to the organ or to a vocal choir. The orchestras at the various courts and churches received more attention than had been paid to them before, and were developed with care. Ensemble music was usually conducted by one member of the group, his conducting being effected either by the hand, by a baton, or by the foot. Ramos de Pareja lists all three methods, and many pictures and etchings bear out the statements of the theoreticians.

Pride in artistic achievements during the era of the Renaissance surpassed even martial pride. Municipalities as well as tyrants and rulers were constantly petitioned by the citizenry for all kinds of artistic projects, which sometimes concerned the rearrangement of streets to suit the placing of a new monument, and sometimes had to do with the engagement of an architect, painter, or organist. The great cities were not alone in constantly endeavoring to enrich their artistic treasures: the small free, or seemingly free, cities, Perugia, Arezzo, Orvieto, and many others, sought to rival the great centers in their own way. The authorities always secured the collaboration of eminent artists, and insisted on new and original works by the leading contemporary masters. Thus, at the consecration of the Cathedral in Florence, Dufay's gigantic motet *Nuper Rosarum* was performed with the utmost display of musical resources; and for the wedding festivities of Ferdinando de' Medici and Christine de Lorraine in 1589 some of the most celebrated musicians, among them Marenzio, Cavalieri, Malvezzi, and Peri, were invited to write the music to the festival play that was to be performed.

While courtly Platonists and adapters of Petrarchian conventions were glorifying love, religion, and martial ardor in highly artistic verses, the Neapolitan merchants, the German artisans, and the Elizabethan shopkeepers found a literature on the same theme no less fascinating, albeit the works that interested them had a somewhat different point of view and emphasis from those that delighted the aristocratic audience. The villanelle, quodlibets, drinking songs, and broadside ballads on current happenings were frequent and provided people with endless amusement. We should not assume, however, that it was only this popular music that indulged in the type of merriment which has elicited the deepest contempt of modern critics, who have approached the Rabelaisian spirit of the era with the codified artistic morals of the Victorian age. Real art expresses typical and genuine inventive-

ness. When contemplating such art the ephemeral weakness of human nature should not obscure the view of the searching eye. The brushstrokes of
the painter, the words of the poet, and the chords of the musician must not
be judged by their minute ramifications; a work of art created by bold and
free spirits should be approached and enjoyed in the same spirit. The inso-
lently impudent and frivolous, yet naïvely sincere and undisturbed style of
the chansons, the fine erotic poetry of the madrigals, with their texts that
make Boccaccio's stories seem tame and harmless, do not, in reality, mean
bottomless moral corruption. Otherwise we could not explain how men of
irreproachable dignity, devout religiousness, and exemplary life took delight
in setting them to music. Moreover, in the midst of the most obscene ditties,
and in the same collections, one can often find sentimental and moralizing
poems. It is evident that the educated public did not see anything fundamentally objectionable in this curious mixture of erotic and sacred poetry.
A beautiful music book written for Cardinal Ferdinando de' Medici between 1562 and 1587, to mention one example, contained motets and Psalms,
three dirges upon the death of Anne Boleyn, and some French chansons
and Italian *villote* whose racy texts stand in curious contrast to the Biblical
words appearing in the sacred compositions. We find a similar unawareness
of incongruity in England before the more puritanic times. Playing in
masques and pageants was a recognized duty of the gentlemen of the
Chapel Royal during the reign of Henry VIII, and there are many references
to such performances. Works like the *Goldyn Arber in the Archyard of
Plesyr* and *The Triumph of Love and Beauty* cannot be taken for religious
pieces; yet the Magister Puerorum Capellae Dom. Regis, holding a position
similar to that of Palestrina in the Capella Julia, was expected to lend a
hand in their performance.[61]

The Consequences of the Reform Movements
Music in the Universities

THE Catholic and Protestant Reformations brought a new spirit into the
world of art and reminded people that they should not squander their time
by indulging in "vain entertainments," and called attention to the moral
aspects—questionable from the point of view of the Church—of Renaissance
art. In the Preface of Tye's *Acts of the Apostles* the object of the publication
is given as being

> That such good thinges your grace might moue
> Your lute when ye assaye:
> In stede of songes of wanton loue
> These stories then to playe.

On the Continent the Protestants considered Lassus an especial pride of Catholicism, and this fact did not affect their admiration; but he must not offend their newly established moral standards. Ronsard declared to Charles IX that "the more than divine Roland seems to have divested the heavens of their harmony to rejoice us on earth"; but this was the homage of an independent artist of the Renaissance. In 1575 appeared the first collection of Lassus's secular works, published in the fortified Huguenot stronghold of La Rochelle. The title, *Mellange d'Orlando de Lassus,* carried an explanatory notice stating that "the profane words of these chansons have been exchanged for spiritual ones . . . ," thus indicating the change of times. It is amusing to see such attempts to "save" the music of Lassus by substituting for the erotic and comic texts religious and serious poems, retaining the music in its original form. Although the pious editor himself recognized that Lassus "composed his music to fit every word of the text, in which art he surpasses every other musician of our time," he did not seem to realize the aesthetic futility of separating this music from its text, which it followed with infinite artistry and sharp psychological observation, establishing a mood not to be applied to any other situation. It is inconceivable that the coquettish chords that accompany lines such as these,

> D'ou vient cela, belle, je vous supply
> Que plus a moy ne vous recommandez?

can fulfill the same role when applied to the pious parody of the original:

> D'ou vient cela, Seigneur, je te suppli'
> Que loin de nous te tiens les yeux convers?

The sincere but heavy and unskilled hands of the editor destroyed the marvelous artistic organism of these chansons to produce puppets dressed in beautiful moral sentences but with no real life in them. It is immaterial whether the original compositions were of a laudable or a deplorable moral character; the work of art was destroyed. Such acts were not restricted to the French and English moralizers. Lassus himself gave permission for a similarly "Christianized" German edition of his works which appeared in 1582 in Ratisbon. But this was not the Lassus of the Renaissance days, the musical *grand seigneur,* serene when writing music for the Church and sparkling, exuberant, and witty when composing chansons and madrigals; it was the aging, unworldly master, entirely under the spell of the spirit of the Counter Reformation.

There is still another field of cultural history which gave music a prominent place in its constitution. University life, ever since its beginnings, had made music a part of the curriculum. We had an opportunity to discuss music in the medieval university, so it remains to see how it fared during the Renaissance. The statutes of the philosophical faculty of the University of Leipzig in the fifteenth and sixteenth centuries mention among the books to be read by the candidates for the magisterial degree the *"Musica* of Muris." The same is true in the venerable old universities of Vienna, Louvain, Heidelberg, Basel, Cracow, Tübingen, Greifswald, Königsberg, Padua, Bologna, and Salamanca. The famous theoretician Salinas, active in Salamanca about 1577, wrote with pride on the title page of his work, *In Academia Salamanticensi Musicae Professor.* We must not think, however, that all scholars were solely concerned with the abstract, mathematical-philosophical aspects of music; there were many lecturers whose prime interest was to bring the theoretical speculations into practical application. At the University of Cologne we find the well-known opponent of Luther, Johannes Cochlaeus (1479-1552), as *magister,* and later as professor of music, discoursing on the choral music of his time. Tübingen counted among its faculty Magister Andreas Ornitoparchus (Vogelsang?) (d. 1535), author of *Musicae Activae Micrologus,* one of the outstanding theoretical tracts of the sixteenth century. In Cracow and Basel lectures were given on the *musica choralis.* With the advent of humanism and the consequent reorganization of the curricula, practical music gained in importance in university life.

Baccalaurei and *Doctores musicae* look back on a respectable ancestry in the English universities, which were among the oldest to bestow academic honors on musicians. While the oldest records of the awarding of the degrees of Bachelor and Doctor of Music date from the fifteenth and sixteenth centuries (Thomas Saintwix, *Mus. Doc.* Cantab., 1463 [?], Robert Fayrfax, *Mus. Doc.* Oxon., 1511 [1504?]), there is little doubt that the degrees are considerably older. It is true, however, that unlike their colleagues in Continental universities, the English *magistri* were mainly concerned with the composition of original music. The "Doctor's theses" submitted by a number of sixteenth- and early seventeenth-century candidates for the degree belong to the treasured glories of English music. In the will of Sir Thomas Gresham (d. 1579), founder of the college bearing his name, provision was made for fellowships (professorships) in divinity, astronomy, music, geometry, law, medicine, and rhetoric. He urged professors to remember that the hearers of the lectures would be "merchants and other citizens," and therefore the lectures should be comprehensible. In music the lecture was "to be read twice every week in manner following: viz.—the theorique part for half an hour, and the practique, by concert of voice or instruments, for the rest of the hour. . . ." The first Gresham lecturer, John Bull (*Mus. Doc.* Cantab.), was appointed in 1596 on special recommendation of the queen; he was followed by William Byrd's son, who substituted for him during his absence. It seems, however, that the generous founder's admonition, to make the lectures easily understandable for the public, was taken too literally, because the subsequent Gresham professors were physicians, ministers, and barristers, utterly unqualified to engage in any form of musical activity.

Toward the end of the sixteenth century the musical scholars gradually disappeared from the universities following the complete reorganization and new orientation of academic life, but in many instances the practical musicians remained, and many famous cantors and organists were connected with academic institutions although they were not regular members of the faculty. The presence of these practical musicians in the university can easily be explained by the extraordinary popularity that music enjoyed with the students. The vogue of music can best be judged from the numerous warnings and regulations issued by the deans and rectors forbidding the students nocturnal excursions with their instruments. The university convocations were accompanied by music, and for the conferring of degrees the academic authorities usually enlisted the services of the town pipers and drummers, the musicians later following the successful candidates to the inevitable banquet.

Music in the New World

LOVE of music accompanied the adventurous conquerors in the New World. One of the first missionaries in the Americas was a Franciscan by the name of Pedro de Gante, born in Flanders about 1480. This Fleming, not only a theologian but an able musician, was of royal blood, probably a half brother of the Emperor Charles V. He received authorization from his imperial kinsman to go to the Indies even before he received the pope's permission to proceed, and arrived in Veracruz the thirtieth of August, 1523. Needing music for ecclesiastic services, he soon discovered that the natives had a natural inclination for song and undertook to teach them the rudiments of liturgic music. In a short time not only the monks sang, but hundreds of Indian voices united in the daily religious service. The indefatigable Fray Pedro learned the Aztec language and in 1524 knew it well enough to found a school, which was later removed to Mexico City and became a center of music. Here in the convent of San Francisco he taught until his death. The instruction consisted at the beginning in reading, writing, the practical arts, singing, and the playing and construction of musical instruments. The fundamental principle of the school being to make converts to the Church and thus to prepare students to take part in the propagation of faith, there was need of precentors, teachers, and sacristans, besides a growing number of skilled workers for the building of chapels and convents. In order to accomplish all these aims it became necessary to enlarge and specialize the teaching of the individual subjects. Fray Pedro made the Indians copy manuscripts so that with practice in writing clear notes they might learn the rules of music and its notation. From that useful process there are preserved copies of truly beautiful appearance, illuminated in colors, in the *Salterios* (Psalters) which date from the first half of the sixteenth century, two invaluable copies of which are in the National Museum of Mexico. At this exercise the students worked for one year, after which they were initiated into the singing of ecclesiastic song. When the students were sufficiently advanced in both plain chant and measured music, they were sent to the small churches to teach, and so successful was their work that in every village there were precentors who exercised their office in Masses and vespers. The first organ built in the school of Fray Pedro dates from 1527. All the churches had organs, played by Indians who studied in the school; and many compositions by indigenous artists, among them polyphonic Masses, are waiting for the searching eye of the musicologists and historians who will, no doubt, soon undertake to explore this fascinating chapter of American history, still largely unknown to us but certainly harboring grateful and important material for the scholar.[62]

*

*   *

THE great historians and philosophers of the culture of the Renaissance, Burckhardt, Symonds, and Nietzsche, impressed on the mind of the modern student the complete break they believed existed between the Renaissance and the Middle Ages. They saw in the Renaissance essentially a return to the world of the ancients. Classical form is exterior, but classical spirit is essence. Classical form has often returned in the past and will return in the future. But the classical spirit has returned very seldom, and never altogether. The world has had a beautiful dream of the sacred primeval era when Pan's pipe echoed in the woods and the flame of sacrificial offerings lit up the Dorian temples. Whenever the tired world has longed for peace and order, harmony and blissfulness, it has turned to this sacred and venerated mythical epoch. This fabulous world reminds us, however, of the hero of the old legend who is in eternal quest for a likeness of his dead wife. When he finds it—her face, eyes, hair, everything seems to be the same—he is convinced for a moment that his quest has ended, but the illusion passes, for the spirit is absent. Classicism has returned frequently in its exterior manifestations, but it has never been the Aphrodite of Cnidus, now dead.

The continuation of antique civilization by the Middle Ages and the Renaissance has influenced Occidental thought up to the present day. It has preserved for us the culture of Greece and Rome; but the significance of this intellectual heritage from the ancients is not limited to its concrete legacy, however important it may be that the basic ideas of Roman civilization still confront us every day in our political and legal institutions. More important than all this is the faith in the propagation of culture and civilization, that classical optimism, which the Renaissance has transmitted to us. To work and to create for all time to come is the eternal longing of mankind, and really great things are produced only by men and epochs whose hands and brains are not weighted down by the idea that the present cannot be saved, and will sink without leaving a trace in the sea of the past.

It was not only great edifices, innumerable monuments and paintings, chronicles and poems, motets and madrigals that the Renaissance gave us. The renewed ambition of the ancients, the new value of the individual's power created figures of an overwhelming intensity of life. Even the most severe catastrophes that visited mankind in those animated centuries, the plague, famine, earthquakes, inundations, the ravages of war and religious strife, fratricidal feuds, and the devastating invasions of the Turks—none could abate the powerful fecundity of the Renaissance which resulted in that rich harvest of a marvelous civilization that does not cease to elicit the interest and admiration of the modern man.

Chapter 10

THE BAROQUE

The Fading of the Renaissance

ONE of the most pregnant lessons of history is that the kernel of the new ideas that seem to arise with each succeeding epoch may always be found in previous times. This is true also with regard to styles.

The last decades of the sixteenth century were filled with bewildering contradictions. Church and state had been shaken to their foundations and were in need of rebuilding. New forces that were making themselves felt in religion, politics, arts, and letters were facing equally powerful forces opposed to them. These were the times of the fully developed reform movements, the religious wars, the establishment of absolutist monarchies, the foundation of the modern science of physics, the appearance of the mystical-natural philosophy of such men as Agrippa of Nettesheim, Paracelsus, and Böhme, and the flourishing of a new scholasticism. A changed Europe emerged from these tormented decades.

Christendom had lost its religious unity and now consisted of two large factions, the north and large parts of central Europe having forsaken Catholicism. The Church could no longer regard the Reformation as an ephemeral heresy, for it had given birth to a new spiritual and religious world which was settling down to a life governed by new laws, creating for itself a definite place under the sun. The regional churches which sprang up following the secession assumed the aspect of national churches supported by the people and defended by the state. The spirit of increased freedom gained ground even within the old Church; although Giordano Bruno was burned and Galileo forced to give up his theses, it was not long before Descartes demonstrated that even the Jesuit-trained savants of Catholic France could free themselves from traditional authority and make doubt in the former conceptions the point of departure for their thinking.

The sixteenth century saw the waning of the political influence of the papacy. The popes of the Renaissance period, especially the great Pope Julius II, made the Holy See into an Italian state and, in so doing, curtailed the universal position of the Church, thus contributing to the success of the Reformation. With the successful prosecution of the Counter Reformation the papacy again rose to the position of a churchly and world power, but by this time half of Europe had been lost to the Church and hardly a country —however Catholic—accepted the absolute domination of the Holy See as in the past. We shall see how, for purely political reasons, a cardinal of the Church, Richelieu, was led to conclude an alliance with German Protestants.

The brilliant world created by the Renaissance, exhilarated by its own richness, paled after the intoxication was over. The subtle ideas of romantic worshipers of antiquity and of courtiers delving into aesthetics did not engender lasting influence. Medieval traditions, ridiculed and dismissed by the ardent humanists of the High Renaissance, began to come to the surface from the depths of Occidental civilization. Gothic elements and forms again appeared in the fine arts of the later fifteen hundreds, reaching, in the first half of the following century, a peculiar second flowering. At the very time when the Renaissance reached its apex, there began a process of disintegration; the scarcely attained classical perfection and balance of form became disturbed, distorted, and ragged. Once more there was a vogue of asymmetry, and architects again became interested in Gothic forms. This curious mixture of the medieval and the modern nourished the process which led to the baroque period of the seventeenth century. This Gothic Renaissance was not restricted to spiritual matters: it was felt in the entire range of culture, and, far from being reactionary in nature, it harbored positively creative forces. The realization of the deep-seated antinomies which were the result of this countermovement necessitated a new formulation and examination, an extension and deepening of the ideas and ideals of the Renaissance. The chaotic situation created by the dissolving Renaissance was cleared by the comprehensive unity of a new style, in which everything strove toward a synthesis and reconciliation. The Gothic elements in the baroque have often been emphasized in recent times, and some historians have taken a position diametrically opposed to the old teachings concerning the Renaissance, considering it an episode in the history of Western civilization which interrupted the natural development of culture. Such a conception would appear, however, as erroneous as the older theories of the complete independence of the Renaissance movement. Even if the appearance of the baroque seems in some aspects to be the return of the Gothic, it is unthinkable without the Renaissance.

As the Renaissance faded all over Italy, the country reflected, more than any other, the change of times. The ideals of the Renaissance were safeguarded for some decades, but its soul was stifled, enveloped in the sweeping waves of the Counter Reformation. Schooling and polish, the rich legacy of form and splendor remained, but the substance had vanished. The humanists disappeared, and the great art and music that remained were drawn within the orbit of the new church spirit. Palestrina's music, turning away from the radiant madrigal, had only one purpose: to serve the Church. The greatest poet of the era, Tasso, morally and mentally crushed, repented the errors of his youth and, like Lassus, humbled himself ceaselessly in his anxiety to redeem himself. It was the excited impulse of the religious struggle, the triumphs and reverses of the Church, the Catholic consciousness, the warm breath of mysticism, ecstasy, the eroticism of martyrdom, dramatic, heroic, burning, and purposeful, which dominated a world formerly devoted to the calm, assured, and finely balanced atmosphere of the Renaissance. The new temper was not restricted, however, to religious and political matters; it permeated all fields of human endeavor, making arts and letters an essential part of the great controversy. The moral refreshment of the Church and of popular life reached every corner of the civilized world, once more held in awe by the elemental powers of the Church, which, shaking itself vigorously, cast away all that was hiding its ancient traditions. The Catholic world created a new uniform culture, offering a spectacle scarcely short of the grandiose and sublime. Religion and theology, unruffled, retained the Church and its traditions as the source of life, work, and faith in the face of all the Biblical and historical criticism of Protestantism. Scholasticism reigned in the universities, and dogmatic and theological discussions occupied even amateurs. The cult of saints and belief in miracles reappeared strengthened. The intense religiosity of mysticism, originating in Spain, was now welcomed by the Church throughout Europe. History and philosophy must serve the Church, philology must help to educate its servants, and music and the arts must contribute to the glorification of its reborn omnipotence. The Church did not suffer independent sciences, mental, spiritual, or natural, and it demanded a new orientation in literature. The fusion of the spirit of the baroque with that of the Counter Reformation, taking place in Italy, soon gained the whole of Catholic Europe, and in whatever country or form the coalition appeared, the leadership was always yielded to the latter. The union was more profound and productive in Spain than in Italy; its results were here more original and more uniform than in France, where the opposing forces were more lively. It subsequently moved up to the north, with a power transcending religious barriers, and retained its essential traits in the following century to reach its height in the pomp and pathos, in the dramatic force, in the ecstasy and fervor, in the overwhelming artistic might of a Rubens, a Rembrandt, a Schütz, and a Buxtehude. Everywhere we can see a more individual life, but everywhere we can also ascertain that this life could not escape the ideas that had been influencing thought since the Tridentine Council. This baroque spirit did not offer anything essentially new; the restoration of the old was its aim. It could not impress itself everywhere, but where it was victorious it surpassed itself to such an extent, and exacted such tributes and energies, that the most fervent peoples which abandoned themselves without reservation to the spiritual, political, and artistic tenets of this maelstrom became victims of its consuming force and disappeared from the stage of history for centuries: Spain, Poland, and what is now Belgium.

Religious Thought as the Motive Power of Early Baroque Art

WEIGHTY changes occurred also in the realm of Protestantism. The victoriously sweeping new faith gradually changed into a fissured structure, an organization completely occupied with its petty affairs. The only faction that retained its propulsive power was Calvinism, especially strong in the west of Germany and in the northern Netherlands. Its powers were not, however, sufficient to support a large political movement of expansion, for the struggle with Spain in the Netherlands and the Huguenot wars in France consumed much of its energies. The Protestant situation was aggravated by constant quarrels regarding matters of faith. Thus the end of the Reformation century saw Protestantism already on the defensive. But the spiritual side of the situation did not correspond to the political picture. Three generations of Protestants grew up in the new faith; they attended schools conducted by teachers earnestly devoted to the new religious-theological literature, and their daily life was imbued with the spirit of Protestantism. The Counter Reformation produced a voluminous pamphlet literature which recalled the militant days of Luther, who had leaned strongly on the printed word. But now the aggressive side was taken by the Catholics, and the Protestants found themselves beleaguered. This literature soon grew beyond the pamphlet stage and produced works of magnitude and importance.

But all this literary activity, important as it was, could not counteract the gains of Protestantism in its heroic period. The English universities, and the majority of the German, Swiss, and Dutch, accepted the new faith, and the princely schools, gymnasia, and other institutions were all overwhelmingly Protestant in the central and northern part of Europe. The difference between the power and ideology of the two faiths is strikingly illustrated by the fact that, except in the case of the English universities, Protestant theology, while occupying a commanding position, could not dictate in matters touching upon education; thus the humanists and scientists enjoyed considerable freedom and immunity. (This was partly owing, of course, to the various sects not being able to agree among themselves.) The Catholic universities declined in the countries with a large Protestant population; only those which came under the influence of the Society of Jesus continued an active and productive life.

The creative work in architecture accomplished by the Jesuits is a matter of common knowledge. The magnificently ornate "revised Gothic" churches built by them have elicited the epithet "Jesuit style," but while not generally known, their activity impressed its stamp on the music of the period no less than on architecture. As soon as the original decrees of Loyola, scorning music, were changed in accordance with the enlarged scope of the Society, the Jesuits, with their usual thoroughness, started to match what the Protestants had been doing in their field. Recognizing the immense advantage of songs in the vernacular as used by Protestants, they set out to provide the common people of their faith with religious songbooks. Naturally these Catholic songbooks were most numerous in the Germanic lands, and German, Austrian, Swiss, and Bohemian Jesuits composed, arranged, edited, and published numerous collections; [1] the French Jesuits were also active, however, and Belgian and Polish songbooks were also fairly numerous. We shall see how the Jesuits subsequently added every form of art to their course of instruction as soon as they became convinced of its usefulness. Following these principles, and encouraged by the Church, the Jesuits were able to impart instruction of remarkable thoroughness, leading to a model, if rigid, education.

Around the turn of the century, a new, powerful generation seized the reins of cultural life. New leaders appeared in the natural sciences, especially in astronomy, in philosophy, and in law; the new, thoroughly modern drama came into being. There were Giordano Bruno and Galilei in Italy; Jean Bodin, the social philosopher, and Descartes in France; Hugo Grotius, the great jurist and humanist in Holland; Francis Bacon and Shakespeare in England; Kepler in Germany, and Comenius, the great educator, in Moravia. If the new theories were advanced in Catholic lands, or elsewhere by Catholics, they called forth the sternest reprimands from the Church. Only the fine arts and music still swore complete allegiance to the Catholic Church and retained within her embrace all their creative powers and productive capacity; the works of pure human intelligence detached themselves more and more from her sphere of influence. But in the domain of arts and music, Catholicism deployed an activity which forever exonerates her from the accusation of a hostile attitude toward art. Catholicism did not welcome religion as a science; its life revolved around the emotional. It demanded complete submission and faith in prescribed norms; it encouraged mystical awe and immersion in the secrets of devotion. And it stood by the faithful, not only encouraging them, but lending a munificent hand to everything that would promote the triumph of faith and gain mastery over the world. Centuries of experience had taught Catholicism that its cult was infinitely enhanced by art and music. As long as the Church ruled medieval life, she ruled art also, and even during the Renaissance the greatest patron of artists and composers was the Church. But the Renaissance was so strongly influenced by secular ideas that the Church had to capitulate to a certain extent, and in many instances art was sacred only in its location or use, not in its nature. The popes of the High Renaissance, from Sixtus IV to Leo X, identified themselves so closely with the spirit of the times that the increasingly secular nature of church art did not seem to offend them. With the turning away of the papacy from the Renaissance spirit, with the Catholic Reform, and under the adverse effects of the Reformation, a new Catholic church art was born.

The pontificate of Sixtus V (1585–1590) may be considered the time at which the early baroque took definite form. The church reforms were rigorously carried out, and the new vigor of militant Catholicism filled the arts with its spirit. New edifices were rising everywhere, and the pope himself sponsored their erection. The strictly religious point of view gained acceptance, but religion took unto itself everything that three centuries of Italian art had produced in virtuosity and technique, in the psychological power of observation and expression. The early baroque was, at first, a period of Catholic churchly art, and it was again the Society of Jesus which gave this art its peculiar traits of character. From the sphere of quiet devotion, the faithful were lifted into the world of the triumphant Church whose cult was celebrated by richly decked clergy under the vaults of a mighty architecture, surrounded by statues and pictures, before scintillating altars ornamented with gold and silver, to the accompaniment of the impressive and resonant music of multiple choirs, orchestras, and organs. In elaborate processions with flags, candles, and torches, triumphal carriages, floats, and arches, with the marchers singing, accompanying soldiers' bands blaring forth with their trumpets, the bells tolling and cannon booming, priests and students, guilds and corporations with their emblems, princes and the populace all united to demonstrate their adherence to the regenerated triumphal Church. Opposed to the soberness of the Protestant, especially the Calvinistic, cult, now all the arts contributed without stint to the service, raising and enhancing, often to excess, their dialectics and expressive faculties. This stylistic change corresponded to the new religiousness, because it was permeated by passionate abandonment to the Church and by the most profound preoccupation with the tenets of faith, but also by the consciousness of the triumph of the Church. All the flame and ardor of these struggles, often, indeed, lost in wild fanaticism, is mirrored in the passionate nature of this art. The Society of Jesus was founded by a Spaniard, a man who came from a country which had for centuries defended the Church against her enemies. The glow of Spanish piety and fervor cast its reflection on the arts of all countries that came under their influence. And as the renewed Catholicism expanded vehemently, its art, in spite of certain weaknesses, followed its triumphal rise.

The German Counter Reformation, having inflicted serious blows on Protestantism, led to magnificent creations of a sacred art. But this German art was too confident of its power and too heavily bedecked with splendor to represent a really profound religious art. Its spirit was not even typically German, as the chief artists were Italians, or Germans and Netherlanders entirely under the influence of the Romanic spirit. Protestant art never got beyond its beginnings. It was not only the horrors of the Thirty Years' War that hindered its development but the fact that Protestantism did not yet manifest a desire for art; it did not endeavor to bring about that union of religion and art which swept Catholicism to the highest artistic achievements. Wherever the Counter Reformation asserted itself and wherever the old faith retained its vigor, new edifices were built in which all the splendor of the baroque was expressed. The Protestant territories were not lacking in artistic achievements: the German Renaissance and the German baroque impressed their spirit on cities and castles in the north, west, and south, but Protestantism as a religion did not partake of this activity. The aristocracy and the wealthy middle classes stood behind this art as the Catholic Church stood behind Romanic art. The cities—the *Reichsstädte*—with their wealth and the ruling princes with their growing absolutist power became, then, after the Catholic Church, the greatest patrons of art in Germany, and in the seventeenth century the country saw the beginnings of a great German art. But the artistic activities of the great cities were stifled during the Thirty Years' War, as the devastating conflagration pre-empted their rich treasuries. The monumental town halls and patricians' residences had all been built prior to these days, and this architecture, as well as other products of the German Renaissance—paintings, woodcuts, book illustrations, and carvings—suffered a temporary lapse. The situation in the realm of art took a turn for the worse when religious fanaticism began to claim a part in it. In its initial determination to assert its independence, Protestantism exhibited a strong dislike for all churchly ornament, considering artistic embellishment of the divine service contrary to evangelical precepts. We have seen how music suffered from this artistic hostility in Germany, Switzerland, Holland, and England. While the last three countries have never recovered from the adverse effects of this antimusical tendency, the special musical inclination and sound psychological observation of Luther laid the foundation for an incomparable Protestant musical culture in Germany. That a religion based on easily understandable precepts and on simple ceremonies did not offer the arts tempting tasks is evident. For Protestantism to accept the frame and spirit that characterized Catholic culture would have been to abandon its ideals; but in clinging to its austere philosophy, it yielded the whole field of arts to the old Church. There were church buildings in abundance, and very few were needed beyond those that had been seized by the new sects. Although the change from a sacramental church with its elaborate ritual to a church centered around the pulpit, with little or no liturgic apparatus, was a fundamental departure, Protestantism failed to create an architecture of its own. Protestant churches remained imitations of church architecture of pre-Reformation times and as such did not express a creative power and spirit of their own. The many products of the goldsmith's, ironsmith's, mosaic maker's, tapestry weaver's, wood carver's, and embroiderer's art, which furnished magnificent *objets d'art* to the elaborate ritual of the old Church, and the pictures, sarcophagi, statues, and side altars—all were banished from the churches as offensive to the puritanic sense of the Protestant clergy. Protestant piety feared that the attention due to God's word would be distracted by vain ornaments and decorations.

There was one field, however, in which Protestantism created an art of its own stamp: music. Music became an inalienable part of the Reformed faiths, and there is scarcely one among its denominations which did not consider music an integral part of its worship. The further Protestant church music developed, the more it became evident that music was the truest artistic expression of Protestantism; it corresponded to its doctrines and aspirations, and it was in this art that all that was missing in the fine arts was fully realized.

The Changing Artistic Ideals

THE High Renaissance embodied calm, assured, and mature human clarity. The strong, happy, and intelligent man who assimilated in himself classical culture was the ideal measure of all things. Proportion, harmony, clarity, comprehensiveness, unity in diversity were the aesthetic doctrines ruling the era. While the first half of the cinquecento was still occupied mainly with the problems of space, with the application and development of perspective, and with the representation of the human body, the second half of the century was more and more interested in the emotional side of action, from which the spatiotemporal unity of the composition develops. What was earlier a pure form of existence, with the artistic problems centering about spatial definition, developed here into a vividly felt phenomenon of action. The Renaissance strove for highest perfection of all parts merged into a quiet organic unity, and the Renaissance artist's feeling for space was like his sense for nature—clear and happy. His architecture was slender, graceful; the palaces, colonnades, and gardens were open, and there was light in every corner. He made himself a hero-ideal, not the courtly armored knight of the Middle Ages but the handsome hero of the ancients.

The baroque changed the atmosphere of this world, and Michelangelo threw all these notions overboard. The strong metaphysical impulse that we knew in the Gothic world reappears in his works, but the opposing motives are not brought into harmonic unison. The shadow of an overwhelming tragedy covers his works. Michelangelo's figures writhe, groan, and sigh. They desire to gain the transcendental spiritual regions, but with their massive corporeality they are even more the prisoners of the earthly, sensuous-spatial, than ordinary mortals. The wondrous gigantic bodies created by his imagination will remain the symbols of captivity in matter, of a longing and desire for transcendental purity. The apotheosis of the sublime becomes again, as in the Gothic, the expression of the spiritual, but in a different sense. In the Gothic era it was naïve objectivity, the expression of the hieratic order. Here it is the expression of the superhuman and miraculous. Architecture also changes. The architectural elements lose their individual constructive meaning and importance and, as with Michelangelo, become the forms of expression of irrational forces. Every column suffers, every pillar groans under the heavy, unbearable pressure. The individual forms are now subordinated to the form of the whole as servants, and beauty is no longer expressed in mild and well-tuned harmonies, but in eruptive power uprooted by passions. Single columns henceforth mean as little as single pillars; they are piled up to emphasize and enliven the space they create. The artistic formation is no longer determined by the materiality of the elements, by their solidity and weight; these elements become living individualities, forms of expression. What was restricted by Michelangelo and the early baroque to the elements of construction invades the whole structure in the high baroque. What we behold is not simply an edifice, but a drama in which the *dramatis personae* are the walls, the columns, interior and exterior. While Italian architecture still retained its rational foundations—it could not cast away such an essential trait of the Latin—these dynamic qualities led to their most violent expression in the German baroque.

The overabundance of decorative elements, the dissolving of organic unity into emotional unity, the drawing on light and shadow as elements of construction also characterize the fine arts. The artists stop adding; they begin to multiply. The Greek painter who became the embodiment of the very soul of baroque Spain, El Greco, created the most convincing symbols of this visionary mood. His often singularly distorted, over life-sized figures seem to come from another world. An almost expressionistic trait—the ignoring of the phenomena of reality—is discernible in them. The magic enchantment and religious ecstasy of the beyond held El Greco's figures spellbound. If we cannot follow the religious abandonment of the artist, his world will be forever closed to us, because this transcendental, ecstatic mood prevails in all his works, even when he shows us a storm over Toledo. This penchant for the transcendental, this same enchanted world, even though less convulsively passionate, dominates the works of Alonso Cano (1601-1667), the chief architect of Granada Cathedral and court painter to Philip IV; of Juan Mon-

tañes (c. 1580–1649), the greatest Spanish sculptor of his period; and of
Francisco de Zurbarán (1598–1662), painter of monastic life and historical
subjects. Contemplating Zurbarán's canvases, we enter into the world of the
Spanish saints. Monks stand before us in life size in an almost rigid oblivious-
ness. Giant missals, chalices, the Crucifix around them, they are murmuring
Latin prayers. Some of them bear an expression of terrifying solemnity on
their faces, while others lift their eyes upward in ecstasy. This is a world
apart, but this is the world which contributed the strongest spiritual incentive to baroque art. The plastic clarity and profound, yet delicate, sentimental
world of the Renaissance faded before these dark, mysterious depths and
excited passions, before this longing for the infinite. The man of the baroque
loves unrest and tension and the overwhelmingly pathetic. The baroque
artist frowns upon strict form and harmony of proportions as being too doctrinal and coercive. It is the new which attracts him, and the more astounding, the more contrary to accepted canons of art, the more it is welcome. He
is not interested primarily in what the Renaissance artist considered beauty
and perfection, and the concordance of proportions no longer interests him
for its own sake: he likes arbitrary disproportion and excessive measures,
for he is striving to give an impression and render a mood; he wants to
present us with drama, the components of which are immaterial as long as the
dynamic force is telling. One of the basic characteristics of this art is a reveling in space and light, in the boundless. We can see this already in Tintoretto,
whose "Paradise" in the ducal palace at Venice is the largest oil painting by
any master painter in the world. This enormous picture, thirty by seventy-
four feet, doubtless required the assistance of a number of disciples, but its
composition was the work of a master clearly under the spell of the early
baroque.

Michelangelo, Caravaggio, El Greco, and the other great figures of early
baroque art had equally bold, fantastic, powerful, and gifted colleagues
among the musicians of the era. The sublime, delicately balanced *a cappella*
ideal of the Renaissance vanished together with the great Netherlandish
musical culture: Italians became the undisputed monarchs—absolute monarchs—of the musical world. It was natural that the rising baroque era
should impress its spirit and style on an art that was so closely associated with
the Church. The return of Gothic elements was not less characteristic of music than of the fine arts. The same boundless torrent of music that we noticed
in the works of Ockeghem, a stream of sonority which was a symbol of
the unutterable, appears in the towering, visionary chords of the Venetians.
Already the aging Palestrina's music, animated with emotion, its mystical
chords here dark, here jubilant, reflects the spirit of the Counter Reformation, and the consuming mystic ardor of Victoria seems to be a musical translation of St. Theresa's exclamations. But these great musicians could not for-

get their musical education. They remained within the bounds of the *a
cappella* style, and their music became the codified symbol of Catholic church
art.

The great master who stood at the end of the Italo-Flemish period and
brought to conclusion the work started by Willaert in Venice was Giovanni
Gabrieli (1557–1612). The dramatic-monumental world of the early baroque
lives in the vast tonal murals of this Venetian's multiple choirs and in the
multitude of instruments that compose his orchestra. The élan and colorfulness, the emotional power and sensuous glow of his music overshadowed the
great influence and prestige of the Palestrinian art; henceforth the Roman
school is relegated, one may almost say, to the archives. The renown of the
great masters, especially that of Palestrina, was still great, but one must assume
that this was owing mainly to his former official and artistic position. That
the understanding of Palestrinian art vanished within the remarkably short
interval of a quarter of a century after his death shows the tremendous power
and vogue of the baroque. Indeed, even former associates of the great Roman
seemed to succumb completely to the new lure of instrumental music. Francesco Anerio edited the Masses of Palestrina with an instrumental accompaniment, and a similar fate befell the magnificent motets of Lassus, while
the *Missa Papae Marcelli* was transcribed and enlarged to a gigantic polychoral composition in the Venetian manner. Another two decades and the
examples of classical vocal polyphony, especially Palestrina's works, were
declared to be dignified museum pieces. A number of eminent musicians,
among them some of the chief figures of baroque art, continued to write occasionally in the classical choral style, but a certain didactic quality is attached from now on to such works and the composers themselves designate
them as written "in the old style." Pure contrapuntal writing is henceforth
considered merely a necessary technical equipment of composers, and up to
our day "strict" style or "strict counterpoint" is looked upon as an inevitable,
if dreary, schooling period for a musician, who, having mastered this medium, can proceed to "free" counterpoint and composition.

The early baroque discovered the great possibilities inherent in the colorful tone of musical instruments, and the growing urge for the monumental,
elaborate, and brilliant carried instrumental music—ever since the most
appropriate medium for the displaying of virtuosity and ornament—to an
astonishingly rapid development. Claudio Merulo and Giovanni Gabrieli
developed ricercar and toccata into logical instrumental-contrapuntal forms
that had no connection with their erstwhile vocal models. The chief instrumental form of the baroque, the fugue, arrived the moment the ricercar
settled down to a monothematic treatment. Another instrumental residue of
the polychoral style was the playing together of single instruments. Two
organs play together in St. Mark's, rivaling each other in virtuosity. This

leads us into one of the most significant fields of baroque music: the *concerto* principle, or concerted music. By transmitting the technique of polychoral writing to instrumental ensembles, Gabrieli laid the foundation of the modern orchestra. His instrumental writing cannot be called "orchestration" in our modern sense, but the purposeful grouping of instruments and the use of specific instrumental coloring was definitely his aim. It is not so much the exact voice leading, the design, which rules these works, but *color,* and the color palette of Gabrieli's orchestra recalls the warm, golden, rich, and transparent *colorit* of his fellow Venetian, Titian.

Thus the pictorial character of baroque art is notably present in music. The increasing tendency to underline important words in the text by suggestive melodic or harmonic passages, the play of light and shadow, the expressive utilization of dissonance and chromaticism, the echo effects of the double choirs are all pictorial as compared to the more linear-plastic quality of Renaissance music. This great stylistic change, which seemingly came with revolutionary force about 1600, has caught the fancy of musical historians. As long as musicography consisted of biography and a chronological sequence of evolution, having for its aim the supreme heights of romantic effervescence, authors could see but the great literary controversy that surrounded and heralded the advent of a new style. Thus the drawing room of Count Giovanni Bardi, Florentine nobleman and accomplished humanist, was made the birthplace of the new style. While the importance of this circle of humanists should not be minimized, new musical styles do not arise from mere literary speculation; there were deep-seated causes for the upheaval, conditioned by the old stylistic incongruity of north and south.

The Netherlandish style remained a musical language fundamentally alien to Italian genius even in its Italianized form and after almost two centuries of active and productive existence in that land. At a time when Palestrinian art was the musical ideal, when the madrigal reached its most polished and graceful finish, the old dance songs of the Italian countryside, frottole, villanelle, balletti, and canzonets, with their traditional Italian folk quality, again claimed a place for themselves. The rhythmical pulsation of these songs changed the whole structure of the formerly evenly flowing, unaccented mensural music of the Flemish and Italo-Flemish styles. Instead of faultless contrapuntal voice leading and an unbelievably subtle and cautious handling of dissonances, which had been the *conditio sine qua non* of the Flemish style, the later Italian madrigal, true to the general spiritual and artistic trend, accepted the dynamic rhythms of the villanelle and the canzonets; instead of carefully balanced harmonic progressions, it reveled in sensuous chromatic alterations and striking harmonic turns. How aggressively the spirit of the canzonets and villanelle, allied with the splendor of the early Venetian baroque, invaded the structure of Italo-Flemish *a cappella* art is illustrated in the *Concerti Ecclesiastici* of the excellent Bolognese composer, Adriano Banchieri (c. 1565–1634), published in 1595, one year after the death of Palestrina and Lassus. These compositions, for double choir with organ accompaniment, display a regularly pulsating rhythm which is acknowledged in the disposition of the organ part, with the treble part superimposed over the bass, and the whole "score" divided into regular measures by bar lines. This rhythmic-dynamic conception is manifest in the new editions of Gregorian melodies, as, with the growth of instrumental music and the waning of pure vocal style and the almost complete oblivion of Gregorian traditions, plain chant became more and more associated with instrumental music, especially organ music. The addition of organ accompaniments to Gregorian melodies, and even the substitution or alternate use of the organ for the voices, was officially sanctioned about 1600. Instead of clinging to the rules governing the use of dissonances, jealously safeguarded ever since Marchettus of Padua even by so progressive a musical writer as Zarlino, composers are ever searching for newer ways of combining harmonies. The whole modern edifice of harmony is before us. When the greatest musical genius of the early baroque, Monteverdi, speaks of a "seconda prattica musicale," and when one of the first champions of the nascent opera, Giulio Caccini, entitles his collection of madrigals and canzonets *Nuove Musiche* (1602), they announced to the world that an entirely new musical style had been born, that they were embarking on a "second," that is, new, musical practice. Giovanni Maria Artusi, a canon of San Salvatore in Bologna, launched a violent campaign against the "new school," entitling his diatribes *A Dissertation about the Imperfections of Modern Music* (1600).[2] Thus the emergence of this modern musical style was fully recognized even before the publication of Caccini's manifesto. The ephemeral and doctrinal discussions of consonance and dissonance based on the point of view of a bygone age and style gave way to lucid and psychologically correct observations. Descartes in his *Compendium Musicae* (1618) recognized the true nature of syncopation and defined it admirably by stating that syncopated tones have an exciting effect, *attentionem excitant*.[3] The madrigals of Marenzio and the other "chromaticists" went far in establishing the new dynamic-expressive style, using a thoroughly modern musical style that was incomprehensible to a man like Artusi.

The full extent of this early baroque orgy in dynamic expressiveness appears in the works of the most "radical" member of the so-called "chromatic school," Don Carlo Gesualdo, Prince of Venosa (c. 1560–1614). There is a singular resemblance between this musician-prince and his contemporary, Caravaggio. Casting aside tradition, the painter created a style remarkable for its vigor, handling of light and shadow, coloring, and emotional depth. Yet his magnificent pictorial compositions are often marred by his emphasis on naturalism. With Caravaggio, Gesualdo appears as an innovator deeply intrigued by experiments; like some of his nineteenth-century colleagues, he seems to have tried his chords and modulations on the keyboard of his instrument and thus arrived at the most sublime or, at times, the most bizarre sounds. It was partly through these instinctive experiments, partly through the limitless application of the new musical doctrines of Vicentino and Zarlino, that this musician of genius created a style in his day and remained unmatched for centuries. The dynamic-pictorial style of the early baroque reaches its most exaggerated peak in Gesualdo's madrigals. The composer is interested solely in expressing the poetic and dramatic content of the text. He does not care for tonal unity; the madrigal becomes in his hands a free sequence of impressions, pictures, and musical outbursts. The beauty of his harmonic language is often remarkable, and the boldness and ingenuity of his modulations rival, if they do not surpass, those of Marenzio and Monteverdi. Many, if not the majority, of Gesualdo's madrigals must, however, be considered closet madrigals, because their frightful, ragged, unvocal writing makes their performance by a vocal ensemble well-nigh impossible.

Romanticism in the Baroque—The Theater

WITHIN the great current of the baroque we can distinguish an ever-increasing prevalence of popular motives and a romantic tendency, which, while originating in the baroque, harks back to the romanticism of the Middle Ages. In Italy the knightly romances reappeared at the very beginning of the baroque, and epic poems, long and tedious, flourished again. The spirit of literature became depleted and too intellectual. Bold and creative inspiration gave way to complicated and artificial rhetoric. The idyls, short poems of a pastoral or rural character popular during the Renaissance, changed into a sentimental pastoral poetry and attained enormous popularity. Another variety of this poetry is known under the name "Marinismo" after Giambattista Marini (1569–1625), whose florid, bombastic style was somewhat akin to the highly artificial style in English literature that derived from the *Euphues* (1579) of John Lily and was called euphuism. The universal prevalence of this literary tendency is illustrated by a similar stylistic movement in Spain called Gongorism, named for Luis de Góngora (1561–1627), the witty and elegant Spanish poet. The intentionally obscure and precious quality of his poetry testifies to the unsuitability of this art to the baroque temper.

In contrast to all this, the resurrected comedies of Plautus and Terence presented age-old Italian popular types. The mocking, licentious verses of the earliest kind of Italian poetry, the Fescennines, returned together with the well-known figures of the ancient *mimus*. The Congrega dei Rozzi (league of the uncouth) was subsequently founded in Tuscany and refreshed the forgotten peasant farce. Ariosto, Aretino, Grazzini, Angelo Beolco, and many others lent a willing pen to this gay and often riotous comedy, but even such lofty thinkers as Machiavelli and Giordano Bruno did not disdain to try their hand at the popular theater. This was the *commedia dell' arte,* extemporaneous raillery, in whose typified figures the desire of the people for fun and persiflage found an outlet. The street singers, impudent and happy scoundrels whose descendants can be seen to this day in Italian towns, sang their own epic songs, parodies of the current chivalric stories. All this was not merely a stylized world of fantasy; it was life itself. The most congenial form of art affording an adequate frame for the expression of the baroque literary spirit was, then, the one which is of all art forms the nearest to life—the drama. The spirit of the Counter Reformation too, the strong desire for regeneration and the penchant for propaganda, found a suitable and sympathetic medium in the theater, which became perhaps the most typical embodiment of the baroque period. The theatrical dominates every form of expression of baroque art. Rembrandt singles out from a narrative scenes which carry the action to climactic points; deeply moving and stirring mental conflicts and visionary scenes are the ones which attract his attention. Be it the sacrifice of Abraham, the awakening of Lazarus, or the blinding of Sampson, each is caught in its most emphatic and decisive moment, and even the landscape becomes dramatic.

As the simple dialogues of the ancient shepherds had developed into the tragedies of Aeschylus and Euripides, the medieval spectacles, mystery plays, and moralities led to the dramas of Marlowe and Shakespeare. Shakespeare's heroes do not hide their romantic-baroque origin; they come from the domain of fairy tales, legends, chronicles, and epic poetry where everything is exaggerated, and most of all, men. The modern reader is not accustomed to seeing Christian romanticism at the bottom of this art; the Christian romanticism which created the baroque is perhaps more apparent to him in Milton's *Paradise Lost* and in Bunyan's *Pilgrim's Progress.* The latter is bound by innumerable threads to the Middle Ages, and its hero, Christian, to Everyman. Yet among the chief sponsors of this new theater we again find Ignatius Loyola and the order he founded. The stage of the whole baroque era shows the marks of this origin, even in those of its branches which were far removed from the Catholic sphere.

We have already mentioned Loyola's *Spiritual Exercises,* designed primarily to educate the members of the order and the Catholic aristocracy. We have pointed out the remarkably practical and psychological technique employed in the *Exercises* to inspire and excite emotion and understanding wherever these forces could be directed toward religious ends; it is also important to note their consistent associations with earthly subjects and allusions to universal-human circumstances. The reading of some of the "contemplations" in the *Exercises* will reveal an artistic construction of such dramatic plasticity that it is small wonder that the dramatic spark generated fire in the young order, eager to lend a most welcome emphasis to its missionary activities.[4] When and how the spark ignited is not yet clear, but the religious situation and the Protestant-humanistic school drama must have supplied a powerful draft. Starting from the south toward the middle of the sixteenth century, the Jesuit theater moved up to the north, conquered the southern German countries and maintained itself until the period of the Enlightenment. Its enormous popularity is more understandable when we consider the fact that the late medieval theatrical undertakings of groups of laymen were not yet forgotten, and that, rekindled, they produced that "play fever" which is an especially characteristic earmark of the baroque. The success of the Jesuits prompted the Benedictines, Cistercians, Franciscans, and Augustinians to follow suit. Enthusiasm for the theater and especially for the spiritual plays, which in the seventeenth century in Germany outnumbered the secular considerably, reached unheard-of proportions. The importance and wide popularity of the Jesuit theater can be surmised from the bitter campaign fought against it and against the theatrical craze in general by the movement of the Enlightenment.

Once we pass from the dramatized processions and religious plays and examine the theater proper, we shall see and realize the profound changes wrought by the spirit of the Counter Reformation in the aims and very existence of the theater. It is not the action of the drama which occupies the author's main attention, but the reaction of his audience. The pictorial and plastic aspects of the Renaissance have disappeared; the theater is no longer an aim in itself; authors and actors extend their hands to the audience and exclaim, "You are the one who is dying here, you are the sinner who will be damned!" In conformity to the new spirit, the old "play stage," separated from the audience, disappeared and the indefinite space of the stage and the auditorium were combined into one unit. The architecture of the old humanistic theater, formerly freely extending, is now well defined and the scenery itself faces the audience like a wall. Andrea Palladio incorporated in the Teatro Olympico in Vicenza (1580) a permanent scenic background, built in architectural perspective well calculated to give perfect illusion. The proscenium, formerly separating stage from auditorium, now housed the orchestra, forming a link between the two. Even the proscenium boxes joined the conglomeration; they often accommodated musicians, and hence were called "trumpet loges." The baroque stage never presented a purely optical picture (that was the contribution of the eighteenth century), because the baroque stage was not independent of the space from which the spectator viewed it. The spectator was a partner, whose role in the show was to look and listen.

The Relationship of Drama to Poetry and Music

THE "dramatic" is usually conceived as being limited to an external happening or action representing opposing human individualities. But there exists also another sort of "dramatic" which we may call internal, a struggle of forces in the individual man's soul. Dramatic poetry can communicate to us, in reality, only the result of these struggles, because it must transform everything into intelligible and concrete symbols. Poetry can represent only momentary mental states, a series of them. Music, however, is capable of presenting these forces in their very struggle, thus giving us a real drama free of all material, tangible, or visible elements. Music is the language of the soul, it is the means of expression of actions and experiences which take place in the secluded depths of the soul. This fundamental characteristic of music makes it a natural expressive and communicative agent of artistic ideas, which are pre-eminently the results of mental experience. The musico dramatic is, then, the correlation of these different mental experiences as they appear in varying individuals. At first glance it seems that this dramaturgical law applies to any drama, and that any one of them could be set to music. A distinguished contemporary composer has taken random excerpts from a well-known American periodical and written interesting music to them; but there is no compelling necessity for such music, and because it is forced to justify its presence, lacking inner necessity, the music is not dramatic. Whenever music is added to poetry or drama for no compelling reason, it becomes a burden: being deprived of its natural sources of incentive, it becomes "free" and romps around irresponsibly, trying to replace its real *raison d'être* by its formal and sensuous graces and by its great ability to characterize. Nowhere is music more clearly a mere addition than in the so-called "grand opera"; and nowhere is music noisier, more aggressively pompous, pretentious, and ostentatious than in the grand operas from Meyerbeer to the present, because it has to divert attention from the falsity of its nature.

But there are many images of the world that are incomplete without music and demand an association with it. There is, then, an extended domain in which music associates itself with poetry and drama, because there *is* a drama which can be fully expressed only through music. This drama cannot be conveyed by music alone in that universal drama which is the classical symphony, whose action takes place in the indefinite, for music has not, strictly speaking, pictorial means of illustration and explanation. It uses other means—forms, rhythms, etc.—to facilitate its comprehension. In order to transform the mental into the corporeal world, music must ally itself with another art or arts. When we think of the famous quartet in the last act of Verdi's *Rigoletto,* where the four principals are placed on the stage simultaneously as a natural consequence of the dramatic situation, we immediately realize that here we have a phenomenon that is the result of this alliance and which actually brought about the alliance of two arts on neutral grounds; for here we are neither in the domain of pure music nor in that of pure dramatic poetry. The four dramatic figures express four different states of mind at the same time, something that can be accomplished through the means of the music drama, for the music unites the outpouring of their various sentiments in a homogeneous constellation and lends it an accent of plausibility. The musical drama has always had its enemies and probably will continue to have them. Many critics feel that in ordinary life people talk and do not sing when they want to express feelings and ideas. But as long as men will jubilate in their happiness, and laugh and sing, as long as they will cry and shout in the agony of pain and unhappiness, opera will be appreciated by many, because opera endeavors not merely to render the phenomena of life, but to give life itself, to depict man as he is, in the realm of passions that are intangible and inexpressible in mere words. It does not want to analyze characters by reasoning, but it places them before our eyes and ears in the making, in their acts.

The Antecedents of the Music Drama

CLASSICAL tragedy originated in the liturgy of Dionysus; it sprang, as has every theater, from a divine cult. To the ancient Greeks it always remained liturgical, even when the immediate ties with the Dionysiac cult had been lost. Italian drama originated in the songs of the *laudesi*,[5] the inherently dramatic nature of religion again producing, inevitably, theater. One would think that the mystery and miracle plays in other countries, emerging from similar origins, would have produced a similar art. But the poetry of the laudi came from the people; it never used the Latin of the Church. The lay brothers, coming from the humblest strata of society, were simple, uneducated people who knew only their mother tongue, but who did know the songs and dances of the people usually not considered worthy of attention by the learned clerics.

The dramatized laudi evolved two new genres, the *maggi* and the *sacre rappresentazioni*. In reality, the two were one and the same, save that the maggi were the rural forms of Italian mystery plays, while the rappresentazioni were urban dramatizations. The maggi retained the unpretentious folk character of the laudi, but the rappresentazioni developed into elaborate and fastidious plays. The art-loving city of Florence—home of the rappresentazioni—endowed them with its customary artistic magnificence, and the chronicles testify to their lavish performances all over Tuscany. It seems as if we were dealing here with a sixteenth-century *Gesamtkunstwerk* embracing the whole compass of art and letters. Parts of the liturgy, a Te Deum, some laudi, dances, secular songs, and artistic part songs mingle with in-strumental interludes, the whole rappresentazione being preceded by a prel-ude. The songs were set for solo voices and chorus, and the dances included all possible varieties. These shows were, in reality, much nearer to being operas than anything else, but the transition from the sacre rappresentazioni to musical drama was a gradual one and produced an intermediate link in the form of the *favola pastorale.*

In its fundamental nature, the pastoral theater is as lyrical and musical as the sacra rappresentazione, because its origin, the Latin eclogue of the Ren-aissance, was equally lyrical. The *egloghe rappresentative* were flourishing in all Italian courts during the High Renaissance and received a stronger dramatic touch from the peasant scenes and farces of the popular thea-ter, and a more closely knit form from the tragedies and comedies of the rising Italian literary stage. Once having entered within the com-pass of the theater, the pastoral plays could not escape the attention and experimentation of the classical scholars and classicistic poets, and they were soon subjected to the Aristotelian rules. With Tasso's *Aminta* and Guarini's *Pastor Fido,* the pastoral play reached a form that was hence-forth to serve as a model to all subsequent authors. The libretti of the first operas depended on these works, from which they took the pretention of representing the renewed tragedy of antiquity. The pastoral play has, then, two lyrical ancestors, a fact which explains its only mildly dramatic nature. It is a mixture of dramatic narration, lyrical poetry, and song, rather than drama proper. Its dialogues and lyrical choral parts swing naturally into music at the very moment when the playful and graceful recitation assumes a little of the pathetic, and it was thus that the pastoral play created a new genre, the melodrama, which carries us immediately into the field of opera. Thus music played an important part in this bucolic poetry from its incep-tion, and we must remember that it was chiefly the lyrical element that evoked music, rather than the dramatic—a curious fact which will confront us repeatedly.

Another important source of the lyric stage was the *intermezzo.* Originally modest scenes inserted in larger festival plays, the intermezzi, thanks to their typical early baroque splendor, soon became the central attraction. But we must not limit interest in the combination of music and theater to the direct ancestors of the opera, or to the first operatic school in Florence. This union, this gravitation of music and theater, was in the air, and many artists and men of letters were occupied by the fascinating problems which it en-gendered. Widely varying forms that lent themselves to dramatic treatment were set to music, including not only the madrigal comedies of Vecchi and the extremely popular dramatic scenes of Alessandro Striggio, but the classicistic tragedy of the Italian theater. Cinzio's *Orbecche,* Trissino's *So-*

Sofonisba, and Dolci's *Marianna* were all performed with music, and it appears that this music was not restricted to the choruses. The elder Gabrieli seems to have preceded many a famed "rediscoverer" of classical tragedy, setting to music Sophocles's *King Oedipus.* Although Gabrieli's choruses were written in a polyphonic style, they had a solo passage and manifested the composer's desire to follow carefully the prosody of the Italian translation in order to give the declamation and the poetry proper relief.

Before it is possible to have drama, however, we must have individualities. The choral settings of the *commedia dell' arte,* such as the madrigal comedies, could not develop into real musical comedies because a polyphonic rendition, even with the help of the consummate craftsmanship of Vecchi and his colleagues, could never fulfill the role of individuals in the action. But along with the general trend toward a musical stage, there appeared a tendency in the technique and expressive means of musical composition toward individualization, or at least the definite favoring of one principal part above the others. It was quite customary to perform madrigals and chansons by giving the treble part to a solo voice, while the other parts were played by one or more instruments acting as a quasi accompaniment. Although such performances were not always graphically indicated during the High Renaissance, there can be no doubt about the widespread custom of monodic performance, because at about the turn of the century we already find solo madrigals expressly written in this manner. Kinkeldey has called attention to the madrigals of Luzzasco Luzzaschi (d. 1607), celebrated teacher of Frescobaldi, which were set for one, two, or three solo voices with a harpsichord accompaniment fully written out.[6] Although published in 1601, the preface clearly indicates that the madrigals were composed several years before that date. The singing of songs with the accompaniment of a single instrument was, of course, not a new discovery; it had remained a fairly common practice ever since the time of the troubadours and Minnesinger. During the Renaissance these accompanied songs provided exquisite music in the Spanish romances and villancicos, sung with the accompaniment of a lute; the sacre rappresentazioni also contained many solo songs with lute or viol accompaniment interpolated into the action.

The new monodic style appeared, then, after many antecedents and modern experiments, almost exactly at the same time in songs, church *concerti,* and in the Florentine opera. Giovanni Battista Doni (1594–1647), jurist, eminent classical scholar, professor of rhetoric, and writer on musical subjects, is our most important source for the animated days of this great stylistic change.[7] He speaks of the new monodic recitative style with great enthusiasm and considers it a decisive step toward the perfect rendering of the text by a single singer. The performance of these monodic songs in the recitative style was, he believed, nearer to natural speech than to singing, and was

calculated to give a more immediate expression of the "affect" than polyphony could. Another category defined by Doni along with the *stile recitativo* was the *stile rappresentativo,* to which belonged all melodies destined
for the stage. Still another term, *stile espressivo,* designated any kind of
vocal music which presented a perfect union of poetry and music, an ideal
correspondence of poetic idea and musical expression, in which the passionate accents of the text found an equally passionate echo in the music. Thus
the war waged against the polyphonic style of the preceding period produced a tangible result, a new style of musical expression, considered by its
practitioners infinitely superior to that of the Renaissance and capable of
conveying the most delicate shades of human feeling and passion. Poets and
musicians worked in close collaboration to build the newly found means of
expression into a definite musico-poetical style.

The Early Music Drama

THE unbounded admiration for the real and imaginary arts and letters of
antiquity resulted in the foundation of learned societies, or academies, which
performed a noteworthy cultural mission in Italian intellectual life, carrying
their influence beyond the Alps and the Pyrenees. After the turn of the
century most of these institutions had lost their original impetus, and, while
some of them retained their original enthusiasm and an aestheticism which
was more refined than creative, in the dynamic world of the baroque they
seemed an anachronism—a group of distinguished men of letters and artists
who, like the academicians of our day, were highly respected by the official
world and gloriously disregarded by living art. "Italy was crowded with poets
and prose writers of every kind, while critics, rhetoricians, grammarians,
professors, academicians sprouted like weeds." [8]

This tendency and atmosphere produced the Florentine Camerata, a
literary and artistic society. Members of the Camerata were, besides the
presiding noblemen Giovanni Bardi, Count of Vernio (1534–1612), and
Jacopo Corsi, the poets Ottavio Rinuccini (1562–1621), Marino, and
Chiabrera, the singers Peri and Caccini, and the musical theoreticians Vincenzo Galilei and Girolamo Mei, to mention the best known among them.
It was the men of letters who guided the activities of this exclusive artistic
club. Count Bardi himself, Mei, and Vincenzo Galilei, all imbued with admiration for the classical world and especially interested in the music of
the ancients, were the protagonists, but Galilei seems to have been the leading
spirit. Versatile musician himself, but one who did not go through the customary schooling of his contemporaries, this highly sensitive and intelligent
aesthete turned violently not only against the great art of the preceding
period, but against the very system of polyphony, which he considered a

desecration of the clear, simple, and lucid artistic creed of the ancients. In 1581 he published a work entitled *Dialogo della Musica Antica e Moderna,* in which he expressed his ideas in a vehemently aggressive style. To make his arguments weightier, Galilei composed several songs for a single voice with the accompaniment of a lute. These works, unfortunately lost to posterity, are customarily considered the ancestors of early opera; but are we actually dealing here, in the early years of the Camerata, with drama?

"I conceived the idea of composing a harmonic speech, a sort of music in which a noble restraint was placed on singing (in the strict sense) in favor of the words." These words, taken from the Preface to Caccini's *Nuove Musiche,*[9] convince us that their author, a singer by occupation but like most singers of the sixteenth century more or less versed in the art of composition, was not so much interested in creating a new drama as in finding a new musical vocal style for the humanistically inclined singer. The whole movement was but a phase of the general tendency to bring poetry and music increasingly closer together. The euphony and sensuous suppleness of verse, the light flow of rhythm, were consciously cultivated during the late Renaissance; poets and musicians vied with each other in their eagerness to achieve a perfect union of words and music. Tasso collaborated with Gesualdo, Chiabrera with Caccini, to make poetry more singable and render music more expressive. There now began a great flowering of melic poetry, in which the poets of the Camerata played an important role. Lyrical poetry and music retained their intimate connections until relatively recent times, but the importance of the musical element in this union underwent fundamental changes. The combination of dramatic poetry and music carried with it an eternal problem, the more or less successful solution of which has occupied all composers since Monteverdi. This was the struggle between the two major components of this musico-literary genre, and for three centuries and a half musicians, poets, and philosophers tried to find the just balance and association of these two elements. For the lyric stage and pure drama are not identical; the requirements of one are not shared by the other, and, unless we acknowledge opera as an independent and in itself finished form of art, having its own laws, we shall err as gravely as did Wagner with his brilliantly written but completely misplaced aesthetics of opera.

The early exponents of the music drama all expressed in the prefaces of their works the firm belief that "the ancient Greeks and Romans sang on the stage the entire tragedy," and this hypothesis furnished the point of departure for the music drama or opera. Their humanistic ardor can, however, neither justify their erroneous historical conclusions as to the nature of classical traditions nor mystify the modern historian, who cannot fail to detect under the thin coat of classical varnish the primordial Italian qualities of the lyric stage. The Florentine humanists searched for the musical drama of the ancients

and found that of the modern world. But were these aesthetes entirely mistaken in considering Greek drama an *opera in musica?* Granted that they
did not know much about the music of antiquity—our own knowledge is
meager enough—they recognized the lyrical quality in Greek drama; they
divined that it was not only the choruses that were sung but that there were
veritable arias interspersed throughout the drama, that at the height of emo-
ional stress the action gives way to a lyrical melodrama which demands music
as the church steeple demands a bell. Greek drama is, indeed, in its fundamental nature a lyrical art, and its lyricism is paralleled in modern times
only by the Italian stage. Thus it can conceivably be regarded as opera, because "opera" implies music and music is synonymous with lyricism. But
there was one more deeply ingrained reason for a kinship between Italian
opera and classical drama: both of them originated from the genius of a
nation. The simple music of the Greek drama and the simple music (relatively simple if compared to the operatic products of other nations) of Italian
opera cannot be judged by the criteria of music in general. The little ritornels
in Monteverdi's *Orfeo* cannot be compared to the gigantic symphonies of
the nineteenth century, and the heroic but amazingly economical recitatives
of Jommelli cannot be held up to the great choral fantasies of the modern
oratorio. They can be judged solely in their own domain, where they will
remain glorious achievements of the lyric stage.

   The problem of relationship between music and drama is curiously dependent upon its country of origin. German genius likes to indulge in dreaming and in metaphysical speculation; hence their lyric drama is not, properly
speaking, opera, that is, a harmonic union of dramatic poetry and music, the
balance being upset in favor of reverie and symbolism. The same applies
to French art, with the difference that the balance inclines to the other factors;
that is, there is too much action. Boileau said that a good opera will never
be composed, "parce que la musique ne sait narrer." But the faculty of
narration which the great French littérateur denied to music is not the
essence of dramatic music. French musicians have often forgotten this last
fact and justified Boileau's criticism by indulging too exclusively in describing actions and exterior happenings. The French theater is more interested
in action than in sentiment; it does not abandon itself to the emotional fluctuations of the drama, since in sentiment it considers above all the practical
sides, those which contribute to the action. Narrative exposition, especially
long tirades, does not seem to fit the operatic, which enters into the action
in medias res, without having recourse to memory, reason, and other intellectual faculties. This does not mean that the opera cannot possibly use narration. If the musician animates his recitation by emotion instead of using
details which can be expressed only by eloquence, the results are sometimes
sublime.

It is only in Italy, however, that we see the "divine marriage of drama and music" accomplished in a truly harmonious way. Italians listen to the opera with ecstasy because it is their real language, a language of pure sentiment liberated from the chains of reason; they abandon themselves to passion without discussion, share pleasure without trying to control it—these qualities favor the flourishing of that peculiar kind of music which we call opera. And opera is, with some exceptions, an exclusively Italian genre, the genre of a people exuberant with life and art. But this, indeed, is not the opera of the reputed originators of the species; this is not the music drama that the Florentine gentlemen expected to re-create by leaning on antique examples.

The Camerata's literary activity was rooted in lyric poetry, and the first librettist of operas, Ottavio Rinuccini, was nourished on the courtly Renaissance poetry of his era, an art which was already manifestly on the decline. In his dramas the accent is on a lyric mood, despite stage setting, the obvious necessity of action, and the avowed aim of resurrecting classical tragedy. Himself the offspring of a noble Florentine family, Rinuccini was a court poet who created his lyric and dramatic works usually in the service, and always in the spirit, of the court. In his songs he glorified the deeds of his princely masters, and his plays were written for their entertainment. At the court of the pomp-loving Medici, the masques, ballets, *carri,* and *canti carnascialeschi* were especially popular, and every festive occasion—marriages, visits of notable personages, or the carnivals—was lavishly staged. Rinuccini collaborated in many of these festivals and was the logical person to carry out the literary end of the Camerata's quest for the resuscitated classical tragedy. In his endeavor to find a form which would merit the name "tragedy," Rinuccini wrote *Dafne,* first performed in the house of Jacopo Corsi, probably in 1594. The date is not yet definitely established,[10] but the event could not have taken place much earlier, as the composition was begun after the leadership of the Camerata fell to Corsi in 1592. The success of *Dafne* was considerable, and it was repeatedly performed in the ensuing decades. Rinuccini made slight alterations, some as late as 1608, at which time the libretto—already set by Peri and Caccini—was again entirely newly set to music by Marco da Gagliano (c. 1575–1642), a composer whom even Peri considered his superior.[11] The famous libretto was finally translated into German by Martin Opitz and set by Heinrich Schütz in 1627, thereby becoming the earliest German opera.

Dafne, generally considered the first opera, was really nothing more than an experiment and remained little more than a dramatized pastoral play after Rinuccini remodeled it in 1597. But even in its simplicity, and in the absence of real drama, this earliest of "operas" outdistances all the earlier attempts at melodramatic composition. The music of the first *Dafne* was lost, so the first really complete opera was *Euridice.* Spurred by the great success of *Dafne*, Rinuccini wrote *Euridice* for the marriage of Henry IV of France to Maria de' Medici, the musical setting being supplied by Peri and Caccini. The first performance, utilizing a version for the most part by Peri, with a few arias by Caccini inserted, took place under Corsi's auspices in the Palazzo Pitti on October 16, 1600. The artistic tenets of the cenacle must have been thought out to the most minute details, for Caccini, taking the same libretto that had been set by Peri, produced similar results, although on close examination of the vocal parts it becomes evident that the musicianly instinct was stronger in Caccini. *Euridice,* which can safely be called an opera from both the literary and the musical points of view, embodied all the aspirations and experiments of the Camerata, the libretto being not merely a dramatized pastoral as was its predecessor, but dramatic poetry of the first water, written in a glorious language. *Dafne* was still called a favola pastorale, but the word "tragedy" appeared in the preface to *Euridice,* to be followed soon in Rinuccini's *Arianna* by the outright appellation *tragedia.* Being a native Florentine, Rinuccini was too deeply rooted in the traditions of the great lyricists of the trecento and the cinquecento to fall victim to the Marinismo, already rampant in Italian poetry. Thus the new lyric stage started under poetic auspices which promised much, although they were, unfortunately, abandoned in the course of operatic history.

Jacopo Peri declared, in the preface to his *Euridice,* that he had observed closely the conversation of people and attempted to render in his music their speech in all shades of quiescence and passion. To achieve this musical dialect he planned that each vocal part should be kept at the same pitch until the meaning of the text warranted a change, at which time the chord upon which the singer's pitch rested also changed. Peri's "orchestra" was small and was not supposed to be in evidence; its role was to support the singer, and the composer explicitly required that the accompaniment be such as not to attract the listener's attention. The chorus, unlike the orchestra, took an active part in the play, and like its distant classical ancestors was the bearer of the contemplative element in the drama. The choral parts of both *Euridices* are written in an agreeable if not masterly style, betraying the hands of noble amateurs; still, they are like oases in the desert of semimusical recitation, for we must admit that the endless recitatives, not offering a single musical melody, created a monotony that to us seems unbearable. All this is speech, not music, yet Peri's contemporaries greeted the stile recitativo with boundless admiration, and, heavy-footed as it appears to the modern student, the work carries the imprint of an earnest artistic endeavor. *Euridice* offers the usual spectacle of a nascent art still struggling for expression, and its composers had the conviction of artists who feel instinctively that they are on the right path.

Peri, Caccini, and Gagliano were earnest artists and claimed, with the other members of the Camerata, that they freed music from the shackles of polyphony; but this seemingly free music was more chained than ever, freezing in the rigid, word-dominated recitative into a mere chanted drama. The new music drama as it confronts us in the first products of the Florentines was neither a reproduction nor a regeneration of classical tragedy. Like Italian tragedy of the cinquecento, it was a learned imitation which, in spite of the excellence of the libretto, remained a pale picture. We forget, however, that the Camerata was the meeting place of poets and artists, among whom there was not a single musician who was a composer by calling and by trade. It is quite probable that the lyric drama would have become a lifeless, artificial, and idealized form like the vers mesuré of the French academicians had not real musicians rescued it from the men of letters. The enormous success of *Euridice,* however, assured the future of the new musico-dramatic genre, and it now awaited the coming of a genius to raise it above the harnessed rhetorical festival play into the realm of music, to lead it away from the archaic-literary reconstruction of antique tragedy, to elevate melody and singing to their rightful place, not as servants of the drama, but as its very soul. If the Florentines wanted to imitate passionate speech, the savior of music drama was to give passion itself. The great genius arrived in the person of a musician who, not being bound by the sacred names of Plato and Aristotle, threw overboard everything that had been forced upon music by learned dilettanti. Opera, the music drama, was born.

Monteverdi

HERE emerges one of those extraordinary individuals who create and organize a new form of art, and whose advent into the domain of thought is analogous to the appearance of a superior species in nature, after a series of unfruitful attempts. Claudio Monteverdi (1567–1643) was not only an exceptional musician; he was great because of the power of meditation and poetical concentration, the seriousness and perseverance which he applied in the pursuit of his ideals. He, and not the Florentine littérateurs, was the first artist to revive the spirit of antique tragedy and create a music drama which was classical and modern at the same time. He was the Aeschylus of music, the creative musical genius whose aim was not the realization of the ideals of the distant past but the expression of the life and ardor that was in him. His grandiose imagination, his colorfulness, the never-abating richness of his musical invention, his tragic rhythm and astounding force of dramatic expression could not find an adequate field in the musical forms of his time. Even the madrigal, of which he was one of the greatest and boldest masters, proved to have too narrow a frame for his passionate ideas. His instincts drove him toward the drama, but after the emotional experiences of the chromatic madrigal, the experiments of the Camerata must have seemed to him primitive in harmony and construction and vague in form. The Duke of Mantua and his family, thoroughly converted to the cause of the melodrama, requested Monteverdi to set to music a drama written by the Secretary of State of Mantua, Alessandro Striggio, son of the noted madrigalist, who enjoyed a wide reputation as a poet.

In setting Striggio's *Orfeo,* Monteverdi drew freely on the great treasury of sixteenth-century music discarded by the dogmatic Florentines; thus everything that could be utilized dramatically from the era of polyphony was fused with the new means of expression offered by the stile recitativo. It was this synthesis of old and new which gave him assuredness where others seem doubtful. But perhaps the most important thing was that Monteverdi was not a man of letters and did not set a text to music in order to satisfy an intellectual desire. In his first opera, *Orfeo,* which we may rightfully consider the first in the history of music, he found a style of such individuality as perhaps no other composer has ever achieved in a first major work. While the elements of the traditional favola pastorale are still discernible in *Orfeo,* its old apparatus is placed in the service of new aims, and we may say that Monteverdi mobilized all the harmonic and orchestral means that were known to his period to help him toward his dramatic end. The orchestra joined in the action, lending its faculties to the psychological expressiveness of music. It ceased to be a noncommittal background; it now helped to establish the mood that prevailed on the stage. While *Euridice* employed only a few bars of instrumental music, *Orfeo* contained fourteen independent orchestral pieces or "symphonies." Later, in conformity with the custom and with the means at his disposal, Monteverdi reduced his orchestral accompaniment to the usual small orchestra, developed the *bel canto arioso,* and forced his recitatives within even more closely defined boundaries, demonstrating that the calm, even, and endless declamation of the Florentines, entirely dependent on the pace of the text, was not the real dramatist's fare. His recitative declamation is never extended, as he senses the lyrical content of the words and interrupts the recitation by short arioso passages. The same desire brought him to melody—not the light and graceful melody of the canzonets, but the boldly arched, purely expressive, sculptured melody that was to haunt composers for a century. To the dialogue he now preferred to add more room for the ensemble of solo singers; in a word, he arrived at a style based on the dramatic succession of closed forms which was destined to dominate opera for two hundred years. Thus Monteverdi's work reaches in a monumental line from the revolutionary madrigal, through the recited music dramas of the stile recitativo, to the new operatic conception of closed forms, embodying and summarizing all the musical tendencies of the early baroque.

After the death of Duke Vincenzo (1612), Monteverdi seized the opportunity to seek a better position. Famed now all over Italy, he obtained one of the most coveted musical posts in Italy, that of choirmaster and conductor at St. Mark's in Venice. At the time of his arrival, opera had not yet been introduced in Venice, and Monteverdi dedicated himself to the composition of church music, an occupation which was his, *ex officio.* Some of his beautiful creations in this field were fortunately preserved and are available in a modern edition,[12] but the stage works, ballets, intermezzi, religious dramas, and operas, which appeared beginning with 1615, are lost to the world. The great epidemic that raged in 1630 dampened the formerly universal enthusiasm for arts and amusements in the Adriatic republic, and the aging master himself turned away from worldly pleasures. He was ordained a priest of the Church in 1632, and retired from the public eye.

The opening of the first public opera house in 1637 and the subsequent enthusiasm of the public for opera electrified the resigned Monteverdi and aroused his creative instinct and dramatic vein. He then wrote his last great operas, which, judging from the two that were preserved, *Il Ritorno d'Ulisse* and *L'Incoronazione di Poppea,* were veritable miracles of dramatic portrayal and artistic rendering of the most profound and moving human problems. *Poppea* has recently been restored to the repertory of some European theaters. With the passionate accents of its music and the wide arches of its freely flowing melodies, it stands alone in the operatic literature; only the *Falstaff* of the seventy-nine-year-old Verdi is comparable, both in its tragic disillusionment and in its bewitching poetry, to Monteverdi's *Poppea,* composed at the age of seventy-five.

Monteverdi has often been likened by modern writers to Wagner, but, if such analogies are at all possible, there seems to be a more intimate kinship between the musician and Michelangelo. They are kinsfolk in their titanic struggle with matter and form, in their ceaseless fight for the deliverance of human powers, in their tragical decrying of the aimlessness of the final aims of human life. They are akin, finally, in the lot of the genius, which is a mysterious and serene loneliness into which the noise of the outside world cannot penetrate, and which can be mitigated by the solace of neither religion nor love. Perhaps Monteverdi often felt in himself the great vitality of a new culture, its victorious rhythms and melodies; but when at the end of one of his beautiful autumnal madrigals he sighed "sono un deserto," he confessed that he felt in himself the eternal loneliness of the desert. This great loneliness taught him that the approach to the human soul is not through classical diction but through sympathy; he tarried at the manifestations of human sorrow because in his eyes sorrow and passion are the real revelations of man. He felt that only the sufferings and indomitable passions of man make him what he is: a tragic being who can live on earth, fighting and falling heroically. "Arianna affected people because she was a *woman,* and Orpheus because he was simply a man," writes Monteverdi in one of his letters (December, 1616); but to make it possible for them to be man and woman, the master reveals them in the throes of passion. Upon hearing the message announcing the death of Euridice the whole world collapses about Orpheus, and the lament of Arianna is the song of a human heart crying in agony for the salvation of death. Or again, in *Poppea* there are love scenes burning with voluptuousness, the voices whispering caresses and then rising to passionate effusions. Peri and Caccini did not even dream of such accents, while we are still living on the heritage of the dramatic breath of the Mantuan musician, who, with Rembrandt, was the great baroque poet of the secret depths of the human soul.

Had the rigid rules of the fanatical Florentine humanists prevailed, perhaps our whole modern music would have received a serious setback, but the Camerata was a curious Renaissance island in the passionate world of baroque Italy; as such, it was an anachronism, incapable of development. What happened illustrates the rule, too often forgotten: the revolutionary, experimental artists are seldom the ones who lead us into the promised land; at the very border the leadership is assumed by the more deliberate and cautious, but also more powerful minds who, unwilling to discard the past, are yet capable of absorbing the present. The men of this temper in baroque Italy did not gaze back into the legendary and nebulous world of the ancients; they were forward-looking modern artists. Once aroused, the musicians of the old line, the real *musicians,* took over the leadership, bringing with them the denounced treasures of centuries of musical art. Counterpoint was reinstated to its exalted position and found entirely new spheres of action in the animated choruses of the music drama. His great mastery of madrigalesque choral writing enabled Monteverdi to make his chorus a most pliable instrument. The uncontrolled flow of recitation is sharply opposed by the aria, which represents melody *versus* declamation. This melody seems to be independent of the rules of prosody and is usually shaped entirely according to the musical requirements. From the dramaturgical point of view the aria should grow from the recitation, the recitative being the dramatic agent carrying out the action while the aria develops the mood in broad lyrical sentiments. This was very well understood by the earlier librettists, and Rinuccini, displaying a remarkable dramatic insight, made the lament of Arianna—the great monologue, we might even say the "great aria," of the opera—the natural focal point of his drama. He gave not oratorical tirades or innocuous madrigalesque verse, but a real expression of sorrow. The musical composition that resulted from Monteverdi's collaboration with Rinuccini created such a stir that every house "that harbored a harpsichord or lute was filled with the plaintive accents of Arianna sung by a trembling voice." A whole chapter of musical history could be named after this lament, admired and imitated by every composer until the end of the century. Its deeply human accents affected not only the Italians but composers of foreign lands, among them a distinguished member of the Bach family, Johann Christoph Bach (1642–1703), whose *Lamentatio* "Wie bist du denn, o Gott," follows the original closely.[13]

When discussing the French Renaissance chanson, we noticed the careful symmetric construction of most of these compositions. The first part was usually repeated after a different middle section, producing a design of form that we may describe graphically as A–B–A. The instrumental canzone appropriated this same method of formal construction, which, under the name of *"da capo* aria"—"from the head," that is, from the beginning—was to play an important role in the music of the ensuing centuries. While a certain limited use of this device can be found in such works as Viadana's *Concerti Ecclesiastici,* the early monodists in general did not pay much attention to it, mainly, presumably, because it did not fit into the system of classical recitation. A musician with as great a sense for rounded form as Monteverdi could not ignore a design so appropriate for musical construction; indeed, short *da capo* songs appear already in *Orfeo.* Such experiments in closed, strophic musical construction added to the great difference separating the art of the musicians from that of the literary men in Florence.

Sacred Opera—Oratorio—Comic Opera
Rome and Venice

THE main seats of early monodic composition were Florence and Rome, the former city also attracting musicians from Mantua and Bologna. The Florentines remained faithful to their original program of "classical" music drama—an almost ascetic cultivation of monotonous recitation, which led to a marked decline in enthusiasm for the new lyric stage. The Romans, occupying at first a more modest position, now began to come into their own. As would be expected, the Roman musical stage stood closer to the sacred drama than to the secular opera. The Jesuits, recognizing almost immediately the great possibilities inherent in the new style, proved to be not only the sponsors of the *dramma recitativo,* but pressed their seminaries and colleges into the service of the new musical theater. Many of the new composers were clerics and members of the papal choir. While Florentine and Mantuan opera was patronized by the local aristocracy, the Roman lyric stage found a powerful support in religious circles. At the beginning of Roman opera, however, we are confronted with a complicated mixture of trends and species which requires some clarification.

The word "opera" had no specific meaning in the century of its appearance unless it was coupled with *per musica,* or *in musica,* meaning a "musical work," in which case it might have various meanings. Only toward the end of the century did the term become localized to the lyric stage and become the equivalent of *dramma per musica,* or melodrama. (The last-mentioned term had not yet assumed the connotation it acquired in the nineteenth century.) Similarly, the term "cantata" (or *cantada*) appeared early and was applied to many forms of vocal music before it gained the meaning we attach to it. In the early seventeenth century it usually signified a narrative lyric poem set to music in the monodic style. The individual parts of the cantata were connected by a recitative called *testo* ("text"). (Later, in the Passions of J. S. Bach, the narrator who recited it is known as the Evangelist.) The cantata served as a veritable school for composers, since within its more modest frame they could safely experiment and build up scenes that were later to be incorporated into their operas. There was also the "oratorio," a term which, beginning in 1640, after a few decades of uncertainty, was applied to the musical form we know today. The oratorio differs fundamentally from the opera in that it does not use stage settings; it appeals to the imaginative contemplation of the listener. The occasional scenic mounting of oratorios, both in the past and today, does not alter this aesthetic consideration. Opera, oratorio, sacra rappresentazione, favola pastorale, cantata, and dramma per musica were not, then, necessarily different species; all were dramas set to music in the new monodic style interspersed with choruses, though the titles of the Roman operas indicate that they have an ancestry going back to more remote times than the stile rappresentativo of the Florentine Camerata.

While the liturgic drama was almost completely absorbed and dominated by the sacre rappresentazione, certain stylistic traits indicate that some elements of the old liturgic drama survived, and reappeared in the oratorio. The history of the oratorio reveals a distinction between the vernacular oratorio, or *oratorio volgare,* usually in verse, and the Latin oratorio, in prose. Both have in common the characteristic traits we associate with the oratorio, but their place in the musical life of the time was different. The earlier Latin oratorio was connected with the official liturgy of the Church, whereas the vernacular oratorio was excluded from the liturgy and the church and was performed in prayer meetings, held in "prayer halls." Despite its official recognition, the Latin oratorio was little known in Italy and, remarkable as it may seem, very little used in Rome. Thus we have to turn to the other, more popular form, the Italian secular oratorio, to find our way in this intricate conglomeration of old and new forms, religious and secular dramas, popular and artistic lyrics.

Desiring to raise morality and piety among the people, Filippo Romolo de' Neri (1515-1595) founded a society of secular priests who held their exercises in his house, and after 1558 in the oratory of San Girolamo. The scion of a prominent family, Neri was interested from his boyhood in religious practices, but he was no ascetic, and always cultivated an atmosphere of kindliness, good humor, urbanity, and culture. He preached, while still a layman, with great success among the Romans; upon being ordained in 1551 he went to the church of San Girolamo, where his informal meetings were attended by men of every sort. Whether the name "Congregazione dell' Oratorio" which the society assumed came from the place of meeting or, as some believe, from the prayers, or *orazioni,* forming the center of their religious exercises, is not yet clear. The success of these spiritual exercises was phenomenal, and as early as 1564 the Florentine colony in Rome requested Neri to take over the leadership of their congregation. Gregory XIII confirmed the statutes of the confraternity, and Neri, revered as a saint throughout his lifetime, conducted it until his death in 1595.

There is a singular resemblance between the life and work of St. Francis of Assisi and of St. Philip Neri. Both were keenly interested in raising the moral, ethical, and religious standards of the people, and both headed popular movements which in reality were reform movements within the Church. The same devout and inspired songs, the laudi which were sung all over the Tuscan countryside centuries before by the Franciscan laudesi, resounded in the prayer meetings of Neri's disciples. The laudi were not well known in Rome and seem to have taken root only after the appearance of Neri and Animuccia, both coming from the Tuscan home of this form of religious music, which was destined for a high artistic career. The *essercitii spirituali* were not Neri's invention. Although mild and friendly like the original Franciscan religious poetry of the laudi, we cannot overlook their close resemblance to the *exercitia spiritualia* of Loyola, whose ardent following was well established when Neri came to Rome. And if the spiritualist-mystical temper gained the upper hand over Neri, whose *essercitii* were in reality a popular and tame edition in the vernacular of the original strict Jesuit *exercitia,* we must remember that the tender and charitable St. Francis had a following that spread the orgy of flagellantism all over Europe. Neri and Loyola were personal friends, and the fact that many of the collections of laudi of the Philippine Congregation bore the imprint of the Society of Jesus, some being published in the Spanish language, testifies to the collaboration of the Congregation with the Jesuits. It was this association which later made possible the rapid development of the oratorio, because the Jesuitic training which fostered the apprehension of figures of the imagination with the intensity of physical reality, prepared the ground for it. While the laudi spirituali of Neri, Ingegneri, Animuccia, and other older composers were simple and quiet, when we reach the first products of Neri's disciples we are faced with the exaggerated allegorical pictures of Jesuit dramatic lyricism in all its intensity.

Neri died in 1595, and only five years later the rooms which had harbored the simple dramatized prayer-songs echoed to the orchestra and choruses of a pompous sacra rappresentazione as the spiritual opera made its appearance.

In 1588 Emilio de' Cavalieri (c. 1550–1602) assumed charge of entertainments at the court of Tuscany. This talented Roman nobleman, inventor of ballets, composer of madrigals, clever and graceful actor and dancer, became attracted to Caccini's recitative madrigals and tried his hand at setting fragments from Tasso's *Aminta* to music in the same style. Next came two complete little pastorals in one act, written for him by the feted poetess Laura Guidiccioni. Encouraged by his success, the "Inspector-General of Arts and Artists" at the Florentine court endeavored to equip the sacra rappresentazione with the technique of the rising music drama. As a consequence, the old medieval mystery play, which had retained its contemplative character, now gained the choral frescoes that we all know so well from the works of Handel, and began its journey on the road that was to lead to the oratorio. Cavalieri's work, *La Rappresentazione di Anima e di Corpo,* was first performed in 1600 in the Oratorio della Vallicella, one of Neri's oratories.[14] The principal characters of the rappresentazione were allegorical personifications —Time, Life, the World, Pleasure, the Intellect, the Soul, and the Body— but from the preface of the original edition it becomes clear that the work was to be performed like an opera, that is, with scenery, dances, etc. Considering this, and the fact that Cavalieri's work had no direct connections with the tradition of the Philippine oratories, we cannot accept Burney's statement, which found its way into all modern manuals on musical history, that Cavalieri's rappresentazione was the first oratorio. This composition was an opera, sacred in content, to be sure, but a stage play like the other Florentine operas; it was the first of those religious operas which flourished for a while, until they were absorbed by the modern oratorio. The significant thing about Cavalieri's rappresentazione was that the spectacular element of the intermezzi, which he so often helped to prepare for festivities, began to displace the ascetic Florentine ideal. Soon the oratorio volgare made its appearance, making use of the lessons learned from both the spiritual and the secular opera; but these oratorios did not employ scenic settings, and they clung to the purely imaginative-contemplative nature of the true oratorio. The recitation of the testo, to introduce and connect individual sections of the work, had to be made impressive and convincing to engage the listener's attention. Once the subject had been introduced, or a significant point in the narrative reached, the chorus was permitted to officiate with its lyrical comments. The participation of the chorus in what we may call the "action," perhaps the most admirable part of Handel's and other modern oratorio composers' art of setting, appears in the oratorio volgare at an early period together with the sudden, dramatic interruptions of the testo or other solo parts.

When we reach the middle of the seventeenth century, in fact about 1640, the original order of the Philippine Congregation has changed. Formerly devoted to prayers and penitential exercises and the singing of laudi spirituali, the oratories now presented oratorios of such proportions that they had to be divided into two sections between which came the sermon. From this time on the word "oratorio" means the musical form rather than the room where it was performed. The full-fledged oratorio became not only popular but offered a certain rivalry to opera. The Latin oratorio in Rome (practiced only in the Oratory of San Marcello) was supported by the pope and by the highest church dignitaries, who did not spare expense to have the performances kept at the highest level, employing a great number of good singers and a large orchestra. These performances were attended by the clerical and secular aristocracy of the city. The people, not understanding Latin, stayed away, and San Marcello's gained the reputation of being the most fashionable meeting place of cultivated minds during Lent. These early oratorios were still spiritual dramas, and a certain theatrical aspect, enhanced by dances and intermezzi, continued to be attached to them; it will not be surprising, therefore, to see the sacred opera emerge from this atmosphere.

The first sacred opera, a *dramma pastorale* entitled *Eumelio,* by the eminent church composer and famous theoretical writer, Agostino Agazzari (1578–1608), was performed in 1606, and was followed by a number of works which culminated in the *Apotheosis of St. Ignatius of Loyola,* by the Italianized German, Johann Hieronymus Kapsberger (d. c. 1650), performed in 1622 in the Jesuit College. Such works were frequently presented in the palaces of cardinals and nobles and prepared the field for the secular opera. Since the Roman opera was almost completely free of literary restrictions, librettists and composers proceeded to create a really practical musical theater.

Roman opera is personified by one great name: Barberini. This was the name not of an artist, but of a family of patrons of art. Passionate lovers of music, the three Barberini princes built a large opera theater of their own. The Teatro Barberini, a sumptuous building rivaling any of the big opera houses of our day and accommodating more than three thousand spectators, opened in 1632 with an opera entitled *Santo Alessio*.[15] Steffano Landi (c. 1590–c. 1655), the composer of *Santo Alessio,* was one of the most eminent operatic composers of the first half of the seventeenth century. A member of the papal choir and choirmaster of the cathedral in Padua, he became the first representative of Roman opera. His works are characterized by noble melodic invention, dramatic force and pathos, all of which made him a worthy contemporary of Monteverdi. With him appears a new tone in opera, a tone least expected in the Eternal City.

While the classical subjects, the *Orfeos, Dafnes,* and *Didos,* retained their vogue for a long time, the national epic poetry of Tasso and Ariosto soon acquired a standing of its own in the music drama, and it was not long before the historical and classicistic atmosphere of the opera was invaded by the spirit of seventeenth-century Italian life. *Santo Alessio* is not a rappresentazione or a simple sacred opera; it is a musical tragedy of the first water. It does not present abstract ideas; the *dramatis personae* are types taken from Roman life and show a keen sense of psychological observation. The scarcely quarter-of-a-century-old opera was already a truly modern, national drama. And the great stand-by of the Italian theater, the improvised farce, finally pushed its way into the opera, after it had successfully invaded the madrigal, within whose sphere, however, it had not been able to develop beyond the still abstract madrigal comedy. The increasingly popular secular opera admitted comical elements, deeply ingrained in the Latin soul but banished by the Florentine archaeologists. Landi was the first composer to insert comic scenes in the drama, and the innovation, enthusiastically received, was responsible for the subsequent growth of the *opera buffa.* As an immediate echo, in 1637 there was performed at the Barberini theater a musical comedy, entitled *Il Falcone,* written by one of the leading Roman composers, Vergilio Mazzocchi (d. 1646), choirmaster at St. Peter's. But the merit of initiative goes to the poet of the libretto, Cardinal Rospigliosi, later crowned pontiff under the name Clement IX. This prince of the Church, who manifested such a fondness for music that he was accused of sacrificing the interests of the Holy See to opera, while perhaps a mediocre pope, was certainly not a mediocre artist. While papal envoy in Madrid, Cardinal Rospigliosi came in contact with the flowering Spanish theater, and his later libretti show a familiarity with the plays of Calderón. It is small wonder, then, that the pastoral drama was soon intermingled with elements that savored of a more modern world. The cardinal's next venture, in which he associated himself with the composers Vergilio Mazzocchi and Marco Marazzoli, resulted in the virtual creation of the Italian comic opera, the *opera buffa.* The three-act comedy, *Chi Soffre, Speri,* performed in 1639, was followed in 1653 by Rospigliosi's *Dal Male il Bene,* the music by Marazzoli and Abbatini, showing astonishing progress made in a few years in the style of the buffoon comedy. The first and third acts end with remarkable little finales uniting all voices on the stage. *Dal Male il Bene* became the prototype of the opera buffa in which the Italians' love of intrigue, their mocking spirit, their splendid sense of humor and raillery, their natural talent for grasping ridiculous situations, all found a natural expression. The opera buffa of the succeeding century was to become one of the most admirable expressions of the Italian temperament.

As we near the middle of the century, opera, oratorio, and cantata seem to have found their individual fields of action and, while still depending on each other, to have embarked on separate careers. The chief Roman masters of the period were Giovanni Giacomo Carissimi (1605–1674) and Luigi Rossi (1598–1653). All the rigidity of the early monodic style has now disappeared, and the infinite flexibility of the musical dialect has fulfilled the yearning of the humanists for a "sweet" and "tender" style which they believed they had found in the fundamentally stiff and unmelodious recitative of Peri.

Carissimi's accomplishments in the field of the Latin oratorio are as exceptional and significant as Monteverdi's energetic intervention in the destiny of the opera. His dramatic musical declamation and his noble melodic invention created a school in the history of Italian music and opened the era of the masters of the "great forms." While Carissimi concentrated his activity on the Latin oratorio, his works were not spiritual operas like those of Cavalieri but real oratorios in the modern sense of the word. Historians and musical writers of the eighteenth century—Mattheson, Burney, and Hawkins—had only the highest praise for him, while the next century considered him the Handel of the seventeenth century. Like all such comparisons, this lacks any scientific basis; still, the two composers have many points in common. As with Handel, the main interest in Carissimi's oratorios lies in the magnificent choruses handled with exceptional skill, and, like the Anglo-German master's choruses, the Italian's always take part in the movemented "action," thus not following set patterns. But Carissimi's choral settings are not polyphonic and he uses very little counterpoint in general, while fugues in particular are entirely missing. The realistic and evocative power of his choruses is extraordinary and reflects the same spirit as Jesuit architecture. This is understandable, for his libretti were written by Jesuits. Carissimi's expressive dramatic power is not restricted, however, to the choral parts; his recitatives and solo songs are equally sweeping and teeming with life. Carissimi's influence was universal. Its traces can be found not only in contemporary Italian oratorio, but in such masters as Schütz as well as in much more recent composers. It is a known fact that when hard pressed for time Handel appropriated whole scenes from Carissimi, whose oratorios constituted the point of departure for his own works in that form of choral music. It is a most regrettable fact that many of Carissimi's works are still unpublished and that a great number of them were lost at the time of the suppression of the Jesuits. The composer was choirmaster of S. Apollinare for forty-six years, and his works were destroyed or sold for wastepaper when the archives of this Jesuit church were disposed of.

Luigi Rossi looms as an important figure in the transition from the recited "melodramatic" opera to the new type, constructed in purely musical "closed" forms. The same classical feeling for rounded form is manifest in his cantatas, of which some hundred are extant, although few of the works of this eminent composer have been published. The light, melancholy grace which emanates from the few cantatas and excerpts scattered in monographs betrays an extremely sensitive and poetic soul. What Carissimi accomplished in the field of the oratorio, or rather, the sacra rappresentazione, was paralleled by Rossi in the cantata.

The Roman musicians brought opera to an impressive degree of structural, dramatic, and technical development. Besides the introduction of the comical elements which paved the road for the opera buffa, the composers of *Chi Soffre, Speri* already employed the light and fast burlesque dialogue that later assumed the name of *recitativo secco*. The acts of *Santo Alessio* were preceded by instrumental preludes of ample proportions, eliciting great admiration and many imitations that led finally to the finely wrought operatic overtures. The Romans reorganized the orchestra, eliminating the great and complicated apparatus used in the sixteenth century, and making the string ensemble the central part and foundation of the orchestra, a principle which was retained henceforth. They did not neglect the individual instruments, however, and their accompaniments allotted important roles to them as well as to the orchestra in general. The recitative shed the last vestiges of its original rigidly declamatory nature and became a pliable vehicle of dramatic musical action, while the solo songs and arias were shaped into well-rounded closed forms. In general, an atmosphere of sound theater and thorough musicianship emanated from the Roman opera and impressed itself on the other schools of opera now rising with astonishing rapidity. Of these schools the Venetian stands out as the most prolific, colorful, and fascinating, retaining the leadership until opera became submerged in the conventionalism of the *fin de siècle*.

Venice, which had retained the character of a republic (at least in regard to the nonhereditary nature of the ruling head of the state), did not have a courtly establishment as the home of opera, as did Florence, Mantua, and Rome. This explains the fact that while it took opera a relatively long time to find its way into the Adriatic republic, once accepted, it acquired an entirely different social status. From the courts of princes, cardinals, and wealthy and noble men of letters it passed suddenly into the public domain. Once the general public gained admittance and contributed financially toward the upkeep of the theater, its tastes and desires had to be taken into consideration. Accustomed to the spectacle of sumptuous parades and open-air performances, and animated by the love of amusement and entertainment so characteristic of the baroque temper, it demanded a musical show diverting and rewarding to eye and ear. Besides being slow and tedious, the Florentine music drama was miniature in its proportions; the performance of *Euridice* took scarcely more than half an hour, assuredly too brief a time for use in the professional theater. Fortunately, the first troupe to come to Venice was a Roman company under the direction of Benedetto Ferrari (1597–1681), and it brought with it the wide experience and developed taste of musicians nourished on the Roman opera. The Teatro San Cassiano opened its doors in 1637 amidst general rejoicing. Ferrari, poet and composer, was also the librettist of the first opera, *Andromeda,* ever performed in a public opera house. Two years later two more theaters were built, partly managed by Ferrari and by the composer of his *Andromeda,* Francesco Manelli, to be followed by many others inaugurating a veritable operatic mass production. Toward the end of the century every parish in Venice had its own opera theater, usually named after the parish church.

Aroused from his retirement, the aged Monteverdi, with his pupil Francesco Cavalli, assumed the leadership of Venetian opera in 1639. We have already mentioned the marvelous compositions of his old age, but the great dramatist was not yet satisfied with his achievements in creating a truly dramatic language. In the preface to his secular oratorio, *Il Combattimento di Tancredi e di Clorinda,* he states that he is endeavoring to establish the dialectics and the technical apparatus of the *stile concitato* in order to find a more adequate means to express the unruly, agitated, and rebellious elements in human nature. And his orchestra rages and trembles; tremolo and pizzicato, which had appeared only a few years earlier in string music, are now introduced into the orchestra, to remain there as mainstays of dramatic accompaniment. But however skillful his orchestral writing, the real significance of Monteverdi's last and greatest masterpiece, *L'Incoronazione di Poppea,* lay in the intensity of dramatization through the singing voice, carried out inexorably in the smallest details. This is opera in its unique and most glorious domain. Whenever in the course of history operatic composers have forgotten this hierarchy of voice and orchestra, they have invariably forced opera into a blind alley from which it must be rescued by true musicians, not given to bombastic grandeur or metaphysical speculation

Pier Francesco Caletti-Bruni, called Cavalli (1602–1676) after he adopted the name of the Venetian patrician who cared for his education, was one of the illustrious musical directors of St. Mark's. His forty-two operas followed the traditions inaugurated by his teacher Monteverdi, and if they do not disclose a genius comparable to that of the master, his strong feeling for the dramatic, his colorful orchestral treatment and interesting harmonic and melodic language enlarged the artistic horizon of opera. Cavalli gave the chorus a more important role than was usual in Venetian practice, and the separation of aria and recitative is almost completely carried out in his works. His reputation was enormous all over Europe, and his *Giasone,* *Egisto,* and *Serse* made the round of all operatic theaters. Yet with all his greatness, Cavalli does not exhibit the artistic integrity of Monteverdi. The quality of his compositions was uneven; among impressive masterpieces we find works that are merely routine. Henry Prunières made the interesting disclosure that, in his hurry to have something finished, Cavalli sometimes neglected to familiarize himself with the text of the scene he was about to set to music. Thus in his *Calisto* he almost finished a duet when the discovery of a third person in the libretto forced him to revise the whole scene.

Cavalli's most famous contemporary and coleader in the Venetian school of opera was Marc' Antonio Cesti (1623–1669), in turn choirmaster in Volterra and at the court of Archduke Ferdinand in Innsbruck, tenor in the papal choir, Franciscan monk, and court conductor to Emperor Leopold I of Austria. In spite of his many escapades and travels, Cesti spent most of his creative years in Venice enjoying the reputation he shared with Cavalli. The two rivals' styles are not lacking in similarities, but Cesti is a more lyrical personality, his melodies are fuller and more mellow than those of Cavalli and it was he who contributed greatly to that melodic quality which makes Italian music irresistible in its sensuous beauty. In his operas the arias are more numerous than the choruses, a fact which reflects the general tendency of the time. Arias and solo recitatives became dominant in the Venetian opera of the mid-century, and the ensemble scenes consisted mostly of duets. Yet the composers, especially Cesti, when writing for such royal and princely theaters as those of Vienna, Paris, and Munich, indulged in the lavish and extravagant pomp of the baroque with a natural abandonment which proves that they were true children of their time. Cesti's *Pomo d'Oro,* performed in Vienna in 1666, required a fabulous apparatus, and this last great choral opera of the Italian *bel canto* cost the imperial household a small fortune to produce.

While the Roman, Viennese, and other operatic performances retained all the expensive scenic, choral, and orchestral equipment of the resplendent baroque theater, the Venetian theaters, managed by "commercial" interests, were confronted with the same problems that our present-day commercial opera houses have to face; and, singularly, the procedure followed seems to have been the same in the San Cassiano theater in Venice in the seventeenth century as it is in the Metropolitan Opera House in New York in the twentieth: no amount of money is spared to acquire excellent "stars" from all over the world, while chorus, orchestra, and scenery must get along with what is left. The chorus was, indeed, finally forced out of existence in the Venetian opera houses, mainly, it appears, because of the expenses involved, the theaters being run by stock companies that had to economize.

Later Seicento Opera

BY this time the theater, especially the musical stage, had become a passion with all the symptoms of a general madness. There were sixty private theaters in Bologna, not counting those in the convents and colleges. In 1678 there were a hundred and thirty comedies performed in private houses in Rome, and from the opening of San Cassiano until the end of the century over three hundred and fifty different operas were performed in the sixteen theaters of Venice.[16] If we note that the city counted a population of less than 150,000, we can form an opinion of the operatic craze of the baroque. To these three hundred and fifty Venetian operas we must add at least an equal number composed by Venetian musicians for other Italian and foreign theaters. Of this enormous number about one-sixth is preserved, all in manuscript. After 1640 very few operatic or cantata scores were printed, partly because the printing press could not cope with the output, partly because of the ephemeral nature of the works. If an opera was accepted by a theater other than that where it was first performed, the original score could not be used, as every opera had to be adjusted to local conditions. It was not infrequent that the libretto alone was retained and music newly composed by the local conductor to fit the needs of the personnel.

The happy balance of all elements that characterized the early opera did not prove to be a lasting blessing. The poets endeavored to continue on the road blazed by Rinuccini, and with the growing popularity of opera found a fairly good source of income in the sale of the libretti, often printed in luxurious editions. The public liked to follow the work from the libretto, and it was customary to carry a small candle that shed enough light for this purpose. The seared and waxy pages of early libretti illustrate the general interest in the literary part of the earlier seventeenth-century opera. But later the melodrama as Rinuccini conceived it disappeared until the advent of the great dramatic poets of the eighteenth century, Zeno and Metastasio. The ideal of the antique drama was entirely abandoned, and opera became a purely superficial art, catering to luxury and amusement. Characterization of the figures of the drama was not even attempted; there were no individuals in the play, only types. The music drama was called *opera seria* (serious opera) but was really never tragic, as the happy ending was mandatory. This desire to satisfy the public prompted the managers of the Venetian opera houses to amplify the existing works, as the earlier operas were considered too short for professional entertainment. Faced with this problem, composers and producers resorted to the old trick of interpolating intermezzi, especially dances, thereby perpetrating a custom already evident in the earlier courtly festivities, namely the introduction of a foreign body into the opera, thus placing the serious composer in a dilemma. The ballet remained in the opera, and was especially welcome in the nineteenth-century grand opera, but it seriously threatened the artistic unity of the lyric stage unless handled with great skill and stagecraft. The solemnly bombastic atmosphere of the stage required a reorientation in the accompanying music, and the melodies became overcharged with ornaments, overloaded with difficulties; the breathtaking sallies of the idolized singers could hardly be duplicated by the nimblest violin or flute virtuosi.

Such vocal acrobatics called for a lung power and endurance not within the province of women; and while the early opera still employed *prime donne,* the sovereign ruler of the operatic stage was now the castrato, deliriously feted by the public. "Evviva il coltello!" (long live the little knife), they shouted, when a seemingly impossible and endless flourish was successfully negotiated by a singer. The secret of their marvelous vocal prowess was that they retained the freshness of their voices as they were in boyhood, when they were emasculated. To this clear and sexless voice was added the powerful larynx and lungs of a grown man, thereby combining two qualities that nature seems to have avoided. The origin of castration for the sake of a musical career goes back to age-old Oriental practices. By the end of the seventeenth century the traffic in emasculated boys, many of whom never became singers of any importance, took on shameful proportions. Although it has never been proved that this unfortunate and despicable practice had the approval of the Church, there is no doubt that it was tolerated, and from the middle of the sixteenth century up to the nineteenth there were castrate members in the Sistine Chapel choir. The castrati rose to the height of their popularity in Handel's days and reigned until Gluck's and Mozart's time. Their influence in the history of opera was tremendous, and the "trouser roles" that appeared in opera in the early nineteenth century, persisting up to Octavian in Strauss's *Rosenkavalier,* are direct issues of its erstwhile popularity. While Italian audiences were held spellbound by the virtuoso singers and the castrati, foreign visitors, especially Englishmen, were utterly repulsed by the whole spectacle, including the opera itself.

I cannot forbear telling you, that I find a certain Confusion and Unpleasant ness in several Parts of their Singing in those Operas; They dwell many times longer on one Quavering, than in singing Four whole lines; and often times they run so fast, that 'tis hard to tell whether they sing or Speak, or whether they do neither of the Two or both together. . . . There is also one thing which charmed them, which I believe would not please you: I mean those unhappy Men who basely suffer themselves to be maimed, that they may have the finer Voices. The silly figure, which in my Opinion, such a mutilated Fellow makes, who sometimes acts the Bully, and sometimes the Passionate Lover, with his effeminate Voice, and wither'd chin, is such a thing to be endured? [17]

This letter, written from Venice in 1688, aptly describes the indignation of a righteous Briton, but the visitors were even more shocked when they discovered that the operatic furor, emanating from Venice and reaching, toward the middle of the century, Italian cities large and small, penetrated every sphere of life. Acting and dramatic scenes were carried to the pulpit to such an extent that foreign travelers frequently remarked that churches could not be distinguished from theaters. The Jesuit professor of rhetoric, Franciscus Lang, author of the Jesuit plays dealing with St. Ignatius's *Exercises*,[18] complains in the preface of the printed edition of his text that he is obliged to publish "merely the dead letters, destitute of the apparatus of the living voice, action, music, costumes, and scenery," because the plays contained in the volume were meant to be a sort of operatic divine service.

With due admiration for the remarkable talents of the musicians of the seventeenth century, it seems that the enormous success of the lyric stage was owing, if not mainly, at least considerably, to the fact that opera, more than any other form of art, was the most adequate, the perfect medium for satisfying the insatiable appetite of the baroque for the spectacular, the enchanting, and the overwhelming. Another cause of its popularity was the universal admiration of virtuoso singing. Many of the leading composers, especially in Rome, were also prominent vocalists. Singers and composers were well paid, and besides receiving a fixed sum for an operatic work—one hundred ducats for an unknown composer, and two to four hundred for a well-known maestro—the composer was paid for his ministrations at the keyboard of the harpsichord for each performance. To procure all the money needed for financing these costly performances the entrance fees were supplemented by donations and the annual lease of boxes. The baroque raised the theater, music, and musicians to a dominating position in the cultural life of the nation, and even social life assumed a stagelike character. The well-to-do families considered it their duty to own a box in the local opera theater, and such boxes were inherited by succeeding generations. The "seasons" of opera, as we know them today, originated with the public opera houses in Venice. There was a main season during the carnival, from December 26 to March 30, followed by the "Ascension season," from Easter to June 15, and as the demand grew a third season was added, from September 1 to November 30. The various rulers and princes, the reigning aristocratic families, appropriated opera as their representative form of art, and the ordinary theater was relegated to the background. Ever since those days great state receptions on the occasion of visiting royalty or heads of state have been centered around gala performances in the opera, and even the free cities, such as the Hanseatic towns, vied with each other in maintaining excellent operatic establishments, as if demonstrating their sovereignty.

The artistic past of Italy made it the predestined country for musical leadership, and Italian music now conquered the whole world. Its triumph was so complete by the opening of the eighteenth century that even in our day, after a century and a half of German, French, and Russian prominence, our musical vocabulary is still largely Italian. It is an edifying spectacle to see the complex resources of Italian genius in the midst of its decadence. All the fervor, inventiveness, and wit of their genius, exhausted by centuries of strenuous glory in all fields of arts and letters, seem to have taken refuge in the new art of opera. The past century, which witnessed pilgrimages to Bayreuth, or our own century of industrialized music, can hardly form an idea of the musical furor of the seventeenth century. But mass production had its fatal repercussions; the aristocratic opera reached its end and great art vanished, later to return in a new form and in a new milieu. The havoc it wrought in its decline was, however, considerable. The more intimate genres, such as the madrigal, declined rapidly as people became insistent on the virtuosity of a solo singer accompanied by an orchestra. The sight of an informal group of madrigal singers, sitting around a table with their part books, was considered savoring "too much of scholastic exercise." This was the opinion of Pietro della Valle, writing about 1640.[19]

And yet in the midst of this bedlam, this frenzy of the musical stage, there were composers of great talent milling about in such numbers as the world has never known before or since. Their works being almost all in manuscript, we can judge only from the few excerpts published in various learned dissertations on operatic history.[20] We must not forget that the general decline was due mainly to overproduction and to the librettists' catering to the lower instincts of the populace in Venice. There were many new elements, introduced mainly from popular sources, that have added considerable wealth to our musical ideas and forms: the lovely Venetian folk songs, issues of the rich frottola literature of the Renaissance, the barcaruola, the siciliana—the latter the pleasantly undulating melody in $12/8$ measure well known from Handel's *Messiah* and Bach's Christmas Oratorio ("Pastoral Symphony"). The introduction of the siciliana is usually claimed, together with the arias with obbligato instruments, for a much later period of operatic music, but both were copiously used by the Venetians. The modern concertgoing public knows these arias in the form used in J. S. Bach's Passions, where the tenor or contralto "concertizes" with an oboe or *viola d'amore*. While the great vogue of these arias started in Scarlatti's time, the battle scenes in the Venetian opera called into existence the so-called trumpet arias in which the voice pitted its brilliant passages against the sallies of the shining brass instrument. These heroic trumpet arias were still favored by many eighteenth-century composers, chief among them Handel. The dramatic scenes of love-death, appearance of divinity, profession of faith, the crossing of Hades, and the especially favored scenes of ghosts, the *ombrae*, became standard equipments of operas set in an almost identical style. Yet they show great skill, ingenuity, and variety within the established traditions. The violin passages of the *ombrae* can still be heard surrounding the part of Christ in J. S. Bach's Passion according to St. Matthew, and the lyrical idyls, lullabies, dream scenes, and rural pictures of these early operas live with undiminished vigor and charm in Handel's oratorios.

In the last quarter of the century a few composers emerge from among the multitude to demonstrate that great art was not entirely lost in the avalanche of ephemeral commercial productions. The outstanding composer between Cavalli and Scarlatti, the head of the next important school of opera, was Giovanni Legrenzi (1625-1690). A composer of great versatility, he was equally at home in the music drama, oratorio, motet, and instrumental music. Unlike his immediate predecessors and colleagues, Legrenzi commanded a contrapuntal technique of remarkable solidity, indicating the line of development that music was about to take. His reputation was of the highest all over Europe, and both Bach and Handel paid their respects to him by using a number of his melodies for thematic material in their own works. Then, with Alessandro Stradella (c. 1645-1682), there begins a new chapter in the history of the lyric stage. The poets seem to have regained their artistic pride, and their human characters, nature scenes, and dramatic ensembles, rising above the meaningless pattern of the average operatic scene, again place the composer in a position to try his faculties at genuinely dramatic music. It is, however, especially in his cantatas that Stradella shows his genius for suave choral writing, the charm of which, again, impressed the alert Handel sufficiently to cause him to annex a number of Stradella's musical ideas and to utilize them here and there as his own. Carlo Grossi, Domenico Gabrieli, Domenico Freschi, and especially Carlo Pallavicino, were the important composers of this revived music drama, which was to become the omnipotent international opera when Alessandro Scarlatti ushered it into the eighteenth century.

The New Technique of Composition and Performance
The Thorough Bass—The Orchestra—Keyboard Music

CACCINI'S *Nuove Musiche* represents a decisive step toward the establishment of modern music; in its seemingly revolutionary pages it consummated a movement which, starting earlier, slowly converted the functional nature of melody. Melody itself now became conditioned by harmony and, what is of great importance, people have listened to it ever since by applying mentally a harmonic foundation or "accompaniment" even if such was not provided. Every tone becomes now the representative of a harmony, a principle which is the complete antithesis of linear-polyphonic conception.

Thus voice leading now results from the succession of harmonies, and harmony itself, no longer the result of the "symphony," the "sounding together," of autonomously conducted musical lines, assumes the directive, compelling the individual voices to obey its design and plans. This is the complete denial of the principles of medieval and Renaissance polyphony. The added harmonic connotation forced the melody to take on another dimension, and it thus became self-sufficient, spatial. The immediate result of these new trends was a change in the hierarchy of musical parts. The two extreme parts, the melody-carrying treble and the fundamental bass, required more attention, reducing the importance and autonomy of the middle parts. This again called for a revised practice of musical setting. Max Schneider and Otto Kinkeldey have demonstrated [21] that the church organists of the sixteenth century, whose duty often required substituting for the choir or for missing parts, were already wont to arrange the bass parts of vocal compositions by marking through the use of figures the general trend in the harmonic successions. Such "scores" are extant from the middle of the sixteenth century, not only in Italy, but in Spain and Germany. What was a mere device to facilitate the organists' labors became, with the appearance of monody, a fundamental principle of the baroque era, assuming the name of *basso continuo,* or thorough bass. Beginning with 1603 the continuo part appears in most new Italian publications, the term *basso continuato* or *basso seguente* having already been used by Caccini in 1600 in the preface to his *Euridice.* Among the influential musicians to indicate the new trend most resolutely was Lodovico Grossi da Viadana (1564–1627), from 1594 to 1607 master of music in the Cathedral of Mantua, the city of Monteverdi and his *Orfeo.* This eminently practical and clear-headed Franciscan monk was the first to realize that the confusing situation created by the absence of certain voices in compositions calling for a number of parts could be remedied by arranging the compositions right in the beginning for a smaller ensemble of parts, with the organ taking an active part in the proceedings instead of making the best of the situation. His work entitled *Cento Concerti Ecclesiastici a 1, 2, 3, 4, Voci con il Basso Continuo per Sonar nell' Organo* (1602) was the first publication of concerted music with the accompaniment of a "following bass." This important and notably practical arrangement which enabled the musical director of a church to cope with any situation without altering arbitrarily the complexion of the work earned Viadana a reputation in modern times as the "inventor" of the thorough bass. Needless to say, such was not the case, as both figures above the bass notes, and the accidentals, are missing in his score, while Cavalieri and Caccini indicated the harmonies fairly accurately by numbers specifying the intervals and also marked sharps and flats. Nevertheless, Viadana supplied the incentive which found a ready following because the thorough bass was the result not of theoretical speculation but of a desire to cope, in a practical manner, with the requirements of current musical practice.

At the opening of the seventeenth century the fusion, or rather the acceptance of the rhythmic principles of instrumental music in vocal music, is almost completed, and the graphical aspect of the modern score is before us. The bar of measure, at first a mere technical expediency to facilitate orientation in the score, now evolved into the regular group measure as we know it today and made possible the unified, superimposed full score. Owing to the systematic rhythmical unity of measures, clearly marked in the score, ensemble playing became much easier and more precise than in the previous centuries, and the conductor, sitting at the harpsichord or organ, was able to direct with assurance singers and orchestra, helping here and there with his instrument and giving cues to the soloists.

The music as it is before us in the manuscripts and printed scores of the seventeenth century gives us, however, a pale picture, a merely approximate idea of how this music really sounded when performed by the virtuosi of the time. The composer indicated the outlines of his work, leaving it to the performing artist to embroider it with ornaments. Many scores contain only the solo part and the thorough bass; the rest, including the instrumentation, was left to the singers, players, and conductor. This leads us to the most typical feature of baroque style: ornamentation, equally prominent in all phases of baroque art. The collective technical term for the improvised ornamentation was "diminution," by which "one long note is resolved and broken into many other smaller and quicker ones" (Praetorius). The musicians of the baroque, whether singers or instrumentalists, considered a sovereign command of improvised ornamentation their chief artistic asset. The excellence and minutely developed technical wealth of the Italian singing schools of the seventeenth century defies any comparison. From the simplest appoggiatura to the most complicated coloratura passages everything was taught methodically and with a clear conception of the physiological requirements of the human voice. Besides the purely technical vocal instruction the singers were trained in the niceties of musical composition. Similarly, every member of an orchestra, especially an operatic orchestra, was expected to be able to invent, on the spur of the moment, a free contrapuntal part over the given figured bass. In this connection the demands of practical musicianship imposed on the conductor were considerable, and it is doubtful whether many of our feted modern virtuoso conductors of a none too elaborate repertory could equal the skill and resourcefulness of their seventeenth-century colleagues. Besides a facility on the keyboard, the conductor had to have a thorough training in musical theory and composition in order to play from the single bass line with ease and fluency. The orchestral instruments were divided into "fundamental" and "ornamental" instruments, the former consisting of keyboard instruments, lutes, and harps, the latter of all string and wind instruments capable of playing melodies and freely running parts. The players of these were experienced musicians with a good command of counterpoint, as their task was to invent and improvise entirely new parts. According to Agostino Agazzari, the first author of a comprehensive manual on the technique of orchestral playing and accompaniment,[22] while the player-composer should endeavor to embellish the parts to the best of his knowledge, he "must beware with great industry and judiciousness not to offend [meaning not to encroach on the part of] the other player or to run with his part." Agazzari, as well as his colleague and translator, the German Michael Praetorius, also warned the players to watch for a balance of sonority to avoid confusion. "Everyone should listen to the other and wait for his turn to apply his runs, trills, and accents." Thus the ornamentation and embellishing of parts was not a privilege of the singers, but was the everyday equipment of all musicians.

At the opening of the century the process of weaning instrumental music from its vocal mother was completed, although the old "neutral" part writing is visible as late as in the fugues of J. S. Bach. What gave a tremendous impetus to this new music was the realization of the essential difference between the sound, and consequently the technical handling, of lute and organ, gamba and harpsichord, cornet and harp. An entirely new conception of sonority fascinated the musicians of the baroque era, and, aided by the considerably improved musical instruments, they started to create a new literature which grew by leaps and bounds. The improvement of the pedal board and keyboard mechanism of the organ gave it added facilities. The stops were being constructed with a view to individuality and contrast, and soon it became apparent that the organ offered possibilities that were virtually unlimited. The various groups of stops could be pitted against each other, and the favorite dynamic trick of the baroque, the echo effect, could be reproduced on the organ at will. The other keyboard instruments endeavored to emulate the organ. The delicate clavichord, somewhat lost in the sonorous world of the baroque, fell behind the harpsichord, which took from the organ its second keyboard and a system of "couplers" to change and combine the stops now at its disposal. While all these innovations increased the range, dynamic possibilities, and general usefulness of this magnificent instrument, the close resemblance of its technique and operation to that of the organ prevented it for a time from having a literature entirely of its own in spite of the great difference of its crisp and brilliant tone from the sustained choral sonority of the organ. The lute, the queen of Renaissance instruments, began to decline in Italy but was to reach a remarkable second flourishing in France and Germany. The family of the viols was also slowly joining the discarded, with the exception of the knee viol, the gamba, which remained for a long time the favored chamber music instrument of professionals and amateurs alike, still being willingly incorporated in polyphonic ensemble playing. Opposed to the soft and quiet nature of the gamba there stood the imperious violin with its strong and brilliant upper register, unwilling to subordinate itself to anything else. Its high register made it especially suitable for the art of diminution, and composers and players were not indifferent to this. At first rated equal to and interchangeable with the cornet, beginning with the second decade of the seventeenth century the violin became the favorite orchestral and solo instrument. Another decade, and it had already evolved a virtuoso literature that boasted of every trick that is usually assigned to more recent times.

The many altar pictures and triptychs depicting the heavenly orchestra of angels are excellent guides for the student of orchestral history. They show the remarkably rich and colorful, if not very systematic, orchestra of the Middle Ages and the Renaissance. A noteworthy detail in these pictures is the presence, in addition to lutes, harps, and their many subspecies, of a large number of organs and other keyboard instruments, that is, instruments capable of playing chords. This was the colorful orchestra of the intermezzi and rappresentazioni, what we may call the "accidental" orchestra, in which the respective choirs of strings, flutes, trombones, bassoons, etc., did not follow a prearranged plan but were used at will, substituting for each other whenever the range and register permitted. The *Orfeo* orchestra of Monteverdi represent the end of the old intermezzo ensemble. The composer of *Orfeo* already indicated repeatedly that certain dramatic effects necessitate a closely defined grouping of instruments. Henceforth the orchestra had to be arranged along more tangible lines. As a rule, up to the appearance of Scarlatti the Italian opera orchestra consisted of a number of violins divided into two, three, or four parts, and one or two bass parts played by the bass viols and gambas, the harpsichord holding the whole ensemble together and covering the fabric of the music wherever it needed helpful intervention. Harps and lutes were occasionally substituted for the harpsichord or played the continuo with it; a chordal instrument was, however, indispensable, for the loosely knit parts required the filling chords of the director's instrument to cover up gaps in the harmonic structure. Trumpets and flutes and other *discant* instruments joined the violins if the situation called for their participation or if the composer wanted to write an aria with a *concertante* instrument. It was especially here that the continuo player's skill was needed, because up to the time of J. S. Bach such arias frequently contained only the vocal part, the instrumental solo, and the figured bass; the whole harmonic accompaniment had to be improvised from the figured bass. The players, twenty to forty strong, and later in the century increasing in numbers, were grouped in the orchestra pit around the harpsichord of the conductor. Every instrumentalist had before him the bass part for guidance in his improvisations if his parts were not written out. While the first player, the "concertmaster," was supposed to indicate the current rhythm by stamping with his foot on the floor, the real unity of rhythm and tempo was safeguarded by the chords struck by the conductor on his harpsichord. If the vocalists or soloists changed the tempo to fit the dramatic situation, conductor and orchestra followed suit. The conductor indicated the dynamic changes and saw to it that the ornament players did not exaggerate their diminutions, thereby covering the singers' voices. The *maestro al cembalo's* role at the head of the opera orchestra was somewhat different from that of the choral conductor. who officiated with a baton, his bare hands, or with any convenient object within his reach, such as a roll of music paper or a handkerchief tied on a stick.

The performances of the great polychoral compositions presented considerable technical difficulties, but we have reliable contemporary testimony that these performances earned unstinted admiration. André Maugars, French viol player in the service of James I of England, translator of Bacon's *Advancement of Learning* (Paris, 1624), a well-educated and competent musician, published in 1639 an interesting report on the state of music in Italy in the first part of the century.[23] The following excerpt will shed light on many questionable points in the musical practice of these experimental times.

. . . this fairly long and spacious church had two great organs erected on both sides of the main altar with room for choirs around them. Along the nave there were eight more choir lofts, four on each side, elevated on scaffolding eight or nine feet high, and separated by the same distance but facing each other. In every one of these choir lofts, according to the custom there, there was a portable organ. One should not be surprised at this because one could easily find more than two hundred of them in Rome while in Paris one can hardly find two organs of the same tone. The master composer beat the principal measure at the head of the first choir accompanied by the most beautiful voices. In every one of the other choirs there was a man whose only duty was to keep his eyes on the original beat given by the chief maestro in order to conform the measure of his choir to it. Thus all choirs sang in the same measure without dragging the movement. During the antiphons one could hear the beautiful symphonies [ensembles] of one, two, or three violins with organ, and some great lutes playing dancelike tunes. These Italian singers always improvise their parts and—a most admirable fact—they never make mistakes, although the music is very difficult. As to the instrumental music . . . there are at least ten or twelve musicians who perform marvels on the violin and some five or six others equally versatile on the lute and the theorbo which they like to play with the accompaniment of the organ, executing a thousand beautiful variations and displaying an incredible manual dexterity.

The early baroque produced an especially brilliant literature of keyboard music, both for the organ and for the harpsichord. Its colossal dynamic range and great variety of color combinations made the organ the baroque instrument par excellence—this in spite of the seemingly archaistic nature of the chief forms of its literature. For fugue and chorale variation were rooted deeply in the old traditions of polyphony. There were, however, the toccatas and fantasies with their excited and rhapsodic atmosphere, their rippling passage work, bold modulations, enharmonic *durezze,* and fascinating ornamental superstructure, all truly baroque to the core. The outstanding master of this new keyboard style was Girolamo Frescobaldi (1583–1644), organist at St. Peter's in Rome. This inspired musician, famed all over the world for his virtuosity and rare gift for improvisation—Baini reports audiences of thirty thousand listening to his playing in St. Peter's—opened a new epoch in the history of instrumental music by placing the keyboard in the service of an extraordinarily personal expressive style. His creative imagination enriched the forms of instrumental music—toccata, ricercar, canzone, fantasy, fugue—with a passionate, almost feverish, poetry and austere pathos. Frescobaldi's style absorbed the revolutionary chromaticism of the early baroque and he used this modern harmonic idiom with more boldness than perhaps anyone else, yet it did not affect his solid and monumental formal designs. In his compositions, tempo and mood sometimes change with a violence found only in dramatic music, but he could subordinate this quality, together with the typically Italian joy in euphony and the sensuous pleasure in dissonance, to a logical and effective construction. The archaic character of ricercar and canzone, deriving from choral origins, changed under his influence into a typically instrumental style. Instead of leading his parts through intricate and often lifeless contrapuntal evolutions, Frescobaldi resorted to a free technique of variation in which the harmonic scheme dominates, although he retained enough of the linear elements to make his constructions coherent and fluent. Every new work shows a more logical and closely knit handling of the thematic material, until in 1624 the publication entitled *Capriccio sopra un Soggetto* (capriccio on one subject) states in the very title the modern principle of monothematic writing by which one musical idea is stated and then developed and presented under many aspects without losing the outlines of its profile. This principle, cherished by all great composers until the advent of the romantic era, replaced the colorful, if not very coherent, succession of a number of themes which characterized the early forms of ricercar and canzone, not yet sure of their independence and artistic standing.

A host of eminent organists and harpsichordists followed in the footsteps of the great Roman organist, among them his personal pupil, Michelangelo Rossi,[24] and Bernardo Pasquini (1637–1710), the latter not only a worthy successor to Frescobaldi's art but a teacher of wide reputation. While all these men were well-trained, versatile, and elegant players and composers, Frescobaldi had no real issues in Italy, and great organ music passed to foreign countries, especially to Germany, where it was to reach its unsurpassed height in J. S. Bach. Frescobaldi's German pupils, among them Froberger and Tunder, transplanted his style to Germany, where it found a rich soil, and every organist of the century became indebted to him. But even as distant a "descendant" as the great Leipzig cantor of St. Thomas's still retained unstinted admiration for the organist of St. Peter's although, in the animated and hectic world of the baroque, composers and compositions usually did not survive the generation of their birth. Some of the conservative humanists accused this ardent musician of musical illiteracy for not knowing the musical doctrines of the ancients. "He carried all his knowledge in his fingers," complained Giovanni Battista Doni; but music was in the blood of Frescobaldi and did not need any philosophic foundation. Like Monteverdi, Frescobaldi was first and foremost a creative musician, fully aware of his powers and not to be waylaid by anything that did not seem relevant to his pure musical invention.

Principles and Types of Instrumental Music
The Italian Violin Schools

BAROQUE architecture was fond of repetition as a method of enhancing and contrasting its meaning and contours. This tendency to echo every idea gains possession of the music of the period, to come to expression in the *concerto* principle, holding under its spell the musical life of the whole seventeenth century. In our day "concert" may mean a recital, or as "concerto" a certain musical species. In the earlier centuries the term was synonymous with ensemble playing—"consort" in England; but—and this is what interests us particularly—in the seventeenth century it stood for a principle of style, and as a principle it means not the co-operation but the opposition, the rivalry, the pitting against each other of musical bodies.

Our finding of a new principle in the concerted music of the baroque period may be disputed, because from the echo of lakes and mountains, from the alternating choruses of Greek tragedy to the antiphons and responsoria of Gregorian music, and wherever two people are singing or playing together, the concertante element is present. It was the baroque spirit, however, which, with its love of virtuosity, display, and ornamentation, caused this elemental principle to become the dominating factor in its music. Contrary to our modern purely instrumental usage, the concerted style took its flight from vocal music. The antiphonal multiple choirs of the Venetians gave the first impetus to its development. The simplest and most natural expression of the concerto principle is the echo. and "echo play" was already the delight of Venetian musicians in Willaert's time, toward the end of the century engendering a style. We have seen how in Maugars's time the churches were provided with a number of choir lofts and galleries to accommodate the various choral bodies and trombone and trumpet choirs to carry out the echo playing. Andrea Gabrieli's *Concerti* (1587) opened the list of works in the concerted style, followed in rapid succession by others. All varieties of vocal music were eager to appropriate the new concerto manner, and a profusion of *madrigali concertate, concerti d'amore, motetti concertate, messe concertate,* and all other imaginable combinations appeared. They were soon supplanted, however, by the so-called "ecclesiastic" or "sacred" concerto as inaugurated by Viadana, and later developed or rather merged into the cantata. The latter was still called "concerto" in preference to "cantata" when J. S. Bach wrote his many works in that field.

Instrumental music soon rallied to the new style, and it was again Giovanni Gabrieli who showed the way by transmitting the principles of polychoral writing to the orchestra. His double orchestra maintained itself far into the eighteenth century; we find it in J. S. Bach's St. Matthew Passion, in Hasse's operas, and in the early symphony. From its very beginning the concerto principle implied the opposition of dissimilar bodies of instruments or voices. The difference could be either in size or in color. Thus Gabrieli's orchestral "sonatas" displayed a choir of higher-toned instruments alternating with a group of deep-toned instruments, such as cornets and high trombones *versus* bass trombones; there were similar compositions opposing stringed instruments to wind choirs; or an instrumental choir to a vocal ensemble. The concerto found an especially grateful field in the opera aria, where the rivalry was keen when a voice opposed its coloratura passages to the equally brilliant runs of a flute, trumpet, or oboe, but the same is true to a lesser degree with regard to chamber music for mixed instruments. The development of the new style was at first tentative; the composers sought to assimilate the "stile moderno," as the concerto was called, with the contrapuntal frame of the existing instrumental forms.

The representative form of early baroque instrumental ensemble music was the *canzon da sonar,* or "play chanson," which was the instrumental variety of the secular part songs of the High Renaissance. The modest beginnings of these instrumental chansons soon absorbed the effects of the polychoral concerted style of the Venetians. Originally written for four or five parts, these compositions now display eight, ten, twelve, and even sixteen parts, requiring the combination of a small orchestra. By 1600 the canzone was so firmly established in both keyboard and ensemble music as a form of instrumental music that the epithet *da sonar,* "to be played," was omitted. Together with the ricercar, which had already asserted its independence, the canzone developed such varieties and cross-species as the fantasia and capriccio, the latter two in their turn evolving a mixed form called "sonata." The seventeenth-century sonata has nothing in common with the species as we know it since Beethovenian times; the term signified merely the purely instrumental nature of such compositions and no specific formal structure was attached to it. Recalling the remarkably neat form of the French chanson—which we must constantly remember—it is not surprising to find that it was the canzone which first showed a regular periodic formal structure, and it was not long before the first signs of symphonic principles in the modern sense of the word, thematic development as established by Frescobaldi in keyboard music, appeared. Indeed, we are dealing in the canzone with one of the far ancestors of the classical symphony. The term "symphony," or rather *sinfonia,* is in fact present in the early seventeenth century; it was at first frequently applied to vocal compositions (*sacrae symphoniae*), such as motets with orchestral accompaniment, but soon it came to designate the instrumental introduction to these vocal works and especially to operas. In this fashion the term was used for another century, and we still find many of J. S. Bach's cantatas opening with a *sinfonia.* Gabrieli's spirit animated the first opera symphonies, but Monteverdi, Cavalli, Cesti, and Landi knew how to endow them with their own personality. After Monteverdi, the "curtain raisers" seem to be somewhat uncertain both in form and in name and were called interchangeably sinfonia, toccata, sonata, and several other terms, but toward the middle of the century the sinfonia took on a definite, well-organized form henceforth reserved for its own use. These symphonies were real overtures, as they endeavored—especially the Venetian opera symphonies—to give a condensed picture of the drama they prefaced. As a rule the main thematic material was selected from among the main scenes of the opera. Not sufficiently known to older historians, these mid-seventeenth-century Venetian opera symphonies have acquired great importance in the eyes of the modern musicologist, not only because they constitute another prime source of origin of the classical symphony, but also because they were the first real program overtures. Thus Gluck will have to relinquish the position of "inventor" of the program overture, a title which he never claimed but which was generously awarded him.

The *sonata da camera* brings, finally, the question of the position of chamber music in this intricate multitude of names, styles, and forms. The principle of chamber music rests on the playing of the individual parts by a single instrument. In this connection the term "da camera," which we translate as "chamber," did not always have the significance we now attach to it. In the early baroque it meant any kind of music not destined for church or operatic use, and thus stood neither for a form nor for a style. Chamber music was obscured for a while by a none too closely defined orchestral practice, but similarly to opera and oratorio the paths of the two began to deviate, reaching, in the eighteenth century, a definite line of demarcation. The acoustic conditions in spacious churches demanded a much larger ensemble than was used for the more intimate chamber music works; moreover, if the violins were to hold their own against the sonorous brass instruments and organs they had to be used in numbers, several to a part. Here we are facing one of the important laws of modern orchestration, the doubling, in unison or octave, of parts. Chamber music, calling for the opposite procedure, effected a reduction in the number of both parts and players, thereby creating a form, the "trio sonata," which became the essence and symbol of baroque chamber music. While absorbing some of the dialectics of the concerto, the trio sonata developed undisturbed into a chamber music form par excellence, because the similarity of the two upper parts (the bass did not count from this point of view) precluded any concertizing. To the Italian mind some form of dissimilarity was essential to the concerted style, and the more the trio sonata gained in formal perfection the more homogeneous became its upper parts. The reduction in the number of parts at the same time prompted the composers to pay more attention to their conduct, which resulted in an increasingly contrapuntal treatment. The circle swung from polyphony to monody, and now music was on the second half of the semicircle, on its way to polyphony; but it was not to relinquish the harmonic foundations it had gained until the advent of the atonal schools of the twentieth century.

The first products of this new, more intimate music that we call chamber music are to be found in the works of Salomone Rossi (1587–1628), a musician of Jewish origin who himself always added "Ebreo" to his name. A colleague of Monteverdi in Mantua, he was one of the first to realize the significance of a true instrumental style, creating little masterpieces in his three-part "sonatas," which ushered in the new form of instrumental ensemble music, the trio sonata. An alert musician, Rossi was engaged in all forms and varieties of musical composition, but the next important figure to consider, Biagio Marini (c. 1597–1665), was a *bona fide* chamber music composer, and perhaps the first professional violin virtuoso among composers. The great variety of his published compositions that appeared between 1617 and 1655 mirrors the whole transition from the imitation of vocal music to genuinely instrumental forms. Thus from *arie, madrigali,* and *correnti* we proceed to *musiche di camera, sonate e sinfonie,* and *sonate da chiesa e da camera,* the latter first appearing as two distinct species. Among Marini's compositions there is an especially notable newcomer, the solo sonata for unaccompanied violin. A number of excellent musicians now joined Marini in building up the trio sonata, which reached its maturity in the second half of the century. Both the "chamber" and the "church" sonata were eagerly practiced by the many eminent violinists of the times. The number and tone of the individual movements reached a definite norm or arrangement and the formerly often rhapsodic character settled down to a logical order, especially in the church sonata, more elaborate and solemn than its sister, the chamber sonata, which with its stylized dance movements shows a similarity to the dance suite. The first of the four movements of the church sonata preserved the character of an introduction, probably owing to the simultaneous rise and development of the opera and cantata overture. The second movement, which may be considered the chief, is usually written in a solid, imitative contrapuntal style, while the third is given to a melodic outpouring of pathos, to be relieved by a fast-moving and spirited fourth movement, often in a dance form of sharp rhythmical steps. The chamber sonata exhibits a less systematic and developed form, but in its string of dance movements it perhaps gave the composer more freedom of contrast and expression. The plastic, classically rounded, and purely instrumental themes and forms, and the dance movements, distilled stylizations far removed from practical dance music, written by Giovanni Legrenzi and Archangelo Corelli (1653-1713), and by Maurizio Cazzati (c. 1620-1677), Giovanni Battista Vitali (1644-1692), Alessandro Stradella, Giuseppe Torelli (c. 1650-1708), and Giovanni Battista Bassani (1657-1716), set the model for a century of instrumental music.

All these composers, while perhaps equally important in the field of opera and cantata, were violinists and, as such, naturally closely allied with the destinies of their instrument and its literature. The master composer among them, who became the embodiment of classical Italian violin music and the one who united all the threads developed by his eminent colleagues, was Corelli. The complicated virtuoso writing of some of his contemporaries, especially the German violinists, with their forced polyphonic texture, double stops, and other effects, was alien to this great artist of the violin. His ideal was the sensuous expressiveness of the human voice; his melodies soar boldly and are filled with noble pathos, with a serious and sublime lyricism keeping a just balance between instrumental sonority and polyphonic construction. The same plastic and finely balanced quality permeates his forms. Experiment and search for form and expression are things of the past; all the effort of the seventeenth century to create an instrumental ensemble music is crowned in his monumental works.

Every art depends on its means of expression, and it is no accident that the great Italian school of violin composition flourished at the time when Stradivari, having finished his apprenticeship, found his own style. The wonderful instruments of the Cremonese school, brought to high perfection by the Amatis, were now even surpassed. Between 1684 and 1700 there took place the important change in Stradivári's craftsmanship, and the "Long Stradivarius" appeared about 1690, after which there was a steady broadening, developing, and arching of the instrument until it reached, in the first decade of the eighteenth century, that unsurpassable grandeur and symmetry which made the very name of Stradivari a symbol. Hand in hand with the growth of the instrument went a steady improvement in the technique of playing it. In this connection the animated operatic *accompagnato* placed serious demands on the players, who, in the sixteen eighties, were not accepted in the orchestra unless they had a sure command of playing in the fifth position. But already in Biagio Marini's time Carlo Farina, a much-traveled violin virtuoso, had works printed (1627) in which the playing in positions was required, together with double stops, pizzicato, tremolo, *col legno* (with the wooden part of the bow), and *sul ponticello* (close to the bridge in order to obtain the strange sounds resulting from the decreased vibration of the strings), that is, technical subtleties usually attributed to much later periods.

With Corelli we reach one of the most fascinating products of baroque orchestral music, the *concerto grosso*. While chamber music went its own way, disregarding the inroads of the concerted manner of composition, the first instrumental concertos, displaying the applied echo principle in the form of a small body of instruments opposed to a large one, appeared in the last quarter of the seventeenth century. But the definitive form of the concerto grosso is the creation of Corelli. Although published in 1712, his twelve Concerti Grossi, *opus* 6, were written and performed several years earlier. The universally accepted apparatus of the concerto—henceforth a form—is now the *concertino*, consisting of two violins and a cello or gamba, and the *concerto*, also called *ripieno*, that is, the whole orchestra. Although these magnificent works were written for church performance, they cannot entirely deny a certain operatic influence, and indeed not only Italian opera but the French opera overture also is represented in them in its original, easily recognizable, form. But what richness of sonority, and what variety of form and expression!—delicately stylized dances, wildly rushing allegros, pleasant drone basses, and broadly flowing largos. The eighth of the twelve concertos in *opus* 6 again became popular in modern times and is known as the *Christmas Concerto*.

The Vogue of the "Colossal Baroque"
Catholic Church Music

WHILE the personal disciples of Palestrina and those of his friend Giovanni Maria Nanino (c. 1545–1607) tried to uphold the great traditions of *a cappella* art, Catholic church music definitely turned its back on the past. In the atmosphere of constant excitement, every year bringing something fundamentally new and interesting into musical life, the "old" art vanished rapidly, although a few outstanding names were still held in reverence. But it was only their names that were revered and not their works, which had to bow before the taste and temper of the baroque. In general, classical choral polyphony was looked upon as a noble relic of the past. The musical setting of the Mass, formerly the highest form of art music, interested only a few composers, but, with the exception of Nanino's circle, these saw in the Mass and motet an excellent medium for colossal polychoral murals. Eight-, ten-, sixteen-, thirty-two-, and even forty-eight-part Masses were composed reflecting all the splendor of the baroque. The monumental choral works of Gabrieli, the polychoral *Sacrae Symphoniae,* represent the height of early baroque sacred art. The great body of singers was joined and supported by an orchestra of viols, trombones, trumpets, cornets, and organs, playing either independently or with the voices. This style, the so-called "colossal baroque," subsided, however, with the general penetration of the concerted style into church music, but not without producing a few truly breath-taking, gigantic works. Among these, the fifty-three-part festival Mass written for the consecration of the Cathedral of Salzburg by Orazio Benevoli (1628) is perhaps the most stupendous.[25]

The new concerted style was soon to appropriate the entire field of church music, a fact which seems a logical outcome of historic trends, but the rapidity with which it progressed is astonishing and illustrates the impetus of the new style. Monteverdi used the basso continuo in motets and a magnificent six-part Mass in 1610. The movement begun by Gabrieli was, then, being enriched by the musical language developed by early opera, because the dark brushstrokes, the dramatic pauses, the rhythmical contrasts, and the emphasis of the dramatic moments in the text betray the operatic origin. With the decline of choral polyphony and the disappearance of the cantus firmus new ways had to be found to retain the liturgic exterior of the Mass. It was at this time that the custom, still current, of dedicating Masses to saints was started. Another way of establishing connections with the liturgic plain chant was to begin the composition with a Gregorian intonation. These Gregorian citations were very popular and, presented first in their simple, unaccompanied original form, gave the baroque artists excellent opportunities to contrast them to the ornamented and highly elaborate structure of the finished composition.

The outspoken preference of the baroque for instrumental music was soon felt in church music, and the Ordinary of the Mass, as well as hymns and Psalms, were equipped with an organ accompaniment. The sudden appearance of musical instruments of all sorts in the church may have puzzled earlier historians, but when we look back upon the old custom of instrumental participation in vocal church music, interrupted occasionally by stern pontiffs but never suppressed for any appreciable length of time, we shall understand that all that was needed was a systematic organization of instrumental-vocal church music instead of an improvised and rather haphazard practice of accompaniment. Neither was the other important new musical device, the thorough bass, unknown to church musicians. We have mentioned above the widespread usage of a primitive basso continuolike practice of accompaniment as reported by Kinkeldey, and it is easy to understand that after Viadana's initiative every church organist was immediately able to reorganize his forces and embark on the organized practice of instrumentally accompanied church music.

A substantial part of the early concerted literature was composed expressly for church use. We know that Corelli, Tartini, and Vivaldi performed many of their works in churches, and, for that matter, the secular instrumental solos played by J. S. Bach during Communion, greatly inconveniencing the master's romantic panegyrists, were but an instance of this old practice. The serenades, berceuses, and songs without words that are played today in our churches by violin soloists accompanied by the tinkling chimes of the modern organ look back upon an old ancestry, though of a more elevated countenance, to be sure. The playing of solos in the church was considered an especially solemn affair, and a large number of the noble Italian violin sonatas were written for this purpose, to be played during the elevation of the Host to enhance the solemn moment. Organists often added a note to their organ compositions designating them to be played *alla levatione,* and Frescobaldi's chief collection, the *Fiori Musicali* (1635), was written for church services and played after the Credo and after Communion. There was a *maestro de' concerti* attached to the personnel of St. Mark's, and for many years the account books carried the salary of two violin players whose duty it was to perform the solo sonatas at appropriate occasions during the services. Masses were frequently preceded by a sinfonia or overture, not only in Italy but in Germany and France. All this corresponded naturally to the solemn pomp of the baroque era, which was especially at home in the church; the alternation of tutti and solo, of forte and piano, of light and shade, all contributed to the pomp and circumstance that the men of this age appreciated and expected to see in church and theater alike.

*

* *

THE historian of music and civilization marvels at the fullness and great artistic strength of church music of the baroque era, but his enthusiasm is seriously contradicted by the adverse opinion of many eminent and competent church musicians who hold that the old motto *ad maiorem Dei gloriam* was exchanged for *ad maiorem Musicae artis gloriam.*

Gravitas, a solemn and dignified tone, was reserved up to our day as a universal if questionable criterion of church style. But the musical elements and forms associated with the ideal of church music underwent constant changes, although always hampered by seemingly unavoidable retrospective tendencies. While this discrepancy was to occupy the northern, especially Protestant, countries for centuries and, in fact, the problem is as vivid today as ever,[26] the strong sense of the Italians for the actual, empirical problems of music, devoid of all metaphysical search, simple, happy, and always ready for practical and creative assertion, solved the question for them. They believed that the best music is the most appropriate homage to God. And yet true religiousness emanates from their church compositions, a religious spirit much more profound, much more sincerely felt than that which comes from the pseudo-archaic imitations of "modern" composers who conform their creative instincts to a well-meaning but dogmatic aesthetics of sacred art. It will remain, then, an open question whether music filled with true and sincere religious spirit but employing the technical means of expression, style, and dialectics of its own times does not impart a more immediate and powerful religious impression and feeling than an archaic music which is held in awe by tradition and intellectual associations.

Western Europe in the Early Seventeenth Century

THE seventeenth century dawned on western Europe heavy with unrest and political strife that had reached a point of crisis. The whole first half of the century was dominated by the gradually materializing united opposition to the world domination of Spain and the Habsburgs. One by one the European powers entered the fray, which, after Germany's terrible exhaustion, shifted to the north, embroiling all of northern Europe. The struggle ended with the victory of France over Spain and established French political hegemony in Europe.

The great European struggle was waged not merely for territorial and political gains: it also involved certain principles of universal importance. Spanish imperialism was the outcome of the spirit of the Counter Reformation and threatened not only the sovereignty of the rest of Europe but the orderly continuation of political thought, about to attempt a new formulation of state and government. A Spanish-Habsburg victory would have effectively destroyed the future intellectual and political freedom of European life. The chief factor in the defeat of Spain was French statesmanship, and a century and a half of activity, financial and diplomatic, against the Habsburgs was consummated when, led by Richelieu, France openly joined the enemies of the emperor and Spain in 1635.

During the twenty years spent at the helm of the government in France, Cardinal Richelieu (1585–1642) engaged himself in a ceaseless fight against all enemies of the crown. Particularists and clericals alike felt the power of this resourceful politician, the first representative of the idea of the sovereignty of the state and thereby the first advocate of monarchial absolutism in France and in Europe. The tendency toward royal absolutism, or rather toward a strong state, embodied in the power of the crown as opposed to the medieval institution of the estates, was a process long evident in Europe and was neither begun nor finished by Richelieu. But to Richelieu the absolute power of the crown was not an aim in itself; in his political philosophy the king was the first servant of the state. The modern conception of the state here comes into being, the state as a living entity, even more real than its ruler, who was often a mere symbol. Here begins, then, the process which was to link state and people, state and nation, in a close body politic.

The towering personality of Richelieu assured the victory of the new philosophy in almost all phases of French political life. The cardinal's remarkable faculties and political foresight are evident in his conduct of the campaign against Spain and the Habsburgs. With a bankrupt treasury and a tired army he had to proceed carefully. Knowing that, singlehanded, France had no hope against an enemy whose possessions stretched from Milan to Brussels, he tried to cement an anti-Habsburg block, at the same time encouraging local dissension among the German and Italian ruling princes. It was then that the much-abused word "liberty" started on its amazing career to remain the chief propaganda slogan to our day. The times of surreptitious diplomatic games having passed, open military intervention was unavoidable; Catholic France took over the conduct of the anti-Habsburg forces. The character of this gigantic feud now became clear; nothing less than the domination of Europe was at stake, a fact which could not be eradicated by the repeated attempts of the pope to reconcile the interests of the two Catholic camps. Political objectives were victorious over religious issues. The deaths of Richelieu and of Louis XIII (1642, 1643) did not change the political picture. The great cardinal did not live to see his work finished, but died with the assurance that Spanish might was mortally wounded and would not survive the middle of the century.

After 1643 the government of France was administered for the minor Louis XIV by his mother, Anne of Austria, and Mazarin (1602–1661), Richelieu's successor. Nothing could more appropriately illustrate the established political doctrine of *raison d'état* than the stewardship of the French state by an Italian and a Spanish woman. But their government rested on quicksand. Owing partly to the financial situation, which approached catastrophic proportions, and partly to the resistance of Parliament, well organized by financiers and officials of the emancipated middle classes which had so successfully opposed Richelieu's plans, the scarcely established absolutist power of the crown was threatened. The cry for *liberté* could not hide, however, the mere desire for selfish privileges, and, a similar desire being manifest among

the high nobility, the world was to witness the coalition of these two diametrically opposed parties in a final battle to wrest the power from the absolutist state. Twice a fugitive, the dogged Italian did not relax the reins; he
survived the great confusion and rivalry of statesmen, churchmen, and generals to see the victory of the crown. By 1653 the uprising was quelled, the
aristocracy bowed before the young king, Parliament was restricted to ju-
diciary functions and restrained from participation in politics and finance.
Thus at the same time when the *Reichstag,* sitting in Ratisbon, acknowledged
the dissolution of the German Empire, the French crown freed itself from
its last shackles; the authoritarian, unified state was fully established.

In its first stage, the absolutist state by no means exhibited the arbitrary
and violent traits we associate with the term; it showed the signs of a period
of transition in which the old mingled with the new. Diplomats, ministers,
and generals were still cautious, ready for compromise; the boundaries of the
rising absolutist states were not yet settled and statesmen and generals often
exchanged service in one state for another. Religious passion and superstition were still uppermost in the people's mind, and the great men who represented the new tendencies were lonely and isolated in their time; but the
forces of the modern world which are still active among us began to penetrate the world, and the terrible times of the Thirty Years' War and the great
struggle for European hegemony harbored in all spheres of human life,
state, economics, arts, and sciences, germs that prepared the coming of the
modern world.

Repercussions of the New Political Philosophy on Arts and Letters
The Louis XIV Style

ARTS and letters of the period mirror faithfully the general trend of civilization; they show the same increasingly nationalistic tendencies, although we
cannot yet speak of national cultures in the modern sense of the word, for
some of the greatest artists and scholars lived in foreign countries or worked
in the service of foreign states. Cultural life was also conditioned by the political withdrawal from the Church and from clerical influence. The divorce
from the denominational sphere of influence is visible in French arts and
letters, all striving for secularization. The reigning baroque style was still
in the service of the Church, but the erstwhile militant Catholic incentive
inspired by the Counter Reformation was considerably diminished. The
baroque retained all its love of splendor and ornamentation, but more as an
established artistic style of the courtly *grand siècle* than as an expression of
church thought.

The strong opposition of forces that characterized French political life of
the seventeenth century was equally present in her artistic life, yet there is

unmistakable evidence of the formation of a national French culture, a culture due largely to the new political thought. Richelieu's France had already resorted deliberately to the modern method of governmental paternalism as regards national culture. The aim was not merely to foster arts and letters but to influence them in accordance with the spirit of the state. The desire to control and marshal even artistic life in the absolutist state cannot be denied. In founding the French Academy—the first meeting of which took place in 1634—Richelieu wanted to organize a group of eminent literary men to put the house of national literature in order. It was supposed to regulate the language by a dictionary and a grammar, and the *belles lettres* by a system of rhetoric and poetics—a grave and dangerous aim. The extension of governmental authority was carried out inexorably in other fields as well. Jean Baptiste Colbert (1619–1683), Mazarin's successor as chief minister, is remembered in history for his establishment of manufacturing industries, giving them state aid and tariff laws, but imposing rigid legal regulations governing the qualities and prices of manufactured products. He also employed the same thorough method when dealing with agriculture or with the arts. Culture was restricted to the upper classes and took on a purely courtly nature. The large masses had no part in it; despised and neglected, they seemed destined to supply the revenues and labor for the glorification of the court and the privileged estates. The monarch's desires set the pace, and his tastes the style; hence the almost uniform character of arts and letters. The throne was surrounded by a multitude of men whose names are high in the annals of the world's literature and art, but their individuality was effectively thwarted, and only the greatest minds were able to safeguard their artistic freedom and integrity in this world which forced even nature to submit to order and regularity, as in the gardens of Versailles.

The divine position of the Roman emperors seems to have returned with Louis XIV. He was surrounded by a cult which elevated him above everyday existence. To serve the ruler was the most gratifying reward of a cowed nobility basking in the reflection of the aureole surrounding the Roi Soleil. A new vassalage was created: not that of free men rallying around the monarch, but of servants who considered it their duty to give up every vestige of personality to conform to the desires of their master. The middle classes, somewhat further removed from the court and the rules, froze to blind allegiance and were happy and content to admire the monarch and his aristocratic entourage from a distance, while the rest of the population had to be satisfied with unconditional obedience. Versailles is the symbol for French classicism of the seventeenth century and for the monarch himself. Here he reigned, supreme, in august majesty, unapproachable, the sun around which revolved courtiers, mistresses, ambassadors, artists, poets, and scholars. But the very uniformity of style, which reduced the number of geniuses to a handful, created national schools of arts, letters, and music. The infinitely polished language, clarity, logic, transparency, formal beauty, and courtly demeanor of this culture exerted an irresistible attraction upon the rest of the world. The political domination of Europe was completed by a cultural supremacy which made Paris the capital of the world.

At the beginning of the seventeenth century, French architecture, in an unsettled state, was under the influence of various foreign styles. With Colbert's energetic measures to discipline the arts and place them in the service of the crown, and with the unlimited means placed at its disposal by Louis XIV, architecture evolved a classical French style of its own. The palace in Versailles in the middle of a park with terraces, fountains, and walks arranged in the most sophisticated architectonic order, with flower beds and lawns covering every appropriate inch of soil, was the epitome of this new style. A cool, noble art it was, unapproachable to ordinary mortals, the ideal of an absolutist royal art. The sculptors and decorators, the cabinetmakers and tapestry weavers, the mosaic makers and goldsmiths contributing their services were all possessed by the same ideal and worked according to a definite program laid down in etchings that betrayed the same cleverness and clear conception of the style to be followed.

In due course the French baroque converted every particle of Italian influence into a Gallic style that obeyed only one impulse: reason. Royal protection and subvention was what made this art great and gave it its stamp, but it was not the king himself who created it. The socio-cultural forces set in motion by Richelieu and Mazarin produced the painter Mignard, the architect Le Bau, the sculptor Puget, the landscape architect Le Notre, before the king started his personal rule. What we call the Louis XIV style was in its fundamentals created by political thought and executed by these artists. Art coming from popular origins was spurned by the court, for the art of the *grand siècle* called for measured earnestness and polite correctness, majestic pomp and pathetic rhetoric, which gave it its classical imprint. Nicolas Poussin (1594–1665), Claude Lorrain (1600–1682), Eustache Lesueur (1617–1655), and Charles Le Brun (1619–1690) were the leading masters of this classicism, exerting a lasting influence on European art.

Poussin's canvases, somewhat pale in their invention, show a remarkably concise composition, though marred, occasionally, by too much insistence on correctness. But there is great idealism in his "heroic landscapes," a classic restraint which made him the idol of French painters for centuries to come. Although lacking in power and cold in color, Lesueur is distinguished for his admirable compositions, graceful, firm drawing, good taste, and sincere expression. Claude Lorrain, a master of the calm atmosphere of idealistic landscapes, carried further the bewitching charm of light effects developed by the landscape painters. The most typical representative of the classicistic art of the *grand siècle* was, however, Le Brun. As an artist he displayed an astonishing versatility, and his rare gifts of organization made him summarize his artistic powers in order to place them—in the spirit of his master Colbert—in the service of the court. As chief painter and artistic arbiter for Louis XIV he developed a grandiose style of interior adornment admirably suited to the splendor of the period.

The various academies discharged their duties well by maintaining an official standard to be respected by arts and letters. The more informal education of artists, writers, and public was taken over by the literary *salons,* which grew like mushrooms and created a literary world in which everyone carried pseudo-classical names, chattered, courted, displayed wit and elegance, sighed and wrote sonnets. It is difficult to conjure up this world and perhaps even more difficult to take its products seriously. Yet the same preciosity which was forever ridiculed by Molière had its assets; the cult of beautiful words, pleasant conversation, delicate verses, and witty letters educated and polished a society which had scarcely emerged from the darkest horrors of a merciless, bloody era. While preciosity remained the dominant tone and style—the great classical dramatists, Corneille and Racine, could no more liberate themselves entirely from this preciosity than their lesser confreres—the reaction it caused gave the world a Molière, a Scarron, and a Cyrano.

Music in the Grand Siècle

THE guiding theme of music in the *grand siècle* was marked by a constant decline of polyphony, inherited from the past century. The same forces seemed to be at work which caused the elimination of the great art of the Renaissance in Italy. The fact that surprises the student of history is the remarkably early and deliberate trend toward monody, a trend which seems to have antedated such symptoms in Italy. The old Gallic traits of the *nation chansonnière* again come to the fore in the songs and *airs* which appeared in the last third of the sixteenth century.

We have mentioned the activities of Baïf's Academy which showed a spirit of striking similarity to the Florentine Camerata. The poets and musicians of the Academy did not content themselves with reforming the *poésie chantée,* but intended to complete it by adding the dance, and thus to resuscitate the ancient drama. This *ballet chanté,* popular in the time of Henry IV, soon demonstrated that some dramatic elements had found their way into this type of musical entertainment. This first phase of the dramatic ballet was followed by the era of the *air de cour,* and until the middle of the century these courtly songs dominated the musical scene. The *air de cour,* starting in the sixteenth century, reached its classical formulation in the publication of Gabriel Bataille entitled *Airs en Tablature de Luth* (1608), the collection being continued by Antoine Boësset, Estienne Moulinié, and other musicians unconcerned with the learned dissertations of the distinguished members of the defunct Académie de Musique et de Poésie. There cannot be a question of humanistic origins in these songs, because the music is absolutely modern and, indeed, not lacking in a certain romantic touch. The *musique mesurée à l'antique,* the product of Baïf's Academy, attempted to safeguard the laws of Latin prosody, but the aesthetes and humanists were once more succeeded by real musicians who knew less about Plato and Aristotle, but understood how to employ all the subtleties of free musical composition and to achieve an extraordinary grace and rhythmic freedom. The parallel with Italian musical history which impresses the student ceases here, however, because while the Italian musicians used their hard-won freedom to build up an incomparable dramatic and orchestral literature, for the French this was the beginning of "an aesthetics of sensualism and hedonism" to which they were to remain unflinchingly attached through the Enlightenment, the Revolution, and Romanticism.

In addition to the more artistic *air de cour,* the chanson flourished with undiminished popularity. It was no longer the finely chiseled form of the Renaissance; the genres were many and the output copious. Love songs and their Latinized sacred paraphrases, *chansons à danser,* drinking songs of a bawdiness that defies the printing press, and *noëls,* Christmas carols converted from secular and operatic music—all these, fresh, spirited, elegant, lascivious, and superficial, formed the contents of the incredible number of publications.

This extensive song poetry could not, however, prevent the slow but steady intrusion of the theatrical into the realm of music. Ever since the early Middle Ages the theater had been a favorite entertainment in France. The performance of mystery and miracle plays, once a privilege of the clergy, passed into the hands of colleges and confraternities of players, which latter survived until the seventeenth century. Marionette plays and ambulant troupes could be found at every fair. Paris had a standing theater in 1600, and by the time of Richelieu it had two, l'Hôtel de Bourgogne and the Théâtre du Marais. The mystery plays declined rapidly, as the public wanted a more sophisticated entertainment, and the confraternities soon found it more profitable to rent their privileged rooms to regular actors' companies. Toward the end of the sixteenth century another great incentive spurred writers and actors toward better plays and performances: a number of Italian actors appeared and offered a serious rivalry to the French troupe currently playing in the old Hôtel de Bourgogne. As we may readily see, Molière practiced a profession that looked back on a long period of activity.

The turn toward dramatic treatment began with the celebrated *Ballet Comique de la Royne* (1581) and continued in the rejuvenated ballet known as *ballet de cour.* The *ballet de cour* hides under its simple title the French bid for the reconstruction of classical tragedy, for, besides the spoken parts and dances, these festive displays contained recitatives, songs, and choruses. At the beginning of the seventeenth century the spoken parts disappeared, and thereafter we are dealing with a French counterpart of the advanced rappresentazione. In conformity with the reigning social and political philosophy, the *ballet de cour* became a state institution, and the king and the peers of the realm did not disdain to take an active part in its performance before large audiences. Beginning with 1640 an overture opened the ballet, and, after a number of *entrées* consisting of dances, instrumental numbers, and choruses, the musicians of the king's band appeared on the scene to prepare for the appearance of the king and the princes of his house in the final *grand ballet* which climaxed the show. The many eminent Italians at the court, headed by the queen, Marie de' Medici, undoubtedly promoted interest in the dramatized ballet with suggestions and advice, as had Rinuccini and Caccini on their visit to Paris in the early years of the century.

Soon after assuming political power, Mazarin invited a little group of Roman singers to give opera performances in Paris. Since there are few references to these performances their success must have been restricted to the immediate circle of the court. The cardinal, anxious to acquaint France with the form of entertainment most admired in his native country—from its very beginning the entertainment of princes in Italy and consequently most suitable for the brilliant French court—sponsored two more operatic performances. In 1645 *La Finta Pazza* was given with lavish splendor, followed during the carnival of 1646 by Cavalli's *Egisto*. One more year and the tenacious statesman attained his aim. Luigi Rossi's *Orfeo,* performed on March 2, 1647, decided the fortunes of opera in France. Thus an Italian cardinal introduced opera into France, where it received an enthusiastic reception by the public at large—and was rejected almost unanimously by men of letters. Violent opposition arose from both religious and political quarters. The Sorbonne condemned the spectacles in the name of religion, and Parliament objected to them because of Mazarin's excessive expenditures, but neither could destroy the triumphal success of *Orfeo*. It is interesting to note that Rossi, the great Roman composer, did not belong to the group of singers imported by Mazarin but was one of the court composers of the Barberinis. The power of the Barberini family was shattered by the political revolution which followed the death of Urban VIII in 1644, resulting in the election of Cardinal Panfili to the pontificate. The new pope, Innocent X, an archenemy of the Barberinis, compelled the latter to go into exile in order to escape persecution. They fled to France, transferring their musicians, poets, artists, and their whole operatic establishment to Paris.

The victory of Italian opera, was, however, short-lived. With the Fronde the Italians saw themselves overwhelmed by the hatred which was directed at anything connected with Mazarin. Rossi's *Orfeo* had nevertheless brought about the foundation of the music drama in France. It exerted considerable influence also on the French theater in general. Its elaborate stage settings enticed dramatists to indulge in similar effects; Rotrou's *La Naissance d'Hercule* (1649) and Corneille's *Andromède* (1650) are good examples. As a matter of fact, the last-named play used the original machinery constructed for *Orfeo*.

Twenty years passed before opera began to show evidence that its roots had taken hold in French soil. Some of the eminent court musicians, Lambert, Boësset, Cambert, all great admirers of Rossi, made timid efforts toward continuing his work. They could not have succeeded in overcoming French prejudice against the music drama without the aid of a clever adventurer, literary man, diplomatist, and a frequent inhabitant of prisons, Pierre Perrin (c. 1620–1675). Profiting by his Italian sojourns, Perrin quickly realized the possibilities that lay in the presence of the Barberini group in Paris, and began to work on the creation of French opera. Associating himself with the composer Robert Cambert (c. 1628–1677), court musician to the dowager queen, he produced in April, 1659, in Issy, near Paris, a work which he entitled with his customary impudence *La Première Comédie Française en Musique Représentée en France: Pastorale,* etc. Cambert's score has been lost, but Saint-Evremond, who knew the musician, expressed little enthusiasm for his abilities.

Judging by these data, the Cambert-Perrin *Pastorale* must have been a very modest contribution to French opera, yet its success was tremendous. French chauvinism played an important role in this success. Perrin was too keen a politician not to capitalize on the prevailing anti-Italian sentiment, and reported with pride that "the spectators were passionately interested in seeing our poetry and music triumph over foreign music and poetry." Encouraged by this warm reception, Perrin then looked for a permanent institution to house his projects. On June 28, 1669, he finally received a privilege for the establishment of *académies d'opéra,* where musical performances in French could be given, in Paris and in other cities of the kingdom.[27] The new theater in Paris opened its doors on March 3, 1671, with the performance of *Pomone* by Perrin and Cambert. Its success was fantastic. A hundred and forty-five performances were given, a fabulous number in 1671. After *Pomone* came *Les Plaisirs de l'Amour,* and with it French opera was firmly established. Molière, the first to realize the possibilities of the new lyric theater, bought the royal privilege from Perrin (at that time spending one of his entr'actes in prison) and, beginning with *Les Fâcheux,* endeavored to unite comedy, music, and the dance, thus introducing a musical element into spoken comedy. He did not change the usual physiognomy of comedy but enveloped it with music. The power of music gave free rein to fantasy, making it possible for the great dramatic poet to finish the *Bourgeois Gentil-homme* and the *Malade Imaginaire* with unbounded Rabelaisian drollery. Had Molière lived longer and had not his experiments been thwarted by that omnipotent political intriguer, Lully, he might possibly have created the French opera buffa. But the presence of music in French comedy was still artificial. We are dealing here with a genius vastly different from the Italian, and should not be surprised to find at first adverse effects. In *l'Amour Méde-cin* we can see the changes brought about by the influence of opera. Molière does not give to the composition of the play his usual minute attention; he counts on the effects of music and the dance to make up for the shortcomings of the more or less improvised play.

Perrin, Cambert, and even Molière soon had to retire before a domineering personality who, Florentine by birth, French by education, yet truly Italian in nature, was to bring French opera to the height of the great and almost forgotten art of Cavalli and Cesti. Jean Baptiste Lulli (1632–1687), or Lully, according to the spelling he adopted in France, was a member of the royal band. At the beginning of his career he was not interested in opera, but wrote ballets, took part in performances as an actor, conducted the orchestra, and, most of all, kept a close watch on the events at court. In 1661 he succeeded in winning the appointment of "superintendent" of the king's music, which assured him a dominating position. At the court he came into contact with Molière and for ten years furnished the music for the comedies and ballets of the great playwright. Noticing the rise of Perrin's opera and seeing his friend Molière paying serious attention to this new form of art, the alert and intelligent Florentine immediately changed his attitude toward opera. It did not take him long to supplant all the other contenders. A secret visit to the prison which was still the home of Perrin assured him of the "abbé's" consent; a few ingenious diplomatic moves with the king, and Molière saw his privilege reduced to almost nothing. After Molière's death the last obstacle in Lully's path was eliminated and he obtained undisputed direction of the Académie Royale de Musique. The Grand Opéra in Paris still bears this title, with the "Royale" suffix changed to "Nationale" to suit the changed regime. Lully wanted, however, a thorough settlement of the situation. Perrin's aides were persecuted by the police; Perrin died in misery; Cambert, forced to retire, went to England and became court composer to Charles II, but was later mysteriously assassinated; and finally, Molière's troupe was driven out of the Palais Royal, which became the seat of Lully's Academy. From this time on (1672–1673) the Florentine was absolute master of the situation.

But this sinister schemer, brilliant businessman, and real estate dealer who gathered up a fortune estimated by Ecorcheville to exceed seven million francs, this inveterate Don Juan who, from his southern home, brought with him, like his compatriot Mazarin, an innate ability for smooth and clever diplomacy, imperative manners, supercilious disdain, and the desire to conquer life entirely, was a musician and artist endowed with supreme gifts. His association with Molière made him a master of the stage, an accomplishment entirely missing in the works of his predecessors. His style has convincing clarity and luminous order, both classical French traits. Lully's works were not called operas but lyrical tragedies, *tragédies lyriques mises en musique,* or simply *tragédies.* His achievement was the creation and development of the form and language of the lyric tragedy, the French opera. He could not have achieved his aims without a truly dramatic temperament and rich imagination, part of his Italian heritage, but the means he used derived from the old traditions of French language and literature. The melodic line of his vocal parts was born from the inner laws of the French language; the rise and fall of his declamation was the result of minute and sensitive coloring of the natural accent of French words. This melodic musical declamation had an intricate rhythm because the composer did not follow the stereotyped formulae of the verses, but analyzed the finer rhythmical pattern of the single words.

French classical drama served Lully as a model. A keen observer, he went to the theater, consulted actors, noted their use of accents and pauses, studied the dialogues, and carried his research into the smallest details. Racine produced *Bérénice, Bajazet, Mithridate, Iphigénie,* and *Phèdre* the same year that Lully began to write operas. The great dramatist must have exerted a powerful influence on this intelligent musician; the expressive dramatic power of his recitatives, not surpassed even by Gluck, shows it clearly. By associating himself subsequently with the eminent if somewhat dry and precious dramatic author, Philippe Quinault (1635–1688), Lully proved how well he realized the importance of the drama in opera. Deliberately falling back on the art of the great Venetian opera composers, he tried to give a musical form to the language of his adopted country. Like Peri, Lully endeavored to shape his music by means of clear and expressive words, but he wanted more than clear words, and like the great Italians, and later Gluck and Wagner, he desired an appropriate and adequate dramatic action. The character scenes which abound in his operas, as well as the orchestral pieces or symphonies, represent lyrical pictures rich in full-bodied and heroic colors, and lived for a century as unalterable types. By including chansons, ballets, and other short pieces in his dramatic action he followed the musical traditions of the French court. Unlike the contemporary Italian orchestra, Lully's orchestra was constantly gaining in color and suppleness, and with the so-called French overture he opened new paths for instrumental music.

In his search for true musical expression, this earnest musical dramatist prohibited the singers from executing extemporaneous embellishments, which he considered ridiculous and distracting, and took care of the most minute changes in declamation or singing by employing frequent changes in the prevailing rhythmic order. Where his Italian colleagues usually adhered to the first rhythmical pattern indicated at the beginning of the aria, leaving the changes to be effected by the singer, he prescribed the course of every note and every accent. In his lifetime he was able to guard the expressive clarity and nobility of the lyric tragedy, but after his death the thousand little embellishments and mannerisms, rampant in intimate music as in interior decoration, found immediate admission into the opera.

If Lully went to the Théâtre Français in order to study the correct declamation of the great dramatic actors, it was for a short time only; then the roles changed. The famous actors, in their turn, attended Lully's Academy, the members of which were considered "the greatest actors and the most perfect models for declamation that have ever appeared on the French scene." [28] Lully's reputation and glory were immense. Italian, German, and English musicians came to study with him, and his music, the confluence of many musical rivers, became the universal language of Europe. In this as in many other traits, the Florentine resembles Gluck, whose art was of a composite nature; but the elements in Gluck were truly cosmopolitan: German, Italian, English, and French, whereas Lully's elements were—disregarding his Italian origin—exclusively French. France could claim no other musician as her son with as much right as she could this Italian who became the embodiment of the spirit of the *grand siècle*.

The Fundamental Opposition of French Thought to Opera

OPERA became the most popular form of theater in France and the great classical tragedy entered into a state of decadence. Poets and dramatists became librettists and turned away from the noble art of Corneille and Racine as the same signs of operatic infatuation began to appear that followed in the wake of opera in Italy. The artistic taste of both the writers and the public seemed to follow naturally the decadence of the classical drama and its conversion into opera.

The influence of the tragédie lyrique caused profound changes in the structure of spoken tragedy. When gods and other superhuman figures entered into the action, their appearance (*descente*) not only called for an elaborate scenic mounting but created unforeseen accidents and denouements which were not the result of the conflicts or passions of the characters, as was the case in the tragedies of Racine. In place of the diminishing human psychology, another sort, fictitious and "divine," was introduced into tragedy proper through opera, creating an artificial atmosphere, an emotional "no man's land" which occasionally reached complete diffuseness in a cloud of words and music. Finally, the tragédie lyrique abandoned the sacred rules of the three unities as the opera libretto introduced secondary, episodic figures to enhance the variety of the spectacle.

The classical theater regulated the number of figures and scenes very carefully. An examination of Corneille's and Racine's tragedies will show a definite ratio between the number of scenes and the number of acts. With the development of the tragédie lyrique the number of scenes grew, for without the addition of extra scenes, the scantier dramatic material of the opera would not have provided legitimate opportunities for all the arias desired. The librettist could not interrupt the recitatives for the sake of arias, because such a procedure would have ruined the drama completely. Therefore he added extra little scenes to the end of each "legitimate" scene by giving an aria to every person as he left the stage. This resulted in an increase of movement on the stage, and the figures of the drama went in and out so as to create opportunities for arias. This procedure was responsible for the decline of the remarkable structure of classical tragedy, for from the lyrical tragedy the custom passed in a short time into tragedy proper. The new conception of artistic "freedom," so different from the measured, sedate beauty of the classical tragedy, gained recognition in a remarkably short time. Dramatists and composers indulged in a courtly art, an art of opportunism; they cultivated the tastes of their patrons and exercised great care when presenting innovations, disguising them in some way in order to avoid the public's disapproval. The period after Lully's death, up to the appearance of Rameau, presents all the aspects of a period of transition. On the one hand, it was dominated by the heritage of Lully, oppressing the imagination of every musician; on the other, Italian influence began to assert itself, taking a position opposite to that of the established French opera. The successors of Lully composed in a style which varied with every composer. Some of them, gifted musicians like André Campra (1660–1744) and his pupil André Cardinal Destouches (1662–1749), were able to sustain some of the splendid qualities of Lully's lyrical tragedies. Louis XIV declared repeatedly that Destouches was the only musician who could fill Lully's vacant place. Nevertheless, French opera was doomed unless a superior genius should come again to its rescue.

Viewed in retrospect, and eliminating Lully, the shining light of the classical music drama in France, we cannot help noting the fundamental opposition of French thought to opera. French opera is, more than any other form of the theater, an expression of decorative art; the decorative effect is its immediate aim. It joined the other arts, so effectively guided by Colbert and Le Brun, in enlivening and decorating the court. The searching for effect forms the basis of the ideas of the French artist. This tradition, unfailingly present in their operas from the very beginning, utilizes all elements employed in the theater by keeping in mind stage effects, singing, instrumentation, the dance, and scenic mounting. One might be inclined to say that the Wagnerian principles, elevating poetry, music, and scenery to the same rank, are not substantially different. We shall see, however, that the overpowering predominance of his orchestra effectively destroyed the highminded aesthetic doctrines of the German master, whereas French opera failed because it consented to an abusive predominance of the decorative element and neglected the essential condition of art, sincere emotion. Nothing can be substituted for it, least of all *reason,* the universal refuge of French opera composers and librettists. Abbé François Raguenet, author of a work that was widely read and was translated into English and German a few years after its appearance (1702), gave an appraisal of French music of the *grand siècle* which, while harsh and pointed, bears out the views of the more dispassionate modern historian: "The Italians find our music sleepy, flat, and insipid. . . . Indeed, the French are always seeking the sweet, the facile, the smooth, and the secure; everything is held in the same tone; or, if the tone is changed occasionally, it is done with careful preparations so as to make the following *air* a natural sequel to the foregoing, as if nothing had been changed in it. There is nothing fiery or audacious about this music, it is even and unified." [29]

Lute and Harpsichord Music

BJÖRNSON'S sarcastic remark that the intellectual life of France is surrounded by a Chinese wall, perhaps even more true of the past than of the present, is nowhere more evident than in the delicate, elegant, ravishing, witty, but rather shallow art of instrumental music. Foreign elements, as in the case of opera, are admitted, but only after they have been assimilated with the traditions and tastes of the French, after which they continue their existence as naturalized subjects, showing scarcely a trace of foreign accent.

The noble and delicate *esprits* who populated the salons could think of nothing more delightful than listening to the silvery chords of the beautiful lutes that came from the workshops of the *luthiers* (a name retained by violin makers even after the disappearance of the favorite instrument of the age of Louis XIV). Anne of Austria was not less fond of playing the lute than were the famous *femmes galantes,* Marion Delorme, whose house was the meeting place for the enemies of Mazarin, and Ninon de Lenclos, who numbered among her lovers such eminent men as Condé, La Rochefoucauld, and Saint-Evremond. Beginning with the *Trésor d'Orphée* (1600) of Antoine Francisque (c. 1570–1605) and the *Thesaurus Harmonicus* (1607) of Jean Baptiste Bésard (c. 1567–?), two excellent anthologies of music from the turn of the century, the publications increased rapidly. Toward the end of the first quarter of the seventeenth century French lute virtuosi acquired a world-wide reputation which attracted many foreign musicians to France. The leading masters among the many good players and composers were the Gaultiers, forming a distinguished dynasty of lute players, many in number and not easy to identify individually. Denis Gaultier (c. 1603–1672) was the most famous of the lot. The tendency toward stylized and organized dance music is crystallized in his works, almost exclusively dance pieces arranged in a suite consisting of *prélude, pavane, courante* (usually several of them), and *sarabande* or *gigue*. Besides establishing the modern French dance suites, Gaultier gave in his lute books precise instructions concerning the technique of the instrument and the interpretation of the ornaments which were beginning to engulf French music.

The embellishments came, most probably, from the English keyboard school and were transplanted to the Continent by the celebrated English musicians in the services of Continental rulers, as well as by Frenchmen long resident at the English court, such as Pierre Gaultier, called the English Gaultier. These embellishments reached, in the form of grace notes, appalling proportions in the second half of the century. As early as 1636 Mersenne, in his *Harmonie Universelle,* cited a perplexing number of *tremblements* (shakes), *accents plaintifs* (sighs), trills, vibrations, *battements* (throbs), which with their innumerable variants minced up the musical line effectively. The *style brisé,* "broken style," of the Gaultiers was eagerly taken up by the many good lute players and composers who succeeded the celebrated family of lutenists. Jacques Gallot and Charles Mouton, both active in the second half of the century, were the outstanding artists of this, the last phase of lute music in France.

Gradually being supplanted by the more sonorous instruments made popular by the opera orchestra, the lute declined and passed, but not without leaving behind the romantic perfume of a sophisticated, if somewhat effeminate, parlor art. Having engendered the dance suite, the system of embellishments which was to dominate instrumental music for generations, and the fine little miniatures, the *tombeaux, dialogues, larmes,* and other musical portraits and genre pieces, lute music was responsible for the first orientation of the *clavecin* or harpsichord art, about to appear with a literature that expresses the essence of French musical art of the century.

At first completely under the spell of the lute, the clavecin literature never entirely outgrew that "vague charm" which characterized lute music. Jacques (Champion) Chambonnières (c. 1602–1672), issue of a family of noted organists, was the master of the musicians we call the "clavecinists." Louis Couperin (1625–1661), François Couperin (1631–1703), not to be confused with his kin, the great clavecinist of the next era, Jean d'Anglebert (c. 1628–1691), Nicolas Antoine le Bègue (1630–1702), and Guillaume Gabriel Nivers

(1617–1714) were the better known composers of the French harpsichord school. They were all clever and elegant musicians, writing in a vaporous and inconsistent style; delightful, to be sure, but promising more than they could fulfill. Their delicately thin ideas, their subtle and pleasant tittle-tattle, are dispersed by the slightest zephyr. The printed score gives us an incomplete picture of the compositions, for they too were embellished by a continuous string of grace notes, the importance of which becomes clear if we translate *agréments,* the technical term by which they were known. These musical trimmings provided the grace and ornament which in those times counted for the essence of art, for those were the days when people's highest aim was to emulate the dances, compliments, laces, silk stockings, and lorgnettes, in a word, the *galanterie,* of the court. The literary currents found an immediate echo in this music. The publication of La Rochefoucauld's *Maximes* (1665) and La Bruyère's *Caractères* (1688) introduced a new element into literature, moral and psychological observation, the literary portrait. The usual literary orientation and approach of the French musicians enticed them to imitations; thus the lutenist Jacques Gallot composed a work entitled *Le Tombeau de Madame,* which was a musical eulogy upon the death of the Duchess of Orléans, and as such a counterpart to Bossuet's *oraison funèbre* written for the same purpose. Similarly the clavecinists gave distinctive titles to many of their innocuous little dances, but there cannot be any question here of program music, because the pattern remained always the same whether the piece was called *La Coquette, La Pastourelle, Harlequin,* or *La Petite Mère.*

The polished and effortless elegance of the French dance suite made it the envy of the world, and by 1670 musicians of all nations adopted it, with its *allemande, courante, sarabande,* and *gigue.* While the form was the same, French keyboard and lute music—this essentially miniature art did not produce chamber or orchestral music—could not be compared with the magnificent instrumental suites of England, Italy, and Germany; like opera, clavecin music was to mark time until the great masters of the eighteenth century should come to its rescue and endow it with ideas, sentiments, and passions.

The Thirty Years' War

PROTESTANT Germany, split into Lutheran and Calvinist camps, watched with grave apprehension the steady gains made by the Counter Reformation. Prevented by petty quarrels from forming a unified front against the victorious Catholic forces, Protestantism at the opening of the seventeenth century was on the defensive in all border states. Opposed to this helpless group stood the Catholic forces led by Archduke Ferdinand of Styria (1578–1637), later the Emperor Ferdinand II (1619–1637), and Duke Maximilian I of Bavaria (1573–1651). Both were born into the atmosphere of

Austrian and southern German Catholic royalty, Jesuit trained, faithful to the Church, right or wrong, and determined to carry the fight to its bitter end. As soon as Ferdinand became of age he embarked on a campaign that started with the revocation of the religious privileges formerly accorded to the Protestants and would have resulted in cruelly severe measures had not the Turkish invasion kept most of the south of Germany occupied with defense operations. Once crowned emperor, Ferdinand decided to emulate his great ancestor, Charles V, by suppressing the Protestants and at the same time fortifying his rule over the German princes; Germany was plunged into a struggle that was to last for decades.

The war would have petered out had not the many issues, territorial, dynastic, and economic, fanned the fire of religious discontent. There ensued a war with shifting alliances and local peace treaties, and the whole conflagration turned out to be a conflict of petty German princes against the unity of the Holy Roman Empire, and against the Habsburgs themselves. What had at first seemed a war for the freedom of religion developed into the final stand of the Habsburgs and Spain for world supremacy, challenged and contested by France, Sweden, Denmark, and England, who joined the Protestant princes of Germany; and the war was fought in Austria, Bohemia, Germany, Italy, the Netherlands, and Spain. How secondary the religious aspect was with the people can be seen from the method of warfare. The military came from both denominations and could be found on either side, looting their own coreligionists without hesitation or pity. There was also France, a great Catholic power, not only siding with the Protestant belligerents and calling even on the Turks for aid, but claiming and assuming diplomatic, and later military, leadership in the anti-Habsburg bloc.

A new phase of the war started when Christian IV of Denmark, fearful of the rise of Habsburg power in north Germany, decided to take up arms against the emperor. England gave a subsidy to aid the opponents of the Habsburgs and sent a few thousand soldiers. King Christian was met and defeated by the most enigmatic of all leaders in the great war, Wallenstein, the Lutheran-born but Jesuit-trained imperial general. The Habsburg and Wittelsbach troops now occupied all of northern Germany, and the forcible Catholicizing of the region started with the same vigor that had characterized the earlier movement in the southern provinces.

Almost the whole of Germany now lay at the emperor's feet; no ruler since the times of the Hohenstaufen had held such overwhelming power. The political import of the war now came clearly to the fore, and the imperial party took up the initiative. The emperor's military forces appeared in Poland, the Low Countries, and Italy, but while their military successes were slight, the antagonism they created was considerable, and the Habsburgs were confronted with powerful opposition from the ranks of their own allies.

Meanwhile the emperor had been prevailed upon to dismiss Wallenstein, who had many enemies in the empire. The high command of the army was now given to the unswervingly loyal Catholic general, Tilly, the best soldier of the old school. But the veteran fighter had to face a great captain of the new school at the head of the finest troops in Europe. Gustavus Adolphus (1594–1632), believing that the establishment of a strong Catholic power in the southern Baltic would threaten Swedish religious and commercial independence, determined to protect his dominions by an offensive campaign. Tilly and Gustavus, the representatives of the old and the new art of war, met in the Battle of Breitenfeld (1631) and the highly disciplined, modern army of the brilliant king-general crushed the irregular mercenary troops of the grizzled imperial field marshal.

The king's victory raised Sweden to the rank of a great power, and Gustavus Adolphus, who had thus saved the cause of Protestantism, determined to carry the doctrine throughout the Holy Roman Empire. Never in world history has one man achieved conspicuous and far-reaching success with such small means. France, the Low Countries, and Venice, all recognizing the exceptional military genius and earnest moral integrity of the great and youthful King of Sweden, offered financial help. Then Wallenstein, hastily recalled by the emperor, met the Swedish king in Lützen, near Leipzig, and although the Swedish forces were victorious, the king was mortally wounded. Wallenstein's subsequent elimination made again possible a unified Bavarian-Spanish-imperial army command, and the Protestant forces led by Bernhard of Weimar were defeated. But Germany was completely ruined, her population decimated, and her natural resources destroyed. Blood-soaked and suffering terrible privations, the country was not permitted to rest, for it was at this point that Richelieu decided to take up the sword openly against the remaining power of the Habsburgs and Spain. This represented the beginning of the last phase of the war, which ended with the break-up of the world domination of the Habsburgs. The Holy Roman Empire became a mere shell in the succeeding centuries.

The dissolution of the old German Empire was consummated in the Thirty Years' War, but the great war was the sequel to this decline, not the cause of it; it was the final act of a drama that started in the sixteenth century. The political decline of the nation was furthered by the undermined structure of economic life. German trade was supplanted by foreign interests, German agriculture has never kept pace with developments in other countries, and the guilds clung to their organizations, although these medieval institutions were manifestly archaic. All this corresponded to the intellectual stagnation of the nation, lost in the ever-narrowing provincialism of the small states. While certain important centers of trade and industry, Hamburg, Frankfort, Leipzig, and Augsburg, still maintained their international importance, the absence of a protective, organized German state prevented a sound economic life, while the intellectual riches of the country were dispersed in the fruitless religious strife that culminated in the Thirty Years' War.

The Catholic world was the loser in the struggle in Germany, for its aim, the spiritual and political conquest of the Protestant world, was never reached. Formerly disunited, Protestantism emerged fortified from the carnage, realizing the values of its new life and capable of transforming itself into a spiritual power equal to its antagonist. The former harmony of Rome and Wittenberg, permitting Protestants and Catholics to live as neighbors, at least tolerant if not very friendly, disappeared as the denominational differences became deeper and the bitterness reached the multitude of the population. The struggle was carried from the pulpit and the theological faculty to all other branches of intellectual life, especially into arts and sciences. Nothing was done, said, written, or printed in the seventeenth century without leaning on divine authority; but every religious party had its own God. Thus the whole cultural life of Germany was split and the cultural intercourse of the two large sections of Germany, the Protestant north and the Catholic south, remained clouded until fairly recent times and, as we shall see, this state of affairs was responsible for seemingly inexplicable paradoxes in the history of arts and letters.

The political uncertainty and lack of orientation is perhaps even more responsible for the failure of German culture in this period, and it opened the doors to foreign influences. Relieved of their former unity, never too closely defined but still kept alive by the imperial idea, the individual members of the empire now started to build up their sovereign states. Austria, Brandenburg-Prussia, and Bavaria were the three large states, surrounded by a number of smaller principalities. But the old generation of ruling princes was gone; a new type, fascinated by the splendor of Versailles and its master, lending a willing ear to the *grande dames* made glamorous and fashionable by their French prototypes, and passionately interested in the new art of European diplomacy, took their place. In their eagerness to emulate Louis XIV they never stopped to wonder whether his armies, court opera, academies, and other expensive institutions could be supported by a small state, and often indulged in imitations that verged on the grotesque, some of the smallest princelings even aspiring to colonies. There were, however, a number of rulers who administered their domains for the welfare of their subjects, and princely paternalism left a profound impression on German cultural life. While the founding of academies and universities was not always prompted by a sincere desire to further arts and letters, and served more to enhance the rulers' prestige, these institutions had the wholesome effect of decentralizing culture and spreading it to all parts of the country. This became a powerful factor in the future intellectual eminence of Germany, whereas France was never able to offset the dominating position of intellectual life centralized around the capital. There was not, of course, any question of a unified German artistic style. Versailles, actually and symbolically, led the foreign influence, but the north looked also toward Holland, while the Catholic south was fascinated by the Italian baroque.

The Reformation did not prove to be a creative force in German art, and the ravages of the war extinguished the little original activity that had been going on at the beginning of the century. "German art was stricken from the annals of the history of art," and almost the whole of the century passed under the dominating influence of foreign art: Italian in the south, and French and Dutch in the north. Nor was the spirit of the Reformation more favorable to literature. Its poetic influence lasted only as long as Luther's fervor flamed behind it. Its forces were diverted by the work of organization, polemical discussions between the leaders, and warring on the dissenters. What was left was consumed by the Thirty Years' War, and its living content was narrowed down to theology. Under the influence of French, Italian, Spanish, and English literature, the German poets and writers slowly recaptured their own tone, that of the latent Gothic. But this was a Gothic stifled by the new rationalism, which, emanating from France, tended to extinguish every irrational force and, in the name of reason, reorganized nature, society, and life.

The old uncertainty was abolished, but what appeared to be order and balance hid an elemental tension which came to the fore when the Thirty Years' War forced its baroque spirit on Germany. Every latent dissension and passion then came to the surface, and where there were no old dissensions, new ones were created. The Counter Reformation introduced the animated theatrical spirit of the Spanish-Italian baroque into the German world, but what created new and ecstatic forms in the Romanic baroque was not easily assimilated by German blood, and increased the already marked tension. The opposition was strongest in the fine arts; poetry, with its intellectual orientation, made good use of the ornaments that accompanied the baroque, but was lacking in that magic power which pervaded the Romanic world. The baroque cannot thrive without a religious background. The stern dogmatism of the Protestant world rejected the Romanic baroque because it identified it with Catholicism. The leading poet of the first third of the century, Martin Opitz (1597–1639), has probably not a single poem that came sincerely and frankly from his heart, but he started modern German secular poetry, organized the German language, and diligently introduced every form of poetry that was popular in the countries which had profited by the rich harvest of the Renaissance. But soon the poets abandoned the cold, autonomous art of Opitz and began to show the effects of the merging of their essentially Germanic "Faustian" spirit with that of the baroque. There were among them gentle dreamers, like Paul Gerhardt (1607–1676), the purest representative of Protestant lyric poetry of the German baroque, whose poetry was permeated by devotion, piety, and religious optimism. "A mighty fortress is our God," thundered Luther, ready for the battle; "I praise Thee with heart and hand," sang Gerhardt in his quiet hymn. Angelus Silesius (Johannes Scheffler, 1624–1677) gave a lyrical summation of the age-old German mysticism in his greatest work, *Der Cherubinische Wandersmann*. But as soon as he leaves the domain of metaphysics his eyes are beclouded and he shows the German's essential forlornness in this baroque world. His contemplation loses its sincerity and then he resorts to the theatrical pomp of the baroque to preach the love of the Crucified.

But the pictorial-musical element—essential baroque in nature—showed the poets the way. It is astonishing to see how far music penetrated this poetry; music, which was to become the embodiment, the only true form of expression, of the German baroque. Even the *da capo* form was used in poetry, taken over bodily from the musical form of the aria. Hans Jacob Christoffel von Grimmelshausen (c. 1625–1676), the great storyteller, was among the first to assert this German baroque spirit, but the elemental sweep of the baroque was reached in the poetry of Andreas Gryphius (1616–1664), the most notable secular lyric poet of the German baroque. Many of Gryphius's poems are veritable dark torrents of words, only toward the end becoming illuminated by a ray which dissolves the darkness. This is the technique of Rembrandt. And now, when we are standing at the threshold of modern German literature and art, music joins and surpasses them, to take over the European leadership, and to rise in the two succeeding centuries to a supremacy as undisputed and imposing as had been the reign of the Netherlanders and Italians in a previous time. It was in music alone that German culture showed a steady advancement, a logical and growing development comparable only to the fine arts of ancient Greece.

The Musical Baroque in Germany

IN Italy and France opera was in the forefront of musical life; but the rank and file of Germans, deeply distressed by the religious wars, turned to religious music. The specific character of Protestant Christianity shaped this music, and the congregation formed the point of departure. Congregation-consciousness speaks with convincing force in the Protestant chorales, which form the basis of this whole art, and in the cantatas and oratorios which are the greatest treasures of Protestant church art. But they are more than art; they give an elementary interpretation of the words of the Bible, the essence of Protestant thought. The church was for the Protestant people of the central and northern German states an asylum, the symbol of protection, and within it they found solace. The solemn music they heard there gave them their much-desired illusion of the peaceful existence in the hereafter, and they did not spare the little money they had left to maintain and foster this soul-saving music. Many an organ was built with community contributions in the trying years of postwar reconstruction. The consecration of each new instrument was an occasion for great rejoicing, and people from all near-by communities took part in the celebration. If the congregation was too impoverished to afford the building of an organ, a music lover fortunate enough to possess an instrument would willingly place it at the disposal of the congregation. The smaller churches were often served entirely by amateur musicians recruited from the ranks of the citizenry, who participated, not only for their love of music but because, being faithful Lutherans, they were convinced that such music is for the glory of God and for the benefit of the congregation. The history of the singing societies (*Kantoreien*) and *collegia musica* demonstrates how eager were the musically educated amateurs to get together and make music in the church. The universal popularity of church music is explained also by the fact that the church was the only place in which any elaborate music was performed, because it took the reorganized or newly formed German courts considerable time before they could emulate the example of Versailles and Vienna, and even after they succeeded in creating and restoring chapel choirs and court orchestras the great majority of the population never had an opportunity to attend the performances. As to opera, it was the entertainment of princes, *ex officio*. The citizens who wanted to hear good music were thus limited to the church, and therefore they gladly sacrificed time and money for their church music.

The pure recitative style did not gain ground so rapidly in Germany as in Italy, but Viadana's works were well known and reprints of his Ecclesiastic Concertos appeared beginning with 1609, providing the German composers with a model they followed willingly. *Sacrae symphoniae, Geistliche Concerte,* became very popular and it was this branch of the monodic style which first acquired citizenship in the north. But the genius of Gabrieli also demanded attention, and the "colossal baroque" found a ready response among German composers, and in its Protestant form offers an interesting spectacle. The Venetian polychoral writing appears somewhat heavier in the hands of the Germans because they added a much more elaborate orchestral apparatus to the vocal choirs. The massive strength that characterizes German baroque music, its somewhat ponderous and measured nature is due to the use of the Lutheran hymns, which form an integral part of this music, reaching final glorification in the chorale cantatas of J. S. Bach.

Michael Praetorius, originally named Schulz or Schulze (1571–1621), issue of an old musical family, became the most important organizer of Protestant church music since Luther first called on Johann Walter to undertake this task. Praetorius knew the Venetians as well as the Romans, and he even tried his solemn spirit on the lilting grace of French dances. His inquisitive mind explored every form and technique of his times and shuffled and melted them, with imposing thoroughness, patience, and skill, into the musical world of the Protestant chorale; in this, he was one of the chief founders of German baroque music. The number of his compositions is fantastic, the collection entitled *Musae Sioniae* alone containing 1,244 settings of the chorales for ensembles, ranging from *bicinia* or "two-part songs" to quadruple choirs. His *Syntagma Musicum* (Musical Treatise) is, with Mersenne's *Harmonie Universelle,* our most important source for seventeenth-century musical history. With typical German thoroughness Praetorius describes every form of musical composition known to him and gives a most lucid and graphic description of the musical instruments built and used in his day.[30]

The old Lutheran chorales, folk songs, and congregational songs instilled in Protestant Germany a love for the simple song for one voice with accompaniment. The Catholic south and Austria, lost in the magnificence of the Italian baroque, did not take up song writing until the very end of the seventeenth century, but the northern masters, even when attempting to write in the new Italian manner, could not detach themselves from the undercurrent of popular taste. The cultural territory comprising the central and northern states never allowed Italian opera such supremacy as had been its privilege in the south, and the organists and cantors enjoyed a reputation and esteem which prevented Italian virtuosi and composers from taking over the leadership unconditionally, as had been the case in Vienna and Munich.

Johann Hermann Schein (1586-1630), one of Bach's distinguished predecessors in the musical directorship of the Thomasschule in Leipzig, opened the ranks of early song writers. While always faithful to his German upbringing, he appropriated the Venetian style in a boldly individual fashion, but he was equally at home in the lighter forms, and starting from the delightful madrigals and villanelle in Hasler's style he arrived at the more homophonous German "basso continuo song." His songs, and those of many of his contemporaries, were written for solo voice with accompaniment, but the polyphonic character of the setting is still evident in the accompanying parts. The German musicians of the baroque era never entirely abandoned their polyphony—a latent Gothic trait that impresses one up to the time of Johann Sebastian Bach—and throughout the seventeenth century they apologized in their prefaces to song publications for not using a *kunstvoll,* "artistic," setting, meaning a more elaborate form of polyphony. For important occasions the many-voiced choral compositions were still preferred to songs, and with this in mind the composers arranged their solo songs in such a way

Peter Brueghel, the Elder (c. 1525–1569), "Kermess"

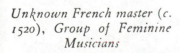

Unknown French master (c. 1520), Group of Feminine Musicians

Caravaggio (1569–1609), *"The Lute Player"*

that additional parts could be sung if desired. This was a complete reversal of the musical practice of the Renaissance, when polyphonic works were reduced to solo compositions with accompaniment.

A combination of the new concerted style with German song composition was inevitable, especially because of the Germans' love of *Gesellschaftsmusik,* of convivial, social music-making, and their preference for instrumental music. The model was the Italian opera aria with obbligato instruments, and the first German specimens appeared in 1634 with Thomas Selle's *Deliciarum Juvenilium Decas,* in which a violin concertized with the voice. It appears that this form of Italian music was most appropriate for the Germans because, while they did not take readily to the vocal coloratura, they liked to adorn the instrumental part, and by adding more instruments to the accompaniment arrived at the orchestral song. The approach was at first somewhat uncertain; preludes, postludes, and ritornelli prefaced and accompanied the songs, and it is hard for the modern listener to feel that they belong to the song proper. But we must not overlook the social significance of this art; the small ensembles which accompanied the songs were played by enthusiastic amateurs who founded convivial musical societies all over Germany. The academies, *collegia musica, convivia,* were all devoted to music, and it seems that some of the spirit of the Meistersinger survived in the evening musicals held in the homes of simple citizens, artisans and small merchants. This eminently gregarious, social tendency precluded a purely solo art, even in the love songs, but perhaps the greatest deterrent to a real song poetry was the lamentable state of German lyric poetry.

At the same time when the rising German musical style, already under steadily growing Italian influence, was threatened by an invasion of French Anacreontic poetry, chansons, and dances, the nation produced a song composer who gave the *Lied* the place it has occupied ever since in German music. Other composers wrote songs among other works, but Heinrich Albert (1604–1657) was a song composer pure and simple. A pupil of his kin, ·Schütz, and a friend of Schein, Albert composed a great variety of songs: simple folk-songlike pieces, more pretentious arias, and, in particular, deeply felt spiritual songs. Since Albert demonstrated a full command of Italian vocal style, his endeavor to create a German song style by using all the foreign elements that could be assimilated must be regarded as a conscious, high-minded, artistic plan.

Another pioneer of the German song was Johann Rist (1607–1667), Protestant clergyman, poet, and amateur musician. Some of his hymns are still sung in the German Protestant churches. The musicians appreciated the help he offered them and rallied around him to form the so-called "Hamburg school." Lübeck, Bremen, Berlin, the Saxon-Thuringian cities, and later Munich and Ratisbon formed song schools on the order of that of

Hamburg, and a host of excellent composers with many publications attest to the popularity of this form of music. Adam Krieger (1634–1666), poet-composer of genius, continued the work of Albert by following his style and form, surpassing the pioneer song writer in the power of expressiveness and the beauty of his melodies. To this generation belonged also Johann Crüger (1598–1662), one of the most famous Protestant hymn composers, whose chorales are still cherished (*Jesu meine Freude, Nun danket alle Gott*), and Johann Erasmus Kindermann (1616–1655), a pupil of Staden and Carissimi, the first of the German composers to apply Italian dramatic dialogue to comical ends. Constantin Christian Dedekind (1628–1715), starting with the first school of song writers but outliving them by half a century, was, perhaps, the most popular figure in this engaging lyric art.

But the dramatic nature of the baroque demanded an outlet, and found it in the German Passion, cantata, and oratorio. The components of the German oratorio were many. We have encountered most of them—the concerto, cantata, and opera—but an important element, the Passion of the Lord, is still missing, as we have not discussed it since medieval times. The earliest extant attempt at artistic polyphonic setting of the Passion was Obrecht's *Passio domini nostri Jesu Christi secundum Matthaeum,* composed shortly before 1505. Despite its title, the Passion uses the text of all four Gospels, no doubt in order to carry the narrative up to the seven words of the Redeemer. Obrecht's Passion is, in reality, a great cantus firmus motet in three sections, but the cantus firmus is divided among the individual parts to symbolize the *dramatis personae.* The words of the Evangelist are usually in the tenor part, the bass personifies Jesus, while other personages are taken by the alto part. Obrecht's simple but monumental setting of the Passion became the accepted model of the motet-Passion. Another variety of the cantus firmus motet-Passion showed a more dramatic penchant by treating the parts of Jesus and the Evangelist in a simple Gregorian recitation style but allotting the animated scenes of the *turbae,* the "crowds," to a polyphonic choir. The first of these "dramatic" Passions was Claudin de Sermisy's *St. Matthew Passion* (1534). The motet-Passion continued to attract the greatest Catholic composers, among them Lassus and Victoria, but with the advent of Protestant music the artistic motet style was reduced to a simple recitation without a touch of the dramatic. This form of the Passion did not satisfy the old-line musicians, trained in the art of choral polyphony, and we soon see the extreme simplicity of the early Protestant Passion of Johann Walter change, in the hands of his successor, Antonio Scandello (1517–1580), an Italian musician living in Germany, to an artistic expression of the Paschal drama. His *Passion According to St. John* (1561), popular all over Germany, restricted the plain-chant recitation to the part of the Evangelist. The other figures of the drama were represented by choruses of varying parts:

Christ was personified by a four-part chorus, and the *turbae* by five-part settings. Cantus firmus constructions were entirely abandoned, for these finely
wrought, varied, and movemented choruses were based on the madrigal,
but on its technique only, because the rough power of the *turbae,* the dramatic presentation of questions and answers, and the soft modulations of
Christ's words, carried this music into an atmosphere saturated with religious
fervor. Scandello's *Resurrection* (1573?) was a direct antecedent of a similar
composition, *Auferstehung,* by Heinrich Schütz, who penetrated to the last
depths of German Protestant religiousness to create, with dramatic energy
and Biblical strength, music for its services that was destined to express
all that German arts and letters of the period were unable to utter.

Heinrich Schütz (1585–1672), who had studied law at the University of
Marburg and was recipient of a stipend, left in 1609 for Venice to study with
the renowned master Gabrieli. The young German musician arrived in what
was then the capital of the world of music, where germinated the epoch-
making changes which were to conquer the music of all Europe. Schütz
drank deeply from the fountain of new impulses and stayed in Venice until
the death of Gabrieli (1612). A year before his departure his first opus appeared, a book of five-part madrigals, bold and intriguing as only Venetian
music of the early baroque can be. Upon his return to Germany he entered
the service of the Margrave of Hessen, but in a short time he was at the court
of the Elector of Saxony; here he occupied the position of court conductor
for fifty-five years, until his death, except for several periods when the religious warfare forced him to seek quiet in other parts of Germany, or in
Scandinavia. A second journey to Italy (1628–29), which again left deep
impressions on the mature master, was followed by several trips to Copenhagen, Brunswick, and Hanover. Deeply affected by the untimely death
of his wife in 1625, the composer dedicated the rest of his life to the composition of church music. His great intelligence, personal integrity, and
staunch character earned him universal affection and esteem. His varied
correspondence with the Duchess of Brunswick shows that his counsel was
sought not only in matters musical, and as a teacher he ranked with the
younger Gabrieli.

Schütz was not only the greatest German musician of his period but one
of the outstanding creative geniuses in musical history. Like some of his
compatriots, he was profoundly impressed by Italian music of the early
baroque, and transplanted monody, polychoral writing, and the concerto
manner to Germany; but the spiritual roots of his art are deeply set in the
German soil. In his cantatas the power of his grandiose imagination brought
to life a series of dramatic visions. His great sense of form and his musical
technique, trained in the classical traditions of polyphony, his earnest Biblical faith, and his universal culture effectively protected him from falling

victim to mere exterior effects. Although familiar with every secret of contemporary Italian music—dissonance, sharp eruptive modulations, chromaticism, *cori spezzati,* echo effects, dramatic recitation, and instrumental illustration—these are never conspicuous and are always subordinated to higher
artistic aims. His artistic development shows a steady growth toward simplification and crystallization. All the foreign elements are melted in an epoch-
making synthesis in the spirit of German Protestant church music. The
manner in which Schütz utilized the picturesque mixture of vocal and instrumental music in the church concerto opened the way for the German
cantata. In his concertos he likes to use dramatic scenes, which he presents,
with a plastic German declamation, within the epic frame of the oratorio,
essentially without staging, but with a power of representation and portrayal
that is unmatched in the whole of musical literature. His pictorial vividness
and capacity to conjure up visions reminds one of Johann Sebastian Bach,
but his avoidance of lyrical reflection and contemplation is in sharp contrast
to Bach's art and to the art of the whole "chorale school" that preceded
Bach, for Schütz very seldom weaves the traditional hymn tunes in his
compositions; his element was the stark drama. His avoidance of the
Protestant hymns lessens his claims to being a Protestant composer, but he
was perhaps even more than that, a Biblical composer who rose above denominational differences to give a universal interpretation of the Testaments.

Like Monteverdi, Haydn, and Verdi, Schütz composed his greatest works
at an age when other people finish their earthly career. The aged master
who lived through the whole gamut of revolutionary upheaval caused by
the stylistic changes coming from Italy, who declared himself passionately
for this brilliant, expressive, and modern music, returned to the great traditions of his Germanic forebears. The *Historia des Leidens und Sterbens un-
seres Herrn und Heylandes Jesu Christi* (1665–66), four settings of the
Passion after the four Evangelists, renounces all the external advantages of
the new style. No instruments are employed, even the recitatives being set
in the old unaccompanied manner. And now he reveals all the greatness of
his mystic Germanic soul, for the dramatic energy and truth of expression
that pour from these *a cappella* choruses, never leaving the bounds of devout
reverence, forsake the love of Italian baroque decoration. This is the voice
of the "Faustian" German, whose fate and life is henceforth a symbol of the
idea of Redemption. Protestant oratorio and Passion are here founded in the
great synthesis of German baroque music, sealing the destiny of German
music.

The peculiar circumstances of the Protestant divine service placed the
organ, in Germany, in a position where it became intimately connected with
the central musical part of the service: the chorale. Charged with the accom-

paniment of congregational singing, the organists came into possession of an infinite treasure of thematic material which started them on the road to a great Protestant instrumental literature, ultimately transcending the denominational line. These chorales remained the chief source of German music long after the cantus firmus technique disappeared entirely from Catholic music. It is natural that church hymns should reign in cantata and oratorio, but we find them dominating concerted music, variations, and the very popular *basso ostinato* compositions with their ever-recurring short, "obstinate" bass themes. The strong assimilating power of the Lutheran chorale is well illustrated by the chorale-like arrangements of compositions taken from the Fitzwilliam Virginal Book and of John Bull's works, widely distributed in Germany. There was also a most curious composition for solo violin with basso continuo by William Brade, in whose title, "Choral," the English composer acknowledges the tastes and sentiments of the country of his residence.

It is surprising to find that an art so typically German and Protestant originated from the most heterogeneous sources. The inspired poet of the organ, Frescobaldi, the famous precentor of St. Mark's, Gabrieli, and the sensitive virginalists of Elizabethan and Jacobean England surrounded its cradle. Among the many artists who visited Italy and returned with a fund of musical inspiration, the most important for the future of instrumental music was the Netherlander Jan Pieterszoon Sweelinck (1562–1621), a pupil of Zarlino and Gabrieli. Sweelinck wrote the final chapter in the history of the great Netherlandish musical culture that lasted for over two hundred years, but he was the product of Venice and his pupils were Germans who disseminated his great fame and influence from Hamburg to Danzig. He had so many of these pupils that contemporary writers called him "the maker of German organists." Although an eminent choral composer, his real importance lies in his organ music. With him the representative form of baroque instrumental music, the fugue, is fully before us, and the traditions of this old master were handed down from pupil to pupil, from Scheidemann to Reinken, and from Reinken to Johann Sebastian Bach, to reach in the latter's monumental organ fugues their final glory. Far as they were from each other in time, the essential qualities of the fugue are nevertheless the same in both. Sweelinck provided the bridge from the variation technique of the virginalists to the art of Samuel Scheidt (1587–1654), whose *Tabulatura Nova* (1624) bids farewell to the old Nordic style and definitely associates music with the new Italo-German baroque.

The rather vague art of diminution of sixteenth-century German keyboard music disappeared under the integrating influence of the chorale, as Sweelinck placed organ music again in the service of the church. Instead of the capricious lines that resulted from the practice of diminution, the chorale paraphrases and variations follow a well-organized contrapuntal plan; the artistic superiority of the German contrapuntal construction over the lighter passage work of their English mentors is incontestable, in spite of the great number of dull choral compositions. The well-thought-out registration and the use of the pedal boards added to the formation of an organ style par excellence, as opposed to the rather ambiguous keyboard styles of the French, English, and Italian composers of the second half of the century, which were apt for both harpsichord and organ, but perhaps more fitting for the first.

Scheidt, a pupil of Sweelinck, proceeded as deliberately as his master to end the prevailing practice of improvising, in the concerted manner, organ accompaniments from the bass-part book of the vocal score, and to place organ music on solid foundations. His *Tabulaturbuch hundert geistlicher Lieder und Psalmen* (1650) is the first real book of organ accompaniment for Protestant congregational singing, and his harmonizations of the chorales are the pride of Protestant church music, second only to those of Johann Sebastian Bach. The first to treat the chorale in an artistic and idiomatic style for the organ, Scheidt became the leader of north and central German organ music. His reputation was such that those who were unable to study with him personally requested instruction by correspondence.

The north could not fail to produce a remarkable organ school under such leadership. The number of church and cathedral organists of the first water is so great that it is well-nigh impossible to deal with them within the limitations of this book. We must mention, however, Franz Tunder (1614–1667) of St. Mary's in Lübeck, notable organist and cantata composer, and his successor and son-in-law, Dietrich Buxtehude (1637–1707). The unruly, romantically colored imagination of Buxtehude, the northern composer, displays a curious mixture of Italian tenderness with the anguish of the German soul, always searching for the ultimate mysteries of life. The *Abendmusiken,* "evening musicals," following the afternoon service in St. Mary's in Lübeck on the last five Sundays preceding Christmas, were famous all over Germany. The "colossal baroque" feted its last feast in these sumptuous performances, for which Buxtehude composed a complete cycle of cantatas. The much-admired height of these musicals was Buxtehude's playing and improvisation, and it is well known that Bach journeyed on foot from Arnstadt to Lübeck in 1705 to hear the master and to study with him. Similar pilgrimages were made by Handel and by Mattheson. Those who think that they are bestowing the highest praise on this great musician by calling him a direct forerunner of Bach err as gravely as the critics who can see in Haydn only a forerunner of Beethoven. Buxtehude's monumental fugues, passacaglias tinged with tender melancholy, fantastic preludes, and virtuoso toccatas are the works of an independent genius; they are endowed with an imagination and inventiveness that are his own and can never be regarded as mere preparation for something to come. His works, compared with the works of Bach, are as finished masterpieces as are the symphonies of Haydn compared with those of Beethoven.

A special place among the adventurous German musicians who peregrinated about the Continent, and returned engrossed by what they had learned in the music-loving countries of Italy, France, and England, is reserved for Johann Froberger (1616–1667). Froberger, a pupil of Frescobaldi, was not satisfied with the usual fare of German musicians in Italy, and visited the leading musicians in Brussels, Paris, and London, returning to his homeland as one of the creators of the clavier suite. The universally adopted sequence of allemande, courante, sarabande, gigue (with occasional *doubles*) was his arrangement, and he also brought home from France the little descriptive program pieces that were so popular in Gaultier's and Couperin's circle. The broad sweeep of his toccatas and the dramatic flashes of his *tombeaux* impressed not only his contemporaries but were still highly appreciated by Johann Sebastian Bach. Jacob Adelung (1699–1762), the learned philologist, historian, and musician, remarked that "the late Leipzig Bach held Froberger in high esteem, although the latter was a somewhat old composer."

The Catholic south was not less prolific in gifted organists, but its most illustrious son, Johann Pachelbel (1653–1706), belongs among the great of Protestant music. The years he spent in the north, where he became a friend of Johann Sebastian Bach's father, added immeasurably to the expressive faculties of the northern organ school. He brought with him the warmth and poetic disposition of southern music, which mitigated the somewhat strict formalism of Scheidt and his disciples. This poetic touch is especially evident in his beautiful chorale preludes, which became Bach's models in this most intimate and artistic form of Protestant musical poetry. With Buxtehude, Pachelbel, and the Alsatian-born Jan Adams Reinken (1623–1722), we enter the high baroque, the period of Bach and Handel. The art of these masters, admired and followed by the two musicians who were to carry oratorio, cantata, and instrumental music of the baroque to their unsurpassable heights, has been overshadowed by the hero worship of an uninformed and ungrateful modern public; but those who read carefully the thoughtful biographies of Bach and Handel cannot fail to notice the sincere reverence and admiration of the younger musicians for their elders, who guided them in their quest for the mastery of form and expression with a sure hand and with proud conviction.

Besides the Italian influence coming through the traditional ports of entry, the imperial court in Vienna and the archiepiscopal city of Salzburg, there was a less noticeable but steady and serious influence coming from

England, especially notable in instrumental music. The English musicians in Germany had been known and appreciated ever since the well-known Shakespearean actor and jig dancer, William Kemp—whose name appears in the earlier editions of *Romeo and Juliet* in place of the characters he played—had visited Lüneburg (1586) and later Dresden and Berlin. These Englishmen were almost without exception instrumentalists, and they brought with them a style and a tradition of pure instrumental music which appealed greatly to the Germans, always fond of the more abstract forms of music. The numerous theatrical groups traveling in Germany were accompanied by emigrants, driven from England by the religious troubles, who settled down in Germany. Thomas Simpson was viola player in the Elector Palatine's band, Walter Rowe an excellent gamba player in Hamburg, and later in the court at Berlin, John Dowland lutenist at the court in Hessen and Brunswick, and William Brade (1560–1630), the most influential of them, variously municipal music director in Hamburg, chapel master at the court in Berlin, and, after a stay in Copenhagen, again superintendent of music in Hamburg. Besides these eminent musicians, known in their own country as well as on the Continent, there were Jordan in Berlin, Dixon and Price in Dresden, Flood in Brandenburg, and many others in Wolfenbüttel, Danzig, Gottorp, Stettin, and Cassel, whose names cannot be found in the most authoritative English reference books. It is regrettable that English historians do not find it worth while to investigate the Continental adventures of their compatriots. A rich and distinguished chapter of English musical history has been neglected here, a chapter as rightfully a part of English musical history as the part played by the Italians in Germany belongs properly in the annals of Italian music.

Unlike the keyboard composers (whose incontestable influence was rather indirect, even though the *Parthenia* composers were known all over the country), these musicians, almost all string players, exerted a direct influence, immediately accepted and assimilated. They were responsible for the development of north German, especially Hanseatic, viol and violin music. Following the example of William Brade, who seems to have been the outstanding personality of the English colony, they set up bodies of string players, and their versatility on the viol won them many disciples. It is sufficient to remark that some of the greatest Germans studied with these English musicians, and Scheidt himself owed gratitude to Brade. The newly organized string ensembles pleased the Germans so much that they began to convert their old and rather ponderous wind choirs into the *capella fidicina,* often designated by its original English name "consort." Praetorius described these ensembles, himself calling them consorts, and was of the opinion that the sound of such a body of instruments is much more pleasant and refined than that of a trombone and cornet choir, heretofore the most popular medium of ensemble music in Germany. The practical activity of the English musicians was accompanied by a considerable number of publications laying the foundation for north German orchestral and chamber music literature, which was to retain its identity in the face of the southern symphonic school until the great classical instrumental composers of the eighteenth century.

The universal admiration for everything that was part of the courtly life at Versailles invited French imitations. In the Rhine country, and even farther inland, French keyboard and orchestral mannerisms began to be felt toward the middle of the century. A more tangible evidence of this influence is to be found in the publications that began to place an emphasis on the French models. Sigismund Kusser (or Cousser in the French version) entitled his collection published in 1682 *Compositions de Musique Suivant la Méthode Françoise,* giving a foretaste of the great vogue of French music and letters which was to capture the disintegrating baroque.

The Italian schools naturally showed greater progress and produced more notable disciples in southern than in northern Germany, but the intermittent visits of such notable Italian virtuosi as Biagio Marini and Carlo Farina left their marks in the English-dominated north. Although the competition of the many Italian virtuosi in Dresden, Munich, and Vienna made it difficult for the Germans to assert themselves, we find among them many good composers and, in the person of Franz Biber (1644–1704), a violin virtuoso and composer admired as was only Paganini in the nineteenth century. The many trio sonatas and virtuoso solo compositions of the Swiss-German, Johann Heinrich Weyssenburg, better known as Albicastro, are valuable examples of the Italian violin style in central Europe, but the sonata da camera was not unknown farther north, as can be seen from the admirable sonatas, suites, and other compositions by Johann Rosenmüller (c. 1620–1684), conductor at Wolfenbüttel, a composer rightly considered the German rival of Lully.

Early Baroque Opera in Germany

OPERA, more than any other form of intellectual life, showed the complete surrender of German courtly taste to Latin civilization. The noisy, sometimes brilliant, but often superficial stream of composers, conductors, players, singers, decorators, architects, and designers of theatrical machinery took complete control of the German princely residences, and from the middle of the seventeenth century Italian opera reigned supreme. Although Germany was impoverished, the foreign artists succeeded in finding there a lucrative employment, for every ruling prince, looking toward Versailles, was ready to pawn his soul to obtain the means to keep a brilliant court.

The chasm that separated this music from that of the people was preserved by the fact that the specially built theaters admitted only the court and invited guests, and not until the middle of the eighteenth century were the doors opened to the public. We see at once how wide and deep was the gulf if we examine the relationship of the German musicians to the Italian visitors. There was no dearth of German talent, but there was no national consciousness within which this talent could prosper. Schütz, on his return from Italy, filled with the spirit of the great art he had come to know there, set the old *Dafne* of Rinuccini to music, to be performed in the tenth year of the war, 1627, at the command of the Elector of Saxony. The score was lost, and it is our great misfortune that we cannot know the first German opera. But Schütz never wrote another opera, and even the greatest musical geniuses of Germany shunned it, confessing themselves unable to achieve the right atmosphere unless, like Hasse or Handel, they resolved to embrace the Italian spirit completely and then spent most of their lives abroad. In the urban middle classes there was enough pride and good will and even wealth left to call for a continuation of the traditions of German bourgeois art. But their undertakings in various fields always bore a slightly pedantic and even comical character, lacking in that aristocratic *laisser aller* which seemed to accompany art in Italy and France. Thus it is easily understandable that the many attempts at German national opera in Zeitz, Bayreuth, Hanover, Leipzig, and other places faltered and quickly fell victim to Italian competition.

The first example of these German operatic essays occurred in Nuremberg, a city which still preserved something of its old burgher civilization. A small group of musicians and music-loving men of letters united in the task of creating German music drama. Among them was the poet Georg Philipp Harsdörffer (1607–1658), a German combination of Count Bardi and Rinuccini, though less aristocratic and esoteric than the Italians. He was the author of "The poetic funnel through which can be poured the German art of verse and rime in vi hours without the aid of the Latin language." And there was the composer Sigmund Staden (1607–1655), son of the eminent Bavarian organist Johann Staden. These two leaders composed in 1644 a "spiritual sylvan poem," *Seelewig*.[31] This oldest of German operas was in reality a sort of *Singspiel*, with the Italian pastoral and the old morality play acting as godparents, but the work, naïve and insignificant, simply proved that the German language was not able to assimilate the recitative style without further extensive experiments.

While the more sedate Germans had difficulty in appropriating the form of music which many of them came to regard as an alluring if foreign art, contemporary documents indicate that musical performances with a stage setting were given in Vienna as early as 1626, although information concerning court ballets and other performances from this period is still missing. The former Netherlandish monopoly of musical positions in the service of the emperor was broken by the constantly widening rift between Protestants and Catholics and by the loss of the Netherlandish provinces, while the influence of the Italians grew, reaching toward the end of the Thirty Years' War a position even more dominating than that of their predecessors. As early as about 1640 we find in the Hofburg an operatic establishment of an excellence that presupposes antecedents. As in the past century, when the best musicians were sought from abroad, Monteverdi was appointed artistic counsel to the imperial court. The only manuscript of the aged master's *Ritorno d'Ulisse* was found in Vienna. Monteverdi's pupil Cavalli wrote for the Vienna opera house one of his first operas, *Egisto,* performed in 1642. After the Peace of Westphalia, musical activity at the court increased and the emperors themselves did not disdain to try their hands at composition; both Ferdinand III and Leopold I were composers of some talent. Vienna developed into one of the most celebrated operatic centers, offering everything that baroque splendor could afford, and the Viennese example was followed, though more modestly, by other south German residential cities. The emperor took his court opera with him to Prague and Pressburg (1648), and to the Reichstag in Ratisbon (1653), where it created a great sensation. This was made possible by the portable theater constructed by the court architect Burnacini, which was transported on barges up and down the Danube.

It was in these days that opera became the accepted accompaniment of high state and court functions. All important events that took place in the imperial family, especially marriages, were celebrated with operas produced with no regard for expense. Cesti's *Pomo d'Oro* stands out, however, even in this fabulous atmosphere of splendor. The great Italian, usually included in the Venetian school, was appointed imperial assistant conductor and stayed in Vienna from 1666 to 1669. *Il Pomo d'Oro* towers above contemporary solo operas. At a time when such writing is almost extinct in Venice this work has magnificent choruses of the power and pathos of Carissimi, and its extended prologue—a whole act—showed the way to Lully. This opera, laden with episodes, leads the spectator in five acts and sixty-seven scenes through heaven, earth, and the underworld, in a continuous succession of elaborate tableaux.

In the three decades following Cesti's activity in Vienna the court opera was dominated by three personages: the poet-composer and future court conductor Antonio Draghi (1635-1700), author of one hundred and seventy-two operas and forty-three oratorios, besides libretti written for Leopold I; the court poet Nicolo Minato; and the theater architect Lodovico Burnacini. This triumvirate jealously safeguarded the high qualities of Viennese opera against the all-too-apparent decline in Italy. The composers' preference for a rich instrumentation and solid contrapuntal writing laid the foundation for the fame and excellence of classical opera in Vienna.

As we advance into the seventeenth century, the northern musical centers, still powerless against Italian opera and unable to produce their own, began to take the matter more seriously, and finally the same civic pride that made them duplicate such imperial establishments as could be set up in their midst, created an opportunity for German baroque opera in Hamburg, where it knew a brief vogue. One cannot help recalling, when comparing the two city-states, the erstwhile eminence of another old maritime city, Venice. But the resemblance gains significance when approached from the sociological angle, for, as in Venice, it was the middle-class population which created the first public opera house in Hamburg. Not visited by the worst horrors of the war and profiting by its old-established sea trade, the Hanseatic Republic, like its Adriatic sister, supported the arts and attracted the best musicians in the country. At the organs of its churches sat some of the best organists of the northern school—Heinrich Scheidemann, Jacob Praetorius, Jan Adams Reinken, and Matthias Weckmann—and in the meetings of the *collegium musicum,* held in the refectory of the cathedral, the best contemporary composers performed their works in the presence of many visitors attracted by the fame of the institution. The German cantata received considerable impulse from the activity of Christoph Bernhard, organist at St. James's. The rich merchants proudly supporting music were also generous to their musicians, rewarding them in a manner unknown in other parts of Germany. The only form of music missing from the city's life was opera.

The first performance of an original German opera in Hamburg took place on January 2, 1678. Underwritten by a number of prominent citizens led by the noted jurist and senate councilor Gerhard Schott, the performances were continued regularly until after his death (1702), when some difficulties were experienced. The opening performance in the "Goosemarket Theater" presented a spiritual Singspiel, *Adam and Eve,* a work still reminiscent of the old mystery play. Thus, with all the external resemblance that bound German opera to the Italian models, the Biblical orientation of the northern Protestants shows the inevitable difference between them and the pseudo-classical southerners. The composer of *Adam and Eve,* Johann Theile (1648–1728), a pupil of Schütz and a musician well known for his church music and great contrapuntal ability, was not a dramatic composer by vocation. Among the less important composers of the first period of Hamburg opera only Nikolaus Adam Strungk (1640–1700), more famous for his violin playing, deserves mention. While not yet threatening German supremacy, foreign works, especially French, began to appear in the repertory. The first period, somewhat placidly bourgeois, was followed by a notable regime when Sigismund Kusser (1660-1727), friend of Lully, brought back with him from his stay in France the great lyric traditions of the Académie Royale de Musique. A restless, gifted man who never stayed long at the same place, Kusser had real talent for organization and a flair for the lyric stage. The task that confronted him in Hamburg was seemingly beyond anyone's capacities. German vocal teaching, unlike the great Italian schools that looked back upon centuries of experience, was at an elementary stage of development. The singers in Hamburg were recruited from the most unlikely sources. Artisans, vagrant students, ex-soldiers, and other questionable individuals formed the bulk of them, and as the *welsche Kapaunen,* the "Italian capons," could not be suffered by the good burghers, they preferred to see the leading feminine roles taken by market women and prostitutes, appearing in their spare time as goddesses and the heroines of humanity. Under the able direction of Kusser the situation gradually improved, but, characteristically enough, the leading soprano, Conradi, famous for her beauty and pleasant voice, was not able to read music and studied her roles by ear. We shall return to the Hamburg opera when the eighteenth century has placed it in the forefront of German music, making its last stand and finally succumbing to the Italian invasion.

New Alignment of Social Forces

THE stylistic changes caused by the baroque had their corollary in the new alignment of social forces. The increasing commercial and industrial activity of individuals and nations provided the middle-class merchants with handsome incomes, and their eagerness to have a culture of their own, already manifest in Renaissance times, now reached a point where they impressed their own accent on the art that came within their compass. Artistic life in this period, especially in poetry and music, was characterized by an "occasional" quality to an extent that we can hardly realize. It strikes the modern student as somewhat ridiculous when the whole population of Olympus is called upon to attend the wedding or funeral of a sedate, God-fearing, and rather simple burgher. But if we pass over the excesses that inevitably attended this situation, we must admit that through its close contact with all the events of life, art succeeded in establishing intimate connections with it, a relationship we lack today. In those days whoever could afford it—and only modest means were required—wanted to commemorate important events in his family life by appropriate works of art. The great mass of printed and manuscript collections of poems and musical compositions for christenings, weddings, funerals, receptions, inductions, and festivals, testifies to the love of art in the widest circles of the population. The income from these sources was considerable and added incentive to the old cantors' and musicmasters' opposition to the Italian musicians, coming to Germany in droves.

The musical life of the middle classes was greatly strengthened by the *collegia musica, convivia musica,* choral societies, and other informal amateur organizations which appeared toward the end of the sixteenth century. In the beginning these societies were devoted mainly to sacred vocal music, the instrumental dilettanti joining them in the seventeenth century. These institutions, as well as the municipal pipers and bands, were the middle-class answer to the courtly chapel choirs and other aristocratic bodies inaccessible to the populace. It is edifying to read in contemporary documents about the devotion and enthusiasm that were lavished on these musical circles. After the peace (1648) we see Schütz helping with advice, money, and music to restore a number of musical establishments which had deteriorated during the war. He also engaged musicians, conductors, and singers who often served for little or no compensation. The meetings of the *collegia* continued, until the second half of the eighteenth century, to perform the best contemporary music available. The players and composers, in perfect harmony, played and sang together, with the "public" taking an active part in the proceedings. There was virtually no audience, for every musically able-bodied person was engaged in the ensemble.

England under the Stuarts—Revolution and Restoration

THE proud position of world power attained by England under Elizabeth was slowly relinquished under the Stuarts, who withdrew from foreign politics to concentrate their interests—shifting and uncertain—to domestic affairs. James I and his son, Charles I, were not insignificant rulers, but they were lacking in that instinct which bound Elizabeth to her people. The new dynasty was foreign to the people, yet it endeavored to introduce an entirely new conception of kingship resembling the Continental form of absolutism. The national church became the means through which the crown attempted to rule the country. The exploitation of the state church inflamed to open opposition the long-latent discontent of militant Protestants, who saw in the Church a sacrilegious political institution. But though the religious motive was weighty, there was also a strong undertow of a democratic-political nature. The differences became more acute under Charles I, who answered the Petition of Rights by dissolving Parliament, and reigned for a decade along absolutist lines. When, however, the Stuart tried to foist on the essentially democratic and strictly Calvinistic church of his Scottish homeland the hierarchy of the High Church, the short-lived absolutism came to an end and the revolution started.

Parliament seized the reins, forcing the king to relinquish his powers bit by bit, and soon the nation was divided into two armed camps. The war brought to the fore a capable captain at the head of an army which relied upon godliness as much as upon arms, an upright and efficient administrator, who, despite his ignorance, stubbornness, and bigotry, was one of the most commanding figures in English history—Oliver Cromwell. The military phase of the civil war ended with the victory at Naseby (1645), but the political struggle continued until Cromwell, at the head of the army, the greatest single factor in politics, declared the independent minority of Parliament the embodiment of popular sovereignty, and established what amounted to a dictatorship exercised by this minority. The king was executed (1649), the monarchy abolished, and England became a republic. But the English people were royalists at heart, and the notion of sovereignty of the people was too advanced for the seventeenth century; the government had no real popular backing. At the death of Cromwell the essential weakness of all dictatorships became evident, and, after abortive attempts to continue the military dictatorship, the restored monarchy was confirmed by Parliament on May 1, 1660. But Cromwell's work left its mark on English social life, in spite of the Restoration. The middle classes, from which he originated, were henceforth to guide the destinies of the nation. A new spirit animated the English people; the modern Englishman was born. Cromwell was convinced that his political course was set by God and believed firmly—as Englishmen did after him—that the greatness and power of Britain is desired by God, that service for the nation is service for God. Under the impact of these events the old England disappeared as if erased by an invisible power.

The new atmosphere of English existence stifled the arts, diverted literature into politics and theology, and silenced the unique musical art of the Tudor era. The post-Shakespearean drama is characterized by a lack of artistic sense, by chaotic, complicated plots, and by a marked decline in poetic language. Even the greatest dramatist of the period, Ben Jonson (1573–1637), had lost the ability to create individuals; his figures are almost types, and his tragedies already show the *doctus poeta* of the century of Hobbes's rationalism. The general decline of moral standards, and the hesitation between pathos, forced sentiment, charm, vulgarity, psychological problems, stirring dramatic motives, and a melodious form, are best illustrated in the plays of Beaumont and Fletcher. The civil war destroyed, then, whatever was left of drama; the theaters were closed, to be opened only after the Restoration.

Poetry also was on the decline. The verses of Abraham Cowley (1618–1667), John Denham (1615–1669), William Davenant (1606–1668), and Edmund Waller (1606–1687), already prefigured that love of finished form which was to characterize the eighteenth century. The exquisite charm and epicurean conception of Robert Herrick (1591–1674) do not seem to fit into this poetry, neat and graceful, but lacking in depth of feeling and passion. The towering literary personality of this era, John Milton (1608–1674), was so completely dominated by the tragic events that most of his literary activity was restricted to political and religious writings. His greatest works appeared only after the Restoration, when this earnest, truly puritanic soul, disappointed in the real world, turned to the world of imagination. In the majestic organ music of his language an impoverished literature received a monument of lasting beauty. But even this ardent conviction and faith was restricted to one man of genius; it did not produce a period of art. The other great figure created by the Puritan movement was Bunyan (1628–1688), whose *Pilgrim's Progress* proverbially rivals the popularity of the Bible.

During the civil war literature withdrew from humanism and emerged from the conflict weakened in power and showing signs of the scientific tendencies. Reason takes the place of the emotions, as could be expected with the ever-growing French influence.

The decline of music is, perhaps, the most tragic, most disconcerting result of the new times. A nation heretofore in the vanguard of the musical world relinquished its most personal cultural riches, thereby suffering a loss which, in comparison with that experienced by literature and the fine arts, seems irreparable. By 1635 the great madrigal art was extinct. That delightful musical lyricism, permeating poetry and forming with it an intimate art of such refinement and aristocratic restraint as will always remain a distant model, gazed upon with admiration by succeeding generations unable to recapture its spirit, vanished in the innocuous and essentially terrestrial-bourgeois music that accompanied masques and plays.

English instrumental music, bold and impressive at the turn of the century, exerted a positive influence on many of the leading Dutch, French, German, and even Italian masters of the early seventeenth century; the same cannot be said of the reciprocal influence coming from the Continent. The first waves of the baroque style that reached England acted as an incentive to more colorful and harmonically refined treatment, but the rapid gains made by foreign, especially Italian, virtuoso solo playing doomed the balanced polyphonic forms to disintegration. John Jenkins (1592–1678), whose fancies appeared toward the middle of the century, closed the history of this typically English form of instrumental music, and after him the fancy rapidly assimilated foreign elements. Jenkins himself published *Twelve Sonatas for Two Violins and a Base with a Thorough Base for the Organ or Theorbo* (1660), which indicates the arrival of the Italian trio sonata on British shores. Because of its retention of polyphonic features that were rooted in the music of the Late Renaissance, the fancy was the only musical form that continued its stylistic development unruffled by the early baroque.

This explains also why ultimately it dried up, whereas Continental instrumental ensemble music, nourished on the concerto style, swung into an unparalleled development.

It is interesting to observe how every important stylistic change in the music of the early baroque was carried out independently in England, the English moves more than once preceding events in Italy and France. Monody was an accomplished fact with the ayres of Jones, Rosseter, and Campion in the very first year of the seventeenth century, while the *ballet de cour* had ancient ancestors in the masques performed in early Tudor times. The same tendency toward a melodramatic treatment that characterized the French ballet is evident in the masque much earlier. Thomas Campion [32] and especially Nicholas Laniere (1588–1665/66), Master of the King's Music, a musician of the stature of the great Renaissance figures of the cinquecento, clever painter, art connoisseur and scenery designer, were the first to attempt composition in the recitative style in dramatic music. Laniere composed the music to Ben Jonson's masque *Lovers Made Men* (1617), and later furnished settings to the same poet's *Luminalia, or the Festival of Light* (1637), in the performance of which the queen and the ladies of the court took part.

One would expect that in a country which excelled in dramatic literature and in music, which looked back on ancient traditions and was still vividly under the spell of a great era of song composition, the circumstances for an operatic culture were especially auspicious. To this must be added the fact that the combination of music with drama was by no means a novelty to Englishmen. As we have related above, the medieval miracle and morality plays contained musical "numbers," but besides a few Christmas and Easter carols, we have no actual documents and must be satisfied with literary notices. During the reign of Queen Elizabeth it was customary for the choirboys of the Chapel Royal to perform some musical pieces. We can form an approximate picture of these little plays if we read the Pyramus and Thisbe episode in Shakespeare's *Midsummer Night's Dream,* which is obviously a parody of these plays performed by the choirboys, and must be imagined in a musical setting. The music in such plays was not continuous; only the sentimental-lyric scenes were set, usually for voice with the accompaniment of a quartet of viols. As a rule the composers were church musicians, and the few extant songs show a remarkable power of dramatic expression and would not suffer if compared with Byrd's *Songs of Sadness and Piety,* written originally for the same combination. The chorister plays did not flourish long, probably on account of the jealousy of professional actors. Music accompanied the plays of the Elizabethan dramatists, or at least was inserted in the supernatural scenes and before and between the acts. Then came the recitative style. English prosody, unlike the German, lent itself well to the new style. *Summa summarum*, everything was in favor of music drama, yet it did not take hold. "The fact was," says Edward J. Dent in his excellent work on *The Foundations of English Opera*, "that in England the spoken drama was already far too highly developed and far too deeply rooted in the heart of the people for its musical counterpart to be accepted as an equivalent, much less a transfiguration of its most powerful emotional workings." There is reason here, and yet it does not altogether account for the situation. With the serious decline of spoken drama and the closing of the theaters during the Commonwealth, the great traditions of the English stage vanished; the considerable influx of foreign music and literature kindled again the musico-dramatic flame, but still to no avail.

The masques, which became increasingly popular in the two decades preceding the Puritans' closing of the theaters, offered the next opportunity for dramatic music. British issues of the *sacra rappresentazione* and the *commedia dell' arte,* the masques quickly acclimatized themselves in England. The eminent architect, Inigo Jones (1573-1652), a pupil of the great Italian theater architect, Palladio, was employed by James I to design settings for the elaborate masques produced at the English court. His fine sketches give a good account of their external features, but no music has survived to help us reconstruct them in their entirety. It appears, however, that music played a secondary role in the masques, which reached an appreciable literary level in Ben Jonson's and Milton's works. But during the reign of Charles I the general artistic decline caused them to sink gradually to a mere sequence of comical dances, in which form they resembled the modern vaudeville. More and more it becomes evident that what is missing here is of capital importance, and of much greater significance than the fact that spoken drama was so highly developed and appreciated in England. English national sentiment refused to accept music as a means of dramatic self-expression; it declined the all-important pure emotional conversion of human passions and sentiments into music, thus preventing music from progressing beyond a pleasant addition, diversion, and ornament to the play.

The Puritans closed the theaters, but it is erroneous to assume that they were absolutely hostile to music. Cromwell himself was very fond of it; Milton, the greatest literary representative of Puritanism, the son of a professional musician,[33] was as passionately devoted to it as was Shakespeare. Although cathedral choirs were disbanded and organs destroyed, in many cases the vandalism had a decided political motive, and was an expression of hatred for the pomp-loving "popish" High Church. Music in the home was often encouraged, and the vast body of Puritans has never questioned the lawfulness of the ordinary practice of the art, confining their prohibitions to music on the stage, to profane music on the Sabbath, and to elaborate music in the church. Cromwell and the leading members of his party did their best to prevent the actual destruction of organs and choir books, and many instruments and scores were not touched. William Prynne (1600–1669), the fierce Puritan writer whose *Histriomastix* (1632) attacked the contemporary stage, himself admitted "that Musicke of itself is lawfull, usefull, and commendable, no man, no Christian dare denie, since the Scriptures, Fathers, and generally all Christian, all Pagan authors extant, do with consent averre it." [34] The initial severity of the Puritan regime having been softened, their suppression of ecclesiastical music actually promoted the practice of secular music. The dramatic authors and composers entertained hopes for the reopening of the theaters. In their eagerness to resume their activity they contrived clever plots to circumvent the official decrees regulating public amusements. Many of them became schoolmasters during the Commonwealth and introduced music, dancing, and drama into the schools. No one seems to have objected to the new pedagogical subjects which thrived, bridging over the interregnum. James Shirley (1596–1666) wrote a number of school plays, or masques, that were set to music by Edward Coleman (d. 1669), Matthew Locke (c. 1632–1677), and Christopher Gibbons (1615–1676), second son of the great madrigalist, but the decisive step was reserved for Sir William Davenant, poet and dramatist, who had the necessary qualifications and experience to undertake the seemingly impending last move to establish English opera.

Having visited Queen Henrietta Maria, who had been living in Paris with her son, the future Charles II, Davenant became acquainted with the teeming theatrical life in Paris. There were the elaborate ballets de cour and the performances in the Théâtre du Marais, utilizing the clever mechanical contraptions of the Italian theatrical machine designers. Since Davenant was in constant attendance on the queen, having fled from England for political reasons, he could not have missed such important occasions as the performances of Italian opera at the court. It occurred to him that what would otherwise come under the theatrical ban might be acceptable, like the school dramas, if equipped with music and the apologetic title of *Moral Representation in Recitative Music*. The incongruous mixture of songs, dialogues, and instrumental pieces that formed *The First Dayes Entertainment at Rutland House by Declamations and Musick: after the Manner of the Ancients*—Davenant's first essay in the new field, set to music by Henry Lawes, Charles Coleman, Captain Henry Cooke (d. 1672), warrior and choirmaster extraordinary, and George Hudson, a rather obscure member of the "royal private music"—has often been called an opera. It hardly deserves the name, but the next venture of the same coalition of musicians on Sir William's text produced a play, *The Siege of Rhodes*, sung in its entirety. Technically this work should be called the first English opera, but while the regrettable loss of the music to all these plays renders categorical statements difficult to make, the very choice of such a "modern" subject, entirely unknown in seventeenth-century opera, strongly suggests that Davenant's main interest was in the reawakening of the English stage. Since regular theater was frowned upon, he cleverly went to the other extreme, and presented a piece sung from beginning to end, a thing unknown in England and consequently far removed from the suspicion of *bona fide* theater. *The Siege of Rhodes* will, then, remain a milestone without markings in the annals of English music and literature. The chief roles were sung by Edward Coleman and his wife. This was the first occasion of the appearance of a woman on the English stage, permitted, no doubt, only because the piece was not called a play but a masque. The experiment obtained a success comparable to the first *Euridice,* prompting Davenant to add, like Rinuccini, more works to his credit. *The Cruelty of the Spaniards in Peru* and *The History of Sir Francis Drake* were the two new "operas" with music by Locke. The music was again lost, but it appears that these plays were much less dramatic in nature and dispensed with the services of female actors.

It is most revealing that the only tangible result of masques and "operas" performed during the Commonwealth was literary and not musical. After the restoration of the monarchy (1660) the theaters opened again and the modern stage took the place of the old Shakespearean theater. This important change was due to the popularity of the musico-dramatic experiments and the modern theatrical notions introduced by them. *The Siege of Rhodes* was revived, and enjoyed renewed popularity. Italian opera was still below the horizon; there was no physical obstacle in the path of English opera, but the English public wanted plays, not operas. Music was welcomed, and even desired, but only in incidental form, and now that it was no longer necessary to disguise the theater in false colors, Sir William abandoned operas and returned to his first love, the drama. During the first decade of the reign of Charles II, indigenous recitative declined rapidly and was practiced only by amateurs. It was more than ten years before another attempt at operatic music was made in England, and it occurred in a vastly different atmosphere.

In the year of the restoration of the monarchy an Italian opera company led by Giulio Gentileschi gave performances at the court, followed in 1661 by French comedians who presented French plays in Drury Lane. Molière was soon a familiar author, and several of his plays were adapted by Shadwell, Dryden, and others. In 1673 a French troupe gave operas in London, and the situation, aided by the presence of a number of eminent foreign virtuosi, was again ripe for a renewal of English operatic experiments. The spirit of the musical stage had not diminished in the intervening years. Incidental music was composed to the revived Shakespearean plays, and the services of orchestras of considerable proportions were enlisted. The "adaptations" of such Shakespearean plays as *The Tempest, Macbeth,* and *Mid-*

summer Night's Dream show a destructive influence of the operatic on the spoken drama, a phenomenon we have seen occur in French literature.

Shadwell and Locke felt secure enough to answer the foreigners with opera in English. Thomas Shadwell (c. 1642–1692), chiefly remembered as the unfortunate Mac Flecknoe of Dryden's satire, was eminently suited for the task, having already tried his hand at refurbishing some of Molière's plays. *The Sullen Lovers,* based on Molière's *Les Fâcheux,* and written, in avowed imitation of Ben Jonson, in 1668, was followed by *Psyche,* after Molière's play of the same title, produced in Paris with Lully's music in 1671. Shadwell had recast the play, and, although he was not a great literary mind, his familiarity with dramatic music made him a creditable librettist. Matthew Locke, the composer, contributed the experience gained in the writing of dramatic music for masques and plays. His incidental music to *The Tempest* is one of the cornerstones of English dramatic music. The result was again as different from Italian and French opera as the outcome of the previous essays. English opera remained within the frame of a romantic play with extensive incidental music. The protagonists, if ordinary mortals, did not sing at all, the music being reserved for spirits, fairies, and other supernatural beings, and for pastoral characters, such as shepherds and shepherdesses. The mortals took to music only when in a highly exalted or a deeply depressed state of mind. Choruses were preferred, especially soldiers' and priests' choruses.

This musical dramaturgy, well expressed in Dryden's preface to *Albion and Albanius,* recognized the fact that opera was an independent form of dramatic art, but refused to admit the one important requisite of the genre: self-expression and characterization in music. "An Opera is a Poetical Tale, or Fiction, represented by Vocal and Instrumental Musick, adorn'd with Scenes, Machines and Dancing. The suppos'd Persons of this Musical *Drama* are generally Supernatural, as Gods, and Goddesses, and Heroes, which at least are descended from them, and are in due time to be adopted into their number." It is evident that under these circumstances there could be no hope for a national English opera. Locke was not flexible enough to penetrate into the spirit of the music drama; he was too much the product of an excellent instrumental school. His melodic invention was rather simple, although he showed considerable skill in instrumental writing. The same is true of William and Henry Lawes, although they were much nearer to Italian influence, having studied with the Italianized Englishman Giovanni Coperario (John Cooper), who was an eyewitness of the birth of opera in Italy.

While the English experiments did not seem to advance the cause of opera, the foreigners made considerable progress in their conquest of the country. Notable Italian musicians settled down in England, among them Giovanni

Battista Draghi, brother of the famed Viennese court conductor, and Nicola Matteis, "the stupendous violin," admired for his "sweet stroke"; and experienced French opera composers like Cambert and Grabu, also permanent residents, began to write for the court in the accepted style of their country. Charles II, not less envious of Versailles and its customs than were the German princes, went so far as to imitate the French king's *vingt-quatre violons* by setting up a similar group in his court. Italian coloratura singing, orchestral and chamber music writing, and even church music, became universally known and began to make serious inroads in English music. Church music, compelled to give up its august isolation, admitted solo passages in the polyphonic anthems. The modest beginnings of Byrd in the field of accompanied anthems now developed into a form which somewhat resembled the German variety of the church concerto. The deteriorated musical bodies of the churches were energetically reorganized; the Chapel Royal, reduced to five choristers without music books, was restored to its former excellence in the unbelievably short time of three years. The brilliant Master of the Chapel was the same Captain Cooke who collaborated with Davenant in *The Siege of Rhodes*. Uniting stern military qualities with an admirable gift for musical, especially vocal, training, Cooke won for himself the reputation of one of the greatest music teachers England has ever known. But his choristers, even this early, were required to sing in Italian as well as in English, and with the consent of the king, or perhaps even at his suggestion, Cooke introduced instrumental music into the church service.

With the memory of French music vivid in his mind, Charles was still dissatisfied with the somber majesty of English church music and urged his musicians to acquire the style of French and Italian church music. To make sure that the music of his much-admired Lully be transplanted into England, the sovereign sent Pelham Humfrey, one of the talented boys of the Chapel Royal, to Paris to study with Lully so that he might improve the quality of English church music. Humfrey (1647–1674) did not disappoint his king, and returned to write some of the finest music of this rapidly declining century. Thoroughly imbued with the spirit of Lully and the French orchestral motet, Humfrey nevertheless remained an English composer, as did John Blow (1648/49–1708), eminent composer and organist, and his pupil Henry Purcell (1658–1695). Blow, maligned by eighteenth-century historians, especially Dr. Burney, and rather unjustly overshadowed by his great pupil, showed a fine understanding of the qualities of Italian music, and Purcell abandoned himself frankly to the lilting grace of French dance music, for which both were seriously taken to task by critics ancient and modern. But this church music, considered too "happy" and "irreverent," was of the utmost sincerity and, consequently, as legitimate as were the similarly condemned "operatic" Masses of the Viennese classicists. Like them, Purcell soared to the most sublime heights in these seemingly mundane works. Church music comprised a large part of his works, and the spirit of the anthems followed him in his dramatic compositions, for the motetlike choruses in *Dido and Aeneas* have no counterpart in Italian and French opera. As a master of English declamation Purcell stands unsurpassed, and will remain—like Lully in France—the model for all English composers to come.

Though Purcell was a church composer by vocation and by profession, his dramatic vein drove him toward the stage, toward the arbiter of contemporaneous drama, Dryden. The result of their collaboration, *King Arthur* (1691), became the most successful solution of the problem of English opera. True to the great dramatic traditions not yet entirely extinct on the English stage, *King Arthur* observes the rights of the drama, and, although the distinction between actors, singers, and dancers is maintained, the work displays a definite dramatic unity. Other notable dramatic works in the same style were *Dioclesian* (1690), *The Indian Queen* (1695), *The Faërie Queene* (1692), and the Shakespearean "arrangements," *Timon of Athens* (1694) and *The Tempest* (1695). It must be admitted, however, that no matter how beautiful most of this music is, it will remain incidental music, in which ornamentation takes the place of dramatic expression and characterization through music. Incidental music to spoken plays is a perfectly legitimate form of art and can lead to compositions of great artistic merit (all of us are acquainted with at least one outstanding example, Mendelssohn's music to *Midsummer Night's Dream*), but it is not opera as long as music merely serves to fortify and illustrate the drama. English opera rejected the socalled "through-composed" style of Italian and French opera, a vital element of opera by which each scene is progressively interpreted by different music to fit the changing mood. Instead, it was satisfied with musical scenes inserted in the spoken play. There was only one instance of a more or less through-composed opera in English music, Blow's *Venus and Adonis,* when Purcell, probably impressed by Blow's experiment, set to work and produced the one great true opera that graces English musical history, *Dido and Aeneas.*

It has often been pointed out that Purcell's music abounds in foreign elements. It is perfectly true that the large number of delicate dances come from French opera, and the sharp psychological characterization of the recitatives from the old Venetian opera of Cavalli. His French style was so pronounced at times that he could insert some compositions by Lully in the body of his own works without being detected. Almost all his dramatic scenes go back to Lully, and the French motet left its marks in his anthem. In the prefaces of his trio sonatas (1683) he himself expressed his regret that English musical training did not give due consideration to Italian music, and announced his earnest desire to express the "seriousness and gravity" of Italian music. But most of these things are negligible, for he remained an English musician with a pronounced personality; compared to his work, everything that his English colleagues created seems pale and unimportant. His melodies are most personal and of an expressiveness found only in a Monteverdi. His unbridled imagination, his free and original forms, transformed every inspiration, however French or Italian in appearance, into his own creation. Conventions meant much to him only as long as they did not interfere with his artistic aims. *Dido and Aeneas* does not soften toward the end in the accepted operatic manner of the French court; Purcell carries the tragedy to its consummation with passion and vehemence. His chamber sonatas and string fantasies, written in the purest Italian style, are Purcell to the core, although they belong to the finest examples of Italian string music. His keyboard music, while less important than his other works, impressed the critical cantor of St. Thomas's so favorably that he himself copied a toccata and a fugue by Purcell. It speaks for their excellence that, until the advent of modern musical style criticism, these two compositions, written about the time of Bach's birth, reposed securely in the great edition of the Bach Society as genuine works of the German master.

A truly divine genius was lost in the young musician, who died at the height of his powers. Baroque in his love for contrapuntal display work and basso ostinato constructions, in his wonderful sense for the theatrical and dramatic, in his obvious pleasure in indulging in sharp dissonances and bold harmonic turns, he gave us, with Monteverdi and Schütz, the essence of his century. The unfortunate times and the orientation of the British mind sealed with his death the fate of English music drama, which might have formulated a musico-dramatic style of Shakespearean stature.

The Baroque in Other Countries
The Netherlands

THE European wars lasting from 1618 to 1660 resulted in the downfall of the world power of Spain and the Habsburgs, elevating France and England to leadership on the Continent. It had become clear as the war progressed that the original motives, religion and patriotism, which animated the various nations in their common struggle to regain liberty from Spain, were superseded by mercantile interests, and the rapidly gaining economic power of France and England ultimately doomed the competing smaller nations to minor fields of action. The important shift in the international balance of power had weighty consequences in the socio-cultural and political life of the rest of Europe. Poland in the east and Denmark in the north lost political importance, and Sweden could not sustain her meteoric rise, for Brandenburg and Russia were looming as future great powers, threatening her on both sides. The Netherlands rose as swiftly as Sweden, but the innate ability of the Dutch for commerce and economic organization created gigantic corporations, such as the Dutch East India Company, establishing factories, warehouses, and fortresses to exploit and guard their possessions. Dutch shipping and commerce flourished and all the hotly debated excesses of capitalism which occupy the liberals of our generation appeared in their most virulent form. But the mercantile greediness of the Dutch achieved what liberal thought failed to establish in bloody wars: religious freedom, for the strongest Calvinistic scruples were laid aside in order to maintain the free flow of goods and money.

The cultivation of arts and letters was inevitably affected by this atmosphere. As would be expected after the similar course of events in England, lyric poetry and music were the first to suffer, but the fine arts, usually the first to attract bourgeois patronage, flourished with unexcelled vigor. Among the great Flemish painters Anthony Van Dyck (1599–1641) and Peter Paul Rubens (1577–1640) were important figures of the Catholic baroque. Van Dyck died as Sir Anthony, court painter to Charles I of England, and Rubens's "atelier was the whole world." He was the greatest painter of the Catholic baroque in the north.

Of an entirely different nature was the art of the neighboring independent Holland. Born and nourished from the Calvinistic soil of a middle-class world in which there were no richly ornamented churches, this art was much more inward, individualistic, and austere than the art of the Flemish school and the colorfulness of Rubens. It embodied much more forcefully the character of the new times, secular subjects being more in the foreground. Baroque it was to the core, but a Protestant baroque. The portraits of Frans Hals (c. 1580–1666) and the landscapes of Jacob van Ruysdael (c. 1628–1682) are less idealistic and more eager to capture reality. Searching character analysis and mastery in the portrayal of facial expression characterize the pictures of Frans Hals, while Ruysdael's woodland glens, mountain scenes, and marines disclose an ardent student of nature who rendered her various aspects with truth and poetic feeling. But they are all overshadowed by Rembrandt (1606–1669), the greatest northern painter of all times, whose power of characterization has probably never been surpassed.

The passionate excitement that filled the epoch of the wars for liberty was followed by the comfortable enjoyment of the blessings of peace. This is well reflected in the arts, now directed toward pictorial effects and a virtuoso technical mastery. The wealth and artistic leanings of the citizenry, as well as the plenitude of creative power, are indicated by the numerous art schools in the cities. European intellectual life was deeply indebted to the Netherlands; Descartes, among others, found a second home there, and

Spinoza an asylum from persecution. The liberal attitude of the country did not allow of the curtailment of intellectual freedom. The centralized absolutist culture of France stood, indeed, in strange contrast to the varied, free, and autonomous intellectual life of Holland.

Thus, as we can see, the religious war for liberty and the subsequent enjoyment of life awakened a multitude of cultural forces in the Netherlands, but the lyric arts, poetry and music, could not prosper, as music especially was too deeply rooted in that marvelous mixture of Gothic romanticism and Mediterranean classicism which characterized the Renaissance in Germanic lands. The fine arts, notably painting, were able to embrace the baroque and adapt it to the spirit of Protestantism, but the centuries-old Netherlandish choral polyphony was too intimately connected with Catholic church music, its mysterious poetry too subtle and too deeply ingrained, to be able to survive if transplanted to a different soil. The last masters to continue the great tradition of Lassus and de Monte, Charles Luython (c. 1556–1620) and Cornelius Verdonck (1563–1625), were already fighting a losing battle. Motet, Mass, and madrigal, the flowers of Renaissance music, retired under the impact of the vehemently conquering new dramatic baroque. They still held to the standards of their traditional polyphonic art, but the Venetian, Florentine, and Roman schools had enhanced the expressive wealth of these choral forms to a point where they burst and disintegrated. There was no possibility left for continuation within the frame of the old art, and compromise seemed to lead to archaism or to formlessness. Verdonck had tried to reconcile the polychoral "colossal baroque" with the principles of his native art, but with his nine-part madrigals he not only defeated the very purpose of this intimate social art, but in his conservatism fell into an exaggeration not shared even by the Venetians. The homophonous facture of the stile rappresentativo, triumphant in the rest of Europe, isolated these composers, and the instrumental style of England, intruding from the other direction, baffled them because there was nothing in the Dutch past that corresponded to this modern and progressive music. In this period of forlornness the genius of the country produced a last great musician, Sweelinck,[35] master of the motet, chanson, fantasy, fugue, and variation, but even he could not establish connections with the ancient traditions of his nation, and with him ends the glorious history of Netherlandish music. His role in this history, beyond his personal history, was not that of the crowning master, for he was a mediator, transmitting the traditions of his native heritage enriched with Italian and English experiences to generations of pupils among whom there were no Netherlanders of note.

Netherlandish musical culture did not cease with the death of its last great master; it took refuge in an intensive bourgeois home music making, well depicted in the numerous etchings and oils of Dutch painters. Lute music flourished for a while, under influences from across the Channel. A few decades later the Italian style became dominant, and at about the time when the Italian trio sonata became victorious over the fancy in England it established itself as the most popular form of instrumental music in Holland. The universal practice of music did not diminish: on the contrary, a veritable avalanche of new compositions appeared; they were, however, but a pale reflection of foreign musical art. The industrial and commercial spirit of the Dutch found a rich field in the manufacture of musical instruments and in music printing and publishing. Dutch harpsichords were famous all over the world, and the instruments built by members of the Ruckers family, apparently impervious to the destructive effects of time, preserved their unsurpassable purity and beauty of tone for many generations. Music publishing developed into an important industry, and the well-equipped printing offices of Antwerp found a ready market all over Europe.

But Holland's heroic period of art was ended. The divine spark was gone, and musical history closed the vast volumes devoted to her great past, never to open them again for further entries.

Spain

HER treasury enriched by the gold of the Americas, her intellectual wealth by the Renaissance, her political power by the Habsburgs, and her faith by the all-embracing Church, Spain entered the baroque period with a national culture of unprecedented intensity and depth. The Counter Reformation feted there its last great cultural glory, as Iberian genius, finding its true self, created two arts which were most suitable for the expression of the baroque spirit: painting and the drama. In our introduction to the baroque era we mentioned Spanish painting as the epitome of the baroque and the artistic expression of the spirit of the Counter Reformation. El Greco, Ribera, Zurbarán, Velasquez, and Murillo left works of art which were masterpieces of realistic handling and penetrating psychology. Their noble sense of color, thrilling power of characterization, and bold scheme of composition raised the Spanish school beyond the boundaries of the nation to be a focus of world admiration. But while the universal significance of this art is an incontestable fact, the national-Spanish and Catholic-churchly forces united here almost indivisibly in the whole physical and cultural life of the Spanish people, endowing it with a unique and inimitable stamp.

Spanish language and literature, highly artistic and very influential in the sixteenth century, in the seventeenth conquered even the ruling power of European aesthetics, French literature. The French *précieux* owe much more to their Spanish prototypes than is commonly supposed; the language of the literary salons reflects the gallant spirit of the centuries-old Spanish troubadours and aristocratic adventurers. The witty ideas and turns of the Spanish *comedia* and its rhetoric gave Corneille and other French dramatists not only the form and means of expression of the modern drama, but many of its subjects, such as the Cid and Don Juan. As a dramatic type, however, the comedia eludes the literary critic's classification. With its lively folklore elements it presents a more or less serious, even tragic, inventive play, rich in epic and lyric motives. Acting under the influence of humanism, the so-called Seville school attempted to win over the Spanish public to the Greco-Roman classical drama, but Sophocles and Seneca have never fared worse than in the home of Lope de Vega, for the Spanish theater sprang from the genius of the nation, as had opera in Italy. It was not created by Lope de Vega, but this great dramatist gave Spanish theater its final and traditional form. His fifteen hundred odd plays, their cleverly constructed plots, well-calculated theatrical effects, and perfect, melodic versification, became the inexhaustible mine for the playwrights of all nations. Even his eminent colleagues, Ruiz de Alarcón and Tirso de Molina, were his debtors. Lope de Vega's legacy fell to Calderón de la Barca, whom we may call the "official" representative of national thought. More learned than his master, and with a distinct inclination toward philosophy, Calderón enriched the Spanish theater with the serious value of contemplation.

As in the case of English literature, one would expect that a country with such a highly developed dramatic art would evolve a national opera as soon as the Florentine principles were communicated to its writers and musicians —if, indeed, it did not create it spontaneously. But exactly the opposite happened. Precisely because of the admirable state of drama, Italian opera could not take hold on the Spanish stage. English genius created its lyric play, which reached its supreme height in Purcell's *King Arthur;* Spain produced its counterpart in that curious mixture of comedy and popular music which is called *zarzuela,* after the castle where its first examples were performed. As in England, these musical comedies (in the true sense of the word) retained throughout the seventeenth century their overwhelming popularity over the operas proper, until Italian opera conquered all Europe in the eighteenth century. Thus as we near the end of the seventeenth century, the originality, the exclusiveness of opera as a purely Italian form of dramatic art, becomes an imposing reality, with France, England, and Spain each developing its lyric stage to suit the national taste and temper.

The first Spanish lyric drama followed the first German opera by two years. Performed in 1629 in Madrid, Lope de Vega's *La Selva sin Amor* (The Loveless Woods) shared the fate of Opitz's and Schütz's *Dafne;* its music was lost. But while the musical score is missing, the libretto and our knowledge of the Spanish theater in general permit at least the reconstruction of the aesthetic principles which motivated the lyric stage in Spain.

There is absolutely no proof that there ever was a lyric drama in Spain, sung from beginning to end, before the Italian operas began to be performed in the eighteenth century. The Spanish theater was, however, literally full of music. Lope de Vega's and Calderón's plays were interspersed with musical "numbers" in a manner not unlike the English plays of the Restoration, and in addition to this, many plays (one could safely call them libretti) were written by the greatest dramatists expressly for the lyric stage. The music that accompanied them—fresh, carefree, infectious with its lively rhythms and melodies, impudent in its romping and unbridled hilarity—came from the great wealth of folk music and popular art music. It was the *cantarcillos* and *villancicos*, the *ensaladas* (*quodlibets*), *farsas*, and *eglogas*, the *tonos*, *tonadas*, and *bailetes* which created the *comedias harmonicas* and *zarzuelas*, the Spanish lyric comedy. It was a folk art, as distinctly and inalienably Spanish as the drama and painting of Calderón and Velasquez. Any attempt to approach this lyric art by incorporating it into the general history of opera will lead to erroneous conclusions. Because of the regrettable state of our knowledge of Spanish music, this field has not yet been touched, save for some cursory allusions in manuals of musical history.

Our knowledge of Spanish music is restricted to a few outstanding composers of the sixteenth century, while the Middle Ages and the baroque are awaiting the musical explorers' spade. The musical contemporaries of Lope de Vega and Velasquez did not attain the Promethean greatness of their colleagues or of their elders of the past school, but they were finished craftsmen and devoted artists who deserve serious study and attention. Appreciation of their worth is, for the time being, restricted to a handful of Spanish scholars, and in the English-speaking world they are acknowledged only by the eminent Spanish historian and musicologist of Cambridge University, J. B. Trend. Some of our largest and most up-to-date manuals on musical history in English, German, and French do not even mention their names. A notable fact that characterizes these composers is their allegiance to their Spanish background, a fact we have noticed in the Spanish lyric theater. This is not the condescending allegiance of many sixteenth- and early seventeenth-century musicians of other nations who quoted here and there a song or used a familiar cantus firmus; it is a musical language deeply rooted in Spanish folk music. They wrote a large amount of religious music, but much of it was not in the accepted manner of Mass and motet, and it was not liturgic. Written on Spanish texts, these *romances,* villancicos, and *folias* usually started with a monophonic verse followed by the full choir in six or more parts. This practice, harking back to the Gregorian intonation of the priest, reminds us of the choral writing in Schütz's Passions.

At the end of the sixteenth century and at the opening of the seventeenth there was a flourishing madrigal school. The brevity of its vogue, singularly reminiscent of the English madrigal school, does not excuse its complete neglect, for the few citations and fragments available in Lavignac's *Encyclopédie* contain music of a remarkably fine texture. Juan Brudieu, Mateo Flecha, and Juan Aranies remain mere names. Unfortunately, the numerous Spanish musicians in the service of the Spanish rulers of Naples and Sicily are also barely distinguishable; future research will undoubtedly unearth a great deal of valuable music and throw more light on the composers. There were also several eminent Spanish musicians still in Rome, in the papal chapel, among them Bartolomé Del Cort, master of the chapel in 1625, and Juan de Santos, according to Burney the last of the famous Spanish falsettists in the Sistine Chapel. The choirmaster of St. Peter's from 1630 to 1648 was a Spanish musician by the name of Pedro Heredia, highly praised for his pure classical style. Others were to be found in many churches and courts in the Low Countries and in Italy.

The great Spanish musical past, bound by a thousand invisible threads to the Church, was doomed to the same fate that befell Netherlandish music; it reached an impasse from which it could not emerge without much hesitation. The times which produced Morales, Guerrero, and Victoria, Milan, Fuenllana, and Cabezón, passed, and the abundance of great musicians was followed by an era of lesser men. But the relative cultural independence of the country and its continued strong Catholic consciousness prevented a sudden collapse like that in the Netherlands and in late seventeenth-century England. The traditions of sacred choral polyphony, especially its reliance on cantus firmus construction, were so strongly impressed on the minds of composers that some of the most gifted musicians were utterly helpless when, in the spirit of the new times, they set out to compose a piece of music without a given theme. In the Franco-Flemish style, the borrowed chanson melody was divested of all its natural and spontaneous charm and was engulfed by the smoothly running, infinitely polished contrapuntal parts; but the Spanish composers, while equally at home in this style, were less internationally-minded than their celebrated Flemish colleagues and absorbed a great deal of the spirit of the folk song. When the great stylistic turn forced a reorientation, the Netherlanders were unable to find connections with popular art. Their great madrigalists, dependent, as we have seen, on the atmosphere of Italy, were stranded when left to their own resources. Faced with the same situation, Spanish music attempted to uphold the great traditions, but when this became increasingly difficult it cheerfully disregarded the precepts of strict contrapuntal writing and fell back on its great treasure of folk music.

Juan Pujol (c. 1573–1626), the great Catalan master, stands at the threshold of this new epoch. Trained in the "old school," he was nevertheless touched by the early Italian baroque, thus forming a bridge between the era of classical choral music and the period we are approaching. Polyphonic church music continued to flourish, and although the polychoral technique, the thorough bass, and concerted music of the baroque were slowly gaining ground, they did not change the austere and inimitably Spanish character of this music as expressed in the works of Sebastian Aguilera de Heredia (c. 1570-?), Juan Bautista Comes (1568–1643), and Juan Barahona de Esquivel (first half of the seventeenth century). The ancient monastery of Montserrat, long famous for its musical priests, preserved its traditions and still harbored within its walls some of the best musicians of the times, among them Juan Romaña and Juan Marqués (first half of the seventeenth century), both highly esteemed for their virtuoso playing and for their delightful harpsichord pieces. The number of active composers is great, but the lack of publications makes it extremely difficult to select the leaders. Mateo Romero (d. 1647), a musician of Flemish origin, enjoyed an immense reputation under the name "El Maestro Capitán," and the church composer Sebastian Lopez de Velasco was found worthy to occupy in 1628 the post that was once Victoria's in the convent of the Descalzas Reales. The outstanding figure among the many instrumental composers in the second half of the century was Juan José Cabanilles (1644–1712), an organist-composer of great fertility and colorful imagination. The universal love of the Spanish guitar, an instrument as typically national as the bagpipe of the Scotch, created a specifically Spanish instrumental style, notably in the dance forms, soon disseminated all over the civilized world. Among these are the age-old *zarabandas* (not to be confused with the elegant eclectic dances that go under the same name in the suite music of the eighteenth century), the *chaconas,* the *pasacelles,* better known in their Italian form, and the *folias,* one of which, called *Folie d'Espagne,* furnished the tune for many celebrated sets of variations from Corelli and J. S. Bach to Liszt.

North America

THE extensive colonization of Central and South America and southern North America by the Spaniards and Portuguese was followed, after considerable delay, by England and France. The almost hermetically closed Spanish territories, extending over Florida, Texas, and a large part of the West, jealously guarded against any intrusion, forced the new colonists farther north, the French going as far as Québec. The settlers converted the territories according to their circumstances and needs, but the country too exerted a reciprocal influence in molding the life of the people living in it. The colonists had their own motives, and the adventurous spirit and courage of a young nation, but the particular circumstances that led them to America were still dependent on the ideas and tendencies of the age. The crosscurrents of the mother country, notable among them the commercial incentive of the merchant and the religious passion of the dissatisfied, accompanied the

British to the New World, creating the two fundamental types of English colonization. The first of these types appeared as the result of the settlement of Virginia. After several unsuccessful attempts, the first permanent British settlement was established at Jamestown, Virginia, in 1607, by the London Company, a corporation which expected to found a commercial-industrial colony. They found the country beautiful and its climate pleasant, but the promised precious metals were not located and the mercantile establishment did not materialize. Lack of food and intermittent epidemics of fever brought the colony to the verge of a collapse saved only by the heroic energy of John Smith. And now these Englishmen gave the land and climate their due, attempting to follow and cultivate with their superior mental and physical equipment what the natives had been doing for their living. Tobacco planting became the economic backbone of the colony, and made it rich and prosperous. This unforeseen eventuality gave Virginia its definite stamp, a stamp which corresponded not to the ideas and wishes of the original colony, but to the natural dictates of land and environment. Instead of the planned commercial settlement, Virginia developed into a plantation colony, and American life began. Making the difference from English life more acute, the sale of twenty Negroes by a Dutch war vessel introduced slavery, an element fundamentally alien to the British mind but readily sanctioned by the newly formed local colonial ideology.

The second type of early American colonist hailed from a vastly different stock, being the product of the intense religious strife of the seventeenth century. Having left England, the Puritans showed their dislike of the adventurous but solid and businesslike merchant settlers while still in Holland, their temporary refuge from England. The mercantile atmosphere of busy Holland was not the right place for the building of God's kingdom on earth, and they decided to migrate to uncorrupted territory beyond the seas. The same company which made possible the settlement of Virginia gave a charter to the Pilgrim Fathers, but the founders of New England did not intend to maintain close relations with the southern colony. They were not from high stations in life and in general were not men of much education, although some of their leading spirits, like William Brewster, were persons of considerable education who had read in Puritanic publications about the organization and conduct of society. The difficulties encountered by the New Englanders were more serious than those which confronted the Virginians, but they stuck grimly to their task, and the news spread to the mother country that there was a place within the British Empire where the worship of God was not hindered by the "sacrilegious rites and discipline" of the Church of England. New settlers, eager to renounce episcopal jurisdiction, came and joined the colonists. The hardships of life and the relentless vigilance against the Indians again demanded a revision of ideas and ideals, and the exclusive

Jan Vermeer van Delft (1632–1675), *"The Music Lesson"*

(Top) Veronese (1528–1588), Detail of the Largest of Veronese's Banquet Scenes. The Musicians Are the Painter, His Brother, Bassano, Titian, and Tintoretto. (Bottom) Bassano (1510–1592), "The Artist with His Family"

ness of the sect and its iron discipline of mind and morals led to intolerance marked by cruelty. On the other hand, however, it engendered a tenacity of purpose and an integrity of character which seem to us almost incredible.

Thus began the other significant phase of American life. It it not necessary to allude to the subsequent colonizations of Maryland and Rhode Island, and still later of Pennsylvania; the religious motives are well known, together with the fact that there were already heroic examples of toleration in the acts of Roger Williams. The formation of the two Carolinas and of Georgia, after the type of Virginia, reminds us again of the molding power of land and environment, for once more the original settlers arrived not only with preconceived ideas but with a model constitution drafted by the great philosopher John Locke that had to be changed in every respect.

The southern states, with their landed gentry, for the most part ruling in complete entente with the High Church, established a typical aristocratic regime based on strictly disciplined servants and slaves who formed the majority of the population. There were few schools, and the middle classes had little political weight. The political structure of the New England society was a theocratic democracy, based entirely on religion, the church being the center of community life. The Puritan mind abhorred slavery and relied on the labor of the members of the community. Their whole life was permeated with religion, God's rule over God's chosen people. To indoctrinate the people with this spirit the churches instituted numerous schools, and in 1636 the first and oldest institution of higher education was founded in New Towne (later Cambridge) by a grant of the Massachusetts Bay Colony. Three years later its endowment was increased by a bequest from John Harvard, and the college was named in his honor. It is a notable fact that the close alliance with Church and state that characterized the early days of this famous institution was maintained, if with less emphasis, until the middle of the nineteenth century.

At the present stage of musical research the musical life of the South in its first century of existence remains almost entirely unknown, but New England's musical history has been examined by several competent historians [36] and presents an interesting picture, at least from the sociological point of view.

Unlike the Spanish priests who accompanied the conquistadors in the sixteenth century and the French Jesuits of the seventeenth, the Puritans, considering themselves God's elects, were not primarily interested in shepherding the natives into their church. They saw in the Indians the Canaanites of the Old Testament and did not wish to contaminate the House of God with them. This same austere and unimaginative spirit endeavored to exclude music from the church, many believing that the tunes of the Psalms were not divinely inspired and ought not to be sung. Their religious life was characterized by simple services in churches cold and unadorned, with lengthy emotion-arousing sermons the essence of the service. Bible reading and prayers in the family group were encouraged. There is no record of the actual practice of singing in the first years of the New England colony, but it is known that the Separatists brought with them Psalm books which, at least before their arrival in America, they were wont to use. Edward Winslow (1595–1655), one of the founders of New England, in his vigorous defense of the colony, *Hypocrisie Unmasked* (1646), described the departure from Leyden in 1620, saying that the congregation, much moved, sang Psalms, "there being many of our congregation very expert in music." [37] Since the singing of metrical Psalms was the only form of congregational singing in the English-speaking Protestant churches (the hymns did not come into general use before the eighteenth century), this statement indicates that the Pilgrim Fathers were not unacquainted with music. But their children, accustomed to the hardships of pioneer life, and seeking to meet the utilitarian needs of a practical world, declined it. The religious motivation should not mislead us, for it was still the gospel of work, founded on the Scriptures, corroborated by the common sense and desires of the middle-class elements, and reinforced by frontier conditions, which was at the bottom of this animosity; the Puritans considered idleness—and what else would music be in their eyes?—a sin second only to adultery, and a danger to society. A society founded on theocracy legislates in terms of moral sins; consequently music, openly liked and practiced by the majority of the Puritans in England, and, as we have seen, by the Pilgrim Fathers on setting sail for the New World, was proscribed by the second generation in America, firmly believing that its prohibition was an act pleasing to God. There was practically no secular amusement or music of any kind, vocal or instrumental, and the churches banished organs, which were introduced only in the eighteenth century. Even the old and harmless merriment of Maypole dancing was looked upon with great apprehension, for " 'twas not the time for New England to dance."

The fact remains, however, that the Pilgrims brought with them Psalm books, notably a Psalter prepared in 1612 by Henry Ainsworth (c. 1570–1593), an able Biblical scholar, for the Amsterdam congregation of Separatists. The Plymouth colony retained this Psalter, but the other New England congregations used the much earlier Sternhold and Hopkins Psalter. This volume, first published as a small book in 1548 or 1549, and with additions made by Hopkins again at the end of 1549, was repeatedly edited until in 1556 an edition was published in Geneva for the benefit of the Protestants who had taken refuge there. This edition contains the famous tunes, among them the "Old Hundredth" (of French origin), which up to this day are cherished by Protestants. By 1562 what we may call the definitive edition of the Sternhold-Hopkins Psalter appeared, to become the most popular Psalm book among

English-speaking Protestants. While an ability to sing tunes "from the book" was widespread in Elizabeth's time, the subsequent editions of the Sternhold-Hopkins Psalter, up to 1607—that is, up to the times when the Pilgrims began to be restless—contained "An introduction to Learn to Sing," with an explanation of the nature of the scales and other elements of music.

There can be no doubt, then, about the meaning of Winslow's remark, whose men, "very expert in music," were fully aware of the age-old indivisibility of the Psalms and music. But the first metrical version of the Psalms prepared and printed in New England, the so-called Bay Psalm Book (1640), the earliest book (aside from an unimportant almanac) printed in the colonies, had no tunes; the socio-theological aversion became tradition. This Psalter, extremely popular, and ultimately replacing the Ainsworth version when the Plymouth settlement was merged into the Massachusetts Bay Colony, was equipped with tunes only in its ninth edition, in 1698, and then with only a little more than a dozen of them. This does not mean, however, that the Psalms were not sung, for as early as 1647 John Cotton published a defense of singing, emphasizing that it is a religious duty to sing the Psalms, and that other "spiritual songs recorded in Scripture" may also be sung without offending public morals. Toward the middle of the century his conception was generally accepted and a simple manner of congregational singing developed. But singing was not supposed to be aided by printed music, for the knowledge of musical notation might encourage the playing of instruments, and it was too reminiscent of the popish vanity of professional choirs. Moreover, the names of the notes were "blasphemous" and "it required too much time to learn them which made the young disorderly, and kept them from the proper influence of the family." [38] To overcome the difficulty a precentor would guide the congregational singing by "lining out the tune," chanting, and with a sort of chironomy, the people singing from memory. This naturally led to confusion; the practice varied in every congregation, and if for some reason joint services were held by several congregations the result was a fantastic cacophony that would be envied by the best surrealists of our day. The inevitable, sad consequence of this practice was a complete deterioration of church music and singing; the different Psalms were gradually dropped until only three or four tunes were used for all Psalms. Under these circumstances the sturdy and varied tunes of the Ainsworth Psalter were also soon forgotten, as they deteriorated for want of printed versions.

At the opening of the eighteenth century voices were heard in favor of a betterment of the musical situation. At the same time German and Swedish immigrants, arriving in the closing years of the seventeenth century and settling in the central states that separated the South from New England, were causing a gradual recovery and a new and friendlier orientation to music which was to inaugurate a new era in American musical history.[39]

Chapter 11

THE LATE BAROQUE

※≫ ≪※

*"Mind possesses a certain character
which depends on the innate temperament of the individual, and by this character the musician is inclined to one type
of composition rather than to another.
For indeed the variety of composition is
quite as numerous as the diversity of
temperaments which come to light in
individuals."*
(Athanasius Kircher, *Musurgia Universalis,* Rome, 1650, *Pars* II, *Cap.*
v, *p.* 581)

Absolutism and the Enlightenment

MODERN history calls the period that extends from the second
half of the seventeenth century to the French Revolution the
"Period of Absolutism." The earnest follower of history will
discover, however, the paradox that a movement admittedly
aiming at the curtailment of personal liberty, the political and spiritual freedom of the individual, coincides with another called "The Enlightenment,"
which may be considered the greatest cultural and spiritual reorientation since
Christianity supplanted the antique world. How can a new conception which
attacked the very foundations of long-established and authoritarian Christian
thought be reconciled with absolutism? Yet the two movements were products of the same times and developed concurrently, influencing each other
considerably until finally the Enlightenment, though not without the active
help of absolutism, gained the upper hand.

Another puzzle will confront the student at the very beginning of his investigations; he will fail to see why absolutism, practiced by the Caesars of
Rome, the rulers of medieval Christendom, and the tyrants of the Renaissance,
should be considered a novelty. In the seventeenth century there were, however, mighty reasons for the accentuated success of absolutism, reasons at-

tributable to the very strata of society which should have conducted the most earnest fight against it. The actual power of monarchs increased as that of the nobility waned. The modern state was slowly emerging; it required a smoothly functioning machinery to carry out plans and administer programs. But few were the countries where the servants of the state and the estates which furnished them placed the *res publica* above their own aims, and the ruler, having identified his dynasty with the state, was left to develop the latter. Thus the exploitation of the country and of its resources for purely dynastic and courtly purposes was a misuse, but in the final analysis it proved to be a necessary stage of political, legal, economic and cultural evolution. We must not forget, furthermore, that all rulers were not worthless despots, that a great many princes and potentates of this era were men of high ability and wisdom, deeply interested in the welfare of their nations. What they created in modern statecraft, national defense, cultural institutions, and social legislation was the invaluable fundament upon which the liberals were later able to base their actions.

The other movement, the Enlightenment, is also of more ancient origin than the seventeenth century, and some historians are inclined to extend its confines to the Middle Ages. Its real impact begins, however, relatively late, at the extreme end of the Renaissance, and the great spiritual movement designated by this name was the issue of philosophy and the natural sciences. Renaissance and Reformation prepared the ground, inasmuch as they questioned the absolute authority of the Church; but neither the Renaissance— artistic and humanistic—nor the Reformation—primarily religious—was a direct antecedent, for the Enlightenment was in no small measure directed against both. "Where reason shall rule neither art nor the Church can determine life." It appears, then, that the Enlightenment of the eighteenth century was the outcome of centuries-long efforts directed toward the secularization of spiritual and practical life, its origin having been a reaction against the conditions of life as dominated and governed by the authority of the medieval Church. By denying this traditional authority modern man expressed his will to form opinions based on unprejudiced and undogmatic thinking and observation instead of relying on the guidance of other minds conditioned by tradition and special allegiances. This new orientation caused a fundamental change in arts and sciences. As Copernicus shattered the old belief in the central position of the earth, as Kepler discovered the planetary system, as Descartes dictated the new rational approach to human existence, as Bayle disavowed all dogmaticism, requiring tolerance even for atheists, and as Newton expounded his mathematical theory of universal gravitation, a free spirit permeated human thought.

The beginning of the eighteenth century does not offer a sharp line of demarcation—the seventeenth flows smoothly into it—but above the confluence rises the baroque structure of Leibnitz's thought, an edifice animated by lawful order and by the dualism of rationalism and irrationalism. The doctrines of Leibnitz were systematized and made accessible to the public by Christian von Wolff (1679-1754), who purged the picture of the universe of all its irrationalistic elements, thus creating, together with Locke, an appropriate philosophical background for the Enlightenment. The changes that took place in the ensuing decades were nothing short of revolutionary. We have seen how absolutism was carried to its apogee by Louis XIV, the king's person becoming the only symbol of the national state and the combination of Church and state threatening to extinguish all individual thought. But the pendulum was to start on its backward swing, and in the very country that furnished the model of absolutism, the reaction was to culminate in an unparalleled upheaval.

While the ideas underlying the Enlightenment of the eighteenth century originated for the greater part in England, the battle for their triumph was carried on in France. At the opening of the eighteenth century we see the leading spirits of that country girded for a war that was to liberate mankind from its shackles. Men and nations struggled in this century for a new formulation of their existence. Old states made their exit and new ones came upon the stage of history. The old order of society, based on hierarchy and feudalism, was being liquidated and the secularization of all phases of life was carried out unfailingly. There remained, however, a uniformity of cultural consciousness, a universally accepted outlook on life directed at the present, dominating the public mind, and filling men with a sense of the omnipotence of triumphant reason. This reason now undertook the creation of a new order, which was to disregard irrational values by relying on absolute thinking—rationalism—or on absolute experience—empiricism. Rationalism gained even the Catholic exegeses, a field least receptive to it; beginning with Bossuet we find the sermons devoid of mysticism, and while the departure was strictly dogmatic, the exposition was supported by an inexorable logic, a profusion of scientific documents, and a total absence of sentimentalism. When in the second half of the eighteenth century the final results of research and thinking were summarized, receiving a synthesis of rationalism and empiricism in the philosophy of Kant, reason, schooled through scientific practice and passing critical judgments, turned finally against itself and recognized the boundaries of its competence in the *Critique of Pure Reason*.

The Philosophical Background

SINCE sensory impressions vary greatly in different persons, the philosophers were inclined to refuse experience as the source of knowledge, retaining thinking as the only reliable way to the realization of the nature of

things. Experience, they said, leads to confusing results; the abstract mind
—*ratio*—detached from the sensory world and immersed in itself is the only
infallible guide. Reason came to be considered the source of all human
knowledge, for it was able to establish the essence of things *a priori,* without having recourse to sensory perception. In fact, some of the rationalists
—Descartes for instance—advocated that the notions of God, the soul, and
causality, as well as moral laws and mathematical maxims, are innate in
man, and consequently are present, *a priori,* in the mind before any observation and experience take place.

On the other hand, empiricism deduced all legitimate knowledge from
experience; there are no innate notions and laws, otherwise we should find
them in every human being without exception. At birth the soul is a blank
slate upon which will be written the letters of external and internal experience (Locke). The validity of our knowledge cannot proceed beyond
the boundaries of experience from which it is solely derived; that is, such
transcendent notions as the existence of God, the immortality of the soul,
and the freedom of the will can never be known to us with exactitude. Thus,
unlike rationalism, `pure empiricism denies the possibility of metaphysics.

A rapprochement of the two schools as to the origin of knowledge is already discernible toward the end of the seventeenth century. Empiricism was
compelled to admit that the raw results of sensory observation do not become experience unless elaborated by the activity of the mind; rationalism
in its turn could not successfully counter the contention that the mental
processes are in reality empty formulae unless they receive content from
contemplation and observation. The reconciliation of the two schools of
thought occupied the greater part of the century. With the full development
of the Enlightenment there was a collaboration between empiricism and
the natural sciences, empiricism gaining some constancy in its conditions and
a clearer formulation of its principles.

The spirit of these times demanded the classification of every problem
either in the domain of the natural sciences or in that of mathematical philosophy. Music as a phenomenon was not exempt from this system of dual
classification and was divided in the baroque era in a scientific-acoustic and
a rational-comprehensible set of problems. The musical writers of this era
were the musicians themselves, thus philosophy and aesthetics of music were
directly connected with creative production. The temper of the period urged
the composers, usually of considerable learning and education, to defend
their art of composition by scientific dissertations about their method; therefore the theoretical and philosophical literature of the eighteenth century
permits us a deep insight into the inner mechanism of this art. We learn the
processes of musical creation and the factors that caused the composers'
imagination to follow a predetermined course; on the other hand we gain

information concerning the criteria of artistic enjoyment on the part of the listener. History and philosophy of art, as practiced in the past century, could not gain or give a true picture of all this because it isolated music from its surroundings and from its extramusical components. The resulting misconception is regrettable not only from the point of view of cultural philosophy but because it is chiefly responsible for the neglect and misunderstanding of the music of the whole baroque era, than which there was none richer and more rewarding in the history of music.

The close connection of arts and sciences brings to a head the old controversial question of whether science is prejudicial to art. It does not seem to be true that imaginative literature or art suffers from scientific interest on the part of the artist. Leonardo, Goethe, and Valéry are convincing instances. One must, however, make a proper distinction between idea and method. Modern psychology has established that ideas are intuitive and come suddenly, the subsequent differences in result being due to their elaboration according to the characteristic methods of philosophy, art, or science. If this be true—the cases of Newton with the apple and Watt with the teakettle seem to confirm it—we must look for the conflict, if any, between science and art in method rather than in idea. The methods of science are those of accuracy and precision, while the methods of art are generalized truth. Truth and accuracy are separate instruments, and the confusion of the two may easily become inimical to art. The answer to the question is, then, that if the artist is master of his generalizing instrument he stands to gain rather than lose by scientific, or any other, knowledge and interest. His imagination is enriched and his actual expression gains vitality from all that is stored in the background of his mind. If his is not an original talent, unable to trust its wings, his meddling with knowledge is fraught with peril, for before knowledge or science can become an adjunct to art it must be converted, not by reasoning, but by the imaginative temperament of the artist combined with the mastery of the means of expression. Both of these the artists of the baroque possessed in profusion, and once we plunge into the almost inexhaustible treasury of this period, we shall find that at the bottom of all these activities was an endeavor to convert the inorganic into the organic, the material into the spiritual, the quiescent into the animated, and the substantial into the functional.

Musical Thought of the Baroque
The Doctrine of Temperaments and Affections

AS far as a phenomenon can be reduced to elements which permit quantitative measuring, it can be analyzed objectively and its physical nature explained. For such a procedure empiricism offers a suitable approach, but it is evident that it cannot lead to a full comprehension of an artistic phenomenon. Although rhythm and proportion, converted into optical and acoustical symbols, offer measurable components of every art, the quality, that is, the essentially aesthetic moment, remains irrational. The criterion of the beautiful sees in rhythm and proportion only the means of presentation of an idea. The realization of such ideas is brought about in the several arts in different ways. Most arts present their general ideas in a concrete example: they represent "something." But while this "something" serves as the first act for the realization of a work of art, the essentially aesthetic moment is the "how" of the presentation; the symbolic is manifested in the concrete. It is quite common, however, that the nature of the representation, the primarily aesthetic element, is overshadowed by the object represented. Unlike the other arts, music presents the symbols as pure abstraction not bound by any concrete content. It can embody the "how" without expressing the "something." It does not present content, as the representation is its very content. This absolute music—defined by no elements outside of musical ones— should, then, be conceived as pure contemplation. It is possible, however, to substitute for these purely musically expressed symbols concrete realities. In its urge to achieve a most objective realization of things, rationalism introduced into music the expression of the realities of life. The Renaissance in its *musica reservata,* in its careful observance of the rights of the text, and in its attempted musical representations of comprehensible actions began to demonstrate an interest in a musical art that was not "free." In the subsequent era, music was increasingly dominated by the spoken word, comprehensible ideas, and concrete actions.

The spirit of the Renaissance eschewed medieval longing for the beyond and reinstated love of life as cherished by the ancients. Man and his natural circumstances became the center of interest. The baroque contributed to this new conception a keener sense for the comprehension of characters, passions, and "affections." The subject of arts and letters was man, the conditions of his mental life, the power of his affections, the divergent character of individuals and nations. This was, of course, fully expressed in philosophy, but it was not less plainly evident in the arts. The musical authors of the baroque are fairly well known to the students of music history, for the number of tracts on composition, figured bass, ornamentation, etc., is considerable; but theories of music based on the technical abilities and limitations of musicians and musical instruments do not properly fit under either of the reigning philosophical processes. Beyond this technical apparatus, offered for practical purposes, there were theories concerning style and aesthetics of music, buttressed with profound philosophical contemplations. Unlike the legion of nineteenth- and twentieth-century theoreticians and historians, the musicographers of the baroque did not define music

and its style by objective-technical precepts, but saw it conditioned by nationality, time, place; briefly, in the diversity of man's bent of mind. Rationalism sought in music as in other arts the "imitation of nature," the
cherished dogma and foundation of its musical thought. We should not,
however, expect this to mean tone-painting or program music, or the imitation of sounds that can be found in nature, such as the rippling of a stream,
the buzzing of insects, or the chirping of birds. While such things sometimes occupied composers, literal imitations form a very small part of the
musical aesthetics of the baroque, the musical thought of which was first
and foremost concerned with rendering and translating into music the
temper, disposition or frame of mind, passions, and mental reactions characteristic of man. The "doctrine of temperaments and affections" which
had already appeared in the anthropological-philosophical literature of the
sixteenth century became the nerve center of baroque music. On previous
occasions we used the term "affect" as a technical term accepted by modern
psychology. In the seventeenth century, however, the Italian *affetti* and the
German *Affekte* had a counterpart in the English "affections," a word
which today is applied to mild feelings, but which formerly stood for the
strongest emotional expressions, distinct from "passions." This can be ascertained from the very title of an *Essay on the Nature and Conduct of the
Passions and Affections* (1728), by Francis Hutcheson, Irish metaphysician
(1694–1746). The same distinction is encountered in writings on music.
"Musick hath 2 ends, first to pleas the sence, & that is done by the pure Dul-
cor of Harmony, which is found chiefly in ye elder musick, of wch much
hath bin sayd, & more is to come, & secondly to move ye affections or excite
passion." [1] It was found advisable to employ the original English word
in spite of the strange impression it makes on the modern reader when used
in this sense, because the foregoing quotation indicates clearly that to the
musician of the seventeenth and eighteenth centuries "affections" and "affective" expressions were definite notions associated with the baroque style,
and cannot be replaced by "emotions" or "passions" as modern usage would
require.

Athanasius Kircher (1602–1680), the celebrated German polyhistorian, one
of the most learned men of the century and the author of treatises on every
conceivable subject, is our best witness for the scientific formulation of the
doctrine of temperaments and affections in the seventeenth century. In his
monumental *Musurgia Universalis,* this eminent Jesuit attempted to give an
explanation for the existence of different styles of music:

Melancholy people like grave, solid, and sad harmony; sanguine persons prefer
the *hyporchematic* style (dance music) because it agitates the blood; choleric
people like agitated harmonies because of the vehemence of their swollen gall;

martially inclined men are partial to trumpets and drums and reject all delicate and pure music; phlegmatic persons lean toward women's voices because their high-pitched voice has a benevolent effect on phlegmatic humour.[2]

These were the *constitutio temperamenti* of the individual man, who is conceived as largely passive, exhibiting a leaning or preference for a certain style. To the *constitutio temperamenti* was added an active agent of style, the *constitutio regionis,* with which we are virtually in the neighborhood of Taine's philosophy of art. The *constitutio regionis* stood for the influence of the environment on the creative musical activity of the population, professing that the combination of temperament and environment will result in a national style.

Toward the third quarter of the seventeenth century the rather vague organization of genres and styles gave way to a classification which was to be followed even by the first generations of the eighteenth. In general the writers distinguished between three styles: the *stylus ecclesiasticus,* the *stylus cubicularis* (chamber), and the *stylus scenicus seu theatralis.* While composers and writers agreed on this classification, musical thought showed two currents in their interpretation, converging occasionally to produce curious combinations. One of these currents, reactionary in content and nature, summarized once more the classic-medieval elements, the other tendency was progressive and seems remarkably advanced even in this forward-looking period. While the first school of thought offered the professional-formal side of the musician's craft in a naïve and uncritical fashion, the rationalism of the Enlightenment invited reflection and reasoning in the second. Although seemingly irreconcilable, both schools had certain things in common.

Among the leading exponents of the first school we find Agostino Steffani (1654–1728), one of the greatest composers of the late baroque, and Andreas Werckmeister (1645–1708), musician and mathematician, better known for his work in furthering the cause of correct tuning. Werckmeister's musical conceptions still rest, to a considerable extent, on purely medieval precepts; hence his extensive mathematical-musical speculations. To him music is *scientia mathematica,* and in his writings we again meet with the Boethian leitmotives: *ratio* and *sensus.* Allegorical, mystical, and astrological discussions and theses, rather strange in this period, abound.

The second school was headed by the Saxon court conductor Johann David Heinichen (1683–1729), whose writings, highly esteemed in his time, remain sound and useful reading in our day and are one of the chief sources of the doctrine of the affections.[3] The picture that confronts us on these lively pages differs sharply from the one painted by the exponents of the other school. Heinichen's tirades against the ancients sound like the radical diatribes of the modernists. He berates their "so-called sense and judgments," and their "overwhelming and exaggerated metaphysical contemplations"; all that matters is "how the music sounds and how the listeners like it," and it is immaterial how it looks on paper. With this we encounter a new criterion, the taste and approval of the public, and, indeed, the French term *goût* now makes its first appearance in musical literature. There is mention of French and Italian *goût, goût der Welt,* or "universal taste," which would be a "happy mixture" of all styles, unmistakably an idea of the rationalistic Enlightenment.

The Alsatian Sébastien de Brossard (c. 1654–1730), learned priest, church composer, and conductor, whose remarkable library, offered to Louis XV, furnished the groundstock for the collection of old music of the Bibliothèque Nationale, is another important representative of baroque musical thought. He was the author of one of the oldest musical encyclopedias,[4] an excellent work rich in documents and information concerning the musical life of his times.[5] A fact of great interest is Brossard's emphasis on the origin of styles, which he places in Italy. His enumeration shows the wide dissemination of the doctrine of the affections and temperaments:

Style means, in general, the particular manner or fashion of expressing ideas, of writing, or of doing some other thing. In music, it signifies the manner in which every individual composes, plays or teaches, and all this is very diversified according to the genius of the authors, the country and the nation: as well as according to the materials, the places, the times, the subjects, the expressions, etc. Thus one is wont to say the style of Carissimi, of Lully, of Lambert, etc; the style of the Italians, of the French, of the Spaniards, etc. The style of gay and joyful music is very different from the style of grave and serious music . . . therefore we have different epithets in order to distinguish among all these different characters, such as ancient and modern style, Italian, French, and German style, ecclesiastic, dramatic, and chamber style, etc. . . . . The Italians have expressions for all that we have mentioned, and we shall explain them in the order of their importance.

The last sentence is of great significance, for *à leur rang,* "in the order of their importance," is meant to apply to the degree of affective communication in the various styles and genres. Consequently we are dealing here with the conception and classification of music which is neither mathematical-symbolical, like that of the Middle Ages or of such baroque theoreticians as Kircher and Werckmeister, nor formal-empirical, like that of the Italians, but an aesthetic conception which attempts to range the musical phenomena according to established laws of evaluation and appraisal. The measure was supplied by the doctrine of the affections, the affections being identified with the content, and their provocation being considered the sole aim and purpose of music.

The music of the baroque sprang from the background furnished by the affections and temperaments; and from its very beginnings preference was accorded to music connected with words and action. While the importance of the literary element was recognized by Zarlino and other earlier musician-thinkers, it is only natural that it was the rising opera which contributed the decisive opportunity for a development of the new principles of musical aesthetics and composition. The literary element dominated this new musical style at the outset so completely that, in the recitative, it dissolved the musical structure. Musical composition lost some of its absolute-musical traits; on the other hand it was enriched by new characteristics and means of expression of a dramatic nature. The danger of delivering music to drama altogether by abandoning its purely musical qualities was a real one. Fortunately the sheer musical genius of such men as Monteverdi was able to retain the intrinsic values of music and place it in the service of new ideals, unscathed and even enhanced, at the very time when the literary amateurs were about to submerge music completely. But the aesthetic interest of his contemporaries was concentrated primarily on the dramatic; they wanted to gain insight through aesthetic sensation, thereby relegating the essential in art to a secondary place. Like philosophical rationalism, this rationalistic aesthetics found its most radical and uncompromising representatives in France. Lamotte-Houdar, the Abbé Pluche,[6] the Abbé Dubos,[7] Batteux,[8] and Voltaire advocated a conception of the beautiful which was independent of sentiments. Boileau's maxim *Rien n'est beau que le vrai* became the guiding principle and soon took the form of "imitation of nature," finding immediate application in music.

This aesthetic orientation viewed art solely from an intellectual angle, Lamotte-Houdar going so far as to deny any merit and necessity for versification in poetry and declaring the essence of poetry to lie in the boldness of the ideas, the truth of the pictures, and the power of expression. As a logical consequence of his beliefs, Lamotte-Houdar wrote his odes and tragedies in prose. It is easy to see in what way music would suffer from such tenets, and while Fontenelle's famous saying, "Sonate, que me veux tu?" may be considered an extreme attitude, valid only in France, it is undeniable that pure instrumental music was placed at a level considerably below that of vocal music. The main objection to instrumental music was that it was not able clearly to express the affections. Since the prevailing aesthetic conception considered the affections the only content of music, this limited affective expressiveness was a serious shortcoming in their eyes. "An instrumental player or composer must observe the rules which lead to good melody and harmony much more clearly and assiduously than a singer or a choral composer, because when singing, the singer or composer is aided by the great clarity of the words, while the latter are always missing in instrumental music." [9] At the same time the old ethical and symbolic connotations attached to musical instruments were transformed and their erstwhile sociological ties disappeared. With Mattheson, the most important theoretical writer of the late baroque, the instruments became integral parts of the general *Affektenlehre,* the doctrine of the affections. He speaks of the "most magnificently sounding trombones, the lovely pompous horns, the proud bassoons, the harsh cornets, the modest flutes, the heroic kettledrums, the flattering lutes, the solid *viole da braccio,* the grumbling bass fiddles," etc.[10] All this should not be confused, however, with the purely extraneous, sensualistic, tone-color characterization of the nineteenth century, although the starting point of the romantic orchestral color palette undoubtedly lies in the affective expression of the late baroque.

Beginning with Mattheson the philosophical conceptions and empirical leanings of the Enlightenment began to displace entirely the many medieval survivals still extant in earlier baroque musical thought. In his very first work, *Das Neu-Eröffnete Orchestre* (1713), the tendency to turn to the educated music lover instead of to the professional musician is apparent. The ideal of the Enlightenment, the universally cultured man, the *homme galant,* becomes the addressee of dissertations. The aim is no longer to justify new theoretical findings by reconciling them with ancient musical doctrines or to introduce musicians into the art and science of musical composition, but to enable the educated person to "form his tastes, understand the technical terms, so that he can discuss this noble science with understanding." With this begins an entirely new era of musical thought.

Rationalism—Irrationalism—Symbolism

THE rationalistic tendency in baroque thinking cannot, however, be applied to music with the exclusiveness and simplicity demonstrated by such exponents of musical symbolism as Albert Schweitzer, the distinguished biographer of Johann Sebastian Bach. What seems to be a hard and fast system in the writings of the theoreticians, in the manuals of composition, and in the recorded statements of composers, is not borne out completely by the compositions themselves. The intuitively creating musician remained "irrational" to a considerable degree even though he was a true child of the baroque, and it is only our unfamiliarity with the baroque style and with the overwhelming majority of its musicians that makes us take the naïve and often puerile "realism" and "symbolism" apparent in the works of even the greatest of baroque musicians for the essential stylistic feature of this art. Music that would reflect, weigh, and reason at every turn would abandon the most precious of its possessions: the immediate, elementally musical invention.

The empirical process of discovering laws of nature is rooted in observation to the exclusion of preconceived theoretical doctrines, while the scientific process follows a planned route. In the course of musical history it was demonstrated that practitioners of either of the two methods could not avoid instinctive application of both precepts. The Pythagorean interval doctrines of medieval theorists, making the third into a dissonance, did not prevent the gradual rise of a new conception of consonance based precisely on the proscribed third, and when Zarlino offered his harmonic system he only codified and equipped with a scientific apparatus a doctrine long in universal use. The empiric origin of such procedures is even more strikingly illustrated by the next phase of harmonic thought. The eighteenth century undertook a scientific investigation of the whole tonal system, emphasizing the physical aspects of the interval doctrine rather than its mathematical aspects. In Rameau's *Traité de l'Harmonie Réduite à Ses Principes Naturels* (1722), the laws of chordal associations were formulated into a system which is recognized today as the basis of modern musical composition. Yet the system was effectively prepared by the practical figuring of the thorough bass, providing a statistical list of the chords in actual use. The most commonly used chords soon became so stereotyped that their arbitrarily established graphical measurements (from the bass) stood henceforth for constant notions such as the sixth chord, the seventh chord, etc. It was not long before the laws of harmony and harmonic progressions, hidden behind the graphic symbols, were recognized and brought into a logical system. Empiricism was able, then, to establish the musical physiognomy of harmony by laws of nature as manifested in the harmonic overtones.

Thus the problem confronting us in the musical thought of the baroque is not so much the attitude of theoreticians and composers, admittedly derived from philosophical sources: it is, rather, whether music developed within its province, by its own powers, and without the conscious application of scientific theories, an artistic will and tendency which was in sympathy with the general trend of culture and civilization.

Viewed from the premises of general aesthetics, it is evident that ever since the late Renaissance music was gradually leaving the sphere of "absolute music," absorbing poetic and pictorial characteristics. While this is instantly discernible in vocal music, it is not less unmistakably present in instrumental music, supposedly least susceptible to extramusical stimuli. The early instrumental paraphrases of songs as well as canzoni and ricercari carried with them the lyric mood of the vocal models. In the simpler examples the periodic construction still showed the formal structure of the original piece of poetry. The dance pieces of the instrumental suites also carried with them a lyric atmosphere recalling the poetic origin of dance songs. But perhaps the most influential agent in shaping the future of free music was the music drama. The music drama impressed itself so firmly on the whole field of musical composition that we can safely say that all important innovations, from the early seventeenth century to our day, can be attributed to operatic influences. The overture shows this clearly, as does the modern symphonic poem, its first cousin, but the seemingly independent forms of instrumental music exhibit it with equal certitude, although more subtly.

The student trying to find his way in this labyrinth is likely to forget a fact of the utmost importance: namely, that the arts, especially music, were struggling for equality with the sciences, for to be classified with the sciences meant to be accorded a higher intellectual rank. Hence we have the many rationalistic codifications of simple musical practice, codifications and summaries which freeze the elastic spirit of living art into inexorable rules and definitions. The formal-structural importance of the affections found, of course, a scientific formulation in musical literature. Manuals containing musical "figures" which corresponded to certain affections began to appear with Mauritius Vogt's *Conclave Thesauri Magnae Artis Musicae* (Prague, 1711), and toward the middle of the century there was offered a thorough exposition of "the doctrine of the musical figures" in Johann Adolf Scheibe's *Der Critische Musicus*. Using Gottsched's *Critische Dichtkunst* as his model, Scheibe expounds the importance of the figures, emphasizing that, far from being mannerisms, they are the components of musical form, decisive factors, and therefore not casual or arbitrary but essential parts of musical composition itself. While these figures seem naïve and are cloaked in a formidable scientific garb—Vogt employs terms like *polyptoton, polysyntheton, schematoides,* etc.—there can be no question that the theoreticians merely tried to express in the current rational-scientific manner what was widely practiced by the musical composers. Wherever we look in contemporary literature we shall find the same anxiety to warn the reader of the presence of the affections for fear he will not notice them. Georg Muffat, in the preface of his *Florilegium,* found it advisable to warn his "friendly reader" that if he finds in these compositions "rough and strange" things he should not ascribe them to a "dry and coarse style"; such flaws are rather due to the fact that "to elucidate certain words, manners, or gestures, one has to compromise occasionally." [11]

All this was taken too literally by a number of authors, chief among them Schweitzer, who attempted to explain the whole art and style of Bach on the basis of symbolism and the doctrine of the musical figures. While his contentions are often true, especially in relation to vocal music, the essence of baroque form lies in far less concrete formulae. Form in baroque music, especially in instrumental music, is to be understood as the consequence of the elevation and exaltation of soul and mood, a circumstance which is not an aesthetic, but a real, psychological elevation and exaltation. That is the reason why the authors standing at the opposite pole from Schweitzer are even more at a loss when they attempt to approach the music of this period by the time-honored methods of nineteenth-century musical theory. The counting of measures and the enumeration of modulations are as meaning-ingless in this era as in the music of Schönberg. The specific formal prin-ciple of the baroque is the statement of the "basic affection" and its subse-quent exploitation by continuous expansion. This means that the basic affection (which does not necessarily express any concrete idea or notion) must be stated in the most pregnant and concentrated manner—the fugue theme—for the rest of the musical composition depends on it. The baroque sonata does not have contrasting themes as used by the symphonists of the classic era, for it is concerned with the exploitation of *one* affection which would be weakened and disturbed by additional material, introducing a different state of mind, idea, or affection. The robust directness, the magni-ficent pathos, the sharp delineation of the opening measures in Buxtehude's or Handel's compositions testify to the affective concentration at the begin-ning of baroque musical form. Once a fugue or a concerto gets under way, it brooks no obstacles, ignores challenges, refuses to pause until it reaches its destination, which is the end; the material is exhausted. Thus baroque form gives free rein to the artist's imagination, and nothing can illustrate more clearly the profound misunderstanding of the essence of this art than the statement found in most counterpoint treatises and histories of music that the fugue is "the strictest form of polyphonic writing," with hard and fast rules governing its construction. Ebenezer Prout in the preface to his *Fugue* (1891) actually mentions the instance of a counterpoint teacher in his time who forbade the study of Bach's fugues because they are "contrary to the rules." It would be difficult, indeed, to find many among Bach's fugues that are built on the same plan. Modern writers have recognized that the fugal form—most representative and highest of baroque forms—may be said to be "a question of texture rather than of design" (Tovey), a conception which comes near to the essence of freely unfolding baroque form. Viewed from the conventional angle of formal theories (usually labeled "classical," al-though with little justification), this baroque unfolding of music seems es-sentially formless, always reaching out for wider expanses and never end-ing; but history teaches us how quickly the understanding of the art of even a recent period vanishes.

If we do not understand the music of the baroque, the latter was not less estranged from the Renaissance, and it is astounding to observe how remote was the second half of the seventeenth century from the great art of the late Renaissance. Italian writers between about 1660 and 1670 speak of Palestrina and Lassus as *gli antichi,* considering their music archaic, written in the *stylus gravis* to the exclusion of any other style. These ancient composers had "but one style and one manner," while the *moderni* have three. Brossard distinguished three musical eras, the *musica antiqua, the musica antiquo-moderna,* which is "modern when compared to the Greeks but ancient when compared to ours," and, finally, music that is *veritablement moderne*. The first era lasted until Guido d'Arezzo; the second, "a sort of grave and serious music for many voices," reigned from Guido's time "until the beginning of the past [seventeenth] century," the third being that "which started about fifty or sixty years ago [Brossard writing in 1703] when musicians started to improve music and make it more gay and expressive and better suited to the text."

There was, then, a fundamental metamorphosis in musical thought already in full swing in the early baroque, shifting the ideal-symbolic toward the concrete-illustrative. The temper of the baroque, the dominating musico-dramatic style, explains the preponderance of operatic aesthetics. The field of action of music was undoubtedly immensely enriched by the tendency toward truth of expression and experience, but, by forgetting that music was originally pure tonal effect free of descriptive or delineative elements forced on it from without, composers and writers came very near to abandoning the fundamental principles of musical aesthetics. Fortunately, the transition period between baroque and classicism was weathered, and when, toward the middle of the eighteenth century, rationalism arrived at the crossroads it admitted that imagination is a thing by itself, and conceded to it laws and properties that were different from those of reason. The new philosophical orientation freed music once more from reflection and reasoning and restored its immanent, absolute-musical powers, launching it into another glorious period of flowering.

Secularism, the Ruling Spirit of the Late Baroque

THE early baroque mind was, as we have said, conditioned by the Church, the resurrected Counter Reformation, and the profoundly religious and passionate fervor of the Jesuits. The militantly religious aspect was the greatest, strongest, and most influential phase of the period, especially in the southern countries, constant in their Catholicism, and for this reason less subject to religious and social wars. Nevertheless, this was only one of the streams of the baroque, preponderant in Italy and in the south. Since its overwhelming pathos was nourished by religious piety, men were enthusiastically engaged in creating churches, exulting in the pomp of the altars and vestments, in the ecstasy of preaching, in the radiant murals of a new and modern mysticism, in the golden ornaments of plastic decoration, and in the fullness of concerted church music.

As we near the eighteenth century another current becomes discernible. Though branching off from the first, this current, more worldly, more rationalistic, preferred to build palaces for autocratic princely will, and to devote material wealth to the dreamy world of fairy interiors, enchanted gardens, and mechanical marvels. This too was baroque, but a more quiet, one might say a more classical baroque, than the first, which, churchly and exalted, had a spiritual kinship with the Gothic. Social life was no longer under the auspices of religious pioneers, great and small, all devoted to ideals, but was dominated by proud sovereigns, princes, nobles, and oligarchs, and filled with a love of power and reason; and this even in Italy. The old spirit of life of the radiant Renaissance was not lost in the mighty shadow of the baroque Church; it was continued in palaces and villas where the art of life was rekindled with the flame of pagan freedom. The old palaces were now enriched with new wings: the original roughly hewn stone blocks were replaced by marble and precious stones; the monumental rooms became articulated by finely proportioned galleries and colonnades filled with pictures, sculptures, and books. Marble staircases, pictorially placed drawing rooms, spacious plazas, formal gardens with terraces, fountains, and winding paths, and classical statues greeted the multitude of guests in this era, which made a cult of hospitality and social life. The descendants of the wealthy merchants became art collectors, were ennobled, rode to hounds or followed the falcons; they read books and indulged in witty conversation.

The new baroque, as expressed in secular art and life, started in the second half of the seventeenth century, and came from the France of Louis XIV. What had been Italian and mythological in the early French baroque— the fountains, the sarcophagi, the opera, or Caffieri's sumptuous gilt bronzes—was changed by the king's fancy to a national art, becoming in another few decades international, the grandiose form of art and life of the civilized world. The new, royal, centralized, absolutist, and rationalist art produced works which were no longer animated by the dynamics of the Italian baroque, but, like the royal palaces, were great, cold, and enduring monuments, revealing symmetry, order, and majesty rather than ecstatic abandonment. The baroque now subjugated nature itself, proclaiming human supremacy over trees, flowers, and the elements. Water was harnessed, that it might spout, give off colors, play music, and propel machinery; it never trickled peacefully according to its nature. Dolphins and swans topped the cascades—not the finny or feathered denizens of sea or lake, but carved from white marble by the will of the artist. The gods of mythology stepped from the picture galleries to populate the avenues of this man-made paradise. Although frozen into stone, they seemed to scurry around eluding satyrs, or embracing women. The garden architect was no longer satisfied to work with trees, flowers, and stones; he now needed clay, glass, and metal. Forged railings and fences, ingenious lamps, kiosks in which even the capricious ivy that covered the enclosure was of iron, testified to the artists' powers over nature and to the king's omnipotence.

The interiors of the French palaces were worthy of the architecture: calm, grandiose, and opulent, but demands for comfort and the seductive elegance of the *cabinets,* destined for conversation and entertainment, gradually mitigated cold pride. Mirrors and glass lamps reflecting a thousand sparks, great scrolls on the walls or under the ceiling, gigantic bronze fireplaces with marble tops upon which rested busts and vases, the graceful products of the porcelain factory of Rouen, the carpets and tapestries of the Savonnerie and the Gobelins all imparted a dazzling wealth to the interiors, enhanced by the legendary art of the cabinetmaker.

This art of the Louis XIV era mirrors the ceremonious life of the court, an atmosphere in which everything was cold, refined, wearing the cothurnus; the very classicism the hothouse of which was the world of the salons and of its *précieux;* related by blood to the soaring verse of Racine, the rhetorical sermons of Bossuet, the tragic pathos of Corneille, to a formal, highly artistic, ceremonious, aristocratic, languishing, and exclusive art, ridiculed by Molière and refined to music by Lully. But what was an exclusive courtly art in the seventeenth century became a universal European style in the eighteenth; the style of cultured grandees, the etiquette, the poetry, the language, the portraits, and the books of this mundane life became a part of Europe's culture. The baroque palace and the life in the salons were repeated in a thousand German, Austrian, Dutch, Polish, Hungarian, and Scandinavian residences; and, although drawn on a smaller scale, the park of Versailles, the ballet, the opera, the pyrotechnics and aquatic artifices, classicistic poetry and sculpture, together with the costumes and manners of noble society, are to be found in every one of them. But the oppressing fame and reputation of the French models notwithstanding, the national traits of the individual countries could not be stifled forever, and tradition, the *genius loci,* the necessities of life, national psychology, and cultural intercourse imposed their stamp on the culture of the late baroque in the European countries in the measure we advance into the eighteenth century. The essence of this style remained, however, valid in all its regional manifestations.

Opera in the Late Baroque

THE opera of the baroque was the art form which united in itself all that this virtuoso era had produced, to become the prototype and embodiment of the baroque spirit. The splendor and the mechanical ingenuity that were lavished on operatic productions of the *seicento* have never been surpassed.

This *seicento* opera was sheer drama, but the *settecento* opera, from Scarlatti to Handel, went through a metamorphosis, the purely musical element beginning to dominate the imagination, forcing the outpouring of human affections into forms organized by aesthetic precepts. The older dramaturgy was not abandoned, and we still find characters drawn with the sharpest psychological observation; but it is undeniable that the beauty and polish of the musical form often take the place of dramatic representation, a fact which explains the coldness and lack of emotional depth of many a great aria. This art created the broad musical gesture filled with pathos; it was an art which gloried in the beauty of the medium of expression, as Scarlatti and his disciples, up to and including Handel, exploited the ultimate beauties of musical melody obtainable from the human voice. This new world of melodic expressiveness not only determined the art of the Italians up to Rossini, but Bach and Mozart are also deeply indebted to it, while a Handel or a Hasse is simply unthinkable without its style-building force. The *al fresco* style of operatic orchestral accompaniment, the *da capo* aria, and the new Italian overture as established by Scarlatti, furnished perhaps the most important groundstock for the classic symphony of the second half of the century. The new style represents, then, the triumph of chiseled melody which knew no law of aesthetics other than its own bewitching and intoxicating sensuous beauty. It was the perfect musical fulfillment of the ideology of the late baroque. The virtuoso singer's coloraturas evoked the same astonishment as the surcharged gilded ornamentations of the baroque architect; the sensuous beauty of the human voice in the *bel canto* was as intoxicating as the visual opulence of marble, gold, ebony, and brocade of the baroque interior. Earlier opera relied on extensive scenic mounting, an operatic conception which was retained in places where the imperial splendor of the earlier baroque continued throughout the first half of the eighteenth century (Vienna, Dresden, Munich, Paris); but the rationalistic Enlightenment cast aside artificial help, confident that inexhaustible melodic invention, the sheer beauty of the voice, and the breath-taking virtuosity of the singer could attain the same end. The resuscitation of the heroic shadows of the ancient world, now enlivened with the blood of the new absolutism, could be accomplished only by means of broad, widely arching, and somewhat cool contours, and this fact determined the style of late baroque opera.

Rome had lost its eminent position in the operatic world with the advent of Pope Innocent XII (1691–1700), a pope universally loved for his charity and piety, but who proved himself a stern reformer, very much opposed to the stage. Following his orders the new Tordinona opera house (built in 1671) was razed in 1697 despite the opposition of many of the music-loving cardinals. The other center of opera, Venice, retained its great enthusiasm for the lyric stage but exhausted the talent of its creative musicians. Thus the hegemony passed to Naples, relatively unimportant in the history of music until after 1650. It was at the approach of the eighteenth century, then, that Neapolitan opera started on its conquering way. German opera succumbed to it in Hamburg, English attempts at operatic creation were nipped in the bud, the many central European court operas came under its sovereignty for almost a century, it introduced opera into Russia, and it competed successfully with the long-established French opera. It was during the flowering of the Neapolitan opera that the Italian *maestro* made the whole musical world his taxpayer. Whoever wanted to study composition and expected to gain fame and wealth went to Naples to study at its famed conservatories with the masters who dictated the musical life of the civilized world. The distinctive quality of the Neapolitan style was due to the inbreeding of composers in the city-kingdom. This should not be interpreted in a derogatory sense, for while these composers taught each other and exchanged ideas constantly, they traveled widely and brought home from their sojourns numerous incentives and impressions. Their close interconnections and the traditional schooling imparted in the Neapolitan conservatories melted, however, all foreign elements into a most homogeneous and finished style.

It is customary to regard this school as responsible for "the degeneration of opera into something like a costume concert," for the libretto became an accidental matter of little or no importance, and everything was concentrated in the person of the virtuoso singer. The singer, in his turn, was little concerned with the original score, and if he did not approve a certain aria he simply substituted another from his own repertory. Before we can continue our investigations we shall have to look into the state of the art of singing, since both praise and invective are concerned with the central figure of Neapolitan opera, the singer.

The singers of the late baroque were subjected to a most complete and rigorous education, not only in tone production but in musical declamation, dramatic expression, musical theory, and composition. The aim of the Italian singing schools was a sovereign command over the human voice. Very soon, however, the very technical perfection they attained made serious inroads into their art; the means became the end. Careful declamation was the first to be abandoned as with the late Neapolitan opera the da capo aria—formerly carefully planned by both librettist and composer—became merely a stereotyped piece of music, often using the same music for different words. The most regrettable development was, however, the entrusting of the embellishments to the singer. It was in this field of vocal virtuosity that the castrati harvested their greatest triumphs. One of their rank, Baldassare Ferri (1610–1680), for whose services a number of sovereigns vied with each other, was characterized by Giovanni Andrea Bontempi in his famous *His-*

toria Musica (1695) as having a beautiful soprano voice of an indescribable limpidity combined with a technique that knew no limitations. Among other noted *evirati* we should mention Francesco Bernardi, called Senesino (c. 1680–c. 1750), one of the highly admired singers in Handel's opera troupe, and Gaetano Maiorano, called Caffarelli (1703–1783), who made such an enormous fortune that he purchased a dukedom, and Carlo Broschi, called Farinelli (1705–1782), whose vocal prowess could not be approximated by any singer or any musical instrument for purity and volume of voice, flexibility, celerity of technique, and exactitude of pitch.

The public's predilection for the castrato voices caused the lower male voices to disappear almost entirely from the Italian opera seria. Even the female voices had difficulty in maintaining themselves, although they found a solution, which, nevertheless, was also unnatural: they took over the male roles. Quantz, Frederick the Great's court flutist, an eminent chronicler of the times, remarked of Vittoria Tesi (1700–1775) that "nature endowed her with a contralto voice of manly strength. She had an innate ability to impress the spectator by her acting, especially in masculine roles, which latter seemed to suit her well." Two of the most famous *cantatrices* of the whole century were Francesca Cuzzoni (1700–1770) and Faustina Bordoni (1693–c. 1770), wife of the celebrated composer Hasse. Bordoni shone especially on account of her immense technical mastery of the singing voice, while Cuzzoni moved her audiences by the fervor and pathos of her performance. The tyranny of these highly paid singers knew no bounds, and most composers had to comply with their wishes.

The flowering of this vocal virtuosity was on the decline in the second half of the eighteenth century, at least as far as Germany, France, and England were concerned. The great strides made by instrumental music restored the composer's authority while diminishing the monopoly of singers, though Italy retained her love for the prima donna and primo uomo. The art of the castrati declined, nevertheless, even in Italy, as people began to realize the monstrosity of this practice; their place was taken by the falsettist, a male singer using artificially produced head tones. There was, however, another weighty reason for the return to a variety of voices ranging from bass to soprano and sung by persons of corresponding character, and that was the ever-increasing popularity of the opera buffa with its flesh-and-blood figures.

The excesses of virtuosity, the rudeness of musical life, and, mainly, the universal lack of information about the music of these times have prompted historians to consider these decades as the most regrettable pages in the book of musical history. But we are doing a grave injustice to this period, teeming with art of the first water, for besides the capricious virtuosi and sensation-hungry public there was a deep and universal musical culture, based on vocal

art, that was shared by large circles of amateurs. This incomparable vocal art
—never even remotely reached in modern times—was employed for high
artistic aims in the chamber cantatas and in the accompanied songs. The
numerous editions of such works indicate how universal was the love of
good choral music. And when we glance over the cantatas of Keiser, written
for *Liebhaber,* for amateurs, we shall see that the great majority of our
present-day professional singers of both sexes would not find themselves
equal to the task of performing them, although such songs were the daily
amusement of music lovers two hundred years ago.

What is true of vocal chamber music is not less true of the despised "concert opera," for, withal, this late baroque opera still rested on an artistic outlook dating back to a period preoccupied with the explanation of love and
of the affections, the period of the Italian and Dutch "manneristic" painters
who gave almost scenic representations of the affections, of Racine, who
converted the affections into a perfection of verse. Similarly, this baroque
opera is mainly interested in the tormented souls of living creatures and in
the enhanced states of affective manifestations. The subjects of these operas
are the same as those used by Corneille, Racine, and Rubens, the heroes of
Greek, Roman, and Biblical history and legend; and these heroes are presented in their moods of rebellion, fervor, and passion which are most appropriate for musical translation and characterization. All this is suffused in
a courtly *galanterie,* delicacy of deportment, and, above everything, pose,
the "great gestures of kings, generals and grande dames" of the era of absolutism. Among the composers were musicians of a lighter blood who,
sensing the growing preference for vocal acrobatics, used their talents to
satisfy the public in the manner it desired. But even the coloratura arias, for
which German, English, and American authors cannot find enough words of
condemnation, were always used for musical ends. Once approached through
the scores, and without prejudice, this notorious Neapolitan opera proves to
be filled with finely chiseled forms, replete with melodic invention of the
utmost expressiveness, with the classic pathos of tragedy and, in the opera
buffa, with ingenious and deeply human comedy. It had neither the fundamentally antimusical, didactic, and antiquarian tendency which characterized early Florentine opera, nor the heavy metaphysics of the nineteenth-
century leitmotif opera; it was a lyric theater such as only Italian genius can
create, with the *dramatis personae* individualized and psychologically justified, and at the same time the dramatic element remaining in perfect entente
with a lyric foundation, making possible and natural the association of
drama and music. This lyric character can be followed in the Italian musical
stage from the sacre rappresentazioni to Rinuccini, from Rinuccini to Metastasio, and from Metastasio to Boito. It is the secret of the opera, and its

perfect blend with the drama has seldom been achieved outside the sphere of Italian opera.

We have as yet no means of forming an opinion of this vast art. The repertory of our operatic establishments is frozen into a routine sanctioned by social convenience, steering a careful "middle course" between old and new. The historical literature on opera is in its very beginnings and reveals little more than names and facts, for the scores still slumber in libraries, only a few specimens being available in modern print. Yet what a fantastic picture is told in the chronicles of the seventeenth and eighteenth centuries! Even the small cities had their opera theaters, and toward the seventeen eighties Esteban Arteaga, the eminent historian of Italian opera, counted forty opera houses within the boundaries of the Papal State alone. Twelve hundred different operas were performed in Venice alone in the eighteenth century. Only the vastness of this operatic culture can account for such startling figures. But it accounts for something else too, which we must discuss before entering on the musical history of the Neapolitan school.

Historians of literature speak of the period after Tasso and before Goldoni and Parini, that is, from the beginning of the seventeenth almost to the middle of the eighteenth century, as an era of decadence in letters. They find a deep hiatus in literary history which they ascribe to various causes. Yet the simplest statistical enumerations of Italian opera will furnish a solution to this problem; for Italian literature was not somnolent in the seventeenth and eighteenth centuries, it was merely diverted from pure letters. The lyric stage fills this hiatus, and oratorio and cantata join comedy and tragedy in keeping the poets and dramatists occupied, thereby depriving literature proper of nourishment. The literary historians do not seem to count the opera libretto as literature. Even Goldoni and Parini are seldom mentioned as librettists, although both of them were rather proud of their contributions to the lyric theater; yet among the music dramas of the baroque one can often find poetry which does not stand an iota behind the best of Tasso and Guarini. Where the literary historians are right is in not considering the lyric drama a literary form in the conventional sense, for, indeed, the opera libretto is a genre by itself, and with its mixture of drama and lyricism, the constant change of meter, its ensembles, finales, and choruses, it belongs neither to pure tragedy nor to comedy. In the early days of opera a libretto was planned with dramatic and musical foresight, but the vulgar and popular spirit that intruded itself upon the public opera houses in Venice, mainly through the intermezzi interpolated between the acts of the opera seria, undermined dramatic poetry, and with the "concert opera" every vestige of sound theater was abandoned. It was this phase of operatic history, known from the derogatory remarks of contemporary opera fanciers and the scornful judgment of posterity, which cast a shadow on the validity of Italian opera. But remedy and salvation were not wanting. A movement to clear the opera libretto of all that was episodic and irrelevant had been started in the seventeenth century by the poet Silvio Stampiglia, but it was left to the two imperial Austrian court poets, Zeno and Metastasio, to find again the aristocratic and noble tone of Rinuccini. It was necessary to reform the opera libretto, but without threatening the prerogatives of music, which was to remain the vital element in the opera. Their reform did not cause changes in the musical character of the opera but restored settecento opera to drama with music remaining the master.

Apostolo Zeno (1668–1750), a widely read scholar, able poet, and well-intentioned playwright, not a musician himself, although well acquainted with the requirements of music, was the first of the two Italian literary men in the service of the Habsburgs to show the influence of French classicism upon operatic dramaturgy. The simple and noble pathos of Corneille and Racine permeated the smallest details of his works not less than those of his successor and rival Pietro Metastasio (1698–1782). The two poets were animated by the same desire, the restoration of the *bonae litterae* in the music drama, and created some of the best opera books in the history of the lyric stage. But their nature and disposition were different. Zeno, more scholarly and less sensitive, naturally espoused the pseudo-classical tragedy, with its noble but rigid heroes, who, in accordance with the prevailing custom, came to a "happy ending." The pseudo-tragic became really tragic in Metastasio; his Aeneas abandons Dido, who in her despair kills herself; his Cato dies the death of a hero; his Regulus returns to captivity although death awaits him there. This is why those who dreamed of a resuscitation of the real music drama, who could not divorce the idea of tragedy and music drama, saw in Metastasio's libretti the realization of their ideal and greeted his works with genuine enthusiasm, acclaiming him the great hero of contemporary literature. Yet Metastasio's philosophy was not touched by the Enlightenment; it remained contemplative and as such was interested only in what directly concerned his subjects. He remained a sovereign artist, primarily preoccupied with purely artistic problems, whereas Zeno often strayed into courtly flattery and academic declarations of love.

Metastasio's diction and verse belong to the best of contemporary Italy; élan, euphony, and consummate elegance in every line, with fine poetic pictures and abundant allegories, but above all with a virtuosity of rhythmic and metric construction which was the composers' joy, permitting them a variety of musical rhythm not usually found in libretti. There was scarcely a composer in the eighteenth century, from Pergolesi to Mozart, who did not set to music at least one of Metastasio's operas, and many a celebrated musician set the same libretto several times.

The Neapolitan School

UNTIL the approach of the eighteenth century Naples, although the home of Gesualdo, Falconieri, and other celebrated composers, was rather associated with the numerous popular canzonets and villanelle, surnamed *alla napolitana*. But toward the end of the seventeenth century the city of Vesuvius began to loom as the capital of the musical world. The great personality who virtually made Naples the Mecca of musicians was the Sicilian-born Alessandro Scarlatti (1659–1725), reputedly a pupil of Francesco Provenzale in Naples and of Carissimi in Rome; but the century-long Neapolitan hegemony was undoubtedly the result of the beneficial merger of southern and northern Italian musical elements and styles as effected by Scarlatti and his followers—half of Italy and Germany. His experiences and positions held in Rome made him well acquainted with the musical life of the Eternal City, where his first opera was performed in 1679. Beginning with *Gli Equivoci* every year saw at least one new opera by Scarlatti, in Rome or in Naples, or in some other Italian city. He composed more than a hundred operas, at least eighty-seven of which are known by their titles;[12] the number of his oratorios is approximately a hundred and fifty, while the cantatas (six hundred) and various types of church music, together with his recently discovered keyboard music, complete a truly imposing oeuvre. Although Scarlatti's case has been ably presented in Edward J. Dent's monograph,[13] our knowledge of his epoch-making importance still rests mainly on circumstantial evidence, as only a few excerpts of his works are available for study in modern editions.[14] This astounding productivity does not mean superficiality or patchwork, for his compositions show a mastery of workmanship and an abundance of original musical ideas. Scarlatti's starting point was the late Venetian opera, then universally admired. It is very difficult to ascertain the influence of Stradella and Provenzale upon Scarlatti, as the lives and works of these masters are not yet sufficiently elucidated, but the Roman influence is shown in his love for the "strict style" of contrapuntal writing, demonstrating the renewed interest in artistic construction noticeable in the high baroque style. In his dramatic works he professed, however, an unconditional worship of the beauty of melody, a complete abandonment to the sensuous charm of the singing voice—an attitude which some of his followers, less royally endowed with inspiration and less well equipped in musical training, carried to extreme one-sidedness.

Modern Italian opera begins with Scarlatti, for he created the typical form of dramatic composition which served all other composers as model and was carried all over Europe by the numerous traveling Italians and the foreigners studying in Naples. Handel, who met him in 1708, remained a devoted admirer of the Neapolitan master throughout his life, studying and imitating his works with loving care. Under Scarlatti's hands the musical forms became more ample, the *recitativo accompagnato* acquired a wider field of action, the da capo aria rose to become the most important single element in the dramatic fabric, and the simple curtain raiser developed into the Italian operatic overture, a worthy rival of the French overture of Lully. His orchestration, always interesting and colorful, was devised in the classic Italian manner, which does not permit it to detract attention from the singing. His melodies are bold and expressive, yet always natural and singable. The rhythmic variety and vivaciousness of his melodic invention is always arresting. His anxiety to give adequate expression to the affections governs the construction of the melodies, and he does not hesitate to break the most beautiful phrase in the middle if the situation calls for a sudden change. Whether it is hesitation, courage, melancholy, rage, or love, the music faithfully follows the text, not only by changed tempi but by effective suggestions in the formation of melody, rhythm, harmony, and orchestration. All that we admire so much in the music of the late baroque and in that of the classical era— the euphony of the Handelian vocal settings, the introspective lyricism of Bach, the lightning-fast *secco* recitatives of Mozart, and the colorful orchestration of late eighteenth-century opera—appears in this extraordinarily gifted composer's works.

Besides the many eminent colleagues and pupils of the master—Leonardo Vinci (1690–1730), under whom the orchestra developed its powers of dramatic commentary, Nicola Logroscino (c. 1700–1763), one of the first to compose elaborate finales, Leonardo Leo (1694–1744) and Giovanni Battista Pergolesi (1710–1736), the creators of the classic comic opera—the chief agents of Neapolitan supremacy were the city's famous conservatories. These institutions were originally homes for the "conservation" of orphans, who received instruction in choral singing and—with due accent on religious exercises—in various trades and professions.[15] At first modest local institutions, with the seventeenth century, when music became the chief occupation and study of the pupils of the conservatories, the schools began to attract attention; and when in the second half of the century such great masters as Provenzale and Scarlatti joined their teaching staff, musicians flocked to them from all over the world. Many of the great composers of the eighteenth century were alumni of the Neapolitan conservatories, where the same great masters who helped to establish the world supremacy of Italian opera trained the pupils in the time-honored old contrapuntal style. This training resulted not only in a sound musical equipment which the young musicians could use to good advantage in their future operatic enterprises, but also in the resurgence of a noble school of church composers, whose chief masters were Francesco Durante (1684–1755), Leonardo Leo, and Antonio Lotti (c. 1667–1740), a pupil of Legrenzi. It is of great interest and significance that the relationship between the seemingly widely divergent fields of church and operatic music was of the most intimate nature. Durante, almost exclusively a church composer, was the teacher of some of the outstanding opera and opera buffa composers of the times; but the two fields retained their respective characteristics, and the same composer who in his comic opera showed remarkable ease in portraying mischievous buffoons by carefree and flippant melodies employed a dignified and elaborate polyphony in his Masses and motets.

When discussing Roman opera in the seventeenth century we mentioned the beginning of the comic opera in the works of Mazzocchi, Marazzoli, and Abbatini. Passing through the hands of the Venetians, who liked to insert intermezzi between the acts of their serious operas, the comic opera reached Naples, where it found a most congenial and brilliant practice. The great popularity of the *commedia dell' arte* and of the Spanish comedy was in no small way responsible for the flowering of the opera buffa, much nearer to the theater proper than to the late baroque opera seria. Since 1504 Naples had been an appanage of Spain, governed by a viceroy with a large armed force and a legion of administrative officers residing in the Italian city, until the early eighteenth century when it passed into the hands of Archduke Charles of Austria. It is only natural that the great theatrical art of Spain was imported into the Italian kingdom in her possession. This explains the presence there of two eminent opera composers of Spanish extraction, Davide Perez (1711–1778) and Domenico Terradellas (1713–1751), who were among the best-known Neapolitan composers. The remarkable unity of the Neapolitan style is again demonstrated in the operas of these composers, for there are no musical traces of a Spanish nature in their works, although their savory humor betrays the Spanish folk theater. The opera buffa, as the Italian comic opera was called, was indeed the opposition of the healthy theatrical and musical instinct of the people to the pompous and garbled concert opera; and the first comic operas were, as later in France, virtual caricatures of the opera seria, until Vinci and Pergolesi elevated them from slight comedy to a true portrayal of life and characters. Being unnatural creatures, the castrati did not fit into the world of the opera buffa, which dealt with life in its broad human aspects. Recitative and aria—always different in nature to a certain extent—were now sharply divorced, the former being devoted to a most faithful observation of human speech, while the latter was entirely dissolved in lyricism. The younger Neapolitan generation, Leo, Vinci, Feo, and Pergolesi became enamored of this lyricism and created a bewitching melodic art that has not lost its freshness up to our day.

Perhaps the most gifted master of the Neapolitan opera buffa was Pergolesi whose short life influenced the future course of a century of musical history as only Monteverdi had before him. The marvelously fresh tone, radiant color, lightness, and melodiousness—undoubtedly inspired by the wealth of popular Neapolitan song—which well up in his comic operas, especially in *La Serva Padrona,* affected his contemporaries like a miracle. But color, gracefulness, and lightness here mean much more than sheer virtuosity; Pergolesi seized the swiftly moving forms of life in their essence. These light and volatile forms shed, in his hands, everything that had been casual and ephemeral, and revealed the poetic reality that lay concealed in them: the profound reality of unchangeable man. This is why Pergolesi could create a really new musical language, could give a new tone to every instrument that came into his hands, for life, in his feverish twenty-six years, threw new forms to the surface every minute, and all that the musician had to do was to listen. The bright spring sun of opera played its warmest rays upon Italy; stage and life were awaiting with open arms the fresh impulses of new forms and expressions. Pergolesi's forms changed the existing frames almost imperceptibly; the musical ideas became more flexible, more clearly articulated, and, almost unnoticed, the method of thematic construction evolved a new melody—both vocal and instrumental—formed by the capriciously playing, scurrying, and jumping tiny motives. All this may be considered a historic reform in technique and form, but that tender, virginal, melancholy, and dreamy lyricism which is never missing even in his robustly comical scenes places Pergolesi among the greatest musicians of the settecento. The score of *La Serva Padrona* seems simplicity itself and the story is innocuous, but when the little opera is performed the listener beholds a masterly rendition of characters in music.

Italian Opera in Germany

THE dissemination of baroque opera in Germany took on impressive proportions toward the end of the seventeenth century. Works successful in Italy were quickly acquired and performed in the numerous princely court theaters. Composers, conductors, poets, diplomats, all were eager to exchange and promote their products, and the effective administration of the theaters was aided by the establishment of the office of *intendant,* or superintendent, inspired by the French *surintendant de musique,* Lully's erstwhile title. These intendants, often music-loving aristocrats, were well informed as to the state of affairs in other institutions and were on the lookout for promising works and musicians.

The main seats of Italian opera in Germanic lands were the three Catholic capitals, Vienna, Munich, and Dresden, but there were numerous operatic establishments in Hanover, Stuttgart, Berlin, Wolfenbüttel, Breslau, Leipzig, the free *Reichsstädte,* and in many of the smaller residences. It was generally conceded that no court, church, or theater could amount to much without the active and personal collaboration of Italian artists. It is most interesting to observe that, although virtually an Italian colony of conductors, castrati, instrumentalists, poets, and architects, Vienna was the only seat of late baroque opera where the great traditions of the music drama were kept alive. Combining an unparalleled faithfulness to the ideals of musical craftsmanship with the dignity of an imperial city, Viennese opera successfully withstood the inroads of the facile variety of Neapolitan concert opera, laying a solid foundation for the great classical school to come. This animated operatic activity called for a new and large theater, and on April 21, 1708, the Josephine Theater, built by the able architect Bibbiena, opened with an opera by Bononcini. The supporting pillars of the magnificent new theater were the composers Johann Joseph Fux (1660–1741), Antonio Caldara (1670–1736), and Francesco Bartolommeo Conti (1682–1732), the court poets Zeno and Pariati, and the architect Bibbiena. The baroque opera lived its last glorious decades under these masters in Vienna. Visitors from foreign countries lavished praise on the splendor of the performances. Lady Mary Wortley Montagu (1689–1762), famous for her witty, lively, and informative letters, called the Josephine Theater so great that one could scarcely behold it; the costumes and settings defied description, and "there could not possibly be anything in this art that would surpass it." On certain occasions the performances were held in the gardens, with the lake serving as part of the scene. Lady Montagu could not suppress her admiration for the naval engagement which took place in one of the operas.

The English visitor does not mention the music that accompanied these sumptuous performances, which would have provoked the envy of Louis XIV, yet the richly set choral passages, the ballets, the elaborate contrapuntal writing, and the rather astonishing dearth of arias won the attention of the musical visitors. It was Fux, the great *Altmeister* of Viennese music, unrelenting in his fine contrapuntal technique, dramatic choral writing, and lively orchestration, who kept the Viennese opera at the high artistic level which had so much to do with the ultimate growth of the classical school that emerged there in the second half of the century. Fux's contrapuntal mastery was proverbial. Mattheson in his *Ehrenpforte* praises his style heartily, remarking that one cannot find "lazy" voices in his part writing. It is at the same time true that the preoccupation with highly artistic settings using the whole arsenal of contrapuntal devices often took the edge from the dramatic interest, and with all their masterful texture the old Viennese master's operas could not compete with the dramatic quality of the Italian opera. This minutely elaborated style of composition, a late flowering of the great art of Cavalli and Cesti, equipped with the ample musical apparatus of the late baroque, the magnificent choruses, the French ballets, and chiseled instrumental parts, impressed the foreign musicians as something archaic in the world of the solo opera. And when Fux wrote an aria in the form of a fugue

—at the time when Bach was following the same procedure in his cantatas— that was more than they could endure; they promptly declared his operatic style to be church music in disguise. While Fux's operas enjoyed high esteem,[16] the manifold duties of the court conductor prevented him from writing many works for the theater. In the field of church and instrumental music he was a master of unquestionable greatness.

The brunt of supplying the court with music drama rested on Caldara's shoulders. The difference between Fux and Caldara lies in the Italian origin and early schooling of the latter. The Venetian musician, composer of eighty-seven operas, thirty-six oratorios, and much fine church and instrumental music, and master of a contrapuntal technique almost the equal of the imperial conductor's, wrote, nevertheless, in a much more flowing melodic style, and his love of euphony and expressiveness carried him away when a conflict with contrapuntal correctness demanded a choice. The third member of the illustrious trio, Conti, was a famous virtuoso on the archlute, or theorbo; his art is reflected in the many arias with lute accompaniment in contemporary Viennese operas, but he was not less famous as a composer of operas. His very first opera, *Clotilde* (1706), carried his renown even to England.

The great wealth of Viennese music in the first half of the eighteenth century surpassed by far the musical and theatrical life in other German lands, mainly because of the love and understanding of music on the part of the Habsburgs and of the Austrian nobility. Charles VI was an accomplished operatic conductor, and there were occasions—Caldara's *Euristo* in 1724—when whole operas were prepared and performed by the high nobility. Not only the solo roles but chorus, ballet corps, and orchestra were manned by them. The imperial opera house was unwilling to compromise on the smallest item in its budget and always had excellent singers gathered from faraway countries, but artists of Austrian origin were encouraged and even preferred. The chief requirement of the baroque opera—the castrato— had to be imported, however, from Italy, the only country that still produced them in the eighteenth century. Beginning with 1700 the payrolls mention cantatrices, whose number and importance increased steadily until their salary mounted even higher than that of the fabulously paid castrati. The magnificent imperial operatic establishment collapsed suddenly in 1740, and the Josephine Theater closed after 1744, to be remodeled into a ballroom. The old baroque opera had outlived its glory, and when the *Theater nächst der Burg* opened a few years later Viennese opera was entering upon that phase of its history which made its very name a symbol of musical art.

While perhaps not so royally endowed as the Viennese, Italian music and musicians were the rule in the other musical centers no less than in the Danubian city. Munich, well disposed toward Italian art and Italian musicians since the sixteenth century, greeted the opera in 1653; thereafter Italian opera remained popular and grew to imposing excellence under the able court conductor Johann Caspar Kerll (1627–1693). After Kerll's departure the Italians took complete command of the musical life of Munich.

The leading musician in the Catholic capital of Protestant Saxony, where opera was introduced in 1662, was a native German, Johann Adolf Hasse (1699–1783), a pupil of Scarlatti and Porpora. No other composer has been so idolized by his contemporaries as Hasse. Italy admired him, calling him simply *il Sassone,* "the Saxon"; Germany was proud of him and placed him high above the "learned contrapuntalists," Bach and Handel; and England saw in him the very symbol of Italian opera. Scheibe and Reichardt, both experienced critics, considered Hasse and his Berlin colleague, Graun, the apostles of a new musical era in Germany, an era which rediscovered and reinstated good taste in music. They found the dramatic style of this Italianized German of such perfection of affective representation that no single scene of his could ever be forgotten. His influence paved the road for many a great composer, among them Gluck, Haydn, and Mozart. He was the most brilliant master of the stylized concert opera in the service of the social conventions of the era of rationalism, and, with Metastasio, the undisputed ruler of Italian opera. About sixty of Hasse's operas are known,[17] together with a number of oratorios and a good deal of church and instrumental music. The nineteenth century judged *il Sassone* harshly. It is true that his operas were the post-Scarlatti type of song-opera, with the bel canto arias as their ultimate aim, but they were by no means mere concert pieces in an operatic garb: they disclosed a melodic invention and a remarkable grasp of the dramatic. His recitatives are models of their kind, and his handling of Italian diction has never been surpassed by the best Italian composers.

Carl Heinrich Graun (1703/4–1759), conductor to the King of Prussia, dominated opera in Berlin, but the dramatic works of this composer—and of most of the Italianized Germans—seem to have been entirely shaped on one well-established musico-dramatic last. They contained a good deal of pleasing and sound music, but the objective was to write well and fluently for the singers, to keep the orchestra occupied in an effective fashion, and to unite, in the important dramatic situations, all available means in a telling manner. Graun's *Rodelinda* was the first Italian opera performance in Berlin (1741) and inaugurated in the Prussian capital an Italian operatic domination lasting almost a century. In its first years the repertory of the newly constructed Royal Opera (1742) consisted almost exclusively of works by Graun and Hasse.

Italian Opera in England

AFTER Purcell's death English opera surrendered unconditionally to Italian music. Thomas Clayton (c. 1670–c. 1730), a former member of the king's band, brought back from Italy a number of Italian arias which he adapted to the English words of a libretto written by Peter Motteux, called *Arsinoë, Queen of Cyprus*. Performed in 1706 ostensibly as a work of his own composition, this opera actually succeeded in smuggling in Italian opera, for Clayton's compatriots considered the work the realization of their wish for a national operatic style. *Arsinoë* was immediately followed by Marc' Antonio Bononcini's *Camilla* which, adapted to English words, proved to be an extraordinary success; Burney reports sixty-four performances in three or four years. By this time the French musicians who had populated the English scene since the ascent of Charles II were disappearing one by one, and the Italians' invasion began, continuing throughout the century. Sensing the coming debacle of the English lyric theater, Joseph Addison (1672-1719), the great essayist, turned to Clayton, who was held to be the worthy successor of Purcell, and offered him a libretto of his own entitled *Rosamond*. Clayton must by now have exhausted his stock of Italian songs, or else he was intoxicated by his great success, for he actually composed the music himself, completely exposing his inability and ending in a miserable failure. The road was now clear for Italian opera, and even the use of the English language was abandoned without a murmur within a few years. At first the Italian operas were adapted in their entirety, but, with the increase of Italian singers ignorant of the English language, the arias came to be sung in Italian (Scarlatti, *Pyrrhus,* 1709). This practice led to an almost immediate domination of the Italian language, for beginning with 1710 English was tolerated only rarely, mostly in the intermezzi. One more year, and the Italian opera became firmly established in the Haymarket Theater at the same time when the English managers of the Drury Lane Theater decided to discontinue the production of English musical works.

The first operatic enterprises coincided with the many imitations and hoaxes that followed the prodigious success of the South Sea Company. Founded in 1711, that company was granted a monopoly of British trade with the Pacific Islands, the riches of which were considered inexhaustible. The business establishment prospered, especially since it extended its operations to the lucrative trade of slaves with Spanish America. Its stocks rose tenfold, and speculation grew to such excessive proportions that a crash was inevitable. In 1720 the "bubble" burst and the fraudulent company collapsed, bringing financial ruin to thousands of people.

The Royal Academy of Music, an operatic undertaking sponsored by the king and by the nobility, evidently patterned after the Académie Royale de

Musique, was founded in this atmosphere, showing signs of the same speculative spirit that characterized other business. One of the directors was Handel, who undertook the assembling of the personnel himself. The season started under brilliant auspices, but rivalry and intrigue, and the phenomenal success of the *Beggar's Opera,* the English equivalent of the opera buffa, gradually undermined the institution. Among Handel's colleagues in the Academy were Attilio Ariosti and Giovanni Battista Bononcini, who, the latter especially, attempted to wrest the command from the German. Very popular in aristocratic circles both for his virtuoso playing on the violoncello and for his compositions, Bononcini found powerful supporters. Handel's duties were difficult enough without the intrigues aimed at his own person and work. The singers, composers, and instrumentalists conducted their own feuds, constantly requiring pacification. Thus, after eight years of splendid existence, the Academy failed in 1728, having produced a number of Handelian operas that became known all over Europe.

Although sorely tried, the robust Saxon started immediately on another project with John James Heidegger (d. 1749), a Swiss impresario in the King's Theater, but this undertaking too went on the rocks by 1732. With a heroic insistence the composer went once more to Italy, whence he brought back singers, and in the face of the worst adversities, with his competitors offering such trumps as Senesino and Farinelli, the imperturbable German now produced a number of new operas. But such feverish energy could not be sustained, and the composer collapsed, together with his institution, which moved in 1733 into Covent Garden Theatre, while the Haymarket stage was occupied by his competitors Hasse and Porpora, backed by a large faction of the aristocracy hostile to Handel. His vitality and creative capacity were, however, phenomenal, and after taking the cure for a short time in Germany he was back again, more eager than ever to enter the fray. He proceeded to turn out operas with a supreme disregard for public demand. Heidegger collected the remnants of his old company and those of the rival establishment, which had since perished, and opened the opera in the fall of 1737, going into bankruptcy almost immediately. Handel turned his attention in the meantime to the oratorio, but he was not yet ready to concede defeat, and in 1739/40 produced his last operas with a hastily assembled, makeshift company.

Born in 1685, Georg Friedrich Händel (later Anglicized as Handel) received the customary education of a German musician. When he arrived in Hamburg in 1703 the world of opera must have been a revelation, after the "cantor's music" to which he was accustomed. But there is no trace of any hesitation on his part, for the young composer entered into the spirit of the theater with the greatest ease, producing two years later his first opera, *Armida.* Having acquired a certain reputation and having mastered dramatic composition, although only twenty-one years old, he left the Hanseatic city in 1706 to go to the promised land of musicians. With the same effortless ease that characterized his debut in Hamburg he adapted himself not only to the Italian style but to the Italian way of living, so different from that of the German Protestant world. Emulating his Italian colleagues, he did not neglect church music and composed several Latin works while visiting in Rome. Back in Florence, he won his earliest acclaim with *Rodrigo,* his first opera composed in Italy. This work earned him the favor of the famous singer Vittoria Tesi, for whom he wrote the exacting title role of his second Italian opera, *Agrippina.* Performed in 1709 in Venice, the work achieved such a stormy success that its creator became one of the most noted composers in Italy. On the occasion of a visit to Rome in the preceding year, the German Protestant had been offered the libretto of an oratorio written by Cardinal Panfili, entitled *Il Trionfo del Tempo e del Desinganno,* which he used in the most substantial of his early works. Handel himself valued it highly, remodeled it in 1737 in London, and brought his artistic career to a close by recasting it again in 1757 into the oratorio *The Triumph of Time and Truth.*

In Rome the composer made the acquaintance of a man whose genius left indelible marks on his style. Agostino Steffani (1654–1728) was one of the great figures of the regenerated baroque opera in Italy at the opening of the new century. An artist of ample inspiration, he was a man of the world, politician, diplomatist, clergyman, papal legate, court conductor, and a prolific composer. This exceptionally cultured man was a composer of the stature of Purcell and Scarlatti, and perhaps the first great representative of the pure aria opera, held in a noble song style, free from undue ornamentation. His role in German music was of the greatest importance, and he fulfilled a mission by tempering the learned, rigid, and ever busily trotting German "cantor's counterpoint" with the simple and noble line of Italian vocal style. The vocal duets of Steffani, both in his operas and, perhaps even more so, in his chamber works, represent the height of three-part baroque counterpoint as exemplified in the trio sonata principle. Upon his suggestion and at the invitation of the Elector of Hanover, Handel took the post of Hanoverian court conductor, lately vacated by Steffani. It was a natural sequence of political events that the Hanoverian court conductor transferred his field of activity to England when the House of Hanover became the ruling dynasty of Britain, remaining there until the end of his life in 1759.

In none of his operas did Handel follow the established pattern of the opera seria, though he was entirely devoted to the solo opera. In the arias he exploited the last secrets of the bel canto, their intensity often leading to romantically colored sallies. The variety in the solo songs is seemingly endless; from little, dramatically terse, and crisp ariosi to great da capo arias, every shade is represented. But even within the established forms such as the da capo aria, Handel always follows the dictates of his infallible dramatic instinct, interrupting the aria with recitatives or even substituting an elaborately accompanied recitation for the middle part of a da capo aria; and his orchestral accompaniment is a constant marvel of dramatic expression. The struggle with his competitors forced a change in Handel's operatic style, and beginning with 1729 the simpler homophonic style of the Neapolitan opera, with its well-calculated sonorous effects, seems to dominate, as if the master wanted to meet his enemies on their own ground. But here and there, as in *Orlando Furioso* (1733), he soars to the ultimate heights of baroque music drama, and in *Serse* and *Deidamia* a philosophical humor appears, couched in a delicate setting, as the master took his leave of opera. Although wronged, calumniated, and hard pressed, Handel rose above all his contemporaries with a wisdom and forbearance that have been paralleled only by two other venerable masters of opera, Monteverdi and Verdi, who, in the ripe old age of lives spent in prying into the secrets of lyric art found its ultimate solution.

Baroque opera was nearing its end all over Europe. The general trend toward a solo opera or "concert opera," facilitated by the lack of choruses which the Neapolitans inherited from the Venetians, undermined its dramatic fabric. The former concerted aria in which the voice vied with an instrument in virtuosity was now carried to such extremes as make the performance of a large part of this repertory well-nigh impossible in the modern theater, for we no longer have singers who can negotiate passages that defy the ability of a flute player or cornet virtuoso. In Scarlatti's and Handel's works the affective expression was still of paramount importance and a serious harmonic and contrapuntal fabric supported the melodies; with the composers of the late Neapolitan school the one-sided emphasis accorded to the exploitation of melody resulted in a comparative neglect of counterpoint and harmony. But while the chorus had disappeared and the da capo aria had lost all its dramatic validity (the recapitulation part being considered the singer's property, to embellish to his heart's content), the opera buffa developed a new, most engaging, and typically operatic form, the ensemble and finale, which was to save the lyric theater by opening up new operatic avenues to the succeeding generation.

Catholic Church Music in the Late Baroque

AS could be expected, the tension, the passions, the affections, the profound pathos, and the musical apparatus created to convey these characteristic expressions of baroque art and life found their way into Catholic church music. And the Church, safe once more in its spiritual power, attempted with its usual sagacity to harness all the wealth of this intensified life that had sprung up with the late baroque. The Puritanic scruples of the Calvinists stifled church music in countries that had formerly been at the head of musical nations; the Catholic Church chose to accept the state of affairs and turn the new dynamic force into channels that would benefit religious life and practice. It goes without saying that the opening of the dikes was attended with danger. The unity of the liturgy was threatened by the large musical apparatus which appeared in the church. The aggregate of orchestra, choirs, and soloists required a reorganization of the musical part of the service, and the choirs were removed from near the altar to the choir lofts. The prima donna made her appearance in the church choir in the company of the hero of the baroque opera, the castrato. The clerical status of the church musicians, so strictly maintained in Palestrina's time, was now altogether abandoned. This permitted, however, an unparalleled development of church music throughout the Catholic lands, for any good musician was eligible for a church position. It provided an opportunity for the many smaller churches which formerly had no musical forces beyond the most elementary necessities, and the many princely and aristocratic households established chapel choirs and orchestras, where formerly only a reigning prince could afford such luxury.

This church music of the late baroque has for a long time suffered from a stepmotherly attitude on the part of both musicians and public, who consider it too secular in nature. Some of the many thousand works erred, no doubt, in the direction of the purely secular, but on the whole this great art is as worthy of the title *ars sacra* as the compositions of the sixteenth century; it has discipline, piety, genuine artistic integrity, and religious fervor. The baroque musician wanted to express himself and his ideals in his church music; the great artists were able to achieve this without jeopardizing the spirit of the *ars sacra*.

Another weighty reason for the neglect and misapprehension was the monopoly of church music so romantically bestowed on Palestrina, beclouding everything that was created before and after the great Roman master. It is manifestly true that without the work and legendary fame of Palestrina serving as a beacon, church music might easily have strayed and lost itself in the whirl of the baroque; but the new era had legitimate new forms and new ideals of its own. Elements that had heretofore been strange were driven to the surface, were grasped with joy and ceaselessly pushed toward perfection. What was sacrificed in the first rush and intoxication—counterpoint, form, poise—was later regained and restored to the new spirit. Thus it happens that a large part of baroque church music is clad in an exterior that recalls an older age, but almost invariably the composers of the older strain courted the new tendency, although never altogether joining its ranks. Secular music became the leader and promoter of church music, a circumstance admittedly perilous, but it was the only possible way to save the *ars sacra* from disintegration or archaic stagnation such as befell the Palestrina imitators of the eighteenth and nineteenth centuries. The most famous opera composers, headed by Scarlatti and Hasse, were devoted composers of Masses and other church music, not only in their modern, opera-born idiom, but also in the *stile antico*.

The presence of the whole operatic apparatus in the church does not necessarily mean a secularization of church music. The reigning aesthetics of affective expression were successfully converted to a church style that was sincere and, apart from occasional ornamental excesses, churchly in the best sense of the word. The Kyrie often employed the da capo aria principle by repeating the music of the first Kyrie eleison after the Christe eleison; the Gloria developed into an elaborate cantata followed by a short, decisive, and generally homophonic Credo; the Sanctus was again a broadly designed cantata of praise, the Benedictus lyric and pastoral, with the Agnus Dei tending to larger proportions. The whole showed the typical Latin sense for fine artistic order and finish coupled with the baroque desire for rendering in music not only the words but the ideas and affections concealed in them. Solo singing in the Mass, especially in the form of independent pieces or movements, did not gain a secure foothold in the seventeenth century; the solo passages were almost invariably closely bound to the surrounding choral parts.

At the opening of the eighteenth century the universally admired virtuosity of the solo singers demanded a place in church music. The road was paved for their introduction by the changed choral writing which opposed concerted double choruses, vying with each other in elaborate passages. The resultant store of new means of expression, ranging from simple *a cappella* settings through coloratura solos, up to monumental choral fugues with the multicolored and flexible orchestra lending an admirable support, was inexhaustible. The richness and variety of the machinery led to a reform in the inner structure of choral writing in the Mass; the latter now approached the style of the concerted motet and cantata, strongly relying on the "terrace dynamics" and echo effects of *solo* and *tutti* of baroque music. The instrumental forms of the late baroque which were often heard in the church in their original form of *concerti grossi* or *sonate da chiesa* became organically incorporated into the fabric of the Mass and the cantata, the Italian and French overture often serving as an introductory *sinfonia* to the Mass, not unlike the cantata overture. In Benedetto Marcello's *Psalms* (1724) the solemn pomp and rhythm of the French overture are transferred to the vocal parts.

The dominating position and influence of the Neapolitan school of Provenzale and Scarlatti in the destinies of opera were equally pronounced in church music. The diligent practice of the *a cappella* art by the Neapolitans stimulated the excellent fugal art of such men as Caldara and Fux. Although this may seem strange in the epoch of the solo opera, we must bear in mind that the sweeping victory of the "monodistic revolution" which set in at the beginning of the seventeenth century had not yet been fully exploited when there began to be discernible the first signs of a revival of the old and once respected art of contrapuntal composition; this was to become, toward the end of the century, the dominating stylistic element of the late baroque. With such masters of the Neapolitan school as Leo, Durante, and Feo, solo parts acquired a permanent place within the Mass as arias, endowing the Mass with a variety of vocal forms which, together with the orchestral elements taken from instrumental sources, created the so-called "cantata Mass." This was still to be employed, unchanged, by the Viennese composers of the classic era. Hand in hand with the introduction of the aria went the use of concerted obbligato solo instruments, a practice well known from Bach's cantatas. All this, together with the unmistakable joy in music making, is what invites censure from the modern Palestrina worshipers. The great crime of these musicians (an offense so movingly defended a few generations later by Haydn) was that, with the church architect of their day, who saw the house of God as an earthly palace, they followed the prevailing genius of their time.

The animated exchange of music and musicians between south and north had beneficial results. The many Italians in German courts and churches and the German students in Italy were responsible for a revival of the *a cappella* art in Germany and for a renewed interest in thematic-motivic orchestral writing in Italian compositions. The stylistic properties of eighteenth-century music was so completely opposed to those of the sixteenth that a continuation of the classical *a cappella* style seemed impossible, and yet the music of the Palestrina era managed to survive the intervening times and occupy a certain modest place in the baroque. However, although it was practiced assiduously in conservatories and in places like the Academia Filarmonica in Bologna, it had but little productive vitality. It goes without saying that survival was made possible only through compromise. As early as the seventeenth century, musicians distinguished between a *stile antico,* reasonably close to the Palestrina style, and a *stile misto,* or "mixed style," which endeavored to blend the former with the *stile moderno.* But neither of these could escape the strong influence of the "affections" of the baroque, and the problem was to reconcile a "modern" sense of style with the old technique of setting. All the baroque composers who were engaged in the revival and practice of the old art endeavored, in reality, to bring about the expression of the affections within the frame of the old technique. Their arrangements and imitations are, therefore, tinted with an unmistakable eighteenth-century flavor, and only very few of them, such as Palotta and Pisari, penetrated into the essence of the *a cappella* style.

Matteo Palotta (1680–1758), a product of the Neapolitan conservatories, was employed by the imperial court in Vienna and must have contributed to Fux's marked love for pure vocal polyphony. Pasquale Pisari (1725–1778) was steeped in Palestrina's works to such an extent that he could write in a fashion that was as pure as his idol's own. Padre Martini called him the "Palestrina of the eighteenth century." These two eminent masters turned back the clock, and while they really understood and appreciated the great art of the past and were even able to approximate it in their own compositions, theirs was a historic, synthetic art, out of touch with life. The others mistook canon, polychoral writing, and other technical and formal elements of the old art for the essence of the *stile antico*. There was one capital departure from the Palestrina style, and that was the addition of an instrumental accompaniment, whether a simple basso continuo played by the organ or an elaborate concerted orchestra.

We have already mentioned the beginnings of this tendency; [18] in the eighteenth century the sense and understanding for the old originals was almost entirely lacking, in spite of the fine compositions of Lotti and Fux. Johann Sebastian Bach himself transcribed Palestrina's *Missa Brevis* and added an ensemble consisting of two cornets, four trombones, bass fiddle, harpsichord, and organ as accompaniment. While the accompaniment was rather discreet and played in the *colla parte* ("with the vocal part") manner of the Renaissance, the accentuation, declamation, and the changes in the cadences entirely altered the physiognomy of the original music. His procedure is perhaps the best proof that baroque polyphony was fundamentally harmonic, based on the harmonic leading tone, while the old *a cappella* art based on the modes was primarily melodic-linear. It is small wonder, then, that the two styles remained irreconcilable and that only a distinctly archaic approach could restore the musical dialect of the sixteenth-century church to the musicians and worshipers of the eighteenth.

The traditional contrapuntal schooling of the Germans and their love of instrumental music made them especially receptive to the elaborate concerted church music that was brought to them by the Italian opera composers serving in southern courts. Johann Caspar Kerll, Johann Heinrich Schmeltzer (1623–1680), and Franz Heinrich Biber were the leading masters of the older generation, and they were followed by Johann Dismas Zelenka (1679–1745), Franz Xaver Anton Murschhauser (1663–1738), and Benedict Anton Aufschnaiter (d. 1742), with Fux towering above them all as the greatest German Catholic church composer of the late baroque. Their Masses were composed with a sure conception of style, with the individual parts held together by judiciously developed thematic material and by dignified instrumental interludes. The serious and festive contrapuntal writing of the southern Germans was combined with the melodic charm of the Italian manner of composition by such Italians as were in German-Austrian services. The inquisitive scholar may find remarkable examples of their art in the volumes of the Monuments of Music in Austria and Bavaria, but the church musician will have to wait for practical modern editions to make this great literature available for devotional use—its real and legitimate purpose.

Religious and Musical Thought of the Protestant North

CATHOLIC southern Germany was culturally overshadowed by the Protestant north. This was owing partly to the peasant character of Austria and Bavaria, and partly to the torpidity caused by the heavy restrictions imposed by the Church. The courts of the Bavarian electors and of the Habsburg emperors were second only to that of Versailles, but the rich and fastidious court life, the fortunes spent on buildings, gardens, opera, and ballet stood in glaring contrast with the spiritual vacuum in which the population lived. The great display at the court, as in most courts of the times, was not calculated to arouse artistic or spiritual interest on the part of the population: it merely satisfied the ruler's appetites and glorified his house.

The politico-historical situation in Germany at the opening of the eighteenth century took a new turn with the emergence of Prussia. The work of the Great Elector of Brandenburg was crowned when his son Frederick assumed the title of King of Prussia. Frederick I (reigned 1701–1713) effected a centralization of power, and absolutism found a realization in the Prussian monarchy as nowhere else in Germany. Frederick's short reign was followed by that of his son, Frederick William I (1713–1740), the first powerful Prussian king. Long considered a parvenu and uncouth barbarian among European royalty, and the father of Prussian militarism, Frederick William was, nevertheless, the able administrator and disciplinarian who made Prussia into a great power. He embodied the essential aims of eighteenth-century royalty: to rule and to work, both carried to the limits of endurance and conscientious efficiency. A man of slight culture—he dismissed the artistic suite that had surrounded his father—his interest was limited to two aspects of stagecraft, the army and the treasury, both of which he raised to unquestioned excellence. The commissions in the army were reserved for the nobility: a Spartan caste, not the courtly aristocracy of Versailles. These noblemen-officers had no time to indulge in the art-loving idleness that characterized the aristocracy of the other German courts; they were hard-working soldiers, drilling their troops from daybreak to night-fall. The king, totally uninterested in spiritual and humanitarian matters, made Prussia into an immense barracks, a northern Sparta, a curiosity to the whole of Europe.

The rise of the middle classes in Frederick William's Prussia was typical of all of northern Germany, and it was this regenerated middle-class civiliza-tion which determined the intellectual and spiritual life of the following two centuries. The word "regenerated" is used advisedly, for once before the bourgeoisie had held a weighty responsibility in cultural life, until its flower-ing in the sixteenth century was ended by the increasing power of the nobility. The Fuggers and the Welsers, merchant-princes who financed the conquering wars of the Habsburgs, had lost their fortunes when the mon-archs refused to pay back the large loans extracted from them, and the Thirty Years' War finished what was left of bourgeois wealth and culture, which yielded completely to a courtly civilization. Mercantilism now re-stored the middle classes to their position in the financial and intellectual world, for only a wealthy bourgeoisie was able to pay taxes. The soldier-king and the other ruling princes saw clearly that the growth of the urban citizenry constituted a prime *raison d'état*. Two powerful forces aided the development of the middle classes: Pietism and the Enlightenment.

The seventeenth century was, as we have seen, the century of great re-ligious controversies. Reformers and organizers came in numbers. They had their followers and their detractors, but no matter how divergent their meth-ods and ideas, they were all possessed by one common desire: to meet more suitably the religious needs of the individual. The development of Protestant thought from the end of the seventeenth century to the middle of the eight-eenth proceeded in the shadow of a great conflict. The rigid dogmaticism of religious thought no longer satisfied a multitude of pious men because it left but little opportunity for the expression of their personal faith. Like the mystics of the Middle Ages, these earnest Protestants of the German baroque endeavored to arrive at a revelation of God through subjective experience not bound to the dogma of the Church. Their sole concern, as op-posed to the orthodox party, was to establish an essentially personal relation-ship with God, and especially with Christ. Among the first to cast this long-ing into a poetic mold was Angelus Silesius, but the tendency broadened into that greatest religious movement of the late baroque era, Pietism.

The second half of the seventeenth century and the first half of the eight-eenth were more active and productive in religious poetry than the century of the Reformation. The number of sacred poets grew, and women of the nobility joined them. They followed in the footsteps of Gerhardt [19] and were led by Philipp Jakob Spener (1635-1705), whose *Pia desideria* (1675) became the program of Pietism. The spirit of medieval German mysticism

seemed to have returned with him—a renewed insistence upon the fundamental Christian idea of not only believing in Christ but living a Christ-
like life. Spener banished learning and oratory from sermons and urged
a more intimate knowledge of the Scriptures.

The gentle and moderate mystics were followed by the energetic Nicolaus
Ludwig Zinzendorf (1700–1760), second founder of the sect known as the
Moravian Brethren. The Moravian refugees, settled on Zinzendorf's estate,
were organized into a community which gave Pietism a great impetus
through the means of missionary work. Germany, Denmark, Russia, England, as well as the West Indies, North America, and even Greenland, welcomed his missionaries. The Moravian colony of Bethlehem, Pennsylvania,
is one of Zinzendorf's lasting achievements. A man of fortitude and ardent
temper, sincerely concerned with the well-being and comfort of his brethren,
Zinzendorf had something of Luther's stature and, like Luther, was often
carried away by vehement feelings. In his theology, immersed in the person
of Christ and in his sufferings, sorrows, in his blood and wounds, one can
see the reappearance of the boundless cult of the Middle Ages fortified with
the emotionalism of the baroque.

But this theology and this poetry were the product of the regenerated
bourgeois spirit. The strong class consciousness of the period did not admit
the middle classes to the exclusive circles of the aristocracy, whose life, art,
and thought remained strange to the citizenry. The majestic pathos of the
baroque, the wealth of art which graced the castles, residences, court theaters,
and monasteries, was thus missing in the thousands of religious poems composed by Zinzendorf and his fellow poets. It is only the predilection for
the "wounds," "blood," and "sufferings" that recalls the early baroque fervor
for emotional excesses, for this poetry often descended into childish puns
and playful blasphemies. It must be said, however, that the essence of the
movement did not consist of such foolishness, and as the eighteenth century
advanced it was more and more restricted. What remained was a saintly
simplicity, which the Pietists considered the most profound wisdom. Religious poetry, marked by this simple "homeliness," took on unheard-of
proportions, and the thousands upon thousands of songs (Zinzendorf himself accounted for two thousand), didactic in tone, took into consideration
the needs of all walks of life. One Mecklenburg pastor collected in 1716
songs for one hundred and forty-seven different professions. In 1737 a Saxon
clergyman published a universal song-book in which songs were to be found
for christenings, marriages, and other family events, others appropriate for
difficult lawsuits, for lameness, blindness, deafness, or for the affliction of
having too many children, and for noblemen, ministers, officials, lawyers,
barbers, bakers, fishermen, teamsters, merchants' apprentices, and many
other professions. In his *Avertissement* the author requested contributions

for a few missing species, such as songs for clowns, tightrope walkers, magicians, thieves, gypsies, and rogues.

The musical side of such religious literature stood entirely under the spell of this "individualized" poetry. From the technical point of view the correspondence is easily recognizable: congregational hymn singing was individualized, and the aria was to gain the upper hand. There was, however, another sequel to the movement that interests us primarily, namely, that in many respects this poetry tried to promote music. Curiously enough, both Pietists and their opponents were filled with this desire, and the observer beholds an extraordinary picture of opposites working toward the same goal.

Viewing Protestant religious history in retrospect, one gains the conviction that music occupied a singularly important position. Music appears to have been an indispensable agent whenever religious moods and feelings were being perpetuated in either the individual or the community. Catholicism commanded infinite means for this purpose. Not only its music and poetry, its architecture and art, but its service, its sacraments, its religious exercises were all permanent and powerful means providing a veritable technique of religious life. Protestantism rejected most of this, retaining religious poetry and music as its chief aids. Bach and Handel still cast over us the spell of the religious feeling of these times; perhaps they and the other great composers of the Protestant baroque offer the only approach to a true understanding of the depth and intensity, the dynamic power of conviction, of righteousness, and of salvation, which was the essence of those heroic times. Religion is carried by historic tradition and legendary faith, but its vividness is in the men themselves who bring their moods and feelings to give substance to every religious aspiration.

Pietism, with its forced subjectivism and its excesses offending good taste and even decency, was entirely contrary to the Lutheran spirit. It recognized and permitted but one form of church music, the simple spiritual song. In the face of the fact that Pietism was the dominating intellectual factor in late baroque Protestantism, we are looking back at a literature of church music that fills us with amazement. Once before in its history Protestant church music had come under the ban of religious thought hostile to art. After recovering from the setback administered by the Calvinistic wing of the Reformed Church, the new stylistic elements brought to the fore by the early baroque were introduced in the second half of the seventeenth century into the music of the Protestant Church. The simple, pious congregational singing envisaged by the fathers of the new church gave way to sonority, dramatic choruses, sophisticated arias with obbligato instruments, recitatives filled with tragic pathos, and opulent orchestral color. The earnest Protestant might well exclaim, "This is not the humility and frugality preached by Calvin, but the proud, ecstatic, dramatic, and propagandistic baroque of the Counter

Reformation." Yet what happened here is a remarkable counterpart to the course of events that culminated in the art of Rembrandt. The formal and technical means of the Catholic baroque were accepted by Protestantism and turned into an art not less gigantic in proportions, not less expressive in emotions, not less lavish in ornaments, and not less profound in convictions than that of the Italian baroque, but fundamentally Lutheran in spirit. And it was individual men, the musicians, who achieved this in the face of a hostile atmosphere, a declining literature, and a declining religion.

Toward the end of the seventeenth century the divorce of congregational singing from art music, a process inaugurated earlier but repeatedly delayed by the innate artistic sense of German Protestant musicians, reached an acute stage. The great musical literature of the Reformed Church fell upon unsympathetic ears, as the great majority of churchgoers were completely estranged from art, the latter having returned to its erstwhile surroundings to entertain the aristocracy and to grace their exclusive worship in court chapels. That this was an accomplished fact is well illustrated by the acquiescence of the church authorities. It was not unusual for them to recommend to such members of the congregation as could not patiently listen to the music to while away their time by reading their prayer books. This recommendation concerned, of course, music other than the *geistliche Lieder,* sacred songs or hymns; thus sacred song and concerted church music went their own ways, although they lived under the same roof. Pietism invited lyric meditation, swelling the number of sacred songs to the astonishing figure of ten thousand by the time the eighteenth century dawned upon Germany. The musicians could not cope with the fertility of the poets, and a great many of the new pious songs were sung to old melodies.

At this point, when Protestant church art was again seriously threatened, this time by Pietism, the artistic genius of the nation came once more to the rescue; it staged a last stand which was to culminate in the most sublime artistic manifestation of Lutheran faith and Protestant tradition. When contemplating this impressive musical culture of the German baroque, with its multitude of motets, cantatas, oratorios, Passions, Masses, Magnificats, and other sacred compositions, one may easily be deceived by the wealth and variety of all this music, for in spite of everything the eighteenth century ushered in an impoverished, declining Protestant liturgy. From the three sources drained by Luther for the melodies of his new church, the first, the old Gregorian songs, ceased to furnish tunes. Having been altered rhythmically to conform to the general rhythmic structure of the German folk song, the plain chant lost its original physiognomy, and its tradition was altogether forgotten. A similar fate befell the second source, the pre-Reformation German sacred folk song. Thus the third source, the German folk song, remained the most important, and its great melodic treasure was made accessible for church use by sacred paraphrase and parody. In the early seventeenth century this was a vivid and living art, as can be seen in the works of Melchior Franck, Vulpius, Schein, Crüger, and others who made the songs the foundation of their truly German art. But this once flowering garden of Protestant church song wilted in the plague and misery of the Thirty Years' War, and after the war-torn years the composers, organists, cantors, municipal and academic musicians, growing in numbers and enjoying the prestige of admired professionals, lost contact with the folk song of older times. As the poem approached the madrigal or even more complicated forms, the music, already influenced by sophisticated art music for over a century, gradually acquired the subjective tone of the individual creative artist. The universality which characterizes all true folk song was exchanged for the personal-individual nature of the art song. Thus there arose slowly from the congregational hymn the spiritual song and the spiritual aria, which ceased to be true congregational songs, for they were the solo songs of the monodic era transplanted into the church. That many of these subjective-personal songs became, through long usage, congregational chorales, does not change the general picture, because in most cases their original rhythm was altered to the isorhythmy of the modified Gregorian tunes and sacred folk songs. The composers of these Evangelical church songs were the same musicians whom we mentioned when discussing the secular song poetry of the period immediately preceding the late baroque, the two domains having no distinct borders.

Pietism, then, carried the disintegration to its completion, and so it happened that when the mature Bach arrived with his works calling for the most profound experience of Christian faith expressed in music, he stood alone, the belated messenger of a Protestantism which was no longer a living force.

The musical Mass was still retained by the Protestants, but only the Kyrie and Gloria were set to music; such a Mass in the Lutheran service was called *missa brevis*. The gigantic B minor Mass of Bach was originally a Lutheran *missa brevis,* the master adding the remaining parts later. As the Mass itself was neither an original nor a sanctioned part of the liturgy in the Reformed Church, its use was somewhat uncertain, and Luther's vision of its practice in his church faded with others of his ideas, neglected or disregarded by his later followers. The new center of the Protestant service was the sermon, which, being an act within the immediate apprehension of the congregation, changed the entire complexion of the service. With the delivery of the sermon the essence and aim of the service was realized, and whatever followed became anticlimactic and relatively unimportant. This led to a separation of communion service and predicatory service as individually complete entities. The Credo had been appropriated earlier in a German version, but the Sanctus and Agnus Dei were now dropped as a natural consequence of the Eucharist having been made a special service. Thus the remaining torso of Kyrie and Gloria became the specific Lutheran "short Mass."

It is a remarkable fact that the second half of the seventeenth century still shows an impressive output of Protestant Mass compositions, no doubt owing to the ability of the composers to detach their works from the form and spirit of the *missa antiqua,* the Catholic Mass. Rosenmüller, Theile, Buxtehude, Zachow, Johann Michael Bach, and Johann Philipp Krieger left many Masses of great beauty and artistic value. Buxtehude's only surviving Mass, a *missa brevis,* and Zachow's *Missa super corale Christ lag in Todesbanden* [20] are two works that should become as widely known as Bach's B minor Mass, especially because of their more obvious Protestant leanings and consummate form and proportions as opposed to the colossal structure of the Bach Mass, totally unsuited for liturgic use. That with the majority of these works we are in the domain of the concerted Mass is well illustrated in the preface to Johann Heinrich Buttsted's *Opera Sacra* (Erfurt, 1720), in which the excellent Pachelbel pupil deems it most important to inform his public that in a Mass of his the violoncello has "especially important parts to play." He ends his preface by saying that "all that remains for me to say is my humble request that the well-inclined music lover should see to it that the instruments be well represented (the violins at least doubled), rehearsed separately, and well played. The words *adagio, presto, allegro* should be respected and the *alla breve* played with celerity."

The intrusion of operatic elements was a slow process, but by the time the Catholic orchestral Mass first reached its height in the southern countries, the operatic influence was distinguishable in the Protestant Mass of the north. Among the first of these elements to appear was the recitative, followed by a dramatic use of the orchestra. At this point the technique of composition approached that of the cantata, and the *raison d'être* of a Protestant Mass, considerably undermined by its unsuitability for liturgic use, became open to serious question. A stately number of Masses belonging to the *majestatico stylo Praenestiniani ecclesiastico,* as the Palestrina style was called, were still composed in the archaic manner of the sixteenth century. We have noticed a similar trend in the Catholic countries, but while works like Fux's Masses called for a true *a cappella* performance most of the northern imitations of the *stile antico* were unwilling to relinquish the participation of instruments, and if they did not have a continuo part, they followed the time-honored custom of having the instruments play with the voices in the so-called *colla parte* manner.

Another important reason for the gradual disappearance of the Protestant *missa brevis* was the radical change in the background of the cantors. The authoritative position of the cantors expired with the passing of the seventeenth century, the eighteenth bringing with it a new artistic orientation.

(Top) Jacob van Loo (1614–1670), "Concert"
(Bottom) Velasquez (1599–1660), "Three Musicians"

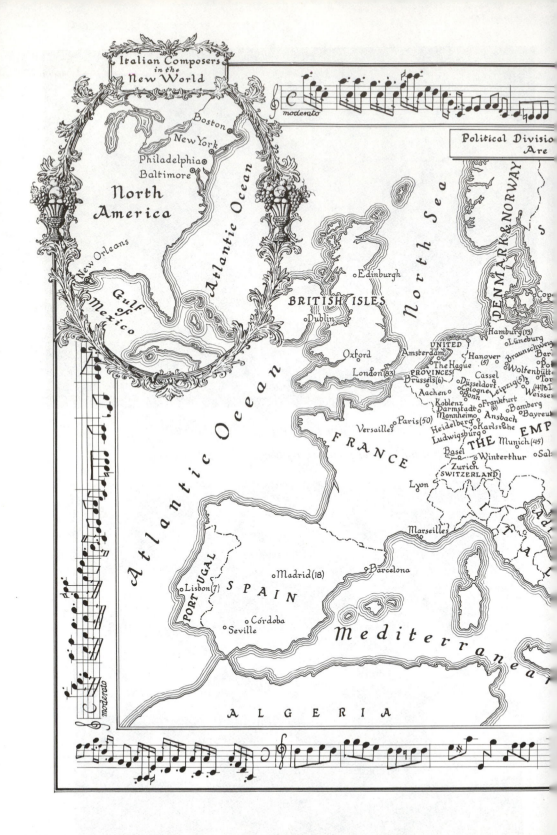

Italian Composers
in the
New World

Political Division
Are

North America

Atlantic Ocean

Gulf of Mexico

Boston
New York
Philadelphia
Baltimore
New Orleans

North Sea

DENMARK & NORWAY

Cop

Edinburgh

BRITISH ISLES

Dublin

Oxford

London (83)

Amsterdam
The Hague
UNITED PROVINCES
Brussels (6)
Aachen
Koblenz
Darmstadt
Monnheimo
Heidelberg
Ludwigsburg
Basel
Zurich
SWITZERLAND

Hamburg (13)
Lüneburg
Hanover (5)
Braunschweig
Cassel
Düsseldorf
Cologne
Bonn
Frankfurt
Ansbach
Karlsrühe
Winterthur

Leipzig (5)
Bamberg
Bayreut

Munich (45)

Berl
Wolfenbütt
Tor
Weisser

Sal

THE EMP

Versailles

Paris (50)

FRANCE

Lyon

Marseilles

PORTUGAL

SPAIN

Lisbon (7)

Madrid (18)

Córdoba
Seville

Barcelona

Mediterranea

ALGERIA

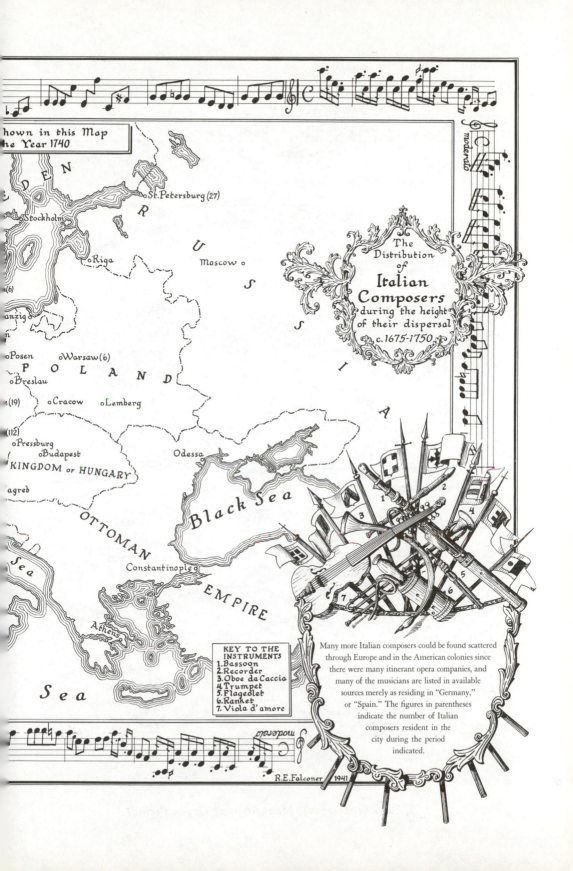

J. S. Bach (1685–1750), Manuscript of Organ-Prelude

The positions were filled by leading musical artists charged with the task of providing the necessary church music. The extraction, leanings, and schooling of these musicians were no longer an issue, and it became immaterial whether they came from the opera, princely orchestras, or academic *collegia musica*. The most remarkable aspect of this new orientation was a certain denominational neutrality. Catholics and Protestants worked together, and for both churches. Thus in Bach's time we find some Protestant composers writing complete Masses, but this means also that the Mass has ceased to be a part of the Protestant liturgy, for these, like Bach's B minor Mass, were written for the Catholic Church.

Rapprochement of Church Music and Opera

THE lines of demarcation between the two great cultural territories of Germandom are now firmly drawn. No other phase of baroque culture shows this division, based on religious geography, more clearly than music. Throughout the baroque, when we use the term "German music" we mean usually the music of the Protestant territories; this applies not only to oratorio, Passion, and cantata, but to solo song and instrumental music, and even to that eclectic child of the baroque, the opera. The German south, with its two musical centers, Vienna and Munich, dominated in the sixteenth century by the crystalline art of the Renaissance, became acquainted with the rising baroque through a continuous and immediate contact with its sources. The ecstatic church music, brilliant opera, pathetic spiritual opera, opulent oratorio, and scintillating Italian violin music were as much at home in Catholic Germany as in the country of their origin. We shall see that the rococo was to follow the disintegrating baroque with the same natural ease. This was, then, an international, world art. The German north was less wealthy, more intimate, and more serious. Although it accepted many innovations from the south, it insisted on national features, thereby lending a certain popular hue to its music in spite of all the learned dissertations and involved aesthetic creeds that surrounded it. This Protestant Germany never permitted Italian opera to attain such prominence as in the south, and—except in Hamburg—opera remained a courtly entertainment largely unknown to the citizenry, which sought its musical pleasures in the church, the university and other musical societies, and in the home. The Evangelical church remained the center of artistic life until under the influence of the Enlightenment the emphasis passed from music to literature. This eventuality coincided with the end of the great baroque period, Klopstock's first appearance and Bach's death both occurring toward the middle of the century.

These fundamental Germanic traits notwithstanding, it was inevitable that opera, slowly reaching every part of Germany, should have repercussions on German Protestant music. The Germans' love of the spiritual-dramatic was well demonstrated in their efforts to create a national opera, for the subjects of these lyric works turned almost immediately to the Bible. Thus the opening of the Hamburg opera in 1678 was celebrated with Theile's *Adam and Eve*. This was followed by other Biblical operas, whose texts bear a close resemblance to the old spiritual plays. Indeed, these eighteenth-century works impress one as the logical continuation of the old form, except that secular elements are more numerous in them than in their predecessors. The increasing tendency *contra bonos mores* of these secular scenes made it imperative to shield the spiritual subjects by keeping them away from the stage, and they were transferred to the church or to such large auditoriums as were appropriate for choral-orchestral performances. The good Lutherans viewed the growth of opera with grave suspicion, and when the spirit of the opera buffa found an adequate parallel in the German *Singspiel* and the Italian humor was supplanted by a much less subtle German coarseness, their wrath caused a number of pamphlets to be printed against the "heathens' operatic orgy to the detriment of the Christian world." The challenge was accepted by the friends of the lyric stage, and the literary exchange was lively. But in spite of such attempts, German opera, pressed in a vise the two jaws of which were Italian opera and Lully, could not keep pace with the rapidly developing music of the German baroque. Hamburg's civic opera as well as the Weissenfels court theater of the Dukes of Saxe-Weissenfels did proudly insist on their national prerogatives, the latter refusing to the end of its existence in 1736 to allow even the interpolation of foreign words. The Hamburg opera, however, was not able to ward off the pressure, and beginning with Kusser French elements appeared in German opera, for the time being to its advantage. It was in Keiser's *Claudius* (1703) that the Trojan horse of Italian opera was brought into Hamburg. Several Italian arias were interpolated in this German opera, and soon the course of events took exactly the same turn that befell English opera—with the difference that it was an almost entirely German personnel which undertook to perform Italian operas in the original language.

The steady pressure of the two foreign operatic cultures produced, then, a German master of the first water, Reinhard Keiser (1673-1739). This highly gifted musician was perhaps the first modern theatrical producer endowed with a flair for publicity and afflicted with the tastes and prodigality of a Broadway theatrical magnate of the nineties. During the height of success, in the years 1697-1702, his extravagances knew no bounds. Lackeys in "aurora liveries" waited on him; coaches drawn by the finest horses carried him to the banquets and receptions which he gave with the generosity of a grand seigneur. Keiser revived the old *collegium musicum,* now called "winter concerts," but instead of the tedious contrapuntal exercises of dignified cantors and organists, he presented elegant singers who performed dashing bravura arias. At the end of the concerts wine flowed freely and choice dishes were carried around in profusion. All this led, of course, to a debacle, but the indefatigable composer, blessed with a facility and endurance equaled only by that of Handel, retired for two years only to reappear with a sheaf of new operas. From 1709 to 1717 he presented twenty-five operas, many of them masterpieces; but the ever-increasing assertiveness of the Neapolitan opera caused a change in style and taste, and Keiser transferred his activity to Copenhagen.

Even the few excerpts available in modern editions [21] make this gifted musician the most significant German dramatic composer before Hasse and Gluck. His dramatic scenes lose nothing by comparison with the most tragic utterances of Handel, and his five- and six-part choruses are worthy of the greatest of the Italians.

The decline of the Hamburg opera theater could not be prevented by the repeated changes made in the management, and even the appointment in 1722 of the famous composer Georg Philipp Telemann as director did not help matters. The soil from which the opera should naturally grow had long been exhausted. The Biblical dramas of the first decades of German opera in the Hanseatic city had sprung from German sources, but the reigning form was now an international mixture based on plebeian taste instead of popular tradition. When, after sixty years of existence, the Hamburg opera closed in 1739, it had seen two hundred and forty-six different operas performed. Two years later Italian opera took possession of the old theater on the Goose Market and under the direction of Angelo Mingotti buried the memory of the first German musico-dramatic theater.

In spite of its auspicious beginnings and the many theaters throughout the country, baroque opera collapsed in Germany, for we cannot consider the imported Italian opera, performed by Italians, a part of German music. Lack of dramatists and lack of public taste for a genre that was fundamentally as alien to Germans as it was to Britons account for this failure. But the consequences of the operatic invasion were far reaching. Musicians acquainted with the opera and cantata of the Italians became weary of the "monotonous congregational singing" and attempted to exploit the elements of Italian dramatic composition—aria, duet, recitative, etc.—which had first appeared in German music with Schütz. It is noteworthy that the most influential musicians active in this movement were those connected with the Hamburg opera, chief among them Mattheson. The old native song literature was supplanted by arias, and even the spiritual songs were nearer in feeling to arias than to anything else. There began, then, a process of rapprochement between church music and opera, aided by such men as Kuhnau, Telemann, and Keiser, but the final fusion was accomplished in the cantatas and Passions of Johann Sebastian Bach, whose two hundred odd cantatas represent the final synthesis of all that the baroque gave to music.

The great task of reconciling the form and style of seventeenth-century concerted church music and eighteenth-century dramatic church music—an ungrateful and most difficult role—fell to Johann Kuhnau (1660–1722), Bach's immediate predecessor as cantor at the Thomasschule. This highly cultured and educated man realized that the times had changed and that the great art of chorale paraphrasing, the cornerstone of Protestant church music, was disappearing. An examination of Kuhnau's cantatas, works of great beauty and merit, shows that this composer, the most progressive of the Leipzig musicians since Rosenmüller, was still wary of the operatic elements, whereas his immediate successor, Bach, used them naturally and without embarrassment. The problem to be faced, then, was the future of the Lutheran chorale as the prime principle of construction in Protestant church music as opposed to the forms and technique of opera. In this struggle the chorale lost. Curiously enough, it was Kuhnau, the unsuccessful opera composer, who was among the first to grasp not only the content of the individual numbers but the cantata text as a whole, and to articulate it according to the poetic intent of the text, yet keep the integrity of the whole intact. Recitative, da capo aria, and other operatic elements appeared and displaced the chorale as form-giving principle, retaining it merely as a traditional ending. Another great master of the transition period was Friedrich Wilhelm Zachow, or Zachau (1663–1712), teacher of Handel, from whom the famous composer learned more than the pupil's share. Zachow's cantatas and organ works [22] disclose a musical imagination, dramatic power, and melodic inspiration which are the marks of a great composer.

The conflict between the old and the new was accentuated when the Pietistic movement declared war on the barely settled body of new church music. The excessive emphasis on Pietistic meditation to the exclusion of theology, arts, and letters aroused the strong opposition not only of the German Evangelical Church but also of many individuals. One of the chief opponents of Pietism was Erdman Neumeister (1671–1756), who in some of his writings placed the Pietists in the same company with the pope and the Turks. This earnest and art-loving clergyman was responsible for a reform in the domain of the German cantata which had far-reaching consequences. His pupils, Hunold in Hamburg, Picander in Leipzig, and Salomo Franck in Weimar, continued their master's work and caused a literary upheaval in the shallow and disjointed cantata texts, providing musicians with books that invited better composition.

Neumeister would not consent to the drastic limitations advocated by the Pietists, entirely against the proclaimed wishes of Luther, and arranged cantata texts which would permit the unfolding of a variety of forms of church music. The contents of these texts came from his Sunday sermons, which he recast in a more poetic form. His first books did not make use of the Lutheran chorales and did not quote Biblical passages, but by calling on both of these in the later "libretti" he gave his cantatas the necessary formal-religious frame. An appropriate Gospel text or one of the older Lutheran songs was usually placed at the beginning or the end of the work, but the body of the cantata expressed the more recent subjective religious thought in recitatives, arias, and duets. Neumeister was determined to remain a cultured Lutheran, proud of the part that art played in the traditional religious life of German Protestants, while at the same time admitting the need for a more personal approach to God, though without trespassing on the limits of good taste and poetic license.

Significant developments took place also in the Passion. In earlier chapters we followed the changes from the chorale-Passion to the motet-Passion in the works of the aged Schütz, where we saw a sound and artistic synthesis of German Protestant feeling with the stylistic features of the early Italian baroque. The next generation witnessed the increasing influence of opera upon the Passion, and now we enter the era of the oratorio-Passion, the oratorio having already absorbed lyrico-dramatic elements. The very year of Schütz's death (1672) represents an important step in this direction, with its first performance of the *Passion according to St. Matthew* by the Weimar-born Johann Sebastiani (1622–1683). Up to Schütz's time the Passion composers held themselves strictly to the words of the Bible, the *introitus* and the *conclusio* containing the only non-Biblical words used in the narrative. The situation now changed, for where Schütz had introduced musical innovations from opera and oratorio into the Passion, his followers began renovating the poetic structure. Nothing could have been more dangerous, for this attempt to disrupt the august dignity of the Biblical text proceeded from and carried with it the weakest part of opera, the libretto. The interpolations were at first rather harmless lyric effusions interrupting the narrative, and when they took the form of the chorale the unity of style was still safeguarded. Sebastiani was the first composer to employ this procedure, but instead of using the traditional hymn tunes he retained merely their text, setting them in operatic fashion for solo voices with continuo and strings. His style was, however, dignified and serious, and we must consider him to be the composer who introduced into the Passion the contemplative element which was to have such importance in Bach's works in this field.[23] With Sebastiani's Passion we are in the domain of the oratorio-Passion, a new form greatly enriched in musical possibilities, but at the same time definitely withdrawn from the sphere of church music proper. The later Passions of Johann Sebastian Bach were intended for church use, but they had no lasting place within the liturgy, for they grew to such proportions that they could not be employed in the service without disturbing liturgical order and balance.

The abandonment of the Biblical words was fraught with real peril. Fortunately, this was soon recognized and steps were taken to remedy the situation, but the world of the oratorio threatened to gain the upper hand. Allegorical figures, recalling the earlier oratorios, appeared in the Passion. One or two of these can be found even in Bach's Passion music (the imaginary "Daughter of Jerusalem" in the *St. Matthew Passion*) and in other works of the late baroque. As we advance into the century, then, the original nature of the Passion changes entirely. Telemann, reputed composer of forty-four settings of the Passion, was the author of the three-part Passion entitled *Blissful Reflection upon the Sufferings and Death of Our Lord,* the title of which, alone, expresses the essential nature of this new type of Passion: reflections and comments about the subject rather than its true and faithful narration. The conversion into the operatic was inevitable and resulted in a purely dramatic style not distinguishable from the current Italian opera. The towering genius of Bach as represented in his Passions may give us the impression that the decline of the Passion was successfully interrupted by him, but we must never forget that Bach's music was not a true expression of his times; he belonged to the old Lutheran world of the preceding generation, a stranger among the Pietists.

The ultimate course of events was clearly indicated in the opera-Passions performed in Hamburg at the beginning of the eighteenth century. *The Bloody and Dying Jesus,* by Keiser, and Handel's first essays in Passion music are good examples of this genre. The Hamburg senator Berthold Heinrich Brockes (1680–1747) created a form which found favor with composers all over Europe. Brockes, being a prominent citizen of the Hanseatic city, was well acquainted with dramatic composition as practiced in the baroque opera. With true baroque feeling and a sense for the dramatic-theatrical, he wrote a work of great sensuous power, presenting the life and sufferings of the Lord in the most touching fashion. *Jesus, Tormented and Dying for the Sins of the World* had an enormous success; translations in many languages followed the original edition of 1712, yet with all its sincerity of religious feeling and conviction, Brockes's Passion was more an opera libretto than a Passion text. Nevertheless, the much-admired work fulfilled a mission, for its author found a way out of the chaos, satisfying the demand for a Biblical text and at the same time retaining the lyric contemplation considered indispensable by the reigning religious thought. The Evangelist became the narrator who linked the individual "scenes" and introduced the chorales by his recitatives. Musicians were grateful for the new arrangement, for the closed scenes of Brockes's book were eminently suited to musical setting; indeed, the Hamburg senator's Passion attained a popularity in

Germany such as few religious works have ever known. His verses, artificial and crude as they often are, express a humble attitude toward nature and a religious interpretation of its phenomena which was new to German letters and prepared the way for Klopstock. Every composer of consequence—among them Keiser, Handel, Telemann, and Mattheson—set Brockes's libretto within fifteen years of its appearance; and Bach himself borrowed some of its lyrics for the arias in his *St. John Passion*.

Johann Sebastian Bach remained faithful to the oratorio-passion but was hampered, like all his colleagues, by the lack of a great poet to arrange his texts. What saved him from the fate of the less fortunate was not only his musical genius, but most of all his pure and sincere religious thought. With him the Passion again became the most profound experience of the Christian soul, a proof and exercise of Christian faith.

Instrumental Music in the Late Baroque

THE colorful wealth of opera, oratorio, cantata, and other vocal music almost overshadows pure instrumental music, yet the late baroque excelled in this field not less significantly than in choral music. Its composers were often those whose names are remembered for operatic or church music.

The high baroque witnessed important changes in the "instrumentarium." The many varieties of hand and knee viols gradually disappeared as the practical advantages of the violin were transferred to the lower instruments of the fiddle family, creating the modern four-stringed viola and violoncello. The number of wind instruments, considerable in the seventeenth century, was also reduced and the types were standardized with the advent of the eighteenth century. The numerous members of the recorder family (fipple flutes) and the side-blown flutes (transverse flutes) were reduced to the two forms in general use today. The shawms (*chalumeau,* hautboy, *Schalmei*), and their many subspecies, high and low, were concentrated in the oboe and bassoon, while horns and trombones took the middle and bass registers, displacing the many other reed and brass instruments formerly employed in the corresponding registers.

At the opening of the eighteenth century the large class of works for instrumental ensembles, comprising solo sonata, trio sonata, and concerto grosso, manifested a tendency toward individualization. Formerly little distinction had been made among these species, and composers usually published an *opus* which contained several or all varieties of chamber and orchestral music under the same title. But now the apparatus of the concerto grosso began to wean its individual members. First to gain freedom and independence was the treble instrument, the last the clavier, main support of the basso continuo. Thus from the concerto grosso will evolve the solo concerto and from the trio sonata the solo sonata. This course of events was, naturally, considerably furthered by the violinists and other artists seeking a more subjective and individual outlet for their virtuosity, but the great development in other types of instrumental music also called for modifications. Among others the French overture of Lully, admired all over Europe, and the Italian overture, or *sinfonia,* of Scarlatti induced the sonata and concerto composers to plan the first movements of their cyclic compositions in a similar manner, thereby establishing a stylistic convention which has retained its vogue to our day. Another important development was the more precise handling of the basso continuo, which often took the form of a completely elaborated and written-out harpsichord or organ part. Side by side with the new species emerging from the older forms, the latter continued their existence, improved and crystallized by the new departures.

In the trio sonata we find the finished, representative form of late baroque instrumental chamber music. It is a cyclic form in four movements—a principle followed even in the chamber sonata, whose dance movements also preferably number four, in well-placed and contrasted order. This judicious arrangement indicates that the dances included in the trio sonata no longer have connections with the dances in the suite form. They have become abstractions of the practical dances and cover a wide range, from simple song-like pieces still very close to the actual dance to pure constructive polyphony. The immediate consequence of this course of events was a rapprochement of church sonata and chamber sonata, and in many cases the difference lay only in the titles given to the individual movements. All experimentation vanished in the mature works of Corelli; in them all search for form and expression terminated in an art of a convincing perfection. The eighteenth century could build on this foundation; all the great Italian composers of the magnificent violin school were, indeed, either personal pupils of the master or continued his art.

The first great personality of the generation after Corelli was Evaristo Felice dall' Abaco (1675–1742), a master of classic form and effortless counterpoint. The musical world into which we enter in his trio sonatas is still that of Corelli, but with a marked advance toward a new contrapuntal, formal, and sonorous ideal. This is, indeed, a more closely knit polyphony, often almost reaching the purely fugal. At the same time this polyphony shows more advanced conception of harmony. The development continued, although the spirit of the great art of Corelli animated even the succeeding generation; it seems, however, as though the classic grandeur and poise of the original school came to an end with dall' Abaco. Trio sonatas were still being composed in the same style, but their architectonic poise gave way to the inevitable love of the Italian for melody, sonority, and virtuosity. And when the opera composers joined their colleagues engaged in the field of chamber and concerted music the new trend received still another stylistic impulse of lasting consequence.

Among the great violinists of the new school of instrumental music were Tommaso Vitali (c. 1665–c. 1740), Tommaso Albinoni (1674–1745), Francesco Maria Veracini (1685–1750), Francesco Geminiani (1687–1762), and Pietro Locatelli (1693–1764), the last two personal pupils of Corelli. These were perhaps the most eminent among a host of great artists. They were all superb musicians, thoroughly versed in the art of composition, and if they abandoned the architectonic poise of their admired master it was not because of a dearth of technique or inspiration. They were great executant artists, in love with their instrument, which itself was a work of art with a veritable soul under the wood and the strings. They abandoned themselves to the sensuous charm of the violin tone and were willing to sacrifice some of the classic purity of the earlier baroque style of Corelli to the more vibrant and emotional style of their own time, the outgoing baroque. The great violinists were, however, by no means the only ones to cultivate chamber music; many of the noted opera composers contributed masterpieces to the literature. Some of them, like Caldara and Porpora, wrote trio sonatas in the classic vein of Corelli, while others, especially Pergolesi, joined the newer tendency. Pergolesi's epoch-making importance is not restricted to his vocal and dramatic music; he is the same inspired master in chamber music, even though some of this music may occasionally seem more important from the historic point of view than for its intrinsic value. With Pergolesi and some of the other musicians of the younger generation the monumental old four-movement sonata disappeared and a new three-movement form, akin to the general structure of overture and sinfonia, appeared. The massive architecture and broad lines gave way to a fluent and graceful play of thematic work: we are in the immediate vicinity of the modern sonata.

The difference between chamber music and orchestral music became more accentuated as the old concerto grosso tended to grant the *concertino* more freedom and importance. The relationship between the two sections of the concerto, *concertino* and *ripieno,* was fairly constant, but as the concertino became enlarged (the number of instruments being raised to four by the addition of the viola) the accompanying role of the larger body of instruments became more accentuated. Besides this trio or quartet of strings there were many other combinations of *concertini.* Vivaldi's concerto for four violins is a well-known example, but there were many combinations for wind instruments also. As a matter of fact, although the great fame of the Italian violin school tends to place the wind instruments in the shadow, they were nonetheless present everywhere and were used with great gusto. It is true that the Germans were more fond of using these instruments than were the Italians, but many of the Italians employed them with great felicity.

Albinoni's and Benedetto Marcello's concerti grossi with oboe are fine monuments of baroque orchestral music. Bach expressed his admiration for these works by repeatedly borrowing material from them or transcribing entire compositions. An excellent example—long held to be a composition of the German master—is Marcello's oboe concerto grosso, transcribed by Bach as No. 3 (D minor) of his sixteen harpsichord concertos for solo instrument without orchestral accompaniment. The greatest master of the Italian concerto, Vivaldi himself, wrote magnificent concerti grossi for a combination of string and wind instruments.

Dall' Abaco's and Geminiani's *concerti da chiesa* again remind us of the close connections of certain forms of the orchestral literature with the church style. These works are impressive in their formal and stylistic beauty, the instruments singing with hymnlike plasticity, but also turning to impetuous fugues that can stand beside the greatest of the period. Acquaintance with the church style and the fine technical training imparted in the conservatories equipped all these composers with a magnificent polyphonic knowledge. The tendency toward broadly woven contrapuntal settings and a love of the fugal are very strong among the Italians, and it is interesting that Geminiani inscribed his *Opus* VII, No. 1, with the subtitle *l'Arte della fuga,* thus preceding by a few years the work by Johann Sebastian Bach which became immortal under the same title.

It was Antonio Vivaldi (1680–1743) who enlarged the solo passages in the concerto grosso until the solo violin became the dominant instrument of the whole ensemble. The new physiognomy required a new organism, and this great master proved to be equal to the task of building it up. His attention was by no means focused exclusively on the virtuoso solo instrument; the accompanying orchestral passages gained in compactness and lived in a domain of their own. Vivaldi's remarkable sense for rounded form led him to the most convincing and plastic idea of handling his tutti passages as quasi ritornels which return in a rondolike manner after the solo passages, picking up the thread where it was last interrupted by the solo. This lucid and logical arrangement so fascinated Bach that he made the Vivaldi form of the concerto his own.

While growing from the same soil that produced Corelli and his school, Vivaldi was a modern, forward-looking master, and the dramatic touch of the opera displaces the remnants of the church style in his concerto. With Domenico Scarlatti he was the greatest late baroque Italian instrumental composer of universal significance, but while his famous contemporary blazed new trails in the miniature world of the clavier, Vivaldi's flaming imagination drove him to the bountiful domain of ensemble music, and under his hands the concerto became a passionate fresco of dramatic contrasts. Yet this revolutionary artist, dramatically animated in his first movements and ardently sweeping in his finales, proved to be a lyric poet of pastoral tenderness in his dreamy sicilianos and other intimate slow movements, while a number of program concertos reveal a romanticist captivated by the sorcery of sonority and color. His daring temper forced him occasionally into extreme ventures, but his innate Italian sense of form stood guard over his fancy, safeguarding form and structure, which always remained essentially artistic and judicious. Vivaldi's influence upon the music of future generations was incalculable, and was still a vivid factor in the nineteenth century. His thirty-eight operas have not yet been examined, and much remains to be learned concerning this original genius.

We have the good fortune of possessing a number of his instrumental works in available editions, but unfortunately the majority of these are offered in distorted form. The transcriptions made by Bach are in a class by themselves. Exhibiting a boundless admiration for the Italian master, Bach diligently transcribed a considerable number of Vivaldi's concertos for organ and harpsichord. While the absence of the sensuous charm of the noble violin tone impoverishes these transcriptions, they still make good keyboard music, though the clavier version of Vivaldi's concerto for four violins is a tour de force without much virtue. If, however, it is thundered by four modern concert grand pianos instead of by carefully and delicately played harpsichords, it becomes a monstrosity as far removed from the original as the dramatized version of a lyric poem. Bach's procedure may be justified on several grounds, especially because a number of his transcriptions are in reality simple piano scores for practical home use, not unlike our piano scores of large works for study purposes; but the liberties that some modern editors permit themselves with the works of a great and original genius will remain the *corpus delicti* of a peculiar phase of our musical history. Some of them, however, go so far as to merit the epithet fraudulent, among them Kreisler and Nachez (Schott) and Mistowski (Oxford University Press).

Instrumental music in the last phase of the German baroque cannot be understood without its Italian antecedents, for in the period from Schütz to Bach both incentive and style came from Italy, and German art would have been unthinkable without the formative power of Italian music and Italian musicians in Germany. In the German trio sonata we find a change in the ensemble which shows that the acceptance of a musical form does not necessarily imply the acceptance of its original sonorous ideal, for the Germans substituted a gamba for the second violin. The full and dark tone of the gamba furnished an element of contrast missing in the Italians' setting for two violins. Among the German chamber music composers we find the rank and file of masters well known in other fields—Buxtehude, Krieger, Erlebach, Johann Caspar Ferdinand Fischer, Pachelbel, and Theile. Until the end of the seventeenth century the much-admired model of German chamber music was Lully, which fact explains the preponderance of dance suites. The inspiring presence of the many eminent Italians in the midst of the German cantors and *Kapellmeister,* and the German organ literature with its wonderful architecture and broad lines, soon called forth similarly wrought chamber music. There was also the same incentive which caused the development of Italian instrumental ensemble music: the appearance of a school of virtuosi. We have mentioned among the eminent violinists of the seventeenth century Strungk and Biber. Their traditions were continued by Johann Adam Birkenstock (1687–1733) and Johann Georg Pisendel (1687–1755), both widely traveled violinists who studied with the best masters in Germany, France, and Italy. The road now leads to Handel and Bach, who summarized the achievements of the instrumental music of the baroque era.

In the literature for orchestra the German composers of the seventeenth century remained faithful to the dance suite; most of their orchestral works were collections of dances for a string ensemble of five parts. But Rosenmüller, in replacing the *Paduana* with a broadly built sinfonia—evidently on the model of the Venetian opera overture—prepared a new orchestral style which came to be regarded as typically German. The German preference for wind instruments is manifest in the subtitles often added to compositions, for the *ed altri,* "and others," appended to the string choir meant wind instruments to be used at the discretion of the performers. The sense for orchestral balance is well demonstrated by the repeated warnings, printed in the prefaces and addressed to the executants, that when using wind instruments the performers were to amplify the string choir proportionately. It was a natural course of events that the outdoor ensembles of wind instruments, very popular in the north, and the delightful dance suites played at the court balls in Vienna, should exert an influence on the future of orchestral style. To this must be added the considerable vogue of the French overture of Lully and of Italian string music which was beginning to filter into Germany.

Thus when the eighteenth century arrived it found a process of integration endeavoring to reconcile all these elements. As in chamber music, the French influence at first claimed all attention; Kusser, Erlebach, and Georg Muffat acknowledged this in the very title of their compositions, labeling them "in the French manner." Most of these works, called *Partie* or *Parthey* (from the Italian partita, i. e., a piece made up of parts or sections), begin with a regular French overture in three sections, followed by a number of dances. The French ballet suite served as model, for many of the dances are program pieces, often with fantastic titles, but the German penchant for elaboration distinguishes them from the original French works; the individual sections are longer and more varied, and the fugal middle parts of the overtures, especially, show a superiority over the Lully type. Other noted composers belonging to this group were Johann Caspar Ferdinand Fischer, Johann Fischer (1646-1721), a pupil of Lully, Rupert Mayr (1646-1712), Benedict Anton Aufschnaiter (the latter two Austrians), and Johann Philipp Krieger.[24]

The French was still the prevailing style in Bach's and Telemann's suites. In the meantime, however, the Italian influence claimed its share, and the concerto began to show its superior artistic qualities within the suite. The opening movement now assumed an importance which was acknowledged by calling the whole suite after this initial "overture" or "symphony." The wind instruments could scarcely be restrained from exhibiting their virtuosity—the exhilarating trumpet parts in Bach's two D major suites are memorable examples—and the fugal movements took on an amplitude that stands in contrast to the simple nature of the dance movements.

In accordance with the seemingly mandatory course of musical history, these tendencies appeared in Austria, the mediator between north and south, and its first distinguished representative was Fux. The suites that make up his *Concentus Musico Instrumentalis* (1701) should be treasured repertory pieces of every orchestra.[25] It is pleasant to see this master of dignified church style use all the wealth of his contrapuntal art in combination with that inimitable Austrian peasant bonhomie which we admire so much in Haydn. Among the other notable composers of this new and progressive orchestral style we should name Christoph Graupner (1683-1760) and his pupil Johann Friedrich Fasch (1688-1758), two of the greatest among Bach's and Handel's contemporaries, highly admired by Bach himself. With Fasch and with Pantaleon Hebenstreit (1669-1750), the suite reached the last stage of its development. On the one hand, the concerto grosso and the solo concerto either invaded the suite or lured the suite composer within their orbit; on the other, the old German suite, the outdoor serenades and *Tafelmusiken,* returned and became significant sources of the classical symphony hovering on the horizon. The output of German concerto literature was copious, but little of it is available, with the exception of those of Bach's works that fall in this category. Georg Muffat, Aufschnaiter, Johann Christoph Pez (1664-1716), Heinichen, Telemann, Graupner, Fasch, Hasse, and Bach were perhaps the most prolific, with Telemann alone accounting for some one hundred and seventy concertos.

It might appear that the historical evolution of chamber and orchestral music was the same in Italy and in Germany, but similar as this development seems there are vital differences beneath the external resemblance. The fundamental difference between the Germanic and the Italian spirit asserted itself in this field as it did in opera and oratorio. The Germans accepted the Italian sonata and concerto with alacrity and practiced them assiduously. Yet while the principle pleased them enormously, most of the German musi-

cians did not conceal their scorn for the "frivolous and flippant" music making of the Italians—a sentiment shared by a number of critics and writers in
Germanic and English-speaking countries today. Needless to say, the modern student should be able to see that these judgments are not based on the
quality of the music, but on a diametrically opposed musical conception. The
Italian violinists reveled in a sensuously beautiful melody, in a broad cantilena which was not allowed to be swamped by any ambiguity. For this reason, their fugal writing seems less accomplished than that of their German
colleagues, but though it is not so intricate as Germanic counterpoint it is
not less artistic. Italian genius demanded clarity and melodic continuity, and
if these were threatened by contrapuntal complications the polyphony was
tempered and smoothed. Not so with the Germans. Rosenmüller had already exhibited a tendency toward an intricate treatment of string writing,
and with the solo sonatas of Strungk, Walther, Biber, and Albicastro, violin
and gamba were practically forced to renounce their very nature. These sonatas, often played on instruments tuned contrary to the accepted manner
(*scordatura*) to permit all sorts of double stops not feasible in the regular
tuning, were polyphonic compositions in three and four parts, scorning even
the accompaniment of the harpsichord. The Germanic urge for immersion
in the ultimate secrets of music forced even these instruments, created primarily for the playing of a single melodic line, to become self-sufficient and
able to vie with the organ, harpsichord, or orchestra. Bach's gigantic *Cha-
conne* appended to a sonata for solo violin carried this amazing polyphonic
art into a sphere from which there was no return. The baroque admiration
for *compositio artificiosissima,* declared by German aesthetes and composers
the goal of true art, celebrated in these works its culmination. Thus, comparison of the two visions of life and art has no validity; the Germans considered "frivolous and flippant" the sensuous, fragrant, melancholy, sweet,
but also dramatic and brilliant melodies of the Italians, clad in an impeccable form and saturated with the pathos of the lyric stage; the Italians in their turn could not understand why everything had to be so
elaborate and ponderous in the German variety of this type of instrumental
music.

There remains still another capital difference between German and Italian instrumental music. We noticed when discussing German opera in Hamburg how the first attempts at a native music drama turned immediately into
works of a religious nature, in fact, into veritable Passions. The same religious conversion appeared in instrumental music, and as early as 1681 Biber
published so-called Passion-sonatas which depicted Biblical scenes. These
works are not program sonatas in the manner of Kuhnau's Biblical sonatas,
but abstract musical meditations on the great problems of Christian life. It
is their tone and their fantastic world, ranging far and wide in the meta-

physical beyond, which characterizes the instrumental music of Germandom. It is still this same unfathomable and mysterious musical world which
is conjured up in Bach's *Art of the Fugue* and in the last string quartets of
Beethoven. The scholar's work ends here, for while the ear still continues to
hear, the intellect ceases to function. We feel everything and we know exactly
where we are, but the light that burns in our heart flickers when we attempt
to force the intellect to translate into concrete formulae what we are beholding. It is impossible to explain this music in terms of technical, formal analyses, for it is lost in the sea of the irrational; any formal elements are merely
particles washed ashore.

Johann Sebastian Bach

MUSICAL dynasties are not uncommon in the history of music, but the
Bach family stands unrivaled and unparalleled, with over fifty of its members actively engaged in the musical profession and a number of them rising
among the great masters of their art. In the second half of the seventeenth
century numerous Bachs occupied almost all the musical positions in Weimar, Erfurt, and Eisenach, and if one of them resigned or died his place
was immediately taken by a cousin or an uncle. The Thuringian territory,
bordered by Meiningen, Mühlhausen, Arnstadt, and Weimar, was the seat
and place of activity of this remarkable family. This relatively small German
country recalls the county of Hainaut, prodigal in musicians of genius
throughout the Middle Ages and the Renaissance.

The oldest member of the family, the baker Veit Bach (d. 1619), was
known for his love of music, but this penchant is much more evident in his
sons, the first professional musicians in the family. Lips (d. 1620), a church
musician, became the founder of the Meiningen line of the Bachs, while
Hans (d. 1626) was one of the famous dancing masters of his time, whose
excellent playing carried him to Gotha, Arnstadt, Erfurt, Eisenach, Schmal-
kalden, and Suhl. Among Hans's children two were of especial note: Johann
the Elder (d. 1673), the sire of the Erfurt branch which gave the city so
many good organists and town musicians that they were called "the Bachs"
even when there was no longer a bearer of the family name among them;
and Heinrich (1615–1692), who settled in Arnstadt. The latter's two sons,
Johann Michael (1648–1694) and Johann Christoph (1642–1703), became
the two most important members of the family before Johann Sebastian. A
third son of Hans Bach, Christoph the Elder, a lesser musician, was the great
Bach's grandfather. His father, Ambrosius (1645–1695), was a town musician in Erfurt and afterwards in Eisenach, where Johann Sebastian was born
in 1685.

Having lost his parents at an early age, the boy's education was entrusted to an older brother, Johann Christoph (1671-1721), a pupil of Pachelbel, who resided in near-by Ohrdruf. The brother introduced him to the rudiments of his future profession, and there was musical instruction in the local lyceum where the youth studied the humanities. In 1700 a scholarship enabled him to enter St. Michael's School in Lüneburg, and he now came in contact with a serious musical culture. The Lüneburg stay of the young student was of decisive importance for his future development, for the choir of St. Michael's acquainted him with some of the best music of the baroque era. A catalogue of St. Michael's library printed in 1676 shows that not only the well-known larger collections of choral works were at the choir's disposal but the printed works of Scheidt, Hammerschmidt, Ahle, Rosenmüller, Crüger, Selle, Krieger, and a number of other great composers, which, together with a collection of over a thousand manuscript church compositions, made up a remarkable choral repertory.[26] As Bach was an indefatigable self-teacher, copying and studying everything that seemed worth while to him, we may assume with certainty his having supplemented the choral performances by borrowing and studying the other scores in the library. Then, too, the organist of St. John's in Lüneburg at that time was Georg Böhm (1661-1733), one of the most eminent organists in Germany. The impressions made on Bach by this fine musician were of lasting importance, and it was owing to his guidance that Bach explored the musical possibilities offered by the neighborhood.

Lüneburg was near Hamburg and Celle. The young musician was able to witness the triumphs of the German opera in the Hanseatic city, and to admire the organ playing of Reinken. In Celle the excellent ducal orchestra introduced him to an entirely different musical atmosphere, for the members of that musical establishment were for the greater part Frenchmen, playing in their dainty and pointed manner the works of Couperin, Marchand, Nivers, de Grigny, and others of their compatriots. Thus the student was not restricted to silent scores but was in the midst of a pulsating musical practice. In 1703 the eighteen-year-old Bach was appointed court violinist in the private orchestra of Prince Johann Ernst, brother of the reigning Duke of Weimar; then, in the same year, he received the more comfortable position of organist of the new church in Arnstadt. Master of a fine new organ, with duties not at all taxing and with a good salary, he was now ideally placed for creative activity. But the little town did not satisfy the musical appetites of the inquisitive Johann Sebastian. The memories of Lüneburg and its varied musical experiences, together with the powerful stimulus of his fine instrument, prompted him to seek the greatest master of that northern German music to which Böhm and Reinken had introduced him, and he decided on a pilgrimage to Lübeck to hear Buxtehude.

The experience of meeting and hearing this great musician was so over-

whelming that then and there the future was determined—for without Buxtehude the greater Bach is inconceivable. The young man found in the old
Lübeck organist an artist of extraordinary personality, rich in ideas, profound in sentiment, impetuous in passion, and romantic in imagination. The
ponderous fugues, the virtuoso preludes with their racing and rumbling
pedal passages, the capricious themes, the dreamy and romantically colored
ciaconas and passacaglias of the old composer fascinated Bach and left indelible marks on his own style. Scarcely less important was Bach's acquaintance
with Buxtehude's cantata style. Small wonder that the organist of Arnstadt
forgot his duties in the face of such an enticing wealth of new impressions.
Upon his return to Arnstadt he was taken to task by the church consistory
for having extended his leave of absence without permission. The church
elders seized this opportunity also to aerate other grievances, but the affair
ended with a reprimand, and Bach was reinstated in his position.

Restless ever since his Lübeck visit, in 1707 he accepted an invitation to become organist at St. Blasius's, in Mühlhausen. Soon after his transfer he
married his cousin Maria Barbara. The Mühlhausen stay proved to be short-
lived, for the town became one of the fiefs of Pietism, and while Bach's pastor was opposed to it, Pietistic feelings ran high in the congregation. This
meant a hostile attitude toward art—something Bach could not suffer—and
within less than a year he moved to Weimar as court organist to Duke Wilhelm Ernst. The compositions of this period show the multitude of his
duties at the ducal court. More than two ponderous volumes in the great
Bach edition are filled with organ music from the Weimar period; indeed,
the majority of his important organ works were composed in the nine years
spent there. A number of cantatas, most of them for solo voice with orchestra, appropriate to the rather small musical establishment at the court,
also date from this time. In spite of their modest exterior, the Weimar cantatas, written on the "reform" texts of Salomo Franck, a disciple of Neumeister, who himself is represented in a few of them, testify to the profound
changes that had taken place in the German cantata.

Musical life at the Weimar court brought Bach into contact with a new
style that attracted him to unexplored fields. Italian chamber and concerted
music was very popular at the court, and in this Bach discovered a type of
music he had not heard before. Curiously enough, the solemn church sonata
seems not to have interested him so much as the *sonata da camera,* and the
concerto in its definitive form as created by Vivaldi. At first he did not try
his hand at original creation but exercised his talents in transcribing for
organ and harpsichord a number of concertos by Vivaldi and other masters,
originally written for the violin or some wind instrument. His curiosity
aroused, this indefatigable student of music proceeded to investigate Italian
instrumental music in its various aspects. His loving occupation with Fres-

cobaldi, Legrenzi, Corelli, Albinoni, and a number of other Italian composers is well reflected in his works.

In his Weimar explorations Bach was aided by a relative and colleague, the municipal organist Johann Gottfried Walther (1684–1748). Walther was not only a highly trained musician whose contrapuntal technique astounded the born master of polyphony, Bach, but the most learned and educated musician of the period as well. His *Musicalisches Lexicon* (1732) was the first bio-bibliographical encyclopedia of music, upon which were based all subsequent works of a similar nature. It still makes good reading and remains invaluable source material for the history of baroque music. Walther's influence is unmistakably present in the ever-deepening contrapuntal problems that appear in the later Weimar works of Bach, and we must consider this little-known but excellent musician responsible for the conception of such works as the *Art of the Fugue* and other monuments of polyphony created by the mature Bach.

The composer's fame now began to spread, and disciples came not only from Thuringia but from other parts of the country. Mattheson himself declared in 1716 that he "saw a few things by the famous Weimar organist, Herr Johann Sebastian Bach, both for the church and for the keyboard, which are of a nature that calls for high esteem for the man." The real admiration was, however, addressed to the organ player rather than to the composer, and the master was repeatedly invited to examine newly installed organs by giving recitals. In his own Thuringia and Saxony he enjoyed a legendary reputation for his improvisation. But all this seemed to weigh little at the court, and, dissatisfied, Bach left in 1717 to become court conductor to the Prince of Anhalt-Cöthen.

The Cöthen period is not yet fully explored, but we know that Bach was conductor of the eighteen-piece orchestra which furnished chamber music to court festivities, in the absence of an operatic establishment. This period produced chamber music and concertos, besides some important keyboard music, including the first part of the *Well-Tempered Clavier*. The Cöthen days formed one of the happiest episodes in Bach's life, yet they ended in tragedy, for his young wife died in 1720. Although respected and honored by the prince, his grief led him to seek a place where he would not be constantly reminded of his home. Somewhat aimless, he first visited the almost centenarian Reinken, who had once inspired him in his early youth. After hearing Bach play on the magnificent organ of St. Catherine's for two hours, with an extended improvisation on the chorale *An Wasserflüssen Babylon,* the patriarch confessed, "I thought this art was dead; but I see that it survives in you." [27]

In the meantime Bach had taken a second wife, Anna Magdalena, and was casting about for a new home with good Lutheran schools. Johann Kuhnau, the cantor of the Thomasschule in Leipzig, having died in 1722, this desirable position was now vacant. The cantorship was not a sinecure, as Kuhnau had learned to his great dismay. The scholars of the institution, directed by their cantor, supplied the music for the city churches, where elaborate services were sung every Sunday. Besides having this obligation to the town churches, the cantor stood in a somewhat official relation to the university and the *collegium musicum*. His official duties also included a number of menial chores, such as teaching grammar to the boys. The services in Leipzig were still archaic at the time Bach applied for the position; large parts of the liturgy were sung in Latin, and some of the congregational singing was done without instrumental accompaniment. Sunday services often lasted as long as four hours. The municipal council, in view of this situation, endeavored to engage a "reform" cantor who would rejuvenate the musical part of the service by bringing it into conformity with the reigning style. Thus the application of the famous organist Bach, also known for his mastery of counterpoint, was not very favorably received.

That he was considered a conservative can be seen from the deliberations that accompanied the selection of a successor to Cantor Kuhnau. The progressive-minded burghers and municipal and church authorities had intended to fill the vacancy with one of the chief representatives of the new art, and it was only after their first and second choices, Telemann and Graupner, identified with the modern Italian style, were found to be not available, that they considered Bach. Councilor Platz remarked in the final session of the committee that "since the best musicians are not available we must select a mediocre one." This judgment was not so much a denunciation of Bach, whom they respected well enough, as a reluctant surrendering of the idea of appointing a reform cantor who would bring new vitality into the old institution.

It was not without misgivings that Bach exchanged the position of a court conductor for that of a municipal music director, and his fears were justified by the ensuing quarrels with the rector of the school, the consistory, the university, and the municipality. To fortify himself with more authority against the petty officials who poisoned his life, he petitioned the king-elector for the title of court composer, sending parts of the B minor Mass and several secular cantatas of praise to the Dresden court. The title was eventually conferred, but too late, for the master had already lost interest in his official work. At the time when Handel was conquering the population with his oratorios Bach seems to have given up the continuous struggle for his artistic principles and retired to the inner sanctum of his home and family. A man of stubborn will and high temperament, he could not suffer the petty persecutions aimed at him by Rector Ernesti and by the university authorities in charge of musical activities, and the steadily declining ability of the students to cope with the musical tasks demanded by his works. A lull in his activities is manifest after 1735, although that same year saw the creation of twenty cantatas; he even relinquished his right to make up the musical program for Good Friday, performing other composers' works. It must have been on such an occasion that he copied parts of a St. Luke Passion by a minor Thuringian composer, a work which was attributed to him before the advent of modern style criticism. Finally he stood alone, with everything he loved and appreciated out of his reach. Even the old *collegium musicum* where he liked to play and conduct his works before a sympathetic and intelligent audience had shrunk to a secondary position; the new concert association founded in 1743 and "frequented by the greatest foreign virtuosi," which was to become the nucleus of the Gewandhaus Concerts, outshone the collegium by espousing the new school coming from Mannheim.

The Leipzig period was, nevertheless, rich in titanic creations: the Passions, the Masses, the *Christmas Oratorio,* a great number of monumental cantatas and organ works, as well as the fugues of the second volume of the *Well-Tempered Clavier,* and other mysterious contrapuntal epics. During the last decade of his life, the master found enjoyment in the musical abilities of his sons and in a few journeys which carried him to Dresden, where he met Hasse, and to Potsdam to a memorable meeting with Frederick the Great. The constant copying of music ruined his eyesight, which failed him altogether in the last year of his life. But the creative urge was still strong, and only a few days before his death, on July 28, 1750, the blind musician dictated to his son-in-law the chorale prelude "Before Thy Throne, My God, I Stand." Buried in the churchyard of St. John's, his grave was lost among the nameless, becoming the object of scientific search on the two-hundredth anniversary of his birth. Learned anatomists and anthropologists identified one of the exhumed bodies as his, and he was laid to rest in a sarcophagus in the same church.

No matter from what angle we approach Bach, tremendous obstacles block our way. The music lover is awe-struck when entering the great palaces of his works, the plan and design of which he can barely divine. He feels himself lost, because while he admires the geometric marvels of the severe architecture, he finds his whole being invaded by a tender poetry which emanates from the meticulously elaborated ornaments of the towering structures. But when he turns his attention to the source of this poetry he sees the walls and columns of an architecture whose order and logic seem to be unalterably constant. The critic is humbled by the unlimited resources and knowledge of the métier and searches feverishly for the outlets through which pour the broad stream of faith, longing, and exaltation. But he too is misled by the dual unity of absolute mathematics and absolute poetry, and in his helplessness tries to dissect these masterpieces measure by measure, counting, sifting, and classifying them, and, failing, he goes to the other extreme of trying to interpret symbolical meanings in every line. The scholar, in his turn, unearthing the creative elements of this music from the Italian baroque and the German cantors' art, tries desperately to solder them together, only to be baffled when everything seems to be neatly joined.

Johann Sebastian Bach offers one of the most remarkable cases in cultural history of isolation from the general artistic tendencies of his time. This is the more striking when contrasted with Handel's enthusiastic espousal of the *Zeitgeist*. Bach's art rests on the traditions of the German Reformation, which reached its highest manifestation in him, in the midst of the era of the Enlightenment. But it is not only this great musician's art which belongs to earlier times: his whole personality is much nearer to the man of the seventeenth century, the earnest German Protestant, unflinchingly faithful to the religion which governed his whole life. He belongs in the company of Gryphius, Fleming, Milton, and the great religious figures of the House of Orange, at the same time surpassing them all by the freedom and imagination with which he could abandon himself to human feelings. He clung with all his faith and sincerity to Protestantism, but he had no use for the denominational quarrels, for the dogmatic discussions, under which Protestant Germany suffered. To him the only living things in religion were its positive forces. Since the Pietists opposed all church music with the exception of the spiritual songs, it is natural that among Bach's cantata text writers there were no Pietists. Still, while avoiding Pietism whose negativism toward life he must have abhorred, Bach was deeply interested in reconciling the rift between the orthodox doctrinaire Lutherans and the popular Pietists; it was for this reason that he collaborated with Georg Christian Schemelli, the editor of a popular spiritual song-book, contributing several original melodies and rearranging others. Yet with all his opposition to Pietistic tenets, Bach's art could not entirely escape the spiritual repercussions of that Pietism which surrounded him. His texts occasionally speak the new language of Pietism, but we must not forget that this language was generally regarded as an expression of deep religious fervor. He was acquainted with the old literature of mysticism, a fact proved by his possession of the writings of Johannes Tauler, a medieval German mystic whose German sermons were highly praised by Luther and whose works have been published in various editions since 1498. On the other hand, he knew poetry only from the hymns and similar religious lyricism which represented a spirit no longer a reality to his contemporaries, who consequently were not impressed by his music, inspired by an outmoded religious poetry.

The Choral Works

THE center of Lutheran religion is the inner struggle of the individual. This traditional subjective religion was transmitted in the Bach family for generations and accepted with the deepest convictions. Its ardor, humility, fear, and soaring hope are embodied in Bach's cantatas with an intensity and effect which make these works the highest expression of Lutheran religiousness.

Bach's art of religious narration is vastly different, musically, from the epic oratorio of Handel. The main difference, however, lies in their conceptions of the dramatic. Handel, the born musical dramatist, is always bent on sharp psychological delineations. Bach, conversely, does not individualize the *dramatis personae:* the characters emerge intermittently from the chorus as typical representatives of the Biblical idea; they are universal, eternal—characters like Bach himself. The variety of his cantatas is great, although certain types can be discerned among them. Thus there are religious pastorals, oratoriolike dramatic scenes, pictorial Biblical episodes, lyrico-epic poems, and, finally, transfigurations steeped in pious contemplation, avoiding dramatic, pictorial, and characterizing effects, but filled with mystic symbolism. The medieval intensity of religious polyphony, reinforced with the drama of the monodic style, is embodied in this music. All the stock devices of the baroque era parade before us in the cantatas: the introductory sonata or sinfonia, the da capo aria, the operatic arioso and recitative, Carissimi's exultation and lament, the chromatic *ostinato* basses with their typical falling interval of the fourth, used from time immemorial, the French overture, occasionally transformed into choruses, the concerto, the scintillating trumpet fanfares, the obbligato oboe and viola d'amore of the concerted arias of the Venetian opera, the multiple choirs of the early baroque, Cesti's and Cavalli's orchestral recitative, Vivaldi's thematic work, and the rhythmical dances of the French instrumental suite given a vocal setting. But all this is dominated by the *Kirchenlied,* the Lutheran hymn.

Unlike his colleagues and predecessors, Bach could never free himself entirely from the chorale and the Scriptures. Kuhnau was forced to do so in order to make possible the introduction of recitative and da capo aria in the cantata. Bach was no longer constrained to sacrifice anything, for he had inherited these elements from Kuhnau, and it was left to him to solidify this new cantata form and make it an essential part of Protestant liturgic tradition. But at the time when the master was finding a final solution, a final relationship between old and new, the chorale and the opera, the chorale had already ceased to be a living force. Having reached a second flowering, after Praetorius and Scheidt, in the works of Johann Schelle (1648–1701), Kuhnau's predecessor as cantor at the Thomasschule, the chorale all but disappeared from the cantata. Until 1727 the emphasis in Bach's cantatas was mainly on the arias, but in his last period he turned away from the monodistic elements and returned to the strict old chorale cantata. This alone must have impressed his contemporaries as an anachronism, and the serene and autumnal character of these works—the choruses often approaching the motet style of the seventeenth century—made them almost forbidding. Bach's mysterious and singularly Gothic nature manifests itself in these compositions almost to the exclusion of the spirit of the times in which he lived. The poignant Easter cantata, *Christ Lay in Death's Dark Prison,* spurning all solo singing and calling on the peculiarly archaic choirs of trombones and viols, carries us back into the distant past. There was not a soul left in Germany who could even divine the profundity of this art, for it expressed the spirit of a bygone age, living only in the writings of Luther and the paintings of Dürer—both legendary heroes far removed from the man of the waning baroque. There is an ironical touch in a petition that Bach made in 1730 to the municipal council; referring to his predecessors Schelle and Kuhnau, he remarked that "art has made great progress, and taste has undergone remarkable changes, therefore the older art of music does not sound pleasing to our ears."

Bach's cantatas give the uninitiated the impression that here speaks one who, rising above earthly confusion, is entirely immersed in the worship of the celestial. But when we become more intimately acquainted with them we are struck by the earthiness of this man and realize that from day to day and from hour to hour he longed for salvation. From hundreds of arias and choruses rings the cry "and deliver me from my sins." In every one of these works he retraces the calvary of redemption. The age-old wisdom of the Orient, "To fulfill our mission, first we must conquer ourselves," was foremost in his mind, as it was in Beethoven's; but while Beethoven, an optimist, was convinced that man can conquer himself in goodness and love, that men can become brothers in joy, Bach, with the dogmatic skepticism of the faithful, was convinced that man will be free in death only. Although he was by no means lost in this skepticism, nevertheless the symbolism of death permeated Bach's whole nature. Here it is the terrible human fate of death, there the abandonment and longing for redemption, which takes possession of his whole being, both penetrating to unfathomable depths of mental anguish. "It was from the first decreed—Man, thou must die," says the dirge in the *Actus Tragicus,* and the finality of this verdict hushes the very life in the listener. But the inevitable can be transformed into a humble Christian supplication, "Now come, Lord Jesus, come," as man realizes that death may bring redemption. What we hear now—"Man, thou must die"—is not the poet's *Weltschmerz* but the judgment of God's emissary. This is repeated inexorably until it becomes unbearable, and then the high soprano voice takes the lead with its "Yes, yes, now come, Lord Jesus, come," and the music is suddenly saturated with a celestial happiness.

In his submission to death and heavenly rest there is not a particle of romanticism; it is a genuine acceptance, entirely possessed by Biblical sobriety. Even in Bach's deepest sorrow there is something of that joy which distinguishes him from the medieval mystics to whom he was distantly related; for it is joy, and not the consciousness of sin, which dominates him. While his representations of the sins and miseries of life are as poignant as those of the greatest artists of the Middle Ages, he did not halt at the deathly earnestness of sin, he did not espouse the medieval belief in the insurmountable finality of sin; instead, he abandoned himself to an indescribable felicity, at times chastely suggested in the most ethereal tones, at times proclaimed with the blare of trumpets. Although the lyric relationship to Jesus as a personal ideal is the attitude of the Pietists, especially of Zinzendorf, such arias, seemingly written for a solo voice, are not soliloquies; they are in reality dialogues, dialogues between death and the plaintive grieving soul engrossed in its struggle with the idea of death. And the spirit of the Gothic returns in them, the medieval Christian mood which opposed sin and redemption, death and divine life, transitoriness and the eternity of existence in God.

Bach's cantatas determined his choral style not only by their sheer bulk, but because they carried him through the whole gamut of musical expression. All the other choral works follow this style faithfully, the difference being only that of proportions. Thus the so-called *Christmas Oratorio* is simply a string of cantatas, while the Passions carry the cantata, and with it Protestant church music, to its ultimate height. While seemingly an entirely different work, the B minor Mass is still a gigantic collection of cantatas, a fact well illustrated by the inclusion in this Catholic work of six individual numbers taken from his earlier German-Protestant cantatas. Thus six sections of the Mass—Gratias, Qui Tollis, Patrem, Crucifixus, Osanna, Agnus Dei—contain music that was originally the embodiment of a spirit diametrically opposed to the Latin text to which it was now fitted without radical alterations or noticeable effort. It cannot be denied that this fact, together with the virtually prohibitive proportions and the great variety of forms and devices employed in the individual sections, makes the Mass somewhat diffuse and heterogeneous. Gigantic concerted motets in the old five-part setting, composed with all available resources of polyphonic mastery, alternate with suave and mellow duets in the vein of Steffani, whose chamber duets were undoubtedly the models followed by Bach; arias are relieved by colossal double choirs, only to be followed by a coloratura aria with an obbligato instrument in the Venetian-Neapolitan manner. The wealth of great music compressed in this score is phenomenal and at times oppressive, but withal the B minor Mass will remain a masterpiece isolated in the whole literature, for it is almost beyond the grasp of the listener and definitely beyond the scope of any divine service, Catholic or Protestant.

The great number of forms within this Mass brings up a question which seems to have caused some anxiety to pious worshipers of Bach, namely, the secular—and, *horribile dictu,* operatic—origin and nature of many of them. A number of authors have taken great pains to deny any secular leanings on the part of this august master of church music, always pointing out that, unlike Handel, he never wrote operas. As a matter of fact, many of Bach's secular cantatas show unmistakable signs of a scenic performance, on the stage or outdoors. Among them are birthday cantatas, the Weissenfels *Hunt Cantata,* the *Coffee Cantata;* and as to *Phoebus and Pan,* this is a comic opera to all intents and purposes. In his *Election Cantata (Mer han e neue Oberkeet),* written in dialect, he gives us a peasant caricature of the most humorous kind. These secular cantatas are diminutive German operas or *Singspiele,* showing that Bach made good use of his Hamburg experiences, and the influence of Keiser can be traced clearly in the most hallowed passages in his Passions.

It is inconceivable that a musician of genius, immersed in the drama of life and religion, should ignore the most powerful and appropriate means of conveying the conflicts arising therefrom, and indeed Bach had a highly developed sense of the dramatic. But the dramatic character of a work like the *Passion according to St. John* is vastly different from the poignant historical-actual dramatization of Handel, for the central figure of the tragedy, Christ, is in himself not dramatized; his person reigns with divine poise and calm. To this supernatural calmness is opposed, however, a restless, passionate world, beholding the sufferings and death of the Lord. The vociferous choral exclamations of the crowd, "Crucify! Crucify!" and the brutality of the soldiers are rendered with tremendous force, yet the person of Pilate is barely traced, and Christ never changes his almost abstract, divine calm. This contrast is worked out by the composer so sharply that at times it reaches truly demonic intensity, and it is this contrast which creates the dramatic atmosphere. The weakening of the Biblical strength of the Passion is nevertheless evident in Bach, and the lyrical effusions of Pietism, interrupting the stark and terse Gospel, often break the continuity, a fact which cannot be excused in even the greatest music. No one felt this more keenly than the master himself, hence his ceaseless search for a poet who understood the great problems of the Biblical drama. It is more than probable that Bach himself arranged the libretto of his *Passion according to St. John,* basing the extra-Biblical additions on Brockes's poems, while the text of the *St. Matthew Passion* was furnished by a Leipzig littérateur, Christian Friedrich Henrici (1700–1764), better known under his pseudonym Picander.

The *St. John Passion,* the earlier of the two extant settings out of the four composed by Bach, is more youthful and impetuous than the later *St. Matthew Passion.* A great number of chorales is woven through its texture, but with one exception the chorale tunes are not expanded into chorale paraphrases or fantasias. *St. John,* considerably shorter than the second Passion, presents the liturgic drama in a more summary, more vehement, and more visually dramatic manner. It is especially in the recitatives, brusquely interrupted by the chorus of the people, that this dramatic quality becomes acute. Less contemplative than the *St. Matthew Passion,* it attains a dramatic violence which is pure music drama. The dramatic atmosphere is deliberately consistent, for, with the exception of the last chorus, Bach made the choral passages part of the recitation, and the crowd of spectators and soldiers takes an active part in the unfolding of the tragedy. The religious commentary is provided by the arias and chorales. This is drama, indomitable and irresistible. But the drama, so poignantly presented in the choruses, recitatives, and ariosos, is interrupted and temporarily suspended by the arias, and it must be said that some of these jeopardize the artistic unity of the work. There is, for instance, the enormously long da capo aria, "O see how his blood-tinted back resembles heaven"—a typical piece of Pietistic poetry usually left untranslated in English and replaced by a new text—which follows a magnificent, terse, and dramatic arioso, "Consider, O my soul." The continuity is all but lost, when the Evangelist picks up the thread and recites how the soldiers placed a crown of thorns upon his head and a purple robe on his shoulders, whereupon the chorus plunges us again into the thick of the drama with its "Hail, King of the Jews!" In the choruses sung by the crowd (the ancient *turbae*), "is manifested the rudeness and blind obstinacy of the people. Bach repeats the same music even when the text changes, giving an ingenious image of the stubbornness of the multitude and its lack of discernment." [28]

The librettist of the *Passion according to St. Matthew* was not a poet of particular distinction, but in his arrangement Bach found the elements he needed: on the one hand the solid churchly tradition, the unaltered narration of the Evangelist, dramatized by the choral settings of the cries of the people and the oratory of the soloists; on the other, the tender reflections upon the Lord's sufferings which corresponded to the feelings of the guilty and thankful soul, longing for redemption. The *St. Matthew Passion* is much less scenic than the earlier setting of the Biblical drama, but its stylistic coherence is markedly superior; and the quality of the lyric commentaries, foreign to the Gospel, is much higher and blends better with the text than in other instances of contemplative Passions. The spirit of the whole is less dramatic, more reflective and epico-lyrical. The unity of the work is the more remarkable because Bach introduces at the very beginning of the Passion an allegorical figure not part of the Scriptural tale. The "Daughter of Zion" appeals to the crowd to behold her betrothed, Christ, who is going to suffer martyrdom. This is a monumental choral fantasy utilizing everything at the composer's disposal: double chorus in eight parts, two orchestras and two organs, joined occasionally by a boys' choir whose song is woven in the fabric of the double choir. The distinctive character of the boys' choir lies not only in the quality of their voices, fresh, and more crystalline than the feminine soprano, but in the fact that they do not sing in the deliberately expressive manner of adults. Their song has an inimitable air of innocent felicity which greatly moves the listener. Underneath, the chorus heaves and tosses like the sea. Through the first chorus the Daughter of Zion bids, "Come, ye daughters, share my anguish, see him." "Whom?" thunders the second chorus, punctuating the request with its reverberating questions; and above the tumult floats the chorale "O lamb of God, most holy," sung by the angelic voice of the boys' choir, imparting a divine calmness.

The recitatives and ariosos in the *St. Matthew Passion* are entirely different from those in the *St. John*. Their accompaniment is much more elaborate, and they are uniformly poetic and of great expressive force. The tender sentimentality that saturates these arias may come from Pietism, but it is infinitely ennobled by the truly poetic soul of the musician communing with the revelations of the Apostle. This infinitely tender poetic wonderment, lost in the contemplation of the Lord's fate, soothes the choruses (so unruly and vehement in the *St. John Passion*), reaching indescribable peace and comfort in the tenor aria with chorus. The plaintive oboe obbligato opens the aria with a ritornel followed by the soloist's short phrase "I would beside my Lord be watching," whereupon the chorus enters, almost imperceptibly, with a gentle lullaby: "Thus will our sins lie dormant." In spite of the many profoundly lyrical and dolorous passages, the second part of the Passion must, of necessity, take a more dramatic tone as the tragedy nears. The crowd asks mercy for Barabbas and crucifixion for Christ, but to make us forget the terrible drama Bach intermingles arias and ariosos of ethereal tenderness, occasionally even dispensing with the basso continuo to make them more intimate and disembodied. Then he leads us to Golgotha, and darkness descends over everything. At this point the Gospel is again abandoned to permit the composer to reflect on the redemption of mankind by the supreme sacrifice of Christ.

We have mentioned repeatedly the serious liturgic and artistic objections to such interpolations in the Gospel and noticed that sometimes even the greatest music cannot save these additions from harming the religious and aesthetic unity of the Passion. In this work, however, Bach succeeded in blending his non-Biblical lyrics with the body of the Passion. Thus the recitative-arioso which follows Pilate's permission for the body to be delivered to the disciples strikes us as almost Biblical. Its final measures, "O let us all regard with thankful wonder his precious death, and on its meaning ponder," seem to close admirably the contemplative parts entrusted to the solo voices. But Bach followed it with an aria which, beautiful as it is, delays the denouement and the last dramatic accents of the chorus demanding a guard for the tomb "lest his disciples come by night, and steal him away." The final chorus, not unlike that of the *Passion according to St. John,* is a gigantic idealized lullaby. Everything has been done, and all the sufferings have subsided and passed into remembrance. Therefore this last dirge takes unto itself the memory of all events and all the significance of the Passion; all the hatred, bitterness, supplication, is a thing of the past, and a serene, transfigured joy, well expressed in the dance rhythm employed, announces to the faithful the message that Christians should derive from the divine tragedy enacted before them.

With the *St. Matthew Passion* we have arrived at the end of the history of the musical setting of the Biblical drama. Bach's works carried the genre to its ultimate and unsurpassable height. The oratorio continued to flourish, and the succeeding generations produced many masterpieces in this form; but the elemental Lutheran faith and strength of conviction which brought about the Passions of Bach vanished, together with the appreciation of the works which so nobly expressed it in music. The very popularity of certain works, contemporary with Bach's compositions or somewhat more recent, testifies to the slight understanding of the great master's creations. Perhaps the best example of both the quality of the postbaroque Passion and the un-discriminating aesthetic and musical judgment of the public is furnished by Carl Heinrich Graun's oratorio-Passion *Der Tod Jesu.* This work enjoyed enormous popularity from its publication in 1760 up to the very beginning of our century, and its influence upon church music and oratorio was con-siderable. As a matter of fact, the soprano aria "Singt dem göttlichen Proph-eten" was still being praised as an incomparable masterpiece at a time when the somber and distilled choruses of Brahms's *German Requiem,* recaptur-ing something of the essence of German Protestant church music, were written. Graun's work belongs to that period of German cultural history which tried to unite under the same banner rationalism and a sentimental-ism which depicted the Passion of the Lord in a series of touching, tearful, and lamenting pictures equipped with edifying running comments. Ram-ler's libretto was as far removed in spirit and insight from the Bible as Graun's music was from the sincerely religious and human music of Bach's Passions, yet *Der Tod Jesu* was acknowledged as a masterpiece while the two works which to us represent the apotheosis of religious music almost perished with the others squandered by Bach's careless heirs. All real "af-fections" are merely skirted in *The Death of Jesus;* the music flows pleasantly, here in the melodic vein of the opera, there in a choral fugue filled with contrapuntal clichés. Some of this music is not lacking in a certain brilliance and feeling, but it does not seem to matter upon what text it was written. To his contemporaries Graun's work seemed the unequaled manifestation of religiousness in music.

The popularity of Graun's church music and the ignorance of Bach's was not due entirely to the infinitely more profound musical ideas expressed in the vocal works of Bach. These ideas were without any doubt far beyond the comprehension of the average musician; not only was the master's vocal style a powerful deterrent in his own time, but it remains so even in ours. Bach's melody and counterpoint are fundamentally instrumental, especially based on the idiom of the organ. This fact explains the complicated texture of his vocal style, its lively ornamentation, its boldly arching lines, its daring, and its harshness. Some of Bach's arias and choral passages would be anathema to Italian masters of the stature of Steffani and Scarlatti, yet the German composer was well acquainted with their works and repeatedly imitated them. With Bach the voice often merely joins the instruments and the individual words of the text lose their significance, whereas with the true vocal composers—the Italians—the situation is just the opposite: the instruments join the voices and sing with them. The instrumental nature and conception of many of Bach's vocal works led to such abstract formations as the inexorably through-composed three-part fugue in the second aria in Cantata No. 54, in which the contralto solo takes one part, the others being taken by the violins and the violas, and the basso continuo lending a constructive hand in the contrapuntal fabric the instant the singing voice pauses. The master's preoccupation with the logical architecture of the fugal structure is such that when in the middle part of this aria the changing text requires new thematic treatment in the voice he lets the voice depart from the fugal development, but the accompanying instruments take no notice of this and continue their predestined course. Another most curious example of instrumental conception forced upon vocal music is the relatively great number of purely dance pieces elaborated into arias. The arias of Cantata No. 194, *Long Expected Festal Day,* hide a complete dance suite. Needless to say, the declamation suffers considerably under such conditions, and in many instances the musical prosody and melodic formation are not derived from the text, but the text is adjusted to the music. Bach often starts with a perfectly natural musical declamation, only to abandon it after the initial measures for purely musical figuration which ignores the literal meaning and natural position of the words, merely retaining their spirit.

Curiously enough, the only department of vocal writing in which Bach was a sovereign and infallible master of declamation and setting was the most operatic of all the elements used in his church music, the recitative.

His faithfulness to the text and the variety of expression, used with the greatest dramatic insight and judiciousness, is unsurpassed even by the greatest of the Italians, acknowledged masters of this style. Bach's recitatives range from the simple *recitativo secco* of the Italian opera, accompanied sparsely by a few chords, through the *recitativo accompagnato* (of which he especially liked the scenes of ghosts, the *ombrae* of the Venetian opera, used in Christ's recitatives in the *St. Matthew Passion*), to the more elaborate ariosos which change the syllabic recitative into melismatic, enhancing the expressive-declamatory delivery by a more active participation of the accompaniment.

The Instrumental Works

WHILE Bach as a vocal composer shows indisputable limitations in spite of his almost oppressive greatness, in his instrumental music he stands before us unrivaled and beyond any criticism, aesthetic or technical. The very fact that the objections raised against many of his vocal works usually center around their instrumental physiognomy indicates that in spite of the overwhelming bulk of his vocal works Bach's real and most personal domain is instrumental music, especially organ music. It is the spirit of the organ which is expressed everywhere, in the cantata-symphonies and in the wondrous polyphonic sonatas for unaccompanied violin; and many of his clavier compositions, especially among the preludes and fugues of the *Well-Tempered Clavier,* stand much nearer to the organ than to any kind of clavichord or harpsichord. The transcription of the two violin fugues (D minor and G minor) for keyboard demonstrates this organlike thinking convincingly. The whole polyphonic structure of the D minor fugue remains intact in the keyboard version, while the second fugue merely receives an extra bass passage.

Thus if we wish to penetrate the gigantic yet graceful, dark yet warm-toned, cathedral of Bach's lifework, we must pass by the main portal. It is through the side door of the sacristy that we must enter, and as we pass through the mystic dark of the winding staircase to the friendly and intimate organ loft, we shall find the place that was the closest to his heart. It is in the lyric poems called chorale preludes that Bach expressed his most personal and profound utterances. They range from illuminated miniatures of a dozen measures to large murals of chorale fantasies and fugues. They are founded on one tone color and on one mood, as is befitting a chamber style, for, taken in the classical sense, the organ is not a coloristic instrument and when it attempts to imitate the orchestra it abandons its very noble nature, as does the string quartet when reaching out for orchestral effects. The instrument may have a hundred shadings, but they must never disturb the fundamentally closed and unified organ tone, and no attempt should be made to minimize the inherent rigidity of the instrument's dynamic fluctuations. Needless to say, the organ is capable of color contrasts, but these have little in common with those of the orchestra. Bach's great variations, fantasies, and fugues are undoubtedly built on contrasting effects, and he was not less fond than his contemporaries of garish oppositions, but the tender mosaics of the chorale preludes offer lyric forms in pictorially closed moods. The terracelike construction of the tonal resources of the organ—an eminently baroque principle—permits the alternate illumination or darkening of the sections or strophes, but an orchestralike coloristic treatment is foreign to this art.

We must keep in mind that the baroque organ and harpsichord were instruments entirely different from our own. They demanded a constancy of dynamics within a given register, thereby alienating themselves from the mimic expression and subjective mood of the human voice, and from the more pliable instruments, such as string and wood-wind instruments. This dematerialized tone of organ and harpsichord creates an atmosphere of its own, pressing for clarity, form, polyphony, motion, antitheses, questions and answers. The baroque organ was particularly well provided with open flue pipes or diapasons, the most characteristic organ stops, and with numerous "mixtures" or combination stops which corroborate the higher consonant harmonic sounds suggested by nature; there were, however, few reed stops, so profusely supplied in our modern organs, which are built with an eye to orchestral possibilities. Unlike the French and English organs, constructed on different principles—the French with a primitive and incomplete pedal board, the English with none—the German organs of the late baroque had a complete pedal keyboard extending two and a half octaves and commanding a considerable variety of stops, including thirty-two foot stops. Thus these instruments commanded a majestic amplitude of tone and a variety of resources.

The chorale is the Ariadne's thread in Bach's works. In the labyrinth of a complicated polyphonic medium it preserves contact with the music of the people. The relationship with popular music is more than external. Bach's own music was as far removed from that of the people as the polyphonic Masses of the composers of the Renaissance who employed cantus firmi taken from popular sources; but the fact that the text and melody of his cantus firmi were as much a cherished reality to him as to the humble peasants in the congregation established an ideological community entirely missing in the dozens of Masses written on the *Homme Armé* tune or on other popular chansons. Only the loving study of the volumes which contain this mystic lyric poetry will enable us to understand the essence of Bach's art.

The chorale prelude was, of course, a well-established and venerable form when Bach first encountered it. Having reached its climax in Bach's works, like the Passion, it was no longer capable of further development. After Bach only one composer, another north German, ever again recaptured its spirit in all its depth and significance: the aged Brahms. While the original purpose of the chorale prelude, to establish congregation consciousness by prefacing, outlining, and explaining the hymn to the church assembly, was still the motive behind them, Bach carried these poetic compositions to a spiritual and artistic depth which could not be fathomed by his contemporaries. Even as a young man he was reprimanded by the consistory of Arnstadt for his manner of playing the chorales: "We charge him with having hitherto been in the habit of making surprising *variationes* in the chorales, and intermixing divers strange sounds, so that thereby the congregation were confounded." [29]

It is impossible to deal at length here with the proud preludes and fugues, which in their lordly splendor and their depth of sentiment are still able to maintain the organ as "queen of the instruments," although for many generations there has ceased to be a literature worthy of the instrument. There are, furthermore, the bold fantasies, the brilliant toccatas reflecting the virtuosity of the German organ school, the stupendous Passacaglia, and a number of single pieces and transcriptions.

Bach's clavier music stems from many ancestors, its lineage going back to Sweelinck.[30] Froberger, whose suite form seems to have been a model followed faithfully by Bach, was another important composer whose influence molded the younger man's style, but perhaps the most lasting influence was derived from the works of Johann Caspar Ferdinand Fischer and Kuhnau. Fischer transmitted to him the Couperin type of French clavier suite and furnished him with a model for the *Well-Tempered Clavier*, while Kuhnau impressed him not so much with his celebrated program sonatas as with his *Clavierübung*. Bach's eminent predecessor in the Thomasschule, whom we have identified as the master who effectuated the transition between the seventeenth and eighteenth centuries, paralleled in his keyboard music his achievements in the field of church music. It was he who adapted the formal structure of the Italian chamber sonata to the keyboard sonata, thereby taking the first decisive step toward the modern piano sonata. As Froberger developed keyboard music by his German suite, Kuhnau carried the development into new paths by his sonatas, published in two sections, the first of which was tacked onto the second part of his *Neue Clavierübung,* in 1689 and 1692. The success of these first sonatas prompted Kuhnau to compose and publish seven more in 1696 under the title *Frische Clavierfrüchte.* His so-called Biblical sonatas which followed four years later (six sonatas belonging to the realm of program music) are somewhat outside the pale of indigenous development, for they were evidently modeled on operatic sources. Their immediate influence was manifestly in orchestral music—such as Telemann's *Don Quixote* suite—and not in keyboard music, although the keyboard piece which Bach wrote commemorating the departure of his brother—his one programmatic work—is undoubtedly fashioned upon Kuhnau's procedure.

The preludes, inventions, suites, partitas, are all genre pieces of endless charm; they are lyric poems, ballads, full of moving content. The *French Suites, English Suites* (which latter are also in the French manner), and the dance pieces which are to be found in the various *Clavierbüchlein* written for his sons and his wife, show Bach's complete mastery of the French style of Chambonnières and Couperin. It is a sheer wonder to see the grave Lutheran cantor, the epitome of German baroque massiveness, clad in the impeccable silk stockings, lace-trimmed jacket, and powdered wig of the French rococo, and moving about in this circle with the assuredness of the very masters whose style he attempted to imitate. The imitations turned out, however, to be works such as no rococo composer could even approach, for over the feathery touch, the agreeably pointed rhythm, and the sweet melancholy of the *style galant,* the German master pours the poetic warmth of a lyricist inspired to meditation where his French colleagues are seeking *divertissement.* In the German suites of the first part of the *Clavierübung* the modern Italian pianistic style of Domenico Scarlatti makes its appearance, and it is interesting to see how Bach, always eager to examine new things, reconciles this new style with the traditional French and German keyboard manner.

The old Kirnberger used to say, "He who knows a fugue by Bach knows really one only." Indeed, Bach made of the fugue, originally a piece of music of more general than specific expressive nature, a character piece as pliable and varied as the piano pieces of the romantic era. Ricercar and canzone were definitely replaced in the last third of the seventeenth century by the fugue, the latter finding its greatest field of action in keyboard music. The southern composers practiced it with a certain moderation, writing rather intimate, or even dainty, compositions. Pachelbel's clever and graceful little fugues on the *Magnificat* [31] afford an excellent example of this style. But in the north, where Frescobaldi's and Sweelinck's art was still remembered, the élan and passion of the early baroque were not only retained but broke all dikes in the robust fugues of Buxtehude. Bach followed in the footsteps of the great German masters of the north and carried the fugue to its zenith. We know, however, that Bach was not less interested in the products of the Italian schools, as he arranged fugues taken from the trio sonatas of Legrenzi, Corelli, and Albinoni. This tremendous treasure of great music he diligently and minutely explored. At first there were many imitations; one can easily detect the rumbling pedal passages of Buxtehude and the fine ornamental open work of Pachelbel. But later everything was completely assimilated and presented to us as the supreme achievement of the baroque.

The organ fugues are, as a rule, more robust and stand nearer to the north German traditions reaching back to Scheidt and Sweelinck. They are superbly idiomatic and utilize the polyphonic-linear possibilities of the instrument as well as its steady sonority. They are also freer and more fantastic than the harpsichord fugues, and the dramatic endings of their uninterrupted, impetuous flow, the themes piling upon each other when the *stretto* sets in like an avalanche, defy description or comparison. The harpsichord fugues are more concise and symmetrical and show the influence of Italian concerted music. Bach's fugues are character pieces, and remain such even when the most complicated polyphonic apparatus is invoked. Hans von Bülow, who coined many a ridiculous bon mot, found an excellent one for the *Well-Tempered Clavier* when he called it the Old Testament of piano music as compared to the piano sonatas of Beethoven, the New Testament.

It is occasionally thought that the *Well-Tempered Clavier* was the first work to demonstrate the practical possibility of composition in all transpositions of the modern major-minor scales. The elimination of the small discrepancy which appears when two identical large intervals are joined had occupied scholars and composers since the end of the fifteenth century. It had been found that perfect tuning, however beautiful in the original key, leads to discrepancies even in the neighboring keys, and when modulations are carried into remote keys the accumulated differences reach appalling proportions, resulting in the worst dissonances. The earlier experiments sought to safeguard the wonderful sonority of perfect tuning, but later it was found that for the sake of practical usefulness some of the beauty of pure tuning must be sacrificed. Finally, Andreas Werckmeister's eminently practical suggestion of dividing the octave into twelve identical intervals gave us the workable arrangement called equal temperament. His system distributed the discrepancy evenly within the seven octaves of our practical musical range, thus making every interval slightly incorrect, but with a discrepancy not commonly noticed unless untempered instruments (such as the violin) play together with a tempered instrument (such as the piano), while the resultant practical advantage is far reaching. Werckmeister provided the solution for the old problem of organists and cembalists, who could now modulate freely in all major and minor keys. Johann Caspar Ferdinand Fischer's *Ariadne Musica* (1715), a collection of preludes and fugues through the circle of tonalities, was the interesting model for Bach's *Well-Tempered Clavier,* which latter was again imitated in a more popular manner by Bernhard Christian Weber (1712–1758) in a collection named after Bach's own.[32] It is erroneous to translate the original German title, *Das Wohltemperierte*

Clavier, as "well-tempered clavichord," because there are weighty reasons for believing that the work was intended for the more substantial harpsichord or cembalo. The German *Clavier* is used in the wider sense of "keyboard," and it seems more judicious to retain the original word, perfectly usable in English.

Between 1726 and 1731 Bach published a collection of keyboard works the title of which, *Clavierübung,* he borrowed from Kuhnau. The collection contains a great variety of works, ranging from suites to the unaccompanied *Italian Concerto* and from a remarkable set of chorale preludes to the great variations over a *ciacona*-bass known as *Goldberg Variations.* It seems as if Bach wanted to present to the world a compendium of the art of the clavier, for every one of the compositions in the *Clavierübung* strikes us as the apotheosis of its respective genre; all are finished, inspired masterpieces in a class by themselves. They were composed in the period when Bach had retired to his study, and these products of the quiet contemplation of the man who had lost interest in the quarrelsome atmosphere of his school and church carry us into regions of polyphony which are scarcely accessible even to the hardiest of musicians and thinkers. The fugues of the second volume of the *Well-Tempered Clavier* had already shown an astonishing deepening of the composer's polyphonic imagination, masterful and profound though it was before. It remained to the works of this last decade to arrive at the quintessence and culmination of all post-Netherlandish polyphony. Indeed, the Latin "riddle canons" of the *Musical Offering* take the baroque master back to the old Flemish masters of polyphony whose spirit still lived in him. This work was written over a theme given to Bach by Frederick the Great on the occasion of his visit to Potsdam. The meeting of the two great Germans was bound to result in something memorable, and upon his return from Potsdam Bach turned the *thema regium,* upon which he had improvised to the Hohenzollern's great admiration, into the composition which, with *The Art of the Fugue,* was to close the history of polyphony as an autonomous style.

The Art of the Fugue consists of a set of fugal variations over a simple, almost insignificant theme. There are fifteen fugues and four canons. Death overtook the master in the 239th measure of a gigantic triple fugue. It is not merely a rhetorical phrase to call *The Art of the Fugue* Bach's last will and testament. Written in open score, it refuses to lean on any specific instrument, in order to preserve the purest, dematerialized spirit of the highest form of baroque art. With it the development of the fugue came to an end. This set of fugues, once considered a cold and emotionless treatise on fugal construction, has recently become increasingly popular and a number of transcriptions, ranging from two pianos to orchestra, have made it known to wide circles. While such transcriptions are not against the spirit of baroque music—Bach himself transcribed repeatedly—the "soulful" rendering of the sinuous contrapuntal lines by a string quartet or wind ensemble distorts their superhuman aloofness, investing the pure motion dynamics, the sheer expansive force of self-generating polyphony, with the petty "expressiveness" of our impoverished musical language; for we have no longer the large canvases, but only the palette with many colors placed upon it. An integral performance of *The Art of the Fugue* is, however, the worst that could be done to it and affords perhaps the best proof that we still have to blaze a trail to this *summa* of the baroque, for the work is a philosophical breviary every measure of which invites reflection and thought. It is only through long and intimate acquaintance with the individual fugues that we can arrive at a true understanding of their message.

After the fugue, the Italian concerto as developed by Corelli and Vivaldi seems to have been the form which most interested Bach, from the time of his first contact with Italian music. As we have seen, the spirit of the concerto invaded even his fugues. The ingenious construction of the concerto, with its three movements and with the logical and artistic principle of rondolike alternation of solo and orchestral ritornel, allowed the composer a great latitude. The slow movement which separates the two fast ones intrigued Bach to such an extent that he attempted to use it in the old and traditionally two-movement forms of organ music, inserting an adagio between toccata and fugue. The so-called *Brandenburg Concertos,* the concerto for two violins, and those for two or more pianos belong to the family of the *concerto grosso.* Written for the Margrave of Brandenburg, the art-loving youngest son of the Great Elector, these concertos testify to the excellence of instrumental ensemble playing in Bach's time, for they demand a virtuoso playing which most of our modern players, commanding a modern technique and performing on perfect instruments, cannot approach without misgivings. In his concertos Bach always remained a faithful follower of Vivaldi, staying within the limits of the established form, whereas Handel, a devotee of Corelli, revealed himself a pioneer in modern orchestral writing, bold, elegiac, and filled with the languishing pathos of the Italians.

Bach's *Brandenburg Concertos* open with that busy and animated tone which characterized commissioned social music, ordered for and performed at official functions, academic convocations, or banquets. It behooved this type of concerto to be spirited, clever, and well built; all introspection was banished, the slow movements usually being harmlessly idyllic. Bach complied with the tradition in the first and third movements in most of his concertos, although their workmanship and the ingenious coupling of solo and ritornel make these movements the highest point in the history of the old concerto; but the spirit of the *Gesellschaftsmusik* vanishes in the middle movements before a bottomless profundity of feeling. The Bach of these middle movements is no longer the consummate instrumental virtuoso; these adagios are Passion music, and belong to the greatest poetic achievements of the German spirit.

The solo concertos for violin, which follow the Vivaldi pattern even more faithfully, are distinguished by the same virtues as the *concerti grossi*, but more than once the master varied the cherished model with freely selected forms within the concerto. Thus the first movement of the E major concerto opens with a great da capo aria, while the larghetto of the double concerto is a slow fugue. Of the numerous solo concertos for violin, only two remain in their original form, but several more are known in piano transcriptions. As a matter of fact, it seems that all of Bach's harpsichord concertos are transcriptions of violin concertos, many of them not of his own composition. The F minor and the D minor, undoubtedly violin concertos in their original form, may be adaptations of other composers' works. Several attempts have been made to restore these works to their rightful medium,[33] an undertaking that is made rather simple by the undisguised string writing in the solo part. By transcribing violin concertos for the harpsichord Bach liberated this instrument, the mainstay of the basso continuo, and permitted it to begin a life of its own. Thus he is the founder of the piano concerto, even though none of the seven harpsichord concertos is a work originally planned for that instrument.

Finally, we must speak of chamber music for a restricted number of instruments, the concertos themselves being chamber music of a more elaborate and ample kind. Here, as in other fields, Bach did not experiment with anything new but carried the traditional and established to its ultimate destination. In so doing he often reached the limits of musical reality and human ingenuity. Nowhere is this more evident than in the sonatas and suites written for an unaccompanied violin. One might think that any composition which forces polyphonic part playing upon a melody instrument par excellence would have to be short and well articulated to avert otherwise unavoidable monotony and sketchiness. Not so with Bach; he waves aside all restrictions and all conventions, unloosens all ties to the rational and empirical, plunging us, with the aid of a little wooden box with four strings on it and a thin rod with horsehair stretched from end to end, into the irrational and timeless. Fantastic preludes, completely developed fugues, and cyclopean variations alternate with graceful dances in these sonatas. Creative imagination fetes in them its absolute triumph over all restrictions and limitations imposed upon it by form, material, and medium of expression.

While Bach's chamber music culminated in the solo sonatas and suites, there are a number of masterpieces of the first magnitude for chamber ensembles with harpsichord. From the declining trio sonata he fashioned the violin-piano, flute-piano, and gamba-piano sonata by entrusting the part played by the second melody instrument to the right hand of the harpsichord player.[34] The sustained active thematic participation of the keyboard instrument makes the performance of these works—marvels of logic and economy of thought and of spiritual concentration—very difficult on the modern piano, the sound of which does not mix well with the string tone. The increasing popularity of the harpsichord promises to restore the balanced sonority of this chamber music, which should come to be regarded as the ideal of the genre.

*
* *

THUS Bach is the end. Nothing comes from him; everything merely leads up to him." Schweitzer's words, taken from the preface to his work on Bach, contain a great deal of truth, but this verdict has to be qualified to become at all acceptable. Bach represents neither the beginning nor the end of musical history. It is perfectly true that many things before his time seem to converge in his art, and it is equally true that no immediate issue to his art can be found. Still, he was not the "terminal point" of musical history, but the crowning glory of one of its greatest chapters, of the epoch which reconciled the polyphonic style of the Renaissance with the monody of the early baroque. While in Italy this process was the result of a gradual reinstatement in the monodic style of polyphonic elements, the merger occurred in the opposite manner in German music, where the operatic elements thrust themselves upon the stubbornly defended traditions of polyphony. Bach was the last great master of this Germanic instrumental polyphony resurrected by the baroque, and with him ends the long period of polyphony which —in spite of a great choral literature—grew from instrumental counterpoint. After him came a new era in which a melodic style based on homophony was to reign. This new style was well on its way when the mature Bach created his works, and it was understandable that with the new music appearing everywhere his own was looked upon as conservative in tone and aim, and was quickly silenced by the youthful eloquence of the rising style. The decline of polyphony was a reality in the first quarter of the eighteenth century. Authors and musicians began to turn against it somewhat as the Florentine literati had a hundred odd years before. Friedrich Erhardt Niedt speaks in a mocking and deprecating tone of the music of the "ancients"; das Wunder-Thier, der Contra-Punct, and the Monstrum des Canons are held up as childish tricks because "music is meant for the ears and not for the eyes." [35] While less sarcastic than his older colleague, Heinichen in his above-mentioned thorough-bass treatise is of the opinion that "once the ordinary fundamental school exercises in counterpoint are mastered, one can fill out three or more sheets with music written in the most correct and legal *stylo ecclesiastico* using a correct theme of a few measures; but in the theatrical *stylo* this would not do, the composer must display everywhere invention, *goût,* and brilliancy."

The eighteenth century did not realize Bach's greatness as a composer. Highly admired as a performer and as a technician in matters of counterpoint, he was considered one of many north German cantors, and to rank him with Graun, Fasch, or Telemann was indeed a high favor. This modest appraisal was not due primarily to a scarcity of available compositions; enough of them circulated in manuscript copies to enable people to see his genius. But he was a church musician, with the great majority of his works vocal compositions for the church, and it was his peculiar vocal style, entirely opposed to the Italian, that deterred people from delving into his scores. His sharp-edged, typically instrumental writing for voices was difficult and ungrateful to sing, and his colossal designs seemed to the critics of the eighteenth century swollen and turgid, if not bombastic. Even his own sons smiled at his old-fashioned contrapuntal writing, at his da capo arias with their elaborate and scarcely singable instrumental ornamentation; they could not but feel that their father's whole musical world was of the past. Johann Adolf Scheibe, a notable musical writer of the century, attacked Bach, in his periodical *Der Critische Musicus,* as the "Lohenstein of music," referring to Daniel Caspar von Lohenstein, a seventeenth-century German dramatist who was famed for his long and gruesome tragedies. And Johann Adam Hiller (1728–1804), perhaps the most enlightened and educated musician of his times, remarked that Bach's cantatas require "special devotees to like them." Yet we must not lose sight of the fact that these men, well trained and clear headed, were partisans of progressive music and not mere "music critics" in the modern sense. Scheibe, like many of his contemporaries, was always ready to admit Bach's greatness; in fact, he often spoke of him as an "extraordinary musician," meaning the composer and not the performer, but Bach's style struck him as out of keeping with the times. The dense polyphonic writing was neither enjoyed nor appreciated by the artists of the Enlightenment and rationalism, whose slogan was the "imitation of nature."

Those of the great classical composers who came into contact with the available works of the old Thomascantor recognized his greatness, and we shall see how much Mozart and Beethoven profited from a thorough study of the *Well-Tempered Clavier* and *The Art of the Fugue;* but a full realization of Bach's genius was not given to them, if for no other reason than that very few of Bach's works were available in the south. It is well known how enthusiastically Beethoven greeted the projected complete edition of Bach's works—which, however, was not carried out in his lifetime. But even Mendelssohn and Schumann, although instrumental in reviving his art, did not fully understand his Olympian greatness. Brahms was perhaps the only one of them to grasp it in all its depth. It took a century before the world realized Bach's significance, and another half century before his music began to be more than dutifully admired as "classic" by the general public.

We are not yet able fully to estimate Bach's position in history and his relationship to his contemporaries. There is no modern monograph on Bach which duly considers his predecessors and collaborators, without slighting great artists by dubbing them "forerunners," and re-examines his period in the light of modern historic research. Monumental works have been written about him, and they are not to be deprecated, but they form only the beginning upon which modern musicology should continue to build. The most imposing single contribution which first attacked the task with the weapons of scholarly research was Philipp Spitta's great biography,[36] a work which will remain the source for all future Bach historians. The uniqueness of Spitta's insight—not yet entirely shared or understood by many contemporary writers on music—was his realization of the greatness of German baroque music, and his virtual discovery of Buxtehude, Pachelbel, Böhm, and a number of other great composers. André Pirro's and Albert Schweitzer's monographs[37] are the other two important essays on Bach the musician, while Charles Sanford Terry's biography[38] added a great deal to our knowledge about the man.

How tightly the scholar's room is still closed, how inaccessible to the millions of music lovers! It is true that the B minor Mass and one or the other of the Passions are performed by choral societies, and a transcription or two of Bach's organ works is played in almost every piano recital; but the Church, for whose greater glory he wrote most of his music, whose service he considered his life work, scarcely takes notice of him, and much too little of his music is played in the home. The large concert hall, the only place where we encounter Bach's music, is not his rightful element; on the contrary, it was the only place for which none of his works was intended. He wrote for the Church and for intimate gatherings. Today neither the Protestant nor the Catholic Church uses his music, save for occasional performances, and such princely and aristocratic "chambers" as exist are entirely estranged from such music. However impressive are the public performances of Bach's larger works, only those will become intimately acquainted with this art who wrestle with it in quiet contemplation, playing the chorales, the chorale preludes, the solo sonatas, and the many other works accessible to the individual.

English Music in the Late Baroque

I SHALL add no more to what I have offered than that Musick, Architecture, and Painting, as well as Poetry and Oratory, are to deduce their Laws and Rules from the general Sense and Taste of Mankind, and not from the Principles of those Arts themselves; or in other Words, the Taste is not to conform to the Art, but the Art to the Taste." [39] These keen words of Addison will help us to approach that chapter of baroque music which, together with Bach and his era, closed the great period. We must, indeed, call on considerable outside help to solve the riddle of the brilliant pages that Handel wrote in the annals of musical history, for one of the highest peaks of baroque music, without which the whole era would be left incomplete, rose in a land where music had ceased to be an art permeating the intellectual life of the nation. We saw Handel as an opera composer in England, but his activity was isolated in the musical history of that country and we discussed it as one phase of Italian opera. We must now turn our attention to the role of music in the history of English culture in the late baroque.

In the early Middle Ages English musical scholars wrote down the laws and theories of music which were read and followed all over Europe. English singers were acclaimed by synods and councils, Dunstable started the great Burgundian school on its way, and the Tudor period boasted a musical culture second only to that of the High Renaissance in Italy. Whatever foreign musical waves reached the British shores had to flow over the breakwater of English musical taste, to continue in the quiet but steady stream of inland waterways. There was hardly a country in Europe that showed such genuine poetic feeling and lyricism, the two prime conditions for the growth of music. But while English music, from Gothic times until the advent of the seventeenth century, had followed its own, specific, and logical development, and while in the culture of the English Renaissance it had occupied a role paralleled in importance only by drama, nevertheless this ancient and distinguished art was not able to carry over into the baroque. England's great and organically developed musical history had ended, despite the fact that perhaps its greatest hero, Purcell, appeared in the second half of the seventeenth century. The practice of music, however, continued, dignified and worthy of the great traditions of the country in the seventeenth century, diminishing and shallow in the eighteenth, and returning to life in the late nineteenth. England never abandoned her love of music; we have seen that even the Puritans were not really opposed to music as an art, and that a form as fundamentally alien to the British mind as the opera had a certain vogue and was actually prepared for by indigenous developments in the masques. There was, furthermore, no dearth of composers who could measure their talents with those on the Continent. But the circumstances, the atmosphere, incentive, and opportunities did not permit music to continue its organic growth. The English people's mind was not so free as the Italian's, their soil not so virginal and undeveloped as Germany's, for over all this music making stood guard the spirit of the industrial, shopkeeping, stalwart Englishmen who made the Empire. Novels, dominated by sentimental coloring, travel descriptions, and the informative articles in the *Gentleman's Magazine* satisfied the demand for entertainment in an era which scarcely remembered the importance and practice of drama and song in "Merry England."

The social ideals that were to dominate English life for centuries to come —ideals which had been slowly taking shape for several generations— crystallized in the emergence of the middle class as an economic and political power in the seventeenth century. Its influence on cultural life was more pronounced in England than anywhere on the Continent. The gospel of work, one of the most significant articles of the bourgeois dogma, was promulgated with great earnestness during the period of Puritan supremacy and paved the way for the later apotheosis of business which has colored the entire outlook of the modern world. However much the stern Puritans of Cromwell's government may have been interested in intricate reasoning on predestination, they were equally concerned over problems of trade and finance. The Restoration did not mean a reversion to Tudor or Stuart cultural life; on the contrary, the bourgeoisie acquired additional importance and prepared for its entry into the ranks of the nobility by buying up the lands of distressed aristocrats. The literature and art of the period are filled with expressions of the realization of the ideals of the middle classes. The arbiter in arts and letters was the most solid stratum of the empire, the middle-class consumer, the same population unit which up to this day dictates the conduct of life in England. These people are slow, shrewd, and quiet-spoken. From generation to generation they do not change their manners, their furniture, their whole environment; they move at a turtle's pace. But the typical Englishman is not cold; hidden beneath his legendary indifference are an adventurous spirit, imagination, and a strong religious sentiment. It is his disciplined purposefulness, his abhorrence of waste in any form, which sealed the sources of music, the most irrational of the arts, where it still allowed poetry and drama, painting and architecture, to flourish. And music is the one art which cannot endure propriety and mere artistry.

Dryden acclimatized the French classical style on the stage, and French pastoral poetry followed the drama, together with the satire, didactic poetry, and the moral fable. The leading master of the latter was Pope, the greatest English poet of the eighteenth century. But even with him the main objective was form; the idea was, so to speak, secondary; all that mattered was artistic expression. The pastoral poems of the "prince of rhyme," as Pope was called, are conventional; they disclose neither sincere feelings nor a poetic conception of nature; they are descriptive, didactic, philosophical meditations. His best-known work, *The Rape of the Lock,* written in imitation of Boileau, acquainted Englishmen with the perfumed, elegant, refined, deceptive, and false atmosphere of the French rococo. The lack of a profound artistic conception is most evident in Pope's transcriptions and editions. His modernized Homer has as little of the Greek classical spirit as his "corrected" versions of Shakespeare have of the Elizabethan. This lack of understanding of the great artistic past explains how musical tradition came to be so completely lost.

Nor was music alone: the drama could not find its way back to the glorious era of its early flowering. We noticed the strong Spanish-French influence in the English drama when discussing the Restoration period. The following epoch added to the characteristic Restoration fertility of wit and brittle artificiality of dialogue a coarseness which invited Jeremy Collier's celebrated denunciation of the English stage. Thus, while poetry and drama failed to carry on the great heritage, in spite of such gifted men as Pope and Congreve, the spirit of the times produced great prose writers, political essayists, and satirists. Swift's sentences, shaped by the cold ecstasy of concentrated hatred to a plasticity of the highest artistic order, poured irony and satire on England and on human society in general. Different in type but scarcely less prominent is the prose writing of Defoe, whose work in the new field of the newspaper and periodical preceded that of Addison and Steele. The great essayists reached their readers chiefly through weekly reviews. Defoe's *Review,* for the most part political, ran from 1704 to 1713; Swift edited the *Examiner* (1710–1711); and Steele's *Tatler* (1709–1711) was the predecessor of the *Spectator,* for which Steele and Addison were jointly responsible. The first daily newspaper appeared in 1702 under the name *Daily Courant.*

This is, then, a brief résumé of the "Age of Reason," or the "Age of Classicism" as it was sometimes called because of the stress placed on the knowledge common to all men, on conventionality, and on the so-called classical "rules" of literature and art. Enthusiasm and individuality were deprecated, while the study of man was exalted over that of nature; reason, manner, and form were emphasized, while imagination and emotions were neglected. It was the age of town life and the coffeehouse, the age of urbanity and poise.

A generation or so before, Pepys had written in his diary his impressions when listening to a performance of *The Virgin Martyr:*

But that which did please me beyond any thing in the whole world was the wind-musique when the angel comes down, which is so sweet that it ravished me, and indeed, in a word, did wrap up my soul so that it made me really sick, just as I have formerly been when in love with my wife; that neither then, nor all the evening going home, and at home, I was able to think of any thing, but remained all night transported, so as I could not believe that ever any musick hath that real command over the soul of a man as this did upon me: and makes me resolve to practice wind-musique, and to make my wife do the like.[40]

But the early eighteenth century frowned upon such abandonment to the emotional powers of music:

Cautions are necessary with respect to Musick and Painting; the fancy is often too quick in them, and the Soul too much affected by the Senses. . . . How can chaste Minds delight in the Languishments of wanton Poetry, made yet more languishing by the Graces of Musick. What great or noble is there in the dying Notes of foreign Strumpets and Eunnuchs? . . . Should Christians squander away so many precious Hours in Vanity, or take Pleasure in gratifying a Sense that has so often been a Traitor to Virtue?[41]

It is small wonder that in this atmosphere Purcell stood isolated. Being an original and powerful representative of the baroque, there were but few threads binding him to the great past of English music, and when he died in his thirty-sixth year there was no English musician who could continue his work. The new century began by offering homage to Italy, to her music and her musicians. English opera, blighted in its first beautiful but tender shoots, gave way to its Italian rival; but even Italian opera, which was and remained an "exotic and irrational entertainment," to quote Dr. Johnson, would not have survived save for Handel's prodigious tenacity. "At present," remarks Addison, "our Notions of Musick are so very uncertain, that we do not know what it is we like, only, in general, we are transported with any thing that is not *English:* so if it be of a foreign Growth, let it be *Italian, French,* or *High-Dutch,* it is the same thing. In short, our *English* Musick is quite rooted out, and nothing yet planted in its stead."[42]

As we have remarked above, the practice of music was not abandoned, and suite, sonata, and symphony were welcomed and found sympathetic treatment in their English adaptations. But English participation in these forms left only slight marks on the history of instrumental music. The church composers preserved the erstwhile dignity of the English tradition, and William Croft (1678–1727), Maurice Greene (1695–1755), and William Boyce (1710–1779) wrote many services and other sacred compositions which testify to a lofty conception of their art. Still, when perusing the pages of the various collections of "cathedral music"—a term used by eighteenth-century editors for anthologies of church music—the works of Tallis, Byrd. or Purcell, interspersed among the many seventeenth- and eighteenth·

century worthies, appear to be mementos of a great art that had all but disappeared. The best known and appreciated among native English musicians
of the period was Thomas Augustine Arne (1710–1778). He was a prolific
composer for the stage, but his musical talents were lyric rather than dramatic. Many of his songs are of a simple moving beauty. "Rule Britannia"
became a famous patriotic song, and his Shakespearean settings do not suffer
from the association with the great poet—a praise that cannot be bestowed
on many musicians more favorably known than Arne.

Handel

IT is a singular fact that the composer who has left the deepest impress on
English music should have been a German who came to England as an up-
holder of a purely Italian art." [43] It is perfectly true that Handel was called
to England to supply the upper classes with operas in the Italian style—this
circle of English society not being interested in English music—and that this
great musician turned to the English oratorio only after his repeated failures
and bankruptcies in the operatic field. It is not less true that he never mastered
the English language, although he lived in England for over forty-five years,
and his declamation followed Italian models so closely that his English choral
settings had to be radically revised in order to make them acceptable and
understandable. Nevertheless, no other composer can claim British citizenship with more right than this naturalized Saxon, as truly an English artist
as Lully was the pride of French music. In spite of his German origin,
Italian training, and French experience, there were many traits in Handel
that not only made him receptive to English influences but actually gave
him a close kinship with English music. The pomp and circumstance of
his processionals and marches was a familiar aspect of the English lyric
stage, together with the trumpet fanfares he learned in Venice; his love of
ostinato basses was the same as the English musicians' predilection for
"ground" basses; his sturdy but not overcomplicated contrapuntal writing
was much nearer to English taste than to the strict contrapuntal construction
of his German compatriots, always on the lookout for canons and fugues;
and his wonderful sense for choral passages of homophonous simplicity, but
carrying terrific dramatic impact, seems to be a direct continuation of the
choral idiom of Purcell.

There is something in Handel's personality which reminds one of Leibnitz's universalism, a certain attitude of the citizen of the world, the internationalism of the European humanist. He acquired his means of expression, his forms, and his technique from German, Italian, and French
traditions, but the climate which ripened this equipment into a great, free art
was that of English civilization and culture. On the other hand it is equally

certain that this varied experience and environment merely served to help deploy his most personal poetic world, deeply rooted in the spirit of old Thuringian-German art, independent of the warming and nourishing civilizations about him.

Handel's art embraces the scintillating forms, colors, and figures of a gigantic creative imagination, the chief characteristics of which are a wholesome power of form, monumental dramatic conception, and a flowing poetic inspiration, abandoning itself in the contemplation of nature and its creatures. Where Pope and his colleagues saw man only in his rational acts, Handel, together with John Gay, Allan Ramsay, and James Thomson, discovered the existence of the universe in which man is only a particle. The same tenderness which impresses us in Thomson's *Seasons*—a work particularly close to the musician's heart—emanates from many a page of Handelian music. To him nature is a great drama, the individual scenes and episodes of which furnish the poet and musician with his materials. Johann Sebastian Bach, who solved his tragic and oppressing problems with a glowing inner force that was probably unknown to Handel, did not experience in his most "worldly," most triumphal moments that carefree abandonment to the beauties of the external world, the lulling wonderment, sensuousness, the mundane pomp, and the naïve, almost intoxicating love of animated crowds that characterize Handel's art. But Handel's was by no means a passive, lyric temperament; his operas and oratorios disclose a dramatic intensity well nigh unparalleled in the history of music. His instrumental works exhibit a synthesis of the most heterogeneous musical styles. The *Concerti Grossi,* which, with Bach's *Brandenburg Concertos,* crowned all efforts of baroque orchestral music, conserved a great deal of the noble tone and brilliant virtuosity of the Italian string style, but the gestures are larger, the melodic arches wider, and the form and logic of construction more monumental in their straightforwardness. Once an allegro movement is started, it rolls along with the impetuousness of a mountain stream, while the broad pathos of the slow movements spins garlands around quietly ambling melodies. His chamber music and keyboard music is many-sided, drawing on a multitude of sources. From the point of view of stylistic and formal development, many of the keyboard pieces are notable for their clear indication of the changing of the older type of instrumental suite into the newer, sonatalike construction, while others, again, are held in an entirely free form. We are coming, then, to a field of composition which, although by no means the only one to win immortality for Handel, is nevertheless associated with his name as the symphony is with Beethoven: the oratorio.

In the section of this chapter devoted to the baroque opera, we have already described Handel's heroic struggle to acclimatize the Italian opera. After repeated failures opera ceased to be his main field of action, and he turned his cyclopean dramatic vehemence toward the oratorio—without, however, abandoning the music drama, merely "shaking the dust of the stage from his feet." This change was brought about by the peculiar circumstances of English intellectual and religious life, and in order to grasp the remarkable conversion we must look into events leading up to it.

No historian could draw a more accurate and appropriate picture of the history of opera in England than did Addison; the following lines, taken from the *Spectator,* represent the keen observations of an eminent man of letters and at the same time reflect English thought concerning opera.

There is no Question but our great Grand-children will be very curious to know the Reason why their Forefathers used to sit together like an audience of foreigners in their own Country, and to hear whole Plays acted before them in a Tongue which they did not understand. . . . There is nothing that has more startled our *English* Audience, than the *Italian Recitativo* at its first Entrance upon the Stage. People were wonderfully surprised to hear Generals singing the Word of Command, and Ladies delivering Messages in Musick. Our Countrymen could not forbear laughing when they heard a Lover chanting out a Billet-doux, and even the Superscription of a Letter set to a Tune . . .[44]

The modern reader cannot fail to be impressed by these words and by the implications which they contain, for they are still valid in our day. Opera is still an alien form to the Anglo-Saxon mind, and the fact that the facile Italo-Greek gods of the baroque had to retire before the bearded, helmeted, and long-winded Germanic gods does not change the situation. While the aristocracy continued to attend the opera, the healthy and unspoiled musical and literary taste of the "average" Englishman turned to the old traditions of the lyric stage in England, causing the emergence of the most important indigenous product of the English baroque lyric theater, the ballad opera.

The *Beggar's Opera* (1728), clever satire on the conventional Italian opera, will remain the most spirited of the species. John Gay (1685–1732), the satiric poet-playwright of society and of the folklore of London's streets, wrote the excellent text, and the music was arranged by a Prussian musician, John Christopher Pepusch (1667–1752), who, like Handel, found a second home in England. The *Beggar's Opera* achieved a sensational success and invited scores of imitations. We shall see how the German lyric theater was to profit by its influence upon Continental music; in England its success hastened the downfall of the Italian opera, already hard pressed by opposition from many quarters. The *Beggar's Opera* presents the sharpest possible contrast to the opera seria, as it consists of the simplest songs and dance tunes of popular origin, the music interspersed with animated spoken dialogues. Pepusch furnished the accompaniments to the tunes and composed a number of "overtures" to the individual sections. The public's joy and very real amusement in listening to an evening of familiar and much-loved music, to a witty and intelligible text in their own tongue, explains the popularity of the ballad operas and their adverse effect on the imported Italian species. Italian opera was defeated, and even the intrepid Handel was obliged to seek another field of action. Once more, at the zenith of his reputation, Arne attempted a bold experiment. Taking one of Metastasio's well-known libretti, *Artaserse,* he translated it into English and then set it to music in the Italian through-composed fashion, with recitatives and arias, omitting the spoken dialogues customary in English lyric plays. The work was successful, but the fundamentally lyric gifts of Arne were only too evident, for only the songs in set forms are remembered.

Handel, in the oratorio, gave England a national substitute for opera. This oratorio was not humble church music, but entertainment of the musico-dramatic kind, though on a higher moral plane, closer to and befitting English taste. Handel glorified the rise of the free people of England in his oratorios. The people of Israel became the prototype of the English nation, the chosen people of God reincarnated in Christendom, and magnificent Psalms of thanksgiving and marches of victory in imperial baroque splendor proclaimed the grandiose consciousness of England's world-conquering power. The Handelian oratorios were entirely the product of English social and spiritual environment, a circumstance instantly obvious if we place any of them beside the master's German compositions, especially his Passion music. For the Pietistic touch, totally missing in the heroic English style, is unmistakably present in the German works, and there is also the searching introspective spirit of the north German Lutheran, entirely different from the self-assuredness of the Anglican. Therefore the road to Handel's oratorio leads through English history.

The Oratorio

THE decline of France and the corresponding rise of England were not merely matters of local interest, restricted to one generation in two countries; they dominated the political history of the world from the "Glorious Revolution" to Waterloo. The intervening hundred and twenty-six years were filled with events of the greatest portent for the socio-cultural development of the world, although more than half of these years were war years.

The Elector of Hanover, great-grandson of James I, being in line of succession, the House of Brunswick ascended the throne of England. George I (reigned 1714–1727) was and remained a foreigner who could not speak the language of his realm and took no interest in the nation's affairs. His son, George II (reigned 1727–1760), while more conversant with English life and institutions, still left the destinies of the country to his ministers. The neutral attitude of these rulers permitted the Whigs, led by Robert Walpole, to establish the definite supremacy of Parliament. Parliament was now vested with powers as unconditional as those of the kings of absolutism; they could, however, be abrogated by elections. When Montesquieu held up to his country the model of the English constitutional monarchy, he saw only the abolition of the absolute monarchy, unaware of the corruption that accompanied the early phases of liberal parliamentarism—for the "modern" practices in democracies of buying votes, distributing "patronage" and pensions, intimidation, and sabotage all flourished on a grand scale under Walpole. It must be said, however, that although the great prime minister has been regarded as a symbol of political corruption, he was far less culpable of direct and personal offenses than most of his eminent contemporaries and successors.

As a financier Walpole achieved conspicuous success, owing, no doubt, to his clear realization of the relationship between political power, party stability, and business. He also realized that peace creates the best atmosphere for good business, and English commitments in the War of the Austrian Succession were against his wishes. But the physical make-up of a world power does not permit isolation and the neglect of international politics as practiced by Walpole. The ultimate aim of British political thought, monopoly of sea trade, could be achieved only by crushing competitors. The logical approach was to continue what William of Orange so clearly saw the necessity of and endeavored to effect, the reduction of French power, both on the Continent and in the colonies. The opportunity presented itself in the War of the Austrian Succession, and the English sovereign took the field and defeated the French in 1743 in the Battle of Dettingen, at the head of British and Hanoverian troops. This was the beginning of a revival of the power politics of William III, and under Walpole's successor the war was continued relentlessly, even though interrupted by long intervals. The Austrian war was followed by the Seven Years' War and the wars in the North American colonies; but the Peace of Paris in 1763 already marked the triumph of England over France, and she became the undisputed "mistress of the seas."

Handel's appreciation of the pathos and grandeur of a struggling people found a most natural echo in the British political philosophy of freedom. He was an eyewitness to the historical events which established British world power, and one of the strongest of all "affections," the politico-historic-religious, reacted on him with tremendous intensity. The musician was not artistically satisfied with the sufferings and joys of private life, nor was the mystical side of religion close to his active-positive nature. His personality rests on a combination of the heroic in music, the energy of an active religion, a rational consciousness of a theism built on the harmony of the universe, and the pomp, solemnity, grandeur, and pathos of the era of absolutism. He could not compose Masses, for he could not be mystical and humbly impersonal. His was a mighty God, whose immense power is the great motive passing through all Handel's works. This solid, strong, victorious attitude, bursting with power, confident of the security of the faithful and their advantageous relations to the Lord, grew from English Protestantism—from the unshakable conviction that this powerful God will stand behind the faithful who are fighting for him, and will help them to realize the Kingdom of God in the model of the British Empire. This does not mean faith in the ruling power of God, in the struggle under him for the victory of the holy in the world—the ideal of the early Reformation; this came from the militant, imperious God of the Old Testament. Handel took his models from the battles of Israel, but his great religious-dramatic works, announcing moral virtue and fortitude, glorified England—the England fired by religious self-confidence, the bold spirit of conquest, and a firm sense of collective solidarity—a country looking back on an ancient and widespread culture and political mission. And the public which spurned his operas turned avidly to his edifying, colorful, and massive oratorios, seeing in their monumental Biblical choruses its own triumphal progress and recognizing in them its own religion, which is not veiled in metaphysics but can be said to *occur,* in a visible, broad, and historic drama. This feeling of the power and triumph of the righteous calls for an entirely different religious tone from that of the mystic who composed *Christ Lay in Death's Dark Prison,* but must not be dismissed—as it often is—by deprecating remarks about its secular nature. Indeed, the *Hallelujah* chorus might be a coronation march, and the bulk of Handel's Biblical oratorios are neither liturgical nor ecclesiastic in tone. But these works are no longer oratorios in the old sense; they are no longer church compositions belonging in the nave of a cathedral—they are stageless folk dramas expressed in music. The chorus is virtually an acting personality, the hero and protagonist of the action. Everything evolves around it, for it embodies the masses of the people, the people which battles, suffers, triumphs, perishes, and is redeemed. And in these folk dramas the existence of the individual heroes receives meaning from the fate of the masses. The solidarity of English Protestantism with the nation's political and cultural aims gave the chorus a natural basis and the role of an ideal public in the drama: a fact still more remarkable if we realize that the spirit which actuated it was the same which was so deeply imbedded in Greek tragedy.

Handel's first oratorio, *Esther* (or *Hamman and Mordecai*), was in reality a masque, while *Semele, Alexander Balus,* and *Susanna* are veritable chorus operas; and *Hercules,* called a "musical drama" by Handel himself, should be considered the highest peak of late baroque music drama. *Deborah,*

Athalia, Saul, Israel in Egypt, Samson, Joseph, Belshazzar, Judas Maccabaeus, Joshua, Solomon, and *Jephtha* are gigantic choral tragedies. The division of the oratorios into three acts shows their operatic origin; on the other hand, the marked decline in solo numbers and in the use of the da capo aria, together with the absorption of the *testo* by the choir, shows a definite stylistic and formal separation. The stupendous polyphonic structure of the massive choirs alternating with powerful homophonous passages, double, triple, and quadruple fugues, the revived apsidal choirs of the old Venetians, occasional *a cappella* passages written with a sure hand, majestic motets, inexorable *ostinati,* grandiose vocal *ciacone,* chorale fantasias, simple choral declamations or choral recitatives, crisp dance songs, and burlesque passages in the madrigal style, all find their place, summarizing with a well-nigh incredible richness and pomp the achievements of the baroque. Italian, German, and French sources are discernible in this ocean of music, but the wondrous beauty of choral setting goes back directly to the great English traditions of choral music, disclosing an intimate knowledge of the anthem and the Service, with Purcell standing there as a revered godfather.

The main force of this new dramatic style was the chorus. Handel reached back to the old choral oratorio of Carissimi, enhancing its dramatic possibilities to the utmost. But it is the spirit of the folk drama which rules here and determines the choral writing, demanding great flexibility in the means of expression. Thus, although the great choruses in the oratorios abound with some of the most complicated constructions of choral polyphony, the style tends often toward a closed, homophonous choral writing based on heavy tone blocks presenting the chorus in a solid, indivisible, monumental phalanx. While the melodies of these choruses are simple, straightforward, and often popular in character, the arias and solo ensembles disclose an inexhaustible treasure of lyric expression. Their broad melodic arches characterize the individual man's sentiments and problems with the same pregnancy which made the Handelian chorus the interpreter of the fate of the masses. The veteran opera composer could not entirely give up arias, duets, and recitatives—they were in his blood—but the emphasis was now on the chorus, with the orchestra also receiving added attention.

The task that Klopstock set for himself in his epic, the *Messiah,* stands achieved in Handel's oratorio. Herder scolded the poet for having neglected narration for jubilation, but he praised the musician's creation as a matchless work of art. The *Messiah* has determined the conception and style of the oratorio to our day. This great influence has its drawbacks; it is distinctly one sided, because from the formal point of view the *Messiah* remains isolated in Handel's output. Nothing could more vividly illustrate Handel's inexhaustible resources and creative power than the fact that he composed three works in succession which deviated from his prevailing oratorio form.

While the majority of his oratorios safeguarded the dramatic form, in *L'Allegro, il Penseroso, ed il Moderato* he gave genre pictures; in *Israel in Egypt* he reached back to the older form of the *historia*, employing the narrator's recitative to connect the individual scenes; and in the *Messiah* he abandoned both aspects, giving us a work predominantly lyric in nature, a contemplation of the life of the Saviour, dramatic only through its intensity of feeling. Immediately after the *Messiah* the master returned to the dramatic oratorio, creating in *Samson* a world in which all moods and characters are expressed in music and all partake of a dramatic present. The contrast between Israelites and Philistines dominates the tragic action. The opposing historic peoples are represented, as usual, by the choruses; grotesque wildness and fanaticism in one, and a single, deep conviction in the other.

The *Messiah* has become the epitome of the modern oratorio. This is understandable, for it unites choruses, arias, and recitatives into a great hymn and conjures up a Christianity without denominational coloring. But we may misjudge the essence of the Handelian style if we confine our acquaintance to the one lyric oratorio among his thirty-two compositions in that form.

Bach and Handel

WITH his conception of Christianity and antiquity as expressed in his music dramas, both Biblical and classical, Handel ventured deep into the era of the Enlightenment and renewed humanism. Bach represents a thoroughly German art, centered around the Lutheran Church and the organist's bench. Handel's workshop was opened wide to all forces and influences—without, however, jeopardizing a particle of his individuality. Bach was a German with roots deeply imbedded in his native soil, Handel a citizen of the world who finally settled down in Britain. This has often been held against the German-born English musician, and the inevitable comparisons between the two giants of the waning baroque usually result in an unstinted glorification of Bach, to the detriment of Handel. Nothing can be more unjust than such a comparison, for the two men represent an ideal contrast and complement—a national and an international personality —which has so often graced German arts and letters. Luther and Hutten, Klopstock and Lessing, Haydn and Mozart, stood together and were opposed to each other in the same way, to the greater glory of art. But above all, it must not be forgotten that with all his international experiences Handel can be regarded only as an English composer, the perfect counterpart of his German colleague.

Bach, parsimonious and prudent, prefacing one cantata by *Soli deo Gloria* and opening another with "206 Thaler 10 Groschen"—the budget of his household—was not fired with worldly ambitions. Toward nature he exhibited a curious indifference. He seemed unaware of the existence of a public and was completely satisfied with his choir loft, the *collegium musicum,* and the entertainment room of a small princely residence. In his life there were no adventures, no hazardous undertakings. This does not mean, of course, that he was submerged in the transcendental regions of music, for he knew every trick of his trade; he was a connoisseur of instruments and an expert judge of the acoustic qualities of buildings, whose advice was sought and appreciated. Though his usually placid, unruffled, and serene nature could on rare occasions give way to stubborn opposition—once leading him to the solitude of the prison cell—the disciplined mind of a sincerely religious and kind man guarded him against excesses. When necessary he stood his ground or even resorted to mild flattery; but when the obstacles became formidable and called for continuous vigilance and political battles, he withdrew and sought relief in his creative work. This may have been temporarily obstructed, but it never sagged and never failed him, even in his blindness. When feeling his end approach, he dictated his profoundly moving chorale prelude "When in the Hour of Utmost Need," but even then he found his spiritual balance and directed that the composition be renamed "Before Thy Throne, My God, I Stand."

Physical and mental faculties were united in Handel to high perfection; both seemed impervious to wear and tear. He enjoyed life fully and at the same time showed an unlimited creative capacity. Adversity and debacle had no meaning for him; the harder he was hit the more determined was his resurgence. His undertakings were hazardous; he gambled with his forces and threw his reserves into the melee before they were needed. Because of the forum of vast proportions in which he appeared, and the large public to which he could address himself—two factors denied to Bach—his fame and influence were tremendous even in his lifetime. He became an institution in England while Bach was a provincial cantor quibbling with the petty school authorities in Leipzig. He was a man of the world who needed applause, who lived in the glare of the footlights, and to whom the outside world, nature, royalty, public, meant everything; and he collapsed when the affliction of blindness made all this illusory. The collapse was not physical. The robust and impetuous artist suffered heroically, but his creative power ebbed away. After finishing *Jephtha* in 1752 he composed very little, merely completing and elaborating earlier works.

Bach approached every new style, every new form, with caution, sampling and selecting, then carrying with him the newly acquired goods for a trial period. Handel gladly accepted everything, instantly assimilating it in a most personal style. Polyphony was for Bach a source of mystic struggle, in spite of his boundless versatility and apparent ease in the most complicated contrapuntal constructions. But it always drove him deeper and deeper, as if in quest of the final secrets of music. Barriers dissatisfied him and he broke them, trespassing boundaries, changing dimensions, and forcing the caesurae to conform to his own points of quiescence. Handel did not wrestle with his creations: his polyphony had an almost Latin clarity and balance; its chief aim was not mysticism but a powerful architectonic of the very elements. Bach's thematic material is heavy with foreboding; we feel that untold vistas will be opened before us as we follow him. Handel's thematic invention is of a plasticity without equal; often a few introductory measures to an aria tell a whole story in the most pregnant and categorical manner.

Bach and Handel appeared at a time when Western music was at the cross-roads. One became the embodiment and final monument of a conception and practice which looked back from the last peak of baroque polyphony to the distant past. The other turned in the opposite direction; he looked into new valleys, and showed new vistas to his colleagues and followers. And the long period of baroque art ended with these two.

*

* *

HISTORIANS and public alike are wont to view the many generations of baroque music as a mere preparation which had for its aim and justification the works of Bach and, to a lesser degree, Handel. This has led not only to the regrettable practice of labeling almost two centuries of music the work of "forerunners," but to the unpardonable error of attempting to find an unbroken lineal development leading up to Bach and Handel. It is difficult for all but specialized scholars to see the absurdity of such conceptions, because the great treasure of baroque music is virtually unexplored, and the writers of such monographs as circulate among the public and in schools have drawn their information from a few sample works published in anthologies. By using Bach's work as a measuring rod these writers have forced an artistic creed on the old masters which was not and cannot be theirs; what has been held up as "primitive" or "crude" in their works was often an artistic orientation fundamentally different from that of the cantor of the Thomasschule. It was this unfamiliarity with both history and music that prompted the author of a well-known manual on the history of English music to remark of Handel's instrumental music that "the great bulk [of it] is mere jog-trot solid conventionalism of the kind that could apparently be reeled off *ad infinitum*, and virtually destitute of any invention worth the name." [45] At the present stage of musicological research it is still impossible to give a concrete and logical history of the music of the baroque era, but our knowledge of the literature and our appreciation of its style are sufficiently advanced to show the absurdity of statements such as that quoted in the foregoing sentence.

The baroque stands vividly before us as an era remarkable for its stylistic unity, for its power to mold all the arts according to its own eloquent spirit. It was its astonishing faculty of assimilation, the fluency of its formal elements, which accounts for the dissemination and fertility of its creed. That the vast reaches of baroque music are still unexplored not only deprives us of great art, but is directly responsible for the lamentable state of present-day music. For the great choral and operatic composers of the seventeenth and eighteenth centuries discovered how to convey "affections" in music, converting drama and religion into sounds the intensity of which remains unparalleled; and in the concertos, fantasies, preludes, fugues, and innumerable other instrumental pieces, imagination revels in the beauty of the tonal world, dissolved in music to a degree which has never since been achieved. To enjoy music begotten by a completely free imagination, music that is bound by nothing, not even by the medium of expression, pure music, has seldom been granted to any generation.

Chapter 12

ROCOCO—STYLE GALANT— EMPFINDSAMKEIT

❯❯❯ ❮❮❮

The Aftermath of Louis XIV's Reign

WHEN Louis XIV died in 1715, after having reigned as absolute monarch for almost fifty-five years, a weighty chapter in the history of France and of the world came to its end. He had raised France to the position of the most unified and powerful nation of his time, not only politically but also culturally. For almost two generations the French king had been the center of Europe; fame, admiration, and recognition were granted him from all quarters. But the bow was overstrained, and the reaction against the unbearable pressure could no longer be withheld. Still, France remained the advanced school of diplomacy, of courtly splendor, and of the art of social life, for her intellectual pre-eminence remained an active force, unbroken throughout the eighteenth century.

The struggle, directed against the absolute monarchy, against the Church, and against the nobility, which was to dominate the whole of the eighteenth century, had already started in the lifetime of the great absolutist king. Pierre Bayle (1647–1706), a member of the colony of liberal émigrés living in Holland, was among the first to champion freedom of thought and of conscience. His *Dictionnaire Historique et Critique,* in sixteen volumes (1695–1697), with its encyclopedic plan, its iconoclasm, leaning to skepticism and satire, and its belligerent spirit, aimed especially against dogmas, provided a treasury for the succeeding generations, and the literary men of the Enlightenment borrowed from it generously. Then came Montesquieu (1689–1755) with his *Lettres Persanes* (1721), which, under the guise of colorful studies of Oriental life, satirized and criticized French institutions. The movement of the Enlightenment acquired content and aim when Montesquieu probed the relationship and causality existing between morals and laws, counseling people against despotic rule and harshness of punishment. This truly enlightened thinker opposed colonization, conquest, and slavery, and fore-saw the possibility of a well-regulated free constitutional monarchy based on parliamentarism.

Montesquieu's role was continued by Voltaire. More outspoken against the Church and more fluent with the pen, he became the first great popu-larizer of history. But Voltaire did not lead his period, he only expressed it. He was the century's greatest stylist, wittiest debater, and most tempera-mental thinker, but as a philosopher little more than a keen-minded bourgeois intoxicated by the first great results of modern research in the rising natural sciences. He questioned dogmas, fought the Church, and played a some-what cautious and involved game with the problem of the existence of God.

It was in the *Encyclopédie* (1751–1776), edited by Diderot and a host of eminent men of letters, that the spirit of the eighteenth century took visible form. Our modern encyclopedias are uninspiring reference manuals eschew-ing all religious and political partiality; their task is to give brief and objec-tive information in all departments of human knowledge. We need these encyclopedias because the vast developments of intellectual endeavor no longer permit anyone to possess encyclopedic information. But the old encyclopedia was meant to be read from cover to cover, for its authors were still endeavoring to impart universal knowledge; more than that, Diderot and his colleagues wanted to give the reader a philosophical conception and world outlook. Every century and every era seeks the truth, and this erratic search is man's beautiful tragedy. But the eighteenth century believed that it was able to find the absolute truth. In careful terms the *Encyclopédie* op-posed science to religion and, tremendously encouraged by the apparent infallibility of the newly born sciences, arrogated to itself the right to answer every question definitively. It took twenty-two years to complete the big volumes with their maps and supplements, and these years were spent in a continual struggle against state and Church. In this great undertaking Diderot marshaled the whole army of his country's "philosophers," but the quotation marks can be omitted from two names only, those of d'Holbach and of Condillac, for the others were lacking in a system of thought. They ignored everything which went beyond the limits traced by experience, and rejected everything which did not serve science and the *res publica*. They wrote about everything on earth with equal facility and with equal convic-tion that they were giving the reader the utmost in correct information. Still, the articles in the *Encyclopédie* can mislead the superficial reader only, and the fact remains that its pages and its authors were among the chief causes of 1789. They enlarged the frame of human thought forever, even though they were not able to fill the frame with real art and profound perspective.

The Drama of the Three Kings

THE three kings of France whose names stand as symbols for their periods might be the center of a magnificent tragi-comedy in three acts. The first is the French baroque; time: the *grand siècle,* the era of Louis XIV; place: Versailles, Paris, and all the aristocratic palaces which wrapped themselves in the haughty pomp of absolutism. Great and uplifting pathos emanates from this ceremonious act, with Lully officiating from the conductor's chair, and a world fundamentally frivolous is moved by its noble grandeur. The next act, still devoted to the regal pomp of French traditions, strikes a different tone. It shows us a stage devoid of earnestness, pathos, and solemnity, with the great traditions made the center of a *galant* world—but whatever we behold here is artistic to the core. This is the rococo, beginning with the Regency and lasting until the latter part of the reign of Louis XV, which presented the world with the most lighthearted, amoral, and beautiful entertainments, pastorals, hunts, and amorous idyls, filled with smiles, sighs, philosophy, conversation, and the delicate tinkling of the *clavecin.* The Church was undermined by the feud between Jesuits and Jansenists, the populace was starving, the enriched middle classes were restive for more political weight—and a few thousand people lived a carefree, luxurious, and prodigal life, even flirting with ideas which were to send them to the guillotine, for even those to whom it meant life did not believe in the moral foundations of the existing order. But this is a symptom which usually appears on the eve of a revolution. The rococo is, then, the art of this aristocratic world, sensuous, pleasure loving, connoisseur, artistic, and sinful to the bottom of its heart. Everything that in the previous era took refuge in the rather sober forms of classicism came now to the surface, abandoning all restraint as long as the etiquette of the *monde galant* was observed. In attempting a critical estimate of the rococo in France we must know that the sanctum of the house was the boudoir, its idol was woman, and its mood was caprice. This was the era of the Mme. de Pompadours and the Mme. du Barrys, the era of unscrupulous morals in which all proportions and measurements were drawn from these feminine models.

Then comes the third act in the play of royal styles, the era of Louis XVI, the finale before the curtain falls on the eighteenth century. Soon after the middle of the century a cooler and more serious spirit returned to the fore from the shadow of the rococo, the classical spirit. In reality never entirely extinct, the embers of classicism retained their glow while kings, finance ministers, cardinals, generals, and courtesans changed; and when in the seventeen sixties the horrible consequences of the boundless prodigality began to be noticeable, the philosophers and moralists fanned the coals to respectable flames. Intellectual currents usually transcend national boundaries, and the whole of Europe now became interested in classicism, in the cult of ruins and antiques. The more fantastic the imagination of the rococo decorator, the more people turned away from it to find pleasure in the contemplation of the calm of classic buildings, to view Giambattista Piranesi's fine engravings of the monuments of ancient Rome, or to read Winckelmann's writings on the art of antique Greece. The objects unearthed in Pompeii and Herculaneum created a veritable classic fever. The Louis XVI style was, however, not a servile imitation of classicism, for it still owed a great deal to the rococo. It was refined and gallant, fond of mild profiles and noble proportions. It is a long way, nevertheless, from the noisy and gaudy interiors of Mme. du Barry's residence to the quiet ensemble of Marie Antoinette's bedroom, with its rosy music on muted instruments. The peculiar charm of this classicism is in its divine childishness, which was not a copy of antiquity but a noble and refined courtly style, created in the belief that it represented the forms of middle-class elegance as opposed to the extravagant excesses of the old art of the aristocracy.

The third act of the drama brings, however, the denouement. The great contrasts that surrounded men forced them to seek a solution. Feudal aristocracy living in luxury while the people staggered under the burden of providing the means for its profligacy, aristocratic sophistication pitted against the simple moral strength of the peasants, Jesuitism warding off the attacks of anticlerical secret societies, the appearance of modern natural scientists combated by the practitioners of occultism—all these contradictions were so extreme that when this accumulated explosive material was touched off it resulted in carnage. The play comes to an end with the roar of cannon from the Bastille, while the *sans-culottes* invade the precious boudoirs. The fearful night of the French Revolution descends upon the scintillating, festive days of the drama of the three kings.

The Rise of the Rococo from the Disintegrating Baroque

THE eighteenth century was engrossed in dismantling the edifice that the baroque had built, and that great monument of style began to crumble before the final stones were carried to its summit. The essence of the new artistic creed, and the idea that animated everything from political philosophy to music, was an urge for liberty: liberation from the rules that had become stereotyped, from the stylistic conventions that had become rigid, from the artistic forms that had become immutable. All this represented a sometimes unconscious, sometimes violently powerful, insurrection against the motive power of the baroque. Born of the Counter Reformation, soaring to breath-

taking splendor with the help of eloquence, fire, sword, and the Cross, and
becoming the artistic expression of absolutism, baroque art and thought became anathema in the eyes of men thirsty for liberty. The cry arose, "Back to
nature," and it resounded with force in France, long under the heels of an
unenlightened absolutism. It was in France that the great battle for freedom
was to be fought, ending in the Revolution, but the first attempts at liberation were artificial, deceiving, and shallow.

The slogan advocating a return to nature was in everyone's mouth, and
everyone was seriously concerned in contributing to this end. The baroque
had merely distorted nature when it compelled trees and flowers to grow
in prearranged shapes and when it regulated the flow and fall of water;
the rococo went further, it created a nature-world of its own with lakes, little reed-covered huts, flocks of sheep, and stacks of hay. But those who lived
in the huts and moved about the meadows were extremely well-groomed
gentlemen wearing silk stockings, silver-buckled shoes, satin knee breeches,
and embroidered brocade coats. The womenfolk bore the refined expression
of marchionesses, wearing the broad-brimmed straw hats of Umbrian shepherdesses, but their arms and shoulders were naked and their crinolines must
have caught on every clump of grass. This whole adoration of nature was
in reality a new game of a decadent society. They played with the little lambs
and goats and were convinced that they had found the way back to nature
and that their pastoral plays represented the utmost liberty in expression.
"Affectation" used to be the word applied to this worship of nature, but the
reproach is misplaced, for affectation really disappeared when everything
was submerged in the illusory world of false sentiments. The illusory conception of nature and the world is nowhere more convincingly presented
than in the fine landscape paintings of the rococo, for with the exception of
Watteau—who was Flemish by birth—the French landscapes were usually
architectural paintings representing well-groomed parks and formal gardens
studded with marble figures, little pavilions, and sentimental, artificial ruins.
Hubert Robert, a well-known and distinguished landscape painter especially fond of such scenes, earned himself the epithet "Robert des Ruines."
This style did not need bold creative architects, powerful dramatists, and
robust musicians; it addressed itself to the decorator. The very name of the
rococo (from the French *rocaille,* and alluding to artificial rockwork and
pierced shellwork) indicates that this style centered around interior decoration, that it became the antithesis of the grandiose pictorial-architectural
character of the full baroque.

Architectonic inventiveness—so bountiful for three centuries—was diminishing; artistic imagination encompassing large architectural masses
with a sovereign command over space ceased to fire artists. Symmetrical
order and articulation were relieved by the free play and the fluctuating

balance of shapes and surfaces, with a tendency to veil the contours of constructive form. The art of representation, the grandiose and solemn execution of allegorical compositions, the heroic and pompous tone no longer appealed to this generation. This society was interested rather in gossiping, conversation, music, and flirting, and preferred the tête-à-tête to the large reception. They no longer built large palaces with imposing façades and elaborate residences with far-flung wings; it was the smaller *hôtel,* the pavilions, pagodas, and garden houses which were in vogue, where one might retire in comfort and elude the watchful eye of the public.

This conception represents a fundamental revision of artistic thought and aesthetic doctrine. The baroque sought to crush, to convert, to exalt, and to bring about redemption; the rococo wished to entertain. To the dramatic intensity, rhetoric, pathos, broad lines, and passionate accents of the baroque, this intimate and interior art—intimate and interior in all the arts—opposed wit, gracefulness, polish, and entertainment, with "variety" as its motto, for nothing was more resented by the rococo than tediousness. In every department of arts and letters taste turned to subjects requiring small, delicate, and graceful treatment. Biblical stories and religious topics in general were relegated to the background. The chief topic of the style galant was love; but love was no longer the great passion which rocks the foundations of man's very existence, nor did it have the strong animalistic-sensuous spirit of the plump women and greedy and impatient men seen on the canvases of the Dutch painters of the baroque. Love was merely a graceful play enacted by exceedingly well-dressed and *soigné* men and charming and elaborately gowned women.

There is, however, a curious dualism in this overdelicate and noncommittal art, for while the superficial ornamentation and rather false and hypocritical social game went hand in hand, the penchant for a true naturalism produced a portrait art of high artistic quality. The painters of *fêtes galantes,* of festivities in fields or groves where exquisite figures are dancing, picnicking, and making love in a poetic, unreal, and fanciful world, could also depict characters whose human qualities were not obscured by the powdered wig, paint, and beauty spots without which no person of standing could do. The greatest master of the early rococo was Jean Antoine Watteau (1684–1721). Settled in Paris, the Flemish master was conquered by the spirit of his environment and substituted for the characteristically robust and blunt the gracefully elegant. Neither François Le Moyne (1688–1737) nor Nicolas Lancret (1690–1743), both eminent painters working in the same manner, was able to touch Watteau's mastery; and even François Boucher (1703–1770), the most highly admired artist of Mme. de Pompadour's retinue, could not equal the poetic thoughtfulness and noble tone of Watteau, although he matched him in technique, inventiveness, and facility. Although

Watteau was unquestionably the greatest artist of the rococo, and the master from whom all others learned, it was not his world which dominated the era of Louis XV and Louis XVI. Among the first to portray the triteness of bourgeois existence, the simple and unretouched reality of the people, Watteau betrayed his Flemish ancestry, his bourgeois origins, and perhaps his bourgeois sympathies, so much out of keeping with the temper of the times in France. For there is a serious sympathy, a compassion, in his bourgeois genre pictures which does not show the social consciousness of the rococo.

It was Boucher who succeeded in bringing Olympus down to earth, into the circle of a frivolous demimonde. Boucher's lifework was the eulogy of woman, but his women were neither the obesely sensual women of the Dutch baroque nor the haughty, aristocratic beauties of the Renaissance; they were lithe goddesses and nymphs, their delicate bodies not yet fully developed, yet aware of the life that throbs in them and knowing something of its secrets. The whole collection of theatrical properties accumulated by the rococo—shepherdesses, goddesses, nymphs, amourettes, rosy clouds, silken garments, delicate boudoirs, and shimmering pools—is placed in the service of Boucher's subjects, the subjects of the rococo: the interrupted tryst, the bathing beauty, the discovered hidden lover, curious maidens, and *fêtes galantes*. The often oversweet tone of his pictures, the meticulous attention he paid to make-up in his portraits, his play with rosy half tones, his sophisticated eroticism, soon made Boucher's decoratively very effective pictures the target of criticism. The reaction against the rococo style, engrossed in the facile gracefulness of its farded and perfumed world, became more articulate with the periodic art shows. Criticism became a factor to be reckoned with, and the encyclopedists raised their voices against the aesthetic principles of Boucher, whose star began to pale.

Boucher's style continued to be cultivated by individual artists until after the Revolution, but the general mood turned toward the moralizing artists of the middle classes, to Jean Baptiste Chardin (1699–1779) and Jean Baptiste Greuze (1775–1805). But the art of Boucher, Lancret, and Fragonard was so thoroughly French that it has remained alive until our own day. For with all the laudable intentions behind the moral principles of Greuze, one cannot help still seeing in the bright eyes and moist lips of the artist's most virtuous women a slight lasciviousness; the sweet, piquant maidens may lower their eyes, but they are willing to dance the gavotte if only someone will ask them. Something of Boucher's spirit remained everywhere, never again to disappear from French painting. His use of diffused light and his treatment of color anticipated the impressionists, and the sweet-scented, nervous delicacy of Renoir is related to him by blood.

Music of the French Rococo

LULLY'S exceptional position in France, the absolute powers he wielded, not less than his universally admired compositions, established France as a great musical power, but when in the eighteenth century French writers still claimed supremacy for their music over that of the Italians (the Germans did not even count in their eyes) they failed to realize that their claims were voiced for something that no longer existed. The sturdy pomp and majesty of Lully's royal baroque, the massive architecture of his music dramas, were undermined by the aesthetics of the rising rococo. The formalism of the *grand siècle* was turned into *sensibilité,* which again established its own intricate code of etiquette, reflecting that artificial, stylized world we know under the name of *style galant.* The one thing that the sensibilité of the style galant could not endure was simplicity; it wanted variety and elaboration, and the ornaments forced an entry into the noble lines of the tragédie lyrique, steering it into the more facile waters of the rococo. The pastoral operas and opera ballets which followed turned the baroque opera into something that was neither heroic nor serene, for it acquainted the public with the same parlor nature they knew from the canvases of the landscape painters. The nobility, led by Louis XV, delighted to take part in the performances, and when they donned their pastoral costumes and played their none-too-difficult parts in the opera or ballet, they were firmly convinced that they were performing the most democratic of deeds.

When glancing over the scores of these operas one is immediately impressed by the impoverished texture of the music. Lully's wonderfully forged melodies were replaced by phrases gasping for breath between the shortest cadences, his careful part writing by sloppy chords, and his expressive basses by an unimportant lower part furnishing only the necessary foundation for the harmonies. The melodies were even more cut up in harpsichord music, where miniature motives were repeated so consistently that the small groups of repeated phrases became a stylistic characteristic of the style galant. Contrapuntal architecture disappeared and was succeeded by a homophonous-chordal accompaniment. The profuse ornamentation employed in the decorative arts seems a mild mannerism compared to its musical counterpart, for the little clavecin pieces, most characteristic of the period, were literally buried under grace notes and embellishments—so much so that often one cannot follow the continuity of the original melody.

What was not curtailed by the efforts of the style galant was dried out by the rationalistic tendencies of the age. Rationalism had already killed lyric poetry in the seventeenth century; the inexorable logic of events added to its victims the other literary forms that depended on verse. The eighteenth century had no significant lyric poetry until the very end of the century produced one true poet—Chénier—only to be mowed down by the Revolution. Its epic poetry was dry and empty, its tragedies in verse rhetorical and philosophical, and its comedies, with the exception of Beaumarchais's two masterpieces, filled with abstract character analyses. Music could not and did not escape this tendency. From every tract, every letter, and every preface we hear the old Boethian precept: *musicus est qui ratione perpensa*. And the greatest French musician of the period—perhaps the greatest in the whole history of French music—Rameau, declared in his very first work that his aim was the restoration of reason in music. The Frenchman remained faithful to the Cartesian traditions, to the critique of knowledge; thus it was the *discours sur la méthode* which mattered, and not the thing-in-itself. But this carried music and lyricism above the timber line, where the rarefied atmosphere required a constant administration of oxygen. The life-giving gas was supplied by literature and other extramusical sources, for, with the exception of a relatively small amount of chamber music, everything depended on suggestive titles, stories, or programs.

The period following Lully's death was decadent. The only composer who successfully approached the master's style in a few interesting works was his own pupil Pascal Colasse (1649–1709); he was well acquainted with Lully's method of composition, for he used to write out the figured basses in his teacher's continuo parts. Marc Antoine Charpentier (1634–1704), the eminent composer of church music, attempted to rival Lully, but his *Médée* proved to be a weak imitation. Colasse's *Thétis et Pélée,* his *Ballet des Saisons,* and the Italian Teofilo de Gatti's *Scylla* (the composer being another pupil of Lully) were the only successful works until the appearance of Destouches. André Cardinal Destouches (1662–1749), soldier turned composer, was a musician endowed with a fine melodic invention and with a sophisticated, although more instinctive than conscious, harmonic sense, occasionally manifest in the boldest use of dissonances. Throughout these new departures, however, the style and construction of the tragédie lyrique remained unchanged until Gluck. Lully's monumental achievement was held in great admiration, but none of his successors could muster a dramatic conception such as the Florentine's, and their works live only in fragments, the elegant dance pieces, overtures, and certain *airs* saving them from oblivion. But while the outward form remained, the content vanished, and the last vestiges of the tragedy disappeared when plot and action became mere pretexts for the ballet, the divertissement.

The ballet-opera became the most popular form of the lyric theater; it was practiced by every composer. Its prototype was created by André Campra (1660–1744) in *L'Europe Galante* (1697). Campra, the most significant opera composer between Lully and Rameau, broadened Lully's operatic scheme by elements derived from Italian opera. His orchestra is more active and more varied and his melodies show more vivacity, but the ornaments and coloraturas—so mercilessly exterminated by Lully to safeguard classical directness and simplicity—he smuggled back into opera. Other more or less successful opera composers were Marais, Mouret, Rebel, Francoeur, Desmarets, Montéclair, and Leclair, most of whom we shall meet in other fields of musical composition.

Owing to the peculiar situation created by Lully, many of the great musical dictator's contemporaries and successors, including perhaps the most interesting among them, will be found, until the performance of Rameau's *Hyppolite et Aricie* in 1733, outside the domain of the lyric stage. Church music and chamber music felt Lully's great influence, but with less force and without political pressure; they were able to assimilate some of that Italian music which fascinated them so much from the distance, and which was not unknown in France. We know from Sébastien de Brossard's correspondence that the choirmasters were well informed about music in Italy and that many manuscripts of Italian church music circulated in France. Unstinted homage was paid especially to Carissimi, whose popularity was so great that former historians were convinced that he had actually been in France. But with all this interest in Italian church music, Italianism remained only a superficial trait in French church music, the masters of which seem to have remained faithful to the traditions of their own sacred art. These traditions do not go back, however, to the great Franco-Flemish schools of the Renaissance but seem to have been founded by Nicolas Formé (1567–1638), whose motets, many for double choirs, presumably followed Venetian examples. Artus Auxcousteaux (c. 1590–1658), Thomas Gobert (d. 1672), and particularly Henri du Mont (or Dumont, 1610–1684), were the chief masters of this very plastic but more decorative than expressive style of church music. Du Mont's compositions were already attempting to dramatize French religious music, a process long since completed in Italy; but the realism and intensity of expression in the Italian cantata and oratorio were barely sketched here, and very little of Carissimi's dramatic power was even faintly indicated.

It was not until Lully's genius for dramatic effect and theatrical pomp was attracted to church music that this type of sacred art came into its own. His *Te Deum* is a magnificent fresco still echoing the tumult and frenzy of the battle, for the victorious outcome of which the thanksgiving hymn rises to heaven, while his *Miserere* is a prayer, moving and pitiful. It is noteworthy that the two important composers in this field, du Mont and Lully, were not native Frenchmen (they were Flemish and Italian, respectively), yet they engendered works which were typically French in character, a course of affairs not uncommon in French artistic history. Once established, the French orchestral motet found a number of good composers

devoted to its cause. Michel de Lalande (1657–1726) looms here as an imposing personality who may well be considered one of France's greatest musicians. With Campra, he is the representative master of the period between
Lully and Rameau. Considerably influenced by the omnipotent and omnipresent "superintendent of music" of Louis XIV, Lalande was nevertheless
able to maintain his artistic independence, presenting in his orchestral motets monuments of French music as it turned from the high baroque to the
rococo. The Italian influence, while not strong, was present in the dialogues
and the concerted arias; but the general decorative and festive tone, avoiding
both mystic meditations and dolorous confessions, makes this music typically French, opposed to both Italian and German church music.

If we turn to the aesthetic and theoretical discussions of French church
music we shall find that the rigid and sometimes meaningless specifications
which in modern times take the place of spontaneous religious inspiration
were present at the beginning of the eighteenth century. Brossard in his
Dictionnaire describes the *stilo ecclesiastico* as "full of majesty, grave and
serious, capable of inspiring devotion and carrying the soul to God," adding
that by virtue of these characteristics this style is "proper to the church."
Thus, henceforth it was not the music itself that might be religious but a
certain preconceived style which was to be proper for church usage—a transition from content to purpose. This music was most appropriate for accompanying the king's religious worship in Versailles: it was well written, sonorous, festive, and dignified, in keeping with the exalted position of the
ruler of a great and brilliant country; it never reminded the king that his
religion was more than a long-established tradition of the nation. Lalande
had many disciples and followers, and church music flourished throughout
the country; but the compositions are dispersed in the manuscript collections
of libraries, and the whole question represents one of those blank spots on
the map of musical and cultural history.

The French violin school, born in the first years of the eighteenth century,
originated from the spirit created by Corelli's sonatas. The French musicians received these works with enthusiasm, but they had already evolved
an instrumental style strong enough to receive the new style as an incentive
rather than as an overwhelming influence. In imitation of the Italian example French composers took to the writing of sonatas, but at first they
remained faithful to the spirit of the suite, their early sonatas being rather
loosely connected dance pieces with an occasional aria thrown in. The old
form of the suite, consisting of allemande-courante-sarabande-gigue (seemingly in four movements but, since the courante was usually a variant of the
allemande, really in three), was practically identical with the Italian suite,
the Scarlatti type of sinfonia, and the concerto. The unifying feature of all
these forms was the ground design of two animated movements separated
by a quiet and restful movement of convincing aesthetic effect.

The French composers of the early rococo, not caring for larger forms and impatient to arrive at what they considered diverting, interpolated little pieces that corresponded to their taste. Thus the French suite was soon filled with minuets, gavottes, bourrées, and opera and ballet pieces in great numbers, and a tendency toward program music became manifest. Unlike the purely French suite, the later sonata under Italian influence shows a much more convincing architecture, and since many of the eminent violinists studied with celebrated Italian masters something of the classic line of Italian string music emanates from the French sonata. Jean Ferry Rebel (1661–1747), Jean Baptiste Senaillé (1687–1730), and Jacques Aubert (1678–1753) were the chief masters of this school, which culminated in Jean Marie Leclair (1697–1764), whose personality dominated the instrumental ensemble music of eighteenth-century France. All subsequent composers, including Jean Joseph de Mondonville (1711–1772), François Francoeur (1698–1787), Gabriel Guillemain (1705–1753), and even Pierre Gaviniès (1728–1800), were greatly indebted to him. But the toying with pastoral effects, so characteristic in both genre painting and genre composition, invaded the larger forms, and the title of many a chamber music work indicates that the music was merely meant to give pleasant and witty entertainment. Guillemain's collection, dated 1743, illustrates this convincingly: *Six sonates en quatuors ou Conversations Galantes et Amusantes entre une Flûte Traversière, un Violon, une Basse de Viole et la Basse Continue.*

The brilliant if not very profound violin school dethroned the old stringed instruments. Even the bass viol, the gamba, universally loved in France, was forced to retire before the violoncello. But this was not accomplished before the appearance of a last great master devoted to its style, Marais. Marin Marais (1656–1728), a pupil of Lully, retained in the five books of his beautiful, somber, and opulent compositions the pure traditions of the baroque.[1]

Of all the varieties of rococo music the most typically French and most representative of the spirit of the times was keyboard music. The earlier clavecinists of the seventeenth century were followed in the eighteenth by a school which commanded a sovereign mastery of the style. Louis Marchand (1669–1732), Jean François Dandrieu (1684–1740), Louis Nicolas Clérambault (1676–1749), François d'Agincourt (1714–1758), and Louis Claude Daquin (1694–1772) were some of the celebrated masters, all brilliant and consummate artists of their instrument. But if one looks for the great preludes and fugues, the bold toccatas, the virtuoso fantasies, and the finely matched suites and partitas of the great baroque keyboard art flourishing at the same time in other countries, he will be disappointed, for what he will find are witty and elegant little pieces, filled with indescribable grace and fine points, piquant rhythms and harmonies, drenched with a shower of little ornaments which linger in the air like confetti. This music is not addressed to the public; it is out of place in the large concert hall, for it was composed for the refined connoisseurs of the aristocratic salons. No less intrigued by the watchword of the era than the painters, the clavecinists effected their own return to nature by composing hundreds of little genre pieces. It testifies to the remarkable power of the cultural and artistic trend that the results were surprisingly analogous, for all the little windmills, shepherds, and shepherdesses were of the same porcelain kind that we discovered in Boucher's pictures.

With all its playful tinkling, this art of delectable musical bonbons beguiled the foreigners beyond imagination. They looked down upon the little harpsichord pieces, but they saw in them something that they would have liked to possess, a certain lightness, suppleness, and agility.

We have omitted until now the greatest of French clavecinists, the cynosure of rococo art, François Couperin, called the Great (1668-1733), for this composer who summarized the artistic tenets of his nation was perhaps the most characteristic genius of the Regency. Being an early eighteenth-century master, Couperin was still bound by many threads to the baroque, and although his art—like all French clavecin music—grew from the delicate atmosphere of lute music, he was not yet addicted to the soft sentimentality of the later style galant; indeed, his little rondeaux are often held in plastic and determined forms which open a large perspective despite their small proportions.

Only insufficient scientific and historic schooling can account for the drawing of so many parallels between Watteau and Mozart, two artists separated not only by generations in time but by great aesthetic and temperamental differences. Watteau's rightful counterpart was Couperin, whose musical genre pieces depicted in sound the same *fêtes galantes,* equally delicate, equally poetic, and equally decorative. For this issue of a respectable dynasty of decent musical craftsmen was a poet, one of the finest poets of the keyboard. And if we remember how the artists of impressionism were related to Watteau and Boucher, we shall understand why Debussy and Ravel could surround the name of Couperin with a veritable cult. Couperin's numerous clavecin pieces, trio sonatas, and "royal concerts" were perfect expressions of the same French musical aesthetics professed by Claude Debussy, proudly calling himself *musicien français;* indeed, few musicians can claim this title with more right than the old clavecinist and his distant kin, the master of the modern piano. Their aesthetic conceptions, French musical aesthetics, advocate music which would charm, entertain, and perhaps move, but without tears and violent passions.

This music, like the paintings of the period, avoided the passionate lyricism of the Italians; its outbursts—if they may be so called—are always controlled, its emotions measured, its sonorities filtered. And since its inspiration is chiefly intellectual—Debussy still relies mostly on poetry—it should not surprise us that every little piece is inscribed with some title. The titles of the many miniature tableaux that Couperin composed would fill a whole encyclopedia, but *la Prude, la Voluptueuse, la Rafraîchissante* are no more representative of the ideas they express in music than are *la Séduisante, le Turbulent, l'Insinuante,* or, for that matter, *les Barricades Mystérieuses.* While his colleagues played with the keyboard, perfectly satisfied with the charming sounds they extracted from it, Couperin sensed that the eternal dance pieces of the suite would finally end in unendurable repetition. He knew that French musical conception does not take readily to thematic-motivic development, the one principle of musical construction which makes possible larger works, even if they are mere dance suites, so he followed the painters and concentrated his great talents on small character pieces drawn with the finest crayon of Watteau and Boucher. That the characters as seen through music were vastly different from what the titles implied, or rather that usually there is little correspondence between the announced subject and its musical realization, does not diminish the merits of this fine and poetic art. The relationship of these pieces to nature and its objects was almost exactly the same as that of Watteau's formal gardens, or Robert's ruins, for they lived merely in the artist's imagination.

The great German masters watched this art with amazement. Bach and Handel studied and copied Couperin assiduously, and Telemann and his colleagues, including Carl Philipp Emanuel Bach, were in their most successful vein when composing in a medium inspired by Couperin's spirit. There is a Gallic air about this composer, distilled and purified of all foreign substance. This is what makes him so attractive and incomparable: he is the embodiment of French music, and while he was not the greatest French composer, he was the one who knew precisely the limits of his art and never strayed beyond them.[2]

Rameau

WE now arrive at the great enigma of French music, the composer whose inspiration was as typically French as Bach's was German and Scarlatti's Italian, who was the one and only French musician to excel in all fields cherished by French thought—a profound and keen thinker, a great composer, and a superb performer—a man whose theoretical writings became the foundation of modern musical theory, whose works are filled with a wealth of invention seemingly inexhaustible, a born dramatist of the first water, and an artist in whose works nothing is left to the hazards of inspiration: Jean Philippe Rameau (1683–1764). This greatest and most French of composers remains a man frequently mentioned as a great thinker, occasionally played as a spirited harpsichord composer, and totally ignored as one of the greatest creative artists of the eighteenth century.

His instincts drove him toward true drama—his magnificent choruses were, indeed, directly responsible for Gluck's similar compositions—yet he was unable to sustain the dramatic flow throughout a whole act, for the rationalistic tendency of the Enlightenment and the allegorical-mythological playfulness of the style galant forced him to descriptive excursions and to divertissement. A disciple of Descartes, he placed so much confidence in the musician's ability to rise above his text that he declared any newspaper could be set to music. His resultant willingness to compose music to the most miserable libretto proved to be fatal for his operas. His most original theoretical findings, misinterpreted and misunderstood by the arbiters of knowledge, the encyclopedists, embroiled him in endless quarrels, and thus the impossible happened: the very people whose aim was to bring the whole world under intellectual control declared that he might be a respectable scholar but could not be a great musician, for erudition kills inventiveness. Rameau wanted to address himself to humanity and was repulsed. After 1745 he ceased to write for the large public, henceforth furnishing divertissements for the court. His gracefulness increased, his settings became even more delicate than before, but he no longer found the warm accents of passion or the generosity of heroism. The menuets, gavottes, and *airs de chant* that he wrote in profusion were prettier than ever, but they were mere divertissements. "From day to day I acquire more taste," he exclaimed to Chabanon, "but I no longer have genius." For once the keen-minded artist-philosopher did not realize that while he created for himself and for humanity he had genius, for he addressed himself to human hearts; as a purveyor of music to a frivolous and dissolute court, all that remained for him was taste, wit, and ability.

With the performance of his *Hyppolite et Aricie* (1733) the fifty-year-old Rameau assumed the leadership missing since Lully's death, a leadership measured not by the success of his opera but by the violent discussion it created. The public was divided into two camps, *Lullistes* and *Ramistes*. The memory of Lully remained so powerful half a century after his death that even a genius of Rameau's rank had to incline himself before it. Deeply affected by the criticism of the Lullistes, who denounced him as an adversary of their great idol, Rameau wrote a long preface to his *Indes Galantes* (1735) in which he expressed his admiration—real, and not pretended—for Lully, but this gesture was of no avail. The composer was so utterly disappointed that he was about to give up the fight when no less distinguished a man than Voltaire spoke in his defense: "I can understand that the profusion of his double crotchets may revolt the Lullistes; but in the long run, it would be desirable that in the measure in which the nation's taste improves Rameau's style [*goût*] should dominate it."[3] Rameau's next opera, *Dardanus,* performed in 1739, caused a terrific controversy; the critics declared it to be so charged with difficulties and filled with the clamor of the orchestra that "for three hours the musicians have not even the time to sneeze." A few more attempts, and Rameau gave up the composition of serious music dramas. He could not cope with the restrictions which the rococo imposed upon the lyric stage and was compelled to accept the gospel of the style galant: divertissement.

Rameau conserved the outline and form of Lully's heroic operas, yet he seldom rose to the dramatic élan and continuity of the Florentine. His very logical and minute method of work, full of intricate detail, prevented him from abandoning himself to the fluctuating drama. To his contemporaries he remained a pedantic craftsman. We should not, however, approach the art of this Frenchman from the angle of conventional opera, for he was a symphonic dramatist, a phenomenon unknown in his period and in the whole of French music. We should consider his works as compositions in which orchestra, dance, and song melt into a multiple phenomenon of sonority. This complexity of sound was the material of his drama, and at the same time its background, its accompaniment, and its governing force. It was this severe but gigantic conception that impressed Gluck, whose dramatic reform was the organic continuation of Rameau's work. There have been, indeed, very few masters of the theater orchestra who could depict and characterize with sound-colors as could Rameau. Lully's orchestra never knew that wealth of harmony, that pomp of color, that sensitive theatrical brilliance which abound in Rameau's operas. Rameau's nature pictures are as impressive as his love scenes and tableaux, but their dramatic catharsis can change into delicate lyricism in his genre scenes. With magnificent dramatic instinct he prepares the entry of his dramatic figures by an orchestral portrait, but this is not the rather naïve dramaturgy of the leitmotif, clinging to every dramatic figure like its shadow; the portrait is painted once only, and never returns again.

In order to be the emancipator of the French music drama this great musician would have needed a more poetic nature, to have been more preoccupied with his texts. Lully realized the paramount importance of the drama and was most careful in selecting and arranging his libretti; Rameau was ready to set to music the most atrocious amateur rhymes. Misled by the traditions and requirements of the rococo opera, Rameau gave the episodes, dances, processions, and theatrical machinery a preponderance in his dramatic works, and the plot is often merely a pretext for divertissements. Everything is exquisite in form and workmanship; there is not one department in which he does not surpass all his contemporaries; but the music drama suffered from all this irreparably.

In Rameau's art there is something firm, deliberate, crystallized, and dominated by logic. A contemporary of the encyclopedists, he was dominated by philosophical conceptions and he imposed them on his observations and on his style. But he had the same limitations as his fellow philosophers, and this is evident in a thesis which seems to be the cardinal maxim of his reasoning. He realized and proved that the physical material of music is identical with its artistic material; therefore the nature of this artistic material is identical with the nature of the physical material of the sonorous world. In the final analysis this would mean that the *corpus juris* of musical aesthetics is acoustics. This doctrine had been sensed and advocated before Rameau, but it took the unique combination of a great thinker and a great creative musician to realize that the more subjective the art of music the more it has to lean on the raw facts of acoustics. Thus, quite contrary to the naïve claims of certain musical scholars, it is not the physicist and theoretician who makes it possible for the composer to expand his powers—it was not a Werckmeister who made a Bach possible—but the demand of the ears and imagination of the composer, whose naturalistic gropings call for scientific clarification and codification. It happened only once in the history of music that both these factors were fruitfully united in the same person; in other instances such union produced mere fantastic dreams and ephemeral music (Scriabin). But the composer and the scholar were not always in accord, and when during the course of his exposition Rameau the philosopher reached a point where Rameau the composer should have claimed the leadership, the philosopher would not admit that in following the lead of acoustics music can never go beyond intentions, even though such intentions can go a long way. For there is a vast difference between acoustics and the sonorous symbols of the mental process induced by acoustics. The laws of acoustics are different from the laws of the stylistic musical effects and consequences produced by acoustics, it being an aesthetic impossibility for the acoustic values to reach musical values.

Rameau's final philosophical conclusions may have been erroneous, but his numerous treatises represent the truly ingenious foundations of modern musical science.[4] He was the first to recognize the inversion of chords which were formerly considered as constellations of sounds measured from the bass. By establishing the doctrine of "fundamental chords" he gave the first impetus toward the modern doctrine of functional harmony, not fully realized until the late nineteenth century. This epoch-making doctrine established the fact that all possible harmonies can be reduced to a limited number of fundamental forms (*accords fondamentaux*) called "tonic," "dominant," and "subdominant," the individual chords being functional representatives of the primary or fundamental forms. This theory ended the former equality of all chords and created a unity of harmonic conception which was both simple and profound. Until his time musicians did not, properly speaking, think in chords—they measured intervals—and to most of them Rameau's conception was sheerly unintelligible. Needless to say, the functional theory was not an invention: musicians of genius use correct harmonies without knowing their scientific foundations; but this indefatigable student of Descartes, Zarlino, Mersenne, Kircher, and other musical scholars was the first to formulate it and to arrange it into a logical system. The modern science of harmony engendered by Rameau exerted incalculable influence, for it changed the whole conception of music and, with it, artistic imagination. In his endeavors to demonstrate the truth of his principles, Rameau encountered serious difficulties. While many of his theories remain the unquestioned achievements of a man of genius, none of his successors have been able to remove the difficulties.[5]

The musician and the theorist being so closely united in Rameau, it is only natural that his musical compositions exhibit the same mastery of logical thinking that we find in the concise sentences of his *Démonstration du Principe de l'Harmonie*. This association of intellect with sensibility, clarity with poise, betrays the classic French composer; it incarnates the criterion of the French spirit—the marriage of reason and feeling. This haggard old man, who was the very image of Voltaire, was not merely the stubborn misanthrope his contemporaries saw in him. Arrived at a ripe age, his great intelligence recognized the real state of affairs, but he too held himself to be a *musicien français,* accepting all that the title implies: "If I were twenty years younger I would go to Italy and take Pergolesi for my model, abandon something of my harmony, and devote myself to attaining the truth of declamation which should be the sole guide of musicians. But after sixty one cannot change; experience points plainly enough to the best course [referring to the overwhelming success of Pergolesi's opera in Paris], but the mind refuses to obey." And thus the greatest musical talent of France remained an enigma which the world will perhaps never fully comprehend.

Rousseau—The Buffoon War—The Opéra Comique

THE development of French music in the second half of the eighteenth century was more closely connected with cultural evolution, with literary and philosophical ideas, than ever before. Previous to this period music and poetry were often in hostile camps, the mistrust of the men of letters being equaled by the jealousy of the musicians. This situation of reciprocal antipathy explains many a failure. Only the court musicians, living in an atmosphere saturated with polished art, had the privilege of collaborating with real poets. But the composers of the rococo did not have Lully's fortune of becoming associated with Racine, Molière, or Quinault; they had to waste their inspiration on texts composed by flighty abbés, pedantic college professors, or grammarians turned poets. Most of these musicians, however—not excepting the greatest of them, Rameau—were not at all concerned with the quality of their libretti. The pseudo-classical tragedy became a mold, mean-ingless and stilted, and composers made use of anyone who could produce a faint variation in the eternal adventures of the heroes of classical mythology. On the other hand, we know of the very limited admiration that a Saint-Evremond, Boileau, La Bruyère, or La Fontaine professed for music. All this changed in the second half of the eighteenth century, and in this domain, as in many others, it was Jean-Jacques Rousseau (1712–1778) who opened the door to new ideas. This unique man, who discovered nature, who started romanticism, who prepared the Revolution—this extravagant man had, fi-nally, the extraordinary audacity to be a musician. Never more than a half-trained dilettante, he arrogated to himself a position in the musical world that was out of all proportion to his talents. Impatient with the representa-tives of French music, he was on especially bad terms with Rameau, who did not make a secret of his low regard for Rousseau's musical abilities.

A memorable occasion, the appearance of a troupe of Italian opera singers in Paris in August, 1752, permitted Rousseau to enlarge his personal antip-athy into a manifestation of universal importance. The Italian company per-formed Pergolesi's *Serva Padrona* and scored a resounding success. Everyone was tired of the opera ballet and of the mythological fables, with their tedi-ous love affairs promoted or thwarted by a god or a sorcerer; people were longing for something that was more in keeping with life as they saw it. The performance of the little Italian opera buffa created an unprecedented turmoil, musicians and public entering into endless polemics directed by the leading literary men of the times, Diderot, d'Alembert, Grimm, and Rous-seau. This controversy, known as "the buffoon war," marks an important phase in the history of music. Louis XV declared himself for Lully and Rameau, the latter now being acknowledged by his former enemies, the Lullistes, as an artist of their denomination; the queen favored the Italian buffoons. As one would expect, Rousseau became one of the champions of the "queen's corner." No one could match his diligence and zeal in detract-ing from the merits and destroying the reputation of French music. Every-thing served to speed him on his course: his insufficiency in the technical aspects of music, his complacency as a self-taught musician, his acute per-sonal antagonism toward Rameau, and also his sincere desire for reform. This explains the tone of his famous *Lettre sur la Musique Française,* by which, according to its author, the "king's corner" was annihilated. The publication of this pamphlet (November, 1753) represents a decisive point both in the history of the opera and in Rousseau's musical life; it is his capital manifesto concerning the sense, means of realization, and the future of the art of music. His other musical writings, however numerous and bulky, have only secondary importance. Shortly before the issuance of the famous letter, at the height of the buffoon war, Rousseau presented an example of his own skill at composition, the *Devin du Village*. He now had both a practical demonstration of his views before the eyes of the public and a biting literary dissertation to support it. The triumph of this little opera was considerable; many composers took it as a model, and even Mozart tried his hand at it in his *Bastien and Bastienne*.

The phenomenal success of Pergolesi's little masterpiece and of Rousseau's play with its meager music, together with the acrimonious denunciation of French music, strikes the observer as one of the most incredible changes in taste. True enough, the ballet-opera was no longer satisfying, and French music had degenerated into a courtly art of decorative playfulness, but it still had imposing assets. In spite of the calendar, which testified that the seventeenth century had passed away long ago, much of the spirit of that glorious era still animated music. Lully's works were still played, Couperin was known all over the country, and there was Rameau, feared and acknowledged, although perhaps not liked. What precepts could Rousseau line up in order to dismiss music which was flesh of the flesh, blood of the blood, of the Gallic national heritage? He said: "Il faut que la musique se rapproche de la nature." This was nothing but the well-known formula of "back to nature," but it was hailed as a revelation and applauded without reservation. When we dismiss the theories and examine Rousseau's music itself we must admit that there is nothing in it to justify an iota of his manifesto; all we owe him is a new scene, for the plot of the *Devin du Village* is situated in a rural milieu. *This* was the innovation. Rustic and pastoral scenes, sheepfolds, peasantry, were now to replace the mythological and heroic scenes of the tragédie lyrique and the ballet-opera. Needless to say, the nature Rousseau pretended to reconcile with music is the same idealized and arbitrary nature which we have found in every department of French artistic and literary thought.

The *Lettre sur la Musique Française* and the *Devin du Village*, together with the repercussions caused by the Italian opera buffa, created, then, what appeared to be an entirely new form of the lyric stage, the French comic opera, with its characteristic traits of good comedy, facility, frivolity, and wit. Yet the *opéra comique* was not a newcomer in French music. Its temporary eclipse was due only to the paradoxical demands of the age of reason, which wanted "sensibilité" in the name of reason. This explains the curious fact that when the *Serva Padrona* was first performed, in 1746, no one paid any attention to it, for the "new" gospel of "back to nature" had not yet been officially proclaimed in music. The causes underlying a natural development toward the type of lyric stage which was eventually named "opéra comique" are deep-rooted and convincing and exhibit the same innate opposition to through-composed opera which we found in England—another proof that opera is an essentially Italian form of music drama, and does not thrive easily in foreign soil. The opéra comique was the form of the musical theater which suited national taste to perfection.

In the preface to Lesage and d'Ornéval's *Théâtre de la Foire ou de l'Opéra Comique* (1721), we find the following definition of the opéra comique: "These works are characterized by the *vaudeville,* a sort of poetry peculiar to the French, esteemed by the foreigners, and loved by everyone, being the most proper means to demonstrate the sallies of wit, to hold up the ridiculous, and to correct morals." Thus the vaudevilles carry us back again to the age-old songs which earned France the title *nation chansonnière,* for the vaudevilles are chansons, and anything connected with them, including the opéra comique, was always considered a national form of art.

The opéra comique came into being through the constant pressure exerted on the "illegitimate stage" by the two privileged royal institutions. The Comédie Française prevented the performance of spoken plays and the Académie Royale de Musique insisted on its monopoly to present all works sung from beginning to end. Thus the *théâtre de la foire* was compelled to find a kind of theatrical entertainment which did not infringe on either of these monopolies. There were, however, several other sources which contributed toward the development of the opéra comique. We have already expressed the opinion that Molière should be considered one of the distant founders of the opéra comique, for his comédie-ballets, together with the somewhat similar plays performed in the *Théâtre Italien,* contributed materially toward the formation of the national genre. In Quinault's operas buffoon scenes were frequent, affording a striking contrast to the heroic-tragic character of the tragédie lyrique and furnishing a comic element quite different from the Italian type. This comic element was really a sort of caricature, a distortion of reality, whereas the comic element in the plays performed at the théâtre de la foire showed reality as it was, with all its incongruities. But then this primitive and vulgar spectacle was real theater. In his preface to *Tartuffe* Molière repeated the ancient maxim of the comedy: *castigat ridendo mores,* a maxim which became the motto of the opéra comique. And when the great connoisseur of the human soul added to the proverb that "it is easy to suffer reproof, but difficult to stand raillery," he defined the aims of that lowly comedy which, for the time being, amused the plebeian public of the fairs.

In 1714 the Academy, itself hard pressed, consented to lift some of its restrictions on music, permitting—not without compensation—the comedians of the fair to sing some songs in their plays. It did not take long before many new songs appeared, and some of the best composers—Campra, Mouret, and even the young Rameau—joined the contributors. Unfortunately, the scores have disappeared and all that remains of these early comic operas are some songs and *couplets* which, however, indicate unmistakably the light, sarcastic, parodizing spirit of these plays. With the appearance in 1732 of the clever playwright Charles-Simon Favart (1710–1792) a new period in the development of the opéra comique begins, for the largely improvised character of the "illegitimate stage" was now invested with all the attributes of good comedy, which, in turn, induced composers to add duos, trios, and other ensembles to their chansons, couplets, and vaudevilles. Favart's translation of *La Serva Padrona* brought the théâtre de la foire into closer contact with the Italian opera buffa, with the result that almost all the vaudeville tunes were abandoned and original music was composed to the whole texts. Thus when we reach the *second* performance of *La Serva Padrona*, Rousseau's *Devin,* and his manifesto, we are really dealing with a type of theater which looks back upon a long and honorable past even though obscured by the tragédie lyrique; and as soon as the public's attention was again directed to this eminently French form of musical entertainment, the opéra comique embarked upon a swift career. The delightful librettos even penetrated foreign countries, and no less a composer than Gluck set several of them to music while still in Vienna.

Until 1762 the théâtre de la foire and the Italian theater were opposed, but a merger of the two institutions resulted in the absorption of the Italians, and in 1790 the Salle Favart adopted the name "Opéra Comique." If the public still had some misgivings about the possibility of original French "buffoon opera," a clever maneuver dispersed all objections. On July 30, 1753, a purported French adaptation of an Italian intermezzo or opera buffa was produced under the title of *Les Troqueurs*. After it had obtained an indisputable success it became known, however, that both libretto and music were the original works of two Frenchmen, Vadé and Dauvergne. Then the usual *deus ex machina* of French musical history presented itself; a foreigner, the Neapolitan Egidio Romoaldo Duni (1709–1775), appeared in Paris to create with his *Fille Mal Gardée* the modern French comic opera. Having written a whole series of works for the theaters of Rome, Milan, Genoa, and Florence, this amiable musician made the acquaintance of the French musical stage while at the court of Parma. With remarkable ease, Duni appropriated the spirit of French comic opera and produced a number of works teeming with life, melody, and a declamation the excellence of which earned him unstinted praise. The French musicians followed suit and soon produced composers of imposing stature.

François André Philidor (1726–1795) appeared on the scene in 1759 and asserted himself as one of the most original and significant masters of eighteenth-century French comic opera. His stage was more realistic, more lively than Duni's, and he leaned more toward parody and had a better command of the orchestra than Monsigny. This was no doubt owing to his familiarity with the Italian opera buffa. Philidor was a man of excellent taste and of wide interests and was recognized as the most celebrated chess player of his time. He traveled around Europe never missing an opportunity to study the music of the countries he visited. Such works of his as *Le Maréchal-Ferrant, Sancho Pança,* and *Tom Jones* belong to the best of the opéra comique. Pierre Alexandre Monsigny (1729-1817) made his debut the same year as Philidor and was equally well received. These two rivals, who carried French opera to a high point of perfection, presented diametrically opposed personalities. Philidor, the professional artist, worked with precision and confidence; Monsigny, somewhat amateurish but highly gifted, original, and inventive, was alarmed at his own mounting success. Indeed, this composer of *Le Déserteur,* one of the outstanding works of the French lyric stage, was so overawed with the extraordinary success of his opera *L'Enfant Trouvé* (1777) that he simply stopped composing for fear of not being able to equal his latest work. The last great master of the classic opéra comique, one who in his later years trod on romantic grounds, was the Belgian-born André Ernest Modeste Grétry (1742-1813). Having studied Italian opera with its masters, he could have become another Hasse, for he was completely Italianized, but upon his return he heard the comic operas of Philidor and Monsigny and rallied immediately to the cause of French music. Neither so original as Philidor nor so fresh as Monsigny, he was, nevertheless, one of the most accomplished masters of the operatic stage. He succeeded in transmitting the lifelike vivacity and characterizing ability of the Italian opera buffa to the opéra comique, and when his admirers called him the French Pergolesi, or the musical Molière, they did not exaggerate his importance. *Richard Coeur de Lion* and *Raoul Barbe-Bleue* are works in which the ideal Gallic mixture of sensibilité and the comical was attained.

Grétry's aesthetic views mirror the doctrines of the era of the encyclopedia. He proclaimed the superiority of dramatic music over any other sort—a doctrine accepted in France until the second half of the nineteenth century— and advocated the imitation of nature. In his writings, important in the history of the times, he revealed himself a true disciple of Rousseau and Batteux. By abandoning the recitative, he judiciously recognized what Addison had earlier expressed, namely, that the recitative is an Italian form of dramatic music, and chose to retain the essential feature of French comedy: pointed conversation. This Belgian musician was so obsessed by the ideas of the encyclopedists that he surpassed the most rabid of them in his writings on music. The strongest of his preoccupations were the search for truth of expression and the coupling of expression with words. Even Rousseau would have been proud to arrive at conclusions such as these: "Vocal music will never be good unless it copies the true accents of the words; without this quality it is but a pure symphony." Not content to stop here Grétry carried his aesthetic ideas *ad absurdum,* declaring that "it would be advisable to add words to the symphonies of Haydn, these works being a vast dictionary of expression from which the dramatic composer should draw.[6]

But Grétry the composer was not affected by his rather far-fetched theories, and his comic operas, in which the singsong of the erstwhile comic opera changed into a finely wrought art form, will remain proud monuments of French musical history. None of the other composers of opera belongs to the illustrious company of these three leading masters, and even François Joseph Gossec (1734-1829), of importance in the history of orchestral and choral music, seems pale and lifeless on the stage. After the Revolution opera continued to thrive on the foundation laid by Grétry and by another foreigner whose imposing figure carries us back into the international arena of Italian music.

New Aspects of Opera Seria and Tragédie Lyrique

FRANCESCO Algarotti (1712-1764), influential Italian author and literary critic, declared in his valuable treatise on operatic dramaturgy, *Saggio sopra l'Opera in Musica* (1750), that in order to preserve and perpetuate itself opera must periodically return to its true principles. That everything was not altogether sound in the reigning opera seria is evident from a work that antedates Algarotti's by thirty-three years, *Il Teatro alla Moda,* by Benedetto Marcello. But it is erroneous to think that all this was merely an academic question raised by literary men, eager, like their distant Florentine predecessors, to change the course of music, for the musicians were quite ready to remedy the situation. Hasse, the embodiment of the stylized concert opera, was casting about for a new librettist, eventually writing a veritable reform opera, *Piramo e Tisbe,* in which the musico-dramatic elements, heretofore employed within individual musical forms, were subjected to a dramaturgical plan.

Charles de Brosses (1709-1777), French magistrate (usually called President de Brosses, because he was the first president of the Parliament of Burgundy), an uncommonly keen-minded polyhistorian, the first archaeologist to write a monograph on the newly discovered Herculaneum, and a contributor to the *Encyclopédie* (languages, music, etymology), has given us a description of the Italian opera of about 1740 which as a page of dramatic criticism would fit admirably into Wagner's *Opera and Drama:*

By wanting to unite too many pleasures opera weakens their enjoyment; thus, with a good many agreeable moments an opera has for me its moments of tediousness, something the good French tragedy does not know. There the interest is created without diversion, growing by degrees, carrying the spectator from act to act without interruption. Partisans of the opera will say that one does not go to the opera for the subject but for the accessories of music and the spectacle, which are preferable to comedy and tragedy. If the Italians believe that they have eliminated the inconveniences which I noticed in our own operas by the choice of their subjects, they are greatly mistaken. To tell the truth, some of their librettos (I am thinking of Metastasio) are admirable and very interesting, but the arias pinned to the end of every scene, not closely connected with the action, these exquisite arias which place Italian music so high above ours, again create diversion; while they enchant the ears they permit the interest to cool off.[7]

These lines were typical of the remarkable critical writings of French men of letters and dramatists, who realized that music was advancing on the wrong road. Among the many prefaces to plays—the favorite medium for essays on dramaturgy—Beaumarchais's are particularly interesting from our point of view. The following sentence from the preface to *Tarare* shows how de Brosses's judgment of the incongruous features of the opera seria was not only shared but was even more illuminatingly presented by the greatest playwright of eighteenth-century France: *Il y a trop de musique dans la musique de théâtre*. This little paradox is a complete treatise on musical dramaturgy. Gluck arrived at the same conclusion—after a lifework spent in all phases of dramatic music—when he said that French opera "reeks of music." In this century of thinkers and theoreticians French thought established, then, *a priori*, by sheer reasoning, the theory of the music drama; it designed a frame which had only to be filled, a plan which had but to be realized. French musicians themselves seldom rose to the height of their dramaturgists; when they did, as in the cases of Rameau and Bizet, their own countrymen disavowed them. It always remained to foreign musicians to come to France and start important reforms by following the dictates of French literary thought. Thus a unique situation was created. The great figures of dramatic music, from Rossi to Wagner, came to Paris and received the lasting influence and inspiration of French thought which enabled them to regenerate music drama again and again.

Christoph Willibald Gluck (1714-1787) was born in the Upper Palatinate but received his early education in the Jesuit school in Komotau, German Bohemia. In 1732 in Prague he studied the violoncello and probably composition with Bohuslav Czernohorsky (1684-1740), who had acquired a good reputation as a teacher and composer. This Bohemian Franciscan friar possessed a well-rounded musical education and knew Italian music from several years' active work in Italy, where Tartini was among his pupils. After a short stay in Vienna in 1736, Gluck had the good fortune to find a patron who sent him to Italy, where he enlisted with Sammartini to finish his studies in composition. Giovanni Battista Sammartini (1701-1775), a composer of great importance whom we shall meet among the founding fathers of the classical symphony. taught him the principles of nonpolyphonic thematic work, of cardinal importance in our modern music. In the works of his youth Gluck proved to be an adherent of the reigning type of opera, the stylized, purely musical, Italian opera of Metastasio. The list of Metastasio's books is familiar; Gluck set many of them to music, and all of them were written with a sure hand and offered successful competition to some of the best opera composers in Italy.

His successes earned him the somewhat dubious papal knighthood of the "Golden Spur," and an invitation to the Haymarket Theatre in London in 1745. The trip through Paris and the stay in London were memorable experiences for the Italian-trained German musician, and their importance can hardly be overestimated, although his English excursion was far from successful. As a matter of fact, it was the lack of response which must have induced this keen observer to reach some momentous conclusions. He found the Haymarket Theatre a mere shadow of its former excellence, and Handel alienated from opera; these weighty facts made Gluck realize, perhaps for the first time, that the opera seria was declining. He soon discovered that real music drama had retired into the chorus oratorio, a sphere unknown to the concert opera. Also, while passing through Paris he had heard Rameau's *Castor and Pollux* and no doubt some of Lully's works and was duly impressed by the dramatic accents and character scenes of this music.

Gluck left London in 1746. *Orfeo,* the first opera to embody his new dramaturgical ideas, was written in 1762. The intervening sixteen years must therefore have been spent in preparing the "reform," for it is sheer folly to maintain that *Orfeo* was the result of a sudden inspiration, the result of a change of heart from the delicious little comic opera *Le Cadi Dupé* which preceded this noble work. The three years (1747–1750) with Mingotti's opera company—one of the "road" companies which in the eighteenth century visited cities that had no regular operatic establishment or had a court opera not accessible to everyone—gave him not only valuable experience in operatic conducting but carried him to such musical centers as Dresden, Prague, Hamburg, and Copenhagen. Needless to say, the conductor of an opera company in the eighteenth century was not a specialist dealing with a certain part of the repertory, but was supposed to provide a part of it himself; consequently this period and the decade spent in the services of the imperial opera in Vienna (1754–1764) produced a good number of operas.

Orfeo ed Euridice, performed in Vienna on October 5, 1762, carried the oldest operatic title in the literature, a title that had appeared on the bulletin board of every opera theater in Europe, yet this work became the symbol of the modern music drama. It is difficult to analyze it dispassionately, for it is surrounded by an aureole almost preventing critical approach. Regarded from the purely musical point of view, *Orfeo* contains really only one innovation which may be called reformational—the abolition of the secco recitative with its harpsichord accompaniment, and its replacement by the animated orchestral recitative. This was not, however, Gluck's invention, as we shall presently see. That the rest of the opera presents a dramatic unity of unparalleled logic and classic proportions is a matter of quality, not of principle. There is no definite change in Gluck's musical procedure—the composer did not even emphasize the reform nature of *Orfeo*—and there was nothing in the work that would have startled an audience accustomed to the opera seria. The results of Gluck's slowly maturing musico-dramatic conceptions were there, however, in spite of the seemingly unchanged exterior. The lifeless figures of the stylized opera seria were replaced by symbolically simplified and monumental character types which led him back to the classical tragedy of antiquity. For his ancient heroes were not seventeenth- or eighteenth-century princes or kings disguised as gods and heroes, but their heroic and sometimes rhetorical pathos had the dimensions and true accents of the tragic greatness that was ancient Greece.

It is often said that Gluck relegated music to a secondary place in the drama, that he made it entirely subservient to poetry. This is no more true than it is in Wagner's case; on the contrary, the whole idiom and apparatus of the lyric stage were reformed by Gluck in order to adapt his music to its superior tasks. Recitative and aria are no longer rigidly separated, and the accompagnato receives added significance, for the music takes part in the whole life of the stage; it takes on its wings every scene, every detail in the drama. The monopoly of the da capo aria is curtailed and great choruses appear to summarize events in truly classic tradition. The orchestra becomes a factor in the drama, and pantomime, large ensembles, and independent instrumental interludes complete the action as integral parts of the plot.

The first opera with the avowed purpose of reform was *Alceste,* performed on December 26, 1767, in Vienna. Noble simplicity, majestic grandeur, and a truly classic equilibrium of accents and gestures make this work worthy of Euripides. The use of the chorus is of telling effect, for, as in Handel's oratorios, it represents the people in its actions. *Alceste* belongs among the greatest dramatic works, spoken or musical, of all times, and should be in the repertory of any institution calling itself an opera house. It should be produced in its original form, not in the version made for Paris in 1776. Gluck, in this opera, penetrated deeper into the problems of the music drama. The poet's intentions were stated in the very title, *tragedia per musica,* and Gluck's accompanied recitative reaches in this work a tragic plasticity which only the great Italian recitatives can equal. The musician's task was to concentrate on the drawing of characters in music, and to this aim he adhered unswervingly, following the poet's words with profoundly earnest devotion.

Paride ed Elena (1770) was the third and last of the so-called reform operas in which Gluck, an artist of great literary and cultural accomplishments, proceeded with the rationalistic, thorough method of his times. If there were any doubts about his intentions in *Orfeo,* the preface to *Alceste* must have dispelled all misunderstanding:

I endeavored to reduce music to its proper function, that of seconding poetry by enforcing the expression of the sentiment, and the interest of the situations, without interrupting the action, or weakening it by superfluous ornament.

The famous preface to *Alceste* was invariably interpreted to mean that Gluck took the field against a worthless, totally degenerate form of the lyric theater. When condemning the opera seria and the tragédie lyrique and citing Gluck as the first man to realize characters musically—"a power all but unknown in the serious opera of his day" [8]—and as the one who gave "the finishing stroke to the antiquated works of Lully and Rameau," [9] we commit a grave act of injustice, at the same time distorting musical history. Such appraisals, contained, unfortunately, in reference manuals of wide circulation and influence, are the result of almost complete ignorance of the great operatic literature before Gluck. It is not necessary to point to Monteverdi, Scarlatti, or Handel, whose works are known at least in fragments, but among the contemporaries of the reformer there were many other opera composers whose works will be revered and admired if we ever reach a knowledge and appreciation of musical literature faintly comparable to that enjoyed by the fine arts and literature; and these are works without which neither Gluck nor Mozart nor Verdi nor the other giants of opera could have arisen. That this will ever come about is placed in doubt by as modern a publication as the *Oxford Companion to Music* (1938) : "It is just possible that the world may come to take pleasure again in these one-time favourites [the late baroque opera], but the greater probability is that they will merely continue to be revived occasionally for the interest of historically minded connoisseurs." [10]

It is almost unbelievable that in times when fabulous sums are paid for little miniatures of medieval painters, when the poems of Renaissance poets are published in facsimile editions, when the plays of Restoration and *grand siècle* dramatists are performed in national theaters proud of their great traditions—that in such times we dispose of our precious musical heritage without even ascertaining its content and value. How irresistible the human qualities of the opera buffa, those works of parody and satire; how wholeheartedly even the victims joined the chorus of laughter! Galuppi wrote a carnival opera for Venice the target of which was the Venetian populace, while a Jewish burlesque was performed in the ghetto to the great enjoyment of the very people whose life and manners were the object of its sallies. With its lifelike characterization, its vivid orchestration, and its ensembles and finales, the opera buffa pointed out the way of salvation to the stagnant opera seria and its masters. Perez's *Solimano,* Terradellas's *Artaserse,* Jommelli's *Didone,* Traëtta's *Ifigenia in Tauride,* to mention a few, contain scenes unsurpassed in the history of music drama. In a few brushstrokes the anguish or joy of a human soul is depicted with such consummate art as the noisy grand opera of the nineteenth century never even faintly approached. These masters were Gluck's superiors when it came to long, sustained dramatic scenes; what they did not possess was Gluck's artistic insight and integrity, and they were therefore prone to make concessions to the detriment of the drama. Comparison of these dramatic scenes with Gluck's reveals that the German master did not even attempt to emulate them; he must have known that his breath was too short to cope with the sheer musical inventiveness and power required to sustain them, and preferred shorter, beautifully rounded songs. But his wonderful artistic sense found a way to remedy his shortcomings and counseled him to form the shorter pieces in groups, connected by ritornels or orchestral recitatives, so that in the final analysis they do present large entities.

The improvement of the dramatic qualities of the opera libretto was only half of Gluck's reform; the other half was musical, the assimilation of the ensemble technique of the opera buffa and the opéra comique, the choral aspects of the tragédie lyrique, and the new Italo-German instrumental music. In carrying out his musical plans Gluck's dependence on his predecessors and colleagues is manifest in every department. The elimination of the secco recitative had taken place in the tragédie lyrique, and as early as Lully the orchestra had accompanied the recitative, although in a very simple manner. The pantomimic element in *Orfeo* is distinctly French, stemming from the early French opera ballet. *Orfeo's* choruses show their sources unequivocally. The wailing chorus goes back to Rameau's *Castor and Pollux,* that of the furies comes from Traëtta's *Iphigenia,* while the echo choruses are derived from Perez's *Soliman.* The oracle part in *Alceste,* in its turn derived from the Venetian *ombrae,* is known to modern audiences from Mozart's *Don Giovanni* (the Commandant) and from Schubert's "Death and the Maiden." The opera buffa is not represented in Gluck's works, but he went through the whole gamut of musical comedy by paralleling the evolution of the French opéra comique. Starting with the customary collection of vaudevilles, he arrived at human comedy. *L'Ivrogne Corrigé* (1760), *Le Cadi Dupé* (1761), and especially *La Rencontre Imprévue* (1764) are not mere episodes in his career but are works of the utmost significance without which the reform operas could not have been written. The consummate technical skill acquired and employed in them, the fine sense for proportions, and the power of characterization were to benefit the whole next generation of opera composers. All these facts demand an examination of the works upon which the musical side of Gluck's reform was evidently based.

The first great Italian composer to heed the new dramaturgical theories advocated by the philosophers arose from the school of the eminent Neapolitan opera buffa composers. This was Niccolò Jommelli (1714–1774), who began his studies under Feo and Leo. His first opera, *L'Errore Amoroso* (1737), showed him to be a promising composer, and within a few years (*Merope,* 1741) he became one of Italy's feted maestri, highly regarded by Hasse and the other princes of the music drama. After a prolonged stay in Stuttgart (1753–1769) as court conductor the celebrated composer returned to Italy, where his compatriots roundly denounced him as an artist totally changed by his Teutonic environment. They greeted him with the same reproach that was addressed to Rameau by his own people: "learned music." (Another century and a quarter, and the same cry was to arise over *Carmen!*) What disconcerted Jommelli's compatriots was his truly masterful dramatic treatment of the accompanied orchestral recitative. Recognizing that the recitative is eminently suitable for intense dramatic action, he developed the accompagnato, the simple orchestral support, into an animated, expressive, and pliable instrument of characterization, effectively supporting the rhapsodic dramatic delivery of the voice. His compatriots were, of course, justified when they discovered in his music a new dialect. Jommelli's excellent sense for the dramatic was bolstered by his acquaintance with German instrumental music, and it is no exaggeration to state that this Italian composer was largely responsible for the development of the rest of eighteenth-century musical history. Without his intervention the great classical school of symphonists might have taken an entirely different turn; on the other hand, it is questionable whether Jommelli could have arrived at his highly expressive idiom without the aid of instrumental music.

Then appeared a new Italian master who confused even more the traditionalists, suspicious of the new dialect, and developed the dialect into a style. Tommaso Traëtta (1727–1779), another Neapolitan, was familiar with the ensemble technique of the opera buffa and pressed it into the service of the opera seria. In his works the age-old, natural musico-dramatic inclination of the Italians, to whom the manipulation of crowds is an innate faculty, triumphed over the temporary eclipse of the music drama by vocal virtuosity; he re-created the dramatic chorus opera. The dramatic recitative and the dramatic chorus were, then, fully rehabilitated while the rest of the world, including Gluck, was still playing the stilted game of the rococo. And in the wake of Traëtta's vigorous music the graceful puppets of the style galant disappeared before the heroes of antiquity; silk stockings, brocade jackets, and lorgnettes were once more discarded for the cothurnus, shield, and sword.

Jommelli's work, while mostly a mixture of German and Italian stylistic elements, still shows the distinct influence of French music drama; the

Italians were mistaken in ascribing his "desertion" solely to the German contrapuntists, for the spirit of Lully and Rameau, and the theories of Diderot and Rousseau, familiar in Stuttgart, had a place in his style. Having noted this French influence in one of the chief representatives of the rejuvenated music drama, our suspicions concerning the source of the musico-dramatic reform will grow when we discover that the court of Parma was the only place in Italy to cultivate the tragédie lyrique. And the court conductor in charge of performances of Rameau's operas here was Traëtta, whose poignant choruses so impressed Gluck that he employed similar effects in his own works.

If the musical elements show a strong French influence, the literary sources were so overwhelmingly French that they raise the issue of a revision of the history and nature of the reform of the music drama. After *Orfeo* Gluck returned to the Metastasian opera seria and to the opéra comique, then suddenly he produced the reform opera *Alceste*. Such a reversion to the older style of composition occurred repeatedly, even after the crowning music drama of his career, *Iphigénie en Tauride,* and suggests an uncommon dependence on the librettist. The circumstance that all three reform operas, *Orfeo, Alceste,* and *Paride ed Elena,* were written by the same poet, Calzabigi, establishes this dependence as a cardinal point in Gluck's work, inspiration, and procedure. He was weak where the poet was weak, and he rose to the most sublime heights when the poet showed him the way.

Ranieri de' Calzabigi (1714–1795) was a man of rather adventurous life, an able poet and a keen thinker, occupied with the idea of musico-dramatic reform before called upon to supply Gluck with dramatic poems for his operas. A critical essay, *Dissertazione su le Poesie Drammatiche del Sig. Abate Pietro Metastasio* (1755), stamps him an anti-Metastasian rebel long before Gluck became articulate. Beginning his essay with a crafty eulogy of the worshiped Viennese court poet, he ends it with an unmistakable denunciation of Metastasio's dramaturgy in favor of the principles exemplified in the French tragédie lyrique. There can be no question that it was this clear-headed man of letters who steered Gluck toward his goal, and there is little doubt that he was responsible for the whole idea of reform as far as Gluck was concerned. It was he who came to the conclusion that Metastasio's *dolcezza* was, in the final analysis, undramatic, for while it might lead to types it could not create characters. Unlike Metastasio's Aeneas and Titus—eighteenth-century noblemen in classical garb—Calzabigi's heroes were timeless, and being timeless they regained something of the classic stature of their forebears. Orpheus again became the noble Hellenic character traced by Rinuccini, which had earlier fired the dramatic genius of Monteverdi.

The student of operatic history cannot help being puzzled by these manifestations of artistic integrity coming from an Italian when the Italian Molière, Carlo Goldoni, writing at the same time, readily sacrificed everything dear to the true dramatist. "When I write for music," he confessed, "the last person of whom I think is myself. I think of the actors, I think a great deal of the conductor, and I want to please the audience. . . ." [11] The solution of the puzzle lies in Calzabigi's sources. "If one is determined to follow in the footsteps of truth," says Gluck in the preface to *Paride ed Elena,* "one should never forget that, measured to the requirements of the subject treated, even the greatest beauties of melody and harmony can become shortcomings and appear insufficient if they are employed at the wrong place." No Italian dramaturgist of the times could have devised this essentially French train of thought; Gluck received it from Calzabigi, but the latter, in his turn, must have obtained it from French sources. The extraordinary molding power of French thought brought to bear upon the operatic reform is not recognized or admitted to its rightful degree. Some historians deny this influence altogether by affirming that Gluck conceived his ideas of reform while still in Italy. This contention suggests an examination of the Italian sources.

Pier Jacopo Martelli, poet and scientist, who introduced the French Alexandrine into Italian poetry, was the leader of the Italian classicists who manifested a certain opposition to opera—an opposition altogether strange in Italy. His book entitled *Della Tragedia Antica e Moderna* (Rome, 1715) contains a chapter on the *dramma per musica*. In it the author describes his sojourn in Paris, where he went to study French literature. The Italian man of letters praises Saint-Evremond highly for his uncompromising attitude regarding the absurdity of the opera as a form of drama and quotes him as saying that "the Greeks created superb tragedies in which some parts were sung; the French write poor ones, the whole of which is sung." In Martelli's opinion the same judgment applies to Italian opera. Saint-Evremond seems to have exerted considerable influence on his transalpine colleagues in aligning them against opera. Francesco Saverio Quadrio (1695–1756), another noted Italian literary critic, and Giammaria Ortes, whose *Riflessioni sopra i Drammi per Musica* was translated into French, frequently quoted from his works. Thus the original movement started by Saint-Evremond found adherents not only among the French but among men of letters of the native country of the opera.

We must mention still another Italian littérateur who, by obviously furnishing Calzabigi with some of his ideas, closes the circle around the reform of opera. Algarotti, whose remark on the desirability of periodic changes in the opera opened this section, was the author of a treatise on operatic dramaturgy which has not lost its freshness and validity to this day.[12] A man of wide culture, his familiarity with literary and philosophical trends of the reigning French school was due to immediate and personal contact with its most illustrious representatives. But Algarotti was not a partisan of the style galant, nor was he an uncompromising rationalist; what he advocated was identical with the Gluckian doctrine, for according to him opera is "a tragedy recited in music" in which music should be the "servant and helper of poetry."

This, then, is the reform as we have it in Gluck, for in a letter to the editor of the *Mercure de France* Gluck himself ascribed the lion's share in the operatic reform to the poet of *Orfeo,* Calzabigi, who was the disciple of Algarotti. This was not a mere act of courtesy. Gluck's whole lifework demonstrates that the composer was dependent on the poet. In those years of unprecedented flourishing of instrumental music Gluck's contributions to its various forms consist of a handful of compositions; church music did not interest him at all, and lyric music, outside of the lyricism of the drama, attracted him only when, at an advanced age, Klopstock's odes provided him with a lyric poetry of a high order.

Gluck's following in Vienna was very modest because the opera buffa monopolized all attention, even displacing, after 1765, the opéra comique. Appreciation of the music drama was not enhanced by the composer of *Orfeo,* and the public stayed away from the performances. Thus when du Roullet, the cultivated counselor of the French embassy in Vienna, his next librettist, advised him to go to Paris, enjoining the directors of the Opera to receive the master "who after mature consideration has come to the conclusions that the Italians erred from the true path of art," he acted as an agent of destiny: the tragédie lyrique was waiting.

The reform of the opera seria had been completed with *Paride ed Elena.* Yet the composer, comfortably well off, and having passed the age—he was now almost sixty—when most people engage in difficult ventures, moved heaven and earth to gain admittance to the Opera in Paris. Having met difficulties, he turned to his erstwhile pupil, the Dauphine Marie Antoinette, and the former Habsburg archduchess intervened on behalf of her esteemed teacher. *Iphigénie en Aulide,* written in French in 1772, was produced in the Académie Royale de Musique on April 19, 1774. *Iphigénie* was followed by French arrangements of *Orfeo* and *Alceste,* and by three new works, *Armide* (1777), *Iphigénie en Tauride* (1779), and the less important *Echo et Narcisse* (1779). The first version of *Iphigenia* was composed while Gluck was still in Vienna, while the second setting, text by Guillard, unquestionably his chef-d'oeuvre, followed after one of the musician's relapses into more conventional music making for want of a true poet to guide him. Between the two *Iphigenias* something happened that seems surprising to anyone following the reformer's career; he turned to an old libretto, *Armide,* by Quinault, which had already been composed by Lully. Far from being an act of complaisance, it shows the master intellect pursuing its plans, a heroic entrance into the lion's lair to retrieve the tragédie lyrique. And at this point it becomes clear why Gluck, at once German, French, and Italian, was destined to effectuate the final synthesis. The highly dramatic chorus opera of the tragédie lyrique and the similar Italian style exemplified in Traëtta's works were in reality not opposed to each other; all they needed was the elimination of the divertissement and the reintroduction of dramatic continuity. An examination of both *Armides* will disclose the consciousness of Gluck's attempt to find his way back to the sources of the tragédie lyrique, for the German musician did not limit himself to Quinault's share in the drama: he borrowed some of Lully's music.

The success of Gluck's great operas in Paris was surpassed only by the controversy they created. The representatives of the pseudo-classical school, such as Laharpe and Marmontel, watched with suspicion these "novelties"; but more liberal and advanced men came to the rescue with enthusiasm. All the bitterness of the "quarrel of the buffoons" was revived when the opposing party enticed Nicola Piccini (1728–1800), one of the great masters of the opera buffa, to come to Paris and place his talents in the service of the anti-Gluck campaign. It is doubtful whether the Italian composer fully realized what he was being used for. His delicate lyricism was far removed from the dramatic pathos of his German adversary. Piccini was one of the earliest artists of that bourgeois humanism which characterized the end of the century, and thus it was not by accident that his best work, *La Buona Figliuola,* derived its text from the representative literary figure of this current, Samuel Richardson, Goldoni having arranged his *Pamela* for the opera. This gifted composer has been unduly penalized by posterity for his participation in the war of Gluckists and Piccinists although, rising above the tumult of the opposing forces, the two composers showed respect for each other, and Piccini finished by accepting the very principles he was supposed to counteract. An uncommonly fine musician, Piccini could not escape seeing the truth, and he was not the only one to succumb. The skeptical Grimm, won body and soul by the Italians, was so moved by *Iphigenia* that to those who exclaimed, "But this is not song," he declared, "I do not know whether this is song, but perhaps it is much more than that. I forget the opera and find myself in a Greek tragedy." [13] The bitter controversy ended with the triumph of Gluck, and the aged composer retired to Vienna to spend his remaining years peacefully, universally admired and revered.

*
* *

SAINT-AUBIN'S etching of Houdon's striking bust of Gluck carries the motto "He preferred the muses to the sirens." No more appropriate tribute could be paid to this artist, than whom few were more devoted to the muses. The parallels drawn between Gluck and Wagner seem to be based on the same motto, but the analogies are superficial, for the two composers had little in common. Wagner, who constantly allowed his orchestra to over-rule his dramaturgical views, and whose music seldom turns to the lyric communing of Gluck, could not see the profoundly classic lines in Gluck's works; he held the composer of *Orpheus* in high esteem mainly because he saw in him the first German master to rebel against Italian traditions. But Gluck had his counterpart, a remarkable counterpart, among his own con-temporaries, in Gotthold Ephraim Lessing (1729-1781), and it seems fitting that this man should have been a dramatist and not a musician.

Lessing the poet and Lessing the critic had their roots in the same in-tellectual substance, although the flowers differed. His essays on drama and art are the first examples of creative criticism. In reconciling the spirit of Shakespeare with the spirit of Greek drama he liberated the stage for the modern drama, and in the wake of his efforts the canons of form of the classical French drama changed into eternally human situations. In his first dramas Lessing created impeccable plays, but his stylizing intellect placed his protagonists in a sort of vacuum. Beginning, however, with *Minna von Barnhelm* (1767) there was a deliberate, convincing change, which in *Emilia Galotti* (1772) and *Nathan der Weise* (1779) reached heroic intensity. There we behold the régisseur-poet, standing behind the scenes, calculating with his supreme intellect the degree of heat necessary to send the passions of his figures to the boiling point and then driving them to a catastrophic end. Like Lessing, Gluck possessed a remarkable faculty for criticism, unerringly recognizing the good and the bad; like Lessing, he was able to suppress the bad qualities and enhance the good, and like his eminent literary colleague he exhibited a manly countenance, industry, and integrity. Like Lessing, he was not endowed with an original creative power commensurate to his abilities, but had an artistic sense which by examining and testing the availa-ble material became creative as it turned the results of knowledge so obtained into works of art. In the results of this process we shall not find values that are entirely new, but rather the fulfillment of something long sought for. The similarity between Lessing and Gluck is again notable if we compare both men to their fellow artists. Klopstock and Wieland were poets of dis-tinctly more potent creative powers than Lessing, and the sheer musical genius of Rameau and Traëtta, the dramatic breath of Handel, were un-questionably superior to Gluck's; and still it was Lessing who gave Ger-man literature the long-expected modern drama, and Gluck who gave the world the modern music drama. Lessing's dramas are the oldest German dramas in the regular repertory of German theaters, as are Gluck's works in the more international world of opera.

One wonders what factors could have made these two serene artists the reformers and apostles of their respective arts. The answer lies in the Apollonian calm and clearness of their creative process, which did not know the Dionysiac intoxication of the genius who abandons himself to the creative urge storming in his soul and finds realization and expression in molds prepared for their sovereign use by lesser talents. Both of these men found their bearings in a maze of conflicting and confusing circumstances, realized the issues involved, reconciled the requirements, concordances, and differences of the contributing factors, and proceeded only after all this had been reduced to a workable, artistically and philosophically lucid, and convincing scheme. "I do not feel in myself the living spring which forces itself to the surface by its own power," remarked Lessing in his *Hamburgische Dramaturgie,* adding that all his artistic deeds required "study and great effort." The same meticulous study and effort characterized Gluck. The thinker was always present, assorting and selecting his material to suit the circumstances. Even in his most sublime, most classical, and most idealistic work, *Iphigénie en Tauride,* the majority of the arias were culled from earlier "ordinary" operas—*La Clemenza di Tito, Le Feste d'Apollo, Telemacco,* and others—a procedure he followed in a number of instances. The fact that these excerpts were modified does not change Gluck's essentially deliberate, critical approach to his task. After he had composed Italian operas in the customary style for a quarter of a century his critical faculties led him to probe the apparent incongruities of the opera seria. Having consulted such literary authorities as could clarify the issues for him, he recognized the problem of the music drama and found the approach to it. He too could say that there was no "living spring" in him, but he too spared no study and effort to force the water to the surface.

Gluck's choice of operatic subjects has often been derided as a regrettable remnant of the old mythological opera seria, but his selection does not betray uncertainty; on the contrary, it was the result of long and careful deliberation. A German-born, Italian-trained operatic composer who could write French comic operas with such delicious felicity cannot be accused of inability to find a new musical style with new subjects. The subjects of his music dramas remained, then, the same, but neither librettist nor composer intended to exploit the dramatic action; each wanted to let the individual man pour out his emotions and feelings. *Orfeo* has a greatly simplified action compared to older versions of the story; in *Armide* the action all but ceases after the first act; in *Paride ed Elena* there is practically no subject or plot. Indeed, Gluck was a psycho-dramatist who gave his greatest in the climactic monologue. This does not necessarily mean that the scene is empty, but at the moment of its presentation all that matters is the one man's sentiments. It will not surprise us, then, to find that in its innermost nature Gluck's art is a noble lyricism, a lyricism which communicates mental states and developments; and it is significant that for a man of his exceptional literary tastes Gluck's favorite poet was Klopstock, to whom even epic poetry meant lyricism.

The contradiction between drama and lyricism is, however, only theoretical, for we have learned to appreciate that it is precisely this lyrical quality which distinguishes the music drama from other varieties of the theater. We have found it in every instance of true music drama, from Aeschylus to the great Italian composers of the baroque. Gluck's dramaticism favors lyric effusion, which it rightly considers a vehicle appropriate for music even more than for true drama; but again we have perfect parallels within this type of drama in Goethe's *Tasso* and Gluck's *Iphigenia*. The Gluckian characters are not like Shakespeare's truly dramatic heroes, acting under the impact of passion; reflections on action and reaction in the human soul, characteristic of the French tragedy, govern them, and one might say, briefly, that Gluck's reform consisted in a turning from the opera seria to the tragédie lyrique. He realized that it was mainly the stilted, lifeless, and undramatic nature of the libretto which prevented opera from fulfilling its original task: the pouring into a poetic mold of the one and eternal theme, the elementally powerful expression of human sentiments and their conflicts.

Carrying his dramatic conception to a logical conclusion, he turned away from the crowned monarch of opera, Metastasio, and forsook the spirit of the opera seria; he demanded that the relationship between poet and musician should be reversed, the latter becoming servant to the former. The resultant changes in the disposition of the musical part of opera were not revolutionary; "simplicity and unity was the historic gain, a permanent gain, of the so-called Gluckian reform of the music drama." [14] Gluck retained the formal aria but insisted that "it is not right to hurry through the second part of a song . . . in order to repeat the first part"; this means that the purely musical-formal element can be retained only to the extent to which it is compatible with the drama. This was the all-important principle of the modern music drama, which meant, not formlessness, but, on the contrary, the creation of new forms—emotional life rendered in musico-dramatic forms, not in purely musical forms. The impeccable taste and judicious conception of a great artist speak from his utterances, which have been interpreted to mean servility of music to poetry. But music is still the master of the music drama; the great deed was to invest it with the seriousness of purpose, the balanced order, the heroism, and the delicacy of classic drama.

The eighteenth century produced a great genius of the lyric stage in Rameau, an artist who, although truly French in his intellectual, scholarly nature, professed a purely musical approach to his dramas. He was therefore rejected by both the literary and the musical parties. The German musician, less gifted than his unsuccessful French predecessor, realized and achieved the dramatic theories of French thinkers "because he had the genius to have better understood French *esprit* and French art than their own musicians." [15] *Musas praeposuit Sirenis.*

Enlightened Absolutism

THE year 1740 marked the beginning of the long reign of two sovereigns whose ascent to the thrones of their respective realms occurred under circumstances that already foreshadowed a general conflagration. Frederick II (1712–1786), King of Prussia, to whom history has given the epithet "the Great" inherited a country with a full treasury, a matchless army, and a good number of promising claims. Maria Theresa (1717–1780), Empress of Austria, succeeded her father to a throne undermined and menaced from every side. The many enemies of Austria, ready to dispute Maria Theresa's right to the crown, considered the situation ripe for intervention and precipitated the War of the Austrian Succession. At this point Prussian ignorance of all international decorum and the ruthless application of force showed itself for the first time in its enormity, as, seeing Maria Theresa's plight, Frederick marched into undefended Silesia.

The two adversaries presented the greatest possible contrast in personality, beliefs, and aims. The king, soldier and philosopher, entirely possessed by the spirit of the French Enlightenment, bent only on securing advantages for his realm, and unscrupulously betraying allies and enemies alike, looked with his calm and penetrating gaze upon all and sundry as servants whose duty was to serve him and the state. The empress, administering her vast empire personally, and surrounded by men, remained a woman, a pious, deeply devout Catholic, a proverbially good mother to her children, and the *Landesmutter* of her many and varied subjects.

Yielding temporarily to Frederick the empress concluded a separate peace treaty with the Hohenzollern in order to be able to devote her attention to France and Bavaria. The French were decisively beaten in 1743, an Austrian army crossed the Rhine, freeing Alsace, and it looked as though the empress would soon emerge victorious from the great controversy, when Frederick struck again, disregarding the treaty he had signed less than a year before, and moved into Bohemia. This time, however, the Prussian met with defeat, for the French treated him in his own fashion, withholding the promised help, and Frederick led his defeated army out of Bohemia. The situation became ominous, but at this moment the political and military gifts of Frederick asserted themselves in all their greatness and the tables were turned. The Austrians were defeated, Saxony's power was clipped, and Prussia irrevocably emerged as a great power. The consequences of these victories were lasting, for with the loss of Silesia Austria was expelled from Germany proper. This was the beginning of the Austrian tragedy, for with the loss of the Germanic territories the non-German population gained in numerical proportion and strength, and the downfall of the Habsburg empire which came so dramatically in 1918 was from now on merely postponed by skillful statesmanship.

The following years passed in feverish activity, the European chancelleries trying to reorient themselves to cope with the new situation created by the two powers in Germandom, Prussia and Austria. The three great powers, Austria, Russia, and France, agreed to work together to reduce the Prussian king to his former modest position of Margrave of Brandenburg. The attack was planned for 1757, but Frederick, learning of the existence of this dangerous coalition, took the initiative. Battle after battle was won by the great soldier-king; still by 1759 he was entirely on the defensive. When the Russian and Austrian armies succeeded in joining forces, the Prussian army was annihilated on August 12, 1759, near Kunersdorf. Two more years and it seemed certain that Prussia's fate would be sealed, when a miraculous change reversed the situation. Empress Elizabeth of Russia died in 1762. Her successor, Peter III, a German prince, was a great admirer of Frederick and did not lose time in making peace with his idol. Having conquered France's whole colonial empire, England came to terms with her old enemy, while France, weakened and realizing the futility of the struggle, seceded from the warring parties. The Austrian treasury, now at its lowest level, did not permit the continuation of an extended war, and so Austria was also ready to negotiate peace.

When the Austro-Prussian peace was signed in 1763 the heroic stature of Frederick, with his firm belief in the victorious outcome of his adventures and with his unshakable confidence in the midst of defeat, became apparent, and admiration and worship of the king rose in a tremendous wave. It soon found expression in a reawakening of German arts and letters, for it was the battles of the Seven Years' War which, embroidered and gilded by romantic hero worship, fired the imagination of German poets and artists. The worshipers did not seek the causes which precipitated Frederick's memorable battles; they did not and could not see that with a victorious Prussia the great struggle for central European domination began.

With Frederick II absolutism entered upon a new and different phase. According to the political philosophy of Louis XIV the sovereign and the state were identical, and he represented the ideal of the king ruling by the grace of God in its most august and forbidding manifestation. Frederick's time was already too much under the spell of rationalism and too secularized in spirit to care for divine justification of the sovereign's position; it considered the monarch and the state earthly institutions to be entrusted to the stewardship of qualified persons. Frederick was acquainted with the writings of Hobbes and Locke, he knew the voluminous French literature on political science, and he was fully aware of the requirements of the times. With him and with the numerous German princes and ruling archbishops of his era began the so-called enlightened absolutism, presenting a seemingly irreconcilable mixture of liberalism and autocracy. Kings and princes, even devoutly Catholic and haughtily Habsburg Maria Theresa, vied with each other in attaching celebrities of the Enlightenment to their retinues in order to endow economic and cultural life with a new spirit. Thoroughgoing autocrats established model governments; rulers great and small, leading the dissipated life of the French kings of absolutism, placed all their weight and resources behind scientific and artistic undertakings. Princes and public servants worked hand in hand for the *res publica*. Even the long-neglected rural population was now protected, and Frederick meted out stern punishment to landowners who did not treat their peasants humanely. Whereas the earlier phase of absolutism rested on mercantilism, enlightened absolutism developed modern agriculture, adapting English theories and methods of cultivation. The various industries maintained the high artistic principles instituted by Louis XIV in his Manufacture des Gobelins, and the porcelain factories of Meissen and Nymphenburg, the silk looms of Dresden, and the jewelry shops of Pforzheim became famous all over the country, with many a smaller potentate trying to establish factories of his own.

This new economic culture was the bulwark of enlightened absolutism, for the rulers wanted their subjects to be industrious and well-to-do, knowing that this was the best way to keep the state treasury filled. The methods used in attaining this aim were often arbitrary and even brutal, but on the whole the policy promoted cultural progress, for the new benevolent despotism was very active in all fields of culture. It organized life minutely in all its aspects, regulating and administering it by a vast police force. Such regulation of private life is repugnant to the modern man, but it wrought sheer wonders in eighteenth-century society. Hospitals and departments of sanitation were created, raising public health to a level not even faintly envisaged by the seventeenth century. All this was not done for humanitarian reasons alone—better health made for better production and income—but the recognition and remedying of needs and problems was a capital achievement.

The same creative spirit that characterized political life enlivened arts and letters. Not since the Italian Renaissance had these enjoyed such universal love and support. The enlightened absolutism was indefatigable in its creative fervor; palaces, castles, theaters, schools, academies, and universities rose everywhere, and artists and musicians were busy delivering the many works commissioned by their employers. This intense artistic activity was, of course, a logical means of glorifying ruler and state, for the poet's and artist's achievements enhanced the reputation of the state and the dignity of the ruler. The universities, neglected in the previous century, received ample support and showed immense activity in academic studies. Scientific and artistic academies, created in every residential city, were responsible for the unprecedented productivity in arts and letters. Many of these institutions, such as the Bavarian Academy and the Prussian Academy, have remained bodies of the highest cultural importance to our day.

Brilliant as all this cultural life was, it represented only a fancy of the king. The idea of human dignity never entered Frederick's mind, and once a passing interest was satisfied the greatest scholar or artist of the century became a mere court attendant. We must not lose sight of the fact that enlightened absolutism wanted enlightenment but not liberty. The whole period was a courtly era, a continuation of the absolutism of the Louis XIV era, and the fame and renown of the ruling house took precedence over all other considerations. If we lift the veil from this brilliant intellectual life and peer behind it, we find that whenever we reach a social situation having no immediate bearing on dynastic interests benevolent despotism was not successful, for secondary and popular education did not keep pace with the wonders achieved by the universities and academies. It was only Joseph II who in his sincere idealism actually endeavored to further popular education.

The Ideals of the Enlightenment and Their Effect on Literature

THE ethical ideals of the Enlightenment crystallized in Lessing's *Nathan the Wise,* a poetic plea for toleration of religious creeds and for judging men for their virtues, not their sect. The play also demonstrated that the Enlightenment had turned its attention to the middle classes and their problems. Henceforth not only in the drama but in other branches of literature and art the bourgeois was to occupy the focal point. The origins of this tendency are to be found, naturally, in England, where in George Lillo's *London Merchant* (1730) and in Samuel Richardson's *Pamela* (1740) were created the first bourgeois drama and the first bourgeois novel, filled with the pride of the newly won social importance of the British middle classes, and at the same time expounding the ethics of the Enlightenment. The reawakening of the middle classes which we noticed at the beginning of the century grows as we advance with the times. The German merchants began to assert themselves not only at home but, through business representatives, in foreign countries. The Central European cities still had their walls and towers, retaining the medieval aspects of urban life, but within a generation this exterior underwent great changes. With the new cities grew the urban **middle** classes, hard-working and industrious, expressing their importance and self-sufficiency in the establishment of their homes. Many family houses, large and small, were built, with comfortable quarters and large parlors. The day's business finished, these merchants and manufacturers turned their attention to different things. They read a great deal, played or sang music, and became interested in pastimes, such as collecting books or antiques, formerly regarded as becoming only to noblemen.

The first consequence of the bourgeois intrusion upon and subsequent domination of arts and letters was a natural reaction against the expansive gestures and the pomp and refinement of a courtly art. The great heroes and frivolous courtiers were out of place in a serious middle-class atmosphere. But though the emphasis on moral fortitude, the opposition to aristocratic prodigality, and the preference for simplicity and economy remained characteristic of the artistic thought of the Enlightenment, the rococo exerted an irresistible attraction for the bourgeoisie, and their intellectual life began to appropriate some of the culture of the aristocracy. This was inevitable, for not since the heroic age of Christendom had nations been tied to each other in a spiritual International such as that of the rococo, impressing on the eighteenth century that international stamp which is so characteristic of its culture. The nobility was still the leader of civilization, but its prerogatives were vanishing in the very measure in which the middle classes became more articulate and wealthier. Rapidly losing the means to sustain the grandeur and lavishness which was once the lifeblood of its existence, the aristocracy no longer looked askance upon the intellectual achievements of the citizenry, although it continued to treat artists as lackeys.

The Germans struggled hard to find their way in this international world, but they could not easily throw off the overwhelming French influence. They tried to create an equivalent to the French *esprit,* but their *Witz* did not come off in German. Exhausted by the great creative era of the baroque, they attempted to regain their productivity by sheer common sense and reason, principles of the French Enlightenment. The creative individual of the Enlightenment was an artisan of a higher order, teaching and entertaining under the constant surveillance of sober reason. The most worthy subject of his art was man, who represented, in his own eyes, the whole of reality. He imitated nature, but his imitation was stylized by reason; he could give scope to his imagination, but he must be prepared to justify every step before the tribunal of reason. The result was comprehensive order, well-proportioned form, controllable content, and an ethico-practical point of view. Within this general picture the German Enlightenment deserves a special place because of its role as mediator between rationalism and Christianity, between a mechanistic explanation of nature and faith, arriving at a synthesis of the two chief European schools of thought, the deductive French thought and the sensualistic-empiric English thought. These two schools opposed and balanced each other; the former was stronger in the first half of the eighteenth century, while the latter was more preponderant in the second.

The men of letters of the transition period continued their optimistic conquest of reality but were not able, for a considerable time, to cast off their baroque heritage. At about this time the moralizing periodicals of Addison, Steele, and other English literary men began to assert their influence on German thought. Their ethically conditioned aesthetics, didactic purpose, and critical attitude toward society found ready acceptance among their German colleagues. The French, being primarily intellectual by nature, were able to utilize the materialism and rationalism coming to them from England, even though this materialism was fundamentally hostile to art, for they could always retire into form, in itself an intellectual element. "Le style c'est l'homme même," said Buffon, but the Germans took all their moral lecturing in deadly earnest. In the absence of true creative spirit, rationalism in Germany limited itself to organization and systematization.

The man who personified the forlorn period following the disintegration of the baroque world of form and expression was Johann Christoph Gottsched (1700–1766). Neither a poet nor an artist, he dedicated his life to the establishment of rational order in all fields of literature, which, for want of a center, control, and authority, had become the prey of arbitrariness and bad taste. In the defense of his ideals Gottsched knew no mercy. With a blind and narrow doggedness he attacked every irrational power, banished it from his own world, and even denied its existence. His literary lawbooks extinguished every trace of the baroque, wiping out imagination and fancy. On the other hand, with his periodicals and ably organized collaborators he succeeded in eliminating the anarchy besetting all branches of literature, especially the theater. By creating "order" on the stage with plays written according to the "rules" he improved literary taste, and his regulation of the language completed his reforms.

But the mechanistic order so created was condemned to collapse the very moment a single monad refused obedience. The decisive attack against Gottsched's law and order came from the German-Swiss men of letters Johann Jacob Bodmer (1698–1783) and Johann Jacob Breitinger (1701–1776). These two men, whose influence upon German thought was considerable, stood as firmly on the principles of rationalism as did their literary opponent, but they were willing to make concessions to irrational powers. The great controversy over the rights of imagination lasted for a generation and ended with Gottsched's downfall and desertion by his followers. No one among the dissidents, with the possible exception of Johann Elias Schlegel (1719–1749), was a real poet, and the most celebrated figure of the times, a literary man enjoying unprecedented reputation, was the Leipzig professor of philosophy, literature, and ethics, Christian Fürchtegott Gellert (1715–1769). The Leipzig poet-savant exerted his enormous influence not only through his works, perfect embodiments of the morals of enlightened mediocrity, but by his whole personality, a pale, somewhat blurred and anemic, but absolutely pure morality which emanates even from his most pedantic works.

With the resurgence of French influence, the spirit of the rococo, especially as manifested in painting and music, took over the leadership. German woods and meadows became populous with the figures of Greek mythology, with the shepherds and shepherdesses that had appeared earlier in French art. The fanciful, stylized, unreal world of the style galant—idyllic, colorful, tedious—supplied the atmosphere of this social art, behind which hid the ironic smile of reason, but the German poets were more sentimental and heavy-footed than their models. Johann Peter Uz (1720–1796) came nearest to French gracefulness, while Johann Georg Jacobi (1740–1814) was more musical and, strongly under the influence of Shaftesbury, gave his rococo world an ethic connotation that has a certain vigor. Johann Wilhelm Ludwig Gleim (1719–1803) was perhaps the most learned of the Anacreontic poets, although nothing was further removed from the genius of antiquity than his playful verse filled with Horatian turns. Christian Ewald von Kleist (1715–1759) was the most virile of these poets, probably because his literary ancestors were English rather than French; the delicate accents with which he sang of nature betray James Thomson. But the German poet whose pictorial musical world, with its dreamy, autumnal atmosphere, was as characteristic of the German *Empfindsamkeit* as was Boucher of the French rococo, was Salomon Gessner (1730–1788), who attained worldwide fame with his poems, and in particular with his idyllic prose pastorals (*Idyllen,* 1756). His choice of the ancient form of pastoral poetry was dictated by his artistic orientation, but his antique form was a mask, his world an intellectual-sentimental dream, his nature not a plastic vision but the timeless Arcady of morbid beauties. It was not homesickness which led him to Hellas, but vogue; it was not the refreshing breeze of antiquity which rustled the foliage of the trees of his nature, but that of German sentimentality; and his whole world was immersed in the gilded haze of the rococo, pictorial and musical.

There was, however, another strain in German thought which, coming from Protestant-Pietistic sources and leaning heavily on English poetry and philosophy, was less ephemeral and more serious. Its beginnings were modest —in Jacob Immanuel Pyra (1715–1744), a rather dry imitator of Pope. But the musical quality we have observed in the German *Empfindsamkeit,* coupled with the greatly admired nocturnal sentimentalism of Edward Young (1683–1765), soon produced a man whose work is like a watershed between rationalism and irrationalism. Friedrich Gottlieb Klopstock (1724–1803) restored to German poetry its wings; after a long absence elemental pathos, baroque ecstasy, and cosmic perspective again emanated from German art. Poetic language had suffered greatly under the onslaught of rationalism, and it was language which first felt the regenerating force of the true poet. Klopstock gave it new blood to replenish its desiccated arteries, and poetry once more found the accents of intimate devotion and flaming passion. Klopstock's chief work was the epic, *The Messiah,* begun in his student days and finished a quarter of a century later. The mystery of Christian redemption, repeatedly taken up by the baroque drama, by the Milton cult, and by the German Passion, was here presented in a new form which created a nation-wide literary sensation. But was this form really new? We now see the *Messiah* as the last gigantic projection of the baroque, in which Klopstock meets the challenge of rationalism with an irrational, antidramatic, musical language. This was the battle of the liberated forces of feeling against rationalism, a battle which, for the time being, gained no decisive victory, for not in literature but in music, the most irrational of arts, was this victory to be won.

Music and the Enlightenment—The Berlin School

KLOPSTOCK'S greatest and most influential achievement was the transplanting into secular letters of the transcendental feelings he found in religious poetry, giving his love lyricism a tender and spiritual tone such as was unknown in his times. This he achieved with the pronouncedly musical quality of his verse, and the same musical quality enabled him to overcome the difficulties experienced by his compatriots when employing antique verse forms. The music emanating from Klopstock's lyricism is still the sonorous music of the baroque and testifies to the deeply ingrained feeling of the Germans for music—the only art in which for the last few generations their creative power had soared into the highest regions.

Latent musical feeling was present, then, in literature, but German music itself, also rallying under the banner of "simplicity" or "return to nature," was less successful in reconciling the massive bulk, heroic tone and proportions, and deep mysticism of its baroque heritage with the aesthetics of the Enlightenment and rationalism. The style galant, the beginning of which we noticed in the first half of the century, was henceforth to dominate the whole of the central and northern part of Germany. Bach's successors at the Thomasschule, Gottlob Harrer (cantor 1750–1755) and Johann Friedrich Doles (cantor 1756–1789), broke the distinguished line of musicians of genius; the great Saxon-Thuringian musical culture which had given Germany so many masters became extinct. The new compositions showed an unbelievably rapid change from the monumental polyphonic style to a simple, uninspired, cerebral music, and the old compositions were discarded and forgotten. Kretzschmar has reported that the catalogue of the library at Cöthen revealed that four years after Bach's death his works (as well as those of his noted contemporaries, Handel, Telemann, Graupner, and the great Italians) had disappeared from the very place where one would expect his activity to have left indelible marks. No other period was ever so possessed by a fanatic interest in the new as the second half of the eighteenth century, and none has proceeded to achieve its aims in a more radical and ruthless manner. As Doles, pupil of Johann Sebastian Bach, declared the fugue to be an antiquated form of scholastic exercise, the miniature art and interior decoration of the rococo, the *sensibilité* of the French, became the *Empfindsamkeit* of the Germans.

But the *sensibilité* as understood by the French contained a goodly amount of etiquette, formality, and restraint, which disciplined their art, preventing it from becoming diluted and unduly "responsive," whereas the incorrigible sentimentality of the Germanic soul broke into tears at the slightest provocation. Where the French created a style, delicate and frothy, but with a fine net of judiciously designed lines, the Germans wanted "mood," "atmosphere," and "feeling." The interior art of the French rococo was still too external and too public to suit German taste, and they endeavored to reduce both volume and sonority in order to attain the "intimacy of a confessional box." Nothing illustrates this better than the exchange of the silvery sonority of the clavecin for the ethereal tinkling of the clavichord, inaudible in the opposite corner of a small room.

The clearly defined artistic aims of the German Enlightenment, its well-planned activity, had as a result the winning of the populace to art. At the same time, it created a new art, seemingly popular. Even the higher society, immersed in the spirit of French and Italian arts and letters, could not escape the influence of the new music which sought to beautify the everyday life from which it grew. The realization that there is no gap between art and the people could be arrived at only through literature, for reinvigorated poetry unfailingly engenders music, which seems to wait for the poet's initiative. This fact was well exemplified in the unimportant but productive and contagious "atmospheric" poetry of Pietism, with its wealth of musical settings and song collections. But rationalism gradually undermined religious faith and the unshakable belief in eternal righteousness. From the second third of the eighteenth century religious lyricism declined steadily, to rise once more, and then feebly, in the spiritual songs of Gellert.

People were aware of the lack of a serious lyricism in their time, hence their great enthusiasm for Johann Christian Günther (1695–1723), the one great lyric talent of late baroque Germany. Sensing that the traditions of the artistic era which had produced him were about to be abandoned, Günther wasted a short and feverish life in quest of a remedy. The warm breath of life is present in almost all of his poems, yet there is scarcely one that satisfies completely. In his heroic odes he made concessions to baroque conventions, but in his love songs he cast aside all decorum and caution, plunging into flaming passions. Music could not immediately follow his initiative, but thirteen years after his death there appeared a collection of songs with which the new era of lyricism began. A group of Günther's friends caused the publication in 1736 of a collection entitled *Singende Muse an der Pleisse*.[16] Philipp Spitta, the well-known biographer of Bach, has proved that "Sperontes," the pseudonym used by the editor of the collection, stood for Johann Sigismund Scholze (1705–1750), a minor lawyer in Leipzig whose interest in music was manifestly greater than his talents. Sperontes broke the spell that hung over German song, but the music of the *Singende Muse* could not rise to the poet's level for it was culled from clavier pieces which were adapted for vocal use, a fundamentally unvocal method. From the musical point of view these compositions are therefore of slight intrinsic value. Yet their historical importance is considerable, despite their shortcomings, for they initiated a series of collections which set a high level for the German song. The first of these was *Sammlung verschiedener und auserlesener Oden* (Halle, 1737–1743), edited by Johann Friedrich Gräfe (1711–1787), likewise an amateur; it included settings by Carl Philipp Emanuel Bach, Carl Heinrich Graun, and Konrad Friedrich Hurlebusch (1696–1765), the latter one of the most gifted song composers of the time. Other anthologies followed, notably the third part of *Neue Oden und Lieder* (1752) with poems by Hagedorn and music by Johann Valentin Görner (1702–1762).

The stylistic requirements established theoretically by the rationalistic school of thought demanded simplicity and prohibited the musician from interfering with the poet. Thus even such imaginative musicians as Telemann were satisfied with setting odes to music, which were performed in a clipped, dry manner. With the improvement of the poets, the musicians themselves improved. Gellert inspired Johann Ernst Bach (1722–1777) to write several fine songs. It is hard for the modern reader to consider Gellert a poet of vibrant feeling, but Bach's *Sammlung auserlesner Fabeln mit dazu verfertigten Melodeyen* (1749)[17] discloses in Gellert's fables a certain poetic conception of nature which excited the composer's imagination, accustomed to abstract and stylized nature poetry. The length of these poems, with their changing moods, demanded a new musical treatment utilizing new material; by following these changing moods in his music Johann Ernst Bach became one of the first practitioners of the modern musical ballad. Valentin Herbing (1735–1766) was the next to bring out a volume of musical settings of texts "by Herr Professor Gellert" (1759).[18] This gifted young composer, who died at so early an age, was especially sensitive to the dramatic content of the poems, and only their weakness prevents his songs from striking us as still impressive. As Friedrich Wilhelm Marpurg, one of the ablest of contemporary musical writers, remarked, Gellert's fables "present objects too small for the art of music." This branch of song literature therefore rapidly wilted. And the public, which turned away from the musical settings of Gellert, remained faithful to the type of French dance songs or couplets which Sperontes had offered in his anthologies. These songs, with their strophic construction, were simple to learn, and the ease with which they lent themselves to instrumental rendition corresponds admirably to German tastes of the time of the *Empfindsamkeit*.

History teaches us that such popular preferences have deep-seated reasons, and if national taste cannot find the medium it desires in its own art it will turn to foreign sources and adapt them to its own usage. The so-called Berlin school fulfilled the role of agent in this case, and once more it was Frederick who, directly or indirectly, caused a new chapter to open in German culture. The whole atmosphere of the Berlin-Potsdam intellectual life favored the creation of such a school. The excellent musical establishments were dominated by a penchant for theorizing, which seems natural in a circle devoted to the rationalistic ideals of the Enlightenment. The king's political aims were pronounced in all matters, including music, and these aims, shared by the Berlin school, did not call for great and entirely original creative geniuses, but for the advantageous employment of useful talents.

The very first publication of the group demonstrates the orientation of the school. Entitled *Odes with Melodies* (1753), and containing songs by Quantz, Carl Philipp Emanuel Bach, Graun, and others, the volume named neither the poets nor the composers but only the two compilers, the poet Ramler and the musician Krause. The motive power behind the activities of the Berlin school was Christian Gottfried Krause (1712–1770), a musical amateur who reminds one of Rist, for his chief aim was likewise education through music. Unlike his Hamburg predecessor, Krause was not interested in the sacred-spiritual; he devoted himself entirely to the secular-popular song. The activity of the first group of the Berlin school was vivid: the decade which started with the first anthology saw the appearance of some fifty collections, accompanied by extended theoretical discussions in the musical journals. But the sober, cool, calculating, and theorizing attitude of these erudite popularizers killed artistic imagination. The arbitrarily set tone of the Berlin school precluded any natural development, and the musicians were entirely unprepared to keep pace with the mighty resurgence of German lyric poetry which began in the latter part of the century, even though individual composers rose to the occasion. Gluck's setting of Klopstock's *Odes* (1780) is one of the exceptional instances of song composition of a high order. While the

poets—Klopstock, Wieland, Voss, and Goethe—acclaimed Gluck's essay at
song writing, the musicians remained indifferent. Then the healthy world
of the lyric stage came to the rescue, again proving that ever since Monteverdi opera has been the most resourceful and original field of music, from
which all other varieties have drawn their nourishment. The stage could not
endure the imaginary and lifeless creatures of the Berlin songs, and the
lively figures of the German Singspiel could not thrive on the Hagedorn
type of witticism. Life demanded its rights in these plays; everyone had to
sing in a manner fitting to him. This suddenly brought home to people
what popular art really meant, minus dead theories, and an avalanche of
publications followed—songs for every age and walk of life.

As we approach the great problem of the song we shall realize the magnitude of the contribution to the cultural and spiritual life of the nation of
that composer who can render a fine piece of poetry into music with relative simplicity, yet retain and absorb its emotional content, for only if this
be done can we speak of a truly national-popular art. The Berlin school
realized the problem, theoretically, but their oversimplified compositions
were failures, for the poetry was too shallow and the music cold and artificial.
The composer who answered the historic calling, and who mediated between the earlier and the later phases of the Berlin school, was Johann Abraham Peter Schulz (1747-1800). The man in whose songs—especially in the
collection entitled *Lieder im Volkston* (1782)—the spirit of popular national
lyricism gained shape with almost Schubertian tenderness, and whose songs
will remain models of a true and noble popular art, was not a simple, home-
spun musician of the people—the Enlightenment did not produce artists of
that type. A highly successful composer of operas, Singspiele, incidental
music to plays, and of melodramas, Schulz was rated Haydn's equal, and as
a writer on musical subjects he disclosed a wide and penetrating acquaintance with the theoretical and aesthetic problems of his art. His essay,
Thoughts Concerning the Influence of Music Upon the Culture of a Nation
(1790)—a work not yet sufficiently examined by historians of art and civilization—indicates the composer's awareness of the great cultural importance
of popular lyricism. This awareness is copiously evident in his musical settings, which opened the windows on the parlor lyricism of the odes, avoiding
all extraneous effect, and succeeding, with their simple and sensitive melodies, in carrying lyric poetry and music into the consciousness of the people.[19] Johann Friedrich Reichardt (1752-1814) and Johann André (1741-
1799), both friends of Goethe, and well acquainted with German literary
thought, though better known as composers for the lyric stage, were the other
notable exponents of the new German song. Reichardt, one of the best-trained
musicians and littérateurs of the times, enriched the new song in every direction. His harmonies were varied and his forms supple but most of all he

made great strides in providing the melodies with a well-co-ordinated and artistic instrumental accompaniment.

It is amazing that the almost simultaneous activity of these three eminent song composers did not change the tone of the Berlin school. The reason lies in the last stand of the partisans of uncompromising rationalism, led by Christoph Friedrich Nicolai (1733–1811), whose *Feyner Kleyner Almanach vol schönerr echterr liblicherr Volckslieder* (1777) was intended to annihilate the new movement toward folk music and poetry advocated by Herder and his followers. Although originally a brother-in-arms of Lessing, Nicolai became a sworn enemy of the new literary and artistic currents, the embodiment of the small bourgeois philosophy abhorring every lofty flight of thought. But nothing could retard the progress of German lyricism, and the second Berlin school, so auspiciously inaugurated by Schulz and Reichardt, ended by producing two significant composers, Friedrich Ludwig Aemilius Kunzen (1761–1817) and Carl Friedrich Zelter (1758–1832). Zelter's chief work, *Lieder, Balladen, und Romanzen,* appeared in 1810, but in spirit and style he was a man of the eighteenth century, and a member of the Berlin group. Many of the songs of the second Berlin school became folk songs in the best sense of the word, sung and revered over all German lands.

Opera and Singspiel

GOTTSCHED'S endeavors to create German national drama did not pass unnoticed by German musicians, but the path of national opera was barred by the Goliath of the lyric stage, Italian opera. The most celebrated German opera composers of the immediate past, such as Hasse and Graun, were completely Italianized, and the few places where a distinctly German orientation prevailed—Hamburg, Bayreuth, Nuremberg, Weissenfels—could not ward off the Italian conquest. Nor could the new theater very well establish connections with the older native opera, because the tone and methods of the latter became obsolete in the era of the Enlightenment. Therefore reform ideas, such as those we usually associate with Gluck, were rife even before the collapse of the baroque opera. "In my opinion," wrote Mattheson, "a good opera theater is nothing but an academy of many fine arts, where architecture, painting, the dance, poetry . . . and above all music should unite to bring about a work of art." This is the first literary record of the Wagnerian *Gesamtkunstwerk*. Mattheson's thoughts were seconded by a number of other writers. There was an unmistakable French influence in the German authors' insistence on simplicity, avoidance of intrigues in the plot, preference for sentiments rather than for passions, observance of nature and reason, and their neohumanistic interest in antiquity. These authors were no less convinced than Gluck that the reforms should start with the literary part of opera, an idea advocated especially by Herder. The new German opera appeared, then, when the composer Anton Schweitzer (1753–1787) allied himself with the greatest poet of the *Empfindsamkeit,* Christoph Martin Wieland. Performed in 1773 in Weimar, their *Alceste,* the first German five-act opera, sung from beginning to end, seemed to be the answer to the fervent hopes for a "great" German national opera, comparable to the opera seria and the tragédie lyrique. The avoidance of castrato roles and of coloratura singing indicates a conscious departure from the Italian music drama; but in the expressive and dramatic recitatives, and in their vehement orchestral accompaniments, the remnants of the heroic baroque opera are present with undiminished vigor. The elaborate orchestration is characteristically German, as is also the occasional clumsiness in the vocal writing. A second notable German opera was produced in Mannheim in 1777: *Günther von Schwarzburg,* libretto by Anton Klein and music by Ignaz Holzbauer (1711–1783). This was another work which professed to ignore certain clichés and patterns only too well known in Italian opera.[20] But while these works breathe a genuinely national spirit—as a matter of fact, they were veritable advance guards of German romanticism—the hold of Italian and French opera was too strong to be overcome within so short a space of time. The technique of this new German opera is obviously a compromise between several styles, although its general disposition differs markedly from both the opera seria and the tragédie lyrique. With the few works of Schweitzer and Holzbauer—we shall meet these excellent composers in other capacities —the new German "grand" opera reached the end of its rope.

We have followed the varied fortunes of the opera and found that it inevitably wound up in an impasse as soon as it ceased to be Italian opera, or opera practiced along Italian lines. We have seen how Addison denounced the validity of the recitative and the Italian principle of continuous musical setting (the so-called through-composed manner) as applied to the English lyric stage, and we have noticed how Rousseau advocated the abolition of the through-composed music drama in favor of a lyric play with music. Now it was Germany's turn to come to the realization that opera is an Italian form which does not necessarily suit the genius of other nations. The arguments advanced by German authors were pertinent and lucid. They rejected the da capo aria and the uninterrupted musical setting in terms that betray a knowledge of the specific operatic criticism that started with Saint-Evremond. They wanted, instead, to reserve the use of music for the high points in the play, restoring the spoken dialogue for the animated exchange of ideas. The opposition to the Italian opera seria was greatly strengthened when these ideas became current, for the natural disinclination of the German middle classes toward a foreign courtly art in a foreign language now turned against the music itself. England found her typical musical theater in the masques and in the ballad opera, both developed before Addison voiced his disapproval of opera. France produced the opéra comique, the first essays of which antedate Rousseau's *Devin du Village*. And now Germany came to the fore with a form of national lyric theater, the *Singspiel*, which had been brewing before the experiments looking toward the creation of through-composed German opera had ended in a fiasco.

Although prepared for by earlier German works written for the lyric stage, and especially by the improvised school comedy, the first German Singspiel was entirely an imitation of English models. *The Devil to Pay; or the Wives Metamorphos'd,* first performed at Drury Lane in 1731, was the most successful ballad farce by Charles Coffey, a popular Irish author of ballad operas whose life and career are almost totally unknown. Reduced to a one-act play, this ballad opera became the most popular entertainment of its kind. The Prussian ambassador to London, von Brock, a gentleman who had proved his literary interests by making the first German translation of Shakespeare's *Julius Caesar,* translated the play into German, and it was performed as *Der Teufel ist Los!* in 1743 in Berlin. While this cannot be ascertained, it is most probable that the original English tunes were used in the German performances, which, although roundly denounced by Gottsched, were as successful as in England, inviting numerous imitations. Among the latter, and of great interest in the development of the German lyric stage, was a version made by Christian Felix Weisse (1726–1804), a well-known poet and juvenile author. This time the composition of the musical numbers was entrusted to a German musician by the name of J. S. Standfuss, fiddler and vocal coach of the Koch troupe, which performed the play in 1752. Nothing is known of Standfuss beyond his name, but his music discloses a composer of originality, with a thorough knowledge of the art of the theater, and with an especially felicitous sense of humor.

In the meantime the great wave of enthusiasm created by Rousseau's *Devin du Village* attracted the Germans' attention. Weisse, on a visit to Paris in 1759, saw a number of French lyric plays composed on the pattern inaugurated by Rousseau, and discovered among these an old acquaintance, *Le Diable à Quatre,* which was none other than a French version of Coffey's *The Devil to Pay*. Weisse retranslated *Le Diable à Quatre,* adding to the eighteen songs of the French version nineteen more, and the whole was set to music by Johann Adam Hiller (1728–1804). The work had such a signal success at its performance in 1766 in the new Leipzig theater that Hiller continued his efforts in this direction. The same year saw the première of his *Lisuart und Dariolette,* the text of which was taken from Favart's *Fée Urgèle,* originally written for Duni. The good schooling and wide reading of Hiller must have triumphed over his original intentions, for the new work turned out to be a full-fledged opera with secco recitatives, da capo arias, and a three-movement symphony. The most astonishing thing about it was its title, for to call a German lyric work in 1766 a "romantic opera" is truly bewildering to the student of theatrical history. But the reaction of the public was not favorable, and the management forced Hiller to return to the erstwhile style of the Singspiel. A year later, in *Lottchen am Hofe* (Favart's *Ninette à la Cour*) and in *Liebe auf dem Lande* (from Favart's *Annette et Lubin*), the Italian operatic elements were greatly restricted in favor of the French type of lyric play; at the same time the English was exchanged for French tutelage. But the genius of Hiller did not rest here, and in his *Die Jagd* (1770, from Sedaine's *Le Roi Fermier*) the foreign musical elements were cast away and the German Singspiel is before us in its refreshing popular guise.

Weisse and Hiller became so popular that they could scarcely satisfy the demand for new works. The librettist was not a great poet, but he was clever enough to make good use of the French originals. The musician, however, can rightly be considered the German counterpart of Monsigny. Hiller's task was not easy. He had to write vocal parts for actors who were not primarily singers, a fact which restricted his field of action; but, excellent pedagogue and true connoisseur of the people that he was, he turned the shortcomings into virtues. The many songs, written in a simple style and making no demands on vocal acrobatics, became real folk songs, not only sung all over Germany but well received in foreign countries. The public was delighted with the change from breath-taking coloratura singing in Italian to amusing texts in German, with melodies they remembered long after the performance was over. Popular approval was as natural and as outspoken as in England, but the German Singspiel far outstripped the English ballad opera, both in quality and in quantity.

Among the more notable composers who followed in Hiller's footsteps were Johann André, the song writer of the Berlin school; Christian Gottlob Neefe (1748–1798), Beethoven's early teacher, a versatile and talented composer; Anton Schweitzer, who, having abandoned his experiments with the German "serious opera," became one of the best Singspiel composers; and Georg Benda (1721–1795), perhaps the most important operatic composer between Hiller and Mozart. The new German lyric theater was materially aided by Goethe, who not only expressed sympathy for the Singspiel but wrote a number of libretti himself.

The youthful Goethe was so deeply impressed with the novel combination of spoken words with orchestral accompaniment in a play with music which he attended that he called it "epoch-making." The work, entitled *Pygmalion*, was a melodrama on Rousseau's well-known text, with music by Anton Schweitzer. The performance took place in Weimar in 1772, while another *Pygmalion* was performed in the same year in Vienna with music by Franz

Asplmayr (1721-1786). Rousseau's libretto was circulating in a German translation before that date, so it is understandable that several composers used it almost simultaneously. Since both the above scores are lost, it is difficult for us to form an idea of the nature of these melodramas. According to Rousseau's conception, words and music in the melodrama "should never go together, but should be heard successively so that the spoken words be announced or prepared for by the music." This is an important statement, because it discloses that Rousseau's idea of a melodrama differed markedly from the works it engendered. The French philosopher—not yet convinced by Gluck that the French language is appropriate for musical setting—wanted, in reality, to create a form of the lyric theater which would bear out his contentions concerning the unsuitability of the French language for operatic purposes. This he expressed clearly when he maintained that "this genre would be an intermediary species between simple declamation and the true music drama."

The initiative thus came from France, but when the development of the melodrama came under the influence of the German theater it took an entirely different turn. The German stage possessed a number of excellent actors even before German drama reached its classical greatness. The resounding success obtained by an actor named Böck in the role of Pygmalion so impressed another by the name of Brandes, active also as an author, that he attempted to write an equally grateful role for his famous actress wife. Selecting the Ariadne legend for his subject, Brandes asked Schweitzer to set it to music; to this the composer of *Pygmalion* agreed, but when the score was almost completed he used it for his own opera *Alceste*. But Georg Benda was so pleased with Brandes's libretto that he composed the music, in "one sitting," and *Ariadne* was produced in Gotha on January 27, 1775, amidst a tumultuous ovation. Benda, who knew Rousseau's *Pygmalion,* did not share the Frenchman's aesthetic ideas, and created in Ariadne a vibrant drama. Whereas Rousseau wanted detached instrumental numbers to support the actors' pantomime, Benda often interrupted the speech by short interludes which did not necessarily accompany the pantomime but rather furnished a musical commentary to the words, and his short pregnant motives gather intensity to the degree in which the emotional quality of the words also grows. These motives undergo thematic developments and are not unlike the leitmotives of the nineteenth-century music drama.

It is no exaggeration to say that Benda's *Ariadne* was the first musico-dramatic work to secede completely from the old opera, for Gluck's reform operas were still purely vocal works retaining the great traditions of the opera. Spoken words and music were used by Benda simultaneously, not consecutively as in the French melodrama; he should therefore be considered the "inventor" of the melodrama as practiced in the nineteenth century.

This must have been the reason for the powerful impression the work made on Benda's contemporaries, among whom Mozart was the first to express unstinted admiration. Following up his success with *Ariadne,* Benda wrote *Medea,* intended for Mme. Brandes's rival, the celebrated actress Sophie Friedericke Seyler. The composer's great talents were even more evident in his later works, which point directly toward the German romantic opera.

The form and texture of these melodramas show a remarkable logic of construction. The changing verses called for similar changes in tonality and tempo, resulting in a long series of small instrumental sections which could have easily ended in unconnected fragments. Benda's dramatic élan and his use of characteristic themes which we may rightfully call leitmotives overcame this difficulty and created musical coherence. Besides remodeling the internal musical structure, Benda developed the dramatic expressiveness of the orchestra to a high degree, and used this flexible body to depict sentiments and feelings the intensity of which could not be adequately conveyed by mere words. The great success of the melodrama caused a mass production which in turn brought about a strong reaction within a decade. Both composers and poets ceased cultivating it, Herder, Wieland, and Schiller declaring the genre unworthy of real artists. But the Sage of Weimar realized the import of Benda's work and collaborated in 1814 with Max Eberwein on a melodrama—*Proserpina*—originally written for Gluck in 1777. "Melodramatic treatment will have to be dissolved in song," said Goethe; "only then will it satisfy entirely."

We should now pause to consider these works and these statements, for their portent is incalculable. On the one hand we notice that the instincts of the German composer for symphonic-thematic work drove him to a treatment which, while very dramatic in mood, had little to do with the lyricism of the human voice, the essence of opera. On the other hand we see the demand made by Goethe for the abolition of what he, as have so many modern critics, considered a hybrid form, speech and music, and its replacement by singing. There was, then, an operatic, musico-dramatic conception present in Germany in the eighteenth century—long before Wagner—which proceeded from poem to orchestra and from orchestra to the voice. This is the antithesis of the lyric drama, the opera, which, true to its own specific nature, originates in singing with the *collaboration* of the orchestra. But the seeds were sown; Benda had made the first momentous step toward the German music drama, and all that was now needed was to superimpose singing voices over the symphonic-dramatic orchestral fabric for the Wagnerian music drama to become a reality. We shall return to the ancestors of the German music drama when we reach its omnipotent "creator" in the nineteenth century.

Although the melodrama declined rapidly as an independent theatrical piece, it won great importance as an episode in play and opera. Two of Mozart's earlier stage works, *Zaide* and *Thamos,* used it effectively, and we shall see it employed with telling effect in Beethoven's *Fidelio,* whence it passed to such works as the *Midsummer Night's Dream* score of Mendelssohn and, finally, to the German romantic opera, one of the sources of Wagner's art.

The Relationship of Musical Theory and Practice

WHILE empiricism and rationalism were recasting knowledge by creating new scientific values, the voice of irrationalism, the protest of intuitively creating artists, was raised against the dogmatic and abstract-scientific attitude of theoreticians and philosophers of music, as had been the case in literature, but the advocates of a new orientation could not muster weapons so strong as those of their adversaries. Schooled in the sciences, the musical scholars of rationalism commanded a facility of logical argumentation which could not be combated by mere intuition. Still, the force of creative instinct was strong in the musicians, who felt that constant reflection would deprive them of the immediacy, the elementally musical in their nature.

Defections came, surprisingly early, even in the ranks of the worthies of the old guard. Mattheson came to the conclusion in his *Forschende Orchester* (1721) that music is an art perceived by the senses and thus, since it does not call on reason, belongs in the domain of feeling. But many of the great thinkers still clung to their conception of music as a science. Among others, the celebrated mathematician Leonhardt Euler (1707–1783) declared music to be a science whose task is to join different tones in such a manner as to create harmonies pleasurable to the ear.[21] Mattheson, however, considered music not a science of harmony and of measurements, but the artistic expression of sentiments, and added that "even instrumental music should never be lacking in emotion." [22] The fact that Mattheson still felt the necessity of qualifying his statement by saying that *even* instrumental music should not be lacking in emotions makes us realize that the German phase of the rococo, the *Empfindsamkeit,* experienced great difficulty in establishing a musical thought of its own. The rationalistic inclination of the men of the Enlightenment pressed for simplification—a tendency well represented in the Berlin school—but there was also an effort to maintain those elements of the baroque which were rationalistically useful. Literary activity in musical theory and aesthetics still consisted largely of essays on the affections, but the tenor of these essays often turned into dialectics and brilliant sophism, reflecting much more the philosophic-scientific inclination of the men of the rationalistic era than an organic continuation of what has been so aptly called "the nervous center" of the baroque. The leading authors, successors of Mattheson and Scheibe, were Carl Philipp Emanuel Bach, Johann Joachim

Quantz, and Friedrich Wilhelm Marpurg (1718–1795), the first two represented by their famous "Essays" on the "true art" of playing the clavier and
the flute, the third by his *Kritische Briefe über die Tonkunst* (1759–1763).

The last vestiges of the psychological doctrine of the affections remained to
the end of the century, at a time when the *style galant* and the *Empfindsamkeit* were being condensed in the classical style of the Viennese school. But
since the doctrine of the affections was the "nervous center" of the baroque,
it could not properly fulfill the same function in a style and conception of
music which was turning against the baroque; moreover, it had ceased to be
a method of aesthetics and a well-regulated science which could be taught
and applied in practice. Instead of seeking the tones and figures most appropriate for the expression of a certain situation, the musician-philosophers
now limited themselves to a psychological comprehension of the impression
made by the object upon the subject. Even this rationalistic-sensualistic theory was soon abandoned in favor of an expressive one; as scientific reflection
diminished, sentiment came to the fore. It was no longer feeling alone that
was demanded of composers; expression and expressiveness were their main
problem and occupied their chief attention.

Baroque mentality established an atmosphere universally shared and understood. The composer of the *Empfindsamkeit,* not supported by this common outlook, was compelled to seek personal outlets with personal expressions. The baroque addressed itself to an already established community of
spirit, whereas the personal expression of a later date had to seek by its own
power to weld the listeners into a community. Thus when Friedrich Nicolai
speaks of the Mannheim taste as "calculated on surprise," or when Reichardt
and Burney speak with wonderment of the famous *crescendo* of the Mannheim orchestra which so electrified the audience that people rose in their
seats, we are actually reaching the point at which the segregated single *affection* turns into *effect*. The affections are, then, still furnishing the motive
power; but the art of the *Empfindsamkeit,* the mincing of music into small
particles, changed the meaning and usefulness of the system. The rationalistic era was not satisfied with the abstract doctrine of the baroque; it broke
down the whole theory into well-defined, typical, single affections which
appear to us as the elements of a modern aesthetics of music. "Flattering,"
"sad," "delicate," "happy," "joyful," "fresh," "serious," "sublime," are some
of the *terminus technici* of the revised doctrine. Once this reduced and ra-
tionalized system was established, it was put into use according to the
prevailing art of the *Empfindsamkeit*. "The player should change—so to
speak—in every measure to a different affection, and should be able to appear alternately sad, joyous, serious, etc., such moods being of great importance in music." [23]

Two distinct tendencies now become apparent, one aiming to endow every small detail with life, expression, and a specific affection, and another which preferred to combine the new freedom and many-sidedness of expression with the steadiness and logic of the old style. In the latter part of the century the various tendencies engendered by the Enlightenment converged into balanced unity and produced, in the short generation of 1780 to 1810, a sublimely perfect musical culture.

The baroque score presented a relatively simple picture, as it seldom contained printed instructions. The performer did not concern himself with small details because his attention was riveted to the "basic affection" that gave the general tone to a composition, which he endeavored to maintain throughout the piece. The *Empfindsamkeit,* having departed from the baroque ideal of a single affection, was now concerned with tempo and dynamics, and with their modifications. A gigantic fugue by Bach might not contain a single word of advice, whereas in the latter part of the century we are told that "since nowadays the finest nuances are used in music and must be indicated in the score, the artistic and technical terms have grown to such numbers that the signs and indications will soon blanket the notes themselves." [24] In this connection it is of great importance to know that the tempo was determined largely by the graphic aspect of the notes: predominantly large note values indicated a slow movement, while a profusion of crotchets and other small notes called for a fast tempo. The inscription *adagio, allegro,* or *andante* designated the character of the piece to be played and aimed to help the performing artist place himself in the mood of the work. When Mattheson speaks of the emotional properties in a ciacona, corrente, gigue, allegro, and presto, it is evident that these terms—some of them mere tempo indications to us—had definite affective connotations to the eighteenth-century musician. The often startling misreading of eighteenth-century works by modern performers and conductors can be explained by comparison of contemporary interpretations of these inscriptions with those of our day. Georg Simon Löhlein (1727–1782), a musician widely known for his clavier and violin methods, advises that vivace and allegro signify a "moderate pleasure"; more abandoned joy is inscribed with allegro assai, allegro di molto, or presto, overwhelming joy with prestissimo, and "raging exuberance" with allegro furioso, while composure is indicated by andante, andantino, or larghetto, sorrow by mesto, adagio, largo, lento, or grave. [25] This is, then, still a form of the doctrine of the affections, for the inscriptions allude to the basic affection which dominates the whole movement, but the emphasis is now on expressiveness. The confusion for the modern performer, unfamiliar with the musical conceptions of the past, becomes serious when the graphic picture of the score and the affective allusion in the inscription do not correspond in the same sense—as, for instance, when he is confronted with a piece printed in small rhythmical values but inscribed adagio.

The use of such graphic inscriptions suggests the battle cry of rationalism, "truth of expression," and neither C. P. E. Bach nor Marpurg was chary in employing them; but again we must realize, when reading the passages that seem to call for descriptive or program music, that what the authors demanded was not the tonal "painting" of objects, observations, or processes, but the translation of sentiments and feelings, the affections. It was the musician, not the philosopher, in Marpurg who spoke when he declared that "the true and best rules are those which are dictated by taste and by the ear." [26] We must bear in mind that the most influential writer on aesthetics, Batteux, whose essay was well known and widely admired in Germany, did not speak of nature as an actual-perceptible phenomenon, but "as it might be." Therefore, although Batteux called music an "imitative" art, he did not mean actual, realistic imitation. There was a great deal of playful, descriptive music making, especially in the would-be-popular songs of the Berlin school, but the German goal was expressiveness, and not pictorial realism. Forkel stated this convincingly: "Every musical expression should be brought about by the inner force of art, by the élan of the ideas, and not by aping external graphic occurrences." [27] Marpurg scorned the pictorial-imitative quality of the music of certain song writers in the following words which remind us strangely of the practices of some of our own overzealous educational experts: "According to these musicians there are four requirements for a complete German song, 1/ text, 2/ music, 3/ a board upon which the story of the song can be painted, and 4/ a stick with which to point at the board while the song is being sung." [28]

The philosopher-composers were well aware of the shortcomings and dangers of the *Empfindsamkeit,* and as early a writer as Mattheson warned the musicians against excesses. The problem of expressiveness became more acute when it touched upon the question of performance and interpretation. C. P. E. Bach remarked that "players who do not attract the sensitive soul of the listener merely stun his intellect without satisfying him," adding that "moving performance calls for a good mind capable of subordinating itself to certain common-sense rules."

The magnitude of the departure from pure rationalism becomes apparent as soon as we consider the aesthetic appreciation of instrumental music. Rationalism found absolute music (pure instrumental music) lacking in meaning and consequently in content. To remedy this shortcoming, it attempted, as we have seen, to change the aesthetic criterion from formal beauty to truth of expression. At this point when the absolute musical elements were being subjected to a process of rationalization fraught with danger, opera came to the rescue, helping pure instrumental music to develop an idiom of its own, as eloquent and expressive as dramatic music itself. To the adherents of the old style of baroque pathos, uninterrupted motor force, and maintenance of a basic affection, the new varicolored operatic idiom coming from Italy seemed as unjustifiable as Stravinsky's new style seemed to the musicians of the early twentieth century, educated on the neatly articulated periods of four, eight, or sixteen measures of the romantic era. Objections persisted far into the high classical period. The Germans, accustomed to the doctrine of the affections, saw in Italian instrumental music, opera symphonies, and chamber music nothing more than pleasant-sounding, sensuous stimuli, lacking in definite expressive aims. The superiority of vocal music for affective communication seemed incontestable to them, although instrumental music was growing about them by leaps and bounds and was greatly appreciated by the public. If among the critics of Italian music one can find even Schulz and Reichardt, it is small wonder that a man such as Quantz, brought up in the well-regulated world of rationalism, could not be receptive to the new "irrational" Italian style. But while the supercilious Prussian court flutist could not find enough words of condemnation for the Italians, the profound changes that had taken place within the last few years are reflected even in his writings. So Quantz recommends the use of dynamic shadings from triple piano (*ppp*) to triple forte (*fff*), explaining that if the playing were held in the sharp alternation of forte and piano (the very principles of baroque terrace dynamics) all the intermediary nuances would be lost. Coming only two years after the death of Johann Sebastian Bach, this statement is no less than astonishing. When we reach the seventeen seventies. the Abbé Vogler (1749–1814), one of the most original minds of the century, and Carl Ludwig Junker (c. 1740–1797), clergyman and musician, author of many books affording valuable source material on this period, state that people were already accustomed to variety both in the music and in its orchestration and that the public did not like a work without the solo participation of all kinds of wind instruments.[29] Schulz, the great song composer, also capitulated, declaring that the new symphony was particularly adaptable to the expression of great, festive, and sublime ideas, and that it embodied the final aspirations of pure instrumental music.[30] Thus, at the beginning of the last third of the century, and before the start of the great classical school, the symphony was recognized as the highest form of instrumental music.

Both praise and condemnation of the new instrumental form seem to have centered about a certain dualism which is noticeable in the style, a dualism of mood and of musical material. Hiller, writing about the "new symphonies," was of the opinion that "it is true that one can find some well written, beautiful and effective movements among them . . . but the strange mixture of the serious and the comical, the sublime and the lowly, which so frequently is blended in the same movement, often creates a bad effect." [31] De Brosses enthusiastically reported "the art of nuances and of *clair-obscur* as practiced by the Italians in 1740 either in rapid succession or by imperceptible degrees. These are reflections, demi-tints, which produce an incredible charm in the coloring of the sounds." [32]

Having lost its connections with the baroque, the *Empfindsamkeit* experimented in two directions to attain coherence and continuity. We have observed its effort to endow every little detail in the music with feeling by rationalizing the affections, but we have also noted that there was another tendency which aimed at a higher order of architecture. As the melodic continuity of baroque music, carried by the impetus of its own motive power, began to lose its generating force, breaking up into separate parts, the situation called for a new aesthetic-formal principle to safeguard unity. Thematic and tonal tension and relaxation became the synthetic elements of form, and the sustained dynamics of the baroque had to yield to a system more appropriate to the structural peculiarities of the new style. The basic affection, the homogeneous, overwhelming spiritual motive of baroque construction, thus disappeared under the pressure of the Enlightenment and *Empfindsamkeit,* and its place was taken by a dualistic principle based on contrasting and heterogeneous materials. It no longer sufficed, as it had in the baroque style, to have a pregnant beginning to set in motion the flow of *melos,* carried inevitably toward its destination by the dynamic current, for the rhythmic and dynamic chains of motives, all subordinated to this general flow, contradicted the sense of the *Empfindsamkeit,* intent on differentiating between components. The new dualistic form rested on the contrasting properties of the two polar points of tonality, the tonic or keynote, and the dominant, the fifth degree of the scale. This polarity, emphasized by the contrasting qualities of themes associated with the tonic and the dominant, created the states of tension and of relaxation which were to become as characteristic of the music of the classical era as the uninterrupted flow of *melos* was of the baroque. The new musical idiom with its many nuances required a new instrumental style, for the presentation of the new type of thematic material and the contrasts inherent in the style could not be accomplished with the objective orchestral technique of the baroque.

Thus we have arrived at one of the greatest stylistic watersheds in musical history. The baroque obtained unity and totality of form by a discursive broadening and a motor continuity which excluded the formation of independent sections. Classicism obtained its unity by organizing parts and sections into a closed form. But the spontaneous, effortless unfolding of baroque music is so natural and self-evident that it dispenses with what our textbooks call form—that is, a graphic, inanimate design, meaningless in its abstraction. With the passing of the baroque a form had to be found, for the natural motive power which created form by merely preventing any slackening in the ever-expanding fabric of music was gone. The history of the great Viennese school is the history of a long struggle for form—for the sonata form. The struggle, starting in the seventeen twenties in Italy, passing through the remarkable if unexplored schools of the preclassical period, never relaxing, reached its most dramatic, most overpowering intensity in the breath-taking development sections of Beethoven's symphonies. It is the most profound paradox of music that Beethoven voiced the most subjective expression of this struggle in such a high degree of innate objectivity of form that the form itself came to be considered an absolute norm, and was treated by the succeeding generations as a prescribed frame for musical composition.

The Antecedents of the Preclassic Symphony

CLASSICAL instrumental style—symphony, chamber music, and sonata—was prepared for through half a century of arduous work by scores of composers in countless works. There are few phases in the history of art so little explored yet so categorically settled in manuals and even in learned dissertations as the preclassical symphony and sonata. Our knowledge of this field was until recently restricted to Riemann's discovery of the so-called Mannheim school; but even this school has not been properly investigated and so is popularly supposed to be an autonomous German school in the Palatinate, whereas actually its members formed a colony of Austrian, Sudeten-Bohemian, and Italian musicians whose activity was a logical chapter in the movement which started in Italy and received encouragement from northern Germany. Riemann's discovery of the Mannheim school [33] was a scientific-historic event of the greatest magnitude, but even so eminent a scholar was satisfied with singling out one man, Johann Stamitz, and a few satellites around the leader, believing that by this the whole preliminary history of the symphony was accounted for. Great art forms do not arise overnight; it takes a long chain of men to bring them to the point where the scholar's magnifying glass is finally able to pick up the thread. Seen under the lens, the continuity of artistic growth, a constant compromise between and synthesis of tradition and life, with the customary slowly receding before the new, asserts itself again and again; its compelling logic often misleads the student to regard it as evolution in the biological sense. Riemann's conception weighed heavily on the musical world and, as far as the majority of our books on music are concerned, is still accepted as exhausting the field. In the meantime younger scholars, following in the footsteps of the grand old man of musicology, have begun to search this uncharted territory, throwing some light on this phase of musical history, the importance of which cannot be overestimated.[34]

The unity and logic of baroque musical architecture, based on the complete representation and exploitation of one "basic affection," was disturbed by the introduction of additional and contrasting thematic material. The difficulty confronting the new principle of musical construction and style was to bring this additional material into a logical relationship with the basic affection, the principal theme. This is, then, the abridged history of the classic sonata. To make the involved process leading from the first essays to the classic form more comprehensible, let us first see what the aim was, halting the process at a point where the principles seem fully established but without having reached the highest peaks of attainment.

At about 1770 compositions in three or more movements, such as quartets, symphonies, *divertimenti,* piano sonatas, etc., usually employed the sonata form in the first of their fast movements. The design of the sonata form can be described as follows. The framework consists of a large ternary cycle: 1. presentation of the thematic material, called exposition; 2. utilization of this material, called "working-out section," free fantasia, etc. (we shall use the term "development section"); and 3. reprise or recapitulation of the first part with certain modifications. Although a more or less extended slow introduction may preface the sonata movement proper, the exposition usually begins with the principal theme, a well-defined melody in the main tonality of the work. This is followed by a transition passage, called "bridge," which leads to the subsidiary or second subject, a contrasting theme or thematic group, usually in the dominant key if the tonic is a major key; if it is a minor key the subsidiary theme usually appears in the relative major key. As a rule, at least in the period under consideration, the principal theme is of a more resolute character, while the secondary theme is more lyrical. With the secondary theme announced, the exposition ends with a short closing section which may consist of a single theme or of a group of closing formulae taken from the transition passage, ending the exposition in the dominant key. The development section which begins here earned its name through the fact that it undertakes to present the thematic material under different aspects, resorting to modulations, melodic and rhythmic changes and deformations, contrapuntal combinations, and other devices to exhaust the capacities for metamorphosis and development inherent in the themes. When this has been accomplished the recapitulation sets in, the tonic key having been prepared skillfully to give this reprise an air of relief and satisfaction. The recapitulation is a more or less exact restatement of the exposition section but, in order to complete the arch, rising from the tonic to the dominant and then falling back to the tonic, and to balance the symmetry of tonal and formal relationship, the bridge passage is altered to avoid a second rise to the dominant; consequently both the subsidiary theme and the closing theme or group will appear in the tonic key. The rise to the dominant is accompanied by a feeling of tonal tension which may be so strong that even the large parts of both exposition and recapitulation devoted to the tonic key often do not suffice to restore tonal equilibrium to complete satisfaction. To overcome this sensation of instability it became customary to add an epilogue called *coda* (from the Latin *cauda,* "tail") at the very end of the recapitulation, the role of which was to affirm and underline the tonic key. The coda may be formed by enlarging the closing section, but it frequently utilizes thematic material culled from the principal subject, presented in a retrospective manner.

The great task of instrumental music, emerging from the polyphonic era of the baroque, was the solution of the principle of homophony as applied to instrumental music. The task was difficult because while in vocal music it was easy to allot a leading part (melody) to a soloist, supporting it with an accompaniment of distinctly secondary importance, in instrumental music the traditions of part writing in ensembles and the involved apparatus of the basso continuo opposed such a radical change. The solution was to come from a single instrument capable of representing the full body of many-voiced instrumental music, but not necessarily restricted to a continuous employment of the whole apparatus of this body. Clavecin music was destined to fulfill this mission because it did not grow from the organ as had Italian and German harpsichord music and consequently was not intimately tied to polyphony.

If we recall the origin of French clavecin music we shall recognize that the rather delicate and capricious manner of writing for the lute, spiritual forebear of the clavecin, was a logical prelude to the ensuing developments. While polyphonic instrumental music employed several independent parts, maintaining their number and function on a constant level, the style galant as exemplified in clavecin music did not cling to a definite number of parts, simply considering the instrument as a medium of expression for the individual, who touched the keys at his will, playing single notes or striking chords following the needs of his musical ideas. With this the rules of voice leading were drastically altered. Hand in hand with the revised principles of part writing went the changes imposed upon the music by the idiomatic technique evolved for the instrument. The short duration of the clavecin tone called for a specific treatment of the melody, which could not be sustained so well as on the organ or in a string ensemble. In order to prevent the melody from being disjointed, its note values had to be divided into small units which would not lose their sonority before the expiration of the time value of the note struck. This problem was not unknown to the baroque, which solved it by the so-called art of "diminution." [35] But baroque polyphony used diminution in all parts, whereas the style galant resorted to the use of embellishments restricted to the main notes of the melody. We have seen how under the decorative urge of the rococo, embellishment gained such importance in music, as well as in the other arts, that every other consideration became secondary. In the case of music this meant that the other parts became mere padding. This technique of setting and playing was, then, quickly appropriated by other instruments, until finally its effects were felt in the ensemble itself. The different parts no longer represented different individuals but the different aspects of one individual.

In considering German instrumental music of the late baroque, we noted the strong influence of French opera and French instrumental music on German composers. The German musicians realized that with the departure of the baroque it became necessary for them to find their own style in the maze of foreign influences, they watched the ardent controversy raging in Paris between the Italian and the French parties and reached conclusions which were to decide the future of music.

The free and easy style of French clavecin music found many adherents, especially among the Berlin musicians. In the meantime the impressions coming from Italy, never lagging, were given a great impetus by one of the most original minds of the eighteenth century. The beginnings of the poly-thematic sonata go back as far as Corelli and dall' Abaco, but their material, while unmistakably polythematic, was still too uniform to present real con-trasts. The first conscious attempt to use contrasting material was made by Domenico Scarlatti (1685-1757). The logic of our contention that the prelim-inary steps toward a new instrumental style originated in keyboard music is borne out by Scarlatti's contribution. This greatest of harpsichord virtuosi was the composer of over five hundred short keyboard pieces, originally called "exercises" but usually referred to as "sonatas." [36] In the majority of cases this is a misnomer, because while the "sonatas" have a definite exposi-tion section, often with two contrasting themes, followed by a development section, the third part, the recapitulation, is too rudimentary to be consid-ered a reprise in the sonata manner. The brevity of this treatment would give the impression of a simple binary form were it not for the capricious tech-nique of pianistic writing, jumping from polyphony to homophony and thereby effectively enhancing the contrasting element, less equivocally indi-cated in melody and rhythm.

The radiant and piquant melody, the colorful and exuberant vivacity, the sudden changes from frivolous playfulness to powerful dramatic accents betray the operatic influence. Being the son of the great opera composer, Scarlatti was reared in an operatic atmosphere. His most illustrious successor in the building up of the modern piano sonata, Baldassare Galuppi (1706-1785), was one of the outstanding masters of the opera buffa, and among the few other important composers of keyboard music Giuseppe Antonio Paga-nelli (1710-1765) and Giovanni Marco Rutini (c. 1730-1797) were also ex-perienced opera composers. Thus it was once again the opera which helped the rest of music to find the means of expression leading to an independent style. This time it was the wonderful celerity, lightness of touch, and humor of the opera buffa rather than the solemn opera seria which affixed its stamp on instrumental music. While the influence of the Neapolitan style is visible in the greatest masters of the high baroque, this influence was only a minor touch in their music, with the exception, to be sure, of operatic music; with the younger generation, however, the Neapolitan elements became all-important factors. With the universal dissemination of Neapolitan opera and oratorio, its formal and technical principles inevitably dominated the scene. In the third decade of the century we see, then, an almost uniform outcropping of works engendered by the three-part *sinfonia* which customarily opened the Neapolitan opera. Italians wrote trio sonatas in the new style (let the reader remember the sweetly melancholy trio sonatas of Pergolesi, mentioned earlier in connection with the first signs of a new motivic-thematic style), while the Germans in the north tried their hand at three-movement clavier sonatas. The opera sinfonia, having acquired such world-wide importance and recognition, now embarked upon an independent career and began to be performed as an instrumental piece divorced from the opera.

This modest newcomer to the august company of the baroque church sonata, concerto, and suite was to displace all of them within a generation. Whether in the south or in the north, in Pergolesi or in C. P. E. Bach, the earliest sonata constructions show unmistakable Neapolitan inspiration by their preference for subsidiary themes in the minor key, a typical mark of the suave Neapolitan style. On the other hand, remnants of the baroque monothematic and monorhythmic style are present. The use of subsidiary themes in the major key and of clearly defined closing sections, timidly introduced by Pergolesi, did not receive much attention until the middle of the century, but after this date it appeared everywhere, although the placing of the second theme in the minor key was retained to a certain extent in Germany and Austria.

At this point we shall deviate from the seemingly logical method of procedure; we shall abandon the instrumental ensemble and return to keyboard music, which, having provided the starting point for the new homophonic instrumental style, reached maturity ahead of the symphony. This may not be an accepted sequence of symphonic evolution, but we shall try to prove that one of the chief sources not only of the form but of the idiom of the classical symphony was the keyboard sonata, notably the sonatas of C. P. E. Bach and his younger brother, Johann Christian Bach.

Carl Philipp Emanuel Bach

CARL PHILIPP EMANUEL BACH (1714–1788), Johann Sebastian's second son by his first marriage, for twenty-seven years court harpsichordist to

Frederick the Great, was the musician whose strong personality and bold initiative consolidated the many earlier attempts at the creation of what was to
be known as the sonata form. It is most unjust, however, to see in this great
master merely a clever innovator of some of the technical-formal aspects of
music, for he was not primarily interested in form, or rather in experimentation with form, and in his music the purely formal side was often less
developed than in that of some of his contemporaries. As a member of the
rationalistic Berlin school he endeavored to convey feelings, to impress his
hearers emotionally. Hence it is rather surprising that his aim should have
been achieved in a field not particularly adapted for such purposes: clavier
music. C. P. E. Bach was the creator of the modern expressive piano style—a
style which, while acknowledging inspiration from various quarters, was not
derived from other instruments or from vocal models, but was indigenous and
idiomatic. In the course of the creation of this idiom he arrived at the new
sonata form by a route not unlike that followed by his Italian colleagues; but
the form was far less important than the idiom and the principle it involved,
for this great master stands out as a beacon in the eighteenth century, the
rays of which illuminated the road for everyone.

If we take one glance at his early piano sonatas we shall understand why
Haydn and Mozart paid such sincere tribute to him. They were deeply indebted to him, for in these sonatas—*opus* 1 (1742), known as *Prussian Sonatas,* and *opus* 2 (1744), the *Württemberg Sonatas* [37]—the musical dialect
of the classical style was established; they had themes of symphonic pregnancy, developments of somber intensity, harmonic intricacies of startling
modernity, and a humor of disarming bonhomie. There is scarcely another
case in the history of music in which prophetic utterances turned into reality
only to be forgotten in the very tumult they created. These sonatas were
widely known and their idiom passed from them into other species. C. P. E.
Bach apparently cultivated two distinct types of clavier sonatas; one entirely
"pianistic" in nature and texture, and leaning more toward the *Empfindsamkeit* of the Berlin school; the other, sounding like veritable piano scores of
symphonies. Nothing of such developed and mature symphonic fabric can
be found in the Mannheim symphonies or in contemporary Italian orchestral
works of any sort. It is small wonder that Bach's fellow musicians were not
immediately receptive to his ideas, but as the century advanced his influence
steadily increased. This influence did not stop with Haydn and Mozart; it
reached through Beethoven, whose piano sonatas were direct issues of the
expressive "dramatic sonatas" of Bach, and extended far into the romantic
era. It is true that the weeds of the rococo style—grace notes, embellishments,
flourishes, and sighs—are present in his music, sometimes in profusion; but
this could not have been otherwise, because no true artist, however revolutionary, can deny his times and environment. Though Bach spent the major

part of his creative years in the center of the German rococo, so great a musical personality as he could not fail to see the faults of the *Empfindsamkeit*. He made use of the ornamentation demanded by his era, but he did not leave its execution to the fancy of the player. The rococo clavier players did not like to let a single note pass without embellishments, but in his treatise Bach recommended moderation, reminding his readers that when too much ornamentation is used the "affections" are clouded, while on the other hand judicious use of grace notes may well serve to amplify the expressive content. Thus the ornamental superstructure was converted into a constructive, integral part of the style. His symphonies, while not less interesting and bold than his clavier works, were less influential in forming the symphonic style. This may sound paradoxical but it goes to prove that the new idiom was first of all a new stylistic principle, a new form of musical logic, coherence, and construction, applied to all forms of instrumental music, of which the symphony, later quasi-monopolizing the criteria of the new style, was only one. This was also the reason for our returning to keyboard music instead of following the course of orchestral music. While the repercussions of Bach's symphonic thought were not immediately felt, we cannot be indifferent, from the point of view of stylistic history, to its chronological appearance, to the fact that the idiom was developed in northern Germany to a high degree at a time when Italian symphonic idiom was just entering its period of formulation. It is true that the subsequent growth of symphony and sonata followed the Italian line of development, C. P. E. and J. C. Bach not coming into their own until the beginning of the classical era; but it is of great importance for us to have now set aside a document which can be used as an "exhibit" at the proper time.

This great musician has become known to posterity as a "forerunner," which in our modern practice of art criticism relegates him to dutiful citation among the yeomen who cleared the underbrush for the oaks. Thus he is always mentioned but never performed or appreciated in his own right. Those who credit him with the "invention of the sonata form" do not know that this worthy son of another great musician was the composer of more than two hundred clavier works, fifty-two clavier concertos, eighteen symphonies, much chamber music and church music—including twenty-two settings of the Passion—and some two hundred and fifty songs. With the exception of some of the afore-mentioned revolutionary piano sonatas, a few brilliant clavier fantasies and concertos, one or two symphonies of provoking originality, and a handful of songs of haunting beauty, nothing is known, not only to the public but to scholars as well. When his works are better known we shall recognize Carl Philipp Emanuel Bach as the outstanding master of the late rococo, of preclassical times, a master who triumphed over the weaknesses of the art and atmosphere of his own period.

We must now return to the other line of descent of the symphony-sonata, rejoining C. P. E. and J. C. Bach at a later period.

Components of the Sonata-Symphony

THE components of the symphony-sonata were many and varied. The cyclic order of movements, fast-slow-fast, harks back, as we have seen, to the Neapolitan opera *sinfonia,* disposed in the sequence of allegro-andante-allegro, to which was later added the minuet as a fourth movement. The da capo aria was responsible for the principle of reprise or recapitulation of the first part following a different middle section, supplying the well-known formula A-B-A, accepted earlier by the concerto. It is impossible to ascertain who caused this important departure in instrumental musical form, but we have noticed that it was already in actual use in the first movement of Johann Sebastian Bach's violin concerto in E major, which is constructed along the lines of a great da capo aria combined with the concerto principle. The symphony owes its rhythmic and sonorous contrasts to the baroque concerto. The terracelike dynamics of the concerto grosso, with its sharp contrasts of forte and piano and its color contrasts of tutti and solo, represent in themselves a dualism most suitable for the new formal aesthetics of pure instrumental music; but the influence goes deeper than mere dynamic and sonorous effects.

The baroque concerto started with a vigorous tutti engaging the whole orchestra; this became the principal theme and section of the symphony-sonata. After the first tutti the concerto usually maneuvered the orchestra to a position where the solo passage played by the concertino entered in a subdued tone, contrasting strongly both in dynamics and in orchestration with the tutti. This passage was converted into the subsidiary group, the repeated tutti passage acting as closing theme or formula. The robust tutti opening of the concerto and the subdued solo passages were in the later concertos of Vivaldi connected by episodes and ritornels. It remained, in the light of the new aesthetics which placed the individual sections in relief, at the same time connecting them logically, to bring these two extremes into a new, less casual relationship. This was done by giving the second section a theme of its own and connecting the tutti beginning—which had developed into the principal theme—and the softly orchestrated second section by a suitable passage, our future "bridge."

The thematic material utilized in the early symphony was usually restricted to fanfares in stately rhythm or to dissolved triads, more energetic and rhythmical, giving that "ready to go" impression we associate with the symphony; the statement was immediately followed by a sequential passage, often a crescendo over a pedal point, which carried the harmonic scheme to a point (the dominant of the dominant) whence it could fall back on the dominant in such a manner as to make the dominant the tonic of a new tonality. Having established the new tonality by key-defining motions, the soft solo passage of the concerto was here transformed into an episode standing in a definite and formal relationship to the first tutti passage. Whether this episode has a perfectly articulated thematic substance is, for the time being, of secondary importance; the main thing is the tonic-dominant relationship and contrast. The last vestiges of the heavy and majestic style of the baroque are still present in these opening measures, which represent the solemn and ceremonious beginning of the Italian opera sinfonia or toccata; but the ceremonial gestures of the baroque are now being rapidly mitigated by the more subjective manners of the rococo and the *Empfindsamkeit*. The Vivaldi type of concerto elaborated two different subjects, the material presented by the concerto and that presented by the concertino or solo. The growing sonata principle, based on dualism and contrast, excluded the possibility of two threads deploying simultaneously; for while it welcomed a number of themes, the association of these with certain positions in the tonality was jeopardized by the introduction of both the main and the subsidiary group in the same key. The only solution was to reduce the tuttis and the ritornels, enlarging and developing what used to be the solo passages, and providing them with a continuity determined by the new principles of thematic construction.

Hand in hand with the structural changes went modifications wrought in the design of the melodic content. Operatic and folkloristic elements, such as the Neapolitan folk song, intruded, as usual, and took over especially the subsidiary and closing groups with their simple, pleasing, and refreshing tunes. The principal themes retained the resolute rhythmical features of the baroque tutti theme, but in the German countries the more suave Italian opera buffa melodies of Pergolesi began to find favor as subsidiary themes, rising to their highest sensuous beauty in Mozart. The nature of the theme followed the requisites of the new aesthetic-formal conceptions. The melody itself reflected the dualism which characterized the symphony, for the unequivocal linear clarity of the baroque melody was no longer sufficient and the new melody had to rely on a harmonic foundation. It was no longer a categorical "form opener" not necessarily needed during the further course of the work; determined and delineated harmonically, rhythmically, and dynamically, it offered the fare for the whole symphonic structure. The contrasting dualism of tutti and solo, forte and piano, unison and polyphony, employed to differentiate between principal theme and subsidiary theme, was now carried into the individual theme groups. If pure dualism had been maintained, the great organic symphony would never have been created. Therefore it became imperative to establish between the opposing complexes a relationship which would bind them into a whole. This necessitated a new grammar and syntax of the language of music.

The early generation of symphonists did not at first know what to do with their newly won freedom from the discursive continuity of baroque music. Lacking the tremendous breath of the baroque, they were winded after a few measures of "free thinking"; the only remedy for the stranded composer was to make a cadence and start all over again. While not a constructive element, the cadence provided at least a sort of articulation. In the better composers' hands this life-saving device was put to artistic use, but the excessive cadencing ruined many a composition and is chiefly responsible for the oblivion which blankets hundreds of works. Having lost the backing of polyphonic motor power, the composers first adopted a very simple technique consisting of repetition of motives coupled with sequential motion. This technique was borrowed from the fabric of the suite, which created its musical texture by weaving motives in repetition, sequential progression, and contrapuntal recasting. This was appropriate to the suite type of construction, which had, instead of sections, only punctuations and caesurae that merely interrupted the orderly flow of *melos* without destroying continuity. (In this connection let us remember that we are not concerned here with the dance movements of the suite, but with the free suite type of construction such as the opening movement in Johann Sebastian Bach's B minor suite for strings and flute.)

The symphonic style, unlike the suite style, called for the organization of independent and well-separated sections; to connect these organically without abandoning their integrity a more flexible technique had to be found. Realizing that motivic work, depending on a single motif, would no longer suffice because its nature does not permit interruption, the composers began to link different motives into thematic complexes which formed a unit even when the individual motives were segregated. Such a thematic unit placed at the head of a composition permitted a much greater variety and latitude than the suite technique. First the smaller sections had to be built up according to the principles of thematic work, for only when the new principle had functioned satisfactorily in the smaller details could the composers embark on the extension of symphonic thought to the whole of the sonata form. The development section, at first little more than a short transition to the recapitulation, profited from the new technique of manipulating the thematic material. It proceeded to dissect this material to its smallest components in order to operate freely with them, dialoguing or dramatically opposing elements taken from the same original thought. A more organic coherence between the individual sections was built up by composing the bridge of material taken from the principal theme, so that the bridge appeared as an immediate continuation of the leading idea. The exposition thus welded together permitted a more fantastic cavorting of the thematic material in the development section. With the enlargement of the development section the recapitulation met what proved to be a temporary setback, probably because of the more lavish use of the principal thematic material in the development. The recapitulation often begins with the subsidiary group, leaving out the principal theme altogether. At the same time C. P. E. Bach's not infrequent derivation of the subsidiary subject from his principal subject shows, for the first time, the archsymphonic instinct of the Germans, which was to find such eloquent expression in the next generation.

The new musical idiom of the early symphonic school altered the function and composition of the orchestra. The motor force of the bass part and the apparatus of the basso continuo carried with them the other parts, but with the gradual disintegration of polyphonic-linear writing the vitality of the bass part sank considerably; instead of being the backbone of the composition, it assumed the modest role of a simple fundamental part supporting the harmonic activity. Liberated from its duty of providing an uninterrupted accompaniment to the whole ensemble, and as the middle parts took over a large share of this duty, the bass became free to abandon its constant rumbling and to take part, melodically, in the thematic development, thereby lightening considerably the musical fabric of the whole setting. In the measure in which the fundamental importance of the bass decreased, the cumbersome apparatus which had enforced its rights became superfluous; the basso continuo had outlived its usefulness. The continuo clavier either disappeared (except in the opera, where it was needed for the accompaniment of the secco recitatives) or was retained as an emancipated instrument, forming new combinations, clavier-string chamber music. The abolition of the continuo was, of course, a gradual process, and although it had lost its structural and even practical applicability, force of habit retained the apparatus far into the nineteenth century.

With the abandonment of the continuo the orchestra lost its "pedals," and something had to be found to restore the continuity of sustained harmony. In the search for this agency a fundamental change in orchestration took place. The ideal instrument to tie together the different groups of the orchestra was the French horn, for its tone, embracing every shade of sonority from barely audible pianissimo to brassy fortissimo, blends with every other instrument or group in the orchestra. These instruments, always used in pairs, became the backbone of the orchestra, their long-sustained notes holding the busily moving parts together. The French horn of the eighteenth century (*Waldhorn* or *cor de chasse*) was, however, an incomplete instrument, capable of producing only the natural harmonic overtones of a given tuning. The players were able to create additional tones by the deft use of the lips and the right fist held in the flaring bell of the instrument, but the muffled

sound of these artificial tones differed considerably from the beautifully clear
and shining color of the "naturals." (The invention of the pistons, making
the horn into a chromatic instrument, occurred after the passing of the
classical school.) The incompleteness of the instrument limited its use to
the natural tones it could produce in the few tunings customarily used at
the time, namely, B flat, C, D, E flat, E, F, and G. This fact determined
the tonalities of the early symphony, for intricate modulations and the use
of keys far removed from those just mentioned were out of the question.
To the horns were later added trumpets—in the same tunings, for they
shared the horn's limitations—and a pair of kettledrums, forming a group
most characteristic of the full orchestral tone of the eighteenth-century symphony. The string body remained the foundation of the ensemble, and the
wood-wind instruments were co-ordinated with the strings, strengthening
the sonority in the tuttis and taking part in the thematic work. This represented a considerable departure from both the closed wood-wind trios that
had been so popular since Lully, and the sustained concerted playing of
single instruments as used in the baroque concerto. The wood-winds were
also used in pairs. The first ensembles usually consisted of the string body
with a pair of oboes and a pair of horns, but flutes, bassoons, and clarinets
also appeared in some of the earliest symphonies.

By 1779, that is, before the beginning of the great classical era which
produced the mature symphonies of Haydn and Mozart, the full symphony
orchestra was ready in its composition as well as function, but we shall first
find it, as usual, in the opera. Gluck's *Iphigénie en Tauride* (1779) employed a great orchestra consisting of piccolo, two flutes, two oboes, two
clarinets, two bassoons, two French horns, two trumpets, three trombones,
kettledrums, and strings. Thus it is ridiculous to attribute either the creation
or the use of the modern orchestra to Haydn or to anyone else of the high
classical era, for one glance at the superb score of *Iphigénie* will reveal a
mastery of orchestration that has lost nothing of its originality and telling
effects. The clarinets, often referred to as introduced by Haydn or Mozart,
were in general use by the middle of the century. Rameau used them in
Paris in 1749, and they were fairly well known throughout Germany, especially in Mannheim, where Stamitz used them at an early date.

Even the earliest of these symphonies disclose that typical orchestral
sonority which we associate with the symphony, and which was due, in no
small part, to the new expressive dynamics that replaced the terrace dynamics
of the baroque. This brings us to one of the vexing problems of the symphonic style, the orchestral crescendo. Crescendo and diminuendo, the swelling and ebbing of tone volume, were, naturally, familiar in vocal music
much before this period; Caccini had recommended the use of shades between piano and forte, called *mezza di voce*. In instrumental music crescendo

and decrescendo signs were employed in the next century by Geminiani, and both Brossard and Walther in their dictionaries (1703 and 1730) printed numerous dynamic signs ranging from extreme piano to triple forte. The orchestral crescendo, an imitation of vocal practices, came from operatic sources. By 1740, that is, definitely before the famous Mannheim crescendo of Stamitz, the operatic crescendo was practiced in all other varieties of Italian music. We have noticed the amazement expressed by de Brosses upon hearing the fine nuances executed by the Roman musicians during his visit in that year to the Eternal City. This keen observer also mentioned that "occasionally while accompanying *piano,* all the instruments in the orchestra would, simultaneously, force their sound until it entirely covered the singing voice, subsequently falling muted (*dans la sourdine*); it is an excellent effect." [38] The crescendo manner reached the German symphonists through Jommelli. The scores of his *Eumene* (1747) and *Artaserse* (1749) contain the explicit instruction: "crescendo il forte." Another source of the new dynamic shadings must have been in France, where in Rameau's score of *Acante et Céphise* (1751) signs, almost in the shape of our modern signs, appear, calling for the swelling and decreasing of tone volume. The appearance of this practice in a printed score indicates its actual use for some time previous. Thus Burney's assertion, invariably copied by modern historians, that Johann Stamitz and the Mannheimers were the inventors of crescendo dynamics must be rejected as based on insufficient information. How this new manner of dynamics was applied to specific effects of composition and the delineation of form is another matter, but we shall see that it was again Jommelli who was the pioneer, transmitting older Italian practices to the Germans.

The Italian and Austrian Schools

HAVING discussed the principles of the rising symphony, let us consider the men who established them. While Pergolesi was almost entirely immersed in the graceful miniature work of the rococo, other musicians, continuing on the path opened by this "child of taste and elegance, and nursling of the graces" (Burney), began to go beyond the little repetitions so characteristic of the rococo, and ventured from the juxtaposition of small groups to a continuous web of motives. The first musician to show a distinctly symphonic attitude was Giovanni Battista Sammartini,[39] who lifted the monotony created by the use of old baroque materials in a treatment unsuitable to them with a rhythmic freedom that instantly enlivened the fabric. The rhythmical differentiation brought about by the thematic dualism is what impresses one most of all when comparing the new style with that of the baroque. In the working out of fine and pointed rhythmic nuances Sammartini became one of the great pioneers of the classical style without whose incentive a Haydn or Mozart would have been unthinkable a generation after Handel's death. Rinaldo di Capua, a once celebrated opera composer (c. 1710–c. 1780) of whose life and works we unfortunately know very little, took the next important step by outlining the contours of the subsidiary thematic group. There was as yet no new idea in this group, which used material already stated, but the delineation of its position was a great formal innovation; it designed the frame of the symphony-sonata. Rinaldo's excellent instinct for articulation was accompanied by the prophetic desire to bind these sections by links that give the feeling of logical continuity.

The symphony of this generation was a fairly well-designed structure, if not particularly profound in content. The difficulties encountered by these composers in deepening their ideas proportionately as they improved technique, idiom, and form can be understood if we remember that this was the era of the rococo, not given to heroic accents, proportions, and forms. In this connection the evolution shows a logical course, and, since the problem on hand was the organization of small details, the early symphony turned naturally to the rococo, a style and conception of art interested primarily in polished detail. Beginning with this date there was, then, a detour toward a compromise that we may call the *"galant* symphony," chopping up the large form and delighting in details until they could be fused into an organic whole. But while the *galant* symphony grew, Rinaldo's tendency toward a large form was not lost; all that his larger form needed was— content. This came from the opera buffa, with its wonderfully pliable technique, its piquant melodies, and its swift orchestral accompaniment. Rinaldo's role in this process remains to be investigated, a task worthy of the labors of any scholar; all we know about the transmutation of the operatic into the symphonic is a short but significant passage in a travel diary which Burney wrote while investigating music in Italy:

Signor Rinaldo di Capua has at Rome the reputation of being the inventor of accompanied recitatives; but in hunting for old compositions in the archives of S. Gerolamo della Carità, I found an oratorio by Alessandro Scarlatti, which was composed in the latter end of the last century, before Rinaldo di Capua was born, and in which are *accompanied recitatives*. But he does not himself pretend to the invention; all he claims is the being among the first who introduced long *ritornellos,* or symphonies, into the recitatives of passion and distress, which express or imitate what it would be ridiculous for the voice to attempt. There are many fine scenes of this kind in his works, and Hasse, Galuppi, Jommelli, and Piccini have been very happy in such interesting, and often sublime compositions.[40]

The task of transforming the highly expressive dramatic-vocal style into an independent and self-sufficient instrumental idiom, begun by Rinaldo, appears achieved with deliberation and serious artistic skill in Jommelli's music; this is the great dramatic composer whom we have already designated as the key man in the early development of the new orchestral idiom. His long motivic phrases were not merely paddings to fill out the empty spaces in a still baffling form, but a conscious attempt at the creation of a large and logical form. The development sections of his sonata constructions are not marked —sometimes they are completely missing—but there appeared something that was to play a great role in symphonic history: the rolling orchestral crescendo, used not only as a means of expression, but as an element of form.

Jommelli takes us away from Italy, for his epoch-making activity took place in Germany. We shall not follow him immediately to Stuttgart, however, for it was not Germany which continued and fulfilled the work begun by Italy, but Austria and Bohemia. It was again Austria which mediated between south and north, reconciling the pure, one-dimensional melodic deployment of the Italians with Germanic instinct for polydimensional organization. The melody-bearing treble, so suavely singing with the Italians, lost its supremacy in German hands, sacrificing coloratura melody to become one of the agents of thematic work, ruled by the periodization, harmony, dynamics, and rhythm of the symphonic web. This course of events was responsible for the unparalleled triumph of German instrumental music in the eighteenth and nineteenth centuries, for in song and melody they could not measure up to the Italians; but once the expressive operatic idiom was successfully converted into an abstract instrumental language, the resulting symphonic mood and tone was theirs, never even remotely challenged by any other nation.

Austria was predestined to become the seat of the great classical school. The more sunny disposition and flexibility of the southern Germans encouraged the intercourse of the many races that made up the empire; Czechs, Bohemians, Poles, Slovaks, Hungarians, and Slovenes, all proverbially musical, mingled with Germans and Italians. This gave an international stamp to the cultural life of the old Austrian Empire, but the musical ties were centuries old, going back to the Flemish and Spanish chapel choirs and to the Italian court operas. Other stylistic elements were absorbed through the intermediary of the north; English keyboard music, French comic opera, German Singspiel, all found their way into Vienna, French *sensibilité,* Italian *dolcezza,* and inimitable Austrian *Gemütlichkeit* uniting in the traditional melting pot that was Vienna. But with all this internationalism the Austro-Germanic element dominated, and the classical school that we usually refer to as the Viennèse school was to remain an inalienable part of Germanic musical history.

The number of good composers working in the Habsburg lands recalls the creative wealth of Renaissance Italy. From Vienna and Lower Austria came Johann Georg Reutter (1708–1772), Georg Matthias Monn (1717–1750), Matthäus Schlöger (1722–1766), Georg Christoph Wagenseil (1715–1777), Ignaz Jakob Holzbauer (1711–1783), Florian Johann Deller (1729–1773), Johann Christian Mann (1726–1782), Franz Asplmayr (c. 1721–1786), Josef Starzer (1726–1787), Leopold Hoffmann (c. 1730–1793), Karl Ditters (later called von Dittersdorf, 1739–1799), Johann Michael Haydn (1737–1806), Franz Josef Haydn (1732–1809), Wolfgang Amadeus Mozart (1756–1791), Johann Schenk (1753–1836), Anton Eberl (c. 1765–1807), Johann Georg Albrechtsberger (1736–1809), Ignaz Umlauff (1746–1796), Joseph Weigl (1766–1846), Ignaz Joseph Pleyel (1757–1831), Franz Peter Schubert (1797–1828), and Carl Czerny (1791–1857). Bohemia, Moravia, and the Sudetenland produced Bohuslav Czernohorsky (1684–1740), Johann Dismas Zelenka (1679–1745), Franz Tuma (1704–1774), Johann Zach (1699–1773), Georg Tzarth (or Zarth, 1708–1778), Joseph Seeger (1716–1782), Joseph Mysliweczek (1737–1781), Leopold Florian Gassmann (1729–1774), Anton Filtz (c. 1730–1760), Franz Benda (1709–1786), Georg Benda (1722–1795), Anton Jiránek (c. 1712–1761), Franz Xaver Richter (1709–1789), Johann Stamitz (1717–1757), Johann Anton Koželuch (1738–1814), Leopold Anton Koželuch (1752–1818), Johann Ladislaus Dussek (or Duschek, 1760–1812), Paul Wranitzky (1756–1808), Wenzel Pichl (1741–1805), Dionys Weber (1766–1842), Johann Baptist Wanhall (or Vanhall, 1739–1813), Wenzel Müller (1767–1835), Franz Anton Rössler (or Rosetti, c. 1750–1792), and Adalbert Gyrowetz (1763–1850).

After reading this rather summary list of composers (many of whom are discussed elsewhere), we may be surprised that the so-called Viennese school, usually limited to Haydn, Mozart, and Beethoven, contained such a plethora of talent and that such a large percentage of the composers came from Slavic provinces. But it was precisely this conglomeration of nationalities and their folklore which created that specific Austrian tone we associate with the Viennese school. And the Bavarians and Rhinelanders (Leopold Mozart, Adlgasser, Beethoven) or the Italians (Salieri) who came to Austria could not help being engulfed by this radiant musical atmosphere, and became thoroughly acclimatized Viennese. The imperial court in Vienna, the archiepiscopal court in Salzburg, and the countless aristocratic households attracted the musicians from the crown lands, not only because of their fame and excellence, but because the constant warfare made the borderlands unsafe. "It will, perhaps, appear strange to some, that this capital," says Burney of Prague, "of so musical a kingdom, in which the genius of each inhabitant has a fair trial, should not more abound in great musicians. It is not, however, difficult to account for this if we reflect, that music is one of the arts of peace, leisure, and abundance . . . now the Bohemians are never tranquil long together [referring to the Silesian Wars]; and even in the short intervals of peace, their first nobility are attached to the court of Vienna, and seldom reside in their capital." [41]

The great company of composers did not stay together in the capital of the empire; they emigrated to Germany, Italy, France, and elsewhere, and Austria became virtually the purveyor of composers to a large part of the Continent, especially to Germany and Central Europe. Thus, among others Zelenka and Jiránek went to Dresden, Mysliweczek to Rome, Zach to Mayence, Tzarth, Stamitz, Richter, Filtz, and Holzbauer to Mannheim in the Palatinate, Dussek and Pleyel to Paris, Deller to Munich, Rössler [Rosetti] to Ludwigsburg, the Benda brothers to Berlin and Gotha, and Josef Haydn to Kismarton and Eszterháza in Hungary. Like a second Naples, Vienna became the metropolis of the musical world, gathering and dispensing music and musicians, remaking the physiognomy of music, and arriving at a style which not only was regarded as the acme of classic perfection, but still had some germinating power left long after its last representatives had died.

The rococo did not triumph so easily in Vienna as it had in northern Germany, where the French influence was most powerful. The forbidding figure of the stern custodian of baroque polyphony, Johann Josef Fux, prevented the wrecking of polyphony and "artistic setting," and indeed the whole Viennese school shows the salutary effects of the conservation of the remnants of the great traditions. The first complete symphony in four movements, including the minuet, was already present in Georg Matthias Monn's symphony in D major in 1740, that is, at about the time when Haydn was eight years of age. Like his colleagues who migrated to Mannheim, Monn developed his instrumental style under the influence of the younger Neapolitan generation (Pergolesi, Sammartini), but connections with the baroque were stronger in him than in his Mannheim colleagues. Neither his invention nor his orchestral sense stands comparison with the genius of Stamitz, but there can be no question as to Monn's priority over the Bohemian symphonist, and his new and independent instrumental language entitles him to be regarded as one of the most important precursors of the classical school. Monn and his fellow composers active toward the middle of the century in Vienna were, then, the first representatives of the German symphony. Theirs was not yet a mature style; the repetition technique of the suite is evident in the numerous sequences, and some baroque spirit can be found in the somewhat trudging basses, but the refined dances of the rococo begin to yield to the more earth-bound Austrian and Bohemian peasant dances, which we know so well from the minuets in Haydn's symphonies. The man who crowned the first period of the German symphony was Wagenseil, but before we carry the Viennese symphony to its logical conclusion we must follow the Austro-Bohemian composers in the Diaspora in Germany.

The Mannheim School

THE most important single group of these composers is to be found at the court of the Elector Palatine in Mannheim. Duke Carl Theodor (1724–1799) was a consistently steady patron of arts and letters and made Mannheim one of the most brilliant centers of German cultural life. During the five and a half decades of his reign he spent the enormous sum of thirty-five million florins on artistic and scientific institutions, museums, libraries, and on his favored musical establishments, hailed as the best in Europe. All the painters, sculptors, and architects, the musicians, singers, and actors, within Mann-heim and its vicinity were employed by the court—a fact of considerable importance in the evaluation of the historic role of Mannheim and its music, for the history of music in Mannheim is synonymous with the history of ducal tastes and desires at the court. Carl Theodor, himself a capable musician, assembled an extraordinary group of musicians at his court, the group later known as the Mannheim school. The school may be divided into two groups: the older generation consisted of the "founders," Johann Stamitz, Franz Xaver Richter, and Ignaz Holzbauer, followed by Anton Filtz and Giuseppe Toëschi (1724–1788); the younger branch counted among its members Christian Cannabich, Franz Beck, Ernst Eichner (1740–1777), and Ignaz Fränkl (1736–1811). There was also a group that flourished after the school had outlived its excellence, Karl Stamitz (1746–1801), Wilhelm Cramer (1745–1799), Anton Stamitz (1753–1820), and Carl Cannabich (1771–1805) continuing the traditions in the face of the complete triumph of the Viennese classical style. All three of the founders were Austrian or Bohemian musicians whom we have already mentioned in the general census of musicians in the Habsburg lands, Stamitz was twenty-four years old, Richter thirty-eight, and Holzbauer forty-two when they joined the court orchestra. These facts preclude the question of an indigenous Mannheim style and school, especially when we discover that the next two composers were also importations from Bohemia and Italy. Let us now see the background which the Austrian and Italian musicians found in Mannheim.

The elector's operatic establishments in and around Mannheim looked back upon a distinguished past,[42] and the tradition of performing the newest operas was maintained during Carl Theodor's reign. Thus in the formative years of the so-called Mannheim school the chronicles list such notable events as the performance of works by the greatest contemporary masters of opera—Galuppi (1749), Hasse (1750), Jommelli (1751), and Pergolesi (1752). The eagerness of Mannheim for new works may seem strange to us, accustomed as we are to time-honored and immutable repertories, but the list is eloquent. Jommelli's *Artaserse,* composed in Rome in 1749, went on the stage in Mannheim within two years. The great success obtained by this somber music drama caused Jommelli's next work, *Iphigenia in Aulis,* to be performed here a few months after its Italian première. Thus the most important intermediary between Italian and German music, one of the great pioneers of the symphonic idiom, was well known and appreciated in Mannheim even before his arrival in 1754 at Stuttgart, not far removed from Mannheim. We are still at a loss, however, to explain the extraordinary reputation for originality enjoyed by the Mannheim school, since we know that its musicians and its idiom came from Austria.

If the idiom itself cannot be ascribed to the Mannheimers, the Austrian musicians assembled in the city merit the designation of a school on another count: their new and perfect orchestral ensemble playing. Stamitz was the first German master to break away from the Italian violin schools, developing a manner of violin and orchestral playing of his own. It was his fiery playing that had attracted Carl Theodor's attention when the young prince heard him in 1742 on the occasion of the crowning of Charles VII in Frankfort. And he did subsequently create a school in Mannheim, as the members of the orchestra were taught individually and drilled in ensembles by him. All witnesses agree with Burney that the orchestra played together in a faultless ensemble, with uniform bowing and a close observance of dynamic signs and the niceties of phrasing. After Stamitz's death his pupil Cannabich raised still higher the excellence of the orchestra, which became proverbial all over Europe.

We have taken away from Stamitz his "invention" and deprived the Mannheim school of the monopoly on the preparation of the classical symphony which it has enjoyed since Riemann; but we can minimize neither the greatness of Stamitz as a composer nor the role of the school, which was not the invention, but the stabilization, of a new form and idiom, and the working out of its orchestral technique. Stamitz endeavored to continue Rinaldo's lead and turn the motivic into thematic work, setting the idea of subsidiary thematic material into the symphony with a firm hand, while his colleagues and immediate successors were still hesitating what to do with the new elements. He approached his task with a vehemence that was well-nigh unparalleled in his times, frightening the timid knights of the style galant. He did not bother with details but cut loose with his orchestra at the first opportunity. Where others experimented gently with a motivic subsidiary group he placed a full-fledged theme, even at the expense of the principal idea, which may have been much simpler. Stamitz established, then, the clear disposition of the sections of the sonata, but their logical-causal connection remained to be perfected, for his ideas were too bold and his technique not fine-grained enough to create that equilibrium of form and content that makes for organic growth. Stamitz had no immediate heirs, but the tremendous breadth of his truly symphonic ideas was not lost; it was only hidden until sympathetic souls, capable of equally bold utterances, were born to listen to this fiery prophet. We are fortunate in having at least one composition by Stamitz that bears out this contention, his so-called orchestral trio-sonata *opus* IV, No. 3, in C minor, published in Hugo Riemann's *Collegium Musicum*. The scherzo in Beethoven's Fifth Symphony was, indeed, modeled after the finale of this modest "trio"; the similarity in both the thematic and structural arrangement as well as in the disposition of orchestral sonority is apparent at first glance.

Next to Stamitz, the leader of the school, the two most important members of the older group were Franz Xaver Richter and Anton Filtz. Richter, who came to Mannheim from his native Moravia, was a singer, violinist, and composer in the ducal band from 1747 to 1769, when he left for Strassburg, remaining there until his death in 1789. Born almost half a century before and dying a scant two years ahead of Mozart, Richter lived through the whole period that led to the classical school, witnessing both the sowing and the harvest. His contribution to the growing style was not insignificant, and he ably seconded Stamitz, but his tone is much less positive and personal than Stamitz's.

Like the younger Neapolitan composers, Filtz was entirely dominated by melodies, at times songlike, at other times impish or coy, but always fresh and beautifully rounded. His melodic wealth was put to thematic use, but with him it was not so much the symphony that mattered as the desire to present his mellifluous ideas in an adequate frame, a curious contrast to the stubborn symphonic instinct of Stamitz. This pleased the composers of the *Empfindsamkeit,* and they made Filtz their idol, the ideal champion of the *galant* symphony. We should not deprecate the contributions of this highly gifted young composer, scarcely thirty when he died, for a good deal of his spirit was to return in Christian Bach and Mozart.

Further Organization of the Preclassic Symphony

THE problem of the symphony had not yet been solved, although it had been approached from various angles. After about 1760 there began the organization of all that had been thrown on the surface by the activity of the earlier symphonists. The musicians of the older generation were somewhat bewildered in the era of interregnum; they tried to hammer together a new form from a multitude of fragments, but the sole member of their ranks who had the breath of genius, Stamitz, died before he could harness his impetuous imagination. The new generation was now occupied with the task of making the sections of the symphony tight and logical. Their problem was the restoration of some of the marvelous continuity by which contrapuntal compositions had formerly been held together, but this time without the accompanying strictness in the texture, and with the addition of freedom and variety of rhythm and voice leading, a cherished innovation of their time. The delicate melodic beauty of the Neapolitans gradually disappeared and was replaced by symphonic terseness, the mark of Germanic musical genius. The dualism of themes and sections remained an essential aesthetic-stylistic criterion, but the isolated formal elements were slowly enveloped by a symphonic organism ruling the whole; the existence and the formal place held by the subsidiary sections must henceforth be justified by their content. The development section, the battlefield of thematic struggle, became the center of gravity of the symphony, and this section already showed all the attributes we assign to the classical symphony: the elaboration of the thematic material to the exhaustion of its last particle, and the stirring up of that irresistible wave which carries in the recapitulation. Imbued with the spirit of the *Sturm und Drang,* composers were no longer satisfied with the content used by the style galant; they were searching for more profound ideas which they might enhance and render eloquent by an appropriate artistic form. Here began the modern symphony. But the road was weary and burdensome, and many a talented artist did not finish the journey. Their tragedy—the tragedy of the *galant* symphony and of the late romantic symphony alike—was that their ideas were too numerous and not pregnant enough, and they filled them with too much minute expression; the symphonic principle was opposed to such diffuseness. After the first memorable start they became stranded, and the musical world passed by them.

But before we discuss the defeated let us follow the successful builders. To these men the importance of invention itself was secondary to the will of finding a way to enhance expressiveness even beyond the capacities of the original idea, of which they must never lose sight, and which must be utilized to the exclusion of every foreign element. And this is the fundamental principle, the cornerstone of the symphony, now clearly realized by the generation of the *Sturm und Drang*. This required, however, a new conception in which form would serve as the means to enhance content. Therefore from this time on the relationship between form and content was much more intimate and causal than before, when form was little more than a frame for such ideas as might be invented. Now the large, bold form envisaged by Stamitz began to take shape and a rich, complex technique of composition filled in the gaps and linked the sections together. Symphony and content became one and the same. With this generation the motivic-thematic technique lost its "worked" aspect and appeared as the product of freely flowing musical imagination.

The greatest master of the oldest symphonic school and the one who connected it with the generation immediately preceding the great classical school was Georg Christoph Wagenseil. This Viennese took over from the Italians the dualistic symphonic form and idiom, but his motivic work shows German qualities; it is more closely knit than the Italian, and the logic of his development goes even beyond Jommelli. Wagenseil now took the important step toward symphonic writing taken by Stamitz a little before, or perhaps at the same time, transforming motivic writing into thematic, that is, into periodized musical ideas, themes that contain several independent motives. Thus the theme, uncertain since the departure of baroque polyphony, became differentiated, offering a selection of motives, and could become the vehicle of ideas and not merely of germs of ideas. Therewith the prerequisites of the classical symphony were realized; the pattern of the symphony-sonata appeared in conclusive shape. Wagenseil's contrasts are superior to those of Stamitz, because they are not merely formal elements but are the result of a dualism predetermined by the nature of the musical material. In his sharp oppositions of minor and major, triad and diminished seventh, we already feel the typical symphonic atmosphere that so fascinates us in the classical symphony.

Wagenseil's work was brought to fruition by Franz Beck and Luigi Boccherini. Beck (1730–1809), a native of Mannheim and a pupil of Stamitz, left his city at a relatively early age, for in 1762 we find him in Marseilles, and it seems that he spent the rest of his life in France, dying in obscurity in Bordeaux. By combining the powerful symphonic gestures of his master with Wagenseil's fine motivic work, Beck achieved the merger that gave the next generation the finished symphony-sonata. It is a great pity that this highly gifted composer did not remain in Mannheim, because he could have continued his teacher's work and thereby prevented the decline of the Mannheim school. He dissipated his energies in a country where for a time he was highly appreciated, but where symphonic thought would never grow strong roots.

The path of the preclassical symphony-sonata, winding over foreign soil with Beck, was crossed, while still abroad, by an Italian whom we shall consider the other outstanding figure of the preclassical sonata, Luigi Boccherini (1743–1805). Boccherini might have become the first "great" symphonist, but he was an Italian; he could not abandon his melodies, although he himself realized that what was needed to carry the symphony forward was a compromise between old and new, and a reinstatement, at least partial, of polyphony. His lyricism was too delicate and could not rise to the heroic power that is so essential in a symphony. Thus the final synthesis was left to an Austrian composer, Haydn. Boccherini remained an artist of the rococo, delightfully sensitive, thoroughly artistic, but too delicate and ornate. For this reason he was supplanted by Haydn, but he was not forgotten, for the thread leads from him—over the heads of the classicists—to the early romantic school. The timid use of polyphony that appears in Boccherini's works is not the architectural counterpoint of the baroque, it merely enlarges the surface upon which the symphony spreads itself; still it was of invaluable help. It made possible the simultaneous handling of several motives instead of the consecutive enumeration formerly used, and it fused the technique of symphonic writing, making it more solid and organic.

We have now arrived in the immediate vicinity of the great classical school. Haydn and Mozart had already contributed a number of works while Wagenseil, Beck, Boccherini, and the other preclassic symphonists were stabilizing the form. These early works of the great symphonists were, however, inferior to the best of the mature masters of the preclassic era. The idiom was now fully developed, and in this connection no monopoly of invention can be claimed for the composers of the later Viennese school.

We still must consider the other movements of the sonata in order to see the state of the symphony-sonata at the outset of the high classical period. The slow introduction that precedes the first movement originated from the desire to preface the usually spirited allegro with a more solemn and serious prologue. The older generation was satisfied with a few chords, but in the late sixties and in the seventies the introduction became more articulate, until in Leopold Anton Koželuch's works we have the classic model, followed by the rest of the Viennese school. The second movement offers no problem, for its aria or songlike qualities hark back to old practices, familiar to composers for generations. Of the two remaining movements, the minuet has been made the object of much discussion. Some authors have endeavored to derive the symphony altogether from the baroque dance suite, pointing, as an unquestionable proof of their contention, to the presence in the symphony of the minuet, whose introduction others persist in attributing to Haydn. As a matter of fact the minuet had been used sporadically both in Italian and in German works for a long time, but its statutory incorporation by Stamitz in the cyclic form dates from about 1745, that is, a good many years before Haydn's first compositions in the symphonic vein. The dance being fundamentally opposed to the symphonic spirit, the minuet was the weakest part of the symphony—a movement inserted between the second and the fourth—and its whole existence in the cyclic form was questionable; indeed, the northern German composers emphatically protested its inclusion. As long as the minuet adhered to the strict periodic construction of the dance, the new symphonic spirit could not penetrate it, and very few of the early symphonic minuets show any distinction. The task was to invest the minuet with some of the properties of the symphonic style, after which its modest measures could permit of alterations and additions. In a number of symphonies the minuet was the last movement, thus embarrassing the composer by its brevity and relative rigidity. From the alternation of tutti

and solo in the concerto came the idea of enlarging the movement by working it over into a rondo, which would permit the insertion of couplets between the tuttis. This developed into the rondo finale. In the meantime the
tendency to break away from the pure dance minuet, already visible in Sammartini, increased noticeably until in the hands of Boccherini's generation
it became a symphonic movement, finely stylized and bearing little resemblance to its ancestor. The last movement enjoyed a tremendous popularity, owing, no doubt, to its derivation from the rapid and amusing ensembles and finales of the opera buffa. It was usually presented in the form
of a rondo, causing endless delight by the clever preparation and introduction of the fresh and coquettish tune employed in the recurring rounds.

The immediate influence of Wagenseil, Beck, Boccherini, Koželuch, and
a number of other composers on the style of the next generation (this can
be seen from the numerous citations from their works in Haydn, Mozart,
and even Beethoven) may create the impression that these composers mirror
the general trend of symphonic evolution. Such was not the case; they represent, rather, high individual achievements. The great majority of symphonists remained within the orbit of the style galant. This was especially
true with regard to the Mannheim school after the death of Stamitz and
the departure of Beck. The second generation of the Mannheim school, led
by the able violinist and conductor Christian Cannabich (1731–1798), created
courtly *Gebrauchsmusik* which today has interest for the historian only.
Their music is smooth and elegant, the themes without a marked profile,
and the shallow inspiration covered with mannerisms. As early as 1777
Leopold Mozart noticed "the stereotyped mannerisms of the Mannheim
goût." The paucity of spontaneous inventiveness was supplemented by external technical elements, and orchestration became a dominant factor as
thematic dualism was replaced by coloristic dualism. For the first time we
now witness the procedure which so successfully camouflaged the impoverished imagination of composers of the postromantic era: the selection of
musical material for the sake of the specific tone color of a single instrument.
The importance of orchestral effects in their works is eloquently demonstrated if we compare an orchestral work of Cannabich with one of his
chamber music compositions; deprived of his sonorous means of creating
contrast, his chamber music discloses a tedious and loosely knit musical texture with both melody and harmony uninteresting and platitudinous. While
it is obvious that the experiments in instrumentation contributed to the
development of orchestral technique, Goethe's warning that whenever technique supersedes thought, art will decline, is as conclusively justified here
as in the orchestral literature at the opening of our century.

Preclassic Chamber Music

THE development of the symphony and the development of chamber music are parallel phenomena, although by no means always identical. The same men who composed symphonies *al fresco* often used a much more subtle technique in their chamber works; on the other hand trio sonata and quartet were often synonymous with almost every other form of instrumental music, from simple sonatas to symphonies and concertos. The same sweeping changes which characterized the new orchestral style, the dualistic principle of the sonata form, the change from motivic to thematic work, and the strong operatic influences, appeared in chamber music. The trio sonata retained its hold for some time, at least as far as the combination of instruments was concerned, but the disparity between the tendency toward more refined writing and that toward orchestral treatment raised havoc until the final divorce between orchestral and chamber music cleared the issues. The rapprochement between trio sonata and symphony took place in the *symphonie concertante,* whereas the differentiated chamber style, definitely renouncing the doubling of parts, found its noblest expression in the string quartet. The overwhelming impressions made on chamber music by Corelli disappeared under the pressure of the new tendencies, but while Sammartini prepared the new sonata style the spirit of Corelli was revealed once more in one of the finest chamber music composers of the times, Giuseppe Tartini (1692–1770). Tartini, whose works are fortunately still known and appreciated, was obviously partial to the baroque solo sonata, and the noble melody that pours from his violin parts does not rely on the new principle of contrasts. But his tone and idiom are definitely nearing the new style, especially that of the symphonie concertante, and in his string quartets he comes in closest proximity to the symphony.

Although the trio sonata retained the basso continuo, with the passing of polyphonic writing the first violin took over undisputed leadership in the ensemble, reducing the other instruments to playing an accompaniment, which, in turn, made the continuo as superfluous as in the symphony. The resultant embarrassment was eliminated in two different ways: the clavier was either retained and, relieved of its menial task, formed new combinations of clavier-string chamber music, or it was abandoned and its place taken by another stringed instrument to make a complete four-part setting possible, which gave us the string quartet. Toward the middle of the century the quartet literature already contained a number of interesting works, while the clavier-string combination produced many of its own; but it seems as if the liberated keyboard instrument took revenge on its former oppressors, for the new clavier sonatas, trios, and quartets often allotted insignificant "accompaniments" to the strings, while the clavier monopolized all attention.

The chamber music of the Berlin school—interesting especially in C. P. E. Bach's works—became somewhat stereotyped under the king's direction; in Mannheim it declined to the level of salon music, but in Vienna it found a fertile field. The string quartets of Asplmayr, Wagenseil, and other of the earlier symphonists all show the vitality of a new art, conscious of the long life ahead of it. They offer, however, a problem to the student, who finds them inextricably mixed with an intermediary form between chamber music and orchestral music. The earlier quartets of the Viennese composers, including Leopold Mozart and the two Haydns, cannot be told from certain compositions called *divertimenti*. A *divertimento,* the general term for a class of compositions including nocturnes, cassations, serenades, etc., is just what its numerous variants indicate, namely, "diverting" entertainment music. As a musical form it takes its place between the earlier suite and the more highly developed chamber music which eventually replaced it. Usually it is scored for simple ensembles, such as a trio or a quartet of string instruments, but the number of instrumental combinations for which it may be written is almost limitless. March and dance movements abound, and not infrequently the slow movement is titled. As the symphony grew, it imposed its principles upon the divertimento, one or more movements of which were constructed along the lines of the sonata form, attaining stately proportions and occasionally weight and serious symphonic countenance. Most of us know this type from Mozart's serenade entitled *Eine Kleine Nachtmusik*. But the main purpose of the divertimento was to take the place of the earlier *Tafelmusik,* or table-consort, to entertain the merry gatherings in the numerous aristocratic households in Austria. It is erroneous to conclude, however, that the divertimento was an aristocratic showpiece of the type used in France or in the court of Frederick, for we must remember that we are now in Austria, far less touched by the style galant than the north, and resounding with wholesome and unspoiled folk music—with which, indeed, the divertimento was saturated. The Vienna Theatre Almanac of 1794 gives eloquent contemporaneous testimony to the popularity and prevalence of this type of music:

During the summer months . . . one will meet serenaders in the streets almost daily and at all hours. . . . They do not, however, consist as in Italy or Spain of the simple accompaniment of a vocal part by a guitar or mandolin . . . but of trios, and quartets (most frequently from operas) of several vocal parts, of wind instruments, frequently of an entire orchestra, and the most ambitious symphonies are performed. . . . It is just these nocturnal musicales which demonstrate . . . the universality and the greatness of the love of music; for no matter how late at night they take place . . . one soon discovers people at their open windows and within a few minutes the musicians are surrounded by a crowd of listeners who rarely depart until the serenade has come to an end.

Hadyn, like the other Viennese composers, used the divertimento as a school in which he taught himself, by experiment and experience, the superb mastery of form and ensemble technique which characterizes his instrumental works. All of his divertimenti testify to a seemingly endless delight in tonal richness and coloring, which at times even dominates the composer's interest in their formal structure. The future of pure chamber music depended on a clarification of the three main genres of instrumental music, and this was accomplished by Josef Haydn, but the unabashed joy, the mocking humor, and the delightful straightforwardness of the many divertimenti of the eighteenth century will remain eternally fresh and fascinating as we slowly begin to appreciate the great art of the past and, cured of the grandiloquence of the nineteenth century, learn to relax and rejoice in the unadultered charms of its "entertainment music."

Chapter 13

THE CLASSIC ERA

※ ※

Ars adeo latet arte sua.

The Return of Classic Thought

THE ideals of arts and letters change with the seasons of civilization. In antiquity it was beauty, in the Middle Ages, goodness, in the era of the Enlightenment, truth, that was written on the banner. But the veneration of truth was soon abandoned with the discovery of the disillusioning fact that the aspect of truth varies according to the angle from which it is approached. Neither would goodness any longer serve, because the Enlightenment had shown that goodness often hides ulterior motives. Men returned, therefore, to the ideal of beauty of classical antiquity. There were many reasons for recalling the beauty and form of antiquity, one of which was the renewed emphasis placed on the universal; another weighty reason was the kinship of the rococo with classicism. Granted that to the rococo poet and artist mythology meant little more than pure ornamentation, the cupids and playful antique gods, and the lovers who carried classical names, did occasionally conjure up the dance of nymphs and fauns and the Olympic felicity of Venus and Adonis. A third reason was that rationalism, not less than the rococo, was bound to rediscover antiquity—if not classical Greece at least Alexandrian and Roman antiquity, for the latter cherished the *doctus poeta* as did rationalism. There was a fourth reason, the rapprochement of Germanic genius to that of Hellas as the ideal of the new Renaissance concluded an alliance with the fresh spiritual forces of Germandom. Germany now gave birth to her most representative minds, minds invincibly attracted to classic thought: Goethe to Euripides, Kant to Plato. The final reason is really a corollary to the preceding: philosophy, art and literary criticism, and philology, following the urge for a classical orientation, created modern classical philology and modern archaeology. The rebirth of the antique through German genius in a constantly increasing intensity and creative force is one of the greatest cultural facts of the eighteenth century.

The atmosphere of German civilization was kept in flux for a few decades by the *Sturm und Drang*. When the movement whose nature was so admirably expressed by its very name assured unlimited liberty to the exceptional creative mind, it found a Johann Georg Hamann (1730–1788) or a Johann Gottfried von Herder (1744–1803) among its champions; when it assailed outmoded traditions, when it probed the ills of society, and when it revalued the accepted tenets of ethics, it rallied around Rousseau's gospel; when it sought a legal foundation to bolster up its arbitrariness it called Shakespeare to witness, for in the latter's "excesses" it found justification for the disposal of such artistic restraints as the three unities. The pathos of the Sturm und Drang was really the transitory mental state of a nation and not a permanent force; therefore it knew extremes only, and its revolutionary tendencies usually flickered out with the exhaustion of the pathos that engendered them.

The representative form of the Sturm und Drang was the drama because the drama turns to the public, and because its patron saint, Shakespeare, was a dramatist. Jacob Reinhold Michael Lenz (1751–1792) codified the dramatic tenets of the period, declaring war on Aristotle, on French classicism, and on everything that impeded the movement. The brutal force of eternal youth asserted itself in his dramas and the greater and lesser idols of the rococo were demolished to make place for the new universal idol, Goethe. The very talented Lenz was even surpassed in vehemence by Friedrich Maximilian von Klinger (1752–1831), whose drama *Sturm und Drang* (1776) gave the movement its name. Johann Anton Leisewitz (1752–1806) united revolutionary content with Lessing's form, while Christian Friedrich Daniel Schubart, the boldest, stormiest petrel of the era, was its greatest lyricist and publicist. It is significant that the last-named, whom we have encountered before,[1] was a musician, and perhaps first of all a musician, for this whole movement was to find its solution in music. The fact that among the literary figures of the era one can find such Anacreontic lyricists as Ludwig Heinrich Christoph Hölty (1748–1776), singing with gentle abandonment of death, of the graves in the churchyard, of the dusk appearing with the setting sun, of the twinkling stars and nebulous moonlight, only accentuates the musical quality that characterizes all this fantastic world. It was in this atmosphere that the great romantic movement filling a whole century was to arise, uniting once more poetry and music in an all-embracing lyricism.

But the apostles of the Sturm und Drang fell victim to the many problems they evoked. The passions whipped up to a frenzy settled and became purified, rude reality was transfigured in the fire of ideals, and creative force and form-building will power united in a common task. The genius recognized the validity of objective norms, boundless humanism gave way to a humanism which sets its own limits. This moderation and equalization ripened into classicism, of which the German phase was the very symbol. In stinct made peace with the law, form triumphed over matter, order over chaos. Classicism beatified life and gave it lastingness by viewing it from the heights of the ideal. It abdicated all its past and future rights, abandoned all disquieting desires in order to be able to live in the timeless present. Its art was devoted to the ideal of plastic beauty which it believed to be absolute; its principal object was man living in consort with nature, man beautiful in body and soul, in bearing and in deed, man who became aware of his own inner harmony, and who was the measure of all things. The centuries-long battle for liberty and form, ideal and reality, German aspirations and the forces of antiquity, came to a standstill, the sentimental irrationalism of the Sturm und Drang emptied into the quiet world of the idea and the result was an aesthetic world picture, a Germandom reborn from the spirit of Greece, purified of its conflicts: a Germanized Hellas.

The Classic Orientation in Arts and Letters

CLASSICISM was not, however, a new tendency associated with the end of the eighteenth century; it merely reached its formulation in the epoch that bears its name. Just as rationalism presented two different aspects in the seventeenth and eighteenth centuries, classicism had a seventeenth-century phase which the rococo could not obliterate. But this earlier classicism, expressed in law and order, was built more on Roman lines than was its eighteenth-century variant, devoted to nature, freedom, and Hellenism, which ended by triumphing over Roman-French classicism. The latter came once more to the fore in the nineteenth century with its monumental architecture, theatrical painting, and historical grand opera, but was alternately superseded by such divergent branches as the Hellenic baroque of Goya, and the romanticists' Grecomania, entangled in Oriental and medieval ramifications. The classical Greek line goes through the eighteenth century unspoiled from Shaftesbury to Goethe. It is present in the Greek figures of Berkeley's dialogues, in Hume's polytheism, in Pope's translations, and in Daniel Webb's writings on Greek art. Richard Bentley (1662-1742) opened the ranks of the learned linguists, and was followed by many others across the Channel. While the great educator Johann Bernhard Basedow (1723-1790) Grecized education, the literary reform which set in at the beginning of the eighteenth century in Italy called on the whole Parnassus in its academies. Metastasio's very name, a Grecized form of his original name, Trapassi, indicates his Hellenic preoccupations, and while Gottsched was still clinging to the Roman classicism of seventeenth-century France the French themselves, clamoring for Greek ideals, took up arms against Boileau. The Hellenist tendency gained in emphasis toward the end of the century, dominating architecture in France, England, Germany, Holland, and Italy, and being reflected in the paintings of David, Mengs, and Carstens, in Canova's sculptures and in Alfieri's tragedies, finding its consummate expression in Gluck's and in Goethe's *Iphigenia,* and earning a scientific eulogy in Wolf's *Prolegomena* to Homer (1795). It was especially in Germany that Hellenism flourished; Klopstock in his earliest odes acknowledged himself a "disciple of the Greeks," and even the Sturm und Drang was immersed in Pindar and Anacreon, hoping for a German Athens as proclaimed in the new humanism of Karl Wilhelm von Humboldt (1767–1835).

In the field of architecture we see a similar orientation in the very midst of the rococo. James Stuart and Nicholas Revett visited Greece around the middle of the century, conducting exhaustive researches in the legendary centers of antiquity, then under Turkish rule. Their findings were embodied in a joint work, *Classical Antiquities of Athens,* of which the first volume, published in 1762, is considered to have had more responsibility than any other single factor for the changed direction in taste. The world was again reminded of the culture of antiquity when the antagonists of the baroque, led by Gottsched, acquired an unexpected and superior brother-in-arms in Johann Joachim Winckelmann (1717–1768), whose *History of the Art of Antiquity* (1764) marks the beginning of modern classical archaeology. Winckelmann examined the ancient art and—taking counsel with Plotinus and Shaftesbury—endeavored to interpret the spiritual content of a work of art and the artistic idea which animates it.

In opposition to the seventeenth-century pictorial baroque, the Hellenic artistic ideal of eighteenth-century classicism tended to plastic clarity. The growing belief in limitation and articulation and the full extent of the departure from the baroque is most convincingly demonstrated in the writings of the early exponents of Hellenism: one has only to read the outraged exclamations of Winckelmann over baroque sculpture or the violent tonal conflicts of Rembrandt. Still, the new plastic ideal did not find its highest expression in architecture and sculpture as had been the case in Greece. While the praise of classical art was universal, the spirit of the antique was not recaptured by the fine arts, for, the many great art works of the period notwithstanding, these artists were searching for the glory that was Greece with the soul of the subjective individual of the eighteenth century, with a mental disposition that was far removed from that of the ancients, to whom glory was a birthright which did not have to be found.

Classicism was convinced that there are forms of art and laws of immutable and eternal validity, and drawing from Winckelmann's abstract and stylized conception of Greece—"a noble simplicity and a quiet greatness"—it professed a belief that universality of content and form is not an unattainable fiction but had been once before realized by Greece and, given the proper

conditions, could be attained again. Architects, sculptors, and painters believed firmly that they had found Ariadne's thread. But having emerged
from the dramatic baroque and having been softened by the playful rococo,
the artists could never equal the serene ideal of Hellas and had to be satisfied
with a compromise. Wherever we glance, toward England, where Robert
Adam (1728–1792) created the graceful "Adam" style characterized by a
harmonious unity between the exterior, the interior, and the furniture;
toward Italy, where Antonio Canova (1757–1822), the leader of Italian
classicism, created his tender and noble figures in marble; toward France,
where Jacques Louis David (1748–1825) revived history in great scenes
whose influence remained absolute until the rise of romanticism; or toward
Germany, where Anton Raphael Mengs (1728–1779) and Asmus Jacob
Carstens (1754–1798) inaugurated the classic school along antique and
Italian models, we behold an art graceful and polished, noble and skillful.
But these artists, unquestionably masters of composition and design, exhausted their imagination in their quest, and their classicism is of a rather
cold logic and sober and reasonable beauty.

The artists of the Renaissance also have been credited with seeking the
rebirth of antiquity, but they drew from the fount of ancient civilization
only to create a world of their own. The fine arts of the eighteenth century,
aided by modern archaeology and aesthetics, approached the task without
the forward-looking attitude of the Renaissance; hence their stalemate. But
something akin to the Renaissance occurred when German genius, yearning
for a Hellas to come and immersed in a creative mood, re-created something
that was not prominent in the hierarchy of classical Greek thought: lyricism;
and lyricism means poetry and music. Contemporary aesthetics, led by Gottlieb Alexander Baumgarten (1714–1762), was more concerned with literature and music than with the fine arts, which seemed content to be dissolved
into poetry and music. When discussing the emergence of German civilization from the late baroque we noticed the preponderance of musical elements, especially in Klopstock. The German Orpheus, as Klopstock was
called, not without good reason, wrote poetry that sounds like music; his
figures are never plastic in the sculptural sense, they dissolve in a cloud of
musical verse. Schiller called this poetry essentially musical "because its intention is more the creation of a mood, a mental state, than the imitation
of definite objects." Such an aim entails an animation which runs counter
to the static plasticity of the antique, a conception of art and life which is
centralized in sentiment, in the humanly subjective which became the
essence of eighteenth-century classicism. This new humanism focused its
attention once more on man and nature, but not with the passionate and
soul-stirring vehemence of the baroque nor the playful superficiality of the

rococo; this Hellenic classicism endeavored to find and represent man—and through him nature—in his natural and particular freedom. Thus classicism again celebrated *la découverte de l'homme,* the spiritual turning away from the celestial to the human, from the universe to the individual; a farewell to the baroque. To the eighteenth century the soul was more important than heaven, and man and his own life more important than the world. And only for man—or rather *in* man—lives Kant's religion, which is purely moral: "We live in the invisible church; God's kingdom is, however, in ourselves." The question was, however, to know man not only in his individual experiences, but in his universal reason, to have this man will and act not only according to his own loves and penchants but so as to make it possible for all others to act likewise; for while it again enthroned individualism, classicism reminded man that he had done enough for and about himself and, that while retaining the gains, he should again think on his place in the universe, to seek for himself a new universality, a new bond of humanity.

The classical precepts evolved by the poets and musicians stood for unity of freedom and order, a remarkable *coincidentia oppositorum,* a self-discipline, a conquest of autonomy such as only the truly great can achieve. They did not want to extinguish the individual in the universal; they wanted to co-ordinate the two rather than subordinate one to the other, and what they achieved was the miracle of universalized individualism. To the nineteenth century this synthesis appeared as form, as an abstract pattern which it believed could be segregated and infused with new content time and again. This idea, happily overcome in literature, was successfully propagated in music, and in the twentieth century people are still being taught to "compose in sonata form." It is no exaggeration to maintain that this conception has been one of the main causes of the general decline of music in recent times. For the rules came to the classicists not as predetermined compulsion but as spiritual law and order, engendered by themselves. Aristotle searched for form, and so did Scholasticism after him, and later the new Scholasticism of the baroque, French classicism. But the forms of this early classicism were static and objective, while the forms of late eighteenth-century classicism are dynamic; they are functions and principles. They are not reduced to restrictive norms, like those of formalistic seventeenth-century classicism or of the archaizing nineteenth century, but they act as executive organs whose lifeblood is the subject. The confusion is perhaps due to the lack of understanding of the place of the rococo in early classicism. As seen from our vantage point it becomes clear why the rococo came between the baroque and classicism; it is not an antithesis but a bridge onto which the strain of the baroque disembogued. The monumentality of the baroque, its passionate mass, could not egress into the relative calm of classicism; it first had to be dissolved, its tumultuous accents had to be tempered by graceful conversation before it could smile on the world with the smile of Greece. Classicism is at the end of the antibaroque movement.

Early classicism still had a good deal of the delicate feminine touch of the rococo, and just as Prud'hon and Canova toyed with the delectable forms and subjects of the rococo before finding their own way and tone, so Haydn and Mozart were in their early phases addicted to the minuets of the era; but the intimacy and playfulness of the century was on the wane as it approached its final decades. The last great champions of the Enlightenment died, Hume in England, Lessing in Germany, and Voltaire in France, and with them departed the rulers, Louis XV, Maria Theresa, Frederick the Great, taking to their graves a whole style of life. And those were the decades which witnessed the revolutions in America and in France. After the smile of the rococo, the satisfied comfortableness of the Enlightenment, the atmosphere is beclouded; Kant's *Critique* appeared in 1781, the year which produced Schiller's *Robbers*. The objectivity of the Enlightenment was overwhelmed by the tempered subjectivity of classicism, its critical rationalism by irrational feeling. How truly all this is reflected in the poet in whom German classicism reached its synthesis, Johann Wolfgang von Goethe (1749-1832). If his first period saw the reirrationalization of German thought, the second, after the revelations of the Italian journey, became the era of poetic sublimation of liberated thought. *Faust* is the closing masterpiece of his life, as it is the summit of German literary classicism, assimilating every stratum from the Sturm und Drang to high classicism.

But the soul of this century and of this era is consummated in music, for its subjectivity had to reach its apotheosis in music. And it is the soul of music itself which in Mozart is revealed in all its purity. All the muses of the century hover about him and find expression in his music; all the youthful delicacy and feminine grace of the century, its smiling comeliness and convivial friendliness, its naïveté and candor, its brightness and naturalness, its *Empfindsamkeit* and fervor, its carefree merriness and playful freedom, its volatile fantasy and vernal freshness, its flexibility, its loving care for the little and the fine. its fondness for variation and for the characteristic, all this lives in him and streams out in sheer perfection and with the same abandoned conviction. But this lovable youthfulness ripens into maturity, and playful freedom and moodiness are harnessed by schooling and discipline, ingenuous feelings are formed by classic measure, ideas are deepened to symbols of universal significance. "Mozart should have composed Faust," said Goethe. With the intuition that only the poet has at his command (his knowledge of music was slight indeed) the octogenarian Sage of Weimar recognized the kinship of *Don Giovanni* to his *Faust*, at the same time acknowledging a unique artistic conception and a realization of the eternally and purely human through music. But it was not necessary to set *Faust* to music. To paint the Faustian picture Mozart the *musician* could not have followed Goethe's ideas, and thus the estuary of the spiritual life of the century poured out into operas, symphonies, quartets, sonatas, Masses, and songs.

The ties between all these species were close and intimate, they were all saturated with the elements of a minutely organized style which gave the classical era homogeneity unparalleled since the time of the Netherlanders. This we have since lost, for in the twentieth century every species tries to eradicate the conventions attached throughout the romantic era to symphony or opera by applying a new technique. But technique alone does not suffice. The classical era surrounded itself with music as with mirrors in which the rays of life were reflected, and thus the music of this era was the music of life. It clung to the outward forms of life, it was present at every occasion in order to make use of it, and from this point of view it was "occasional music." But it no longer was, as in the past, the servant of any particular occasion, the means with which man served cultural aims, sacred or secular, of worship or of entertainment. On the other hand, this music did not yet pretend to give the world a philosophy and guide the life of nations; it accompanied life, running parallel with it, always reflecting in the glass the riches of life. This music did not originate in closets: it moved in the open, in fresh air, at all times; hence its symmetric growth, its sound and flexible body. It was the incarnation of the Apollonian art which the century had hoped for and which it never quite realized it had found—in music.

Haydn

KANT once defined genius as "the talent which gives art its rules." The musician who opened the classical era was one of these men of genius, who, moreover, was permitted to accompany a new world of art from its inception to its supreme flowering. He absorbed everything on his way, yet always remained his own self, and once he assimilated something was again at the head of the movement. He started with popular ministrelsy and arrived at the consummation of art. With him music shed its courtly etiquette and playfulness to become a most personal expression, the expression of the Austrian peasant, of love of life, of the colorfulness of nature, moving about in a kaleidoscope of wit, humor, joy, and sorrow. From the Italians, he took the beauty of a rounded form, from the Germans their counterpoint, but with all his skill and artistry he remained the Austrian peasant.

Born on March 31, 1732, in Rohrau near Bruck in Lower Austria of purely German parentage,[2] Haydn grew up in a humble but music-loving family. His first musical education is hardly worthy of that name although he was a member of the cathedral choir of St. Stephen's, for the imperial choirmaster, Johann Georg Reutter (1708–1772), was not interested in anything beyond the daily routine. Metastasio having recommended him to the good graces of a lady, the latter in turn introduced him to Nicola Porpora, the composer, who was also the greatest vocal teacher of his time. Intercourse with persons so closely connected with the operatic stage must have had its repercussions, and indeed Haydn wrote the music to a *Singspiel* entitled *Der Neue Krumme Teufel* (1751).

It seemed natural that the young musician, saturated with vocal, especially operatic, music, should take up the career of an opera composer, the major field of musical activity of his time, but events took a different turn. In those days the best music was cultivated by the aristocrats. The Kinsky, Schwarzenberg, Esterházy, Erdödy, Liechtenstein, Lobkowitz, and other noble houses of Austria, Bohemia, Hungary, and southern Germany often surpassed the imperial court in the art of music. Through the intermediary of his two eminent Italian patrons, Haydn made the acquaintance of a number of these ardent music lovers, who became attracted to the young man. One of their rank, Karl Joseph von Fürnberg, invited him to take charge of music on his estate, Weinzirl, near Melk. From the services of this rather modest noble-man he passed, in 1759, into the more elaborate court of Count Ferdinand Maximilian Morzin in Lukavec, near Pilsen. The course of events aptly illustrates both the musical practice of the times and Haydn's genius for making the best of circumstances. Von Fürnberg's finances permitted only a very small musical establishment, so Haydn proceeded to write string quartets. The combination intrigued him, and the first essay was soon followed by seventeen more works. Count Morzin provided a small orchestra for him, and, rising again to the situation, Haydn composed his "first" symphony in 1759. After a short stay in Lukavec, Haydn was appointed conductor of the orchestra of Prince Paul Anthony Esterházy, premier peer of Hungary, a wealthy, art-loving aristocrat. The prince died in 1762 and the latifundium fell to Prince Nicholas Joseph, even more devoted to music and himself a fair practitioner. This apparently dynastic love of music on the part of the Ester-házy princes [3] had made their residence one of the most brilliant musical centers, especially after Nicholas Joseph built in addition to the ancestral manor in Kismarton (Eisenstadt, in German) a magnificent castle which he named Eszterháza. Even the French visitors compared this palace, with its beautiful theater and vast parks, to Versailles. The prince liked Haydn and his works and encouraged him; in his turn Haydn was devoted to Nicholas and realized the unique advantages of his position. "As a conductor of an orchestra I could make experiments, observe what produced an effect and what weakened it, and was thus in a position to improve, alter, make additions or omissions, and be as bold as I pleased; I was cut off from the world, there was no one to confuse or torment me, and I was forced to become original." [4]

By the middle of the seventeen sixties Haydn was already well known and his compositions were sought in England and France, while the Austrians called him the "Gellert of music," undoubtedly intended as the highest of compliments.[5] Haydn was not the first great German musician recognized outside his country, but in Hasse and Graun the world at large saw Italians, Handel became an Englishman, and Gluck was identified with French opera. Haydn remained, however, a typical representative of German instrumental music and it was with his quartets and symphonies that the great vogue of German music began. Out of loyalty to his prince the musician refused all invitations to leave Kismarton or Eszterháza, but when Prince Nicholas died and his successor disbanded orchestra and opera, assuring Haydn a generous pension, he felt free to undertake artistic tours. At the age of sixty he was a man youthfully climbing uphill, toward greater works of art. Vienna became his home but his sojourn was interrupted by two voyages to England, in 1790 and in 1794. Haydn could have occupied in English musical life the position once held by Handel, but he was not a man of the world. Unlike the Saxon, equally at home in Italy, Germany, or England, this Austrian could not stay away from his Vienna.

The once so productive composer had lost his incredible fertility and had to struggle with his genius, but the youthful freshness, the virile power of the *Creation* (1799) belied the composer's sixty-six years and the three years its composition took. The following year saw him at work on another oratorio, the *Seasons*, after which the effects of age curtailed his creative activity. A few more veritable gems of vocal quartets, then (after 1803) he ceased to compose altogether, looking forward to death with calm serenity and pious conviction.

Earlier Works

THE young composer had begun his career in the midst of the rococo and the *Empfindsamkeit,* and his first years of active creative work were spent in trying to reconcile his popular Austrian musical invention with the conventions of an aristocratic art opposed to his own instincts. In these first works, a dozen or so string quartets, divertimenti, and serenades, we see nothing of the future logic of musical construction and—most remarkable— nothing of the masterly thematic work of the archsymphonist. The unsettled state of chamber music mentioned in the previous chapter is even more evident in these works than in those of his older colleagues. Elements from the trio sonata, suite, symphony, concerto, and especially the divertimento are milling around in the quartets, written in the sequential and repetitious patchwork manner of the style galant, pieced together from short motives, and without a definite feeling for continuity. The distribution of the musical material is also precarious and not in the spirit of chamber music. The first violin claims an undisputed and oppressing monopoly throughout, the other three instruments seconding it with an unimportant accompaniment. This is obviously due to the influence of the concerto. But in some of the slow movements there appears a tone filled with a hymnlike solemnity that recalls Klopstock, a tone and mood that stand out in this inconsequential and playful environment. Stamitz and Wagenseil were unquestionably the superior masters of the new style, and not until the first years of the sixth decade of the century are there any indications that Haydn would ever even approach them. Beginning with the fifteenth quartet and the second symphony the symphonic instinct works wonders—wonders indeed, for Haydn did not start out with the imperative and explosive gestures of Stamitz but, motivated by the same southern German instinct for the symphonic, embarked patiently upon the progress of organizing the microscopic motivic idiom of the style galant into a symphonic fabric of causality and continuity. The process was a long one and grew imperceptibly until it reached the stage of thematic development; once Haydn arrived there, however, and met the line of construction carried by Wagenseil and the Mannheimers, his minutely organized motives within the thematic web gave his symphonic idiom an iron logic and coherence which stand well-nigh unsurpassed in the whole literature.

One can well imagine the profound impressions experienced by Haydn when he discovered that his subconscious penchants had already been realized in bold and pregnant compositions, Emanuel Bach's piano sonatas. These came to him as a revelation, for in them he found a positive answer to his instinctive questions. What he saw in this music was not only the emancipation of part writing from the bonds of scholastic polyphony and the transference to man-made instruments of the expressive vocal style of the lyric stage, but also the ultimate aim of musical composition. Now he understood what Emanuel Bach meant when he advised his readers that the musician's duty is "to move the heart."

As we have already seen, the instrumental ensemble works of Haydn's first period are almost entirely in the sphere of the divertimento, and the composer does not show any evidence of acquaintance with the new, dualistic sonata construction. In the last few of the first eighteen quartets there appears a new tone, not so much in the material itself as in its organization. The careless accompanying parts take their task more seriously and begin to be interested in the thematic material. The Austrian peasant touch which appeared earlier in the works of Wagenseil and Zach is even more pronounced in Haydn, and the more he develops as an artist the more he loves his realistic peasant *Ländler,* and the jokes and surprises which endear him to us in his later works are not missing in these earlier ones. It is significant that in the next three series of quartets, six to a set, Haydn abandoned the designation "divertimenti," and with these compositions we reach the characteristic string quartet style. That he was perfectly clear concerning the nature of his new orientation is evident from the fact that long after he had found his definitive chamber music and orchestral style he continued to write divertimenti along principles opposed to the new style. The four-movement cyclic form is now before us, and the characteristic individuality of the movements is such that they can no longer be exchanged as before, when the first and last allegro or presto movements were virtually alike in tone and spirit. The first presto now tends toward a moderate allegro with pregnant and clear-cut themes, while the finale retains the more exuberant, often humorous and coquettish quality of the divertimento or the opera buffa finale. He has not yet arrived at the use of dualistic thematic material; on the other hand he offers an ingenuity in his formal schemes that ought to be made the object of thorough study for those who hold the sonata form to be a hard and fast pattern. Nearly every one of these quartets presents a different solution of the formal problems. It must be emphasized, however, that the second or subsidiary theme is not a matter of value, but is often merely a matter of existence; that is, if a symphony-sonata has no second theme it is not necessarily of a lower artistic quality, as can be readily seen in some of Haydn's latest and most accomplished works, which were built upon one theme long after he became accustomed to using the dualistic principle.

At the end of this phase of his artistic growth Haydn had defined the boundaries of chamber music, divertimento, and symphony, at the same time reserving a specific style for the piano sonata. This is the memorable point at which an idiom, formerly indiscriminately used in all sorts of instrumental music and especially developed in the keyboard works of the two famous sons of Johann Sebastian Bach, becomes definitely attached to a genre, the quartet and its more ambitious cousin the symphony. But they are no longer interchangeable, as each type has its own store of formal and thematic elements. In the last of the quartets of this period, and especially in the group designated *opus* 20, the sure and steady stylistic development comes to a halt; the composer arrives at a crisis in his artistic career. Some of the compositions making up the set, still in the musicianly style of the previous quartets, solve their problems with resourcefulness and originality, but in the others there is a profound excitement, a struggle for expression and for orientation. The utterances are bold and passionate, for their composer is at the crossroads and is experiencing the same romantic upheaval that agitated Goethe before he was able to master his own self to reach his resolute, transfigured classicism. Arrived at this point, Haydn realized that a major element was missing in his style, the absence of which prevented the final integration of his idiom and form. The composers of the preclassic era had not been able, not even Emanuel Bach, to rid themselves entirely of the drawbacks of the style galant. Haydn recognized that what was needed was a more judicious part writing which in turn impelled him to a reinstatement of polyphony in musical construction. This, we might say, represented the final and decisive step toward the achievement of the classical ideal of instrumental style.

Haydn was now almost forty years of age and looked back on a series of quartets and symphonies in which he had acquired a sure technique, ability to form his material, and a wide range of expressiveness. Still, he ceased to compose quartets for a decade. To us the road traversed by the composer may seem short, but to him it wound around many hills and even mountains, covering a wide territory from divertimento to symphony. And now comes the crisis of the Sturm und Drang, and the dramatic, passionate, and at times demonic tone that appears in his mature works appears here to give battle to the style galant. It became necessary to pause and to marshal forces.

The early symphonies have until recently remained unknown to the public at large, but with the slowly appearing volumes of a proposed complete and scholarly edition of his works [6] they are now available in every major library. These early symphonies do not show a methodic application of the principles of thematic development; nevertheless, as with the quartets of the same period, there are a number of noteworthy compositions among them. Up to about 1770 they seem to call on, or at least to permit the participation of, a continuo harpsichord, but after that date the experience gained in the exacting writing for the string quartet bears fruits in the symphony: the technique of carrying the thematic material through all parts is applied to the orchestra, and the instruments are liberated, taking part as responsible individuals in the development of the symphonic idea. This is a modern orchestral idiom but—and this cannot be emphasized strongly enough—all orchestral effects result from the manipulation of the abstract musical idea and are in its service. The symphony has caught up with the quartet, and seems to have occupied Haydn's mind during the long pause in quartet writing. It was during these ten years that Haydn experienced, besides the influence of his own recently acquired mastery in symphonic writing, the powerful influence emanating from the works of his young spiritual disciple and friend, Mozart. This influence is not expressed in borrowings or imitations, but in a flexibility, in a sensitiveness, which gave his rhythmic, energetic, and angular musical language added variety. When in 1781 his *opus* 33 appeared, he himself remarked in the subscription invitation that the works comprising it were composed "in an entirely new and particular manner." With these works the string quartet is present in its classic garb. The long pause ripened his ideas and the last remnants of the style galant disappeared.

A similar concentration of his faculties is exhibited in the symphonies of his middle period. Here again the last vestiges of the operatic origin of the idiom, still so obvious in the Italian symphonies and occasionally even in Mozart, disappear, or, rather, are dissolved and converted, in a purely instrumental style of great vitality. The same is true with regard to the other ingredients of the symphonic idiom, the concerto and the trio sonata. The better known symphonies of this period are *La Chasse* (No. 73 in the complete edition), *L'ours* (No. 82), *La Poule* (No. 83), *La Reine* (No. 85), a nameless symphony in G major (No. 88), and the *Oxford Symphony* (No. 92), all written for Paris where Haydn's symphonies were greatly in demand. The titles did not originate with the composer and should not be interpreted as indicating program music; they were merely nicknames appended by the French, always fond of literary, descriptive designations, and were derived from certain characteristic rhythms or melodies which they associated—not without some lively imagination—with such things as the cackling of a hen or the ambling gait of a bear.

Later Works

WITH the Oxford symphony (1788), so named because of its performance in Oxford on the occasion of the conferring on Haydn of the honorary degree of Doctor of Music in 1791, the composer arrived at his final period of creative activity. The quartets, symphonies, Masses, and oratorios composed in the next dozen or so years are the works of the consummate master. The path was still laborious but every inch gained was consciously utilized. The requirements of a higher order of symphonic construction eliminated the simple rondos in the finales, replacing them with finely developed sonata-rondos worthy of the artistic quality of the initial movements. The typically German love for variation appears in the middle movements, the sets ranging from rollicking travesty to the cantus firmus treatment in the *Emperor* quartet. The slow prologues that prefaced his later symphonies gain in depth and dramatic intensity. Consisting often in but a few grave and at times cryptic measures, they invariably are steeped in thoughts and visions, occasionally dreamy, then again romantically emphatic. These epigrams show the great symphonist in a soliloquy, weighing the issues before embarking on their exegesis. They moved later composers profoundly, and no one appreciated them more than Beethoven. In these works, especially in the quartets *opus* 76 and in the symphonies written for London, Haydn reached the ideal balance of homophony and a specific modern instrumental polyphony, thematic and melodic rather than rhythmic and motivic. This gave him a freedom of imagination heretofore unknown. What a fantastic cavorting of melodies, rhythms, syncopations, dynamic contrasts, general pauses, hesitations, sudden explosions, distortions, their maze skillfully manipulated by the subtle employment of the high art of double counterpoint carried into the smallest particular. Detail in composition—and the real artist shows in details especially the most thorough craftsmanship—is derived from the whole and leads back to it. What makes Shakespeare's characters great is that the poet develops, above all, those traits in their nature and mentality from which their destiny, their rise or fall, originates. It is in this way that dramatic actions achieve their sense of unity. Haydn proceeds in the same manner, but his characters and figures are abstract. In his development of the thematic element he gives the essential by eliminating everything that is secondary or that has no bearing on the destiny of his subjects. The detail serves him in working out the character of his motives, in leading them into a situation which enables them to present the solutions of their destinies as inevitable natural phenomena.

In his mature symphonies and quartets, Haydn carried the symphonic principle, the art of developing a pregnant idea through all imaginable metamorphoses, to such a high degree that, according to Brahms, it was thereafter "no longer a joke to write symphonies." The themes were whittled down to their most elemental and plastic simplicity, permitting an unlimited thematic use. With the insight of genius, Haydn seizes upon the idea which is most fitting to be elaborated. With unbroken flow and complete disregard of material unessential for his purpose, the development unfolds with a logic that can hardly be described. So great is the power of symphonic consistency that although Haydn had long since appropriated the dualistic sonata principle, it sometimes becomes possible to dispense with the introduction of a second individual theme. Scarcely any composer ever approached this inexorable logic of symphonic construction, and even Beethoven surpassed it in dimensions only.

Haydn is habitually called the "father of the symphony" and the "founder of the string quartet." Needless to say, this is incorrect both historically and in principle—as we have seen in the foregoing chapter—for the symphony has had an interesting past and has counted among its practitioners eminent composers of individuality and creative power. Among Haydn's contemporaries there were also symphonists of an original vein, and as to the string quartet, Dittersdorf had produced fully developed specimens of this type before Haydn caught up with him. Haydn's great contribution was the synthesis of all this into a style of convincing logic and permanent validity, an accomplishment that makes him a contemporary and worthy brother-in-arms of Kant. Kretzschmar was fully justified in considering his stylistic reform "one of the greatest achievements in the whole history of the arts."

Haydn's popular tone, unspoiled by all his mastery of the technique of composition, endeared many of his melodies to the simple country folk.

We have noticed, when discussing the works of the creator of the new lyric song, Johann Abraham Peter Schulz, how such nobly popular tunes are assimilated by the people. As Schulz's songs became folk songs so did many of Haydn's melodies. There can be no question of his repeated use of popular material, German, Bohemian, Croatian, Hungarian and even Gypsy tunes, but all attempts to make this Austrian, the incarnation of the Viennese School, a Croatian, Slavic composer are without the slightest foundation and represent a flagrant misreading of musical styles, not to mention the disregard of amply demonstrated historical facts. In an exhaustive and well-documented article written on the occasion of the two-hundredth anniversary of Haydn's birth, Carl Engel disposes admirably of this legend, created by Kuhač and perpetrated in the English-speaking world by Hadow and Parry. Citing "the peculiar charm of eighteenth-century Vienna, the distinctive luster of the Kaiserstadt," Engel has pointed out the "Alpha and Omega of Haydn," and he is absolutely justified in seeing in the so-called Croatian peasant "a more typically Viennese composer than Gluck, Mozart and Beethoven." [7]

Of great significance was Haydn's relationship to Mozart. The unparalleled friendship and mutual influence of these two great musicians is known to all. Yet what a difference in nature, character, and conception! Haydn, the untutored, virtually abandoned child who had to fight his way to mastery, and whose only principle could have been *non scholae sed vitae discimus,* and Mozart, the man of the world, who enjoyed such a splendid education. Paris—London—Latin abstraction and English empiricism—Johann Christian Bach—then Italy—Martini—Hasse—the great singers. The Italian dreams followed Mozart through his whole life as they haunted Handel and Goethe, and they crystallized, as in Handel, in a passion for the human voice—in singing. This passion was so powerful that vocal elements intruded into his instrumental style. Haydn's genius lived in the instruments; his poetical life became the life of oboes, horns, and violins. He plays on his instruments; Mozart sings on them. Haydn's orchestra is exuberant with life, with his instruments jumping about capriciously. In his magnificent symphonies, Mozart is always under the spell of the voice; there everything sings, even his allegros. It is small wonder that with such a disposition Haydn became one of the purest representatives of German musical culture, of which instrumental music is as typical as is vocal music of the Latins. Thus, although his career began with what should be considered one of the earliest examples of the southern German Singspiel, his operas, with the exception of *L'Isola Disabitata* (1779), do not exhibit uniform and sustained dramatic composition, although many of them contain remarkable sections which served Haydn as excellent preparation for his later choral works. We shall discuss Haydn's role in operatic history on the pages devoted to late-eighteenth-century opera, as we shall treat his Catholic church music together with that of his contemporaries. There is, however, one field of choral music in which Haydn can claim a whole chapter to himself: the oratorio.

The two great oratorios, written at an age when other people acquiesce with resignation to the laws of life, testify to the undiminished youthful powers of invention of the aged musician. More than that, they represent a milestone in the history of the oratorio. Haydn was acquainted with the works of Johann Sebastian Bach and Handel before he visited the country where the oratorio was the subject of a veritable cult. What must have impressed him in England were the wholehearted performances of Handel's works, backed by the optimistic Protestantism of the English. In his youth, German literature had enjoyed its springlike blooming, contemplating nature with religious joy and peaceful admiration. But neither Brockes, nor Haller, nor Kleist possessed a spirit as naïvely and fervently abandoned to the miracles of nature and life as Haydn, and it was the musician who was to express fully that religious conception which words could convey only incompletely. The text of the *Creation* came from England. Handel had already seen it but his mighty dramatic fantasy, fond though it was of nature and its contemplation, found it too pale for his liking. It was based on a poem by Milton, but the spirit of Shaftesbury and of the English poets of the cult of nature had lent unmistakable accents to the Biblical story of the creation, which is unfolded here in large choral hymns. Haydn's treatment of the text evoked a great deal of criticism and many smiles. The fact that Beethoven was among those who smiled should not mislead us, for the naïve painting of lightning and thunder, of rain and snow, of the flow of the river, and of the appearance of the various animals is entirely submerged in the general mood and blends perfectly with the rest because only the musically feasible was attempted and emphasized. And then man emerges, and the naïve descriptive music changes to give us a portrait of loveliness, Eve, only to rise to the accents of human tragedy.

Narrative description and nature poetry were here a form of worship of the Creator. Divine benevolence appeared in the beauties of the world. This was still the conception of the Enlightenment which required a simple musical language. The most life-bound of the great German composers found this tone, and the wondrous beauty of the world speaks to us in his *Creation*. Haydn was able to express his religious feelings in their sincere freshness in music, for his beliefs were one with his subject. In their conception of nature, Shaftesbury and Goethe praised love as the peak of nature; this is what Haydn expressed in the music of the last part of the *Creation*.

Following the tremendous success of the *Creation,* the sixty-seven-year-old musician embarked upon the composition of another oratorio, the *Seasons.* Handel's distant inspiration is again evident if one recalls *L'Allegro, il Pense-*

J. S. Beck (German, c. 1765), "House Concert"

Performance of Lully's Alceste in Versailles, 1674

North America

New York

Lititz

Germantown
Philadelphia

Atlantic Ocean

NORWAY AND DENMARK

North
Sea

BRITISH ISLES

Dublin

Political Boundaries: 1740

Atlantic Ocean

London

The Hague
Amsterdam
Leyden

Boulogne
Ghent
Brussels
Louvain
Cologne
Bonn
Coblenz
Mainz

Paris (25)

THE

Ludwigsburg
Strasbourg

FRANCE

Basel

Berne
Thun
Zürich
SWITZERLA

Lyon

Mil

Bordeaux

PORTUGAL

SPAIN

Mediterr

R.E.Falconer

SWEDEN

RUSSIA

o St. Petersburg (7)

o Moscow

o Riga

Baltic Sea

o Königsburg
Danzig   PRUSSIA

o Schwerin

Weissenburg   o Warsaw (5)

o Berlin (8)
Potsdam
o Leipzig (7)   POLAND
o Dresden (17)
o Bautzen   o Breslau (4)
o Gera   o Hirschberg
Jena   o Leitmeritz
o Saatz
o Bayreuth
EMPIRE
o Rudolfstadt
o Regensburg   Pressburg
o Munich (16)   o Eisenstadt

KINGDOM OF HUNGARY

o Venice
o Trieste

Adriatic Sea

ITALY

o Rome (6)
Naples (5)

ean Sea

The Distribution of Austro-Bohemian Composers, Members of the So-called Viennese School ~ c. 1700 ~ 1775

This map gives a fair picture of the dissemination of the style of the so-called Viennese school. It is not, however, complete since many composers cannot be definitely identified as to their country of origin, while the residence of others is too vaguely stated in the available sources. The figures in parentheses indicate the number of Austro-Bohemian composers resident in the city during the period under consideration.

(Top) Watteau (1684–1721), "The Music Lesson"

(Bottom) John Zoffany (English, 1733–1810), "Itinerant Musicians"

roso, ed il Moderato, but the German Singspiel helped Haydn to avoid the pitfalls of Italian dramatic composition, admittedly not his forte. The contemplative nature of the composer who liked to talk and to recite found an ideal sphere in the tableaux that make up the *Seasons.* They are, to use Kretzschmar's words, genre paintings, idylls painted with the finesse and exactitude of the Flemish masters. Again the occasionally Philistine tone may have elicited a smile from the robust composer of *Judas Maccabaeus,* but the two oratorios do not suffer even when compared to Handel's.

A career which began in the domain of light opera came to an end in the admirable, exceedingly vital choruses of the oratorio. The solid edifice which rises between them is instrumental music. "These works constitute an ideal language of truth; their parts cohere with vital necessity" (Goethe) and in them he "can amuse and shock, arouse laughter and deep emotion as no one else can do" (Mozart).

*

*   *

HAYDN'S warm and human solicitude for the men under his care and his love of children earned him the name "Papa Haydn," often used in a truly filial spirit by Mozart. That this epithet addressed to the kindly man was extended by later musical writers to the artist shows the lamentable ignorance of the spirit of his music and of his times. Such animated and vivacious flight of musical imagination was beyond the understanding of the second half of the nineteenth century and is still entirely strange to the twentieth-century listener, schooled as he is on the ponderous music of the late nineteenth century. Haydn's works occupy a definite position in our musical life, a position which could not be filled by anyone or anything else. Love of life, wholesomeness, clarity, purity of feeling, noble and profound sentiment, inexhaustible humor, and impeccable craftsmanship are the characteristic traits of his art which should be treasured by us in whose art they appear so seldom.

Mozart

SALZBURG was a bit of Italy in a German land, the blissful clarity and brilliant architecture of the south imbedded in the calm earnestness of a German province. It was here that Wolfgang Amadeus Mozart was born on January 27, 1756. Mozart's life is the most enigmatic example of the history of a genius. We need not repeat here the many well-known anecdotes about the abilities of the precocious youth; it seems to the distant observer as if music appeared in the frail child as a cosmic phenomenon. There have been other youngsters who played an instrument adroitly, but at the age of eight, Mozart not only was an accomplished piano, organ, and violin player, but had a knowledge of musical composition such as one would expect from a man seasoned in the profession. He was perhaps the only child prodigy whose peregrinations in various lands did not spoil his taste and originality but, on the contrary, proved to be highly beneficial. Like Lassus and Handel, he united the musical treasures of all nations of his time. This could easily have led to a mixture without character, but like the two other great composers, Mozart did not imitate anyone or anything; the external appearance of music was but a means of expression to him, never technique. Technique and form are meaningless without content; his world of expression is inseparable from his form, and this is the secret of the perfection and unity of his music. It is not enough, however, to say that content and form balance each other in Mozart's music, for this unity is style, and while the style is constant the variety of its manifestations is as great as the number of his works. Mozart never created really new forms but by regarding the existing styles not as unities but as phenomena which contribute toward a general style, he created a universal all-inclusive style which stood above all subspecies. Such a universal style is possible perhaps in music only, because the diversity of languages in literature and the concreteness of the subject in the fine arts prevent a final synthesis.

If we want to grasp the real greatness of Mozart and if we want to understand the profound secret of the power of redemption of his music, we must always remember that this man suffered the pains and agonies of a noble soul frustrated and contemptuously humiliated. The inexhaustible capacity for love which was the dominant trait in his nature prevented the sufferings from striking the dominant tone in his works. The public in Mozart's time found his works heavy and complicated compared to those of his famous contemporaries. "His ears are of iron," they said. Nowadays we smile when we read this criticism of the eighteenth century. Mozart heavy? Mozart lacking in clarity? Mozart, who to the public of today is the model and symbol of gracious beauty and transparent harmoniousness! We smile, but we may not realize that this smile reflects a new but nonetheless misguided prejudice. The public which sees in Mozart the poet of gracious naïveté and the master of fine musical laceworks knows and likes but a very small part of his universal genius. They consider this small part the very essence of the Mozartean spirit. How many are there who still see his art through the glass of rococo romanticism; how many are there, who, when listening to this music which reveals the deepest regions of the human soul, recall only powdered wigs, silk stockings, and minuets. The taste of our generation has its roots in the romantic musical literature of the late nineteenth century. The musicians of that era expressed their thoughts by large gestures, using a complicated, at times even enormous, technical apparatus. Because of this fact the assumption arose that deep poetical feeling cannot be expressed without an intricate medium. Wagner's less important contemporaries and immediate successors reflect this spirit of the times. They tried to simulate deep and ponderous thoughts by using a grandiose musical architecture richly ornamented.

If we can liberate ourselves from this pseudo grandeur we shall see that everything that seems childlike and simple in Mozart's music is in reality an infinitely intense and complicated cosmos, and we shall realize the meaning of the Ovidian motto at the head of this chapter: "So art lies hid by its own artifice." This music seems simple because the content is presented in the most natural and plastic form, attended by a compelling logic of construction. The wonderful harmony of spiritual conception and practical execution is so astonishing that the superficial student is misled by its very perfection. We must not forget that Mozart was the child of an era customarily called the "golden age" of musical art. Such a golden age—as was the *cinquecento* in the art of painting—offers to the genius the richest treasures of the various artistic forms. He has only to stretch out his hands and select the proper material to build up his own art. The child of the golden age need not experiment, he need not demolish the form material he is offered in order to build a new edifice out of the ruins. He simply takes the gifts of his epoch, intact, and, as a self-evident matter, utilizes them at his will. Mozart grasped the form material of his epoch, the rich and colorful creations of German, Italian, and French music of the eighteenth century, with the liberty of the artist of the golden age. He shuffled them like a pack of cards and the result was a strikingly original and individual world.

Mozart's birthplace was the second seat of music in Austria, and while its musical life was modeled after that of Vienna, it possessed an unmistakable local color. All branches of music were well represented in Salzburg. Eberlin, in charge of the archiepiscopal court chapel, was a man of the older generation, still imbued with the severe polyphony of the baroque (one of his fugues was for a long time considered the work of Johann Sebastian Bach); Adlgasser, a pupil of Eberlin, less austere and more versatile, represented the younger generation, in sympathy with the new style; above all there was Michael Haydn, whose music, coming from a humble and religious soul, affected young Mozart deeply. The most lasting influence, however, emanated from the child's father. Leopold Mozart (1719-1787) was an excellent musician, a noted violinist, and a respected composer. A man of education, he was the author of a *Versuch,* in this case dealing with the playing of the violin, a work which, appearing in the year of Wolfgang's birth, remained a highly esteemed violin method for almost a century. The father's excellent pedagogical insight can be seen in the remarkably rounded musical literature he gave his children, drawing on French, Italian, and German compositions both southern and northern. At the age of four to five, Wolfgang played the harpsichord and the violin, and, music being his natural language, he started composing virtually before he could write. He was not yet six when his international career as an artist started.

The family embarked on a tour of Austria, western Hungary, and northern Germany. After a short rest a more extensive tour carried them farther afield and acquainted Mozart with some of the leading musicians of his time. Thus in Munich he heard Luigi Tomasini (1741-1808), later Haydn's trusted concertmaster; in Ludwigsburg he met Jommelli and Pietro Nardini (1722-1793). The effortless cantilena of Nardini's superb violin playing must have greatly agitated his innate sense for melodic beauty, but he was of course too young to grasp Jommelli's significance. Another surprise awaited him in Mannheim, where his admiration for the ducal orchestra knew no bounds. Visiting a few more German cities, the Mozart family touched Brussels and then stopped in Paris. It is difficult to reconstruct the impressions a mere child might have gained in the French capital in 1763, but the musical impressions were again distinctive. Johann Schobert (d. 1767), a German who settled in Paris, seems to have been the dominating single experience in Mozart's French sojourn. This feted hero of the Parisian salons was one of the most original musicians of the eighteenth century, uniting in his versatile compositions the aspirations of the Mannheimers with the romantic and rhapsodic, intensely emotional tendencies of the Sturm und Drang. Musically related to Emanuel Bach, Schobert is also often astonishingly akin to the young Beethoven. His particular field was keyboard music and chamber music with harpsichord, in which he found new accents and new forms that rivaled the innovations in Mannheim, in northern Germany, and in Vienna. Mozart's genuine admiration for the eccentric musician is attested by his first four piano concertos, which were refurbished sonatas by Schobert, whom we must consider as one of the child Mozart's most influential teachers.[8] It must have been Schobert's works that acquainted Mozart with fantasy and poetry in music, and it is a remarkable coincidence that this should have happened in Paris.

Continuing their travels, the Mozarts arrived in London in April, 1764, to stay there until August of the following year. The Parisian impressions were deepened by the musical experiences in London. Italian music, which dominated the London scene, introduced Mozart to the happiness that reigns in the domain of pure music divorced of all reality. This also served to bring into relief the stylized and more mathematical beauty of the French forms of music. Curiously enough, it was in England that he must have realized that this pure music was his homeland. In the King's Theatre he heard the operas of Piccini, Hasse, Galuppi, and many other composers, and Handel's memory was still vivid, but it was again in the music of two Germans, Carl Friedrich Abel (1725-1787) and Johann Christian Bach (1735-1782), that the creative impression made itself felt.

Abel, son of the famous gamba player Christian Ferdinand Abel, for whom Johann Sebastian Bach wrote his gamba suites, was himself an eminent gamba virtuoso and a former pupil of the elder Bach. As a composer he was an adherent of the Mannheim school, and Mozart found his symphonies so interesting that he copied several of them, presumably for later reference and study. One of these copies found its way among Mozart's works, where Köchel, Mozart's first cataloguer, assigned number 18 to it. While Abel's orchestral style interested him, the real fascination came from the youngest son of Johann Sebastian Bach. No other composer's individuality and music left such deep marks in Mozart's artistic development as did this "renegade" son of the Lutheran cantor of the Thomasschule. After his father's death, Johann Christian stayed with his older brother, Emanuel, with whom he also continued his musical studies. At the age of nineteen he left for Milan. His complete conversion to Italian music and life was symbolically demonstrated by his embracing of Catholicism. This German worshiped Italian ideals of beauty and form with singular tenderness and became the consummate master of the style galant, but of a style galant born from the union of a German father and an Italian mother. His melodies, polished with emery, were captivating and seductive, and his construction fused with infinite skill and artistry the contradictory elements in opera and instrumental music. Christian Bach divined young Mozart's genius and spent some time in examining and advising him, to the boy's great pleasure.

His feeling for form and beauty of sound inevitably drove Mozart toward Italian music, and when in December, 1769, father and son went to Italy the thirteen-year-old musician must have received the Italian experiences as the fulfillment of an instinctive yearning. The Italian journey was a triumphal tour; at every place he was acclaimed and at every place he received added stimulus by meeting and hearing the best of Italy's musicians and music: Locatelli, Hasse, Sammartini, Martini, Farinelli, Nardini, Jommelli, Paisiello, di Majo, Caffarelli, Vallotti, and many others. The aged Padre Martini (1706–1784), the greatest teacher of his times and perhaps of the whole century, a distinguished composer, theorist, and historian, undertook his instruction. Well acquainted with the spirit of Italian music before visiting the country, he was completely ensorceled when actually partaking in the life which produced this music. The beautiful mirage he had beheld in London had turned into warm and pulsating life, and it was in the midst of this new atmosphere that he must have come to the realization that "passions, whether violent or not, must never be expressed in such a way as to excite disgust, and even in the most terrible situations must never cease to be *music*." [9] This remained his creed throughout his life.

The daily contacts with phenomenal singers soon convinced him that this beauty of music he had made his creed was not to be fully attained in instrumental music, but must call on the human voice. Like the Saxon Handel before him, this Austrian became enchanted by the sorcery of singing, and song was henceforth to dominate his whole musical imagination. The temper of the times and his own dramatic instincts made him turn to the paramount form of vocal composition, the opera. It is significant that the young musician, filled with the freshness of life, was more attracted by that branch of the Neapolitan opera seria which at that time had already benefited from the rejuvenating influence of the opera buffa. Jommelli, the representative of the majestic music drama, and Hasse, the last great champion of the more rigid dramatic poetry of the aria opera, filled him with admiration, but he could not follow them because he felt instinctively that the stage should be allotted a more active part in the opera. His first essays do not show the sure hand of an Italian master, but if he is not yet able to infuse real life into the figures of the drama, if he does not yet live his own life in them, his stage nevertheless already begins to come to life. It was undoubtedly in Italy that he received the stimuli that led to his unsurpassed ability of characterization of life and men in music. From the sharply drawn forms and types of the Italian operatic idiom, from its plastic expression, he learned how to espy the significant and characteristic moments from life. Arrived at this point in his artistic development, he began to feel that the freshness and suavity he had admired in Christian Bach and Sammartini was only a small part of the musical universe and something more concrete and concentrated was needed to express his ideas in their plenitude. Padre Martini's counterpoint lessons came as a revelation: now he began to understand the power of polyphony. A whole series of contrapuntal compositions followed his discovery.

So many vital changes and discoveries must have repercussions, and indeed the youthful composer experienced his first internal dissensions, so admirably translated in the tragic, dramatic pathos of his Mass in C minor (K. 139), written in Salzburg between the second and third Italian journeys.[10] After his final return from Italy this dissension grew into a romantic crisis the like of which Haydn experienced as a mature man. The slow movements of his six string quartets (K. 155–160) show us a different Mozart, still an adolescent but already knowing that life harbors disillusionments and that man is at the mercy of fateful forces that are beyond his power.

No matter how deep the Italian impressions were, Mozart did not forget his Austrian homeland. Among his compatriots there were several to whom he was attracted and whose music elicited his admiration. There was Wanhall, who enjoyed the reputation of a "bold and wild composer," Gassmann, himself a pupil of the famous Bolognese Padre, whose operas first show that engaging mixture of the Austrian and the Italian which became Mozart's second nature, and above all, the gentle Michael Haydn. Then came a new revelation: Joseph Haydn, in whom he suddenly discovered the genius in music. Formerly he divined, through the impeccable formal and melodic beauty of Christian Bach, that the heterogeneous can be fused into unity, but now he learned that this is not enough, and that in order to achieve completeness in the work of art one has to live it to the very end. His symphonies took on an amplitude and a logic, and, armed with the certitude of the artistic mastery of the problems encountered, he permitted his subjective feelings a wider range. In the G minor symphony (K. 183) the great Mozart is before us. Hammered out of one piece of metal, this symphony is sheer perfection in conception and realization, but in its incomprehensible mixture of sensuous melodic beauty and demonic passion it also shows the tragic Mozart. It is saddening for the student of Mozart to discover that at such a tender age a person can call himself the child of sorrow. Through Haydn he also discovered that the instruments have souls, and now began an avalanche of instrumental compositions: concertos, symphonies, quartets, sonatas for the new hammer pianoforte, and, most of all, divertimenti and serenades, the richness and variety of which defies description. These are "occasional pieces" written for occasional ensembles, but it is precisely in their occasional, *ad hoc,* quality that the idealism of Mozartean music manifests itself most palpably; for reality, while given its due, is enveloped in the sobriety, humor, and irony of the ideal world. Such occasional music provided him with an opportunity of lifting the curtain to look into the little particular corners of life.

As his position in Salzburg did not improve, Mozart resigned from the archbishop's service and took to the road once again in the company of his mother. After a few stops there came a longer rest in Mannheim, where many old friends awaited them. The Mannheim stay brought Mozart together with a stimulating group of musicians: Holzbauer, the Abbés Vogler and Sterkel, and Cannabich, not to mention the attraction of the fabulous Mannheim orchestra. In March, 1778, Mozart was in Paris again, but the Mozart who now scrutinized Paris and its music was a different person from the child who took everything in wonderment. There can be no doubt that the opéra comique and Gluck's and Piccini's works still elicited great admiration, but on the whole he did not make a secret of his low opinion of French musical life. The literary aureole that surrounded music in France and the theoretical and aesthetic controversies between Gluckists and Piccinists were entirely repellent to his purely musical imagination. His operatic plans fell through, but the Parisian visit produced, nevertheless, remarkable instrumental works. Although the rationalistic tendencies of French music were far from his taste, the cold aesthetic sobriety of the French once more reminded him of the great artistic advantages of a homogeneous style. There was also the opéra comique with its lively, unspoiled music and excellent declamation which could not have left him indifferent. The concentration of his style, the fusion of heterogeneous elements, is especially noticeable in his opera seria *Idomeneo, Rè di Creta* (1781), which seems to be the threshold to his mature style. While Mozart's conception of the opera seria is still somewhat uncertain, the manner in which the French elements are reconciled with the Italian traditions announces the musico-dramatic genius par excellence.

The national Singspiel theater planned by Joseph II came into being, and Mozart, now living in Vienna, was commissioned to compose a German stage work. *Die Entführung aus dem Serail,* a libretto once before set to music by André, was selected and with Mozart's collaboration so changed that operatic elements of larger proportions could be included. Shortly after the successful performance of the *Entführung,* in July, 1782, Mozart married his own Constance, and it was also in this year that the intimate and mutually stimulating friendship with Joseph Haydn began.

The four years following his Singspiel are the years of the mature man during which the free artist exercised his calling as an everyday profession, uniting the practical and ideal aspects of art. On the one hand, he built his art systematically from material taken from life; on the other, he used his art to organize his life. There were many problems of reality to be faced: marriage, the raising of a family, and finding a place in society. The intimate social intercourse within his family life, and with friends and colleagues, resulted in a multitude of occasional songs, canons, *terzetti,* and other miniature masterpieces which find their equal only in Goethe's *Gesellige Lieder.* His life now was varied. Piano pupils, public concerts, so-called "Academies," and supervision of the printing of some of his works, and other functions and gatherings occupied his time, and every one of these "occasions" called forth a bevy of works.

The highly developed Viennese musical life with its aristocratic background was a natural greenhouse for chamber music. Under the influence of Haydn's so-called Russian quartets, Mozart composed six quartets (K. 387, 421, 428, 458, 464, 465), dedicating them to his older friend and mentor in terms of deep affection. The younger musician emphasized that it was from Haydn that he learned "how one should write quartets," but after listening to the new compositions, the sincere and generous master of the quartet said to Leopold Mozart, "I declare to you upon my honor that I consider your son the greatest composer I have ever heard." In his earlier chamber music, Mozart carried the *Gesellschaftsmusik* of the eighteenth century to its most differentiated sphere; with his D minor piano concerto, G minor piano quartet, C minor piano concerto, C minor piano sonata and fantasy, a new and singularly darkened tone seems to dominate. The genius whose shadow covered this new orientation was Johann Sebastian Bach, but we must not search for concordances and reminiscences, for it was not in concrete examples that Bach's genius affected Mozart. The counterpoint he had learned from Padre Martini had earlier strongly affected him and he had quickly acquired considerable facility in polyphonic composition. In the house of Baron van Swieten, the distinguished amateur who translated for Haydn the English text of the *Creation,* he now learned to appreciate polyphony as expressed in the works of the last great masters of the baroque. Van Swieten was a fervent admirer of Bach and Handel and organized concerts at which their works were performed before gatherings that comprised the best musicians in the capital. Mozart must have realized that this music was the embodiment of that German musical spirit which lingered in his subconscious imagination and which occasionally took more concrete expression in his church music. Now the polyphonic culture of German music was before him in all its greatness. His intense interest in his new discovery resulted in a number of works, starting with the transcription of some Bach fugues for string quartet (K. 405), following through such works as the magnificent fugue in C minor for two pianos (K. 426), and ending in the last Mass in C minor, unfortunately incomplete. The Mass followed the *Entführung,* and it is not without significance that the composer's entry into a new period of his creative life through the German Singspiel was seconded by a sacred composition in which the echoes of life from the previous work were dissolved in the spirit of German polyphony. Yet the great number of unfinished compositions written in this style shows that the Viennese and Italian allegiance was stronger, that the German heritage was still more desired than appropriated. It was not until the end of his life that Mozart succeeded in reconciling the two styles, poles apart, and could call the German his own.

Now the theater again attracted him powerfully—the theater, which has always been a symbol of the life that is in his music. The operatic situation in Vienna was entirely under the control of the Italian clique which had the emperor's ear. Even the success of the *Entführung* did not change the situation, for the Singspiel and the German troupe occupied a position distinctly secondary to the court opera and were slowly engulfed by the Italians. One more attempt, the performance in Schönbrunn of the little one-act occasional play *Der Schauspieldirektor* (February, 1786), and Mozart gave up the composition of German lyric plays to meet the Italians on their own ground. The competition was still formidable but the obstacles were not only those placed in his way by competitors; he himself experienced great difficulty in finding his medium. We know from his letters that he read no less than a hundred libretti before he found, in the person of the Italian poet and playwright Lorenzo da Ponte (1749–1837), a man of letters who understood his intentions and was willing to arrange Beaumarchais's *Le Mariage de Figaro* to suit his fancy. Performed on May 1, 1786, *Le Nozze di Figaro* was fairly well received and earned nine performances. Its fame reached Prague, where it was produced in December amidst such applause that the management invited the composer to appear in person in the Bohemian capital. For the first time since his childhood, Mozart knew what real success and acclaim meant, but perhaps the most important result of the trip was the incentive to follow up *Figaro* with another opera. On his return to Vienna, he found that *Figaro* had already been superseded by Martin's *Cosa Rara,* and the *Entführung* by Dittersdorf's *Doktor und Apotheker*. Mozart, whose operas had the reputation of being "heavy" and "difficult," had lost his vogue entirely. His family life and his financial situation also left much to be desired. Most of his children died in infancy, his wife squandered the little money he earned, and then came the irreparable loss of his most cherished friend and counselor: Leopold Mozart died. In this time of sorrow and decline he composed one of the greatest masterpieces of all times, *Don Giovanni,* first performed in Prague on October 29, 1787. Conducted by the composer, the work carried the audience away and the echo of the applause reached the emperor himself and after many delays *Don Giovanni* was finally produced in Vienna in May, 1788. Considered confused and dissonant, *Don Giovanni* found only one sincere and appreciative admirer—Haydn.

As Mozart's operatic fame waned, his instrumental works too ceased to interest the public, and his last great symphonies did not receive public performance. With the changed circumstances the physiognomy of his art underwent a gradual change. A peculiar, intensely subjective hue seems to dominate his music; it is already evident in the magnificent D major symphony (K. 504) and even more clearly in the string quintets (K. 515, 516). While all these masterpieces were being created, he felt how the basis of everyday reality upon which his art rested was fading, as life raced past him; he sensed that this life was not so much a reality as a fictitious home created by his music. The resignation which had accompanied him unconsciously since his childhood now appeared to him as a tragic and inescapable fate. The very first measures of the G minor string quintet utter this conviction, and neither the sparkling final movement of the quintet nor the cherubic grace of the *Kleine Nachtmusik* (K. 525) can dispel the tragedy, for "where there is much light the shadows are deepest"; they merely accentuate and recall his fundamental love of life. It was in these days that he found the demonic champion of love of life, Don Juan; and as his hero was really a lonely wanderer amidst the populous scene of his escapades, so Mozart retired more and more into his music. Most of the chamber music and piano compositions of this period he seems to play for himself. Then comes his last divertimento, the E flat major string trio (K. 563), and over the most sociable form of music descends the spell of solitude. The three stringed instruments speak of the poet's most subjective dreams and desires, of his sorrows and tribulations, for they know that they are alone, that their "entertainment" is for themselves.

The last three years of Mozart's life passed in growing need and despair. A trip to Berlin did not result in a position, although the King of Prussia received him with honors. During this journey, when stopping in Leipzig, Mozart heard Bach's motet *Singet dem Herrn ein neues Lied,* and the musical horizon opened up anew to his wondering eyes. A successful revival of *Figaro* finally moved Joseph II to commission his court composer to write an opera. *Così Fan Tutte,* composed on an original libretto by da Ponte, was staged on January 26, 1790. In the wonderfully wrought ensembles of this opera buffa the unruly demons of passion had to bow before the superior force of classic art. The instrumental works of this period all profess this same classic ideal: the piano sonata in D major (K. 576), the B flat major piano concerto (K. 595), the iridescent clarinet quintet (K. 581). Profound harmony, serene equilibrium, crystalline transparency characterize these works. In this last style period of the master, in the quartets (K. 575, 589, 590), in the quintets (K. 593, 614), in the piano sonata (K. 570), in the clarinet concerto (K. 622), there is a concentration of expression, a severe melodic design aided by a polyphonic texture, resulting in a stylistic unity in which poetic thought is completely converted into musical form.

The man whose artistic life had reached the summit could not much longer continue his struggle with everyday life. He must have sensed his approaching end, for his last year was spent in feverish creative activity. The point of gravity of this final phase of his career centered as usual around a lyric drama, the *Magic Flute,* written in collaboration with the actor and theatrical manager, Emanuel Schikaneder (1748-1812). With this work, Mozart returned to the German Singspiel and in the recitatives found the dramatic vocal and declamatory style upon which rests all subsequent German lyric drama. The *Magic Flute* is often compared to the second part of *Faust* and to the *Tempest.* Both comparisons are well taken, for one cannot help thinking of *Faust* when beholding this amalgamation of all musical civilizations. Mozart united in his lyric drama all the symbols of human dreams and desires, and this permitted him to employ such widely divergent forms and moods as the simple folk song and the majestic chorus, the sensuous Italian arioso and the severe chorale-fugue, the demonically scintillating coloratura song and the hymns of humanism. But, like Prospero, the musician knew that the figures he conjured up were merely the creatures of his desires, in spite of their lifelike behavior. He knew that resignation was his lot; he did not step forward to lead the battle with his subjective personality as a Beethoven might, his glance turned inward. "Oh dark night, when wilt thou vanish? When will there be light falling on my eyes?" sings Tamino.

There was nothing left for him but to work on his Requiem Mass, commissioned by an anonymous patron, but death did not permit him to finish this poignant eulogy of the beyond. The voice of the hopeless lover of life broke after the first few measures of the *Lacrymosa*.

*

*   *

WHENEVER Goethe spoke of the nature of genius—which he did especially in his later years—he mentioned Mozart, who appeared to him as the human incarnation of a divine force of creation. There have been few men in all arts and letters in whom genius was so purely creative, so completely creative, as in Mozart. This creative process had in him something of a divine certainty and serenity. His letters are the precious documents of this unique personality.[11] Writing to his father on July 31, 1778, from Paris, Mozart complains that he does not like to give instruction in music and is always relieved when a lesson is over. "Unless you wear yourself out by taking a *large number of pupils,* you cannot make much money. You must not think that this is laziness on my part. No, indeed! It just goes utterly against my genius and my manner of life. You know that I am, so to speak, soaked in music, that I am immersed in it all day long and that I love to plan works, study, and meditate." [12]

Ever since the distinguished Bonn scholar, Otto Jahn, published his romantically colored Mozart biography (1856–1859), the world has been wont to consider him a musician who, in Wagner's words, created "with undisturbed naïveté, in a process entirely free of reflection," a misunderstanding of both the artist and his work as startling as Voltaire's celebrated sentence on Shakespeare, whom he took for a "drunken savage." Perhaps the chief reason for our lack of understanding of Mozart's art is that the only approach to it leads through opera, admittedly the least-known province of classical music. Opera became the preferred medium of musical expression for Mozart. This is understandable, for it offered the greatest variety. Even with a bad libretto, it permitted the whole gamut of human feelings to be brought into play. The fact that his operas were written on commission contributed to the judgment of the Wagnerian circle, which considered these works occasional pieces, denying specific dramatic gifts to the composer of *Don Giovanni*. But such views were due to an ignorance of musical history. No one in the eighteenth century would have thought of composing a work without having in mind a definite performance by a definite company of artists. This was not a matter of "artistic indifference," as contrasted to l'art pour l'art of the romantic era, but an established policy which had definite artistic advantages. Between the operas, Mozart like all his colleagues wrote many other works, for composition was to him synonymous with life; still, from his letters, from the many testimonials of his contemporaries, and most of all from his works themselves it becomes clear that Mozart clung to opera with every fiber in his body. It was this love for the musical stage which continually directed his attention to Vienna, not only because of the excellent operatic theater of the capital, but because of the constant rumor that Joseph II intended to create a haven for the German national Singspiel. Haydn was the born symphonist and quartet composer; to Mozart these fields were but part of his universal musical imagination, dominated by the lyric stage. And, again, the child of the golden age does not set for himself stylistic ideals to be rigorously followed; he writes music as it comes to him, whenever it is needed, the only condition being that this music be the expression of life. Thus divertimento and quartet, sonata and symphony, are equally welcome and one is not absorbed by the other.

Instrumental Works

MOZART'S early chamber music reflects the molding influence of Wagenseil, of Schobert and the Mannheimers, and of Johann Christian Bach. It is fresh, unspoiled music, already notable for vivacity of imagination. It is astonishing to see how immediate and effortless, one might say instantaneous, is his orientation as compared with Haydn's careful and conscious sampling and weighing. The string quartets and symphonies written in Italy have nothing in common with the divertimenti: they are Italian to the core, singing in abandoned suavity the melodies learned from Sammartini, Tartini, and Christian Bach. A process of stabilization makes itself felt, however, in the next group of works, undoubtedly under the influence of Haydn's earlier quartets. The dualistic principle is missing, but the unity of mood does not require it, and once more we must remember that contrasting themes are not a matter of value, nor are they indispensable; the customary allusions to "primitive forms" are therefore without any foundation. On the contrary, the unity of mood would have suffered in these particular instances, and the general design virtually excludes contrasting material.

The series of chamber music works of the earlier periods are punctuated by divertimenti (which generic name includes serenades, cassations, etc.), the number and variety of which is legion. The Mozartean divertimento is, as we have remarked, not a stepping-stone to quartet or symphony, the occasional elaboration of a serenade into a symphony notwithstanding; it is an independent type of music sharing the process of spiritual and technical maturity with the other works, though remaining within its own sphere. An incomparable sphere it was, the purest music making of all times. The earliest examples of this subdivision of Mozart's art were simple, innocent, and devoid of problems. Retaining their essential joy in mere existence, they became works of art in their own right. Displaying sonata constructions, courtly dances, here and there a contrapuntal movement, adroit variations, searching slow movements, concertante passages, and exuberant finales, they are neither chamber music nor orchestral music but rather the quintessence of Austrian musical entertainment in the noblest sense of the word. This pure music making could not be continued by the free-lance master in Vienna; it seems that in abandoning Salzburg and the court he lost his faith in the music which symbolized it. Some of the last serenades remained unfinished, for behind them stood a symphonic concentration unsuited to their nature. With the conversion of the Haffner serenade into a symphony and of the C minor serenade (K. 388) into a string quintet (K. 406), the metamorphosis is an accomplished fact.

The same animation that dominates Mozart's operas, the same lively exchange of ideas and personalities, and the same virtuoso polyphonic summary of characters live in his chamber music. Outside impressions may be strong—they are acknowledged in the dedication of the six quartets (K. 387, 421, 428, 458, 464, 465) to Haydn—but all stimuli are converted into a personal idiom and form. The difficulties which he experienced with Bach's polyphonic style, resulting as we have seen in a number of unfinished works, were solved by the example of Haydn's resolution of a new and free instrumental ensemble polyphony. Still, while the principles were developed by Haydn, Mozart's solution is again entirely original. With the newly won mastery of polyphony and form came a differentiated harmonic language and an ever-increasing range of tonal sonority.

Ever since the Middle Ages when we first encountered it, polyphony has assumed different aspects in different style periods. We have seen it in its absolute and independent form in the old *motetus,* in the infinitely complicated canonic writing of the Netherlanders, in the ethereally balanced vocal settings of the Roman school of the sixteenth century, in the robust harmonic counterpoint of the high baroque, in the scholastic fugues of the declining baroque, and in the new instrumental polyphony of Haydn. With Mozart we discover an entirely new variety, or rather a new blend of polyphony and homophony, best exemplified in the finale of the Jupiter Symphony. When we say a blend we do not mean an interpenetration of homophony and polyphony—that was Haydn's contribution—but a literal blend of the two types, each retaining its individuality. This curious mixture appears much earlier than the Jupiter Symphony, and is present in the quartets dedicated to Haydn. Here, in the finale of the first of the set of six, we see a fugal beginning, very much like that of the Jupiter finale, relieved, with the instancy of lightning, by an entirely homophonous passage. Hardly had this change been consummated when the fugato reappears, this time enriched with a complementary subject and developed into a veritable double fugue only to surrender, at the height of its intensity, to an impudent and mischievous little ditty that might have been one of Figaro's asides. This is again the creation of the musico-dramatist to whom life is capable of embracing every mood and climate; no rules of chamber music style apply to this imagination and none can be deduced from it; it will remain the personal property of its creator.

At the time of the *Abduction* the symphonist comes of age. Not that Mozart's earlier symphonies do not contain much valuable music, but the young composer's heart was closer to the divertimento and to chamber music. The reason lies perhaps in the fact that his models, the Italian opera-symphony and the post-Stamitz symphony of the Mannheim school as exemplified by Cannabich, steered him into an atmosphere of festive rhetoric, not flexible enough in mood and technique to suit his nature. It was in the melodious slow movements that he gave his best, and this again is understandable, for here his mentor was Christian Bach, the incomparable melodist. Now the missing flexibility is found in Haydn, whose symphonic style changed Mozart's whole outlook and taught him the art of logic and continuity.

Between chamber music, divertimento, and symphony there was a specific territory ruled over by the pianoforte. The piano was Mozart's first and favorite instrument, and it is only natural that some of his most personal utterances were reserved for it. We shall discuss his magnificent sonatas in the subsequent chapter and shall now examine the works that fall in the category of ensemble music.

Arrived at his mature style, Mozart, fond of his instrument and eager to possess works of his own for performance, experimented a great deal with various combinations. The sonatas for piano and violin, trios for piano, violin, and cello, or piano, clarinet and viola, quartets and quintets for piano and strings, or wind instruments, as well as concertos for piano and orchestra, composed under this influence attest the sensitive musician's seemingly unending search for balance; for indeed the tone of the hammer piano refuses to blend with any other instrument or combination of instruments. Anyone who has heard Bach's violin-harpsichord sonatas performed on the modern piano will understand this problem, because the impression created by this ensemble is that the violin plays for itself while the piano goes its own way. (This, of course, is not the case when performed on a harpsichord, whose plucked tones blend readily with the violin.) The heterogeneous nature of this instrumental combination is not less acute in modern works, and viewed from this angle one can understand why the string quartet became the epitome of chamber music. While Mozart's ability to blend the various ensembles with the piano is manifest and successful in all the works mentioned, he came to the conclusion that the piano trio constitutes the most suitable ensemble in chamber music calling on the keyboard, and in its own field should assume the role played by the string quartet. The style had to be idiomatic for all instruments concerned, at the same time holding fast to a sonorous unity. This he achieved by abstaining from the strict thematic treatment employed in his quartets and quintets for homogeneous instruments, replacing it with a free, almost improvisatory piano setting, surrounded by more closely knit string parts. Thus the piano was always able to avoid literal imitations of thematic material when such imitation would disturb the euphony of the setting. Works like the somber piano quartet in G minor (K. 478) and the piano trio in G major (K. 496) show how this improvisatory pianism developed into a style of convincing authenticity.

Another and entirely different task faced Mozart when he combined the piano with the orchestra, for the problem of tonal equilibrium was joined by other factors that had to be overcome. Looking at the earlier piano concertos, one is aware that with all the brilliance and skill lavished on them, Mozart was prevented from penetrating to greater depths by the unavoidable social role of the concerto. The rococo had made it social music (*Gesellschaftsmusik*) par excellence; its tone and content were predetermined by the tone and artistic capacities of this society. More than in any other field of music, Mozart's initial ventures in the concerto were imitations, or even outright arrangements of piano compositions by such masters of the style galant as Christian Bach and Schobert. It is the more surprising to find that the engaging violin concertos, composed at the age of nineteen, while not among his most profound works, rise to considerable mastery with the fourth (D major) and fifth (A major) of the set of five. In the second group of his original piano concertos the virtuoso-composer found his bearings, and we are immediately confronted with a work (K. 271, E flat major) which constitutes one of the original departures in the eighteenth-century concerto literature. Mozart's dislike of patterns made him enter the solo instrument in the second measure as if to announce that henceforth piano and orchestra would be on equal terms. Indeed, his concertos departed considerably from the earlier type: they were much more symphonic in nature, and the dialogue of piano and orchestra, representing opposing forces of equal importance, eliminated the sectional continuity of the rococo concerto. In the subsequent concertos one begins to feel that the barriers of convention are demolished and Mozart is writing music not only to his satisfaction but to his enjoyment. The subservient orchestral support is a thing of the past and its place is taken by a symphonic ensemble every member of which is eager to get in the fray.

The many experiments with the piano taught Mozart the art of blending it with the orchestra, and in the slow movements of the concertos, beginning with the three written in 1782 (K. 413, 414, 415), we perceive the exquisite *bel canto* of the vocal composer entrusted with success to an instrument not especially suited for it. The blending of solo instrument and orchestra is no longer a problem in the succeeding concertos (K. 452, 453, 456, 459), and the composer's fantasy gains untrammeled freedom. If there was anything left of the *Gesellschaftsmusik* in the previous concertos, the last vestiges of it disappear in the D minor concerto (K. 466). With the very first measures—strangely rumbling muffled basses accompanied by hesitating syncopation in the upper parts—we know that we are in Don Giovanni's abode. The whole tone material of this concerto is dramatic and passionate and, at the end of the orchestral exposition, one is almost surprised to hear the entrance of the solo piano, but for an instant only, because the composer does not permit us to wonder about the miracle of opera in the concerto, everything becomes perfectly plausible. The formal and stylistic consolidation is so firm in the following great works (K. 467, 468, 482) that when the intensely symphonic and dramatic C minor concerto (K. 491) is created the master is able to cope with the tremendous tension and to keep it within the possibilities of the concerto. The orchestra now is entrusted with tasks that Mozart's century had never heretofore dreamed of; every instrument must vouch for itself, for it is a leading actor. Another remarkable stylistic detail is Mozart's use of the variation principle within the concerto. The last movement of the C minor concerto, a set of variations based on a deeply moving theme, represents the highest point attained in this particular type.

In his last symphonies Mozart abandons his former habit of using unrelated material in his development sections, and everything now is organized in the best symphonic traditions established by Haydn. It is significant, however, that again he has set his own rules, for while the development sections are strictly thematic, the material utilized is often taken from the subsidiary themes, little appendages of the closing theme, or a chance motif from the second theme. The D major symphony (No. 38) has an extraordinary introduction, and one wonders whether it was dictated by sheer imagination and concentration, or whether the composer resorted to it deliberately. The introduction is, namely, a complete operatic scene—without the vocal parts. Its mood fluctuates with the typical immediacy of the stage; festal and friendly opening chords make us think of a pleasant scene to follow, but the atmosphere becomes darker, the orchestra begins to hammer fateful chords, and the chromatic inner parts beg for mercy, with submission finally secured amidst the veiled threats of trumpets and kettledrums. The allegro emerges from this oppressing scene with difficulty, the syncopated accompaniment covering a pleading melody. Once the theme gains the surface everything becomes determined and defiant and a lively contrapuntal debate ensues. The introduction offers the most striking illustration of the history of the symphonic idiom, for in it flares up, undisguised, the passionate world of the music drama. At a time when the transliteration of the operatic elements into a self-contained instrumental style is an accomplished fact, Mozart permits us once more to see with X-ray clarity the skeleton through flesh and sinew. It may be significant that Mozart omitted in this unruly symphony the customary minuet, returning to the old Italian form of three movements, for even the andante is saturated with the dark mood of the first movement, and the seeming merriness of the last presto has to conquer tempestuous obstacles.

The last great chamber music compositions with piano, violin sonatas and trios, were followed by still another stylistic find: the string quintet. The addition of one more instrument to the quartet may hardly seem enough to cause an entirely new style; one is prepared for added color and sonority, but to Mozart it meant freedom of imagination. If we recall Brahms's remark about Haydn's symphonies we shall understand how Mozart felt about the older master's quartets. No matter how individual his conception and realization, the road led to the Rome of the string quartet: to Haydn, who had established a tradition that could not be evaded. The quintet was a little-known medium; Boccherini's delightful compositions for this combination had failed to create a school, and Mozart was free to manipulate this type of chamber music to his liking. He exchanged Boccherini's second cello for a second viola, and with this apparatus proceeded to go his own way. This way was the path of *Don Giovanni,* for the breadth of the first quintet in C major (K. 515) and the tragic conflicts of the G minor (K. 516) cannot be compared to anything but the universality of *Don Giovanni.*

The concertos written in this period, among them the unusually large C major concerto (K. 503), the so-called Coronation Concerto (K. 537), and the last work of this type, the B flat major concerto (K. 595), are distinguished by more brilliant pianistic writing and by a singularly bold harmonic idiom, but they do not reach the fervor of some of the earlier ones. It is his very last concerto, an isolated work for clarinet and orchestra (K. 622), written a few days before the first performance of the *Magic Flute,* in which the symphonic concerto principle is carried to its summit. The character of the solo instrument is exploited as far as was technically possible, and the instrument sings in rapturous melodiousness. The texture of this composition is so closely woven that the clarinet is required to play throughout the tutti passages.

The last three symphonies, the ones universally known to us, were composed a year and a half after the D major, in the short interval of three months. They represent three totally different moods and aspirations: the E flat major happy and proud, the G minor passionate and sorrowful, the C major, the broadest, the richest, the most classic expression of his symphonic art. They encompass a wide range of sentiments: the first overflows with radiant optimism, sure of its power and beauty, heroic and exuberant; the second, written in the key of the somber quintet and of the dark arias of the Queen of the Night, strikes passionate accents such as Mozart had seldom shown in instrumental music; and the third, worthy of the epithet "Jupiter" attached to it, is an overwhelming monument of musical architecture and contrapuntal mastery. Yet with all their differences in mood and their adherence to their respective aims, they show the unpredictable nonconformist, the archdramatist, for the shadow of Don Giovanni is suddenly conjured up in the last notes of the festive introduction to the E flat symphony, childlike felicity interrupts the cutting dissonances of the minuet in the G minor symphony, and the festive flourishes of the overturelike beginning of the Jupiter symphony are immediately halted by hesitating and pleading questions before the orchestra can cut loose with its blaring trumpets and rolling drums.

At the end of this creative period, after the quintets, Mozart returned again to almost all types of his earlier instrumental music. The trios and quartets, the divertimenti and serenades are, however, the works of the composer of *Così Fan Tutte;* their style is distilled and codified. With a few more quintets, among them the most consummate expression of Mozartean chamber music, the apotheosis of melody, the clarinet quintet (K. 581) and the equally accomplished although less weighty E flat major quintet for strings (K. 614), we arrive at the end of the roster of his instrumental works, now to enter the mysterious hinterland of opera from which they claim their descent.

Theater and Opera in the Classic Era

WHILE symphonies and quartets were being produced in countless numbers in the classic era, the theater, both dramatic and lyric, again became the focal point of the temporal arts, not because it offered a spectacle and representation as in the baroque, but because it permitted action, a free deployment of man's individual powers. This classical theater and opera championed characters who were sculptured individuals in contradistinction to the baroque tragedy with its idealized types. It searched more deeply for the inner actions of man, for heroism in the soul; its protagonists act under the impulse of more subjective dynamics, as heroism and even tragedy appeared to the man of the classic era under aspects quite different from those of the preceding rococo. Tragedy and epic poetry were too weighty for the rococo, and what the latter produced in this field was nothing more than an eviscerated baroque drama. The heavy burdens of Calderón and Racine were thus disposed of and were replaced by explosive bombast and effective emptiness, well illustrated in Voltaire's tragedies in verse. The outstanding works of the dramatic stage were Scipione Maffei's and Metastasio's neoclassic dramas, but even these were at their best when turned into music dramas. The colorful pomp and natural power of baroque epic poetry were also successfully diluted by such works as Voltaire's *Henriade.* The rococo did, however, produce great comedy, for the wittiness, gracefulness, and spirited élan that emanate from the superbly formed plays of Beaumarchais and Goldoni remain the finest that Latin imagination created in the eighteenth century. The clever and resourceful intriguer, Beaumarchais's Figaro, who does not recognize difficulties, became the symbol of the second half of the century. The frothy lightness of his figure rises above everything that is heavy and burdensome. Goldoni's versatile mistress of the inn (*La Locandiera*) joins the company of the gay barber without suffering in wit and cleverness by the inevitable comparison; and although somewhat different, the fairy plays of Carlo Gozzi (1720–1806), called *fiabe* and written with the purpose of equaling Goldoni's success, were, in fact, equally accomplished. It was this extremely witty and lifelike portrayal of characters in the latter part of the eighteenth century which brought about a change in the conception of the drama by reviving Molière's precept, *castigat ridendo mores,* and nowhere was this more noticeable than on the lyric stage.

The opera seria was definitely on its last leg in Italy. Gluck's *Orfeo* and *Alceste* were presented in various Italian cities without making any perceptible impression and disappeared from the repertory after a few performances. As a matter of fact, judging from the joking allusions and parodies which they occasioned, one must conclude that these "reform" operas appeared ridiculous to the Italians, who refused to acknowledge the necessity of an operatic reform movement. They looked askance not only at Gluck's operas but at those of their compatriots, Jommelli and Traëtta, rejecting the Germanic and French elements they instinctively felt at work in them. What they objected to in the music and even more in the libretto was a certain Teutonic turgidity, for, as Arteaga and other aesthetes have repeatedly declared, celerity is an essential quality of life and consequently of the music drama. The ceremonious and circumspect proceedings of the Gluckian opera were too artificial and pathetic to suit their taste. This opinion was shared by those Germans accustomed to Italian opera, and in the light of the foregoing we shall understand why the Viennese, devoted to the opera buffa and the Singspiel, called *Alceste* a "de profundis," lamenting its excessive slowness. That Gluck was pleading most eloquently for Monteverdi's ideal no one seemed to realize, nor, indeed, could they, for this ideal had been forgotten. This was, however, inevitable, for the imagination of the people —and in Italy the operatic public was not made up of archdukes and archbishops—could not be satisfied with mythology: they wanted to see themselves on the stage. Thus the future of opera depended on the development of the opera buffa.

It would be erroneous, however, to assume that with the decline of the pure opera seria the drama was entirely displaced by comedy. The younger Neapolitan opera school continued to flourish, barely touched by the events abroad; its expressive range was altered, enlarged, and made more flexible by the influences emanating from the opera buffa. This neo-Neapolitan school boasted talents of the first magnitude whose dramatic gifts glowed unimpaired by the merger of idioms, by the captivating melodiousness and capricious mobility that came to them from the opera buffa. Francesco di Majo (1740–1771), dying, like Pergolesi, in his youth, was like his illustrious predecessor a mature and finished opera composer in his first works. A pupil of Martini, he was one of the last representatives of the expressive, purely musically conceived opera style of Hasse, a master of the bel canto, of elegiac melodies that haunted his confreres, especially Christian Bach and Mozart, throughout their life. It was notably his sensuous chromatic melody which impressed Mozart. It must be borne in mind that di Majo and the other great composers of the school were equally at home in the opera seria and in the buffa, a fact which accounts for their versatility. Since Goldoni had changed the course of operatic history, giving the opera buffa a new form by raising its popular elements to a literary status though safeguarding the traditions, a rapprochement of the two species took place. The Goldoni-inspired Venetian opera buffa, practiced with great success by Galuppi, Giuseppe Scarlatti (1723–1777), Domenico Fischietti (c. 1725–c. 1810), and the young Gassmann, seems to have undergone a stylistic reorientation toward 1770. The new opera buffa which began to dominate the theater in Venice and Naples produced two great leaders, Piccini and Paisiello, in whose works there appeared a new tendency toward an admixture of more lyricism with the comical, and a more elaborate and active participation of the orchestra.

The classical phase of the opera buffa started with Piccini's *Buona Figliuola,* a comedy in music of such humorous and human qualities—here sentimental to evoke tears, there comic to rouse unbridled laughter—that it was played in Rome for two years without interruption. The composer, whom we have already met as an involuntary tool in the hands of a political party, was unhappy in Paris and, like Mozart, was repelled by the French attitude toward music. "Lonely, transplanted to a foreign country where everything seems strange," Piccini wrote to Marie Antoinette, "intimidated by a thousand difficulties, I have lost all my courage." When he was about to resign and return to Italy, his *Roland* was performed amid the greatest acclaim, and deservedly so, for the work should be counted among the finest of music dramas. Composed with dramatic élan, fine delineation of characters, and with a wealth of melodies, it presents a hero every inch as demonic, superhuman, and fearless as Don Giovanni. The merger of opera seria and opera buffa is accomplished in his works, and while the new designations which cropped up during the period of transition—*opera semi-seria, dramma giocoso*—continue to be employed in title pages and theater bills, they have lost their literal meaning. The interpenetration of the two types caused changes in the formal structures. The opera buffa took over the chorus and the larger design of the seria, while the latter accepted the elaborate orchestration and the spirited ensembles of the buffa, shedding or at least altering its own da capo arias and other elements retained from the baroque opera. The most distinguished representative of this "reformed" serious opera was Antonio Maria Gasparo Sacchini (1730–1786), better known as a member of the Gluck circle in Paris. We must regard him, however, as a full-blooded Italian composer who had left his mark on opera before, toward the end of his life, he joined the Gluckists. The chief agent of dramatic action, the accompanied recitative, is employed in his Italian operas with great skill and force, and he likes to combine recitative and aria in complementary forms bound together by the identity of the basic musical material.

Giovanni Paisiello (1740–1816), pupil and later member of the faculty of the Neapolitan Conservatorio di Sant' Onofrio, distinguished himself at an early age with successful operas and by the end of the seventeen sixties conquered Naples. A few years later his fame rivaled that of Piccini and of the other idols of the time and he was invited by the Empress Catherine II to assume the directorship of Italian opera in St. Petersburg. It was there that he wrote several of his most popular operas, among them *Il Barbiere di Siviglia* (The Barber of Seville), 1782, one of the most universally admired works in the whole history of opera. On his return from Russia, Paisiello visited Vienna, dedicating several works, among them twelve symphonies, to Joseph II, finally entering the services of Ferdinand IV, King of Naples. The subsequent years (1784–1799) carried him to the zenith of his artistic career. Works such as *La Scuffiara, La Bella Molinara, Nina, Pazza per Amore,* seized upon life with a wonderfully realistic fantasy, turning it into music with dramatic force, robust humor, and unerring craftsmanship. His characterizations and his comic scenes betray a strong popular impulse, and this, as well as his operatic technique and vivid orchestration, brought him close to Mozart's style. Indeed, the latter, befriended by Paisiello, owed much to him.

Paisiello's successor in St. Petersburg, Domenico Cimarosa (1749–1801), was the former's peer as a composer of operas; his *Matrimonio Segreto* (Secret Marriage, Vienna, 1792) can be compared only to Paisiello's *Barber of Seville*. It made the rounds of every opera theater in the world and if it were given in its original form without the customary modern "restorations," it would become a favorite of present-day operagoers. Like most Italian opera composers active after Mozart, he learned a great deal from the Austrian master.

It seemed as though the prodigious operatic era of the seventeenth century had returned in the latter part of the eighteenth, for even the world-famous leaders could not enjoy undisputed supremacy, so great was the number of eminent composers. Piccini and Paisiello found formidable rivals in Gennaro Astaritta (active 1765-1793), Giuseppe Gazzaniga (1743-1818), and Johann

Gottlieb Naumann (1741–1801), to mention a few of their competitors. The last-named was one of the few Germans successful with serious opera in Italy. Little known today, Naumann was one of the most famous German composers of his time, vying with Haydn and the Bach sons for international honors. He was an accomplished composer in every field of music but he was especially noted for his operas.

"Before I begin my work I try to forget that I am a musician," declared Gluck. By this he meant that, contrary to operatic traditions, he strove to be "more a painter and a poet than a musician." The Italian composer's approach is different. What he wants from the libretto is not "literary value" but an opportunity to perceive a certain inspiring and intensive picture of life, from which with the aid of music he can create something of his own. The plots, forms, and principles of the many operas may be similar, yet every work gives a different picture of life. The public—and not only in Italy—could not satiate its pleasure in seeing such animated, lifelike musical plays. The greatness of Italian opera was determined by the mimic force and talent of the genius of the Italian people. To them music is a natural expression of physical and spiritual life; the *dramatis personae* think in tones, and tones are their language. With this, music advances beyond the domain of the drama, which in the final analysis is but an enhanced imitation of a real action. The opera is divorced from the reality of life; consequently it has evolved a style whose forms have their roots in purely musical soil. Aria, duet, quartet, and other formal elements, when segregated and lifted from their context, seem ridiculous aesthetic abstractions compared to the constant flow of dramatic life. They are completely vindicated when we realize that a world divorced from reality cannot obtain its principles from the latter and must turn for law and order to the element from which it springs. This gives Italian opera its strength, for it is completely identified with music. The Italian composer builds everything, characters, situations, and action, purely by music. The main characters are presented in well-defined musical forms, contemptuously referred to by modern critics as the "set numbers," but every one of these numbers is a self-contained scene in which the idea and mimic expression are completely absorbed in a musical form. This music can achieve what the spoken drama can only indicate, the simultaneous and instant representation of temperament, character, mood, and expression. Being apart from, even above reality, the music drama can give us pure human characters, the most immediate outpourings of a human soul, while spoken drama must always retain a certain measure of plausibility which imposes restrictions. The relation of the figures of the drama to the action is also purely musical, and in it opera rises to the height of the dramatic, into spheres that cannot even be touched by the spoken drama. The music drama is distinguished from the spoken drama by its ability to permit a number of persons to express themselves simultaneously. The great Italian opera composers—and the foreigners who identified themselves with Italian opera—constructed their animated scenes by presenting some or all of their protagonists at the same moment, each deporting himself in his own manner, venting his rage or shouting his joy in his most personal fashion, asking questions while others are being answered, and sustaining views and moods perhaps diametrically opposed to those of the others. This can be achieved only through music, for it is the musical form which, embracing all these diffuse elements, gives them back to the listener as an aesthetically un-paralleled single effect, binding the variety of characters into the unity of life. Thus opera alone is able to give us the accumulated richness of life con-centrated in moments of utter tragedy or all-absorbing mirth, undivided in its fullness.

Mozart is the supreme master of this art, never surpassed and seldom approached. The very first ensemble in his *Don Giovanni,* with the dying commandant writhing in pain, the imperturbable knight laughing at the misery unfolding before him, and Leporello, his servant, trying to find a way of escaping from this dangerous situation, is a scene of such dramatic in-tensity, with murder, death, fear, lust, defiance, and cunning all condensed in a few measures, as can hardly be matched in the whole history of the theater. The spoken drama can only present such scenes in succession; the music drama concentrates them, enhancing their impact tenfold. Another great advantage for the increased dramatic force of the opera is gained by the collaboration of the orchestra, which is capable of upholding and main-taining the mood, thereby permitting the greatest mobility on the stage. This purely musical principle of construction made Italian opera inde-pendent of its text, and it is this quality which differentiates it from the Ger-man music drama. No matter how trivial the text, through music every word receives an entirely different meaning and weight.

Mozart's Italian Operas

SCHILLER wrote to Goethe on December 29, 1797, "I had always placed a certain confidence in opera, hoping that from it will rise as from the choruses of the ancient feasts of Bacchus the tragedy in a nobler form." "The hopes you placed in the opera," replied Goethe, "you would find fulfilled to a high degree in the recent *Don Juan (Don Giovanni)*." The great dramatist's judgment of *Don Giovanni* holds true of the whole op-eratic oeuvre of Mozart. The greatest musico-dramatic works are usually the creations of men advanced in age and looking back upon an impressive past of experience—Monteverdi, Rameau, Gluck, Wagner, Verdi. With Mozart (as with Pergolesi and di Majo) it is the incredible prodigality of youth that is at work, tossing out masterpieces composed with the sure hand of his elders. Still, at his debut the youthful musico-dramatist found himself faced with many problems. In his earlier vocal works, especially in church music, he soon overtook the Neapolitans, but the opera seria presented difficulties not conquered in the first works. *Mitridate* (1770), *Ascanio in Alba* (1771), *Lucio Silla* (1772), and *Scipione* (1772) represent more or less unsuccessful attempts to master the music drama. There is no guiding operatic conviction in them, and they show that their composer was not an Italian, saturated with the traditions of opera.

All this had to be learned. The technique of Italian dramatic composition he soon mastered, curiously enough at the same time that his Italianate instrumental style began to change under the influence of the German symphonic style. His second visit to Paris acquainted him with Gluck's works, then in the center of French musical life. It has often been said that Gluck's operatic art was continued by Mozart, and that it was Mozart who handed it down to Beethoven. We shall see that Gluck's dramatic style was merely another style to Mozart, like the opera seria, opera buffa, or the Singspiel. He took from it whatever he could use in his own art; he gained stimuli, nothing more. It is easy to find numerous Gluckian reminiscences in Mozart's music, and sometimes they are significant, but from such details—however important—to the acceptance of Gluck's dramatic principles there is a wide gulf never bridged by the young master. His conception of the role of music in the lyric drama remained diametrically opposed to that of the composer of *Alceste*. The music drama was for Gluck the form of expression of his artistic convictions. To Mozart it was expression itself; his personality lies in the music. To Gluck—admittedly "trying to forget that he is a musician"—the drama was supreme, with the accompanying music completing the picture. For Mozart the drama is there only to give music opportunities; it is absorbed and completely recast in the music, which remains supreme.

In *Idomeneo* (1781) Mozart found his bearings if not his definitive style. Written by the Salzburg court chaplain, Abbate Varesco, the libretto of this opera was designed on Metastasian lines, but it no longer mattered what conventions or patterns were followed by the libretto, for Mozart parted with the opera seria tradition of composing situations created by the plot; he was intent only on psychological characterization of the *dramatis personae*. This opera, now almost forgotten, contains sublime pages, pages that would honor the greatest of operatic composers, excelling especially in individual sketches within the ensembles. The Gluckian tone which is noticeable in this work more than in any other of his operas made it somewhat stiff and static, and Mozart, finally realizing that the opera seria was too stylized and too close to the literary ideal of the drama to suit his own preferences, with *Idomeneo* abandoned the seria forever. We are justified in saying "forever," because *Titus,* the one opera seria written at the end of his life, was a halfhearted and unsuccessful venture, engaged in under duress. Like his great Italian contemporaries, Mozart felt that the admixture of the tragic and the comic, embracing the whole range of human emotions, was the atmosphere in which he could best express himself, and he was at home in this wide world of sentiments, capable of sympathy with every shade of it, for he could sincerely say "I deem nothing human alien to me." He did not want to organize his nation by dedicating gigantic dramas to the genius of the race, to be performed in a temple set aside for the resurrected gods and heroes of its mythology; he came to express the world and its living creatures, representing every character and idea with the directness and simplicity that characterized his classic times.

Don Giovanni is perhaps more overwhelming and the *Magic Flute* more profound, but Mozart's love of life fetes its most harmonious exuberance in *The Marriage of Figaro* (1786). Here he abandons himself without reserve to the whirl of life. There is no supreme hero in this opera to dictate the tempo of life. Don Giovanni sets the surrounding world to an intoxicating dance but the characters in *Figaro* are made to dance by the world in which they live. All the personalities of the opera fight and love on an equal footing. Each is a sculptured individual, yet there is a common resemblance—their common humanity. There is no sharp social difference to separate them, as in *Don Giovanni,* their importance on the stage is not meticulously divided, as in *Così Fan Tutte,* and their symmetry is not based on contrasts, as in the *Magic Flute;* they are placed on the stage as life would have thrown them there, the one central power around which they rally being "almighty love that creates and preserves everything."

In order to realize this picture of life, Mozart turned to the adventurous Venetian, Lorenzo da Ponte (1749-1838), imperial court poet in Vienna, an able and highly cultivated man of letters. It was not da Ponte however who suggested the subject, and one cannot but ask what caused Mozart to select Beaumarchais's comedy, for the brilliant political satire with its strong rationalism did not offer a particularly musical theme. Beaumarchais's revolutionary ideas could not have appealed to him, and Mozart was not sufficiently interested in social philosophy to attempt a musical setting of the social ideas expressed in the original comedy. What must have attracted him was the *result* of Beaumarchais's satire, that is, partly his virtuoso and thoroughly artistic theatrical conception, partly the elimination of social conventions. Aristocrats and servants deport themselves on this stage as humanly equal persons, thus presenting life in its naked form. This real stage, with its human figures free from all external coercion, is what permitted

Mozart's fantasy to soar with equal freedom. What he gave us in *Figaro,* in this opera buffa, was a profound picture of life, free of all caricature. This life, to be sure, is full of fun and comedy, with unexpected turns caused by the miscarriage of human plans and calculations, but the humorous situations do not change the heroes into puppets: their sentiments are real sentiments coming from the bottom of their hearts; their anger is just as real as their merriness. The composer whose music animated these figures was engrossed by the world he conjured up on the stage, but he was not merely smiling, for the spirited jokes, the general hilarity, are the echoes of a rich and fascinating inner life. If we want to understand Mozart's masterpiece we must always remember that the jubilation that greets us even before the curtain goes up, in the first measures of the overture, is not the sign of carefree amusement; it rather suggests Boileau's lines,

> Heureux qui, dans ses vers, sait d'une voix légère
> Passer du grave au doux, du plaisant au sévère.

Da Ponte's arrangement of the play is a masterpiece of a lyric libretto. The keen-minded and experienced poet eliminated all political connotations to give Mozart a text that was a pure comedy of life. Yet, except in Prague, the opera was misunderstood and denounced; even Joseph II, connoisseur though he was, found it heavy and lacking in finesse. In modern times it has been regarded as an innocent light comedy, while literary circles complain, as they did in Mozart's time, that the opera is entirely different from the original play, that it disfigures Beaumarchais's wonderful satiric comedy.

The Marriage of Figaro is, indeed, a different piece, but the difference is not in the words. The composer's music changed the hearts of Beaumarchais's personages. Among the many commentators past and present there is one who has grasped this metamorphosis: Stendhal. Guilty of more than one inept statement on music, the poet in this case divined with fine intuition the intentions of the musician.

Dominated by his sensibility, the musician changed into real passions the rather light fancy which in Beaumarchais amused the amiable inhabitants of Aguas-Frescas. . . . Count Almaviva's caprice for Susanna becomes a veritable infatuation. Rosina's inclination toward Cherubino might become very serious, it savors of the trouble that precedes great passions, Bartholo's character as well as Figaro's is marked by entirely new traits, in the French piece Cherubino is sketched, in the opera his soul is entirely developed. . . . One can say that Mozart distorted the play as much as it was possible, but . . . he changed Beaumarchais's picture entirely . . . all the characters were turned toward the tender or the passionate. Mozart's opera is a sublime blend of wit and melancholy such as there is no other example.[13]

The point of gravity in *Figaro* is in the ensembles, the aria ceasing to be the main form of characterization. Whenever it is needed, however—as in the case of the lone opera seria figure, the countess—it is used with the tragic pathos of old, most convincingly dramatizing the rather passive, suffering role of the heroine. The vivacious and elaborate orchestral idiom of the opera buffa, the use of a motif of accompaniment developed symphonically, reaches in *Figaro* its ideal perfection, affecting operatic composers for half a century to come. Every pause between phrases or during the singers' natural breathing respite is filled with music as if an electric current were igniting the instruments into song. Powerful and omnipresent as this orchestra is, it never loses sight of its duties, aiding and abetting the drama without disputing the sovereignty of the voices.

Despite its moderate initial success, soon after Mozart's death *Figaro* reappeared in a number of imitations. Most of these operas were the work of obscure composers such as Johann Tost (*Figaro*, 1795), Pietro Persechini (*Le Nozze di Figaro*), Luigi Ricci (*Il Nuovo Figaro*, 1833), but one can find among them eminent musicians of the stature of Ferdinando Paër, a rival of Rossini (1771–1839, *Il Nuovo Figaro*, 1797), and Marcos Portugal (1762–1830, *Le Nozze di Figaro*, 1797), the great Portuguese composer. We should also mention an English adaptation called *The Marriage of Figaro* (1819), by Henry Rowland Bishop (1786–1855), one of England's best-known musicians in the first half of the nineteenth century.

The opera buffa had received a monument of eternal validity, and now Mozart turned his dramatic gifts toward the tragic aspects of life. It is most significant that the road to tragedy led through comedy, for this keen observer of human nature discovered that the essence of life is its manysidedness.

Da Ponte did not invent the libretto of *Don Giovanni:* Chrysander has called attention to the fact that he used a libretto written by Giovanni Bertati (1735–1815), a noted librettist, and author, among other works, of Cimarosa's *Secret Marriage*. It would be erroneous, however, to consider this a plagiarism, for in the eighteenth century poets and musicians felt free to take and use whatever came their way; the important thing was what became of the borrowed goods. There can be no question that da Ponte's *Don Giovanni* is infinitely superior to Bertati's, and quite different in nature and scope. Da Ponte was not a mere purveyor of libretti to whom any composer could apply for a text to be turned out speedily in the fashion of the day; on the contrary, he not only wrote in a style and spirit he considered congenial to the composer, but even selected his subjects with regard to the composer's personality.

Exuberant love is carried to overflowing in this opera. Its hero, the supreme champion of love, rises above the turmoil of existence to perish tragically because his passions flare beyond the limits of life, challenging the powers that reign beyond it. Love is exemplified in its passionate and demonic aspects in the hero of the drama who dominates the whole work; but love, from the lofty and reverent ardor of Don Ottavio to the calculating coquetry of Zerlina, is in possession of every one of the other figures. They are all vastly different and so are their amorous inclinations, but as the atmosphere of love pervades the whole play it fuses everything. The old Spanish play presents to us a world which knows and recognizes love as the highest moment in human life, its ultimate value. This determines and justifies Don Juan's stand toward life. The spectator is so completely enveloped in the magic of love, mirrored to him from all sides, that the natural measure he usually follows in human relations vanishes, together with all scruples he might entertain toward the diabolical greatness of the hero. The existence of Don Juan hinges on one question: can he fit himself into the world of order and conventions? Fundamentally there is only one obstacle in his way, his own passionate and insatiable nature. Like Faust, his only real kinsman, he does not recognize the boundaries of humanity, and, clashing with the order of things, must perish. Mozart divined the last secrets of Don Juan's character, and cast it in music with incomparable fidelity. Life is everywhere, crowded and eventful, until it is whipped up to such intensity and speed—the champagne aria—that one can scarcely follow the rapidity of thought and mood. The opera begins with the banalities of everyday life, with Leporello complaining about the hardship of serving his unpredictable master. From this solid ground we are immediately plunged into sheer drama—the murder of the commandant—the atmosphere of which lingers through the rest of the play.

The arias, recitatives, and ensembles of this opera all follow the best traditions of the musical stage giving the leading characters ample opportunity to distinguish themselves. *Don Giovanni* shows the influence of Gluck, Grétry, Handel, and other great masters, just as *Figaro* and *Così Fan Tutte* exhibit copious study of the works of Christian Bach, di Majo, Piccini, Paisiello, Anfossi, Gassmann, and others; but everything is melted into the master's most personal dramatic idiom, even though the formative atmosphere, the beatification of the intoxicating glorification of flesh and blood is Italian—Italian opera.

Strange as it may seem, there arose a controversy over *Don Giovanni,* some authors claiming it to be a comic opera while others insisted that it was a tragic work. There are marked comic characters and situations in the opera, and Mozart himself tried to satisfy the existing conventions, which called for a happy ending and expiation, by assembling—*after* the catastrophic end of Don Juan—all personages of the opera who had suffered from the perished hero's acts, making them express their satisfaction over the righteous turn of affairs. If the comic interludes and the added final scene could transform a tragedy into pure comedy, many of Shakespeare's most terrible dramas could be classified as comedies. The more thoughtful conductors and stage directors omit the final scene, for they recognize that the master was forced to tack the anticlimactic end to the real finale.

The uninitiated might think that in his last opera buffa, *Così Fan Tutte,* Mozart returned to the simple schemes of the operatic ventures of his youth, that the flesh and blood and vitality of the characters in *Figaro* are again exchanged for puppets. But Mozart no longer counted on the warm reality of life; after the year of *Don Giovanni* he could not return to it, and leads us into a world in which life is but a mirage. The comedy of life that is enacted on the stage presents well-known types of men in their accustomed frivolity; they flirt with each other's fiancées, the mischievous maid and the incorrigible bachelor pursue their intrigues and jokes, but the puppet men do not realize that they are projected into a sphere beyond the small world of the stage. In none of his operas has Mozart so severely divided reality from the ideal as in *Così Fan Tutte,* a delightful caricature, delicately stylized like a marionette play. The absolute forms of music, which he has placed with unmatched skill in the service of dramatic realism, proclaim here their sovereignty and their own authentic laws. This is the opera of ensembles, of a perfectly balanced and euphonious musical style no longer disturbed by the noise of the world.

Mozart and the Singspiel

THE memory of the years of play and study spent in his Austrian homeland before his Italian journeys was never obliterated by Mozart's later experiences, and it was to this heritage of his youth that he returned with his *Zauberflöte,* the *Magic Flute.* As its name indicates, this was a German opera, and it used to be the consensus of opinion that here Mozart finally realized his "true allegiance" and decided to continue Gluck's work. Gluck's reform operas did not entirely escape the attention of the Viennese musicians. Gassmann's *Amore e Psiche* (1767) is a veritable imitation of *Orfeo,* although the ensemble finales betray the influence of the opera buffa. On the whole, however, Gluck's ideals, so eloquently cultivated by French composers and some Italians living in or creating for Paris, found as little echo in Germany as in Italy, and were ignored, especially in Vienna. The members of the Viennese school, while occasionally showing influences that can be traced to Gluck, did not stem from him and did not arrive at his dramaturgical conclusions. In their German operas they showed themselves the adherents of the Singspiel, and it is to this source that we must return to gain an understanding of the *Magic Flute.*

The German Singspiel, product of the indestructible musical and theatrical appetites of the people, came into being, as we have related, in the seventeen sixties, to oppose to the international Italian opera a new, native, and popular form of the lyric stage. The many folk songs inserted in Hiller's Singspiele made them very popular, and a large and enthusiastic public clamored for more works. Hiller's influence reached Vienna relatively late, but, once acclimatized, the Singspiel there experienced its greatest triumphs. The Viennese Singspiel leaned more on the Italian opera buffa than on its northern German relatives. This is a logical consequence of the general Viennese ignorance of music from the Protestant north; there was, also, a certain aversion to this northern style. The original Singspiel presented a consistent, even though small, form in which were already assimilated the various elements from which it had originated. In Vienna a new mixture was inevitable. The infiltration of Italian elements was as characteristic of the Viennese Singspiel as was the French touch in its north German ancestor. The fact that the opera buffa was highly developed in Vienna and was practiced with great success by native composers contributed, of course, to this mixture of styles. There were, furthermore, Austrian composers who wrote Italian operas in the buffa style with great felicity, while some Italians did exactly the opposite, cleverly and adroitly writing typical Italian works in a Viennese garb. In spite of the far-reaching Italian influences the strongest element in this Singspiel was the improvised comedy of the Viennese popular stage.

The Austrian branch of German literature led a modest existence, the court, ever since the late Renaissance, having favored Italian men of letters. The royal and aristocratic vogue of Italian poetry and drama nevertheless could not stifle the tastes of the public, and the popular theater, especially in Vienna, flourished unmolested and developed by assimilating such foreign stimuli as penetrated the protective cordon of the suburban theaters ruled by a curious traditional figure, "Hanswurst."

The jester appeared in German folk drama in the sixteenth century, increasing in popularity when the wandering English comedians acquainted the Germans with their "clown." The jester, often charged with the improvisation of his lines, commanded the public's attention because in him crystallized the popular comical figures of Germandom. A distant kin of the ancient *mimus* and a descendant of the medieval *Spielmann,* jongleur, and minstrel, he was a composite creature, servant, messenger, spy, intrigant, sorcerer; always hungry and thirsty, always ready for mischief; a coward, yet boasting the minute he opened his mouth. Comedy, tragedy, and opera all opened their doors to his various aliases, of which the better known were Pickelhering (Pickle-Herring), Harlekin (Harlequin), and Hanswurst (Jack Pudding), especially the last-named. Pickle-Herring was as obviously of English origin as Harlequin was a descendant of the *arlecchino* of the commedia dell' arte, but Hanswurst, although related to both, was an old German figure.

English, French, and Italian folk comedy found a most fertile field in Vienna, famed since the Middle Ages for its farcical proclivities. The Austrian capital had, in the opening years of the eighteenth century, a permanent popular theater in which Hanswurst reigned supreme, the darling of the Viennese public. No literary influence could change his original character; he accepted only such things as agreed with his nature. As time went by almost everything changed around him: the stage was modernized by the use of ingenious machinery, redundant tragedies and elaborate operas replaced the simple plays, and the Alexandrine acquired citizenship in the domain of prose; but the smutty jokes stayed, to the great joy of the public. No matter what he was called—the famous Viennese actor, Joseph Kurtz, gave him the name Bernardon—he remained the old Hanswurst, and when toward the middle of the century the serious literary theater tried to assert itself by attempting to crowd out the Viennese farce, it found its way barred by the jester. Whenever a serious play was offered in which there was a lowly figure, Hanswurst appeared under his mask, improvising lines of his own. The long drawn-out struggle ended with his extermination. When the French troupe playing in the court theater, the Burgtheater, was replaced in 1772 by German actors, the repertory turned to Shakespeare, Lessing, Goethe, and Schiller; literature was victorious over farce and Hanswurst was buried without honors. This, at least, was the course of events in the annals of the aristocratic stage in Vienna, but if we follow the retreating folk drama into its real habitat, the suburban theater, we shall see that neither the farce nor Hanswurst was permanently dead.

The Leopoldstädter Theater, founded in 1781 by Carl Marinelli, became the chief seat of the old Viennese farce. There the public could satiate its appetite for jokes, enjoy the popular caricatures of Bohemians, Hungarians, and other non-Germanic elements of the empire, and admire the tricky theatrical machinery capable of re-creating all the wonders of the fairy tales. It is not difficult to recognize the old Hanswurst in a certain Austrian peasant boy named Casperle who seemed to be present in every play reviving the old gags of his popular ancestor. The most famous actor during the initial seasons of the Leopoldstädter Theater was a comedian named La Roche, a lineal descendant of Stranitzky, Weiskern, and Kurtz, the famous impersonators of the Hanswurst of old, now called Casperle. The new Hanswurst, with La Roche, was so popular that the theater was simply called *das Casperletheater*. Northern visitors found the Viennese German *Singschauspiel* atrocious. The *Berlinische Musikalische Zeitung* expressed wonderment that the public should applaud "this miserable fellow, who is not entirely without some comic ability, but whose utterances would offend any decent person. It appears, however, that the Viennese public finds all this very enjoyable." [14] The reproach reflects the usual disdain of the northerner for the unbridled love of life of the southern German. Vienna was with good reason considered the symbol of a happy, carefree, hospitable, and artistic city, the atmosphere of which was eminently suited for the lyric stage.

Joseph II, always alert to utilize everything for the promotion of German culture, realized that the Singspiel could become to the Germans what the opera buffa was to the Italians, and therefore he ordered the establishment of a national Singspiel theater in Vienna. The institution opened on January 16, 1778, with *Die Bergknappen,* by Ignaz Umlauff (1746-1796), a born Viennese, whose plays enjoyed extraordinary popularity.[15] It was in this theater, and at the emperor's command, that Mozart's *Entführung* was produced in 1782. The libretto, written by Gottlob Stephanie, director of the theater, with additions by the composer, was one of those Turkish pieces that became popular in the time of Eugene of Savoy. It was not an original work but a refurbished version of *Belmonte and Constance, or the Abduction from the Seraglio* by Christoph Friedrich Bretzner, whose libretto had been set to music by André. With the *Entführung* the Singspiel really became the German comic opera, light, sunny, pleasing, sentimental, fantastic, and filled with wondrous music.

It was after a long absence from the Singspiele of his youth, after considerable activity in the field of Italian opera, and after the masterful pages of *Idomeneo,* that Mozart returned to the German lyric stage, and it cannot be denied that there are in the *Entführung* stylistic discrepancies of which Mozart was never guilty in his later works, or which, if deliberately used, as in the *Magic Flute,* were blended with consummate skill. Mozart's initial uncertainty in this form of the lyric stage is convincingly demonstrated in the relative lack of characterization. Among the men in the play only one is molded with his customary distinction: Osmin, the paunchy keeper of the harem. Thus in the otherwise charming and comical ensembles, such as the trio at the end of the first act, the simultaneous development of characters is almost entirely missing. It is only Osmin's part that detaches itself from the ensemble; Belmonte and Pedrillo merely sing some fine music. The women are somewhat better designed, and Constance's elegiac aria in G minor actually rises into almost heroic spheres, faintly indicating the tragic arias in the same key that were to come in the *Magic Flute.* Concessions were made for Signora Cavalieri, the impersonator of Constance. A pupil of Salieri, this Viennese singer (Austrian despite her Italian name) was endowed with an extraordinary coloratura voice and it was for her "fluid larynx," as Mozart himself stated, that he wrote two coloratura arias in the purest Italian manner, which were distinctly at odds with the other songs.

Dramatically the greatest mistake was the role allotted to Selim Pasha, a figure who spoke throughout the play. His sober voice answering Constance's soaring coloraturas has always something disillusioning about it. On the other hand, the sharp eyes of the born dramatist are evident everywhere. Thus when the two men, Belmonte and his servant, question their ladies about their doings in the harem, the rather veiled allusions of Belmonte are entirely differently treated from the straightforward questions of Pedrillo. The women's reactions—the lady's tears and the maid's slaps—are also true to life. The scene where Osmin imbibes against the laws of the Prophet shows Mozart in his natural element, the painting of life.

The master of the opera is present in all his greatness in the quartet which ends the second act. While it has not the individualistic stamp of the Italian ensembles, this quartet carries a remarkable double action, with two couples —one aristocratic, the other plebeian—presenting their amours simultaneously. Neither the ideas nor the gestures of the two pairs have anything in common, yet in the music they unite and present their case at the same time, each in its own way. The last act contains a veritable collection of gems of songs, among them the popular triumph song of Osmin, which, although comical, depicts convincingly the state of mind of the man, at heart a jailer, who would like to see the prisoners hanged even though he happens to entertain amorous feelings toward one of the women.

With all its shortcomings, we have the right to consider the *Entführung* the crowning piece of the eighteenth-century Singspiel. Dramatically and poetically faulty, it was recast in music that breathes life and youth. In the history of German art the *Entführung* is a companion of Goethe's *Werther*.

The national Singspiel was launched on a career that well-nigh threatened the existence of Italian opera in Vienna. The Viennese attitude toward the Singspiel was much more serious and artistic, in spite of its robust humor, than elsewhere. Where other places called on the participation of actors and amateur singers, Vienna commandeered its best singers, a superb orchestra, and a group of experienced church choristers. We should not think, however, that all this started with the *Entführung,* for the Viennese comic opera and Singspiel attained a very high degree of excellence in the works of Gassmann. These works, even his Italian operas, although closely related to the Venetian opera buffa, nevertheless showed an independent local style, especially notable in the fine orchestration, that should not be underestimated and the influence of which is unmistakable in Mozart. It was this high artistic level of the Viennese opera buffa which contributed to the rejection of Mozart's first dramatic essay, *La Finta Semplice*. Still, the national institution was not long-lived and in five years it was ready to capitulate. A new troupe of opera buffa had in the meantime been recruited in Venice to stage a comeback of Italian opera. A contributing factor to the decline of the national Singspiel theater was the attitude of the emperor, who, from the political point of view, desired a German national opera; but his musical tastes were nevertheless closer to Italian opera, and he was prone to listen to Salieri and to the Italians, who convinced him that his experiment was doomed. Once more the Singspiel, this time located in the Kärntnertor Theater, registered a great success with the works of Dittersdorf, whose *Doctor and Apothecary* (1786) was one of the most beloved lyric plays in the whole history of the German stage. Great gifts of characterization, a robust, at times obscene, humor, especially marked in the ensembles and finales, and a spirited and piquant orchestration distinguished Dittersdorf's Singspiele. As his art grew it shed the Italian elements of both opera seria and buffa. In the great solo scenes of his stage works there is a notable tendency toward parody of the pathos of the opera seria, a tendency that seems to underlie all non-Italian national schools of lyric theater.

There were many other excellent and successful composers devoted to the Viennese comic opera—Mozart and Dittersdorf had raised the Singspiel to this status. Wenzel Müller (1767–1835), Joseph Weigl (1766–1846), Johann Schenk (1753–1836), whose *Village Barber* (1796) rivaled the success of Dittersdorf's *Doctor,* and Paul Wranitzky (1756–1808) are a few of those whose works made Vienna toward the end of the century a unique musical metropolis.

The native opera flourished, then, with unabated vigor, yet in a few years the Italians regained every foot of territory ceded. The new Italian opera troupe was led by Antonio Salieri (1750–1825), a discovery whom Gassmann brought back from Venice to Vienna, where he enjoyed a great reputation until the end of his life. An intriguer like his seventeenth-century compatriot Lully, this able musician was even accused of poisoning Mozart, a fact that can be as little substantiated as Lully's alleged murder of Cambert. There can be no question, however, of Salieri's malevolent interference with the success of his Austrian colleagues. His fine musicianship told him to concentrate his malice on Mozart, whose lamentable fate was due in no small degree to the Italian's machinations. Arriving in Vienna at the time of the short-lived supremacy of the German comic opera, he lost no time in composing a Singspiel, *The Chimneysweep* (1781), but on the whole the Viennese opera remained a minor adventure in the works of this universally admired musician, who was considered not only the leader of the resurrected Italian opera in Vienna, but the lineal successor of Gluck in the field of the serene music drama.

The establishment of the national Singspiel theater came too late to succeed, but, while it was difficult to invest the Singspiel with the exalted status of Italian opera, under more popular guise and without aristocratic patronage it enjoyed a tremendous vogue in the Viennese suburbs. It was in these suburban theaters that the fantastic and romantic predilections of the Viennese burlesque plays, noticeable in less accentuated form in the Singspiel and the comic opera, came to full fruition. The ingredients of the eighteenth-century Singspiel were many and varied—from the opéra comique to the fairy poetry of Wieland, from the commedia dell' arte to the opera seria. The remarkable and unexpected consequence of this mixture was, however, its turn toward the bona fide operatic. The farce with its modern theatrical machinery presided over by Hanswurst-Casperle was combined with the fairy tale, producing the *Zauberstück,* of which one particular form was the *Zauberoper,* or fairy opera. The mechanical apparatus of the fairy opera was employed whenever the opportunity arose; thus there were special versions of *Macbeth* and of *Don Juan.* Joseph Martin Ruprecht's *Das Wütende Heer* (1786) impresses one as a veritable preliminary study to Weber's *Freischütz,* while in Wranitzky's *Oberon* (1790) and Wenzel Müller's *Sonnenfest der Brahminen* (1790) the lowly Zauberstück developed into the most important and immediate predecessors of the *Magic Flute.* The success of all these works was tremendous and it was from them that the *Magic Flute* and *Fidelio* sprung, a fact which solves the riddle of Gluck's comparatively unsuccessful attempts at winning the Viennese to his operatic reforms. For these Viennese, composers and public alike, were all musicians, blessed with a vivid imagination, but an imagination centered about music and grown out of life; philosophical theories of drama and music never entered their minds. Mozart's German stage works do not give us anything essentially new as far as the technique and general aspects of these operas are concerned, but in the *Entführung* and in the *Zauberflöte* he carried the Viennese lyric theater to its final development.

Schikaneder's libretto for the *Magic Flute* was based on a tale by Wieland and on the Viennese fairy operas, among which *Oberon* by Ludwig Giesecke, a member of Schikaneder's troupe, was a direct source. In reality a mere adapter of still another work based on Wieland's *Oberon,* Giesecke was later claimed, without justification, to be coauthor with Schikaneder in the preparation of the *Magic Flute.* Other sources were Perinet's *Caspar der Fagottist oder die Zauberzither,* and Hensler's *Sonnenfest der Brahminen,* both set to music by Wenzel Müller. The last two works were not unlike the many Magic Islands, Magic Lamps, and Magic Mountains which enjoyed such popularity in Schikaneder's theater. At the bottom of all the secondary sources was a famous old novel, *Séthos,* by the Abbé Jean Terrasson (Paris, 1731), consulted apparently by Wieland himself. Both libretto and music were in an advanced state when Schikaneder and Mozart discovered to their chagrin that the production of *Caspar the Bassoonist or the Magic Zither* necessitated a refurbishing of their own work. The changes were extensive, involving a complete about-face of some of the characters. There was, however, still another important element that intruded upon the apparently naïve and childlike fairy opera, the ideals of Freemasonry.

We have previously mentioned the rise of Freemasonry in the Protestant countries and noticed that the leaders of cultural life as well as some of the political leaders joined the movement. The nature of Freemasonry was bound to antagonize Catholicism and, indeed, toward the middle of the eighteenth century measures were taken against it. The repercussions of the Enlightenment were, however, still powerful, and the lofty ideals of the Masons elicited great admiration not only in the Catholic middle classes but even among the high nobility and members of the imperial house. Maria Theresa did not allow the order to function officially, but refused to persecute its members, who gathered secretly. Under Joseph II Freemasonry entered a period of virtual flourishing, aristocrats, artists, and professional men embracing its tenets. Among its adherents were Haydn and Mozart, both pious Catholics but true children of the reign of the high-minded Habsburg.

For a long time the *Magic Flute* was held up as the model of an incomprehensible libretto, yet its symbolic ramifications hide the very real sentiments and humor of two dreamers, the actor Schikaneder and the musician Mozart. The verses are often trivial, but the dramatic intentions are always well thought out, and every one of the figures of the drama is the representative of some definite idea; their characters are planned throughout. A curious mixture of good and evil arrests one's attention: the demonic Queen of the Night has three ladies in waiting filled with the desire to do charitable acts, while the serene high priest entrusts Pamina to a sinister slave of the temple. Profoundly symbolical is the departure of the prince and the birdcatcher Papageno, the semidisguised Hanswurst-Casperle. The noblest and lowest of creatures can seek the highest ideals together. Occasionally, as during the ordeal which the probationary lovers must undergo, the old Hanswurst-Casperle becomes irrepressible, claiming precedence over the real heroes of the drama, but this was an essential feature of the Viennese comedy from time immemorial.

The action embraces three concepts: the Masonic thoughts of the priests of humanity, trying to recruit new followers among men of noble ideas; the realm of the Queen of the Night, opposed to the priesthood of Freemasonry, a province of hatred, sorcery, superstition, and seduction; and, finally, the world of those incapable of being elevated to humanism, who must seek and find happiness and goodness in their own simple ways. The swift dramatic style of *Don Giovanni* could not be applied to this atmosphere, so Mozart built a musical organism of an entirely different and most peculiar character. He realized the musical essence of all three groups and gave them expression in purely musical terms; music seems to be the natural language of all these men.

This natural power of the tones, surging from everything and from every-where, calls for a certain simplicity faithfully reflected in the music; but this simplicity is not that of children, it is monumental like the lines of Egyptian architecture. Such simplicity is also present in the purely human parts of the opera, the waking of first love in two young souls. This was Mozart's most personal, most cherished subject, and Tamino's first love aria is almost like an echo of Cherubino's arias. Characterization is carried through to the smallest detail. Simple persons and simple events are treated with simple harmonies and orchestration and with appropriately popular melodies, but as their mental equipment becomes more complicated the harmonies and melodies as well as orchestration become more elaborate and varied. The Queen of the Night appears in the music as a mysterious twin personality; earnest and compelling as night itself, then again full of horror and fearful sorcery. In the scene where she appears to Pamina, her eccentric, bewildering passion is developed into the superhuman. The two birdsmen are, in the vivacity of their little souls and in their timidity, drawn with masterful tenderness. Like the birds, they are timid, frightened by every rustle but overjoyed by every ray of the sun. When Monostatos the Moor lecherously watches the sleeping Pamina, Mozart's music becomes erotic, but when Sarastro proclaims that in these sacred halls revenge is not known, he lavishes on his melodies all the human kindness that a sincere artist can muster. The Italian opera seria style and the hair-raising coloratura passages emphasize the strange and fantastic nature of the Queen of the Night in an otherwise simple German surrounding, Papageno and Papagena babble in the buffa tone, the three ladies sing their songs full of sentiment in the manner of the Singspiel, Tamino and Pamina represent the romantic-expressive, Mozart's most typical style, while Sarastro and the priests call for a harmonic-contra-puntal idiom almost unknown in the opera of the fin de siècle.

Beginning with the nineties Mozart's operas held every musician spell-bound, Germans and Italians alike. Performances he had desired so much in his lifetime now became numerous all over Germany, and the *Magic Flute* especially created a profound impression as people began to realize what it meant for the German lyric drama. One year after its first performance Schikaneder celebrated the hundredth repetition of the *Magic Flute* in the Theater an der Wien. Noticing the Germans' powerful reaction to this sub-lime Singspiel, the Italian troupes in Germany had it translated and, as *Il Flauto Magico,* performed it wherever they went. Around the turn of the century it was customary to write a sequel to especially successful operas and Singspiele, and the *Magic Flute* did not escape this honor, repeatedly bestowed upon it. Even Goethe tried his hand at these imitations, but the most celebrated work was Peter von Winter's *Pyramids of Babylon,* written to a libretto furnished by Schikaneder himself. Schikaneder continued his fairy operas with great success, collaborating with composers of note, among whom were Süssmayr and Weigl. The enterprising author-actor tried to interest Beethoven himself in one of the plays, and the existence of sketches indicates that the latter was weighing the idea seriously.

Mozart's Operatic Conceptions

SPEAKING to Eckerman about the public reaction to his own stage works, Goethe remarked that while the large majority of theatrical audiences will always be satisfied with what they see, the initiated will not miss the more profound meanings, "as is the case with the *Magic Flute*." But the great connoisseur of drama overestimated the initiated: while praising the "beautiful and charming music" in Mozart's dramatic works, the generation that grew up under the aegis of the nineteenth-century music drama showed little understanding for their "more profound meanings." Kretzschmar, the eminent German musicologist and historian of opera, declared that "Mozart's greatness would not suffer if *Così Fan Tutte* had remained unwritten . . . one could take it for a work from the times of the first operatic essays." [16] Krehbiel, noted American critic and musical writer, also particularly interested in opera, found that "Papageno had to have music . . . and Mozart doubtless wrote it with as little serious thought as he did the Piece for an Organ in a Clock in F minor." [17] This appalling misconception is enhanced by the singularly inappropriate comparison drawn between Papageno's simple and warmly human ditties and the colossal organ fantasia which must have been known to Krehbiel by the title only, otherwise he could not have taken this severe contrapuntal essay for a music box piece.

Mozart has himself stated his conception of the interrelationship of the elements of opera: "I should say that in an opera the poetry must be altogether the obedient daughter of the music." [18] This aesthetic creed prompted Wagner and the apologists of the Wagnerian music drama to consider eighteenth-century opera with a benevolent smile, admitting that the music is "charming" but could have been written for any other occasion or combination. Mozart's cardinal operatic principle, and that of Italian opera in general, did not, however, weaken the drama; on the contrary, the exigencies of the stage were always uppermost in his mind—every scene, the attitude of every figure, is always carefully weighed. In doing this Mozart displays a sovereign knowledge of the theatrical; one would think that an expert régisseur is behind the scenes. The following passage, taken from a letter addressed to his father, permits us a glimpse of the musico-dramatist, working on his *Entführung:*

. . . Osmin's rage is rendered comical by the accompaniment of the Turkish music. In working out the aria I have given full scope now and then to Fischer's beautiful deep notes. The passage "Upon the Prophet's beard" is indeed in the same tempo, but with quick notes; but as Osmin's rage gradually increases, there comes (just when the aria seems to be at an end) the allegro assai, which is in a totally different measure and in a different key; this is bound to be very effective. For just as a man in such a towering rage oversteps all the bounds of order, moderation and propriety, and completely forgets himself, so must the music too forget itself. But as passions, whether violent or not, must never be expressed in such a way as to excite disgust, so music, even in the most terrible situations, must never offend the ear, but must please the hearer, or in other words must never cease to be *music*.[19]

Another of Wagner's judgments concerning Mozart and eighteenth-century opera, expressed in his *Opera and Drama*, is still widely shared and prevents an unbiased study of these works. "Nothing seems more characteristic to me concerning Mozart's career as an opera composer than the careless indiscrimination with which he approached his task; it did not occur to him to ponder over the aesthetic scruples underlying the opera; on the contrary, he proceeded with the composition of any text submitted to him with the greatest lack of self-consciousness." If the nature of Mozart's works is not sufficiently eloquent to contradict these assertions, factual data can be opposed to them in abundance, for Mozart studied his texts carefully, and once he accepted a libretto there was no end to conferences with the librettist, who was compelled to change scenes, sentences, and even single words, if the musician did not find them to his liking. "The first act [of the *Entführung*] was finished more than three weeks ago . . . but I cannot compose any more, because the whole story is being altered—and, to tell the truth, at my own request." [20] Had he been so careless in accepting "any" libretto he would not have read, before deciding on *Figaro*, "a hundred books," none of which found favor with him.

Mozart is the greatest musico-dramatic genius of all times. This unique position he owes to a temperament which approached everything, every situation, and every human being with absolute objectivity. He did not want to become the German nation's teacher and eulogist, as did Wagner; he did not, like Beethoven, want to reach the highest ideal tone; nor did he, like Handel, want to be God's voice. Every situation and every individual appeared to him as music, his whole conception was purely aesthetic, and music was his language. He preserved the old and great virtues of Italian music, and in his universal genius these united with German transcendentalism, embodying the plans, desires, and hopes of the outgoing century.

Chapter 14

THE PERIPHERIES OF EIGHTEENTH-CENTURY MUSIC AND ITS PRACTICE

⋙ ⋘

Spain

AS WE have related, the sad life and death of the unfortunate King Charles II of Spain was followed by turmoil in the form of a devastating war of succession. The Duke of Anjou, who ascended the throne as Philip V (1700–1746), never forgot that he was a grandson of Louis XIV, nor did his influential Italian queen, Elizabeth Farnese, suppress the memories of her homeland. The king's neglect of national culture, together with the repeated partition of the riches of the once mighty imperium, definitely ended the significance of Spain, both political and cultural. Under Philip began a systematic reduction of national art, a process faithfully continued by the Spanish Bourbons.

The first years of the eighteenth century passed in a bitter struggle between native music and Italian art, pouring into the country across all frontiers. Spanish music had fallen too far below its erstwhile excellence to offer successful resistance to Italian penetration, especially since the royal court sided with the foreigners. The struggle, particularly intense between the two lyric theaters, Spanish and Italian, occupied the first two decades of the century and national art finally was dealt the deathblow with the appearance of Farinelli, the world-renowned castrato singer, whose art captured the melancholy King Philip, rousing him from his lethargy. Philip's admiration and munificent disposition toward Farinelli was shared by his successor, Ferdinand VI (reigned 1746–1759), and the singer's power and influence grew to dominate a full quarter of a century of Spanish music. During this time national art retired into a small circle, and to the outsider the history of music in Spain seems to consist of the history of Italian music in Spain. As the century advanced and new rulers assumed the kingship, the decline of national music became more general. The court of Charles III (reigned 1759–1788) was one of the great centers of European artistic life, where a host of foreign artists found a home. Luigi Boccherini arrived there in 1768, becoming a figure as dominant as had been Farinelli. He retained this position under the next sovereign, Charles IV (reigned 1788–1808), and remained in Spanish services until his death in 1805.

The decline of Spanish music and the lack of appreciation of its past grandeur become more understandable if we realize that, in another field, Lope de Vega and Calderón were considered barbarous playwrights whose works had to be adjusted by literary men trained in the pseudo-classic drama and its Aristotelian precepts. It is not surprising, then, that a similar procedure was followed with regard to the lyric stage. When the Italian opera troupes arrived in Madrid (1703) and in Barcelona (1709) they found the Spanish lyric theater still holding its own against the pro-Italian policy of the court. The "barbarous" vernacular opera was forced to retreat, but before surrendering it attempted to stave off the invader by emulating its style. *Angelica y Medoro* (1722), the first opera written in the Italian style, was the work of the poet Don José de Cañizares and the Italian composer Francesco Corradini. Cañizares was one of the last representatives of the great Spanish theater of the past century, but he was already thoroughly under the influence of the pseudo-classic drama and Italian operatic poetry. The fact that one can find a number of *operas españolas* should not deceive us, for only their language was Spanish; the libretti were imitations of the works of Zeno and Metastasio and the composers were for the most part Italians. The Italians were, however, not entirely in command, for such works as Joaquin Martinez de la Roca's *Cassandra* and Juan Sisi y Mestre's *El Oráculo Infalible,* while not measuring up to the standards of Italian opera, enjoyed a certain vogue.

The Italian theater made its entry with the finest of operas. Against such splendor the native genius was helpless, but it could fall back on the impregnable defenses of the music of the people. Thus, history again repeated itself: the Spanish musician's opposition to Italian opera and to the castrato singer resulted in a protest akin to that expressed in the ballad opera, the opéra comique, and the Singspiel.

The reaction resulted in two movements, one prepared consciously by a man of letters perceiving the futility of a naturalization of Italian opera as clearly as had Addison and Rousseau, the other the result of an upward swing of popular music, developed into the so-called *tonadilla.* Don Ramón de la Cruz (1731–1794), the most popular Spanish author of the eighteenth century, learned poet, and witty playwright, endeavored to adapt the principles of opera to the Spanish lyric stage. While perfectly familiar with the operatic dramaturgy of Zeno and Metastasio, de la Cruz realized that the starting point should be the old and typically Spanish *zarzuela.*[1] The revived zarzuela was much nearer to the opera than to its seventeenth-century form, but it still permitted to a certain extent the survival of the native lyric theater. De la Cruz's collaborator was Don Antonio Rodriguez de Hita (d. 1787), as familiar with Neapolitan operatic music as was his librettist with its literary aspects, but equally independent of his sources and animated with the desire for a national art. Their works, *Briseida* (1768), a sort of "zarzuela seria," and especially *Las Labradores de Murcia* (*The Laborers of Murcia,* 1769), full of lively Spanish national color, represent the best in this genre. It is a remarkable and not sufficiently appreciated fact that the Spanish lyric theater produced a national opera of full value at the same time that the opéra comique and the Singspiel were making history in their respective countries. It is most regrettable that the artistic climate of the country was unfavorable for the growth of the revived national lyric stage, which became swamped by mediocrity.

The other outstanding figure in the attempted restoration of the national lyric theater was Don Luis Missón (d. 1766), famous virtuoso on several instruments and creator of the tonadilla. Originally a little scenic chanson in the form of a duet, the tonadilla developed into a sort of intermezzo not unlike the Italian works of that type inserted in the Neapolitan opera. Its character was, however, distinctly Spanish. The tonadilla consisted of a little prelude, recitatives, airs, and a final *seguidilla* or *tirana*. The wealth of Spanish popular music, the tunes and rhythms of which became so famous in the nineteenth century and were frequently borrowed by composers of other nations, appears in the tonadillas, forcefully contributing to the preservation of the spirit of national art.[2]

The controversies which plagued Spanish music at the opening of the eighteenth century were not restricted to opera; they flared up with violence among church musicians. Although the foreign influence was not less oppressive, the issue in this case was raised by Spaniards, and took the form of a rift between progressive artists and academicians. In church music the century in its opening decades offered a musician of genius, Don Francisco Valls (1665–1747), choirmaster of the cathedral at Barcelona. His was an alert and bold spirit, and it was his contrapuntal Masses which precipitated the unparalleled dispute embroiling a multitude of musicians. Even the few excerpts of his art available in print[3] disclose music of moving beauty. A flood of pamphlets appeared against and in defense of Valls, but he stood his ground.

Neither he nor his lesser colleagues were able to prevent, however, the general decline of church music—a decline the more incomprehensible because the cathedral choirs and other musical bodies, excellent since the Middle Ages, had at their disposal financial resources that would have seemed fabulous in any other country. The Italian operatic style was an entirely alien idiom to these musicians, and by trying to acclimatize it in their churches they ruined the last vestiges of their great past. This church music impresses one as mere improvisation, devoid of the traditions of musical construction. Among the simpler native forms, the ever-popular *villancicos* disappeared and were succeeded by the *letrillas* and *gozos,* canticles of a rather questionable artistic quality. These compositions, usually in honor of the Eucharist and the Blessed Virgin, were the answer to the increasing demand for nonliturgic songs in the vernacular. The theatrical atmosphere kindled a great love for the oratorio, which took the place of the old auto sacramentale. Valls himself composed oratorios, as did Luis Serra (d. 1759), Antonio Sala (d. 1794), and Juan Francisco Tribarren, choirmaster of Málaga Cathedral. These musicians were able to withstand the foreign influences, but others, such as Don Antonio Ripa (c. 1720–1795) and Don Pascual Fuentes (d. 1768), succumbed to the prevailing spirit. Prominent in the latter group was José Pons (1768–1818), whose theatrical and bombastic style sealed the fate of the magnificent choir of Valencia Cathedral. Some of these musicians were not lacking in talent and were admired even in Italy, but they had lost all connections with their own past and, not being able to assimilate Italianism intimately enough, became eclectics without a profession of musical faith.

The output in instrumental music and the activity of players were by no means negligible in the eighteenth century, and the famous Escolania of the Abbey of Montserrat still harbored and educated a number of capable musicians, but the quality of this music was mediocre. One great artist appears alone in the midst of the diligent artisans, the Catalan Fray Antonio Soler (1729–1783), whose brilliant harpsichord sonatas make it doubly regrettable that the bulk of his works is still in manuscript.[4] Among the other instrumental composers the more notable were Don Fernando Ferrandiere, guitarist and violinist, whose *Art of Playing the Spanish Guitar* (1799) attests the continued popularity of that instrument; Antonio Ximenes, whose violin sonatas were published in Paris about 1780; and Don Carlos Francisco de Almeyda, whose quartets were successful enough to be printed by Pleyel in Paris in 1798.

Glancing over this rather modest harvest, one is inclined to think that the creative genius of Spain failed to rise to the level of the international musical art flourishing all over Europe; yet the decadence was due not to a lack of interest or even talent, but to the unfortunate socio-cultural circumstances. Spain was still a music-loving country. Although the theater declined, the taste for dramatic performances of all sorts, serious and light, sacred and secular, opera, drama, cantata, serenade, and oratorio, remained vivid. The archives of the city of Madrid alone guard the manuscripts of some two thousand tonadillas which represent the repertory of the two municipal theaters. The practice of music was not less conspicuous in social gatherings, where chansons with the accompaniment of a guitar or a harpsichord were performed. The great vogue of Boccherini's and Haydn's chamber music is indicative of the general dissemination and high level of instrumental ensemble playing.

Among the Spanish musicians who migrated abroad more than one became world-famous. We have encountered several of them as the feted masters of Italian opera: Domingo Miguel Bernabé Terradellas, originally a pupil of Valls, Davide Perez, and Vicente Martin y Soler, known as Martini Lo Spagnuolo. The musical scholars shared the composers' fate; those who stayed at home remained obscure. But Antonio Eximeno y Pujades (1729-1808), called the "Newton of music" by his enthusiastic followers, and Esteban Arteaga, the learned historian of Italian opera, were known in all civilized countries. These two brilliant writers were Jesuits, compelled to leave Spain with the expulsion of the order. They went to Italy and published their chief works in Italian and Latin, from which they were translated by others into Spanish.

Thus the Italian musical conquest of Spain, abetted by the ruling classes, became as real and as devastating as a military occupation and, aided by the stubborn conservatism of certain musicians of the old school, caused a universal decline of native music—a disintegration, which, with the political, cultural, and military humiliation suffered in the ensuing Napoleonic wars, left Spanish music all but extinct.

England

THE final exchange of world supremacy from French to British hands was the decisive event of the eighteenth century. The rise of British world power was, moreover, not merely a political event of grave consequences: it changed the course of cultural evolution. A seafaring and merchant nation, Britain began to lay the foundations of her modern industrial position, and became the world's workshop. Karl Marx called the process of technical and economic transformation which began in the eighteenth century, and which promoted the third estate in Western civilization to a new social class, the "industrial revolution." The middle classes demanded freedom of industry so that not only the master craftsman but the entrepreneur could engage in industrial ventures without being bound by the exclusive prerogatives of the guilds. The new industrial spirit became filled with the ideas of the Enlightenment. Serving the interests of both the state and the people, it established a remarkable and unique union between the ideal and practical aspects of life. Out of this union was born English liberalism, much admired by the rest of Europe. Besides the founding of the British Empire and the industrial revolution, the English Enlightenment was the third great historical fact of universal importance communicated by England to the Western world of the eighteenth century.

The Enlightenment pursued, it is true, the same ideals on the Continent —political, religious, economic freedom, the autonomy of the individual— but while French and German thinkers entertained theories, the English, equally bent on theoretical speculation, were always empiricists at heart, disinclined to abstractions. This attitude was the main source of English liberalism and remained a fundamental characteristic of British thought. The French never ceased to be theorists, not even during the Revolution, while the British mind, imbued with its unique respect for authority and tradition, yet animated with a positive and forward-looking political ideal, created a *modus vivendi* for both the state and the individual which filled the political philosophers of the world with envy and admiration.

Victorious wars, colonial aggrandizement, and momentous social and economic changes notwithstanding, England's *grand siècle* was a much quieter century than France's eighteenth. The reigns of Queen Anne and the three Georges were far removed from the revolutionary and regicidal atmosphere of France, for English temperament reflected faithfully the spirit of the empire-building nation. With the quiet measure of empiricism English philosophy ranged far and wide in the cultural life of the country, and even literature was able to retain a friendly and calm exterior in the face of the unruly tenets emanating from across the Channel to the British Isles. The men of letters could be sensitive and sentimental where the French were cool and calculating; they could be satirical, yet they were far from the radical ideas of the French, intent on destroying the existing social order. England's eighteenth century was the century of the enriched bourgeoisie, of merchants and shipping men, of manufacturers and diplomats, of squires and entrepreneurs. The notables of this society—its beautiful women, delicate children, and fat-cheeked men—were painted on great decorative canvases by the famed portrait painters of the period, Reynolds, Gainsborough, Raeburn, and Lawrence; the men sitting there with a serious countenance, the women with a sensitive expression; beautiful draperies, landscapes, and rosy clouds surround the figures, the whole proclaiming the era of plenty. There was individuality of style and great technical merit in these canvases, the works of truly great painters; but, while decorative and charming, these portraits are frequently artificial in pose and expression, as if demonstrating that art was not gushing from the very sources of inspiration.

The bourgeoisie became the nation's kernel, wherein the future was germinating. Between the aristocracy, morally corrupt and enriched by colonial trade, and the populace, steeped in misery, they led a diligent, virtuous, and religious life. They constituted the reading and musical public, and writers and musicians created for them and about them. The most appropriate medium of such a society is the novel—by nature democratic; its language is the prose of everyday life, and its subjects are likewise the subjects of everyday life. It operates through the media of observation and experience, with a resultant soberness and trueness to life. Up to our day the bourgeois public at large likes books which do not unduly excite passions and the imagination, and do not remove the reader far from his own world of experience. It likes to contemplate its own virtues and condemn the moral laxity of the aristocracy. Accordingly, the writers preached morality and flayed and caricatured immorality, creating the novel, moral and satiric, but thoroughly unromantic.

We have discussed the beginnings of the novel with Richardson. Its influence was as tremendous as that of English political thought; Diderot, Lessing, Voltaire, and Rousseau owed a great debt to the eighteenth-century English novel, although its characters were actuated by their authors' moral precepts rather than by their own personalities. Laurence Sterne (1713–1768) and Tobias Smollett (1721–1771) continued the novel, and, although finer analysts than Richardson, their works are eternal observations, filled with clever ideas and remarks. The authors carry on a witty conversation, they entertain and fascinate, but the novel itself remains static and does not develop. In Sterne's *Tristram Shandy* the hero is born in the third volume, and three more elapse before he is dressed up in his little garments. All this literature would remain entirely obscure to the modern reader were it not for Henry Fielding (1707–1754), who did not place his figures under the glass case of comfortable middle-class existence but drove them outside, into the alcoholic vapor of the tavern and the mud of the highway, where they must come to terms with life. His wonderful sense for realities made him the founder of the realistic novel and the greatest novelist before Dickens.

One more book from this period remains alive, a novel by Oliver Goldsmith (1728–1774). There is a great deal of inconsistency in *The Vicar of Wakefield,* but the author warns the reader in his preface that this is immaterial, provided the work is properly entertaining. The novel is planned in a manner that will bring the moral lessons into proper relief in every chapter. The characters themselves are monuments of virtue and the prototypes of middle-class conventions. This work became the model of the English novel precisely because it was engendered by English middle-class life and ideals.

It is of great interest and significance that the dominating literary figure of the period was a literary critic and scholar, Samuel Johnson (1709–1784). His belletristic efforts are negligible and his judgments old-fashioned, like those of most literary historians. Yet this dictator of English letters is fully entitled to the admiration that has been bestowed on him by following generations. His *Dictionary* (1755) is architectural; the massive assuredness of its plan, the virile correctness and faithfulness of its execution, and its intellectual breadth of conception can hardly be matched. The same qualities characterize the *Lives of the Poets* (1781), in spite of the prejudices that color the individual evaluations.

As we continue our search for the creative expression of English culture in the eighteenth century we are constantly impressed by the order and conservatism that prevail everywhere. We have mentioned the role played by English architecture in the development of the classic style, but in the second half of the century the growth of the population and the industrial revolution called for increased activity in the building of dwelling houses, both for the aristocracy and for the upper middle class. Social needs produced, then, a typically English style of architecture, commercial, civil, and governmental. While privacy and convenience were the chief motives, the desire for elegance was expressed even in the somewhat stereotyped modest dwellings.

It was in the interior decoration of these dwellings that eighteenth-century English art produced its most notable original creations. Here again we must not expect interior architecture of large proportions, a tuning together of surfaces or their large-scale decoration; for, with the exception of some great aristocratic residences and other buildings constructed in a rather formal style, the English house had a finely arranged harmony which evoked that friendly, subdued, homelike atmosphere that characterizes English dwellings. The peculiar language of English interior decoration speaks to us through its furniture, which embodied all the Flemish, Gothic, Chinese, rococo, and antique influences that made themselves felt in architecture, but which the English master cabinetmaker's modern and practical sense fused into an eminently valid style. A certain technical expediency was here at work, coupled with a noble sense for decoration, the property of a civilization long interested in the dignity and decorum of its dwelling places.

A civilization so constituted must needs be lacking in the atmosphere of lyricism; a philosophy of life so deliberate and practical spurns the irrationalism which permits the flourishing of music. The river of the art of music, once flowing in abundance, then ebbing to a small stream at the time of Handel's arrival in England, now barely covered the river bed. Another major reason for the decline of music was the lack of architectural imagination, without which literature and music are prone to fall into loosely connected sections or stereotyped frames. There is no plan and no system of construction in *Tristram Shandy;* Sterne allowed descriptive literature to turn into a diary of sentiments almost impressionistic. Fielding's heroes are always on the move, and the narrative flow is dependent on their stops at various and numerous places. His style is epic in character, with a penchant for burlesque. Johnson's *Rasselas* is lacking in plot and even in incident, the place of both being taken by moralistic reflections. Smollett's constructions are also conspicuous for their weaknesses. The eloquence of the written word might still save literature to a considerable extent, but music had nothing comparable to fall back on. Dent recognized this "national indifference to constructive principles" in his admirable work on English opera. "The French, we may say, aimed at erecting a palace: the English at an agglomeration of irregular buildings which could never attain formal beauty, but only picturesqueness." [5] But even picturesqueness disappeared from English music, save for popular music—once despised, but now recognized as the only vital and truly native aspect of English eighteenth-century music.

The composers tried to preserve the noble traditions of English church music but, with the exception of a few isolated works, this fell victim to unimaginative archaism or to bombastic grandeur, transplanted into the church from the oratorio. Among the more notable composers we should mention the following. John Christopher Smith (1712–1795), Handel's amanuensis, wrote operas, oratorios, and instrumental music. His "Shakespearean operas," *The Fairies* (from *Midsummer Night's Dream*) and *The Tempest,* though now forgotten, were once very popular for their songs. James Nares (1715–1783), Master of the Children of the Chapel Royal, enjoyed a reputation as a composer of harpsichord music, church music, and glees. Charles John Stanley (1713–1786), of whose musicianship Handel had a very high opinion, wrote cantatas, oratorios, and some instrumental music. Blind from childhood, he was endowed with a fabulous musical memory and became an excellent organist, later succeeding Boyce as Master of the King's Band of Music. Benjamin Cooke (1734–1793), pupil and successor of Pepusch as conductor at the Academy of Ancient Music, and organist of Westminster Abbey, was the author of anthems, services, and hymns, as well as of some instrumental music, but he is best known for his many beautiful glees, canons, and catches. The keyboard improvisations of Joseph Kelway (d. c. 1782), a remarkable harpsichordist and organist, earned him the unstinted admiration of leading musicians, including Handel, himself an acknowledged master of extemporaneous playing. One of the best composers of anthems was Jonathan Battishill (1738–1814), who also wrote fine songs and glees. William Shield (1748–1829) is remembered chiefly for his excellent songs, although he was the author of many operas.

At the time when the novels and plays of Sterne, Fielding, Goldsmith, and Sheridan, together with Johnson's *Dictionary,* had become the literary fare of the general public, an unpretentious anthology made its appearance. Thomas Percy (1729–1811) edited the *Reliques of Ancient English Poetry* (1765), based on an old manuscript collection of English and Scottish ballads and folk songs. These works rekindled interest in earlier English poetry (Johnson ignored the poets of the Renaissance, beginning his history with

Cowley's period), at the same time heralding the coming of romanticism. Percy's intentions were not philological or antiquarian—he corrected and completed the fragmentary parts—but his real aim was the popularizing of the English poetry of the past. The modest bishop prefaced his collection with a foreword which strikes one as a virtual apology for collecting these simple poetic trifles. The conviction that these popular poets might some day be considered more significant than the learned littérateurs of the eighteenth century was only timidly indicated. Percy's anthology was preceded by James Macpherson's *Fragments of Ancient Poetry,* well known for the controversy it created regarding its authenticity.

And now the ballads of the bards dispersed the clouds; the sun shone again on a lyricism reborn from naïve popular fantasy. Warm humanity and a loving contemplation of nature emanate from the poetry of Thomas Gray (1716–1771), Robert Burns (1759–1796), and William Cowper (1731–1800). Anglo-Saxon and Celtic genius unite in an incomparable art, not self-conscious and restricted to a narrow circle, but drawing the smallest events and simplest sentiments of life into the orbit of universal human interest. Animals and flowers are treated with equal love, while the depths of the popular soul are bared with benevolent humor, awakening our sympathy for its earth-bound figures.

Music could not follow poetry to the Parnassus that was reopened; it had drifted too far from its traditions. Editions of the great music of the past were not wanting, however. Samuel Arnold (1740–1802), organist of the Chapel Royal, issued an edition of *Cathedral Music* in 1790 which was a continuation of Boyce's similar anthology. (He also edited a forty-volume edition of Handel's works in full score.) John Stafford Smith printed a collection entitled *Ancient Songs* (1779), culled mainly from the celebrated Fayrfax Manuscript of the early part of the sixteenth century. Joseph Ritson (1752–1803), the antiquary renowned for his erudition and unmatched critical ferocity, actually discovered Wynkyn de Worde's song-book, along with other early musical manuscripts. The numerous singing societies helped to keep alive the traditional British fondness for singing, and their repertory contained many a masterpiece of the heroic age of English music. There was even a much-admired dissertation on the indivisibility of poetry and music. John Brown (1715–1766), clergyman, poet, and musician, was the author of the work, which, translated into French, Italian, and German, made the rounds of European musical circles. *A Dissertation on the Union and Power, the Progressions, Separations, and Corruptions of Poetry and Music* (1763) took up arms in favor of an expressive lyricism in music. The musical response was, however, incommensurate with the great revival in lyric poetry. The great strides made in instrumental music diminished the receptivity for lyricism, while at the same time the preference for large-scale choral compositions that inevitably followed Handel's activity created an inclination to turn the smallest song into epico-dramatic proportions. Transcriptions, and additions grafted onto vocal works entirely unsuited for such treatment, ruined many a masterpiece; thus Benjamin Cooke added choruses and accompaniments to Pergolesi's delicate *Stabat Mater*.

Viewed from the lofty height of lyric poetry, the musical harvest of the period seems scant indeed, yet the lyrical revival made itself felt in music, notably in the sudden flourishing of the *glees*. The great vogue of these unaccompanied part songs was an evident corollary to the popular lyricism spreading over the country. Modern writers have made various unsuccessful attempts to classify certain vocal compositions of the preceding generation, of Arne and Boyce, as glees; but these were ensemble pieces from operas. Nor can the glees be traced back to the madrigal, whose finely wrought contrapuntal parts obeyed entirely different artistic impulses than the homophonic-chordal construction of the glees, abounding in sharply defined cadences. They undoubtedly hark back to indigenous music that preceded the Elizabethan madrigal, and it was in this rather simple form of music— seldom very artistic but of considerably higher quality than the corresponding *Liedertafel* literature in Germany—that the great musical heritage of England found a modest existence. While its ancestry cannot be documented at the present state of musicological research, this ancient origin can easily be followed in the *catches*, faithful companions of the glees and equally popular in the eighteenth century, but in more or less continuous vogue since the Middle Ages. We have encountered the catch, originally a round (*rondellus*), or rota, in the famous "Summer Canon" composed about 1240; its present name comes from the Florentine *caccia*, the fourteenth-century canonic song. In the early seventeenth century the catch was very popular, as can be seen from such publications as *Pammelia* (1609) and *Deuteromelia* (1609), both collected and edited by Thomas Ravenscroft, and *Melismata* (1611), by Thomas and William Ravenscroft. The title of the first collection expresses the robust and popular nature of this music. *Pammelia: Musicke's Miscellanie, or Mixed Varietie of Pleasant Roundelayes and Delightful Catches of 3, 4, 5, 6, 7, 8, 9, 10 Parts in One. None so ordinarie as musicall, none so musicall as not to all very pleasing and acceptable.* The next important collection was John Hilton's *Catch that Catch Can* (1652), with others following until the middle of the nineteenth century. Besides a great number of simple rounds, there were many catches that display a remarkable ingenuity of construction, calling for contrapuntal artifices and clever manipulation of the text, which in turn required accomplished musicianship from the singers. It was in these catches and glees, together with the songs, of which John Stafford Smith, Shield, Battishill, and Cooke composed a number of arresting examples, that musical lyricism enjoyed a limited flourishing.

Samuel Webbe (1740–1816) was England's greatest lyric composer of this era, a musician whose three hundred odd catches, glees, and canons represent the finest of the species.

The most notable and successful lyricism of the period not connected with the glees is to be found in Charles Dibdin's sea songs, which so powerfully influenced the national spirit. The merchant vessels of the seafaring Briton and the frigates of the navy were glorified in these songs, popular beyond measure. Their effect on the spirit of the navy was so stimulating that their creator received acknowledgment from the government in the form of a pension. Dibdin (1745–1814), composer, poet, playwright, novelist, and actor-singer, was perhaps the most original figure among the many musicians creating assiduously but without the compelling urge of inspiration. This adventurous and restless son of a parish clerk had in him something of the originality and effrontery of the earlier composers of popular music. None of the operas written by his colleagues exhibited so much life and truly English spirit as his operettas and plays, among which *The Waterman* (1774) and *The Quaker* (1775) are best known and would be thoroughly enjoyable even today. Like the generation of Gay and Pepusch, Dibdin showed a strong penchant for parody, and in his plays and puppet shows he ridiculed prominent contemporary figures. It was this spirit that prompted his *Oddities,* a sort of musical variety show, and other song scenes or monodramatic entertainments which made him famous all over the country. The songs, of which he wrote more than a thousand, were the backbone of all his compositions, operettas and varieties alike, and in them he demonstrated a genuine lyric gift, remembered in "Tom Bowling," to mention the most famous of these simple yet pregnant tunes.

The variety and excellence of English musical life in the last third of the century made a deep impression on visiting artists and—as we have seen with regard to Haydn—exerted a beneficial creative influence on them.[6] But the brilliancy hid a decline of original composition, which became universal. Davey in his *History of English Music* points with a certain pride to the achievement of Richard John Samuel Stevens (1757–1837), the first composer who "succeeded in adapting the sonata-form to the glee," not realizing that this amounted to a deathblow, for vocal music has its own formal laws, and to impose the frame of a large instrumental species upon an essentially small lyric form shows a complete lack of sense for lyricism. This lack of lyric feeling and the reverence for academic music thus claimed as their victim the most original product of English music in the eighteenth century. The oratorios continued to be popular, but toward the end of the century, when the performances originally conducted by Handel, and after his death by John Christopher Smith and Samuel Arnold, came under the management of John Ashley (c. 1740–1805), they degenerated into "selections" that contained a little of everything. It must be said, however, that Ashley was responsible for the first performances in England of Mozart's Requiem and Haydn's *Creation*. The famous concerts in 1784 commemorating the birth of Handel (the old style of reckoning time placed Handel's birth in 1684) put an army of performers in the field. The performances were continued in subsequent years and the last commemorative presentation, in 1791, the one attended by Haydn, employed over a thousand singers and instrumentalists.

As the production as well as the appreciation of stylistic properties declined, England acquired the reputation of a "country without music" so unjustly emphasized on the Continent until recent times. The animated musical life and the wealth of the still music-loving public made Britain the paradise of foreign musicians. The munificent patronage which attracted foreign artists was considerably enhanced by the highly developed establishments for the printing and trade of music and the manufacture of excellent musical instruments, especially pianofortes. The composers, accustomed to most shameless acts of piracy on the part of Continental publishers, were greatly pleased by the relatively sound business practices of the British music merchants. The great migration toward England started shortly after the middle of the century when various members of the Mannheim school arrived to take up residence in England. Leopold Mozart with his young son went in 1765 to visit Johann Christian Bach, known as the "London Bach," and innumerable French, Italian, Spanish, and German musicians followed. But it was not until the last quarter of the nineteenth century that the creative spirit in English music aroused itself from its lethargy, a lethargy usually conveniently ascribed to the attrition caused by the titanic figure of Handel, but which was in reality the natural sequel of socio-cultural conditions.

America

TOWARD the end of the seventeenth century when musical life was stagnating in the culturally superior regions of America, the middle states, lying between the two sharply defined cultural centers represented by Virginia and Massachusetts, offered a more or less undisturbed continuation of European customs and institutions. This accounts for the early settlement of non-British colonies, especially German and Swedish, in their midst. These peoples brought with them a disposition and outlook on life that was favorable for the growth of music, but besides their favorable inclinations they also brought with them actual music. Both the Swedish and the German churches were known for their hymns and instrumental music. The Gloria Dei Church near Philadelphia is supposed to have been the first church in the English colonies equipped with an organ (the Spaniards had them much earlier), and its pastor is known to have requested the dispatch of harpsichords from his homeland. These people had an unquestioned advantage over the puritanical New Englanders and the indifferent Southerners in that music was to them not a sinful and frivolous diversion, but a heritage to be cherished. It was not long, however, before they too found themselves opposed by a sect, mild and humanitarian and not cruelly austere as were the New England Puritans, but equally opposed to music: the Quakers. We witness here a curious reappearance of the old Lutheran-Calvinistic controversy about music which we watched develop in Germany and in the lands that leaned toward one or another aspect of Calvinism. The original reasons for the controversy had changed and the Germans had themselves drifted far from the artistic ideals of Luther, but they had clung to their love of music as the issues of Calvinistic factions had retained their dislike, or rather their distrust, of it.

These Germans were not less earnest and severe about their religious tenets and ethical ideals than their Anglo-Saxon hosts, the followers of William Penn; indeed, in many ways they showed a much more harsh and intransigent attitude toward life and religion than the Quakers; but their music they were not willing to abandon. Justus Falckner, the first German minister ordained in America, complained that while the uncivilized Indians showed a distinct liking for music, the "melancholy, saturnine, stingy Quaker spirit" refused to be won over. Soon these Germans furnished active composers, perhaps the first, to American music. Conrad Johann Beissel (1690–1768) came from Germany and settled, about 1720, in Germantown, Pennsylvania, already a flourishing German colony. At first allied with the German Baptist, or Dunker, denomination, he subsequently carried on independent missionary work. In 1731 he founded at Ephrata, Pennsylvania, a Seventh-Day Baptist colony, a semimonastic religious community which became famous in colonial times. The colony included men and women who, despite the austerity of the settlement, carried on a remarkable cultural life centering about two activities dear to Germans, printing and music making. At least four hundred of the chorales sung in Ephrata, many of Beissel's own composition, were printed, most of them in the *Turtel Taube* (*Turtle Dove,* 1747), the Ephrata hymnal.

Another Pennsylvania settlement that left its mark on American musical history was the community founded in Bethlehem in 1741 by religious refugees from Bohemia and Moravia under the leadership of Bishop David Nitschman and Count Zinzendorf, the founder of the Herrnhut sect, who came to America to supervise the establishment of the colony. The Moravians came from a part of Central Europe that had particularly fine musical traditions, and their music classes and community singing started as soon as they had a roof over their heads. They brought with them musical instruments and used them freely in their churches. It is by no means accidental

that the small Moravian colony in Pennsylvania should have become in recent times the seat of a unique Bach cult, with yearly festivals participated in
by the simple and the learned alike. The German Protestant musical memories of these people were handed down from generation to generation.

We must bear in mind, however, that the Germans were recent arrivals,
the recipients of a musical tradition and practice interrupted only for the short
time needed for the erection of dwellings and churches. Theirs were self-
centered communities which did not cultivate or encourage intercourse with
other settlements, least of all with forbidding New England. Thus it is not
surprising that while in the Ephrata Cloister four- and six-part chorales were
sung, while in Bethlehem anthems with instrumental accompaniment reverberated in the churches, in Massachusetts ministers, congregations, and
magistrates were still debating whether music should be tolerated at all, even
in its simplest form. The ragged singing offended the ears of even the mildly
musical, and some kind of reform and organization was imperative. The
initiative was taken by a few enlightened clergymen who braved the ingrained hostility of the people to music; they tried to improve matters by
urging the use of notes. This effort met, as before, with great opposition, as
the pious were still appalled at the possibility of surreptitious music making
on instruments once people learned how to read music. There was also the
perennial denunciation of popish vanity, any organized choral singing being
considered a distinctive mark of Catholicism. In 1712 the Reverend John
Tufts of Newburyport published the first colonial instruction book on singing, *A Very Plain and Easy Introduction to the Whole Art of Singing Psalm
Tunes,* which enjoyed a surprisingly wide circulation, reaching its eleventh
printing in 1744. The book contained thirty-seven tunes in three parts, but
the good pastor defeated his own intentions by concocting a most complicated
sort of tablature instead of a simple musical notation. Another of the champions of singing by note was the Reverend Dr. Symmes of Bradford, Massachusetts, author of several dissertations on singing. His *Reasonableness of
Regular Singing, or Singing by Note* (1720) refuted the argument that reading music by note would lead to the employment of instruments in the
church. Symmes's arguments seem to have been based on sober and irre-
futable observations. There was little likelihood, he said, that people would
spend money for organs or organists when they were too stingy even to have
a bell to call people together on the Lord's day. In another decade the rabid
opposition began to weaken, partly because the more enlightened leaders'
counsel prevailed, partly because the theocratic democracy of the seventeenth
century began to lose its absolute power as the boundaries of mental occupation were extended. The mother country's mercantilistic politics were
causing a certain economic pressure that was a source of grievance but at
the same time forced the beginnings of American political thought. Toward

the middle of the century most churches had choirs, and even secular music was no longer opposed. The Boston *News Letter* actually announced a public concert in that city in 1731—the first on record in colonial America—and by 1754 the city possessed a concert hall where concerts of "Vocal and instrumental Musick to consist of Select Pieces by the Masters" were performed. One more decade, and Boston became the seat of regular subscription concerts.

While opposition to music in Pennsylvania was equally stern among the Quakers and the Presbyterians, its practice was smoldering in Philadelphia, supported by other denominations, especially the Church of England. Since the Quakers, unlike the more severe New Englanders, did not invade the privacy of the family, musical life grew in the intimacy of cultured homes, and in many a Philadelphia parlor amateurs gathered to play chamber music. Italian and English music of the leading seventeenth and early eighteenth-century composers was well known and liked.

The southern cities, unfettered by restrictions, offered an inspiring spectacle. Charleston and Williamsburg, most aristocratic and most British of the colonial centers of wealth and culture in the South, were proud of their music, which echoed the latest fashions in England. The first recorded performance of an opera in America, in 1735, took place in Charleston. *Flora, or Hob in the Well,* one of the most successful one-act ballad operas, performed some two hundred times within twenty years in London, was the memorable piece. Nothing could characterize more eloquently the difference between the North and the South than the fact that this ballad opera, first performed in London in 1729, reached Charleston six years later. Williamsburg, Virginia, owned a permanent playhouse as early as 1722, and some authorities vouch for an even earlier date. Maryland also welcomed concerts and theatrical performances; in 1752 the Kean and Murray Company offered there the *Beggar's Opera,* a performance particularly notable for its use of an orchestra instead of a mere spinet. Charles Theodore Pachelbel, a German musician related to the great seventeenth-century composer of the same name, gave concerts in New York and Charleston in 1736, when such events were almost unheard of in New England.

It is only natural to look for the first native composer who was part and parcel of the nation's culture among the aristocratic dilettanti of the middle states and the South. Francis Hopkinson (1737-1791), jurist, author, and statesman, professed among his many avocations a particular fondness for music. This signer of the Declaration of Independence was a patriot in the best sense of the word, and in some of his literary and musical compositions—especially in the satirical "Battle of the Kegs"—he taunted the British very effectively. It is generally agreed that his song, "My Days Have Been So Wondrous Free" (1759), is the first-known composition by a native American, and that his *Seven Songs* (1788) was the first book of music published by an Anglo-Saxon composer in the New World. While these works have little more than historical importance, their freshness places them high above the cumbersome products of the professionals, clinging to outmoded musical precepts. Hopkinson himself was aware of the historical importance of his efforts and expressed this belief in a letter of dedication to Washington.

While New England relented in the matter of church music and even permitted public concerts, the puritanical antagonism toward the theater so vigorously expressed in Increase Mather's writings in the seventeenth century was unabated. Two years after the Reverend Mr. Tufts's brave manifesto on behalf of singing in the church, Samuel Sewall, one of the judges in the Salem witchcraft cases, was aroused by the acting of a play in the Council Chamber. Although an open-minded man who had publicly repudiated his views on witchcraft and taken the blame for the executions, he was still horrified at the thought of histrionic exhibitions. The opposition was still vigorous toward the middle of the century, and when some visiting actors from England, assisted by local amateurs, performed Thomas Otway's *Orphan* in a Boston coffeehouse, indignation knew no bounds. The *Orphan* was a tragedy in blank verse—not one of the coarse and licentious Restoration comedies (of which Otway wrote more than one), but a stark drama of passion and love in which many critics see almost Shakespearean qualities. Thus the objection could not have been raised on purely moral or ethical grounds and hence the violent aversion to the theater could not have been based purely on religious prejudice. One sentence from the law passed in the wake of the indignation created by the public performance of the *Orphan* will convince us that the gospel of work and production and the horror of waste in time or materials, which we discovered conveniently enshrouded in a pious religious dialect in the creed of the middle-class Englishman of the seventeenth century, was still at the bottom of this aversion. The law prohibiting all forms of theatrical entertainment stresses the dangers of such spectacles as "tend to discourage industry and frugality"; the likelihood that impiety may increase greatly is also mentioned, but only after the hideous thought that people's regular occupations may be disrupted by attending plays. The same spirit actuated the zealous Philadelphians, who in a similar law, passed the same year, spoke of "idle persons and strollers in the character of players." Here the wrath of the magistrates was aroused by the presentations of the Kean and Murray Company. The "disorder" was terminated by the departure of the London theatrical company to New York, but in 1754, an undertaking much worse in scope from the Quaker point of view followed: Lewis Hallam, an English actor and manager, arrived at the head of a troupe which performed ballad operas. A few years later a season of plays and ballad operas was repeated but the pressure was too strong; Quakers,

Presbyterians, and even Lutherans joined forces, compelling the local authorities to interdict the spectacles. The affair was carried to the king, who set the prohibition aside, but it was not until 1766 that David Douglass, who married Hallam's widow and became the head of his company, returned with the troupe. Henceforth the theater remained undislodged, though not unmolested, until the Revolution.

A generation after the antitheater law of Boston the theater was still not considered entirely acceptable, although the civil authorities and the ministers were no longer disposed to enforce the law at any price. There began, then, a timid movement resorting to subterfuges, not unlike those used by playwrights during the Commonwealth in England, of offering most decent and high-minded "moral readings" or interpretations. It took several years, however, before Bostonians were permitted openly to enjoy their theater. Beginning in 1793, ballad operas appeared regularly in Boston's two permanent theaters, and the stern New Englanders apparently released all their repressed theatrical ardor at once, for the few years that separated them from the nineteenth century saw no less than one hundred and fifty odd ballad operas—a respectable number for the most seasoned opera-going city.

There were, besides the importations from England, new "operas" composed along the model of the ballad opera. Hopkinson's *The Temple of Minerva* (1781), called an oratorical entertainment, Hewitt's *Tammany* (1794), and Pelissier's *Edwin and Angelina* (1796) were the most notable American products, although the two last-named composers were not native-born.

The Pennsylvania Germans continued their musical activity, and to the *Singstunde* ("singing hour") they added in 1744 the *Collegium Musicum* in imitation of the thriving student organizations for the performance of music in vogue in German universities. In 1765 a similar *collegium* was set up in Lititz. It has been pointed out that such activity in a settlement which, as late as 1800, numbered only fifty houses, is evidence of an extraordinary interest in music.[7] This remarkable musical life, considerably superior to anything else in the country, though on the whole isolated and entirely Germanic, began to produce composers of instrumental ensemble music and concerted choral music. Of this generation of American Moravians, John Frederick Peter (b. 1746) seems to have been the most eminent; he was a composer of chamber music as well as organist of the Moravian congregation.[8] But in a country dominated by English thought and customs, a little band of foreigners, absorbed in themselves, could not be expected to make a lasting impression; the music of the Moravians will therefore always remain an episode interesting to the historian but of little importance to the musical destinies of the country at large.

Those destinies were shaped by people of an entirely different character and ability. Some of them were clergymen engaged in the congenial task of providing their congregations with hymns and Psalms. Of these, James Lyon (1735–1794), a Presbyterian minister, acquired fame with his hymn book *Urania* (c. 1761), which included hymns of his own composition. There was, however, another type of composer, less urbane and less educated but possessed by a fervor not to be found in the mild clerics. William Billings (1746–1800), a Boston tanner with the imagination and fiery energy of an Evangelist, was the most colorful representative of the inspired amateur musicians laboring for the cause of music in America. Historians have called him "self-taught," but in reality he was not taught at all, for the bad "introductions" in the hymnals that were within his reach could hardly impart any knowledge of music. This did not dampen Billings's enthusiasm, and in 1770 he published the *New England Psalmsinger,* which, as Howard appropriately remarks, "announced his musical declaration of independence" from all restrictions. His enthusiasm prompted him to venture into the field of contrapuntal music, producing most extraordinary concoctions devoid of any system or even sense. The artisan turned professional musician ended his career by composing an instruction book on the fundamentals of music entitled *The Continental Harmony* (1794), written in the customary dialogue form. Billings was ridiculed by earlier historians, stupefied by his "fuguing pieces" and other fantastic and not very coherent stunts, but this crude musician with his contagious enthusiasm accomplished more in the way of promoting music in America than the relatively highly trained Moravians or the timorous hymnologists. His lusty works are to be found on the printed programs of almost every late eighteenth-century American musical assembly.

When discussing the history of music in England in the second half of the eighteenth century, we noticed the invasion of foreign artists that grew in the measure in which English music declined. The migratory Continental musicians soon discovered that the New World offered great possibilities, while Englishmen, displaced by Italians, Germans, and Frenchmen, remembered their kinsmen across the seas and sought a better livelihood in America. The timid infiltration toward the middle of the century grew to a considerable immigration after the Revolutionary War. To this we must add the increasing mobility of the musicians, formerly restricted to one place but now going freely from Philadelphia to Boston and back to Charleston, with a resultant quickening of musical life. Even before the middle of the century organ and spinet makers were established, starting a new trade in the country. Johann Gottlob Klemm (1690–1762), a Saxon organ builder, was active in New York and Pennsylvania, while Gustavus Hasselius, a Swede, manufactured spinets in Philadelphia as early as 1742. After the middle of the century various more accomplished musicians began to arrive from England, among them William Tuckey (1708–1781). This former choirmaster of Bristol Cathedral was not only a well-trained musician but a clear-headed and patient organizer whose first act was to develop a good choir by imparting musical instruction to the children in the school maintained by Trinity Church in New York. His forces were able enough to stage a performance, with orchestra, of Handel's *Messiah* in 1770, a memorable date in the history of American music. By this time the works of Purcell, Arne, and Boyce were known and appreciated by concert audiences, and now the Italians and Germans joined the English composers. William Selby (1738-1798), an English organist from London, arrived about 1771 and soon became the main light of music in Boston. Sonneck attributes the rapid progress of music in this city—a generation before Selby's arrival almost barren of music—to the influence of this enterprising musician.

Among the later newcomers the most influential were Alexander Reinagle (1756-1809), an Englishman of Austrian parentage, and Henri Capron, a French cellist, active in Philadelphia after 1786. In 1792 several members of the London Professional Concerts arrived together, among them James Hewitt (1770-1827), a prolific if not original composer, publisher, and orchestra leader who founded a dynasty of musicians who exerted considerable influence on American music. The same year saw the arrival of Raynor Taylor (1747-1825), an Englishman who composed a number of ballad operas while in America, and Victor Pelissier, a versatile Frenchman, a born player and the author and arranger of many "operas." A number of other musicians, actors, and singers arrived toward the close of the century, finding a musical life that must have amazed the old residents in New England who still remembered the Draconic measures enacted against music in their youth.

The repertory was first dominated by English compositions, but the fare became more varied with the influx of foreigners and with the gradual expansion of American music. The foreigners brought with them the most recent music. Reinagle played Haydn in 1786; James Hewitt, Jean Gehot, B. Bergmann, and William Young, the four musicians formerly with the London Professional Concerts, banded together to offer works by Haydn, Pleyel, Stamitz, and Wanhall. As a matter of fact, Haydn's works were known to the Moravians at the incredibly early date of 1761, and at Bethlehem in 1795 there was a regular string quartet especially devoted to Haydn's chamber music. In the library at Bethlehem are manuscript copies of works by Mozart dated 1785, that is, in the master's lifetime, when his instrumental compositions were unknown to most Europeans outside his immediate surroundings. At about the time of the Revolution, Psalms and hymns were produced in increasing numbers, and in 1795 there appeared a collection that was practically an encyclopedia of psalmody. The compilers were Oliver Holden (1765-1844), Samuel Holyoke (1762-1820), and, for good measure as also for good harmonization, a German by the name of Hans Gram. Both Holden and Holyoke are remembered for their pleasing hymn tunes, while Gram can claim the historic right to the first printed orchestral score on this side of the Atlantic.

With the settlement of the great issue that had been agitating the public since the conclusion of the French wars in 1763, the cultural life of the nation began to be organized around the natural objects of human interest. The era of political and spiritual fermentation produced mainly political and polemical tracts, but it also saw the birth of such popular songs as "Yankee Doodle." During the Revolution musical activities, especially the theater, were discouraged and even forbidden in view of the serious times, but after the cessation of hostilities musical life started with renewed vigor, with subscription concerts and permanent theaters rising everywhere. That Hopkinson's *Seven Songs* elicited admiration from Washington, Jefferson, and many other personages not themselves musicians, testifies to the general appreciation of music toward the end of the century. Indeed, music became such an honored endeavor that when Washington visited various cities during his inaugural tour he was frequently entertained at public concerts. Thus the opening of the nineteenth century ushered in an era in which music, like literature, was fully prepared to embark on a career of national significance.

Eighteenth-Century Conception of Vocal Music

SPEAKING of English musical tastes and theories in modern times, Edward J. Dent made the following remarks:

Wagner and Brahms once accepted by the leaders of musical thought in this country, it was hardly possible to avoid accepting as a general principle of musical criticism the supposition that whatever was German was good, and whatever was Italian was bad. To that they added the subsidiary principles that as a general rule sacred music was superior to secular, and instrumental music to vocal, exception being made only for polyphonic choral writing, solo singing of a strictly declamatory type, and of course German *Lieder*. These principles once established, it was only natural that eighteenth century Italian opera should be regarded as the concentrated expression of all that was most evil in the art of music.[9]

This excellent analysis is valid not only for England but for America and, to a certain degree, for Germany as well. With its strong literary orientation, the nineteenth century—and our own, which still derives its aesthetic tenets from the preceding era—found most of the vocal music of the eighteenth century (opera, cantata, oratorio, and Mass) incongruous and primitive. Its opera, the various authors stated, was based on libretti devoid of literary value;

dramatic action, plausibility, and logic; it was entirely dependent on the singers' caprice and presented a disjointed sequence of "numbers," that is, recitatives and arias, among them the much-maligned da capo aria. In the cantata and oratorio Bach and Handel were the supposed victims of text writers, and the Masses with their operatic physiognomy were considered a caricature of church music. It stands to reason that a style which attained the greatest homogeneity in instrumental music, a homogeneity universally recognized even by us, will not have failed in the other chief types of music. And indeed, the old "number opera" was as accomplished in its artistic conception as the modern music drama; but the aesthetic factors were purely musical and not literary, and consequently the application of nineteenth-century dramaturgical principles to the older opera led to a general misunderstanding and flat condemnation of eighteenth-century lyric art—a condemnation meted out indiscriminately to the hasty and careless as well as to the thoroughly artistic opera.

Church music, especially that of the classic era, was even more roundly denounced than opera. As we listen to these sacred compositions we readily perceive and enjoy their purely musical values, for we are dealing with the art of a period whose general principles and a number of kindred masterpieces are well known to us; but the liturgic and social aspects require a historical conditioning to a degree approximating the elaborate studies recommended for the comprehension of the church music of the central Middle Ages.

It apparently has never occurred to critics that the eighteenth century could not possibly have envisaged a vocal art along nineteenth-century lines, and that consequently its point of departure as well as its aim is at variance with our own. According to Wagner, the lyric drama is a work in which music should take a distinctly secondary role and be governed by the literary conceptions of the dramatist, seconding the latter, if necessary, to the point of self-effacement. Arteaga, the great eighteenth-century historian of Italian opera, who echoed the beliefs of his contemporaries, declared that the poet must surrender his rights unconditionally to the musician. This is the great issue.

Eighteenth-century opera was not a literary form, and consequently it did not know the type of dramatic action we require from today's opera composer. By action it understood something entirely different. Except in the finales, the action was usually left to the secco recitatives, and the composer's fancy rose to its highest flight after the factual occurrences had taken place, giving the protagonists' most intimate reactions in arias and ensembles. This was a purely musical conception, but a conception not an iota less artistic than that professed in our modern literary music drama; the only reason for our not recognizing its validity and integrity is our inability to listen to this music with the same understanding that we bring to the appreciation of eighteenth-century painting. It is futile to "rewrite" the libretti of these operas, as has been done repeatedly, to "save an opera for modern audiences," for that amounts to treating the symptoms instead of the malady. The Zenos, Metastasios, and Da Pontes do not need doctoring. It is we who need reconditioning. Music was the great concern of these people, and the poet was not allowed to impose his artistic personality in a collaboration in which he was distinctly an agent of the musician. From this angle one can understand the relative failure of Gluck's so-called reform operas. Yet what Gluck achieved was by no means the subservience of music to poetry, as he had announced, but a more concentrated, pregnant, and economical employment of music in the lyric drama. His operas were still dramas of sentiment and not of action; only his diction was more resolute and his general musical construction more closely knit. The great musico-dramatist himself could not help being musician first, once he was carried away by his imagination; and we shall see how an even stronger mind, Wagner, frequently became completely submerged in his music, forgetting all self-imposed laws of dramaturgy once the fervor of creation took possession of him.

But in these cases, especially in the late nineteenth-century music drama, such temporary abandonment of the prevailing literary-aesthetic doctrines by reversion to a purely musical conception caused stylistic inequalities all too noticeable, while the older opera presented a form of art intact and irreproachable in its adherence to its own precepts. How little the action mattered in this opera is convincingly demonstrated by the earlier composers' habit of entrusting the writing of the action-bearing secco recitatives to their pupils. It was not until the second half of the century, notably after Hasse's exemplary use of the recitative, that the lyric drama gradually acquired the qualities we know from the classic opera buffa. The very gradual change from the purely musical conception of all forms of vocal music to the literary began at the end of the late baroque, reaching its completion in the late nineteenth century, when its influence was strong enough to make itself felt in pure instrumental music and was carried *ad absurdum* in certain forms of program music. The poet was then no longer incidental, nor even a mere librettist lending his services to music; he took the lead, and the musician could not challenge his authority.

The "literarization" of music really began in earnest with the emergence of the great poets and dramatists of the classic era. But we should not consider this a one-sided tendency, for, beginning with Klopstock, poetry in its turn showed a musical disposition heretofore unknown. This was a natural reaction to the cool rhetorical correctness of French rationalism, so efficiently championed in Germany by Gottsched. As the new tendency was due not alone to a new conception of music but to a realignment of poetry and music, the change in aesthetic theories had to be wrought in the country where the new literary movement had originated—in Germany. On an art dominated by the genius of Italy, therefore, the repercussions were relatively mild. Abert has pointed out the interesting fact that in 1791, when the literary orientation in vocal music had already been well established, the older conception was still conspicuously present in individual cases, such as the *Magic Flute;* hence one can understand why this, the consummate "musical opera," has drawn the harshest criticism from modern authors: "bad text," "no continuity," "too much unmotivated contrast," "senseless coloratura passages," etc., that is, all the criteria which we have quoted as totally irrelevant in the preliterary musical opera. Mozart and the Italian opera buffa do reflect the new literary orientation, but, as we have seen, they still convert the literary elements into music. After the passing of their century the balance began to be shifted as the spoken drama forced its laws on the lyric drama. This was especially true in Germany, while Italian opera retained the principles of the old "musical opera" for a long time; in fact, one might say it has never really relinquished them.

The technical means of the eighteenth-century opera corresponded admirably to its aesthetic ideals. In the aria the great composers of the baroque opera gave the most remarkable portrayals of human sentiments transformed into music. In doing so they dispensed to a considerable extent with the poet's services. The fundamental dynamic scheme of the baroque, sharp contrasts without gradual transition, was faithfully carried out in the arias themselves, which usually depict contrasting moods. This quality naturally contributed to the "isolated numbers" so much condemned by another era, which expected a psychological growth of dramatic conflict. Unity in the opera dominated by arias was created by a logical disposition of tonalities and by the architectural use of thematic material—eminently musical elements that have lost their structural meaning in the modern opera, where literary factors take charge of both continuity and cohesion. Leichtentritt has discussed the symbolism of tonalities in Handel's operas,[10] but the constructive force of tonalities in opera extended throughout the century and was still predominant in such works as the *Magic Flute,* in which E flat major is allocated to the humanitarian ideal underlying this opera, F major to the priests and their world, C minor to the sinister powers, and G major to the buffoon element. While this use of tonalities may be almost meaningless to us, Beethoven still professed a limitless admiration for it, holding up the *Magic Flute* as an unsurpassable masterpiece of musical logic.

The da capo aria is never questioned in Bach's cantatas and Passions, while it is always held up as a ridiculous convention in opera, imposed upon it by singers. Such opinions leave out of consideration the obvious correspondence between the ternary sonata form, with its recapitulation, and the da capo aria built on the same principle. The da capo aria, with its general rules of tonal relationship and modulation, was as much a structural law in vocal music as the sonata form in instrumental music in the latter part of the century. This was a fact acknowledged not only by the composer but by the librettist, who arranged the text to fit the musical principles of the da capo aria. The employment of coloratura passages, motives of accompaniment, or occasional descriptive imitations does not change its fundamental, purely musical organization. This basic principle led to another custom in eighteenth-century music gravely deplored in modern times, namely, the "senseless repetition of words." But since the plan was purely musical, the composer, aiming to render the state of mind of a dramatic figure in music, was always wont to dilute his text if he needed more music to express his ideas. If a present-day composer should resort to such a procedure he could rightfully be accused of an inartistic attitude, for he is setting words to music, whereas the older composer was turning a text *into* music.

As the more static baroque opera of sentiment turned toward the classical opera, which already required action, it was naturally the recitative, the link between the individual numbers, that was charged with the carrying out of dramatic action. The *recitativo accompagnato* therewith began its ascendancy, to become the most effective agent of dramatic action. In the cantata and Passion the inherent lack of action caused the recitative to develop in a different manner, absorbing lyric and epic elements, especially in the *testo* part, and showing a more songlike character than its operatic counterpart. This change in the role of the recitative necessarily occurred at an earlier date in the oratorio because of the importance of the narrative, which took the place of the action. At this point the musical setting of the individual words in the operatic accompanied recitative gradually reached the careful composition of the almost ariosolike recitative of the cantata, oratorio, and Passion, developed to the highest artistic standards by Johann Sebastian Bach.

The same musical instinct that activated the lyric drama brought about a rapprochement between church music and opera, even in the north German Protestant cantata and oratorio. It was not so much that the musicians, including Bach and Handel, were inspired by the poet as that they compelled him to accommodate their musical imagination. Thus it is again entirely out of order to "improve" the literary quality of cantata texts. However, when discussing church music of the eighteenth century, we cannot proceed as simply and directly as in the case of opera, because a number of factors, such as theology, liturgy, philosophy, and tradition, must be taken into consideration, whereas the opera could follow the dictates of aesthetic convictions. There is also the wide gulf that separates Protestant from Catholic church music, which again demands different standards for each.

Protestant Church Music

THE Enlightenment wrought havoc in the various Protestant liturgies. Man and his happiness became the focal point in the thought of the Enlightenment, a conception which sharply differentiates eighteenth-century thought from that of previous times. The investigation of man's mental life became the most popular of scientific and philosophical occupations. The program of the times is embodied in Pope's statement that the true object of human thinking and research is man himself. Progressing along this path, the thinkers of the Enlightenment came inevitably upon the great obstacle of religion, and before anything else this had to be redefined and explained. Religion changed into moral conviction, largely under English influences. To the moralizing Deists, following the writings of Shaftesbury, Toland, and Bolingbroke, the existence and nature of God could be proved rationally from the course of nature and without the aid of supernatural revelation. God became the Most Gracious, who opened the way of happiness to man; to live virtuously was to serve and praise God. This simplified formulation of religious life, perhaps the most typical characteristic of the Enlightenment, culminated in Voltaire's celebrated statement: "Si Dieu n'existait pas, il faudrait l'inventer."

Old-fashioned theological thought was turned into artistic-aesthetic philosophy by Shaftesbury. The harmony that he perceived in the beautiful he held to be present in the universe, which, like the philosophers of the Renaissance, he conceived as a work of art. God, whose activity is reflected in this universe, becomes an artist, and religion a profession of membership in the universe. The loftiness of this conception was not understood by Continental philosophers for a generation or two, for their rationalistic orientation was insistent on knowing the practical advantages of a reorganization of the philosophy of life. Then came the great disaster of the Lisbon earthquake (1755), which shattered the long-cherished belief in Leibnitz's formula and strengthened the materialistic tendencies especially noticeable in the encyclopedists. Religion gradually changed into ethics. This attitude was not a form of atheism; it merely broke with the Church and its formalism. Both orthodoxy and Pietism were attacked by the Enlightenment, and under the onslaught of liberal reasoning Church and religious life declined, for tolerance dulls the edge of the weapons of a militant church. Luther's *Volkskirche,* the people's church, became a thing of the past when secular interests rose above religious in setting free the human spirit.

All this had repercussions of the utmost importance in music, for, like other aspects of religious life, music too drifted away from the Church. Bach's music, especially in his Leipzig period, lost all connections with the people; it became art music of the most exalted spiritual kind. But while

Bach was still a musical apostle of Protestantism, summing up the essence of Luther's church in a region where few could follow him, Handel, Telemann, Graun, and the other notable Protestant church composers were merely setting religious texts. Theirs was no longer church music. As man became emancipated from ritual, proclaiming his right to worship in his own fashion, the music supplied for his devotion divorced itself from the bonds of the liturgy. Even when Latin songs were composed by Protestant musicians, they were no longer liturgic, although they had a certain spiritual tone—the tone of religious musical pieces. The new ethico-humanitarian ideal was not a churchly ideal. As expressed in music it was lofty and, since it leaned to Biblical texts, was connected with religion. But Handel's oratorios are not church music; they represent the new religious ideal which is equally present in classic drama and in the noble mythological music drama. The old Lutheran tradition of the German cantors became extinct, and oratorio, cantata, and Passion turned to the music drama as they had in England. We have followed the history of oratorio and Passion and noticed how the Pietistic-contemplative element displaced the Biblical; now they were looking for a new dwelling and found it in the concert hall and theater. The most famous Passion of the late eighteenth century, Graun's *Tod Jesu,* which remained popular throughout the nineteenth century, was first performed in a theater. A number of oratorios by the leading composers of the postbaroque era still showed high musical values, as would be expected from such men as Carl Philipp Emanuel Bach and Johann Abraham Peter Schulz, but they were secular in spirit and nature, constantly drawing away from the Church and preparing for the advent of the romantic oratorio.

The lack of a liturgy, the theological and philosophical insecurity, and the retention of traditions without compelling convictions led to a well-nigh complete disintegration of Protestant church music. This should not be taken to mean a complete absence of music, for this was not the case, but the specific genius of Protestant church music became extinct. The "spiritual songs" which displaced the magnificent treasure of Protestant church melodies led to the arbitrarily set, gloomy, and dragging congregational singing that was a caricature of the sturdy and lively chorales of the heroic age of the Reformation. Church elders and municipal councils sought to simplify the services, making them "a matter of the heart" instead of "external splendor." In the midst of this general decline organ music could not sustain its ancient glory. The chorale preludes, jewels of Protestant instrumental church music, shrank, undoubtedly under the influence of the spiritual song, to little song-like pieces, and it was only in the freely conceived toccatas, preludes, and other nonliturgic pieces that a few composers produced works of some note. Among these we should mention Johann Ludwig Krebs (1713–1780), a personal pupil of Johann Sebastian Bach; Johann Peter Kellner (1705–1772), well acquainted with Bach and Handel; Franz Vollrath Buttstedt (1735–1814); and Daniel Gottlob Türk (1756–1813).

With the appalling ebbing of German Protestant church music, its practitioners, the able cantors, disappeared and were replaced by incompetent and unimaginative officeholders. The extreme circumspection of municipal and church authorities cut the allowances to such an extent that in many churches the choirs had to be disbanded. Other factors responsible for the decline of the church choir were the increased popularity of the *collegia* and *convivia musica* and the general supplanting of choral by instrumental music. The schools failed to replenish the thinned ranks of the choristers as instruction in singing was likewise neglected, and in many instances the student choirs were also discontinued. It is well known how Bach's life was embittered at the Thomasschule by constant friction with his superiors and by his inability to secure adequate personnel for his musical establishment. One can imagine the conditions in the smaller communities when the citadels of Protestant church art had to struggle against such heavy odds. The great Singspiel composer, Johann Adam Hiller (cantor at the Thomasschule, 1789–1801), who was always interested in church music, wrote in the *Berlinische Musikalische Zeitung* (March 3, 1793) that he was almost helpless in the face of the neglected musical liturgy and it was not within his power to change matters for the better. Klopstock, who recognized the low level and the shortcomings of the divine service, attempted to further the cause by rewriting some of the songs. The effects of this well-meant act were disastrous, for the many minor poets, cantors, and schoolteachers who, emboldened by the great poet's example, took upon themselves the task of refurbishing the sturdy old Lutheran church songs were convinced that the songs had to be adjusted to the tastes of their generation. Both Herder and Goethe condemned this "vandalism committed in the name of the Enlightenment."

Catholic Church Music

THE historian cannot help wondering at the rapidity with which the German south wrested the leadership in music from the north when the great baroque era had passed away. It was perhaps the sobriety of the Enlightenment, deeply impressed on the Protestant lands, which was chiefly responsible for the new balance of power, for the Enlightenment did not affect the Catholic south nearly so much as it did the other half of Germany. In this case as in others, the Church with its political sagacity knew how to assimilate the most heterogeneous elements, at the same time defending and assuring its fundamental existence, and incidentally preventing any sharp interruption in the flow of intellectual and artistic currents.

The aged Maria Theresa died in 1780. The new emperor, Joseph II, burning with ambition and with a desire to create a homogeneous Austrian empire, now had no one to oppose him. The empress had always shown consideration for established customs and traditions. Joseph wanted to abrogate all privileges in order to establish a single centralized government. No monarch since Charlemagne was so earnestly devoted to his task, and no monarch has ever brought to this task such fanatical tenacity of purpose. Joseph had no children, no friends, and no avocations. He trusted no one and attended to everything personally. An essential part of his plans was an edict of tolerance, placing all religious denominations on the same footing. The curious contradiction between Enlightenment and absolutism is especially glaring in this measure, for while the emancipation of Protestants in a traditionally Catholic country seemed a heroic gesture of liberalism, Joseph was too keenly aware of the advantages of a state religion for a centralized government to abolish the privileged role of the Roman Church. The Church remained, then, the religion of the land, although seriously disciplined and supervised by the crown. Religious orders were suspended, and processions and holydays, diminishing labor and production, were reduced. Perhaps the most radical step undertaken by the earnest monarch, the Apostolic Catholic ruler of a Catholic empire, was the establishment of civil divorce. Joseph's judicial reforms were equally far-reaching, and what the powerful Prussian king could not achieve without weighty compromises the bold Habsburg obtained with a simple stroke of his pen: serfdom was abolished in the land of wealthy aristocrats and prelates.

All this was too much to endure by a society not ripe for such reforms. Clergy and aristocracy rebelled; even the populace, for whose very benefit the reforms were enacted, turned against the emperor, and troops had to be sent to enforce the orders. In the midst of this turmoil Joseph died, in 1790, his last years saddened by the realization that his great work could not be consummated. Leopold II restored the old order, and the Church, threatened politically but with its houses of worship filled even during the height of the controversy by the multitude of humble and unshaken peasants, burghers, and aristocrats, regained everything it had lost. In contrast to the uncertainty of Protestant ecclesiastical organization and liturgy, the Catholic Church could always resume its activity virtually at a moment's notice, for its world-wide following was united in the same ritual, the same language, and the same dogmas. Its existence and influence no longer threatened, the Church was characteristically willing to accept and adopt the new philosophy within its own framework to its own purpose.

That after Bach's death the scales swung clearly toward the south was attributable not only to operatic predominance, but to the persistence of the traditions of Catholic church music, the focal point of which was the Mass. In spite of the wealth of great music that surrounded the sermon, center of the Protestant divine service, the latter could and did dispense with any music other than simple hymns; the Mass, on the other hand, was music itself, and its minutely organized liturgic form invited organic musical thinking which produced besides the strictly liturgical necessities a great deal of other music, churchly in purpose but free in imagination. In the midst of the Enlightenment, Catholic church music was not declining, nor was it stagnant or archaic. The same love of music for music's sake which triumphed in the opera saturated the Mass. The masters of the Neapolitan opera were its masters, followed by the radiant Singspiel composers and the great symphonists of the classic era. Their music was neither impious nor antiliturgic. Instead of clinging to expressive media of bygone ages which had lost their meaning to men of the eighteenth century, Catholic church composers utilized the wealth of their secular music, notably opera and symphony, placing them in the service of the Church. This they did with genuine devotion, turning the liturgical text into music with the same fervor that characterized their secular music. In doing so they proved themselves fellows of the high-minded and true artists whom we admired in the great masters of church music of the beatified *a cappella* period, for they too drew on the great musical wealth of chanson, madrigal, canzone, and ricercar, giving in their church music a synthesis of the music of their times.

Yet eighteenth-century music today comes under the same ban that falls upon the opera of that century. The Masses of the great composers are held to "correspond neither to the liturgy, nor the ideas, exigencies, or artistic traditions of the Catholic church." [11] A century of arbitrarily established church style has so blinded us that we fail to see in sacred music the same idealism which we recognize in arts and letters and which characterized the classic era. It was present in the alliance of intimate Austrian Gemütlichkeit with religious devotion. The former was manifested in the engaging serenade music of Salzburg, the latter in concerted church music. Serenade and Mass were good neighbors; earth and heaven were near to each other. The very fact that the objections raised to opera and Mass are almost identical should indicate to us that there must be some logical system operating in both. As in the "musical opera," text and music in the earlier eighteenth-century Masses corresponded only loosely as far as the musical setting of the words is concerned, and, since the construction was dictated almost entirely by musical logic, there were often unnecessary and even disturbing repetitions of fragments of the text. It would be erroneous, however, to conclude from this that the spirit of the text was not reflected in the music. The cultic and liturgic aspects were at first surrendered to the musical (operatic and symphonic); and as the composers were preoccupied with the great stylistic-formal problems demanded by secular music, in the midst of its struggle for a new synthesis, liturgic order and propriety were overruled by the will and urge for plastic musical construction. This is the same phenomenon that accompanied the emergence of the symphonic idiom from its many constituents. Opera, concerto, and symphony struggled here, and in their preoccupation they occasionally all but forgot the liturgic requirements.

The new stylistic element, the principal factor of construction, was naturally in church music the same thematic work which ruled the orchestra, both operatic and symphonic. The changes therefore had to emanate from the orchestra, and this led to the introduction into church music of such important formal elements as the sonata and the rondo. Searching for the originators of this tendency, it will not surprise us to find them among the same men, Pergolesi, Jommelli, Hasse, etc., who were the leading masters of the opera and the rising new instrumental style. These Italians and Italianate Germans were too much devoted to vocal music to err in the wrong direction; the Austrian school, however, was compelled to reconcile a multitude of tendencies before it could arrive at a definite solution and style. Fux's school still lived in a number of composers, and the Italian school had had an uninterrupted representation ever since Caldara. Some of the German composers, such as Gassmann, embraced the pure Italian style, but on the other hand the Singspiel and the symphony did not fail to exert their powerful influence on church music. The symphonic instinct seems to have been the strongest, and many Masses of the early classic period belong, properly speaking, in the field of instrumental music; their individual sections are "movements" presented by a symphonic orchestra with the voices in the background. Many a *Kyrie* and *Gloria* opens with a veritable overture, the voices entering at points where the symphonic fabric permits some harmonic fortification.

The confusion created was considerable, and a solution seemed far less likely than in the opera. The classical urge for perfection, formal beauty, and propriety of expression and purpose overcame the difficulties. The grouping of the individual parts of the Mass now became carefully planned, and, if not through-composed or held together by other means, it was customary to repeat the music of the first *Kyrie* (thus gaining the rounded form of *Kyrie* [A]—*Christe* [B]—*Kyrie* [A]), or the final sections of the *Gloria* and the *Credo*. As the years passed the sonata form intruded upon the *Kyrie*. The Mass then often started with a slow introductory section not unlike the solemn symphonic preamble, and continued with a regular allegro movement. Later the sonata form was extended to the other parts of the Mass. Solo arias as well as such choral parts as the *Gloria* were set symphonically. Occasionally several sections formed a large sonata form with a fugue at the end as a monumental coda. Nothing could illustrate more aptly the purely musical instincts and conceptions of the century than this transformation, inevitable under the pressure of a progressive musical thought. In contrast to the opera and oratorio, where the prevailing musical conception found a logical use in the da capo aria, the liturgic text in Catholic church music did not permit its application, and most arias were in a simple duple form, only those whose text permitted recapitulation reverting to the da capo form. The symphonic orchestral accompaniment was used with great skill and, we may add, with great prudence by the classical composers. The symphonic background remained a background, and the fine instinct of the composers, trained in both aspects of music, found a remarkable solution. Retaining a markedly polyphonic treatment for the choruses and reducing the solo and coloratura arias often to mere passages within a section, they created a finely balanced style which, while using all the devices of opera and symphony, could rightly be considered an independent and typical church style of the period.

The new symphonic-polyphonic Mass, like the string quartet and symphony, reached its perfection in the hands of Haydn and Mozart. The earlier Masses of both masters share the conception of church music prevalent in their time: namely, that while the general mood follows the meaning of the liturgic text, the setting depends entirely on purely musical reasons, disregarding both prosody and continuity of recitation, with individual syllables or words, or even whole passages, repeated at will. In this period there was a difference between the solemn extended Mass, the *missa solemnis,* and the short and simpler *missa brevis,* not to be confused with the incomplete Protestant short Mass consisting of *Kyrie* and *Gloria.* Mozart's little Masses represent the highest in churchly chamber music. His earlier sacred compositions, following the examples of Eberlin and Adlgasser, were at first less positive in their style than were his instrumental compositions. With his moving to Vienna and leaving behind the traditional atmosphere of Salzburg, a change is noticeable in his church style. On the whole, sacred music now became a minor field in his creative work, but something of the earnestness and profundity of the baroque emanates again from the choruses of the C minor Mass, although the idiom is far from being strictly polyphonic. The young master did not copy any of the devices of the great church composers; he merely assimilated their spirit, translating it into the modern language of his times. And he did not hesitate to set in the same Mass a gigantic eight-part ciacona over the traditional falling chromatic bass, and some breath-taking coloratura arias in the Neapolitan style. This Mass (K. 427), which we have mentioned among the unfinished works, is a monument of the new classic church style, worthy of the greatest traditions of Catholic music. In his last ecclesiastic composition, the Requiem Mass, musical logic and faithful liturgic setting of the text strike a judicious balance and produce the most consummate creation of church music of the Viennese era.

Nine little and eight great Masses (1768–1782) permit us an insight into

Mozart's religious nature. Bach's majesty and Beethoven's ecstasy were equally far removed from him, but what he gives us in his church music, pure humanity, must not be placed below either of the others. The spirit of German classicism illuminated by the reflection of Italian memories emanates from these Masses, and the image of Christ appears in them, moving, pure, and beautiful as only the early Christians could see him. Mozart's confessions of Christianity are expressed not only in his Masses. The earnest Catholic who on Corpus Christi Day walked piously in the procession with a candle in his hand set a Protestant chorale ("Ach Gott vom Himmel, sieh' darein") in the *Magic Flute*. The atmosphere is that of the New Testament, a profoundly religious confession enveloping the spirit of Freemasonry. But the Freemasonry of Mozart's time manifested, unwittingly, the universal human desire to find a sincere relationship with religious matters. The trio of the three genii strikes a peculiar, penetrating, convincing tone, and the transcendental is symbolized in the majestic chords of the wind instruments. Immortality is announced in the aria and chorus "O Isis and Osiris," the eternal love embodied in Jesus is expressed in the choralelike aria "In these sacred halls," and the humanity of Christ is conjured up in the priests of Freemasonry.

The Requiem Mass, with its serene contrapuntal writing, its gripping dramatic utterances, and its seraphic implorations, would have crowned the history of the classic orchestral Mass, but it remained tragically unfinished. The aged Haydn took it upon himself to affirm the artistic place of the Mass. Haydn's great melodic gifts and his imperishable popular invention are present in his Masses of the earlier period. His well-written, melodious choral songs do not resort to polyphony, with the exception of specific contrapuntal movements such as choral fugues, in which case the whole movement is contrapuntal. The leading role is assigned to the voices, the orchestra lending its assistance with occasional thematic participation. In his *St. Cecilia* Mass, Haydn uses the dramatic recitative in the *Et incarnatus est* with telling effect. The formal origins of this device are, nevertheless, unmistakable when he follows up the recitative with an aria. In general Haydn was not so much interested in the solo parts as most of his contemporaries, using the four solo voices in an ensemble which he opposes to the tutti of the full choir. This procedure is a remnant of the church music of the southern German baroque, which in its turn derived it from older, Venetian-Roman sources.

Home from his second London journey, the sexagenarian again returned to the composition of Catholic church music. The works he created after a pause of fourteen years constitute, with Mozart's C minor Mass and the Requiem Mass, the final achievements of classic church music. The two poles, symphonic orchestra and polyphonic choir, were intensified and at the same time brought closer to each other, for as the orchestral idiom became

invested with the breadth of the symphony, the choral settings became increasingly polyphonic, with a tendency toward fugues, especially double
fugues. The *Kyrie* from Mozart's Requiem and a number of sections from
Haydn's six great Masses, written between 1796 and 1802, testify eloquently
to this. These Masses (named, in order of their composition, *Heilig, Pauken,
Nelson, Theresia, Schöpfung,* and *Harmonie Messe*) use the full symphony
orchestra. While their general tone is naturally symphonic, lavish use of
polyphony characterizes them, with numerous canons and elaborate fugues.

The religious ideal, the image of Christ, was conceived by Haydn in the
popular manner. He told Giuseppe Antonio Carpani, his first biographer,
that "at the thought of God his heart leaped for joy, and he could not help
his music's doing the same." This surely does not indicate a thoughtless mixture of sacred and secular but an idealized and entirely homogeneous outlook on life, in which both tears and laughter have their logical place. So we
shall understand why a *Crucifixus* in Haydn's setting is more moving than
dolorous, why in the *Agnus* of the *Kettledrum* Mass he strikes bellicose tones,
and why the *Gloria* shines with pomp and jubilation.

The classic era saw a tremendous growth in church music. The great productivity in Catholic church music affected even the north, and it is most
interesting to observe the Protestant composers' rapprochement to Catholic
musical life. Joseph Alois Schmittbauer (1718–1809), a pupil of Jommelli in
Stuttgart and, after 1776, conductor in Karlsruhe, was one of these composers who tried to write works that could be used by both denominations.
His oratorio, *The Friends at the Grave of the Saviour* (1783), was so arranged as to make it acceptable for Catholic services. The high ideals of
Haydn, Mozart, and, a little later, Beethoven, Schubert, and Cherubini were
soon undermined by the mass production which caused a sad decline of
Catholic church music in postclassical times. Every organist of the smallest
village church considered it his duty to compose Masses literally by the hundred. Even the revival of the great treasures of old church music and the
advent of an earnest neo-Catholic school of composition were not able to
stem the tide of a totally insincere and uninspired Catholic church art, and
it cannot be denied that its influence seems to be as powerful as ever even
today.

Eighteenth-Century Musical Practice—The Constructive Role of the Orchestra—The Art of Performance

OUR modern musical practice is based on the printed score, which gives a
relatively unequivocal picture of the music, aided by more or less precise instructions as to the manner of performance. Thus if the modern artist indulges in what is usually called a "new reading" or interpretation, he departs

from the printed instructions so profusely given since the late romantic period in original compositions, and supplied in instructive editions of the music of the older masters. By "new reading" of a score we understand tempi, dynamics, and articulation that are considerably at variance with the score, and not the innate right and duty of the artist to give us his own conception of a work he is attempting to present to us. With all the freedom accorded to him, the true student and connoisseur will not take the second theme of a classic sonata at a perceptibly reduced tempo, play a lively chorale prelude in the manner of a funeral dirge, or accelerate a witty and gossipy symphonic finale to a mad scramble of racing instruments, although such offenses are not only committed but even encouraged by the modern "interpretative" school.

In the first half of the eighteenth century the burden placed on the interpreter was considerably more onerous, for he was actually charged not only with the execution of a composition but with the final elaboration of the score. The composer wrote down the outlines of his musical ideas, leaving conductor, singers, and instrumentalists to invest the bare lines with embellishments and orchestration to suit the occasion. The operatic scores of the period offer the greatest difficulty to the modern student, for they are little more than general directions for the use of the conductor. In many instances the bass was not even figured, leaving the choice of harmonies to the whim of the continuo player. If we add to this the convention of "custom-composed" roles (a convention that persisted throughout the century) we shall understand why the resurrection of the earlier baroque opera is almost beyond possibility. Organists and musical directors were expected to master contrapuntal improvisation. Handel's organ concertos, interpolated in his oratorios, were universally admired for their wonderful polyphonic elaboration, yet the printed scores seem almost insignificant and certainly do not give the remotest idea of how they were played. Similarly, Buxtehude's, Reinken's, and Bach's improvisation of fugues and ciaconas was legendary. Improvisation on the organ and clavier remained a highly treasured art to Beethoven's time.

Since the organist or director was usually a trained composer, his elaboration of the score was generally in conformity with a musicianly and cultivated taste. Not so with the feted singer. The castrato or prima donna would deliver his or her aria, embellishing the return part of the da capo aria with improvised flourishes which disagreed with the accompaniment as often as not. Such composers, however, as were in a position to crack the whip over the singers, either because they were musical plenipotentiaries in a court or opera managers such as Handel, insisted on respect for their music and generally sketched out the ornamentations themselves, practicing them with the singers until they were sure of their parts.

While opera and Catholic church music, often performed by the same forces, were to a considerable degree at the mercy of the singer, Protestant church music (excluding, of course, such nonliturgic works as the Handelian oratorio) remained free from arbitrary distortions. This was natural in view of the fact that the German cantors virtually lived with their pupils (who made up the church choirs), supervising both their training and the performances closely. The cantor's authority was supreme and he encountered no difficulty in upholding it, for the number of performers engaged in church music was usually small, seldom more than four singers to a part with an orchestra of perhaps twenty.

After the middle of the century improvisation as an integral part of musical practice began to decline rapidly. While it was still popular in the north, Leopold Mozart in his very influential violin method (*Violinschule*) frowned upon arbitrary acts indulged in by players, emphasizing that it was the composer's prerogative as well as his duty to indicate the embellishments by writing them out in exact notation. The instrumentalists soon accustomed themselves to the new order of things, but embellishments and cadenzas were still frequent in opera. It is well known how Weber clashed with the singers of his troupe in Dresden in the early part of the nineteenth century. The most earnest war on "cleanliness in singing" was started by the intrepid and inexorable Gluck, who succeeded in Paris in putting the fear of God into the singers. While Mozart abolished all embellishments in Vienna and Prague, with the exception of some cadenzas, in Italy Burney still found the vogue of virtuoso absolutism undimmed.

The enormous gains made by instrumental music during the eighteenth century elevated orchestral music to a position where it almost rivaled opera itself. The orchestra was not yet a body of heterogeneous instruments placed together and used at will; it was closely allied with the musical material and served as one of its chief agents of construction. The baroque orchestra followed the polyphonic parts with the constancy of organ stops; indeed, orchestral writing was related to organ registration. The strings and the basso continuo, a large homogeneous body of instruments, were the foundation of the orchestra as the diapasons were the principal foundation stops of the organ. The wind instruments were added to the strings somewhat as the reed stops were to the diapasons, that is, either as solo stops, usually retaining a dominant position for the duration of the piece or movement, or as dynamic (but not coloristic) support joining the strings. Tone color, dynamics, and form were thus closely bound in a structural unity. Baroque orchestral writing favored choirs of strings, wood winds, or brasses, a division which corresponded admirably to the terrace dynamics of the musical style of the period. The modern author on orchestration usually characterizes the baroque composer's handling of his orchestra as "primitive," but the accusation can easily be refuted by examination of the remarkable consistency of the principles of construction. In the Protestant north the wind instruments, especially the brasses, were preferred, the strings complementing them in the same fashion in which the wind instruments joined the predominant strings in the Italian-dominated south. This relationship was abolished with the gradual change from baroque to rococo. A shift from the polyphonic to the homophonic, with a resultant decrease in the importance of part writing, left the treble part as the virtual representative of the musical idea. This highly expressive and flexible treble part, with its embellishments and figurations, required a different treatment; the choric orchestral ensemble became broken up. As Italian opera and string music had in the meantime conquered the world, displacing the more angular and robust baroque style of the north with its sensuous and vibrant cantabile qualities, the opera aria, the glorification of the human voice, became the model for all music.

In the preceding chapter we followed the intricate process of "the birth of the symphony from the spirit of the opera." Nowhere is this more faithfully mirrored than in the orchestra itself, which, having abandoned the sharp terrace dynamics of the baroque style, undertook to carry out the new stylistic principle of graduated transition dynamics (the famous "Mannheim crescendo") and to reconcile the operatic *accompagnato* and the *bel canto* with the ideals of pure instrumental music. This required a regrouping of instruments. The string choir remained the fundamental body of the orchestra, but its constituent parts were now clearly differentiated. The wind instruments ceased to be treated as bodies of equivalent standing with the strings; they were now required to blend in the scheme of a pliable, unified, yet colorful ensemble. Consequently such instruments as the trumpet, formerly a melody-bearing instrument, were demoted to the modest place of tonal reserves, called upon to reinforce the sonority whenever needed. (We shall see how in the second half of the nineteenth century the demoted instruments regained their erstwhile prominence.)

We have already discussed the elimination of the basso continuo and the harpsichord and the replacement of the missing "orchestral pedals" by wind instruments. By the time of the advent of the great classical symphonic school the orchestra had been completely reformed and presented a wonderfully mobile and flexible body, capable of a great variety of tone color and dynamics, and totally different from the tenaciously constant baroque ensemble. But orchestral "effect" and tone color, however varied and rich, were never an end in themselves, for the classical style subordinated all details to the one central idea of organic creative growth, in which mere effects had no place unless they were in definite and logical relationship to the whole. This does not mean that the classical symphony does not abound in ingenious orchestral effects, but the latter are invariably motivated by the musical material and not by the technical possibilities of the instruments. The occasional "tone painting" indulged in by all composers, from Bach to Mozart and up to Beethoven and Schubert, is infinitesimal—and, one might say, ephemeral—in the great body of baroque and classical instrumental music, and cannot be taken as an index of the prevailing style. Orchestration and tone color serve to solidify and set off the architectonic construction. This is true of the baroque as well as of the classic period, for just as it was against the principles of strict and continuous polyphonic part writing to interrupt linear progression, so the tone color of the baroque instrumental ensemble preferably remained the same for a given movement or part. Contrarily, the dualistic sonata form, with its differentiated sections, demanded a treatment that would properly enhance the antithetic qualities that characterize this type of formal construction. The enormous growth of subjective expressiveness in the nineteenth century forced the instrumental ensemble, from string quartet to symphony orchestra, to emancipate tone color until the latter superseded everything, becoming in the works of the impressionists a formative agent and in many instances the chief aim of composition. The great classical masters looked upon the orchestra as an agglomeration of individual instruments, every one of which could be called, at a given moment, to make its own contribution without impairing the essential unity of the symphonic ensemble, which frowned upon undue individualism.

The orchestral idiom was, as we have said, entirely dependent on the musical idiom proper. This may sound rather obvious and appear to be valid in any era, but in reality it was not the case in subsequent periods. The composers of the classic era knew the idiomatic qualities of their instruments and always endeavored to exploit them—if this was feasible within their general musical scheme. Haydn and Mozart and their many colleagues were most skillful in bringing about an ideal balance of the two; Beethoven made the instruments suffer if they could not accommodate his musical ideas; and still later composers readily altered the ideas themselves to suit the technique of the instruments. The preclassical symphony used a simple orchestration, endeavoring to delineate the form by a judicious deployment of sonorities. In the meantime the florid runs, the syncopations, and the large stock of traditional devices taken from the current operatic scenes of "rage," "lament," "exorcism," "revenge," etc., enriched the expressive capabilities of the orchestra, lending it a vivaciousness unknown to the generation before Haydn. Some of these clichés lived on virtually unchanged and are admired by us as typical examples of pure symphonic style. Thus the imitation of the heartbeat in moments of anguish and surprise, especially popular in the opera buffa, was still causing profound tension in the bass pizzicati at the beginning of Schubert's *Unfinished* Symphony (although nineteenth-century composers were probably not aware of its origin). Specifically operatic elements were the unison and the doubling of parts in the octave, both over-done in the late romantic symphony, but used with subtle effect by the composers of the classic and early romantic eras. These two devices became integral elements of the symphonic style. The unison shows its origins clearly both in the humorous effects in the works of Haydn and Dittersdorf, and in the dramatic pathos and sensuous glow of unison passages in Mozart's instrumental compositions. The Viennese school liked to couple violins with bassoons, violas with oboes, and other combinations at the distance of one or more octaves, a procedure well seasoned in the accompaniment of arias.

The dualistic principle of the sonata also asserted itself in the orchestration and was especially manifest in the alternation of sonorous qualities. Contrasts were obtained by different groupings of instruments, something the baroque would not condone within a movement, but which Pergolesi had already applied in the opera buffa. The increased subjectivism of the Sturm und Drang demanded an instrumental language that could express passionate accents with the effectiveness of the opera. Jommelli and the Mann-heimers prepared the ground; their vehement tutti beginnings, not essentially related to the thematic material but effectively preparing for the mood and form of the composition, still live with undimmed vigor in such works as the *Eroica* Symphony. The classical masters now began to build up tone clusters by alternating and combining the various choirs of instruments, a procedure which would indicate a return to baroque orchestration. This time, however, the purpose in falling back on the choric grouping was not merely the creation of antiphonal effects; the baroque principle of contrasting dynamic complexes was now co-ordinated with the finely differentiated and flexible orchestra of the classic era, forming an admirable combination of the two manners. In general the terrace dynamics and the correspondingly sharp color scheme were replaced by graduated dynamics. This has been interpreted by some modern conductors to mean that every phase has to be extensively shaded. The classical composers were explicit in their instructions and do not require additional "interpretations." If there are no instructions, their absence is not the sign of neglect; it was the composer's wish to keep his tempo and dynamics constant.

We have seen how the dualistic sonata was guided from its infancy by certain orchestral devices such as tutti and solo. The further development of the symphonic idea was always followed, indeed made possible, by similar changes in the orchestral dialect which greatly helped to define and articulate the sections and materials so important in the symphony. The wood winds acquired more and more independence and took part in the increasingly delicate and important thematic evolutions. The true rococo style had been satisfied with a loosely woven two- or three-part construction surrounded with padding; the classical symphony orchestra operated with a full, detailed, and continuous part writing extended to all instruments. To what extent this was carried out can be gauged from works like Mozart's *Jupiter* Symphony, in whose finale even the unwieldy brasses and kettledrums take pride in contributing to the thematic-polyphonic fabric. Canonic elements appeared in the minuets and trios, and the new instrumental ensemble polyphony, the advent of which we noticed in the earlier chamber music of the classical masters, was now judiciously seconded by appropriate orchestration. At the opening of the high classic era in the seventeen eighties, sonata and symphonic orchestration, form, technique of composition, and sonority determined each other collectively. While Gluck was still reluctant to mix the colors of his orchestral palette beyond certain dramatic requirements, the Viennese masters, especially the Singspiel and opera buffa composers, showed themselves past masters in placing a colorful orchestration in the service of musical architecture, and this skill facilitated the effecting of the subtle changes necessary in the recapitulation section of the sonata-symphony. Never before nor after were design and color scheme so perfectly united as in the instrumental style of the classic era.

The orchestral music of the greater part of the eighteenth century was still a "chamber" art, conditioned by the sociological requirements of the times. The customs of French social life, accepted the world over by the aristocracy and imitated by the upper middle classes, called for ensembles that could be manned by a relatively small group of professionals. The numerous amateur organizations of the bourgeoisie, especially the *collegia musica,* were also intended for convivial music making on a rather intimate scale. The average orchestra in Austria, Germany, and England in the third quarter of the century counted about a dozen violinists, two or three violists, and the same number of cellists and double bass players. To this group might be added flutes, oboes, bassoons, horns, trumpets, and kettledrums, but the standard equipment consisted of two oboes, two horns, and strings. Even so, many a symphony bears the note *oboi e corni ad libitum*. In the eighties the range of the individual instruments, and with it that of the orchestra, was greatly enlarged. The virtuoso writing for wind instruments bespeaks a great development in the technique of their playing. At about this time the orchestra began to expand to cope with the demand for more sonority. The impetus came from Italian opera and from French concert life. Leopold Mozart, reporting on the performance of his son's *Mitridate* in Milan in 1770, says that the opera orchestra consisted of fourteen first and fourteen second violins, six violas, two cellos, six double basses, two flutes, two oboes, two bassoons, four horns, two trumpets, and two harps; that is, an orchestra of almost modern proportions. At about the same time the celebrated Mannheim orchestra consisted of eight violins to a part, four violas, two cellos, two double basses, three flutes, three oboes, two clarinets, four bassoons, and five horns. The old discrepancy between strings and wind instruments is still manifest, especially if we count the duke's field trumpeters and drummers, not mentioned in the records but known to have played in the orchestra. The *Concert Des Amateurs* under Gossec again shows a balanced ensemble. As the century advanced the number of performers grew steadily. Handel employed about sixty singers and instrumentalists for the original performances of the *Messiah,* while the centennial memorial performances in the seventeen eighties drafted eight hundred and even a thousand participants. Berlioz, whose fantastic orchestral projects advocated in his book on orchestration seem to us bordering on the ridiculous, would have envied the twenty-six oboe players and the twenty-eight bassoonists, twelve French hornists and twelve trumpeters who played in this immense and unwieldy ensemble.

In spite of the frequent mention of large instrumental and vocal ensembles in the eighteenth century, the more intimate character of its orchestral music demands a small orchestra and its choral works a moderate number of singers. While our concert halls naturally require an amplification of sonority, Schweitzer has recommended for the performance of Bach's works a judicious compromise: a chorus of some one hundred to a hundred and fifty voices and an orchestra of about fifty to sixty players. For the Mozartean symphony an orchestra of about forty should be employed.

At the beginning of the eighteenth century a number of treatises appeared discussing the art of conducting. They were especially numerous in France, where a thoroughly modern conception of the measure and of its indication by means of a baton had prevailed since Lully's time. Besides the baton, used especially in the opera, the conductors often employed a tightly rolled sheaf of music paper or their bare hands. Conducting with a roll of paper survived until the early nineteenth century; Weber led his concert in London in 1826 in that fashion. The Germans as a rule followed the Italian example of conducting from the harpsichord, and only when very large ensembles were called upon did they resort to beating the measure, for they eyed the French system with great suspicion. It was only after the middle of the century that the more modern French method found adherents in other countries. The contemporary theoretical works reflect the confusion between the Italian and French systems, but their polemical tone subsided as the more modern French manner of conducting gained wider acceptance.

The methods of conducting church music, opera, and instrumental music were quite different. In the better endowed court operas there was usually a harpsichord for the conductor and another for the continuo player, who also accompanied the secco recitatives if the conductor did not discharge that function. If singers broke away from the orchestra or dragged their parts, the conductor straightened them out with his clavier. These were all important technical matters, but the chief role of the conductor directing from his harpsichord was the articulation of the music by his harmonies, dividing long notes, emphasizing the beat to keep all the performers informed of the general rhythm, and playing the part of any singer or instrumentalist temporarily lost in his score until he caught up with the ensemble. The accompanied recitatives with their fiery, dramatic passages presented marked difficulties. They progressed in a rhapsodic manner and the conductor had to be on the qui vive, falling in with his chords, followed by the orchestra, before the last syllables of the preceding sentence were sung, in order not to miss the usually exciting chords and runs that punctuated the singer's part and prefaced each utterance. The conductor's duties were so manifold and absorbing that it was almost impossible for him to look after every detail. The concertmaster was obliged to come to his assistance by indicating the measure, either by dipping his violin or by beating with his bow. This alliance of the concertmaster with the clavier director became the typical method of conducting in the major part of the eighteenth century. The *maestro al cembalo,* or *Kapellmeister* (as a rule the local composer), was the more important, while the concertmaster helped him in the preparation of the orchestra and supervision of its proper functioning during the performance. In the second half of the century, and the nearer we approach the end, the conductor was slowly developing into the modern type; that is, he was less concerned with his own compositions, as his duties called for the performance of a variety of others' works. At the opening of the nineteenth century Weber, for instance, was prevented from producing more than one of his own works within a given period.

The double direction of concertmaster and conductor remained the rule throughout the century and was still employed in the Beethovenian era. It goes without saying that such division of office often led to rivalries and discords, especially when, beginning with the seventies, the continuo-playing conductor became an archaism. Then began the ascendancy of the violin-playing concertmaster, who took charge of the conducting of symphonies, while the opera director retained his position in front of his harpsichord. Thus Mozart still conducted his *Entführung* from the clavier. In large choral works the old double direction was, however, retained. Beethoven's Ninth Symphony was still performed under the leadership of the piano-playing conductor and the gesticulating concertmaster, with Beethoven beating the measure. The afflicted master did not realize that players and singers obeyed the two other directors' instructions.

The concertmaster of a fine orchestra tuned his violin to the harpsichord and then made the round of the orchestra, checking the pitch of every instrument. Great pains were taken to arrange the orchestras so that the conductors could be seen by all. In the celebrated theaters in Vienna, Dresden, Stuttgart, Paris, etc., the conductors took pride in a judicious arrangement of their forces. In orchestral concerts it was customary for the musicians to play standing, but later the "Viennese manner" of sitting on benches or chairs gained universal acceptance. Almost every writer in the first half of the eighteenth century protested against the noise made by the choir directors in the churches. They stamped with their feet, hit their desks with the paper rolls, and in general "drowned the music." Mattheson and others pleaded for a visible use of the baton instead of its all too audible employment. Unfortunately the "gros bâton de bois bien dur" mentioned in Rousseau's *Dictionary* was so big and heavy because it was often used not merely to whip the air but to pound the rhythm on some hard object to keep the chorus together. The noise made by the conductor earned him the title of "wood chopper."

There can be no question but that some of these performances were noisy affairs. The contemporaries' complaints and such anecdotes as the one that Lully's death was caused by an injury sustained from a blow by his heavy "baton" have led to the widespread belief that the "ancients" had no conception of conducting, their music making being a haphazard sawing on the strings and whistling on the wind instruments kept together by luck, prayer, and the wood chopper's blows. An eminent modern conductor, Serge Koussevitsky, has declared that "orchestral conducting was born at the end of the nineteenth century and really flourished only in our time." [12] Needless to say, such extreme views must be ascribed to blissful ignorance of the music lying outside the sphere of the modern concert industry. The orchestras of Mannheim, Dresden, Berlin, Paris, London, and numerous other musical centers were trained to high perfection by their able concertmasters and conductors. The string body of the orchestra was drilled separately by the concertmaster, who taught the members a homogeneous technique of playing and saw to a uniform use of the bow. As to the conductors themselves, strict discipline and a high degree of accuracy in execution and ensemble playing were already the order with Lully. Fux, Hasse, Graun, and Stamitz were equally renowned for their painstaking rehearsals and performances. The members of the older school, especially Johann Sebastian Bach, lavished great care on the realization of the figured basses. Whenever possible, Bach wrote them out in elaborate four-part setting, but as the traditions waned and the baroque style began to be diluted, most composers and conductors were satisfied with a rather rhapsodic continuo part, restricted to filling the harmonic gaps in the setting. The conductors examined their scores conscientiously to master their practical difficulties as well as to familiarize themselves with the "affections" expressed in them. In operas and oratorios they knew every word in the text and studied the degree of expressiveness required from the accompanying music. Rector Gessner describes the infinite care Bach took when rehearsing with his small band of singers and players, giving cues and indicating the pitch to the singers, playing the fiddle or the harpsichord, or singing, if it was necessary to make things clear. Mattheson relates how everyone feared the rehearsals under Kusser in the Hamburg opera. So meticulous was this excellent musician that he commanded unsatisfactory performers to go to his home, where he "went over every single note" of the singers' parts until satisfied that they understood his intentions.

With the high classic era the difference between the work of art and its interpretation was reduced to a minimum; at least the graphic aspect of the score was faithfully reproduced in actual sound, and the performers' arbitrary changes now affected not the melodies and harmonies themselves, but only dynamics, tempo, and perhaps orchestration. It became the more imperative to follow the score faithfully, and on this such conductors as Gluck sternly insisted. Handel and Jommelli were feared, but Gluck was dreaded by the members of the orchestra, who demanded and received double pay when he was in charge of a performance, as the hardship of the rehearsals was considered unique. "No pianissimo was delicate enough for him and no fortissimo strong enough." The legends that circulate about the tyrannical requirements of Toscanini pale next to the minute care and solicitude for the utmost faithfulness to the original score enforced by Gluck. He measured the balance of sonority by wandering about the auditorium, listening to his orchestra repeat certain passages, and when the instrumentalists seemed to attain the desired effect every singer came under his scrutiny, followed by exacting demands as to the handling of the stage. Twenty, thirty, or more rehearsals were the custom in Paris, and the finish and élan of the performances astounded all qualified critics. The high-minded master was not satisfied with embodying his convictions in his scores; he insisted that their content be observed to the letter, thus becoming the first great modern conductor a good century before the alleged birth of orchestral conducting. In view of the exemplary competence of the composer of *Orfeo* and *Alceste* it is the more regrettable that his works were, and still are, continually tampered with. From Berlioz, Wagner, and Strauss to Bodanzky, conductors believed that they must reorchestrate these superbly craftsmanlike scores and rearrange the vocal parts.

Mozart was another exacting conductor, infusing his enthusiasm into both orchestra and singers, and laying great stress on good acting.

Among the first to eliminate the harpsichord from the orchestra and conduct standing or sitting in front of a conductor's stand was Reichardt. Although roundly denounced from all quarters, Reichardt's attitude demonstrated that the clavier director would have to cede his place to the baton director, for, as Rellstab wrote in 1789, the accompaniment of a harpsichord was no longer a necessity—only bad singers required it.

The Social Aspects of Eighteenth-Century Music

MODERN historians usually call the eighteenth century the era of the Enlightenment or the century of absolutism. We have touched upon the apparent contradiction between these two notions, which in reality stood in a causal relationship. Another seeming paradox in the era of absolutism was the extension of middle-class influence to all domains of life, its serious ways contrasting with the elaborate social life of the aristocracy. Arts and letters, under this influence, turned away from the scintillating gracefulness of the rococo to the earnestness of classicism. The manifestations were not merely artistic, for there reigned a conviction that the new orientation carried with it a moral uplift, abandoning the "immorality" of courtly art for the recaptured serenity of antiquity, the symbol of which was seen in the Greek column, once more an architectural creed. People surrendered willingly and with relief to a more sober life, divining that by abstinence from the strong beverage of the baroque they could regain their cultural health and be rid of the spiritual hang-over that was the aftermath of their indulgence.

While the spiritual trend and mood was unquestionably a corollary to the increased social and political expansion of the middle classes all over Europe, the barriers between the different social strata were still marked and typical of social life. Nobility and lesser landowners were separated by a deep chasm, and there were caste distinctions within the ranks of each. The rules of social intercourse and etiquette were rigid and were observed by the middle classes not less faithfully than by the nobility. The patrician burgher knew how to assert his superiority over the small merchants and tradespeople. Personal dignity and polite behavior were essential requisites for all and varied in degree only. The nobleman had his footmen and lackeys and insisted on his title; the wholesale merchant must be addressed in a manner that distinguished him from the well-to-do head of a business house, who, in turn, stood above the small shopkeeper. The nobleman studied at the universities or academies but did not take a degree—considered a professional attribute; instead, he went on an extended tour of Europe. Arts and letters flourished, but their representatives held a very low position in the social hierarchy. University professors, very active in all fields and often consulted by the reigning nobility or municipal governments, were treated as servants, and if their advice did not please a king or duke they were thrown into prison. An illuminating example is the case of Johann Jacob Moser (1701-1785), Germany's greatest publicist and the first to apply to the discussion of international law the modern equipment of a learned jurist. Although his writings numbered hundreds of volumes, and every student of law and every German official as well as head of state relied on his opinions, his duke threw him in a dungeon for five years when their views happened to differ on one occasion. The smaller the principality or country, the more wretched was the lot of artist and scholar. Even Goethe, who served an enlightened monarch, often complained of the lack of liberty and the menial tasks assigned to him.

The social position of the musicians sank to the lowest, except in Italy, always appreciative of her artists. They were mere lackeys ("valet de chambre" was the title of the French court composer), dressed in uniform and ranked with the servants in the princely household. As a matter of fact, butlers, gardeners, gamekeepers, and cooks in an aristocratic residence were engaged with an eye to their musical abilities. Haydn's orchestra in Eszterháza consisted partly of such servants, while at other places the entire musical establishment was recruited from the household personnel. It is true, however, that many of these were competent instrumentalists or singers.

Commissioning musical compositions belonged to the noble duties of the aristocracy until and including the Beethovenian era. The commissions came in great numbers, and the composers responded with a large output; the smallest group was about half a dozen sonatas or concertos united under one cover, but a whole dozen was not unusual. Even the young Beethoven was still in the habit of composing sonatas and chamber music by threes, and there is a group of string quartets, *opus* 18, which contains six works. But, unfortunately, the composer's labors were usually wasted and were appreciated only by succeeding generations, because the commissioner most often did not provide for a performance. On the contrary, absolutism and monopoly of possession manifested themselves notably in the arts and letters, for the renown and dignity of a noble house demanded a library well stocked with musical works by noted composers, and these musical libraries remained closed to the public. The emblem of exclusive aristocratic art, opera, remained Italian until the end of the century, because there were no national-popular foundations for it in other countries, while in Italy it was a truly national form of art, shared and enjoyed by the whole population. The court establishments remained, as a rule, inaccessible to the public, and it was only toward the end of the century that court orchestras and opera houses were opened to the citizenry. They then had to pay admission fees, while formerly they had been guests of the local prince or lord on rare festive occasions. The original courtly and patrician musicales gathered together a group actively engaged in playing or singing and others who listened to the performance as guests of the house. Similarly, the student organizations, the *collegia musica,* entertained themselves actively without catering to an audience beyond a few friends and colleagues.

This devotion to music remained general throughout the century, but the new social order brought about another form of public music making. As the bourgeoisie advanced its claims, it found a field of action in the public concerts which it opposed to the exclusive aristocratic circles. While the first real concert organization was the *Concerts Spirituel* in Paris, founded in 1725, the beginnings of public concerts with admission fees charged to the audience go back to the seventeenth century. John Banister (1630–1679), leader of the king's band, seems to have been the first musician to organize public concerts on a profitable basis, according to announcements inserted in the *London Gazette* on December 30, 1672. After his death another member of the royal band, Robert King (d. after 1711), obtained a license to establish a similar undertaking in 1689. Allied with Johann Wolfgang Franck (b. c. 1641), one of the important seventeenth-century German composers of opera, he gave "Conserts of vocal and instrumental music" between 1690 and 1693. Thomas Britton (1643–1714) was perhaps the most curious figure in the London musical world. By trade a humble coal merchant—or, as he was called, "the musical small-coal man"—he was a man of considerable learning, possessed by a passion for music. His business establishment, located in a rented stable, provided the gathering place for noble amateurs and for some of the best musicians of his time. Handel and Pepusch, as well as the members of the audience, reached the upper story through a staircase that was little more than a ladder. The meetings soon developed into what virtually amounted to regular concerts, as a subscription price of ten shillings was charged. At the time of Britton's death concerts were common in London, as can be seen from the London press of the period.

Having received his letters patent from Louis XIV in 1672, Lully saw to it that his "privilege" was interpreted in the absolute sense of the word. It is significant of his formidable power that when more than half a century later Philidor resolved to satisfy the general demand for musical entertainment, he still had to seek permission from the heirs of the great musical dictator. Permission was granted with the following restrictions: the new concert organization could hold public performances on the religious holy days (about thirty-five during the year) when the Académie Royale de Musique (the Opéra) was not in session; Philidor furthermore had to pledge himself not to present even a fragment of a French opera nor any vocal piece with French words. A large room in the Tuileries having been arranged for the purpose, on March 18, 1725, the first Concert Spirituel took place amid great applause.[13] The programs were not restricted to choral and orchestral works; virtuosi, both vocal and instrumental, soon appeared, to the great delight of the audience. With the acceptance of foreign virtuosi, foreign music other than Italian made its entrance into French musical life, notably the heretofore totally unknown products of Germany. The concerts continued with fair regularity, although endangered by frequent financial difficulties and by the death of Philidor (1728) and some of the subsequent directors. By means of incessant negotiations, exacting leases, and other financial burdens imposed upon the organization, the Académie Royale finally obtained its desire, control by the Opéra itself.

Concert organizations existed in other French cities, notably in Lyons, Marseilles, Nantes, Troyes, Dijon, Nancy, and Strasbourg. These were conducted in the spirit of civic service, with complimentary *billets* sent to the local worthies, civil, military, and ecclesiastic authorities. The military commanders were given tickets to be distributed among such of their soldiers as were interested in music. But the best concerts of the period were given by Riche de la Pouplinière's private establishment, especially after the middle of the century, when it counted among its performers and patrons all the great musicians, French and foreign, who visited Paris. The immense wealth of the *fermier général* permitted him to import the musicians needed for the performance of such novel works as those of Johann Stamitz which called for horns, then unknown in the Parisian orchestras.

During the "hostilities" of the buffoon war the Concerts Spirituel profited from the excitement by performing, in 1753, Pergolesi's *Stabat Mater*, which remained a standard fixture of Holy Week until the end of the century. By this time the personnel of the society counted some fifty singers and forty instrumentalists, with a large organ installed in the hall. This respectable force was employed in the performance of symphonies and oratorios, the ban on singing in French having been tacitly overlooked. Beginning with the seventies the Concerts Spirituel became the model and envy of the world. All the great traveling virtuosi were welcomed there, and the inclusion in the programs of the works of Gossec, Handel, Stamitz, Wagenseil, Haydn, Mozart, Jommelli, Piccini, Johann Christian Bach, Toeschi, and many others indicates the remarkable variety of the offerings. The great success of the undertaking inspired other ventures, among them the Concert des Amateurs, which, under the able leadership of Gossec, attained exceptional importance in the history of orchestral music.

In Germany, meanwhile, Doles, the Thomascantor, enlarged the old *collegium musicum* in Leipzig, giving public performances in the Inn of the Three Swans until 1763, when Hiller took charge of the undertaking, henceforth called *Liebhaberkonzerte*. In 1781, the civic pride of the merchant city having been aroused by the popularity of the concerts, Burgomaster K. W. Müller appointed a committee of twelve to organize twenty-four yearly concerts to be given in a concert hall in the Gewandhaus, the Cloth Hall. Hiller continued to be the leader of the new society. Vienna followed suit with the *Tonkünstler-Societät,* the first German institution of professional musicians, founded in 1771 after the model of the Concerts Spirituel. Its first leader was Florian Gassmann, the celebrated Viennese composer. Karl Friedrich Christian Fasch (1736–1800), son of the great composer Johann Friedrich Fasch, transplanted the Concerts Spirituel to Berlin by calling to life the *Singakademie* in 1790, with which he revived choral singing, fallen into desuetude in Germany.

The modest beginnings of concert life in England progressed with equal vigor. In 1765 we read about the excellent performances given under the leadership of Johann Christian Bach and Karl Friedrich Abel, both of whom were mentioned in connection with Mozart's visit to London. After Bach's death Abel continued the concerts, but a new organization similar to the Viennese Tonkünstler-Societät, known as the Professional Concerts (1783), eclipsed his reputation. Led by the famous violin virtuoso, Wilhelm Cramer, the Professional Concerts offered subscription series in the Hanover Square Rooms. These, in their turn, were supplanted by a new body formed by their concertmaster, Johann Peter Salomon (1745–1815), an eminent violinist, fine-grained musician, and able impresario. The Salomon concerts presented Haydn to England and inaugurated the brilliant musical life of the end of the century.

The growing mass of music consumers changed the whole aspect of musical life. The international exchange of composers and compositions that forms the backbone of modern musical life started on a large scale. In the second half of the century the compositions of the members of the Mannheim and Viennese schools were played all over Europe, their quartets and symphonies being printed by several publishers and pirated by others, a state of affairs which bespeaks a great demand. The number of traveling virtuosi grew steadily, and the cult of *Wunderkinder,* so popular in the nineteenth century, got under way.

The love of music reached proportions that cannot be realized by the public of the twentieth century. The aristocratic bands played all day, and it was not unusual to perform half a dozen or more symphonies or concertos at one sitting. Concerts took place in all imaginable locations: in inns, taverns, theaters, churches, and aristocratic palaces, between the intermissions in oratorios, in parks, and in the great halls of the universities. The most significant element in this new musical life, and the one largely responsible for its intensity, was the large fraternity of musical amateurs. Composers, who formerly addressed themselves exclusively to princes and archbishops, now turned to *Kenner und Liebhaber,* connoisseurs and amateurs; there was even a periodical, appearing in 1769, entitled *Der Musikalische Dilettante,* devoted to their service.

Orchestras engaged for concerts were usually *ad hoc* ensembles made up of music-loving amateurs; only toward the end of the century could Mozart or Beethoven count on the collaboration of a professional theater orchestra. But even among the concertizing artists dilettanti were not rare. Toward the middle of the century almost every town, castle, university, and church had its orchestra, and many musical associations gathered for weekly musical exercises. The Academy of Ancient Music was one of the oldest of these associations. Established in 1710 in London, it counted among its members distinguished amateurs and professionals united in the study and performance of vocal and instrumental music. The Madrigal Society, founded in 1741, while not the earliest in England, can claim the honor of being the oldest society in continuous existence. The great vogue of vocal chamber music in England is reflected in the Noblemen and Gentlemen's Catch Club (1761), with a select membership of royalty and aristocracy complemented by eminent professionals. A similarly exclusive club was the Anacreontic Society, established in 1766. The Caecilian Society, devoted to music more or less religious in nature, began its career in 1785, acquiring great merit in the propagation of Handel's and Haydn's oratorios. The colonies were not far behind the mother country in their zeal for music. The first musical society founded in America was the St. Cecilia Society in Charleston (1762), followed by the Harmonic Society in New York (1774).

These and the many *collegia* and *convivia* on the Continent, the innumerable chamber music ensembles in the homes, and the private and church orchestras, consumed an amount of music which spurred the music publishers to modernize their industry. John Cluer (d. c. 1730) seems to have been the originator of the beautifully engraved editions that came out of England in the early part of the century, while John Walsh (d. 1736) succeeded in issuing at low prices Continental music reprinted from Dutch editions. By stamping pewter plates instead of engraving on copper, a much more expensive method, he could compete with the many Continental printers, at the same time offering superior products. The Leipzig firm of Breitkopf & Härtel, long famous in the printing business, started the extensive printing of piano reductions and arrangements of operas and Singspiele which provided the dilettante with literature for the home. This was made possible by the invention of typesetting by the head of the firm, Johann Gottlob Immanuel Breitkopf (1719-1794), which reduced the costly process and made possible a sort of mass production. The house of Breitkopf & Härtel also organized the trade of music along modern business lines, keeping a large stock of printed and manuscript scores and issuing periodical catalogues remarkable for their thematic indexes.

In Bach's time the dilettante's task was such as would frighten most present-day professionals. He had to play from a figured bass and improvise a good deal of his part. After the middle of the century the music came to him in a finished form, and if he mastered his instrument to a degree he could play almost anything; his only problems were technical. Therewith disappeared the creative element from the music lover's activity. As the old art of improvisation, continuo playing, and "mental counterpoint" disappeared, little was left to the imagination; the scores carried ample instructions for every detail. The professional musicians soon felt the repercussions of this trend. As their technical ability increased, their formerly universal musical training and knowledge decreased. Quantz, Leopold Mozart, Emanuel Bach, and their colleagues were not only the authors of treatises summarizing the technical and theoretical properties of an instrument, or the practice of the general bass; they testified to the comprehensive knowledge of the well-trained musician, characteristically cultured and catholic in taste. No matter what his instrument, the musician of the earlier eighteenth century was acquainted with the whole field of music and was expected to be conversant with everything musical. With the rapidly increasing influence of the dilettante and the dissemination of music in the middle-class home, the high cultural level of the executant musician was constantly lowered, with the resultant rise of the specialist. The orchestra violinist knew how to play his instrument well, but he was little concerned about the rest of his art.

The general tendency in intimate music making in the home was away from the vocal chamber music of the earlier centuries and toward instrumental music. It was at this time that piano playing became a social requisite, such as the cultivation of the lute had been during the Renaissance. To the number of active participants and amateur-connoisseurs we must add a new factor, the passive participant, the listener, whose tastes and desires were henceforth to demand acknowledgment from both composer and performer.

Musical Criticism and Historiography

THE variety and wealth of this musical life demanded guidance, needed equally by composer, performer, amateur, connoisseur, and listener. The answer was musical criticism. Musical criticism is determined by sociological factors, for it deals with musical life. The performance of a composition transforms a mute score into reality; the critic deals with both aspects. Musical life follows the metamorphoses of social life, and criticism in the modern sense could develop only with the increasing availability of the art to human society. Rationalism prepared the ground, for it taught people to approach all manifestations of culture with a critical appraisal. The public was no longer a courtly aristocracy bound by traditions, nor even a specific stratum of the middle classes; it was a mixture of all. The social barriers were not lowered, but an interpenetration of the spiritual values affected in common by the Enlightenment was inevitable.

There were many polemical pamphlets and learned dissertations on certain technical or speculative phases of music, but Mattheson's *Critica Musica* (1722–1725) was the first periodical to assume a critical attitude. Its title should not be interpreted too literally. The criticism, applied to the whole body and organization of music, did not echo the musical life of the period but was, rather, the position and orientation of one individual, still primarily a scholar, who was eager to teach and to enlighten. Another of the early editors was Lorenz Christoph Mizler (1711–1778). A pupil of Bach, a philosopher, mathematician, and physician, he was a musical scholar of parts and is remembered as the founder of the Association for Musical Science (1738), a society which listed among its members the leading musicians of the period. Although touching on criticism, Mizler was still a scientist who considered philosophy and mathematics the most important prerequisites to music. With Scheibe [14] the theoretical and practical lines of music converged, as the author of the *Critical Musician* differentiated between science, that is, music itself, and art, its performance. The writers now began to realize that a purely rational conception of musical phenomena was insufficient and tended to question the role of mathematics as advocated by Mizler. The great stylistic revolution of the eighteenth century from the contrapuntal to the homophonic, and from style galant to classicism, is mirrored in their writings, hesitating between intellect and sentiment; but Marpurg's warning that criticism should consist not only in emphasizing shortcomings but also in detecting the beautiful and accomplished was beginning to be heeded. The growing concern with musical life and a corresponding estrangement from mathematics invited the critics' interest in the aspects of musical life that were distinctly outside the sphere of speculation, presenting sociological, political, national, literary, and technical problems. They began to campaign against Italian opera in Germany and in England, then they took up the whole question of opera: its "bad libretti," the ridiculous acting of the singers, the castrati and their privileged position, the shortcomings of staging. The sociological implications are noteworthy, for what was criticized was the residue of a former aristocratic musical civilization, now felt to be incompatible with the ideals of the middle classes. The books, no longer dedicated to the ruling potentates, were addressed to connoisseurs and amateurs, which was a much larger public, dominated by the nonprofessional music lover. This new public demanded a new manner of writing.

Toward the middle of the century the "critical" literature increased. Marpurg published his *Critische Musicus an der Spree* (1750), *Historisch-critische Beyträge für Aufnahme der Music* (1754–1760), and *Critische Briefe über die Tonkunst* (1760). In Marpurg we are dealing with a scholar and littérateur far superior to his immediate predecessors. While not less learned than these, he declared that his writings were more in the interest of the practical than of the theoretical side of music. With him we are virtually leaving the field of musical scholarship to enter into musical life proper. This statement requires, however, qualification. By musical scholarship preceding the mid-eighteenth century we mean mathematical-philosophical speculations and not the thoroughly scholarly exposition of musical theory. Therefore, when Marpurg disavowed any interest in the "theory" of music he referred not to the theory of composition but to the theoretical speculations on mathematics, physics, and kindred subjects. Indeed, with him began the first critical appraisal of published compositions.

All the men mentioned so far were active musicians with a varying degree of talent. Then came a real composer, Johann Adam Hiller, a man of excellent education and convinced of his mission as was only a Gluck, a Weber, or a Wagner. His Singspiele were intended for the public, and so were his writings. As his Singspiele were the antithesis of aristocratic opera, so were his writings in sharp contrast to the baroque literature on music, for they were imbued with the spirit of the new social doctrines emanating from France, aimed at a middle-class public. Instead of complicated philosophical parables, his *Wöchentliche Nachrichten und Anmerkungen die Musik Betreffend* (*Weekly Reports and Remarks Concerning Music,* 1766–1770) gave his readers a sympathetic discussion of the artists' compositions; the generous attitude was maintained even when the type of music under discussion was not to the critic's liking, as was the case with the works of Bach, Handel, and Gluck. And now another modern phenomenon appeared in musical writings: the reporting of musical events.

Johann Friedrich Reichardt was, after Hiller, the most significant writer and critic of the century. He was a man of the world who corresponded with Goethe and engaged in polemics with Kant and Fichte; besides being an eminent composer, he was endowed with a sense of humor and was well read in every field. The rationalistic approach was left even further behind in his *Musikalische Kunstmagazin* (1782), a journal almost romantic in tone. The artist was idealized here and placed on the pedestal once occupied by the scientist—who alone, according to Guido's famous poem, understands true art, while the mere musician "sings whereof he knoweth not, a mere brute is he." [15] This was, then, the chronicle of a new musical life, the life of the bourgeoisie; and since this implies the end of the former international courtly art freely exchanged between the ruling classes, it is natural that reports from foreign lands were of value and interest to the middle-class readers, accustomed to a German musical life and ignorant of the world at large. Both Hiller and Reichardt published accounts of what they learned from their travels through Europe. The rationalism of the doctrine of the affections had presented the critic to the public in the nonpartisan third person. With Reichardt the first waves of early romanticism displaced the last remnants of a doctrine that had lost all significance to the musician of the classic era. Reichardt addressed his readers in the first person and dared to confess in print that he was so moved by the overture to Benda's *Ariadne* that he scarcely noticed the curtain and the beginning of the first act. The modern personal element, the subjective attitude toward art and the artist, had now come, and with it modern musical criticism.

These enlightened musicians and critics endeavoring to bring music to the people also recognized the dangers inherent in popularization as compared to the decreed excellence of courtly art, and they insisted that the more widespread the practice of music and its literature becomes the more imperative it is that this variegated musical life be directed by qualified people. At the end of the century there appeared Johann Friedrich Rochlitz (1769-1842), a thoroughly trained musician and man of letters, the first professional musical writer and critic who had no other occupation and held no office. We shall see his great influence and initiative in the Beethovenian era.

The individual literary ventures soon attracted enough attention to entice the Hamburg music publisher, Westphal, to sponsor the *Magazin der Musik,* headed by the first professional music editor, Carl Friedrich Cramer (1752-1807), whose only concern was the literary conduct of the periodical; the business end was handled by the far-flung connections of the publishing house. Most of the eighteenth-century journals were not long-lived, because the organization of musical life was at a turning point. Authors and editors were well aware of this, and planned their papers rather as fascicles of a book; whenever a periodical ceased to appear, the fascicles were gathered up, bound together, and issued in book form.

On the heels of the critic came the historian. In former periods the history of music was made, not written; all literary efforts were limited (in so far as they were historical and not theoretical) to the discussion of the music of the ancients. At the beginning of the seventeenth century a certain historical tendency had become noticeable in Calvisius's *Exercitationes Musicae Duae* (1600) and in the first volume of Praetorius's *Syntagma Musicum* (1615), but the first chronicle of music was the work of Wolfgang Caspar Printz (1641-1717). Entitled *Historische Beschreibung der Edlen Sing und Kling Kunst* (1690), this engaging book was a typical baroque mixture of scholarship and fantastic playfulness. Old legends, Biblical and medieval, mingled here with cloudy information concerning the composers of the older centuries; the approach was essentially literary and uncritical and the aim the usual eulogy of the glorious art and science of music. This same tone, largely borrowed from Printz's work, dominated musical historiography until the middle of the eighteenth century.

In the meantime the scientific attitude of the Enlightenment had taken possession of musical historians. It is only natural that this new tendency should have made its appearance in France. Pierre Bayle's monumental *Dictionnaire Historique et Critique* (1697) set the new scientific method for every branch of learning and bore fruit in the field of music. Pierre Bourdelot (1610–1685), Abbot of Massay Abbey in the Char Department, France, collected material for a history of music which he elaborated in co-operation with his nephew Pierre Bonnet (1638–1709). The work was finally published in 1705 by Bonnet's brother, Jacques (d. 1724), under the title *Histoire de la Musique et de ses Effets depuis son Origine jusqu'à Présent.* True to the French method of philosophic-scientific investigation, the maze of legends and uncritical anecdotes was here scrutinized and brought into order and continuity. Whatever the shortcomings of this work, it represents the first serious attempt at systematic musical history.

The preliminary and tentative essays—including Padre Martini's work, which was of monumental proportions but again failed to go beyond the times of the ancients [16]—were all overshadowed by the two English histories of Burney and Hawkins, prepared independently and published by coincidence in 1776. Charles Burney (1726–1814) called his work a *General History of Music,* while Sir John Hawkins (1719–1789) used the more formidable title of a *General History of the Science and Practice of Music.* Both works addressed themselves to an intelligent public, that is, to what would correspond to the German Kenner and Liebhaber, at the same time safeguarding the principles of research and the utilization of original sources. Burney was a man of considerable learning and an accomplished musician, and his work surprises one today with its freshness. While he never minces words and is always liberal with his own opinions, the organization of his material (collected in libraries and on a number of fact-finding expeditions to the Continent), the delineation of periods, the establishment of schools headed by outstanding masters, and, most remarkable, the constant allusions to contemporary cultural currents, make his *History of Music* an incomparable scholarly achievement.

Hawkins was not a musician. He was a distinguished jurist and author, biographer of Dr. Johnson. His great five-volume work has often been rated below that of Burney, yet the latter, who published the three remaining volumes of his own essay after his competitor's complete history had appeared, made good use of Hawkins's ideas. Burney the musician was more artistic in the performance of his task, but Hawkins was the more meticulous scholar, with uncompromisingly earnest judgments, the soundness of which is still admirable. Instead of opposing the two excellent treatises, they should be considered as complementary, thus forming an invaluable source of information for the study of the eighteenth century.

Burney has been accused by modern writers of having given "whole pages to long-forgotten and worthless Italian operas, whilst the great works of Handel and J. S. Bach remain unchronicled; the latter indeed is almost ignored" (Grove). But again, this is demanding of the eighteenth-century scholar the reflection of our own ideas, which is patently impossible. Burney tells us what he ferreted out in Germany and Italy, and certainly few people in those days would have given preference to the cantatas of the obscure old cantor in Leipzig, whereas an opera by Galuppi (forgotten but scarcely "worthless") made the rounds of all theaters. With all his concern, assiduous work, and insight into the nature of music, Burney still echoed the views of the true Englishman of the Enlightenment, to whom music was "an innocent luxury, unnecessary indeed, to our existence, but a great gratification and improvement of the sense of hearing." Hawkins, on the other hand, seriously condemned the "vulgar notion" that the ultimate end of music is amusement. He regarded the art as a phenomenon which must be approached by scientific thinking "to demonstrate that its principles are founded in certain general and universal laws."

The Germans learned from both the English and the French intellectual currents. Much less experienced in public life than the two western nations, and always given to abstractions, they immersed themselves in a philosophical exploration of all the problems of life and existence. They deepened the doctrines of the Enlightenment and emerged from its impasses. This was one of the most important achievements of German classicism. Thus it was within Germany that Hawkins's desire for scientific thinking and for the exploration of the "general and universal laws" of music found an echo in Forkel, a musician at Göttingen University. Göttingen belonged to a state whose ruler was the King of England. The political relationship had its repercussions on cultural life, and English thought was unmistakably present in the principles of research. English thought and the revolutionary ideas filtering in from France combined with the traditional and dogmatic academic learning of the German university, diluting and humanizing the latter, and producing a school, especially in historiography, that was unique on the Continent. The scholars, working in perfect entente, undertook the ambitious task of presenting a new summary of the history of science, allotting every field of learning to an acknowledged specialist who, nevertheless, was governed by certain principles binding on all.

Johann Nikolaus Forkel (1749–1818), doctor of philosophy and director of music at the university, undertook the task of writing the history of music. Forkel's work was facilitated by the large amount of research placed at his disposal by Martini, Burney, and Hawkins in their essays. Other important additions to the existing literature were the *Essay sur la Musique Ancienne et Moderne* (1780) by Jean Benjamin de Laborde (1734–1794), a scholar who followed in the footsteps of the admirable French school of scientific investigation, and the various works of Gerbert. The first volume of Forkel's *Allgemeine Geschichte der Musik* appeared in 1788, the second, carrying the history of music to the mid-sixteenth century, in 1801. What distinguished the Göttingen doctor from his predecessors was that he was a scholar professing a conception of the history of music based on cultural philosophy seconded by aesthetic-psychological considerations. To him music was the highest manifestation of the language of sentiment, a God-given blessing to humanity; hence his sharp criticism of Burney's *History*. The philosophical basis of his conception of history was the evolutionary theory advocated, following Leibnitz and Herder, by the celebrated historians of Göttingen. This conception, the firm belief that music and the other arts are steadily growing from a lower to a higher order, really landed him in Burney's domain. His conclusions, reached after the most painstaking research and exemplary collation of material, were invalidated by the preconceived attitude of the scholar of the Enlightenment. In the final analysis the music of the Middle Ages and the Renaissance was to him as primitive as it was to Burney, and polyphony, preferably of a sacred sort, the final aim and the crowning glory of musical art. But Forkel must still be counted among the founding fathers of modern musicology. His *Allgemeine Literatur der Musik oder Anleitung zur Kenntnis Musikalischer Bücher* (1792), together with the works of Gerbert, opened the way for modern research.

Unlike the rather austere Forkel, Martin Gerbert (1720–1793), Abbot of the Benedictine Monastery of St. Blasien, strikes one as one of the great medieval polyhistorians. Searching through the libraries of Germany, Italy, and France, and corresponding with the important musical and ecclesiastic scholars, especially with Padre Martini, he acquired a knowledge of medieval music unequaled by anyone before him. Such works as his *De Cantu et Musica Sacra* (1774) and the invaluable collection of medieval theoretical writers, *Scriptores Ecclesiastici de Musica Sacra Potissimum* (1784), still take first place on the bibliography of every modern medievalist.

Failure of the Enlightenment to Produce an Art of the People

THE central motive in the movement of the Enlightenment was the deification of man's mental life and the urge for the secularization of every other aspect of life. The aim was to render every authority answerable to reason, and the latter was to derive absolute norms from experience. The realization of this ideal was much more feasible in the sciences than in cultural life in general. Still, while the original goal was not reached in arts and letters, the attempt to realize it caused significant changes. Secularization of cultural life was accomplished to a marked degree, but sovereignty of the individual as contrasted to the sovereignty of the scientific mind was not attained, for the very good reason that most people—knowingly or unknowingly—want to base their opinions on some authoritative source. Thus sovereignty of the individual was converted into sovereignty of the people, of the nation. At first the absolute monarch personified the nation, but later a differentiation set in within the nations. The notion of "the people" had changed.

In the Middle Ages the people represented the whole nation, comprising all estates, as opposed to the possessors of scientific knowledge, the clergy. Beginning with the end of the fifteenth century, scientific knowledge having been appropriated by certain upper classes of lay society, the term narrowed down to denote the rest of the population whose naïve mental life was not yet disturbed. The people had their own music, and the upper classes had theirs. As the upper strata of society acquired cultural wealth there arose a dualism in art music—still conditioned, however, by the Church. The aesthetic elements of popular music and art music were divergent from the very beginning. The people, knowing nothing of Boethius, followed their inclination toward the major-minor tonality. They also adhered to systematized rhythm and meter instead of to the complicated mensural theory of art music; their dance songs and their poetry gave them natural rhythmic patterns. All this popular music was very modest in proportion and restricted in range. Medieval historians have barely taken notice of its existence, while modern use of folkloristic material is seldom lacking in a certain preciousness or antiquarian taste strangely contrasting with modern harmonic and orchestral devices.

Yet the impact of this unsophisticated music on art was tremendous. We have seen how the unspoiled musical instincts and cherished traditions of the people of the north called polyphony to life, how their reluctance to listen to the Latin service made them interpolate words in their own tongue into the liturgic text, and how they came to equip these words with music of their own. We have seen how the harmonic instinct of the populace as reflected in the songs of Italy converted the great Flemish contrapuntalists, giving rise to the magnificent madrigal art of the Renaissance. We have seen how the Catholic Church tried unsuccessfully to prevent popular elements from intruding into its music, and how Protestant church music was associated with popular music from its inception. And we have seen how popular unwillingness to accept life in a stilted form created the opera buffa, the ballad opera, and the Singspiel, the constant source of rejuvenation of the lyric stage. We should expect that with the socio-cultural changes of the Enlightenment music would finally produce a sovereign culture of the people, but the growth of musical culture on profane soil no more led to an exclusive style of the people than emancipation from the clergy led to a secularization of life. In both instances the Enlightenment accomplished only the first step toward this aim. In music the result was an international art called classic, while the process of secularization, reaching a sudden and dramatic fulfillment in the French Revolution, was again followed by a relapse. In the meantime the bourgeoisie began its artistic ascent by opposing to the international courtly art its own organizations.

Once again popular music had to be content with a compromise with formal art music, lending its freshness and unaffected grace to the master craftsmen skilled in the art of composition. The indestructible vitality that throbs in the works of the "Viennese" school is nourished by the tunes and rhythms of the Austrian, Bohemian, and German peasants. As we are leaving the eighteenth century to enter the century of romanticism, we must take leave of this spirit, for the spontaneous influence of popular music, its effortless blending in symphony and opera, will cease when romanticism discovers the people and makes use of their resources deliberately and with varying degrees of success and faithfulness.

Chapter 15

THE CONFLUENCE OF CLASSICISM AND ROMANTICISM

※》 《※

Classicism versus *Romanticism*

THE century of the Enlightenment closed its process of emancipation with a cataclysmic storm of liberation, yet the new century opened under the aegis of a new Caesar. From the maelstrom of the rights of man emerged the boldest of tyrants; the liberty of the masses, so earnestly desired and so exuberantly feted, ended in the reign of one individual. The reaction which usually sets in after such oscillations from one extreme to the other was surprisingly different from the expected, for instead of a reversal to the liberal tenets of the Enlightenment, the political movement ended with the establishment of national monarchies as the universal type of state in Europe. Imperialism reigned as a new Caesarism, but saturated with the spirit of nationalism. So strong was the renewed imperial idea that it was felt even by Japan, Mexico, and Brazil. The state was now identified with the empire and the people with the state, of which they were the support both morally and by furnishing the armies, which were formerly mercenaries. In the eighteenth century the people were the spectators, in the nineteenth they became the actors. Socialism, during the Enlightenment a sort of literary Utopia of a few individuals, became a world factor: first an idea, then a party and a reform, and finally a world outlook. Liberalism continued as a heritage of the eighteenth century, but, flanked by two powerful neighbors, it had to take a relatively mild middle course. At first it was naturally attracted to the left, toward socialism, and until the 1848 revolutions liberals and socialists formed an almost united front, but the attraction of nationalism made itself felt, as the liberals identified themselves with the nationalistic wars for liberation from foreign bonds.

With the advent of the nineteenth century, "Europe" became more than a geographic term. The political ideal of the new century was unification not the dynastic particularism of eighteenth-century absolutism, but a federation of available territories and resources. As early as 1812 voices were raised for the formation of a united German Reich, and the hopes of Baron Heinrich Friedrich Karl von Stein (1757–1831), the great Prussian statesman, for the nationalization of Germany were prevented only by the Congress of Vienna. The federal idea led to the conclusion of alliances and to the holding of congresses, which, beginning with the Congress of Vienna, in 1814, disposed the future of the world by sitting in judgment. In 1819 Claude Henri, Count of Saint-Simon (1760–1825), the French social philosopher, wrote about the "reorganization of European society," while the great powers assembled at the Congress of Aix-la-Chapelle created the "concert of European nations." The United States, realizing the implications of the alliances, proclaimed the Monroe Doctrine, while the various Slavic nations dreamed of a return of the Slavic world.

How remote all this was from the ideals of the Enlightenment! The intimate aristocratic atmosphere of the eighteenth century, with its courts and salons, was forgotten in the large assemblies of parliaments, alliances, confederations, syndicates, and trade-unions; its small residential cities, fine palaces, and dwellings overshadowed by metropolises, barracks, factories, warehouses, and tenements. Everything was organized in ever-growing proportions. One would expect all these tendencies, to which one might add a renewed clericalism and the new movement of internationalism, to result in a complete suppression of the individual, for they were all aimed at the most effective organization of the multitude. Indeed, Saint-Simon preached the abolition of inheritance in order to bring about a leveling of society, and even strongly individualistic England experienced the beginnings of a cooperative movement promulgated by that fearless and admirable social reformer Robert Owen (1771–1858) in *A New View of Society* (1816). Capitalism, coming of age in the nineteenth century, tried not only to amass and rule money and goods, industry and communications, but endeavored to create a monopoly of these by international business relations. Both men and materials were collectivized, and small industries were swept away. From 1804 to 1830 the guilds of artisans in England shrank to one-third of their former size, and small landowners were similarly reduced. Even in agrarian France, commercial and industrial centers were formed with a resultant growth of cities. And even socialism, apparently the antithesis of capitalism, was not opposed to mass production and collectivistic economics; on the contrary, it wanted to "expropriate the expropriators."

Religion and philosophy also joined the cause of efficient organization, the former uniting the various Protestant denominations and renewing a militant Catholicism, the latter expounding new universal doctrines, as Hegel spoke of the *Weltgeist,* the world spirit, and Humboldt of the cosmos. Herder opened the century with a desire for the union of the arts, and Wagner closed it by fulfilling his wish. Indeed, romanticism was engrossed with the idea of the fusion of all arts; its poets painted, its painters made music, and its musicians painted and wrote dramas. The great historical canvases of the romantic painters needed literary elucidation, while, correspondingly, mural painting blended with architecture. In the Pre-Raphaelites, music and poetry converged almost indivisibly, Daumier was a veritable painter-journalist; the novelists Stendhal, Balzac, Gautier, and Mérimée depicted their subjects with the exactitude of character painters; Goethe, E. T. A. Hoffmann, Stifter, and Mörike painted and composed. Kleist thought to find the secret of poetic form in counterpoint and pretended that his dramas were composed musically, the protagonists being more "voices" than figures. Swinburne's haunting, intoxicating, and unrestrained lyrics are melodic in a musical sense, and the poet wanted them to be considered musical in nature; Whistler called his paintings "symphonies and nocturnes, harmonies in tone." On the other hand, the musicians turned to poetry and drama, and one of their ranks capped the whole century with his formidable, all-embracing Gesamtkunstwerk.

The nineteenth century reveled in friendship, idealized in the relationship of Schiller and Goethe and in the Schubertian circle, which included, besides a number of musicians and amateurs, Grillparzer, the dramatist, and von Schwind, the painter. Instead of the salons of the eighteenth century, clubs and associations of every imaginable sort, religious, political, artistic, and scientific, were the natural gathering places. This was also the time of the organization of political and economic parties and leagues: the Anti-Corn-Law League, formed at Manchester in 1838 to secure reform of the laws; Chartism, a movement in England for universal suffrage and Parliamentary rights (1838); the Gustavus Adolphus Union (1832), a society founded by the German Protestant churches to aid their sister institutions in Catholic lands; and innumerable others.

This dynamic era of action and organization, which tried to seize upon and unify everything, we call the period of romanticism. The urge for binding, for union, remains the essence of romanticism, and love and friendship—again forms of association—were its chief subjects. The romanticists were the poets of the apotheosis of love and the most passionate champions of friendship—Shelley wanted to be drunk of love, which to him was the only law of the world, and sang in *Queen Mab* the golden age of the omnipotence of love—but they carried both from intimacy to extensity, from individualism to universalism. This fanaticism that swirled everything into unity, that found all ideas kindred, was a direct answer to the cool and deliberate articulation of the Enlightenment. Romanticism strove to restore life and ideas to their erstwhile and natural unity, which was severed by the Enlightenment. The Enlightenment separated and limited; romanticism bound and united. But all this we must reconcile with its extreme subjectivism, usually cited as the sole characteristic of romanticism. The romanticists lived on the subjective, but by widening it from the individual to the social they created subjective universalism. Soul and matter, spirit and nature, melted into love and the love of the infinite. An ideal wonderland was envisaged in which everything was reconciled, heathenism with Christianity, past with future, heaven with earth, man with beast. To express their souls in lyricism was not enough for these dreamers; they wanted to envelop the world with their soul, the romantic ego wanted to go out into the world, into the universe of spirit and nature. Romanticism started with the cult of the ego, and yet to the extent that it grew it tried to escape from itself, finding the subjective too isolated and meaningless unless brought into relation with the universal. One of the fundamental traits of romanticism is a longing for the infinite. It never accepts the present without reservation, always searching for something else and always finding indications that that something is better. One might say that a romanticist becomes a romanticist only when he experiences the desire to be different from what he is, when he is filled with longing.

Romanticism did not know classic measure and poise. The object of its artistic efforts was not man in his ideal isolation, for it always saw man in his relationship to infinite nature, to infinite space, with man as the center of sensation, as the focal point of all sentiment. Everything was animated by this relationship, and through it received life and meaning. Nature became revelation, the expression of human experience; thus romanticism abandoned itself to nature and lived wedded to it. Hölderlin and Novalis, Byron and Shelley, Schubert and Weber, all sang and thought with nature, unlike the men of the Enlightenment, who loved in nature the idyllic only. But the romanticist was filled with nature, in which he immersed himself, feeling himself mystically, pantheistically one and the same with it.

Romanticism permitted the real to remain valid but liked to attach to it mysterious connotations. Thus it did not suffer mere reality, full, true reality; fantastic seeing and spiritual experience were its guides. The true romanticist could not and would not be a naturalist. He declined the naturalism which, announced by the Sturm und Drang, returned again a century later in the so-called postromantic period, for this he considered false and inartistic. The conception which saw "reality" in every segment of nature and life appeared to the romanticists too narrow, too uniform, too everyday, and—untrue. They felt that life had much more to offer; hence their flight from the so-called realities, hence their search for other civilizations through which they could prove the fundamental correspondences of humanity, hence their urge to unite arts and letters into a universal medium. They rediscovered the Middle Ages and discovered the Orient, both seen through history as homogeneous cultures.

As the romanticists extended their studies, turning to the civilizations of the Orient, they realized that every true culture of the past was founded on religious mythology and received its impulse and nourishment from religion. The worship of the classic world of antiquity had already passed its peak and was not mystical enough; therefore they endeavored to evolve a new mythology from forces that could still be made living and universal, and so they inevitably returned to Catholicism. They became convinced that every other system of philosophy is limited compared to Catholicism, which embraces man's whole existence and permeates into its smallest particle. None of the philosophical systems could offer this, for in their eyes the other systems did not organize models of existence; they merely offered certain formulae. Romanticism surprised Rome by directing toward the Mother Church an endless stream of German converts, re-enforcing the propaganda carried out by the Catholic romanticists, de Maistre, Lammenais, and Chateaubriand. What tempted these Germans was the universality of the *una sancta* Church which they missed in their own Protestant religion. In their zeal they condemned the Reformation as humanity's second falling into sin, lavishing praise on the Society of Jesus as the symbol of the unselfish service of Catholicism.

All this, of course, had little to do with true Catholic piety; it was the escape of restless and overwrought spirits to the soothing bosom of the age-old community of the Church, sure and imperturbable—a "holy anesthetic," Gundolf called it. Thus Catholicism seemed to offer fulfillment to romanticism's longing for the infinite, but when we read the many fiery professions of faith it becomes evident that the romanticists were too subjectively human in their idealism really to abide by the unilateral requirements of the Church. They Catholicized, but they were not Catholics; what they desired was merely a union of all faiths, a totalization of love and friendship. What they expected from religion was the elevation of man from finite to infinite life; religion was to them nothing but a segment of the romantic cult of the infinite.

Romanticism was not a new movement. Its three fundamental traits, youthfulness, longing, and intoxication, have transcended all historical and geographical barriers as ever-recurring human qualities since classical antiquity. But if this be true, what is romanticism? A period in which the romantic became dominant? One might say so, but the idea of romanticism must then be taken in its more profound meaning, for it has become a household word as badly misused as "classicism."

The romantic is a universal phenomenon of all times, all zones, and responding to various names; it was at the bottom of the Gothic period and was a living force in earlier, pre-Christian civilizations. It can be followed everywhere in human history, sometimes dominating, at others accompanying, a period of culture. The romantic was, then, not a discovery of the romanticists; it was merely a rediscovery, a reawakening of an ageless human quality under a new name; a new resumption of earlier romantic energies, a new attempt at the solution of the romantic problem, undertaken at a definite time and at definite places, at first under Protestant and later largely under Catholic influences. The romantic was still living in the second half of the nineteenth century, though not in its erstwhile ampleness, for life in itself is romantic and always has been; but it was no longer romanticism. The rekindled liberal movements of 1848 pushed romanticism into the background, and it has never again come to life in its original guise. The weak pseudo-, post-, and neoromantic rivulets, silted up by the bourgeois-idyllic, cannot be seriously considered as worthy successors of the great currents of romanticism, even if they were legitimate offspring. The many grandchildren and great-grandchildren inherited little from the mighty maternal stream; romanticism was not reborn in them and could never be begotten by them, for there remained little of the profound integrity of the artistic, cultural, national, and religious efforts of romanticism. This late romanticism no longer led, it abducted; it ignored the most important problems of life and fled into an atmosphere where life would not challenge it; it became aestheticism. This is no longer life itself, but an attitude toward life; this neoromanticism is life in a pleasing selection. No matter how many truly artistic moments there are contained in it, they are only moments, for on the whole it is an artistic formula, artistic atheism.

Romanticism was not a sort of chaos like the Sturm und Drang, nor was it a demoralization of classicism as it is still often regarded. It rested on definite precepts from its very inception. Taking its departure from the rationalism and radicalism of the Enlightenment and the Revolution, from the Sturm und Drang, and from the abstract idealism of classicism, which it found to be an insufficient concept of life, it set out to develop a cultural ideal. Europe accepted romanticism as a new order and built on it a great civilization; but after the middle of the century this civilization became tragically disorganized because it had abandoned its original patrimony for the sake of *Weltanschauung,* world outlook, the term significantly coined by the era. Its poetry turned to drama and its fantasy found the theater the most congenial medium because the theater unifies, and addresses itself to, the multitude. Thus the century culminated in the theatrical universal art of Wagner, which brought the passions to a *Totalausdruck,* the sum total of all human passion and experience.

The centrifugal forces engendered by the irrational elements taken over from the Sturm und Drang, slumbering in the womb of classicism, came into their own in the romantic era. Nevertheless, romanticism should not be taken as the antithesis of classicism, nor was it a mere reaction to it, but rather a logical enhancement of certain elements which in classicism were inherent and active, but tamed and kept in equilibrium. For the irrational elements which now surged on the surface were nothing but the subjectivistic tendencies we have been encountering since the close of the seventeenth century. It is only in their vehemence that we feel a direct opposition to classic measure. And thereby the stylistic relationship between classicism and romanticism seems determined.

Romanticism did not create an entirely new style; it merely developed certain forms in a one-sided manner, displacing others or giving them new significance or new functions. What separates romanticism from the Sturm und Drang is the positive and constructive nature of romanticism as opposed to the destructive urge of its predecessor. The romanticists were irrational not in their aims, but only in their means, and romanticism is no more mere lawlessness than classicism is sheer form and order. Romanticism is not, then, an adversary of classicism. To the romanticists, Goethe and Beethoven seemed to have embodied most of that which was dear to them and toward which they were working; in combining the deification of Goethe and Beethoven with their own ideals, they merely carried the accomplishment of classicism into the unrealizable.

The Romantic Movement in Germany

THE romantic movement was different in every country. Conservative England, always fond of gains made through experience, did not care for the complicated mental processes rife in Germany. France held fast, as in the seventeenth century, to her classical ideals. Sturm und Drang and romanticism touched her superficially only; her own romanticism in the nineteenth century may have been kindled by outside influences, but it was essentially nourished from native sources. Although France was the center of the upheaval, the revolutionary spirit made an about-face there with startling rapidity. Freedom was turned into order, in 1797 a royalist majority was at work, in 1799 Napoleon was elected First Consul and Christian worship and the old calendar were reinstated. In England, too, poets such as Coleridge, Wordsworth, Southey, and Landor abandoned their youthful revolutionary ideals of freedom and equality and turned to a conservative romanticism. In Germany, however, the romantic strain was old and vital. This remains true despite the classic ideal of the end of the eighteenth century, here more majestic and productive than in any other country; for if we look at the base of Hellenism in Germany we shall find that the only uncompromising priest of Greek classicism was Winckelmann. No one else, not even Goethe, remained unflinchingly faithful to the ideal. While many writers and artists approached the classic ideal, in others a strong romantic tendency was present, as the German, unlike the Frenchman, could never subscribe to the sanctity of artistic doctrines.

But there were other reasons why romanticism had its first and greatest flourishing in Germany. Great spiritual movements operate according to the rules of natural forces, that is, they throw their weight at the point of least resistance. At the end of the eighteenth century the least resistance among the western nations was offered by Germany, strictly speaking the youngest of European civilizations. This youth proved to be a blessing, for, compared to the political life of older civilizations, hers was so rudimentary that a participation in the shaping of the world's history was not likely. We know that even in the midst of the wars for liberation, Goethe placed his only hope for the development of Germandom in its spiritual genius. Unlike France, Germany did not carry the heavy burden of seventeenth-century classicism, and she had passed through the upheaval of the Sturm und Drang, the discoveries of which she could salvage for the treasury of romanticism. Her sons were emancipated without a revolution because they were free and their great and variegated civilization spelled order and creative force. Their revolution came only after the passing of classic arts and letters, after the death of Goethe and Beethoven. The French revolutionaries fought for their freedom with the "mentality of slaves," as Cousin has said; they were not free men but slaves who broke their yoke. The Sturm und Drang, one might say, was a revolution, but it did not reach a climax; on the contrary, it ended in classicism of the purest water, in order and harmony. It became heroic in arts and letters, not on the barricades.

The first period of German romanticism was rather theoretical, even in its artistic creations. Programs and manifestoes, battles to lay down principles announced an artistic movement before its real advent. This predirected activity of the writers of the early nineteenth century would have made them deliberate and doctrinal but for the fact that the program was not followed, and also that personality cannot be stifled even by its own program. Kant's synthesis quieted the restless search of German philosophy for a reconciliation of will and intellect, nature and freedom, subject and object. But Johann Gottlob Fichte (1762–1814) made the synthesis problematic again by deducing the universe from the creative function of the absolute ego. The ego recognizes objects of nature as relative to it, as instruments to be used for its progressive realization. This was the first philosophical exposition of the metaphysical longing of romanticism. Fichte's philosophy was complemented by the natural philosophy of Friedrich Wilhelm von Schelling (1775–1854). According to him, nature was to be looked upon as an organism, and a unity of plan was to be sought in considering the production of organic life. This, he and his followers professed, would bring back man, detached from nature, into a metaphysical bond with her, for the laws of nature and the laws of the spirit are identical. The universe thus became an organic whole; what was still needed to complete the metaphysical firmament of the new outlook on life was to find a way to God again and to restore religion to its central position, then the domain of romanticism would be fully equipped. This last decisive step was made by Friedrich Schleiermacher (1768–1834).

The literary program as a program was first announced in the works of the Schlegel brothers. August Wilhelm Schlegel (1767–1845) founded, with his brother Friedrich Schlegel (1772–1829), the Athenaeum (1798–1801), around which rallied the seekers of the new thought. The elder Schlegel, the greatest critic and translator of German romanticism, was able to arrange in good order the results of the collective work of romantic theory and practice. His Shakespearean translations are the triumphant crowning of the struggle for the romanticization of the German language and of the world of Goethe. His championing of the *Nibelungenlied* gave the Germans their own *Iliad* and awakened interest in the German people for their old poetry. His *Lectures on Dramatic Art and Literature* (1809–1811) outlined the future path of the movement, not only by means of the principles expounded in them but also by means of their new conception and appreciation of world literature. The younger Schlegel's development is a faithful mirror of the whole movement. Taking his departure from Goethe's vicinity, he was first attracted by aesthetic-artistic problems, which he followed by historical, sociological, and philosophical studies, to arrive, guided by history and religion, at a cultural Catholicism.

Among the brothers-in-arms fighting devoutly with the Schlegels was Ludwig Tieck (1773–1853), the only one among the early romanticists who conquered the fragmentariness of the movement by poetry. He played on every string of the Sturm und Drang, then, under the mask of rationalism, declared war on his previous excesses, and wound up, in his stories and fables, as the poet of romantic miracle and music. Tieck, whose influence on future generations was incalculable, was himself strongly impressed by Wilhelm Heinrich Wackenroder (1773–1798). Dying at the age of twenty-five, Wackenroder left no large works, but what little he wrote had epoch-making consequences. With impatient fervor he proclaimed the rights of art above those of reality; his appreciation of art is prayerful, his picture gallery the temple of devotion. *The Outpourings of the Heart of an Art-loving Cloister-brother* (1797) is a great protest against rationalism and formalism, a denial of Lessing's order and Winckelmann's ideal of plastic beauty. Wackenroder discovered for the romanticists the Gothic world which provided them with that medieval fiction they desired so much, but with the Gothic world he also provided a literary approach to aesthetic-cultural Catholicism which became one of the prime moving forces of the movement. This glowing young man was the first to recognize and proclaim the kinship of Germandom and music, and his own prose was saturated with musical elements. He was also the first to exhibit that hatred of the Philistine, the romantic horror of the gray, everyday spirit who cannot understand art.

The chaotic richness of Jean Paul (Johann Paul Friedrich Richter, 1763–1825) is representative of the complications of the romantic soul. But in him there is nothing left of Greek classicism; his intensely musical language is not dampened by classic measure, and his soul is nourished by unruly Pietistic ideas. There is a great deal of the conventionalism of the older German and English novel in his works, but the world of small merchants, village parsons, petty lawyers, and schoolteachers, though still present, slowly opens its gates to romantic lyricism. The men change, they are born with a longing soul, they discover that they have an inner world. Jean Paul's lyricism and even his prose are rooted in the cultivation of this "impressionism."

The true and great lyricist of this early romanticism was Novalis (Friedrich von Hardenberg, 1772–1801), the embodiment of that lyricism in which Hegel saw the essence of romanticism. In his hymns language, reborn from the mystery of death and love, discards the fetters of rhythm, rhyme, and molded surface. His novel, *Heinrich von Ofterdingen*—which, although fragmentary, is the greatest monument of early romanticism—tries in the magic atmosphere of the fable to achieve the impossible: the restoration of the broken metaphysical unity of life. The naïve mysticism, the fervent Catholicism, the poetic, fantastic, and subjective illumination of the Middle Ages began with him. His novel created the mystic "blue flower," the unattainable blue flower, which became the symbol of romanticism.

Early romanticism had two dramatists, Zacharias Werner (1768–1823) and Heinrich von Kleist (1774–1811). Werner's dramas were born from the crossing of romantic music with Christian mythology and thus were exposed to every current, suffering every contradiction, the most irrational stylization and the heaviest realism. While not the founder, Werner was the most effective representative of the romantic drama of fate. Kleist saw the ideal aim of dramatic art in the reconciliation of antique form with modern content, but like all the early romanticists he merely found the road to Hellas without traversing its entire length. The sheer beauty of his novels and dramas and the consuming fire of his imagination make him one of the great figures of the world's literature. His characterizations are unsurpassable in their penetrating fidelity, but he does not draw them with the calm superiority of the artist, for he always struggles with himself, often straying into pathological regions. His style and diction are surcharged with an explosive tension, the fever of a constant pursuit in which his soul drives itself toward the unattainable.

Ernst Theodor Wilhelm Hoffmann (E. T. Amadeus Hoffmann, he called himself, 1776–1822) was the most complicated and capricious personality of early romanticism, a truly great artist but a dissonant soul whose irony was turned against his own self. Magnificently tender and poetic stories and fables alternate with horror novels in his works, in which the intertwining of romantic and realistic imagination provides a bridge between the two tendencies. His influence on both these directions in German literature was enormous. This extraordinary man was a musician, and with him music—a powerful component, as we have seen, of every form of romanticism—demanded its own recognition.

Poetry is not the best means of expression of the German genius, partly because this genius is too rationalistic, partly because it is too abstract. Its rationalism is not practical, like that of the English; it is theoretical, with its final threads leading not into the immanent (Newton) but into the transcendental (Leibnitz). Therefore drama and novel, the forms of realism, are well represented in English literature at an early period, whereas in Germany they come on the scene comparatively late. German lyricism, on the other hand, rises to great poetry only when it approaches the beloved intellectual sister, Greece, as in Goethe or Hölderlin, or if philosophic thought fertilizes the poet's fantasy, hindered in its endeavor to soar into the transcendental by the restraint of rationalism, as in Schiller. Where, however, rationalism could not clip the wings of imagination, German genius created the greatest: in religion, the most transcendental of domains; in philosophy, where reason and transcendentalism run parallel, enhancing each other; and finally and most intensely in music, where rationalism either disappears altogether, as in Mozart or Beethoven, or is converted in some sort of philosophy, as in Wagner.

"Without music," says Ludwig Tieck in his *Phantasien über die Kunst,* "earth is like a barren, incomplete house with the dwellers missing. Therefore the earliest Greek history and Biblical history, nay the history of every nation, begins with music." The early romanticists held that only music fully embodied their poetic ideal. They derived speech from music, considering the various languages "individualizations of music." In the latter half of the century Nietzsche proclaimed the origin of tragedy from the spirit of music, believing that when words are exhausted and are no longer able to convey the artist's sentiments, they turn into music again, thus closing the circle. Music begins where the language ends, said Wagner, whereas a century earlier Voltaire had maintained that what is too stupid to be said is sung. "No color is so romantic as tone," said Jean Paul, and Schumann called music "romantic in itself." E. T. A. Hoffmann also believed that music is the only truly romantic art and addressed Beethoven as a romanticist, while Hölderlin was ashamed of his language, which he found poor and expressionless compared to music. No other art could express the longing for the infinite, no other art could bring men into such close contact with the universe, and no other art could provide so direct a way from the multitudinous to unity—to the achievement of the romantic ideal, the union of all arts, the Gesamtkunstwerk; and even when achieved, it was this urge toward this goal which made the romanticists seek to couple word with tone so that music could become a world philosophy. "Music is the art of the arts," said Wackenroder, "for it is able to detach the sentiment of the human soul from the chaos of earthly existence." Music became to romanticism the symbol of infinite unity.

The Classic-Romantic in Literature and Its Counterpart in Music

AS soon as we turn to our specific subject, music, we realize that we are faced by a grave contradiction. We have just enumerated the many testimonials that music is the romantic art par excellence, only to discover that we have not yet reached the end of the great classic period in music. And now, with this in mind, we must take another glance at literature. When classicism was at its apex, romanticism was barely getting started. The ballads of Wordsworth and Coleridge appeared in 1798, and Tieck and Wackenroder published their first works when Haydn was rising to the summit of his art. The consolidation of romanticism came later in the century, when the last giants of classicism, already affected by early romanticism but still saturated with the mighty instinct for order, discipline, form, and synthesis, departed. While the alternation of classic and romantic is acceptable to most historians of culture and art, it is equally true that there are instances when the two are not alternating but are running concurrently, confronting but also penetrating each other. Such was the case at the beginning of the nineteenth century. We cannot make the imaginary line drawn by the changing centuries visible, for it would cut into classicism, which stands there as a necessary and logical beacon to guide both the departing ship of the eighteenth century and the incoming ship of the nineteenth. Perhaps the greatest strength of classicism, its greatest mission, is fulfilled by the act of bringing the two vessels into waters safely navigable for both. They sail past each other and "speak each other in passing," heaving to under the protection of the beacon. And the acme of classicism, Goethe and Beethoven, was attained in that interval when the ships spoke to each other.

In Hegel, Schelling, and Schleiermacher, classicism and romanticism met, in Beethoven classicism became romantic, and in Schubert romanticism became classic. The classicists in general often appeared romantically inclined in their youth and again in their old age. Schiller began as a real exponent of the Sturm und Drang and called his own *Maid of Orleans* a "romantic tragedy." Thus we should not categorically oppose the two tendencies. The Sturm und Drang was certainly a romantic preamble, and it appears that classicism provided the bridge between preclassic Sturm und Drang and postclassic romanticism; for the classicists too were born from the former, and the first generation of romanticists were to them as younger brothers.

As we examine the literature and the music of the early romantic era, we begin by discovering one fundamental difference between the two: romanticism produced a philosophic-aesthetic literature which practically set its program before the movement developed; the musicians did not present such a program and did not form a school to fulfill the theories advanced. It was only later that a certain esprit de corps became manifest under literary influences. On the other hand, the lack of a program and of its acknowledgment by the composers belonging to various periods of the romantic movement caused great confusion in style criticism and classification. If Weber, Chopin, and Schumann are accepted as full-blooded romanticists, we certainly cannot enroll the composer of the *Unfinished* Symphony and of the glorious C major Symphony in their company. The boundaries were constantly extended in both directions; the Sturm und Drang phenomena in Mozart have been called romantic, together with the melancholy pathos of Tchaikovsky, and finally Bach; in like manner, Richard Strauss and Elgar have been claimed for the same movement. What we so loosely call romanticism is not the romanticism of the great figures of the heroic period of the movement, but the mood established by the composers of the second half of the century; for, again, we must remember that in contrast to the classic era the movement did not culminate in the synthesis of the great masters, but proceeded from the outstanding composers through a leveling process to the lesser. It is the same confusion of "romantic" and "romanticism" that we discussed at the beginning of this chapter. There is little of the profound preoccupation with the problems of romanticism of Chopin or Schumann in Grieg or Tchaikovsky; they may be distinguished composers in their own right, but romanticism was no longer an ideal to them, only an artistic métier.

We usually consider the new forms of vocal music, the art song and the romantic opera, as representative of the whole romantic era, and other musical products are customarily measured by comparison. But if this is valid we are again baffled by Schubert, who was not in quest of the mythical blue flower, of the unattainable, but reveled enthusiastically in the attained perfection. While the longing of a Chopin or Schumann is indescribable, Schubert experiences the absolute, the finished, the unsurpassable. In him the German song reached its pinnacle. There was, however, another Schubert, the composer of incomparable instrumental music, and this romanticist gave us the greatest, the richest post-Beethovenian symphonies, written with the sure hand of the classic symphonist although undeniably saturated with romantic elements. Such breadth, such mastery of symphonic thought, was with this exception denied to the romanticists, and only one composer in the whole succeeding period, Brahms, could match it. But while Schubert's symphonies were written in the immediate and actual neighborhood of Beethoven and were fresh and positive, in a springlike bloom, the four magnificent symphonies of Brahms are autumnal, heavy with resignation, the Indian summer of the symphony. While Schubert was still able to sail lustily into symphonic struggles, not shying from the consequences of their vastness, Chopin and Schumann were unable to cope with them, and Mendelssohn was virtually afraid to face them. This inability was almost tragic in Schumann, always so gallant and full of hope.

It took a long time for an artist to come to the fore who was willing and able to face the realities and to assume toward them an unflinching attitude. This was Brahms, but he belongs to still another period. The romantic spirit ranges freely in his works and his indebtedness to his romantic predecessors, in particular to Schumann, is never minimized, but he no longer piles up experience upon experience in breathless haste. The romantic element is accepted, but the composer is not dissolved in it. We are beholding a new struggle, the struggle of the romanticist against the very sap that nourishes him, the romanticist who wants to rise above the shackles of romanticism—for this they became to him—in order to compose, to build and shape, like a classicist. The profoundly human qualities of his music, its intensity and impact, impress us as deeply as Beethoven's, for our compassion and fascination are again aroused as with the Titan of the nine symphonies, but for totally different reasons. For Brahms did not succeed. He could not achieve the impossible, he could not recapture the serenity of the classicist as he could no longer really believe in their tenets. Hence the resignation that envelops his works, the pessimism which is his outlook on life. He was no longer a romanticist, yet he could not become a true classicist. The true romanticist might be melancholy and reticent, but he was so in works congenial to his lyric genius, that is, in compositions that did not try to fill in large forms no longer understood by the post-Beethovenian generation. Men like Chopin and Schumann, by following their romantic instinct, reached the highest spheres of musical poetry.

In the midst of the final splendor of classic symphonic architecture there appeared another romanticist of the purest water, entirely free of formal doubts and scruples and as profoundly convinced of the righteousness of his cause as was Beethoven. The musical romanticism of the forest, this most Germanic of romantic moods, was the creation of Carl Maria von Weber. The *Freischütz* and its sister works shower us with the contents of a treasure chest, the riches of which were gathered up by every succeeding composer, not the least among them Schubert. These riches are not mere coloristic effects, they are realities, even facts, a wholly new musical climate.

The woods and groves, the fairylands and gnomes of early romanticism, waned; the domain of the romanticist became his innermost soul, his sentiments. No vestiges of a real world remained, and nothing coarse disturbed the spiritual quality of the music. This was a true idealism, but it, in its turn, had to give way. The worshipers of "form" killed it. The priests of l'art pour l'art crippled art, for the form they championed was merely a pleasing arrangement of surfaces, not an inner necessity striving for articulation. Form, real form, is the mastery of matter, but what is brought into submission is alive, as much alive as the force that reigns over it. This is the lifeblood of form, for this is its ethics.

While the epigonous composers established the comfortable world of forms and idioms that still manages to keep alive, men imperious and egoistic, and fully aware of the realities of life and art, appeared and, led by Liszt and Wagner, disavowed ethereal and other-worldly existence. They were great and bold artists who recognized the futility of living on the crumbs of a bygone era, who knew that every true art must find its own forms and means of expression—and they set out deliberately to find them. They were aware of the world around them, and, instead of trying to forget it, they drew it within their orbit. Wagner was not listening to celestial whispers, he himself decided on the future; with tremendous concentration of energies he aimed at nothing less than the attainment of the ultimate possible. Superlatives were the real fare of these men, and success a matter of course. The composer no longer struggled: he created and commanded; he gave the law, for it was himself. He had only one duty, to impose himself. This was not the active creative force of Beethoven or the dreamy longing of the romanticist for the unattainable, but the restless and ruthless urge toward the limits of the humanly attainable. These limits were known to Wagner, who never lost sight of them; and now we realize that such forceful, purposeful, dynamic, sensuous, and premeditated ideals are in contradiction to the longing for the endless, the ethereal, and the disembodied which actuated the romanticists. Isolde, dying, glorifies *höchste Lust,* the highest ravishment, and the paroxysm of sensual orgy overflows all bounds. This is possessing, not desiring; the blue flower is wilted by the desiccating heat of consuming passion.

Compared to classical maturity, romanticism seems youthful. This youthfulness is its most typical characteristic; its heroes either die or fade when young. Romanticism is also fragmentary because of its urge for the infinite and its insistence on color and on the union of many diverse elements. The classicist also worships unity. To him contrast and unity, separation and wholeness, individuality and universality, subject and object, man and world, all can be reconciled and brought into a unison; but while these opposing forces are balanced in the classic, they are tossing about in the romantic. Nothing is considered more poetic by the romanticists than the mixture of the heterogeneous. Winckelmann's century emphasized contour and design, the romantic era, color. The romanticists were colorists not only in painting but also in music, in poetry, and even in their Weltanschauung. This colorism was not, however, joy in the variety of existence, as in the Renaissance; it was, rather, an expression of the intoxicating fullness of experience. The superabundance of adjectives, of colors, of harmonies—that is, of decoration—weakened the substance; it did not permit things to appear as they were, but illuminated them with a general mood. Romanticism sought not the limited, actual phenomenon, but only its image. Intensification, enhancement, and enlargement were inborn with the romanticists; they spoke of the poetry of poetry and of the philosophy of philosophy. The urge for the absolutistic colossus, for the monumental, possessed the nineteenth century from the time of Napoleon and is manifest everywhere, in the poet's conception of Cain, Mazeppa, and Don Juan, as well as in the *Symphonie Fantastique* and *Thus Spake Zarathustra*. Even the sensitive poet of impressionism, Baudelaire, wrote Wagner that what impressed him most in his music was its greatness and vastness. But the greatness they worshiped was not so much a mathematically measurable majesty as a dynamic majesty—oppressive, powerful, and intolerant—and this was embodied in one heaven-storming individual, Berlioz.

Classicism stands firmly on the earth for it does not cross the threshold of the absolute and does not attempt the final explanation of existence; therefore it was not interested in metaphysical speculation. This speculation announced itself as soon as the ground under man's feet ceased to be solid, when his life became problematical. The dependence of the German mind of the nineteenth century on philosophy to stimulate and expand artistic endeavor often inhibited the creative genius of the artist. "All art should become science, and all science art" was their motto, and they considered poetry the key to philosophy, whereas a few decades before Kant had categorically denied poetry admission to philosophy. Romanticism left the Enlightenment's cult of man behind, for it found man too human, and art above him. To the classicist it was man who elevates the artist, and thus his process was an ethic one. The romanticists proceeded from revolution to restoration, following the times and experiencing its ravages. The classicists continued serenely in their own sphere, taking in the unfolding new century, struggling profoundly with the Promethean temptations; but the struggle was in their innermost soul, and what they gave us was harmony, heroic harmony, and this penetrated and transfigured every gesture. Only music could achieve this, and as the eighteenth century found its fulfillment in music, so the nascent nineteenth century still found its purest and noblest tone in music—the Titanic music of Beethoven.

Beethoven

THE mood that possessed Germany in the era of the Sturm und Drang provided the atmosphere for the young Goethe and the young Schiller. The conflict between man's natural claims and convention was realized and presented in various forms—*Götz von Berlichingen, Werther, Die Räuber, Kabale und Liebe.* They derived their peculiar energy from the forces of their times—an era whose strongest incentives for a new life were in the spirit of opposition against existing ideas and institutions. Men found themselves in social circumstances that led the nation from economic slavery to a free modern order, from princely autocracy to a participation of the middle classes in the government, from the domination of the nobility and the courts to an assertion of the rights of the citizenry. In the ensuing campaign wide possibilities of progress opened up, with new aims on the horizon. More than anyone else, Ludwig van Beethoven (1770–1827) lived in this movement and was carried by it.

There are natures which can walk erect only, to whom life would be worthless otherwise. In every note and every word of Beethoven, from the time he first became articulate, this erect stature and proud majesty of soul spoke with convincing assuredness. He felt, he knew, that his was a creative power to which all opposition in the matter with which he dealt must succumb; he formed it after his will and filled it with the contents of his soul. Thus was born a peculiar music, music that was the incarnation of strength and integrity. There is in these sounds nothing of the dreamy weaving of sentiments which casts such a spell over the musical lyricism of the romanticists; the emotions in them are sired by great and fully conscious intentions, governed by ideas, hence their unheard-of unity. The main impression they create is of greatness. No other musician has ever approached this gigantic, never-slackening will power; no one has ever coerced so impetuous, demonic a nature into following the dictates of his will under all circumstances, converting its energies into sheer creative power. This trait, the salient feature of his mental disposition, was, then, enhanced and conditioned by the temper of his times. The elemental necessity of his soul to rise above the individual through great, objective aims distinguishes him from his older classic brothers. But there was also the difference in the age, for, unlike the others, Beethoven did not grow up in the subjective Sturm und Drang era; when the young man came to Vienna, attention was focused on the more universal problem of social freedom. There is always something in him which stands above his personal fate; he was the poet of the ideal. In this idealism he identified himself with the point of gravity of his period, which stood for a friendly progress toward the realization of the dignity, freedom, and beauty of man, which it palpably believed capable of achievement. It is only natural that a man of such active nature, always proceeding from preconceived ideas, will take a stand relative to every great force of his time, will utilize it or will oppose it.

The most classic of dramas, Goethe's *Iphigenia in Tauris,* announces the redeeming force of pure humanity, Euripides's *deus ex machina* conquered by humanity. The exhilarating problem now was to elevate the individual into the universal. Egmont and Tasso perish, but Faust succeeds. Faust, the Promethean man, beholds Arcady, although his path has led over the dead body of Margarethe. He is Goethe himself, reaching the eternal peaks of knowledge through the wild Walpurgis Nights, now acquiescing in law and order, whose barriers he stormed with such vehemence. He is the universal, the eternal man who lives the whole gamut of human experience, the Everyman, not saved by divine misericordia but by his eternal humanity, which destroys Satan. As in Goethe and his Faust, one beholds this genius in Beethoven.

Eighteenth-century classicism sought immersion, appeasement of the heart. Beethoven's harmonies, like Schiller's, are eruptive; these men were no longer made for a quiet life. The urge for freedom that dominated the second half of the eighteenth century lived in Beethoven as in the other classic geniuses. This humble son of a menial musician discarded the wig and raised his head as the first modern artist who felt himself the equal of princes, profoundly convinced of the dignity of man and fanatically believing in freedom. And his music echoes this personality tenfold. Goethe himself was stunned and frightened by this "untamed personality," and by this "grandiose, great, and mad music." Every one of Schiller's dramas, from the *Robbers* to *William Tell,* is a formidable protest; in all of them a single person or a whole people champions an idea. The heroic ideal which permeates Beethoven's whole being is the same, the heroism of the liberty-loving German classicism, and this keynote is manifested in every one of Beethoven's musical gestures. How truly heroic and uplifting they are as compared to the decorative and dazzling but exterior and even unconvincing fanfares of the French school of the Empire. The French were burnt out: all they could do was to stylize or be theatrical. Beethoven's Coriolanus and Egmont, his anonymous heroes of the Third Symphony, the *Sonata Appassionata,* and the Mass in C are worthy of the ancient epopoeia, for they stand at the summit of human nobility. Beethoven proved convincingly that true idealism is heroism; with him we reach the limits of the classic conception of the heroic and perhaps the ultimate limits of heroism expressed in music. He came as the herald of the nineteenth century, the musical prophet of will power. He rose from the spirit of the war for freedom, and, threatened with what for a musician is worse than death, he beseeched God to give him strength to "conquer himself." The firebrand and bacchant became a classicist through self-discipline.

Beethoven was to a certain degree drawn to the spiritual sphere of romanticism. There can be no question as to the numerous threads that lead from him to the romanticists, but to count him among the latter amounts to a fundamental misreading of styles, for Beethoven grew out of the eighteenth century; the whole immense wealth of that century was concentrated in him, and what he did was to make a new synthesis of classicism and then hand it down to the new century. The romantic elements in the early Beethoven do not contradict his pure classicism, for the effects of the Sturm und Drang created a "romantic" crisis in all the great classicists. In his very first trios and piano sonatas that appeared as *opus* 1 and 2 (after a considerable number of earlier compositions, which were left unnumbered), the uncertainty as to his future course gave way to a definite profession of faith in classicism, clearly visible in his espousing of the ideals of three great classic masters, Haydn, Clementi, and Cherubini. It is in the nature of the classic genius that it organizes itself and everything around it. How much of the eighteenth century still lives in Goethe and Beethoven, how much of the naïveté and fresh straightforwardness of the Enlightenment—and how truly were they still designers and not painters.

All classicism rests on equilibrium—not a rigid but a living equilibrium of forces and functions. All classicism seeks relation, proportion, and form, achieving unity in the identity of form and material. The whole nature of classicism is a middle path, but not because of half measures or indifference, for the equilibrium is the result, and not the point of departure. The scales between the contending forces never stand still. The romantic is what overflows from the boiling cauldron of the overheated style of the period and forms its own world. It usually dissolves the classic elements. The sharply designed contours of classic melody are loosened; classic harmony abdicates its structural functions and becomes vacillating, even aimless, while on the other hand exhibiting a colorfulness and variety unknown to the classicist. The temptation to follow romantic voices was not missing in Beethoven, but there stood his tremendous will to mold, to carry the gospel of thematic logic to the limits of human power and understanding. These limits he reached at the end of his life, at the time when romanticism was a victorious reality. Unconcerned digression in tonalities without provision for a safe return is unknown to the classicist. He is always watching his compass to conduct his modulations and developments. This does not in the least mean a lack of variety or a stifling of the imagination. On the contrary, it requires the greatest architectural skill and fantasy. The bolder the modulations, the more admirable the logic that is brought into play.

The romanticists took over these principles and established a whole code of formal laws, but the essence of tonal logic, its really form-building qualities, were lost. We are only too conscious, especially in the larger sonata forms of the romantic composers, that after an indulgence in rich harmonic adventures they suddenly resort to their code of formulae and force their way back, for there must be a recapitulation and the subsidiary material must be brought back in the tonic key. We often say that Beethoven burst the forms, but such a statement is really meaningless, for with the classicists form is result and not aim. What seems to be enlargement and variant from the traditional is, in reality, new and does not rest on arbitrary acts but on necessity in order to frame the composer's thoughts. Thus, from Beethoven's point of view, it is as much "according to the rules" as the conventional form seems to the pedant. The romanticists were carried away by rhythm; seizing the natural emphases, they abandoned themselves to the pulsating alternation of certain patterns until, in the later works of Schumann (to cite one example), such patterns dominate whole compositions. Beethoven places his sforzati with dogged determination on the offbeats. Weight and accent do not appear to him as simple natural phenomena; they must be organized and elaborated according to his will. Nothing escapes his iron fist; no rhythmic pulsation is permitted to flow past uncontrolled, and even if meter and rhythm develop "naturally" they are merely permitted to do so. But all this is the unique privilege of the classicist; Haydn and Mozart were equally masters of their music. They were not led; they commanded.

The romanticists searched every corner of their world, they infused themselves with its beauties, but they did not attempt to rearrange their universe; they surrendered themselves to it. Beethoven remained a classicist, and no matter how many threads lead from him to romanticism and from romanticism to him, he never became a romanticist. He never changed his belief in the duty of the creative artist, and while, in his last decade, the temptations became more intense and required Herculean self-discipline, the works of this period acquired a peculiar greatness from the inexorable will power which kept them intact. Occasionally this severe regimen caused an acute hypertrophy of will, rising to the highest tonal regions where tonal sensation proper, dominated by the energy of the élan, was all but lost. But no matter how deeply he was stirred or carried away, the rudder never slipped from his hands to whirl masterless.

The great problem of nineteenth-century music was the union of poetry and music. The romanticists hoped to include mimicry, painting, and architecture in the universal art. The union of music and poetry was not new; for hundreds of years lyricism had been synonymous with it, and the dance had been wedded to music since time immemorial. There is, then, a line in art that tends toward the Gesamtkunstwerk. Yet this universal art is not the crowning of all arts, for music possesses a wide field where a greater verbal clarification of expression is not a gain. One might even say that the essentially musical is opposed to association with another art, for, as Schopenhauer has said, music conveys the idea itself, whereas the other arts present only its images. The limitations placed on music by such associations are of a varying degree, but one thing is certain: the most advanced form of this universal association of arts, the Wagnerian drama, cannot satisfy all our artistic desires.

To Beethoven the association of words with music was of minor importance. His music remained, with a few exceptions such as *Fidelio,* instrumental music, even when a text was involved as in the Ninth Symphony, and his music is not enriched by such associations. Music was with him, as with the classicists in general, the immediate expression of creative activity; the creative problems that his imagination conjured up appear immediately as pure music. Later in the century the original incentive became literary, a literary conception conveyed by music. Beethoven created heroism in his *Sinfonia Eroica,* whereas Strauss conceived the life of a hero and proceeded to tell it in music in *Ein Heldenleben.* The innermost content of Beethoven's works cannot be expressed in words, for this content is the idea itself. Program music played an infinitesimal part in the works of the classic composers of the eighteenth century. Whenever a symphony was labeled with a program, as were Dittersdorf's descriptive symphonies, it usually ended in naïve playfulness and imitation. Whenever Beethoven resorted to poetic allusions—in the sonata called *Les Adieux,* or in the *Pastoral* Symphony— every scrap of descriptive or associative material was incorporated organically in the body of the work. There is only one bona fide program composition in his oeuvre, the so-called *Battle* Symphony, a purely exterior *pièce de circonstance* and perhaps his most insignificant work.

The problem is of an entirely different nature when the relationship of words and music is association in a mutual task. In the foregoing chapter we discussed the purely musical conception of vocal music in the eighteenth century and the gradual development toward the literary. In the romantic era, the literary approach dominated all domains of vocal music, with the exception of Italian opera. Music joined a literary text, which was in charge

of the shaping of the creative ideas. The duty of music then became to enhance poetic expression by adding to it what words cannot express.

The great Ninth Symphony with its choral finale created a controversy
that, after more than a century, has not yet abated. The romantic apologists,
led by Wagner, based their theories largely on the existence of this choral
finale; Wagner declared that the very fact that Beethoven had to resort
to human voices proved the insufficiency of pure instrumental music. "A
human voice, with the clarity and confidence of speech, makes itself heard
above the uproar of the orchestra," said Wagner, and he did not hesitate
to claim that his own works, derived from this choral finale, began where
Beethoven ended. The numerous "choral symphonies," from Spohr and
Mendelssohn to Mahler, testify to the profound impression made by the
Ninth Symphony on subsequent composers; but they also prove that this
symphony, like many other works of Beethoven's regarded as romantic
compositions, was really not understood.

The listener not preoccupied with claims and counterclaims cannot fail
to perceive the essential unity of the four movements. To him the entry
of the voices does not change the general impression and certainly does not
entail a fundamental change in principles. The employment of the chorus
in the Ninth Symphony represents as little the union of poetry and music
as the singing of the birds, the rippling of the brook, and the thunder make
the Sixth Symphony into simple program music. Everything in the *Pastoral
Symphony* is symphonically conceived, and no sooner does the lightning
flash than its motif is thematically utilized and engulfed in the symphonic
fabric. The same purely abstract symphonic conception rules the Ninth
Symphony. The sufferings and trials of humanity we experience in the first
three movements with the greatest intensity, although the chorus, announcing the joy of mankind, joins in the fourth movement only. The same human beings who sing here in words were present for Beethoven in the
previous movements where he speaks of their tribulations in a purely instrumental language. And now he turns to them: "O Friends, not these
sounds! Let us sing pleasanter and more joyful ones." Now they must sing
with him, the human voices singing with the symphony. No one could call
the final movement of the Ninth Symphony a setting of Schiller's ode, for
the music did not arise from the poem. Rather the poem joined the
music. The disposition of the finale is fully determined in the purely orchestral introduction followed by a set of variations that precede the vocal entry.
Nothing happens here that Beethoven has not done before. Instrumental
recitatives occur in some of his earliest works; they were common in the
eighteenth century, and the reintroduction of themes from previous movements is one of the features of the piano sonata *opus* 101. The theme in
itself, the theme of the "Ode to Joy," is a typically instrumental thought of

purely symphonic qualities. Thus, by the time the voices enter, the whole course of the finale is determined. The text itself mattered little to Beethoven once he was actually proceeding with its musical elaboration. The first and most startling appearance of the human voice, the baritone solo alluded to by Wagner, sings Beethoven's own words. He selected but a few of the twenty-four verses that make up Schiller's ode, and these he arranged in a wholly arbitrary manner; there was only one thought in his mind, to distribute the words to suit the requirements of the music.

This is, then, the antithesis of the union of poetry and music so fervently advocated by romanticism. The edifice of the classic symphony remains unshaken, entirely undisturbed by the voices. Like its sisters, the choral symphony unveils a drama of a personal, inner life in a form so pure, so free of all the accessories of life, as to be unmatched in any other art.

Life

WITH the phenomenal success of the child Mozart still vivid in the memory of the musical world, Johann van Beethoven decided to turn the unmistakable musical talents of his son Ludwig to profitable employment. At the age of eight the child appeared in public as a pianist, and three years later he was taken on a short concert tour. His first musical instruction was entrusted to van den Eeden, the Flemish court organist at the electoral court, a Methuselah of a musician, to the many-sided but dissolute tenor Pfeiffer, and to a few other insignificant musicians who happened to be in Bonn. These men could contribute but little to the youth's musical education, while his general education was thwarted by the dismal pecuniary and moral conditions in his family. The hardships of his youth taught him independence at an early age, and the lack of guidance instilled in him that thirst for self-education which accompanied him throughout his life. Cultural life in Bonn was well suited for self-education, for the electors were enlightened, music-loving princes of the Church. The young man had access to good church music, orchestral music, and opera. Since the prevailing interest centered around the Mannheim school, Haydn, and Mozart, his musical tastes were well formed in spite of the most rudimentary professional instruction. In 1779, Neefe [1] was appointed court organist, and therewith Beethoven came under the influence of a well-trained and experienced musician, a man of culture and good taste, who acquainted him with the keyboard works of Johann Sebastian and Emanuel Bach. Neefe divined the youth's exceptional talents and in an article published in 1783 predicted his career as successor to Mozart. He was also instrumental in publishing Beethoven's first essays in piano composition.

In the meantime, Beethoven's skill increased sufficiently to permit Neefe to employ him as his assistant organist in the church and as harpsichordist in the orchestra, to which was added the post of viola player in the theater. A number of compositions written for various occasions rounded out the activity of the young musician, whose social life also improved through acquaintance with Franz Wegeler, an intelligent medical student. Wegeler became Beethoven's lifelong friend and performed a great service to the musician by introducing him to the widow of Court Councilor Emanuel von Breuning, in whose refined home he forgot all the miseries of his own family.

In 1792, Beethoven settled in Vienna. His hopes of studying with Mozart had been shattered by the latter's death in the previous year; thus he approached the other great leader of the Viennese school, Haydn. The old and the young master could not see eye to eye. Haydn was not made to be a teacher, while Beethoven was a born antagonist. He therefore took clandestine lessons with two experienced musicians, Johann Schenk and Antonio Salieri, both occupying foremost positions in the musical world. After Haydn's second London journey the instruction was not resumed and his other teachers were supplemented by Johann Georg Albrechtsberger (1736–1809), an eminent composer and authority on counterpoint, whose teaching, especially his fugual exercises, left a deep impression on Beethoven. Salieri, with whom he was on friendly terms, continued to teach him the principles of dramatic composition until 1802.

We dwelt on the brilliant musical life of the Habsburg capital when discussing Haydn and Mozart. The same aristocracy which sponsored the older composers now took Beethoven under its protection. But the young musician who arrived with letters of introduction from Count Waldstein was no longer merely a favored servant like Haydn, who had to wear a princely uniform not markedly different from a lackey's garment: he was received in the aristocratic palaces of the Lichtensteins, Schwartzenbergs, Lichnowskys, Brownes, Erdödys, and Brunswicks as an honored guest. His brilliant piano playing, especially his improvisations, soon earned him a reputation that eclipsed many world-famous Viennese pianists, but his aristocratic patrons were well-educated amateurs and realized that the composer in Beethoven should receive encouragement over the virtuoso. Prince Lichnowsky's house quartet was placed at his disposal, and later the prodigal Prince Lobkowitz made it possible for him to experiment with an orchestra. Under such circumstances, Beethoven's genius could develop without any compromise; its limits were determined by himself only.

Yet there was something in his music which was incompatible with the atmosphere of the aristocratic salons, a certain heretofore unknown ampleness of tone and gesture that broke through the circle of the privileged few and wanted to appeal to the multitude. On March 29, 1795, Beethoven ap-

peared for the first time before the Viennese public, playing his piano concerto in B flat, and in the same year appeared his *op. 1*, three piano trios,
followed in the next year by three piano sonatas. His creative activity expanded in the next few years, producing piano sonatas *op. 5, 7, 10, 13
(Pathétique)*, 24, and 26, six string quartets, the septet, two more piano
concertos, the First and Second Symphonies, the ballet *Prometheus,* and the
oratorio the *Mount of Olives.* In 1803, Beethoven moved into the building
of the Theater an der Wien to collaborate with Schikaneder, the librettist
of the *Magic Flute,* on an opera. Although the plan was frustrated by
Schikaneder's bankruptcy, Beethoven continued his connections with the
theater and signed a new contract, the result of which was the production,
November 20, 1805, of his opera *Fidelio.* The occupation of Vienna by the
French prevented careful rehearsing, the general atmosphere was rather unfavorable, and the opera was withdrawn after three performances. A revival the next year proved equally unsuccessful.

His operatic setback did not affect his instrumental works, which continued to be very successful. The Third Symphony, the great piano sonatas
op. 27, 28, 30, 31, 53 (Waldstein), and 57 *(Appassionata),* the piano variations in C minor, violin sonatas, among them the *Kreutzer* Sonata, the
three Rasumowsky quartets *op. 59,* and the two piano trios, *op. 70,* appeared in these years. In March, 1807, Beethoven gave two concerts in
which the first three symphonies—already known to the public—were supplemented with the new Fourth, the *Coriolanus* overture, and the G major
piano concerto. At about this time the Viennese Liebhaberkoncerte, modeled
on the Parisian Concerts des Amateurs, began its public concerts, at which
Beethoven often appeared as conductor of his own works. In acknowledgment of his growing reputation, he now gave a big concert in the Theater
an der Wien on December 22, 1808, presenting to the packed auditorium his
G major piano concerto, parts of the C major Mass, and the Fifth and Sixth
Symphonies, together with the Fantasy for piano, orchestra, and chorus,
op. 80. This enormous creative activity was very little hampered by attacks
directed against the "novelty" in his works. The new dimensions and accents seemed far more objectionable to the musicians than to the amateurs
and the public, and Beethoven appealed to the latter, for he felt the need
to communicate his ideas to the masses and to make music a factor in the
cultural life of humanity.

Beethoven's intercourse with the hereditary nobility of the Austrian Empire was free of a patronizing attitude, and he was on intimate terms with
a number of them. (The celebrated letter to the "immortal beloved" was
addressed to one of the titled ladies, probably to Countess Brunswick.) During the winter, he lived in the midst of this society, and only in the summer
months did he retire to some quiet suburban place. Gentlemanly deport-

ment and attitude in itself did not attract him, for his nature always strove for liberty in every form, but he accepted it willingly as a means for gaining freedom of movement in life. When, however, the spirit of rebellion against conventions was upon him, his "bad manners" shocked even his closest friends. Yet even in his most boorish moments, the tone of goodness and love made itself heard as if waiting for an echo from life. He knew how much less men could give him than he had to offer, and his impulsive nature occasionally showed disdain which could be atoned by humiliation only. He loved man as he felt man should be, but the man thrown before him by the chance of existence was a different matter; toward him he often exhibited superiority or even superciliousness, to which was later added suspicion. All this was greatly intensified by a terrible physical infliction, the gradual loss of his hearing, the first symptoms of which manifested themselves in his late twenties. In the next decade it became apparent that his ailment was incurable, and in his last period he became totally deaf. His tremendous will power was put to a trial and he emerged the victor, but something of the poet's oracle never again left him: "He who loves humanity learns to hate humans."

In the further course of his life, prosaic reality was relegated to the lowest plane. Since it now had little to do with his mental life, the warm-hearted artist became almost cynical in his business dealings. But again this attitude helped materially to increase the economic security of the modern musician, who could now claim rights where formerly a publisher was the sole arbiter. Having assumed a cold and rigid attitude toward everyday life, Beethoven turned with even greater fervor toward the elect of spiritual life. Books had always been his faithful companions; he delighted to read the Greek classics as well as Goethe, Schiller, Klopstock, and the new literature on natural sciences. Now he sought personal contact with poets and writers. He made the acquaintance of Bettina von Arnim, Clemens Brentano, Varnhagen, Tiedgen, Rahel, and other literary figures, and he also met Goethe. This literary interest was immediately reflected in his compositions, a number of songs, choruses, and incidental music to Goethe's *Egmont* and to Kotzebue's *Ruins of Athens* and *King Stephen.* Among the instrumental works of this period were the piano sonatas *op.* 78, 81, 96, the piano trio *op.* 97, the Seventh and Eighth Symphonies, and the quartets *op.* 74 and 95. His affliction prevented him from appearing as a pianist, and when the E flat piano concerto was first performed, in 1818, the solo part was entrusted to his young pupil, Carl Czerny.

In the last period of his life, at a time when his fame spread all over Europe, Beethoven avoided the public and lived almost like a hermit. His visitors had to converse with him in writing, and the once proud and erect man became untidy and was willing to associate himself with such simple bourgeois minds as Schindler, his faithful secretary, for the remainder of his life. But while outwardly giving the impression of an unkempt, elderly, and deaf musician, his creative faculties and energy were not only unimpaired but were ready to proceed further and further. The misery of his physical condition, the endless annoyances caused by an ungrateful nephew whom he treated like his own son, could make the man despair but not the composer. The last great piano sonatas, *op.* 101, 106, 109, 110, 111, the Diabelli variations and the Bagatels, the cello sonata *op.* 102, and a number of musical epigrams in the form of canons opened his last style period. Then two colossal creations, the Ninth Symphony and the *Missa Solemnis,* materialized from among the many plans for large oratorios, operas, and symphonies. By this time the public had ceased to know the retiring composer, although his name was a symbol in Vienna, but once more Beethoven was permitted to experience the esteem and affection of the Viennese. This was at the first performance of the Ninth Symphony before a deeply moved audience. After this last communication, he buried himself once more in the solitude of creation to write his last works, the five great quartets *op.* 127, 130, 131, 132, and 135. After long and intense sufferings, he died on March 26, 1827.

The Earlier Works

THE central thought in Beethoven's works is the symphonic, but sonata, chamber music, and symphony all belong together stylistically, as all of them are dominated by the dramatic dualism of the classical sonata form. The contrasts which agitated his whole being found a most adequate and congenial expression in the sonata form. This explains the relatively secondary place of lyricism in his language. It was the predominance of lyricism, the romantic trait par excellence, which frustrated the romantic symphony. Beethoven not only wanted and was able to write sonatas and symphonies; he had to write them, he needed this medium.

The first Viennese works published under *op.* 1 are the works of the finished master; the C minor trio, third of the set, is Beethoven in all his greatness in spite of the slight Wertherian touch that clings to it—and that was to depart soon after he mastered his first romantic crisis. We must guard against finding in these works of the first period, up to and including the First Symphony, "great progress" when compared to similar compositions by Haydn and Mozart. Equally untrue and unscientific is the attitude often encountered wherein the forms of these earlier works are held to be still the traditional ones used by Haydn and Mozart, only their content being different. This criticism may be summarized in the opinions regarding the First Symphony as written "entirely in the manner of Haydn and Mozart." The symphony shows certain technical aspects which naturally tie it up with the symphonic style of the eighteenth century, but such connecting links are a prime necessity of stylistic evolution. From the bold beginning on a seventh chord, every movement in this symphony is original, and the "greater" Beethoven lurks everywhere. The chamber and orchestral music of the early Viennese period may mislead the uninitiated, but even he cannot fail to see the new and original when meeting Beethoven eye to eye in the piano sonatas.

We have watched the emergence of the keyboard sonata and followed its course northward until, in the hands of Emanuel Bach and Schobert, it became a flexible and dramatic medium. Then came Mozart. He learned from Emanuel Bach how to seize upon a mental moment and develop it logically, his logic improving with acquaintance with Haydn's quartets and symphonies. Haydn himself was the composer of incomparable piano sonatas, which, together with those of Mozart, are today somewhat obscured by the virtuoso literature of the public concerts, though the real pianist will treasure them as the quartet player treasures their quartets. In the meantime the harpsichord was displaced by the hammer piano. The first composers to use the new instrument were Wagenseil and Kozeluch in Vienna, Schobert in Paris, Christian Bach and Abel in London, with Bach playing it in 1768 for the first time in public, followed by Clementi. Toward the end of the century, the harpsichord ceased to be an instrument for concert purposes and remained in use in the opera orchestra only where it served to accompany the recitatives. Mozart was the first real virtuoso on the "pianoforte," but in 1780 Haydn himself adopted the new instrument, as is evident from the dynamic instructions given in his keyboard compositions after this date. Piano sonatas retained the character of divertimenti for a long time, and it was not until 1770 that this mood and style inherited from Wagenseil disappeared from the piano works of Haydn and Mozart, although even after this time they occasionally returned to it for specific reasons. Beethoven owed a great deal to the keyboard music of his older Viennese colleagues, but not nearly so much as in other fields. Emanuel Bach and Clementi, especially the classically finished piano sonatas of the latter, gave him his definite orientation.

Muzio Clementi (1752–1832), with Cherubini the last great Italian master of classical instrumental music, was one of those artists who survived their own time. He started cautiously, trying to find his way in the traditions and strong impressions created by Domenico Scarlatti and the other great Italian keyboard composers. Then he made the intriguing acquaintance of Christian Bach and Schobert, and by 1782 the great classic sonata composer, Clementi, is before us, with masterworks that are worthy companions of Haydn's and Mozart's piano sonatas. But this gifted composer did not stop here, and soon we notice emanating from his sonatas ideas, tones, and moods that take us into the Beethovenian world. Indeed, Clementi was responsible for rescuing the piano sonata—somewhat overshadowed by the great development of chamber and orchestral music—and thus enabling the young Beethoven to get a firm start. Clementi's influence is not limited to certain melodic borrowings, clearly present as late as in the *Sonate Pathétique,* but appears in the pianistic setting and in the variety and logic of the development sections. This is what has prompted some authors to attribute "surprisingly" Beethovenian touches to Clementi's sonatas.

Like the symphony, the piano sonata reached its culmination in Beethoven's thirty-eight works of this type. Tremendously impressed by Clementi's sonatas, Beethoven started out, as usual, with traditional forms and idioms, but soon he exhausted them and melted and recast them. He did not use the implements of revolution, but if the lawful carrying out of his plans was thwarted he did not hesitate to take an untried way. Although an entirely new element—the expression of dark and demonic moods—appears in the *Sonate Pathétique,* it is in this sonata that Clementi's inspiration was most fruitful, and Beethoven even borrowed thematic and harmonic patterns. But he proceeded on his own way, and the classic sonata was soon enriched with variants. The so-called *Moonlight* Sonata and the A flat sonata depart from the accepted pattern and return to the older divertimento type with their fine variations and darkly majestic funeral marches. This is, however, no reversion; it is, rather, another example of the freedom from formal conventions characteristic of Beethoven.

Beethoven was aware of the fact that with the development of the symphony the concerto would have to merge with the former unless its symphonic background were to become a mere support, or rather pretext, for the exhibition of virtuosity. Thus relatively early in his career he ceased to write concertos, but not before giving us works that crowned the history of the species: the violin concerto (1806) and the last two of his five piano concertos, in G and E flat. It is interesting to note that on one occasion, in the slow movement of the Fourth Concerto, he suddenly reverted entirely to the solo and tutti of the baroque concerto. This is of course not an imitation, for the tone is conspicuously romantic, but the spirit is that of the old concerto. In this connection it seems significant that Brahms, whose beautiful violin concerto was a direct issue of Beethoven's, struggled immeasurably with his two piano concertos, which are more symphonies with obbligato piano than concertos in the accepted sense.

In his first quartets Beethoven did not simply continue where Haydn stopped; this was impossible, for such mastery as the aging Haydn displayed can be won only by a lifelong development. Thus the quartet style had to be evolved once more from the start. The road was not easy and entailed a great deal of experimentation, reflected in the variety of thrusts into the peripheries of chamber music, the center of which is the quartet. The young composer essayed his hand at wind ensembles, piano trios, violin and cello sonatas, then string trios, and finally he arrived at the quartet. By the time the first group of quartets (*op.* 18) was created, Beethoven had surveyed the whole territory of music, establishing various parcels for himself. The piano sonata remained his most personal medium, one in which he could experiment to his heart's content. Its antipode was to be the symphony, the summation of the experiments. The string quartet took a middle position until the latter part of his life, when it became the synthesis of everything. His quartet style, enriched by a polyphonic ensemble technique learned from Haydn, reached its first summit in the finale of the third Rasumowsky quartet in C. After this culmination it was no longer possible to continue in this vein and a pause became necessary.

As Beethoven's art matured, his constructions increased in dimensions. In the development sections of his sonata forms he now occasionally introduced material not presented in the exposition. This was undoubtedly done to give the far-ranging modulations scope, so that after distant regions had been traversed such new themes might play a part not unlike that of the subsidiary subject reached after the bridge. In this fashion large development sections were fused without jeopardizing the elemental effect of the recapitulation. This was not a violation of the symphonic ideal. On the contrary, it prevented the necessary modulatory operations from becoming a mere formal requisite. The new themes appear in the midst of the tumultuous thematic development as points of quiescence, after which the restless pursuit of the original aims continues unabated. Accordingly, such new themes are usually noble cantilenas, such as the ones in the first movements of the Third Symphony and the violin concerto. The enlargement of all dimensions necessitated a much more elaborate coda, which is often so extensive that it almost impresses one as a second development section. While these modulations know no restrictions, there are among the most complicated and extended works others which are models of laconic massiveness.

The epitome of this new thought is the Third Symphony, one of the incomprehensible deeds in arts and letters, the greatest single step made by an individual composer in the history of the symphony and in the history of music in general. This should not be interpreted as belittling the previous symphony, in every way comparable to the others, but the *Eroica* simply dwarfs everything in its boldness of conception, breadth of execution, and intensity of the logic of construction. Beethoven himself never again approached this feat of fiery imagination; he wrote other, perhaps greater, works, but he never again took such a fling at the universe. Every component is unusual and novel but singularly appropriate for his purpose, which is not the cult of one person but that of an ideal, of heroism itself. The celebrated story about the original dedication of the work to Napoleon does not in the least alter this fact.

Instead of a long introduction, the heroic and impatient character of the first movement is condensed into two furious chords, after which a maelstrom of an allegro starts its onward rush, punctuated by the sforzati of the enraged orchestra. The slow movement, a funeral march, is almost graphic in its profound mourning, but it mourns a hero who even in death rises with clenched fists and makes us forget the initial calm and sorrowful tone, until toward the end everything collapses and the almost incoherent stammering of the orchestra makes us realize the catastrophe. The scherzo is upon us with a swiftness, here murmuring, there flashing, that we are scarcely able to follow, and the symphony ends with a variation cycle, or rather several cycles of variations, which, appropriately to the heroic tone of the work, employ a theme first used by Beethoven in his ballet *Prometheus:* a dithyrambic and glorious finale.

The Fourth Symphony is again an entirely different type, one of the happiest and loveliest works of Beethoven. Its slow movement is perhaps the most intimate symphonic song ever placed in a large orchestral work. The Fifth Symphony does not require discussion; it will remain *the* symphony, the consummate example of symphonic logic.

Thayer's keen observation that in his Sixth Symphony Beethoven wanted to meet his competitors and colleagues in their own field is altogether plausible, if we consider the great number of program symphonies of the late eighteenth and the early nineteenth century. But we have already emphasized that this is not program music in the realistic sense of Berlioz, for program music begins where the construction is directed by extramusical, whether literary or other, forces. The *Pastoral Symphony* is a true classic symphony; even the most descriptive of its movements, the Scene by the Brook, is entirely dissolved in bewitching sonorities, in an undulating flow of tones which fills one with unspeakable peace. Indeed, this is not program music as it was later understood, but the sheerest musical poetry expressed in tones, not in ideas. The title page gives the gentle warning that the symphony is "more an expression of feeling than painting," and Beethoven's short inscriptions prefacing the individual movements speak of "cheerful *impressions* received on arriving in the country" and of "happy and grateful *feelings* after the storm."

Drawn toward the opera all his life, Beethoven faced a conflict which started with the first notes of the overture of his only opera. The French school, which he greatly admired and followed in many aspects of his operatic work, placed an emphasis on the dramatic elements as constructive factors even in the overture. Therefore their overtures, dealing with materials taken from the opera, did not always follow the precepts of symphonic construction, notably disregarding the dualistic sonata principle. The more or less literal recapitulation of the first part of the sonata allegro was often unsuited to a certain dramatic plot. In the second *Leonore* overture, Beethoven, mindful of the anticlimactic nature of a literal recapitulation after the trumpet call signaling the arrival of the liberator, dispensed with it. This is a unique instance in all his large sonata movements, and he did not repeat it again. The symphonic architect was not satisfied, however, and in still another overture, the third, he restored the recapitulation, only to reject the overture altogether as unfit for an operatic prelude. The fourth overture, entirely different in nature and scope, finally took the place of all others, and it serves its purpose admirably. The other three remained symphonic poems in which the word "symphonic" must be taken at its full value.

Wagner's opinion, shared by many modern critics, that the opera itself is a trifle compared to the third *Leonore* overture, is not taken seriously by any connoisseur of opera, for *Fidelio* is closest to Schiller's classic drama; it is carried by the same lofty ideas which unite people of the most diverse personalities. *Fidelio* is the expression of the same classicism which in Schiller's last plays combined personal feeling with the pathos of humanity, with liberty, with the struggle for the noblest aims, and with the confidence of their ultimate victory. Beethoven saw in the subject of his libretto the highest ideal of the times, a noble humanity, the co-operation of good men for its realization, the kinship of souls united by sympathy for the oppressed, and the sublime joy over the triumph of righteousness. If *Fidelio* is not so homogeneous as Mozart's great operas, it is because the heroic quality of the text is not sustained. Beethoven wanted from his librettists books of great historic or moral portent. In the first part of the opera, where he has to deal with everyday events, he is obviously ill at ease, but the very minute he can divine the message of even such happiness as is symbolized in the homely warmth of a bourgeois family, his fantasy catches fire (quartet scene). As the drama progresses, the dramatic musical unity becomes pronounced and in the second act attains great and convincing intensity. There are few contrasts in the dramatic literature that move us so profoundly as the bright sunshine after the scenes in the dungeon, the song of the prisoners, trembling and whispering when they first emerge, and then growing into a thanksgiving hymn, an ode to freedom.

The opera should be restored to its original form, that is, some of the discarded numbers should be reinstated and the ridiculous tradition of playing the third *Leonore* overture in the entr'acte abandoned. Beethoven knew better than anyone else that this overture is a powerful and finished drama in itself and cannot preface another drama. If the third *Leonore* overture is unsuitable as a curtain raiser—and without any doubt the *Fidelio* overture is the best prelude to the opera—it will be most disruptive when placed between the acts. Beethoven himself was aware of the independent nature of his overtures. On one of the violin parts of the discarded first *Leonore* overture he wrote "Characteristische Ouvertüre"; indeed, he found the character overture a particularly appropriate medium for the portrayal of heroism. Among these "symphonic poems" the heroic ideal is notably well expressed in *Egmont,* with the basic mood sustained in a blaze of tonal glory and jubilation despite the tragic end of the hero. With fine intuition the chief feminine figure, Clärchen, is not involved in the overture, for she is only an episode in the main object of the work, the fight for freedom. Another great and most concentrated heroic-symphonic poem is the overture to *Coriolanus.*

The Seventh and Eighth Symphonies, the symphonic landmarks of the next years, are again as contrasting as possible. The Seventh, a Dionysiac orgy of vast proportions, is too well known to require discussion. The Eighth, somewhat neglected and misunderstood, is an essay on humor in music, a parody on the symphony itself. The first movement, starting without preliminaries, is a sunny and vigorous symphonic picture, proclaiming all the glory of the species. The second, with its witty imitation of the ticking of the metronome, is unique in the annals of symphony for its gracious humor, and the third, significantly inscribed "Tempo di minuetto," pokes fun at Biedermeier docility. Everything goes wrong in this movement: it has difficulty in getting started with its overemphasized and heavy-footed tentative lines; then the horns, trumpets, and tympani, missing their cue, hurl their ponderous tones at the wrong places and get entangled in the cadence. The finale, one of the longest Beethovenian movements, romps about with unrestricted merriment. Suddenly, in the midst of the swift but subdued flow in C major, the full orchestra crashes in with a resounding C sharp and pandemonium follows. The Homeric laughter ceases and the composer gives us immediately a calming and ingratiating melody, but only to sooth us, for there is an endless store of surprises waiting for the listener.

Beethoven's chamber music of this period does not reflect the tremendous driving urge of his symphonies and sonatas. His cello and violin sonatas and string quartets, all finished masterpieces, are quieter and more measured, yet they are filled with novel tones and with singular melodic beauty. The slow movements show a distinct romantic leaning, especially haunting in the mysterious slow movement of the piano trio, *op.* 70, no. 1. But the lyric mood and freedom of form are balanced by the architecture of the finales, with their wonderful disposition of tonalities, crisp and clear voice leading, and much of that euphony that characterizes the finales of the late eighteenth century. Occasionally, as in the scherzo of the E flat quartet, *op.* 74, the tremendous dimensions and relentless intensity of the symphonies make themselves felt, but on the whole Beethoven keeps away from the typically symphonic.

As we are nearing the last of these compositions we begin to realize that chamber music is about to acquire a new attitude and a new meaning. The somber quartet in F minor is entitled *Quartetto serioso*. The clipped and pregnant sentence that starts it has something irritable and violent about it, and up to the ending, which reassures and brings peace, the quartet remains unruly and inscrutable. With this quartet Beethoven was through with his chamber music style, but before abandoning the past altogether he once more united his beloved personal instrument, the piano, with strings, in the last piano trio, *op.* 97, the last violin sonata, *op.* 96, and the last two cello sonatas, *op.* 102. And again the problems are forgotten in the magnificently flowing music, with its broad melodies and rich sonorities. Organic growth and logic of construction are everywhere, with the thematic material reigning supreme, but the variety of rhythm and a deeply felt curious polyphony indicate a latent new conception. Then, after a pause, come the last two cello sonatas: stubborn, wild, and fantastic compositions filled with suppressed emotions which, contrary to the preceding trios, quartets, and the violin sonata, are neither relieved nor resolved. The romantic crisis is upon him in all its earnestness but the archclassicist is on guard and opposes the disrupting forces with an almost baroque polyphony. Only the strength of this polyphony is baroque, however, for no baroque composer could have written such a bizarre and cross-grained fugue as that in the second sonata—almost unplayable. This was the end of the road; Beethoven had to return or blaze a new one for himself. He elected to pause, and for a period of ten years he abstained from chamber music.

The Later Works

OPUS 101 opens the series of the last piano sonatas; this is a work of almost romantic freedom and apparent sketchiness, yet it is classic to the core, though the logic of construction is so concentrated and seamless that the caesurae between the individual sections are completely covered. The following sonata, *op.* 106, written while the *Missa Solemnis* and the Ninth Symphony were in their early stages, rivals these in the magnitude of its plan and content. Every one of its movements is a sheer marvel of endurance, of the unflagging adherence to the working out of symphonic-thematic ideas. The slow movement is the longest of its kind and the final fugue the first of those polyphonic edifices peculiar to the late Beethoven. A work like this sonata cannot be repeated, and the following two, *op.* 109 and 110, are less gigantic in dimensions albeit equally searching in content. Their sonata construction is exemplary in its precise and yet almost undetectable architecture. The last of the piano sonatas is strangely reminiscent of the early *Pathétique* Sonata; it is in the same key of C minor and opens with the same broad pathos, but what follows is different. The concentration of emotions and energies is such that all conventions had to be thrown overboard, and the majestic first movement was followed by a relaxation in remote spiritual regions. Nothing could be said after these celestial utterances, least of all a witty scherzo or a robust finale.

The enormous proportions, both physical and spiritual, of the great baroque composers return in the *Missa Solemnis*. In the midst of the strong literary tendency of romanticism, the faithful declamation of the text once more becomes secondary, as in the baroque, in order to make possible its full realization in music. It is neither by accident nor by technical insufficiency that Beethoven arrived at this style; he worshiped Handel and admired Bach and, receiving their message, passed it on in his own way. As Bach in his B minor Mass leaves behind all churchly thought (we must not be misled by the Catholic liturgic text, the B minor Mass remains a collection of cantatas), so the *Missa Solemnis* transcends Catholic liturgy. Yet the work is Catholic and liturgic, and is expressly so acknowledged by ecclesiastic authorities. "In contrast to Bach's B minor Mass, which does not suffer from the atmosphere and garish light of the concert hall, the *Missa Solemnis* is never quite at home there. In a church, on the other hand, where the divine office is of prime importance, full justice can never be done to its music. Thus, in common with many other great works of art, it has grown up in a realm that lies beyond the bounds of practical possibilities." [2]

To the Christian whose supreme law is obedience, the Beethovenian attitude seems repellent, for submission is preceded in him by a struggle with doubts; faith is gained through a Faustian trial. Nevertheless, Beethoven was a pious Catholic, not a romantic pantheist, and he had nothing but contempt for the romantic converts. He read Thomas à Kempis and other religious writers, and studied the works of Palestrina with devotion. The religious education of his nephew caused him endless concern and he often consulted the parish priest to make sure that everything was being done for his ungrateful Karl. What seems strange to us, accustomed as we are to the attitude of the late nineteenth century, is the spirit of the Catholic Enlightenment which survives in Beethoven. His warring on a meek and mechanical treatment of the sacred text and his seeking for the meaning of every word of the liturgy (he had the text translated into German to make sure that nothing escaped his attention) betray the Catholic Enlightenment of the late eighteenth century, which, while not favorably looked upon by theology, is nevertheless Catholic and valid.

At first the younger man could but follow what his times, traditions, and education decreed, and his C major Mass (1807) is a faithful and sincere companion to Haydn's late Masses. This superb work, undeservedly neglected, is filled with the heroic ideal of the *Coriolanus* era. This is, to be sure, an unusual adjective to use in connection with a Mass, but the composition was again the vehicle of most personal thoughts. The proud heroism of the divine creature that is man is proclaimed here in a liturgy made human. In the *Missa Solemnis* faith is conquered and regained, and, despite its immense power and stupendous proportions, the Mass remains a liturgic work and, unlike its gigantic counterpart, the B minor Mass, shows no trace of diffuseness. Its tone is churchly and there are no concert elements in it.

The diffuseness of Bach's B minor Mass, is, as we have noticed in the chapter devoted to Bach, due to the sequence of heterogeneous "numbers." Each one of these numbers is a masterpiece of the highest order, but they are arrayed like so many individual cantatas. There is no compelling unity watching over the whole, there is not even a relationship between the two *Kyries*. The *Missa Solemnis* is planned and fused from the first to the last tone. Wagner recognized this when he called it "a purely symphonic work bearing the true stamp of Beethoven's mind." The symphonic unity of the classical Mass of Haydn is carried here to ultimate cohesion and perfection. The symphonist has again restored that "leitmotivic" unity which gave such magnificent continuity to the polyphonic Mass of the fifteenth and sixteenth centuries. Within this severe construction Beethoven has given free rein to his imagination. Every nuance, every suggestion in the text is followed faithfully by the music; the articles of faith are set, one by one, according to their order of importance. In the *Et incarnatus est* he even recaptures the ecstatic mysticism of Palestrina, abandoning his tonal scheme in favor of a modal atmosphere, and in the *Dona nobis pacem* the music turns martial, the trumpets blaring and the drums rumbling. This has been found objectionable by the devotees of "official" church music, who declare Beethoven devoid of any true religious feeling. But the martial tone was not unknown in the Masses of the era of the Enlightenment, and the whole subjective conception—much more so than in the first Mass—is a repercussion of the Enlightenment's tendency for independent thinking and interpretation rather than acceptance of traditional devices. The man accused of being impious wrote in his score at the beginning of the *Credo*, "God above all—God has never deserted me." Truly moving words from a man visited by the worst affliction a musician can suffer.

Nevertheless, in one aspect the *Missa Solemnis* went beyond the limits of church music proper and really entered another field of religious music, the oratorio. This was no doubt owing to the subjective conception of the text. The kinship with the oratorio is evident not only in the large dimensions of the individual parts which make it, like the B minor Mass, unsuited to liturgic purposes, but in numerous other details. Significantly enough, the fugue theme of the *Dona nobis pacem* Beethoven took from Handel's *Messiah* ("And he shall reign forever and ever"), and the beginning of the *Kyrie* too has a good deal of the spirit of the majestic anthem choruses. Beethoven himself was aware of this quality in his *Missa,* and even recommended its performance as an oratorio. This did not, however, imply an abandonment of the original purpose of the work. What he really wanted was to make the Mass, which he considered his supreme achievement, available for Protestants as well as Catholics. This attitude again shows the enlightened Catholic who, imbued with the ideals of humanity of the eighteenth century, is eager to conceal the differences between the two great factions of Christendom rather than to emphasize them.

With the *Missa Solemnis* and the Ninth Symphony the possibilities of the large orchestral and choral forms were exhausted, and although Beethoven made plans for a tenth symphony, a third Mass, and large oratorios, he himself came to realize that he had reached the limits of large musical architecture. And now all the types of music he had cultivated earlier seemed to have been carried to their ultimate destination. As he looked back upon his lifework, the tired man realized that the relentless dynamic pounding of the musical universe had demolished its visible barriers, that the battering ram had no more objectives left. Yet his creative power was still unimpaired and was still aiming at the final synthesis. But this he would have to seek outside the Dionysiac, in the rarefied atmosphere of the purely spiritual. What he attempted now was no less than the union of all that could not be united before, all that could not be developed further in its own right, the abstract with the particular, line with sound, polyphony with street song. Only one medium was suitable for such thoughts, the incorporeal string quartet, which he had abandoned fourteen years before. He returned, therefore, to the quartet, but instead of sonorous string writing, he enveloped himself in abstract ideas and, like the aging Bach, turned to the last secrets of polyphony.

A new miracle unfolds before us, a new polyphony in which the nonthematic parts live a life of their own, yet the whole becomes impersonal or, rather, above the personal, as rhythm and melody are concentrated to such an extent that they become principles. At the same time the cyclic unity grows even beyond the single works, encompassing the second, third, **and fourth** of the five late quartets in one incomprehensibly great cyclic unit; the substance of these three quartets is the same. This unity which transcends the individual work is not altogether new, and it is true especially in the string quartets of the Rasumowsky series, but what was merely suggested there is a concrete reality here, visible in thematic and rhythmic concordances.

The dualistic sonata form is modified, if not left behind, in these works, for the idea must be given freedom beyond thematic conflicts; and as the contrasting thematic principle of the sonata form is abandoned to permit a free unfolding of the idea, the dividing line between the traditional movements is often deleted to permit more organic connections. Yet we must guard from considering these works "free fantasias," and even if our rules do not seem to fit the formal structure of the late quartets we must seek to find the unity we unmistakably hear in these works but which our eyes perceive with difficulty. "Beethoven nowhere submits to the laws of musical form with such Spartan rigor as in his individual and strongly imaginative last sonatas and quartets." [3] This was Brahms's opinion, the opinion of a great musician steeped in the study of Beethoven. And indeed his judgment is true, although the "Spartan rigor" should not be translated into expositions, recapitulations, and codas; they are still there but disappear from sight as opposition is succeeded by juxtaposition, and subordination by co-ordination. Variation and fugue, the freest and at the same time most logic-bound forms of expression, became the final symbol of the idea. What he once achieved in the final fugue of the third Rasumowsky quartet is now carried out into the unsubstantial, the dimensions themselves being eliminated, the triumph of pure music over construction.

The Beethovenian Style

WHILE a division of Beethoven's creative years into three style periods is customary and feasible inasmuch as every artist has one period each of youth, maturity, and old age (the latter not necessarily implying an oppressive number of years), one must be careful not to attribute exclusive characteristics to each of these periods. Beethoven was one of those composers who carried an idea in his imagination for years and even for decades. Some of the most typical "innovations" of his final period are present in lesser known works of his youth. There is also the remarkable fact that at the time he created the largest of symphonic constructions, he also arrived at a concentration and poise expressed in the smallest possible forms, the epigrams in his last quartets and the Bagatels for piano.

An invaluable aid in studying Beethoven's mind and process of composition is furnished in his sketchbooks, happily available in modern editions.[4] They disclose a fundamental trait valid in all three periods, namely, that what Beethoven wanted he demanded with absolute unconcern as to the medium or the performer. When technical restrictions interposed themselves between an idea and its realization, he did not hesitate to violate even ordinary common sense, especially in his vocal writing. It is idle, however, to think that Beethoven "could not write well for the voice," for if called upon he could master the Italian vocal style, as can be seen in the two dramatic scenes for voice and orchestra, the aria "Ah Perfido!" and the terzetto "Tremate, Empi Tremate!" He was also the composer of a number of very fine songs. We might just as well say that he could not write for the piano or for other instruments dear to his heart, for certain movements in his sonatas cannot be adequately played. What Beethoven hears with his inner ear, and what he coerces into a graphic score, he wants executed no matter whether this is feasible or not. No Italian or French musician would take such an attitude, for this inconsiderateness is German. That his deafness had anything to do with his stubborn insistence on the carrying out of his ideas can be believed only by people who do not know the creative process in music. Demonic impetuosity and arbitrary disregard of propriety can give way, however, to the most tender intimacy. His slow movements, the prayerlike adagios in the C sharp minor Sonata, in the *Appassionata,* in the *Emperor* Concerto, and especially in the last piano sonata with its seraphic trills, embrace us with a loving song; here moving, plaintive and tearful, then again, as in the violin solo in the *Benedictus* of the *Missa Solemnis,* soaring heavenward, uplifting and consoling. A profoundly kind and gentle soul, deeply wounded and yet daring to give itself to fervent abandonment, speaks to us from these tones, a pure and rich human heart. No one else could pass from one extreme to the other without losing his bearings, but Beethoven is never lost; his elemental power saves him alike from sentimentality and from excess. No matter how soft and tender, he always remains the giant; he can never appear small. In a few measures he can illumine the depth of his soul as if with lightning. The most complicated states of mind he can project with unexampled concentration. One need only recall the little introduction to the fugue of the *Hammerklavier* sonata. At the same time his sorrow, joy, or humor envelops whole movements of tremendous proportions, the sorrow of the adagio of the *Hammerklavier* sonata, the passion of the first movement of the last piano sonata and of the quartet *op.* 132, the humor of the Diabelli variations. Sorrow, passion, and joy he does not choose romantically, for every state of mind so expressed mirrors the whole of life. His enthusiasm is at times lost in touchingly naïve pictures. Thus he converted the tenor solo in the Ninth Symphony, which exhorts men to go their way like conquering heroes, into a march such as one could hear in the Prater, the

Viennese amusement park, the voice being accompanied by "Turkish music," wind instruments with triangle, cymbals, and drum. On the heels of this moving scene follows a choral bedlam, a reeling, intoxicated revelry such as no other musician has ever produced.

Beethoven's themes are not merely invented and then shaped into compositions with a masterly hand; their constructive possibilities are inherent. Not every musical idea lends itself to symphonic elaboration provided sufficient skill is brought to bear on it; the result may be quite artistic, but it will never be a faultless masterpiece unless the germs of the whole are contained in the idea. To write a symphony one has to be a symphonist and must have symphonic ideas, that is, ideas which are not only capable of symphonic elaboration but demand it. Nowhere else is the axiom that idea and style are determined by each other so true as in the classical symphony. We are wont to regard composition as a process beginning with the invention of a theme, which is then followed by a logical elaboration. The classic composer, and especially the symphonist, proceeds in a different manner. His themes are the most concentrated expression, the compressed power of all that which seems to us derived from it. But—and this is the essence of symphonic thought—only in their elaboration is their nature revealed.

The most convincing, the most miraculously concentrated symphonic structure in the whole musical literature is Beethoven's Fifth Symphony, the fulfillment of the symphonic ideal. This is in no way disproved by the mighty ones which followed up to the Ninth, which stands as the great memorial to the classical symphony that was. The first movement of the Fifth Symphony is built on a theme consisting of four notes supplied by two tones. This surely is the minimum of a musical theme. The hammering strokes of the orchestra seize us with weird, irresistible force; there is no letdown in their progress, and the inexorable logic of thematic development is interrupted by the plaintive little recitative of the oboe only to plunge us again into the headlong turmoil which ceases only at the end of the movement. Then and only then, after having heard the whole movement, shall we understand the meaning of this theme, for now it is no longer a motto but the quintessence and the summing up of the whole.

The same utmost concentration characterizes the scherzo of the Ninth Symphony, where three notes form the chief motif. It is incredible that such terse and laconic germs of ideas can lead to the vastness of a symphonic movement, and yet never for an instant are we permitted to lose sight of them because they are not merely the point of departure but the essence, the governing force itself. The demonic frenzy to which his symphonic developments lead frightened some of his more sensitive contem-

poraries, and as fine a musician as Carl Maria von Weber heard the violent
torrent of tones and rhythms of the Seventh Symphony as if listening to
the work of a madman.

Like all the Viennese composers, Beethoven was fond of the variation,
which permitted a wide margin for the imagination, at the same time binding it around a pivotal theme. The principle of the variation acquired significance in the high classic era. Before that time, and not counting the
ostinato variations of the baroque, the variation had appeared rather modestly in the dance suite and in the divertimento. The cycle of variations as
a musical form dates from the turning point of the preclassic era, and it
will not surprise us to find it in the divertimentolike compositions of that
period. Mozart wrote a number of early works of this type. But the variation also appeared in individual movements of sonatas and symphonies,
many of these compositions being, indeed, in reality still divertimenti; one
has only to recall Mozart's celebrated piano sonata in A major (K. 331).
In the high classic era, the variation grew from mere playful alteration
of a given theme to the so-called character variation. Haydn, especially
fond of the variation technique, developed the character variation to a
point where it rivaled the sonata itself. A simple melody was now presented
under aspects of great diversity, usually ending in an elaborate coda. In
the slow movement of the Fifth Symphony, Beethoven faithfully followed
the Haydnian precepts, but later his variations acquired dimensions and a
constructive unity unknown even to Haydn, master of the art. Sets of
variations like the C minor, the *Eroica,* or the Diabelli variations are large
cyclic works, fully equal to the most extended four-movement compositions; indeed, they virtually contain all the elements of the traditional
sonata capped by a fugue as a finale. The great classicist speaks in the
Diabelli variations, for the theme, a miserable little waltz, would seem to
deter rather than inspire anyone to further meditation. Yet Beethoven
built on it a musical cathedral matched only by the similarly supernatural
ciacona of Bach for solo violin, both incomprehensible in their vastness.

The same study that led Beethoven to the variation and his constant urge
for concentration directed him toward the fugue. He knew and admired
the masters of the baroque, but his was neither an imitation of the baroque
fugue nor a scholastic toying with a bygone device. It was wholly original,
and it reacted on his voice-leading technique in general. One year before
his death, he mentioned proudly his new manner of voice leading, as exemplified in the C sharp minor quartet. This technique, known as open
or pierced work, was not really new, and one might say that the medieval
hoquetus[5] already embodied its principles, but Beethoven gave it new
scope. Unlike the customary setting which allots a phrase in its entirety to
one instrument, this musical open work articulates the phrase by giving its

elements to a number of instruments, and every instrument contributes a word or two to the phrase which is thus assembled from several musical parts.

*

* *

WE still do not realize the tremendous impact of Beethoven's music on the succeeding generations. We know that instrumental music was under his spell for the rest of the century, but there is still no department of music that does not owe him its very soul. Beethoven endowed pure instrumental music with the most intense and expressive dramatic accents, an expressiveness that cast its reflex on dramatic music itself. A circle closes here; opera-born symphony now helps to create the language of the modern music drama. The tremendous power and sharp edge of this music, its fervor and warmth, but above all, its animated contrasts were eminently dramatic. Wagner thought that the great influence emanating from Beethoven was due to his having trespassed the limits of instrumental music and embraced the faith of the union of voice and instrument, but this his own works belie on every page. For no matter how sublime creations, it was not *Fidelio,* the *Ode to Joy,* and the *Missa Solemnis* that gave this new music drama its idiom, but the symphonic thought which actuated Beethoven even in his choral works. The sonatas, quartets, and symphonies are what inspired the dramatists, for they are dramas even if they have nothing to do with the stage. This does not contradict the absolute rejection of all programmatic associations, for words are powerless to describe what takes place in them. We do not need, and cannot here afford, lengthy technical explanations; everyone who has heard the tempestuous introduction to the *Walküre* will instantly realize the implications, for this is a symphonic idiom pure and simple, and we shall see how this same idiom dominates the Wagnerian opera despite all claims to a purely literary-dramatic plan and inspiration.

Beethoven was the musician who found the way to the last confines of classicism and thus passed from the realm of the beautiful into that of the sublime. In that region such criteria as "taste" are no longer valid, because in its atmosphere feeling and sentiment are topped by ethic will power. Beethoven thus created for himself a heroic style which unleashes subjective forces unknown to his classic brethren. While he opened wide the doors, he did not enter the new halls; he remained a true classicist to whom force is form. But what gave him his unique position in the world of music— even in the whole history of civilization—is that at the same time form also served as force. This means that his form is not externally binding but stands for deployment; this form means forming, an active creative process which acknowledges limitations, for it is not borderless, it demands content. Beethoven's whole art is the triumph of power over material, a triumph of function over substance, subject over object. Form is essentially subjective with him, and the subject essentially forming. And the more Beethoven advances into the early romanticism of the nineteenth century, the more classic he becomes; Janus-faced, looking at once backward, expressing the ultimate apotheosis of classicism, and forward, beckoning to the future, a guide and teacher of the nineteenth century.

"Take a hundred century-old oak trees, and write his name with them, in giant letters, on a plain. Or carve his likeness in colossal proportions, like Saint Borromaeus on Lake Maggiore, that he may gaze above the mountains, as he did when living; and when the Rhine ships pass, and foreigners ask the name of that giant form, every child may answer— It is Beethoven, and they will think it is the name of a German Emperor." [6]

Schubert

SCHINDLER relates how Beethoven, on his deathbed, exclaimed when perusing some songs by Schubert: "Truly he has the divine spark." In spite of Schindler's occasional unreliability, there is no reason to doubt the authenticity of this story, for Schubert was the unique early romanticist whose inspiration had its roots in Beethoven, who came the nearest to Beethoven, and who at the same time was the greatest individual personality next to him. There he stood with the archclassicist in that peculiar period in which classicism and romanticism converged, at times called the classicist of romanticism, at others the romanticist of classicism, sharing to a certain extent the ambiguity that surrounded Beethoven.

This last of those divinely gifted musicians under whose hands every pebble became harmony had a short and simple life. Born in Vienna in 1797, Franz Peter Schubert received his first musical education from his father, an elder brother Ignaz, and the choirmaster of the church in the suburb where the family resided. They taught him the rudiments of violin and piano playing, as well as his "general bass." The family was musical, and perhaps the most important factor in Schubert's life and education was the love of music in his home, where chamber music playing was a daily event, where music illuminated the drabness of everyday existence. His own compositions often reflect the character of this music making for one's own enjoyment; their agreeableness, the enjoyment of the sheer beauty of the elements of music, the loving care bestowed on details, all go back to the discoveries he made every day while playing the viola in the family quartet. Like Haydn before him, Schubert was received in 1808 into the imperial chapel as a choirboy, the position carrying with it instruction in the choir school, or *Convict*. This institution had an excellent student orchestra in which Schubert played first violin, occasionally acting as assistant conductor. On the advice of the Convict's music teacher, Schubert took up studies with Salieri, and although the studies were continuous from 1812 to 1815, and undoubtedly familiarized him with many aspects of composition, the Italian musician's eclectic international spirit was strange to him and the counterpoint he learned from him remained a cloak thrown over his fundamentally harmonic, popular, German musical imagination.

In his first instrumental works, Schubert was entirely under the influence of the Viennese school, but even in his very first songs, "Vatermörder," "Hagars Klage," and others, written in 1810–1811, rich in formless potpourries of moods, there appears an entirely original and personal type of melody and harmony, though, indeed, the originality is evident mostly in its excesses. Schubert's development was decisively influenced by his early acquaintance with a group of highly cultivated young poets and writers who introduced him to the atmosphere of romanticism, whose ideals were in such contrast to the complacent spirit of his own environment. In order to escape military service, he took the post of assistant teacher to his father, the school principal, a heavy burden to his artistic temperament which he had to endure for four years. Afterwards he severed all relations with ordinary middle-class life to live, devoid of all regular income, mainly on the good will of his friends. These friends were generous and faithful, but their generosity was sharply limited by their very modest means.

Schubert's precocity is well illustrated by the composition of some of the gems of the musical literature in the years 1814–1816, among them "Gretchen am Spinnrad" and the "Erlkönig." Most of his early instrumental works were written for the excellent Viennese dilettante groups, and he himself was often welcomed in well-to-do music lovers' homes as a good pianist, especially notable for his improvisation of Viennese dances. The first influential admirers of Schubert's genius were the Sonnleithner family, distinguished jurists and music lovers, the poet-playwright Grillparzer, and the excellent singer Johann Michael Vogl (1768–1840), who became the enthusiastic apostle of his songs. During the summer months of 1818 and 1824, Schubert acted as music teacher to the daughters of Count John Esterházy on the latter's estate in western Hungary. The Hungarian sojourn won him another spirited friend, Baron Karl von Schönstein, a fine tenor and an indefatigable propagator of Schubert songs. It also acquainted him with Hungarian and Gypsy music, echoes of which often appear in his own compositions.

In order to improve his precarious financial status, he made several attempts at writing operas, but all proved to be unsuccessful. His forlorn economic existence was compensated for by the warm circle of friends who organized so-called "Schubertiads," spirited reunions combining music with literary discussions, dances, and gay excursions to the countryside. At this time he sought the acquaintance of Goethe, in whose lyricism he found the greatest inspiration for his songs, but the poet left his letter unanswered. In 1823 his frail health forced him to enter a hospital, where he wrote the greater part of the song cycle *Die Schöne Müllerin*. The next theatrical venture, *Rosamunde*, written on a flat and tedious libretto by Helmina von Chézy, the future librettist of Weber's *Euryanthe*, fared a little better than its predecessors, but success was still wanting. In 1826 he applied for the position of assistant court conductor, but his petition was declined, as was another application the next year for a similar post in a private theater. Finally, in his last year of life, his friends arranged a benefit concert of his own compositions which netted him some much-needed money; but Schubert was already in the throes of death. The *Winterreise* cycle was even now overshadowed with heavy depression, from which, summoning all his powers, he escaped into the wondrous beauty of the C major symphony and the C major quintet. At the summit of his creative power, he felt the need of more study and early in November, 1828, sought instruction with the renowned contrapuntist Simon Sechter. But it was too late; he became bedridden and died on the nineteenth of the same month in his thirty-first year. His last wish, to be buried near Beethoven, was fulfilled.

A true poet who ennobled Viennese gaiety with a peculiar melancholy, in his outward appearance he was unprepossessing, gauche, and lacking in refinement. His contemporaries had no idea of Schubert's significance. His most important works were either unknown to them or not properly understood. They appreciated his talents and found genuine pleasure in many of his songs and piano pieces, but that they did not grasp the greatness of his achievements is evident from Grillparzer's epitaph: "Music has here entombed a rich treasure, but much fairer hopes." The parochial romanticism of the early twentieth century, which made operettas out of melodies plucked from his songs and symphonies (*Blossom Time*), feted in him the prodigal melodist, picturing him as an innocent Biedermeier figure, spending his time in merry company in the Viennese cafés, quite at a loss as to what to do with his inexhaustible invention. Schubert was, however, neither a Bohemian nor a seeker of light company. Far from being a Biedermeier character, he joined the men of letters who, suffering from the fetters of bourgeois docility, fled into their own world of poetry in which they could express their ideas freely, bold and revolutionary ideas, filled with secret desires. The composer of the "Gruppe aus dem Tartarus," "Die Stadt," "Der Doppelgänger," was not the poet of lavender-scented homely felicity, comfortably shielded behind shutters from the glare of life; a deep and

furrowing pathos and passion is harnessed in them, on the verge of erup-
tion. The conflict of the romantic soul was visited upon him, the conflict
which arises from the failure to take up the fight with the contradictions
of life. But the same man who looked up to Beethoven as to a gigantic
monument of a bygone age, who built the bridges that enabled the romanticists to reach distant shores, who was as sensitive and impressionable
as any of the romanticists afflicted with the mal du siècle, was, nevertheless, a Beethovenian creature. He did not continue Beethoven's work, for
that was impossible, but—the only musician in the whole post-Beethovenian
world—he could keep pace with him, if not for years, then at least for
certain long days. His egocentric nature was that of the romanticist, as
was his faith in sudden inspirations, his love for a color patch or a harmonic turn, but his nature was not always passive, for music lived in him
like a mystic, natural force. His sensitiveness knew no limits, and in the
"Wegweiser" and the "Doppelgänger," in the D minor quartet and the
Unfinished Symphony, he descends to the bottom of the fantastic and
visionary as does only Novalis.

A great many misconceptions surround the lifework of this great musician. The title "Father of the song"—in itself entirely incorrect—which
customarily appears after his name in reference manuals alone prevents a
just appraisal of a musician who was one of the outstanding composers of
instrumental music. Even the songs selected as typical from his many hundreds are usually the ones nearest to the Biedermeier conception. In this
connection, one might say that while as a song composer he does not really
show a steady development—some of his most magnificent songs dating
from his youth—as an instrumental and choral composer he exhibits a
well-nigh incredible development from "play music" to large-scale symphonic architecture, and from balladry to the great orchestral Mass.

Although the music of the nineteenth century offers a movemented and
varied spectacle, with a multitude of forces and components at work, we
have seen that what determined its course was the changing relationship
of words and music. We followed the slow process from the purely musical
approach to the words to the literary approach to the music, noting that
all this took place in opera, oratorio, and cantata. This being the case, one
can understand why the song, or rather the *Lied,* reached its real flourishing in the early romantic era—a literary era par excellence in the history
of music—for a song cannot be treated in the same manner as an opera
libretto; poetry has vested rights in it that cannot be ignored. The eighteenth century neglected the song as being incompatible with a purely
musical approach to vocal music, and of the different types of vocal music
the song was the least important in that era. Songs flourished in the Berlin
school and up to Sperontes because this school was based on literary pre-

cepts; but in the following classic era, exclusively musical in its aims and means, the song ceased to be a musical type of primary importance. We should guard, however, against considering the German romantic song a new form of music. It is true that, beginning with Schubert's time, the German song occupied such a special place in the musical literature of the world that its name, *Lied,* was accepted and introduced in other languages as if demonstrating that "song" or "chanson" does not adequately express its particular nature. But the songs of Schulz, Reichardt, Zelter, and Zumsteeg, together with many fine "numbers" from the Singspiele, represent a rich and estimable literature, fully answering the description reserved for Schubert's songs. Max Friedländer's important work on the German song in the eighteenth century [7] gives a good idea of the fallacy of regarding the romantic song as a new phenomenon. Thus the Lied was not new, either in technique or in principle, but the complete discarding of aesthetic theories and preconceived attitudes, the casting of every song in an independent mold, did inaugurate a new era.

Schubert, who recognized the new order of things, the new relationship of poet and musician, was far more creative in the purely musical sense than any other song writer, with the occasional exception of Schumann and Brahms. Had he accepted the romantic dictum of the poet's absolute supremacy, merely providing music to the text, he would not have created the modern song; but by consciously elevating such purely musical elements as harmony and instrumental accompaniment to equal importance with poem and melody, he brought to bear upon the atmosphere of the song the force of an overwhelming musical organism, a force sufficient to establish a balance between poetry and music. This balance he observed and safeguarded with the unlimited resources of a true genius. It is this relationship to the poet which explains Schubert's power over all poetry. Significantly enough, he set forty-one poems by Schiller, whose verse was always considered to be "impossible to compose." Yet Schubert almost invariably succeeded in conquering the philosophical and rhetorical that characterizes these poems by the force of the musical rendering. This immersion in the elementally musical resulted in the miraculous union of voice and accompaniment—neither a simple harmonic assistance, as in the songs of the older song writers, nor orchestrally conceived incorporation of the vocal part in a quasi-symphonic structure, as with the modern song composers. His instrumental accompaniment, especially in the song cycles *Schöne Müllerin* and *Winterreise,* acts in a manner not unlike Mozart's opera orchestra, furnishing the mood, the soil from which grows the vocal flower. Hence the uninterrupted enchantment of these song cycles; the accompaniment holds us permanently in the mood of the idea while the voice, especially in the *Winterreise,* gives us its various images. Paradoxical as it may seem, for this very reason and despite the great importance of the accompaniment, Schubert's melodies are such finished entities that they can be sung unaccompanied and will still give perfect aesthetic satisfaction. Only certain songs of Schumann and Brahms rise to such musical integrity, for while there were many fine song composers after Schubert who divined the secret of the Lied, the balance was gradually upset in favor of the literary element, thereby ending the history of the true song. In Hugo Wolf's songs, for instance, the high degree of animation and excitement is due to a poetic text, and in the final analysis his way of composition is a reproductive art in the literal sense; something already created is again revealed through the medium of a personality with the aid of another art. Wolf embodies the ideal of the ancient Greek rhapsodist, who performed a poem in a declamation enhanced by music. Schubert's dependence on the poet is not absolute; his song is the same "poesy in tones," as Beethoven's "dichten in Tönen," even though it is determined by the words. But his creative power is of a purely musical nature; the poem is merely an incentive to his own creative activity. While the literary quality of his song texts often influenced their musical value (a sign of the romantic era), this quality was not essential to him. Some of his most sublime melodies were composed to poor poems, but his ability to find in every instance the right antidote and his recognition of the boundaries of the song show how deeply he was rooted in classicism. In this highly literary period he could no longer disregard prosody, and his setting of the individual words is exemplary; but this was also attributable to the fact that the individual words successfully expressed the general mood in the many fine poems of Goethe and other great poets, which offered him the kind of musical treatment that became his second nature. How strongly the musical idea prevails over the image given by the poem is best seen in Liszt's transcriptions of the songs—unadorned faithful piano transcriptions which still make veritable little symphonic poems, although the text is missing, because Schubert was able to project the idea, that is the purely musical, through the image of the idea, the poem. It has often been said that Goethe's rather poor musical taste is sadly evident in his rejection of Schubert's settings of his poems in favor of Zelter's much simpler melodies. But does that not rather imply that Goethe felt that while his verse still dominates Zelter's song, Schubert would turn it wholly into music, thereby robbing the poet of his own property? This attitude is perfectly understandable from the point of view of Goethe, who could only see his ideas vanish into music, not divining what his lyricism made possible in the field of music.

No other musician's works convey the impression of the outdoors as do Schubert's. In his wanderings in and around Vienna, in Upper Austria,

Styria, and western Hungary, he picked the wild flowers of folk music with both hands and gave them back to us in his songs and dances, arranged in wonderful bouquets. Nature inspired a large part of his lyric output, from simple songs like "Wohin?" or "Am See," to the hymnic "Meeresstille" or "Die Grenzen der Menschheit." His song cycles created in the Lied an organism planned and realized to a degree of unity that only the great classic instrumental forms had known before him. His choral works are entirely under the spell of his song lyricism, yet in some of them he arrives in the vicinity of the lyric drama. Schubert was more successful, however, in a musical dramaticism which did not require a theatrical setting. Only one of his numerous operas, *Fierrabras* (1823), exudes a dramatic spirit; the others contain much fine music but little of the dramatic.

The song writer in Schubert was uninhibited and original from the very beginning, but the instrumental composer struggled for classic clarity. The earlier piano sonatas are diffuse and restless; Schubert is almost desperate in his attempts to free himself from the oppressive shadow of Beethoven. The construction also is beclouded by the romanticist's discovery of the charms peculiar to the piano. Technical expediency and the sonorous qualities of the instrument, while not ignored, are never permitted undue influence upon the construction of a composition in Beethoven's works; pianism, if admitted, is made to conform to the whole. In Schubert, it becomes a constructive factor and the only saving grace of the earlier sonatas; but it could not prevent the development sections from falling apart. The master who wrote the great symphonies and quartets could never find the same security in the piano sonata; the romanticist who succeeded in conjuring up the broad symphonic organism of Beethoven succumbed here to the cultivation of detached moods. Many of the movements of his sonatas are of a bewitching beauty, some of them profoundly moving, and here and there is a well-knit sonata construction; but the movements seldom hold together, they share no unifying, guiding idea. On the other hand, the lyric piano pieces, *impromptus* and *moments musicaux,* inspired by similar works by Johann Wenzel Tomaschek (1774-1850) and Johann Hugo Worzischek (1791-1825), two excellent and poetic Czech composers, show Schubert at his best. Every one of these pieces (the numerous little dances, for instance) is a bit of genre painting, the exquisite lyric confession of a musical poet.

In chamber music and symphony he was again confronted with the towering figure of Beethoven, but already in the Second Symphony, in B flat (1814), the youngster attempted to emulate the large Beethovenian gesture, and again in the Fourth, more tragic in intention than in outcome. It is interesting to observe how Schubert found his way to one of Beethoven's sources of inspiration, Cherubini, in particular the latter's *Medea*. The *Tragic* Symphony shows its imprint together with those of Beethoven's *Coriolanus* and *Egmont,* which in their time were equally under the spell of *Medea*. In the particularly felicitous Fifth Symphony, in B flat, Schubert returned again to the Haydn-Dittersdorf-Mozart circle, although every tone in the work is inalienably his own. While the quartets of 1812 are definitely experimental, by 1814 the great master of the string quartet is before us, earnestly striving to find his relationship to the classics. His frequent use of Austrian and Hungarian popular tunes and moods demonstrates his allegiance to Haydn, as the elaborate coda which appears almost as a second development section shows the Beethovenian idea. It is true that in his chamber music and in his symphonies he did not always follow the symphonic lineage of Haydn and Beethoven, for instead of concentrating on the exploitation of a laconic symphonic idea he often reached with both hands into the inexhaustible treasure chest of his melodic invention; but he could still muster enough discipline to prevent diffusion, and he still breathed the air of the symphonic atmosphere that surrounded Beethoven. If we examine Mozart's occasional prodigality in his symphonic structures we shall realize where Schubert's maternal ancestry came from; but the paternal, the Beethovenian, was in evidence too, and after about 1820 it became dominant, as can be readily seen in the so-called *Unfinished* Symphony. His greatness becomes fearful if we realize that this wonder of a symphony was written in 1822, in the immediate vicinity of the Ninth Symphony. Here is a composer, inspired and overawed by Beethoven, who dares to follow the Titan to dizzy heights, returning unscathed with a work every tone of which is his own, and which can be placed next to those of Beethoven without paling. Never in the subsequent history of music did this happen again. The symphony is fortunately too well known to require discussion, but it is high time that its name be changed. The sentimental conception of the tragic death of the composer in his youth termed this symphony his last, interrupted by the stony hands of fate. In reality, at least two great symphonies followed (one of them unhappily lost), and the only reason for Schubert's not finishing the earlier symphony —he began and abandoned a scherzo—must have been the same that prompted Beethoven to be satisfied with two movements in his F sharp, E minor, and C minor (*op.* 111) piano sonatas: the mood was completely exhausted. Far from regarding it as a magnificent torso, we should treasure the B minor symphony as a consummate work of art, free from all formalistic restrictions.

And then we arrive at the last great symphony, the C major, not only Schubert's last, but the last mighty classical symphony which like a bastion guards the exit of the hallowed precincts of the greatest era of orchestral music. What magnificent and truly symphonic élan, what a wealth of pictures drawn from the heroic-capricious, utterly classic, symphonic theme! The little development within the exposition—a genuinely Beethovenian touch—where the powerful trombones announce the coming storm while the wood winds chirp in happy abandonment, impressed every German composer in the nineteenth century. The andante is a most complicated composite movement utilizing a plethora of material with an assuredness that makes it appear as simple as a song, and the scherzo is a worthy counterpart of the boldest of Beethoven's, although most of its melodies are popular Viennese tunes blended with the symphonic pregnancy of the chief motif in a manner that leaves one speechless. The finale of this symphony moved Schumann to comment on its "heavenly length": "How refreshing is this feeling of overflowing wealth! With others we always tremble for the conclusion, troubled lest we find ourselves disappointed." [8]

The D minor quartet is again a work which braved the Beethovenian magnet and passed by, emerging as the greatest Schubert. It is the triumph of the reconciliation of classicism with romanticism. The variations on the familiar song "Death and the Maiden," which gave the quartet its name, once more resurrect this favored medium of the classic composers in all its glory, and the tremendous momentum is never lost to the very end of the frenzied last movement. It is not speed but the impact that grows, for it is again force that speaks in these themes—force which generates form, a force that makes itself felt in the smallest particle of a composition, giving it the unity of classicism.

His early Masses are the works of a pious Austrian Catholic, unobsessed by doubts or by metaphysical speculations, writing church music intended to fulfill practical needs. While these early Masses exhibit the same inequalities that characterize the other works of this period, they are distinguished by a genuine, unaffected warmth and a fine lyric tone. Paralleling his ascent as symphonist and chamber music composer, Schubert the church composer rose to supreme heights in his last great Masses in A flat and E flat. Schumann said that "he who is not acquainted with the C major symphony knows very little about Schubert"—a remark which should be extended to cover these Masses.

Like Johann Sebastian Bach, Schubert may seem to be the crowning master of a long period of a certain type of music. Yet, like Bach, he remains eternally new. His songs carried the German Lied to its zenith, as Beethoven's instrumental works carried those types. They encompass a world in which simple folk songs and philosophical professions of life, simple tunes and broad dramatic scenes, live together. The man who plucked "Heidenröslein" challenged the universe with his "Prometheus," revealing with a shudder the "Grenzen der Menschheit," "the boundaries of humanity." But he was the one in whom the Beethovenian lineage ended; symphony and chamber music disintegrated after him and did not find a true disciple until Brahms. Schubert owed more to Beethoven than to anyone else. The great classicist appeared to him enthroned on Olympian heights, and so great was his reverence that he never dared to speak to the man he often saw in Vienna. Beethoven's death shook him to the depths of his soul and hastened his own passing. He felt no shyness with Beethoven's compositions, however, and he incurred his debt to the great symphonist willingly and with a clear artistic conscience, for he knew how to use it for his own purposes, remaining independent and original where he approached nearest to his idol.

In the first movement of the D minor quartet there is a real polyphonic spirit, that of the free ensemble polyphony of the Viennese school; other movements, like the andante in the B flat piano trio, are the purest, most pristine expressions of romanticism. There are, to be sure, elements in his instrumental music that one does not encounter in the works of the classic composers, such as a certain lyricism, songlike constellations which threaten the formal design, but in most cases he finds a way to maintain balance and cohesion. The harmonic element also unquestionably acquires with him the importance we associate with romantic music, and there is a wide exploitation of chromaticism; yet with all his overflow of melodic wealth, the often apparent absence of a guiding hand and of an imperative will, everything seems naturally coherent and simple. And this unity is not restricted to the individual movements, as in most of his piano sonatas, for in works like the A minor quartet (1824) it encompasses the whole composition. The often repeated accusation of formlessness cannot be maintained save in some instances and only from the point of view of formalistic aesthetics. Form and content fit perfectly more often than not, giving the sense of equilibrium experienced only in the true classicist. That this equilibrium is not always obtained in the manner sanctified by a theoretical code does not in the least change the essential impression it makes; the problems which he attacked often do not exist in this code. In the "Erlkönig," for instance, the harnessing of the dangerous mixture of dramatic, epic, and lyric elements within the frame of a simple song for voice and piano, producing a composition of unexcelled unity, testifies to his power of creative forming. His limited literary and artistic horizon did not prevent him from penetrating regions unattainable to the most highly educated of his successors. Schubert often tried to penetrate behind the meaning of the words, using the sharpest harmonic or melodic characterizations, but even in works like the quartet bearing the suggestive title of his song there is not the slightest attempt at program music; on the contrary, this work is the ideal translation of a literary content into an absolute form of instrumental music.

We accept this miracle of a musician as something natural and are far removed from knowing what we really possess in his art. From the prodigal gifts he left us we do not even know the majority of his songs, let alone the other works. The forty large volumes of the complete edition of his works (1885–1897) permit us a panorama of his activity, which touched on all fields of music—music that is youth itself, beautiful as only youth can be, free, and full of the natural solemnity of unspoiled idealism. Such men must die young to bequeath to the world the legacy of youth incarnate.

French Opera During Revolution, Directoire, and Empire

CARL Maria von Weber (1786–1826) appears as the response to the desire for German opera which had animated German musicians ever since Schütz, and which became the symbol of romanticism, toward which all musicians strove. "My morning and evening prayer," said Schumann, "is for German opera." The movement toward the fulfillment of this dream is discernible half a century before Weber's time, in the Singspiel. Yet this earnest musician was obsessed with the passion to create a German opera as if there were no such thing in existence—this, although thirty years before the *Freischütz* there was the *Magic Flute* and a little later *Fidelio,* and no one had more admiration for them than Weber, who as an operatic conductor was often in charge of their performance. But he, the romanticist, one of the first of those composers whose literary education matched their musical training, turned sharply against the international-universal musical style of the eighteenth century, deliberately seeking that which distinguished the German from anything else. Weber's *Freischütz* (1821), an immediate artistic echo of the patriotic and religious enthusiasm of the wars of liberation, signified the victory of the German romantic opera over the French revolutionary and empire opera, admired and followed by all other early nineteenth-century composers, including Beethoven. What Mozart and Beethoven were not able to achieve, this man of infinitely more modest talents accomplished; he brought about a closer relationship between the German people and German music, summoning the spirit of the German forest to the German operatic stage. But to understand the magnitude and the portent of Weber's role we must examine the opera he vanquished, the French opera of the eighteenth and early nineteenth centuries, which exerted such great influence on the German lyric stage, and which remained a favorite with the German public throughout the political upheavals.

Gluck's musico-dramatic principles continued to be regarded as a sort of canon by French composers and by such foreigners as tried their fortunes in France, although the inroads made by the opéra comique threatened the very existence of the music drama. Among the French, Jean Baptiste Le Moyne (1751–1796) and Gossec composed some noteworthy works, but they were overshadowed by the Italians, Piccini, Sacchini, and Salieri. Sacchini's *Oedipe à Colone* (1787) is worthy of the great traditions of the tragédie lyrique, and Piccini's *Roland* we have called a true companion to the classic dramas of Gluck. Salieri was not comparable to his two compatriots, but his great routine and technique of dramatic composition assured him a high position in the operatic world and his influence was extensive. Still another foreigner in Paris was Johann Christoph Vogel (1756–1788), whose *Toison d'Or* and *Démoophon* belong among the best dramatic works of the period. This uncommonly talented young German composer could have become Gluck's successor but for his early death.

While the foreigners were still dictating the style, Grétry continued the cultivation of the spirited dialogue opera, developing it methodically in numerous works. Grétry was responsible for the creation of two types of opera in which the French national tone once more asserted itself over that of the foreigners; one was the fairy opera first presented in his *Zémire et Azore* (1771), the other the so-called "rescue opera," the ancestor of which was his celebrated *Richard Coeur de Lion* (1784). Both these works inspired an avalanche of imitations in France and in Germany. We must not forget, nevertheless, that Grétry gave his best in the field of the comic opera,[9] in spite of the great influence of his more ambitious dramatic works in which the vaudeville spirit gave way to loftier aspirations.

As we near the end of the century the old vaudeville-comic opera and the through-composed dramatic opera evince a tendency for fusion, and in Méhul's *Euphrosine* (1790) the rapprochement becomes a fact. Continuing his efforts, Etienne Nicolas Méhul (1763–1817), whose great talents were praised by the aged Gluck, composed a short opera entitled *Stratonice* (1792) in which the comical element is entirely missing. Beginning with this work the term "opéra comique" becomes ambiguous, often causing confusion, for henceforth the term was applied to any musico-dramatic work which contained spoken dialogues, whether comic or tragic. (Even much later *Carmen* was still called an opéra comique.)

When the Revolution shook the land, French music nurtured a number of ambitious composers, and even the older men, such as Gossec and Grétry, felt rejuvenated by the movemented times, displaying novel ideas and a freshness of imagination. Besides Méhul, already mentioned, the most important composers were Luigi Cherubini (1760–1842), a thoroughly Gallicized Italian, Nicolas Dalayrac (1753–1809), Charles Simon Catel (1773–

1830), Jean François Le Sueur (1760–1837), François Adrien Boïeldieu (1775–1834), and Henri Montan Berton (1767–1844). These were all excellent musicians, brought up in the old traditions, who now had to obey the will of the people and readjust their artistic creed. The professionals were joined by Claude Joseph Rouget de l'Isle (1760–1836), the soldier-musician who without the martial events would have remained obscure but, carried away by the grandeur of the ideals, gave the nation its much-admired anthem, the "Marseillaise." The resilient mental capabilities of the French helped them to overcome the ravages of the revolutionary years, and it is significant that the theater seems to have been one of the agents of comfort and diversion. The theaters of Paris, of which there were some sixty, were never so popular as during the Terror. A contemporary ditty expressed this graphically:

> Il ne fallait au fier Romain
> Que des spectacles et du pain;
> Mais au Français plus que Romain
> Le spectacle suffit sans pain.

"In the morning the guillotine was kept busy, and in the evening one could not get a seat in the theater," remarked Madame Cherubini to Hiller. The Republicans now discovered music, and with the customary zeal of the liberators, whose first duty is always to force their convictions on the liberated, commanded all musicians to compose revolutionary and patriotic songs and teach them to the people. Everyone seems to have complied, for among the composers mentioned in contemporary notices we find all the great names in French music, with Gossec apparently the most enthusiastic partisan of the new regime, judging from his many songs and hymns. The populace was herded into the squares in large masses, where they were taught the latest revolutionary songs.

The former simplicity and directness of French music was overwhelmed by the bombastic grandeur that remained an unfortunate characteristic of French music until the late nineteenth century. The execution of Louis XVI was commemorated in gigantic musical festivals. The opening of the Council of Five Hundred on the memorable twenty-first of January, 1796, the third anniversary of the king's death, was preceded by the singing of a choir of five hundred conducted by Cherubini; and the Opéra, for which (as the Académie Royale de Musique) the king and queen had done so much, did not fail to give a yearly gala performance in honor of the event. While the antireligious persecutions were not relaxed (Le Sueur was arrested for having "made music for Jesus Christ"), Robespierre put through the Convention an edict permitting the belief in immortality and the worship of an impersonal Supreme Being, whom it was decided to honor by a three-day-long Fête de l'Etre Suprème, June 6, 7, and 8, 1794, in the National Gardens (Tuileries). The teachers of the Institut National de Musique, the future Conservatoire, knowing full well the imprudence of ignoring decrees of the Convention, sent a petition to the Committee offering their services, at the same time pointing out the value of music for the people. Among the signatories of this document were Le Sueur, Gossec, Méhul, Berton, Cherubini, and Dalayrac, that is, all the important composers of the time. An invitation followed to set to music a "Hymn to the Eternal Being," text by Marie-Joseph Chénier. The diligent professors, not satisfied with the simple task of composing the music, took pains to initiate the people in the secrets of higher art, now made democratic. Thus in the last days before the Fête they could be seen, armed with a flute, violin, or some other instrument, in certain popular meeting places practicing with the citoyens and citoyennes. Standing on a table or an overturned cart, they played and conducted until the monster performance was whipped into shape. The "Hymn" was sung by twenty-four hundred singers, the refrains by the whole populace to the accompaniment of cannon. The dimensions of the performances kept on growing, although in a purely external fashion. Méhul used three orchestras and choirs, after which Le Sueur added a fourth. There was nothing left for Berlioz but to add a fifth, which he did thirty years later in the *Tuba Mirum* of his Requiem Mass. The din of the orchestra became so loud that it covered the voices of the singers, to the chagrin of those composers who were lyrically inclined. Grétry drily remarked that every operatic performance, no matter what its subject, seemed to re-enact the demolition of the Bastille.

In February of the year of terror 1793, Le Sueur's *La Caverne* was produced with tremendous success. The fantastic and gruesome nature of this opera, filled with jagged arias and wild and noisy ensemble scenes, fitted the temper of the times admirably; Le Sueur virtually gave the revolutionary era its musical style, followed by all Frenchmen and imitated by the foreigners. *La Caverne*, performed everywhere in France, reached its hundredth performance in a little over a year, adding another six hundred to the record before it was dropped. Two years later Méhul essayed a *Caverne* of his own, but without much success. Le Sueur's *Paul et Virginie*, also composed during the Terror, did not please as much as *La Caverne*, but the descriptive sea storm that seems to have been its pièce de résistance found many admirers and was responsible for many a musical tempest, such as the one in Berlioz's *Fantastic* Symphony.

Once the model was accepted and musicians of greater talent engaged in its cultivation, the horror and rescue opera yielded powerful works. Dalayrac, one of the most popular composers, whose fame rivaled that of Mozart, registered great success with his two horror operas, *Raoul de*

Créqui and *Les Deux Savoyards*. Catel, Méhul, and Berton contributed a number of other equally well-received works, but the composer who raised this type of opera to true music drama, the one among the many who was a worthy successor to Gluck and Piccini, was Cherubini, a composer admired and studied with the greatest reverence by every musician in Europe. Schooled on the vocal polyphony of Palestrina, this earnest seeker of perfection found a setting in France that was ideally suited to the development of his innate talents. To his contrapuntal studies he added a knowledge of the fine instrumental music of French classicism. The new German instrumental music of the Mannheim and Viennese schools was well known in Paris, and the purity and nobility of the old Italian string style remained intact, practiced by the Italian-trained French violinists Leclair and Gaviniès. Giovanni Battista Viotti (1753–1824), the most eminent violinist of his time and one of the best composers for his instrument, resided in Paris for several years as director of the Théâtre de Monsieur (afterwards the Théâtre Feydeau). In his position as aide to Viotti, Cherubini's delicate task was to adapt Italian operas to suit the French taste. This required changes in the text and corresponding alterations in the musical score, which he carried out with great skill. This, and the earlier experience gained under Sarti, who entrusted to his young protégé the composition of the "minor characters" in his operas, equipped Cherubini with a technique of dramatic composition that became the much-admired model of musicians, from the numberless minor opera writers to Beethoven and Schumann. The first performance of his *Lodoiska,* July 18, 1791, repeated two hundred times in the same year, was an event in the history of the lyric stage that ranks with the presentation of Gluck's *Iphigénie* and Mozart's *Don Giovanni,* and its reception was surpassed only by that accorded to *Les Deux Journées* (1800), generally conceded to be Cherubini's finest opera. Although *Les Deux Journées* unquestionably merits this designation, *Medea* is perhaps his most impressive and poignant horror opera, composed with a dramatic intensity that knows no compromise. The dark forebodings and feverish activity of the opera are evident with the first chords of the overture; it is a piece that held the greatest composers spellbound. Indeed, who will not recognize in the somber *Medea* overture the source of inspiration for Beethoven's *Egmont,* to mention the most outstanding example?

This fiery yet disciplined musical aristocrat and uncompromising artist was a noble idealist reveling in the portrayal of heroic women. The terrorists may have forced him to undignified acts, but the fortitude and integrity of his chief figures, all women—Lodoiska, Elisa, Medea, and Constance—reflected his true and compassionate soul. These wonderful characters were matched only by Leonore, their kinswoman, for none of the French composers around him, however distinguished, could muster such intensity of feeling coupled with consummate craftsmanship.

Cherubini's operas, indeed all his music, represented a real classicism, for they were classic in spirit and execution, the Grecomania of the Revolution having exhausted itself in ostentatious inscriptions. To take one example, Le Sueur's *Télémaque* (1796) was filled with "classic" intentions and allusions, which begin in the overture, designated as being "in the hypodorian tone, in spondaic rhythm, and using mesodic melody."

Under the impact of the social upheavals, the opéra comique was slowly transformed from farce to bourgeois opera, a course of events facilitated by the abolition of the privileges usurped by the Académie Royale de Musique. The Théâtre de l'Opéra Comique could now perform "serious" works without being persecuted. With Méhul's *Mélidore et Phrosine* (1795) the melodrama joined the new mixture of operatic types and styles. In the light of our acquaintance with the German melodrama we should not be surprised to find orchestral commentaries between the spoken dialogues, which, in turn, soon led to leitmotivic technique of composition. And now we must proceed with the utmost wariness, for we are nearing the juncture of a circle. In his essay entitled *De la Musique Mécanique et de la Musique Philosophique,* Berton gave the program of the musical "revolution." The aim was to combine Gluck's dramaturgical theories with the symphonic ideal, especially as manifested in the logical thematic work of Haydn. This was stated unequivocally, and Haydn's "art of developing a motif and presenting it in all imaginable shades" was cited as the specific example to be followed. The consequences of this reasoning were far reaching. For some time the French had already employed certain recurring motives. Of great significance for the future were Grétry's experiments with such recurring motives, and *Richard Coeur de Lion* is, in a way, a veritable leitmotif opera. The recognition and discussion of the leitmotif as an agent of dramatic construction goes back to Count de Lacépède (1756–1825), distinguished scientist and man of letters, whose *Poétique de la Musique* (1785) seems to have been widely known. With the adaptation of a symphonic-thematic technique, the leitmotif received a new scope and was to overshadow every other consideration. An instrumental operatic style arose which gradually surrendered the prerogatives of the singing voice to the orchestra. The beginnings of this tendency are most interesting. Méhul's *Ariodant,* performed in 1799, seems to have been the first significant work among the full-fledged leitmotif operas obeying the new symphonic-dramatic principles.

The opera is based on one fundamental motif—the composer called it "cri de fureur"—which, developed symphonically, dominates the whole lyric drama. This basic motif, customarily called "trait chromatique" as it was usually a short chromatic theme, became the stylistic mark of the school. With superior mastery Méhul synchronized the dramatic development with the symphonic treatment, and Catel and Berton proved to be equally versatile operatic symphonists, although lacking Méhul's warm musicianship.

The circle begins to close here; the orchestra, nurtured by the lyric drama and now rich in experience gained from its own independent life, is about to overpower its erstwhile ruler and in the Wagnerian symphonic leitmotif opera will all but swallow the remnants of the lyric drama. But while the symphonic opera grew, supported by literary testimonials and dissertations, it was not destined to reach its fulfillment at the hands of Latin composers. The ancient musico-dramatic instinct of the Italians once more broke through with all its might, steeped in tragedy, passion, and pathos, yet appearing in the most sublime classical forms in Cherubini's operas. The inscrutable Florentine-Parisian, acquainted with all the secrets of Italian, French, and German music, fusing them into a sovereign classicism, recognized the advantages of the leitmotif technique and used it—but with circumspection, for he never allows the lyric drama to be threatened by the eloquence of the orchestra.

French opera did not follow the course it had set for itself toward the end of the eighteenth century; life as well as art had changed under the imperial command of Napoleon. The democratic spirit of the French opera was incompatible with the empire, and the old "glorification opera" had to be resuscitated to extol the glamour of emperor and empire. As a good operatic establishment had been considered a necessary fixture of a royal household ever since the early seventeenth century, Napoleon, always jealous of his imperial prerogatives, assembled in the court theater in the Tuileries an excellent troupe. The Italians enjoyed his full and munificent protection, although he often consulted Le Sueur and Méhul, with whom he was on friendly terms. From his dealings with these musicians one would surmise that he was far from being the Boeotian historians like to depict him concerning matters musical, but he demanded absolute obedience even in artistic points; this he could not get from Cherubini, hence his dislike of the greatest French composer of his reign. The unbending nature of the two Frenchmen by adoption, eying each other in silent defiance on the occasion of a congratulatory visit paid to Napoleon by the faculty of the Conservatoire, impressed the witnesses so much that they referred with awe to "ce regard qui c'était croisé avec le regard de Bonaparte." Finally Napoleon succeeded in finding the composer and director who was to his taste in Gasparo Spontini (1774-1851), a pupil of Piccini and of the Neapolitan conservatory "della Pietà." A towering artistic personality, true musical Napoleon, and born tyrant, Spontini was purposeful and ruthless, his activities always directed toward success. He revived the old opera of homage in a modern guise by treating historical subjects in such a manner that they appeared as a rather transparent eulogy of contemporary events. In his first opera written for Paris, *La Vestale* (1803), the ancient tragic greatness of Italian music drama was revived with one stroke. The subjects selected invariably offered opportunities for the deployment of great pomp, glittering ceremonials, and a life based on effect and splendor, seemingly exuded by the subject itself.

Spontini's strength lay in his faith in himself; he was convinced that he was giving not only his best but the best. This belief grew into a sort of megalomania which earned him many enemies. On the other hand, the haughty contempt of this imperial composer wrought benefits of no mean importance. The manner in which he enforced the rights of composer and conductor, making the two the undisputed rulers in the theater, made it possible to abolish the humiliating preposterousness of singers and officials. *La Vestale* was followed by *Fernand Cortez* (1809), likewise greeted with acclamation, and when the regime changed Spontini's reputation was so secure that he retained his position under Louis XVIII, until in 1820 he accepted the invitation of the King of Prussia to join his court in Berlin.

Powerful, modern, and animated, Spontini's music drama was the embodiment of the Napoleonic spirit. He succeeded in combining the old Italian music drama with the horror opera and with the Gluckian lyric tragedy. The blaring trumpets that greet the arrival of the hero in *Lohengrin* are his, as are all similar scenes in French and German operas up to the middle of the century. The musical scene in France was dominated by him and after his departure there came an inevitable lull until the advent of the romantic grand opera, which, however, owed much of its make-up to him.

Early Romantic Opera in Germany

GERMAN opera was destined to fulfill the desire of romanticism for a universal art. The acknowledged leader in the romantic art world having been music, the universal art, the Gesamtkunstwerk, could take shape only under musical auspices. We know that such was the course of musical history, but we also know that the fulfillment actually came after the romantic era proper had passed. If this fact seems puzzling, the antecedents of German romantic opera are more than puzzling, and one has great difficulty in finding the thread leading up to Weber, only to lose it almost immediately after the death of this symbol of German romanticism.

When we turn away from France, the cradle of nineteenth-century operatic movements, to follow them into Germany we are startled by the picture confronting us. After witnessing the triumph of German instrumental music all over Europe, we find the operatic field in the undisputed domination of Italy. In the first two decades of the century the important operatic posts in Germany were still filled by Italians—Salieri in Vienna, Paër and Morlacchi in Dresden, Spontini in Berlin—and it was not until the eighteen twenties that the situation changed. But while conductors and the theatrical personnel were slowly Germanized, as far as the works themselves were concerned the whole of the first half of the century was still dominated by foreign opera. Like Hasse and Mozart, Mayr, von Winter, Gyrowetz, Weigl, Meyerbeer, and as late a figure as Otto Nicolai, German composers went to Italy to study and compose in the Italian manner. In Dresden the Italian opera survived until 1832, six years after Weber's death; in Munich a new Italian opera, supported by the state, was maintained even after the middle of the century. Vienna was to all intents and purposes still, or rather again, an Italian operatic colony. From 1821 to 1828 the management of the Kärntnertortheater and of the Theater an der Wien was united in the hands of Domenico Barbaja, a famous impresario, who at the same time retained the management of La Scala in Milan and of the San Carlo Opera in Naples. He was truly the head of the greatest operatic trust in the history of music. In this atmosphere Beethoven and Schubert had small hopes for recognition as opera composers; the others, the Weigls and Gyrowetzes, wrote Italian operas. And when Rossini came the whole country was at his feet. We should not be misled by the fact that this enthusiasm has been ridiculed in many a historical monograph, for it was genuine, shared by all. The philosopher Hegel, passing through Vienna in 1824, prolonged his stay and was reluctant to resume his journey so charmed was he by Italian opera.

Since opera was like a battlefield of cultural and political currents, faithfully reflecting the issues at stake, opera in Germany soon echoed the tone of French revolutionary opera. Its impact was considerably diminished there, however, for the political prerequisites were different. Apart from a few unimportant imitations, Beethoven's *Fidelio* remains the only valuable German contribution to the species, although the elements of the horror opera were vividly utilized in the German romantic opera. While the revolutionary opera proper did not take deep roots in Germany, German composers were fascinated by the post-Gluck school of Méhul and Cherubini, as they were dazzled a little later by Spontini and the empire opera. The newness of this imperial style, steeped in pathos and pomp, its full and rich orchestration, highly dramatic recitatives, and exemplary vocal writing impressed them tremendously. If we add to the seemingly inextricable maze of Italian and French music and musicians the cult of Mozart and of the

German Singspiel, very considerable at the opening of the century, we shall understand the historian's dilemma, a dilemma made infinitely more acute by the views held by the composers themselves.

As long as classical antiquity furnished the subjects for Italian, German, and French opera, composers of these nations, joined by some Spaniards, could unite in the practice of an international art; but as soon as romanticism began to investigate the medieval past, each of these nations discovered that it possessed a history of its own. Here begins, then, a new national orientation. But while the need for a new orientation was recognized in theory, in practice we can find no trace of it, save in the libretti. Yet the composers were convinced that they were actually creating in the new idiom and, what is more astounding, imputed a full-blooded romanticism to their elders. E. T. A. Hoffmann was the first to eulogize Beethoven in penetrating writings, in which he feted him as the fulfillment of all that for which romanticism was longing. Discussing Cherubini's *Lodoiska* on the occasion of its performance in Dresden (1817), Weber remarked that the dominating artistic tendency "in our time is romanticism," which he believed to be present in Cherubini's works. To make the confusion more complete, Hoffmann praised Mozart as "the inimitable creator of the romantic opera" and considered Haydn, Mozart, and Beethoven romantic composers "whose works, with all the differences between them, breathe the same romantic spirit." Even Spohr named Mozart as his chief operatic model, an attribution he repeated several times in his autobiography.

We need not reopen the question of Mozart's operas—their essentially classical eighteenth-century nature is established beyond doubt—but in view of the persistent allusions to Beethoven as a romantic opera composer we must take another glance at *Fidelio*. *Leonore,* as it was first called, had its roots in the bourgeois Singspiel and in the French rescue opera. The libretto was a conventional story about "conjugal love," four variants of which had been set to music before Sonnleithner arranged it for Beethoven. Of these settings Beethoven knew those of Pierre Gaveaux (1761–1825), a French singer and composer whose *Léonore, ou l'Amour Conjugal* was first performed in Paris in 1798, and of Ferdinando Paër, whose *Leonora, ossia l'Amore Conjugale* was produced six years later in Dresden. Emulating his models, Beethoven's choir of revenge, singing ominously behind the scenes, and the trumpet calls signaling impending rescue are all typical products of the revolutionary opera in vogue at the turn of the century. The greatest single influence hovering about *Leonore* was, however, Cherubini. On the whole *Fidelio* is little more than a translation of Bouilly's *Leonore.* Bouilly was the librettist of Cherubini's *Les Deux Journées,* the creator of those heroic and noble characters Beethoven admired so much in Cherubini's opera. This was essentially the same heroism he eulogized in *Coriolanus* and *Egmont,* in the Third Symphony and the C major Mass, the classic ideal of heroism rendered in classic music.

In its first version *Fidelio* shows the guiding hand of the same great classicist who admired so much the disposition of tonalities in the *Magic Flute,* who, like his revered model, Cherubini, used the leitmotif with discretion, always guarding the beauty of form and the logic of design. When *Fidelio* reappeared in 1814 the atmosphere in which it had originated, the era of the horror and rescue opera, had passed away; the romantic opera was making its first essays while the opera buffa celebrated its last triumphs. Despite the great advantages gained by the rewriting of the opera, the difference in time caused stylistic inequalities. As we have remarked before, the opera should be restored to its original form. Erich Prieger succeeded in piecing together the first version of *Leonore,* performed in Berlin in 1905. That this version has not become popular is owing to the exceedingly difficult and high tessitura of Leonore's part, but the same expert hands which so often distort the works of the classical composers could easily remedy this shortcoming.

The classical opera composer builds, and his constructive intentions are felt in the smallest details. The romanticist is naïve and intuitive; he may have very decided dramaturgical ideas, but his musical realization of a plot or of characters follows no architectural plan. But one element is always deliberately utilized by him: tone color. From the first horn quartet in the *Freischütz* overture this element dominates Weber's music and is applied everywhere with loving care. The scenes emerge from the depths of sheer tone color, of primal sonority, to rise and take coherence and consciousness when uniting with the words; "beauty born of murmuring sound." We must, then, leave Beethoven and his *Fidelio* and search for other connecting links.

Among the first romanticists there lived and created a host of respectable musicians. They were neither true romanticists nor classicists; some of them studied with Mozart and Haydn, others with Abbé Vogler, still others with Beethoven. Thus they were imbued with respect for the precepts of classicism, for the logic of tonal relationship and thematic design. But while they obviously endeavored to follow in the footsteps of their masters, the nascent musical idiom of romanticism was strong enough to becloud classical design, condemning them to oblivion, for they really did not belong to either camp and did not stand for any definite artistic principles. This is the key to the puzzling interregnum between the *Magic Flute* and the *Freischütz*. These pseudo-romanticists observed and noticed the classic elements but misinterpreted them; they did not realize that technique and idea are not synonymous. What is remarkable in the situation is that the first generation of romanticists itself not only accepted the tenets and idiom of the great classical composers but felt a kinship with them. We have quoted Hoffmann and Spohr, both professing their belief that they were the spiritual descendants of the "romantic" opera composer Mozart. This merely illustrates, however, their conception that *all* music is romantic; they shared the littérateurs' opinion of music as the romantic art par excellence.

E. T. A. Hoffmann's operas, even his *Undine,* greatly admired by Weber, were romantic in their subject matter, but the music was still in a vein nearer to the classic than to the romantic. When discussing Hoffmann the composer we must beware of drawing too heavily on Hoffmann the romantic poet. His musical career preceded his literary, and his compositions do not show the originality and fantasy of the man of letters. His musical style grew from a study of the older operatic schools from Handel, Feo, and Durante, from Gluck, and particularly from Mozart and the Singspiel: a typical transition style, to which was later added the influence of Beethoven and Cherubini. The frequent tone painting, the use of leitmotives and of melodramatic treatment, undeniably romantic in nature, had their repercussions on Weber. The same conflict of classical and romantic tendencies is manifest in Louis Spohr (1784-1859). He belongs to those musicians who joined the romantic movement because as well-read and educated persons they were carried away by the literary romanticism. But his nature was anything but romantic; popular music and Weber's romanticism of the German forest were as repellent to him as a noble and "undisturbed" musical language was attractive. His rather soft nature urged him to a calm and clear conception of life and art. The romantic element is present in his music, especially in the later operas, in a striving for orchestral color and the characteristic harmonic expression, with which he prepared the advent of the late romantic colorists. These operas are, however, merely the continuation of the German fairy opera. They are important and remarkable, but from a historical point of view only, for they did not achieve the dramatic quality of Weber's music because of the lack of that naïve conviction and abandonment that characterize the true romanticist. His Biedermeier sobriety did not permit an uncontrolled flight of imagination. Literary preoccupations, which he took for romanticism, are evident in Spohr's effort to make the contents of his instrumental works tangible by programmatic allusions; but the theater demands more than mere allusions.

Hoffmann's *Undine* (1813) and Spohr's *Faust* (1816), while not romantic operas in the full sense of the word, were the chief precursors of the *Freischütz.* Weber found in their subjects, in their leitmotivic technique, and in their orchestration the last ingredients needed for his own, entirely new, romantic opera.

A true romanticist, Weber announced his aesthetic creed before actually embarking on its practical realization. The romantic ideal of the "artistic whole" is repeatedly expressed in his writings, yet his operatic works are still within the traditional sphere. His first sources were German Singspiel and Italian opera. The early works show plainly the mixture of styles, but also a sure instinct for the theatrical and for vocal music in general. Historically speaking, Weber's songs precede those of Schubert, yet they already mark the great difference between classic and romantic vocal music. Marked by a fine simplicity, they deserve a permanent place in song literature, especially the gay ones with their genuine humor. They could, however, be martial and stirring as are his patriotic songs for men's voices. While Beethoven continued the classical piano sonata, Weber, following especially Johann Ladislaus Dussek (1760–1812) and Leopold Koželuch (1752–1818), the first a bold harmonist and the second already touched by that light melancholy which enveloped romanticism, was already in romantic waters. Fascinated by the sonority of the piano tone, he was willing to loosen the contours of his melodies and the design of his forms. These early sonatas have been strongly condemned in the name of the classical piano sonata, but such arguments are irrelevant. The sonata form does not really exist in them, as it does not in the works of the somewhat later romantic sonata composers; the fact that there are first and second themes, developments, recapitulations, etc., is merely a superficial convention, for these works obey entirely different impulses. No wonder that Weber steadfastly refused to admit any indebtedness to Beethoven, for in truth there was little in common between the two.

However brilliant, especially in his piano concerto and other instrumental works, Weber remains first and foremost the opera composer who set himself a goal, German national-popular opera, which he succeeded in reaching, virtually sacrificing his life in the endeavor. The initial insecurity evident in his multitude of styles soon passed; his teacher, Abbé Vogler, showed him the road, making him infuse this mixture with a German spirit. Vogler understood the import of the *Magic Flute* and of the German vocal speech idiom it announced, and attempted to continue and develop it in his own opera *Samori*. Another of Weber's important counselors was Danzi, a repository of the Mannheim traditions. And what the great lovers of nature of the classic era worshiped as spectators, this sensitive musician lived, becoming part of it. *Freischütz, Euryanthe,* and *Oberon* dissolve in nature like the visions of the great romantic poets. What Hoffmann merely indicated in his text Weber poured out in heartfelt music in the *Freischütz*. The soldiers, returned from the wars of liberation imbued with the newly won pride of German patriotism, found in the popular story drawing on the typically German legends and superstitions, in the rustling of the forest, in the sounding horns and popping muskets of the hunters, and in the merry dance of the peasants, all that for which they went to war. The Metastasian characters still lingering in almost every opera in the late eighteenth century were here replaced by figures as German as the former were Italian.

Weber the man and artist was the antithesis of his great contemporary, Schubert. Instead of lyric immersion he leaned toward brilliancy and effect; hence his preference for the stage, his real medium, which he served in three capacities: as composer, conductor, and critic. In principle he strove for the same aim that fired Wagner, but his road was barred by the surrounding armada of French and Italian opera, and by the plague of German opera, the German libretto. Only with the greatest strain of his intellectual capacities was he able to arrange the libretto of the *Freischütz,* prepared by a mediocre playwright and poet by the name of Kind. These, however, were not the only reasons that prevented his achieving what it remained for Wagner to fulfill; the proximity of the Singspiel was a decisive factor. The critics reproached him for his "popular" taste, and he struck out toward the promised land, the German opera seria; but his real home was the forest and the meadow, the home of German folklore, the Singspiel. Not satisfied with the *Freischütz,* he tried to rise to higher spheres, for the romantic desire for the all-embracing German music drama was foremost in his mind. Thus came *Euryanthe* (1823), epitomizing the heroic chivalry of medieval romanticism and well-nigh determining Wagner's *Lohengrin,* and *Oberon* (1826), whose fairy music opened wide the gates of the realm of romanticism. While the *Freischütz* is still a Singspiel with spoken dialogue, *Euryanthe* endeavors to combine the Gluckian music drama with the new German vocal style and with the new orchestral technique. All scenes are through-composed, and the orchestra supports the action with its explanatory leitmotives and psychological tone painting. Still, there is a great difference between *Euryanthe* and *Lohengrin,* for while Wagner's musical dialect merges aria with declamation, Weber's scenes, however unified, remain songlike arias and ariosos. Thus *Euryanthe,* already sadly deficient on account of its miserable text, could not maintain itself. While it is filled with fine music, its stylistic inequalities are pronounced.

Such scenes as would oppose the figures of the drama to one another, creating dramatic tension by actual and visible conflict, are secondary with Weber; his preference is for songs and choruses, for the characterization of situations and moods. Although always conscious of the requirements of the stage, dramatic continuity was not a strong point with him. The *Freischütz* became what it is because it did not require dramatic continuity, and, if we forget the general mood and subject of the opera, we soon discover that poetry is still "music's obedient daughter." If we add to this the dramatic insecurity of *Euryanthe* we find that instead of being a comrade in arms Weber was one of Wagner's antipodes. But we cannot forget the mood, and we cannot ignore the subject. The *Freischütz* will remain one of the highest peaks ever attained by German opera. This proud position it owes to its genuine roots in the saga and song of the German people. The symphonic orchestra with its leitmotives, tonal splendor, and subtle instrumental symbolism (clarinets for Agathe, low flutes for Samiel, etc.), the stirring dissonances of the harmonic idiom, and other elements of the "high music drama" cannot eradicate the essential kinship of this opera with the Singspiel.

Thus Weber, while a romanticist of the first water, rightfully belongs in this period which was still so closely bound to the late classic era. With Beethoven and Schubert, he completes the unique convergence of epochs, styles, and philosophies, for he does not belong to the lyric romanticists of the next generation nor to the classicists or classical romanticists of his own time. Equally distant from Beethoven and Schubert and from Schumann and Chopin, he was the first German composer to answer the prayer for a national-romantic opera, which became a symbol not only of a type of lyric drama, but of German romanticism, German aspirations.

Chapter 16

ROMANTICISM

⇢⇢⇢ ⇠⇠⇠

A theme! a theme! great nature! give a theme;
Let me begin my dream.

(Keats)

Aspects of Romanticism

WHEN a nation brings its innermost nature to consummate expression in arts and letters we speak of its classic period. Classicism stands for experience, for spiritual and human maturity which has deep roots in the cultural soil of the nation, for the mastery of the means of expression in technique and form, and for a definite conception of the world and of life; the final possible compression of the artistic values of a people. Romanticism is always a youthful movement, a program, a slogan, deliberately used as such for propagandistic purposes, the expression of a desire oriented toward the future. In his preface to *Cromwell* (1827), Victor Hugo declared the maxim of "artistic freedom" to be the first requisite of the times and defined romanticism as "liberalism in art." This liberalism naturally tended to foster in the men who proclaimed it a political counterpart which often drew art into the service of revolutionary activities.

The political and patriotic literature of the wars of liberation was the echo of the philosophical-historical outlook of romanticism. It produced no new forms, relying rather on borrowings from folk song and from Schiller. Its pathos was the political moment. Among the earlier poets one can find true romanticists—Max von Schenkendorf (1783-1817), still dreaming of the medieval German Empire, Theodor Körner (1791-1813), fallen on the battlefields, expressing his patriotism in his poems (*Lyre and Sword*) with a glowing fervor that is unique in the history of German literature—but many were merely guardians and virtuoso practitioners of romantic forms and ideals. August von Platen (1796-1836) and Friedrich Rückert (1788-1866) were able, at times, to conjure up the purest accents of romanticism, but, as Platen expressed it in his beautiful poem *Tristan*, "he who had once beheld beauty, is affianced with death." Their language and versification are impeccable and infinitely artistic, but their sacrificial offerings made on the altar before the image of beauty, their deity, were not consumed by fire.

Was classicism followed by romanticism as the new century opened? We have answered this question by considering the first decades as the confluence of the two, but a phenomenon such as Brahms at the end of the century should make us wary, as there must have been a latent line of classic, or rather classicistic, composers throughout the stormiest days of romanticism. The many lesser contemporaries of Beethoven were little influenced by him and continued to write in a settled classicistic idiom. In this they were not unlike their successors at the end of the century who wrote in a "romantic" idiom oblivious of the great changes taking place around them. Beethoven was as distant from romanticism as was Bach from the rococo, but the reaction of the respective generations that followed them was fundamentally different. The rococo rejected Bach, who was virtually abandoned and almost forgotten for a century, whereas the romanticists believed Beethoven to be one of their rank and by "romanticizing" him were able to assimilate and utilize much of the great heritage of the classic era. Thus the musician who was the symbol and epitome of the classical symphony and sonata, least suited for the ideology of romanticism, was made the standard-bearer of a movement to which he did not belong. There must be, then, a conflict in romantic psychology expressed in the survival of nonromantic cultural artistic elements which either continued to be active or were assimilated, stylized, or misinterpreted. This conflict was one of the factors that ultimately led to a crisis of the whole movement.

In Mendelssohn's time classicism was no longer an inner necessity; it was merely a component of higher education and culture, approached from without as was the art of classical antiquity. The greatest and final problem of the romantic artist was the reconciliation of the classic form with the new mentality. The manner in which the artists answered this challenge depended on whether they adhered to the average cultural ideals of the educated middle classes or whether they wanted to force upon it a new ideal.

We have mentioned the curious fact that although as a poet Hoffmann was a full-blooded romanticist, his music is classicistic and largely derivative. Unromantic music composed to romantic texts is the order in the many now forgotten operas of the period. In Hoffmann's case recognition of this fact was made difficult by the poet's acknowledged fame as a romanticist, and by the slight knowledge of his music; but there were a number of musicians living in the midst of the romantic movement who were really expatriates and whose music illustrates the ballast of foreign goods carried by the rising era. Among the notable pseudo-romanticists let us mention two typical cases, Paganini and Onslow. No matter how romantic his life, Niccolo Paganini (1784–1840), the famous violin virtuoso, follows in his music a clear and unequivocal articulation that bespeaks the classic models, notably Viotti. George Onslow (1784–1853), a great favorite of the romantic era, all his sweetness and tenderness notwithstanding, is merely a product of the French-German classicistic merger, not unlike his more distinguished compatriot Elgar who at the end of the century fused in his music both the German and the French romantic and realistic schools.

Romanticism attempted, as we have seen, the restoration of the cultural elements and forms of bygone periods, especially the Middle Ages. It hoped to revive the medieval soul; failing that, it had two alternatives: to deal, like the rationalist, with concrete signs, or to intellectualize atmosphere and mood. In Walter Scott the two tendencies merged: he satisfied the romantic desire without warring on rationalism. His German disciple, Willibald Alexis (pseudonym for Wilhelm Häring, 1798–1871), endeavored to acclimatize Scott's conception in Germany. Using Scott's procedure, he depicted great episodes and crises in the history of Brandenburg from the Middle Ages to the dissolution of the Holy Roman Empire. The force of all this historic interest was weakened by abstraction and by rigid form. Among the German writers there were only two who, aware of the dangers, attempted to break through the stereotyped forms in order to weld the individual soul with a historic atmosphere: Philip Joseph von Rehfues (1779–1843), also a disciple of Scott, and Johann Wilhelm Meinhold (1797–1851); but even they were not successful in conveying the dynamics of historical life, despite their excellent reconstructions. The ideal of the romantic drama, too, proved to be unattainable. The intellectualized romantic subject matter became allied with the grand pathos of Schiller. Karl Immermann (1796–1840) opened the line of poets who began the process of intellectualization of their own romanticism. Whatever poetic value there is in their works is, however, of romantic origin. And then romanticism became the twilight of the gods. The poet realized that he could not change fate, and his fervid optimism turned into pessimism, changing the form of dramatic struggle. The hero defended himself desperately against the leveling force of reality, but his struggle was tragically futile. The new form broke with Schiller and reached back to Shakespeare, or to the German past, to the Sturm und Drang. Christian Grabbe (1801–1836) and Georg Büchner (1813–1837) were the representative figures of the latter trend. Their genuine and powerful talent collapsed too early, and German drama lost in them two of its greatest dramatists. These men belong to the romantic era, but the piling up of horrors in their plays shows their dependence on the Sturm und Drang. Opera could not escape the repercussions of this literary trend, but while Grabbe and Büchner could be so vivid and so intensely convincing that "they could make even military strategy poetic" (Immermann on Grabbe's

Napoleon) the romantic opera was lost in the sinister passions and robber romanticism of the Sturm und Drang. Hundreds of operas were composed between the *Freischütz* and *Lohengrin,* the crowning of German romantic opera, but only Wagner's *Flying Dutchman* and *Tannhäuser* survived, besides a few works of lighter, more Singspiel-like nature.

The same search for the German past that animated the literary men led romantic music to Bach, and from him to the forms and materials of earlier periods. Mendelssohn's performance of the St. Matthew Passion in 1829, one of the great events in the history of music, gave this movement its start, and oratorios, a cappella choruses, and fugues began to be composed in large numbers. But in spite of such unbounded enthusiasm, this generation was not vitally affected by the knowledge of Bach although his indirect influence was considerable. Even Schumann, who had a fine sense for counterpoint, and Mendelssohn, the "rediscoverer" himself, an equally deft polyphonist, were only superficially affected. It remained to Brahms to grasp the essence of baroque polyphony. The resuscitated oratorio was no longer moved by Handel's dramatic élan or Haydn's loving contemplation, and polyphony was present there as an archaic device, especially empty and meaningless in the choral fugues. Only the lyric parts live, but they of course are typical romantic territory. Rochlitz and Wagner both declared the oratorio completely outmoded in the eighteen thirties, and only a handful of the many works composed during the romantic era survive. Mendelssohn's two fine works in this genre, *Paulus* and *Elijah,* represent a most ambitious artistic plan. Emulating Handel (and to a lesser degree Bach), Mendelssohn, a follower of Schleiermacher's romantic philosophy which saw in religion the sum total of existence, endeavored to unite once more the period's religious and musical aspirations. As was to be expected, he met an especially warm welcome in England, where he was feted as the second Handel. Yet Mendelssohn's religious music leans on the great baroque masters only outwardly; it recalls, rather, the homophonous-melodic style of the Italian choral composers of the seventeenth century, for its chief quality is soft melodic design based on a homophonic foundation. Schumann's *Paradise and Peri* remains the chief secular oratorio of the romantic era. Schumann himself considered it his greatest work. The oratorio, like his *Faust,* contains parts remarkable for their beauty, but the choruses are lacking in impact, in that epic and dramatic fullness which was the mark of the earlier oratorio. The best parts are the songlike solo passages, and thus it is again lyricism that makes them live. However, although not divining the essence of polyphony, these two sensitive artists contributed to the foundation of a new contrapuntal style. Mendelssohn's piano fugues, organ works, and some of his choruses, Schumann's poetic pieces in fugal style for the piano and the canonic studies for the pedal piano (an instrument equipped with a pedal keyboard), all created a polyphony, which while remaining throughout the romantic period a hothouse art, made possible the revival of religious music and organ music which in Brahms reconquered something of its ancient glory. We must beware, however, of drawing far-reaching conclusions on the reappearance of polyphony. With a classicistic romanticist like Mendelssohn, the antiquarian tendency explains both its presence and its skillful use; with Schumann, the embodiment of romanticism, we must be prepared to find more symbolic than actual correspondences. "I learned more counterpoint from Jean Paul than from my music teacher," said Schumann, and indeed, with all his enthusiasm for Bach, he did not see the latter in his true light, but in that fantastic-mystic twilight which for the romanticist enveloped polyphony. Elaborate polyphonic voice leading symbolizes in his works, fine though they are, the meditation of the lonely dreamer. We might repeat that, as in poetry, whatever value we discern in this polyphony is of romantic origin. This immediately becomes painfully evident if we look at the appalling desert of fugues and canons every composer considered it his duty to turn out en masse. "The emptiest head thinks it can hide its weakness behind a fugue; but a true fugue is the affair of a great master." [1]

Romanticism undoubtedly grew from subjectivism, which it increased to overflowing. But romanticism was also bound with many ties to the Revolution. The Revolution emancipated the middle classes and in so doing yielded cultural leadership to the petty bourgeois spirit, with its eyes set on the practical, and with its urge for a continuation of the movement of the Enlightenment according to its own precepts. Napoleon's star was still rising when the Prussian statesman Schulenburg symbolically opened the period we have come to call Biedermeier by proclaiming in Berlin that "peace and calm are the first duties of the citizenry." A little later the throne of the roi soleil was occupied by the citizen king, Louis Philippe, who exchanged the Napoleonic eagle for umbrella and overshoes. And when the Napoleonic eagle rested securely under the rock of St. Helena the victorious middle-class spirit could safely enjoy the peace and calm that were decreed to be its duty.

Gottlieb Biedermeier, the humorous Philistine character and imaginary author whose verses appeared in the *Fliegende Blätter,* the favorite family magazine of the small bourgeoisie, gave the name to a whole period of culture, a period which left indelible marks on romanticism. The psychological foundation of the Biedermeier era is a simplification of classic forms and a retreat from romantic pathos, a tired flight into bourgeois quietude, modesty, and simplicity. The word has become a stylistic term for furniture of the period from about 1816 to the middle of the century, but the phenomenon itself is European. The Biedermeier style was of course not a conscious artistic tendency and not even a slogan, and we cannot separate certain writers and musicians from others by calling them Biedermeier artists; there were many, however, who show Biedermeier traits, no matter what their school. *The Vicar of Wakefield* and *Hermann and Dorothea* were already the heralds of the Biedermeier world, more definitely expressed in Chênendollé's sentimental lyricism, in Chamisso's *Frauenliebe,* and in Kotzebue's plays. Biedermeier literature reached its artistic heights in Dickens's bourgeois sentimentalism, in his lovingly described family scenes and plumpuddinged Christmas dinners. Biedermeier art painted the life of the burgher and of the landed gentry. It depicted their surroundings accurately in the smallest details; nothing was omitted and nothing was neglected, every wrinkle in the clothing and every spot on collar or cuff was faithfully recorded. This art no longer searched for the eternal present; it sought the actual present; the notion of the symbolic was extinguished. What had importance was the tangible, the immediately seizable, the matter of fact.

There is a remarkable telescoping of the real and the desired in the Biedermeier world picture; it feigns an ever-happy, shadowless existence, an eternal, radiant Sunday. There is no dust and no unevenness on its objects and no concern or solicitude on the faces of the people; order and satisfaction are everywhere. It was not that the artists of this era did not realize the vicissitudes of life; they knew them well, but they took refuge in the illusion of this seeming fairyland in order to escape the outside world. They abandoned metaphysics for fables and reduced religion to mythology. The world became relieved of divinities and populated by sober and very real people without any penchant for metaphysics or for the infinite, entirely devoted to the present. One must admit, however, that after the frightful tension of the Revolution and of the Napoleonic years, after having conquered their rights through heavy sacrifices, the middle classes were entitled to a siesta, the Biedermeier. Nonetheless, there was still evident a great deal of the gold of the cultural past in the alloy of the Biedermeier, for the bourgeois spirit had its roots in the strong and high-minded Enlightenment still echoing in young Germany. This modern Enlightenment in its turn had roots in antique thought transmitted by the classic era. Bourgeois spirit is urban spirit and as such is distantly related to the classic polis ideal; thus a stream of Hellenism and humanism watered the nineteenth century, flowing from the undimmed classical studies of the intelligentsia. And the much-despised Philistines were, of course, not ordinary Philistines, for a goodly number of the red corpuscles of romanticism flowed in their veins. The Biedermeier Philistine demanded a world ruled by order, common sense, and good nature, obeying the laws promulgated by Schulenburg in order to preserve all past accomplishments and cultural acquisitions.

The Biedermeier trait was more or less strong and innate in all the secondary figures of musical romanticism. Spohr, Marschner, Kreutzer, Lindpaintner, Reissiger, Flotow, and others seldom showed the poetic tone and enthusiastic conviction of the true romanticist, while on the other hand the realism toward which some of them inclined was only half hearted. Not so with the leaders. The bourgeois spirit in Mendelssohn was a conscious one; [2] in his circle the enjoyment of music was "plaisir" and good music "charmante," he adored "elegant fluency" and was somewhat terrified by such force as was embodied in the Ninth Symphony. Therefore he could not reciprocate Schumann's admiration, for with all his love and esteem for the creator of the imaginary David's League, Schumann seemed to him confused and adventurous, almost an eccentric engrossed in finding the answer to unanswerable riddles.

In its zeal for "restoration" romanticism rediscovered the "Era of Woman." These were the times when Mme de Staël traversed the Continent as an intellectual prophetess, when Queen Louise in Prussia and Archduchess Sophie in Austria gave the tone in politics, when the dancer Lola Montez all but ruled Bavaria, when Baroness von Krüdener devoted her life to preaching Pietism all over Europe, wielding enormous influence and inspiring the formation of the Holy Alliance. Comfortableness and agreeableness emanated from the home ruled by woman, and with her reign friendliness and amiability gained even the cooler north, its literary salons and its arts and letters. Domesticity dominated everything; dwellings were no longer filled with pictures and busts but with innumerable knickknacks, the chief ornament of a middle-class home. In music, piano playing, an especially "da camera" art, took the first place, seconded by romances and songs. This music no longer echoed the storm of world history; it played on the sweet and delicate strings. The prima donna and the aria were still greatly admired, but instead of the heroism and humor of the classic era, the tones were either sentimental or were lost in mere tonal acrobatics.

The trivial sentimentalism we associate with much of this music is again of socio-cultural and literary origin. One of its chief exponents was August Friedrich Kotzebue (1761–1819), a dramatist of great abilities and endowed with a freshness of imagination, but one who, divining the secret instincts of the public, was content to use his great talents to satisfy them. If the slogan of the times was sentimental morality, the figures in his plays were fairly dripping with it, although all the beautiful tirades were mere words covering a dissolute world. But this was effective and flattering; the good citizens, who felt and acted like Kotzebue's heroes, could leave the theater with the feeling of virtue. Kotzebue's theater was matched in the novel by August Julius Lafontaine (1758–1831), the most popular German novelist of the first part of the century, and by the almost nauseating pseudo-romanticism of Heinrich Clauren (pseudonym for Karl Gottlob Heun, 1771–1854).

In the strong antiromantic tendency at the beginning of our century, this sentimental vein was considered to be the essence of romanticism, and its prevalence in many works cast an ignominious shadow over the whole era. Yet we have seen how many currents traversed the romantic movement, how much noble poetry was mixed with bourgeois sentimentality. We must not forget that the musical literature of the romantic era is still little known, that we confuse the moonlight romanticism of the late nineteenth century with the true species of the first half of the century, that quiet and finely wrought lyricism is not synonymous with sentimentality, and that the supreme in music is not necessarily expressed alone in the gigantic orchestral and dramatic works to which the pseudo-grandeur of the fin de siècle has accustomed us. Romantic ardor was helpless and stood with clipped wings before the architectonic logic of the sonata-symphony, but where it recognized the boundaries of its own domain, where it liberated itself from tradition and from the cultural ideals of the petty-bourgeoisie, it created art of the highest quality. It was against the Biedermeier, against Philistinism, that Schumann and Berlioz took the field; the difference between the two crusaders was not in their intentions but only in their approach, Schumann being much more idealistic and less vehement than the impetuous and bellicose Frenchman. That the Philistines themselves were opposed to true romanticism and to lofty classicism alike can readily be seen. Kotzebue, a fanatic reactionary in politics, was a zealous adversary of all that was poetic and forward-looking in romanticism, while the more placid Spohr, the embodiment of the righteous and dutiful bourgeois office holder, although no mean artist, found that the Fifth Symphony of Beethoven "does not form a classic whole, the theme of the first movement is lacking in nobility, the adagio is too tiresome, the trio is too baroque and the finale meaningless noise."

What unites the various currents that make up the romantic era is a general literary orientation, for, as we have said, romanticism was primarily a literary movement. Hoffmann, Weber, Schumann, Berlioz, Liszt, Wagner, and their lesser contemporaries were men of an extensive literary and philosophical schooling, many of them holding doctoral degrees in philosophy; they were able writers, critics, poets, and playwrights. The literary orientation is expressed in the predominance of lyricism in both vocal and instrumental music. Schumann's preference for song cycles testifies to an outspoken literary sentiment, as do Mendelssohn's *Songs Without Words* and Schumann's and Chopin's many piano pieces, all of which have in common a lyric unity which we may well consider the typical trait of romanticism. The romantic urge for the "poetic whole" is behind the tendency to demand the playing of symphonies written in the regular four-movement form without rest between the individual movements. Mendelssohn and Schumann took pains to arrange the details in some of their symphonies to facilitate such presentation. That even the Wagnerian poetic-dramatic material was a direct result of the German literary movement is seen in the not infrequent attempts on the part of other, earlier composers to use the same subject matter. The story-telling poets of romanticism, the folk songs and sagas, the fairy tales, inspired this art and made it sharply different from the previous large-dimensional classicism. Mendelssohn's title, *Songs Without Words,* indicates plainly the source of inspiration, but while the classicistic penchant of Mendelssohn permitted merely a hint at the intermediary role of the new Schubertian song, Schumann acknowledged the poetic nature of his instrumental lyricism by giving suggestive titles to his piano pieces. The inscriptions are, however, merely poetic acknowledgments of the character of the piece, placed by the composer on the finished composition, and the high artistic value of this romantic lyricism lies in the spontaneity of its creation, in the absence of reflection and of programmatic tendencies. An immense chasm separates these composers from the other factions so uncritically called "romantic" which demanded concrete poetic meaning from music, elevating reflection to a constructive principle. "I should not like to be understood by everybody," said Schumann, and this, perhaps, may be the best motto for the romantic era.

Mendelssohn—Schumann—Chopin

THE classic personality is firm and undivided; the romanticist has a double personality, so convincingly personified by Schumann's Florestan and Eusebius, the two creations of his fantasy who put into perceptible and visualized literary form the dissension in the romantic artist's soul. The romantic ego is eternally in formation, for it is that endless striving itself which is its soul. Novalis thought that "to develop his individuality man must take unto himself several individualities and then assimilate them." This constant preoccupation with the assimilation and reconciliation of contending personalities fills the lives and works of the three great romantic composers who gave the era its stamp.

Felix Mendelssohn Bartholdy (1809–1847) was the grandson of the great Jewish philosopher Moses Mendelssohn and son of a wealthy banker and of a mother of exceptional culture and refinement. The Mendelssohn home presented a family of character and integrity, equally devoted to each other and to the noble and artistic in life. As far as sheer talent is concerned, Mendelssohn belongs to the class of the Pergolesis, Mozarts, and Schuberts, but in the child of an era that regarded intellectual culture an integral part of the composer's trade, these natural gifts were equally manifest in other fields. The wealth and solicitous care of the family provided him with the best teachers available in Berlin, and the youth was soon equally proficient

in music, linguistics, and painting. Music, however, took the place of chief
interest, and under the surveillance of Zelter and having at his disposal every
combination of ensembles in the regular house concerts, the seventeen-year-
old composer created works of incredible maturity and genius, among them
the radiant octet for strings and the bewitching overture to Shakespeare's
Midsummer Night's Dream. Through Zelter he learned to appreciate Bach,
and there followed the memorable performance of the St. Matthew Passion
(1829), the first of many other notable premières and revivals which made
Mendelssohn the great authority in the thirties and forties to whom composers and scholars appealed for advice and encouragement. His London
concerts in 1829 carried his fame all over the world. In the next year he
visited Italy, France, and again England, but acquiescing to his father's
wishes he sought a permanent position. Thus we find him successively in
Düsseldorf and Leipzig, where he became conductor of the famous Gewandhaus concerts and one of the founders and leading members of the conservatory. Leipzig remained until his death the focal point of his activity,
interrupted only for his numerous guest appearances in the European capitals.

Artistic creation originates from an interplay of unconscious and conscious
building forces, the creative artist beholding with amazement the products
of his imagination as if they had been given to him by another person. Once
he collects himself he sets his intellect to work to make the invention mallea-
ble. In Mendelssohn the conscious elements are conspicuous, and this is what
distinguishes him chiefly from his other romantic contemporaries. Endowed
with great melodic gifts and with a craftsmanship given to few, this remarkable and many-sided musician is usually remembered as the sentimental
composer of *Songs Without Words,* yet he was by no means a devotee of
the soft and sentimental tone that characterized this period. His intellect
and intuition warned him that glowing passion and the tone of profound
emotions were not in his make-up, therefore the emotional content in his
works is carefully articulated and toned down. How fully he was aware of
this is well expressed in his ironic designation of himself as a Philistine, compared to Berlioz. It was with this disposition that Mendelssohn approached
the greatest problem of romanticism: form. To him the sonata form was
not an empty shell suitable to frame musical ideas as it was to Berlioz, nor
was it used with the lack of understanding for its real function common to
most of the other romanticists, for the wonderful artistic sense of this fine
musician led him to the essence of classic music. But while he understood the
meaning of the classical sonata-symphony, under his hands the classic spirit
became a noble gesture, acquired but not assimilated. Schumann greeted in
Mendelssohn the reconciliator of the classic and romantic outlooks, the one
great artist who resolved the disharmony of the times, but this was the ad-

(Top) M. von Schwind (German, 1804–1871), "The Symphony"
(Bottom) Thomas Eakins, "Music" (Art Institute of Chicago)

Renoir, "At the Piano" (Durand-Ruel)

miration of the great dreamer embattled with the insoluble problem of the romantic symphony, who, like every other musician past and present, could not help admiring the effortless elegance of the Mendelssohnian large form. His plan to reconcile classical construction with romantic content was doomed from the beginning, for although his wonderfully polished and fluent writing lent itself admirably to any type of construction, be it fugue or symphony, the lack of conflicts and the cautiously held reins make this highly refined and cultivated music only classicistic. Mendelssohn became the leading composer of this classicistic romanticism, which paralleled the art of Peter von Cornelius (1783–1867) and Julius Schnorr von Carolsfeld (1794–1872), the German historical painters who looked back to the early Italians for inspiration. In the hands of his lesser followers this art froze into sentimental academicism; what was brilliant craftsmanship and noble and truly artistic conception became mere formalism accentuated by sentimental pseudo-romanticism. It was against this pseudo-romantic school and not against Mendelssohn that the neo-German school led by Liszt and Wagner declared war, but posterity made the poetic composer of the *Midsummer Night's Dream* music expiate for the sins of his time.

There can be no question that in many of Mendelssohn's works there is missing that real depth that opens wide perspectives, the mysticism of the unutterable. A certain sober clarity permeates his music, not the clarity of mood and conviction, but that of the organizing mind. His balanced proportions are the result not of a classic outlook on life but of a remarkable intellect and refined taste. In the romantic era most of the great musical personalities ceased to live in harmony with their social environment, espousing revolutionary ideals. Mendelssohn's personality was opposed to a secession, for to him an artistic understanding with the prevailing social order was an emotional necessity; therefore he took into consideration the will of the public instead of opposing it like Chopin, Schumann, or Berlioz. While we cannot help noting the limitations in Mendelssohn's music, largely due to his nature and his social philosophy, his frail figure becomes gigantic if we glance at the musical world around him. What he created is not overwhelming, it does not carry us away; he was not one of the very great, but he was and remains a master, and he has given us much that fills us with quiet enjoyment and admiration. With all his formal dexterity and classicistic penchant, Mendelssohn will remain a romanticist, for the elegiac, at times pessimistic, tone, the tendency for dark tints, is that of the romanticist. The dual personality of the romanticist is present in Mendelssohn, but it does not lead to internal struggle, sapping the physical and creative strength of the artist. Calm and clarity accompanied him throughout life; a certain inborn feeling for orderly expression was seldom missing; the two personalities lived together and found expression alternately. He knew his position exactly and he knew the drawbacks and the advantages of being placed at an artistic watershed. As his friend Devrient said, "He wanted to do only what was congenial to his nature, and nothing beyond."

Mendelssohn's great admirer, Robert Schumann (1810–1856) passed his youth in the typical romantic enthusiasm divided between music and literature. His literary taste was developed in the reading of Goethe, Jean Paul, and Byron, and the young man wrote poetry at the same time he composed piano pieces and Psalms. He was the prototype of the talented, sentimental, romantic youth, falling from excess to excess and filled with conflicts. Life meant to him fervor and dreaming; nevertheless, to fulfill his mother's wish he went to Leipzig to study law. Nothing could have more quickly convinced him of his true vocation than his antiromantic law studies, and soon he found a capable music teacher in the person of Friedrich Wieck (1785–1873), under whose direction he started systematic studies in piano playing. In 1829, while in Heidelberg, he came under the influence of the romantic Palestrina worshiper Thibaut,[3] and his artistic horizon was further enlarged by a trip to Italy. Hearing Paganini, he now decided on the career of a virtuoso. By 1830 he had definitely abandoned his law studies and plunged with such energy into his piano studies that he ruined his right hand by violent exercises. The career of a virtuoso thus being frustrated, Schumann turned more toward composing, and from then on his musical and literary abilities grew swiftly. One of the first notable acts of the new music critic was the celebrated article in the *Allgemeine Musikalische Zeitung* on Chopin, and in his own journal, the *Neue Zeitschrift Für Musik* (1834), the romantic movement acquired an eloquent apostle. Declaring war on the "salon composers," he admonished his compatriots to heed the great traditions of the German past.

Clara Wieck, the daughter of his first piano teacher, one of the most distinguished woman musicians in history, and an understanding and enthusiastic propagator of his music, became his wife after an epic courtship in 1840. This happy year yielded a prodigious harvest of music, and Schumann now set out to achieve the dream of every romanticist, the reconciliation of the Beethovenian traditions with the tenets of romanticism. Accordingly, several large choral, orchestral, and chamber music works appeared in succession. When Mendelssohn founded the Leipzig conservatory in 1843, Schumann was appointed to the faculty, but his introspective and dreamy nature was not made for teaching, and within a year he relinquished his position. All similar ventures ended in failure, especially after the first signs of mental disorder appeared. In 1846, Clara presented his piano concerto amid jubilation, and none of the ensuing years was without some resounding success, but beginning with 1851 his mental capacities declined noticeably and fatigue and certain pathological traits appeared in his works (D minor violin sonata, G minor trio). While his fame grew steadily—Leipzig organized a Schumann week—his mental and physical health declined rapidly. The *Faust* overture, and an article on Brahms, similar to his prophetic announcement of Chopin, were his last lucid works. Two years later, lingering death caught up with him.

Schumann united in his person the richness of the poetic imagination of the romanticist with the sensitive reaction of the musician. He is more nervous and responsive, reflective and sensuous, and richer in minute and delightful details than Schubert, but he never attains the latter's elemental grandeur and natural force. Unlike Schubert, Schumann was not rooted in the music of the people, from which he borrowed only occasional naturalistic effects and tones. Every experience in life found artistic echo in him. Friends, colleagues, loves, and his own self, all are fictitious personages in the mysterious company the purpose of which was to solve the riddle of life by music. Thus he created the imaginary circle of the "Davidsbündler," David's League, foe of the Philistines. Although the members of the League were imaginary, Chiara really stood for Clara, his wife, and Felix Meritis for Mendelssohn. The two most important characters, Florestan and Eusebius, embodied his own dual personality, the vehement and strong, and the gentle and poetic. At times, under the influence of Mendelssohn, he attempted to serve the cause of the educated bourgeoisie of his time, but the mating of the traditional with romantic aspirations produced mere academicism. The sober middle path was to Mendelssohn a natural avenue through which he arrived at finely wrought classicistic forms; but Schumann was not able to find his bearings on this road, as is plainly shown by the large movements of the piano quartet and quintet, the finales of his symphonies, the cello concerto, and other works. Schumann learned much from Mendelssohn but did not accept the polished ease with which he straddled the problematic, for the pursuit of the problems and secrets of life was indispensable to him. His imagination was kindled by the dusk and the night, by everything mysterious, puzzling, and ghostly. His favorite authors were E. T. A. Hoffmann and Jean Paul, the poets of caprice and fantasy.

Like the other romanticists of his era, Schumann was master of the song form and its kindred varieties. What he and Chopin called a sonata form was merely a fantasylike elaboration of the spirit of song lyricism, vocal and instrumental. He had, nevertheless, command of all romantic types of music with the exception of the opera, but while his pregnant individuality emanates from every sentence, he is not so invariably original as Chopin: strong threads tied him to Beethoven and Schubert and he learned much from Spohr and Moscheles. One of his most original traits was his penchant for complicated rhythm, which fascinated Brahms so much. Occasionally he carried the relentless playing with a rhythmic pattern to great excess, and while such obstinate passages—often whole movements—are unquestionably monotonous and even irritating, one cannot simply dispose of the practice by calling it a sign of helplessness or of his mental aberration, for with Schumann it was a stylistic-symbolic peculiarity which even had a constructive function. His harmonic language is again original and varied; the characteristic chromatic passing tones and the unorthodox resolution of foreign tones are still strongly in evidence in Wagner's music, especially in his love lyricism.

Frédéric Chopin (1810–1849), the son of a French father and of a Polish mother, was again one of the youthful giants who appear on the scene of musical history with a finished personal art. His great talent soon drove him toward the musical metropolises; in 1829 and 1830 he earned acclaim in Vienna and Munich, then, like many other Polish emigrés, he settled down in Paris. The twenty-year-old composer electrified the young musicians of Europe; Schumann's celebrated manifesto of 1831 greeted in him one of the heroes of romanticism. He became the idol of the distinguished Parisian salons and a much-sought piano teacher and performer. With all the fame and brilliancy surrounding him, his life was uneventful. The hypersensitive musician's doom was accelerated by the stormy love affair with the imperious and domineering George Sand; his delicate soul seared, he offered little resistance to the tuberculosis that attacked him in the prime of life.

Chopin was one of the creators of the typically romantic musical idiom and as such one of the most original and remarkable creative geniuses in musical history. Among his mature works there is not one that relies on traditional forms or devices, for he remade the musical universe for himself, retaining only the necessary outer frames of musical form. This universe, more than any other romantic composer's, is the complete antithesis of the classic, especially Beethovenian, world. The large-dimensional architecture with its balanced economy is foreign to this art, capricious, arbitrary, always fascinating and characteristic down to the smallest detail. The elements of Chopin's art are not subjected to a higher law of form; the enchanting melody and multicolored harmony weave their own fantasylike form that corresponds admirably to the nature of this music. This art is original, independent. Chopin had few ancestors and many followers. There are some germs that came from Beethoven's last sonatas, and more tangible influences and ideas from Field, Dussek, Hummel, Kalkbrenner, and from the idolized Mozart, but when these were absorbed they became thoroughly original. His melodies were also influenced by Italian opera, especially by Bellini, but the sensuous element thus received was distilled and somewhat dematerialized.

The romantic style flourished in Chopin's art with such abundance that his successors found everything prepared for them. The Chopin imitators and followers filled the rest of the century and were by no means extinct by the twentieth century. Scriabin and Rachmaninoff were still entirely under his spell, but while they were not able to derive from Chopin's heritage more than ephemeral compositions, dated at the time of their creation, the same ideas engendered original responses in Liszt, Wagner, and, to a certain extent, in Brahms. Berlioz may have been the ideological founder of the post-romantic school, but the musical material proper did not come from him; one of its chief contributors was Chopin, whose free constructions and melodic and harmonic idiom furnished the main ingredients to romanticism itself. Without him the music of the second half of the nineteenth century is hardly imaginable. His originality is so compelling, every one of his ideas and phrases has such unique aroma, that perhaps no other composer can be so quickly identified. Such originality is inimitable, and one glance at Scriabin's preludes will show that only certain characteristic external turns are reproduced, but not the essence, which is a poetry that makes the most secret strings of human moods reverberate. The range of his sentiments is astonishingly wide, running from light, almost ethereal melancholy to scintillating fireworks and hymnic exaltations. His musical ideas are so pregnant and characteristic that one suspects hidden programs behind them, but his characterizations are never descriptive, nor even epic; they are purely lyrical confessions.

That most of his works were written for the piano, and none does without it, is typical not only of Chopin but of the period which discovered the poetry of the piano. In spite of important stimuli coming from Hummel and Field, Chopin's pianistic style was wholly new, and he was the first great composer to whom the modern piano became the only possible means of expression. Liszt's own technique is based on Chopin's, but where Chopin always clung to a pure pianism, Liszt exploited the coloristic and orchestral possibilities of the instrument.

Chopin composed relatively little, and, like Heine, subjected that little to the most rigorous artistic criticism, filing and polishing incessantly. Yet the essentially improvisatory character of his music, its freshness and immediacy, are never disputed. A composer who took cognizance of the outside world only when it affected his nerves and mood, Chopin spoke of himself and to himself; he composed confessions. His melancholy and sentimentalism exude a bewitching redolence, for everything is truly lived and experienced. *Mal du siècle* and *Weltschmerz,* however strong, never cause fragmentariness or distraction in his music, for the artist is always on guard and when, in Heine's manner, he plays with spirited surprises, these never turn to biting irony. His preference for dance forms was not merely for their stimulating motion and freshness; it had deep-seated symbolic meaning. The lonely artist who lived his whole life in the turmoil of society enlivened and populated with these dances the solitude of his creative fancy.

It was the maternal blood that predominated in Chopin, and he was the first great composer in whose music the national Slavic element came strongly to the fore, whence it passed into the main stream of European music. The Polish blood throbs with particular vigor in his warlike polonaises, whose boldly arching melodies are of bent steel. The knightly mazurkas glow with fiery gestures; sweet languor and coquetry live in the waltzes. Besides these spiritualized dance forms there are fantasies, scherzos, and ballads, impromptus, preludes, and sonatas, the lyric effusions of a sometimes demonically mysterious, sometimes enticing and cajoling sirenlike, but always warm and gracious heart. The spirituality which through his lyricism became a universal language celebrated its highest triumphs in the sparkling études, but the nocturnes are the dreams of his solitude, confiding to the night the deepest longing of a man outwardly spoiled by good fortune but in reality, like many of his romantic contemporaries, a virtuoso of suffering.

Stylistic Criticism of Romantic Music

STYLISTIC criticism of romantic music offers the greatest difficulties to musicology, still in the early stages of its modern orientation. On the one hand romantic music clings to the formal stylistic factors of classicism, on the other it seeks to eradicate boundaries and architectural logic. The loosening and flexibility of the coloristic, freely unfolding melody, the differentiated harmony, rich in dissonances and leaning to a veiling of tonal relationship, resulted in a wide variety of refined tonal and sonorous sense; the immensely enriched rhythm, lending itself to many combinations and indulging in the reversal of strong and weak beats, the intimate, egocentric, dreamy, oscillating and fantastic mood complexes, all created a conflict not only with classicism but within the romantic style itself.

"We have lately had few orchestral works of consequence; . . . many have been absolute reflections of Beethoven; and it is scarcely necessary to mention those tiresome manifestations of symphonies, with power enough to shadow forth the powder and perruque of Mozart and Haydn, but not indeed the heads that wore them." [4] This remark of one of the chief symphonists of the romantic era, Schumann, must be taken at its full value, as an unconscious admission of the consequences of the romantic conflict which caused the decline of sonata and symphony. The sonata form became simply a framework that held the release of emotions within bounds, remaining, however, outside the actual musical substance, and therefore always in evidence. In the eighteen twenties the disintegration of the classic "large form" was symbolically announced by the custom of performing in concerts single movements from symphonies. This outward sign corresponds to the episodic compositions of the era, such as the violin potpourris of Spohr. The romantic sonata is no longer a drama, the clashing of forces, a great struggle between antithetic materials, but a large frame in which the themes are only matters of relative importance to the course of the whole composition. Hence the development section lost its erstwhile role and importance, for it no longer served as the battleground for the clashing forces and consequently lost most of its expansive force. This lack was thought to be remedied by a greatly enriched harmonic language, but this very thing killed, or at least crippled, the other fundamental principle of symphonic thought: the logic of tonalities. The fundamental relationship in the sonata form was changed and even revised. The subsidiary theme, with its lyricism, acquired an importance that overshadowed the principal subject, dwarfing the evolution of the thematic material. The development section appeared negative, as if it had exchanged roles with the exposition, for the concentration displayed in the latter, notably in its second half dominated by the subsidiary subjects, precluded a development that could enhance the mood. The one great symphonist of the late nineteenth century, Brahms, recognized this clearly. "The great romanticists continued the sonata form in a lyric spirit which contradicts the inner dramatic nature of the sonata. Schumann himself shows this contradiction." [5] Schumann, together with composers of the nineteenth century, was often misled by the symphonic élan of classicism, but the relentless pursuit of thematic material turned with them into a headlong steeplechase. We must guard against mistaking excitement and sequential climaxes for symphonic development. And even when the romantic symphonist embarked on thematic development proper, he was usually satisfied with playing with the contours of the idea. If we compare the contemporary works of Spohr, the Rombergs, and Friedrich Schneider with Beethoven's and Schubert's symphonies, we shall find them to be full-blooded examples of sentimental romanticism, all showing the mutual trait of the romantic symphonist (a "negative trait," as Bücken called it), the lack of symphonic thought and logic. It begins with the themes themselves, unsymphonic and rambling. They might be, and often were, beautiful melodies, but almost invariably they were entirely unsuited for symphonic elaboration. Even though occasional shorter movements are written in a masterly fashion, no other type of music shows the deep rift between the two styles and musical conceptions so clearly as does the symphony.

The most conspicuous shortcoming in the romantic sonata and symphony is the lack of unity and cohesion. At certain points the symphony yawns and stagnates, and the best interpretation cannot prevent the sensation of broken continuity. Instead of offering a conflict, the dualistic sonata themes are merely antithetic, with the lyric second theme dominating, robbing the development section of its dramatic role. Some composers, Schumann among them, tried to solve the problem by loosening the outlines of the sonata form, reducing it to a large ternary song form. All this is usually designated as a disintegration of form, but it is more than that, for form in itself is abstract and it is still present in this music in the shape of a pattern. What was lost was inner unity, architectonic coherence, logic of harmony and melody. The construction of a movement is no longer based on a motivic theme out of which grows the whole structure. The lines are drawn freely, without much regard as to what precedes and what follows them; the harmonies cease to maintain a planned relationship, and lead a capricious life; the melodies became ample and songlike, too unwieldy for symphonic elaboration, and too numerous for clarity; episode upon episode follows in a multicolored sequence, often necessitating extramusical means, such as programs, to give a sense of cohesion and continuity.

Thematic logic is the *sine qua non* of sonata construction, and requires specifically symphonic thematic material. This fundamental requirement the romantic sonata lacked. The many singularly beautiful and expressive melodies we so often hear in romantic symphonies and quartets seem to contradict such a statement, but these are seldom the short, concise themes of classicism, and a large, widely articulated subject precludes symphonic development, for its components cannot be detached without giving the impression of fragments. On the other hand, an extended subject does not lend itself to a flexible thematic treatment. We must constantly bear in mind the unsurpassable prototype of the symphonic theme, that of the Fifth Symphony of Beethoven. The romantic theme has no inner tension and is carried by harmony, which, however, provides only changes in color and no development in the symphonic sense of the word; the romantic theme is passive, it is not a force, merely a phenomenon. And when it girds itself for action it still does not build, it swings and soars beyond workable symphonic proportions, requiring harmonic appendices which prevent a logical tonal relationship, the other essential feature of symphonic thought. The departure from a causal relationship of tonalities led to the elimination of clear articulation marked by cadences, with a resultant gain in harmonic variety and expressiveness. The many episodes thus gained all led a harmonic life of their own, giving free rein to the composer's fantasy, which reveled in a wealth of ideas, sonorities, and colors. But every accidental episode weakened the essential unity of the symphonic fabric, and while in the instrumental lyricism of the piano literature it created a new art of unmatched beauty, in the larger forms it proved to be fatal. The expansive force and possibilities of the romantic theme are virtually exhausted with its announcement; it circles repeatedly around itself without growing, thereby causing a stagnation which often becomes almost offensive. The subsidiary subject in Franck's D minor symphony, to mention a typical example, refuses to move; the composer tried it in various registers, but every time he finished by arriving at an impasse. This lack of expansive force called for substitutes, which came in the form of a plurality of ideas, another antisymphonic trait, for it leads to diversion, to a lessening of logic. The frequency of nonessential new departures arrests the flow of development, and as a matter of fact the latter exists in most romantic symphonies in name only, for it is usually an isolated section trying to comply with a formal tradition.

The deep-seated cause of these symptoms lies in a gradual change from pure and specific instrumental thematic invention to one more nearly akin to vocal. The literary orientation of romanticism favored vocal music, and, directly or indirectly, instrumental music absorbed much of the characteristic style elements of vocal music. This is already evident in Schubert, not only in his use of some of his famous songs for thematic material in instrumental works, but in his shaping of other, original themes. Most of the time he succeeded in finding, however, a happy balance between the two, but in the romantic symphony the preponderance of songlike elements often resulted in mere colorfulness.

Mendelssohn and Schumann wrote few symphonies, Chopin none; the great fertility of the classic era had passed. The new generation of composers stood under the awe-inspiring influence of Beethoven, but the temper and style of the period was opposed to the symbol of classicism, the symphony. Two of Mendelssohn's symphonies enjoy undiminished popularity—the A minor, called *Scottish,* and the A major, called *Italian.* Both are distinguished by freshness and by wonderful orchestral colorit, yet they are entirely compatible with symphonic thought. The *Scottish* is the more romantic of the two, with its balladlike tone and the exalted ending, which seems to have tempted many a romantic symphonist. (The finale of Brahms's First Symphony is still one of these hymnic final movements.) The nature of its material and the too square-cut form prevented a really arresting development, but there is much fine music in the symphony. In the *Italian* Symphony Mendelssohn was able to free himself to a considerable degree from the song lyricism which constricted his freedom of action, and the impetuously rushing first movement exhales real symphonic spirit. While not penetrating to unfathomable depths, this is one of the most accomplished symphonic movements of the romantic era; in its development section the swords are drawn from their sheaths and the contending opponents eye each other with serious intent to give battle. The middle movements in both symphonies are large orchestral ballads, noble in tone and achieving their purpose with taste. The finale of the A major symphony is a wild Italian *saltarello,* written with the greatest orchestral virtuosity. This movement and the fine scherzos in both symphonies lead us to Mendelssohn's most original and personal creations, the fairy scherzos. One of the most entrancing of these is found in the *Midsummer Night's Dream* music; even the overture to this play is really a big sonata-scherzo. While in Weber's *Oberon* the fairyland of romanticism is only seen through a veil, Mendelssohn takes us into its very center. His is, however, not a mysterious or fearful fairyland; in its demitint the gnomes and elves play around merrily, full of good will. After Mendelssohn came a legion of imitators who "made the fairies dance," but no one could even remotely match his shadowy lightness.

Schumann's First Symphony, written in the happiest period of his life, sparkles with a life and optimism truly deserving of the title *Spring Symphony.* As it was written in an uncommonly short time it is relatively free of the obstinate rhythmic patterns and dearly won connecting links that characterize Schumann's larger instrumental works. The young composer, living and creating in the shadow of the great symphonic school, instinctively used melodic material that had symphonic pregnancy and possibilities. The next symphony, although known in its second version as No. IV in D minor, is much better in the original score, which is now available to conductors, for as the orchestration was thickened, the symphony lost some of its freshness. The first movement of this symphony is one of the most difficult to perform; Florestan and Eusebius carry on an animated exchange of ideas, varying incessantly both mood and motives, sometimes within a few measures. The symphony begins with a hauntingly beautiful introduction that recalls the meditation of the classical symphonic introduction. Another introduction precedes the last movement. These preambles and short transitory passages are masterly and are filled not only with wonderful imagination, but with specifically symphonic thoughts. The middle movements are tender and poetic, for here, in the domain of instrumental lyricism, Schumann was at his inimitable best. The last two symphonies show fully the inability of the true romanticist to cope with the exigencies of the symphony. The C major symphony, the Second (in reality the Third), with difficulty undertakes the development of a theme unsuited to such tasks, and the finale collapses entirely. The two less ambitious middle movements are again considerably superior in every way. The *Rhenish Symphony,* the Third (fourth), starts out with exuberant enthusiasm but moves with leaden feet. The development consists largely in transposed sequences. All of Schumann's symphonies contain much beautiful music, but, in romantic fashion, their beauty is in their details.

The ability to "orchestrate" is denied to Schumann by most of his biographers. We must not forget, however, that "orchestration" as divorced from composition is a recent development, the pastime of composers and conductors who, lacking in original ideas, convert piano and organ music into would-be orchestral works. The older musicians, and their modern colleagues endowed with inventiveness and imagination, *composed* in an orchestral idiom, that is, their original ideas and aims were in an orchestral medium. Any able-bodied musician can learn how to orchestrate, and Schumann was no exception to this rule. It is a different matter, however, to try to force essentially unorchestral ideas into a symphonic garb. Schumann's pianistic-lyric fantasy did not produce material that lent itself to good orchestral use. Yet when he succeeded in steeping himself in an atmosphere other than song-like or pianistic, as in the overture to *Manfred* or in the A minor string quartet, his writing became idiomatic and free from unconvincing twists and turns.

It is perplexing to think that by the middle of the nineteenth century the number of compositions of more than ephemeral merit written in the symphonic idiom, once the pride of an era and the supreme aim of its composers, had shrunk to a handful. True enough, we do not know the period extending between the Ninth Symphony and the *Rhenish* Symphony in all its aspects, and the existence of a symphonist of the ability of Kalliwoda [6] should warn us against making categorical statements; but as we look around, the symphonic panorama is indeed melancholy in its sparseness. Among the minor composers only one can claim the title of symphonist: Spohr. Yet even this conservative musician, a self-confessed "disciple" of Mozart, found himself constrained to look for literary support to revitalize the symphony. Spohr's "program" symphonies are not at all related to those of Liszt or Berlioz; they merely have a title which suggests a mood. On the whole they do not go beyond the well-established bounds of the symphony-sonata as practiced in Beethoven's earlier period. His programless C minor symphony is by far his best work in this field. The symphony entitled *Die Weihe der Töne* tries to illustrate in a series of examples the many connections between life and music. This idea, serious and musically acceptable, is displaced by a stylistic toying in his *Historic Symphony,* while the composition called *Iridisches und Göttliches im Menschenleben* (1842) merely makes enough noise to put Berlioz to shame.

The decline of the symphony was paralleled by that of the concerto; indeed, the picture is even more desolate when we turn to this genre, once a vehicle for the most personal utterances. While most of his fellow composers were engaged in the composition of empty fireworks, while Weber and Mendelssohn were writing piano concertos of merit but of no really outstanding qualities, while Chopin was struggling with a medium totally alien to his genius, Schumann, sensing the futility of continuing on the road once traveled by Beethoven, deliberately left it at the first crossing. His A minor concerto, originally written as a fantasy, is the only great and original piano concerto of the period. All virtuoso passage work is eliminated in favor of a consistently free and poetic language, and, as Mendelssohn did in his beautiful violin concerto, Schumann prevented the soloist from disfiguring the work with meaningless acrobatics by writing the cadenza, entirely in keeping with the general tone of the composition, and constituting an integral part of it. Mendelssohn's violin concerto, one of his most personal and finished works, is, with Brahms's violin concerto, the only contribution to the genre in the post-Beethovenian nineteenth century worthy of the great tradition of the concerto. It remains one of the outstanding concertos of the violin literature.

The classic era established an orchestral and chamber music style that gave a specific physiognomy to each of its components. The string quartet differed from the symphony, and likewise the piano trio differed from the string quartet. Romanticism eliminated the hard-won stylistic independence. The expressive media characteristic of chamber music with or without piano were the first to be deprived of differentiation, as specific chamber music became simply instrumental music for various ensembles. The further the century advanced the more the quintessence of chamber music, the string quartet, exhibited orchestral tendencies. This was already plainly shown in the showpieces called *quatuor brillant* of Rode, Romberg, and Spohr, and in the latter's double quartets written for eight players. Among the chamber music composers of the romantic era, perhaps the only one who remained faithful to pure chamber music without the participation of the piano was Spohr, but he, unlike the other champions of romanticism, was a violinist. Significantly enough, Mendelssohn, himself a brilliant pianist, wrote the majority of his chamber music works for string ensembles without piano. His quartets, quintets, and the string octet are pure chamber music, written with a fine instinct for style and a genuine feeling for ensemble work. This music is always interesting and fascinates with its elegance, craftsmanship, and balanced sonority, but when Mendelssohn ventures into the atmosphere of Beethoven's "great appassionato," he fails, for that was given to Schubert only. The great pathos of the Beethovenian mood is, however, almost reached in the two magnificent piano trios of Mendelssohn, although these works are not imitative in the least. A movement so compact and so convincingly launched as the first in the D minor trio was not matched by any composer of the romantic era until Brahms. Schumann was justified in calling the work the "master trio of the present era." Both trios are purely instrumental and not songlike, and the piano, in the best Mozartean traditions, avoids a constant and intimate thematic participation in order not to create a conflict of unblending sonorities.

Among Schumann's quartets, that in A minor is his best and one of the best of the period. On the other hand the piano quintet and the piano quartet, brilliant and proud compositions, are carried by the momentum of the piano. One cannot help feeling that these compositions would be perfectly satisfactory for piano alone. His other works for piano and one string instrument are almost outside the realm of chamber music proper. The two large violin sonatas are extended fantasies or rhapsodies for piano with violin, dangerously extended for their uncertain construction. Thus chamber music shared the fate of the piano sonata, dissolving into virtuoso, rhapsodic, or program pieces. Schubert had already written some works of this type, a fantasy for violin and piano, and an adagio and rondo concertante, but they were mere experiments, for the bulk of his great chamber music compositions stands as the incarnation of the art called "da camera."

The romantic composer likes to linger over single effects; he revels in sonorities, in colors, instrumental and harmonic; an unusual rhythm fascinates him; the rippling tone of the piano, the velvety smoothness of the human voice, beguile him. The classic composer always views the whole; even when he is engaged in breaking up his material in his symphonic developments, details exist to him only in relationship to the whole. It is this quality which separates the two philosophies of art, and the loss of any elevation from which the whole could be surveyed has been held by critics to be the principal shortcoming of romantic music. This, as we have seen, holds true with regard to the large forms of classicism. One cannot, however, maintain this judgment in a general sense, for the dwelling on details, the harmonic, melodic, and coloristic refinements, enriched music immensely, and in the smaller, predominantly lyric forms romanticism created an art fully equal to the greatest in the past. The stylistic mark of this romantic lyricism, vocal and instrumental, is the concentrated expression in single melodies, the delineation of a situation, and the establishment of a mood in a few measures, which is then retained for the duration of the piece. There is nothing here of the dualistic sonata form, for there are no contrasts; a characteristic subject is presented in a songlike form, usually small but sometimes becoming quite ample by the combination of several smaller entities or by fantasylike elaboration of the whole or of certain parts. The theme or motif expresses a state of mind or mood which is permitted to live its full life within the modest frame. The lyric "musical moment," though largely the creation of Mendelssohn, is before us most typically in the pieces strung together by Schumann in cycles—*Kinderszenen, Kreisleriana, Carnaval;* every piece complete and independent in itself, projects a different mood, here frolicking, there lapsing abruptly into earnest meditation. Even the piano sonatas are merely three or four pieces strung together, and indeed the romantic piano sonata is this and nothing else. The composers of the classic era preferred to present such varying states of mind together within one large form, where their conflicting nature furnished them with the dramatic quality so necessary to the dualistic sonata. With some romantic composers these *moments musicaux* tend to be stereotyped; thus Mendelssohn and Field do not show great variety, although within the type they give fine pictures. On the other hand Schumann and Chopin, less consistent in restricting the piece to one idea although maintaining the unity of mood, are inexhaustible in variety. The canzonet-like slow movements in Mendelssohn's quartets, or in the violin concerto, the dreamy *notturno* of the *Midsummer Night's Dream* music, together with the beautiful-sentimental *Songs Without Words* created a new type of romantic instrumental song, a type which cannot bear imitation without being compromised. In his songs and secular choruses, Mendelssohn joined the popular tendency inaugurated by Weber, but his German folk character is rather of the parlor, lacking in real earthliness. Few of his songs reach the level of the great romantic song composers, for he hesitated to follow the poet into deeper regions, but some are worthy companions to similar songs by Schumann and Franz.

Schumann reached his creative peak in his songs, in spite of the value and wealth of his piano music. His legendary love story he translated into a lyricism second only to Schubert's. The year 1840, when he was finally united with Clara Wieck, was the birth year of *Myrthen,* the Eichendorff song cycles, his settings of Heine's *Liederkreis* and *Dichterliebe,* Rückert's *Liebesfrühling,* Chamisso's *Frauenliebe,* and a number of others, a bounty unparalleled in the annals of music. We have noticed Schumann's marked literary penchant. No matter how purely lyrical his songs, in the cycles especially, their succession gives us a picture of the development of mental experiences. In the union of poetry and music and in the emphasis on the psychological moment, Schumann undoubtedly goes beyond Schubert. (This, of course, does not necessarily mean a higher flight of the song.) Voice and instrumental accompaniment form an indivisible unity. The piano stands in the most intimate relationship to the text and to the voice, often contributing more to the expression of the mood than the voice itself; the many delicate postludes are a case in point. In this connection Schumann showed the way to the modern song.

Although distinctly non-Germanic in his romanticism, we must place Chopin in the company of Schumann and Mendelssohn, for he was their spiritual brother, understood and loved by them, whereas his French milieu (with the exception of Liszt and Heine) was never very close to him. More elegiac and sentimental than Mendelssohn, but also more fantastic, sensitive, and exalted, creating with a surer hand than Schumann, Chopin was the truest instrumental lyricist of romanticism.

Instead of dizzy heights, romanticism sought friendly depths; instead of heroic struggle, it craved loving immersion. It wanted to associate itself with nature, to crawl in its innermost regions, for it was there that it believed the purest human heart could be found. The poet in his sanctum sits by his lamp, reading and singing, and the whole of romanticism reads and sings with him. They sing even when they read, they sing always. All their poems are texts to be set to music, and the melodies hover about them. Not everyone hears these melodies, for not everyone understands romanticism; but Mendelssohn.

Schumann, and Chopin heard them, and they proved that the soul of romanticism is music, that music, the art of pure sentiment, is the crowning of poetry, of lyricism. And romanticism appreciated the fact that music and lyricism are inseparable; with all its senses, with all its thoughts, poetry, experience, and faith, romanticism longed for music, it wanted to become music. This it hoped to achieve in the Gesamtkunstwerk, but as we look back from the end of the century we realize that when the "blue flower" was found romanticism ceased to live. Perhaps the little scherzo from the *Midsummer Night's Dream,* the Heine songs, and the nocturnes and mazurkas, small as they are compared to the vast dramas of the Nibelungen, are the works which fulfilled and pre-empted romanticism, after which all romanticism seems archaic or futile.

The Grand Opera

THE international art and style typical of the eighteenth century disappeared as German music acquired undisputed leadership in instrumental music and as Italian opera lost its monopoly. Although the Germans protested against the presence of Italians in their midst, Rossini and Bellini soon had the world, including the Germans, again at their feet. Nevertheless, Italian music, while still admired, ceased to be the sole dictator of style. French music soared to a redoubtable position on the wings of the French romantic movement, and henceforth we must deal with a triangular rivalry in which every party vindicated its claim to equal rights.

The nineteenth century saw the victory of French opera as French librettists, and later French musicians, assumed a leading role in the operatic field. Beginning with the eighteen twenties the Italian librettists regarded French literature as an inexhaustible source from which they did not cease to draw. It will be noted immediately that the Italians, although mediocre playwrights, were thoroughly familiar with the needs and problems of the musical stage and furthermore were writers endowed with musical gifts. In France the authors who furnished libretti for operas were utterly uninformed as to musical problems. They could not select or vary their rhythms and they burdened their melodies with verses which contributed a great deal to the monotony of the art of the empire; this, despite the fact that most of these authors attended the performances of the Théâtre des Italiens, the popular Italian opera in Paris, where they must have noticed that when the verses were carefully scanned half of the composer's labor was saved. Along with this awkwardness in poetic composition was a conventional aesthetic conception which subjected the dramatic métier to certain formulae. They did not apply these theories to their own works only: their incontestable leadership made it possible for the French dramatists of operatic fame to carry their principles into the works of foreign poets, and they mutilated translations of operatic texts to a point where there was little left of the originals. At the same time they condemned everything that did not meet their requirements.

The discrepancy between text and music reached its height in the chief product of the lyric stage of French romanticism, the grand opera. The great composers of the seventeenth century, together with Rameau and Gluck, were forgotten, Mozart and Beethoven were rejected, and Rossini, utterly disgusted, put aside his pen, while grand opera triumphed as a supreme spectacle. The apparatus grew larger and larger, the orchestra doubled its size, and the display of noisy crowds and tumultuous "dramatic" actions and sentimental tableaux became the sole aim of composers and poets. Voltaire's sarcastic remark, so unjust in Gluck's time, became a bitter truth toward the middle of the nineteenth century: "One goes to see a tragedy to be moved, to the Opéra one goes either for want of any other interest or to facilitate digestion." It was against this grand opera, supreme ruler throughout the nineteenth century and still unmistakably the inspiration for many a so-called modern opera, that Wagner, Verdi, and Debussy took the field. The public and the literary world suddenly discovered the great artistic value of opera. The attitude of men of letters changed radically. Lully and Rameau had stood in the center of violent attacks; the best minds of French letters had proclaimed that opera was an incongruous and impossible form of art, a bastard progeny of poetry and music. Grand opera, a form of theater which presented a perfect picture of everything frowned upon by the great figures of French thought, now caused a change of opinion that defies explanation. Men of letters, heretofore opposed to opera, which in the works of Lully, Rameau, and Gluck approached almost the Greek ideal of drama, endorsed with enthusiasm works that were written and composed for the use of bourgeois merchants. If we recall that only a few years earlier these same men witnessed the triumphs of the revived music drama of the Gluck disciples, Méhul, Cherubini, and Spontini, and the inimitably French art of the opéra comique, and that one of the eminent representatives of the latter, Boïeldieu, was still in their midst creating his best-known opera, *La Dame Blanche,* in 1825, we are at first entirely at a loss to understand this course of events. As usual, however, the reasons are not purely musical and must be sought in the general cultural life of the nation.

With the passing of the stormy days of the Revolution and of the Napoleonic era, the romantic period began. The origins of French romanticism are not to be found in literature, even though the movement itself was entirely literary; we shall find them in life, in the history of France. Indeed, much can be ascribed to historical and psychological causes rather than to the romantic movement in England and Germany, which admittedly exerted a serious influence upon French romantic thought. The children of the men of the Revolution and the Napoleonic era, who witnessed in their youth the horrors of the upheaval and the glory of the empire, heavily taxed their imagination, the only thing left to them. The sons wanted to use the same gestures in their private life that their fathers used on the barricades or on the battlefields. Reduced to inactivity by historical events, the French nation spent the two decades between 1825 and 1845 in imagining what no longer could be achieved. Since it no more could live the great adventures, it indulged in reading about and listening to them. It was in this atmosphere that both romantic drama and grand opera, closely interrelated, started; and this explains the importance that romanticism attached to the theater, and also the decline of instrumental music, the complete extinction of the fine symphonic school that started so auspiciously with Gossec, Méhul, Cherubini, and others. For decades to come, with the exception of Berlioz, who declared himself to be "three-fourths a German," music became to the French synonymous with the lyric stage.

The new aspirations and political and social preoccupations, the invasion of the bourgeois spirit, the pursuit of money and pleasure, abolished the sincere atmosphere of the first fervors of the romantic movement. The bourgeois spirit found great satisfaction in two genres of art: the pseudoclassic drama and the grand opera. The dramatists of the first period of romanticism still wrote dramas on classical patterns. After two centuries of classicism people hesitated to throw off the yoke of tradition. Chateaubriand and Mme de Staël attempted to turn their eyes toward the Middle Ages and to the literature of the north, but the great majority continued to look toward Athens and Rome. Auger, the diligent academician, attacked dramas as romantic that did not yet represent the species. Imagination, fantasy, free construction, ample, varied, and surprising action first appeared in the melodrama, the "tragedy of the canaille." "Romantic drama was already thirty years old when Dumas and Hugo achieved their success. Otherwise the dating from *Hernani* to the *Burgraves* seems incredibly short. Romantic drama originated in the melodrama at the end of the Revolution and after remaining for thirty years in a popular form at the small Parisian theaters, became a literary genre with its entrance into the Comédie Française in 1830." [7] The seemingly great distance between the melodrama and the historic drama was bridged with remarkable ease in a short time, and thus the task of romantic drama was considerably simplified.

The battle for the romantic drama progressed, although the resistance of the conservative dramatic stage was strong. A new edition of Letourneur's translation of Shakespeare (1816) and a French edition of Schiller (1819) gave a new impetus to the cause of the romantic movement, and romantic drama finally took form in the year of Beethoven's death, 1827, in Hugo's *Cromwell*. *Cromwell* was a closet drama. It was written in verse and in keeping with the laws of the classic unities. There was still a long way to travel from the book to the stage. The 25th of February, 1830, marks the date when, with *Hernani,* the romantic drama obtained its first decisive victory. This phase of romanticism ended with the failure of the *Burgraves* in 1843. Hugo and his followers, now in control of the stage, eliminated the last vestiges of the classic tragedy. Construction ceased to be the means of unity in romantic drama; the aesthetes of romanticism believed that poetry would take its place. While the classic tragedy was somewhat rigid, while its rhetoric was a hindrance to action, its sacrifices were well rewarded at the decisive points. Here, in the final tragic dialectic, classical tragedy reached heights which were beyond the power of "free" drama. Corneille's and Racine's dialectic puts dramatic life into the hero standing in the center of the conflict. Their type of man sometimes seems too abstract, and so are his feelings, but classic rhetorical pathos was capable of carrying the expression of abstract feelings to a point of majesty unequaled by modern drama. What gave its chief value to French classical tragedy was the carrying of dramatic logic to the utmost limit. By insisting on absolute liberty in form, romantic drama elevated circumstance to the position of an important factor in the plot, and thus made room for illogical accidents, preventing the working out of a logical dramatic web. Another weakness of the romantic drama was its obvious symbolism. Some authors gave away the key to their symbolism prematurely, others used figures that do not constitute appropriate symbols and fail to create individual characters. On the stage everything at once assumes a definite symbolical meaning, even against the writer's intentions. With the utterance of his first inconsistency he changes the impression he had created and forces the listener to change his conception. We must really be intoxicated by the flow of colors and sounds to identify the various Hernanis as one and the same. Hugo brings about this state of intoxication by the lavish use of stagecraft, costumes, crowds, the brilliant, though often false, application of local color; most of all, however, by his language, his verse, and his lyric rhetoric.

When classical tragedy wanted to ascend to poetic pathos it set an artificial distance between life and itself. The subject matter of the bourgeois drama was too near to the romanticists and appeared trivial to them. The natural pathos of its figures is not dramatic, its plots seem arbitrary, it does not and cannot have the poetic resonance of tradition. This may have been the reason for the preference for historical subjects displayed by the romanticists. Historical atmosphere served as substitute for mythology. It could create the necessary "distance," bring about monumentality, and obliterate trivialities; it could produce new pathos. Thus the most important element in classical tragedy, which we have called "distance," was still present in the romantic drama. This history-created distance, however, seemed not only much more obvious than its predecessor, but less firm, requiring the assistance of facts, of historical accuracy. This historical perspective used something that occurred in the past instead of something occurring in the present; thus romantic drama always substituted one real occurrence for another real occurrence, it never substituted symbol for reality. Classic tragedy was based on psychology, no matter how anachronistic the term may seem when applied to the seventeenth century. Mere historical atmosphere can never reach such depths and distances. In the *Burgraves,* Hugo attempted to resuscitate medieval Germany, the world of Barbarossa and his feudal lords. In spite of the minute care for historical truth, the profuse application of erudition, there is a constant anachronism. We realize that the hero is not really the medieval emperor but Napoleon, that the whole play is really the "Return from the Isle of Elba" in medieval costume.

It is here, in this historic atmosphere, that we seem to find the origin of the grand opera. It was a necessity, a logical outcome of trends in French literature, and thus French literature is once more responsible for the creation of a musical type.

When listening to *Le Roi s'Amuse,* the only concrete impression we experience is a negative one—the absence of music—and, indeed, certain of Hugo's dramas are better known to the world at large as opera books than in their original literary form as French plays. *Hernani* and *Le Roi s'Amuse* served Verdi as the books of *Ernani* and *Rigoletto, Ruy Blas* has been turned into a libretto several times, Balfe's *Armorer of Nantes* is based on *Marie Tudor,* Mercadante's *Giuramento* is a setting of *Angelo. Lucrèce Borgia,* the final act of which is a perfect grand opera scene culminating in the bacchanalian lyrics of the supper party with the dirge for the dying chanted by the approaching priests, was used to excellent account in Donizetti's *Lucrezia Borgia.* Hugo was right when he opposed his works' being utilized for libretti. He realized that the musician's version of his drama would be superior to his plays. *Rigoletto* is, indeed, a better *play* than *Le Roi s'Amuse;* Verdi's music fills in the gaps in the action, it animates the moments when the figures of the drama do not have anything to say, and it forces the singer to lend the necessary intonation to the words. The affiliation of grand opera with romantic drama, their common origin, is, then, unmistakable; but if grand opera and romantic drama grew up together, there must have been a time when their ways parted.

La Muette de Portici (1828), by Daniel François Esprit Auber (1782–1871), opened the new era in the history of French lyric drama, the era of the grand opera. The Restoration received the first products of the new operatic genre with enthusiasm. The subjects used by grand opera were different from those of the old music drama, the tragédie lyrique, or the opéra comique. They were historical, dealing with fairly modern history; Biblical and classical themes disappeared almost entirely. With them disappeared the tragedy proper, and the romantic drama took its place. The critics praised in *La Muette* the quality of dramatic interpretation; they believed they saw in the new drama the continuation of the almost two-hundred-year-old traditions of French opera. They had to admit, however, that the principles used in grand opera were not "exactly" the same as those prevailing in the time of *Alceste* or *Iphigénie*. Instead of subordinating music and every other component of the drama to the exigencies of the text, this new drama subordinated everything to music. This was not, however, the musical conception of the eighteenth-century classic opera, which turned a libretto into music, realized a text in music, but the attitude which Beaumarchais lashed with such biting irony: "Ce qui ne vaut pas la peine d'être dit, on le chante" (What is not worth saying is sung). Auber's contemporaries thought that they restored the musico-dramatic genre and continued its traditions. This belief was responsible for the surprising blindness of the critics and the public. Dramatic power, so poignantly presented by Rameau, Gluck, and Cherubini, was reduced to meaningless exterior effects; a tremolo in the orchestra sufficed to make the public of the Restoration believe themselves listening to psychological characterization. *La Muette,* in itself a work that contains much good operatic music and is carried by real élan, opened the way to the long string of grand operas which represent in music what the bourgeois drama represents in literature.

While undoubtedly the "first" grand opera, *La Muette* must be considered a false start, for soon after its great success Auber abandoned the new road, returning with his *Fra Diavolo* (1830) to the heritage of Grétry and Monsigny. If we recall that every new operatic style in France was originated by a foreigner—Lully, Duni, Gluck—we shall not be surprised to find the real founder of the grand opera in a person coming from a different musical climate. There is another fact we must also remember, namely, that every one of these operatic periods was launched by literary preparations entirely French in nature and spirit. We shall find both if we continue our comparison of classic and romantic drama.

Stage technique was always cherished by French playwrights, but the tendency to emphasize this aspect of theatrical art manifested itself at the very beginning of the century of romanticism. The extensive use of technique indicates that life itself does not intensify the typical conflicts that arise in it. How simple were the situations presented in Molière's plays, and how penetrating their picture of life, of real life. The reign of the *science des planches,* "the science of the boards," originated with Eugène Scribe (1791–1861). Perhaps the whole of modern dramatic art is indebted to him;

partly because he reigned for a long time as a sovereign master of the theater in France and abroad, partly because the course of the theater in the second half of the century was due to the reaction to his authority. Thus, accepted or opposed, his influence was manifest. To the writing of dramas and libretti Scribe brought the unexampled skill acquired in the writing of a hundred minor plays and vaudevilles. His knowledge of the stage and of what could be done there, and how to do it, has never been equaled. The world-wide acceptance of the French theater and opera libretto in the second half of the nineteenth century was due to the perfection of his methods. Scribe and his disciples, the melodramatic playwrights, devoted themselves to the construction of a self-acting plot; once constructed, this plot could be dressed up quite as well in English or German as in the original French. Scribe's knowledge of the profession was such that it was almost an art in itself. Dumas Fils remarked once that a dramatic author with Balzac's knowledge of the human soul and with Scribe's familiarity with the requirements of the stage would be the greatest dramatist of all time. Every musician in France and abroad was eager to obtain a libretto from the man who excelled in inserting arias and ballets in seemingly impossible places in the dramatic action. Auguste, the celebrated head of the *corps de claque* in the Opéra, expressed his enthusiasm for the neatness of Scribe's libretto technique in a memorandum to the administration: "every aria and almost every duet can be made," that is, the applause could be started conveniently without the interference of some troublesome postlude or connecting link.

While Scribe's works reflect the conventionality and prudishness of the French public of the eighteen thirties and forties, French romanticism was not lacking in the tendency we observed in Germany toward finding an outlet, or rather a more universal medium of expression, in music, but it could not meet music in transcendent regions like German romanticism. Its reunion with music was limited to external things. It was in these days of romantic efflorescence and longing for music that a certain Jacob Liebman Beer came to France. He had only to add to his family name that of one of his benefactors and to Italianize his first name to become the famous composer Giacomo Meyerbeer (1791–1864). With excellent instinct Meyerbeer divined the possibilities offered by the times. This highly cultivated and gifted man, exceedingly well-trained and ambitious musician, jealous artist, indefatigable worker, clever and patient diplomatist, watched with keen eyes the intellectual spectacle unfolding before him. With a sure hand he first succeeded in segregating all elements which in the past had hampered the success of a national French opera. Then he deliberately set out to utilize the weaknesses of the French character. By addressing himself especially to the intelligence of the French, by associating himself with

Scribe and learning from him the "accessories" and the theory of the little causes which lead to great effects, by embracing the religious currents then in vogue, Meyerbeer succeeded in conquering the French public at his first attempt. Thus this Prussian Jew was responsible for the form of music which was unanimously called *genre éminemment français*.[8] He estimated the intelligence of his public at its correct value, and was also perfectly aware of how much the contemporaries of Auber and Adam could endure when it came to music. His theater became a sort of grand spectacle where the most bizarre figures paraded to the accompaniment of cleverly calculated music. Processions, councils, princesses on horseback, cardinals and heretics, figured in shipwrecks, cannonades, tumbling cathedrals, with choirs of demons and corteges of phantoms.

It is amazing to compare the judgments of his works made by his compatriots and by his adopted countrymen. Mendelssohn called the ballet of the nuns in *Robert le Diable* "a veritable scandal," and Schumann wrote that "the world has rarely seen such a conglomeration of monstrosities"; Wagner thought that the secret of Meyerbeer's music was "effect without cause or reason." Such was the opinion of the Germans, accustomed to *Don Giovanni,* the *Magic Flute, Freischütz,* and *Fidelio*. The opinion of contemporary France was entirely different. Balzac considered the *Huguenots* "as true as history itself," and did not hesitate to declare it the embodiment of the Lutheran ideal. George Sand saw in the hero of this same opera "one of the greatest dramatic figures, one of the most beautiful personifications of the religious ideal ever produced!" It is hard to account for the laudatory opinion of French critics. The major part of the French public of Meyerbeer's time knew no other music than that performed on the contemporary lyric stage. Concert life as such was in its very beginnings, for the Revolution interrupted the earlier organizations, which in any case were too exclusive to reach the public at large. The public lived in the conviction that Scribe and Meyerbeer gave them the *grand musique;* the opéra comique and everything else was the *petite musique agréable,* and only the grand opera represented great art with its dramatic climaxes.

Robert le Diable (1831) marks an important date in the history of music. With this work Meyerbeer and Scribe created the grand opera, for the modest beginnings of *La Muette* had been forgotten. The grand opera is called a genre, but legitimate genres of literature and art have a foundation in nature; they correspond to as many aspects under which things can be contemplated, to as many natural moods and expressions of sentiments and aspirations of the artistic soul. The grand opera has its foundation not in nature, but in the nature of Scribe and Meyerbeer. Scribe's opera libretti fill twenty-six volumes in the complete edition of his works; that alone is comment on the extent of his influence. Meyerbeer's influence upon the course of opera was not less conspicuous. That he was one of the ablest musico-dramatists in the whole history of opera is undeniable. Scenes like the poignant duet between Valentine and Raoul in the *Huguenots* can be composed only by a truly gifted musician. And as far as orchestration and dramatic accompaniment are concerned, Berlioz and Wagner owed much more to Meyerbeer than they were willing to acknowledge. But on the whole he used his great gifts to conceal with superb craftsmanship the emptiness of an art devoid of artistic integrity and entirely calculated on effect.

With the success of the grand opera and of the bourgeois drama, the theater became a profession in which hard competition made people sacrifice their ideals. Almost every one of the contemporary critics complained about the alarming concessions made by the playwrights and musicians to the provincialism of the public. In this atmosphere the opéra comique, the lively, witty, thoroughly artistic and thoroughly French creation of the lyric stage, which in Boïeldieu's works still furnished remarkable masterpieces, reached a point where a crisis seemed inevitable. On the one hand, the opéra comique declined to the lowest level of vaudeville literature, while on the other there was a tendency, under the influence of the grand opera, toward more operatic treatment of both libretto and music, and the better composers took this route, which eventually led them into the field of opera proper. Reinforced by this more ambitious type of opéra comique, grand opera continued its triumphal progress. Meyerbeer and Jacques Fromentin Halévy (1799–1862), whose *La Juive* (1835) shared the enormous success of the *Huguenots,* seemed to fulfill the expectations and ideals not only of France but of the whole world. The Germans forgot all their indignation, and the King of Prussia invited Meyerbeer to become general director of music in Berlin. Opera at the middle of the century had become a pompous spectacle enhanced by music. Everything in it was calculated to appeal to the senses, not only the arias sung by the prima donna, but the number and beauty of the dancers in the corps de ballet, the variety of the staging, and the splendor of the scenery. And now, when the lyric stage degenerated to the status of pure spectacle, the literary world acclaimed it as the only form of theatrical art to be enjoyed by discriminating people. There were still some writers devoted to the great traditions of the French theater, but they could not escape the pernicious influence of the new idol of dramatic form, the grand opera. It is astounding how opera, once responsible for the decline of classical tragedy, was again strong enough to bring about the practical destruction of French drama.

| Figure-toi, lecteur, que ton mauvais génie | Imagine, reader, that your evil genius |
| T'a fait prendre ce soir un billet d'opéra. | Has made you take a ticket for the opera tonight. |

Te voilà devenu parterre ou galerie,	Behold you now become parterre or gallery,
Et tu ne sais pas trop ce qu'on chantera.	And you aren't too sure what they are going to sing.
Il se peut qu'on t'amuse, il se peut qu'on t'ennuie;	Maybe you'll be amused, and maybe bored;
Il se peut que l'on pleure, à moins que l'on ne rie;	Maybe people will weep, if they don't laugh;
Et le terme moyen, c'est que l'on bâillera.	And the mean term will be that they yawn.
Qu'importe? c'est la mode, et le temps passera.	What matter? 'Tis the fashion, and the time will pass.

(de Vigny)

Italian Opera

IN this general complacency, when the public obtained what it wanted and the great masters were forgotten, there appeared a curious figure who with his Rabelaisian laughter promised to halt the decadence of opera. But he was utterly misunderstood, and this time even by those who praised him to the skies. This was Gioachino Rossini (1792–1868).

At the time of Rossini's appearance the great traditions of classic opera were paling and various factions were waging a battle for hegemony. The antagonists were Germans, French, and Italians. French libretti were becoming more and more influential, and the attraction of Paris as the musical capital of the world lured even the Neapolitans to France. While the French libretto was gaining an undisputed rule the impressive shadow of Metastasio was still noticeable far into the nineteenth century. With the change in the literary orientation came a new trend in operatic music. In Italy this was personified by Johann Simon Mayr (1763–1845), a Bavarian who, like Hasse, became entirely Italianized. Everything he learned from the great classic school of his homeland he transmitted to his adopted country, especially the newly won technique of the pliable symphony orchestra, which he transplanted to the opera and developed to a degree that fascinated every composer in Europe. Neither Spontini nor Meyerbeer could have arisen without his school, and the supposed inventor of the modern orchestra, Berlioz, owes him the lion's share. Then English romanticism, which had found such a resounding echo in Germany and France, reached Italy, where it struck sparks of a different nature. The Italian does not imitate; if something really engages his fancy he will match it with something of his own. Byron's and Scott's characters and the romanticized Shakespearean heroes retained their names only in Bellini's and Rossini's operas. They are not at all the romantic figures we have known in their literary form, but the music that surrounds them—Italian to the core—is romantic. The same is true of the operas of the type of Donizetti's *Lucia,* but since we are not yet sufficiently acquainted with the nature of Italian romanticism and since the operatic history of the first half of the nineteenth century still needs a great deal of elucidation, it is difficult to reconcile these works with their counterparts in Germany and France.

Rossini approached the scene with a clear knowledge of the situation. This, but only this, he shared with his great opponent, Meyerbeer. His *Tancredi* already shows that Rossini's music is not servile to the text, nor does it govern the opera in the older Neapolitan manner. Romantic tendencies manifest in the earlier operas are harnessed by a classic wit and pregnancy, and in the *Barber of Seville* (1816) he gave the world a work worthy of Beaumarchais and Mozart. Indeed, with his inexhaustible melodic gifts, his masterly characterizations, his uncanny knowledge of the stage, Rossini stands close to Mozart, and the *Barber,* sadly disfigured and completely misrepresented in modern performances, is a worthy companion to *Figaro.* No one could withstand the charms of this music, sparkling with spirit and caprice, overflowing with merriment, melodies, and a firework of rhythm. The whole world was at Rossini's feet. Schopenhauer declared that he now understood the elemental powers of music, and Hegel could find only ecstatic words. Cool Germany lost all sane measure. When Rossini visited Vienna in 1822, Beethoven was outshone, Mozart forgotten, and Schubert ignored. It is by no means an exaggeration to claim that with the *Barber* the history of comic opera, or rather that of the opera buffa, came to an end. It was the last brick in the edifice built by Pergolesi, Mozart, Cimarosa, and Paisiello. Donizetti and a few other composers contributed some fine specimens to the opera buffa after Rossini, but the universality of the classic opera buffa flared up only once more in all its greatness, generations later, in Verdi's *Falstaff.*

In *William Tell* the Italian composer demonstrated what he owed to French art and literature, to which he was now drawn more closely without, however, losing his originality. This was perhaps the first time in his prolific career that he resisted his prodigious facility of creation. He held in check his improvisatory imagination, illuminating it with the light of reflection and study. It took him six months to "build" his opera, an interval of time which usually saw the production of several operas. *William Tell* was a mixture of music drama, opera seria, and grand opera. The old revolutionary opera lived in it, re-enforced with the pathos of the opera seria, the character painting of the opera buffa, and the bombast of the grand opera. After the production of this work something seemingly inexplicable happened. At the age of thirty-seven, at a period when he had hardly reached the full development of his powers, Rossini ceased to compose operas. During the remaining thirty-nine years of his life he produced nothing more for the stage, and nothing else of importance except the *Stabat Mater.* An encyclopedia of music in general use attacks this problem in the following way: "There can be only one plausible explanation of Rossini's thirty-nine years of inactivity, and this is his inveterate and unconquerable laziness." The article in question also lists thirty-eight operas, a dozen cantatas, and a multitude of short pieces of music when enumerating Rossini's output up to his thirty-seventh year. One surely cannot accuse the composer of such an impressive list of works of "inveterate laziness," yet Rossini is always held up as the incarnation of a gifted but lazy and unscrupulous artist devoid of all integrity. Had the author of the article in question thought twice about his own statement, when he reported Rossini attending the first performance of the *Huguenots,* he might have found a more plausible explanation for Rossini's silence. Rossini witnessed the immense success of Meyerbeer's grand opera and realized that his own art was no longer needed. He stopped writing and lived the life of a frivolous, ironical epicurean. He returned to Bologna shortly after the performance of the *Huguenots* and on the way home stopped in Frankfort, where he met Mendelssohn. The conversation of the two musicians is recorded in Ferdinand Hiller's *Mendelssohn,* from which one can see that Rossini was outspoken about the grave concern he felt for the future of the opera.

In Rossini's works one can discern the current of a free and happy civilization, based on the gracefulness of a natural aristocracy. While not always free from negligence and improvisation, they reward us with a sane, vivacious, and broad sensibility coupled with a clear and decided spirit. His melodic gifts were matched by his orchestral writing, a wonder of mobility, sonority, and color, always constructive in the classic sense. After leaving his congenial environment, he was not at all perturbed at facing the immense room of the Paris Opéra, changing his refined orchestration overnight to suit both the ampleness of the theater and the grandiloquence of the prevailing French style. His hands had not lost their infallible security, and no lesser critic and enemy than Berlioz paid tribute to his marshaling of noisy and bombastic sonorities in *William Tell.* The elaborateness of the orchestral part, however, was never allowed to obscure his musical thoughts. Every opera composer of his time was indebted to him, as composers of the next generation were to Liszt, and most operas echoed Rossinian turns, as most orchestral scores of the so-called neo-romantic era were a dictionary of thoughts and devices originated by Liszt.

After Rossini, Italian opera drew nearer to the orbit of the romantic grand opera. Gifted composers were not lacking, but the prevailing musical creed forced them to find their aesthetic bearings in the public's taste. The opera composer did not give himself, he sought himself in the mirror of public vogue and, as in the era of the concert opera, he had to count upon the spoiled interpreters of his art, the singing stars. Operatic life turned from the stage to the auditorium; the coloratura soprano and the heroic tenor advanced to the footlights, raised their arms, opened their mouths, and shouted at the public. All the composer had to do was to follow a few well-tried recipes, and if he had melodic gifts he could write a successful opera. But the Italians' operatic genius was able to overcome even these oppressive conventions and the superficial taste of the public. Their wonderful sense for the beauty of the human voice gave their melodies that broad, elastic, flexible, freely arching line which is the birthright of the lyric stage. The soul of this melody is in love with the reality of the human voice, and while it is the slave of this love it also fires it with passion and exuberance. The fervor of this intoxicating singing voice is present even in the recitatives, and it created a new type of ensemble (for instance, the sextet in Donizetti's *Lucia*) in which the individual parts vie with each other and inspire each other to higher flights. The eclecticism of the nascent grand opera was poorly suited to the Italians, and on the other hand, in their own field, the old traditions were loosened and the great popularity of the singers forced them to concentrate on virtuoso arias. In this musical atmosphere they had only two sources of inspiration, Rossini's wonderfully free dramatic construction, still intact, and Mayr's new operatic and orchestral technique.

Severio Raffaele Mercadante (1795–1870) and Giovanni Pacini (1796–1867) continued Mayr's school. Both of them were famous and successful composers of opera whose contributions to modern orchestral and musico-dramatic technique have great historic significance, but their music was not enduring. It is a different matter when we approach the two chief composers of Italian opera in the romantic era, Gaetano Donizetti (1797–1848) and Vincenzo Bellini (1801–1835). Both were born to the operatic stage, both were imbued with the great traditions of Italian opera, and both realized that the principles of their national art were threatened by the new ideals emanating from Paris. Both attempted to save the old operatic ideal, but in their approach, they disclosed vastly different personalities.

Bellini seized from the musical wealth of his period one detail, the cult of melody, upon which he built an entirely personal art. Donizetti, still engrossed with the glory of the classic opera, endeavored to follow it in all its aspects. The times had changed, however, and only in fragments was he able to rise to the heights to which his genius entitled him. An aria, a scene, and sometimes a whole act show us an opera composer compared to whom the champions of the grand opera sink to ignominious insignificance; but Donizetti was unable to maintain uniform excellence and was unable to give the nineteenth-century Italian opera its laws. To do this was reserved for a stronger personality: Verdi. For when Donizetti succeeded in writing a finished masterpiece, *Don Pasquale* (1843), he did not give us of his innermost soul as did Verdi in his *Falstaff;* he merely composed a brilliant and consummate opera buffa in the best Italian traditions. Similarly, *La Fille du Régiment* (1840) is a French opéra comique of eternal freshness, wit, and grace, but the very ease with which this gifted musician turned from opera buffa to the entirely different opéra comique, finding unerringly the style true to the species, did not give him time enough to listen to his own voice; before he could ponder the issues he had a finished work in score. His facility and melodic inventiveness were beyond comprehension, satisfying public appetite for melodies and the demand of the singers for virtuoso arias. One bankrupt opera manager beseeched Donizetti for help, whereupon the composer set about to find a suitable subject, worked it out himself into a libretto, composed the music, and prepared and conducted the production, thus saving the theater from its impending doom, in nine days. The last act of his *La Favorite* is perhaps the most brilliant example of his dramatic expressiveness, yet it was the result of a few hours' work.

While Rossini lived as part of his era, he was at the same time above it. Donizetti was not a sufficiently strong individuality and he was submerged in his time. His *Maria di Rohan* (1843) is an imperfect predecessor of Verdi's profound music dramas, while his *Don Pasquale* is a perfect successor of Rossini's opera buffa. These two works establish, then, with absolute clarity his place in operatic history, exactly halfway between Rossini and Verdi.

Bellini did not find the "eternal singing of arias" as one-sided as his modern German and English critics, for when he sang he did not spare himself; everything sang in him, his whole soul bathed in the happiness of the flowing melody, warm, scented, and caressing, filled with desires, memories, passions. He, unlike Wagner, did not want to eliminate the aria from the opera; on the contrary, he wanted to endow it with that importance and completeness, that natural and true expressive force which justified its central position in the opera. And no one valued him for it more than Wagner. Bellini's music does not reflect the metallic strength of the baroque opera nor the concise and swift dramatic pace of the classic opera; *La Sonnambula* and *Norma* (both 1831) are the works of a romanticist with a penchant for melancholy, softly elegiac melodies which captivated all musicians who recoiled from Meyerbeer. Wagner expressed great admiration for him, and in his earlier works Bellini's influence is manifest, but Liszt and Chopin are not less his debtors. These melodies and arias are not patterns; on his stage there are no puppets but real dramatic figures, living men and women whose language is melody, most beautifully and convincingly expressed in the love duets. The influence of the grand opera did not ruin the charm of Bellini's style. *I Puritani* (1835) shows how well he approached the task of merging the styles of Italian and French opera. It was his early death that prevented a lasting reconciliation. Being less affected by French influence than Donizetti, Bellini proclaimed once more the pure lyrico-dramatic ideal of Italian opera. His clinging to the traditions was not mere conservatism, for what he retained were the principles only, and these are still alive in the aged Verdi. His undiluted Italianism carried him to dramatic scenes such as the serious opera had not known in his time. His early death was mourned by all musicians and deprived opera of one of its great hopes.

German Opera

AFTER Weber's *Freischütz* the desire in Germany for a national opera never died, but for a long time the opera theaters jealously watched the French and Italian lyric stage, giving preference to works that achieved success in Paris, Rome, Venice, or Milan. This attitude is attributable not only to the relative youth of German opera; it has its roots in opera itself. Since opera is to a much greater extent than any other form of music the product of a social culture, its traditions are more powerful. German composers, never easily mastering the difficulties inherent in the lyric drama, could not match the long experience and innate theatrical instinct of Italians and Frenchmen. An examination of the repertory of German opera theaters from the Congress of Vienna to the 1848 revolutions will disclose the indisputable superiority of Italian and French works over the native German. From about 1830 to 1849 there were performed in Germany forty-five French and twenty-five Italian works, against twenty-three German, of which only nine were by composers living at the time. The latter were restricted mostly to the places where the composers were conductors.[9] Among the "living" composers only Spohr, Marschner, Lortzing, Kreutzer, and Flotow were able to offer any competition to the foreigners, until after the middle of the century, when Wagner changed the situation. But even when Wagner reversed the tables, he had to count on an immediate rival in the young Verdi, conspicuously present in the repertory of German theaters.

Goslich lists about one hundred German opera composers active from around 1800 to Wagner's later period.[10] From this large list only a few survive with a handful of operas. Operatic history between Mozart and Weber is still enshrouded in darkness; the only ray we see is *Fidelio,* but the period between *Freischütz* and *Lohengrin* is perhaps even more confusing and will require much research and study. This was the period of the composing conductor (as opposed to the eighteenth-century conducting composer) for which the Germans coined the apt term *Kapellmeister-musik;* indeed, a special chapter should be reserved in all manuals of music history for the *Kapellmeister* opera. There are at least five hundred known operas composed by German musicians between the *Freischütz* and *Lohengrin,* and a good number of these were performed, usually in the theater where their author wielded the baton. Nevertheless, in the revised edition of his *Memoirs of the Opera,* George Hogarth, English musical writer and critic, generally acknowledged as a sound chronicler of contemporary events, remarked in 1851 that "at the present day there is not a single German composer of note who contributes to the support of the national opera. The musical theatres are chiefly supplied with German versions of pieces imported from Italy and France." This statement, while significant, should not be interpreted literally; still, it shows that, apart from the old operas of Mozart, Gluck, Dittersdorf, Weigl, Gyrowetz, Weber, and Winter, the few works of Spohr, Marschner, Lortzing, Flotow, and the even fewer of Lachner and the young Wagner were so thinly distributed among the amazing number of theaters giving operatic performances in Germany that they failed to make a particular impression on a foreign visitor. In 1857 there were about seventy traveling opera companies, twenty-three court operas, and about one hundred municipal and other permanent institutions performing opera.[11] While still setting the style, the court operas found rivals in the municipal and private theaters, which, with their less cumbersome administration, proved to be very successful, often overshadowing the princely establishments. Many of the notable composers of the romantic era served as conductors in these institutions, contributing to the emancipation of German opera while the courts still favored the Italians. Thus Weber was conductor in Breslau and Prague, Hoffmann in Bamberg, Spohr in the Theater an der Wien in Vienna, Lachner in another Viennese private theater and later in Mannheim, Marschner in Leipzig, Mendelssohn in Düsseldorf, and Wagner in Magdeburg and Königsberg—all private or municipal opera houses. The preference for Italian and French opera was supported by the dearth of good German singing actors. ("I wish," remarked Florestan, "I could read something of the dramatic situation, something of the music's joy and pain, in German eyes; fine singing, issuing from an inexpressive, colorless, wooden, or marble face, leads one to doubt the existence of any inward feeling; I mean this in general.") [12] Yet the voices calling for original German operas were never muffled, everyone was waiting for the German operatic Messiah, and the German musical journals continued to denounce "foreign trash," maintaining that German composers ought to be able to match them.

German romantic opera often rose to great dramatic intensity, but the

Singspiel was still lurking in the background, for the most intense scenes were often followed by some strophic song, soldiers' quartet, hunting quartet, or drinking scene. All composers tried to imitate the lilting grace of Italian operatic melody, but by this time they were too Germanic really to feel the Latin elegance and finesse. The Rossinian sallies of Spohr and Marschner usually sounded more grotesque than graceful. A certain robust romanticism with a demonic tinge dominates Marschner's operas, *Vampyr* (1828), *Templer und Jüdin* (after Scott's *Ivanhoe*, 1829), and *Hans Heiling* (1833); if, however, we look a little closer we shall find that the demonic is rather decorative. Lord Ruthwen and Hans Heiling thrive on sound human passions; the blood that flows in their veins is the warm blood of living, earthly, human beings. It is regrettable that the original romantic fervor of this composer ebbed into Biedermeier sobriety; his three chief operas had, however, considerable influence on Wagner. Both Marschner and Spohr had in common that love of chromaticism which ultimately culminated in Wagner's *Tristan*, but while this sensuous-erotic chromaticism forms a natural language in Wagner's music, its intermittent and arbitrary use by the earlier composers is often offensive. It must be said, nevertheless, that in his *Jessonda* (1823) Spohr penetrated to the very frontiers of the *Tristan* dialect.

A much more coarse-grained romanticism, the robber romanticism so beloved by the people, lives in *Das Nachtlager von Granada* (1834) by Konradin Kreutzer (1780–1849), the only one of his thirty operas which is still alive, thanks to its effective choruses and songs.

Amidst the ambitious musico-dramatists there appeared two men, Otto Nicolai (1810–1849) and Albert Lortzing (1801–1851), who, in a lighter vein, offered works lacking in the conflicting stylistic elements that are often too evident in Marschner and Spohr. The spirit of the Singspiel and of the Viennese opera buffa reaped its last triumphs in these amiable works, modest but fully worthy of the great traditions. Nicolai once more revived that engaging combination of Italian opera buffa with German Singspiel which had delighted the late eighteenth century. His *Merry Wives of Windsor* is the only "German buffa" in this period of somber subjects, and perhaps the only romantic opera that attempted to follow in Mozart's footsteps. Unfortunately, it remained an isolated case. Friedrich von Flotow (1812–1883), who tried to bring about a similar fusion of French opéra comique and German Singspiel, created a sort of French Biedermeier. *Alessandro Stradella* (1844) and *Martha* (1847) have many delightful melodies, but on the whole Flotow tends to a sentimentalism that often dilutes the good qualities of his musicianly talent.

Lortzing was the embodiment of the German petty bourgeois of the times preceding the 1848 upheavals, an upright citizen, honest artist, good family man, happy and contented, full of warm feelings, and animated by the poetic mood of an era which considered art the chief ornament of life. But while Lortzing and his fellows welcomed art into their life, they did not experience it particularly profoundly. Great, strong, and passionate tones are not to be found in his operas, yet they are valuable both for the absence of these tones and for the welcome contrast they afford to more pretentious works. Lortzing's operas began their vogue on the German stage when Wagner began to dominate it, and for the next half century he was the most performed composer next to Wagner. From a purely artistic point of view it would be ridiculous to compare *Zar und Zimmermann* (1837), *Hans Sachs* (1840, which figures among Wagner's sources for his *Meistersinger*), *Wildschütz* (1842), *Waffenschmied* (1846), and his one romantic grand opera, *Undine* (1845), with the great Wagnerian music dramas, but the great vogue of these delightful comic operas in the face of the Wagnerian triumphs testifies to the healthy taste of the public. As in the old days, gods and mythological figures, symbolism and metaphysics, tired the music-loving multitude; they wanted some variety and recreation, they wanted to see human figures on the stage, human intrigues, failures, and merriment. These Lortzing gave them in profusion by finding a tone of entertainment that was a worthy parallel to the opéra comique. Besides possessing remarkable musical gifts, Lortzing knew every secret of the theater and arranged his witty libretti himself. This modest German composer was a master whose works are still fresh and thoroughly enjoyable, a worthy successor to Hiller and Dittersdorf, who enriched the Singspiel with elements taken from German romantic opera and French opéra comique.

What the whole nation desired so fervently found fulfillment not in German opera but in the work of one man, Richard Wagner. Romantic opera culminated in his *Lohengrin,* but with this same opera began a new era; therefore we shall first explore the cultural trends that brought forth Wagner and the period which nurtured his art.

Chapter 17

FROM ROMANTICISM TO REALISM

—»» ««—

Realism as a Philosophy of Life

EVERY transition period produces talents whose predestined role is the demolition of the old and the formulation of the new. These are sometimes literary critics and essayists, sometimes poets and novelists, and occasionally all are engaged in the same task. Of the former was Ludwig Börne (Löb Baruch, 1786–1837), who demanded the timely and beatified the experience of the present moment. He preached hatred of Goethe, the poet of timelessness, and turned his irony against romanticism. His aesthetic beliefs required the artist to avoid solitude, for the artist must be alert to be able at every moment to pour into a mold the fever and disquietude of social movements. The opaque, romanticized reality was de-romanticized by the great lyricist of the transition era, Heinrich Heine (1797–1856). In his first period he was entirely romantic, but after moving to Paris (where Börne himself transferred his activity), the moral-social program of Saint-Simonism changed his whole philosophy of life and art, and his poems exude the irritability of a Europe panting between two revolutions. His love lyrics are set against a new background of intellectualized romanticism, Saint-Simonism, the salons, streets, and environs of the city. In his most beautiful verses there is, however, a retrospective glance, an idyllic calm after the struggles preceding others to come; a cultural lyricism. Real romanticism is always optimistic, it believes in its visions and hallucinations, in the omnipotence of its desires; therefore no disaster can disillusion it. Heine's romanticism in his last literary period is not this; here a deep and dark hopelessness glows in the tragic light of futility. The dissolution of an infinitely sensitive, feminine era speaks in the soul of a fine lyricist whose heart was bleeding although he wore the cap and bells of the satiric jester.

The romantic urge for expansion drove everything out from the interior, from the narrow studio into the open air, the élan carrying with it the closeted middle-class spirit into the streets and fields, and it seemed as if in the late eighteen forties romanticism as a spiritual force was about to

843

come to an end. The problem of the times was the problem of the masses, of society, and the spirit that animated life was a social spirit. The social implications already manifest at the beginning of rationalism became more accentuated when the romantic movement entered into the phase that came to be called realism. Toward the middle of the century socialism developed into *Weltanschauung,* into a socio-cultural ideal, and was beginning to be regarded as the Kingdom of God on earth. A congress of communists in London asked Karl Marx (1818–1883) and Friedrich Engels (1820–1895) to prepare the *Communist Manifesto* (1848), a document which became basic in the doctrine of communism. In the same year Karl Johann Rodbertus (1805–1875), German economist, author of *Overproduction and Crises,* took office in the Prussian National Assembly solely because as a conservative socialist he wanted to help in the preparation of the transition from capitalism to government-owned property, a transition which he believed to be imminent. The clash between Christian ideals and those of capitalism called forth another variety of socialism, Christian socialism, whose leaders pleaded for the laboring classes in journals, pamphlets, and novels, and, themselves clergymen, sought to enlist the Church in their struggle for social reforms. And it was in these days that Auguste Comte (1798–1857), the founder of the positivistic school of philosophy, placed sociology, to which he himself gave this name, at the highest point in his classification of the sciences.

Gustave Courbet (1819–1877), the great French painter who became director of fine arts during the Commune, declared that "realism is an essentially democratic art." And the subjects of his pictures exhibited in 1855 were factories, railroad stations, and mines. Daumier's caricatures of the bourgeois, Millet's eulogy of the toiler, showed the same powerful urge toward the proletarian, and thus realism dragged the third estate down into the fourth. But all this does not mean that the romantic root died, it merely stopped growing upward and continued to spread on the flat ground, for romanticism is not altogether opposed to realism; the social orientation had its beginnings in the romantic movement, and subjective moments cannot be denied in nascent realism. "Art is a bit of nature seen through a temperament," said Zola himself.

Realism came as a changed philosophy of life, therefore it affected all fields of human activity. Realism can be natural and obvious, as in Homeric poetry or in folk tales, for there neither the narrator nor his public sees a fundamental difference between functions of a higher and of a lower order, between details that should be emphasized and those better omitted. They find equal pleasure in the representation of all phenomena of life. Similarly natural and self-evident is the drastic realism of Rabelais. At a later period realism became, however, a conscious endeavor, developing into a slogan aimed at idealistic, or rather pseudo-idealistic, characterization, which it opposed.

in the name of truth. Thus modern realism started out with the philosophically debatable conviction that life can be depicted "as it is." Still, realism does not always stand for objectivity. While it selects certain details to be viewed from the greatest proximity, this act leaves the widest field for subjectivity. The inevitable consequence of viewing things from proximity deflects, however, the artist's or writer's interest from the whole, from form, and will drive him toward the types of art which have the freest, the least integrated form: the novel and program music. The romantic genre par excellence was lyricism, whether in lyric poetry proper, in epic poetry, drama, or symphony. Drama, which in the hands of Hugo and his satellites flirted with realism, made great strides toward a more consistent application of the principle; similarly the "atmospheric" overtures of Mendelssohn (*Hebrides, Meeresstille*) prompted musicians to seek a more realistic rendition of nature in music. But just as the really artistic dramas continued to be ground between the millstones of romantic subjectivity and a certain objectivity indispensable in the drama, so the composers ran afoul of the great problem of the inherent forms of music.

Politics and social philosophy were forced upon art by the rush of events and also by a natural reaction to the secretive idealism of romanticism. Political intent overshadowed poetic will, but it did succeed in tearing the veil spun of pathos and fantasy hung between the heroes of the historic drama and the public. Stendhal (Henri Beyle, 1783–1842) was among the first to leave the warm and colorful landscape of pure romanticism, but he was not yet a true realist; the subjectivity of the romanticist breaks through his theatrical nature. And the most objective, the most realistic painter of humans, Honoré de Balzac (1799–1850), the novelist who dethroned love to give in unending analyses life "as it is," still has a romantic undercurrent in his hostile attitude toward society; romantic pathos often shimmers through his bitterness and sardonic praise. And with all his realism Flaubert retained a great deal of the romantic spirit in the Oriental splendor of his *Salammbô,* only he watched with keener eyes, observed and analyzed in a manner no romanticist could.

Realism is, then, not the antipode of romanticism but rather its continuation, its further expansion, as romanticism had been the continuation of classicism. Realism is the realization of romanticism; it arose from broken idealism, from a sobered romanticism, from a mental descent which corresponded with a sociological descent. As a reaction against pseudo-idealism realism played a health-giving role, for it brought art closer to life. It also enriched the scope and means of expression of arts and letters enormously, and much of this wealth was retained even after the arts and the public turned against it.

The Search for the All-Embracing Universal Art

AT the present time there are only three of us who belong together because we are alike." [1] The three fellow artists alluded to in Wagner's letter were Richard Wagner (1813–1883), Franz Liszt (1811–1886), and Hector Berlioz (1803–1869), the three dominating musical figures of the fiery new romantic-realist school. What moved Wagner to consider three totally different human and musical individualities as kindred spirits? The only answer is that they were bound together by the common origins of their art, by the survival of romanticism in realism, and by the essential failure of their respective missions. All three wished to avoid the pseudo-classic idiom in order to escape artistic servility, and all three were in quest of the unattainable romantic ideal, the universal, all-embracing art work. In every other respect their arts were substantially different and their approaches diametrically opposed. Wagner sought to unite everything in opera, Berlioz endeavored to bring everything including opera into the symphony, and Liszt dreamed of a new type of music, "humanistic music," which would unite the dramatic element of the theater with the devotional element of the church. These are eminently romantic ideas, but their pursuit and realization led far from the original aims. The life and activity of these three musicians passed in the sign of the crisis of romanticism, proceeding in an overwhelming crescendo until the final achievement and collapse in Wagner's *Tristan*.

The romanticists were idealists, insatiable idealists, who could not suffer any definite ideal because that would have limited their idealism; they loved all ideals. Berlioz, Liszt, and Wagner were equally absorbed in the romantic ideal, but they approached it consciously, with well-planned systems, philosophic or musical. The romanticists were unsystematic, they were aphorists who thought in short lyric forms. The realists knew only large structures governed by some sort of system: *idée fixe,* or leitmotif. None of them was given to writing intimate pieces, not even chamber music, and only some of Liszt's piano pieces and perhaps a song or two approach pure lyricism. Romantic lyricism was fragmentary, but the fragments were not a symbol of forlornness, they were not spiritual atoms but monads; every idea, no matter how small, was an individuality, and thus it could and did reflect the whole in miniature. Wagner started out with *Siegfried's Death*, but finding that he could not condense his plans and ideas in one large music drama he enlarged it into a colossal tetralogy in which systematic guidance is needed for the uninitiated, crushed and awe-inspired by its vastness. But romanticism must by nature be fragmentary because it is that longing for the infinite, and the infinite cannot be expressed, only indicated. Berlioz attempted to prescribe exactly the route to be followed by the listener's soul, and Wagner erected a temple in which the ultimate aim of romanticism, the Gesamt kunstwerk, could be presented to the nation in whose honor and for whose everlasting glory it now stood achieved.

The romanticists also knew Dionysus, Nietzsche's and Wagner's god, but they sought the bacchanalian in the spirit only, to obtain freedom for their fantasy. They merely called for wine: they did not actually drink it. They sought the feminine to the extent of sentimentalism; Wagner sought the masculine to the extent of brutality; what he chose as his lifework was to masculinize culture and art. The romanticists sought not so much woman as, through her, love, and the essence of romanticism was love. All three great musicians of the following generation inherited a great deal of this zest for love, but love in their life and art became a wild, burning passion for possession, that is, an antiromantic love. To the romanticist love was virtue. "Every unworthy feeling is faithlessness toward the beloved," said Novalis, and Schlegel believed that "true love should be like a secret, a miracle." Wagner sees, feels, and thinks erotically, his love knows no obstacles, it is consummation and annihilation. The mythical "blue flower" was the romanticists' symbol of love in the color of longing; Wagner courts with sword and love potion, he tramples over the flower, forcing and subduing.

Romanticism searched for a world outlook upon which it could build its new art. It hoped to find this in mythology, and one can safely assign to mythology a central position in romantic thought. In this connection one can say that Wagner and Berlioz continued the romantic trend, standing at its end. There is, however, a fundamental difference between the romantic and the realistic conception. Goethe, Schiller, and the first generation of romanticists, Hegel and Hölderlin and the others, recognized in Greek mythology the symbolism of pure humanity, the representation of the universal in the particular. They saw in its individual figures the representatives of ideal humanity. They did not want a return of Greek mythology; they wanted a religion which would breathe the same spirit of love and beauty, a new religion of nature elevated to the religion of the ideal. "Young Germany," as the movement of which Wagner was one of the leaders was called, was also searching for a new world outlook, but its aesthetic Weltanschauung was to be free from all mythological form and—true to the spirit of realism —was to express itself in the forms of living life. An artistic tendency which breaks with the old forms and which wants to establish immediate connections between art and life has no room for mythology. A modern, realistic artist can use mythology only as aesthetic fiction. Taking his ideas from the works of a modern historian, Göttling,[2] Wagner attempted to endow the myth with its primeval mystic atmosphere, at the same time making it the vehicle for his philosophic beliefs. Such a retrogressive-progressive transliteration from history to myth and from myth to philosophy was, however, impossible to achieve even for a man of his exceptional mental powers—a fact that did not escape the sharp eyes of Hegel's greatest disciple and successor in aesthetics, Friedrich Theodor Vischer (1807–1887), one of the most individual and gifted thinkers of his century, the first and still the only independent critic of the Wagnerian mythology.

At first Wagner was undecided on the subject matter of his dramas. The historic atmosphere of the romantic drama attracted him, as did the big tableaux of the empire opera of Spontini and the grand opera. He even consulted Scribe. After he turned his back on the Parisian scene and produced his German romantic operas he was still undecided whether to turn to history or to mythology. Among his planned works were *Frederick I, Siegfried, Jesus of Nazareth*. Finally he decided on the legend, "after coming to the full realization of the fact that pure history is insufficient for the purpose of art." This was, indeed, a remarkably clear realization of the essential shortcoming of romantic historism, but what could be offered in exchange? Like Carlyle, Renan, and Taine, Wagner felt that modern life is opposed to the creative mission of man; that it is passive, lacking in will, and therefore inhuman. He felt that man was gradually becoming a servant of life, whereas his destiny was to be life's master. He felt that the divergence between action and thought was swinging man to his doom, and he resolved to lead mankind back to the unity of action and thought, of body and soul, to creative action which does not know problems separate from life. Like Nietzsche, he felt that mankind was in need of a new mythology, a new, and at the same time old, mythology, therefore, he reached back to the primeval creative force of the ancient Germanic myth, repopulated Valhalla, the dwelling place of the German gods and heroes. With the magic of his music he wanted to resuscitate the world of pure will and pure passion, a world in which the problems of modern life would not become arrested in the prison of thought but might find complete expression in deeds and acts. Art must be placed again in the center of religious cult as the mouthpiece of a pure, heroic, divine action. Music, poetry, mimicry, and the plastic arts must all unite to create this neo-ancient faith. It was this new, universal, and heroic art, the worshipful wish, the supreme hope of romanticism, that he wanted to offer in his music drama.

The creator of the new music drama and mythology learned from his historical studies that a myth arises from the collective religious imagination of the multitude to furnish material for the aesthetic imagination of the gifted individual. He accepted this and appropriated the material as the rightful subject of the creative artist. But in modern times collective imagination no longer creates materials; the modern genius therefore turns to nature and to history. In the original myth the gods were actual creatures, feared and revered; to us they are aesthetic fiction. Wagner's history-born mythology purported to bring forth the new world of creative passion, but what it really brought was the passion of the stage. The gigantic poetic and musical voices of this heroism often covered deep-seated lies with their wonderful resonance. This new mythology's appearance on the stage could have been natural, but its weakness was that it appeared staged, that it wanted to impress rather than to create. In the final analysis the Wagnerian world is mere stage mythology which with an arsenal of effective means, chief of which is music, conjures up the false splendor of a fictitious world. When we examine Wagner's works following *Lohengrin* we shall discover that in his moments of exaltation he not only relaxes his adherence to his subjects but virtually abandons them. From the concrete dramatic he turns to the abstract musical. He wanted to bring life and art closer, but the real world is left behind in his music dramas and the listener loses all connection with the world, and even his bearings as to the action unfolding before him. This is, then, nothing other than the last and final sphere of romanticism, the world of dream, and perhaps the embodiment of Hölderlin's motto of romanticism: "Man is a god when he dreams, a beggar when he thinks."

If all this is true we are still dealing with a romantic opera and not with the "art work of the future," and the application of the name "opera" to these music dramas—perhaps the greatest sacrilege in the eyes of the perfect Wagnerites—is entirely justified. It remains to be seen, however, whether the musical setting of these romantic opera libretti bears out the contention. But the disciple of Schopenhauer was fundamentally a musician, and even the formidable dialectic and enthusiastic zeal of the philosopher who wanted to raise a monument to the genius of his people could not suppress the romantic musician in him. "I can no longer look at the poem without the music," he wrote to his friend Röckel, and while he believed that this was merely because his "poetic intent becomes clear only through the music," the tonal stream flowing from the deep E flat that opens the *Rhinegold,* that is, from the very beginning of the tetralogy, belies this argument; this music surges with the irresistible power of the tide, until his intellect interrupts it. It is unbelievable that the maxim of Wagner's musical dramaturgy, that music is merely the means of expression in the service of the true aim, the drama, and as such must be satisfied with a secondary place, has been, and still is, taken seriously. That would mean that the dramas alone are self-sufficient works of literature. All of the mature Wagnerian dramas (with the exception of the *Meistersinger,* an almost "old-fashioned" opera) are altogether preposterous, totally unsuited for a theatrical performance without music, whereas his music, unlike any other operatic music, is the favorite and most reliable stand-by of the symphonic repertory. Thus the alleged operatic reform raised music to a position in the lyric drama where its supremacy became so omnipotent that it could be detached from the drama proper to live its own life. Even the most undramatic seventeenth- or eighteenth-century "concert opera" could not afford this, for the disjointed and illogical da capo arias were still lyric pieces for voices; they could not live without the human voice and without the text.

What Wagner the realist, the philosopher, the dramatist, and the symphonist did was to utilize everything romanticism had produced and cherished and then in a most unromantic fashion unite all in works of gigantic proportion. Musical romanticism reached its peak and its ruin in him. He achieved the final aim of romanticism, the Gesamtkunstwerk, but what he and his apologists proclaimed—that the Gesamtkunstwerk means the end of the individual arts, that both absolute drama and absolute music have lost their raison d'être—was made invalid by the uncompromising reign of music in his dramas. Pure drama and pure music stand unimpaired; Ibsen and Brahms could rise in the very hour of Wagner's triumph.

Of infinitely smaller stature as man of letters and as musician, yet endowed with undeniable gifts in both directions, Berlioz was likewise a firm believer in the Gesamtkunstwerk and wrote his own dramas. "My score was dictated by Virgil and by Shakespeare," says Berlioz in his *Mémoires* when discussing his opera *Les Troyens*. The work is, however, merely a series of episodes taken from Virgil and arranged in "tableaux." It lacks continuity and a guiding idea, and only to a limited extent fulfills the requirements of the drama, even if one takes the term in its most liberal interpretation. Having cut up the *Aeneid* into small particles, Berlioz was much more preoccupied with the problem of providing picturesque scenes, large choral frescoes, and poetical tableaux for his music than with expressing his passionate conflicts in dramatic actions. This attitude explains the interminable scenes of clair de lune, and other exquisite but meaningless scenes, which were obviously inserted in the text in the best grand opera traditions, and during which the drama—if there was one—remains in the background. The musical numbers —for that they are, *horribile dictu!*—are very lyrical in character, but they are never dramatic and one should not hesitate, even on the merits of his *Troyens,* to declare that Berlioz has a less than minor place in the history of the lyric drama. Even his most conscientious panegyrist, Hippeau, admitted this otherwise hotly debated fact. "It is enough if we say that Berlioz's dramatic art has nothing in common with Wagner's formidable creations; his sole object was the traditional form of the opera—a sort of romantic opera which the master hoped to oppose to Italian opera." [3] *Les Troyens* consists of a series of pieces, or rather numbers, among which there are admirable ones. but they are incongruous, lacking in continuity and in dramatic action. Serious objections must also be raised to his proud statement concerning the united inspiration which emanated from Virgil and Shakespeare. The duet sung between Dido and Aeneas follows closely the celebrated lines of

Lorenzo and Jessica in the last act of *The Merchant of Venice* ("In such a night . . ."). Such aberrations destroy even the good moments that can be found here and there in the opera. It is hard to understand how a confessed admirer of Shakespeare could have transformed the admirable comedy, *Much Ado About Nothing,* into the incarnation of platitude which was called *Béatrix et Bénédict.* It proves only that he did not understand Shakespeare, whom he took for a fellow romanticist, for a Byronian. French dramatic criticism assigned Berlioz an important place in the history of the romantic stage; [4] he is also often considered a forerunner of Wagner. It appears, however, that the first contention cannot be substantiated, and the second is entirely unfounded as far as the lyric drama is concerned—on the contrary, the claims should be reversed. When Berlioz began his sketches for his *Troyens,* the scores of the *Rhinegold* and the *Valkyrie* were finished. Liszt and the Princess Wittgenstein, who belonged to Wagner's intimate circle, knew every page of these scores, and they mentioned them frequently in their correspondence with Berlioz. It seems more than plausible that Berlioz attempted to create a trilogy of his own following Wagner's example. This is borne out by the fact that the original version of the work called for three complete operas, of which two were roughly sketched, *La Prise de Troie* and *Les Troyens à Carthage.* Berlioz later reduced the work to one *bona fide* grand opera.

As we continue our investigation of the remarkable *coincidentia oppositorum* manifested in the romantic-realists we arrive at the last fundamental issue: religion. "Our whole life is a divine service," said Novalis, and, truly, romanticism saw its final destiny in abandonment to the divine. It could not be otherwise; it had to pray and worship, for religion was to it the highest sanction of society, the strongest agent between the individual and the universal. This belief was what drove the romanticists to Catholicism, what sent the Protestant pilgrims to Rome, for having rediscovered the Middle Ages they realized the regenerating power of the Mother Church. Thus the romanticists were responsible for the renewed Catholic movement in the nineteenth century, for Catholicism seemed to them the fulfillment of their longing, and the embodiment of *quod semper ubique et ab omnibus creditum est.* Their Catholicism may have been only a step toward the achievement of the omnipresent romantic desire for union—in this case for the union of all denominations—but Christianity itself was the foundation of their religious thought.

As a poet Wagner was Christian neither in thought nor in intent; he was a pantheist, for his god was inaccessible, divided among a number of creatures, in demiurges, mortal and immortal, who were in charge of the world's destiny. His figures act against the tenets of Christian morals and are fundamentally hostile toward the gods. He imputed sexual life to these

divine creatures—in itself one of the oldest pre-Christian elements of mythology—and the very subject of the *Valkyrie* is incest, sacred incest between
two semidivine personalities, and the offspring of this union is Siegfried,
who was to regenerate the world. Another of the age-old primitive and innate feelings, the kinship of man with animals, is embodied in the basic
idea of the Wagnerian religious philosophy. "Wagner is certainly the poet
who has most accurately expressed this primitive feeling of mankind, which
is, indisputably, one of the most solid bases of the different forms of totem-
ism. To his descendants and to his enemies the god Wotan identified himself with the wolf; living like a grim recluse and pursued by all in the
woods, he took the name of the wolf." [5] Wotan's descendants retain the
characteristics of the clan, incest between the two children of the wolf making its appearance as the inevitable consequence of primitive and utterly
un-Christian feelings.

All these ideas have an honorable ancestry and were part and parcel of
some of the greatest poets, but they are definitely outside the pale of Christianity. Then came a sudden change, a typically romantic turning toward
the Christian religious ideal. What had appeared earlier rather decoratively
in the garb of romantic opera, and had been given up after *Lohengrin,* now
became the desire for self-effacement, for renunciation, for purification and
dissolution in the eternal, in *Parsifal.* The influence of Liszt and his family,
their warm and mystic Catholicism, played an important part in this conversion. But was it a real conversion?

Parsifal incarnates the hero who resigns earthly life under the profound
force of pity, and who by this resignation cleanses life of sin. The dynamic
Wagner, the Dionysiac Wagner, the Orphic Wagner, the musical interpreter
of pure creative will, suddenly speaks the language of Christian piety, and
speaks in false tones. The materialist such as he, the realist who hears the
tones of eternal poetry from the battling swirl of life, cannot find redemption in religion. The man who arrived at the idea of redemption through
the naturalistic materialism of Feuerbach, who believed with Schopenhauer
that life is made up of willing and attaining, and that satisfaction, even of
the intense want, would result in emptiness, whose heroes therefore die in
the paroxysm of satisfaction—for this same man only art, not religion, could
be the most profound revelation. Thus *Parsifal* could become not the drama
of Christian redemption, but only the artistic substitute for religion which
Wagner believed he could represent by pure ethics surrounded by a
nebulous religious aura. But even this he could not attain despite the many
magnificent musical passages in the opera, the uncertainty leading to a
work of monstrous proportions not at all justified by the content.

While the religious atmosphere of *Parsifal* made it a sacrosanct and un-
assailable work of liturgic strength and dignity, this conception is shared

only by the Germanic and Anglo-Saxon musicians and operagoers; by the former because of their readiness to attribute metaphysical meaning to everything that lends itself remotely to *Vergeistigung,* "spiritualization," and *Parsifal* admittedly does so to a high degree, by the latter because their innate and inconquerable suspicion of opera is allayed by the religious subject. (We have seen how long it took Handel to discover in what form Britons are willing to accept opera.) Not so the musicians and music lovers of other cultural traditions, who are free from metaphysical leanings and who approach music leaving the imponderables unpondered. They all admitted the great beauty of much of this music, but most of them were repelled by the turgid and artificial symbolism of the drama itself.

Nowhere in Wagner's music is a more serene beauty attained than in the prelude to the third act of Parsifal [writes Debussy] and in the entire Good Friday episode; although it must be admitted that Wagner's peculiar conception of human nature is also shown in the attitude of certain characters in this drama . . . Klingsor is the finest character in *Parsifal* . . . this crafty magician, this old gaol-bird, is not merely the only human character but the only moral character in this drama, in which the falsest moral and religious ideas are set forth, ideas of which the youthful Parsifal is the heroic and insipid champion. Here in short is a Christian drama in which nobody is willing to sacrifice himself, though sacrifice is one of the highest Christian virtues! [6]

What the brilliant Frenchman who passed through a Wagnerian period found merely ridiculous and insincere the more naïve and inexperienced young Stravinsky, not yet acclimatized to this world, thought unendurable. "Is not all this comedy of Bayreuth, with its ridiculous formalities, simply an unconscious aping of a religious rite? . . . It is high time to put an end, once for all, to this unseemly and sacrilegious conception of art as religion and the theater as temple." [7]

Church Music and the New Symphonic-Dramatic Tendencies

ROMANTICISM having been an insurrection against the Enlightenment, it had to oppose the essentially sober religious tenets of the latter with a renewed mysticism and with a militant Church. We have noticed the religious tendency in romanticism from its inception, and we have seen that this had to take the form of a regenerated and intensified Catholicism. The re-establishment of the Jesuits as a world order by Pius VII in 1814 led to a quickening process of Catholic rehabilitation. The alliance of renewed Catholicism with the forces of romanticism supported both the romantic desire for the reawakening of the past and the creation of a new art in conformity with the Zeitgeist. But the peculiar nature of Catholicism, its veneration of tradition, resulted in a latent struggle between tradition and progress, forcing many compromises. Under Wackenroder's influence and inspired by the cultural Catholicism of the leading romanticists, a group of German painters, imbued with the revived idealism of the Middle Ages, attempted to recapture the medieval attitude and feeling. In the early years of the century they journeyed to Rome, where they formed a society calling itself the Brotherhood of San Isidoro, after the abandoned Franciscan monastery where they established themselves. Later they came to be called the German Lay Brothers, or Nazarenes. Some of the most eminent painters of Germany—Overbeck, Veit, Cornelius, Schnorr von Carolsfeld—were members of the Brotherhood and their influence was felt all over Germany, to which some of them ultimately returned. At this time interest in old choral music —a corollary of the Nazarene movement—was renewed, and with the activity of Thibaut and Baini a veritable Palestrina renaissance began in the second quarter of the century.[8] The movement spread and gradually assumed the aspect of historism. It was especially in Germany that this reconstructed, timeless, a cappella art flourished. Composers like Eduard Grell (1800–1886) and Heinrich Bellermann (1852–1903) were able to recapture the technique of the great choral composers of the past; Grell's sixteen-part a cappella Mass is a work of remarkable purity. But all this was little more than pious antiquarianism and a hothouse art which could not leave the protecting glass roof to be transplanted in the open garden. The restoration of the past was greatly aided by the growing science of musicology and by the beginning of such great publications of early ecclesiastic music as Commer's *Musica Sacra* (begun in 1839) and his *Collectio Operum Musicorum Batavorum* (1840), the vanguard of many vast collections of music that saw the light during the next half century. Libraries and cathedral chapters set about purchasing manuscripts and early printed music books dispersed or even discarded during the secularization of the era of the Enlightenment, institutes for church music were founded, and cathedral and church choirs were enlarged and trained with care and discipline. The most important repercussion in Catholic church music was the revival of interest in the Gregorian chorale and the recognition of its supreme position in church music. While modern historic-scientific knowledge of Gregorian music was still in its infancy, and organ accompaniments of the most heterogeneous sort made their appearance in large numbers, the Benedictine Congregation of Solesmes, under Abbot Guéranger, had already begun its epoch-making collection and restoration of plain chant.

The restoration movement and the Palestrina renaissance, consolidated and organized by the Cecilian Societies, created a church style that excluded more recent music not only in form and spirit, but even in its musical idiom and technique, universally acknowledged in all other fields of music. An international style arose which, being rather characterless, could hope for general acceptance all over the world. The archaic and fundamentally lifeless nature of this music and its remoteness from the true sources of a living religious art are best seen in the fact that its devotees failed to realize that all church music of the past great periods was in the forefront of contemporary art, and that aside from certain necessary stylistic and liturgic considerations, national characteristics could no more be excluded from church music than from any other kind of music.

The two Catholic composers of the great triumvirate, Berlioz and Liszt, were both affected by the religious aspects of the romantic movement, but their reactions were as different as their music and their personalities. Both started out from the revolutionary church music of Le Sueur, but while Berlioz retained throughout his life the basic traits of this music Liszt overcame its bad aspects by merging his essentially modern music with the revived Gregorian spirit and with the Cecilian movement, thereby creating an *ars sacra* of entirely modern and individual stamp, which, nevertheless, was within the requirements of the liturgy. Ursprung, speaking both as a priest and as the leading historian of Catholic church music, found an admirable comparison when he likened Liszt—*mutatis mutandis*—to Obrecht.[9] Like the great Netherlander, Liszt used Gregorian themes which under the powerful emotional pressure of his temperament occasionally went beyond the sphere of liturgic expression, but always found a way back to fervent submission.

The generation of young poets rallying in the eighteen twenties around the throne and the Church in France learned from Chateaubriand's *Génie du Christianisme* to love religion. This new religious ideal soon allied itself with political ideas when rising romanticism decided that classicism, which it opposed, was wanting in religious feeling, concealing behind its mythology and antiquarianism a "heathen spirit." It was not long, however, before the Catholic royalists succumbed to the attraction of the political thought of liberalism, and under the powerful guidance of Felicité Robert de Lamennais (1782–1854), who preached that the Church could have no liberty under a royal government, swerved to an exaltation of the *concensus gentium,* a democracy supported by free speech and free press, as opposed to royal-Gallican absolutism. They came to the conclusion that a true religion must support the requisites of freedom. Saint-Simonism, although by this time discredited as a movement, contributed to the development of the new church thought, whose repercussions were soon felt in arts and letters and led to Hugo's definition of romanticism as liberalism in art.

The country which gave the greatest impetus to the movement of the Enlightenment naturally registered the most marked decline in church music. Cherubini was still there, but his magnificent church music does not belong to this era; its noble classic lines belie the calendar. The movement inaugurated by Lamennais exerted its strongest influence on Liszt and other foreigners residing in Paris, and we shall presently see how profoundly the new Catholic thought affected their music. The representative French composer of the romantic era, Berlioz, was not drawn into this circle; he was devoted to the "grand goût de l'antiquité," which was in reality the revolutionary-Napoleonic grandiloquence, the "grandiose-antique," of Le Sueur and Spontini, the very "heathenism" the romanticists deplored, and not the classic ideal of Hellenism. Indeed, the inclination toward the immense evident in Berlioz goes back to the composers of the Revolution and of the Napoleonic times, who participated in the great outdoor celebrations employing battalions of singers and players. The germs inherited from Le Sueur developed in Berlioz's virile imagination, and he was ready to match and surpass anything his elders did on the Champs de Mars. When first beholding St. Peter's in Rome he decided instantly to match its gigantic architecture with a church music of similar proportions, a "colossal oratorio entitled the *Last Day of the World.*" The plan ultimately materialized in the Requiem Mass and in his Te Deum, two works purely dramatic and entirely removed from the liturgic—as truly veiled Napoleonic homages as Hugo's *Burgraves*. Although in other instances the homage was not evident or not even intended, a certain military tone is always present in these choral works as if they were still glorifying the Emperor.

Berlioz had neither feeling nor respect for the liturgy and did not hesitate to revise the liturgical phrasing where it did not agree with his purposes. The Requiem Mass will remain a work of genius, if of a somewhat morbid genius, but is altogether outside the pale of church music. It requires an enormous body of players and singers, with special batteries of brasses and drums. All that Berlioz saw in the *Missa Pro Defunctis* was the sinister implication of death, the melancholy of passing; he saw the bodies of the dead in hecatombs but did not care whether they had ever had souls; the resurrection merely gave him an opportunity for dramatic pictures. Few great composers ever uttered *dona eis pacem* in such perfunctory tones. Yet the work often rises to great heights, and the terror of vast catastrophe is effectively conveyed, at times with truly gripping intensity. The effect is often obtained, however, by sheer material weight, and if stripped to its essentials the music not infrequently reveals meaningless fanfares. One might say briefly that Berlioz's Requiem Mass is a magnificent experiment in sepulchral sonority. His Te Deum is equally powerful, equally uneven, and equally lacking in liturgic-religious spirit and inspiration. Strangely enough, the only music of Berlioz that impresses one as religious in spirit and tone is his nonliturgic oratorio *L'Enfance du Christ*. The monstrous orchestra of the Mass and the Te Deum is replaced here by a delicate and chaste ensemble, handled with understanding and finesse. There are again admirable pages—the second part, the Flight from Egypt, is enchanting almost throughout—but many also are grotesque and devoid of musical substance.

Berlioz's lack of understanding of matters spiritual, his incapacity for meditation, made this fiery musician the antithesis of a church composer. His unruly acoustic imagination permitted him no peace, his orchestra knows no respite, it is constantly on the move, from color patch to color patch, here ethereal, there coarse and vulgar like the worst Rossinian imitator's noisy opera orchestra. In his Memoirs Berlioz said of the *Tuba Mirum* of his Requiem (which has five orchestras) that its "grandeur was so terrible" that one of the choristers had a nervous collapse during the performance of this movement. The critics also spoke of a "triumphant success," and the modern eulogists marvel at the virtuoso orchestral technique displayed in this score; no one ever seems to associate this gigantic work with prayer for the departed souls. "He who offers God a second place offers him no place." Indeed, "grandeur and success" are the rightful text of his introit and not *ad te levavi animam meam*.

In his essay "On the Church Music of the Future" (1834), Liszt pleaded for a renewed church music that should lead men back to an appropriate observance of the divine service. Music he held to be predestined to fulfill this task, because of its historic place in Christian worship, and because of its power to move and inspire. This new music, recognizing as its sources of inspiration God and the people (an idea obviously originating from Lamennais), can exert its beneficial influence everywhere, within and without the church. Indeed, this will be its new significance and aim, its content and substance, to lead mankind to the true worship of God. This new art he called "humanistic music," a kind of music which unites the means of the theater and of the church, which is at the same time dramatic and holy, majestic and simple, strong and calm; it will be the *fiat lux* of the art. "Come, hour of deliverance, when poets and artists will forget the public and will know one slogan only: man and God." That these notions of the youthful musician reflect the romantic conception of the universal art is obvious. Liszt never abandoned the idea of "humanistic music" and we shall see how it is reflected in other types of his compositions, culminating in his oratorio *Christus*. Patently, both our modern instrumental church music and the *Parsifal* idea owe their inception to this first essay. Liszt's taking the cloth surprised the world in his lifetime and still mystifies those who see his lifework and personality through the *Second Hungarian Rhapsody*. In reality his religious preoccupations began with his essay on church music, and his intentions to enter the priesthood were marked at the beginning of his career; thereafter, every time the enforced life of the virtuoso became unbearable he was on the verge of abandoning everything for the peace of an ecclesiastic life. Throughout his life he was an ardent and active Catholic and strongly given to mysticism. The religious sentiment slowly gained the dominating position in his mind, until he entered the service of the Church, devoting his newly won ecclesiastic status to the furthering of church music.

The following years saw him composing much church music, Masses, litanies, as well as many Psalms and other greater and smaller works. Among these the outstanding are the large orchestral Masses which with their splendor and with their sudden submissiveness recall the regal pomp of the baroque Mass, opening in the history of the symphonic Mass a new chapter. There are also the two great oratorios, *Christus* (1866–1867) and *Saint Elizabeth* (1862). The mystic-religious was not missing in Liszt's secular compositions; the very first symphonic poem, *Ce qu'on entend sur la Montagne,* and the last movement of the *Faust Symphony* are two eloquent examples, but in these works his new spiritual orientation created a new style.

Both oratorios are diametrically opposed to the Handelian oratorio, for they are entirely Catholic in spirit, the subjective confessions of a religious soul. Handel's oratorios were folk dramas, while Liszt's aristocratic-Catholic church music is a modern equivalent of the *sacra rappresentazione,* far removed from the spirit of the Protestant oratorio. The occasional performance of these two oratorios on the stage is entirely misplaced, for they retained one important element of the oratorio—the fantastic-contemplative —which suffers when translated into the concrete-real. There is a fundamental difference also between Liszt's original conception and the *Parsifal* idea which it engendered, for the "union of theater and church" advocated in Liszt's essay was not to be taken in its literal sense. By the theater he meant drama, a rightful and ancient component of church music, and not the theatrical. Medieval elements, both Gregorian and polyphonic, so external and unconvincing in Gounod's and Franck's oratorios (although the sincerity of the composers is beyond doubt), are here blended most successfully with the technique of the modern symphonist. The spirit of the medieval liturgic play is resuscitated, for over the whole there hovers a religious ecstasy that is truly Catholic and medieval without being archaic. While the lengthy orchestral interludes of these oratorios often drift into tone painting, and while there are sections that are almost operatic in their vivid dramaticism, such elements have often been present in Catholic church music and are altogether compatible with its spirit. Catholic also is the unmistakable and unconcealed joy of life, expressed especially in the instrumental parts; far from destroying the mood, they contribute to the remarkable unity that characterizes these works. The new "Metagregorian" idiom created in *Christus* had far-reaching effects on the future of church music and also constituted one of the strongest incentives to such works as *Parsifal*.

Berlioz

IN the first chapter of this book, in our discussion of the semimythical, semihistorical music of ancient Greece, we encountered among the many legendary stories a fact proved by documentary evidence: a piece of program music known as the Pythic Nome.[10] Ever since those remote days program music has appeared sporadically as a type of musical composition. Descriptive and symbolic elements were present in the music of the medieval mystery plays, in the instrumental accompaniments of the ars nova, in the great renaissance chansons of Janequin, in the Biblical sonatas of Kuhnau, in Telemann's suites and overtures, in Bach's celebrated *Capriccio,* in the symphonies of Dittersdorf and Beethoven, and in countless other compositions. In spite of this ancient and persistent current, program music as an aesthetic principle upon which a composer might base his whole art was a product of the post-Beethovenian times and appeared notably in Berlioz's symphonies as an entirely new tendency. What had been a rather unimportant and occasional indulgence in the past was raised by Berlioz to a constructive principle of composition.

While literary romanticism in France immediately recalls a cluster of names, the period produced only one musician of note, Hector Berlioz, who in his "instrumental dramas," as he called his symphonies, ranged himself alongside Hugo and the other champions of romantic drama. He shared their preference for wild, demonic, and horrifying subjects and moods, a preference which often resulted in the transference of the point of gravity from the internal, from the subjective, to the external, the fascinating object. This, in its turn, called for pictorial and decorative imagination, focused on the peculiarity of the phenomenon. The striving for literary expression and for the picturesque constitutes the most characteristic trait of French musical genius of all ages, and the possibility of a poetic interpretation remained the chief criterion by which an audience judged a musical composition, vocal or instrumental. This ancient French desire, made more acute by literary trends, drove Berlioz toward the composition of symphonic music that was imposed upon a more or less clearly defined program, while at the same time the universal romantic urge for the Gesamtkunstwerk induced him to convert the symphony into a "drama without voices" by assigning to poetry a role equal to that of the instrumental part of the work. Thus Berlioz must be considered Wagner's rival, engaged in the same task but achieving it in a manner poles apart.

Berlioz sincerely believed—as did his two great confreres—that the roots of his art lay in Beethoven's symphonies, that he was continuing the symphonic ideal, which he interpreted as the embodiment of a poetic idea in music. This he believed he could achieve through program music, not realizing that his conception was the antithesis of symphonic thought. Berlioz's whole plan was literary, whereas the symphony responds to the abstract-musical only. We must recall that the *texture* of Beethoven's music obeys purely abstract musical impulses even in his so-called programmatic works, in the Third and Sixth Symphonies, in the sonata *Les Adieux,* or the A minor quartet. It is manifestly impossible to retain a sonata construction with its formal sections and then submit it to an extramusical program which determines the course of procedure. We remind the reader that this very problem was encountered by Beethoven in the Leonore overtures and his final decision was to drop the "program." This is the reason that compelled us to say that "the program was imposed upon" Berlioz's symphonic music instead of saying simply that he wrote program symphonies; for, in spite of the lengthy story with which he might preface a work, Berlioz did not go beyond the time-honored principles of symphonic construction. The first movement of his epoch-making *Symphonie Fantastique* displays all the signs of a conventional "first movement" with its slow introduction, sonata allegro, first and second subjects, exposition, recapitulation, and so forth. The descriptive and "fantastic" elements came as additions and were stretched over the eighteenth-century symphonic frame. They did not represent anything new, for in Berlioz's early period the slogan of "musique caractéristique" was already common, and represented an acknowledged aim of French composers. Neither was the use of leitmotives new; we have seen that it was common practice in operatic music at the close of the eighteenth century. The leitmotif as a means of recalling dramatic situations had its roots in the old ritornel placed between arias or individual scenes of the oldest operas, but now it grew to be the symbol of personalities which it identified not only thematically but with certain definite instrumental colors, as in the case of the solo viola associated with Harold in Berlioz's symphony of that name. Strict adherence to this principle places the composer in a position where his natural musical instinct is often curtailed and a purely musical continuation of an idea is thwarted by a preordained process. A dramatic-psychological variation of a theme, a change dictated not by musical-formal impulses but by programmatic exigencies, must, of necessity, clash with musical logic. A man with the musical gifts of Wagner could face this dilemma and assert his will over the material-technical obstacles, but with Berlioz—and to a lesser degree with Richard Strauss— one is painfully aware of the breaking down of originally well-conceived musical ideas by forcible thematic and other changes which deflect the natural flow of music. Berlioz's thematic invention was his weakest side and very often led him to trivialities that prompted some critics to declare him fundamentally unmusical, an opinion palpably untrue, but easily understood if one considers his willingness to distort musical logic for the sake of an extramusical cause. It is noteworthy, however, that among the critics were not only Mendelssohn, Schumann, Liszt, and Wagner, but also the enthusiastic defender of French music who so proudly signed himself "musicien français," Debussy. "Musicians are alarmed at the liberties he takes with harmony—they even call them blunders—and his 'Go-to-the-devil!' style." [11]

Berlioz's symphonies present a tragic conflict of mind and instinct. His dramatic intentions are deflected by his inability to shake off inherited and outmoded formulae of composition, for as the poetic-dramatic ideas, the program, were applied to any well-articulated formal construction the result was necessarily a failure. The spirit of the "old symphony" stood in his way every time he faced a large form. Thus the chief movements in his symphonies inconvenienced him considerably, and it is astounding to see to what primitive sonata constructions he resorted. The sonata movements of these symphonies go back to the preclassic type of "concertante" symphony such as was practiced by the Mannheimers, a type which operated with ritornels instead of through-composed sections. All other movements are symphonic poems or scenes in which he was much more at ease, and here, in these movements, when his fiery imagination was given free rein, with merely a suggestive poetic or dramatic title attached to the piece, setting the mood rather than endeavoring to depict· a precise action, he composed music of the greatest originality and compelling genius. The "Witches Sabbath" and the "March to the Gallows" in the *Symphonie Fantastique,* "Queen Mab" in *Roméo et Juliette,* and most of the *Damnation of Faust* present something really new, sonority; sonority for its own sake; sonority which engenders ideas. The violence of his mental experiences was such in these compositions that he was able to invest insignificant melodic inventions with breath-taking intensity. His orchestra seizes one with a colorit that is never static but always dynamic, bent on moving the listener and carrying him away. Hence the great variety of contrasts in his orchestral writing, from brutal mass effects to the most delicate whispers. Certain clichés are, however, present in almost every one of these symphonic scenes, and in the midst of his most extravagantly romantic utterances there is a classicistic streak that never left him. It is this latent streak that defeated his principal symphonic movements, but it also helped him to his most accomplished creations, such as the fourth movement in *Roméo et Juliette,* entitled *La Reine Mab, ou la Fée des Songes.* Below the romantic title there is a simple word—"scherzo"; and indeed, the movement is a *bona fide* scherzo in which Berlioz abandons any intention of indulging in an exegesis of Shakespeare, permitting his fancy a freedom it seldom enjoyed. The result is bewitching, and one wonders what might have become of this fiery musician had he not succumbed to the violent aesthetic prejudices which he enforced with inexorable severity. This "scherzo" is incomparable and un-forgettable. It lives in the memory of every musician as bold music of eternal freshness.

By conveying to the hearer his ideas in sober and precise words and thus conditioning his receptive imagination, binding it to definite associations, Berlioz forced him to an intellectual control and articulation of the music. Instead of letting him receive the emanations of the composer's feelings directly as a subjective experience, he compelled the listener to take an ob-jective attitude which precluded spontaneous feelings. As the program tries to steer the listener's imagination in a certain direction, the composer had to resort to a more characteristic, colorful, and animated musical language, to more realistic, almost visual effects. The constant search for this ex-pressiveness of visual strength was what enticed him into musical aberra-tions that caused even Debussy to call him a "musical monster, an excep-tion, . . . the favorite musician of those who do not know much about music." Berlioz called the *Symphonie Fantastique* an "instrumental drama," and the other symphonies followed this quest for the romantic ideal, the universal art work. We have noticed that Berlioz approached the task from an entirely different angle than Wagner, for he sought to create the music drama in the symphony. The fact that in doing so he at times employed voices and choruses should not mislead us. There is a passage in the pro-gram prefacing the score of *Roméo et Juliette* which is as significant as Gluck's celebrated preface to *Alceste* or Wagner's declarations in his *Opera and Drama*. "The sublimity of this love made its description so difficult for the composer that he was compelled to give his imagination a freedom which would not allow the positive sense of the sung words. Therefore he took refuge in the language of instrumental music, a language, which with its greater richness, its greater variety, nay its limitlessness, was to lead, in this case, to incomparably more powerful effects." This is assuredly a per-plexing document: a symphonist defending his resorting to pure instru-mental music in a symphony! No wonder that Saint-Saëns called him a "living paradox." Yet the ideas expressed in this preface are neither incon-sistent nor are they typical of the mental-musical make-up of Berlioz only. A composer devoid of feeling for real lyricism and endowed with a power-ful sonorous-pictorial imagination will naturally tend to an instrumental language. We have seen to what wonderful creations the uninhibited de-ployment of such an imagination could lead in Berlioz, and we shall see how the apostle of the music drama, Wagner, virtually adopted the tenets expressed in this preface at the critical moments in his stage works.

Despite his convictions, Berlioz realized that the *drame symphonique* was not feasible, for the drama requires several individuals, who in turn would require a multitude of musical symbols—we must not forget that the *idée fixe* is not a leitmotif but a "leitmelody," symbolizing a person. His rather primitive and homophonous motivic-thematic technique could not cope even with the relatively simple thematic complexes of the sonata form, therefore the maximum he could attain in this direction was *Harold*, a solo drama, which gives us the moods of one man projected against various phenomena of the world. In the other symphonies we lose sight of the *dramatis personae*. His quest for the unattainable romantic ideal had to be continued, however, and in the *Damnation of Faust* he sought to "extract the musical essence from Goethe's *Faust*." The idea and much of the music was not new; *Eight Scenes from Faust* formed, in fact, his *Opus* 1, composed in 1828–1829, preceding the *Symphonie Fantastique*. Seventeen years later he returned to the eight pieces which he now arranged into a "dramatic legend," a type between his dramatic symphony and the music drama proper. The earlier pieces were already astoundingly original and interesting; the experienced composer made them more so in his second version, and the dramatic legend is replete with fascinating music. Significantly, the best pieces are again those which allow a freedom of fantasy and are only loosely connected with the "essence of Goethe's *Faust*." This essence is very curiously conceived by Berlioz, confessed admirer of Goethe, who treated the German poet's ideas with the same license he applied to Shakespeare and Virgil. Therefore we must not be surprised to find the German hero transferred to the plains of Hungary in order to make possible a "plausible" use of the famous old Hungarian battle song, the Rákóczy March. The adventuresome literary spirit and the old penchant for the *style énorme* (Berlioz demands two or three hundred child singers for the choir of the Seraphim) are more than compensated for by the singular and at times sulphurous eloquence of much of this music.

With the *Damnation of Faust* a decisive step was taken toward the music drama proper, and now Berlioz changed his line of attack, invading the stage proper. Unlike his first opera, *Benvenuto Cellini* (1835–1837), libretto by Wailly and Barbier, the late operas, *Les Troyens* and *Béatrice et Bénédict*, were his own literary creations. Thus the antipodic rival of Wagner entered the Wagnerian orbit as musico-dramatist in the fullest sense of the word. We have seen that this apostle of Gluck and of dramatic truth succumbed at every turn to the very abominations he exorcised so mercilessly in others. Dances, arias, ariosos, recitatives, pantomimes, pompous marches, and other stand-bys of the grand opera abound in his dramatic works, and he never hesitates to interrupt the dramatic continuity for an effective instrumental piece or long aria. The dramatic intentions and their vocal realization always proceed from the music and only to a lesser degree from the text. Thus in this department of his activity Berlioz is again beset by a conflict between old precepts, no longer valid in his time, and novel intentions. Unlike his symphonies and other instrumental music in which he rises to greatness only when he frees himself from the fetters of classic symphonic thought and form, his operas are at their best when he reverts to the dramatic accompanied recitative of his predecessors.

At the end of his artistic career this man of vulcanic personality and fierce imagination looked back with profound discontent at the sum total of his efforts, seeing everywhere unfulfilled promises and unattained goals. His glowing and untamed subjectivity prevented creative unity. The wealth of inspiration, the seriousness and strength of artistic conviction, are impressive and manifest despite the unevenness of quality and the rigidity, at times even flatness, hiding behind great gestures, but there is not one finished work in his musical legacy. "Berlioz's best is wonderful; his worst is appalling—and the twain, with the degrees between them, are inextricably confused together." [12]

Liszt

SPEAKING of Schumann's piano pieces, Liszt remarked that they raise the question of "pittoresque" music which some people think can rival the painter's brush. This seemed to him absurd. "It is obvious that things which can appear only objectively to perception can in no way furnish connecting points to music; the poorest of apprentice landscape painters could give with a few chalk strokes a much more faithful picture than a musician operating with all the resources of the best orchestra. But if these same things are subjectivated to dreaming, to contemplation, to emotional uplift, have they not a peculiar kinship with music; and should not music be able to translate them into its mysterious language?" [13] These are the words of a composer commonly closely associated and identified with the musical and artistic aims of Berlioz. They suggest that we approach the works and writings of this enigmatic artist with critical eyes and an open mind, for the contradiction between this statement and the customary evaluation of Liszt seems to be so great as to suggest deep-seated misunderstandings.

Liszt was educated in France, where he went at the age of eleven. Not only was a large part of his musical equipment acquired there, but his literary and philosophical culture was entirely conditioned by French thought, as we have seen in the pages devoted to his church music. As a young man he insisted that the intellectual culture of musicians must be improved before a truly modern art could be launched. Thus the greatest of virtuosi battled for philosophy and musical criticism at the same time that he wrote the operatic fantasies which today prevent a clear appreciation of his true role in the history of modern music. Soon after his arrival in Paris, Liszt became interested in the literary and political movement.

which impressed him deeply. This is evidenced by his frequent quoting from Hugo's *Cromwell,* the manifesto of romanticism, and by his concern with Lamennais and Saint-Simon. The immediate result of his studies was the afore-mentioned essay on church music. Despite all his theoretical and philosophical preoccupations, Liszt's compositions up to about 1840 (with the exception of a little opera, an overture, and a few sketches) consisted of piano compositions and transcriptions. At about that time his activity shifted to vocal music, and the number of piano compositions dropped abruptly. After a few more years his work centered round the orchestra; he then almost completely abandoned composing for the piano, though still retaining his liking for vocal writing. Such sharply defined periods cannot be considered merely accidental; indeed, the first period may furnish the clue to an understanding of Liszt, of a new musical idiom, loosely attached to the era even more loosely called romantic.

While the mere fact that his whole activity was confined to the piano suggests a unity of purpose, this first period of Liszt's harbors many a conflicting tendency. He was attracted by the modern piano and realized the infinite tonal possibilities of the perfected instrument; he sensed that immediateness of communication was now possible to the pianist, that the piano could compete with the orchestra, that the pianist had become a sovereign.

The promotion of sonority to an element of inspiration is perhaps the most important single factor in musical romanticism. The romantic composer could express within the seven octaves of the keyboard ideas that had called for a whole apparatus in the past. Indeed, we see that the leading romantic composers, Schumann, Chopin, and the young Liszt, preferred composing for the piano to any other medium of expression. One competent author goes so far as to question whether romantic piano music and romantic musical style are not synonymous terms.[14] There were weighty reasons for preferring the piano to the orchestra. The orchestra of the late Beethovenian period could not keep pace with the development of the technique of composition. A few composers rebelled against the burden of technical restrictions and came very close to creating a new style. Weber manipulated his strings in a truly "Wagnerian" fashion; Simon Mayr, in his Italian operas, showed a thoroughly modern treatment of the wood winds; Pacini and Meyerbeer inaugurated a veritable cult of the brass instruments. Yet most composers could not go beyond the accepted orchestral language because this idiom was synonymous with the classic musical speech; orchestral style, the symphonic style, was the classical style par excellence, as Berlioz had learned at his own expense. This explains Liszt's initial aloofness from orchestral ventures. He who was consciously striving for a new idiom recognized the oneness of classical musical language with orchestral dialectics. He saw the cause of failure in the post-Beethovenian symphonists, for he recognized the impossibility of expressing modern ideas in traditional forms and declared that form must be the result of the expression of the idea. But the road to the new idiom was not clear; the explorer had to start out on the broad highway to find his way to the forks.

Liszt began by taking orchestral compositions and translating them into the language of the "universal instrument," the piano. This activity immediately raises a weighty psychological problem which is one of the important factors in the complex question of romanticism; the desire for improvisation and virtuosity arising from the identity of composer and performer. These two elements are really indivisible, and the more so the greater the executive abilities of the composer. The romanticists believed in improvisation because it came closest to their ideal of instantaneous creation. The unbounded admiration for Paganini, shared by all and sundry, was not directed toward his music—obviously derivative and lacking in substance—but to the superhuman prowess of the virtuoso. In this connection we must bear in mind that what those who attended Paganini's recitals heard was not even remotely approximated in the printed score, for Paganini improvised freely, and this active creative process unfolding before their eyes and ears was what fascinated all romanticists. Schumann and Brahms (the latter under Schumann's influence), confined to the poetic atmosphere of German romanticism, expressed their homage to Paganini in a few transcriptions and fantasies, but on the whole their music was not unduly affected by Paganini's hypertrophy of fantastic zeal. Liszt, however, lived in Paris, where Berlioz, Meyerbeer, the grand opera, the melodrama, in a word, the *style énorme,* reigned, where a score of piano virtuosi tried to emulate the magician of the violin. If we read contemporary testimonials we must come to the conclusion that Liszt's performance of his own fantasies and rhapsodies must have been similar to Paganini's free improvisatory playing, hence their devastating effect. "Épater le bourgeois" was one of the slogans of bellicose French romanticism, and nowhere was this tendency displayed with more acumen than in Liszt's earlier piano works. The formal principle of classicism gave way to dynamic and sonorous pictures caught in the moment of their conception. The tendency toward the sonorous was manifest at the beginning of the century and was expressed by Reicha in his *Philosophisch-praktische Anmerkungen* (1803).[15] The dialectical unity of classical music was replaced by a unity of mood. The incompatibility of sonatalike constructions with such precepts of composition is obvious and explains the failure of the romanticists in the symphonic field. The same situation can be observed in romantic literature, especially in romantic drama. Like the sonata form, the three unities of the classic drama did not fit in with the new atmosphere, so Hugo threw the traditions overboard. Deprived of constructive formal elements, romantic drama bared its weaknesses. The romantic hero, once left unsupported by the intoxicating effects of the writer's rhetoric, disintegrates. Hugo brings about this state of intoxication chiefly by his phenomenal art of verbal expression. The liberation of the language, the use of the *mot propre* instead of classic paraphrase, enriched the language immensely. In fact, such language becomes almost music, by virtue of its rhythm, cadence, and color. It might be interesting at this point to quote Flaubert, who became so fond of the sonorous qualities of words that he made the following statement in a letter to George Sand: "It is hardly necessary that words express ideas. So long as one assembles them in harmonious sequence, the object of art is served." The situation was, then, remarkably similar in both camps; but it was also chaotic enough to prompt Dumas to say that "on one point everyone was agreed: if they did not know yet what they wanted, they knew at least what they did not want."

Here Liszt emerges as an independent innovator, the first musician who saw clearly that even Chopin's admirably original method of composition would not suffice for the foundation of a new style, for the new art which was lurking about the classic scene could not rise from the ruins of the old; it had to break completely with the past and to develop its own aesthetic principles. He threw himself wholeheartedly into this new world of sonority, and the individual pieces of his *Années de Pélerinage* testify to the new art at which he arrived through his transcriptions. Let us single out one piece from the many fine compositions in this collection: *Sposalizio*. The whole composition is based on one sound phenomenon: a chord. From it Liszt derives both his melody and his accompaniment. He presents this dissected chord sometimes slowly and majestically, sometimes fast and imperiously, and at the end the arabesques, formed from the same material, envelop a melody in the middle parts. The very same arabesques return in one of Debussy's early piano pieces, showing an unequivocal continuity in the development of style and Liszt's role in the formation of "modern" music.

"To me it is highly significant," said Wagner, "that the very pianoforte player who in modern days has shown us the highest summit of virtuosodom, who in every respect has been the wonder-worker of the pianoforte —Liszt—should now be turning with such momentous energy to the sonorous [tönende] orchestra." [16] Indeed, a new phase opened in Liszt's creative activity as the circle closed; the composer who disdained the orchestra by transplanting its riches to the keyboard, returned to the orchestra with new experiences and demands. Liszt's great innovation and achievement consisted in proving that it was possible to create a well-rounded and logically organized piece of music without forcing the ideas into the established frames of traditional forms. This he achieved by following a program, hence the popular term "program music"; but this misused term meant to him something entirely different from what it meant to Berlioz. He came to program music through the same notion of "humanistic music" that in his earliest youth made him think of the romantic ideal of uniting the various arts.

The musician who is inspired by nature exhales in tones nature's most tender secrets without copying it. He thinks, he feels, he speaks through nature. But since his language is more arbitrary and more uncertain than any other . . . and lends itself to the most varied interpretations, it is not without value (and most of all not ridiculous, as it is often thought) for the composer to give in a few lines the spiritual sketch of his work and, without falling into petty and detailed explanations, convey the idea which served as the basis for his composition. . . . This will prevent faulty elucidations, hazardous interpretations, idle quarrels with intentions the composer never had, and endless commentaries which rest on nothing.[17]

Had composers and critics from Berlioz to Honegger read this truly enlightening and prophetic passage and had they studied attentively Liszt's works which embody his aesthetic views, modern music might have escaped the impasse into which such works as the *Sinfonia Domestica* or *Rugby* carried it. Among all the "program musicians" of the nineteenth century Liszt was the only one to realize the meaning of the words with which Beethoven prefaced his Sixth Symphony: "More the expression of sentiment than painting." This motto, which Liszt accepted wholeheartedly, defines very clearly the difference between program music and tone poetry. There is, to be sure, a certain amount of tone painting in his works (as in Beethoven's *Pastoral* Symphony), but this never takes the upper hand. The literary or pictorial subject is completely dissolved in music. "After hearing one of Liszt's new orchestral works, I was involuntarily struck with admiration at its happy designation as a 'symphonic poem.' And indeed the invention of this term has more to say for itself than one might think, for it could only have arisen with the invention of the new art-form itself." [18] Here was an excellent judge, Wagner, who sensed the advent of a new art form. He was the more qualified because he was familiar with the work of the other noted experimentalist, Berlioz. The whole development of modern orchestral music is credited to Berlioz. In the light of more recent and dispassionate research, this is manifestly unjust to his contemporaries. While it is obvious that Berlioz contributed a great deal to modern orchestral technique, we must distinguish between this technique and the music proper. It appears that we should look for other sources than Berlioz alone, if we want to piece together the history of the modern orchestral idiom.

The symphonic poem really started with the character overtures of Beethoven. *Coriolanus, Egmont,* and the *Leonore* overtures transcended the frame and purpose of the opera overture and grew from the role of curtain raiser to self-sufficient and independent one-movement symphonic pieces. Weber's overtures to his operas cast in a symphonic form the essence of the drama, and as such were the other main source of the symphonic poem. These overtures are the finest and the most original orchestral works of the early romantic era, infinitely superior to the classicistic symphonies of most of the romantic composers. Mendelssohn added several excellent specimens to this genre, but while some of these, such as the splendid overture entitled *Hebrides,* were still within the sphere of symphonic music proper, like the earlier character overtures, only a few years later we find definite evidence of the type which was to become the symphonic poem. This was his overture to the *Beautiful Melusine* (1837), a long orchestral piece subdivided into five sections. The first section displays an entirely new idiom, both in the musical material and in the orchestration. The idiom consists of melodies which are used throughout the orchestra in their entirety with complete disregard of their adaptability to certain instruments. This is what gave the enormous "interdepartmental" mobility to the modern orchestra. Mobility does not mean speed only—every type of orchestral music of every era knew speed—it means a fluency obtained by the unrestricted participation of all members of the orchestra in the development of the material. When the clarinet starts out with its typical string arpeggio in the *Melusine* overture we are almost instantly placed in the atmosphere of the *Rhinegold;* indeed, Wagner's admiration for this overture was more than platonic. The arpeggio wanders from part to part and the wood winds and horns carry on the narrative in the same fashion that we see later in Liszt's and Wagner's scores. While programmatic, this music is not program music, and herein lies its great importance, for it succeeded in departing from the symphony without sacrificing its great cohesive force.

The two leaders of the new orchestral style went into action against the symphonic framework. That is, one of them attacked it and wrestled with it; the other accepted the ideas embodied in it and finished by creating an entirely new species. Wagner recognized that "Liszt's way of looking at a poetic subject must needs be fundamentally different from that of Berlioz." [19] The difference is evident even in the externals. Liszt seldom utilized specific orchestral effects for their own sake, while Berlioz used even the shortcomings of instruments for characteristic effects. Liszt never liked extravagant subjects, the products of an overheated romantic imagination, and his reverence and understanding of great literature recoiled from tampering with an author's ideas. While he sketched characters with consummate artistry—one need only recall the three "sketches" in the *Faust* Symphony— he never invited the listener to follow in his music an unfolding action. The metamorphosis of "leitmelodies" takes place in his works without any attempt at concrete visual-descriptive allusions. In the final analysis he was the composer of absolute music, and as such again entirely different from Berlioz, who wrote "absolute" music in moments of self-negation. Where Berlioz struggled with form, poetic program, and, most of all, musical logic and continuity of progression, Liszt built with a motivic thematic concentration only to be found in the greatest symphonists.

We have already mentioned the Beethovenian precept of program music and Liszt's agreement with it. The symphonic poems *Hungaria* and *Festklänge* have no program at all. Among the others, *Mazeppa* is the only one which presents descriptive music, but even in this score all descriptive elements are incorporated in the general musical scheme and are elaborated as *musical material*. Our observations can be corroborated by the fact that in his essays and letters Liszt does not allude to programmatic descriptions. On the contrary, we find remarks that speak eloquently for a purely poetic-musical conception. "Sheer feeling, unadulterated, lives and glows in the music, without pictorial transformation, without being linked to action or thought." [20] This attitude contrasts strangely with the efforts of Liszt's commentators, who, in their naturalistic interpretations, devised all sorts of conflicting descriptions of the meaning and content of his music. His melodies (as we can see in *Sposalizio* or in *Les Préludes*) are generally founded on a terse and seemingly simple basic figure or motif. This motif is then elaborated and even the accompanying figures develop out of it; an eminently symphonic conception. Individual melodies derived from this basic motif are handled sometimes in a similar manner, sometimes in a contrasting fashion, and sometimes all of them meet in a sort of apotheosis at the end, a procedure followed by Wagner in the *Meistersinger* overture. Liszt followed this procedure so consistently that one must see in it a new principle of form, free form.

Another indication of an autonomous principle of form and development in Liszt's works is his application of the same technique to instrumental compositions that had no title or programmatic indications whatsoever. We may look upon the B minor piano sonata as in direct line of succession to the last C minor sonata of Beethoven. Such harmonic tension and nervosity appeared here for the first time in modern instrumental music, having existed up to this sonata only in dramatic music. This fact may have led critics to hunt for a hidden program, failing to recognize this new element as a constructive principle of a new form—a form which is not determined by orderly groups of four, eight, or sixteen measures. The same is true of the E flat piano concerto, which again solved the problem of the modern concerto. Its compact theme, together with that of the B minor sonata, recaptured the pregnancy of classic symphonic thought in an entirely original and modern fashion. The freedom of his constructions is well reflected in their unconventional exterior form; they have one, two, or three movements, the number determined solely by the nature of the source of inspiration. But this freedom does not mean license, it merely breaks completely with the classic precepts of formal construction, thereby accomplishing what Berlioz had intended but failed to realize.

Among the fourteen symphonic works the *Faust* Symphony (1855), consisting of three "character pictures," is the most outstanding by virtue of the wealth of ideas and of their remarkable elaboration. The fact that Liszt called the three movements character pictures shows that his intention was not a musical setting of Goethe's *Faust,* although that dramatic poem was his source of inspiration. Again this bespeaks an attitude diametrically opposed to that displayed by Berlioz in his *Roméo et Juliette.* The first movement of the *Faust* Symphony shows Liszt in all the greatness of his imaginative power, and this movement constitutes one of the most original solutions of the problem that agitated the whole romantic era: the future of the sonata-symphony. For the movement is in sonata form, but in a sonata form that obeys the spirit rather than the letter of the law. The second movement, a wonderful idyllic sketch of Marguerite, also in a sonata-like frame, is at once astounding and convincing in its freedom and originality. Instead of a development section, the middle part returns to the thematic material associated with Faust in the first movement, as if Marguerite has been awakened from her dream seized by doubts. The third movement, Mephistopheles, is a demonic tone poem befitting its subject, ending in a mystic psalmody before which the satanic tones must retreat. When listening to this symphony one realizes the true meaning of program music, that it can become a principle of musical composition of convincing aesthetic validity. But while this music is suggested and laid out by poetic inspiration, it is governed by purely musical factors, and this is its secret, the secret of true program music. The *Dante* Symphony, steeped in passionate accents, rises, nevertheless, to ethereal and other-worldly spheres paralleled only by the best in *Parsifal,* upon which it had no small influence.

It has often been said that Liszt's manner of composition was casual, that he jotted down his ideas *ad hoc,* following the route traced by the program. A deeper study of his writings will convince us that his whole conception and philosophy of music was based on very definite and solid ideas which he expressed repeatedly, and which contradict the popular and erroneous conception of his art as mere slapstick symphonies or gypsy reveries. It is most illuminating to compare the views of the two brothers-in-arms in the fight for the "New German school." Wagner too wanted to write a *Faust* Symphony; the *Faust* overture was supposed to constitute the first part of it. His plans were not carried out. "Already I had theme and mood for it:—then—I gave the whole up, and—true to my nature—set to work on the *Flying Dutchman,* with which I escaped from all the mist of instrumental music, into the clearness of the drama." [21] Thus the dramatist took refuge in a region where, according to him, the hazy mist of instrumental music does not distort the clarity of thought. This idea was shared by Berlioz, who clarified his thoughts by precise commentaries, literary or musical. But Liszt, that often maligned composer of program music, professed great admiration for the "misty" regions of instrumental music: "The composer of instrumental music, by virtue of the nobility of sentiment and the grandeur of form, is well able to mount to greater heights than any other; yes, he may rise to such an elevation that no program can follow him." [22]

Franz Liszt occupies a unique position in the history of modern music; most of our accomplishments in the field of harmony, orchestration, and construction originated in his inquisitive and inspired mind, yet the dispute which started when Liszt turned his back on the piano to devote himself to composition is carried on with undiminished vigor by a legion of admirers and detractors. His willingness to support magnanimously every worthy undertaking even if his artistic preferences did not correspond with those of his protégés, his dazzling life as a virtuoso, his romantic love stories, his religious inclination, his brilliant literary essays, all created a compound personality which made it difficult to form a clear picture of both the man and the artist. The tragedy of his life, and the reason for his not becoming the savior of nineteenth-century music, and with it of modern music—a position to which he was entitled by virtue of his great genius and unexampled originality—was that he could never cast aside the ballast of his early manhood. There was the virtuoso, the pianist extraordinary, who had the public of the civilized world at his feet. But in reality it was he who was the slave of the public. "Were he no famous man, or rather, had not people made him famous, he could and would be a free artist, a little god, instead of being the slave of the most fatuous of publics, the public of the virtuoso. This public asks from him, at all costs, wonders and foolish tricks; he gives it what it wants." [23] The same man who played the fantasy on *Robert the Devil* played to his friends the piano sonatas of Beethoven, which, according to Wagner, "have first been made accessible to us by Liszt, and till then were scarcely understood at all." The transcriptions, fantasies, and rhapsodies of the early period are a typical sign of the romantic endeavor for the union of arts. This was display music, purporting to show that the modern piano can match both opera and orchestra. It is a tragedy that these compositions were taken by public and critics for the typical products of Liszt's creative imagination, for their very popularity contributed to the development of the innate bombastic strain in Liszt. The mysterious relationship between the virtuoso artist and his instrument, which he regarded as part of his own being, was another romantic trait, and the young romanticist swore to "give up the study of the development of piano playing only after I have done everything at all possible, everything that is attainable for me." But there came a time when he felt that "perhaps I am deceived by the mysterious trait that binds me so much to the piano." [24] This, however, seems to have come too late. The eclectic nature of his melodies, caused by the leveling influence of much travel, the rhetoric of the virtuoso, repetitions, interjections, and exclamations, the forced work of the hard-pressed world patron of music, pianist, composer, conductor, teacher, philosopher, conservatory president, and priest, prevented his art from attaining maturity in the peace that it required. Therefore his works are uneven, and the great compositions are easily overshadowed by many *pièces de circonstance*. But his extraordinary ability to draw a situation or a character with a few strokes often fascinates even in the weakest passages, and warmth of expression and the elementally musical qualities of his invention seldom failed him. He may become noisy, bombastic, even border on vulgarity, but he always remains essentially musical. In Liszt's garden we see many noble plants which inclement circumstances prevented from bursting into bloom, but while many of them bear no flowers, not one of them is without deep roots.

Wagner

GREAT creative personalities often see the essence of an age with a clarity denied to the masses, a clarity so vivid that when subsequent events confirm their visions in some manner, humanity, slower at arriving at a realization of its present, hails them as prophetic. It is tragic that we notice the peculiar tempo of the life of an era only when it begins to lose its intensity, when it begins to cool, when it all but belongs to the past. It was thus in the nineteenth century. The new middle-class society began to organize a new order of capitalism, technology, the reign of the machine. Individuality protested against uniformity and regimentation, against insignificance, against mental sterility and the rule of the mechanical. There were individuals who felt that creative will and ability which brought about the great periods of the past had begun to vanish from this world. They believed that the human race was suffering from a mysterious illness of which the mechanical and the uniform were symptoms only. They thought that by entering the era of capitalism and of the machine, humanity not only entered into a new era but arrived at the beginning of the end of the *genus humanum*.

Thomas Carlyle (1795–1881) proclaimed in his writings on the French revolution, on Cromwell, on Frederick the Great, and on heroes in general, that the cause for the decline of humanity and of its creative power lay in the disappearance of the heroic spirit, the spirit of incentive. On the other hand he maintained that the cause for the waning of the heroic spirit was the lack of religiousness.

Unlike Carlyle, Hippolyte Taine (1828–1893), also a great historian, and equally deploring the disappearance of creative force and initiative, tried to interpret human culture in terms of outer environment, explaining the individual by the formula of race, milieu, and the moment. Opposed to democracy, like Carlyle, he even denounced the achievements of the French Revolution. Though subordinating the individual to the mass, Taine also looked to an elite for guidance, at the same time advocating observance of traditions.

Ernest Renan (1823–1892) was perhaps the most attractive personality, and in many ways the most popular among the great connoisseurs of the past who criticized the present. Doubts and historical criticism rent the seminarist's cassock and drove him out into the world. Continued studies enabled him to apply the rationalistic approach of the scholar to the study of religious history. In his celebrated *Life of Jesus* no miracles are performed, nothing is said about the hereafter, the life of an incomparable man is related. This Jesus perhaps never lived in time, yet he lives at the bottom of the soul of everyone as an unfulfilled promise, as the moving illusion of a beautiful world into which we flee from the treachery of the real world.

Despite the great differences in their approach, there were many common traits in Carlyle, Taine, and Renan, and while the British Protestant and the French Catholics could not easily see eye to eye in the interpretation of religion, they all agreed in the need for leadership and in their disdain for democracy. Like his two confreres, Renan distrusted the mediocrity of democracy and believed in a cultured, responsible aristocracy of mind.

Besides these three great historian-philosophers there were other notable critics of the times dreaming of the greatness of the past and waiting for the regeneration of the declining human race. Jacob Burckhardt (1818–1897), a Swiss-German grand seigneur of erudition and intellectual history, shared with Walter Pater (1839–1894) a hatred of the regimented world of modern civilization and a boundless admiration for classical antiquity and the Renaissance. Those among the critics who showed socialistic leanings, John Ruskin (1819–1900), and particularly William Morris (1834–1896), saw in it a means of gaining larger freedom for the individual. The cult of the great man for whose sake nature seems to exist is the central idea in the writings of Ralph Waldo Emerson (1803–1882). Like Plato, this New England philosopher believed that the basis of virtue is belief in truth, that the coercion of fate exists only for the coward, that the determined and heroic soul knows no obstacles. According to him lack of will enslaves society, for what makes man is not knowledge but will; the individual should be faithful to himself and follow the voice of his own soul and conscience.

All these men contributed forcefully to the shaping of the spirit of the nineteenth century, but the most powerful minds among the "hero-worshipers," whose personality and influence overshadowed that of all others, were two Germans, Nietzsche and Wagner.

Friedrich Nietzsche (1844–1900) was the greatest thinker of the second half of the nineteenth century, whose influence was decisive not only in philosophy and aesthetics, but in philology and literature as well. In his works he fought for the new man, demanding, like his English and French "coreligionists," the reorganization of human society under the guidance of exceptionally gifted leaders. Nietzsche's "superman" theory, which called for the reign of a human stratum steeled in self-discipline and striving for perfection, was grossly misunderstood by his period. Even at the beginning of the twentieth century, literature and the theater were abounding in demonic human beasts, supposedly above all moral precepts in the sense of Nietzsche's superman. The profundity of his ideas, their moral truth, and their great poetic qualities are now better understood and admitted, even by his enemies. Although mistrusting metaphysics, strongly present in both Schopenhauer and Wagner, Nietzsche became an adherent of both because of his belief that Schopenhauer and especially Wagner stood in direct relationship to the spirit of classical Greece. Hence his centaurlike book on the origin of the tragedy. (This idealistic train of thought he gave up when he turned to positivism.) The frail young scholar, who spent his youth among books, saw in Wagner the powerful high priest of Dionysus, the imperious ruler of life, the lawgiver of modern art, life, and philosophy. Thus we arrive at the man who not only criticized and prophesied, not only exhorted and roused, who not only delineated the program and called for the heroes, but who achieved all this and became the hero incarnate, the superman, whose compelling personality and tremendous works had an unprecedented effect on the intellectual life of a long period: Richard Wagner (1813–1883).

At first it seems surprising that in the galaxy of thinkers a musician should be the dominating figure, but romanticism considered music the romantic art par excellence, assigning to it a special place at the top of the hierarchy of arts and letters. Since music is the most illogical of arts—despite the strict technical requisites of musical logic—and since it has nothing to do with concrete symbols, it is able to give not only the idea itself, as Schopenhauer maintained, but the will, the "thing in itself" so highly coveted by all philosophers seeking the Kingdom of God on earth. All romantic philosophy is artistic and aspires more strongly toward art than toward science. Yet not art, but passion, lost in the infinite, in the boundless reaches of imagination, is the essence of romanticism, and it is this essence which seeks expression in art, dissolving, in the final romantic analysis, itself, and life, and the world, in music. This romantic dream of the cosmic nature of music was taken up in earnest by Schopenhauer, who proclaimed music to be a substitute for the world: "music is the melody whose text is the world." Schopenhauer saw the embodiment of these ideas in Beethoven's symphonies, for in them speak all human passions, a spiritual world devoid of all matter. How then, might we ask, could the romantic synthesis, the romantic longing for music and for the universal art, culminate in the Wagnerian opera, professedly a drama with the assistance of music? Did not Schopenhauer himself say that "music is much more powerful than words; music and words is the marriage of a prince with a beggar"?

Fundamentally, and all his remonstrances notwithstanding, the strongest component of Wagner's creative power was the musical, and music remained his strongest means of expression even on occasions when the words require all attention, in the dramatic crises. Therefore the leitmotives, contrary to almost universal belief, do not really represent characters or situations; they are part of the abstract idea of the drama. Thus, speaking rather generally, the leitmotives assume the role played by the thematic material in the symphony, with the difference that, deflected from its true field of activity, the Wagnerian "symphony" cannot be satisfied with the few motives needed for the symphony but has to operate with a multitude of ideas. This is a negation of the basic principles of symphonic thought, and at the same time its ruthless application in the lyric drama to the detriment of the human voice and the drama itself violated the spirit of the lyric drama. Such arbitrary and deliberate opposition to aesthetic laws must lead to failure, and in principle the Gesamtkunstwerk was a failure. The amazing part of the matter, and the one which demonstrates Wagner's genius and creative power, is that while none of his mature operas, with the possible exception of the *Meistersinger,* is free from the consequences of the fallacy of his assumptions, none of them is without its moments of supreme beauty and greatness. The innermost content of the Wagnerian drama is the symphonic poem of a philosophic world problem; what we see on the stage is merely the elucidation of the idea in a symbolized dramatic form. Wagner himself claimed that his music drama did not continue Gluck's, Mozart's, and Weber's work, but arose from Beethoven's Ninth Symphony. After reading the *Ring* Schopenhauer declared that Wagner might be anything else, but not a philosopher; and Christian Friedrich Hebbel (1813–1863), the most powerful tragic dramatic poet since Schiller and Kleist, who admired Wagner's music, thought that "Wagner's reform plans rest on a fundamental misconception of the nature of the drama." In another letter he compared Wagner's music to his dramas as warm, flowing blood to desiccated arteries.

Both Wagner and Nietzsche proceeded from the belief that the Gesamtkunstwerk had once been the pride and possession of a whole people—the ancient Greeks—and that, unfortunately, many centuries of Christian civilization, dictated by the Church, had interrupted the natural development of this art. But the universal art work they were confident could be resuscitated would, once established, prove to be the only possible form of art, all individual arts must vanish. Nietzsche saw in Wagner the man capable of bringing about the regeneration of arts and letters in the spirit of ancient Greece; in Wagner's spirit he saw the emanation of the eternal, the genius (which latter notion later developed into the "superman"). He believed he had found in *Tristan* the reborn ideal of the Dionysiac drama.

In dem wogenden Schall	In the swaying sound
in dem tönenden Schall	in the ringing echo
in des Welt-Atems	in the wafting all
wehendem All—	of the world's breath—
ertrinken—	to drown—
versinken—	to sink—
unbewusst—	unconscious—
höchste Lust!	highest rapture!

In these verses, and much more so in the music that illustrates them, is embodied the *conditio sine qua non* for the Dionysiac "consuming fire death," the dissolution of the individual in the fire of fulfillment, in the "highest rapture." Tristan and Isolde die, for in death they are united:

So starben wir,	So we died,
um ungetrennt,	that we, unparted,
ewig einig,	forever one,
ohne End',	without end,
ohn' Erwachen,	without awakening,
ohn' Erbangen,	without anxiety,
namenlos	namelessly
in Lieb' umfangen,	embraced in love,
ganz uns selbst gegeben,	given wholly to ourselves,
der Liebe nur zu leben.	might live on love alone.[25]

This is "death music" without the slightest trace of the macabre, for it is really music glorifying life that is eternal, music in which everything individual is sublimated into the "world's breath." The love death is not tragic—neither in Senta, nor in Brünnhilde, nor in Isolde—for it means final abandonment to and final fulfillment of consuming desires. Death, the complete disintegration of the individual, is identical here with the ecstatic rapture of the transports of voluptuousness. The poet tries to trans-figure his heroes, but the musician cannot restrain the triumphant erotic music which engulfs everything. Wagner was a full-blooded dramatist, but he was no "tragedist." The last act of *Tristan* is music *sub specie aeternitatis,* the last amen in the Missa Solemnis of love. In it romanticism culminates and falls, for in it the longing of a century reaches its fulfillment and then perishes in the embrace, like Tristan and Isolde.

Never since Orpheus has there been a musician whose music affected so vitally the life and art of generations. Yet this influence was not com-mensurate to the intrinsic value of his music; Bach's or Beethoven's, in-comparably more significant, never created such revolutionary, expansive consequences. There must be, then, various reasons, not only musical, that made Wagner the universal prophet of European culture of the turn of the nineteenth century. Wagner himself wanted to be more than a great musician; the new music he created was for him merely the path to the complete reorganization of life in his own spirit. His music, besides being art, is protest and prophecy, but Wagner was not satisfied with lodging his protest through his art; he used every means at his disposal, which meant that the ordinary means of music were not sufficient for his purposes. Mozart's or Beethoven's music left it to the listener's soul to respond to the emotions music evoked in him; the listener partook in the creative act, for he had to create his world and images in the light of this music. The Wag-nerian music refuses to permit this freedom to the listener, it prefers to give him everything in a finished form. It is not satisfied by merely indicating what transpires in the soul, it attempts to give a complete account. Using the most accomplished and many-sided musical language, with clearly rec-ognizable symbols, he gives a finished program, not only sentimental, but mental, with which he can fascinate the modern intellectual listener. This *Totalausdruck,* the complete expression of passion and experience, is re-sponsible for the intoxication the Wagnerian music creates in the listener, for his possible reactions are already included in it, and his creative partici-pation is not required. He who wants to affect and move at any price must study the means capable of bringing this about, and Wagner studied them so assiduously that they became part and parcel of his own being. There has seldom been a human life presenting such an artistic web of conscious untruth and self-deceiving, pathetic world conceit. Nietzsche, in a work dedicated to the exaltation of his idol (*Wagner in Bayreuth*), recognized this when he said that "viewed from close proximity and without bias Wagner's life appears in many ways as a comedy, as a very grotesque comedy." No one understood better than Wagner how to transform petty feelings into bombastic presentations, to inflate lowly and sometimes sordid little interests into matters of national importance, the destiny of the German people. This is the point where both his life and his art assumed a potential danger for the future of German culture.

It is in the nature of German mentality to "spiritualize" (*vergeistigen*) natural instincts and interests into abstract problems of Weltanschauung. The spirit of the Wagnerian mythology and legend fanned this tendency and coated this characteristic German penchant with a quasi-religious ointment. By mixing new charm potions in the German mental vapors Wagner contributed as much if not more to the rising superiority complex of the Second Reich as Bismarck. Nothing illustrates this more appropriately than the well-known picture of Emperor William II, standing with his Lohengrin helmet before a swan, the knight of the Grail of German imperialism. The Wagnerian heroes and Wagnerian music called to life not only a new world of natural passions, but a world that concealed these very human passions with mythological-religious untruths. These lies at times invaded even *Tristan,* written in the white heat of true passion, and the *Meistersinger,* the one of his mature works in which humor, whimsical gentleness, human wisdom, and human love dominate to the exclusion of sorcery and incest. His genius was so used to acting that the most beautiful flowers of his natural creative power could not be tied into a bouquet without the addition of some artificial ferns. The pictures in Wagner's art are retouched, and so are those of his life, in itself a stage production filled with the same gestures and sounds as the mythology. As a born actor he wanted to imitate man at his most effective best, in the highest regions of passion, for his extreme nature saw in all other circumstances feebleness and lack of truth. But the danger of constantly reveling in the intoxicating, in the sensuous, in the ecstatic, in continuous animation, is great, for it inevitably leads to the prostration of the aftermath.

Young Nietzsche came entirely under Wagner's influence. As a true romanticist, Nietzsche started out from the Goethe cult, feting in him the genius, which notion grew into the mythical. The same measure he later applied to Wagner. Like all devoted listeners of Wagner's music, he was entirely delivered to the powerful sensuous attraction of this music, to which came the equally strong attraction of a rich and colorful personality. The profound depths of his beloved classical antiquity seemed to have been reopened to him by Wagner, and Nietzsche saw in his music the omen of the birth of a new era, tragic and heroic, for he believed that the tragic myth of ancient Greece was similarly born from the spirit of music. He saw in Wagner the herald of the new Dionysiac man. Nietzsche's first great work, the *Birth of the Tragedy from the Spirit of Music,* was dedicated to this Dionysiac spirit which he believed he had found in Wagner's music drama. Thus Wagner found a disciple, a fellow philosopher. But this disciple was much more dangerous than his many enemies. As long as there was contact between the creative activity of these two, the younger man's friendship and admiration was boundless, for he presupposed his own ideas, aims, and views in the other's acts. A break was inevitable as soon as Nietzsche's critical faculties were brought into play and he began to examine his own ideas. There was seldom a man more devoted to friends than this strange philosopher, but he had an almost morbid ability to sense a false tone, an insincerity. Such uncanny clairvoyance is the characteristic of those fanaticists of truth who educate themselves by vanquishing the many evil inclinations and passions seething in themselves. Surrounded by satellites, some excellent musicians, and many adoring women, Wagner's powerful intellect was thirsting for a thinker of his own caliber, and he rejoiced in finding him in his friend Nietzsche; but the disciple had to abandon his master the very minute he discovered that Wagnerian heroism was the heroism of an actor, that the Wagnerian mythology was theatrical myth. He was among the first to read Wagner's autobiography, then available only to the circle of friends; the first doubts must have arisen then, for he must have felt the insincerity which he denounced later in scathing words. "That which is circulated as Wagner's autobiography is fiction, if not worse, intended for public use. I must confess that every point we know from Wagner's description I regard with the greatest suspicion. He was not proud enough to utter the truth . . . even in biography he remained true to himself—he remained an actor." The first Bayreuth festivals disillusioned him further, for he expected the rebirth of the solemn fervor of the Greek tragedy, the first manifestation of the dignity of a new humanity, instead of which he found the eclectic atmosphere of the typical international music festivals, with a motley public eager to attend sensational productions. This was not Wagner's fault, but what was his fault was that his whole personality fitted entirely into the atmosphere. What finally embittered Nietzsche beyond measure was Wagner's last work, *Parsifal,* for *Parsifal* did not correspond to his Dionysiac ideal drama, which he thought was also Wagner's aim. *Tristan* he considered close to the ideal, but *Parsifal* was false, the Dionysiac ideal transformed into a theatrical fairy opera for the edification of the sanctimonious bourgeois of the new German Reich. This was a deadly disappointment that shook him profoundly, for nothing was more hateful in his eyes than religious hypocrisy, the great compromise with the "slave spirit," the psychology of the multitude. Up to this time all of Wagner's religious utterances were cynical, offending merely Nietzsche's sense of tact. In *Parsifal* he saw the actor's bow before the public's wishes and tastes. In his *Menschliches, Allzumenschliches,* appearing at this time, Nietzsche pointed out the shortcomings and inconsistencies of Wagner's creations, and the master suddenly realized that instead of a disciple he had nurtured an enemy, and the two parted. Nietzsche could never survive his great disappointment, which was one of the chief causes of his ultimate insanity.

In 1873 Nietzsche said he did not think that Wagner believed in anything but himself, and "he who believes in himself only is no longer honest toward himself." This was a keen observation and entirely true, but although Wagner was not honest to himself or to anyone else, and although fundamentally speaking his universal art was a failure, his iron will and his tremendous mental powers prevailed; his all-puissant attempt to assert himself and to dominate succeeded. He became the lawgiver, his glance took in all circumstances, and all pettiness disappeared in the vastness of his creations. Taken separately, his drama and poetry are weak, his acting is often mere rhetoric, his music often of the greatest, often merely labored; but taken all together he is formidable and unique. His artistic language is a theatrical language, it does not suffer a small place. It is the voice of a people, the voice of Germandom which wants to be heard in all four corners of the world, and it was heard and it was heeded. Nothing was neglected to achieve this, and no act of his was unmotivated, no chance words ever left his lips, and no sentence in his writings is idle. His dominating characteristics, intractableness and tameless immoderation, penetrated every fiber of his art, and his penchant for demagoguery, with which he combined a ruthless tyranny, together with his lack of any chivalry or magnanimity toward colleagues and rivals, earned him legions of enemies.

Wagner's writings, whether on historical, aesthetic, musical, literary, or political subjects, are always passionate and egocentric. Almost every book or article is polemical, directed against people or things in the path of his plans and ideas. In his discussions he utilized everything that lent itself to his purposes: history, philosophy, politics, or religion. As source material it must therefore be carefully scrutinized, for controversial matters are always settled summarily in favor of the critic, Wagner. Still, his theoretical activity, his writings, no matter how debatable and how contradictory to his own actions, not only remain always interesting and provoking, but they were absolutely necessary for the creation of his new world in which his music dramas were to be launched. This explains why his writings were not restricted to music but dealt with many aspects of culture and civilization. We must approach these writings with the understanding that they are descriptions of a promised land; in them Wagner said what he desired and what he believed in, albeit the artist in him created something entirely different. As a musical writer and critic Wagner considered all previous efforts at the creation of music drama as abortive. A more intimate knowledge of the history of music would have taught him that the Florentines, the French composers of lyric tragedy, Gluck and Weber, as well as many musical writers, advocated the same principles as he. But Wagner's artistic activity cannot really be explained from his writings.

No man or artist can be separated from his predecessors, and Wagner himself began his creative work under the influence of the reigning musical forces. He started out with the old fairy opera (*Die Feen*), whence he progressed to the historic grand opera (*Rienzi*), then came the romantic opera (*Flying Dutchman*) in the wake of Weber and Marschner, which reached its height in *Tannhäuser* and *Lohengrin*. At this point a great stylistic and ideological change set in, a change marked by sharpness unprecedented in the history of arts and letters. The revolutionary year of 1849 gave us the Wagner who altered the course of history. It is probable that Wagner would have arrived at his ultimate destination without the political upheaval; still, it is hard to imagine how this could have happened without the trials caused by the heavy punishment inflicted for his ridiculous and rather harmless participation in political events. The insurrection had little effect, and the "democrat" who harangued the rebels on the barricades became the most enthusiastic admirer of Wittelsbachs and Hohenzollerns, and a loud backer of the War of 1870, which cost him the friendship of many an upright admirer. But while the political consequences of his "leftist" activities thus ended in a reactionary refrain, the insurrection did set free a man. If we read his letters from exile we shall see that the émigré was an entirely different man from the Dresden *Kapellmeister*. Everything that bound him to the past was dissolved. Having been expelled from the social and human community of German art he became free of its conventions, standing outside the artistic world and no longer partaking in its development. His enormous strength manifested itself in the fact that he did not try to regain the lost connections but set out to create a world of his own in which his art could grow unmolested. And so Wagner became the most eminent representative, the consummate master, of the period which was the culmination and the aftermath of romanticism. He united in himself all the restraining weaknesses of his century, developing them actively into Promethean works of tremendous intensity: the highest pathos of passion, the darkest pessimism, uncontrollable sensuous fervor, and a tormented desire for fulfillment and redemption, all carried to a point where the boundaries of the world and the beyond are no longer recognizable. The forming of an artistic personality of compelling power and originality under these circumstances will remain one of the most extraordinary feats in the whole of cultural history.

The Gesamtkunstwerk

THE technical and spiritual foundation of the Gesamtkunstwerk was the ·new musico-dramatic unity, resting on the forms of old German alliterative poetry, the *Stabreim,* and on fundamental musical themes handled in a symphonic manner. Alliteration served as a structural element in the early Teutonic verse and followed a well-defined pattern in which the normal line had four strongly accented syllables, the third accented syllable alliterating with the first or the second or with both. Each consonant alliterated only with itself; each vowel alliterated with itself or with any other vowel. Wagner, who studied the principles of the Stabreim assiduously,[26] employed it, with certain modifications, with such determination that at times the overabundance of forced alliteration makes his verse devoid of sense. The fundamental musical themes are identical with the leitmotif principle. As a principle the leitmotives, or rather the recurring motives of reminiscence, were not, of course, new. They were already present in some of Keiser's operas and we have seen to what degree the French operatic school perfected their use toward the end of the eighteenth century. A little later Spohr, Marschner, and Weber were fully aware of their potentialities, but it remained for Wagner to employ the system integrally as a dominating stylistic-constructive factor. The constant manipulation of predetermined thematic material inevitably leads to a symphonic technique, while the singing voices must follow the prosody of the text and require an entirely different treatment. Consequently, the point of gravity passed from the voices to the orchestra, not bound by the technical and aesthetic limitations of the voice and responding with ease to abstract musical requirements. This tendency we have noticed in the melodrama,[27] where the orchestra took charge of the dramatic expression. Its motives of reminiscence, which had helped to underline and connect important happenings and characters, were now developed psychologically to express the mental process of the figures of the drama. These leitmotives, as they were now called, were employed with the aid of a symphonic technique of ample proportions.

Wagner extended the old operatic accompagnato by abolishing or postponing cadences; thus his orchestral accompaniment carries on for long stretches without interruption or rest, while above the orchestral parts the voices are deployed in a sort of speech-song. It would be ridiculous, of course, to maintain that Wagner was the originator of the principle of the orchestral commentary utilizing the thematic material of the vocal roles, but he was the first to demand that the motives of the orchestra should assume the pregnancy of "gestures." The melodrama had shown clearly the ability of orchestral music to give expression to mental processes when the words were unable to do so, and Weber and Marschner had already made full use of the highly developed expressive orchestral language of Beethoven, in this sense preparing Wagner's advent.

To the wonderfully expressive symphonic idiom of the classic and early romantic era Wagner could now add an infinitely more flexible and modernized orchestral technique, of which he will remain one of the greatest wizards of all times. And this modern orchestra takes command, imperiously and with complete disregard for restrictions from any quarter, expressing itself completely and translating unequivocally the composer's intentions and feelings even when those on the stage are hindered from doing so by the limits set by the action and the drama. The orchestra tells the truth always; when in Gluck's *Iphigenia* Orestes pretends to be calm, a singular restlessness coming from the orchestra invades everything. To the critics Gluck answered: "Orestes is the one who lies, the violas do not lie; Orestes killed his mother!" And the monopoly of expressive power which the orchestra began to arrogate to itself grew steadily in Wagner. Even in the comparatively early *Tannhäuser* the parting scene between Elisabeth and Wolfram (Act 3, scene 1), a dramatically all-important moment, is without words, everything is left for the orchestra to express.

As the voices relinquished their prerogatives the *Sprachgesang,* the dramatic speech-song—prepared in the recitatives of the German baroque, in Mozart's *Magic Flute,* and in Löwe's ballads—proceeded to abolish the difference between declamatory recitative and the lyric arioso and aria. All this is fully accomplished in *Lohengrin,* together with the elimination of the "set forms" of duet, aria, finale, etc., in favor of literary-dramatic scenes. The grand opera elements of Wagner's youth do not really disappear entirely—there are dances, marches, investitures, prayers, processions, etc., from *Tannhäuser* to *Parsifal*—but they are made plausible and, in the case of the *Meistersinger,* employed purposely. The finales are partly discarded, partly merged with the rest of the act. In the earlier operas the composer's musical instincts struggle with his dramatic intentions. In Senta's Ballad, in the Rome Narration, in the Song to the Evening Star, he is still composing arias, and the compelling force of musical logic is seen in the frequently faulty declamation, a "sin" committed by the very champion of the absolute supremacy of drama over music, probably because at that time his technical mastery was not yet sufficiently strong to abide by his aesthetic creeds. The diction is, however, already much better in *Tannhäuser* and is finished in Lohengrin, for the orchestra asserted itself sufficiently to carry the brunt of the musical material, leaving the voices to their speech-song.

With the full development of Wagner's leitmotivic technique the initial lack of security disappeared and a rich orchestral fabric woven with a sure symphonic hand enveloped the whole opera. It has become customary to label minutely every scrap of music in Wagner's operas. and most Wagnerian commentators solve every problem by calling attention to the presence of a certain motif which in itself is supposed to clarify the issues at stake. The various "guidebooks" and "motivic tables" made possible the growth of an enormous literature of Wagneriana, for the system appears to be foolproof and—leaves nothing for the imagination. Fortunately the situation is not so simple and so stereotyped. There are long passages during which the "system" is obviously being enforced, but whenever Wagner's inspiration carries him away, what takes place is the free symphonic unfolding of a polythematic dramatic material, as in the leitmotivic passages in the operas of Méhul, Cherubini, or Beethoven. Some of these "symphonic poems"—and there are many of them—are of a convincing power and beauty such as the history of music has seldom known, although we do not usually associate such music with the opera. On the other hand it is undeniable that the possibility of "understanding" every move, dramatic or musical, by the application of a system of identification has been largely responsible for the popularity of Wagner's music, a popularity which has disastrous effects on the understanding and appreciation of music that does not lend itself to exact cataloguing and identification. Many of the leitmotives make good symphonic material and, indeed, this supposedly formless mass of music, obeying purely dramatic dictates, shows innumerable little sonata expositions in the best symphonic traditions; the symphonic logic is especially keenly demonstrated when new motives are being introduced. There are also rondo and strophic forms and many other definite constellations responding to purely musical logic.

Wagner's operatic aesthetics and theories were not the soil from which his art grew, but they often imperiled his original and natural musical instincts, which were those of a symphonist. His musical language, if examined without the halo of the music drama, establishes his place among the heroes of music, and not among the gods. His periodization is always clear and on the whole follows romantic precepts such as one can find in Schumann. Wagner pushed forward the major-minor tonal system to its limits, but never ventured outside it. However, in his ever-evolving, swirling modulations one is often at a loss to discover a basic key, for the ordinary key relationship is abandoned with the thinning out of cadences. Yet neither harmony nor modulation is ever illogical or drastic. His marked tendency away from diatonic melody and harmony to chromaticism is a musical manifestation of the romantic urge to dissolution in the infinite; it stands for freedom, freedom from the shackles of tonality, from voice leading, from the classic cadence, and from the form-determining factors of tonality. This "freedom" first manifested itself in melody, and later invaded harmony itself, where it found a wide field in the treatment of altered chords either left unresolved or resolved in an entirely unconventional man-

ner. Chromaticism as a means of realistic characterization was amply used
in earlier times. With Wagner's immediate predecessors, Spohr and Marschner, it reached a stage at times almost touching the intensity of Wagner's
harmonic-melodic dialect. The composer of *Tristan* then carried it to a
point where the very existence of the whole romantic era was put on trial;
a century of music reached in this surcharged harmonic world its crisis.
Allied with chromaticism was another harmonic factor of great importance in the crisis of romantic music, enharmonic transliteration, through
which freedom from tonal logic was even more emphasized. The incessant
modulations, the constant wavering of tonality, was the supreme attempt
of the musician to follow the aesthetic ideals of the dramatist, to give an
adequate portrayal of the restless, glowing, and insatiable passions that fire
the drama. The leitmotivic treatment was supposed to give the work a
unity which would more than compensate for the loss of pure and abstract
musical logic. It is a profound paradox that the same man who derided
Italian opera for its "catalogue of arias" offered in exchange a veritable
filing system. The crisis was reached in *Tristan,* after which Wagner returned to a broader and less nervous and swollen style.

In his essay on the "Music of the Future" Wagner remarked that the
distance covered between *Tannhäuser* and *Tristan* is much greater than
that between his first compositions and *Tannhäuser*. This is, indeed, true,
and accentuates the remarkable change in the man Wagner which we
discovered after the Dresden period. *Rienzi* is a full-blooded grand opera
with all the blaring and brassy glory of Spontini's trumpets, the ballets and
sword dances of Meyerbeer and Halévy, with other elements coming from
Spohr, Marschner, Méhul, and Auber. But in the *Flying Dutchman* there
appears a tone that was his and no one else's. In the second act of this opera
all the ghosts of *Rienzi,* the *Huguenots,* the *Vestale, Hans Heiling,* and
Jessonda fade, for they have met their master. *Tannhäuser,* its overture, the
processional of the guests in the Wartburg, are still very much in Spontini's
style, but the Venusberg music has a good deal of Berlioz's lightning orchestral writing. This opera still has many lyric "numbers," even though
they are well enough connected to give an uninterrupted dramatic action
in the literary sense envisaged by Wagner. While there are still "prayers,"
"songs," and "choruses of pilgrims," what mattered was that despite the
grand opera elements Wagner succeeded in creating a dramatic atmosphere
that gains in intensity up to the end, for there is a real dramatic tension
engendered by the two diametrically opposed personalities of Elisabeth and
Venus fighting for the hero.

The continuity of dramatic composition grew to imposing steadiness in
Lohengrin, and is well illustrated by the fact that the celebrated passages
from this opera that appear in Wagnerian albums and other anthologies all

need some kind of makeshift ending provided by the editor, without which the piece would merge with the next "number." *Lohengrin* represents the culmination of the romantic opera. In it the foreign elements are fused with the sound orchestral-symphonic inventiveness of the German, the orchestra glorying in its sensuous power but the singers still singing rather than discoursing. From the very first measures of the overture we are aware of the emergence of a new orchestral virtuosity, a virtuosity that no longer counts on weight and force alone but which can rise to the most translucent regions.

After *Lohengrin* originated the works which earned Wagner the position he held and still holds in the musical world: the *Ring des Nibelungen, Tristan,* the *Meistersinger,* and *Parsifal.* The writing of the four dramas comprising the *Ring* progressed in a curious manner. First came *Götterdämmerung,* then, finding this gigantic piece too summary, Wagner prefaced it with *Siegfried,* which in turn needed additional preparation for which the *Valkyrie* was written, then the whole trilogy was introduced by the *Rhinegold.* The musical setting of the dramas proceeded, however, in the opposite, that is, the correct, order, interrupted, at the end of the second act of *Siegfried,* for twelve years. During the pause Wagner created two works of totally different scope and nature, yet when he returned to the continuation of the *Ring* he was able to finish it in a manner that does not show the slightest hesitation or change in style. The peculiar growth of the dramatic story of the *Ring* doomed its unity from the outset; Wagner could not master it dramatically, and it is a sheer wonder that the musician triumphed over the long and rambling repetitions by the power of his symphonic eloquence.

Wagner's preoccupation with Schopenhauer's philosophy and his love for Mathilde Wesendonk made him put aside the quarreling Germanic gods and heroes, and under the impulse of his great passion he composed his most powerful, most romantic, and most fervent drama, *Tristan* (finished 1859). Without the undeniable moments of ennui and save for its excessive length, this greatest of erotic love poems of all times would be a work of almost miraculous unity of style, mood, and expression. It still remains one of the most powerful and absorbing musical compositions in the recent history of music. *Tristan* is, nevertheless, a peculiar music drama. Its sultry language, full of complicated polysyllabic words which cannot be understood unless the listener knows them by heart and has decoded their meaning, makes it the more impossible to listen to the drama itself, but we do not need the drama, and when we are tired of looking at the static stage in the third act, and when our ears begin to buzz with almost senseless alliterations, all we have to do is to sit back and listen to the music, for the orchestra "does not lie." From the beginning of the third act to

Tristan's death the restlessly appearing motives develop; here intertwining, separating, and again enlacing, there struggling with each other only to embrace again in an orgiastic death grip.

Tristan carried the sensuous expressiveness of music to its ultimate limits, and the terrific erotic power of this music poisoned the minds of the composers of the succeeding generations. No one could escape its devastating influence, yet no one could even remotely match, let alone continue it, for after the Dionysiac "love-death" nothing is possible but undisguised sexual lust.

This passionate symphonic orgy, in which all characters melt in the fire of the music, was followed by a real *play*, the *Meistersinger*, a drama with characters who act and keep on acting and being characters throughout the drama. The accomplished scholar that was Wagner assembled centuries of legends, consulted many philological and historical sources, blending and transforming them with literary skill. This Hans Sachs is not a lecherous and vindictive demiurge or a lovesick knight, but a Lutherlike ancient German burgher, nurturing a profound and sincere affection with sublime resignation. Walther von Stolzing recaptures the romantic ardor of Walther von der Vogelweide, honoring and worshiping his beloved, Eva, a tender and subtle woman who has never even dreamed of the dangerous charms of Venus-Isolde. And the misanthropic Beckmesser, the stalwart German master-craftsmen, the prankish apprentices are all sterling human characters. Only a Mozart was able to change so completely from one operatic work to another, for the blood-boiling chromaticism of *Tristan* with its shifting, dark tonalities, its eternally postponed cadences, disappeared here before a sturdy diatonic idiom and a radiating C major sunshine. The German past is reborn in the *Meistersinger* in chorale, fugue, basso ostinato, German song, lute music, cantus firmus motet. And the old operatic art of ensembles, processionals, dances, is again admitted to its rightful place, and the result is a spectacle that warms one's heart. The listener is scarcely aware of the still excessive length of the opera, for humor, lyricism, and whimsical meditation, banished in the mythological works, as well as character portrayal and, most of all, some undisguised singing, keep the attention focused on the stage.

To go ahead composing, with the mighty but unperformed scores of the *Rhinegold, Valkyrie, Tristan,* and *Meistersinger* buried in the drawers of his desk, required a Herculean artistic integrity against which all of Wagner's insincere acts pale to insignificance. But with all his determination his situation was desperate, when a royal patron changed all this into a sudden Canaan. Ludwig II of Bavaria, youthful fairy-tale prince, rescued the distressed composer, placing his kingdom at his disposal. Under his protection and with the assistance of the best singers and instrumentalists,

Hans von Bülow conducting, *Tristan* was performed in 1865 before a most illustrious gathering of musicians. The days of triumph and glory were, however, few. Wagner's objectionable private life, his always tactless behavior, his political past, his strong influence on the mentally unbalanced king, engendered a political move which forced him from the Bavarian capital. But the king's munificence followed him into Switzerland, whence he repaired with von Bülow's wife, Cosima. Then came the exhilarating year of 1870, and the old revolutionary watched with pride and satisfaction the emergence of the German Empire. Now the times were ripe for a revival of his great plans, the erection of a monument to the genius of Germandom. This monument was to be partly his music dramas, partly a temple for their performance. Next year Wagner moved to Bayreuth, where he intended to build his festival theater of German art. On May 22, 1872, the cornerstone was laid, to the strains of his own Imperial March, followed by a performance of Beethoven's Ninth Symphony. The old self-vindication, the oft-proclaimed mandate received from Beethoven, had to be emphasized again with the very work which is supposed to have constituted the point of departure to the "art work of the future." Four years later the theater opened with three complete performances of the *Ring*. The lifelong ideal came to fulfillment, and the only dissonant note that accompanied the celebration was the serious deficit of 150,000 Marks. The Bayreuth festivals were, indeed, in grave danger of faltering because of the adverse financial returns.

Then the master, imperious and unrelenting as ever, summoned his powers to create something intended to crown his lifework and at the same time be beyond the reach of ordinary controversy or criticism because of its subject matter: *Parsifal*, "Christianity arranged for Wagnerians" (Nietzsche). The world beheld with awe the Catholic mysticism of this Protestant Freemason turned atheist. There were, however, doubters, chief of whom was, as we have seen, Nietzsche. Having known Wagner for years as a cynical atheist freely airing his disbelief, he could not ascribe this sudden conversion to the known strong Catholicism of Cosima, for in intimate circles Wagner did not spare his wife's religious ideals. (It is a known fact that the editors of Wagner's letters eliminated much of Wagner's often violently anti-Christian diatribes.) With his highly developed and sensitive intuition Nietzsche sensed in this changed religious conception purely materialistic motives. He knew how dear to Wagner's heart was the success of Bayreuth, and he knew the disappointing financial results of the first festivals, but he also knew that Wagner's sharp mind could not overlook the new piousness of new Germany, acting on behalf of God and emperor. Wagner's whole life and his whole art were an unwavering assertion of the Dionysiac belief in eternal rapture and not in its denial, the

Christian ideal. Was it possible that the same man who in the *Tristan* music found and expressed the greatest secrets of life would now voluntarily shut his eyes so as not to see them? It was not, and, indeed, *Parsifal* is sincere only in the passages where the composer's imagination triumphed over the self-imposed religious-metaphysical bonds, where the irrepressible creative force of the musician overcame the calculating preoccupations of the thinker; everywhere else *Parsifal* is false and mere theatricalism.

Parsifal was first performed on July 26, 1882, and created a deep impression. The decline of Wagner's creative power of invention is often recognized in this work, in which Wagner lost all sense of proportion; at times, however, his music here rises to its highest and becomes incandescent. Despite its subject and aim, and coming after a long pause, *Parsifal* resembles *Tristan* both in its language and in its chromatic musical idiom, both of which he discarded in the *Meistersinger*. A strange and alarming perfume, narcotic and enervating, emanates from this romantic, operatic Christianity, which, combined with the doctrines of Buddha and Schopenhauer, was to weigh heavily on the future of German civilization.

Since the advent of grand opera all musicians, especially those of minor importance, had shown great interest in the opera because it gave them such excellent opportunities for grateful pieces. There are the overture, the big scenes and arias, the dances and ballets, the choruses, all offering a large variety of forms and types which every composer liked to exploit. All this does not, of course, mean dramatic music, but simply the conventional operatic setting of a given text. While the musicians were occupied with the ephemeral task of providing music to the libretti, turned out freely after the honored model of Scribe, no one was concerned with the problem of the lyric stage, for a problem it remained even after every successful solution. Thus opera became an occasion to make music in which text and dramatic action had no other aim than to make the mood of the music visually intelligible. With his powerful intellect and fine artistic instincts, Wagner recognized that this attitude would lead to a complete degeneration of opera; in fact, he declared that this state of affairs had actually been reached in contemporary Italian opera. He maintained, as had Gluck, that this lamentable situation was caused by the fact that "the means of expression—music—has been taken for the sole aim and end, while the true aim—the drama—has been neglected for the sake of particular musical forms." Wagner, indeed, was convinced that the "natural line of evolution" must progress from the number opera to the music drama. Yet the actual sequence of events was not as represented by him and by many writers on music, nor did it follow dramatic precepts. The line of development remained practically unbroken in Italy, the home of opera; in Germany it became a corollary to the great symphonic development of the classic era. The road forked in the Beethovenian era. We are wont to consider the overabundance of virtuoso singing the plague of true music drama, whereas the real danger lurked in the orchestra pit. With the enormous development of the symphony and the symphony orchestra the desire for through-composed opera grew in Germany—a desire clearly exhibited in the melo-drama—but it did not disturb the classic composers, nor even Weber, who used all the resources of the modern symphony to write number operas in which the voices dominated. Still, the greater role assigned to the orchestra decided the future of German opera, especially since it was accompanied by a dearth of dramatic talent and the natural inclination of the German for abstract symphonic thought.

We have mentioned Wagner's claim to Beethoven's heritage and found it inadmissible in the light of his brief. Yet this claim is not unfounded if we change Wagner's own reasoning.

Wagner did not write operas. He opened in his works infinite horizons, he gave us a philosophy which also deals with men and matters. Monteverdi and Mozart gave us men, and men only. Wagner took his stuff from leg-ends and sagas and then made his heroes into symbols, into embodiments of his philosophy. Mozart's hero is simply man; it is his joys and sufferings that occupy him exclusively, the mystical and mythical are not his concern. From Monteverdi to Mozart the great opera composers did not compose abstract music; they rendered in music the soul of their dramatic figures; they composed character dramas. Wagner ceased to write character dramas and attempted to view the myth in its primeval form, as an idea, a philoso-phy. This abstraction led to types and away from characters. We have seen how "reason," supreme ruler in the Enlightenment, surrendered in the clas-sic era to "feeling"; now feeling was about to surrender to metaphysics. The chief characters in Wagner's operas, the great heroines, are too easily lost in a rarefied atmosphere, becoming more mythological than human. They may be impressive in their greatness and in the elemental power of their love, but not in tenderness, grace, and womanliness. In his first opera, *Die Hochzeit,* a noble lady, her honor threatened by the knight she secretly loves, kills the very object of her love. The man's death remains a mystery until the time of his burial, when the woman, joining the mourners in prayer, slumps to the ground, dying of grief. Thus in 1832 in this unfinished youthful opera, the motive of love-death and the first kinswoman to Senta, Elisabeth, Elsa, Isolde, and Kundry are before us. She is a type, an idea, the embodiment of the Dionysiac rapture. But orgiastic passion can be satisfied only in ever-new sacrifices until the last and highest—Isolde. That after this supreme sacrifice and lethal passion he could present us with the tender figure of Eva will remain a solitary artistic accomplishment in the annals of music. It also makes us wonder what secret powers agitated this remarkable genius to divert his great talents from their rightful path.

Despite his intentions Wagner's heroes seem to be individuals divorced from their surroundings. He does not accentuate their individuality and is satisfied with the indication of their main traits of character. But his heroes are not "accessible." The individuality of the Shakespearean heroes does not separate them from their surroundings, it is always expressed in communications; only Hamlet tends to monologues. Every great figure in the French classic drama likes to open his heart to his confidant. Wagner's figures are not always solitary, but when two or more figures are pitted against each other and the symphonic melos engulfs their personalities into one stream of music, they are but figures and not dramatic characters. Even *Tristan and Isolde* does not become a personal confession embodied in the *dramatis personae,* and yet the work is entirely the result of Wagner's stormy personal experiences. The passionate confessions are entirely in the music, not in the figures of the drama. They are present and take part in the tremendous tonal drama, but they are helpless, entirely carried by the symphonic torrent. At the height of passion it becomes irrelevant what they say, for they are pawns, they lose their identity, they dissolve, undramatically lost in music, in pure music. Thus it happens that the crowning glory of this opera, the consummation of the music drama, the love-death, is today one of the most popular symphonic pieces, performed in concerts without the figures of the drama, without the vocal parts. And the scene is entirely satisfactory and tremendously moving, for it is actually a symphonic piece, it is a drama in the Beethovenian sense. This is unthinkable in the true lyric drama; not one scene from *Don Giovanni, Iphigénie,* the *Barber of Seville,* or *Otello* could be so treated; without the voices they would be meaningless and even incoherent. But in *Tristan,* as in the major part of the other Wagnerian dramas, it is the orchestra which provides the world in which the men on the stage live, and they and their voices are not absolutely indispensable. Viewed from this angle, we must admit that Wagner's claim is valid, for his music is more abstract-symphonic than operatic, the surging power of his music comes from the wordless symphony. After 1849 it was no longer Gluck, Marschner, and Weber whom he followed, but that Beethoven in whom he saw the end of instrumental music, in whose Ninth Symphony he so triumphantly pointed out the compelling necessity of the addition of human voices to instrumental music, arrived at the end of its resources.

The supreme conflict in Wagner was between the poet and the musician. Musical criticism up to our day has been willing to accord to him his claims to the priority of the poet. This is true as far as the earlier operas are concerned; up to and including *Lohengrin* he was entirely under the influence of literary romanticism, leaning on what he and the world at large conceived to be Gluck's reform of the lyric stage. But as the master matured, the musician came to the fore, and in spite of the now more voluminous and forceful literary activity, especially in the form of dramatic essays and criticism, the irrational power of the musician all but swept it away. *Tristan* is an unpalatable drama, its language is often so dark and surcharged that without the music it would be unendurable. In one of the most glowing scenes, the love duet in the second act, there is no action, no continuity, not even sense or poetic form; it is a storm of passion whipped up to sheer ecstasy—by the music, which rules as undisputed as in any of the long da capo arias of the early eighteenth century, based on the weighty text "I love you." The abstract symphonic instinct of the musician lost contact with the professed dramatic poet; his characters cease to be delineated and even lose their humanity, they are no longer alive. The philosophical preoccupations of their composer endowed them with ideals but not with plastic individuality. It is only in the *Meistersinger* that the metaphysical background is not strong enough to obscure the figures of the drama, who live there more than in any of the late works. And this music drama is the nearest thing to an opera, that is the secret of its homogeneous excellence. Wagner was, then, not the creator of a new opera, the "music drama"; with all his originality, with all his greatness, he was at the end of the short history of German opera, which after his death all but collapsed in the efforts of powerless imitators. His music dramas administered the death blow to opera as his orchestra swallowed up the stage, the singers, and the whole opera. He took the song from the mouths of the singers and gave it to his orchestra. If opera ever was an "impossible," unnatural genre of art, it now reached the height of impossibility. But we must never forget that even the composers of the Florentine group in their most austerely declamatory moments regarded the human voice as the principal means of expression in the *dramma per musica,* and opera was and will remain a lyric theater in which characters deport themselves on the stage expressing their feelings in song. In the great ballroom scene in *Don Giovanni* Mozart projects the whole world on the stage. Over the general tone of the festive occasion and the innocuous music of the little dance orchestras playing for the assembled company we hear the sovereign grandezza of Don Giovanni welcoming his guests, the dramatic accents of the three masked strangers seeking revenge, the buffoonery of Leporello, the shrewd coquetry of Zerlina, the peasant distrust of Masetto, all mixing together and gloriously alive in a musical world so real and plausible that compared to it even the most animated of Wagnerian ensembles, the finale of the *Meistersinger,* appears as a theatrical tableau.

Perhaps the birth of tragedy from the spirit of music manifested itself in a much purer stage in a work like *Don Giovanni,* for this is music which is music before anything else and yet fulfills the requisites of the drama as fully as this can ever be achieved. The romantic speculations on an all-inclusive art work, the universal Gesamtkunstwerk, remained speculations. In reality they inflicted grave damage to both romantic poetry and music, for music must remain the supreme master in any association in which it enters. Wagner's attempt at the final solution of the problem of the lyric drama was unsuccessful; he retarded and almost strangled opera. But the opera's real home again came to the rescue and, by restoring the great qualities of Italian opera to their full sovereignty, at the end of the century demonstrated, in Verdi, the unimpaired triumph of the three-hundred-year-old music drama, proclaiming the glory of the human voice, of human drama.

Chapter 18

COUNTER CURRENTS

⇛⇚

Brahms

THIS chapter, an entr'acte in the extended drama of romanticism, has been entitled "Counter Currents." We must here treat those musicians who disagreed with the prevailing tendencies or who were not able to rise to the powerful main current. It is true that there are counter currents in every period and in every art, but the dissenters are usually the stragglers, and it is seldom that a great artistic personality can be discovered among them. In the case of the great artists who seem to have arrived belatedly and who do not fit into the general picture of their period we usually find either supreme unconcern coupled with great creative activity—Johann Sebastian Bach—or disdainful silence—Rossini. When the dissenters take up arms against the representatives of the dominant philosophy they are usually more convincing in their diatribes than in the art they can oppose to the victorious style. This time, however, we are faced not only with the usual army of disgruntled minor composers, embattled theorists, frustrated virtuosi, acid critics, and stubborn philosophers, but beyond and above them with three of the greatest composers the world has known—Brahms, Bizet, Verdi. This is assuredly a curious situation, rendered even more perplexing by their vastly differing art and personalities. They had, however, something in common: all three were opposed not so much to the prevailing musical style as to the literary and philosophical orientation of this music; they wanted to restore music to its own kingdom. This identity of purpose makes it possible for us to deal with them in the only manner that does justice to them and to their roles in the history of music.

Among the succeeding generations of romanticism the attempts made to claim Beethoven's heritage appeared as a struggle for the possession of a world, like that waged centuries before for the fabulous treasures of Peru. There were many who appreciated the Peruvian works of art for their precious metal only; they broke them into pieces to be able to bring them home in their small ships. Others broke them too, but for different reasons;

895

they melted the pieces anew, fashioning designs to suit their own taste. So now in music: what had been a miraculously homogeneous union of symphonic, dramatic, and coloristic elements was segregated again into its components, despite the romantic slogan calling for closer union. Wagner became a dramatist, Bruckner a symphonist, Berlioz a colorist; none of them wrote chamber music, piano music, or songs; they were, in fact, incapable of intimate communing. They were neither classicists nor true romanticists.[1] Then once more there emerged a musician who tried to be universal like Beethoven, who was equally at home in all domains of music (excepting opera) and who again knew what "da camera" stands for, what the majestic symphony, the ample oratorio, and the all but forgotten organ demand as their true and rightful patrimony: Johannes Brahms (1833–1897). Among all the composers after the death of Schubert, Brahms was the only one to bring home a Peruvian masterpiece almost intact. No one among his fellow composers approached as near to the Beethovenian ideal, and no one was able to reconstruct true symphonic thought as he did; but that one word "reconstruct" qualifies his whole art.

The great art attained by Brahms makes his works classically poised, but one feels that this calm and poise hide something, a tragic philosophy, a developed world outlook of pessimism and resignation. His soul was sick, but he discovered the illness and tried to combat it with discipline, for his illness was the romantic ill, the overflowing richness of the romantic soul. Therefore he tried to limit it, bind it, balance it with art and study. The struggle was profound and the relapses frequent. At eighteen this soul was already the soul of a man, its art a manful art, and in his early thirties Brahms gave the impression of undisturbed classic perfection. The great composer of the last phase of romanticism was, at that time, close in spirit to the musicians of the classic era as was no other musician after Schubert. His art was like a ripe fruit: round, sweet, and flavorsome. And who would think that the sweet peach has a bitter pit? The composer of the German Requiem realized the great tragedy, the crisis of music. He heard the fiery words of modern progress, "Look forward and forget the past," and he became a singer of the past, believing, perhaps, that by singing of the past he might serve the future.

Let us not read anything into Brahms, but let us notice that what had been impossible to achieve spontaneously—order in the feverish world of the dramatic realists—could be done by applying the brakes of art, and that Brahms set out to learn how to manipulate them. He studied assiduously and found that mastery could be learned from the great musicians of the preceding generations; hence his great interest in old music, his collection of books and manuscripts, and his studies [2] which are literally musicological essays. But he learned also that the taming of the imagination demands compromises and sacrifices. This explains Brahms's extraordinary sense for the past, which, like his noble sensibility, is an aristocratic trait. The aristocratic soul carrying the past within itself becomes in its own creative efforts a conscious propagator of the art of the past, and from every one of his works the spirit and glory of bygone ages will echo. In such a soul the pictures of the present cannot appear in their simple and natural colors, for the ever-present past will cast a peculiar reflection which renders these colors entirely personal and individual. Such an infinitely sensitive and complicated soul is inclined toward reticence; therefore his music does not give immediate impressions but nourishes itself from memories discreetly veiled, therefore his art is less lyric and dramatic than epic. At the bottom of this epic poetry there is a secret but undeniable subjectivity, yet its appearance seems objective. His sensibility enables him to perceive the finest in the past, and, in the face of his antagonism toward the present, his solicitude to render these impressions faithfully is unlimited.

This conscientiousness was Brahms's tragedy, the tragedy of all sensitive, aristocratic souls devoted to tradition. Moral conscientiousness is not always a virtue; most often it is inborn as one of the characteristics of the honest bourgeois spirit. The infinite pains taken by Humperdinck, Rheinberger, Fauré, Stanford, and Parry in preparing their scores was not a matter of moral fortitude, it was their very nature. They were sincere because they were simple and did not have anything to conceal. Not so with Brahms. To him whose whole soul is scarred by hidden wounds sincerity is a bitter conscientiousness; to him who carries the past in himself the essence of conscientiousness is a faithfulness and a moral obligation to the past, for the dissension between past and present means new wounds and eternal remorse. This is at the basis of that extraordinary sensitiveness which made Brahms's life the life of Hamlet, made him hesitant and chaste ("the chaste Johannes," Wagner called him), for he to whom every seemingly innocent action may become the source of new regrets shuts himself in and shuns action. If, however, he is enticed onto the field of action, he longs for his solitude as the sick man for his bed. And he endeavors to live a blameless life, a life that can remain blameless only if others are not intimately involved in it. Thus Brahms remains a genius in the mask of a morose middle-class professional man.

A great admirer of Schumann, the young romanticist began his career with compositions for the pianoforte, but among these are three sonatas (*op.* 1, 2, 5)—most unusual for a romanticist, especially in his youth, for the reigning type was the "moment musical," the small lyric form, and, as we have seen, even in the larger forms the romanticists either coupled several smaller pieces or expanded a songlike construction to a larger work by free, fantasylike elaboration. It is astounding to see how clearly the romantic elements were confronted—and almost rejected—by the young Brahms. These piano compositions spurn the wonderfully developed romantic piano style. They have a peculiar pianism of their own, and the great conflict—Beethoven's shadow—that accompanied him throughout his life is evident here, at the beginning of his career. While he endeavored to take his departure from Beethoven's late piano sonatas to create a style of his own, his labored pianistic writing shared only the unpianistic qualities of some of the Beethovenian movements. More than once one is conscious of a deep-seated desire for symphonic expression, making these works, as so admirably described by Schumann, "veiled symphonies." While Brahms took to the composition of piano music and mixed chamber music with relative ease, his approach to the two greatest forms of the classic era, string quartet and symphony, was most cautious and time-consuming. This fact is of great significance in judging Brahms. For in reality he was a romanticist and, like Schumann, instinctively drawn to the smaller, intimate forms. In his last years, after the great symphonic and choral works, he immersed himself in the arrangement of folk songs and in the composition of chorale preludes for the organ. What drove him toward the large forms was a longing for, an invincible attraction to, the great art of the German past and perhaps a desire to save it. In his *Fall Wagner* Nietzsche expressed an opinion on Brahms, which, although one-sided, exaggerated, and unjust, touches upon the kernel of his nature: "If we discount what he imitates, what he borrows from the great old or exotic modern styles, what remains as his most personal is his longing." But longing implies a certain softness, and Brahms's sharp eyes did not overlook the fact that it was this very softness of the romantic yearning that played havoc with the musical architecture of large forms, and he resolved to fight these tendencies in himself. Formlessness he recognized as the most detrimental consequence of romantic dreaming and yearning; therefore he built solid breakwaters around the surging waves of his imagination. It is a sign of the greatness of the man and the beauty of his art that this form which he imposed upon himself he learned to love as no other musician in or after his time.

What is discreet in musical lyricism may become indiscreet in the larger forms of instrumental music, and Brahms was horrified at the thought of giving free rein to his imagination or to his penchants. He mercilessly eliminated from his instrumental music all ornament and mere eloquence and was especially opposed to the sensuous coloristic euphony of the modern orchestra. Fully aware of the enormousness of the problem, the mental anguish Brahms experienced in the many years of preparation for his first quartet and symphony must have been intense. He destroyed all sketches, unfinished and even finished compositions. The number of quartets written before the three that finally were allowed to reach the printer was

great, but not one survived. The musical scene in which the aspiring symphonist found himself was not encouraging, for, aside from the bold symphonic poems and other new orchestral music, the many symphonies still
being written by his fellow composers were either breaking into innumerable fragments or, with the exactitude of an Oxonian doctoral composition,
putting all the "rules" of the symphony to practical use. Brahms was perfectly aware of the fact that the age of the symphony had passed with
Schubert, but his profound admiration and longing for that heroic age,
his sincere belief in his being a sort of Elijah of that era, and his tremendous artistic integrity fired him to challenge fate itself. The severity
of his conception, his profound faith in the great classic symphonists, and
the deliberately archaic quality of his symphonic music aroused the other
camp, the neo-German school. They could not understand how one of their
contemporaries could shun almost everything music had acquired in the
generation of Wagner and Liszt. Hugo Wolf, at that time music critic of
the fashionable Viennese *Salonblatt,* expressed their wonderment in the
following words: "The leaders of the revolutionary movement in music
after Beethoven (in which Schumann indeed expected a Messiah and
thought he had found him in—Brahms) have passed by our symphonist
without leaving a trace on him. . . . Brahms writes symphonies regardless of what has happened in the meantime."

Brahms was conscious of the romantic streak in his nature but even
more of the fundamental opposition of romanticism to symphonic logic;
therefore he was not satisfied with a minute thematic and architectural
logic, he wanted to buttress his symphonic edifice with such elements of
contemporary music as would lend themselves to symphonic use. In his
First Symphony we see the application of the "idée fixe" in the form of a
motto which binds the symphony above and beyond the logic of thematic
work. This idée fixe he elaborates with one of the great devices of classical
art: the variation. This device, or rather principle, applied by the classic
composers in the slow and final movements of their quartets and symphonies, now appears in Brahms's big sonata constructions, adding a new
element of cohesion to symphonic construction. The idée fixe is not restricted to a single movement but attempts to bind the whole of the work.
His symphonies retained the Beethovenian principles even to the extent
of modulation and tonal relationship, markedly absent in the romantic
symphony proper. He clung to the dualistic sonata in every one of his
works and even enforced this principle in the basso ostinato variations of
the Fourth Symphony. His intimate knowledge of certain phases of musical history was as thorough as any musicologist's of his time. It was this
familiarity with the problems of the past that made him hesitate to approach the large symphonic forms. The D minor piano concerto, for in-

stance, was planned as a symphony, then, as the composer felt his inability to sustain such a large symphonic structure, was reduced to a sonata for two pianos. A few years later, the composition having assumed a pianistic complexion but still showing its orchestral origins, Brahms converted it into a piano concerto. The finale, which originally defeated the symphonic plan, was replaced by a rondo, but it still does not rise to the level of the first movements. The noble and tragic work remains a unique hybrid, a symphony with obbligato piano.

His quest of the symphonic led Brahms to the sources of the classic symphony. The two serenades for orchestra testify to his experiments, but more eloquent examples are afforded by the middle movements of his large symphonies, loving reconstructions of the heroic age of classic orchestral music. Reconstruction is, to be sure, not meant here in a literal sense, for the gracious serenade in the third movement of the Second Symphony is the original composition of a great musical poet, but it is, nevertheless, a conscious and deliberate attempt to conjure up the radiant divertimento of the eighteenth century. Where other composers aped the past, labeling their works written in "the olden style," Brahms unostentatiously and with profound conviction actually echoed the past. Similarly, the last movement of the Second Symphony breathes the exuberant spirit of the finales of Haydn's symphonies. The scherzo Brahms avoided in the first three symphonies, for the demonically swift and irresistible scherzo was the epitome of classic symphonic art, and unless carried by truly symphonic élan it inevitably turned into graceful play. Mendelssohn wrote some fine and altogether artistic scherzos, but Brahms understood that the essence of this type of music was boldness and not gracefulness, and so he preferred to return to earlier types of symphonic middle movements until by writing scherzos in chamber music he learned to handle them adequately. Schubert had already felt this, for he kept on composing minuets for a long time before he dared to venture a symphonic scherzo. Brahms's scherzos in his chamber music works are, however, often worthy of the finest Viennese traditions. It is very significant that the "scherzos" of the first three symphonies are all marked with moderate tempo designations, such as "allegretto grazioso" and "quasi andantino." They are melodic and quiet, recalling the spirit of the classic minuet; only the Fourth Symphony has an impetuous scherzo.

In the first and last movements of the symphonies and other large works the frame is often more extensive than originally conceived, because the form is expanded in all directions through elaboration. In order to fill the immense spaces thus created—Brahms exhibited a veritable *horror vacui* —the content had to be enriched artificially. This is why those large movements are so "difficult to understand," but it is also in these extensions that his great artistry, his polyphonic and variation technique, shows itself in all its potency. Traces of hard work are often manifest, especially in the first movement of the Second Symphony, where additions and changes are readily perceivable. His main themes are often derived from counterpoints set against the idée fixe or motto theme (First and Third Symphonies), and while the music so obtained is unquestionably of great artistic merit it is lacking in a certain freshness and immediacy of inspiration. But where his inspiration is left undisturbed by his penchant for complications and by the willful interference of the learned connoisseur of the past, he gives us the highest that orchestral music had known since the death of Schubert. It is most significant that such passages (like the coda in the first movement of the Second Symphony) are usually filled with the deepest sorrow, with the noblest resignation, for he knew that they rightfully belong to another world. The pessimistic tone becomes at times so acute that one actually hears the strains of funeral music (the trombones in the second movement of the Second Symphony).

The Fourth Symphony, the greatest of the series, is the most melancholy and the most archaic of them. Melancholy, seldom missing in Brahms's art, is here the dominating mood, penetrating every fiber of the work. This great autumnal picture opens with a theme of extraordinary length and complexity which would have defeated any other composer of the second half of the century. The romantic tendency is present, the composer's wishes and plans notwithstanding, for the laborious first theme is followed by a celestial second subject, a lyric melody which comes as a relief and tends to overshadow the principal subject. As if to counteract the general archaistic mood Brahms suddenly turns to a bold scherzo in $\frac{2}{4}$ measure, concise, swift, and symphonic to the core. The culminating point of the symphony, and perhaps of Brahms's whole art, is the last movement, in which the composer leads us into the immense halls of baroque music. This most archaic of all movements is a great *ciacona,* a cantus firmus movement in a late nineteenth-century symphony! But the man who wrote it was one of the great German masters of the art of variation, who from his northern homeland had brought with him the memories of the orchestral suites with their wind and string choirs, the big organs of Lübeck and Hamburg Cathedrals, the robust, fantastic, and lordly art of Buxtehude, Reinken, and Bach, to weld them in his new home with the fine-grained symphonic writing of the Viennese school. The cantus firmus returns thirty times without interruption, and this seemingly rigid skeleton is incorporated in a sonata construction to give us music that evokes searching thoughts. The wonderful contrapuntal and variation technique of the master gives us picture after picture of profound meditation, and the sepulchral trombones again appear (fourteenth variation) to remind us that this is a Requiem Mass for the eternal rest of the soul of the symphony.

Brahms's whole creative activity was planned with care and circumspection. Thus the smaller choral works ended in the Requiem, the piano trios and quartets in the symphonies. After he finished his Second Symphony the works of the late period set in, rich in experience and assuredness. But even now the august precedents were never lost from sight, and whenever he embarked on a new venture he tried to find immediate connections to his great forebears. Whenever he realized that his contribution lacked sincerity or originality, or where he deemed the precedents unsurpassable or even unapproachable, he chose to direct his efforts elsewhere. Thus, unlike Schubert, he abandoned the piano sonata early in his career, restricting himself henceforth to shorter pieces. The quartet was also given up for want of finding its true tone. His C minor quartet is already plainly symphonic in texture and sonority, and the stern self-critic could not have condoned this deviation from his revered models, which he acknowledged to be Mozart's quartets, that is, works particularly "da camera" in style. The violin sonata did not figure among the earlier works; the keen observer did not miss the spectacle of confusion and helplessness that followed Beethoven's last works in this genre. Then he picked up the thread where Beethoven's last G major sonata had dropped it and wrote a work in the same key (*op. 78*), following this with two more sonatas. All of these are masterpieces, but while Brahms was able to restore the stylistic unity of the genre, so completely lost in works like Schumann's violin sonatas, he sinned as badly against euphony and clarity as any of the romanticists. His piano parts are tremendously overloaded and swollen, and if they do not bury the violin part, they make it very difficult for the stringed instrument to join the proceedings as equal partner. This pianistic hypertrophy is less oppressive in other works written for piano-string ensemble, but he was particularly felicitous when using wind instruments in his ensembles, or when writing for full-bodied groups such as quintets. Among these works the quintet for strings and clarinet is a composition of incomparable nobility of thought and sound.

Brahms fortified and condensed the rhapsodic chamber music style of romanticism, recapturing the spirit and tone of chamber music by fusing and organizing his works into an order that makes him appear, compared to his contemporaries, a classicist. Unlike his romantic colleagues, he did not believe in creating from chaos, for he alone really understood Beethoven. Still, the dilemma of the "classicistic romanticist" could not be altogether overcome, and occasionally one is plainly aware of the intellect trying to force the imagination. One glance at the first theme of the celebrated F minor piano quintet—to mention one case—will reveal its synthetic nature, for the second half of this theme is obviously "worked" and is in itself undistinguished and even expressionless. Another one of these synthetic themes is that of the first movement of the quintet *op.* III.

Although occupying a central position in his art, the song remained as problematical to Brahms as the symphony. Instead of approaching it with the circumspection he displayed toward quartet and symphony, he solved the situation for himself by evading the issues. As the romantic song grew in the nineteenth century the instrumental part gradually assumed a paramount importance, especially through the influence of Liszt's pianistic writing and Wagner's manner of orchestral commentary. Ignoring this tendency, Brahms placed the singing voice in the foreground and did not permit the accompaniment to arrogate rights beyond its essential subordinate role. It is noteworthy that, despite his great admiration for Schumann, as a song composer Brahms stood much nearer to Schubert; in his own words, "There is no song of Schubert from which one could not learn something." His deliberate shunning of the expression of a mood in favor of an unequivocally clear and direct declamation carries him far afield from Schumann and even more from Wolf. Beginning with his first song, *Liebestreue, op.* 3, a sad, pessimistic composition, unhappy love is the subject of the majority of his serious songs. He was markedly partisan to the strophic form, and set some children's songs and folk songs which in their simplicity and heartfelt sincerity belong among the greatest that this art has produced.

In the second half of the century the choric song, formerly a secondary field for the great musicians, who did not offer competition to the innumerable minor specialists, found in Brahms a composer who dedicated himself to it with the earnestness that characterized his great works. On the composition of both magnificent polyphonic motets and simple harmonic dance songs with piano accompaniment he lavished equal care, and nowhere does he show the careless voice leading in the middle parts that mars so many of even Schumann's choruses. His choral works culminate in the German Requiem, which will remain his most beloved work, a Protestant Office for the Dead such as German music had not known since the days of its great Biblical composers of the baroque era. Unlike the Latin Requiem Mass which prepares the souls for the *Dies Irae,* this German Requiem comforts the bereaved, an unspeakable peace envelops the whole work, and only once, in the terrifying unison passages of the mysterious funeral march, are we reminded of the tragedy of death.

Hans von Bülow's fantastic bon mot, the "Three B's," grouping together Bach, Beethoven, and Brahms, became a household word in popular and unenlightened musical criticism. No matter how ridiculous from the point

of view of history and aesthetics, the conception of the Three B's is an
interesting phenomenon, for it is one of the few aesthetic axioms that
penetrated large strata of the music-loving public. Brahms's art is fundamentally different from the unequivocal positiveness and heroic directness
of the other two; his musical world has its own human species, its own
fauna and flora, a climate in which the others would not and could not
thrive. It would be patently impossible to draw a parallel between the
great baroque master and this late nineteenth-century musical recluse;
however incompatible the association, one can at least discuss Brahms together with the other member of the triumvirate, Beethoven. But they are
entirely different. Beethoven resented the word "to compose," he claimed to
be a musical poet (Tondichter); Brahms composed in the literal sense of
the word. Beethoven always and everywhere gives the development of one
feeling into another. Brahms unravels one mental state at a time; he
perhaps resembles Ibsen, while Beethoven is Goethe's counterpart. An art
so strongly conditioned by the past, so fervently clinging to the classic
ideals, is incapable of stylistic changes, it only deepens, mellows, and gains
in wisdom. Beethoven, forward-looking and bent on conquering, went
through a great stylistic metamorphosis, sometimes from work to work;
but Brahms matured without radically altering his course, for he was
riveted to the sum total of this great stylistic curve, constantly before his
eyes. Thus Brahms as we know him in his great works is the same, stylistically, as in his first compositions. The very currents that stream backwards
from Brahms surged forward in Beethoven. Since the times could no longer
furnish him the antitheses Beethoven once found, he could only conjure
them up. And thus classicism became in him a beautiful gesture, whereas
in Beethoven it was fulfillment and synthesis. His tragedy was that Beethoven's shadow followed him everywhere.

Brahms was the Lord Keeper of the seal of classic heritage in whom all
threads united once more before they were lost in chaos. He fought for
form, sought it, and created it, whereas Beethoven experienced form as the
result of his creative activity. Yet this earnest, incorruptible, and devoted
artist, proud of his achievements and profoundly convinced of the righteousness of his cause, was always aware of the true state of affairs, ironically
summing it up in a letter written in May, 1878: "That people in general
do not understand and do not respect the greatest things, such as Mozart's
concertos, helps our kind to live and acquire renown. If they would only
know that they are getting from us by drops what they could drink there
to their hearts' content!"

Bizet

TOWARD the middle of the nineteenth century the fire and expansive power of French romanticism subsided. Literary taste tired of the uncritical flight of imagination, of the eternal stories whose complicated artificiality belied life, and demanded a new orientation more in conformity with the phenomena of life. Thus naturalism came as a direct opposition, a conscious reaction, to romanticism. The soil was well prepared by Comte's philosophical school and by such influential publications as a French translation of Darwin's *Origin of Species* (1862), Renan's *Life of Jesus* (1863), and Claude Bernard's many volumes on experimental medicine. It was this same atmosphere which produced the romantic realists, Balzac and Flaubert, who immediately preceded the "founders" of naturalism, Edmond Goncourt (1822–1896) and Jules Goncourt (1830–1870), who, in their own words, "wrote true novels although the public preferred false and artificial ones." Their style is rich and nervous, often somewhat bizarre as they constantly strove to be artistic. They wanted to paint human beings and human aspiration with the visual accuracy of a portrait. A faithful disciple of the Goncourts was Alphonse Daudet (1840–1897), the poet of the novel, whose naturalism was still tempered by a delicate sentimentalism and a fine sense of humor that remind one of Dickens. The real champions of the naturalistic novel, however, were Guy de Maupassant (1850–1893), one of the great masters of the French art of narration, whose lucid prose resurrected the finest traditions of the French language, and Emile Zola (1840–1902), whose novels became, under the influence of scientific and sociological studies, documents of human life and customs.

While naturalism produced an impressive number of poets and novelists, it never really succeeded in conquering the stage. The Goncourts and Zola experimented with drama, but their attempts remained mere experiments. Even in the most arduous and triumphant days of naturalism the theater remained faithful to the bourgeois drama and to Scribe's technique, and the stage was ruled by Emile Augier (1820–1889), well-meaning if somewhat provincial champion of middle-class ethics; Alexandre Dumas, fils (1824–1895), the orator of the theater, whose plays are the exegeses of theses; Edouard Pailleron (1834–1899), delightful and resourceful chatterer; and Victorien Sardou (1831–1908), gruesome but always effective. The only really eminent dramatist among all these very successful playwrights was the unsuccessful Henri Becque (1837–1899), who did not take sides, did not harangue his public, but presented everyday life with absolute objectivity and merciless fidelity.

This lack of vigor in the French theater was caused, to a degree not realized by literary historians, by the intrusion of music in the spoken theater. Toward the middle of the century the great success of musical comedies and the grand opera tempted other Parisian institutions to invade their field; almost every theater was ready to produce plays with music. The "judicial" principles of Lully's time and the monopoly system used against the théâtre de la foire seem to have returned.[3] The younger Dumas was obliged to add several chansons to *La Dame aux Camélias* to meet the requirements for music imposed upon such leading theaters as the Nouveautés, the Gymnase, and the Vaudeville. At other times the Gymnase had to renounce all its rights to musical productions in order to be able to perform Balzac's *Mercadet.* The reading of contemporary memoirs and letters convinces us that the chaotic legal situation considerably affected the artistic level of the theater. On the other hand we may notice that simple drama without music was often considered inferior to the musical plays. "We must admit that the idea of a 'William Tell' without music does not seem admissible to us," wrote the *Mercure Galant,* January, 1846, on the occasion of the production of a play by Virgile Boileau.

Still another factor which tended to weaken the theater was the excessive indulgence in local color. One of the characteristic traits of romantic men of letters was their disdain for the present and their worship of the past and the strange world of the Orient. "He needed a camel and four dirty Bedouins to tickle his brains into creative action," said Zola of Gautier, a bon mot which would seem rather far-fetched had not Gautier himself exclaimed in a letter that he is "consumed by ennui, and has a nostalgia for Asia Minor." Later in the century a group of poets of southern origin, among them Roumanille, Aubanel, and Mistral, founded a society for the resuscitation of Provençal literature. The society was called the "Félibrige" and its members the "félibristes." With them the love of folklore and of the exotic which had manifested itself earlier in the century became popular all over the country.

The great popularity of the musical stage and the predilection for exotic subjects produced one of the most dramatic operas in the history of the lyric stage, a work that towers above all plays and operas of the period: *Carmen,* text by Meilhac and Halévy, music by Bizet. The musical talents of Georges Bizet (1838–1875) manifested themselves so early that at the age of nine we find him in the Conservatoire studying piano with Marmontel and composition with Halévy, his future father-in-law. Not yet twenty, he was the winner of the Prix de Rome, and his sojourn in the Villa Medici began with an Italianate opera, *Procopio,* followed by several symphonic works. After he had returned to Paris he composed the operas *Les Pêcheurs de Perles* (1863) and *La Jolie Fille de Perth* (1867), without, however, attracting attention. The following one-act lyric work in a lighter vein, *Djamileh* (1872), was better received, and the work is indeed filled with delightful "light" music, so incongruous in the world of the grand opera. Bizet expected a definitive success from his incidental music to Daudet's *l'Arlésienne,* but its reception was icy and Daudet's friends worried lest the bad impression created by the music cast a shadow on the play itself. As it turned out, Daudet's play is chiefly remembered for Bizet's music, music of such freshness, limpidity, and piquancy as the second half of the century had seldom known, music that should be cherished by a world addicted to weighted harmonies, stereotyped rhythms, labored melodies, and artificial colors. Curiously enough, the two orchestral suites made from the music to *l'Arlésienne* are classified as "light music," and are usually performed by park bands, "pop" orchestras, and other popular organizations; the august philharmonic societies play them only in their matinées for children.

Bizet's most important work, *Carmen* (1875) met with a near failure, and its composer, already suffering from a heart ailment, died a few months later. The epitaph that was placed upon the grave of Schubert, lamenting not so much the passing of the musician as the "much fairer hopes" that were entombed in his grave, although the young Viennese master died as the mature and accomplished composer of a legion of masterpieces, should have been carved upon the tombstone of this admirable musician, who had just found his bearings when death overtook him.

Carmen represents a totally new orientation, not only in opera in general but in Bizet's own musical style. Its subject was taken from Prosper Mérimée's well-known short story of the same title. Meilhac's and Halévy's versification does not go beyond the Scribean ideals of poetry, but there are numerous scenes in prose, and as a whole the libretto is not inferior, nor is the original savage and lifelike beauty of Mérimée's story destroyed. Here we are facing a musico-dramatic work of unique force, of poignant *vérité dramatique,* the lyrical parts of which disseminate a tender and suave melancholy in which nothing is stylized, everything is presented with almost brutal force and naturalness. Here is a folk drama of such concentrated power as was unknown in the grand opera and appeared only a generation later, albeit with vastly diminished artistic conviction and creative power, in the Italian veristic school of Puccini, Leoncavallo, and Mascagni, whose model was Bizet's *Carmen.* It was this drama, swift and undisguised in its music, with its overheated southern temperament, dazzling and vital orchestra, wonderful harmonies, inescapable melodies, that called forth the enthusiastic homage of Nietzsche, who saw in *Carmen* the eternal model of the lyric drama. This homage was at the same time the indictment of Wagnerian operatic aesthetics.

Carmen was rejected by the French public and the musical world. The same people who admired the realistic and naturalistic novel and drama rejected the very same elements in this music drama, which for sheer power and plausibility towered above anything which that generation produced. In order to understand the attitude of the critics we should quote from the article devoted to *Carmen* in the authoritative *Dictionnaire Lyrique* of Clément and Larousse, which appeared shortly after the presentation of the opera. It is an important document of nineteenth-century operatic conceptions. "Bizet's opera contains some beautiful fragments but the strangeness of the subject drove him to bizarrerie and incoherence. . . . It would be necessary to rewrite the libretto, eliminating its vulgarities and the realism which is unbecoming to a lyric work. Carmen should be made into a capricious Bohemian girl instead of being a harlot, and Don José, a vile and odious creature in the present libretto, into a man possessed by love. . . ." In *Carmen* we behold a stark drama and pulsating life on the stage, but such a story and such sensuous and powerful music were not noble enough for the authorities on the lyric stage, accustomed as they were to the platitudes of the grand opera. Such a dramatic atmosphere might be accepted in spoken drama, but an opera must never transgress the code of musico-dramatic aesthetics as conceived by the reigning French operatic style; it must be "joli, clair, bien ordonné." *Carmen* will remain one of the greatest creations of the musical stage, a work whose popularity is not excelled by any other lyric drama, for it is the ideal drama, enjoyed by connoisseur and uninitiated alike. Although the following lines were written less to praise Bizet than to spite his former hero, no one could give a more admirable summary of its qualities than the fiery philosopher who once thought he had found the ideal of the music drama in the Wagnerian opera:

Yesterday—would you believe it?—I heard Bizet's masterpiece for the twentieth time. Once more I attended with the same gentle reverence. How such a work completes one! . . . This music is wicked, refined, fantastic; and withal remains popular,—it possesses the refinement of a race, not of an individual. Have more painful, more tragic accents ever been heard on the stage before? And how are they obtained? Without grimaces! Without counterfeiting of any kind! Free from the life of the grand style! . . . Fate hangs over this work, its happiness is short, sudden, without reprieve . . . I envy Bizet for having had the courage of this sensitiveness, which hitherto in the cultured music of Europe has found no means of expression—of this southern, tawny, sunburnt sensitiveness. . . . And finally, love, love translated back into nature! . . . Love as a fate, as a fatality, cynical, innocent, cruel, and precisely in its way *Nature!* . . . I know no case in which the tragic irony which constitutes the kernel of love is expressed with such severity, or in so terrible a formula, as in the last cry of Don José with which the work ends: "Yes, it is I who have killed her, I—my adored Carmen!' [4]

Verdi

THE Austrian rule of Italy following the Napoleonic wars created a tremendous political reaction in the country, already seething with patriotism and liberalism engendered earlier by the French Revolution. National thought received another powerful impetus from French romanticism, for the cult of the past and of the exotic offered a great variety of subjects which expressed, *sub rosa,* the desires and aims of the suffering patriots. It was this same romanticism which directed the attention of Italian literature, steeped in the classics, toward other European letters, both old and new; Ossian and Shakespeare, Goethe and Walter Scott, all found their way into public favor. Having hitherto been addicted to a pseudo-classicism, Italy now built bridges to the spirit of western Europe, never again to lose these newly won connections. Italian romanticism triumphed with Alessandro Manzoni (1785–1873), in whose works the classic taste was definitively displaced by an inimitably Italian atmosphere. What Tasso sought as the internal perspective of his *Jerusalem Delivered* Manzoni found in his epic novel, *I Promessi Sposi,* a work which encompassed and accommodated religious ethics and national aspirations. With its patriotic fire and the enticing attraction of the exoticism of bygone ages, *I Promessi Sposi* recruited a great and enthusiastic public which supported the many historical novels and dramas that came to be written following its unprecedented success (though most of these have neither public nor success today). Among the other members of the romantic school there were some fine poets and writers: Giovanni Berchet (1783–1851), author of the beautiful, balladlike *Profughi di Praga;* Silvio Pellico (1789–1854), whose books on his sufferings in the Austrian political prisons (*Le Mie Prigioni*) hurt the oppressors more than the battles lost; and Giuseppe Giusti (1809–1850), the most interesting and temperamental spirit of Italian patriotic lyricism. But again, most of their works can no longer be enjoyed because of the historico-political ramifications, and many of them—especially the brilliant verse of Giusti—cannot be understood without commentaries and concordances. This same period and these same sentiments are reflected in contemporary Italian opera, and it is in the works of Giuseppe Verdi (1813–1901) that we shall find the highest expression of Italian arts and letters contemporary with the Wagnerian era—in these operas, because the heroic tinge of the music does not pale even with the oblivion of the political events that evoked them, because this music is eternally human, bold, dramatic, full-bodied, and Italian in every atom.

Verdi was born into a period of indecision in Italian opera. The style of Donizetti, Mercadante, and Bellini was cultivated by innumerable minor composers, but while those three great musicians were able to reconcile their Italianism with the French grand opera without abandoning their ancient national traditions, the younger generation united the typical Italian facility of invention with the showmanship of grand opera, a marriage that resulted in the shallowest and most ephemeral style. It is the more remarkable that, after a few false starts, Verdi found his own way regardless of the models before and around him. *Nabucco* (1842), while still showing signs of the perilous neighborhood of French-Italian conventional opera, exhibits an energetic conduct of melody, a fresh rhythmic and metric articulation that were unknown among most of Verdi's compatriots of his generation. Then the nationalistic movement, approaching revolutionary intensity, carried him away. The deeply religious patriot took to subjects that in the face of strictly enforced censorship nevertheless conveyed an allegorical meaning to his compatriots waiting for deliverance from the Austrian yoke. *Ernani* (1844), *Giovanna d'Arco* (1845), *Attila* (1846), *I Masnadieri* (after Schiller's *Robbers,* 1847), made his name synonymous with the Italian cause, and when in his *Battaglia di Legnano* (1848) the knights swore an oath to repulse Italy's tyrants beyond the Alps the public's frenzy knew no bounds. The animated days of 1848-1849 saw him in Paris, whence he eagerly followed the movement for independence. This period of Verdi's creative activity ended with *Luisa Miller* (1849), after which the now famous composer retired to a country estate in his home county, living, to all appearances, the life of a country squire, raising livestock, hunting, and representing his district in Parliament.

But this same retiring provincial landowner, who spent his free time reading Shakespeare, Schiller, and the Greek dramatists, surprised the world by writing *Rigoletto* (1851), *Il Trovatore* (1853), and *La Traviata* (1853), three of the most universally known operas in the history of the lyric stage. All three were composed in the grand opera tradition, and once again we may see the world-wide influence of the French school, for the libretti themselves were fashioned from celebrated French plays. If, however, we examine the works we cannot help seeing that besides posing the question of the romantic grand opera—"Does the libretto present opportunities for effective scenes?"—Verdi remembered the all-important question of the classic music drama, adding, "Can the scenes be linked by a convincing and logical musical development of characters?" And he carried out his plan in the age-old Italian tradition, in melodies, sung by human voices, melodies which originated from a dramatic or lyric situation and fit only one specific situation, melodies the plasticity and dramatic expressiveness of which should not be approached and cannot be appreciated from the point of view of the German symphonic opera style. None of the grand operas ever attained the sincere and profound pathos, the lyricism, and the virile artistic conviction that issue from these works. But there is much more than that: there is a masterly arrangement of motives, a logic of harmonic and tonal relationship which made Verdi the true and worthy successor of the great classic opera composers and a formidable rival of Richard Wagner. The arrangement of motives should not be taken in the Wagnerian sense, for Verdi does not apply a system of leitmotives; he uses only certain recurring themes as Cherubini and Beethoven had done.[5] Such a motif, for instance, is the murder motif in *Rigoletto,* or Violetta's "life motif" in *La Traviata.* More important than these motives are the motivic and tonal relationships which dramatically connect the various details, furnishing the internal pillars of construction. The Gypsy scenes in *Il Trovatore,* Azucena's arias, as well as Leonora's and Manrico's music, are all connected with innumerable fine threads.

The Verdi of the eighteen fifties was no longer satisfied with giving every person his dramatic tone; mere character was no longer sufficient, he wanted to delineate the dramatic task of each character. Herewith he began to draw away from the grand opera and went through a veritable purgatory, the stations of which were *Les Vêpres Siciliennes* (written for Paris, 1855), *Simone Boccanegra* (1857), both in the grand style of the Paris opera with the imposing orchestral accouterment of the Meyerbeer school, *Un Ballo in Maschera* (1859), in which a new Verdi is before us, and finally, in 1867, the powerful if not homogeneous *Don Carlo.* The struggle with the foreign elements steeled his determination and cleared away his scruples; the distilled new style appears in *Aïda* (1871), more lavish in pomp and fanfare than the most spectacular grand opera, but the dazzling exterior is merely one aspect of a grandiose conception of drama in which passionate accents and delicate genre scenes represent the two poles between which the drama takes its course. Then came a long interlude interrupted only by the magnificent *Requiem Mass* (1874, although begun earlier) on the death of Manzoni, in which Verdi proved himself to be a direct descendant of the great composers of dramatic, concerted church music, Scarlatti and Durante.

The seventy-three-year-old composer broke his silence with *Otello* (1887), a work which bears the stamp of genius at its pinnacle. Beginning with the opening "storm chorus," a scene of such elemental power as modern opera never knew before or after, to the indescribably sad last song of Desdemona and the tragic end of Othello, this score is one throbbing story of the catastrophe of a great love. The old form of the opera, so contemptuously buried by Wagner and his apologists, returns here raised to undreamed of heights. And it presents us with a miracle: another *Othello,* not Shakespeare's, but one that is its equal; drama and opera, independent entities, and each the peak of its species.

Drama is a mystic duel between man and his fate, and the question is merely whether their meeting will call for words or whether they will cross their weapons silently; whether the dialogue alone will reflect the true problems or whether the expressive but less concrete flash of a gesture, the all-comprising, arrowlike lightning stroke of one sentence will become the symbol of a moment of fate. The "gestures" predominate in both *Othellos;* that is the reason for the embarrassment of the explainers, for any formula they may put forward is, of necessity, false where the matter defies any formulation. *Tristan* can be defined, *Otello* never, for "the rest is silence," for fate does not armor itself with words, it escapes from every word and is present only in the sum total of all circumstances, all words, and all gestures. Verdi's symbols are therefore not symbols in the sense of this or that "meaning"; they mean everything and nothing concrete, they are musical and not intellectual. They are symbols because they seize a man and his fate from such depths that every man and every fate sounds with them as distant overtones; they are symbols because every feeling appears in its extreme, because the eternally human is carried to infinite perspective.

Verdi remained in this wondrous opera the same inexhaustible musician that he had been since *Rigoletto,* with nowhere a paling of inventiveness, nowhere a slackening of intensity, such as might be expected in a man of his age. But to all this was added the consummation of a vigorous old age, the subtle wisdom of experience which embraces a whole life. A rich and just life, filled with deeply felt humanity, is transfigured in this unique work to an image of truth and beauty.

"E finito!" wrote Verdi on November first, 1886, to Arrigo Boito, announcing the completion of *Otello,* and the world thought, indeed, that the septuagenarian had arrived at the end of his long and glorious career by giving the world the consummate musical tragedy of modern times; but he did not rest. He could not rest, because he knew that the regeneration and reaffirmation of the great traditions of the opera was not complete. Returning to a field he had not cultivated for some forty years, at the age of almost eighty, he began where Mozart and Rossini had left off in their thirties to give us—an opera buffa. *Falstaff* (1892) is, indeed, an opera buffa, but the laughter in it is not Donizetti's harmless merriment but the laughter of wisdom, the amusement of a great and experienced connoisseur of life who had lived through generations and learned their changing ways. *Falstaff* is Verdi's bitterest exposure of life, yet it is also its most triumphal defense. With profound sorrow the aged composer unveils the tragic fate of the dreamer in the prosaic realities of life. *Falstaff* will always remain timely and actual because it is the final fulfillment of a will and desire to create the ideal form of the lyric drama. It is a brother to *Figaro.* Verdi himself has said that in this work he created the "eternally true type of the jovial scoundrel"; and this he has done entirely in music, by means of his music, although one must acknowledge that there is scarcely a better libretto in the whole operatic literature. But the composer well knew that while the drama is very important in the opera, music should always assume the leading role. Soul and character should be sketched by the drama, but they must be realized and rendered by music.

It is true that this Falstaff, the celebrated knight, hides in the laundry basket upon the arrival of the vengeful husband of the woman to whom he has just sworn eternal love. But the prose of life is gray and covers ignominiously the dreamer of beauty and greatness. And what would the world which constantly reminds Falstaff of the drabness of everyday life be without him? Falstaff and his kind are the yeast in the world's bread; they have to be kneaded to release the life and energy which is hidden in them. They teach us the love of life, they shout optimism, and the bitterness of humiliation merely doubles for them the value of the triumphs and pleasures of life. No convention is binding for them; in their own eyes they are free, independent, strong, and full of vitality.

And there is something else in this cavorting comedy, something that is real and true, not caricature but the meaning, the most beautiful meaning, of life. A pair of young lovers is this bit of reality and dream. They do not sing great love duets, they meet only for chance moments to strike the gentlest, the most intimate sounds of love lyricism, for the next minute they are dispersed by the great comedy of life. But this minute is eternity. Anne and Fenton . . . around them roars the whirl of life stirred up by human folly, but they are completely abandoned to the sorcery of the moment. They are brief, these passages of love music, brief and passing like youth itself, but they were always present in the poetic soul of the eighty-year-old Verdi, a soul eternally youthful and eternally devoted to love.

Operatic criticism, originally misdirected by Eduard Hanslick (1825–1904), followed the example of this influential critic, who thus can claim the distinction of having misjudged both leading musico-dramatists of the later nineteenth century. A number of German, English, and American writers saw in the young master a naïve continuator of the "Italian opera with hurdy-gurdy melodies and a guitarlike orchestral accompaniment," while the mature Verdi earned their plaudit as a man who overcame his errors by wisely imitating Wagner. No lesser man than Hermann Kretzschmar saw in Aïda and Otello a Wagnerian conversion. Verdi could not assimilate Wagner's dialectics, spirit, and Weltanschauung. Wagner's work was diametrically opposed to his aims; it was the crowning of a movement from which Verdi detached himself more and more. Wagner's oeuvre is closed and secluded; it does not point to any direction. Verdi's is open and cuts a broad path for the future. While Verdi admired Wagner greatly, he could not accept anything essential from the German master's style, for he recognized that the difference between them was the enormous gulf between Italian and German genius. "Do you think that under this sun and under this sky I could have composed *Tristan* or the *Ring?*" [6] Certain technical details in orchestration cannot be accepted as constituting an "influence," for Verdi never in a single instance jeopardized the lyric drama by permitting the symphonic orchestra to encroach on the privileges of the human voice, on which his musico-dramatic architecture entirely rests. There are other weighty differences between the two leading opera composers of the postromantic era. Verdi never merged aria and accompanied recitative to obtain the Wagnerian "endless melody," although he brought the two nearer to each other; his innate sense for articulation protested against the formlessness and unvocal nature of such a procedure, and he never ceased to consider the accompanied recitative the true vehicle of dramatic action, pouring out his love songs in arias and ariosi, that is, in real songs. In his last period he did not employ many clear-cut arias and tended to chains of ariosi which follow closely the evolution of the drama. His orchestra gained in power and eloquence and, under the influence of Boito's stimulating spirit, dramatic subtleties hitherto unknown in his works appeared. His method and approach remained, however, fundamentally different from the ponderous, metaphysical, problem-seeking enterprise of the master of Bayreuth. No fundamental issues of world outlook were raised; man and his fate remained his object, and everything was solved with innate musicianship and Latin grace. Verdi was neither a philosopher nor an essayist, yet every one of his letters contains observations and aesthetic judgments that are more convincing and go deeper than any of his great rival's dramaturgical studies. "Opera is opera, and symphony is symphony," he remarked on one occasion, and this lapidary sentence penetrates to the marrow of the problem of opera.

Man and artist are singularly united and complemented in Verdi, and it is well-nigh impossible to understand one without knowing the other. And again, what a difference between the insincere and domineering Wagner, always craving publicity and issuing "manifestoes to his friends," and the retiring, severely upright, and incorruptible Italian maestro, who refused a small fortune rather than make minor changes in one of his libretti. The ruler of a little empire—his estate employed some two hundred hands—he looked after the well-being of his charges with the benevolence of a father. When the times were hard he raised their wages and the not inconsiderable earnings of his model farm—he was a competent agriculturist—were invested in foundations to help needy musicians. The great modesty which actuated him in his philanthropic acts was equaled by the artist's calm and absolutely sincere conviction of the nature and place of his

art in the world of music. Yet all he said after the most overwhelming successes was "Il tempo deciderà," "Time will decide."

Verdi was the last great figure of Italian opera, and with him ends the
lineage that started with Monteverdi. Over and above all restrictions of
time and environment he once more solved the three-hundred-year-old problem of the lyric drama, of opera. True enough, he sought help for his supreme efforts, and sought it throughout his life, but the genius who made
possible his final triumph was not Wagner—was not, indeed, a musician
at all. It was Shakespeare. After many efforts he found a man who could
bring his lifelong idol, whom he considered "the greatest authority on the
heart of man," within his reach. Boito, himself an excellent musician and
man of letters of great qualities, divined the composer's intentions and furnished him with libretti that will always be associated with the best of Rinuccini and Metastasio. *Tristan and Isolde,* Wagner's most powerful music
drama, is really a great ballad made up of symphonic and lyric poems and
scenes. Love in itself does not offer conflicts, and what causes Tristan's and
Isolde's sad fate comes from without, induced by means far from being
subtle; theirs is merely a catastrophe, not a tragedy. Aided by Shakespeare's
spirit, Verdi tore out live threads from life, lacing them anew in his own
manner, through music. Being more human than Wagner, he is much nearer
to us and to our faculty of understanding and enjoyment. Wagner drew
ideals; Verdi, men. Wagner preferred mythological figures, for it was in the
German past that he hoped to find his own ideals; Verdi was ready to take
any subject that provided him with living characters and was not at all interested in the authenticity of the accessories of his plots. Wagner's conception called for great heroes. Verdi builds up not the hero but the passions
of which he is carrier and victim; his men are like ourselves, fundamentally
weak and self-deceiving, of consequence only in their passions and not in
their acts. Wagner's heroes appear to us in the theatrical glare of the footlights; they seem unchangeable, we cannot take away from or add to them,
and we cannot exchange their swords, spears, horned helmets, and wolf-
skins for anything else. Verdi's men and women can be divested of their
exterior, of their sixteenth-century ruffs, Egyptian tunics, Venetian armor,
and Gypsy robes, for Rigoletto's pathetic impotence, Aïda's unflinching love,
Iago's diabolic cunning, Othello's consuming, senseless jealousy, and Azucena's half-demented vengefulness will still remain. These constant elements
in man Verdi has given us in music, in opera, which exemplifies the essence
of the lyric drama: the transliteration of human emotions from a literary
sketch into pure music.

Chapter 19

THE PERIPHERIES OF NINETEENTH-CENTURY MUSIC AND ITS PRACTICE

➤➤➤ ⬅⬅⬅

Germany

AS we turn away from the commanding musical personalities of three-quarters of the nineteenth century and turn to the rank and file of composers, we notice such a multitude of trends and individuals that it is difficult to scrutinize them in an orderly procedure. To the marked regionalism and factionalism of south and north, Catholic and Protestant, we must add the widening gulf between realists and pseudo-romanticists, "opera" and "music drama," the new barriers and distinctions created by the national schools, the ever-increasing cult of the virtuoso, and the grave changes wrought in the practice and very existence of music by the industrial organization and exploitation of the art, its artists, and its public. The second half of the century saw German symphonic supremacy successfully challenged, and while the Wagnerian music drama restored German prestige this was seriously rivaled by the grand opera and by Verdi. Similarly, the offensive thrust executed by Richard Strauss was almost immediately countered by Debussy and by the new interest in Russian music.

Examining the musical scene in Germany we discover to our astonishment that the majority of her musicians were not aware of the changes that were taking place both in music and in international musical relations and politics. Old musical lineages were continued unaffected by the passing of generations, and curious islands of style existed even within the various factions. The north German symphonic school maintained its independence through the reign of the Viennese school. It was more pathetic-formal, serious, and calm than the Viennese, its forms showing a steadiness and solid workmanship superior to the average run of the many compositions of the Austro-Bohemians. But it was also somewhat dry, leaning to contrapuntal scholasticism, whereas the Viennese played with vivid folk tunes. The Viennese composers were not unfamiliar with counterpoint and could make good use

916

of it when the situation demanded polyphonic treatment. We have seen that the new ensemble polyphony of Haydn and Mozart was perhaps the most important single element of the new classic symphonic style, but the northerners clung to their counterpoint as to their most cherished patrimony and filled their symphonies with imitation, canon, and fugue, the learned part writing often threatening to drown the original intentions. After the triumphs of the Viennese school the northern school could no longer maintain its austerity, and a rapprochement was inevitable, the movement crystallizing in Brahms.

This naturally presupposes a strain of symphonic academicism that survived throughout the century. To us, knowing a scant dozen symphonies from the period falling between the deaths of Schubert and Brahms, this strain may seem tenuous, but to the nineteenth century this symphonic literature was a reality, for the symphony enjoyed undiminished favor among composers, who turned out work after work. Among these musicians there is a group noteworthy for its clinging to the classicistic ideals of Mendelssohn tempered with the romanticism of Schumann, yet at the same time weighted with the academicism of the north German symphony. This group is really a continuous link of composers the beginnings of which go back to the immediate surroundings of Beethoven—Johann Wenzel Kalliwoda (1801–1866)—continuing through the Schumann-Brahms era—Hermann Götz (1840–1876), Hugo Ulrich (1827–1872), Robert Volkmann (1815–1883)—far into the twentieth century—Albert Dietrich (1829–1908), Friedrich Gernsheim (1839–1916), Max Bruch (1838–1920), Felix Draeseke (1835–1913), and Robert Fuchs (1847–1927). These names represent merely a fraction of the many symphonists active in the latter part of the century, but even among the leaders only Kalliwoda, Götz, and Volkmann could interest the modern world. Some of these composers partially assimilated the technical means of expression coming to them from the neo-German school and the French program symphony, but their whole conception remained purely musical, unaffected by literary or other extramusical influences. In clinging to the old principle while using a somewhat new vocabulary, they could not escape eclecticism and their works soon became dated. The three musicians mentioned in particular, however, deserve to be better known. There is a certain vigor and earnestness in them that offsets the obvious hothouse nature of this art, and in Kalliwoda and Volkmann there glows at times something of that symphonic essence that Brahms alone could recapture in the post-Beethovenian era. It might be said, parenthetically, that Brahms was well acquainted with the works of Volkmann, who was also the composer of some excellent chamber music and of a set of fine variations on a theme by Handel, and that this quiet Saxon composer played a certain role in his musical development.

The other branch of symphonists, stemming from Berlioz and Liszt, counted among its adherents Joachim Raff (1822–1882), Joseph Rheinberger (1839–1901), Hans von Bronsart (1830–1913), Alexander Ritter (1833–1896), Richard Strauss (b. 1864), and Siegmund von Hausegger (b. 1872). Again, the group is far from being homogeneous despite the organized leadership of the Weimar circle. Its members all wrote "program music," but almost all these works were in accordance with Volkmann's precept that the composer should be satisfied with creating in the listener's mind the desired mood and impression by purely musical means; if in so doing some contours of his "action and plot" are recognized "this should be considered only a gratifying accident." Some of them, like Raff, returned to the safety of the old stereotyped form before getting halfway across to the Lisztian camp, while some of the others were lost in grandiloquence or experimentation. The fact that the Allgemeiner Deutscher Musikverein, Liszt's national society for the promotion of contemporary music, declared itself for the orientation represented by these composers and gave preference to their works in the important concert organizations could not save them from oblivion. Only one of the group emerged, as we shall see, as a real master to dominate the end of the old and the beginning of the new century: Richard Strauss.

We have accounted for the main tendencies in the German postclassic symphony and dealt with its composers with the exception of those who will lead us into the twentieth century. But we have not touched upon a peculiar phenomenon, standing, not above and beyond, but outside the times, living in a small-town clerical atmosphere, but in his soul reveling in the pomp of Wagner's orchestra, in the epic breadth of Schubert, the boldness of Beethoven, and in the baroque opulence and fervor of the monasteries along the Danube, combining, in his Masses and symphonies, the childlike mystic religiosity of the Middle Ages with the verbose and swollen plenitude of the postromantic idiom—Anton Bruckner (1824–1896). Bruckner's art is monumental yet manneristic, original yet always reminding one of Schubert, Beethoven, Wagner, serious yet naïve, often poignant yet equally often hapless. Bruckner knew no difference between sacred and secular, life and art; that is why the works of this medieval Catholic cast into the turbulent world of the Wagnerian era are all similar in content and proportion, why they are all large and hymnic. He does not search for any other inspiration than his own, but he unconsciously accepts everything that corresponds to his taste, giving his confessions without attempting to conceal his pious simplicity of mind, his technical gaucherie. There have been few artists so completely untimely, but there have also been few who reflected in such concentrated manner the good and the bad of their period.

This medieval soul living in the nineteenth century, struggling with the problem of finding an artistic relationship to God, dedicating a symphony "to the good Lord," petitioning the emperor to discipline the "ugly critic Hanslick," found an adequate and congenial expression for his mystic soul in his Masses, which with Liszt's similar works are undoubtedly the most significant concerted Catholic church music in the romantic and postromantic eras. But his symphonies from the first epic utterances are torrents of music, great hymns, broad and inundating, therefore offending the essence of symphonic thought: logic and economy. He is a perpetual eulogizer, always the same, always saying the same thing in the same way, with the sameness of the majestic river. Certain of his symphonies have no individuality, no particular mood; his whole symphonic poetry is one large poem. The church organist and composer of Masses who turned symphonist never really abandoned his first calling, and his symphonies are perhaps best characterized as the monumentalization of his organ improvisation. The many choralelike "scenes," frequent thematic quotations from his own Masses, the long pedal points, all hide the church musician's embarrassment in a field which he made his own after much hesitation and relatively late in life. This ardent follower of Wagner and the neo-German school held fast to the "rules" of the symphony as laid out in the Beethovenian era, but the chorales, the many pauses (especially in the Second Symphony, admiringly called by German writers the *Pausensinfonie*), the tremolos and pedal points supported by solemn brass fanfares are blood clots in the symphonic vein, strangely opposed to his many excellent symphonic ideas. There is a strong Beethovenian influence, particularly noticeable in the slow movements and the scherzos, but as the slow movements are all kindred in mood and tone—the slow movement from Beethoven's Ninth Symphony seems to hover about all of them —the scherzos are even more alike in their tone and technique, even though both tone and technique are excellent, earthly, and lacking in the somewhat wearying hymnic quality of the other movements. The scherzos in particular are rustic and healthy, genuinely symphonic and Austrian. The orchestral setting steers clear of all extravagance, is always euphonious and sonorous, the strings singing with abandonment, the horns and the Wagnerian tubas bugling their mellow chords, the trombones and trumpets proclaiming, and the wood winds playing their solos and counterpoints chastely and reverently —truly a musicianship to warm everyone's heart. Like Brahms and Verdi, and his admiration for Wagner notwithstanding, Bruckner attempted to cleanse music of the extramusical literary components forced on the art by romanticism; but the symphony was no longer a living force, and what Brahms could achieve with the utmost discipline of thought through a clear comprehension of the conflicts involved he could match only in certain details, here a beautiful slow movement, a bold scherzo, a dreamy-romantic exposition, but not one symphony can entirely avoid the shoals. It is characteristic of the devoted and self-critical musician that he was never satisfied with his scores, editing and correcting his symphonies so often that today it is hard to say which is supposed to be the definitive conception.

In the second half of the nineteenth century, in a period entirely given to pragmatism, to the cult of power and success, the figure of Bruckner—as that of his French colleague César Franck—appears as a historical paradox. Misunderstood, misinterpreted, and even obscure, they fixed their gaze on the ideal, with ineffable gentleness and incomparable serenity. They were two "primitives" left behind from the Middle Ages, and like all primitives they were believers and mystics. Believers they were with disarming purity and fervor. Like their hearts, their religion was pure love and pity; their God, whom they glorified in their works, was not the terrible and powerful God of Luther nor the Jansenist God of Pascal, but a God who is too loving to inflict punishment. The religion of these men was a sentiment, not an idea, a complete abandonment to Catholicism such as the world of the arts had not known since the Middle Ages.

German opera contemporary with Wagner was insignificant, whether accepting the new musico-dramatic tenets or opposing them. Those who embraced the Wagnerian ideal did not go beyond his theories, while those who recoiled from it could not shake off the vestiges of the long Italian influence and of the alluring opportunities offered by the grand opera. Some succeeded in writing typical grand operas, but few survived the decade that saw their birth. With Engelbert Humperdinck (1854–1921) the colossal Wagnerian myth was toned down to fairy tale. *Hänsel und Gretel* (1893) and *Die Königskinder* (New York, 1910) are the two best works in the Wagnerian idiom, distinguished by remarkable craftsmanship and a thorough knowledge of the limits of the composer's powers. This, and the happy leaning on folk song, assures these operas a respectable place in the operatic literature even though their effect is more pleasing than convincing. It is characteristic of the dislocated aesthetic judgment and one-sided operatic culture of our times that these works are usually performed for children, with a minor cast, a reduced orchestra, and an assistant conductor officiating.

Only two composers of opera escaped the magnet while actually living within its sphere of attraction; they were Hermann Götz, whom we have mentioned among the symphonists, and Peter Cornelius (1824–1874), poet-composer, nephew of the great romantic painter of the same name. Both recognized Wagner's greatness but both approached him with critical eyes. They were willing to follow him up to *Lohengrin* but refused to accept the gradual disappearance of lyricism in the later works. They were both gifted composers of a decidedly lyric nature, and could not give up what they considered the cornerstone of the musical stage. It must be said, however, that while their operas contain much fine music, they are doomed for lack of real dramatic power and expression. Both composers gave their best in the comic variety of opera, Götz in the *Taming of the Shrew* (1874) and Cornelius in the *Barber of Baghdad* (1858).

Chamber music, although less ephemeral in quality than the symphonic output, shared in general the latter's features, both good and bad. Still, there is an extensive literature that deserves to be better known. Piano music, on the other hand, deteriorated materially. Gone was the keyboard poetry of the romantic era, which was replaced by austerely academic sonatas, bravura pieces, or—even worse—by a bountiful second flourishing of the Biedermeier which was now little more than salon music. The best of these keyboard composers, again stemming from the Mendelssohn-Schumann lineage, tried to save their integrity by frankly acknowledging their indebtedness and then holding their own within these self-imposed limits. Thus Theodor Kirchner (1823–1903) was entirely under Schumann's spell, admitting his filial admiration in the titles of his compositions—*New Dances of David's League, Florestan and Eusebius,* etc. Yet his was a fine personal talent and his piano miniatures are undeservedly neglected. Another composer whose gifts for instrumental lyricism were pronounced was Stephen Heller (1813–1888), but others had higher ambitions and aimed at larger works. Since their master, Brahms, saw fit to abandon the large solo sonata at the beginning of his career, one should not be surprised that these minor composers who ventured into this field are now all but forgotten. Like Brahms, some of them came to the conclusion that the variation principle offers large structures without the pitfalls of the sonata, and an avalanche of "themes with variations" followed. Unlike Brahms, however, they did not realize that a mere reharmonization of the theme may offer a pleasant divertissement but does not make for constructive variations. Nowhere is the classicistic, and one might almost say antiromantic, spirit more convincingly demonstrated than in Brahms's variations. The magnificent *Handel Variations* earned their name from the theme borrowed from Handel, but the model that stood before Brahms was Bach, the *Goldberg Variations,* with their basso ostinato. "The bass is more important than the melody," said Brahms to his pupil Jenner. The chief device of the romantic variation—reharmonization of the theme—is entirely missing in his variations, always linear-architectural in conception. This does not imply a lack of variety in his harmonic scheme— on the contrary, his harmonies are remarkably colorful and expressive—but they lean on the bass line and the individual variations are poetic metamorphoses rather than harmonic travesties.

The *Lied* became the most popular type of music during the second half of the century, with legions of more or less unimportant pseudo-romantic composers devoted to its production. Nevertheless, some of the songs of the composers of these generations salvaged much of the excellence of the great romantic period, particularly distinguished for its song lyricism. Musicians such as Robert Franz (originally Knauth, 1815–1892), Adolf Jensen (1837–1879), and Cornelius were proud of being true lyricists, and all of them tried to escape the Wagnerian orbit by fleeing into one where they were safe from his oppressing influence. Franz, a tender poetic soul, never showed a development in artistic stature. His absorbing study of Bach and Handel determined his own art. Form became to him, as to Brahms, the one solid and visible mooring in the flight of phenomena. The spirit of the polyphony of the past and the modern melody born from language are united in his songs in a new organism which, however, is formally conceived, and therefore subject to rapid fading. Jensen is a likable master of miniatures, but his songs often verge on tearful sentimentalism while at other times he affects a gallant devil-may-care attitude not altogether convincing. The subtle and refined lyric gifts of Cornelius found a congenial release in his songs, undoubtedly the finest in this period, and entirely and purely lyric in the best traditions, without anything derivative about them.

All these composers felt safe and secure in their own bailiwick, yet that they were open to contamination can be seen in Jensen's later songs, in which true and forthright song lyricism is already receding under the pressure of the overworked harmonic idiom coming from the Wagnerian dialect. Realism and the rapprochement to the music drama offered themselves as a natural sequel to the general tendency in the main theater of musical life, and the musician to give this tendency scope and impetus appeared in the person of Karl Loewe (1796–1869), virtually antedating Wagner. Loewe built the bridgehead from song to the music drama; his ballads could be regarded as narrated music dramas. The ballad transforms all action into narrative, to which it ties the lyric confession, creating the effect of a dramatic dialogue. The whole received by this procedure a basic lyric character which views even the action from the hero's subjective angle. The peculiar nature of this unique conception is especially interesting in his longer ballads, which he divided into several sections or songs held together by the bonds of the accompaniment, in which he employed certain characteristic figures, always changing in conformity with the prevailing mood. This is in reality a sort of leitmotivic principle. Though not particularly original in his invention, Loewe's songs are uncommonly fresh, filled with a musicianly warmth of feeling and an innate sense for nobility of expression. While his ballads reflect a tone of realism and while the dramatic touch is very definite, this realism is always healthy and is never lost in excesses, and the dramatic never really threatens the lyric quality of the song. His idiom is simple and he often takes to strophic forms albeit displaying great artistry in finding different and often exceedingly subtle strophic constructions.

France

IN the latter part of the nineteenth century the musical despot in France was the opera, the *genre national* so auspiciously launched by Scribe and Meyerbeer. *Musique* was synonymous with the lyric stage, and no one paid serious attention to anything else. The century saw the gradual ascent of the bourgeoisie. This bourgeoisie owed its power—despite incontestable qualities of action—mainly to that tenacity of purpose which enabled it to conquer wealth and, with the help of this formidable ally, to gain power and a commanding position in the political administration. What type of lyric theater was needed in the world of these indefatigable workers, prudent, thrifty, and shrewd citizens?

After Rameau, aristocratic and courtly music disappeared together with the society of *gentilhommes* and *capitaines en dentelles,* for whom such music was written. But the third estate became accustomed to well-being and luxury, and exercised the right of the ruling class; it demanded caressing melodies, pleasant stories and plots which would help to obliviate the worries of daily existence. Dramatic tirades, the harsh cries of passion, and the sorrowful accents of tragedy and suffering gave way to the *couplets de plaisir,* and Jules Massenet (1842–1912) and his *Manon* appeared. These bourgeois wanted amorous cantilenas, and Charles Gounod (1818–1893) with his *Roméo et Juliette* and Ambroise Thomas (1811–1896) with his *Mignon* came on the scene. These rulers without a past desired the glamour of chivalry and knighthood, and they obtained Ernest Reyer (1823–1909) and his *Sigurd*. All the explosive material accumulated during the stormy days of romanticism was safely doused with water and thus rendered harmless. There is nothing in the music of Gounod and Thomas to indicate that they were contemporary with Bizet; everything is, to quote the supreme artistic maxim of this French music, *joli, bien ordonné.*

Massenet was essentially an imitator in whose numerous works one can follow the history of opera in the second half of the century, that is, the history of successful operas, the difference being only that in his hands they were emasculated and sentimentalized. The repentant Mary Magdalen was followed by a gallery of hetaerae, Herodias, Manon, Sappho, Thaïs. A more conventional love story was offered in *Werther; La Navarraise* followed Italian verism, *Cendrillon* the German fairy opera, *Le Jongleur de Notre Dame* the mystic-symbolical lyric drama. The diversity of these works, to which we may add a considerable number of others, is fabulous, ranging in their subject matter from prehistoric antiquity to the French Revolution. If we disregard, however, the titles and the figures of these operas, we see that this historic encyclopedia can be reduced to a single type, which is a sort of amorous epic poem. Massenet was the poet of beautiful sinners and sang of their love. *Manon* is the outstanding example of this poetry, the music of which is also reduced to one type, be it the expression of the incense-diffusing worship of *La Vierge,* the sensuous charms of *Thaïs,* or the reckless courage of *Don Quichotte;* a workmanlike, clever, and scented mixture of little character and much sentimentalism, an atmosphere of sighs, caresses, spasms, and tears. Thomas, with his impersonal mixture of styles, remains unconvincing and trite, but Gounod excelled in some ingratiating scenes and pictures although the Faustian is not of course to be taken seriously in his version. The other composers of opera who enjoyed a great vogue in their time all followed in the same tried path, and most of them (with such exceptions as Leo Délibes, 1836–1891) are now rarely heard even in France. The spectacular grand opera found still another staunch champion in Camille Saint-Saëns (1835–1921), whose *Samson et Dalila,* with its facile and well-coated melodies, is still part of the repertory in many an opera theater.

In the meantime the Wagnerian wave reached France. The scandalous fiasco of *Tannhäuser* in 1861 was avenged by the enslaving of the spirit of French opera. A phenomenon such as Wagner can be neither denied nor avoided: it must be overcome, that is, it must be absorbed in a manner which does not erase the composer's individuality, but rather strengthens it. If the Germans themselves were unable to overcome their lord and master it is small wonder that none of the French composers who embraced the Wagnerian faith, not even Franck and d'Indy, could succeed. Realism of a native sort was, however, more successful, for Bizet's *Carmen* produced another school whose technique was that of the grand opera, but whose artistic integrity and seriousness of purpose, if not its talents, were considerably above those of the other group. Alfred Bruneau (1857–1934) enlisted Zola's help (*Le Rêve*), but the hopes he raised with his first work did not materialize. Much more definite success was attained by Gustave Charpentier (b. 1860), whose *Louise* (1900) is the only one of the French grand operas of this period that offers real theater and a sense of the present. *Louise* is a true daughter of Paris. Despite a rather slight musical inventiveness, the old French esprit here returned to a certain extent, owing, no doubt, to a healthy theatrical instinct that eschewed all pseudo-mysticism and mere display.

It seems that although naturalism in literature waned toward the end of the century its influence upon the theater still prevailed. At the time when poetry and the novel repudiated, if not the doctrine as a whole, at least the banal and coarse aspects of naturalism, the theater seems to have clung to the original formula. The drama does not enjoy such liberty of conception as the novel. A school which pretends to substitute truth for convention on the stage may doubtless abolish certain artificial conventions, but it usually replaces them by others. Such a school will have to meet and face, sooner or later, the fundamental conventions which are inherent in the theatrical genre.

By clinging to the formula of naturalism and by trying to reconcile this formula with the rules and conventions of the stage, French drama drifted more and more toward what we may call journalistic playwriting. Emile Augier (1820–1889) and Victorien Sardou (1831–1908) were the first representatives of this tendency. In many ways Sardou, the author of *Tosca* and *Fédora,* suggests Scribe, the skillful contriver and arranger. Scribe was slowly passing out of sight as Sardou came into prominence; but without Scribe he was scarcely likely to have attained the position he occupied. In their many successes, in their willingness to suit the public taste rather than to serve any rigid rules of true art, in their bourgeois respectability, in their mastery over stage technicalities, in their frequent borrowing of material from a neighbor, in the dexterity with which they could play with the audience—in all these respects the two dramatists were alike. But Sardou was really a journalist playwright; he tried to put the newspaper on the stage. Rarely content to rely on his dramatic framework, good as it might be, he sought to set it off by an appeal to the temper of the time, so as to appear as its reflection. To enable him to combine this dramatizing of editorial articles and the latest *chronique scandaleuse* with the proper presentation of a strong situation, Sardou devised a new formula of dramatic construction. Here was a literary development that was bound to invite a parallel current on the lyric stage, but French opera refused to follow suit. Realism and naturalism continued with Bruneau's *Messidor* (1897, book by Zola) and then, as so often happened in the history of French music, Sardou's formula was realized and executed by foreign musicians, chief among them Puccini.

While opera dominated musical life in France, the second half of the century produced a school of composers which attacked the undisputed reign of the grand opera. The emergence of this school, the leaders of which were César Franck, Edouard Lalo (1823–1892), and Camille Saint-Saëns, was greatly aided by the concerts directed by Jules Etienne Pasdeloup (1819–1887). This excellent and forward-looking orchestral conductor created a veritable renaissance of French music, acquainting the public with the works of Berlioz and Wagner as well as with those of the great German classicists. The foundation of the Société Nationale de Musique (1871) finally made it possible for the newer French composers to present their works to the public, and it was thanks to these efforts that music other than theatrical became again acceptable. Since the public at large had nothing but contempt for anything but operatic music, Franck spent fifty years of his life as an obscure teacher and organist. After the first successful performances of some of his earlier works with the help of the Société Nationale, he received a professorship at the Paris Conservatory, after which his creative spirit took new flight. Franck's activity not only gave French music new vitality but largely determined its future course, for it was he and his disciples who at a time when young French composers could think of nothing but opera led them to the appreciation of instrumental music. In chamber music and symphony he transmitted to France the spirit of German polyphony, and although the polyphonic ideal could not triumph over the romantic-harmonic, French music gained new values.

Aside from his oratorios Franck is remembered chiefly for his one symphony in D minor, several symphonic poems, a violin sonata, piano quintet and trios, a string quartet, a piano concerto called Symphonic Variations, and a number of keyboard works. These compositions reflect his preoccupation with German polyphony, the best and most engaging example of which is the last, canonic movement of the violin sonata, and show also the composer's desire to build, to capture the symphonic form for French music. But both of these lofty aims were to be achieved in an atmosphere which by nature was opposed to them. Franck's musical idiom proper derived from Liszt and Wagner. The conflict faced by the German symphonists, lost between inherited form and new idiom, weighed upon Franck's whole art, intensified by further recession from the original symphonic idea. Using their idiom, Franck attempted to restore the very thing Liszt and Wagner were attacking and eliminating. If we add to this the racial antagonism of the French toward *musique savante,* that is, polyphony and symphonic logic, we have a picture before us as tragic and as moving as that presented by that other mystic, Bruckner. And indeed, here too we have movements abounding in great beauty, but the contradiction between hymnic ecstasy and symphonic flow and continuity, polyphonic-linear profile and eternally shifting chromaticism, tonal logic and hypertrophy of modulation, was too destructive to permit the emergence of an *oeuvre* that would offer both a personal and a stylistic synthesis. As in Bruckner, the organist never disappears under the cloak of the symphonist (although in Franck's case the organist wrote some of his best works for his own instrument). On the other hand the improvisatory nature of his music, his tendency to "pull stops" and to switch from manual to manual (the development sections in his sonata construction, notably in the symphony), and the temptation of the nineteenth-century organist, long estranged from true organ music, to permit his fingers to slide about chromatically, are always in evidence. Yet he has his supreme moments—the scherzo in the string quartet, or the organ variations in B— when the great issues are forgotten, when only the music speaks, unencumbered by theories, reminiscences, and problems.

The many disparities in Franck's style, its felicitous moments as well as the squirming chromatic meanderings, made this art especially attractive to the young twentieth century, for it expressed that which the declining Western world desired so much: faith in the midst of uncertainty. The ecstatic yet sensuous and disquieting quality of Franck's music pleased the overrefined aural senses of the public, no longer capable of subsisting on diatonic harmonic logic; at the same time they beheld the saintly devotion of the man, his indifference to success and financial returns, his apostolic zealousness to move a public indifferent to pure music, and his love of the faithful disciples gathered around him. Franck has been at once perhaps the most overrated and the most calumniated of composers of recent times. To quote a typical example we might call on a distinguished British musical critic. "Franck's symphony is a great work," wrote Cecil Gray in 1915. "A new addition to the great chain of mountains, the legacy of the last two centuries, it stands somewhat apart from its fellows, but from the summit one can dimly discern through the veiling mists the faint shadowy beginnings of the new range, less austere and dignified, perhaps, but full of a mysterious and haunting loveliness." Then came the new apostle, the new light on the symphonic horizon, Sibelius, and the cry arose, "The King is dead, long live the King!" and the same writer, who now held Sibelius the greatest symphonist since Beethoven, fortified his point by referring to Franck's symphony as "the unapproachable model of everything that should be avoided in symphonic writing."

We can hardly speak of a Bruckner school, but Franck and his numerous disciples formed a school which developed almost heedless of the march of time. They cultivated a polyphonic style at a time when part writing was a principle at the mercy of harmonic progressions, they wrote symphonies and quartets on classic formal patterns when the rest of the world was frantically searching for new forms, they stuck stubbornly to a leitmotivic and symphonic treatment of the lyric drama when others did their utmost to throw off the Wagnerian yoke. It is understandable, then, that besides a good deal of pleasurable music the school, aside from its master, produced little of more than ephemeral value. The leading figures of the school were Vincent d'Indy (1851–1931) and Ernest Chausson (1855–1899). D'Indy's was a fine lyric and poetic disposition fatally adulterated by the Wagnerian faith and by the penchant for contrapuntal elaboration imparted to all his pupils by Franck. Polyphony was a mystic ideal to Franck, but once we examine his fugues—to take the most obviously polyphonic constructions in his works— we shall see that they are all fundamentally homophonic, a sort of pseudo-polyphony in which parts disappear before their mission is fulfilled, and in which the excessive modulation through chromatic alteration creates the impression of linear movement. Not so with d'Indy; he was no mystic, he took his part writing in earnest and worked hard at it. Hence some of his finest lyric inventions are distorted if not thwarted by a constant desire for elaboration and complication. The neatness of workmanship he nevertheless always preserved is admirable. Chausson, equally gifted but more original, unhappily died at an early age before he was able to emancipate himself from Wagner and Franck.

Franck did not produce, among his disciples, one musician of his own caliber; they were possessed, they were bewitched by the German Klingsor. D'Indy's *Fervaal* is an echo of *Tristan* and *Parsifal,* the *Chant de la Cloche* was inspired by the *Meistersinger,* Chausson's *Viviane* and his Symphony in B flat are filled with the brassy glory of *Tannhäuser* and the riding Valkyries—music far removed from the genius of France. Yet the Franck school had great significance as far as the future of music in France was concerned. The many excellent musicians, composers and performers, who rallied around the master were instrumental in the creation of the Société Nationale, the Schola Cantorum, and the Chanteurs de Saint-Gervais, societies and institutions founded for the purpose of bringing back the French public to the appreciation of *music,* old and new. Thus whatever the shortcomings of this school, its intentions were the noblest, the same for which Parry and Stanford were fighting across the Channel: the restitution of music to its erstwhile and ancient dignity.

Returning to the other factions, we find a different atmosphere. Saint-Saëns is the perfect type of the eclectic musician of talent. His musical gifts matured on the study of the classics, but nothing in the new musical movements escaped his attention; he knew everything and used everything. Active in all branches of music, he was equally at home in all of them, for his positive, intelligent, reasoning, and precise mind—the antithesis of Franck's —always advised the creative musician in him. But his clever music lacks conviction and ardor and today is faded. Lalo's strong sense for coloristic orchestration and harmonization was decisive in turning the younger generation in this direction, a process materially aided by Emmanuel Chabrier (1841–1894), whose symphonic works, such as *España,* are a curious mixture of preciosity and an almost Russian blatancy. The older school produced one more composer, perhaps the most reasonably forward-looking among the immediate predecessors of the impressionists, Paul Dukas (1865–1935). A progressive, Dukas nevertheless did not take the decisive step that would have carried him into Debussy's retinue. He was essentially a fin de siècle artist, perhaps the French equivalent of Richard Strauss. Learning from everybody, he was able to maintain his individuality where the others succumbed to one or the other current, or like Saint-Saëns maintained a diplomatic status in the various styles. His Symphony in C is a homage to the past, but his symphonic poem *The Sorcerer's Apprentice* is a brilliant orchestral scherzo, again reminding us of a similar orchestral rondeau by Strauss, *Till Eulenspiegel.* The similarity is not to be sought in the quality of their music, essentially different, but in the striking analogy of their positions. With all his genuine artistic gifts and integrity, a composer so peril-ously situated between stylistic watersheds could not maintain himself. Like Strauss in Germany, he reached the limits of his powers at an early age, but after that, unlike his German colleague, he valiantly renounced further efforts and devoted his time to teaching.

We have arrived, now, at the period when the transition schools must give way to a master who really gave the world a new art and a new tone, around whom the rapidly disintegrating art of Western music was to stage a rally: Debussy. But Debussy was a man of the twentieth century despite significant compositions created at the end of the nineteenth, just as d'Indy, who sur-vived him by a dozen years, was essentially a product of the nineteenth. Before we can discuss impressionism—in the next chapter—we must again pause and try to comprehend a man as enigmatic, as isolated and untimely as was Bruckner in Germany.

Gabriel Fauré (1845-1924) stands chronologically between the genera-tion of Franck, Lalo, and Saint-Saëns and that of Dukas, Debussy, and Ravel. Universally admired and worshiped by Frenchmen of all musical denomina-tions, and held up by French writers on music as the embodiment of French musical genius, Fauré appears to the foreigner as perplexing a case as that of Reger and Mahler, for the world at large cannot even remotely concur in this attitude and evaluation. What the French call in Fauré's style *souplesse* strikes the German or American as verging on the salon style, even though they may concede that the intentions are noble and lofty. Although many of the leaders of twentieth-century French music were Fauré's devoted pupils, he himself has nothing in common with even moderately modern tendencies. His chamber and orchestral music is dignified in tone and spirit, but it is often monotonous and monochromic, using the same classic patterns which no longer could adequately serve Schumann and Franck, the two sources of his style. Many of his songs are, however, exquisite and masterly, disclosing a sense for lyricism that compels admiration.

England

THE animated musical life in England of which we spoke when discuss-ing the close of the eighteenth century, and which continued at the opening of the nineteenth, could not hide the attrition of the native creative forces. Musical institutions flourished, the universities continued to train their stu-dents in exemplary, if academic, fashion, and a steady stream of foreign virtuosi and composers kept the level of the practice of music on a high plane, but the decline of English music in the narrower sense of the word was complete. Only in church music were there some active figures, such as Samuel Wesley (1766-1837), nephew of the founder of Methodism, a composer strongly influenced by the great Italian vocal composers of the past centuries, his son Samuel Sebastian Wesley (1810–1876), who inherited his father's gifts as organist and composer, Thomas Attwood Walmisley (1814–1856), and Sir John Goss (1800–1880). These composers were distinguished by uncommon musical culture—the elder Wesley championed J. S. Bach's cause at a time when the Germans were hardly aware of his greatness—they were excellent performers on the organ, and their Services and anthems still echo the venerable traditions of the English choral schools. But their art can be best characterized as respectable, a kind of dignified and suitable churchly *Gebrauchsmusik*.

Among the other composers only one secured a place for himself in the romantic movement. William Sterndale-Bennett (1816–1875), admired by Mendelssohn and Schumann, could have become a great composer and a full-fledged member of the Leipzig romantic clique of which he was a welcome guest. His early works—his best—were very promising, but he later succumbed to the infinite reticence of the Englishmen of the Victorian era, a reticence which constantly prevented them from fully giving themselves to anything. Bennett's style is an intellectual style, polished with great care and in its general tone even more cautious than Mendelssohn's. The inevitable consequence of such an attitude is sentimentalism, the symptom of suppressed and sterilized feelings. Bennett's colleagues and contemporaries were all of essentially provincial stature, and the best of them excelled in music pleasing and artistic enough, but of little propulsive power. Robert Lucas Pearsall (1795–1856), after having done some desultory studying and composing in Germany, returned to England, where under the influence of the Elizabethan madrigal school, then vigorously resuscitated by the Bristol Madrigal Society (1837), he composed a few dozen excellent part songs. Henry Hugo Pierson (Hugh Pearson, 1815–1873), who also sought the heaven of romantic art, became so fond of musical life in Germany that he resigned the important Reid Professorship of Music in the University of Edinburgh to live the rest of his life, his name slightly adjusted for German pronunciation, as an esteemed colleague of the large German fraternity of musicians gravitating around the Leipzig idols. His works do not materially differ from the average output of the many forgotten German worthies, and he shared their fate. The subsequent Mendelssohn worship in England obliterated even the modest contributions of these composers, and the diary of English musical composition would have been dull for decades but for that department of music which is always so scornfully treated in the histories of "serious music," the "light opera." Opera was virtually dead in England, but Michael William Balfe (1808–1870) and William Vincent Wallace (1812–1865), although of Irish birth, brought back the liveliness of the English lyric stage, which shuns the through-composed opera and loves good songs and amusing plots. *The Bohemian Girl* and *Maritana* are neither great art works nor are they written in a refined style, but their great popularity is well deserved because they are English to the core, and are so without pretense or apology.

The decline of music reached its lowest point during the first part of Queen Victoria's reign. Then, in the last quarter of the century, a remarkable revival took place. The musical reawakening was led mainly by two noted musicians, Sir Charles Hastings Hubert Parry (1848–1918) and Sir Charles Villiers Stanford (1852–1924). Both followed the usual course of training which eventually led to Leipzig or some other German musical center, resulting, in the earlier part of the century, in a declaration of faith in Mendelssohn and Schumann, or in the latter part, in Wagner and Liszt, or in Brahms. In Parry's and Stanford's case the difference was that the alternative conjunction gave way to an inclusive one. Of the two, Parry was the more profound thinker and Stanford the more accomplished musician. The new movement was initiated in 1880 by Parry's *Prometheus Unbound* (Shelley), followed six years later by Stanford's *Revenge* (Tennyson), inaugurating a cult of the choral ballad. The underlying idea, that of setting the poetry of the great of English literature instead of turning to manufactured libretti, was new; it testifies not only to a refined literary-artistic taste, but also to a confidence in creative power altogether missing in most English music of the nineteenth century. Parry's especially congenial field was the choral; the oratorios *Judith, King Saul, Job* are his representative works. Stanford was active in all branches of music, composing operas, symphonies, and chamber music, yet his reputation rests mainly on his choral works. This is understandable if we remember that choral singing had been a highly developed national art in England ever since the Middle Ages, and its traditions never really disappeared even during the post-Handelian stagnation. Stanford's Irish origin makes itself felt in his melodies and lends a peculiarly personal touch to his music.

The non-British student of music passes over these works with polite praise, for indeed, with all the solid knowledge of the métier, the integrity and seriousness of the artists, and the loftiness of their aims, the impact of this music is slight, the product of exceptionally sensitive and highly cultured men. And it is undeniable that this music cannot become common property of the world. But for the Englishman, and for the student of English culture and civilization, there are values in this music, or rather in the life and work of Parry and Stanford, that place the two in an entirely different light. Both were men of great intellectual culture, professors respectively in Oxford and Cambridge; they maintained intimate contact with the leaders of British thought and, saturated with a devotion to their art, dedicated themselves with the wise and far-sighted vision of statesmen to the restoration of music to England. They were guided by the same lofty idealism that actuated Huxley, Carlyle, and Gladstone, and Oxford and Cambridge became the centers of musical life in England. Most of the succeeding generation which after the turn of the century revitalized English music came out of their school.

Sir Arthur Sullivan (1842–1900) stands apart from the Parry-Stanford movement. A pupil of Sterndale-Bennett, and a lifelong student of Schubert, Sullivan was a prolific composer. Among his choral and orchestral works there are many which are fully equal to those of the leaders of the new English music, but what distinguishes him from all the others and what endeared his music to millions instead of the elite of academically trained connoisseurs was the popular-bourgeois spirit he espied in Schubert and which he succeeded in transforming with the invaluable help of his able librettist, Sir William Gilbert (1836–1911), into an inimitably British idiom that typifies late Victorian times. His "comic operas" became an institution in England and the English-speaking world, but they were well received even in countries where the association with "the good old times" was not inevitable.

As English music became rekindled all the types of post-romantic composers and compositions we have met in Germany and France appeared in a British edition. Arthur Goring Thomas (1850–1892) wrote some grand operas in the Gallic vein; Sir Alexander Campbell Mackenzie (1847–1935), a fertile if not an impressive composer, was a great educator active in all branches of music and one of the elder statesmen who raised the Royal Academy of Music to its excellence; Sir Frederick Hymen Cowen (1852–1925), symphonist and song writer, captured some of the grace of the Mendelssohnian fairyland. But the nineteenth-century revival was summarized by an earnest composer who occupies a position analogous to that taken by Fauré in France, Sir Edward Elgar (1857–1934). Elgar is one of the few English composers in whose music the Wagnerian and Brahmsian influence was complicated with impressions from Liszt, Strauss, and Verdi. A romantic classicist of solid musical attainments, he is universally beloved by all England but, like Fauré in France, fails to communicate this enthusiasm to the non-British public. His symphonies and chamber music all suffer from the same mixture of archaic formal pattern, brilliant orchestration, and opulent harmonization that characterizes the pseudo-romanticists in all lands who came on the scene at a time when romanticism was more a memory than a reality. At his worst he is weighted by an overstuffed splendor (violin concerto), at his best he is arresting by virtue of impressive craftsmanship and musicianly imagination (Enigma Variations), not lacking in élan and mood. His choral works we shall discuss later.

Toward the end of the century began the great work of the rediscovery and collecting of folk song in the British Isles. Irish, Scottish, and Welsh songs had been popular since the late eighteenth century, and it is well known that even Haydn and Beethoven were commissioned to harmonize and elaborate them, but this was, naturally, not a work to be done by foreign composers. Enthusiastic musicians and scholars now brought out publications which made accessible a wealth of appealing, elementally musical tunes, the proud possession of an ancient musical civilization temporarily beclouded but not suppressed. It was this treasure, together with the general discovery of the great literature of English music of the Middle Ages and the Renaissance, which made possible for England the recapture of a strong position in the world of music by the musicians of the nascent twentieth century.

America

THERE is a certain similarity between English and American musical history in the nineteenth century. Both countries weathered foreign musical colonization, conquered the invaders, and established their own artistic commonwealth; both reached their objective through the deliberately planned and far-sighted work of enlightened musical statesmen; both gained their freedom through the road of German romantic and postromantic music; both remained partial to the Anglo-Saxon conception of choral and instrumental music, to which opera, then the chief vehicle of Continental composers, is an alien medium; and the decisive efforts of both were directed by a geographically restricted academic group, Oxford and Cambridge in England, New England, particularly Harvard University, in America. But the manner in which they established their own musical world was different. Emerging from the Leipzig-Weimar-Bayreuth atmosphere, England fell back on the centuries-old treasure of British folk song and on the ancient glory of Elizabethan art, making possible the existence of the modern school that came into being after the restoration and revitalization achieved by Parry, Stanford, and Elgar. American music entered the new century with the country's socio-political institutions barely settled, and with a handful of amateurs and some mediocre professionals to guide it. Another weighty difference lay in the fashion they disposed of the German influence. England outgrew it, America assimilated it, a fact that is only logical in view of the circumstances of the growth of the Republic.

The foreigners whom we observed migrating to America toward the end of the nineteenth century were still coming in fair numbers when the earlier generation had already acquired a certain American national consciousness. Among the later arrivals the Hanoverian Gottlieb Graupner (1767–1836) deserves attention. An excellent instrumentalist (oboe), he founded in Boston the Philharmonic Society (1810), an organization composed of amateurs and a few professional key men devoted to the practice of the instrumental music of the late eighteenth century. Later Graupner was one of the founders of the

Handel and Haydn Society (1815), one of the oldest distinguished musical societies in the United States. Both these organizations invited similar undertakings in other cities.

Then the native musicians began to assert themselves, especially in New England, and it was from this New England stratum, now free to enjoy the pleasures of music, and characteristically sobering down the uncontrollable temperament of Billings and of his music to a more dignified (and better harmonized) type of hymnody, that Lowell Mason (1792–1872) emerged. Mason was more than a mere musician eking out a living (as a matter of fact his profession earned him a fortune, the first American musical fortune): he was an educated American gentleman who steered music toward the foundation of American culture, the public school. This scion of an old American family, whose hymns are still liked and sung all over the United States, hesitated for a time to abandon the business career of a banker, but with his keen intelligence he realized it to be within his power to shape the destiny of music in America, and thereafter no amount of opposition could deter him—not even the fact that instead of receiving compensation he had to shoulder the expenses of his experiments for some time before school boards were convinced of the feasibility of teaching music to the children. Mason's record is impressive. Besides establishing musical instruction in the public schools of Boston, he did not lose sight of the necessity of training the teachers who were to administer this instruction; therefore he established "Conventions" of music teachers, periodical gatherings where teaching and the exchanging of ideas promoted the cause of music immensely. These conventions, and the million or so copies of his books sold to the public, accomplished an American aim in an American manner. The Mason family became a sort of musical dynasty, active in composition and teaching, in the music-publishing business, and in the manufacture of pianos (Mason and Hamlin), giving the country many outstanding public figures. Daniel Gregory Mason (b. 1873), a grandson of Lowell Mason, is today upholding the distinguished family traditions as composer, writer, and educator.

Among Lowell Mason's collaborators Thomas Hastings (1784–1872), George James Webb (1803–1887), an Englishman by birth, William Batchelder Bradbury (1816–1868), and Henry Kemble Oliver (1800–1885) made a name for themselves. Isaac Baker Woodbury (1819–1858), whose hymns were very popular, complemented Mason's work; his volume entitled *Self-Instruction in Musical Composition and Thorough Bass* inaugurated another American institution, home study.

Toward the middle of the century all the sizable American cities had their musical societies, around which revolved an animated musical life. Several important new organizations came into being, such as the Philharmonic

Orchestra of New York City, founded in 1842 by U. C. Hill (1802–1875).
The first program of this orchestra consisted of Beethoven's Fifth Symphony,
Weber's *Oberon* overture, an overture by Kalliwoda, vocal excerpts from
Oberon, Fidelio, the *Entführung,* a duet by Rossini, and—in the Continental
manner—a piece of chamber music, a quintet by Hummel; a thoroughly
artistic and progressive program, considerably superior to the typical fare
offered by many contemporary European organizations. While some of the
concerts, especially the piano recitals, reflected the taste of the European capitals—fantasies on Irish songs, potpourris from current operas—the musical
literature presented by these early nineteenth-century musicians was thoroughly commendable. Even opera was flourishing and the American public was familiar with the works of Paisiello, Mozart, Beethoven, Weber,
Boïeldieu, Auber, Donizetti, and Bellini. It is remarkable how soon some of
their works were taken up in a country where a few generations before legislation protected the people from the evil charms of music. Rossini's *Barber*
was played in New York in 1819, three years after its Italian, and six months
before its Parisian, première. Weber's *Freischütz* was given in New York in
1825, while Mendelssohn's oratorio *St. Paul* reached the same city in 1838,
only two years after its original German presentation. The Germania Society
performed excerpts from Wagner's *Tannhäuser* in 1852, that is, at a time
when Wagner was still little known in most of the European musical centers.
It bespeaks the common sense of the organizers of these early opera performances that they presented the works in English, a practice the later abandonment of which accounts in no small measure for the distance still maintained
between the average American music lover and opera. When Da Ponte,
Mozart's celebrated librettist, took up residence in New York, it was to be
expected that this enterprising poet-adventurer would enter the musical
scene, and indeed he invited an Italian opera troupe to give a season in New
York, for whose performances a sumptuous opera theater was built in 1833.

Ballads and popular songs were also greatly relished and a number of
native composers, among them descendants of the Hewitt family which we
met among the eighteenth-century pioneers, as well as some musicians who
came from the home of the popular ballad, England, produced them in
quantity. But all of them, and most of the composers of "art music," were
overshadowed by Stephen Foster (1826–1864), who became the embodiment
of American minstrelsy.[1]

With the flourishing of musical life there began in earnest the parade of
foreign virtuosi. Singers—Jenny Lind, Henriette Sontag—violinists—Ole
Bull, Edward Reményi—pianists—Henri Herz, Sigismund Thalberg—came
and conquered. But American virtuosi also began to find their way to the
public. Louis Moreau Gottschalk (1829–1869) measured up in every respect

to the Continental knights of the keyboard. As a piano player he was hailed all over Europe, and his sugary compositions as well as eccentric behavior equaled the best in Paris and London.

Besides the visitors, earning their money and then departing, there was, especially after the revolutionary year of 1848, a steady influx of immigrants, many of them skilled and able musicians who greatly accelerated the tempo of American musical life. As many of these immigrants were Germans, a distinct Germanic trend was now noticeable in American music, supported by such organizations as the excellent little orchestra of the Germania Society, and by individuals like Anton Philipp Heinrich (1781–1861).[2]

Music followed the westward-expanding frontiers with a rapidity and constancy that fill the student of American cultural history with amazement. One decade after Lowell Mason's system was accepted in the Boston public schools the Chicago schools introduced music in their curriculum, and by the middle of the century there were oratorio and singing societies in Milwaukee, Cincinnati, and St. Louis, opera and symphony in Chicago and San Francisco. The works performed in the new opera houses of these new cities were also new; Bellini's *Sonnambula* was presented in Chicago in 1850, Verdi's *Ernani* in San Francisco in 1853. In the late sixties began the traveling of whole bodies of musicians. The Germania Society had earlier visited the eastern cities, giving hundreds of concerts, but in 1869 we find Theodore Thomas with his New York orchestra as far west as Chicago.

The leader of the new generation of American musicians came from the Mason dynasty, Lowell Mason's son, William (1829–1908), who was among the first Americans to associate with the leading musicians of his time. A pupil of Liszt, and a resident of the Rome of the neo-German school, Weimar, he returned to America as an uncommonly well-trained and experienced musician who continued his father's missionary work by extending it to the field of instrumental music, and whose subsequent influence on American music was incalculable.

In the last quarter of the century the major symphony orchestras multiplied. New York City now had two permanent orchestras, adding to the existing Philharmonic Orchestra the Symphony Society founded by Leopold Damrosch in 1878, and there were several temporary and traveling orchestras. But opera still remained a rare luxury, despite the establishment of an institution of the first magnitude, the Metropolitan Opera in New York (1883), and was enjoyed by a handful of cities only. To the venerable old societies, such as the Handel and Haydn Society, were added new and enterprising ones offering annual performances and festivals. The man who was largely responsible for the excellence and popularity of orchestral music—a man of vision who discharged his duties with the highest artistic and cultural intentions, that of elevating the public to his level instead of giving it what it desired—was

Theodore Thomas (1835-1905), who came to America from his German home in early boyhood. Thomas ranged all over the country and left his impress on every musical organization of every city he visited, showing them the way, giving them the ideals to work for. There was a Handelian trait in this indefatigable man who met adversity with renewed energy, who was uncompromising in his artistic beliefs, and who, although hardly a composer, was the best and most understanding friend of the composer, old and venerable or young and aspiring.

William Mason's example was followed by his confreres. They went to Germany, to Leipzig, Weimar, Dresden, and the other musical centers, then the musical metropolises of the world, coming home imbued with the spirit of German music. Thus the Germanization of American music, already greatly promoted by the many Germans who had settled in America, was even more emphasized by these Americans, in general as competent as, and in intellectual attainments clearly superior to, the immigrants. The result of their studies was the formation of a group of men who engaged in the composition of the larger forms and types of music without apology or self-consciousness. They began to impress the old world of music, receiving encouragement and genuine praise and admiration from the Lord Overseer of the neo-German camp, Liszt, as well as from the more gentle followers of the Mendelssohnian denomination. John Knowles Paine (1839-1906), George Whitefield Chadwick (1854-1931), Arthur William Foote (1853-1937), Edward MacDowell (1861-1908), and Horatio William Parker (1863-1919), all were sound and cultured musicians; and if the modern world, indiscriminately hostile to the "Victorian era," looks upon them with a somewhat condescending smile, it forgets that the last two at least were the Rheinbergers, Faurés, or Parrys of America, that is, they rank with the eminent men of their period. They were no giants—even the old musical nations, Germany, France, and Italy had them but singly—yet they were fully as representative of the culture of their homeland as were the others of their respective countries and bear comparison with the best of them. Such comparisons must remain, however, mere rhetorical phrases, for the customary likening of Macdowell to Grieg, and of Parker to Franck, usually results in questionable equations. To both of these fine musicians could be applied the judicious words of Howard:

MacDowell need never be put forward with the chauvinism he hated so heartily himself. He is probably the first of our creative musicians for whom we need make no allowances for lack of early training. None of his limitations were caused by his being an American. Whether he shall eventually be judged great or small, he may be considered simply as a composer, without our being kind to him because he was our countryman. And after we have put him under the magnifying glass, stripped him of the idealization that has been wrapped about him by admirers more zealous than wise, he will emerge with several of his banners still flying.[3]

Of these banners, MacDowell and Parker carry one that flies higher and with more color than those carried by their European colleagues of the same stylistic vintage. They were the heralds of a new, growing civilization, springing from a musical soil hardly tilled, yet equaling the feats of those who had behind them the unbroken past of centuries of great music. What seemed similar to the extent of inviting comparison is really as different as the new world is from the old, as spring is from autumn, hope in a future from acquiescence in a moribund past. It remained for the twentieth-century American composer, who exchanged the German for French tutelage, to prove whether these expectations were justified.[4]

Nationalism in Music

THE eighteenth century was the century of internationalism, the nineteenth was the era of reaction, the century of romanticism, of the Gothic renaissance, of the discovery of the charm of exotic lands, of the renewed vogue of foggy, mystic, pessimistic philosophies. It was this century which presented the problem of nationalism in arts and letters, a problem which colored its whole artistic output. The large literature since devoted to the so-called national schools of music has attributed specific values to their mere existence as opposed to the "international" schools of the past centuries. A certain literature or art may become part of the world's art, following its currents, expressing faithfully its ideals, assimilating its traditions, using its forms and means, without possessing independent and absolute value. Such a literature or music may well be one of the small epigonous arts which simply swell the quantity of world art without adding something new or vital to it. In the domain of arts and letters only qualitative additions represent value, and from this point of view a "national" literature or music carries universal value and importance only if the new tones and new colors it contributes to world art are not mere local color. We must, however, make this qualification: originality, new colors, and new tones do not imply a raw and wild nationalism; furthermore, not every nationalism is able to fit itself into the unity of a larger culture, and nationalism is a positive gain for world art only if it can absorb and be absorbed. World art, culture in general, is the great concert of the peoples' souls; every coarsely national tone will create a dissonance until it is attuned to the universal spirit. To add a new tone to this concert, to give a new hue to the multicolored panel of world art—this is of the greatest service.

The world art value of individual works is not in direct ratio to their specifically national nature. On the contrary, a work of art can play a role in world art in the measure in which it represents something universal, something that does not belong only to the nation which produced it. One might add that if a work of art contains few or no national traits, that in itself does not deprive it of universal importance. Alexandrian literature was remote from everything we call national; the Latin literature of the Middle Ages was not even bound by language to one nation; the great polyphonic sacred music of the Renaissance showed stylistic unity, from Flanders to Sicily; and the eighteenth century created an international literature along French lines. The creators themselves, be they the humanists, Franco-Flemish composers, or the author-adventurers of Casanova's century, were international figures. All this fortifies the theory that universal and national artistic values are different, although both can be present in the same work. Art which is concerned with the specific problems of one nation can no more represent universal values than one which expresses a single, remote, and specific aspect of national art and life can give an account of the whole national art. On the other hand, the most intensely nationalistic rendition of the problems and tribulations of a people can become universal art if it is shaped objectively, as a type of the universally human, if it has connections with the commonwealth of men. The assimilation which leads to real world art takes place when internal form and color are national, but the content is universal. Opposed to this stands the type of national art in which the content is one-sidedly—and consequently meaninglessly—national, while the forms are colorlessly cosmopolitan.

The two values we have segregated—national character and Western-universal import—are always present to some degree in every art. In some national arts, notably in Russian music, there is, however, a constant friction between the two, preventing the definitive emergence of one or the other. Throughout the short history of Russian music two tendencies seem to be at war; one attempting the conservative preservation of national traits by excluding all Western influences, the other frowning upon the conservative and attempting to join the West body and soul.

Artistic phenomena can be roughly divided into three classes: genres (or types), works, and individualities. Besides receiving genres from the great treasury of world art, every art is capable of developing new national genres adapted to its own specific circumstances. But these genres have universal significance only if they prove to be useful receptacles for ideas and ideals of the culture of the world. Since the development of a literary or artistic genre is not the accomplishment of any one person but of a whole art or literature, and since national arts always develop the various genres according to their own specific needs, it stands to reason that such genres of universal significance and possibilities are produced only by arts the necessities of which coincide with those of world art. That is, they are either *the* world art, as in ancient Greece, or they impose themselves with the aid of a universally disseminated style to become the art of not only a specific racial or politico-geographical entity, but that of the widest cultural circle; Franco-Flemish vocal polyphony, Italian opera, Viennese symphony. Keeping all this in mind we shall not be surprised to find that such a markedly national art as Russian music has not given music a single new genre. Yet its individual composers occupy a high place in the music of the nineteenth and twentieth centuries. This curious circumstance again poses a new set of problems.

The conditions necessary for the rise of a musical culture differ in the various circles of civilization. A large territory with a long historic past, as that of Europe, naturally falls into zones and periods of culture in which some peoples disappear from the arena of music while others take their place. Such disappearance may be temporary—Spain or England—or else may be seemingly permanent—the Netherlands after the middle of the seventeenth century—and there are peoples and nations whose social organization precludes altogether the formation of a musical culture. The latter situation can be observed in modern times in nations with a feudal social structure dominating an overwhelmingly agrarian, peasant civilization—Roumania, Bulgaria—and where the middle classes are inarticulate on account of their small number. Needless to say, the absence of an original musical culture does not mean that a great musical genius could not arise from their midst, but the real market for the products of these artists is not within the tents of the country fairs of their fatherland but in the stone buildings of the musical metropolises. Thus we have observed that the art of a Tchaikovsky or Stravinsky became the cultural commodity not of Russia but of Europe and North America.

At this point we must make a distinction between the practice of music and musical culture. Music was and is being practiced by all peoples which have risen to the cultural level of articulated speech. This practice may exhibit a creative aspect, reaching a highly advanced stage in folk music; on the other hand it may merely concentrate on the diligent practice of the musical products of other cultural circles, as during some phases of English and American musical history. But folk music lacks the consciousness which characterizes musical culture—witness the engaging folk music of Scotland and Roumania and the absence of original art music in those lands—while the assiduous and luxurious practice of foreign music tends to bar the scene to the heralds of a national musical culture who grow up in the meantime, as we ourselves can observe in the United States of America. The fact that up to a certain time a nation has no musical culture does not mean that its lack is permanent. To cite one instance, the Scandinavian countries whose music was a mere colonial variety of the art of the German and French "mother" countries until recent times show evidence of the beginning of an autochthonous musical culture. As we glance back at history we notice that Italy's original musical culture appeared in the fourteenth century, at a time when England and France boasted a centuries-old art of music. One must also envisage the possibility of predominantly agrarian countries changing under the impact of historical events their socio-cultural structure, thereby calling to life the producer and consumer of music.

To define the "national" in music is not an easy task. Almost two centuries ago Gluck declared in a Parisian periodical that his desire was to eliminate the "ridiculous difference" existing between the various kinds of national music. But what Gluck meant by this term was the formal-structural differences of musical styles, not the sheer feeling of solidarity with the maternal soil that every true artist, even those whose personality is the most marked, will communicate. Shakespeare and Beethoven, whose heads and shoulders tower above their fellows, rest their feet on the secure ground of their respective national communities. We call music a universal language whose vocabulary, grammar, and syntax are shared by all peoples. Let us overlook, for the time being, the fact that the development of Western art music was the work of a relatively small number of nations, and let us oppose to this seeming universality the apparently inexplicable opposition by other nationalities to the music of certain composers considered in their respective countries the embodiment of their spirit and musical thought. Reger is well-nigh unpalatable to Frenchmen, while Fauré means little to the Germans; Bruckner fills Americans with boredom, while all of continental Europe, with the exception of Finland, is astounded by the deification accorded to Sibelius by America. This can mean one of two things: either the music of these composers does not fulfill the conditions we mentioned as essential for world art, that is, they only represent a particular segment of their own national art, or the universality of the language of music is mere fiction. The latter explanation seems to be disproved by the world-wide appreciation of that most Germanic music of Bach, that inimitably French music of Debussy, and that poignantly Russian music of Moussorgsky.

The deliberate annexation of elements considered representative of a certain nation's music seems to be an important asset of all national schools of the nineteenth century. The use of popular elements in the earlier romantic era was always a superficial procedure. These elements never showed organic growth within the work; they were, rather, quotations or mere local color and, as such, isolated. Western art music acquired a certain pseudo-national physiognomy when the musical material it annexed came from civilizations outside the main trunk of Western art music. One of the best-known and earliest of these instances is the music of the Gypsies. Living among many nations, their music reached the body of Western art music only when they came into contact with the southern fringe of the great domain of German music. We shall not now discuss the old question of Gypsy versus Hungarian music, but the many pieces or movements labeled "Hungarian" that became so popular from Haydn to Brahms appropriated these national elements in a distinctly unnational manner. If a painter tried to represent a historic event he at least attempted to approximate the costumes of the period; but the German musicians using the Gypsy motives did not even keep the costumes, for in order to be able to use freely the Gypsy material, its components had to be changed arbitrarily, thereby robbing the original material of its essential traits. It is evident that the utilization of national music in such a manner will never result in significant masterpieces, for the foreign elements have the function merely of spices. The national element must be used in accordance with what Beethoven called *dichten in Tönen,* poetry in music. But when this *dichten,* this poetry in musical tones envisaged by Beethoven, turned out to be in fact a literary element, when it became real subject matter, the situation changed. Again, we shall not now attempt to discuss whether this state of affairs represents progress, whether the fact that the content of music was lifted from the purely abstract-mental into the empiric atmosphere of the surrounding world and thus became more corporeal did not jeopardize the most fundamental powers of music. Beethoven's poetry in music became tone poetry. The tone poem (not necessarily orchestral program music alone) attempts to express the definite experiences of a definite human being, that is, a special empiric phenomenon in tones. With this the idea ceased to be the content itself; as Schopenhauer so sharply emphasized, the content became the image of the idea. Whether the idea originated in the most personal experience of the composer or was taken from the surrounding world is immaterial; the decisive point rests in the fact that music now expressed something that can also be communicated through a purely intellectual procedure.

It goes without saying that such music still retains a manner of expression that is its exclusive property, and that its representation of, let us say, Byron, will differ from the poet's. But by identifying itself with Byron, an individual, it gives up its original power, that of expressing the Byronic itself. Beethoven's Third Symphony may have been originally dedicated to a hero, Napoleon, but it was the eulogy of heroism; Strauss's *Heldenleben* depicts the life of one hero. Thus we are dealing, to quote Schopenhauer once more, with the image of ideas rendered, according to the composer's abilities, either more externally illustratively, or more internally mentally. With this "concreteness" of its content, music loses the universality of this content, for there are few universal world problems which have found expression in some concrete shape such as literature that would win recognition from all peoples as typical expression and representation.

As tone poetry developed it became more and more re-creative, communicating musically the contents of sagas, myths, poems, and pictures, the character of great personalities, the nature of great events, in short, experiences that became apprehensible realities. This course of events naturally engendered a desire for enhanced distinctness, even obviousness, for sharper characterization of musical expression, which, in its turn, called for an increase in the means of purely musical expression. And then suddenly all music grown out of a closely defined environment, under specific circumstances, won a heretofore unsuspected importance. Henceforth it was not restricted to the lending of mere thematic material but became the means of characterization. Thus it is no accident that the flourishing of the so-called national schools came on the heels of the disintegration of the romantic school, rising into eminence with the romantic realists, the "tone poets," the program musicians.

The symptoms were not so easily noticeable in Germany, Italy, and France, for the great creative musical activity of these countries was centuries old and their musical properties were always kept alive; but even in these old musical lands there was a decided change caused by the pointed emphasis on the popular-national elements, which the composers no longer tried to assimilate with the highly developed idiom of their art music. The picture is vastly different, however, with the composers of such countries as had heretofore failed to take part in the great development of Western art music and which evolved, owing to their isolation, specific melodies, peculiar rhythms, and a harmonic idiom that seems to be resting on principles different from those commonly accepted. These composers refused to follow the internationally developed musical idiom, trying, instead, to adapt it to the peculiarities of their own native music. Nor were they satisfied with the popular aspects of their native art, and unlike the composers of Gypsy dances and finales *all' Ongarese* they strove to develop their own national dialect beyond the popular and the incidental into legitimate and autochthonous art works. There appeared then, almost miraculously, schools of Russian, Bohemian, Scandinavian, and other music, causing a great enrichment in the means of musical expression; and although in the majority of cases these means were purely external it is undeniable that the enrichment of means and forms can also lead to an enrichment of the mental and artistic sphere, for by providing new means the possibilities of rendering spiritual experiences are enhanced.

The period of "nationalism" in music was a short one. Speaking in lexicographic parlance, the various "fathers" of the music of their countries— Glinka in Russia, Smetana in Bohemia, Grieg and Sinding among the Scandinavians—are all recent figures, the latter within our own memory. The high-water mark was reached at the turn of the nineteenth century, apparently coinciding with the collapse of the so-called postromantic era, as impressionism salvaged and arbitrarily appropriated many of the new and heretofore characteristic means of expression, making out of them a new international style the components of which suited Debussy as well as a Falla, a Respighi, or a Delius.

Russia

IN the modern concert repertory Russian music occupies an enviable place; yet if we analyze the statistics of works performed and generally known we discover that they are restricted to the output of the era which we call romantic. This Russian music which we hear in the concert halls and opera houses recalls the wars of certain Oriental nations which fight their national battles with arms made in European factories, and Tchaikovsky reminds us of one of those Oriental captains who study European tactics throughout their lives. He was well at home in this Western world and utilized what he learned at Saint Cyr and Potsdam in his own strategy and method, which more than any other represents to the rest of the world the Russian in music. We are further surprised to find that Russian folk song and church music, much older than art music, often appear in the latter as a foreign body. An excursion into the neighboring fields of Russian literary and cultural history will, however, dispel the mystery and will make us realize that prior to the nineteenth century music was a foreign commodity in Russia, a luxury imported for the use of the upper classes, and that its practice was monopolized by foreign musicians. It was only at the beginning of the nineteenth century that Russians began to realize that folk song and liturgic cantilena are the inexhaustible resources of art music.

Peter the Great (1672–1725) was the creator of new Russia, rousing the immense country from its lethargy. His greatest merit, and at the same time his greatest crime, was that he defied the orderly process of history, forcing upon his country a pace of modernization that was to remedy in a few years the negligence and indolence of centuries. By ruthlessly fastening Western customs and institutions upon Russia, and by deprecating and eliminating national traditions, he greatly widened the gulf between liberals and conservatives, the aristocracy and the people. It is incontestable that Peter did much for the civilization of Russia, even though this civilization cost the lives of many of the beneficiaries, but the accent was on material progress, not on culture. The cleavage between the Russian national and the Western orientations which we notice in Russian music of the romantic era is already evident in literature during Peter's reign, but while the traditionalists did not produce gifted writers, the pseudo-classicists aping the West had the great merit of acquainting Russia with French and English literature.

The reign of Catherine II (empress, 1762–1796) brought new and significant changes. The Western influence in Peter's time was somewhat external as far as the arts and letters are concerned, the tsar being more interested in engineering and statecraft, but this Russianized German princess was possessed by a veritable Gallomania, corresponding brilliantly with the leaders of the French Enlightenment. Her intense admiration of everything French was contagious, and soon the whole of the Russian intelligentsia reflected French thought. But one thing was missing in this French thought, the real spirit of the Enlightenment, for the empress was a true despot, and while demanding literary acknowledgment of her humanitarian ideals, she suppressed ruthlessly every attempt to better the people's lot. The pseudo-classic school flourished more than ever, but the French *poésie légère* did not come off in the heavy Russian medium and appeared coarse and gauche. The novel, however, began to show at least a trace of the future greatness of Russian literature. Toward the end of the century pseudo-classicism was relieved by sentimentalism, a reaction against the aristocratic courtly art. The curious contradiction in the Russian mentality is, however, sadly evident in the work of the most influential writer of the movement, Nikolai Mikhailovich Karamzin (1766–1826). Karamzin's novel *Poor Lisa* was the model of all future sentimental novels, depicting the misery of the poor and innocent country girl betrayed by the wealthy society lad. Yet this same author in his voluminous *History of Russia* revealed himself an ultra-conservative adherent of absolutism and serfdom. With Vasily Andreyevich Zhukovsky (1783–1852) the German romantic movement reached Russia and soon became the dominating literary-artistic current. The poet of sentimental friendship and love, Zhukovsky, a fine lyric talent, is one of the most sympathetic figures in Russian literature; his understanding of foreign letters and his exemplary translations widened the horizon by breaking the unilateral French influence.

Whatever of the great and beautiful had been created by the genius of Russia in the past centuries was summarized by her greatest poet, Alexander Sergeyevich Pushkin (1799–1837), whose importance as a prose writer is overshadowed only by that of his verse. All the literary men of the succeeding generations took their assignments from him, master of the fantastic and at times erotic fable, of volatile and musical verse, of impeccable form, keen wit, and critical insight. But there is something more in Pushkin's art, a musical resonance, that attracted all composers to him, and like Klopstock, who guided German music into its great classic phase, it was this Russian poet who inspired the course of music in the Russia of the romantic era.

When at the end of the seventeenth century the wall that separated Russia from Europe began to crumble, music found its way to Moscow together with other importations of Western civilization. Beginning with this period, but especially during the reigns of the Empresses Anne, Elisabeth, and Catherine, Italian music contributed materially to the glittering pomp of the court. Many of the greatest Italian opera composers supervised the practice of

Italian opera personally; Galuppi, Traëtta, Paisiello, Sarti, Cimarosa, and others appear in the annals, and from this list it is evident that Italian music enjoyed unchallenged monopoly. With the increasing Russian national consciousness timid voices began to be heard in favor of the use at least of Russian local color in these works. Sensing a possible source of competition, the Italians tried to satisfy this desire by adapting some Russian tunes in their operas. We have seen how they similarly took to the opéra comique and the Singspiel to forestall competition.[5] Catterino Cavos (1776–1840) was among the first to turn to Russian folk song, but his harmonizations were, of course, entirely incompatible with the nature of the tunes. Yet we might say that Cavos set the model for the rising school of Russian composers, a school composed of well-to-do dilettanti. Among the composers of this era only two are remembered: Dimitri Stepanovich Bortniansky (1752–1825), a pupil of Galuppi, and Alexis Verstovsky (1799–1862), a pupil of Field and of a number of other teachers. The former, fairly well trained during his sojourn in Italy, wrote some pleasing Italianate church music. The latter, composer of many vaudevilles and operas, acquired fame through his opera *Askold,* a sort of vaudeville-Singspiel which, despite its very primitive and patchy construction and elementary orchestration, was extremely popular, thanks to its many pretty melodies.

The first significant figure in a thoroughly aroused musical world was Michael Ivanovich Glinka (1804-1857). Studying at first with some German musicians residing in St. Petersburg and for a short while with Field, he then came in contact with Bellini and Donizetti while spending a few years in Italy to restore his frail health. After Italy he went to Berlin, where he submitted for the first time to systematic musical training under the able theorist Siegfried Dehn (1799–1858), later the teacher of Cornelius and Rubinstein. But the course of studies was short-lived. Returning to Russia, Glinka came under the influence of the national literary movement and his poet friends literally ordained him to compose *the* national opera. *A Life for the Tsar* was first performed in 1836 and was received with great enthusiasm. His next opera, *Russlan and Ludmilla* (after Pushkin's tale, 1842), did not fare so well as *A Life for the Tsar,* although from the purely musical point of view it shows progress and better workmanship. The disappointed composer again sought the company of great musicians abroad. In Paris he and Berlioz showed a warm admiration for each other's music, and his association with the French program symphonist was bound to result in symphonic works, of which *Kamarinskaya* is a notable example. Back again in Russia, Glinka's new operatic plans went awry and his last years were spent in a growing uncertainty as to the rightful idiom of Russian national music.

In Glinka Russian folk music became fertile. The pseudo-folklike quality of the music of the early nineteenth century does not entirely disappear in his works, but it is nevertheless superseded by a romantic, popular-national tone that has a certain strength of style. It would be a mistake to think that he invented a new form of opera, for he simply accepted the classic and early grand opera with its arias and choruses, but he filled them with his spirit and the spirit of his country. It is very significant, however, that in his works he harmonized the Russian folk songs and folk song-like material by pure instinct without being able to find a theoretical key to his procedure. His death came during his search for a solution of his problems, a search that had carried him back to Dehn in Berlin. Glinka's vocal works, operas, songs, and church music, are considerably superior to his instrumental compositions, although the confessed admirer of Berlioz was well versed in orchestration; but the instrumental works, with a few exceptions such as *Kamarinskaya,* present the cosmopolitan classic-romantic mixture of styles practiced by all minor composers of Europe and America.

Glinka's faithful brother-in-arms, Alexander Sergeyevich Dargomijsky (1813–1869), was the other outstanding figure of this generation of Russian composers; in fact, the two musicians constitute the school. This entirely untaught amateur was at first immersed in Italo-French opera, and his first stage work, *Esmeralda* (composed in 1839), owes everything to Rossini and Auber, while Hugo's *Notre-Dame de Paris,* the source of his libretto, could hardly impart a Russian atmosphere. Dargomijsky's subsequent friendship with Glinka converted him to the national cause, and the older composer lent him his notebooks containing the results of his studies with Dehn, Dargomijsky's only source of instruction, thus acquainting him with the technical aspects of his chosen vocation. Dargomijsky offers the extreme example of the sterilizing effect of the uncritical espousal of foreign tenets, in this case the one form of vocal music that invariably baffled all non-Italian composers, the recitative. In his later works, notably in his operas *Russalka* and *The Stone Guest* (Don Juan), the purely musical element is totally submerged in abstract dramaturgical doctrines and the lyric drama emerges as a forbidding new *stile recitativo* of arid monotony, even though this recitative occasionally reaches remarkable pregnancy. Of a much more engaging nature are his songs, admired and beloved throughout Russia.

"The music of coachmen" was the verdict of the fashionable opera-going society on that memorable December day in 1836 when Glinka's *Life for the Tsar* was first performed. A few years later even the aristocracy and the literati shared the opinion of the populace that this work represented the beginnings of a national art music in Russia; they realized that there is "national truth" in music and heeded Turgenev's warning that they must bow to this truth, which is nothing but the self-esteem of a racial-ethnic entity and the belief in its vocation to develop into an independent cultural force. It was through national pride that Borodin, berating the circumstances which made Russians and Russian musicians appear in the world's eyes as mere consumers, now counseled against changing the consumers into producers by simply adjusting their musical output to Western patterns. "We are self-sufficient," he said, meaning that this new Russian music should be addressed to Russians only. What now took place in music was again a residue and corollary of the literary movement which had split between a Slavophile and a Western school. The former, embracing partly conservative, partly democratic ideals, searched for the true type of an independent national culture yet at the same time idealized the Muscovite past and advocated Russian Messianism. It hated the West and idolized the *moujik,* the Russian peasant, as the source of all earthly wisdom and goodness. The greatest exponents of this school were Alexander Nikolayevich Ostrovski (1823–1886), a powerful dramatist, Feodor Ivanovich Tyutchev (1803–1873), zealous apostle of the unshorn power of the Tsar and a poet the Russians hold second only to Pushkin, and Feodor Mikhailovich Dostoyevsky (1821–1881), the novelist whose compassion and pity for the sufferings of his people created those demon-possessed or angelic personalities which are the wonder of modern world literature. The Western school, on the other hand, was convinced that Byzantine-Slavic civilization was no longer capable of development and must therefore be abandoned for the culture of the West. Its chief representatives were Nikolai Alekseyevich Nekrasov (1821–1878), poet and editor of the leading Russian literary magazine of this time, Ivan Sergeyevich Turgenev (1813–1883), the famed author of *Fathers and Sons,* and Ivan Aleksandrovich Goncharov (1812–1891), the keen-eyed painter of the indolence of the Russian gentry. The two schools influenced each other mutually and in a sense their products were complementary. These great literary men gave a faithful picture of their Russia in all her cultural oscillations, surpassing in their powerful realism and characterization anything the West could offer.

The new Russian music came in the wake of the socio-cultural orientation set by literature and similarly resolved into two groups, one pan-Slavic and nationalistic, the other dedicated to Western musical rapprochement. The great popularity of Russian music with Western audiences can be ascribed to the cosmopolitan school, the first apostle of which was Alexander Serov (1820–1871), an enthusiastic follower of Wagner, who curiously succeeded in writing music that does not show an atom of Wagnerian influence but was rather akin to the Meyerbeer type of spectacular grand opera. As if to emphasize the Western orientation and the knowledge of the métier it involved, the musicians belonging to this group exhibited a conscious academicism which, indeed, stood in contrast to the essential dilettantism of the nationalist school Anton Rubinstein (1829–1894) and Peter Ilich Tchaikovsky (1840–1893) were the leading figures in the Western school. Rubinstein, a brilliant pianist but an entirely imitative follower of the Leipzig circle of Mendelssohn and Schumann, hardly deserves the title "Russian composer," but his activity on behalf of music in Russia, including his founding of conservatories, was responsible for the wide dissemination of music and the subsequent excellence of musical institutions in his vast country. The first significant pupil of Rubinstein's St. Petersburg Conservatory, and Russia's first full-fledged "professional" composer, was, then, Tchaikovsky.

This composer, who in his first symphonies was totally unable to find the symphonic tone—his works in the lighter vein are far more successful from the stylistic point of view—ended his career with two symphonies which in popularity rival those of Beethoven. His artistic development in the latter part of his life was remarkable and compels admiration. The Fourth Symphony is still largely antisymphonic. While some of its thematic material is engaging and well presented and the orchestration is interesting throughout, there is no trace of development in the symphonic sense, but merely a succession of repetitions and a sequence of climactic runs that often become hysterical. The slow movement has one of Tchaikovsky's typical songlike melodies, presented with dignity and simplicity; the scherzo fascinates with its clever orchestration, but all the good is lost in the coarse band music of the last movement, swelling an innocent Russian dance tune into a wild Sarmatian bedlam. But the Fifth and Sixth Symphonies show an astounding growth in his stature as a composer. The "sonata" themes are more compact and the primitive Russian repetition and variation technique is supplanted by a more organic fabric. The *Pathétique* Symphony, especially its lyric "theme song," is perhaps the most sure-fire piece of symphonic music ever composed. The fact that the otherwise remarkable, remarkable in Russian music, symphonic treatment which precedes the appearance of this theme is simply wiped from the listeners' memory and experience until it is brought back forcibly and with violence, thus destroying symphonic thought and plan, is forgotten in the stream of melancholy-sensuous sentiment that pours out warmly from the frenetic strings massed into one broad melody. The second movement shows the best side of Tchaikovsky's innate musicianship and craftsmanship, for it succeeds not only in maintaining the somewhat unusual ⁵⁄₄ measure throughout, seldom accomplished without the appearance of a tour de force, but in making the hearer unaware of the presence of the Russian repetition technique which takes the place of development. Every theme and motif is repeated time after time with little change, yet the composer succeeds in giving the impression of bona fide variations, largely through his masterful orchestration. Indeed, his handling of the orchestra is in general remarkable, ranging from delightful and caressant filigree work to blatant mass effects. It is undeniable that the latter, the perfect vehicle for modern conductorial extravagance, is the strongest factor in his great popularity with Western audiences.

Tchaikovsky does not belong in the company of the great of music; to call him the "modern Russian Beethoven" is footless, Beethoven being patently neither modern nor Russian—but neither can he be lightly dismissed. Russia never had a musician of stature who was more thoroughly international. The nation forms part of the external world, it is a concrete fact and in a sense a restriction; Tchaikovsky's music is divorced from this external reality, it is abstract and generalized. That is why he cannot be held up as a Russian composer par excellence as opposed to those "unpatriotic" writers and musicians whose main subject was the excoriation of the weaknesses of their nation. With all their denunciation of Russia, the latter are truly national artists because their feelings originated from the circumstances of Russian life. Tchaikovsky's feelings have no bearing on the external (that is, national) world. Artistic imagination and language are, however, the mirror of the relationship existing between the creative artist and the external world, from which it follows that Tchaikovsky's imagination, though brilliant, is rather restricted and one-sided. Yet his musical language, while cosmopolitan in technique, is not lacking in individuality, as is Rimsky-Korsakov's; on the contrary, it expresses a powerful individuality with abstract but brilliant accents, with pictures that are not colorful but shining. This language is not pictorial but it is intense, it is not imaginative but persuasive, it is rather uniform, without a national or picturesque hue, molded in cosmopolitan form, but it can be soaring, burning, and full of élan. Only occasionally, under the spell of a terrifying mood, does he find more forceful expression and more variety, but even then these moods do not assume the strength of pictures. His musical versification is hymnic, swollen, and uniform, like Milton's, one might say, if the comparison of values did not immediately invalidate the simile.

And yet Tchaikovsky is thoroughly Russian in the less tangible aspects of nationalism; in the tearful sentimentalism of his melancholy, from which he can pass without warning into the most gross and brutal gaudiness. It is perhaps characteristic that although entirely under German-French influence he avoided Wagner and even Brahms, while he was strongly attracted to the classicistic romanticists of the Mendelssohn circle and to the sentimental wing of the French school. The Russian in Tchaikovsky is not to be credited to the many Russian themes and motives used in his works, but to the indecision in his artistic character, to the hesitancy between mood and purpose which characterizes even his most mature works. A good example of this weakness in his artistic personality can be found in the famous third movement of the *Pathétique* Symphony, a remarkable combination of scherzo and march which makes for an exciting piece written with considerable virtuosity. But no amount of artistry can entirely cover the underlying idea, fundamentally undecided and undistinguished, neither pathetic nor heroic. The movement's effect is, nevertheless, electrifying. This movement epitomizes his whole art, for the same can be said of his other major works; the rousing piano concerto in B flat, pouring out the typical frenetic unison melodies at the very start while the piano is pounding away impatiently until its turn comes; the violin concerto, vacillating between sensuous cantilena and offensively vulgar ornament; the ballets and suites, on the whole thoroughly enjoyable because of the restraint the composer imposed upon his orchestra and his vocabulary; and the symphonic poems or program overtures, noisy and hysterical beyond measure. These are all the works of a tragically perturbed soul, deeply stirred yet curiously bombastic, sincere yet overwrought, lacking the strength that is the result of artistic discipline, but withal musician to the core.

The other school, which, unlike Tchaikovsky's, spurned the great musical heritage of the West, at least in theory, descended partly from that naturalism which appeared in literature with Gogol and in music with Dargomijsky, partly from the pan-Slavic movement already foreshadowed by Glinka. The five musicians banded together in St. Petersburg comprised a curious group. Mili Alekseyevich Balakirev (1837–1910) was the mentor, organizer, and teacher of the others: Alexander Porfirevich Borodin (1834–1887), professor of chemistry in the medical academy, Modest Petrovich Moussorgsky (1839–1881), army officer, Nikolai Andreyevich Rimsky-Korsakov (1844–1908), naval officer, and César Antonovich Cui (1835–1918), a military engineer. Balakirev, although self-taught like the rest of the school, was the only one of them who possessed the semblance of a professional knowledge of music, perhaps the only reason for his presence in the group, since creatively he was little more than a salon composer, as was Cui, curiously untouched by the national melos, and, despite the avowed aims of the group, playing with French imitations. Still, the genuine enthusiasm of Balakirev, as well as his initial instruction, was responsible for the careers of the other musicians, who ultimately surpassed him but who always regarded him affectionately as their erstwhile teacher. Although still obviously an amateur in the noblest sense of the word, Borodin's is a much more arresting personality. Of his rather modest musical output—he was also the author of important chemical treatises—two symphonies, two quartets, one opera, and a symphonic sketch, together with a few songs and smaller pieces, acquired wide popularity. The early symphony and quartet surprise mainly by their sheer existence, that they could have been composed by a man barely familiar with the rudiments of composition. The later works, especially the opera *Prince Igor,* are at times beguiling, especially the fresh melodies and powerful choral scenes. Perhaps the most popular among Borodin's works is the symphonic sketch *In the Steppes of Central Asia,* which fascinates with its impressionistic harmonic and orchestral idiom, placing its composer, as it were, between Liszt and Debussy.

Borodin is the third member of the nationalist school whose whole equipment seems to be Western and who, although opposed to the other camp, could assert their nationalism only in local color. The situation does not change with the fourth, a celebrated and accomplished member of the "Five." Although he too took the field with the slogan of Russian national music, it is only the beautiful fables that Rimsky-Korsakov set to music that are truly and exclusively Russian in spirit; his music cannot even bear comparison with the spirit of this engaging literature and with the great writers who graced the world's literature with their Russian contributions. Rimsky's soul was not occupied by the somber and fateful shadows of the tragedy of his people; the eternal and mysterious *active* forces that are at the bottom of the Russian soul and which agitated a Moussorgsky or Dostoyevsky were unknown to him, who leaned rather toward the passive, storytelling nature of the Russian, always colorful, but always devoid of problems. This type of imagination, which does not find its inspiration in true life, which perhaps is afraid of it because it knows that it could not respond to its exigencies, always flees into the world of the fabulous. All the color, pomp, and lulling intoxication of the Slavic fairy world return in the scintillating, phosphorescent, often sensuously opulent orchestral and operatic works of Rimsky-Korsakov, but the color and élan is that of the picture books which grownups read with such pleasure to their children, but which without the enraptured listeners lose their spell. What paucity of ideas and feelings, aside from the folk tunes, in the most fetching of his orchestral poems, *Scheherazade*—it reminded Debussy "more of a bazaar than the Orient"—what grand opera pose and trick in *Coq d'Or!* And if the beguiling apparatus of the storyteller, the orchestra, is taken away there is a complete collapse. Rimsky's chamber music and other works for intimate ensembles or solo instruments are not within the realm of serious music; they might be taken for the works of an unpromising beginner.

And thus we come to the last member of the group. Moussorgsky is the founder of modern musical realism and naturalism, but we must not take these terms in too narrow a sense, for while his ability to convey "dramatic truth" is overpowering in its directness, he sought this dramatic truth in the poetry of the human soul. The blind and fatal forces of life are so real and menacing in Moussorgsky's world because these crushing and unbridled forces lived in his creatures and were not merely pleasant Russian tunes arranged in nice bouquets as with his fellow members of the "Five." Like Wagner, Moussorgsky was a psychologist, but unlike the German, who attempted to seize the active forces of the human soul in an artistic unity, he, like his great literary colleagues Gogol and Dostoyevsky, was attracted to the forces and passions smoldering formlessly at the bottom of the human soul. These forces and passions seldom or never take an active form, yet they often steer a human life to ruin. It was the rendition of these formless instincts which led Moussorgsky into spheres where no other Russian musician, only their great writers, could follow; spheres where the elemental passions of man flourish with miraculous clarity and immediacy, where they are not veiled or falsified. The approaches to such worlds lead through the children and the people, and through them to humor and to nature, all of which Moussorgsky knew intimately. *Boris Godunov* is the greatest musico-dramatic masterpiece of Eastern Europe. It is not merely a tragedy of conscience but the universal tragedy of the Russian people cast in a musical folk drama. Moussorgsky penetrated into the spirit of his people with an elemental, fatelike force, conjuring up the problems of both the masses (the choruses in *Boris*) and the individuals (the songs) with a freedom and intensity of expression denied to all other Russian composers. That is what made this "dilettante," experimental composer, whose large works were all finished, reorchestrated, or otherwise completed by Cui, Rimsky, and others, the greatest musical genius of Russia.

Russian literary and artistic life took its beginnings with the Christianization of the eastern Slavs toward the end of the first millennium. The new cultural movement started under the aegis of the gospel, and no matter what excesses it witnessed during its course, the spirit of charity, of defending the helpless and consoling the bereaved, and the denunciation of tyranny and vice which characterize Russian literature are directly attributable to this early phase of Slavic civilization. The great Russian writers took up the struggle with the forces of darkness; they bared their hearts, and read the Gospels while awaiting execution. They proved that suffering is also a gift of God, that we need it to cleanse our souls. They depicted the beast and the angel in the human, and their pity tried to redeem the former. They believed intensely in their mission and even in their aberrations—Tolstoy condemned not only modern civilization but even the cult of the beautiful—they showed the mistakes of genius. They seldom arrived at a definite philosophical outlook, but on the other hand they never abandoned the search. Above all, they were always consummate artists.

With the exception of Moussorgsky, there is no trace of this spirit in Russian music. It was not that the Russians lacked musical gifts, all the Slavic nations are proverbially musical, but their musical gifts were first exploited at a late date and with a suddenness that caught them unawares. Their musical necessities did not correspond with the necessities of a world art, and the cause of their young art was impaired when it established contact with the dying Western romantic movement which they took for a nascent era. The hotbed of every musical culture is intimate music, chamber or vocal, played in the home. It was on the madrigal, motet, consort, on the lute and harpsichord suites, on the ayres and songs that our tremendous musical literature of recent centuries was built; the Russians started with symphony and opera. Yet even these had long passed their heroic age when the Russians discovered them; Rimsky-Korsakov's First Symphony, the first Russian symphony, was composed in 1864. Modeling their own on the late romantic symphony, they shared the inconsistencies of a type of music that carried on an inherited form which could no longer adequately serve their idiom. The sonata form, formerly indivisible from the content, became with the romanticists a prearranged pattern to be filled out. Thus the somewhat worn but still dignified garments of the classical parents were handed down by the romanticists to the Russian grandchildren, who once more readjusted them to their own stature. But the repeated tailoring tripled the seams, now visible everywhere.

It is no wonder that this suddenness of a musical culture found the nation unprepared and the majority of its composers were dilettanti. The fact that some of these amateurs, such as Rimsky, ended by acquiring an impressive technical equipment does not alter the situation. Rimsky himself admitted in his autobiography, *My Musical Life,* that at the time of his appointment as professor at the St. Petersburg Conservatory he had "never written one counterpoint nor heard of the existence of the $\frac{6}{4}$ chord." On the whole their ability to shape and form is very modest, their favorite method being literal or sequential repetition and a rather primitive sort of variation. They displayed, however, a remarkable sense for the orchestral palette. The critics usually mention the "superb orchestral language," not realizing that with that they have exhausted their criticism of the music. Truly, the language cannot be rich all by itself, for behind its richness there must be ideas and convictions. The extensive use of folkloristic elements lent to Russian music an interesting exotic touch, yet, their fine tunes notwithstanding, their music is cosmopolitan, not only in its exterior but in content, with the emphasis on the Western and not on the truly national traits. On the other hand the Russian's passion for the indiscriminate use of folk material and its naturalistic variation contributed materially to the final disintegration of the symphony. While this orchestral music was fundamentally influenced by the schools of Berlioz and Liszt, in Tchaikovsky's case by the Mendelssohn-Spohr-Volkmann circle, their operas show a more marked regionalism. But again only Moussorgsky's two operas, or rather musical folk dramas, realize with grandiose power the national and naturalistic aspirations of the new school.

Borodin's statement, "We are self-sufficient," we interpreted as meaning that the new Russian opera was addressed to Russians only. This is true of his own *Prince Igor,* as it is true of most Russian operas excepting those that are obviously within the orbit of the international grand opera, such as *Coq d'Or* or Tchaikovsky's *Onegin.* Thus we should really change the old dictum that, unlike Russian orchestral music, well known all over the world, Russian opera was not able to maintain itself abroad; it did not want to maintain itself. The problem, to be sure, is not solved by this realization, for such a pronounced emphasis on the national can only be the result of a reaction, the reaction of the long-time consumer become producer, and it hides a fundamental provincialism. The really great works, no matter how primitive and how much doctored—*Boris Godunov*—are accessible to the whole of the world. And this world, which had exhausted its own musical resources by the end of the nineteenth century, avidly seized upon the exotic music coming from Russia. This music was intriguing and yet easy to understand; it was full of melody, at that time beginning to be scarce in Germany as well as in France and England; and, most of all, it did not require a reconditioning of the Western musical mind, for it used the latter's current musical language. But the music so eagerly adopted was not the music of Moussorgsky, for that was not merely "Russian" but a bit of Russia, and it had to wait for another decade or two until the great Russian novelists introduced the world to the Russia of the brothers Karamazov and Anna Karenina.

Bohemia

"EUROPE'S conservatory" was Burney's characterization of Bohemia. We have seen how intimately Czech and German-Bohemian musicians were connected with the so-called Viennese school, and we have found them to be among the founders of the new instrumental lyricism that preceded Schubert.[6] But we have also seen, and Burney is again our witness, that like the Bohemian aristocracy, which rallied around the imperial house and really supported the art of the empire, the musicians were part and parcel of this great school, which assumed international significance.[7] The important Bohemian musicians of those times, from Czernohorsky to Tomaschek, cannot be detached from the general current of European music, for there was nothing consciously national about their music. This is true despite the past history of Bohemian music, a history not only much more ancient than that of Russia, but one which kept pace with the development of Western music. King John of Bohemia welcomed Machaut to his court in the fourteenth century, and in the following two centuries Franco-Flemish musicians were frequently visitors in the country. The Hussite movement temporarily dampened the universal love for music, but the Bohemian-Moravian Brethren, although of Hussite origin (the sect was founded in 1464) fostered popular singing, which soon became so famous that in 1519 a German translation of the sect's songbook appeared. Toward the end of the sixteenth century a number of large songbooks were printed with many hundred songs. Their popularity was not restricted to Bohemia and Moravia; the German and Hungarian borderlands knew and loved them. Emperor Rudolf II (reigned 1576–1612) made Prague the imperial residence and the Bohemian capital became the meeting place of famous musicians; Gallus, Hasler, Regnart, Philippe de Monte were some of the outstanding composers associated with Prague.

The centuries-long Austro-German rule began to show cultural repercussions, for in the seventeenth century the admixture of German and Bohemian elements was pronounced. Many a musician celebrated in that period of German music, Demantius, Hammerschmidt, Biber, originated in Bohemia. It is small wonder, then, that by the time we reach the Viennese school the Bohemian musicians give the impression of forming a branch of German musical history. In Prague musical life was co-ordinated with that of Vienna and the German capitals. At the turn of the eighteenth century the Bohemian composers were still without exception contributors to Austro-German musical literature. Gyrowetz, Kozeluch, Reicha, Vanhal, Wranitzky, musicians whom we have known as members of the school that also included Dittersdorf, Haydn, and Mozart, were as much part of the musical life of the Habsburg capital as the three who are symbols of Austrian music.

The new national orientation began almost exactly when the first Russian attempts at the creation of national music were made, and was prepared by theoreticians, pedagogues, and executant musicians, until in Bedrich Smetana (1824–1884) and Antonin Dvořák (1841–1904) the nation found indigenous composers whom it could oppose to the great in the neighboring musical empires.

Smetana is called the "father of Czech music," and if such title can be justified it is true, inasmuch as he was the first to draw deliberately from the amply flowing source of Bohemian folk music, where his noted predecessors merely allowed their natural environment to enter the musical picture. In his operas he forsook the well-tried fare of the international grand opera and reached for saga and the life of his homeland. But, and this is the most important fact in his art, these elements represent positive values in this art and not mere local color, even when used in program music. Smetana wrote eight works for the lyric stage, of which, significantly, only the comic, Singspiel-like variety was successful, where the great treasure of Bohemian folksong and dance could be utilized without giving the impression of mere exoticism. *The Bartered Bride* will remain one of the most engaging pieces in the repertory of the lyric stage, equally enjoyable in Bohemia and in America. As a symphonist the earlier Smetana belonged to the Lisztian circle, as can be seen from the titles of his symphonic poems; but, with all due regard to the fine craftsmanship he exhibits in these compositions, they do not give us the genuine Smetana. The composer discovered his heart as a symphonist after his experiences with the national opera and proceeded to cast it in an orchestral epic the six cantos of which depicted six aspects of the Bohemian countryside. Completely dissolved in the history of his nation, in its heroes, mountains, valleys, and streams, *Ma Vlast* (My Country) is a captivating narrative which, even though not possessing the force of an inner message, will remain an oasis in the program music literature of the late romantic era.

As Smetana accepted the principles of the neo-German school, so Dvořák was attracted to the noble ideals of the "Brahmins" without denying his newly won national consciousness. If Dvořák lacked Smetana's dramatic strength and descriptive talents, his chamber music was born from a musical imagination, ample and fertile, reflecting a healthy temperament, a simple yet by no means shallow sentiment and inventiveness, a fine sense for form, and a balance between sentiment and expression. Everyone liked this music, and everyone was satisfied with it, except Dvořák himself, who felt that the world saw in him not so much an individual composer in his own right as a representative of the new music of Bohemia. He resolved to present his personality in sharper relief by using materials and subjects untouched by the people, which he could shape by the force of his own musical imagination. Thus the musician who for a quarter of a century counted among the devoted practitioners of "absolute music" joined the ranks of the program musicians. He did not succeed, despite his ardor and seriousness of purpose, for his was an essentially naïve nature, not equal to the task of the tragic greatness his subjects demanded. On the other hand, his innate sound musicianship did not permit the extramusical elements to take command over his music making, and thus his symphonic poems were unconvincing, as were his dramatic operas, although again the Singspiel-like lighter operas were quite pleasant.

Dvořák affords convincing proof of the idea expressed at the beginning of this chapter that nationality may give the composer a material world, but great and lasting works will arise only if the content comes from the depths of a positive personality, in which case the geographic and ethnic restrictions are immediately lifted. This is well illustrated in the great and deserved popularity of his Fifth Symphony, *From the New World,* the inspiration of which came from his stay in America.

When comparing the music of the Bohemians to the Russian and Scandinavian schools, that is, to the other national schools that arose in the nineteenth century, one immediately becomes aware of the natural ease and unaffected spontaneity with which the Czechs move in their idiom as opposed to the preciosity of the Scandinavians and the indecision of the Russians. There is also the difference in musicianship, always sound and thoroughly workmanlike even in the lesser members of the school, whereas the amateurish cast is never missing in the Russians with the exception of their outstanding "professional," Tchaikovsky, who, however, was the least "Russian" among them. Launched under such auspicious beginnings, it remained to the twentieth century to prove whether this vital and sincere national art could be continued in a manner worthy of the "fathers."

Scandinavia

OF an entirely different nature again is the national music of the Scandinavian countries, with a folklore the richness of which is scarcely surpassed by any nation's. Where popular poetry flourishes song is never missing, even though written monuments may not be extant. The Norsemen whose small vessels braved the ocean were the boldest and most adventurous people of Europe, and perhaps the most song-loving. They preserved for posterity the old Germanic legends, and Danish poetry was a highly developed art in the time of Canute (c. 995–1035), King of England and of almost the whole of Scandinavia. Although this poetry is lost, Anglo-Saxon literature has preserved its remnants, which show that the rich folklore of the north belongs to the oldest literary stock of Western civilization. But the historian's difficulties mount as soon as he advances beyond generalities, for he cannot separate the sister nations. Swedish literature proper does not begin until the thirteenth century, and Denmark and Norway formed one nation from 1307 to 1814, with Danish and Norwegian literature and the arts developing together and making any division impossible. During the Middle Ages Scandinavian literature flourished together with Latin letters, until the Reformation, with the great polemical literature it created, induced a more marked development in the literary language of Denmark and Sweden, Norwegian being still entirely submerged in the Danish. The various currents of Western thought all found their way into Scandinavia, eliciting response in kind, but nothing could curb their wonderful popular lore. Thus it is the more surprising that their art music did not show any eagerness to develop until very recent times. This should not be ascribed to isolation from Western music, as was the case in Russia until the eighteenth century, for the number of distinguished and influential musicians who resided for a time in the Scandinavian countries is great and among them are names that represented progress and bold initiative all over Europe: Coclicus, Dowland, Schütz, Gluck, Schulz, Sarti, etc. This again illustrates that the Scandinavian countries went through the usual stages of musical colonization, Flemish, English, German, and Italian, until in the nineteenth century the same national movement which separated Denmark from Norway, and which created the Russian and Bohemian schools of music, caused a sudden emergence of nationally colored art music.

We use this term advisedly, for this music was merely nationally colored. Almost all the Scandinavian composers of the romantic era studied in Leipzig, a few in Dresden and Berlin, and brought home the spirit of German romanticism, which they adapted to their particular needs. The representative composer of Denmark, Niels Gade (1817–1890) was entirely submerged in the spirit of the Leipzig composers, especially Mendelssohn and Schumann ("Mendelssohnacidic Schumannoxide" was the neo-Germans' chemical formula for Gade), while the first Swedish national composers, Johan August Söderman (1832–1876) and Andreas Hallén (1846–1925), were disciples of the neo-German school, only Ludwig Norman (1831–1885) and Albert Rubenson (1826–1901) resorting to a more pronounced use of folkloristic elements. The national tone is somewhat more accentuated in the works of Wilhelm Stenhammer (1871–1927), Hugo Alfvén (b. 1872), and Olaf Peterson-Berger (b. 1867), but on the whole all these composers belong to the large group of decent musicians who live and create on the sun porch, the large windows of which let in some of the rays of the sun that warms the countryside.

Among the Norwegian musicians Halfdan Kjerulf (1815–1869) was among the first to emphasize the Norwegian tone with songs and choruses that employed folkloristic elements. This modest music has the virtue of staying within self-imposed limits, but the next musicians, Johan Svendsen (1840–1911) and Christian Sinding (b. 1856), attempted to acclimatize the idiom of Berlioz and that of the neo-German school. The music of both these composers is pleasing and workmanlike, but cosmopolitan and shallow, without a marked profile. Of a much more positive nature is the musicianship of Edvard Hagerup Grieg (1843–1907), who is largely responsible for the vogue of Scandinavian music in Europe and America. At first he was carried by the same romantic current that dominated Gade's works; in fact, he belonged to the same Leipzig circle that nurtured all other Scandinavian composers, but under the influence of a young and very gifted musician, Richard Nordraak (1842–1866), who introduced him to the folk music of Norway, there came a decided change, which, in the field of lyricism, led Grieg to piano pieces and songs, delicate and appealing. Much of his chamber music is also under the influence of this lyricism, and there are some fine genre scenes among them. But the large forms are wanting, for he lacked not only the concentration but even the will to master architectural construction; the ideas are too lyric and are quickly lost in mere sequential miniature work. His soft lyric disposition, when coupled with the austere and stark dramatic personality of Ibsen, resulted in a notable score, the incidental music to *Peer Gynt*, for the softness of the composer's music came as a welcome contrast to the play, overwrought with ideas and forebodings, and provided tender moments of quiescence.

*   *   *

Fatigued romanticism greeted the national schools with admiration and relief, for the rapidly declining Western schools, immobilized by Wagner, perplexed by Brahms, and whipped up by Liszt, could not find a way out of their impasse. The slightly exotic perfume emanating from Russia and the Scandinavian countries acted as a tonic—Bohemian music, being much more integrally Western, though at the same time thoroughly and unostentatiously national, did not seem exotic, and young composers gloried in the typical harmonic turns of Grieg and in the piquant orchestration of Rimsky-Korsakov. Often the folk elements—left unused for centuries—became so numerous and so easily apprehensible that the composer's own mental world became submerged in them, and it is undeniable that the compositions reflect more the richness and flavor of this newly discovered external world than the soul of a positive personality. This contributed to their exploitation, and the rising style of impressionism soon appropriated these elements, again creating an international style under French auspices. Thus early, Grieg and Moussorgsky were reconciled in Debussy, and the period of nationalism was practically over even before the last representatives of the various schools departed, but their pleasant music remained to furnish the repertory of the modern concert industry with a literature that under the guise of "modern music" could be held up successfully against the music of the twentieth century.

Nineteenth-Century Musical Practice

THE rather chaotic situation in ensemble playing that arose in the first third of the nineteenth century was the result of the changed musical equipment of the instrumentalists and the conductors. A generation or so before, musicians were trained in the principles of composition and the execution of the thorough bass, and they had to assume complete responsibility for their parts while the conductor actually carried the performance from and with his harpsichord, dictating tempo and dynamics, but also accompanying and helping with his playing. Now the player's only responsibility was to follow a part in which everything was minutely designated for the performance, with individual interpretation greatly reduced. The conductor, on the other hand, was no longer an active performer, or if so, he often was a violinist, not necessarily wedded to the daily practice of playing his scores—not mere parts—on the keyboard. Thus at first there was an estrangement between the conductor and the orchestra of which he used to be a member, and there came an interregnum during which the players, lacking in the schooling of their elders although perhaps better instrumentalists, looked out for themselves without much regard as to what their neighbors were doing, while the conductors were trying to find a technique of rehearsing and conducting to hold together their heterogeneous and often unwilling groups. The advantages of the new system became acknowledged as capable conductors began to officiate in the more important musical centers. Musicians and the public began to realize that by concentrating his attention on the players alone and not dividing it between them and the playing of an instrument the conductor could achieve better co-ordination and unity; the orchestra itself, the whole body of players, became his instrument. In the eighteen thirties conducting with a baton became known and accepted almost everywhere.

It was during this interregnum, when a great many mediocre musicians occupied important positions, that bad programs and indifferent playing were the order. The lack of authority of these men over the many dilettante orchestras that sprang up as a consequence of the voluminous orchestral literature created by the classic school led to slipshod performances, mostly without rehearsals. We have spoken of the popular belief, generally endorsed by modern critics and conductors, that conducting is a new art. We have also mentioned the impeccable performances staged by eminent eighteenth-century conductors.[8] It was during the few decades when the piano-playing director was weaned from his instrument that there occurred the lapse into amateurish and haphazard playing which gave rise to this blanket condemnation; but a high level of excellence was soon restored. It is a great misfortune, of course, that among the victims of the interregnum there had to be a Beethoven.

The beginning toward restoration was made—as once before, in Stamitz's time—by some excellent violinists who drilled their men with authority. Chief among these were Ignaz Schuppanzigh (1776–1830), famous as the leader of the string quartet which gave the first performances of Beethoven's quartets, an excellent performer, teacher, and conductor; and Louis Spohr and François Antoine Habeneck (1781–1849), followed by such men as Ferdinand David (1810–1873) and a legion of other "concertmasters," who taught the musicians a uniform technique and style of performance. The violinist-conductors, such as Habeneck, often used the bow of their instrument to conduct, playing with the ensemble if everything seemed to go well, but Spohr already insisted on the use of the baton, even though his London public was aghast at the sight of the little ivory stick he produced from his pocket. Weber and Spontini were the first modern opera conductors, as Spohr and Habeneck were the first in symphonic music. Weber introduced the baton in the opera and originated the system of preparation still in use in the lyric theater, that of having piano rehearsals with the soloists and the chorus and separate ones for the orchestra, the forces meeting in final and dress rehearsals. He was a born executive and like Spontini also assumed the role of stage director. Spontini made the Berlin opera into a marvel of perfection. Contemporary memoirs speak of the terror that this iron-fisted tyrant inspired. When he entered the orchestra pit every bow was poised over the strings, every horn and flute raised to the lips of the players anxiously waiting for the big ebony baton to start its gyrations. Wagner himself, a sworn enemy of Italian opera, had nothing but admiration for Spontini, for he recognized in him something of his own, that ability and desire to make opera into a multiple work of art with drama and music, stage and orchestra one unit. Spontini rehearsed and rehearsed until everything was crystal clear, then during the performance he gave his forces free rein, merely supervising the flow. Denounced as a musical Napoleon, he indeed abused his powers and exacted more from his men than they were supposed to give, but all this was not for the personal glory of the conductor, but for the work performed. Spontini and Weber were sovereign masters of their theater, and their solicitude for the best possible performance knew no limits. They studied the score, the libretto, the capabilities of the individual singers, the mise en scène, the properties, and were not satisfied until everything was tuned and co-ordinated. It was not at all unusual to hold a dozen dress rehearsals. Weber also had the unique distinction, unhappily lost in modern times, of writing admirable program notes for his own performances.

Mendelssohn, the antithesis of the opera conductor Weber, was a typical symphonic conductor, with whose administration begins the great period of the Gewandhaus Concerts (1835) and that of German orchestral concert life. His programs, their variety, the solicitous examination of contemporary scores sent to him for performance from all over the country, and his constant search for the discovery of old masterpieces have never been equaled. This august musician educated both the critics and the public in the highest sense of the word; he did not merely entertain them. In the meantime the casual Viennese also found a teacher who led them back to their former standards of excellence. At the head of the newly founded Philharmonic Concerts (1842), Otto Nicolai, the composer, a thoroughly modern and competent conductor, offered exemplary programs in exemplary performances. He did not tolerate fragmentary symphonies or mere virtuoso pieces, and while the programs were still long and varied, even the smaller numbers and vocal pieces were carefully selected.

Since the great classical literature of orchestral music originated in Germany, it seems natural that the many theaters and orchestral organizations of that country furnished the standards of performance for the rest of the world. But the French influence became strong in the second half of the century because Berlioz and Liszt, who represented the musical spirit of France, were the acknowledged leaders in Europe, and Wagner himself depended on them to a considerable degree. All these celebrated musicians who transmitted the French conceptions to the rest of the world are indebted to Habeneck. Wagner says that Habeneck's performances at the Conservatoire opened for him the road to Beethoven. This is indeed a high tribute, and it is also a logical consequence of earlier developments. Germany had many provincial capitals harboring court establishments. Its many operas and orchestras were the pride of a decentralized and widely disseminated musical culture. France was practically synonymous with Paris, where all new efforts received concentrated attention, with the best talents of the country officiating. Stamitz, Schobert, Gluck, the many great Italians, Haydn, Mozart were all well received and many of these composers tried their new and bold ideas in the French capital, where such original departures were appreciated. Then came the world-dominating French opera, with such eminent experts in performance and production as Spontini and Meyerbeer directing musical life while Cherubini stood there as the guardian of classic moderation. Habeneck's orchestra consisted of sixteen first and second violins, eight violas, twelve cellos, eight double basses, four flutes, three oboes, four clarinets and bassoons, with a full complement of brasses and percussion: the Wagnerian orchestra, one year after Beethoven's death! This ensemble he directed in the old concertmaster style, by playing his violin and giving cues with the bow. The orchestra needed little prompting during the performance because the rehearsals were thorough and exhaustive, Habeneck playing, on his violin, every phrase to the members of the orchestra until they responded. Difficult works were literally studied for years; the Ninth Symphony of Beethoven was rehearsed and polished intermittently for three years. The most authoritative critics of the times considered these performances unsurpassable. Berlioz learned the métier from Habeneck but developed it in wholly original fashion. His personal appearances all over Europe, as well as his writings on conducting and orchestration, became basic factors in the modern art of interpretation.

The Mendelssohn-Spohr school of orchestral conducting, spirited but inclined to glide over difficulties, was superseded by the dynamic school of Weimar. Liszt, holding forth in the capital of neo-German music, was not a German and was not educated in the German school of interpretation. Besides his legendary musicianship—Cornelius and others considered his rehearsals the finest musical education—he brought to his task Habeneck's precision and Berlioz's fire, that is, the best qualities of the French school, undoubtedly superior to the German. But the manner in which he conducted was as much his own as his pianistic technique. He insisted that his orchestra master all the technical details so that during the performance he

could concentrate all his attention on phrasing and shaping, leaving the individual artists to their own resources. This is a notable conception and a
dignified and high-minded artistic principle, altogether lost in our day when
even the little oboe recitative in the first movement of Beethoven's Fifth
Symphony is "conducted," making the members of the orchestra into mere
organ stops. Liszt's beliefs can be summed up in one remark: he wanted to
make the conductor "seemingly superfluous."

Liszt was the first conductor to indicate, by gestures and facial expression, phrasing, dynamics, and everything that is essential in a spirited performance. Wagner followed suit, and the devoted band of musicians who
watched the rehearsals and performances conducted by this phenomenal
artist whose glance beheld everything and whose facial expression and histrionic talents of communication were pronounced exceptional by the best
actors, emerged as the first group of modern, thoroughly competent, and
devoted masters of the baton. The theater and its atmosphere were in
Wagner's blood as in Weber's, and in his younger years he discharged his
conductorial duties in exemplary fashion. But it was not so much his actual
conducting as his writings and the manner in which he supervised the
preparations at Bayreuth that influenced the art of orchestral and musico-
dramatic interpretation to the marrow. As usual we must deduct from his
writings the invectives, accusations, and the all too obvious suggestions that
only he and his party really understood the art of conducting. This done,
we are dealing with the keenest of judgments and technical counsels. His
analyses of problems presented by certain works (*On Conducting,* 1869)
are penetrating and lucid, his recommendations eminently sound and practical, and his constant care for co-ordination of stage and orchestra, singing, acting, and accompanying show him to be thoroughly familiar with
everything the old and the new schools—Gluck, Weber, and Spontini,
Berlioz, Meyerbeer, and Liszt—had contributed to the art of conducting
and interpretation. Wagner's and Liszt's teachings and spirit were still alive
and virtually intact in the first quarter of the twentieth century in a number of devoted disciples: Hermann Levi (1839–1900), the Viceroy in Bayreuth; Hans Richter (1843–1916), who carried the Gospel to England;
Ernst Schuch, lawgiver in Dresden; Anton Seidl (1850–1898), Wagner's assistant in Bayreuth, who laid the foundations for the Wagner cult in
America; Felix Mottl (1856–1911), ambassador at large; Arthur Nikisch
(1855–1922), the famed director of the Gewandhaus; Karl Muck (1859–
1940), the aristocratic conductor of the Boston Symphony Orchestra;
Richard Strauss, Gustav Mahler, and Felix Weingartner. They all knew
that an orchestra must be precise and homogeneous, prompt to react to
the conductor's wishes, but they also knew that this precise and polished
orchestra will have a soul only if its individual musicians know not only

their parts but also the role of their parts in the body of the composition.

The twentieth century opened, then, with orchestral and operatic interpretation developed into a devout and supremely musical art, yet it elected to give prominence to the school of another disciple of the Wagner-Liszt era. Hans von Bülow (1830–1894), brilliant pianist and orchestral director, the first conductor of *Tristan* and the *Meistersinger,* is to be credited with the working methods of the modern concert conductor. His regimen was severe, for he did not stop at rehearsing with the string and wind sections separately but worked with single desks of players. As one of the first traveling virtuoso conductors he soon made the German orchestra the envy of the world. This gifted artist was prone, however, to use his great talents and technique with complete disregard of the composer's wishes and directions expressly stated in the scores. His extensive and arbitrary changes in orchestration, tempo, and dynamics gave the world an example to follow and contributed materially to conducting later becoming an aim in itself, not necessarily taking its inspiration from the compositions performed. Although von Bülow was undoubtedly the chief single factor in this course of events, Berlioz's warning to composers that "the most dangerous of your interpreters is the conductor" rests on old experiences. Arbitrary changes were already indulged in by Habeneck, and subsequently by many other conductors, among them artists who were capable of the utmost fidelity and integrity if they were so inclined. Rimsky-Korsakov, Wagner, Reger, Mahler, and Weingartner, to name a few, were all busy disfiguring the scores of the older masters. That they reorchestrated Beethoven's symphonies or Gluck's and Weber's operas would be a serious enough breach of respect for a fellow artist's inalienable property, but they tampered with the ideas themselves. No one would dream of adjusting the "primitive" or "incorrect" perspective of the great medieval painters, yet the same thing is done to the greatest of composers by their present-day interpreters. To what regrettable maiming and counterfeiting this inexcusable interference can lead is best illustrated in that glorious passage in the first movement of the *Eroica* symphony where the horn anticipates the recapitulation by two measures, thus creating an indescribable atmosphere of repressed impetuosity. The strings are still removed from the main tonality, but the horn already tries its martial main theme which thus clashes with the harmonic texture of the prevailing tonality. This was found offensive by champions of modern harmony, who corrected what they considered faulty writing by arbitrarily changing the second violin part, eliminating the very element of surprise and impatience which the composer sought. We might mention the furnishing of dialogue operas with recitatives—a practice still maintained in such important institutions as the Metropolitan Opera House in New York—the orchestration of the accompaniment of intimate songs, and even the refurbishing of entire works. *Boris Godunov* is completely misrepresented in its present form, as are many of the operas of Gluck, Weber, and Rossini, to say nothing of the multitude of symphonic works.

Another scourge of modern concert life, the presentation of orchestral arrangements of works written for single instruments or small groups instead of the original literature conceived for orchestra, also goes back to the beginnings of the century. Habeneck, whose devotion to Beethoven was unquestioned—he played Beethoven's quartets in Paris as early as 1802—did not hesitate to offer the master's piano sonatas in an orchestral garb; thus Weingartner's foot-loose orchestration of the *Hammerklavier Sonata* follows well-established precedents. The phenomenal memory of von Bülow, who conducted without a score, invited others to emulate him. In recent times Toscanini, another special case, gave new impetus to this custom, which has disastrous effects on lesser minds. Many of the best musicians of the late nineteenth and the early twentieth century opposed this practice, which naturally greatly limits the conductor's repertory. It must be said that despite his occasional interference with perfect scores—he was one of those who corrected the *Eroica,* reorchestrated Gluck, Beethoven, and Weber—Wagner decried conductorial extravagance; but perhaps the strongest protest came from Verdi, he of the "one hundred rehearsals." The aged master lamented that no sooner did the composers end the preposterous privileges of the prima donna than they were faced with the high-handed conductor who deigned to accept their works for performance on his own terms.

At the beginning of the century the orchestra changed its whole complexion with the invention of the ventil mechanism for brass instruments which made trumpets and horns into chromatic instruments capable of playing in any key. The horn tone, which soars over all barriers with which the classic style surrounded it, became the symbol of the modern orchestra, which it saturated with its glorious sonority. The composers became intoxicated with its wonderful timbre, ranging from scarcely audible piano to hymnic opulence, and Berlioz and Liszt began to give it and the other brass instruments melody-bearing parts. It remained to Wagner to exploit all the possibilities offered by these instruments. By assigning meandering inner parts to the horns he made his orchestra incandescent, while the imperious melodies of the trumpets, the massed might of the trombones and tubas, filled the next generation with awe. Wagner took over Liszt's already large orchestra, enlarged it by adding a fourth wood wind to the original three, four horns to the existing quartet, a fourth trombone, a bass trumpet, and a few other instruments, and, by using the coloristic effects of the individual instruments melodically, created a language of his own, much imitated but matched by few. In Beethoven's earlier period the symphony orchestra had already been standardized along the lines of Gluck's *Iphigenia* orchestra: two each of flute, oboe, clarinet, bassoon, horn, trumpet, and kettledrum, with the trombones and a second pair of horns optional. Some such orchestras were well balanced, especially the Italian opera orchestras, but many were short of strings. Beethoven demanded "at least four first and four second violins, two violas, two cellos, and two bass viols," which means that the balance between strings and wind was weighted in favor of the wind instruments, whereas in our modern orchestras an equally anomalous practice prevails: the twelve wind instruments of the classic complement are often pitted against sixty or seventy strings. A little later, and especially in the opera orchestras, the situation improved considerably, and orchestras with eight, ten, or twelve violins to the part, four to eight violas, cellos, and double basses, were quite common. After the middle of the century the great, multicolored, extremely mobile modern orchestra was the order in the musical centers. Its string players were able to play the solo concertos and were accomplished virtuosi, from the concertmaster to the double bass player; its wood winds rivaled the violins in agility, and its brasses, heretofore unwieldy and unpredictable, were handled with confidence and security. This marvelously pliable, gigantic instrument became one of the wonders of modern civilization, manipulated with supreme skill by conductors whose métier became an art developed and administered in the manner of virtuoso playing.

Public concert life began in earnest in Beethoven's time. The many musical institutions, choral societies, orchestras, conservatories, and music festivals that saw the light in the first third of the century announced a new and widespread musical life. This expanded activity demanded a great number of executive musicians, and the composers who in previous times took care of the performance of their works no longer could satisfy the demand: composer and performer became distinct, the latter now coming into his own. A significant change in musical style and taste was the increasing popularity of instrumental music over vocal music for professional performance. The great classic symphonic school finally tipped the scales— balanced in the eighteenth century—down on the instrumental side. It goes without saying, however, that Italy and France could not be alienated from their opera, England and America from their hymns, church music, and oratorios, and the Germans from their glee clubs or *Männerchöre;* but on the whole instrumental music, especially in the numerous cities in central Europe, was favored. Recitals in the modern sense began only in the eighteen thirties, with the generation of Liszt, Thalberg, and Clara Wieck Schumann. Before their time a solo recital on the piano or the public performance of a piano sonata was a rarity. Concert performances were always given from the score, and it was largely the example of Paganini (who did not need a score, for he usually departed from the written version) which prompted the other virtuosi to discard it. The concert programs presented in the first quarter of the century would suffice for several evenings in our time. Beethoven's celebrated concert on December 22, 1808, offered the Fifth and Sixth symphonies, the Choral Fantasia, two movements from the Mass in C, the piano concerto in G, the dramatic scene *Ah Perfido,* and free improvisation on the piano by the composer. The concerts in the second third of the century reflect the decline of understanding for the great symphonic forms. Symphonies were seldom performed in their entirety, and even if only two movements were played, they were usually separated by an Italian operatic aria from the current successes of Bellini or Donizetti. Paganini would give a concert for the background of which he would select a Beethoven symphony, performing between the movements his own breathtaking glissandos, harmonics, and double-stops. Mendelssohn, Nicolai, and a number of other eminent conductors succeeded in bringing order into this haphazard concert making, but if we read Schumann's critiques we must admit that even the Gewandhaus concerts were often endurance tests for both players and public.

Piano playing began to claim the lion's share in intimate domestic music, but the great popularity of ensemble music in the home, perhaps the greatest contribution of the classic era to musical culture, was still intact, which explains the reason for the many printed arrangements of operas, oratorios, symphonies, and overtures for ensembles ranging from two flutes (there is a printed edition of the *Creation* for two flutes!) to string quartet and quintet, or for mixed ensembles. However, public chamber music concerts, notably quartet playing, began early in the century. Habeneck in Paris (1802) and Schuppanzigh in Vienna (1804) gave quartet recitals, followed by Pixis in Prague (1808) and Baillot in Paris (1814).

With the romantic era the piano reached its full glory, occupying the position of universal instrument which it has held ever since. Outgrowing its domestic environment, perfected by French, Austrian, and English makers, and with a notable American innovation, the steel frame, by the time of Liszt the instrument was ready to withstand the belaboring that seems to have been its fate. But it was also capable of rendering the poetic and delicate lyricism which characterizes the pianistic output of the romantic era. Still, it was not the latter that dominated the concert halls, for the fine genre pieces of Mendelssohn, Schumann, and Chopin are not meant for the glittering auditorium. The customary piano recital was made up of potpourris, variations, polonaises, fantasies, and, until the middle of the century, free improvisation. This atmosphere, and the competition of the famous heroes of the Parisian salons, forced Liszt to the composition of the rhapsodies, fantasies, and potpourris which contributed to his fame but weighed heavily on his later creative efforts. Once his supremacy was assured, Liszt began to play more and more the rich pianistic literature of his time and of the classic era. According to Wagner he was the first to acquaint the world with the later sonatas of Beethoven. Liszt's initiative was followed by his disciples and enemies alike, and in the second half of the century the programs were greatly improved by a host of eminent artists. Still, it was relatively late in the century before the great keyboard literature of the eighteenth century together with Beethoven's sonatas acquired full citizenship in the concert repertory, and von Bülow's playing of preludes and fugues from the *Well Tempered Clavier* was still considered a mark of exceptional artistic courage by the critics and something of a punishment by the public.

The era of the traveling virtuoso began with Paganini. Although the pianists seem to have been the leading artists, violinists and singers were not less popular, and if they gave fewer full evening recitals, they were always welcome between other numbers in a concert. Many of the traveling virtuosi liked to entertain the public by imitating the sounds of animals or certain objects, playing blindfolded, eliminating several strings from their violin, etc. Paganini himself excelled in these artistic pleasantries. Others indulged in playing storms and battles on the organ, a specific art the vestiges of which can still be heard at expositions and conventions. That phenomenon which we associate with modern times, the "one-program virtuoso," was already flourishing in the earlier nineteenth century. To quote one instance, the Italian cantatrice, Angelica Catalani, whose repertoire consisted of a dozen arias, traveled all over Europe for years offering serious rivalry to the greatest of musicians, among them Liszt and Wagner. Toward the end of the century began the "specialization" of artists into "Beethoven players," "Chopin players," "Wagnerian tenors," conductors of Russian music, etc. But all this activity and musical turmoil, for such it was, could not efface the supreme art of those musicians to whom interpretation meant a dissolution of the performer in the art work, who looked upon their duties as ministry in the service of art.

Besides solo recitals and orchestra concerts, nineteenth-century musical life created another institution of significance, the music festival. The effect of the famous Handel memorial performances in London at the end of the eighteenth century and of the monster ceremonies of the revolutionary and Napoleonic times in France did not go unnoticed, and large festival orchestras and choruses appeared in all countries. The music festival even then boasted an honorable past in England, where the ancient cathedral cities of Gloucester, Worcester, and Hereford had combined their choral forces in yearly performances since the early eighteenth century. Similar events took place during the following century, at times assembling several thousand singers and players. The concerts of the Vienna Friends of Music in the forties employed from seven hundred to a thousand instrumentalists and choristers in the performance of Haydn's *Creation*. A similarly large number of performers, in this case the assembled choirs from twenty surrounding towns, is recorded in the Broadway Tabernacle in New York in 1839, followed by impressive festivals in Boston, Worcester, and Cincinnati.

The great popularity of choral music was a corollary of the romantic movement, and as such it came rather suddenly, for choral music was all but extinct in the latter part of the eighteenth century on the Continent. English historians have overlooked this change in Continental musical life for the very good reason that "unmusical" England had never abandoned her age-old choral singing, and while Handel and Haydn came as a revelation to the Germans, the same two composers' oratorios owe their existence to English love for this type of music. After the passing of the great Saxon-Thuringian school of Protestant church music Germany was so unprepared for the revival of choral singing that in Leipzig, for instance, the *Creation* could be performed only with the assistance of the pupils of the Thomas gymnasium, while in 1802 in Dresden the *Seasons* had to be performed in Italian, for in the absence of German singers the organizers were compelled to fall back on the chorus of the resident Italian opera. We have mentioned the timid beginnings of choral societies toward the end of the eighteenth century, but such societies were possible in the larger cities only. A diligent cantor, Georg Friedrich Bischoff (1780–1841), conceived the idea, probably in emulation of British traditions, of combining the forces of several small communities for the purpose of musical festivals. The first of these was held in 1810 in Frankenhausen, Thuringia, under Spohr's direction, and was followed by so many others that by 1830 festivals had become a characteristic mark of musical life.

The middle-class social music making of the romantic era created the *Männerchorvereine* or German glee clubs, for chamber music, the typical attribute of the classic period, no longer sufficed in this era, partly because the able dilettante had begun to disappear, partly because the vogue of poetry required a musical acknowledgment in social life. The name *Liedertafel* (song-table) was first adopted by the twenty-four male members of the Berlin Singakademie and demonstrates the social connotations of these societies, the membership of which was made up of a cross section of rather serious middle-class professional men. The artistic level of the compositions sung—mainly the products of the membership—was, however, shallow; the free and convivial atmosphere of the male choirs as opposed to the more formal mixed choirs made them very popular and they ended by becoming small bourgeois "warbler clubs," without the slightest claim to artistic laurels. The northern Männerchor movement met a similar movement in the south and in Switzerland, except that in this part of Germandom the movement was frankly popular from its inception. This was the more understandable because folk song itself was much more alive in the south than in the north; all that was needed was a conscious utilization of this wealth of music. Perhaps the most successful mediator between folk song and Liedertafel was Philip Friedrich Silcher (1789–1860), who collected many folk songs and published them interspersed with his own, in arrangements for various vocal combinations.

There was still another interesting connection between this popular choral music and the past when staid tradespeople and burghers made music. When the last Meistersinger school in Ulm disbanded in 1839, its emblems, flags, and songbooks were bequeathed to the local Liederkranz, "song wreath," the Meistersinger recognizing that the nineteenth-century citizen's choral society was their distant descendant. By 1834 the Swiss choral societies numbered twenty thousand organized members, and their number in Germany was tenfold. The various Liedertafel banded together and organized festivals, and their federation began to publish its own journal in 1862.

An important feature of the German male choral societies, which if investigated would furnish the historian of the animated years of 1848–1849 with interesting material, was their political role. The reaction following the Napoleonic wars suppressed political unrest with force. The people voiced their political desires and ideals in music. The stirring tunes of Weber written to Theodor Körner's lyrics (1814) opened the long line of political songs. There was a veritable pan-Germanic movement among the singers; thousands of men sang of German glories of the past and of the German future, and their songs reached and stimulated millions of their compatriots. Under these circumstances the great song festivals acquired important political significance because they brought together thousands of Germans from the various unfederated and at times hostile states. The Würzburg (1845) and Cologne (1846) song festivals already savored of a Grossdeutsch event. Recognizing the implications, Austria steadfastly refused to sanction the formation of such societies, and it was not until 1843 that the first Viennese Männerchor was founded. The cultural mission of both the great choral societies and the smaller glee clubs far outshone the quality of the musical literature engendered by them. With the exception of a few isolated works, the oratorio after Haydn declined completely, while the bulk of the Männerchor literature cannot even be considered from the point of view of art.

The social significance of this gregarious music making had long before been recognized in England, and her catches and glees continued to flourish in the nineteenth century. The quality of this music also declined, but it was still within the realm of art, and the gradual revival of the Elizabethan madrigal made people conscious of the need of lyricism instead of neat vocal writing. The fine choral and vocal composers of modern England were the direct issues of this movement. In the United States the Anglo-Saxon tradition of choral song was strengthened by the German singing societies, with a resultant number of organizations that would compare favorably with the Swiss federation's. The quality of the musical literature they used was, however, even below that of the German Liedertafel. This same type of music served the many college glee clubs until a few thoughtful and enlightened educators and scholars, familiar with the high artistic and cultural mission of the old *collegia musica,* madrigal clubs, and university chapel choirs, decided, practically in our own time, to brave the wrath of the entrenched partisans of "good old choral music." The outstanding leader in this crusade, perhaps the most uncompromising foe of this "literature" and at the same time a connoisseur of the great art of choral music, is Archibald T. Davison of Harvard University, who, aided by similarly inclined men and by his well-trained university singing societies, has performed a cultural mission in American music the repercussions of which have been felt all over the country.

We have seen that beginning with the latter Beethovenian times the practice of music shed the last vestiges of improvisatory and complementary additions to the written score. Beethoven especially was absolutely unequivocal in indicating his intentions in notation, in dynamic signs, phrasing, and even explanatory remarks. The romanticists followed suit, and in the later nineteenth-century score even the preference for certain individual strings, fingerings, as well as the desired number of players, instruments, and their seating arrangement, were indicated in great detail. The question of tempo was also settled, at least in large degree, by the invention of the metronome, generally attributed to Johann Nepomuk Mälzel (1772–1838) but actually of much earlier origin, even though Mälzel's clockwork mechanism housed in the familiar pyramidal box displaced all other tempofixing devices. The great art of improvisation of the past centuries, which reached its summit in Beethoven, disintegrated rapidly after his time into harmless variation and figuration of given themes. Free improvisation was still very popular at concerts, however, and such musicians as Liszt and Chopin made brilliant use of it, while in America William Mason liked to end his piano recitals with improvisation on a theme given to him by the audience; but on the whole the practice fell into desuetude. Improvisation, or rather well-prepared improvisation, continued to be used in the free cadenzas in concertos. Some of these, such as Joachim's cadenzas to Beethoven's violin concerto, are written with taste, moderation, and understanding, but as time passed new ones came to be written by performing artists in the nervous harmonic idiom of modern times, with a resultant grotesque discrepancy between the body of the work and the appended, often inordinately long cadenza. The more explicit the printed score became, the more the artist's initiative and creative freedom was curtailed, although it is undeniable that many of the composer's intentions—perhaps the most important ones—cannot be expressed in notation or writing, and can be realized and communicated only through the skill and sympathetic understanding of the reproducing artist. While the nineteenth-century composers endeavored to make their own scores as self-explanatory and safe from modification as possible, editors of older music launched volume after volume of the "classics" readjusted to the tastes of the time. Brahms once said that the so-called instructive or practical editions are seldom concerned with art. What seems at first a gross exaggeration is unhappily confirmed by such caricatures as von Bülow's edition of Scarlatti's sonatas, Riemann's accompaniments in his *Collegium Musicum,* and Bodanzky's version of Purcell's *Dido and Aeneas.* The *Urtext* editions—that is, the publication of scores without additions by the editor—begun by Breitkopf and Härtel will, as more of the masterworks appear in that form, materially aid in restoring these works to their original physiognomy; the frequent publication of facsimiles also indicates a sound approach to the problem.

Nineteenth-Century Musical Thought
Theory—Aesthetics—Philosophy—Science

UNTIL the nineteenth century the teaching of composition was done in a way that corresponded to instruction in the fine arts: in actual practice, under the direction of active masters in their workshops. Such counterpoint treatises as those of Fux and Martini were consulted by musicians already well versed in their art, while the various books on thorough bass served more to improve the consultant's ability to play accompaniments than to teach him composition proper. The systematic theoretical-practical teaching of composition began when the number of nonprofessionals advised by Mattheson and the other eighteenth-century theoretical writers reached such proportions as made detailed personal instruction impossible, calling rather for class and mass instruction. This stage was reached at the beginning of the second third of the nineteenth century, and ever since there have appeared works attempting to summarize the individual branches of music, harmony, counterpoint, form, etc., in single universal manuals of composition. The number of manualists, starting with Antonin Reicha (1770–1836) and François Joseph Fétis (1784–1871), and continuing with Salomon Jadassohn (1831–1902), Ebenezer Prout (1835–1909), Hugo

Riemann (1849–1909), and d'Indy, is considerable, but unlike the earlier masters who taught music they tend to teach technical expediency, and as a result the student becomes proficient in only the technical means of many-voiced construction and orchestration, unquestionably a positive asset but not markedly different from the skills learned in modern schools of commercial crafts. This instruction teaches a métier, not an art. The old English tradition of teaching composition as part of the college curriculum, which has also been transplanted to America, tended to emphasize the academic tone and nature of the music of the postromantic era. An academic degree now is supposed to attest the qualifications of a musician, who wastes his valuable time in passing tests, writing "fugues" and "eight-part counterpoint" instead of living the life of an artist in the company of more mature colleagues in free schools of music. The fact that a few prominent composers of recent times were the products of Oxford or Cambridge, Harvard or Yale, does not contradict the desirability of studying with active masters unfettered by academic routine. The long stagnation of English music and the difficulties encountered by American music have been due to a not inconsiderable degree to the thwarting of the forward-looking instincts of young composers by academicism.

Musical theorists of the nineteenth century did not pay much attention to the epoch-making discoveries of Zarlino and Rameau, the system of harmonic overtones, the nature of consonance and dissonance, tonal functions, or the parallelism of major and minor tonalities. The practical teaching of harmony was (and still is) based largely on eighteenth-century principles of the thorough bass, no doubt because of the simplicity—almost mechanical—of teaching the rudiments of voice leading and harmonization unencumbered by intellectual considerations. However, the musicologists continued Zarlino's and Rameau's teachings and researches, developing them into the so-called system of harmonic dualism, that is, the opposition of major and minor tonalities. They were further concerned with another important problem in musical aesthetics, the treatment of consonance and dissonance.

Until the seventeenth century—that is, until the time when our major and minor keys came into general usage—the difference between the keys was not determined by the quality of the tonic triad. In contrast to this harmonic conception the modes were considered as scales in which half and whole steps of tones were variously arranged. The antithetic nature of major-minor is, then, seemingly a relatively modern phenomenon, and its problems were not really solved until the later nineteenth century. Yet the antithesis of major-minor is actually much older and may be expressed by a formula showing that the intervals of the most pronouncedly major key will, if reversed, give the most pronouncedly minor key: *C D E F G A*

B C—C B♭ A♭ G F E♭ D♭ C. The minor key thus derived affords the basic scheme of the ancient Greek Dorian (the ecclesiastic Phrygian) scale. Despite these age-old differences and the fact that the theoreticians derived the minor chord from the inversion of the major, the musicians created them from the bass tone up just as they did the major chord. Later, especially after Joseph Sauveur's *Principes d'Acoustique et de Musique* (1701), which established the doctrine of harmonics or overtones, the scientific world became aware of the natural derivation of the major chord from a fundamental tone. It also realized that such an acoustic derivation cannot be claimed for the minor chord, that the latter is not a physical phenomenon. It is interesting to note how the creative musicians instinctively felt this difference, and although they treated the minor keys as they did the major ones, Zarlino declared the latter better sounding than the former, and Rameau and Tartini still considered the major key more forceful, a view confirmed in the closing of compositions in a minor key with a major chord (Picardy third). Subsequently the two types of triads received complete *aesthetic* equality which rested precisely on their antithetic nature, major and minor keys being opposed like light and shade. But aesthetic equality does not correspond to physical facts, and the nineteenth century was engrossed in the unraveling of this problem.

Arthur von Oettingen (1836–1920), German physicist and musicologist, was the first to prove that the consonant quality of the major triad cannot be entirely explained from its physical properties, for the basic tone has several dissonant overtones, and furthermore the tempered scale can be considered true from the practical point of view only.[9] To make things more complicated, the minor chord, considered psychologically, is as consonant as the major, making it seemingly futile to attempt to explain and justify both chords as physical consonances. As a consequence the dualistic system, strongly defended by Riemann, gave way to the monistic, which, however, was qualified as being biforked. In substance the new scientific theory endorsed the long-standing practice of musicians, who saw an essential difference between the major and minor keys in the quality of the interval of the third in the tonic chord, and who in their harmonic architecture treated the minor key along the principles accorded to the major, the relationship of the three primary tonal functions, tonic, dominant, and subdominant, being the same in both. By the time this question was decided upon, the practical aesthetic application of the clair-obscure quality of major-minor had lost a good deal of its force, since the latest development in harmonic thought and idiom freely mixes major and minor as well as the older systems of scales.

The science of acoustics, so named by Sauveur, its first noted exponent, was further developed in the eighteenth century by Euler, Tartini, and others. Ernst Friedrich Chladni's *Akustik* (1802) opened the long sequence of works in the nineteenth century. His discovery of the modal lines was followed by the application of calculus and logarithm to acoustic problems by Charles Edouard Delezenne (1776–1866), and by Charles Cagniard de la Tour's (1777–1859) utilization of the siren for determining the exact number of vibrations, while Félix Savart (1791–1841) probed the acoustic properties of instruments. Arrived at this point, modern scientific research was no longer satisfied with the purely physical attributes of sound and introduced physiological acoustics, which inquired into the process taking place in the ear and in the nervous system attached thereto. Hermann von Helmholtz (1821–1894), one of the greatest scientists of the century, summarized the physical and physiological researches of the past in his epoch-making work entitled *On the Sensations of Tone as a Physiological Basis for the Theory of Music* (1863).[10] His great work laid the foundations for modern physiological research in the field of music. Of especial interest are his findings relating to consonance and dissonance, and to tone color. John Tyndall (1820–1893), British scientist, published his much-read volume *Sound* four years later, and this influential work was followed by the *History of Musical Pitch* (1877–1881) and other notable essays by Alexander John Ellis (1814–1890). Another milestone was reached with the publication of the *Psychology of Tone* (1883–1890) by Carl Stumpf (1848–1936), who attempted to revise and extend Helmholtz's theories, holding that the scientific system of musical theory rests on acoustic-psychological facts rather than on physiological laws, thereby opening an entirely new scientific discipline. At the opening of the new century, which gave the work of these eminent scholars enlarged scope by offering them new and perfected instruments for their researches, acoustics had established two main branches of inquiry. One studied the sound itself, its laws of production, its constitution and propagation, its relationship to the organs of phonation and audition; the other was occupied with the rapport between science and art, and with the practical application of the scientific doctrines, such as the construction of instruments and of rooms where music is performed.

Since the great problems of musical aesthetics formed the subject of the ardent controversy among the various factions of romanticism, pseudo-classicism, and the appendages of the great romantic movement, we have already touched upon them while discussing the manifestoes, programs, aims, and achievements of the century. The aesthetics of music is created by the composers, and as long as it is *practiced*, that is, translated into actual art works, it is not difficult to follow, but once there is an attempt to make deductions and abstractions, to formulate into concrete statements the theories hidden in them, the task becomes all but insurmountable. It is this difficulty which beclouds the theoretical writings on aesthetics of the century of romanticism.

Nineteenth-century aestheticians started with an oppressive heritage, for their chief legacy came from Kant, who based his theories on a hierarchy of the arts which cannot be defended on scientific grounds. The early romantic philosophers, Schelling, Schlegel, and Schopenhauer, countered by dipping into metaphysics, connecting the content of music with the eternal essence of the universe. Their transcendental conception was approximated by two of the most influential writers in romantic literature, Jean Paul and E. T. A. Hoffmann. Schopenhauer and Hegel raised the theories of Michel Paul Gui de Chabanon (1730–1797) concerning the content of music [11] into higher spheres, but they could not avoid a certain conflict that was bound to occur between the spirit of their source, a product of the era of rationalism, and the metaphysical inclinations of their own time. Thus Hegel's discussion of instrumental music resulted in a one-sided formalism, while Schopenhauer outdid Kant when he declared—in typical romantic fashion —that the possibilities and faculties of music raise it above all the other arts. The next generation opposed to the content aesthetics of the earlier romanticists positivistic, empiristic-psychological conceptions. The exponents of this school of thought, Johann Friedrich Herbart (1776–1841), Gustav Theodor Fechner (1801–1897), and Friedrich Theodor Vischer (1807–1887), attempted to deduce the essence of music from its external characteristics, thus offering a parallel to the classicistic school of composition. In the latter part of the century the various schools were no longer intact and the leading thinkers showed compromise theories. Naturalistic aesthetics—a line of thought to which Wagner adhered to a certain degree —found its extreme advocate in Friedrich von Hausegger (1837–1899), whose *Music as Expression* (1885) is the most orthodox and uncompromising aesthetic pamphlet of neoromantic musical aesthetics. Relying on the ability of music to depict, represent, and elucidate, this school of thought liked to place the aims it believed could be reached by means of this ability of music in a literary, social, and moral light, thereby searching for the essence of music in extramusical moments. The metaphysical orientation, another of the compromise philosophies, culminated in Eduard von Hartmann (1842–1906), the philosopher of the "unconscious," by which term he meant any natural effect which has no demonstrable natural cause.

The most influential work among the many voluminous essays of the opponents of the naturalistic, symbolistic, and metaphysical aesthetics was a little pamphlet entitled *On the Beautiful in Music* (1854), by Eduard Hanslick (1825–1904). A polemical sketch rather than a philosophic treatise, this book took sharp issue with the content and feeling aesthetics of the romantic era. Thoroughly convinced of the righteousness of his cause, Hanslick sought the other extreme. Denying music all ability and even tendency to represent and picture anything outside its own field, he constructed a severely formalistic aesthetics which saw in musical creations merely the play of "sounding forms." With all its shortcomings, Hanslick's work was valuable for the future of musical aesthetics, for it greatly diminished the fantastic nonsense and sentimental speculations on the effect and aim of music rampant in the romantic and postromantic era. The success of the little book was astounding. By 1922 it reached its fifteenth German edition, and translations circulate in all modern European languages as well as in Japanese.

At the close of the century musical aesthetics, never well defined or delineated, was at the mercy of at least four different schools of interpretation. The mounting popularity of the scientific approach ranged the mathematical, physiological, and psychological orientations in one large camp, within which the mathematicians sought the source of beauty in music in the analysis of sound; the physiologists, leaning on the authority of Helmholtz, were confident of finding the laws of beauty in the sensory effects of music; while the psychologists acknowledged music as the language of sentiment and endeavored to explain it by the study of the impressions it creates in the human soul. There was, finally, a fourth group, having a camp by itself, often referred to as the "musicians' party," which, following Hanslick, saw the beauty of music in itself, professing to discover the unique criterion in the perfection of forms. Each of these schools contributed a great deal to the sum total of our knowledge, although each of them is more or less hopelessly mired in its own domain. The mathematicians' theories work well enough when applied to tones or intervals, but they are meaningless in the face of complete art works. Since some of Helmholtz's findings regarding auditive perception have been superseded, the physiologists, bent on recapturing their position, have extended their researches into territories that have little in common with music as an art, and are at present constantly moving away from their erstwhile goal. The psychologists, the largest and most heterogeneous group, especially active in Germany and America, and intoxicated with the seemingly endless possibilities offered by a young and relatively untried science, are firmly convinced that they can find the answer to every question and a solution to every problem. But psychology cannot assume the task of solving problems of aesthetics, for here it is only an auxiliary science to aesthetics. That neither of these two disciplines was able to arrive at definitive conclusions is to be attributed in good measure to the indiscriminate overlapping of their respective provinces. The fact that few philosophers possessed a musical equipment that could be considered more than dilettante, whereas true philosophers are rarely found among the musicians, made for more confusion and disagreement. Some of the thinkers, such as Schopenhauer and Nietzsche, often displayed a profound insight into the final essence of music but became lost in the technicalities; conversely, such keen thinkers as Schumann, Liszt, and Wagner were too artistically inclined to submit to a true philosophical discipline and were only too ready to side-step logic for emotion.

As the scientific orientation became dominant in the last quarter of the century, a vast literature, especially prolific in the least accessible and most speculative field of psychology, appeared, mostly in German. All shades of opinion had their champions, and instead of being clarified the issues became more abstruse. The simple and rather innocuous thoughts of Hanslick engendered such far-fetched and incoherent theories as Busoni's *Plans for a New Aesthetics of Music* (1907); on the other hand the philosophically inclined were rewarded by a new system of aesthetics, the so-called phenomenological, which starts out from the work of art as a finished, given phenomenon, and examines its nature; while between the Germanic extremes stands the cool and incisive Gallic logic of Charles Lalo (b. 1877), who in his *Esquisse d'une Esthétique Musicale Contemporaine* (1908) summarizes the state of research in acoustics, psychology, and aesthetics of music with imposing skill and impartial erudition.

Musical Criticism

WHEN at the close of the eighteenth century the great publishing firm of Breitkopf and Härtel entrusted the editorship of its newly founded periodical, the *Allgemeine Musikalische Zeitung,* to Johann Friedrich Rochlitz, whom we mentioned among the musical writers of the outgoing century,[12] it acted so in the belief that this man, a professional writer and critic not identified with any faction or trade within the large musical fraternity, was best qualified to direct a journal devoted to music. But Rochlitz is not merely an interesting personality, the first representative of a profession that was to influence musical life profoundly; he is a symptom, the visible memento of a fundamental change taking place in the social order of the musical world. His life and work meant that music had become a necessity of life, that there was a large enough public interested in it to warrant a constant and regular service of information and criticism for their guidance.

The eighteenth century established the model of the musical periodical upon which the nineteenth could build its own journals, but no sooner did the new century make its preparations than the rapid development of the daily press upset all calculations, placing the musical publicist in an entirely new situation. The Germans' penchant for literary and aesthetic elucidation, their far-flung, decentralized musical life, and the great number of newspapers appearing in their many cities account for the early development of musical criticism in that country; these factors also explain the preponderance the Germans held in this field until the end of the century.

A graduate of the Thomasschule and pupil of Cantor Doles, later student of theology and literature at the university, Rochlitz entered upon his profession, that of an independent musical journalist, with exceptional qualifications. He was not a critic acquainted with music only by following it from without; he lived with music and musicians and was not unmindful of the cultural currents of his times. Rochlitz knew Mozart and Hiller, Beethoven and Schubert, Weber and Spohr, Salieri and Zelter, but he also knew Mendelssohn and Schumann, and appreciated and encouraged the fledgling Wagner. Perhaps the most remarkable testimony to the man and the writer was given by Beethoven, who wanted Rochlitz to be his biographer. Aside from the musicians, he also knew and corresponded with Schiller and Goethe, Herder and E. T. A. Hoffmann, as well as with a number of French and Italian literati, and as a member of the board of directors of the Gewandhaus Concerts he took an active hand in steering the musical life of the city of Leipzig, then among the first musical metropolises of the world. Under his editorship the *Allgemeine Musikalische Zeitung* became the oracle of musical life in Germany, reigning unchallenged until Schumann's *Neue Zeitschrift für Musik* (1834) wrested the leadership from the paper declining under his undistinguished successor in the editorial office. Nothing could more honor this able and enlightened critic, whose opinions were respected by both artists and public, than the following sentence from his review of the first performance of Beethoven's Second Symphony, none too well received by his colleagues: "This work of a genius will remain living when a thousand famous works now popular will be long buried."

Musical journalism in the daily papers began with Friedrich Rellstab (1759–1813) and his son Ludwig (1799–1860). From 1808 to 1813 the elder Rellstab regularly wrote critiques and articles on music in the Berlin daily *Vossische Zeitung*. From his father he had inherited a music-printing firm, to which he added the first circulating library of music. Although he belonged to the older, rationalistic school of Marpurg, his counsel was sought and appreciated. The younger Rellstab, active in the position his father occupied at the *Vossische Zeitung* from 1826 to 1860, introduced into musical criticism an element which was later to dominate the "Sunday articles"— *feuilletonism*. He was a good journalist whose many writings, concert critiques, novels, travel stories—later collected in twenty-four volumes—all reflect the actuality of the day on which they were conceived. He also was among the first to take violent exception to men or music he did not like. Such diatribes against the Berlin musical tsar, Spontini, landed him in jail, a reprimand that our present-day critics happily do not have to fear. Ludwig

Rellstab's activity was of the utmost importance for the future of public musical life. With him the music critic emerged as a power to reckon with, for he addressed himself to the public in the widest sense of the word, that is, not only to experienced music lovers, but to all readers of the paper. From this time on musical criticism became a middle-class, democratic profession. A well-trained musician and writer, Rellstab acquitted himself of his task brilliantly; his judgment was sound and his style easy and entertaining. The public followed him with avidity and confidence, and the musical column of the *Vossische Zeitung* exercised an authority respected and feared.

With Carl Maria von Weber and E. T. A. Hoffmann began the branch of musical criticism—that of the romantic artist-critic—which differs markedly from the office discharged simultaneously by the professionals, Rochlitz and Rellstab. All these men, Weber, Hoffmann, Schumann, Berlioz, Liszt, Wagner, and Hugo Wolf, were endowed with literary gifts and represented—in varying degree—the romantic ideal of the union of arts which would abolish the difference between poetry and music. For the expression of so lofty a purpose the ordinary technical equipment and language of musical writing did not suffice, so they drew on poetry and philosophy, a course which inevitably carried some of them far afield. All of their writings are interesting, many of them poetic and high-minded, but, with the exception of the earlier romanticists, they were musical "politicians," passionately interested in their cause and consequently not eminently suited to sit in judgment on their colleagues. They administered their papers or columns—Weber deftly appraised the public of the work he was doing in the opera house where he was conductor, and Schumann's *Neue Zeitschrift* was a militant periodical, as were some of the others—as the organs of an artistic party, demanding loyalty of its adherents and proselytizing in the other parties. This musico-political zeal could engender the crassest sort of intolerance—Hugo Wolf—but it often gave evidence of the most moving recognition of the fine and great in others—Weber, and especially Schumann. The expert professional evaluation, literary skill, and magnanimous and high-minded attitude that characterized the musical criticism of the romantic era, culminating in Schumann, have never since been equaled. It is true that at times they were carried away by their romantic ardor, but they had the power of reflection. With delightful aphorisms and poetic similes, but also with penetrating and dramatic strength, they achieved the impossible, to talk about music so that the impression such talk leaves does not pale hopelessly in comparison with the music it discusses.

The professional musical criticism of non-composing musicians and musical writers developed together with that of the artist-critics. The latter were musicians, emotionally wedded to the art work, the former thinkers and aestheticians, approaching everything with critical eyes; the former drew on their artistic instinct, the latter on well-formulated principles. After Rochlitz, Eduard Hanslick was the first important professional critic. Although he started out as a jurist, his ample musical studies removed all taint of the dilettante. Hanslick and the Hanslicks were men with a good general education, and literary, aesthetic, and musical schooling; but what they represented was the typical product of a middle-class civilization and had no roots in the genius of the people, race, or country whose artistic products they criticized. In their writings they showed themselves partisans of a sober and one-sided rationalism, the seriousness of which does not as a rule transcend the mental capacities of the average intelligence of good middle-class readers, though they had a sense for sarcasm and witticism which made their writings good reading.

"The Bismarck of musical criticism" was Verdi's word for Hanslick, and, indeed, we are dealing here with a new sociological implication, that of the power of the press to influence public opinion. Hanslick's column in the Viennese *Neue Freie Presse* was a supreme court of justice before which were haled musicians and their music. His relentless prosecution of the Wagnerian circle earned him an unenviable reputation, and no present-day critic omits chastizing and ridiculing him. Hanslick had undeniable limitations; as an aesthetician he was rigid and dogmatic, but as a critic he showed within his limitations sound qualities and considerable literary skill. His dislike for Wagner and Bruckner was matched by admiration for Schumann and Brahms, and he never lost an opportunity to write approvingly of their works. One cannot dismiss him, therefore, simply by calling him an ultra-conservative misanthrope. He later collected and edited his critiques and articles in numerous volumes, of which *From the Concert Hall* (1870) and *The Modern Opera* (nine volumes, 1879–1900) contain much valuable material. Hanslick attacked Wagner with vehemence and hatred, yet fundamentally he was not an enemy of this music; as a matter of fact, up to *Tannhäuser* he backed it entirely, and with certain limitations *Lohengrin* and the *Meistersinger* were not less acceptable, nor did he dispute the greatness and power of much of the music in the other works. What he fiercely opposed was Wagnerism and all it stood for, its aesthetics, its philosophy, its fundamental negation of the lyric drama. His sober mind was appalled by the swollen, erotic vapor in *Tristan,* by the cosmic-German implications and leaden mythology of the *Ring.* This is what led him to aberrations as regrettable as those committed by his opponents. Like many other critics, he was under the erroneous impression that by supporting and endorsing Brahms he professed faith in a classicism which he could successfully oppose to the violent realism of the neo-German school. There are other things in his writings that should make his condemners wary. In his autobiographical essay we read the following sentence: "I consider it the duty of the critic not to discourage production, to recognize the genuinely felt and the spontaneously spirited in the art of the present and not degrade it superciliously by opposing it to the products of a defunct era. Different times create different conditions which necessarily change artistic values and tastes." [13] It must be said that no professional critic—certainly not Hanslick—erred in the violently malicious, uncritical, and wholly unreasonable tone of such artist-critics as Hugo Wolf, the "wild wolf" as he was called by the shocked readers of his column in the *Wiener Salonblatt,* the nineteenth-century Viennese equivalent of the *Ladies' Home Journal.* Even though attached to one tendency or another, they planned and weighed their criticism, the others simply cut loose with purely subjective impulses.

The activity of the critics outside of Germany was neither so widespread nor so varied as in the homeland of philosophers and pamphleteers. In France, François Joseph Fétis (1784–1871) founded the *Revue Musicale* in 1827, a periodical the serious tone and aims of which were unmatched in the world. Fétis also conducted a column in the *Temps* while Berlioz wrote his brilliant articles in the *Journal des Débats* from 1835 to 1863. Berlioz was the first exponent of the witty and satirical criticism which characterizes French musical journalism, and his influence was still strongly reflected in Debussy's writings.[14]

Up to the end of the nineteenth century musical criticism in England was virtually monopolized by two men in commanding position. Henry Fothergill Chorley (1808–1872), a man of excellent journalistic abilities but almost entirely self-taught in matters musical, was critic of the *Athenaeum* from 1833 to 1868, while James William Davison (1813–1885) held a similar position on the *Times* from 1846 to 1879. Both critics were extremely cautious, never venturing beyond the tidal waters of the Mendelssohnian sea. The great influence wielded by the two, especially by Davison, who besides being the critic of the greatest British newspaper also edited an important musical journal, the *Musical World,* contributed materially both to the one-sided Mendelssohn worship and to the closing of the British musical mind toward new ventures. It was only beginning with the writings of Parry and Stanford that the spell was broken and the way opened to modern British literature and criticism of music.

Unlike their British colleagues, American music critics of the past century were especially noted for their progressive attitude. John Sullivan Dwight (1813–1893), founder of *Dwight's Journal of Music* (1852–1881) and of the Harvard Musical Association, championed Schumann, Wagner, and Brahms against much adverse feeling. After his journal ceased publication he joined the staff of the Boston *Transcript* as its first music critic. William Henry Fry (1813–1864) represented the artist-critics. A composer of parts, among the few earlier American composers to write both grand opera and symphony, he was music critic of the New York *Tribune*. A diminutive Wagner, he berated his compatriots for their acquiescence in the inferiority of American music as compared to the products of Europe and for their reserve toward contemporary art. John Rose Green Hassard, who followed Fry in office (1866–1888), was an eloquent champion of Wagner and other contemporary composers.

At the time when English musical criticism was spurred by the two distinguished leaders at Oxford and Cambridge, the United States boasted a galaxy of critics and writers whose activity continued far into the twentieth century, and whose many works disseminated the understanding of music from coast to coast: Henry Edward Krehbiel (1854–1923), New York critic and author of a dozen books on musical subjects; Henry T. Finck (1854–1926), noted for his work on the New York *Evening Post,* and author of several works on the composers of the romantic era; Philip Hale, Boston critic and the author of exemplary program notes for the concerts of the Boston Symphony Orchestra; Richard Aldrich (1863–1937), New York critic, who amassed one of the finest music libraries in the country; and James Gibbons Huneker (1860–1921), the most accomplished essayist among the critics, a littérateur whose writings are marked by pungent satire, audacity, and originality.

The elder Rellstab used to say that everyone who judges something is a critic whether or not he knows whereof he speaks, but he counseled those who do not know to restrict themselves to the expression of their likes and dislikes rather than to indulge in evaluations. This admonition really anticipated the course of events, but the old critic saw clearly into the future, for alongside the artist-critics there arose a guild of professional writers who considered their office to be that of the *Merker,* the Meistersinger judge, enemy of all progress and flight of fantasy, the smug and stubborn bourgeois worthy, always ready to invoke the guaranteed endorsement of the departed masters and the moral support of the angels in heaven. Their number was great and their influence pernicious, often retarding and seriously hampering art. In former times the artist was considered the witness of everlasting truth and beauty and not a quasi defendant standing before a judge. It is significant that by far the largest number of these critics did not come from the ranks, they were jurists, literary men, theologians; and while among the earlier practitioners there were men of high intellectual attainments who were able to transmit to their musical writings a good deal of the skill acquired in other fields of endeavor, toward the end of the century musical criticism, or rather musical journalism, became—with due allowance for exceptional individuals—the province of writers whose musical and intellectual culture barely covered the day's necessities. The twentieth century

opened with the same cleavage that once had separated the musical connoisseur from the public, and which had been partly eliminated by the universal
practice of music in the home during the classic and the early romantic era,
and by the enlightened literary activity of the critics of the earlier part of
the nineteenth century. Musical criticism now addressed itself to two groups
of people: one, exceedingly small, the "connoisseurs" of old, that is, the professionals or professionally trained; the other the countless millions of the
"public." The first group, with its own writers, had no use for the second,
while the second regarded the products of the learned critics with understandable aversion. As it has come to be viewed more recently, musical
criticism stood in the first place for a report on performance and only in a
restricted sense for an aesthetic appraisal of the composition. This was an
inevitable consequence of the requirements of modern journalism, the essential aim of which is reporting, but the combination of reporting with applied
aesthetics proved to be a task mastered by few. Musical criticism as divorced
from reporting should be concerned with one thing only, to lead us to the
work of art. It calls ȯn a positive and serious ethical and artistic conception;
it does not measure by prearranged values but always takes its departure from
the artistic creation itself, for, as Goethe has said, the artist creates his own
laws. In this musical criticism the aim is not so much judgment as knowledge,
the bringing of the critic and his reader nearer to the enjoyment of art.
And the task of this criticism is to detect and convey what the artist wanted
to do and not what he should have done. "Criticism should not be a scissors
which gets snagged on a wart only to cut an artery, it should rather be a
plow that plows a furrow only to sow in it seeds that will grow fruits." These
words of Hebbel allude to the most admirable property of criticism, the incentive that the composer derives from it for further creations.

Musicology

WHEN the University of Freiburg in Switzerland opened its academic year
in 1920, its newly elected *Rector Magnificus* pointed proudly to the fact that
musical scholarship had in the past century regained the prominent place
in the life of the university that it had held during the Middle Ages and the
Renaissance. The newly elected head of the university was neither a theologian nor a philosopher; he did not represent the medical sciences nor was
he a member of the law school. He was a musicologist, Peter Wagner (1865-
1931), the great scholar of Gregorian music.

The youngest discipline of the *Universitas Litterarum,* musicology, some
of whose subdivisions in the fields of physics and philosophy we have already
discussed, has its place in practically all the universities of Europe, and a
number of American universities have established chairs devoted to this

subject since the first American professor of musicology, Otto Kinkeldey, was appointed at Cornell University in 1930. Before the revival of musicological activity at the beginning of the nineteenth century, however, the academic study of music had been dormant for generations. (The musical instruction imparted in the English universities was of a purely practical nature, making no pretense to being academic work in the sense of philology, history, or the sciences.) Musical scholarship, once an integral part of the university curriculum, was looked upon with contempt by the guild of professionals who opposed the scholar with the well-known slogan that disappointed composers like to hurl at the critic: "He who can does, and he who can't criticizes." The labors of the musical scholars and historians of the eighteenth century, Hawkins, Burney, Gerbert, Laborde, Martini, and Forkel, awakened the desire of German scholars to be again represented in the famous institutions of learning. It was not, however, until 1826 that the first academic lecturer was appointed in the University of Bonn in the person of Carl Heinrich Breidenstein (1796-1876), followed by Adolf Bernhard Marx (1795-1866), appointed in Berlin in 1830. Both of these men had received a thorough academic training in other disciplines, they were jurists and philologists, and attempted to transmit the principles of scholarly research to the newly opened field of musicology. This the old guild members and thoroughbass experts resented bitterly, as can be seen from letters addressed by Zelter to Goethe. Zelter made the most derogatory remarks about "the new music professor Breidenstein," whom he counseled "to do something before he starts speaking." Goethe's musical adviser, who expressed the consensus of opinion of the practical musicians, could not conceive of a person's talking or writing about music without being a composer or virtuoso. There is another remark of Zelter's which should interest us, for it could have been said a hundred years later: that Forkel's history of music [15] ended at the date where it should have begun. After these first professors there came a pause until Hanslick occupied his chair at the University of Vienna in 1861, after which chairs were gradually created in all important Continental universities.

The pause between the appointments of Marx and Hanslick did not affect the research work begun in the latter part of the eighteenth century and which now began to yield works the scientific usefulness of which is still considerable. Fétis, in 1829, published a *Mémoire* on the merits and achievements of the Netherlands composers which, together with a similar work by Raphael Georg Kiesewetter (1773-1850), opened new vistas in the knowledge of musical history. In 1834 there appeared the first modern musical biography, Winterfeld's *Gabrieli*,[16] compiled with exemplary erudition and painstaking research. Winterfeld's work was followed by Jahn's Mozart biography, written in the typical style of romantic hero worship, but the next important publication, *Händel* (1858), by Friedrich Chrysander, was one of those masterworks upon which all future scholars will have to base their work. The first heroic era of these scholarly biographies ended in Philip Spitta's monumental life of J. S. Bach (1879–1880), distinguished by that solicitude for the preliminary men and events which lead up to the life and work of such a great master which has ever since been followed by competent biographers. An especially honorable place among these savants must be reserved for an American consular officer, Alexander Wheelock Thayer (1817–1897), for his great Beethoven biography [17] which forms the ground stock of the whole voluminous literature of Beethoveniana.

Modern lexicography started with a work of astounding proportions, Fétis's *Biographie Universelle des Musiciens* (eight volumes, 1835–1844), a work which with all its inaccuracies still is of great service to musicologists. Later in the century came the well-known dictionaries of Sir George Grove and Hugo Riemann, supplemented by reference manuals of hymnology, liturgy, bio-bibliography, and many other works dealing in an encyclopedic manner with the special fields of musical research.

The study of musical history was given an entirely new turn by the appearance of an extended essay on this subject by August Wilhelm Ambros (1816–1876). Although left unfinished,[18] Ambros's *Geschichte der Musik* (1862) is the first modern work of its kind, distinguished by exceptional scholarship and erudition and by a soundness of judgment that has retained its provocative freshness until our day. With the vast field of musicology thus opened wide, diligent research work started in all its corners. Of the numerous scholars and their works we shall mention only a few of those whose initiative led the others to new sources of knowledge. François Auguste Gevaert (1828–1908), Fétis's successor, engaged in the study of the music of antiquity and of the early Christian centuries. The former subject received a great impetus with the publication of *Musici Scriptores Graeci* by Karl von Jan (1836–1899), the first important edition of classical treatises dealing with music since Meibomius (1652), while Gregorian music was virtually revived by the unceasing labors of the Benedictines, expert guardians and scholars of church music since the Middle Ages. Among the many monasteries in Germany and France, that of Solesmes is the best known for the stupendous work of collecting, collating, and editing the vast material pertaining to plain chant. Dom Prosper Guéranger (1805–1875) and Dom Joseph Pothier (1835–1923) were their leading scholars in the nineteenth century, the latter's disciple, Dom André Mocquereau (1849–1930), continuing their work in the twentieth.

The tremendous interest aroused in the music of the Middle Ages and the Renaissance by the works of Fétis, Kiesewetter, and Ambros soon yielded important monographs. Edmond Vanderstraeten (1826–1895) published *La Musique aux Pays-Bas* (1865–1888), in eight volumes, filled with interesting information (besides a goodly number of mistakes). Franz Xaver Haberl (1840–1910) and Sir John Stainer (1840–1901), the latter aided by his son and daughter, explored the schools of Dunstable and Dufay, while the latter part of the fifteenth century and the sixteenth were probed by Michel Brenet (1858–1918), Adolf Sandberger (b. 1864), and Felipe Pedrell (1841–1922). Hermann Kretzschmar (1848–1924) and Hugo Riemann (1849–1919) started the elaborate stylistic study of types and periods of music, their activity leading up to the enormous musicological literature that opened the new century. By this time the many German scholars had been joined by eminent musicologists of other nations, and while heretofore their contributions had been sporadic or restricted to such special work as that of the Benedictines of Solesmes, they now formed an integral part of the international fellowship of musicologists. Harry Ellis Wooldridge (1845–1917), a man and artist of unusual accomplishments and one of the leading musical medievalists of his time, published the first anthology of early British music, *Early English Harmony* (1896), and was the author of the first two volumes of the *Oxford History of Music* (1901, 1905), these two volumes rising head and shoulders above the succeeding ones. Pierre Aubry (1874–1910) was another medievalist, especially notable for his studies in musical philology, while Romain Rolland (b. 1868), the distinguished French poet and writer, was the author of a fundamental essay on the early phases of opera.[19] After their time the volume of musicological research reached such proportions as to prohibit even their mere enumeration within the scope of this work. Our bibliography gives eloquent testimony to their achievements.

Contrary to popular opinion, especially in England and America, where musicians still look at these scholars with the suspicion that greeted Breidenstein, their vast labors were not restricted to musical philology, of no use to the humble lover of music; musicology rediscovered, unearthed, and made available today the immense wealth of the music of past centuries. This is its chief aim and purpose. Aside from important eighteenth-century publications, which were rather collections of examples, the publication of large series called "Monuments of Music" was a corollary of modern musicological research. The first attempt at such a collection came rather early. Forkel assembled an important group of sixteenth-century choral works and was engaged in correcting the proofs when the French troops occupying Vienna in 1805 seized the plates and melted them into bullets; all that remains is a set of carefully corrected proof sheets. Another interesting early collection of church music appeared in London, entitled *Selection of Sacred Music* (1806, *et seq.*) and edited by Christian Ignatius Latrobe (1757–1836). Such special anthologies appeared afterwards in goodly numbers, edited by Rochlitz, Dehn, Commer (*Musica Sacra*), Proske (*Musica Divina*), Delsarte (*Archives du Chant*), and others, until with Chrysander's *Denkmäler der*

Tonkunst (1869) there began the publication of large collections of music not restricted to any one field or nation but rather aiming at comprehensiveness. The publications of the German Society for Musical Research (1869–1905) furnished the first of these gigantic undertakings, followed by the hundreds of volumes of Austrian, German, Spanish, English, French, Dutch, and Italian "Monuments."

Besides the anthologies, there appeared collected editions of the works of the great masters. The first attempt at such a complete edition was made in 1786 by Samuel Arnold,[20] who published a thirty-six-volume edition of Handel's works, but the time for such enterprises came only with the rise of scholarship in the modern sense. Societies devoted to the works of the masters, such as the Bach and the Handel Societies, were responsible for the issuing of the complete works of these masters, publications beginning in 1850 and 1859 respectively and continuing through the rest of the century. Palestrina, Schütz, Lassus, Purcell, Grétry, Mozart, Beethoven, Schubert, Schumann, Chopin, and a number of other great composers all had their works collected, sifted, collated, and edited in big folio volumes during the century. Some of these editions are complete, some are still being issued.

As musicological research broadened, the cognate subjects also received much attention. We have dwelt on the acoustic, physiological, and psychological discoveries of the century, but there is still another field of great importance to be mentioned, comparative musicology, that is, the study of musical systems and literatures lying outside the domain of Western civilization, as well as musical anthropology and ethnology. The beginnings of these studies also reach back into the eighteenth and the early nineteenth centuries, but the failure of the earlier scholars to view such music as the natural expression of other civilizations rather than as exoticism seen through Occidental standards did not permit a thoroughly scientific discussion until the advent of the twentieth century. The great activity of all these scholars led to the foundation of scientific societies, united in the International Musicological Society (*Société Internationale de Musicologie*), founded in 1899 (dissolved at the outbreak of the war in 1914), with numerous national and international organs devoted to musicology.

Chapter 20

THE ROAD TO THE PRESENT

※》》 《《《

New Notions of Tonality

THE end of the nineteenth century was shaken by a tremendous upheaval, intellectual, social, moral, and artistic, directed sharply against the tenets of romanticism.

There was a reversal of the notions of pictorial space, of form, and of tonality, a reversal which was a corollary of similar revaluations of space and time in modern physics. The theory of relativity denied the existence of an absolute space and time, considering the two mutually dependent, and pronounced that the emission and absorption of energy is not continuous as it had heretofore been thought. Impressionism represents the first stage of the dissolution of geometrically constructed pictorial space, although it still adhered to the system of optical projection originated by the Renaissance. While the other arts endeavored to revise geometrical canons of perspective space, music was engaged in emancipating itself from the major-minor system of tonality, similarly imposed upon it since Renaissance times, but, as with painting, the break was not complete: it did not reject the principle of tonality itself. The strongest original incentive toward a new tonal sense came from Liszt, who appropriated the state of intertonality reigning in the development sections of the classic sonata form, making it the foundation of his whole formal-tonal architecture. He was also the first to employ a "neutral tonality" based on the whole tone scale which subsequently became one of the earmarks of the impressionistic style, and to create a great elasticity in the interpretation of tonality by deleting enharmonic differences and by advocating the simultaneous use or mixing of two tonalities. To this widening of the tonal sense was added the renewed use of the medieval ecclesiastic scales and the folk idioms of the national schools, all contributing first to an extension and reorganization of the old system and later to its disintegration.

Liszt's initiative bore its most delicate and artistic fruits in Debussy's music, volatile, tender, and poetic, in which harmonic subtleties abound. The Germanic wing, to which belong in a certain measure Franck and other composers who embraced the faith of the neo-German school, re-acted differently, for it had to reconcile the new harmonic thought with its hereditary instinct and desire for polyphony. French writers always refer to Franck as the modern master of polyphony, while their German col-leagues like to see in Max Reger (1873–1916) the composer who, by uniting the styles of Bach and Brahms, regenerated polyphonic thought in an in-dividual style. But his counterpoint is largely a pseudo-polyphony. He carried the chromatic contrapuntal subjects of Franck, entirely conditioned by shifting harmonies and thus being more by-products than original musi-cal ideas, to the ultimate dissolution of harmony in horizontal embroidery of the individual parts. Since these harmonies are constantly shifting, the motion of the constituent "voices" is so continuous that it gives the impres-sion of linear counterpoint.

The process of disintegration was to end in so-called atonality. This slogan of the modern musical movement is thought capable of covering all aber-rations, when, as a matter of fact, as usually employed it is meaningless. In general the partisans of modern music employ it to denote a tonality which differs from the older major-minor variety, while the enemies of modern music use it as an accusation which implies that modern composers write music that no longer has any semblance of cohesion. In both cases the use of the term is misleading: new tonality does not mean a lack of tonal unity, for without such unity there can be no music. Music rests on melody, and every melody has a certain construction regulating the relationship of the various pitches. Only that music could be called atonal whose melody would show no system of relationship between its various pitches; but such music no longer belongs within the domain of aesthetics, that is, it is no longer art, it is not music, it is merely a conglomeration of unrelated sounds.[1]

The vogue of tone painting gave to harmony, rhythm, dynamics, and color preference over melody, which no longer was suitable for themes because with its periodic definition and articulation it restricted the pictorial element, now supreme. After prolonged indecision (demonstrated at the very be-ginning of the movement in the awkward melodies of Berlioz, hesitating between periodization and articulation in the Beethovenian sense and free tone painting) a new type of melody appeared, conditioned so as to permit a free utilization of all the nonmelodic elements.

Form in art is the sum total of those means with the aid of which an artistic soul seeks to reveal itself. In a more restricted sense and applied to music, form is the recognizable architectonic articulation of compositions. The postromantic and impressionistic schools sought form in the unity of mood, therefore they were constrained to eliminate the thematic and rhythmic character differences. Their musical idiom does not operate with isolated thematic material and its groups, as did the classic and romantic, but with motives which are developed without sharp caesurae into a universal fabric or endless melody. In this universal fabric theme, bridge, exposition, and development show no difference in texture, and the growth of the composition does not take place in the organization of these groups, for the individual motif regions or spheres are connected with each other as links of equal importance and function. Only by the bringing into play of great contrasts, which provide the necessary articulation, can such a musical architecture take the strength of "form." Wagner employed it in his operas, and Liszt in his instrumental works, but both of these men had a great wealth of dramatic, epic, and lyric ideas and moods at their disposal, whereas the postromantic symphonists had only lyric talent. Thus in its last phase the symphony and the sonata became extended fantasies which were attempts to combine a freely handled, predominantly lyric fabric with the *pattern* of the sonata form, now entirely meaningless.

The indistinctness of mood and contour of the music of the fin de siècle, its groping gestures, caused an asymmetry of musical phraseology which was vaguely akin to free verse. The developing lines are broken, the harmonies like to tarry in the no-man's-land between tonalities, and although some central key is never really abandoned, constant chromatic and enharmonic modulations prevent an unequivocal tonal skeleton, a condition again leading to abrupt and broken form. All these uncertainties demanded an antidote, and a guidance for the performer, which was supplied in the form of the most minute dynamic, agogic, and other instructions which now literally covered the score.

Instrumental Music

THE post-Wagnerian period found music in confusion, with the best minds either exhausting themselves in the search for a breach in the Wagnerian wall, or deceiving themselves and the world with virtuoso verbosity. The mental incapacity of the period drove the artists in all directions, from eroticism to religious mysticism, from eccentric individualism to demonstrative collectivism. They tried to force heaven and hell for the desired redemption, passing in review Bach's religious firmness, Beethoven's heroism, Wagner's erotic Nirvana, and Brahms's ethic-artistic steadfastness, to find a new departure, a style and form of their own. While Debussy translated the poetry of the intimate quiverings of the soul, the hedonistic intoxication of colors, while Strauss proudly displayed his sensuous force in the glittering diplomatic uniform of the knight of the world, while Hugo Wolf set miniatures in music whose delicacy was like that of a mimosa, the others produced works the majority of which are belligerent professions of faith in the cultural weapons of old Europe, made at a time when these weapons were already discarded by the new armies of modern music. Thus they merely echo the pseudo-martial spirit of the old traditional militia, marching on Governor's Day, the barrels of their rifles filled with a protective coat of grease against rust and deterioration. They beheld the wonderfully artistic world of true romanticism, a world filled with life and poetry, and they thought themselves part of it, believing that the same fire burned in their bosom that once consumed their elders. However, their romanticism was conceived not in the storm of life but in the nostalgia of a decadent epoch, and therefore as soon as the breath of reality touched it, the burning fire of their ideals became the glowing log of the electric fireplace. They all had small ideas and little lyric gifts, yet they all insisted on casting them in the largest possible frames.

Symphony and tone poem, chamber music, and piano and organ literature found their representative composers in Gustav Mahler (1860–1911), Max Reger, and Richard Strauss (b. 1864), three musicians who stand apart from the multitude of satellites. They typify the prevailing tendencies and embody the spirit of the dying nineteenth century without appreciably entering into that of the nascent twentieth, although one of them, Strauss, is still active as these lines are written.

The ability to manipulate musical elements can be carried to the highest technical virtuosity by sheer intellectual force. But these elements, such as orchestration, can be mastered without necessarily entering the creative field proper. It was not for the first time that composition was little more than a highly developed technique of the métier—the fugue literature of the late and postbaroque era is one earlier instance—but the composers of the late nineteenth century differ from the diligent fugue writers, and also from the purveyors of post-Mendelssohnian romances, in that they exhibit a certain idealism. They believed that a direct ratio existed between the size of the apparatus of expression and the ideas to be expressed. They were convinced that by utilizing all available tonal resources they could create compositions of matching artistic value. The embodiment of this outlook, which did not spare labor or devotion in assembling the strongest and most varied means of expression, which pitted intellect against matter, was Gustav Mahler. As a type, his attitude toward art was not only noble but it had greatness. Thus the attitude was not that of the twentieth-century "orchestrator" who believes in his métier only, but that of an artistic personality of uncompromising earnestness and integrity.

The disharmony of the declining century looms with tremendous intensity in Mahler. With monastic devotion he tried to give form and shape to all the contradictory instincts of his time, but all he could summon was an almost religious sincerity which cannot be challenged by the grandiloquence, and even hysterical Titanism, that often mars his best efforts. He strove for monumentality with every sinew in his body, and to this end he used every means at his disposal. Like an excellent régisseur, this great executant and re-creative artist, one of the greatest conductors of modern times, gathered together all available means, and it cannot be denied that the external impression of the performance of such a work as his Eighth Symphony has something grandiose about it. This impression cannot be separated from the work, which suffers greatly when, as in phonograph recordings, the performing apparatus is not visible. For in this external presentation is offered the inner musical construction. There is in the background a great organ, in front of it, on stands, a large choir of children, and at a somewhat lower level, several hundred male singers, then, grouped around two pianos, two large female choirs. In the middle is a gigantic orchestra, comprising, besides all varieties of instruments of the modern orchestra in multiple numbers, piano, harmonium, mandolin, bells, *Glockenspiele,* and a wide variety of percussion instruments, the whole topped by a special brass choir. It is sad, however, to be compelled to admit, in the face of the deployment and adroit handling of such forces, of such unsparing energy, inexorable will, and intellectual effort, that the only great thing in these creations is the intention, that as a matter of fact the composer of these gigantic works was at the bottom of his heart a lyricist, foundering in the epic vastness of the symphony. One wonders whether Mahler himself did not realize this—why, otherwise, the sorrowful *Lied von der Erde?* Often there are some convincing and spellbinding details, but they cannot cover the lack of cohesion and aesthetic unity. Both the mental-musical bankruptcy of postromanticism and the fruitlessness of the enormous concert apparatus of the end of the century reached their most characteristic stage in Mahler's Eighth Symphony. The Titanism, and the desire to give the forlorn world something to cling to, prompted him to select the sturdy old hymn, *Veni Creator Spiritus,* and the closing scene from the second part of *Faust* for his texts, thus making the *Symphony of the Thousand* into a monster cantata; but nothing could raise this tragic work above a post-Wagnerian theatricalism, although it has its moments of inspiration. Mahler poured his essentially lyric gifts into some fine songs, but otherwise there was no soil under his feet, only the music of Schubert, Beethoven, Bruckner, and Wagner; his smile is lifeless, his irony bitter, and his humor forced.

The case of Reger and of the so-called contrapuntal school presents another aspect of fin de siècle confusion. Nevertheless, although the symptoms are seemingly entirely different, the malady is the same, namely, that the creative force springs more from the technical than from the spiritual. This is at once painfully evident when we consider the music of the less complicated members of the school, if an inclination to "write counterpoint" can be considered a tie strong enough to form a school. Two extremes can be quoted in this connection, the *Fantasia Contrappuntistica* of Ferruccio Busoni (1866–1924)—a work obviously the result of the composer's editorial activity, a pale and entirely unjustified interpolation in his edition of Bach's keyboard works, which was nevertheless hailed as "the crowning of Bach's *Art of the Fugue"* (Moser)—and any of the "symphonies for organ" of Charles Marie Widor (1845–1937), contrapuntally belabored products of a flat and scant musical imagination, the bastard nature of which is evident from the title alone.

Reger's output cannot be grasped and judged with such ease. We have already mentioned the nature of his polyphony, its being essentially the result of rapidly alternating harmonic progressions. This is the German equivalent of impressionism, and as such Reger is the real German counterpart of Debussy; but while Debussy follows his own principle of growth, Reger is in an eternal quest for ideals that once animated the great masters of the German past. He searches and searches, but every time he thinks that he has found the object of his quest, he discovers that it is something entirely different, and the search begins anew. This constant wandering does not permit his art to grow deep roots, it makes his music feverish and unhealthy. He tries to steady himself by clinging to the wonderfully sound and fertile art of the German baroque, but that art has only a symbolic meaning for him. While his colleagues were strongly affected by literary currents, Reger remained curiously "illiterate," living in a neobaroque vacuum. This is especially notable in his two hundred odd songs—among them a number of fine and moving ones—which disclose a total lack of feeling for literary values. This explains why Reger's works, no matter how interesting and remarkable in many ways, affect one's nerves rather than one's soul. If we recall the music and musicians of the eighteenth century we might say that perhaps Reger's unconcern with other than musical values heralds that return to music as music which evidently was the only salvation of an art completely enveloped by literature. And indeed, the pure musicianship, the marvelous self-sufficiency we so much admired in the composers of the baroque and the classic eras, was secretly admired even by the staunchest adherents of the neo-German school; but such absolute musicianship is entirely dependent on the invention of musical materials, and this inventiveness is altogether missing in Reger and in his colleagues. His most successful works are variations on borrowed themes, chorale preludes, and other works in which there is a *cantus prius factus*. Variation is one of the oldest and most elemental types of music, beloved and practiced by all musicians since the early lute and keyboard composers. Unlike Beethoven and Brahms, Reger and his confreres approached the variation in a purely formal fashion, as if justifying Hanslick's aesthetic maxim that music is mere sonorous motion. Their variations on a given theme are not metamorphoses of the spiritual and poetic content, but a mere musical play with a given material. Even this is not new and had been done by earlier composers in a most satisfactory and artistic manner, but such literal variations demand a clear tonal and formal logic, offering many aspects of the same material, justified by the mastery of musical setting. With Reger the uncertainty of the tonality, the eternal chromatic modulations, destroy the logical foundations of all such music making. There is no compelling artistic creative urge in most of this music; the great technical skill of the plodding fugues, the various shades of gray in the slow movements, and the nervously excited allegros that he wrote in profusion differ in mood only, not in ideas.

And finally we arrive at music which can no longer be heard, only read. Such a composition is Reger's gigantic *100th Psalm,* at the end of which there is an eight-part fugue accompanied by a great and animated orchestra, and into this sea of tones the composer tosses the chorale "A Mighty Fortress Is Our God," played by a brass choir. Opposed to the metallic sound of the brasses the song of the hundreds of singers appears as an inarticulate stammering. One can see the singers' mouths move, but one no longer can follow the song, the melodic lines are lost. All this is not due solely to a hypertrophy of sonority and a paucity of musical material: it is mainly the result of a total absence of spiritual conviction and planning. The chorale is merely a gesture here and is resorted to simply to swell the sonority.

While other composers tortured themselves with the problems of life and art, Richard Strauss freed himself from all mystic and metaphysical ties and proceeded to utilize everything the century had produced in a technical synthesis, thus becoming the greatest virtuoso and technician of the declining century. "Virtuoso" is not meant in a derogatory sense, for virtuosity carried to such a degree is art. Moreover, unlike Ravel, who in his later years became a mere orchestrator handling his many-headed orchestra with supreme skill but without much spiritual conviction, and ended by orchestrating other composers' works (Moussorgsky) or writing stunts appropriate for the modern cinema theater orchestra (*Bolero*), Strauss relished this virtuosity with the conviction that comes from an old family of musicians. It is true that in his synthesis of the century's music there is nothing of the spiritual content of classicism and romanticism, none of their problems nor of their joys, but instead an appropriation of all their means of expression, developed with the utmost ease and with a healthy and sober musicianship to a pliable virtuoso technicism. It is noteworthy that Strauss began his career with Mendelssohn, another impeccable craftsman, his earlier works being veritable Mendelssohnian clichés; then under Alexander Ritter's influence he was converted to the cause of the neo-German school, to become, beginning with the nineties, the leader of its left wing. This progression was entirely natural, for mysticism was alien to his soul (one should not be misled by *Zarathustra,* for that is mysticism with a glossary) and he seized upon the actual and visible only. Therefore he explored all styles with gusto, always emerging, unlike Mahler, unscathed; instead of carrying oppressing memories he made off with a bag of new tricks, for Strauss had the powerful physique and the rhetorical skill of a tribune of the people, persuasive and dynamic, and armed with these formidable weapons he entered every debate offered at the musical crossroads. Thus he tried out every possible lead for a continuation of the neo-German school. There were no scruples of conscience to bother him, no preconceived theories, social responsibility, or binding Weltanschauung, for he is a musician who likes music and likes the world as it is and not as it should be. We might say, and indeed it is often evident, that Strauss attempted to cover his shortcomings with a ready rhetoric, but he loved life and wanted to live, whereas the others gravitated toward the cemetery.

The uselessness of writing symphonies, quartets, or piano sonatas was apparent to Strauss after a few essays in those media; his instinct warned him of the impossibility of reconciling the ideas and ideals of the music of his time with these inherited forms. At the same time he realized that Liszt's was the only possibly *new* direction to follow. Since he was no dreamer and since, outside of perceptible reality, there was no life for him, he could not follow Liszt, the composer of programless tone poems, hence his espousal of the realism of Berlioz; but—with the exception of certain aberrations in his later years—this realism was accomplished· with consummate musicianship that more closely followed Liszt's precepts than those of Berlioz. And thus virtuosity became art in him, for there is no modern composer who handles the orchestra with so sure a hand, with more élan and musicianship; his orchestra seems virtually happy to play. His realism encompasses everything, from jovial humor to hysterical perversity. Where other composers reflect the nervous and decadent in works that aim to give a positive faith in art and life, Strauss approaches this state of mind deliberately—*Salomé*—rendering it as a form of observed realism and not as the result of a painful and torturing experience. Unlike Liszt's tone poems, Strauss's music requires not only a title but a detailed knowledge of the program, which the listener must follow from point to point. The minute explanations and comments on the subject matter are integral parts and aesthetic factors of the work, without which sense and coherence suffer. The great problem of form that defeated most of his contemporaries Strauss solved by these programs, the episodes of which he marked with characteristic motives fathered by the Wagnerian system. This was not an eminently musical solution, for it is impossible to impute to music the expression of fate (*Death and Transfiguration*) and experience (*The Life of a Hero*). Music can express the feelings caused by a stroke of fate or awakened by certain experiences, for our feelings are the sum total of our experiences, but our multifarious feelings lend themselves to few typical formulations. If the greatest power of music is that it is able to convey the idea of all things, unrestricted by the images to which—as to life itself— all the other arts are bound, it is conversely true that it is not within its power to transform the idea into a concrete and comprehensible phenomenon. There were many composers in the nineteenth and the early twentieth centuries who realized the futility of this procedure, but when they fell back on "absolute music" they met inevitable defeat in the equally futile attempt to use forms and idioms of a bygone age. Thus Strauss's solution proved to be more workable than the pseudo-sonatas and was, of course, much more readily intelligible to everyone. Then there was his phenomenal orchestra, ready to follow his intentions, for what he put on paper was true to the author's plans and sounded well under all circumstances; and his thematic inventiveness, usually banal but always frank and often spirited, was the mark of an uninhibited soul. Strauss carried the Wagnerian technique to its apogee; compared to him all the other followers of the Bayreuth Moloch seem victims rather than disciples. But there are, of course, the shady sides of his art, for the brilliant orchestral scherzo-rondeau *Till Eulenspiegel* was later followed by the aimless and frameless mural of the *Alpensymphonie,* which more than any composition up to Honegger's steam engine epic showed the complete bankruptcy of this type of program music. The other symphonic poems all have their good moments—notably *Don Quixote,* a set of variations, that is, a work with a more or less delineated "form"—but are often lost in the attempt at the musically unattainable—*Zarathustra.*

Strauss has been compared to Hasse, and the comparison is well taken, for this nineteenth-century compatriot of the eighteenth-century idol was a born master who loved his craft, knew his public and how to satisfy it, and, like Hasse, who witnessed Mozart's triumphs, he survived by a generation the era to which he rightfully belongs, watching from his well-entrenched position the march of twentieth-century music.

Opera

OPERA too, at the turn of the century, presents a divided picture. On the one hand the Wagnerian domination was complete to the extent that its apostles would brook no individuality nor stylistic "defection." They took the only product of an independent spirit, Cornelius, valiantly trying to hold his own in the neo-German sea, and after his death in the name of charity and righteousness reorchestrated his operas in the Wagnerian spirit. On the other hand the verism of Sardou and Bruneau quickly recruited followers in Leoncavallo, Mascagni, Puccini, d'Albert, and a number of lesser composers; but with Puccini's *Girl of the Golden West* (1913, book by Belasco) the tendency was already in full decline, although occasional attempts at veristic music drama are made even in our day. Richard Strauss stands between the two tendencies, trying to combine the advantages of both. The usual wariness that the symphonist exhibited toward preconceived stylistic philosophies was relaxed in his operas, and after a few false starts in the orthodox Wagnerian manner, Strauss endeavored to combine the "music drama" (as the Wagnerian style is still called by musical authors) with the Mozartean "opera." Needless to say, this was a dangerous undertaking, and although his prodigious technical skill succeeded in converting the recitative into a swiftly moving orchestral fabric and the aria into a broad cantilena, the former modulating incessantly, while the latter remains faithful to one main tonality and uses tunes of a popular nature, the picture is not convincing and in the *Rosenkavalier* actually becomes precious; Mozart and Johann Strauss rouged and lipsticked. The comedy is excellently handled and the musician's virtuosity sparkles, but what were small but genuine diamonds in *Figaro* are large rhinestones in the *Rosenkavalier,* and the graceful pairs dancing in the Redoutensaal to the tune of the Viennese waltz king seem to have indulged in something different from the traditional champagne. Among the other works *Salomé* is particularly noteworthy for the faithful musical translation of the atmosphere of the "libretto," which in this case is the original book. The orgiastic tendency of the period reached its height in this work, and in certain parts of *Electra*.

Although Strauss carried the Wagnerian technique to its ultimate destiny and doom, he did not share his model's pretensions as to the role of the stage in the opera; his orchestra remains in undisputed and undisguised control, dictating mood as well as form. In fact, he systematized what Wagner did in his moments of exaltation: the dramatization of the symphonic poem. Thus Strauss's operas are orchestra operas even more than are Wagner's. His melodies can be offensively banal, studded with stereotyped harmonies that at times descend to the level of Barnby's hymns, marring some of the climactic scenes. His vocal parts do not translate characters in music, they merely summarize what takes place in the soul of the dramatic figures, and they struggle throughout to maintain themselves against the onslaught of the eloquent orchestra.

The leading figure in the other operatic community, uniting the grand opera with verism, was Giacomo Puccini (1858–1924). Idol of his public at the turn of the century, Puccini was another full-blooded opera composer, more familiar than any one of his contemporaries with the secrets of theatrical effect and success. This sure instinct—evident even in the selection of his libretti—was the substantial heritage bequeathed to him by the great past of Italian opera, but Puccini did not remain unconditionally faithful to the tenets of this great tradition. From Verdi's art he learned more the externals than the essence, and from the school of *verismo* he appropriated a love of the brutal, often trivially "thick" effects; on the other hand he learned much from the French, from Bizet's dramatic economy, from Massenet's sentimental lyricism, and from Debussy's opulent color. Real dramatic concentration he achieved only toward the end of his life, but his technique of effective theatrical writing, his understanding of the singing voice and its place in the lyric drama, his wonderful sense for new colors, ideas, tricks, and above all his rich melodic invention, piquant harmonies, and clever but unostentatious orchestration, qualities which appear in his earliest works, attest the hand of a born and distinguished artist. The exotic colorit which gradually veiled his stage, the decadent drugs which he used to accelerate the blood circulation of his theater, the burlesque, bizarre, and grotesque elements he salvaged from the old and inexhaustible mine of the opera buffa, found a real master in him. But the old masters' healthy humor as well as Verdi's true romanticism paled in him to the declining stimulant of exoticism; what was ardent passion on Verdi's stage is more like hysteria on Puccini's. The youthful ardor, verve, and lyricism of *La Bohéme* were soon drowned in enervating *raffinement;* beginning with *Tosca* and *Mme Butterfly* the costumes are more noticeable, as is the forced use of local color, but these works still make good theater and are essentially operatic. Toward the end of his life Puccini again found himself in the macabre but virtuoso humor of *Gianni Schicchi,* a modern opera buffa written with deep insight into the problems of the musical stage.

With Strauss and Puccini opera exhausted what possibilities had been left by the main types of nineteenth-century opera. It became evident that the Wagnerian music drama was essentially one man's work and style and could not be continued since it was not timeless and universal. Wagner's heavy shadow was like Attila's horse; the grass did not grow where it passed. A legion of imitators followed in his footsteps, but since they were merely the heirs of a complicated and rather naïve system of dramaturgy they failed to carry the music drama one inch from the place where Wagner left it. In Italy, although Verdi reaffirmed the great traditions of opera, the prevailing tendency leaned toward the grand opera and its veristic variant, and France remained, in general, wedded to the school of Massenet, with such composers as d'Indy straying into the Wagnerian camp. (Debussy's *Pelléas et Mélisande,* being a unique work, demands specific discussion and will be treated separately.) The typical grand opera pattern of works like d'Albert's *Tiefland,* Rabaud's *Marouf,* Dukas's *Ariane,* and Busoni's *Turandot* cannot be camouflaged by what is called "modern music."

The reasons for this stagnation were many. Among them was the failure of composers and librettists to understand that opera has its own aesthetics and that it cannot be approached and understood from the point of view of the spoken drama. Music intensifies emotional values to such a degree that the changing emotional state of the acting operatic figures appears as if seen through a magnifying glass. A spoken drama cannot, therefore, be set to music without alterations. The value attached to the libretto has followed the fluctuating importance of the relationship between drama and music at the various epochs of operatic history. There seemed to be a belief among the composers of the last generation that a drama which is to be set to music must move in the so-called sentimental-emotional sphere, by which was understood a world of flabby lyricism not dependent on causality. But they overlooked the fact that since music has a tendency to switch from the actual content of an action to its sentimental implications, this actual content must possess an especially pregnant meaning. The action again must show a certain pantomimic plasticity because of the difficulties of clear enunciation in singing. Such facts compel the thoughtful librettist carefully to plan his plots and action in detail and then to retain the most important moments of the action. The purely narrative parts are always tedious on the operatic stage and are successful only if kept in a lyric vein to characterize a figure. All important happenings should occur with pantomimic clarity on the stage, and nothing should be left for speculation. The episodic tableaux and side alleys have tempted many a composer and librettist to indulge in coloristic hors d'oeuvre, invariably to the detriment of the intelligibility of the whole. Artistic economy is opposed to the introduction of motives which cannot be utilized organically in the main body of the action. Episodic figures may interest the listener momentarily, but he may be annoyed if he cannot fit them into the course of the drama. On the other hand, it is equally faulty to place on the stage figures whose presence there is merely for the sake of dragging the action out of an impasse. Eighteenth-century opera was able to carry on action in music with the rapidity and colorfulness of actual life, in the so-called *secco* recitatives. Eighteenth- and early nineteenth-century composers were also perfectly willing to have spoken dialogues inserted into the fabric of the opera, reverting to music when the situation and the psychological moment permitted or required it. Nowadays we are ashamed of spoken words in an opera house; we hide them; we forget that opera is theater with music, not a pretext for singing. While the recitatives connected the individual scenes, the large and animated finales of the classic opera were also teeming with action and life, which disproves the theory that the recitative is the only possible musical expression of dramatic action. All these facts contribute to the dramaturgical laws of the opera, which do not permit too much lyricism or too much narration in the text proper.

While critics and composers did not notice that the world was weary of both the psychological leitmotif opera and the empty grand opera, that it was yearning for a lyric theater again, good theater, without metaphysics in every line of the text and hidden meanings in every harmony, salvation was promised from that department of the lyric stage, the comic play-opera, which always rescued the lofty music drama whenever it reached a blind alley. That truly Shakespearean comedy of Verdi, *Falstaff,* came as a revelation to all composers who understood and loved the stage. After the orgies of his large music dramas, Strauss returned to the eighteenth-century play-opera and in his *Ariadne* tried to give a modern German version of the opera buffa, reducing his orchestra and permitting the figures of the drama to sing. After a lifetime of realistic *comédie larmoyante,* Puccini rejected the guidance of Scribe and Sardou and, turning his back on grand opera, reappeared with a little modern opera buffa, the above-mentioned *Gianni Schicchi,* nurtured on the great traditions of Italian opera. These works may not yet represent great art, but they represent a certain artistic integrity and a grasp of the necessary and impending realignment of the operatic front. But this was merely a beginning, a slogan which it remained for the twentieth century to put into action.

Dance Music and Operetta

THROUGHOUT its history music has allied itself with the dance, an alliance natural and inescapable since rhythm is a vital element common to both. It was especially in the popular realm that dance and music were cultivated together, a large part of the folk song of all nations consisting of dance songs. Then, beginning with the late Renaissance, the great development and refinement of social life promoted the dance from a harmless amusement to a sophisticated social game. As older instrumental music grew out of the positive articulation of dance music, this new, higher order of the art of dancing produced instrumental forms of great variety. Curiously enough, the immediate development of these new instrumental forms did not take place in the dance halls; the dances were stylized and continued as independent instrumental pieces. A series of such stylized dances gave us the suite, one of the highest species of instrumental music of the baroque. All this was, however, an autonomous, highly developed and refined art; dance music proper declined, and was reduced to a very modest existence. This is understandable, for an artistic, minute choreography imposes formal restrictions, and it was only after the strictly organized figural dances gave way to "free" square dances that further development could take place in real dance music. The robust minuets and *Ländler* of the south German and Bohemian composers are, indeed, different from the courtly dances of the rococo, and while many of them have a symphonic air about them, equally as many are unmistakably peasant dances, just as were the ones that Schubert collected on his forays in the Austrian villages.

Art and civilization are, as we have repeatedly discovered, always most intimately connected. Dance music is entertainment music, it emphasizes more pointedly than any other type of music an almost corporeal sensuousness. Art music reached for the dance with the avowed intention of providing accompaniment for it only at a time when, after the Napoleonic era, the people's desires for amusement and entertainment became marked. Vienna, long experienced with the popular dance music of its music-loving racial mélange, was the logical seat for this new art, but the "first" striking example of modern artistic dance music came from the pen of Carl Maria von Weber. *The Invitation to the Dance* (1819), dreamy, yet impudent and chivalric, must have banished, almost instantly, the lingering remnants of the style galant which had become as outmoded as wigs and dress rapiers. With the *Invitation,* then, began the new dance music, immediately producing two different types, one, the character piece, the other, the straightforward dance, both largely under the aegis of the waltz. It is unnecessary to dwell again on the many engaging dance compositions of the era, from Chopin to Brahms; they belong to the highest sphere of art. But it is another matter with the minor composers, for with them there was a gradual and steady descent into the realm of salon music. The dances of the Scharwenka brothers, Philip (1847–1917) and Xavier (1850–1924), and of Moritz Moszkowski (1854–1925), are pleasant, but of a somewhat watery romanticism.

The history of the waltz is a bit of Viennese history. Josef Lanner (1801–1843), Johann Strauss, Sr. (1804–1849), and his son, Johann Jr. (1825–1899), summarize its whole development. Beside these three important composers all the others are ephemeral. The somewhat sentimental moonlight romanticism of the period of reaction is reflected in Lanner's works, soft and dreamy, but the elder Strauss is full of fire and life. The formal construction of their waltzes is identical, consisting of five sections with an introduction and a coda. Lanner's compositions, however, emphasize the lyric melody, while Strauss likes sharp rhythms and piquant orchestral colors. After Lanner's death Strauss became the sovereign but was immediately challenged by his son, who had his own band. And again music obeyed social dictates. The Austrian metropolis became the center of an international society. The original citizenry, with its famous laisser aller temperament, its gregarious musicals in comfortable homes, withdrew before a glittering eclectic society gathered in sumptuous ballrooms. Everything became more festive, elegant, nervous, and spirited; the bouquet of the Austrian wild flowers was replaced by Parisian perfume. It is remarkable, indeed, that the younger Strauss was able to retain the best from the older style, uniting Lanner's soft melodies with his father's vigorous rhythm, and at the same time enlarging the form internally and externally. With unheard-of fecundity and facility Strauss composed hundreds upon hundreds of dances, but his art remained fresh and young, and this freshness safeguarded his waltzes from losing their original aim and purpose, that of dance music. Nevertheless, the decisive step that led from the ballroom to the theater was still taken by him: the waltz turned into the Viennese operetta.

Strauss's *Indigo* (1871), the first operetta, carried in itself all the germs which were to ruin this type of the lyric stage: senseless action, insipid content, insincere sentimental feelings, characterizations that at their best are caricatures, miserable versification in the songs, and laboriously invented jokes made enjoyable by peppery seasoning. Today it is impossible to divorce these attributes from the operetta, and the genre cannot bear comparison with the old Singspiel which discharged similar functions. It was a great misfortune that Strauss never obtained a good libretto, for his fascinating musical talents triumphed in the *Bat,* which will remain the best German operetta. Something that all subsequent operetta composers could not understand, the dramatic in the dance, is offered here with consummate artistry. The dance becomes a dramatic mood, most convincingly presented in the masterly musical pantomime of the prison warden in the third act, which is a worthy counterpart to the Beckmesser scene in the *Meistersinger*. From the other of Strauss's sixteen operettas we should mention the *Gypsy Baron,* in which the endeavor to create a genuine comic opera is thwarted mainly by the libretto.

None of Strauss's colleagues and successors could match his art. Karl Millöcker (1842–1899) was perhaps the only serious artist among them. Two among his many operettas, *Bettelstudent* and *Armer Jonathan,* are filled with delightful music. After him the operetta was lost in the products of the Viennese theatrical export commerce, ruled over by Edmund Eysler, Leo Fall, Franz Lehár, and Oscar Straus (not related to either of the Strauss families). It was with the latter that the industrial exploitation of musical comedy started. A theater was leased and a successful operetta played a hundred or a thousand times, until its appeal or its public was exhausted. We may deplore this state of affairs, but it is evident that the great success of this lowly lyric theater would not be possible did it not satisfy a popular demand, a natural demand whose artistic gratification is refused by the representatives of our "higher" art. This desire on the part of the wide majority of the public is still the same that called into existence Singspiel, opéra comique, zarzuela, and ballad opera. Pepusch, Hiller, Lortzing, and many other able composers understood the problem and answered the challenge with works of popular and artistic appeal, but as long as there are no composers to follow in their footsteps, and in those of Monsigny, Sullivan, and the French composers we shall mention presently, the popular lyric stage will be dominated by products coming from the artistic gutter of the metropolises.

Unfortunately the damage is not limited to the lyric stage. The many songs that passed from the Singspiel and opéra comique into the public domain contributed greatly to the treasury of folk song. The people like to sing, but their spontaneous creative activity has long since evaporated, and what they have retained is only their groping and easily misdirected love for song and music. It is to be hoped that universal musical instruction in the public schools will establish a taste for good music, fulfilling one of the foremost tasks of modern education.

The French *opérette* started under entirely different circumstances, for the incentive was literary rather than musical, a fact which assured an initial excellence not enjoyed by the Viennese variety.

Meilhac and Halévy, the able librettists of *Carmen,* founded their partnership in 1860, and one of the first successful plays of the literary firm was the book of *Fair Helen* (1864), followed by several others, all set to music by Jacques Offenbach (1819–1880). If we consider the fact that these operettas are the most widely known, the most popular, and perhaps the best of Offenbach's works, there is no need to insist on his indebtedness to his librettists, or to point out how important a thing the quality of the opera book is to the composer of the score. So long as Meilhac and Halévy furnished Offenbach's books for him, the result was always a work of art, with a certain restraint which art demands. As soon as he went to other librettists, the products of their collaboration became vulgar. What Meilhac and Halévy kept subordinate, or at best suggested, was by their imitators paraded and emphasized. In short it is not unjust to say that a vast share in the credit for the creation of the modern opéra comique belongs to its first librettists.

The son of the Jewish cantor of the Cologne synagogue, Offenbach went to Paris at an early age. After some studies at the Conservatoire he became a member of the orchestra of the Opéra Comique, afterwards conductor and régisseur of his own works in different theaters. Offenbach's music is characterized by a radiant, fresh spirit, elegance, and a light, ironic tone. He can be frivolous, biting, and arrogant, but also genuinely moving. The adventurous-flirtatious elements in his works seem somewhat cynical, especially to German and Anglo-Saxon audiences, yet this great expert of the human marionette theater that was the Second Empire merely felt that the figures of this era were too small to inspire tragic greatness. Having partaken of the frivolous and lighthearted life of Napoleon III's Paris, and having ridiculed it with biting sarcasm and humor, he himself seemed to enjoy making part of it. That he also could see the sadness under the cover of revelry is well demonstrated in the *Tales of Hoffmann.*

Offenbach approached his task with a musical equipment and technique which remained the unsurpassed, even unequaled, model of the modern operetta. His small, finely wrought forms, lilting or slightly lascivious dances, ingratiating and impudent melodies, remarkable declamation whittled to a fine point, rhythmic verve, and brilliant, piquant, yet supple orchestration have not lost an iota of their freshness. Nor would the plays show age, *Orpheus in Hades, Parisian Life, The Grand Duchess of Gérolstein,* and a number of others, if in our time the actors and stage directors did not over-lay the action with forced contemporary asides. *Fair Helen,* for instance, is the humorous parody of a whole system of government and of theology, and, allowing for the variations made with comic intent, surprisingly Greek in spirit. The cheap parodies of many late nineteenth-century play makers are not to be mentioned in the same breath with this scholarly fooling.

Among Offenbach's successors the most notable was Charles Lecocq (1832–1918), whom the Parisian public considered his rightful heir. Although less original than Offenbach, his music is attractive and exceedingly well made. Offenbach's influence was not restricted to France but was even felt in Vienna, where the Dalmatian-born Franz von Suppé (1819–1895) success-fully applied the superior technical and formal means of the French operetta to the erstwhile form of the Viennese. Retaining the typical Viennese local color, Suppé wrote delightful works, more nearly akin to the comic opera than to the operetta, and not at all related to the shallow products of the Austrian operetta industry.

Church Music

IN Liszt's two oratorios [2] the spirit of Catholicism reappeared in a type of music that since the late baroque had been especially identified with Protes-tantism. It is understandable that their echoes were heard in Catholic lands, and for a while we witness the flourishing of the oratorio in the hands of Catholic composers. While new and towering over their immediate progeny, Liszt's oratorios were really the result of a trend in French music and were notably influenced by Berlioz's *l'Enfance du Christ,* as the oratorio always retained a certain vogue in France, rekindled after the Napoleonic times by the romantic mystics. Saint-Saëns, for example, composed a Latin Christmas oratorio in 1854, that is, before Liszt's influence was felt. In general these French oratorios are distinguished more by the purely instrumental parts than by the choruses. More notable is Franck's chief choral work, *Les Béati-tudes,* although its badly diluted handling of the text bespeaks a lack of epic strength without which the oratorio sags. Similarly powerless, although not lacking in certain lyric qualities, are the oratorios of Edgar Tinel (1854–1912) and Peter Benoît (1834–1901). All these composers were under the spell of Wagner and ignorant of the choral schooling of the Handelian era—only Brahms possessed that. They leaned toward the decorative from which the step toward the theatrical, incompatible with the northern-Protestant con-ception as opposed to the southern-Catholic, was not far removed. Still they did not take this decisive step, leaving it to Gounod and especially to Massenet.

Handel made the oratorio a national institution in England, even though up to the end of the nineteenth century the successful composers were foreigners. National traits are discernible only in Sullivan's cantatas and oratorios. No matter how well Mendelssohn's soft melodies corresponded to English national taste, the neo-German school with its song-speech was soon welcomed along with an emphasis on the role of the instrumental accompaniment. The uninterrupted cult of good choral singing protected the compositions of de Cowen, Mackenzie, Stanford, and Parry, but their music is lacking in power and often lapses into mere academicism, overcome to a certain degree only by Elgar. His *Dream of Gerontius* is the one English oratorio of the period to leave the confines of the British Isles for more than passing visits, but again, epic strength is missing, for this oratorio is dominated rather by loveliness. There is a great deal of music in the *Dream of Gerontius* that is merely well worked, which is the more surprising because in the quiet and meditative scenes, such as the death of Gerontius, Elgar can give himself without technical and stylistic clichés. His melodies, the clear architecture and euphony of his choruses, recall Mendelssohn. Similarly good workmanship, fine choral writing, lyric feeling, but also a lack of epic strength characterize Horatio Parker's notable oratorio *Hora Novissima*.

One might think, when considering this meek literature of cantata and oratorio, that the great forms of nonliturgic Protestant church music, once the pride not only of a church but of a whole musical civilization, had all but disappeared. This was not the case, however, for such music, together with *a cappella* motets, anthems, and various other types, among them Masses written for Protestant use, were composed in profusion throughout the nineteenth century from Mendelssohn to Reger. What had departed was the spirit of Protestantism, the conviction, sense, and desire for churchly thought which in the past inspired great sacred art. The whole of the century dissipated its religious energies in trying to regain it, but only two of its composers were worthy of the great traditions of the past, Mendelssohn and Brahms; for the rest we might say that the church was the refuge for all the music unfit for theater or concert hall. The sentimental "Catholicizing" of the Protestants of the romantic era and the historical efforts of a period becoming conversant with the products of the great past, also took their toll, the former by implanting the sweetly sentimental tone of Bortniansky, Franck, and Rheinberger—to name three typical representatives of this type of church music—the latter by falling into the other extreme of mere counterpoint writing. English and American composers succeeded in combining both. The strong attraction of historism is especially evident in the Catholic Reger, whose church music is almost exclusively intended for Protestant services. The mirage he followed was the Lutheran chorale and all that it meant to the sturdy church music of the baroque. But historism is not creative, living art. All the impressive scholarship that rediscovered for us the great art of the past, the many educational institutions, schools for church music, university chapel choirs devoted exclusively to the best in sacred music, and all the belief in rules, all the vows for purity and nobility in church music, cannot replace conviction, for the problem of church music is the problem of the church itself. We may give correct and highly artistic performances of the great church art of the past and thereby accomplish a serious cultural deed, but religion is neither retrospective nor archaic, it must be living to inspire a living art.

The absence of a uniform liturgy caused the decline of Protestant church music, whereas the world-wide validity of the rites of the Catholic Church insured it against the ravages of the times. This does not mean that Catholic church music was superior to contemporary Protestant music, for it shared liberally in the other's decadence, but there was always a well-defined ideal to which it could return; thus the same search for the recapture of the spirit of church music which occupied Protestantism throughout the nineteenth century, and which was not less intense in Catholic circles, received a certain scope from its very beginning. But the archaism that characterized the Protestant efforts was not less evident.

We have had occasion to discuss the romantic Palestrina renaissance and the rise of Caecilianism.[3] A movement so strongly conditioned by preconceived religious-aesthetic creeds was perforce lacking in critical insight, and the much needed reform of plain chant, undertaken by the influential church music center in Ratisbon, was unfortunately based on the *Medicea*[4] and other sources, whose distorted nature was known to scholars. But the scholars were not heeded and the serious reform activity was misdirected for a whole generation. The already pronounced preference for the none too well-defined *a cappella* ideal of the Renaissance was buttressed by the wealth of music appearing in the great musicological editions, and by a revival of the cult of strict modal counterpoint which enthroned Fux and his *Gradus ad Parnassum* as an infallible authority in all matters of composition.[5] It goes without saying that such an orientation could produce but archaic churchly *Gebrauchsmusik*.

In the Romanic countries the desire for a regeneration of church music was much less affected by historism and by a dogmatic worship of archaic polyphony. French and Italian church musicians turned first of all to Gregorian song and, largely unconcerned with polyphony, were busy in France with the publication of all sorts of incongruous organ accompaniments to the chants, and in Italy with the serious preliminary studies which were to lead to the significant reforms of Pius X. In accordance with this spirit Pius IX renewed the *schola cantorum* at the Lateran in 1868, and institutions for the study and teaching of church music were founded in Milan, Rome, and Venice, the latter by the Patriarch Sarto, the future Pope Pius X. The serious reform ideas appeared with the first of these institutions. In 1882 there was held in Arezzo a congress for liturgic song, ending with the foundation of an international society for the improvement of church music; Leo XIII issued a decree restricting the use of instruments and of the organ (1884), and Patriarch Sarto a pastoral letter (1895) which gave a foretaste of his memorable encyclical that was to come in 1903.

In the meantime the spirit of the German Caecilia movement reached France, where it found a receptive group of composers rallying around the newly founded Schola Cantorum. But the French composers were not given to archaic *a cappella* polyphony, and remained true to their former ideals, concentrating on churchly instrumental music rather than on choral writing. Thus while the country churches practiced a marchlike "Gregorian" song accompanied with atrocious chords, the great churches in Paris boasted some of the finest organists of the world.

The old Caecilians were still fully occupied with the battle against "chromaticism in church music," the French playing their sophisticated organ pieces during the Mass and singing their own brand of plain chant, when the quietly working Benedictines of Solesmes began to publish the results of their epic labors: the first volume of the *Paléographie Musicale* appeared in 1889. Their work so impressed the authorities that when the thirty-year privilege of the Ratisbon publishing firm Pustet, which carried out the principles of the German chorale school, expired in 1901 it was not renewed. A few months after assuming the pontificate in 1903, Pius X issued his celebrated *Motu Proprio* which sought to restore church music to its traditional dignity by accepting the Solesmes restitution of plain chant and at the same time making a certain compromise with Caecilianism. Thus along with a reform of the practice of the Gregorian chorale and a renewed canonization of the Palestrina style, there was promulgated a ban on "theatrical style," on women in the church choir, on the use of instruments, and even on the use of the organ. Women were replaced by boys, the organ was assigned a much more modest place in the service, and among the instruments only those of the wind variety whose tone was considered akin to that of the organ were tolerated.

Pius X's reform is comparable only to that attributed rightly or wrongly to Gregory I. Beginning with 1905, the volumes of the *Editio Vaticana* provided the Catholic world with a practical and authoritative edition of the Solesmes corpus of plain chant. What made this edition notable, and the pope a worthy successor of his great medieval precursor in office, was the practical and artistic decision not to cling to archaeological subtleties—these were left to the scientific folios of the *Paléographie*—but to select from among the many existing variants of the melodies those which were most traditional, that is, living. The great cultural and religious importance of this revival is not substantially beclouded by the fact that the musicological world is far from agreeing with certain properties of the restored plain chant. There are especially grave misgivings about the rhythmical principles employed by the Solesmes school. Another question of paramount importance is the accompaniment of the melodies. For while it is undeniable that the only correct way to perform Gregorian chant is by unaccompanied singing, and while lately we have recaptured in some small measure the ability of our distant ancestors to follow and enjoy a pure one-dimensional musical line, centuries of many-voiced music have so conditioned our musical perception that we hear harmonies even if they are not present. This question will have to be decided upon by scholars of wide musical, theological, and cultural experience and must not be left, as heretofore, to the whims of wayward church organists.

The twenty-nine points of the *Motu Proprio* betray the spirit of an ecclesiastic who did not legislate on the administration of church music merely *ex officio,* but who made a lifelong study of music as an auxiliary to religion. The enlightened pope also knew that there are temperamental and traditional-cultural differences between the many nations that constitute his flock. The serious and in many ways severe articles of the encyclical represented more a desire than a law, and the pope delegated authority to the bishops to rescind such provisions as they thought could be dispensed with in the interest of their diocese. This was a tacit admission of the impossibility of completely restoring that which no longer was a living force. To exclude the tremendous literature of Catholic church music since Palestrinian times would have been an unjust act, damning the memory of men who honored and served their church with a devotion fully the equal of their consecrated elders; their only sin, that they expressed themselves in the artistic spirit of their time, was shared by Perotinus, Dunstable, Dufay, Palestrina, Lassus, and Byrd, but what was a living religion and art in the times of these venerable composers appears to the forlorn modern man as archaism, an arbitrarily established religious-artistic code. What the pope envisaged was a strengthening of the spirit of Catholicism by recalling and restoring the great liturgic art of the past. He hoped, perhaps, that by this infusion some of the liturgic strength of the heroic age, lost in the romantic and postromantic eras, would again be captured by the new century. As the restrictions were gradually relaxed by diocesan authorities, these hopes did not materialize, for the same reason that they could not materialize in Protestant music. The great concerted church music of the seventeenth, eighteenth, and early nineteenth centuries, once more rekindled by Liszt and Bruckner, died down almost immediately to the pale glimmer of the Rheinbergers and Perosis, and after it was again permitted to burn, all that was left was the ashes.

The Song

THE strong literary orientation inaugurated by romanticism, and the rapprochement, nay, union, of poetry and music which it fostered would lead one to expect the postromantic period to be especially felicitous in its song literature. The events belie this expectation.

In discussing Schubert we came to consider the song as the ideal balance between poetry and music, as the vehicle in which poetry retains its nature and fully conveys its content while music forms a judicious entity. Nevertheless, the perfect song represents a shift of the point of gravity into the musical sphere. It is by no means true that the sung word is more penetrating and impressive than the spoken; on the contrary, the musician's rendition will often be distinctly weaker than that of a good reciter, since the purely sensuous beauty of the singing voice may render the ideas colorless. But the true song composer can do something more than replace the beautiful speech melody of verse with a sung melody: he can recast the whole situation, he can give us the poet's moods and ideas, not with, but in, music. This is what Schubert did, and Schumann, and Brahms.

Under the growing pressure exerted on all branches of music by the literary, realistic, and dramatic trend in the second half of the century, the ideal balance between poetry and music struck by the great song writers of the romantic period was gradually but deliberately altered to give us the modern song. Its beginnings lay in those of Schumann's compositions in which the texts (the Eichendorff poems, for instance) offer various moods as units between which there is a latent development of feeling. Schumann composed musical transitions to the various moods, especially in his preludes and interludes, which latter no longer fulfill formal purposes but are independent means of creating atmosphere. They open the world from which the poem originated, carrying us into regions where the voice can no longer be articulate. This is the road to Hugo Wolf (1860–1903).

The romantic song composer, inspired by a poem, transformed it into a song, and this song was no longer the property of the poet. Wolf wanted something else. He did not recast mood and idea, but attempted to guide the listener's soul toward the poem. He was able wholly to immerse himself in poetry; for the duration of the composition of a song he became one with the poet, whose poems were henceforth virtually his own creations. So completely did he identify himself with each poet that once he exhausted the moods, imagery, and atmosphere of one poet he never returned to him. His whole creative activity, with its sharply determined stylistic groups, is itself determined by the poets. Thus he set six poems by Gottfried Keller, fifty-three by Mörike, fifty-one by Goethe, twenty by Eichendorff, forty-four from the Spanish songbook of Heyse and Geibel, and forty-six from the Italian songbook of Heyse, while three poems by Michelangelo stand at the end as a sort of curiosity. Each of these groups of poems represents a period in his creative activity, usually followed by complete spiritual exhaustion until another poet's world was again assimilated. Music as such was never an aim to him, only a means to enhance the poem. He was a rhapsodist, albeit a rhapsodist who used his instrument not only for the purpose of accompaniment but as an independent medium for creating moods. The poem is declaimed in an animated speech song, with impeccable prosody, but it is the piano which takes over the task of realizing the mood and following its fluctuations. The musical essence of the composition is in the piano part, and it was entirely proper for him to call his works "Songs for voice and piano," and not "Songs with the accompaniment of the piano." This accompaniment is a musically independent factor free from the vocal part yet entirely subordinated to the text.

Wolf's dependence on the poet has often been interpreted as a lack of artistic individuality. This is palpably erroneous; the reasons are much more deep-seated. If we again turn toward the poems, we shall soon notice that the most frequently composed poets, Heine and Lenau, are missing. We shall also discover that Wolf almost never resorted to subjective lyricism. From among the many poems of Goethe he selected those in which we hear a third person speaking from a definite situation. This is true of most other songs of Wolf and it is for this reason that he turned to Mörike, whom other composers shunned as not being so "musical" as the typical lyricists like Heine. This method of composition is fundamentally dramatic—dramatic lyricism; the composer first visualized the situation presented by the poet and then placed the singer in it. These situations presented almost operatic roles, which, of course, cannot be changed arbitrarily, and Wolf was steadfastly opposed to the transposition of his songs from low to high voice or vice versa. What we are facing here is another aspect of the Gesamtkunstwerk. Wolf is the prototype of the littérateur-musician to whom the form of a song is entirely determined by the "inner music" of the poem. While historically he descended from the German romantic song composers, his musical idiom and his aesthetic beliefs stem from Liszt and Wagner; he used the piano as Wagner used his orchestra, and the piano ruled the song as Wagner's orchestra ruled the stage. Yet Wolf never handled the voice in the instrumental fashion of many of his colleagues; the melodies are all vocal and not difficult to sing (aside from the difficulties of intonation created by his complicated and shifting harmonies); moreover, the piano part, despite its paramount role, is never permitted to cover the voice.

While Bruckner stood somewhere between the Middle Ages and the nineteenth century, Wolf was a child of his era in every fiber of his body, a tragic phenomenon of the declining century who took his themes from the spiritual store of German classicism, elaborating them in a peculiarly nervous and sophisticated manner, to afford highly valued musical delicacies for the intellectual gourmet. He tried to combine Schumann's lyricism with the declamatory style of the Wagnerian circle, using their chromatic enharmonic idiom to the point of saturation. It is noteworthy that his least characteristic songs are those written in the more stereotyped song forms, while in the others he revealed himself a master of lyric genre painting whose sensitiveness for the smallest gestures, for the most intimate feelings, and even for mere allusions is unparalleled. The scale of his sentiments is truly limitless, from the most delicate mirth to religious submission, expressed with almost impressionistic lightness of touch, yet at times with eruptive force. All subsequent song composers were indebted to Wolf, and while many good songs have been composed—we have mentioned such a fine lyricist as Fauré—the modern song reached its limits with Wolf. His lyric Gesamtkunstwerk carried the principle of the instrumentally dominated song to its confines, for his melodies are often the result of his exceedingly rich harmonic manipulations, the song rising from the tone painting of the accompanying piano. After this ultra-refined and sophisticated style there was only one possibility left: to replace the piano with the orchestra. And with this step, taken by Mahler and Strauss, among others, ends the history of the song, for such a medium and such an environment are entirely opposed to the essentially intimate character of song lyricism. The concert hall naturally encouraged the dramatic tendencies in the song, the singing voice became more and more declamatory, and its part was either buried under an avalanche of music or merely recited by a "speaking voice."

Objection to certain aspects of the modern song is directed against neither the often decried "lack of melody" in the singing voice nor the symphonic enlargement of the accompaniment, but mainly against the false conception of the "musical" in the song. Most modern composers seek the musical not in the lyric ground tone of the poem but in the externals of the individual words. This, however, offends the very essence of music, which is the "idea" itself, and not its images. We must not be misled into thinking that this conception is due solely to the repercussions of the program symphony and to the vogue of the Wagnerian orchestral commentary, which paint the words and the poetic ideas in music. They undoubtedly contributed much to the complete about-face in song composition, but the well-intentioned and docile song composers who surrounded the great romantic composers had already sinned as gravely as their colleagues, the symphonic-lyricists, against the natural laws of the song as codified by Schubert. For if a musician invents a melody that roughly corresponds to the speech pattern of the poem, is quiet if the poem is quiet, energetic if the poem demands more force, he has merely composed a piece of music in a certain form; there can be no question of a musical consummation of the poem. It is possible, however, for such consummation to be achieved in the modern song. When a closed and symmetrically designed melodic line is abandoned, when the human voice declaiming the text is lost in the melos carried by the instrumental accompaniment, the musical element can still be supreme, and can consummate the lyric mood of the poem. The first example is usually an ingenuous play with lyricism, the second may be a great masterpiece of a symphonic poem with voice, but neither of them is a genuine song.

The Last Stylistic Synthesis of the Century
Impressionism

> . . . la chanson grise
> Où l'Indécis au Précis se joint. . . .

ROMANTICISM bequeathed to Europe, together with subjectivism, the notion of the genius, a notion unknown to the Biedermeier period. In his writings Delacroix emphasized that the imitation of nature alone cannot lead to art, it is merely one of the latter's fundamental media; only genius can fathom inner causes and reasons, and in the final analysis every work of art is the product of imagination. The latter is, however, something different from the fantasy of romanticism, it is rather the sum total of man's experiences and observations, his artistic temperament. Such a conception was bound to lead to extreme subjectivism, which would not even tolerate the constancy of a studio; the painters fled into the open, into the *Plein-air* of nature, declaring color the carrier of life; and since they endeavored to apprehend life in its minute momentary aspects, they reduced color to its finest particles. The final aim was an art bent on seizing the impressions of volatile, scurrying moments. Only in this way, they believed, could the essential many-sidedness of life, as it was now understood, be rendered. The final solution was offered by impressionism, but the foundation was laid by Delacroix himself.

Delacroix destroyed the form created by mid-eighteenth-century classicism and by the earlier nineteenth-century realistic painters. In his pictures there are no definite lines and surfaces, there is no rhythm carried by great formal complexes, no composition which could be objectified in laws or formulae.

Contour and silhouette have lost most of their own qualities, the forms are dissolved into color patches. If we still want to find rhythm in these pictures we must seek it in the innumerable color particles, in the most subjective oscillation of the subtle color patterns. This rhythm, flickering restlessly, can no longer be abstracted from content and form; it rests on the relationship of theme, form, and color, receiving its validity exclusively from its creator. Compared to any older style of painting, a canvas by Delacroix is a field of ruins, but from these ruins there emanates a life of the greatest intensity and immediacy. The partitioning of surface and form into innumerable brush strokes of varying nuances gave the representation a new vitality, life of the most acute instantaneousness. Such things as plastic formations have no meaning for Delacroix; they are no longer symbols, the bearers of metaphysical connotations, as with the romanticists; they are elusive, merely indicated by hasty brush strokes. What disembodies them is light. Many of the romanticists— such as Turner—had already allotted an important role to light, but in their works light still illuminated objects; now, in Jean Baptiste Corot (1796-1875), light, color, and object become one, henceforth everything exists in light.

The work of art now appears as a new manner of the expression of the ego: not so much the expression of its feelings as that of its will. The creative genius is embodied in an autonomous will no longer restrained by anything. The creative artist no longer abandons himself to his subjects with devotion, as did the conscientious painters of the Biedermeier; he does not play with them, as did the painters of the rococo, for to him the subject is a mere means to immortalize his autonomous individuality. To embrace an ideal, as was necessary in the classic era, or to be in communion with the eternal-infinite of the romanticists, was given to few at the end of the nineteenth century. After the peak of subjectivism, impressionism seems to have come as a reaction. Early impressionism is represented in the art of Gustave Courbet (1819-1877). An individualist, Courbet recognized neither tradition nor convention, but his art has not the subjectivity of Delacroix's. To him there was no longer a soul, only bodies and the apprehensible present with which he struggled every time he painted. His only aim was to render their materiality in illusory realism, and in that he forgot everything else. The same is more or less true of his eminent colleagues, Constant Troyon (1810-1865), Jean François Millet (1814-1875), and even Adolf Friedrich von Menzel (1815-1905). The impressionists carried the whittling of the momentary to its extreme, making the picture the distillation of an overexcited eye, but by forcing themselves to react again and again in the same concentrated yet fleeting manner the impressions of the moment became schematized. This is already apparent in the work of Alfred Sisley (1840-1899), Claude Monet (1840-1926), and especially in Camille Pissarro (1830-1903), despite the unabated excellence of their artistry. Man to them is the accessory in the landscape and represents a passing act of nature, with no claims to specific rights and privileges. Between them and Delacroix lies the last great artistic rally of the century, vibrant in color, bathed in light, and full of "atmosphere."

Impressionism in painting stands for an art of representation which is pictorial in the fullest sense of the word, the antithesis of the plastic-linear. The more the pictorial sense of the nineteenth century developed, the more color was victorious over design, the "how" over the "what," quality over matter. Subject, composition, and detail were to impressionism of secondary importance; its subjects are lacking in clarity, their contours are wasted away, and what dominates is a planar, uncertain color oscillation with no pretense at corporeal roundness (a fact which explains the relatively small role played by sculpture in the movement) or at composition in the sense of clear-cut forms. The latter is rather the juxtaposition of objects than compositional arrangement. The impressionist portrait treats the subject as if seen for a fleeting moment, when passing by. It is satisfied with the impressions gained at this first glance and forgoes everything that might make us desire to stop to get better acquainted with the person on the canvas. This, and the consequent avoidance of everything that is not seen and optically apprehensible, that requires interpretation—such as a man's mental life—limits its action. The sensuous, corporeal, and actual stimuli of color and light become the main subjects, while the importance of the concrete subject is minimized. Needless to say the concreteness of objects cannot be altogether eradicated, and the great color virtuosi of the period did not attempt to eliminate tangible subjects. Paul Cézanne (1839–1906) and Pierre Auguste Renoir (1841–1919) could paint forcible portraits and sensual, poetic, and superbly modeled nudes, the flesh tones and texture rendered with the greatest skill, while Edgar Degas (1834–1917) showed an unexcelled mastery in the portrayal of the human form in motion. But fully to achieve their aim the impressionists customarily selected relatively unimportant subjects that invited no associations. *La nature morte,* still life, which requires neither interpretation nor association, was one of their favored subjects—fruits, flowers, vases; and if they painted men in the open, they were often mere patches in the fascinating play of colors. The coloristic urge is so strong that even the shadow is colored. This reveling in light and color does not necessarily entail the use of a wide color scheme; it is sometimes restricted to one tone, like the "colorless" gray of Whistler, which the artist handles with consummate skill by manipulating his light effects and transitional shades. All this kept impressionism from dealing with several humans in a homogeneous group; polyphonic composition was as alien to them as it was to the musicians of their stylistic orientation.

Yet impressionism is not formless in the sense of having no stylistic logic. It is rather beyond both form and formlessness; it is free of "form," its particular beauty lying in its ability to enhance the effect of that which remains when the intellectual associations are suspended; and since the criterion of style is impressionability and harmony of sensory perception, it possesses a style of the most refined quality.

Impressionism in Music

THE term "impressionism" is generally applied to the graphic arts, but, as usual, music and poetry, philosophy and ethics, the thinking and acting of the whole period, echo similar tendencies. As in painting, impressionism in literature existed before the period so named. Stendhal's description of the Battle of Waterloo seen through the inexperienced eyes of the hero of the novel (*La Chartreuse de Parme*) is an early example, for the novelist, like the impressionist painter, describes only that which he has actually seen in a given moment, dismissing such correct information as he may have on the true state of affairs. Although Brunetière called Daudet's works impressionistic, the real field for this style in literature was lyric poetry, for the poet works with color patches, arresting passing events. The poets of impressionism are many and show a great variety of individualities, but they all struggle against rhyme, verse, and strophe and demand "free rhythm" (the term itself paradoxical), so that they will not be bound by architectural elements, so that they can have their own poetic pointillism. But poetry and drama cannot here compete with painting and music, for words and verse always have a meaning, they always induce associations. Nevertheless, the greatest poets of impressionism, the French—such as Paul Verlaine (1844–1896) or Arthur Rimbaud (1856–1891)—could create almost purely musical-pictorial moods in which sonorous words take the function of colors. Their arrangement of consonants and vowels induces almost the same sensuous pleasure as the color oscillations of the painters, or the chain dissonances of the musicians.

> Les sanglots longs
> Des violons
> De l'automne
> Blessent mon coeur
> D'une langueur
> Monotone.

This is music, tone painting, but it was Ronsard's thought, "de la musique avant toute chose," which this same poet, Verlaine, repeated; and indeed, a style in which moods are not only dominating but are enhanced by a preference for the accidental, the uncontrollable, the unique, was especially suitable for music. Led by French musicians, musical impressionism soon recruited an international following around its banner, with Debussy the flag-bearer.

The new style evolved from the disintegrating postromantic and national schools, seized upon certain elements in the music of Bizet, Franck, Wagner, Grieg, Borodin, and Moussorgsky, and reacted sympathetically to influences emanating from contemporary poetry and painting. Its international portent is well illustrated in the "membership" of the school, which includes, among others, Maurice Ravel (1875–1937), Cyril Scott (b. 1879), Frederick Delius (1862–1934), Joseph Jongen (b. 1873), Ottorino Respighi (1879–1936), and Manuel de Falla (b. 1876). Russian impressionism, headed by Scriabin, appears to form an independent wing.

Musical impressionism shares many traits, even technical ones, with literary and pictorial impressionism. It exhibits the same disinclination toward a logical compositional grouping of ideas, the same pictorial-planar preference for the juxtaposition of different colors and sonorities which are not held together by definite lines and which give the desired effect only if "viewed" from a certain distance. The unifying effect is no longer achieved through grouping and building but through the similarity of the sections, their character and mood. Thus it is not the order but the mood of the particular sections which achieves "form," for it calls not on memory, but only on a faculty of sensory impressionability. The chief component of this music is a programmatic atmosphere; a mystic, opaline quality, dreaminess, mood-impressions, instead of causal continuity or logical relationship of ideas. Now music becomes illustration, the illustration of a mood announced in the title. It no longer counts on form in the conventional sense; it is held together by the suggestive mood announced by the poetic—that is, extramusical—title. Still, this is not program music, nor is it descriptive music; it is, rather, poetry translated into music, the "landscape poetry" of French literature and painting. A really descriptive and narrative program music would mean the negation of the spirit of impressionism, for the more extramusical moments there are in a composition, following a prearranged plan, the more characteristic episodes it has, which latter induce definite associations, to the detriment of mood and atmosphere.

The technique of impressionism may be characterized by a neglect of elements heretofore considered constructive, in favor of instrumental coloring and harmonic piquancy. The clear articulation of a musical phrase turns into a swinging, undulating repetition, into a sounding mosaic comparable to the lapping of waves or the rustling of leaves. The coloristic-pictorial element dominates even the harmonic structure, for the phenomenon of merging tones is superimposed on the principles of tonal-chordal architecture, which again results in a changed role for the dissonance, whose use and desirability now depend entirely on its value as color agent. As the pointillists knew that the juxtaposition of multicolored dots creates a very definite color sensation on the retina of the beholder and mixed their dots according to a systematic and well-calculated plan, the composers were similarly aware of the acoustic and psychological qualities of their instruments and harmonies. Pointillism in painting has its counterpart in music, in the chords which unite many far-removed intervals, chords of the ninth, eleventh, thirteenth. The more of these, and the farther removed, the less are they capable of merging, creating instead a vibrating, oscillating, glimmering sound complex, trembling and nervous, caressing the senses. By shifting these harmonies, the most trivial melodies can be made interesting without changing one note in them. We have seen this procedure employed, to a certain degree, by Franck, a special case being the second theme in the first movement of his symphony. There the egocentric theme, incapable of symphonic pregnancy and development, is foundering helplessly, yet the composer averts a seemingly inevitable collapse by constantly shifting colorful chords under the melody, which thereby, although remaining unchanged, appears to take on new aspects. Impressionism carried this technique much further and banished real part writing almost entirely, using generally one principal part colored by chords. Impressionist harmony is the last stage in the disintegration of romantic homophony.

Like color and light in painting, the last aim of impressionistic music was sonority and tone color; everything that in a fleeting, momentary impression excites the ear, satisfies and intoxicates it. The cult of harmonic progressions and coloristic effects extinguished melody; this is the reason why orchestral music, the symphonic poem, is much nearer to the spirit of these times than chamber music, and among the solo instruments the piano, capable of both harmonic and coloristic subtleties, is the overwhelming favorite. It was no longer the full chords, the massed sonorities of the gigantic orchestra that interested the impressionist composer, but the soft, strange, muted sonorities, produced not by reducing the enormous orchestral apparatus of the post-Wagnerian period, but by handling it with the utmost delicacy. The mighty trombones and the stentorian trumpets are muted, the shrill wood winds are used by predilection in their lowest registers; the strings are divided into many parts, the violins into four, eight, or ten sections, climbing into regions formerly exceptional for the best solo players, the cellos taking the role of the violin, the violas assuming the bass; the ear-shattering cymbals are lightly touched on the edge, kettledrums and snare drums are discreetly muffled, and the whole is drenched with the silvery confetti of harp, celesta, triangle, and Glockenspiel, with the tam-tam faintly rumbling in the distance. And this orchestration, shimmering in a thousand colors, achieving a remarkable crescendo of sensuous effects by the subtlest means, without having recourse to violent colors, harmonies, or dynamics, now takes the place of thematic construction.

We stand here at the frontiers of logical consciousness. Everything we have looked for and honored in musical composition seems missing in this music. The fugue, once the symbol of a whole era, with its pregnant diction and logical voice leading, requiring divided attention together with simultaneous apprehension, is the very antithesis of the impressionistic style. But the spirit of the symphony and sonata is not less alien to it, for the essence of all these types of music is causal relationship achieved by the grouping of many small musical units into larger ones and finally into a great system of architecture. The same objections that were raised against impressionistic painting by the patrons of the *Salon,* against the symbolistic-impressionistic poets by the *Parnassiens,* were aimed at the impressionist musicians. Pictures, poems, and music were denounced for the indistinctness of their subjects, for their lack of melody and design. But the denunciators of a new art or style see only that which this new art has dethroned, heretofore revered and held inviolate. They never realize that the abandonment of the means of expression, forms, and devices which are the property of a particular style is a necessity for a new style if it hopes to express the spirit of its own era; that this turning away from the traditional is a prime requisite for an art eager to give something positively new and vital. It is this new and vital that the biased critic does not see. Thus when the painters and musicians assert that they did not intend to draw unequivocal contours and profiled melodies, that their aim was a dissolution in color, that they wanted to create aesthetic enjoyment through color rather than through design, they have every artistic and moral right to do so, and it is totally irrelevant whether their creations fit the criteria of a previous artistic code.

There is, however, another objection, less technical than the one advanced in the name of design, form, and melody, but infinitely more important: that which we consider great art always endeavors to give us more and to mean more than aesthetic pleasure, for great art is never satisfied with ornamenting life, it strives to redeem life, to be its quintessence. With the exception of the one great poet of musical impressionism, Debussy, in whose works this coloristic mood and atmosphere gained an almost plastic shape, the others wanted merely to entertain, and it is this absence of higher spiritual forces—abundant in poetry and painting—that doomed the music of impressionism to an ephemeral course, placing it at the mercy of succeeding movements deeply convinced of their cultural mission.

Claude Achille Debussy (1862–1918) started his career vacillating between the two extremes that dominated French musical life: Massenet and Wagner. While still a pupil at the Conservatoire he traveled through Europe, visiting England, Italy, Austria, and Russia. In the eighties the Wagnerian ikon was turned toward the wall, for through his friends, Erik Satie and Chausson, who acquainted him with such utterly different music as Moussorgsky's operas and songs, he realized that there was a way to dispel the Bayreuth magic.

Massenet's influence also paled although it never entirely disappeared, for there is a bit of Massenet in every Frenchman of whatever generation. Intercourse with the leading exponents of impressionistic and symbolistic poetry and painting, and the great discovery that there had once been a French art such as he dreamed about, the art of Couperin and Rameau, matured and gave direction to his instincts. Having thus discovered his voice, he astounded the world with an orchestral *Prélude* to Mallarmé's poem *l'Après-midi d'un Faune* (1892) the originality of which was unexampled in a period ruled over by energetic musical personalities. The *Prélude* was immediately followed by a string quartet, and later by a lyric drama, *Pelléas et Mélisande* (1902), works which confirmed his great and original talents. He, and no longer Richard Strauss, now deserved to be considered the leader of modern music. But it took many years of struggle before the private cause of a little band of admirers assumed the aspect of a world-wide movement which saw in Debussy the prophet of new music.

Debussy stands at the end of the long century of romanticism; at the same time he was the first great master of the new music of the twentieth century which we so loosely call "modern." Although he abhorred the egocentric hero worship of postromanticism, as well as the overdimensional proportions of the Wagnerian era, it is undeniable that he took his start, especially in regard to his harmonic equipment, from that era. But while he developed the inherited harmony in an entirely individual manner, his instinct told him to shun the outlived "forms"—especially the sonata form—still carried by the late romantics as an inalienable trust fund of the classic era. It was only toward the end of his life, after a quarter of a century of experience in free musical construction, that he turned to a more severe musical architecture. While his constructions are entirely different from the conventional, they show the bold and well-proportioned conception which once was the mark of the great Latin masters. He thirsted for pure music and, freeing himself from all mental complications, endeavored to achieve his end by purely musical means.

Debussy's music reflects the differentiated mental world of the oversensitive, restless, and complicated soul of the turn of the century, yet it is free of that period's whipped-up passions, tearful sentimentalism, and noisy naturalism. His pictures are never naturalistic scenes, no matter what their title; every external happening, every poetic inspiration, turns into musical experience. Debussy was a lyricist of aristocratic restraint, but his demeanor cloaks an intense, warm, sensitive, and allusive musical temperament which accomplished that which was given to few if any composers of his time: a harmony of feeling and intellect. He was a French composer, as French as Couperin and Rameau, from whom he learned the essence of French spirit in music, and he was proud of being so, for he realized fully the task of emancipation that falls to him who recognizes the genius of his own people. He was equal to this task, the only great and absolutely original composer of the turn of the century, gloriously alive and independent, unconcerned with the life-and-death struggle that consumed the energies of the dying schools of the postromantic era.

Debussy epitomizes impressionism in music. This is indeed true, but the fact that he has been lumped together with the many other composers who claim membership in this school by virtue of brilliant tonal canvases tends to place him in an unfair light. For while it is true that he was a brother of Cézanne and Verlaine, and that his inspiration was almost without exception kindled by some poetic stimulus, unlike the naturalistic virtuosity of the other musicians the musical shape the stimuli took in his works was free of all extramusical substance. "All his senses were tributary to his musical inspiration . . . but there is always something more than mere sensation in what he gives back for what he has absorbed. In transmitting Nature into harmony, he has made sonorous his own emotions." [6] He approximated Cézanne's palette with his orchestra (*Nuages, Fêtes, Sirènes*) and with his piano (*Pagodes, Reflets dans l'Eau, Poissons d'Or*), Verlaine's musical verse with his poetic recitation (*Fêtes Galantes*), but he also knew how to endow this dazzling game of light and shadow with life and poetic expression (*La Mer, Ibéria*) and to pour it into molds the unconventionality of which is not less fascinating than their finished roundness (*Préludes*). His late works are in a noble and distilled style, the nature of which still remains to be grasped, as can be seen from the rather ambiguous adjective "neoclassic" which musical writers have bestowed upon this, his last style period, unfortunately left unfinished.

Symphonic poem, chamber music, and song accompanied him throughout his life, and he found new tones, new forms, and new expressions for all of them, but opera tempted him only once. *Pelléas et Mélisande* (book by Maeterlinck) does not resemble any other piece ever performed in a theater. It is absolutely original in its endeavor to repudiate any melodic design, any precise or tangible musical or instrumental scheme. The singing is reduced to psalmodic declamation which comes very near to natural spoken language, and the orchestra is left with the task of depicting and expressing everything. The Wagnerian principle, one might say, but the music in this unique "opera" does not take part in the drama, it follows it. At times it stops to discover the thought behind the words, to construct a frame in which the action may evolve. The pages of this score do not present definite and concrete ideas, they are a unique association of complex sensations. The sensations are new because no one before Debussy had created such an intimate association of subject, frame, form, and timbre. In *Pelléas* the psychology of the action emanates entirely from the drama itself. Debussy departed far from Wagner, who with the aid of his orchestra and the combination of motives created a symphonic music drama. In spite of certain motives which recur occasionally, characterizing Golaud or Mélisande, unity, homogeneity of inspiration, emanates from the drama and not from the musical structure. The orchestra follows the text almost word for word and excels in the descriptive pages, but it always remains music of the poet and of the impressionistic painter; it never becomes music of the thinker.

In his youth Debussy was a frequent visitor to Stéphane Mallarmé's salon. The poets who assembled there, although constituting talents of greatly diversified personal aims and beliefs, endeavored to banish from poetic inspiration subject, development, and composition. They wanted to break with the inherited forms, to save the purity of sentiment in its literary expression, to condense in it the elusive mobility of life. To achieve this aim the school did away not only with the rules of traditional prosody, but also neglected the requirements of syntax and disregarded the habitual usage of the language itself. They did not seek in their language the intellectual and objective function of words: they sought their sensuous, musical, and plastic functions. Debussy transplanted into music the aesthetics of this new poetry. He attempted to create the musical equivalent of a literature permeated with ambiguity—intriguing, deceiving, yet attractive ambiguity, which Maeterlinck succeeded in assimilating without important changes. But this essentially lyric quality is not suited to the drama; Pelléas, Mélisande, Golaud, Arkel, Geneviève, and little Yniold do not move about much and act very little; they are rather figures than personages. They are figures which speak and feel. Debussy's music lent color to their pale cheeks and created a shadow around their transparent bodies, but they still remain two-dimensional.

Pelléas et Mélisande belongs among those rare works of art in which music dissolves in a synthesis of poetic and plastic beauty, always sought and seldom attained by poets and musicians. But it also belongs to those works which show most clearly the fragility of such an art. Pre-Raphaelitism could create a perfect illusion—for the moment; today it is dated. Maeterlinck's dramas will be dated soon, if they are not already. Music which is so faithfully adapted to a poetic work of essentially transitory character may perish in the adventure.

"The Decline of the West"?

CLASSICISM rested on the ideal unity of form and content, with a musical architecture based on harmonic logic. The romanticists emphasized the individual components, the formal details, trying to achieve logic and unity by enhancing the importance of the elements of sentiment in the content, the juxtaposition or opposition of which became so marked as to acquire constructive form. This enhancement and emphasis reached its height in the "symphonic orgy"—Strauss's own characterization of certain operatic scenes —of the latter part of the nineteenth century, and ended in that disintegration which characterized the mental life of the dying epoch. Then came the last stylistic synthesis, which we have summarized under the term "impressionism," although the school included impressionists, plain "romanticists," and symbolists. One cannot, in fact, distinguish sharp lines of demarcation between systems and groups; ideas and inspirations are exchanged, theories are neither clearly conscious nor well drawn up, the most domesticated composers show a desire for emancipation, the most independent bear the mark of servitude. Fauré occasionally reflects Saint-Saëns, the young Debussy is close to Massenet, behind Ravel one espies Chabrier and Strauss, while certain composers show a curious mixture of adverse schools. In this *schola musicorum* the catechumens sometimes exhibit more audacity in the treatment of the traditions than the emancipated, full-fledged faithful. Then, to crown the confusion, the man whom all of them acknowledged as their leader and master, Fauré, is a composer of the tamest old-fashioned romantic hue, whom the generation of Schumann would not have denounced for his progressivism.

Expressionism was later to come as a quasi reaction against impressionism, turning away from the latter's forms and contents, and emphasizing, with marked excess, man's solitude and isolation, his seeking of the truth. Impressionism voices the influence of the external world on man in a pronouncedly subjective manner; expressionism seeks to cast into musical forms the most mysterious, intimate, and uncontrollable movements of the creative process, as independent of external influences as possible. The impressionist abandons himself; the expressionist seeks the utmost concentration. The chief technical means of impressionism were coloristic; expressionism believed in the linear. Impressionism is naturalistic and homophonous to the point of being a sort of modern organum; expressionism is abstract and contrapuntal. Against the worldly, hedonistic nature of impressionism, expressionism opposed the unnatural, the clashing, the torturing. While impressionistic music is almost always tonal, that is, it moves within the bounds of the tonal system of romanticism even though pushing its frontiers far beyond those known to the previous schools, expressionism turned sharply against the tonality traditions of romanticism, trying to build upon new systems of both tonality and harmony. In its most uncompromising utterances expressionism carried the antiromantic zeal to the point where it refused to recognize sentiments, thus basing its new aesthetic doctrine on the mental state of emotional suspension. We shall not enter into the discussion of this stylistic current, because it is still in the making and would carry us beyond the scope of this book, but one cannot help noting the fallacy it covers, for the loud advocates of the aesthetics of impassivity really champion the emotion of avoiding emotions. The contradictions do not end here; in fact, they begin with the name itself, for expression is the chief visible means of all art, since it mirrors the impression. While theoretically "impression" (the influence of the external world, coming from without) and "expression" (the influence of the internal world, coming from within) can be separated, the work of art itself is created by the presence of both of these elements in the artist's soul; there is no style which would be the result exclusively of either. If the impressive elements dominate in the creative mental sphere a naturalistic style is likely to result, while the prevalence of expressionistic elements will result in an abstract style; but these terms should not be used to differentiate the notions of program music and absolute music. These styles are, moreover, often mingled together, making the confusion that reigned at the turn of the century forbidding.

Lack of spiritual ideals, submission to materialism and technicalism, and a resultant hunger for sensation and bluff, created an atmosphere in which philosophical and aesthetic judgments were vacillating and a normal and purposeful development of artistic individuality was made exceedingly difficult. This decadence of culture ended in the World War of 1914. New life could be infused into the music of this rapidly disintegrating world only by an even more nervous, sophisticated, and surcharged emphasis on the already overtaxed elements of effect and technique. Experiment then became the final aim, as is so tragically demonstrated in the works of Alexander Scriabin (1872–1915), whose whole art, nay, whole life, was a mere experiment, a supernatural dream, and whose mind, possessed by demonic forces, penetrated deeper and deeper into the mire of mystical speculations, hallucinations, and dementia. The mystic of the early Christian centuries received from Scripture and from the Church an unshakable structure, the secure walls of which could withstand the flow of the most ardent lava of ecstasis. The modern mystic does not receive anything from any source; he has to find not only his forms but he has to create everything, God and Satan, the world and the beyond, the Redeemer and the Antichrist, the saints and the damned; he must himself write the Bible. There was no halt for Scriabin, the modern mystic, for there was nothing that would bind him; such an artist is not interested in national or social aims, in the music of the people, not even in purely technical or formal problems, for he already knows everything and wants everything, and like Icarus soars toward the sun.

Scriabin's new harmonic system proved one thing only: that tone alone no longer suffices, and that the refurbishing of the tonal system cannot furnish the solution. Nor was the already immensely rich color scheme of the modern orchestra sufficient; Scriabin and his followers wanted actual light and actual color. In his last works Scriabin freed himself entirely from the shackles of tonality, proclaiming that he had found the answer to the riddle of cosmic music. The great unity of sensations, visions, and hallucinations emanates from the orchestra of *Le Poème du Feu* (1913), its "color piano" inundating the unruly maze of tones with its "color fire." And then he took the final step toward the universal music of Nirvana, the union of sound, color, drama, song, religion; the universal mystery play which would be the crowning of human art. But by this time that meteor of Scriabin's spirit has passed beyond the atmosphere of the planets, continuing its path in the eternal darkness of the unknown spaces.

The enormous technical dexterity, the mammoth orchestra, were the products of an era whose desire was to exhibit the power of matter. Public concert life, accepting the prevailing system of capitalism, developed into a major industry with international ramifications that rivaled the metal or textile industry. Despite the countless number of concerts given, only a fraction of the musical literature is actually performed. Paradoxical as it may seem, it was this abundance of concert life which prevented the dissemination of modern music, for, as every industry works on the profit basis, the international concert business could not afford to enter into doubtful enterprises and, capitalizing on the reluctance of the majority of the public to listen to anything unfamiliar, drafted a veritable code to be followed in every country, leaving space for such modifications as the idiosyncrasies of the individual countries demanded. The musical public of Beethoven's time was much more receptive to new ideas than later generations. For to accept the *Eroica* symphony within a few years of its composition over the protracted opposition of the musicians was indeed a remarkable proof of musical intelligence. But the public of those days was reared on "contemporary" music, as the innumerable quartets and sonatas were written for their use. Chamber music and piano sonatas are meant to be played for small audiences, virtually surrounding the players, and songs lose their charm if more than a few dozen people listen to them. Modern concert life forced these intimate types of music onto the platform of the great concert hall, since the public today cannot make its own music, and it is economically impossible to maintain hundreds of quartets so that they can play in congenial surroundings for small groups.

But it is no longer always the work of art that entices the public to the concert; many go to hear the virtuoso, player or conductor, and the program is of only secondary importance. While the conductor's real duty should be "to make himself seemingly superfluous," as Liszt once remarked, the modern orchestra leader is inclined to think that the composer exists only to permit him to set off his wizardry. And with few exceptions he has little respect for the composer's property. The enormous length of the Wagnerian operas and the symphonies of Bruckner encouraged the habit of cutting the scores even in the lifetime of these composers. The scissors were used indiscriminately and on all occasions until recently a more enlightened press started a campaign against such unscrupulous practices, but it is by no means unusual to hear in our own day a violinist play a concerto with piano accompaniment in which the orchestral tuttis—integral and indispensable parts of the work— are cut to a few measures.

As scientific research and literature on music expanded into a vast field of endeavor, its standards and products reaching new excellence at the opening of the twentieth century, musical criticism, so spirited, varied, and high-minded in the romantic era, declined because of the restrictions imposed upon it by modern journalism. The critics of the romantic era, and to a certain extent Continental critics until recent times, studied their scores before and after the performance and, after due deliberation, went to press a few days or even weeks later. This the modern critic is seldom able to do, especially in the United States, and so despite the very high level of our journalism, this confusion between critic and reporter persists except in the case of a very few leading papers. Modern journalism requires artistic events to be classified as "news" and presented to the public the morning after the performance. Thus the critic is obliged to write a sizable article without time for reflection and study, practically on his way home from the opera or the concert hall. This would do if the morning article were simply a report on the quality of the performance, but the same procedure is employed when a new opera or symphony is to be appraised, which is manifestly unfair not only to the composer and the public, but to the critic himself. The single hearing of a new work does not entitle anyone, not even the most accomplished musician or scholar, to express a definitive opinion, and few of our thoughtful critics want to do so, although the majority are perfectly willing to discuss a whole opera after one hearing. This confusion of reporting with art criticism is materially responsible for the unholy division the young century set up between great art and the concert industry.

* * *

Talleyrand used to say that only those who lived before 1789 knew the sweetness of life. What he meant was that the French Revolution first unleashed the forces that would ultimately engulf the individual's life to subordinate it to the *res publica,* to the masses. And the masses, their weight, their importance, their desires, and their power, were responsible, even if indirectly, for the helpless foundering of culture at the beginning of the twentieth century; for the culture of the century of romanticism was not designed for them, they acceded to it only in the expectation of assimilating it or replacing it by their own.

The main fact of this period of capitalism was the enormous increase in population, more than doubled in Europe despite the vast migration to America, a country which developed beyond all imagination. Such a large mass of people is, however, not merely a matter of its own existence: it is the cause for seemingly detached social and cultural moves, it creates new problems of life. Thus man's needs became the needs of the masses, and to satisfy these needs there had to be a new technique of production. This was furnished by modern industry. The mechanization of culture through industry is the chief characteristic of the new century; its extent cannot even be gauged, for it is well on its way to transforming even inorganic nature. Industry drives to collectivism and away from private life, for it requires associations for its exploitation. Everything tended from the single, small, individual, and qualitative, toward the colossal, universal, impersonal, and quantitative; from individual enterprise to corporations, cartels, syndicates, conventions, and trusts. The dissolving of the human being in the mass apparatus of life, in machinery and bureaucracy, in the mere effort to insure an existence, submerges the individual and tends to extinguish creative art. This proved itself to be the greatest era of virtuosity, of re-creation, the victory of talent over genius. The nineteenth century seemingly accepted the doctrine of Jeremy Bentham, the great English social philosopher, who taught that the individual's happiness depends upon the happiness of the greatest number. But this principle is not clear, since it deals with unknown quantities; for "happiness" varies subjectively in every individual, while "number" is a vague notion. At any rate, number, or quantity, or collectivity does not mean quality. The masses as such have no fantasy, and they have a tendency not to tolerate fantasy, greatness, and individuality; but most of all, the masses as such are not creative, it is only the individual who is. Thus we have arrived at the undeniable fact that at the opening of the twentieth century the impending collapse of bourgeois civilization threatened to rob humanity of its spiritual forces by leveling it into the mass civilization of modern industry. Collectivism in its various forms has given no evidence of having the strength to create art.

The question of modern music is, then, not a matter of dissonance, the use of erratic melodies or peculiar sonorities, but a philosophical one, that of a new outlook on life. Artistic creation requires positive mental forces, and the greatness of the modern creative artist depends on whether he has the power to overcome the volcanic upheaval of the times without being consumed. The romanticist created from an insatiable urge to express his innermost feelings, he saw the chief aim of the world in his ego. This ego collapsed at the end of the century. The classic individuality saw the individual's task in heroism resting on transcendent convictions, but this heroism could not prevail, for the individual was lost in the chaos of contending forces; the overheated atmosphere choked off the individual's breath. It seemed as if the intense pessimism with which social philosophy at the turn of the century looked into the future was justified, that by gulping up the individual the masses were to be victorious, sounding the death knell of art. Nineteenth-century historians and philosophers saw the march of events and, like the distinguished and aristocratic interpreter of the cultural deeds of princes and tyrants, Burckhardt, lamented the inevitability of life's being dictated by the masses, the masses which would never conceivably "vote millions every year for half a century to build St. Peter's."

The chief document of this pessimism is, however, Oswald Spengler's fanatically cruel and brilliant book, *The Decline of the West* (1918). Spengler sees the bourgeoisie declining into the proletariat, intellectual culture into physical well-being, the European commonwealth of nations into Bolshevism, and spiritualism into materialism. He maintains that what ruined Western culture was liberalism, which destroyed authority, that the decline was already noticeable when Beaumarchais's arrogant comedies which made fun of the code of the highest strata of society were found exceedingly enjoyable by these very strata who were supposed to rule and lead the people by their authority. From this time on humanity was divided into two camps, clawing at each other until they should be mutually annihilated. Spengler does not say who is on the right side, although his unconcealed admiration for such men as Metternich makes it easy to draw up a list, but the left side, the camp of the culprits who ruined the culture of the West, contains every name that once stood for the betterment of mankind since the authority of Odin and the old gods of Valhalla was so boldly challenged by a carpenter's son. Spengler offers a solution, but his remedy, despite the brilliant writing and composition, is repellent, for it is not only purely materialistic and anti-intellectual, but emphasizes the animalistic in man, the "triumph of blood," the superiority of the "race." This would lead us back to the collectivism of the masses, this time synonymous with "race," whereas salvation can come only from the freedom of the individual; for freedom means differentiation and independence of mind, it creates individuals, whereas any form of social regimentation calls for uniformity of civilization, limiting individual inventiveness, killing art.

But theoretical programs for a new order of humanity are not sufficient to create a new art, because art is the product of genius, and requires the faith of Columbus. If this faith is strong the shores will loom up before his eyes watching ceaselessly for land, for even if there were no coast beyond the horizon, his creative force would raise it from the bottom of the ocean. The philosophers who feared the coming reign of the masses, who deplored that millions would no longer be set aside for half a century to build St. Peter's, forgot that there was once a democracy that built the Acropolis. Nor is "mass" necessarily identical with "canaille." Superficial identifications have not only falsified history but have at times actually ruined peoples and civilizations. As classical democracy did not destroy the old culture but founded a new one, so its modern counterpart will find its own art; for democracy, recognizing no conflict between the individual and the good of the *res publica,* tries to assure him all possibilities for the development of the force and vitality that is in him.

The music of the new century will rise from the civilization of democracy and has, indeed, already sprung from the unspoiled and untapped energies of the New World and the countries of the peripheries of Europe, which heretofore were outside the main territory of Western civilization. At the end of the period of romanticism, when the reaction engendered by its long rule and disintegration found Western music in a hopeless tangle, the first heralds of this art appeared, who with their barbaric vigor and uninhibited strength frightened an enervated world. Their coming, and the rise of a new culture from the new civilization of the twentieth century, was prophesied by the most powerful and marked individuality of the previous two generations, Wagner: "I could not but be aware that in that new birth of art from life another power must lend its creative help, a power which must manifest itself as *the conscious willing of that art.* To wake this conscious will in those who feel dissatisfied with our art of today appears to me as the principal task for the artist and critic of the present; for only from the fellow longing of others, and finally of the many, can spring the force to feed his higher effort."

NOTES

⇛⇚

(For abbreviations consult Bibliography)

CHAPTER ONE

1 "Greece" is used here in the accepted sense as the conglomeration of the various tribes which inhabited the mainland, the isles, and Asia Minor.

2 In his *Republic* Plato shows a certain hostility to art, on the ground that art is based on the purely physical world.

3 We are equally unfortunate with the popular music of medieval Greece, but we are quite familiar with the rich folklore of modern Hellas, some of which shows unmistakable signs of great age.

4 "The Muse loved him above all other men, and gave him both good and evil; of his sight she deprived him, but gave him the gift of sweet song." *Odyssey,* VIII, 62 (tr. A. T. Murray).

5 *Iliad*, II, 595.

6 Another version attributes his blindness to his having looked upon the bathing Athena.

7 *Odyssey*, I, 154.

8 "Lyre" is used here exclusively to denote these two instruments. The term was later applied to a variety of instruments. It was synonymous and interchangeable with a number of plucked and bowed instruments such as the lute, fiddle, hurdygurdy, etc. When Alfred de Musset says "poète prends ton luth" he means the classical lyre. The "lyra" or "lira" which we encounter so frequently in the Renaissance was a predecessor of the violin.

9 Horace (*Epod.*, 9, 5) speaks in a derogatory way about the simultaneous playing on the aulos and the cithara.
Sonante mixtum tibiis carmen lyra,
Hac Doricum, illis barbarum.
This is one of the last survivals of the old precepts which forbade the mixing of the sounds of the two instruments.

10 Dances figured in the services of worship in early Christendom, and the spiritual *tonadillas* of Spain testify to their vogue in the seventeenth century.

11 Like the *Râga* of the Hindus or the *Maqâm* of the Persians.

12 The literal meaning of κροῦσις is "to strike the string."

13 Plato mentions (*Laws,* VII) ἑτεροφωνία and describes it as simultaneous melodic variation between song and its instrumental accompaniment. Cf. Guido Adler, *Ueber Heterophonie, Peters Jahrbuch,* Leipzig, 1908.

14 There are some indications that in later periods there may have been duets.

15 It did not disappear entirely in modern times, and we still have one serene, isolated descendant of ancient Greek tragedy in Goethe's *Faust. Faust* still has choruses, and they should be sung, for they call for music and they have music besides the *Glockenklang* and *Orgelton.* With the majestic *Dies irae, dies illa,* Goethe actually conjures up the Middle Ages.

16 Cf. Schiller's letter to Körner, May 25, 1792. "Feelings [*Empfindung*] originate in me without definite or clear subjects; the subject is formed only later. A certain musical mood and sensation [*Gemütsstimmung*] occurs first and the poetical idea follows." Ed. Jonas, III, 202.

17 Not all of these ideas are original with the Greeks. Herodotus mentions a similar selection of music by Egyptian priests, and we know of analogous practices in China. This is but another proof that we are dealing here with age-old Oriental cultural elements.

18 It is true, however, that our explanation of the ethos of certain scales is valid in a general sense only, for there can be no doubt that in late classical times the tradition became very hazy and that there was a considerable diversity of opinion as to the exact pitch or key when speaking of "manly" or "lascivious" tones. But the ethos doctrine lived nevertheless and is by no means confined to antiquity. The Middle Ages took over the Greek names and applied them, loosely, to the new church keys or scales. Luther was still of the opinion that the hypolydian scale should be used for the Gospel tone "for Christ is a gentle Lord, and His words are lovely; therefore let us take the 6th

tone for the Gospel. . . . Since St. Paul is a grave apostle, we will set the Epistle in the 8th tone." We shall see later how the Renaissance revised these theories and how the characteristics attributed to the various scales and pitches were later standardized when, about 1700, the church keys were "officially" succeeded by our modern major-minor keys.

19 Inscriptions on monuments indicate that the thymelic agones were still practiced in the third century A. D. They ceased probably only in 526, when Emperor Justinian forbade all theatrical performances. Antiquity produced a considerable literature on the agones (*peri agonon*).

20 Ἡ Ἀρμονια ἐν τῇ Ἀρχιτεκτονικῇ Ποιήσει, Athens, 1926.

21 See Clouds, 332.

22 Cf. *The Oxyrhynchos Papyri,* ed. and tr. B. P. Grenfell and A. Hunt. Egypt Exploration Society, London, 1922.

23 This piece is supposed to be an original composition, but the possibility exists, of course, that it is merely an old melody fitted out with a new text.

CHAPTER TWO

1 Byzantine music is one of the domains recently invaded by musicological research. Its history and complex notation are now the subject of intensive examination, and with the publication (now in progress) of the *Monumenta Musicae Byzantinae* (Copenhagen) and the *Trésor de Musique Byzantin* (Paris) we shall soon possess more abundant material concerning the music of Eastern Christendom.

2 Under "Byzantine" we shall now understand the family of nations—Syrians, Armenians, Abyssinians, Russians, Bulgarians, and other races—which accepted the Greek Orthodox Church. Unlike Western Christendom, Eastern Christendom did not have a universal liturgic language: every country used its own, but the spirit of the Greek Church prevailed; hence we are justified in using the collective term "Byzantine" even when speaking of modern times.

3 Of ancient Jewish music we have only a pale picture. On the one hand, it is certain that the present-day Jewish temple music has only remote connections, if any, with the music of ancient times. On the other hand, recent research conducted among the isolated Jewish tribes in Asia —which remained in almost primeval condition while their brethren migrated

to the West—has proved that there is an affinity between Christian and Jewish psalmody. A. Z. Idelsohn's publications furnish important material for the study of this complex question. The situation is further complicated by views held by other scholars, who see in this Hebrew music the influence of the Greek nome and the Hindu *Râga*. If the melodies discovered and published by Idelsohn are identical with ancient Palestinian melodies, it is remarkable that they disclose a predominance of Greek modes. At any rate, it is of interest to note that Clement of Alexandria (c. 200 A. D.) already saw the model of ecclesiastical singing in Jewish diatonic music, and that Saadia Gaon, the great Jewish scholar of the tenth century, professed an aesthetic system which is singularly similar to the ethos doctrine of the Greeks. Cf. A. Z. Idelsohn, *Jewish Music in Its Historical Development,* New York, 1929.

4 The antiphonal character of singing and the use of two organs is of great importance and may help to rectify an erroneous statement frequently encountered in essays on musical history. The use of an antiphonal double choir goes back to ancient Hebrew traditions and was continued in Syria. With the acceptance of the Syrian liturgy in Milan, antiphonal singing was introduced into Italy. One outstanding late monument of this practice survived in Venice, where, in the early sixteenth century, St. Mark's possessed two organs placed in two choir lofts. If we consider the fact that the architectural design of St. Mark's is Byzantine, the church having been rebuilt with the assistance of Byzantine architects (the Gothic additions date from the fifteenth century), and also that such organ construction is mentioned by the last Byzantine historian, Phrantza (or Phrantzes), at the time of the fall of Constantinople, we must conclude that the musical settings using double choirs and two organs, considered a characteristic trait of the musical style of the baroque, were not due to an "accident," as the presence of the two organs in St. Mark's is usually called, but to the survival of a musical practice of Byzantine origin which was still a living art in the time of Adrian Willaert, the great organist and choirmaster of St. Mark's in the second quarter of the sixteenth century.

5 The Byzantine system and the eight modes or scales of the Gregorian system are not identical, but the relationship between the two is obvious.

CHAPTER THREE

1 Seneca, *Epistolae*, 84, 10

2 Cicero, *De Orat.*, III, 98.

3 Three hymns by Mesomedes are available in almost any larger manual on musical history. Cf. *Musici Scriptores Graeci*, ed. von Jan in the *Teubner Classics*, p. 454.

4 ". . . *preparare ab imis sonis vocem ad summos.*" Quintilian, XI, 3, 22.

5 "*Numerius Furius, noster familiaris, cum est commodum, cantat, est enim pater familias, est eques Romanus, puer didicit quod discendum ferit.*" Cicero, *De Orat.*, III, 86.

6 Suetonius, *Nero*, I, 49.

CHAPTER FOUR

1 *Augustine's Confessions*, tr. William Watts, Loeb Classical Library, book 10, chap. xxxiii, p. 165.

2 The most recent manifestation of this spirit can be found in the acts of Pope Pius X (pope from 1903 to 1914), who discouraged the use of any music later than Palestrina in the services of the church.

3 Ammianus Marcellinus, XIV, 6.

4 *Les Origines du Chant Liturgique*, Paris, 1890.

5 The keeping of vigils was abolished early in the Middle Ages because of the riotous behavior of the people.

6 M. Gerbert, *De Cantu et Musica Sacra*, I, 128.

7 *Apology*, paragraph 61, *et seq.*

8 See above, pp. 2, 20, 23, 47.

9 Cf. the Hymns of Mesomedes, above, pp. 19, 33.

10 St. Augustine, *op. cit.*, book IX, chap. vii.

11 *Ibid.*, book IX, chap. vi.

12 The authorship of the *Te Deum* is now attributed to Bishop Nicetas of Dacia (c. 335–414).

13 See Gerbert, *op. cit.*, I, 33.

14 The *scholae* were often synonymous with orphanages: "*schola cantorum, quae pridem orphanotrophium vocabatur.*" Cf. Ambros, *Geschichte der Musik*, II, 13.

15 *Inst. Mus.*, I, 33.

16 "*Sine musica nulla disciplina potest esse perfecta; nihil enim est sine illa.*" Isidore of Seville. Cf. M. Gerbert, *Scriptores Ecclesiastici de Musica Sacra*, I, 20.

CHAPTER FIVE

1 Cf. G. H. Hörle, *Frühmittelalterliche Mönchs- und Kleriker-Bildung in Italien*, Freiburg (Breisgau), 1914, p. 20, *et seq.*

2 *Les Origines du Chant Liturgique*, 1890.

3 *Deutsche Vierteljahrsschrift*, V.

4 Cf. P. S. Bäumker, *Geschichte des Breviers*, 1895, p. 293.

5 The most complete collection of sequence texts is to be found in G. M. Dreves, *Analecta Hymnica* (1886–1911), vols. L, LIII, LIV. The melodies were treated by Wagner, *Einführung in die Gregorianische Melodien*, vol. III.

6 An interesting phenomenon is the reappearance of the tropes in Protestant church music toward the last quarter of the seventeenth century. They can be followed with the German cantata into J. S. Bach's time. The recitatives interpolated into the Lutheran chorales are real tropes. Cf. the recitative *Er ist auf Erden kommen arm* in Bach's Christmas Oratorio.

7 *Kirchenmusikalisches Jahrbuch*, 1911, and *ZfMW*, XII, XIII.

8 Cf. Spanke, "Das Fortleben der Sequenzen in den Romanischen Literaturen," in *Zeitschrift für Romanische Philologie*, vol. LI.

9 See above, p. 28.

10 Several tracts on music have been ascribed to Odo. See Gerbert, *Scriptores*, I. While it is not possible to uphold Odo's authorship, the fact remains that the tracts were written during his administration.

11 Cf. *Revue de l'Art Chrétien*, 1888, III.

12 *Micrologus*, Prologue, in Gerbert, II, 3a.

13 *Ibid.*, p. 44a.

14 E. de Coussemaker, *Scriptorum de Musica Medii Aevi*, 1864–1876, I, 6.

15 *Ibid.*, p. 253.

16 Gerbert, II, 214.

17 See Johannes Wolf's edition of Grocheo's *Theoria* in *SIMG*, I, 83.

CHAPTER SIX

1 *La Comédie Latine en France au XII*e *Siècle*, Paris, 1931.

2 *Drames Liturgiques au Moyen Age*, Rennes, 1861.

3 Magdalen is still pronounced, in the old English colleges bearing her name, Môdlin; hence maudlin, i. e., tearful.

4 *Op. cit.*, p. 285.

5 Cf. B. Monod, *Le Moine Guibert et son Temps*, Paris, 1905.

6 See Henry Copley Greene, "The Song of the Ass," in *Speculum*, October, 1931.

7 See Paul Lehman, *Die Parodie im Mittelalter*, Munich, 1922, p. 200.

8 Songs taken from the *Carmina Burana* form the main part of songbooks used by German students today. Many of them have been delicately translated by John Addington Symonds in his book entitled *Wine, Women, and Song* (1884). See also the excellent translations in the various volumes of medieval poetry by Helen Waddell, and the recent modern edition of the *Carmina Burana* by Alfons Hilka and Otto Schumann, Heidelberg, 1930.

9 See especially Alfred Jeanroy, *Les Origines de la Poésie Lyrique*, 3rd ed., Paris, 1925.

10 Taken from the collection of Coussemaker. English paraphrase by M. Hadas.

11 See Grocheo, *op. cit.*

12 Cf. Pierre Aubry, *Estampies et Danses Royales*, Paris, 1906.

13 Jeanroy, *Histoire de la Langue et de la Littérature Française*, p. 387.

14 Adam's *Jeu* has been edited by Ernest Langlois in the *Classiques Français du Moyen Âge*, Paris, 1923–24.

15 Chambers, *The Medieval Stage*, II, 234.

16 See Anglade, *Le Troubadour Guiraut Riquier, Étude sur la Décadence de l'ancienne Poésie Provençale*, Paris, 1905.

17 See V. de Bartholomaeis, *Le Origini della Poesia Drammatica Italiana*, 1924.

18 *Kirchenmusikalisches Jahrbuch*, 1894, p. 33.

19 The extant works, mostly fragments, of these poets are published in Vogt's *Des Minnesangs Frühling*, Leipzig, 1920, and in F. v. d. Hagen's *Minnesang*, Leipzig, 1923.

20 *ZfMW*, VII, 65.

CHAPTER SEVEN

1 The terminology used in connection with music for more than one voice is confusing. Simultaneous sounding of two or more tones does not necessarily mean polyphonic independence of parts, which latter represents the composition of simultaneous but melodically independent and individual parts or voices. In order to distinguish between the two varieties we shall use the term "many-voiced music," or simply "polyphony,"

for the first species, and "contrapuntal polyphony" for the second.

2 See Marius Schneider, *Geschichte der Mehrstimmigkeit*, I, *Naturvölker*, Berlin, 1934.

3 Giraldus Cambrensis, "Descriptio Cambriae," in *Rerum Britannicarum Medii Aevi Scriptores*, I, xxxvi.

4 The MS. is now in the library of Corpus Christi College in Cambridge. Cf. *Publications of the Henry Bradshaw Society*, vol. VIII.

5 Cf. *Oxford History of Music*, vol. I, 1901 (Wooldridge); *Musical Times*, London, June 1, 1932, and August, 1933 (Handschin).

6 Cf. Gerbert, *Scriptores*, II, 230.

7 Published in the first volume of Coussemaker's *Scriptorum*.

8 The rhythmic modes should not be confused with the Greek and medieval system of diatonic tonalities. In early medieval music the term *modus* had a purely rhythmic significance. By disregarding this fact writers have often created confusion in their discussion of medieval musical theory. Cf. "Rhythmic Modes," in Grove's *Dictionary*.

9 See Guido Adler, *Handbuch der Musikgeschichte*, Berlin, 1930, I, 234.

10 Robert de Lasteyre, *L'Architecture Religieuse en France à l'Epoque Gothique*, Paris, 1926, I, 361.

11 Cf. H. G. Farmer, *The Arabian Influence on Musical Theory*, London, 1925.

12 His treatise is published in the first volume of Coussemaker's *Scriptorum*.

13 Coussemaker, *Scriptorum*, I, 182.

14 See above, p. 72.

15 Cf. *Speculum Charitatis*, in Prynne's translation.

16 Cf. *Polycratus*, I, 6.

17 See Heinrich Besseler's articles in *AfMW*, VII, 180, and VIII, 207.

18 Cf. Higini Anglès, *La Música a Catalunya fins al Segle XIII*, Publicacions del Departament de Música, Institut d'Estudis Catalans, vol. X, 1935. Biblioteca de Catalunya.

CHAPTER EIGHT

1 Cf. A. Machabey in the *Revue Musicale*, Paris, February, 1929.

2 Coussemaker, who published it under the title *Messe du XIIIe Siècle*, Tournay, 1861, was misled by its archaic qualities and placed it in the thirteenth century although it originated in the fourteenth.

3 Edited by Friedrich Ludwig, Leipzig, 1926–1934.

4 See the excellent study by Leonard Ellinwood in the *Musical Quarterly*, April, 1936.

5 *The Works of Francesco Landino*, ed. L. Ellinwood, Cambridge, Mass., Mediaeval Society of America, 1939.

6 See ballad No. 33 in Ludwig's edition of Machaut's works.

7 Two manuscripts of *Les Echecs Amoureux* are known, one in Paris and the other in Dresden. First published by H. Abert in K. Vollmöller's *Romanische Forschungen*, vol. XV.

8 Guillaume de Machaut, *Oeuvres*, ed. Chichmaref, I, 10.

9 *House of Fame*, 809–816.

10 Modern version taken from *Wyclif's English Works*, ed. F. D. Matthews, *Early English Text Society*, 1880, p. 191.

11 *Purgatory*, II, 101–117.

12 See *The Digby Plays*, ed. F. F. Furnivall, *Early English Text Society, Extra Series*, 70, pp. 100, 107, 145.

13 Cf. André Pirro, *La Musique à Paris sous le Règne de Charles VI*, Strasbourg, 1930, p. 19.

14 See Felipe Pedrell, *Jean I d'Aragon, Compositeur de Musique*, in *Riemann Festschrift*, Leipzig, 1909, p. 231.

15 See Sir John Hawkins, *op. cit.*, p. 207.

16 See André Pirro, *op. cit.*, p. 31.

17 See J. Jusserand, *English Wayfaring Lives in the Middle Ages*, New York, 1920, p. 212.

18 S. E. Faral, *Les Jongleurs en France*, Paris, 1910.

CHAPTER NINE

1 See above, p. 157.

2 See Gabriel Pérouse, "Georges Chastellain, Étude sur l'Histoire Politique et Littéraire du XVe Siècle," Académie Royale de Belgique, *Mémoires* (Lettres), 2e Série, VII.

3 See Manfred Bukofzer, *Geschichte des Englischen, Diskants und des Fauxbourdons*, Strasbourg, 1936.

4 A large selection taken from the six codices was published in *DTOe*, XIV.

5 Coussemaker, IV, 153.

6 Hugo Leichtentritt, "Was Lehren Uns die Bildwerke des 14–17 Jahrhunderts," etc., in *SIMG*, 1905–06.

7 Arnold Schering, *Die Niederländische Orgelmesse im Zeitalter des Josquin*, Leipzig, 1912.

8 Coussemaker, IV, 76.

9 Otto Kinkeldey, "Music and Music Printing in Incunabula," in *Papers of the Bibliographical Society of America*, XXVI (1932), 113.

10 Both available in modern reprints, the *Gründlicher Bericht des deutschen Meistergesanges* re-edited by R. Jones, Halle, 1888, and the *Singebuch* revised by G. Münzer, Leipzig, 1906.

11 Facsimile edition (together with Paumann's chief work, *Fundamentum Organisandi*) by K. Ameln, Berlin, 1925.

12 The motet, entitled *Non Moriar Sed Vivam*, was published by Breitkopf & Härtel, Leipzig, 1917.

13 See *AfMW*, July, 1920.

14 A substantial number of these chansons is available in the volumes of Henri Expert's collection entitled *Les Maîtres Musiciens de la Renaissance Française*, Paris, 1899–1908.

15 See note 4, Chapter Two.

16 The *ricercare*, although hardly distinguishable from the fugue proper, was still among the musical forms used by the composers of the early eighteenth century. It is significant that in his *Musical Offering*, which contains various treatments of a subject given him by Frederick the Great, J. S. Bach included two *ricercari*, and the subtitle of the work is an acrostic play on the word *ricercar*: "Regis Jussu Cantio Et Reliqua Canonica Arte Resoluta."

17 See Otto Ursprung, *Jacobus de Kerle*, Munich, 1913.

18 Of a projected sixty-volume edition, twenty-one volumes have so far appeared, published by Breitkopf & Härtel in Leipzig.

19 Justus Thibaut, *Ueber Reinheit der Tonkunst*, Heidelberg, 1825.

20 Charles Gounod, *Memoirs of an Artist*, tr. E. A. Crocker, Chicago, 1895, p. 99.

21 Richard Wagner, *Beethoven*, tr. E. Dannreuther, London, 1893, p. 33.

22 Carl v. Winterfeld, *Johannes Gabrieli und sein Zeitalter*, Berlin, 1834.

23 Curt Sachs, "Die Streichbogenfrage," in *AfMW*, 1918.

24 Cf. notes 6 and 7; also Otto Kinkeldey, *Orgel und Klavier in der Musik des 16. Jahrhunderts*, Leipzig, 1910.

25 Gerbert, III, 352.

26 See the English translation by C. W. Beaumont, London, 1925. An earlier but less extensive treatise is *L'Art et Instruction de Bien Dancer*, printed by Michel Toulouze at about 1495 in Paris. A facsimile of the only recorded copy, with a bibliographical note by Victor Scholderer, London, 1936.

27 Preserved Smith, *The Age of the Reformation*, New York, 1920, p. 689.

28 A detailed account of the type of verse form used by Ronsard may be found in the *Revue d'Histoire Littéraire de la France* (1900) in an article entitled "Ronsard et les Musiciens du XVIᵉ Siècle" by Charles Comte and Paul Laumonier.

29 See Waldo Selden Pratt, *The Music of the French Psalter of 1562*, New York, 1939.

30 See Felipe Pedrell, *Hispaniae Scholae Musica Sacra;* Don Hilarion Eslava, *Lira Sacro-Hispana;* Higini Anglès, *El Codex de la Huelgas.*

31 See Guillermo Morphy, *Les Luthistes Espagnols du XVIᵉ Siècle*, 1902.

32 Cabezon's works appeared in Pedrell's *Hispaniae Scholae Musica Sacra*, vols. 3–4 and 7–8.

33 Louis B. Wright, *Middle Class Culture in Elizabethan England*, Chapel Hill (N.C.), 1935, p. 185.

34 In *Oxford History of Music.*

35 Ed. F. C. Hingeston, London, 1858, p. 314.

36 Cf. "Un Poème Inédit de Martin Le Franc," in *Romania*, XVI, 383.

37 *Oxford History of Music*, 2nd ed., II, 158.

38 *Ibid.*, p. 159.

39 W. H. Grattan Flood, *Early Tudor Composers*, London, 1925.

40 Jeffrey Pulver, *A Biographical Dictionary of Old English Music*, London, 1927, p. 180.

41 *King's Music, An Anthology*, by Gerald Hayes, London, 1937, p. 76.

42 Published in the *Rolls Series* by H. T. Riley, London, 1863.

43 See H. G. Farmer, *Music in Medieval Scotland*, London, 1930.

44 The part dealing with the reign of Henry VIII was edited by C. Whibley in 1904.

45 J. H. Westrup in *Oxford History of Music*, 2nd ed., II, 348, 372.

46 Nos. 354–365 in *Oxford Choral Songs from the Old Masters.*

47 Charles Burney, *A General History of Music*, London, 1776, II, 551.

48 J. Stainer, *Early Bodleian Music*, London, 1902; L. S. Myers, *Music, Cantilenas, Songs*, etc., London, 1906; J. A. Fuller-Maitland, *Carols of the XVth Century*, London, 1891.

49 See E. H. Fellowes, *The English School of Lutenist Songwriters*, London, 1920.

50 The list is printed in Gerald Hayes's anthology, *King's Music*, p. 86.

51 Published by J. A. Fuller-Maitland and W. Barclay Squire. (1894?)

52 Ernest Walker, *A History of Music in England*, London, 1924, p. 136.

53 W. H. Hadow in W. H. Grattan Flood's *Early Tudor Composers*, Preface.

54 The only available complete edition of Zarlino's works is the publication entitled *Tutte l'Opere del R. M. Gioseffo Zarlino da Chioggia*, Venice, 1589.

55 See Raphael Mitjana, *Francisco Guerrero*, Madrid, 1922, p. 12.

56 See Franz Haböck, *Die Kastraten und ihre Gesangskunst*, Leipzig, 1927.

57 See E. Fremy, *L'Académie des Derniers Valois*, Paris, 1887, p. 40.

58 See R. v. Liliencron, "Die Horazischen Metren in Deutschen Kompositionen des 16. Jahrhunderts," in *VfMW*, 1887.

59 See Wright, *op. cit.*, p. 603.

60 Kinkeldey, *op. cit.*, p. 166.

61 Some of these Gentlemen of the Chapel Royal, such as William Crane, were also engaged in the import and export business, transacting deals of imposing magnitude.

62 See Charles S. Braden, *Religious Aspects of the Conquest of Mexico*, Durham (N.C.), 1930; Ruben M. Campos, *El Folklore y la Musica Mexicana*, Mexico City, 1938; Eleanor Hague, *Latin American Music*, Santa Ana (Cal.), 1934.

CHAPTER TEN

1 Cf. Wilhelm Bäumker, *Das Katholische deutsche Kirchenlied in seinen Singweisen*, Freiburg, 1911.

2 Giovanni Maria Artusi, *L'Artusi Ovvero delle Imperfettioni della Moderna Musica*, Part I, 1600; Part II, 1603.

3 Cf. the chapter entitled *De Ratione Componendi et Modis.*

4 Franciscus Lang, S.J. professor of rhetoric in Munich toward the end of the seventeenth century, recognized the origins of the baroque theater in his work entitled *Considerationes Melodicae, seu Spiritualia S.J. Ignatii Exercitia*, published posthu-

mously in 1727 in Munich. Cf. Josef Nadler, *Literaturgeschichte der deutschen Stämme und Landschaften*, Ratisbon, 1923.

5 See above, p. 114.

6 Otto Kinkeldey in *SIMG*, IX, and the same author's *Orgel und Klavier in der Musik des 16. Jahrhunderts*, Leipzig, 1910, p. 157.

7 Important excerpts from his work are included in Angelo Solerti, *Origini del Melodramma*, Turin, 1903.

8 Francesco de Sanctis, *History of Italian Literature*, New York, 1931, II, 638.

9 A collection of arias and madrigals for one voice with thorough bass (1602, 2nd ed. 1607, 3rd 1615), the title of which became a motto for a whole era, not unlike de Vitry's *Ars Nova*.

10 Cf. O. G. Sonneck, *Dafne, the First Opera*, *SIMG*, XV.

11 An abridged version of this opera was published by Robert Eitner in vol. X of *Publikation Aelterer Praktischer und Theoretischer Musikwerke*, Leipzig, 1881.

12 *Tutte le Opere di Claudio Monteverdi*, edited by G. Francesco Malipiero, 1927.

13 The composition, erroneously attributed to J. Ph. Krieger, was published in *DTD*, 53–54.

14 Facsimile edition of the score in *Collezione di Prime Fioriture del Melodramma Italiano* (ed. Mantica), Rome, 1912.

15 We have, fortunately, good descriptions of the Barberini palace, and of the performances given therein, by a French traveler, Jean Jacques Bouchard. Cf. *Revue d'Histoire et de Critique Musicales*, January, 1902.

16 See Arnaldo Bonaventura, *Saggio Storico sul Teatro Musicale Italiano*, 1913, p. 99.

17 M. Misson, *A New Voyage to Italy*, 4th ed., London, 1714, V, 362.

18 See note 4 in this chapter.

19 The interesting and informative *Discorso della Musica dell' Eta Nostra* of this author was published in a modern edition by A. Solerti, *op. cit.*

20 See Romain Rolland, *Histoire de l'Opéra en Europe avant Lully et Scarlatti*, Paris, 1895; Hugo Goldschmidt, *Studien zur Geschichte der Italienischen Oper im 17. Jh.*, Leipzig, 1901; Andrea della Corte, *L'Opera Comica Italiana nel 1700*, 1923.

21 Cf. Otto Kinkeldey, *op. cit.*, and Max Schneider, *Die Anfänge des Basso Continuo*, Leipzig, 1918.

22 *Del Suonare Sopra il Basso con Tutti Stromenti et Uso Loro nel Concerto*, Siena, 1608. Copious excerpts in F. T. Arnold's monumental work, *The Art of Accompaniment from a Thorough-Bass*, London, 1931.

23 *Response Faite à un Curieux Sur le Sentiment de La Musique d'Italie. Escrite à Rome le premier Octobre 1639*. Cf. E. Thoinan, *André Maugars, Célèbre Joueur de Viole*, Paris, 1865.

24 Unfortunately the many compositions included in anthologies under his name are the work of another Rossi, a contemporary of the young Haydn.

25 Published in *DTOe*, vol. X(I).

26 Cf. Archibald T. Davison, *Protestant Church Music in America*, Boston, 1933.

27 For the full text see Nuitter & Thoinan, *Les Origines de l'Opéra Français*, Paris, 1886.

28 Titon du Tillet, *Le Parnasse François*, Paris, 1725.

29 See L'Abbé [François] Raguenet, *Parallèle des Italiens et des François en ce Qui Regarde la Musique et les Opéra*, Paris, 1702.

30 Modern editions by Eitner, in *Publikationen der Gesellschaft für Musikforschung*, vol. XIII (*De Organographia*); by Gurlitt, in *Publikation der Hist. Sektion des deutschen Orgelrats*, Kassel, 1929 (facsimile edition); and by Bernouilli, Leipzig, 1916 (*Tomus Tertius*).

31 The score of this opera was published in *Monatshefte für Musikgeschichte*, XIII, 53.

32 See above, p. 288.

33 See Ernest Brennecke, *John Milton the Elder and his Music*, New York, 1938.

34 P. 274, edition of 1633.

35 See above, p. 399.

36 Cf. John Tasker Howard, *Our American Music*, New York, 1930; Waldo Selden Pratt, *The Music of the Pilgrims*, Boston, 1921.

37 Pratt, *op. cit.*, p. 6.

38 See George Hood, *History of Music in New England*, Boston, 1921.

39 At the time of this writing there appeared the first series of *Early Psalmody in America*, New York, 1938. Prepared under the direction of Carleton Sprague Smith, this publication of the New York Public Library bids fair to fill an important gap in the history of American music.

CHAPTER ELEVEN

1 *The Musicall Grammarian,* by Roger North (c. 1728), edited by Hilda Andrews, London, 1925, p. 15.

2 Athanasius Kircher, *Musurgia Universalis sive Ars Magna Consoni et Dissoni,* Rome, 1650, VII, 545.

3 Johann David Heinichen, *Neu erfundene und gründliche Anweisung,* Hamburg, 1711.

4 Brossard, *Dictionnaire de Musique,* Paris, 1703.

5 Cf. Michel Brenet, *Sébastien de Brossard d'après des Papiers Inédits,* Paris, 1896.

6 L'Abbé Pluche, *Spectacle de la Nature,* Paris, 1732.

7 L'Abbé Dubos, *Réflexions Critiques,* Paris, 1719.

8 Charles Batteux, *Les Beaux Arts, Réduits à un Même Principe,* Paris, 1743.

9 Johann Mattheson, *Der Vollkommene Capellmeister,* Hamburg, 1739, p. 82.

10 Johann Mattheson, *Das Neu-Eröffnete Orchestre,* Hamburg, 1713, I, 266.

11 Cf. *DTD,* II, 19.

12 Cf. Edward J. Dent's list in *SIMG,* vol. IV.

13 Edward J. Dent, *Alessandro Scarlatti, His Life and Works,* London, 1905.

14 One of his important operas was published in Eitner's *Publikationen* (vol. XIV), some church music in the well-known anthologies of Proske, Rochlitz, and Commer, and a few instrumental works by various modern editors.

15 In Venice there were similar institutions called "hospitals."

16 His most celebrated opera, *Costanza e Fortezza,* is published in vol. XVII of *DTOe,* also in the *Smith College Archives* (No. 2), Northampton, Mass., edited by Gertrude Parker Smith.

17 See Carl Mennicke, *Hasse und die Brüder Graun als Symphoniker,* Leipzig, 1906.

18 See above, p. 324.

19 See above, p. 392.

20 The former was published by the Bärenreiter Verlag, Kassel, 1928; the latter in *DTD,* 21–22.

21 *Croesus* and *l'Inganno Fedele* in the *DTD,* 37–38; *Octavia* in the Appendix to the complete works of Handel.

22 Published in *DTD,* 21–22.

23 Sebastiani's *Passion* is published in *DTD,* XVII.

24 The French influence is demonstrated in an interesting publication by Jules Ecorcheville, *Vingt Suites d'Orchestre du 17e Siècle,* Paris, 1906. The volume, derived from a manuscript in Kassel, Germany, contains compositions for the most part by German composers entirely dominated by French taste and style.

25 Two suites from this collection are printed in *DTOe,* IX, 2.

26 The list of these manuscript compositions was published by Max Seiffert in *SIMG,* IX, 593.

27 Bach's two chorale preludes on that hymn tune, especially the one with the double pedal part, are so typically north-German-Netherlandish, closely paralleling Reinken's style, that one may safely consider them the kind of music which elicited the patriarch's praise. Cf. the organ works of Bach in the *Peters Edition,* VI, 32, 34.

28 André Pirro, *J. S. Bach,* Paris, 1924, 6th ed., p. 182.

29 See the document quoted in full by Philipp Spitta, *J. S. Bach,* English edition, London, 1899, p. 315.

30 See above, p. 399.

31 Cf. *DTOe,* VIII, 2.

32 See Johann Kaspar Ferdinand Fischer, *Sämtliche Werke für Klavier und Orgel,* ed. Werra, Leipzig, 1901. Bernhard Christian Weber, "Das Wohltemperierte Klavier," in *Publications of the New Bach Society,* XXXIV, 1, Leipzig, 1933.

33 Cf. J. B. Jackson's restoration of the *F minor* concerto (transposed into *G minor*), London, Oxford University Press, 1915. The *D minor* piano concerto was transcribed by R. Reitz, Leipzig, Breitkopf & Härtel, 1917.

34 The fact that Bach himself called these works sonatas for *cembalo concertato e violino solo* indicates that we are still dealing with a sort of trio sonata for violin, harpsichord, and thorough bass, and it is probable that in Bach's time the *cembalo concertato* itself was accompanied by another harpsichord.

35 Friedrich Erhardt Niedt, *Musicalische Handleitung,* vol. III, Hamburg, 1717.

36 Philipp Spitta, *J. S. Bach,* Leipzig, vol. I, 1873; vol. II, 1880; English translation, London, 1884–1885.

37 André Pirro, *L'Esthétique de Jean-Sebastien Bach,* Paris, 1907. Albert Schweitzer, *Jean Sébastien Bach, le Musicien Poète,* Paris, 1905; expanded German edition, Leipzig, 1908; English translation of the latter, London, 1912.

38 Charles Sanford Terry, *J. S. Bach*, London, 1928.

39 *The Spectator*, ed. by Gregory Smith, New York, 1906, I, 109.

40 *The Diary of Samuel Pepys, 1660–1669*, ed. by O. F. Morshead, New York, 1926, p. 506.

41 *The Ladies' Library, Written by a Lady*, published by Richard Steele, 4th ed., 1732, I, 16.

42 *The Spectator*, I, 71.

43 Ernest Walker, *A History of Music in England*, 2nd ed., London, 1924, p. 183.

44 *The Spectator*, I, 69.

45 Ernest Walker, *op. cit.*, p. 194.

CHAPTER TWELVE

1 Lionel de la Laurencie's study, *L'Ecole Française de Violon de Lulli à Viotti* (Paris, 1922–1924), is the outstanding work on the relatively little-known French violin school.

2 Owing to the fact that French organ style differed little from French harpsichord style, and that practically all clavecinists discharged the duties of an organist, their works will be found in organ collections as well as in clavecin books. See Félix Alexandre Guilmant, *Archives des Maîtres de l'Orgue*, with important prefaces by André Pirro; *Les Clavecinistes Français* (Durand), and Couperin's keyboard works (Durand).

3 Letter to Thieriot, 1735.

4 See *Traité de l'Harmonie Réduite à ses Principes Naturels* (1722); *Démonstration du Principe de l'Harmonie* (1750); *Nouvelles Réflections sur la Démonstration du Principe de l'Harmonie* (1752).

5 Cf. Matthew Shirlaw, *The Theory of Harmony*, London, n.d.

6 *Mémoires ou Essais sur la Musique*, Paris, 1789, I, 130, 244.

7 Cf. Le Président de Brosses, *Lettres Familières Ecrites d'Italie en 1739 et 1740* (fiftieth letter), Paris, 1858.

8 See *Encyclopaedia Britannica*, art. Gluck (Tovey).

9 See Grove's *Dictionary*, art. Gluck (Chouquet).

10 *Oxford Companion to Music*, art. Opera.

11 From Goldoni's preface to his opera libretto *Statira*, Venice, 1756.

12 *Saggio sopra l'Opera in Musica*, 1750.

13 *Correspondance Littéraire* (1753–1790), complete edition 1877–1882, VIII, 34.

14 Hermann Kretzschmar, *Geschichte der Oper*, Leipzig, 1919, p. 206.

15 Romain Rolland, *Histoire de l'Opéra en Europe avant Lully et Scarlatti*, Paris, 1895, p. 230.

16 Reprinted in *DTD*, 35–36.

17 *DTD*, 42.

18 *DTD*, 41.

19 Twenty-five of Schulz's songs were published by the Steingräber Verlag in 1909.

20 Reprinted in *DTD*, 8–9.

21 See Leonhardt Euler, *Versuch Einer Neuen Musikalischen Theorie*, 1729.

22 *Der Vollkommene Capellmeister*, Hamburg, 1739, chapter 12, paragraph 30.

23 Johann Joachim Quantz, *Versuch einer Anweisung die Flöte Traversiere zu Spielen* (1752), reprint, ed. Schering, Leipzig, 1906, p. 108.

24 Christian Friedrich Daniel Schubart, *Schubarts Leben und Gesinnungen von ihm selbst im Kerker aufgesetzt*, 1791–1793, II, 94.

25 Georg Simon Löhlein, *Anweisung zum Violinspielen*, 1781, p. 104.

26 Friedrich Wilhelm Marpurg, *Historisch-Kritische Beiträge zur Aufnahme der Musik*, 1754–1762, I, 416.

27 *Musikalisch-Kritische Bibliothek*, Gotha, 1778, I, 74.

28 Marpurg, *op. cit.*, I, 149.

29 Vogler's most informative work is his *Mannheimer Tonschule* (1778–1781), while Junker's remarks may be found in his *Tonkunst* (1777).

30 Schulz wrote a number of articles on music in the encyclopedic *Allgemeine Theorie der Schönen Künste* (1771–1774), edited by the Berlin philosopher Johann Georg Sulzer (1720–1779).

31 *Wöchentliche Nachrichten*, 1768, p. 107.

32 De Brosses, *op. cit.*, p. 372.

33 Cf. the essay preceding Riemann's edition of the Mannheim symphonists, *Sinfonien der Pfalzbayrischen Schule*, DTB, III-1; also VII-2 and VIII-2 (1902–1908).

34 See Robert Sondheimer, Wilhelm Fischer, Guido Adler, Bernhard Rywosch, Franz Tutenberg, etc., in the Bibliography.

35 See above, pp. 359–362.

36 Scarlatti's keyboard compositions appeared in ten volumes under the title *Opere Complete* in Milan, 1906 (ed. Longo).

37 Both collections available in modern reprints in Nagel's *Archiv*.

38 De Brosses, *op. cit.*, II, 379.

39 See above, p. 554.

40 Charles Burney, *The Present State of Music in France and Italy*, London, 1771, I, 285.

41 *Ibid.*, II, 11.

42 A most interesting and revealing picture can be gained from the list of operatic performances printed in the second appendix to Friedrich Walter's *Geschichte des Theaters und der Musik am Kurpfälzischen Hofe*, Leipzig, 1898. .

CHAPTER THIRTEEN

1 See note 24 in preceding chapter.

2 Sir Henry Hadow, basing his statements on allegations made by Francis Xavier Kuhač (1834–1911), Croatian composer and historian, perpetuated in the English-speaking world the legend of Haydn's Croatian origin. In his work, entitled *A Croatian Composer* (London, 1897), he made the following statement: "He [Haydn] could not have written of set habit in the German idiom; he was Slav by race and Slav by temper, and his music is too genuine to present itself in foreign guise. It is from this point of view that we should understand him; not by loosely classifying him among a people with whom he had little in common, but by regarding him as the true embodiment of his own national spirit" (p. 84). Such regrettable aberration is difficult to explain unless political or other motives prompted the author to disregard elementary requirements of scholarship. The question was unequivocally cleared by E. F. Schmid, "Joseph Haydn," *Ein Buch von Vorfahren und Heimat des Meisters* (Kassel, 1934), and by D. Bartha in the *Acta Musicologica* (October, 1935). A rather comical anticlimax to this unnecessary controversy is furnished by Kuhač, whose original family name was the good German Koch, later changed to the Croatian form.

3 Paul Esterházy, Prince of the Holy Roman Empire (1635–1713), was the editor-compiler of *Harmonia Coelestis seu Melodiae Musicae per dedecursum totius anni adhibendae ad usum musicorum* (Vienna, 1711), a work of unique importance in the history of old Hungarian music, as it constitutes the oldest document of the merger of native idiom with Western art music. Although not as active as their ancestor, most of the younger members of the family exhibited a more than amateurish acquaintance with music.

4 See Georg August Griesinger, *Biographische Notizen über Joseph Haydn*, Leipzig, 1810.

5 See above, p. 576 f.

6 Published by Breitkopf & Härtel, Leipzig.

7 *Musical Quarterly*, April, 1932.

8 Cf. Theodore de Wyzewa and Georges de Saint-Foix, "Un Maître Inconnu de Mozart," in *Zeitschrift der Internationalen Musikgesellschaft*, 1908. A selection of Schobert's works appeared in *DTD*, 1909.

9 See below, p. 674.

10 The letter K, an abbreviation of Ludwig Ritter von Köchel's name, followed by a numeral, is the accepted symbol for the chronological catalogue of Mozart's works. Köchel's *Chronologisch-Thematisches Verzeichnis Sämtlicher Tonwerke W. A. Mozarts* (Leipzig, 1862), a work of imposing scholarship, made possible the publication of Mozart's complete works. Although a third edition of the catalogue, edited in 1938 by Alfred Einstein, added considerable new material to our existing store of knowledge, causing in many cases a shifting of the chronological order, we shall quote the old numbers since they appear on the printed editions.

11 Mozart's letters as well as important ones by members of his family are now available in an edition excellently translated, collated, edited, and documented by Emily Anderson, London, 1938.

12 Translated by Emily Anderson, in *The Letters of Mozart and His Family*, London, 1938.

13 The fact that the work from which the quotation is taken (*Vie de Mozart, Haydn, et Metastase*, Paris, 1814) was largely a shameless plagiarism should not diminish the acuteness of this observation.

14 1794, p. 142. The article was written by Carl Spazier, the noted editor of the journal.

15 *Die Bergknappen* is printed in *DTOe*, XVIII, I.

16 Hermann Kretzschmar, *Geschichte der Oper*, Leipzig, 1919, p. 241.

17 Henry Edward Krehbiel, *A Book of Operas*, New York, 1920, p. 62.

18 Mozart to his father, October 13, 1781. Cf. Emily Anderson, *op. cit.*

19 *Ibid.* Letter to his father, September 26, 1781.

20 Same letter.

CHAPTER FOURTEEN

1 See above, p. 422 f.

2 See José Subirá, *La Tonadilla Escenica,* Madrid, 1930.

3 A short excerpt in Lavignac's *Encyclopédie,* p. 2331, in the volume on Spanish music; another composition in Eslava's *Lira Sacro-Hispana.*

4 Twelve of Soler's sonatas appeared in Joaquin Nin's anthology entitled *Seize Sonates Anciennes d'Auteurs Espagnols.* Paris, 1925.

5 Edward J. Dent, *Foundations of English Opera,* London, 1928, p. 125.

6 A very interesting picture of this can be gleaned from the excellent work of Carl Ferdinand Pohl, *Mozart und Haydn in London,* Vienna, 1867.

7 See Theodore M. Finney, "The Collegium Musicum at Lititz," in *Papers Read by Members of the American Musicological Society,* privately printed by the Society, 1938.

8 The New York Public Library, on the initiative of the Chief of its Music Division, Carleton Sprague Smith, has published a number of Peter's works, choral and instrumental, as well as some by his colleagues.

9 Edward J. Dent, in *SIMG,* XIV, 501.

10 Hugo Leichtentritt, *Händel,* Leipzig, 1924.

11 See Paul Henry Láng, "Haydn and the Opera," *Musical Quarterly,* April, 1932.

12 Cf. the preface to David Ewen's *The Man with the Baton,* New York, 1936.

13 See Michel Brenet, *Les Concerts en France sous l'Ancien Régime,* Paris, 1900.

14 See above, p. 442.

15 See above, p. 87.

16 A fourth volume, intended to deal with the early Middle Ages, remained unfinished in manuscript.

CHAPTER FIFTEEN

1 See above, p. 582.

2 Walter Riezler, *Beethoven,* New York, 1938, p. 188.

3 Cf. Hans von Bülow, *Schriften,* III, 445.

4 Cf. Gustav Nottebohm, *Beethoveniana,* Leipzig, 1925; Nottebohm, *Ein Skizzenbuch von Beethoven* [1865], ed. Paul Mies, Leipzig, 1924; Paul Mies, *Beethoven's Sketches,* London, 1929. The publications of the Bonn Beethoven-House (*Veröffentlichungen*) also contain much valuable material, especially vols. 2, 3, 4, and 5.

5 See above, p. 139 f.

6 Robert Schumann, *Music and Musicians,* tr. F. R. Richter, 5th ed., London, n.d., I, 25.

7 *Das Deutsche Lied im 18 Jahrhundert,* Leipzig, 1902 (one volume of music).

8 *Op. cit.,* I, 54.

9 See above, p. 552 f.

CHAPTER SIXTEEN

1 Schumann, *op. cit.,* I, 73.

2 See his letter to Ferdinand Hiller, February 26, 1835.

3 See above, p. 233.

4 Schumann, *op. cit.,* I, 51.

5 Quoted in Oswald Jonas, *Das Wesen des Musikalischen Kunstwerks,* Vienna, 1934, p. 191.

6 See below, p. 917.

7 James F. Mason, *The Melodrama in France from the Revolution to the Beginning of Romantic Drama,* Baltimore, 1912, p. xii.

8 See Lavoix, *Dictionnaire du Conservatoire.*

9 See Julius Cornet, *Die Oper in Deutschland und das Theater der Neuzeit,* etc., Hamburg, 1849, p. 56.

10 See Siegfried S. Goslich, *Beiträge zur Geschichte der Deutschen Romantischen Oper,* Leipzig, 1937.

11 See F. C. Paldamus, *Das Deutsche Theater der Gegenwart,* Mayence, 1857.

12 Schumann, *op. cit.,* I, 40.

CHAPTER SEVENTEEN

1 *Wagner-Liszt Briefwechsel,* Leipzig, 1910, II, 267.

2 See Karl Wilhelm Göttling, *Über das Geschichtliche im Nibelungenlied,* Rudolfstadt, 1814, and *Nibelungen und Gibelinen,* Rudolfstadt, 1816.

3 E. Hippeau, *Berlioz et Son Temps,* Paris, 1892, p. 225.

4 See Romain Rolland, *Musiciens d'Aujourd'hui,* Paris, 1908, chapter on Berlioz.

5 Denis Saurat, *Literature and Occult Tradition,* London, 1930, p. 30.

6 Claude Debussy, *Monsieur Croche the Dilettante Hater,* London, 1927, p. 110.

7 Igor Stravinsky, *An Autobiography,* New York, 1936, p. 60.

8 See above, p. 233.

9 See Otto Ursprung, "Die Katholische Kirchenmusik," in Bücken's *Handbuch der Musikwissenschaft,* Potsdam, 1931.

10 See above, p. 9 f.

11 Debussy, *op. cit.*, p. 151.

12 J. H. Elliot, *Berlioz*, London, 1938, p. 204.

13 Liszt, *Gesammelte Schriften*, II, 104.

14 See Kurt Westphal, "Der Romantische Klavierstil," in *Die Musik*, XXII, 2.

15 See E. Bücken, *Anton Reichas Leben und Kompositionen*, Munich, 1912.

16 *Richard Wagner's Prose Works*, tr. W. A. Ellis, II, 123.

17 Liszt, *op. cit.*, II, 130.

18 Wagner, *op. cit.*, III, 243.

19 *Ibid.*, p. 250.

20 Liszt, *op. cit.*, IV, 30.

21 Wagner, *Letters to His Dresden Friends*, p. 300.

22 Liszt, *op. cit.*, IV, 31.

23 Wagner, *op. cit.*, VIII, 137.

24 Liszt, *op. cit.*, II, 151.

25 Translations by M. D. Herter Norton.

26 See Hermann Wiessner, "Der Stabreim in Richard Wagners Ring des Nibelungen," in *Germanische Studien*, vol. 30, Berlin, 1924.

27 See above, p. 583.

CHAPTER EIGHTEEN

1 Bruckner's single chamber music work, a string quintet, and the handful of Berlioz's songs do not modify the validity of this fact.

2 See the interesting compilation of his studies on the use of consecutive fifths in the old masters, Universal Edition, Vienna (Schenker).

3 The general confusion is well expressed in a curious contemporary treatise on theatrical legislative practice, Lacan & Paulmier, *Traité de la Législation et de la Jurisprudence des Théâtres*, Paris, 1853.

4 *The Complete Works of Nietzsche*, VIII, 2 ff.

5 See above, p. 791 f.

6 Verdi was in the habit of making copies of his letters, which afford a veritable mine of information. See G. Cesari and A. Luzio, *Giuseppe Verdi, I Copialettere*, Leipzig, 1913.

CHAPTER NINETEEN

1 See J. T. Howard, *Stephen Foster, America's Troubadour*, New York, 1934.

2 See W. T. Upton, *Anthony Philip Heinrich*, New York, 1939.

3 John Tasker Howard, *Our American Music*, New York, 1939, p. 380.

4 While we included popular balladry in our section on American music, we shall not attempt to deal with folk music in America. The music of the American Indian does not belong within the orbit of Western civilization, while the large body of Negro, cowboy, mountaineer, and other folk music, undoubtedly of vital importance to American music, has not yet been sufficiently studied to permit scientific and historic evaluations of a definitive nature. With the development of comparative musicology in America the many prejudices and misapprehensions attached to this field of music are being effectively eliminated by a number of distinguished scholars. Cf. George Herzog, *Research in Primitive and Folk Music in the United States*, in "Bulletin 24" of the American Council of Learned Societies, Washington, 1936.

5 See above, p. 669.

6 See above, p. 606 f.

7 See map no. 3.

8 See above, p. 717.

9 A. Oettingen, *The Harmonic System in Dual Development*, 1866; 2nd ed., *The Dual Harmonic System*, 1913.

10 English translation by A. J. Ellis, London, 1873.

11 *De la Musique Considérée en Elle Même*, Paris, 1785.

12 See above, p. 728.

13 E. Hanslick, *Aus Meinem Leben*, Berlin, 1894, p. 308.

14 See Claude Debussy, *Monsieur Croche Anti-Dilettante*, Paris, 1923.

15 See above, p. 730 f.

16 See above, p. 234.

17 A. W. Thayer, *Ludwig van Beethovens Leben*, 1866. Later editions were edited and supplemented by Riemann and Deiters. English edition, New York, 1921 (Krehbiel).

18 The last complete volume (III) carried the history of music to the death of Palestrina, the fourth, barely reaching Frescobaldi, was later completed by Leichtentritt (1909), and a fifth volume containing important musical examples was added by Kade in 1882. A number of other emendations and editions cannot be considered from the scientific point of view.

19 See note 20, Chapter Ten.

20 See above, p. 684.

CHAPTER TWENTY

1 Even the so-called twelve tone system of Schönberg and his disciples has a "tonality" represented in certain concretely defined basic melodic steps. Cf. *Musical Quarterly*, January, 1936 (Hill); *Arnold Schönberg*, ed. M. Armitage, New York, 1939, containing a number of essays on the subject.

2 See above, p. 858.

3 See above, p. 854.

4 See above, p. 235.

5 Besides reinstating Fux, the movement also produced textbooks of its own, such as the treatise of H. Bellerman, *Der Kontrapunkt*, Berlin, 1862.

6 Oscar Thompson, *Debussy, Man and Artist*, New York, 1937, p. 23.

BIBLIOGRAPHY

-»» ««-

Several important books have appeared within the last year too late to be consulted. Of these, perhaps the most significant from our point of view is Gustave Reese's *Music in the Middle Ages* (New York, 1940).

It has been found impractical to list the often very important essays prefacing the musical anthologies, such as the *Denkmäler der Tonkunst;* most libraries have analytical cards for these collections.

LIST OF ABBREVIATIONS

ActaM	*Acta Musicologica*
AfMW	*Archiv für Musikwissenschaft*
AHB	*Handbuch der Musikgeschichte* (Adler)
DTD	*Denkmäler Deutscher Tonkunst*
DTOe	*Denkmäler der Tonkunst in Oesterreich*
DVfLG	*Deutsche Vierteljahrsschrift für Literatur und Geisteswissenschaft*
HdMW	*Handbuch der Musikwissenschaft* (Bücken)
MfMG	*Monatshefte für Musikgeschichte*
ML	*Music and Letters*
MQ	*Musical Quarterly*
MT	*Musical Times*
PJ	*Jahrbuch Peters*
RM	*Revue Musicale*
RMI	*Revista Musicale Italiana*
SIMG	*Sammelbände der Internationalen Musikgesellschaft*
StzMW	*Studien zur Musikwissenschaft*
VfMW	*Vierteljahrsschrift für Musikwissenschaft*
ZfMW	*Zeitschrift für Musikwissenschaft*

Abbott, W. C. *The Expansion of Europe*, New York, 1938.
Abert, H. "Antike," in *AHB*, I.
——— "Les Echecs Amoureux," in Vollmöller, *Romanische Forschungen*, v. XV.
——— *Gesammelte Schriften und Vorträge*, ed. Blume, Halle, 1929.
——— *Jommelli als Opernkomponist*, Halle, 1908.
——— *Die Lehre vom Ethos in der Griechischen Musik*, Leipzig, 1901.
——— *Mozart*, Leipzig, 1923–24.
——— *Die Musikanschauung des Mittelalters*, Halle, 1905.
——— "Paisiello's Verhältniss zu Mozart," *AfMW*, I, 1918–19.
——— "Piccini als Buffokomponist," *PJ*, 20, 1913.
——— *Robert Schumann*, Berlin, 1920.
——— "Wort und Ton in der Musik des 18. Jahrhunderts," *AfMW*, V, 1923.
Abraham, G. *A Hundred Years of Music*, New York, 1938.
——— *On Russian Music*, New York, 1939.
——— *Studies in Russian Music*, New York, 1936.
——— "Weber as Novelist and Critic," *MQ*, 20, 1934.
Adam, A. *Dernier Souvenirs d'un Musicien*, Paris, 1871.
——— *Nouveaux Souvenirs d'un Musicien*, Paris, 1859.
——— *Souvenirs d'un Musicien*, Paris, 1857.
Adam de la Halle. "Jeu de Robin et Marion," ed. E. Langlois, in *Classiques Français du Moyen Age*, Paris, 1923–24.
Adams, H. *Mont-Saint-Michel and Chartres*, Boston, 1913.
Adler, G. *Handbuch der Musikgeschichte*, 2nd ed., Berlin, 1930.
——— "Haydn and the Viennese School," *MQ*, 18, 1932.
——— "Internationalism in Music," *MQ*, 11, 1925.
——— "Schubert and the Viennese Classic School," *MQ*, 14, 1928.

Adler, G. "Über Heterophonie," *PJ*, 15, 1908.
———— "Die Wiener Klassische Schule," in *AHB*, II.
Agoult, M. d'. *Memoiren, Erinnerungen an Franz Liszt*, ed. Ollivier, Dresden, 1928.
Agricola, M. *Musica Instrumentalis Deudsch* (1528), ed. Eitner, Leipzig, 1896.
Alaleona, D. *Studi sulla Storia dell' Oratorio Musicale in Italia*, Turin, 1908.
Alembert, J. d'. "De la Liberté de la Musique," in his *Œuvres et Correspondances*, ed. Henry, Paris, 1887.
———— *Fragments sur la Musique en Général, et sur la Nôtre en Particulier*, Paris, 1773.
Algarotti, F. *Dell' Opera in Musica*, Naples, 1762.
———— *Saggio sopra l'Opera in Musica*, Naples, 1756.
Allen, P. S., and Jones, H. M. *The Romanesque Lyric*, Chapel Hill, N. C., 1928.
Allen, W. D. "Baroque Histories of Music," *MQ*, 25, 1939.
———— *Philosophies of Music Histories*, New York, 1939.
Allgemeine Theorie der Schönen Künste, ed. Johann Georg Sulzer, 1720–79.
Altmann, W. "Meyerbeer-Forschungen," *SIMG*, IV, 1902–03.
———— "Spontini an der Berliner Oper," *SIMG*, IV, 1902–03.
Amelli, G., ed. *D. Thomae Aquinatis De Arte Musica*, Milan, 1880.
American Council of Learned Societies. *A Bibliography of Periodical Literature in Musicology and Allied Fields*, No. 1, Washington, D. C., 1940.
Andrees, G. *Mozart und Da Ponte*, Leipzig, 1936.
Andres, H. *Beiträge zur Geschichte der Musikkritik*, Greifswold, 1938.
Anglade, J. *Le Troubadour Guiraut Riquier, Etude sur la Décadence de l'Ancienne Poesie Provençale*, Paris, 1905.
Anglès, H. *El Codex de la Huelgas*, Barcelona, 1931.
———— "La Música a Catalunya fins al Segle XIII," in *Publicacións del Departament de Música*, Institut d'Estudis Catalans, Barcelona, 1935.
———— "La Polyphonie Religieuse Péninsulaire Anterieure à la Venue des Musiciens Flamands en Espagne," *Kongressbericht*, Liége, 1930.
Angus, S. *The Mystery Religions and Christianity*, New York, 1925.
Arbeau, T. *Orchesography—A Treatise in the Form of a Dialogue*, transl. Beaumont, London, 1925.
Arend, M. *Gluck, eine Biographie*, Berlin, 1921.
Arienzo, N. d'. "Origini dell' Opera Comica," *RMI*, II, 1895; IV, 1897; VI, 1899; VII, 1900.
Armitage, M. *Arnold Schönberg*, New York, 1939.
Armstrong, A. J. "Operatic Performances in England Before Händel," in *Baylor University Bulletin* No. 4, Waco, Texas, 1918.
Arnold, F. T. *The Art of Accompaniment from a Thorough-Bass*, London, 1931.
Arnold, T., and Guillaume, A., eds. *The Legacy of Islam*, London, 1931.
Artusi, G. M. *L'Artusi Ovvero delle Imperfettioni della Moderna Musica*, Part I, 1600; Part II, 1603.
Arundell, D. *Henry Purcell*, London, 1927.
Aubry, P. *Estampies et Danses Royales*, Paris, 1907.
———— *Trouvères et Troubadours*, Paris, 1909.
Auda, A. *La Musique et les Musiciens de l'Ancien Pays de Liége*, Brussels, 1930.
Augé de Lassus, L. *Boïeldieu*, Paris, 1908.
Augustinus, A. *Confessions*, transl. W. Watts, in Loeb Classical Library, Book 10.
———— *St. Augustine on Music*, Books 1–6, transl. R. C. Taliaferro, Annapolis, 1939.
Auriac, E. d'. *Théâtre de la Foire*, Paris, 1878.

Bach, C. P. E. *Versuch über die Wahre Art das Klavier zu Spielen*, new ed. Niemann, Leipzig, 1906.
Bäumker, P. S. *Geschichte des Breviers*, 1895.
———— *Das Katholische Deutsche Kirchenlied in Seinen Singweisen*, Freiburg, 1911.
Bagier, G. *Max Reger*, Stuttgart, 1923.
Baïf, J. A. de. *Œuvres en Rime*, ed. Marty-Laveaux, Paris, 1881.
Baini, G. *Memorie Storico-Critiche della Vita e dell' Opere di Giovanni Pierluigi da Palestrina*, Rome, 1828.
Balet, L. *Die Verbürgerlichung der Deutschen Kunst; Literatur und Musik im 18. Jahrhundert*, Strasbourg, 1935.
Balmer, L. *Orlando di Lasso's Motetten*, Bern, 1938.
Banchieri, A. *Conclusioni nel Suono dell' Organo* (1609), new ed., Milan, 1933.
Banning, H. *Johann Friedrich Doles*, Leipzig, 1939.

Barclay Squire, W. "John Dowland," *MT*, 37–38, 1896–97.
———— "Purcell's Dramatic Music," *SIMG*, V, 1903–04.
———— "Purcell as Theorist," *SIMG*, VI, 1904–05.
Bartha, D. *Benedictus Ducis*, Berlin, 1930.
———— "Zur Abstammung Joseph Haydns," *ActaM*, 7, 1935.
Bartholomaeis, V. de. *Le Origini della Poesia Drammatica Italiana*, 1924.
Batiffol, P. *Saint Grégoire le Grand*, Paris, 1928.
Batka, R. *Die Musik in Böhmen*, Prague, 1906.
Batteux, C. *Les Beaux Arts Réduits à un Seul Principe*, Paris, 1747.
Baumstark, A. *Missale Romanum, Entwicklung, Urkunden und Probleme*, Paderborn, 1930.
Baxter, J. H., ed. *An Old St. Andrews Music Book*, London, 1931.
Beaumarchais, *Œuvres Complètes*, ed. Fournier, Paris, 1875.
Beaumont, C. W. *Complete Book of Ballets*, London, 1937.
Beck, J. B. *La Musique des Troubadours*, Paris, 1910.
Becker, C. H. *Christianity and Islam*, London, 1909.
Becker, G. "Goudimel et Son Œuvre," *Société de l'Histoire du Protestantisme Français*, No. 8, 1885.
Beckman, G. *Das Violinspiel in Deutschland vor 1700*, Leipzig, 1918.
Bédier, J., and Aubry, P. *Les Chansons de Croisade*, Paris, 1909.
Beethoven-House, Bonn. *Veröffentlichungen*, 1920.
Bekker, P. *Beethoven*, London, 1925.
———— *The Changing Opera*, New York, 1935.
———— *Die Sinfonien Gustav Mahlers*, Berlin, 1921.
———— *The Story of the Orchestra*, New York, 1936.
Belaiev, V. M. *Mussorgsky's Boris Godunov and Its New Version*, London, 1928.
Bellerman, H. *Der Kontrapunkt*, Berlin, 1862.
Benn, Fr. *Die Messkomposition des Johann Joseph Fux*, Vienna, 1931.
Berend, F. *N. A. Strungk*, Munich, 1913.
Bergmans, P. *La Typographie Musicale en Belgique au XVIe Siècle*, Brussels, 1930.
Berlioz, H. *A Travers Chants*, Paris, 1862.
———— *Les Années Romantiques*, ed. Tiersot, Paris, 1904.
———— *Evenings in the Orchestra*, New York, 1929.
———— *Gluck and His Operas*, transl. Evans, London, 1915.
———— *Memoirs, 1803–65*, transl. Holmes, rev. E. Newman, New York, 1935.
Bernardin, N. M. *La Comédie Italienne en France et les Théâtres de la Foire*, Paris, 1902.
Bernet-Kempers, J. *Clemens non Papa und Seine Motetten*, Augsburg, 1928.
Bernouilli, E. *Aus Liederbüchern der Humanistenzeit*, Leipzig, 1910.
Besseler, H. "Musik des Mittelalters und der Renaissance," in Bücken, *HdMW*, 3.
———— "Studien zur Musik des Mittelalters," *AfMW*, VII, 1925.
———— "Von Dufay bis Josquin," *ZfMW*, XI, 1928–29.
Bethune-Baker, J. F. *An Introduction to the Early History of Christian Doctrine*, London, 1929.
Bidou, H. *Chopin*, transl. Phillips, New York, 1927.
Birge, E. B. *History of Public School Music in the United States*, Boston, 1928.
Blume, F. "Evangelische Kirchenmusik," in Bücken, *HdMW*.
———— *Das Monodische Prinzip in der Protestantischen Kirchenmusik*, Leipzig, 1925.
———— *Studien zur Vorgeschichte der Orchestersuite im 15. und 16. Jahrhundert*, Leipzig, 1925.
Böhme, F. M. *Altdeutsches Liederbuch*, 2nd ed., Leipzig, 1913.
Böttger, F. *Die Comédie-Ballets von Molière und Lully*, Berlin, 1931.
Boileau, *Œuvres Complètes*, Paris, 1873.
Boissonade, P. *Life and Work in Medieval Europe*, New York, 1927.
Bonaventura, A. *Saggio Storico sul Teatro Musicale Italiano*, 1913.
Bonaventura, M. *Verdi*, Paris, 1930.
Bonavia, F. *Verdi*, London, 1930.
Bonnet, E. G. *Philidor et l'Evolution de la Musique Française au XVIIIe Siècle*, Paris, 1921.
Borren, C. van den. *Alessandro Scarlatti, et l'Esthétique de l'Opéra Napolitain*, Paris and Brussels, 1921.
———— *Guillaume Dufay*, Brussels, 1926.
———— *Orlande de Lassus*, Paris, 1930.
———— *The Sources of Keyboard Music in England*, London, 1913.
Boschot, A. *Histoire d'un Romantique: Berlioz*, Paris, 1906–13.
Botstiber, H. *Geschichte der Ouverture und der Freien Orchesterformen*, Leipzig, 1913.
Bottrigari, H. *Il Desiderio* (1594), ed. Meyer, Berlin, 1924.

Boucher, M. *Claude Debussy*, Paris, 1930.
Boult, K. F. *Berlioz's Life as Written by Himself in His Letters and Memoirs*, London, 1903.
Bouvet, C. *Les Couperin*, Paris, 1926.
────── *Massenet*, Paris, 1929.
Braden, C. S. *Religious Aspects of the Conquest of Mexico*, Durham, N. C., 1930.
Brancour, R. *Massenet*, Paris, 1922.
────── *Méhul*, Paris, 1912.
Brandes, G. *Main Currents in Nineteenth-Century Literature*, New York, 1923.
Brandes, H. *Studien zur Musikalischen Figurenlehre im 16. Jahrhundert*, Berlin, 1935.
Brandi, K. *Deutsche Reformation und Gegenreformation*, Leipzig, 1927.
────── *The Emperor Charles V*, New York, 1939.
Brenet, M. *Claude Goudimel*, Besançon, 1898.
────── *Les Concerts en France sous l'Ancien Régime*, Paris, 1900.
────── *Haydn*, London, 1926.
────── "La Jeunesse de Rameau," *RMI*, IX–X, 1902–03.
────── *Les Musiciens de la Saint-Chapelle du Palais*, Paris, 1910.
────── *Musique et Musiciens de la Vieille France*, Paris, 1911.
────── *Sébastien de Brossard d'après des Papiers Inédits*, Paris, 1896.
Brennecke, E. *John Milton the Elder and His Music*, New York, 1938.
Bricqueville, E. de. *Le Livret d'Opéra Français de Lully à Gluck*, Paris, 1887.
Brinkmann, H. *Entstehungsgeschichte des Minnesangs*, Halle, 1926.
Brossard, S. de. *Dictionnaire de Musique*, Paris, 1703.
Brosses, Le Président de. *Lettres Familières Écrites d'Italie en 1739 et 1740*, Paris, 1858.
Brunetière, F. *Les Epoques du Théâtre Français*, Paris, 1906.
────── *L'Evolution des Genres dans l'Histoire de la Littérature*, Paris, 1898.
────── *Histoire de la Littérature Française Classique*, Paris, 1912.
────── *Manuel de l'Histoire de la Littérature Française*, Paris, 1897.
────── *Victor Hugo*, Paris, 1902.
Brunschwig, M. *L'Abbé du Bos*, Toulouse, 1904.
Bruun, G. *The Enlightened Despots*, New York, 1929.
Bruyr, J. E. *Grétry*, Paris, 1931.
Bryant, A. *Samuel Pepys*, Cambridge, 1933–38.
Bryce, J. *The Holy Roman Empire*, New York, 1926.
Bücken, E. *Anton Reichas Leben und Kompositionen*, Munich, 1912.
────── *Handbuch der Musikwissenschaft*, Leipzig, 1928–34.
────── *Der Heroische Stil in der Oper*, Leipzig, 1924.
────── "Musik des 19. Jahrhunderts," in his *HdMW*, 6.
────── "Musik des Rokokos und der Klassik," in his *HdMW*, 5.
Bührmann, M. *Briefe Deutscher Musiker aus der Romantik*, Kiel, 1934.
Bülow, H. von. *Briefe und Schriften*, Leipzig, 1911.
Bukofzer, M. *Geschichte des Englischen Diskants und des Fauxbourdons*, Strasbourg, 1936.
────── "Über Leben und Werke von Dunstable," *ActaM*, VIII, 1936.
Bumpus, J. S. *A History of English Cathedral Music*, London, 1908.
Burckhardt, J. *The Civilization of the Renaissance in Italy*, New York, 1937.
Burke, U. R. *History of Spain*, New York, 1900.
Burney, C. *A General History of Music*, London, 1776–89.
────── *The Present State of Music in France and Italy*, London, 1771.
Bury, J. B. *The Eastern Roman Empire*, London, 1912.
────── *The Idea of Progress*, London, 1920.

Calvocoressi, M. D. *Glinka*, Paris, 1913.
────── *Moussorgsky, The Russian Musical Nationalist*, London, 1919.
────── and Abraham, G. *Masters of Russian Music*, New York, 1936.
Cambridge Medieval History, Cambridge, 1911–32.
Cambridge Modern History, Cambridge, 1902–12.
Campos, R. M. *El Folklore y la Musica Mexicana*, Mexico City, 1938.
Carmina Burana, ed. Alfons Hilka and Otto Schumann, Heidelberg, 1930.
Cecil, G. *The History of Opera in England*, Taunton, 1930.
Cesari, G., and Luzio, A. *Giuseppe Verdi, I Copialettere*, Leipzig, 1913.
Chamberlain, H. S. *Wagner*, London, 1897.
Chambers, E. K. *The Medieval Stage*, 1903.
Chapman, C. E. *History of Spain*, New York, 1931.

Chappell, W. *Old English Popular Music*, ed. Wooldridge, London, 1893.
Chase, G. "Origins of the Lyric Theater in Spain," *MQ*, 25, 1939.
Chastellux. *Essay sur l'Union de la Poésie et de la Musique*, Paris, 1765.
Chouquet, G. *Histoire de la Musique Dramatique en France*, Paris, 1873.
Chrysander, F. *Georg Friedrich Händel*, Leipzig, 1919.
Clément, F., and Larousse, P. *Dictionnaire des Opéras*, Paris, 1905.
Closson, E. *Grétry*, Turnhout, 1920.
Cobbett, W. W. *Cyclopedic Survey of Chamber Music*, London, 1929–30.
Coeuroy, A. "The Musical Inspiration in English Literature of the XIXth Century," *MQ*, 6, 1921.
———— *La Musique Française Moderne*, Paris, 1922.
Cohen, G. *Histoire de la Mise en Scène dans le Théâtre Religieux Français du Moyen Age*, Paris, 1926.
Coleridge, A. D., ed. and transl. *Goethe's Letters to Zelter, with Extracts from Those of Zelter to Goethe*, London, 1892.
Colles, H. C. *Brahms*, London, 1908.
Collet, H. *Le Mysticisme Musical Espagnol au XVIe Siècle*, Paris, 1913.
———— *Victoria*, Paris, 1914.
Collezione di Prime Fioriture del Melodramma Italiano, ed. Mantica, Rome, 1912.
Collins, R. W. *A History of Medieval Civilization in Europe*, Boston, 1936.
Comte, C., and Laumonier, P. "Ronsard et les Musiciens du XVIe Siècle," in *Revue d'Histoire Littéraire de la France*, 1900.
Cooper, M. *Bizet*, London, 1938.
Cornelius, P. *Literarische Werke*, Leipzig, 1904.
Cornet, J. *Die Oper in Deutschland und das Theater der Neuzeit*, Hamburg, 1849.
Corte, A. della. *L'Opera Comica Italiana del 1700*, 1923.
———— *Le Relazioni Storiche della Poesia e della Musica Italiana*, Turin, 1936.
Cotterill, H. B. *Italy from Dante to Tasso*, London, 1919.
———— *Medieval Italy*, London, 1915.
Coulton, G. G. *From St. Francis to Dante*, London, 1907.
Coussemaker, E. de. *L'Art Harmonique aux XIIe et XIIIe Siècles*, Paris, 1865.
———— *Scriptorum de Musica Medii Aevi, nova series*, Paris, 1864–76; reprinted 1908, and Milan, 1931.
Coxe, W. *Memoirs of the Life and Administration of Sir Robert Walpole, Earl of Oxford*, London, 1797.
Cram, R. A. *The Substance of Gothic*, Boston, 1925.
Cucuel, G. *Les Créateurs de l'Opéra-Comique Français*, Paris, 1914.
———— *La Pouplinière et la Musique de Chambre au XVIIIe Siècle*, Paris, 1913.
Cummings, W. H. "John Blow," *SIMG*, X, 1908–09.
———— *Henry Purcell*, London, 1923.
Cunningham, W. *Christianity and Politics*, Boston, 1915.
Curzon, H. de. *Meyerbeer*, Paris, 1910.
———— *Rossini*, Paris, 1920.
Cysarz, H. *Von Schiller bis Nietzsche*, Halle, 1928.

Damerini, A. *Tommaso Traëtta*, Milan, 1927.
Dampier-Whethan, W. C. D. *A History of Science*, New York, 1935.
Dauriac, L. *Meyerbeer*, new ed., Paris, 1930.
Davis, H. W. C. *England under the Normans and Angevins*, London, 1909.
Davison, A. T. *Protestant Church Music in America*, Boston, 1933.
Day, C. L. *The Songs of John Dryden*, Cambridge, Mass., 1932.
Debussy, C. *Monsieur Croche, the Dilettante Hater*, New York, 1928.
Degen, M. *Die Lieder von Carl Maria von Weber*, Freiburg, 1924.
Dehio, G. *Geschichte der Deutschen Kunst*, Leipzig, 1926.
Delmas, M. *Bizet*, Paris, 1930.
Dent, E. J. *Alessandro Scarlatti, His Life and Works*, London, 1905.
———— "Ensembles and Finales in Eighteenth-Century Italian Opera," *SIMG*, XI–XII, 1909–10 and 1910–11.
———— *Foundations of English Opera*, London, 1928.
———— *Mozart's Operas, A Critical Study*, London, 1913.
———— "The Operas of Alessandro Scarlatti," *SIMG*, IV, 1902–03.
Deutsch, O. E. *Franz Schubert, Die Dokumente Seines Lebens und Schaffens*, Leipzig, 1913–14.
Dickinson, G. S. *The Pattern of Music*, Poughkeepsie, N. Y., 1940.

Diderot, D. *Le Neveu de Rameau*, Paris, 1823.
Dietz, M. *Geschichte des Musikalischen Dramas in Frankreich Während der Revolution*, Vienna, 1886.
Digby Plays, The, ed. E. F. Furnivall, *Early English Text Society*, Extra Series, 70.
Dilthey, W. *Von Deutscher Dichtung und Musik*, Berlin, 1933.
Doorslaer, G. van. *La Vie et les Œuvres de Philippe de Monte*, Brussels, 1921.
Doren, R. van. *Etude sur l'Influence Musicale de l'Abbaye de St. Gall*, Louvain, 1925.
Douen, O. *Clément Marot et le Psautier Huguenot*, Paris, 1878–79.
Dow, E. W., and Seignobos, C. *The Feudal Regime*, New York, 1931.
Dreves, G. M. *Analecta Hymnica Medii Aevi*, 1886–1922.
Droz, E., and Thibault, G. *Poètes et Musiciens du XVe Siècle*, Paris, 1924.
Dryden, J. *Works*, ed. Scott and Saintsbury, London, 1882–93.
Dubos, Abbé. *Réflexions Critiques sur la Poésie et la Peinture*, Paris, 1715.
Du Cange, C. *Glossarium*, ed. Favre, Niort, 1883–87.
Duchesne, L. *Early History of the Christian Church*, New York, 1926.
Ducros, L. *French Society in the Eighteenth Century*, London, 1926.
Dudden, F. H. *Gregory the Great*, New York, 1905.
———— *The Life and Times of St. Ambrose*, London, 1935.
Dufrane, L. *Gossec*, Paris, 1927.
Dunhill, T. F. *Mozart's String Quartets*, London, 1927.
Dunning, W. *A History of Political Theories*, New York, 1921.
Dupré, H. *Purcell*, New York, 1928.
Duruy, V. *A History of France*, New York, 1929.
Dyson, G. *The New Music*, London, 1926.
———— *The Progress of Music*, London, 1932.

Early Psalmody in America, Series 1, "The Ainsworth Psalter," ed. Carleton Sprague Smith, New York, 1938.
Ecorcheville, J. *De Lully à Rameau, l'Esthétique Musicale*, Paris, 1906.
Edelstein, H. *Die Musikanschauung Augustins nach Seiner Schrift "De Musica,"* Freiburg, 1929.
Ehrenberg, R. *Capital and Finance in the Age of the Renaissance*, London, 1928.
Ehrichs, A. *Giulio Caccini*, Leipzig, 1908.
Einstein, A. "Alessandro Stradella," in *Sandberger Festschrift*, 1918.
———— "Anfänge des Vokalkonzerts," *ActaM*, III, 1931.
———— "Annibale Padovano," in *Adler Festschrift*, 1930.
———— "Dante im Madrigal," *AfMW*, III, 1921.
———— *Gluck*, New York, 1936.
———— *Heinrich Schütz*, Cassel, 1928.
———— "The Madrigal," *MQ*, 10, 1924.
———— "Die Parodie in der Villanella," *ZfMW*, II, 1919–20.
Ellinwood, L. *The Works of Francesco Landino*, Cambridge, Mass., 1939.
Elliot, J. H. *Berlioz*, New York, 1938.
Emerton, E. *The Beginnings of Modern Europe*, Boston, 1917.
Emmanuel, M. *César Franck*, Paris, 1930.
———— *Reicha*, Paris, 1937.
Encyclopedia of the Social Sciences, New York, 1929 ff.
Encyclopédie de la Musique et Dictionnaire du Conservatoire, Paris, 1920–31.
Engel, C. "Schubert's Fame," *MQ*, 14, 1928.
———— "Die Wagnerdämmerung," *MQ*, 14, 1928.
Engel, H. *Die Entwicklung des Deutschen Klavierkonzerts*, Leipzig, 1927.
Epstein, P. "Zur Geschichte der Deutschen Choralpassion," *PJ*, 36, 1929.
Ernst, G. *Brahms*, Berlin, 1930.
Eslava, H. *Lira Sacra-Hispana*, Madrid, 1869.
Euler, L. *Versuch einer Neuen Musikalischen Theorie*, 1729.
Evans, E. *Tchaikovsky*, New York, 1935.
Eximeno, A. *Dell' Origine e delle Regole della Musica colla Storia del suo Progresso*, Rome, 1774.

Fairchild, H. N. *The Romantic Quest*, New York, 1931.
Falk, M. *Wilhelm Friedemann Bach*, Leipzig, 1913.
Faral, E. *Les Jongleurs en France*, Paris, 1910.
Farga, F. *Salieri und Mozart*, Stuttgart, 1937.
Farmer, H. G. *The Arabian Influence on Musical Theory*, London, 1925.

Farmer, H. G. *Music in Medieval Scotland*, London, 1930.

Fassini, S. *Il Melodramma Italiano a Londra*, Turin, 1914.

Favart, C. *Mémoires et Correspondance*, Paris, 1808.

Fay, B. *Revolution and Freemasonry*, Boston, 1935.

Fehr, M. *Apostolo Zeno*, 1912.

Fellerer, K. G. *Palestrina*, Ratisbon, 1930.

———— *Der Palestrinastil und Seine Bedeutung in der Vokalen Kirchenmusik des 18. Jahrhunderts*, Augsburg, 1929.

Fellowes, E. H. *The English Madrigal*, London, 1925.

———— *The English Madrigal Composers*, London, 1921.

———— *English Madrigal Verse, 1585–1632*, London, 1920.

———— *The English School of Lutenist Songwriters*, London, 1920–32.

———— *Orlando Gibbons*, London, 1925.

———— *William Byrd*, London, 1936.

Ferguson, D. N. *A History of Musical Thought*, New York, 1935.

Ficker, R. von. "Die Früheren Messkompositionen der Trienter Codices," *StzMW*, XI, 1924.

———— "Formprobleme de Mittelalterlichen Musik," *ZfMW*, VII, 1924–25.

———— "Die Musik des Mittelalters und Ihre Beziehungen zum Geistesleben," *DVfLG*, 1925.

———— "Polyphonic Music of the Gothic Period," *MQ*, 15, 1929.

Finney, T. M. "The Collegium Musicum at Lititz," in *Papers Read by Members of the American Musicological Society*, 1938.

Fischer, W. "Instrumentalmusik von 1450–1600," in *AHB*, I.

———— "Instrumentalmusik von 1600–1750," in *AHB*, I.

Flaubert, G. "Correspondance," in *Œuvres Complètes*, IX–XII, Paris, 1904.

Fleischer, O. "Denis Gaultier," *VfMW*, II, 1886.

Fletcher, J. B. *Literature of the Italian Renaissance*, New York, 1934.

Flood, W. H. Grattan. *Early Tudor Composers*, London, 1925.

———— "An Eighteenth Century Essayist on Poetry and Music," *MQ*, 2, 1916.

———— "The English Chapel Royal under Henry V and Henry VI," *SIMG*, X, 1908–09.

Florimo, F. *La Scuola Musicale di Napoli*, Naples, 1880–84.

Flower, W. N. *George Frederic Handel, His Personality and His Times*, New York, 1922.

Flueler, M. *Die Norddeutsche Sinfonie zur Zeit Friedrich des Grossen*, Berlin, 1908.

Font, A. *Favart, l'Opéra Comique, et la Comédie-Vaudeville au 17e et 18e Siècle*, Paris, 1894.

Foote, H. W. *Three Centuries of American Hymnody*, Cambridge, Mass., 1940.

Forkel, N. *Über J. S. Bachs Leben, Kunst und Kunstwerke (1802)*, ed. Müller-Blattau, Augsburg, 1925; transl. C. S. Terry, London, 1920.

Forsyth, C. *Music and Nationalism*, New York, 1911.

Francke, K. *A History of German Literature*, New York, 1927.

Fremy, E. *L'Académie des Derniers Valois*, Paris, 1887.

Friedell, E. *Cultural History of the Modern Age*, New York, 1930–32.

Friedlaender, L. *Darstellungen aus der Sittengeschichte Roms*, Leipzig, 1920.

Friedländer, M. *Brahms's Lieder, An Introduction to the Songs for One and Two Voices*, London, 1928.

Frere, W. H. "The Winchester Troper," *Publications of the Henry Bradshaw Society*, VIII, 1894.

Frotscher, G. *Geschichte des Orgelspiels und der Orgelkomposition*, Berlin, 1935–36.

Fry, R. *Flemish Art: A Critical Survey*, New York, 1927.

Fürstenau, M. *Zur Geschichte der Musik und des Theaters am Hofe zu Dresden*, Dresden, 1861–62.

Fuller-Maitland, J. A. "The Age of Bach and Handel," in *Oxford History of Music*, 4, London 1931.

———— *Carols of the XVth Century*, London, 1891.

Gaartz, H. *Die Opern H. Marschners*, Leipzig, 1912.

Gagey, E. M. *Ballad Opera*, New York, 1937.

Gaiffe, F. *Le Drame en France au XVIIIe Siècle*, Paris, 1910.

Galilei, V. *Dialogo Della Musica Antica e Della Moderna*, Venice, 1581.

Galpin, F. W. *Old English Instruments of Music*, London, 1910.

Ganassi, S. *Regola Rubertina (1542)*, ed. Schneider, Leipzig, 1924.

Gastoué, A. *L'Art Grégorien*, Paris, 1911.

———— *Le Graduel et l'Antiphonaire Romains*, Lyons, 1929.

———— *L'Orgue en France de l'Antiquité au Début de la Période Classique*, Paris, 1921.

Gatti, G. "The Academy of St. Cecilia and the Augusteo in Rome," *MQ*, 7, 1922.

Gautier, T. *Histoire de l'Art Dramatique en France*, Paris, 1858.
————— *Histoire du Romantisme en France*, Paris, 1874.
Gebhard, F. *Die Musikalische Grundlagen zu Luthers Deutscher Messe*, Halle, 1929.
Geiringer, K. *Brahms, His Life and Work*, New York, 1936.
————— *Joseph Haydn*, Potsdam, 1932.
————— "Wagner and Brahms," *MQ*, 22, 1936.
Gennrich, F. *Formenlehre des Mittelalterlichen Liedes*, Halle, 1932.
————— "Das Formproblem des Minnesangs," *DVfLG*, IX.
————— *Rondeaux, Virelais, und Balladen*, Dresden, 1921–27.
————— "Zur Ursprungsfrage des Minnesangs," *DVfLG*, VII.
Gerber, R. "Die Deutsche Passion von Luther bis Bach," in *Luther-Jahrbuch*, 1931.
————— *Der Operntypus Hasses und Seine Textlichen Grundlagen*, Leipzig, 1925.
Gerbert, M. *De Cantu et Musica Sacra*, 1774.
————— *Scriptores Ecclesiastici de Musica Sacra*, 1784; reprinted Milan, 1931.
Gérold, T. *Histoire de la Musique, des Origines à la fin du XIVe Siècle*, Paris, 1936.
Gevaert and Volgraff. *Les Problèmes Musicaux d'Aristote*, Ghent, 1903.
Giessler, R. *Die Geistliche Lieddichtung des Deutschen Katholicismus im Zeitalter der Auf-klärung*, 1928.
Giraldus Cambrensis. "Descriptio Cambriae," in *Rerum Britannicarum Medii Aevi Scriptores*, vol. 21, Part 6.
Glareanus. *Dodecachordon* (1547), ed. and transl. P. Bohn, Leipzig, 1888–90.
Gluck-Jahrbuch, ed. Abert, Leipzig, 1913–18.
Göttling, K. W. *Nibelungen und Gibelinen*, Rudolfstadt, 1816.
————— *Über das Geschichtliche im Nibelungenlied*, Rudolfstadt, 1814.
Goldschmidt, H. *Studien zur Geschichte der Italienischen Oper im 17. Jahrhundert*, Leipzig, 1901–04.
Gombosi, O. J. "Bemerkungen zur l'Homme Armé Frage," *ZfMW*, X, 1927–28.
————— "Ghizegem und Compère," in *Adler Festschrift*, 1930.
————— *Jakob Obrecht*, Leipzig, 1925.
Gordon, P. "Franz Grillparzer: Critic of Music," *MQ*, 2, 1916.
Goslich, S. *Beiträge zur Geschichte der Deutschen Romantischen Oper*, Leipzig, 1937.
Gounod, C. *Memoirs of an Artist*, transl. E. A. Crocker, Chicago, 1895.
Grande, C. del. *Espressione Musicale dei Poeti Greci*, Naples, 1932.
Graves, C. *Hubert Parry*, London, 1926.
Greene, H. C. "The Song of the Ass," in *Speculum*, 1931.
Gregorovius, F. *A History of the City of Rome in the Middle Ages*, London, 1894–1912.
Grétry, A. E. M. *Mémoires ou Essais sur la Musique*, Paris, 1789.
Griesinger, G. A. *Biographische Notizen über Joseph Haydn*, Leipzig, 1910.
Grillet, L. *Les Ancêtres du Violon*, Paris, 1901.
Grimm, M. *Correspondance Littéraire (1753–90)*, 1877–82.
————— *Le Petit Prophète de Boehmisch-Broda*, Paris, 1753.
Grocheo, J. de. "Theoria," ed. J. Wolf, *SIMG*, I, 1899–1900.
Gros, E. *Philippe Quinault, Sa Vie et Son Œuvre*, Paris, 1926.
Grossmann, W. *Die Einleitenden Kapitel des Speculum Musicae von Johannes de Muris*, Leipzig, 1924.
Grove, G. *Beethoven and His Nine Symphonies*, London, 1906.
————— *Dictionary of Music and Musicians*, 3d ed., London and New York, 1927–28; reprinted New York, 1935.
————— ————— Supplementary volume, New York, 1940.
Gründlicher Bericht des Deutschen Meistergesanges, re-ed. R. Jones, Halle, 1888.
Guignebert, C. *Christianity, Past and Present*, New York, 1927.
Gurlitt, W. *Leben und Werke des Michael Praetorius Creuzburgensis*, Leipzig, 1914.

Haas, R. "Die Musik des Barocks," in Bücken, *HdMW*, 4.
————— "Die Oper im 18. Jahrhundert," *AHB*, II.
————— "Die Wiener Ballet-Pantomime im 18. Jahrhundert und Gluck's *Don Juan*," *StzMW*, X, 1923.
————— *Die Wiener Oper*, Vienna, 1926.
Haberl, F. X. *Bausteine zur Musikgeschichte*, Leipzig, 1885–88.
Haböck, F. *Die Kastraten und Ihre Gesangskunst*, Leipzig, 1927.
Hadden, J. C. *Haydn*, New York, 1934.
Hadow, H. *A Croatian Composer*, London, 1897.

Hagen, F. von der. *Minnesang*, Leipzig, 1923.
Hagen, M. *Dietrich Buxtehude*, Copenhagen, 1920.
Hague, E. *Latin American Music*, Santa Ana, Calif., 1934.
Hall, H. *Court Life Under the Plantagenets*, London, 1890.
Handschin, J. "A Monument of English Mediaeval Polyphony," *MT*, v. 73–74, 1932–33.
———— "Ein Mittelalterlicher Beitrag zur Lehre von der Sphärenharmonie," *ZfMW*, IX, 1926–27.
———— "Die Musikanschauung des Johannes Scotus (Erigena)," *DVfLG*, 1927.
———— "Die Rolle der Nationen in der Mittelalterlichen Musikgeschichte," *Schweizer Jahrbuch für Musikwissenschaft*, V, 1931.
———— "Über Estampie und Sequenz," *ZfMW*, XII, 1929–30.
———— "Über den Ursprung der Motette," *Kongressbericht*, Basel, 1924.
———— "Was Brachte die Notre-Dame Schule Neues?" *ZfMW*, VI, 1923–24.
———— "Zur Geschichte der Lehre vom Organum," *ZfMW*, VIII, 1925–26.
———— "Zur Geschichte von Notre-Dame," *ActaM*, IV, 1932.
Hannas, R. "Cerone, Philosopher and Teacher," *MQ*, 21, 1935.
Hanotaux, G. *Histoire de la Nation Française*, Paris, 1920.
Hanslick, E. *Aus Meinem Leben*, Berlin, 1894.
———— *Geschichte des Konzertwesens in Wien*, Vienna, 1869.
Harnack, A. von. *The Expansion of Christianity in the First Three Centuries*, New York, 1904–05.
———— *A History of Dogma*, Boston, 1903.
———— *Monasticism*, New York, 1910.
Harris, C. A. "Musical Allusions of Great Writers," *MQ*, 2, 1916.
Haskins, C. H. *Studies in the History of Medieval Science*, Cambridge, Mass., 1927.
———— *Studies in Medieval Culture*, London, 1929.
Haydon, G. *The Evolution of the Six-Four Chord*, Berkeley, Calif., 1933.
Hayes, C. J. C. *Essays in Nationalism*, New York, 1926.
Hayes, G. *King's Music*, London, 1937.
———— *Musical Instruments and Their Music (1500–1750)*, London, 1928–30.
Hazlitt, W. C. *The Venetian Republic*, London, 1915.
Hearnshaw, F. J. C., ed. *Social and Political Ideas of Some Great Thinkers of the Renaissance and the Reformation*, London, 1925.
Heinichen, J. D. *Neu Erfundene und Gründliche Anweisung*, Hamburg, 1711.
Helmholtz, H. *On the Sensations of Tone as a Physiological Basis for the Theory of Music*, transl. W. A. Ellis, 3d ed., London and New York, 1895.
Hennig, K. *Die Geistliche Kontrafaktur im Jahrhundert der Reformation*, Halle, 1909.
Henry, L. *Dr. John Bull*, London, 1938.
Herder, J. G. *Sämtliche Werke*, Berlin, 1877–1913.
Hertzmann, E. *Adrian Willaert in der Weltlichen Vokalmusik Seiner Zeit*, Leipzig, 1931.
———— "Studien zur Basse Danse," *ZfMW*, XI, 1928–29.
———— "Zur Frage der Mehrchörigkeit," *ZfMW*, XII, 1929–30.
Hervey, A. *Saint-Saëns*, London, 1921.
Herz, G. J. *S. Bach im Zeitalter des Rationalismus und der Frühromantik*, Leipzig, 1936.
Herzog, G. *Research in Primitive and Folk Music in the United States*, Washington, D. C., 1936.
Heurich, H. *John Wilbye in Seinen Madrigalen*, Augsburg, 1932.
Heuss, A. "Die Dynamik der Mannheimer Schule," in *Riemann Festschrift*, Hesse, 1909.
———— *Die Matthäus Passion*, Leipzig, 1909.
———— "Zachow als Kantatenkomponist," *ZfMW*, X, 1927–28.
Hiller, F. *F. Mendelssohn-Bartholdy, Briefe und Erinnerungen*, Cologne, 1874.
Hippeau, E. *Berlioz et Son Temps*, Paris, 1892.
Hobson, J. A. *The Evolution of Modern Capitalism*, London, 1926.
Hörle, G. H. *Frühmittelalterliche Mönchs- und Kleriker-Bildung in Italien*, Freiburg (Breisgau), 1914.
Hoffmann, E. T. A. *Musikalische Dichtungen und Aufsätze*, Stuttgart, 1922.
Hoffmeister, K. *Dvořák*, London, 1928.
Hohenemser, R. *Cherubini, Sein Leben und Seine Werke*, Leipzig, 1913.
Holz, G., Saran, F., and Bernouilli, E., eds. *Die Jenaer Liederhandschrift*, Leipzig, 1901.
Hood, G. *History of Music in New England*, Boston, 1921.
Horst, K. *Barockprobleme*, Munich, 1912.
Howard, A. *The Aulos or Tibia*, Boston, 1893.
Howard, J. T. *Our American Music*, rev. ed., New York, 1939.

Howard, J. T. *Stephen Foster, America's Troubadour*, New York, 1934.
Howes, F. S. *William Byrd*, London, 1928.
Hübner, A. *Die Deutschen Geisslerlieder*, Berlin, 1931.
Hughes, A. *Worcester Medieval Harmony of the 13th and 14th Centuries*, Burnham, Buckinghamshire, 1928.
Hugo, V. *Œuvres Complètes*, Paris, 1899.
Huizinga, J. *The Waning of the Middle Ages*, London, 1927.
——— *Wege der Kulturgeschichte*, Munich, 1930.
Huré, J. *Saint Augustin Musicien*, Paris, 1924.

Iacuzzi, A. *The European Vogue of Favart*, New York, 1932.
Idelsohn, A. Z. *Jewish Music in Its Historical Development*, New York, 1929.
——— "Parallelen zwischen Gregorianischen und Hebräisch-Orientalischen Gesangsweisen," *ZfMW*, IV, 1902–03.
Indy, V. d'. *César Franck*, London, 1909.
——— *La Schola Cantorum*, Paris, 1927.
International Cyclopedia of Music and Musicians, Oscar Thompson, editor-in-chief, New York, 1938.
Irving, W. H. *John Gay's London*, Cambridge, Mass., 1928.
Istel, E. "Carmen: Novel and Libretto—A Dramaturgic Analysis," *MQ*, 6, 1921.
——— *Die Komische Oper*, Stuttgart, 1906.
——— *Das Libretto*, Berlin, 1915.
——— "The 'Othello' of Verdi and Shakespeare," *MQ*, 2, 1916.

Jahn, O. *W. A. Mozart*, transl. Townsend, London, 1891.
Jan, K. von. *Musici Scriptores Graeci*, Leipzig, 1895.
Jean-Aubry, G. *La Musique et les Nations*, Paris, 1922.
Jeanroy, A. *Histoire de la Littérature Latine*, Paris, 1891.
——— *Les Origines de la Poésie Lyrique*, 3d ed., Paris, 1925.
Jeans, J. *Science and Music*, Cambridge, 1937.
Jeppesen, K. *Counterpoint, the Polyphonic Style of the 16th Century*, transl. G. Haydon, New York, 1939.
——— *Die Mehrstimmige Italienische Laude um 1500*, Copenhagen, 1935.
——— "Die Neuentdeckten Bücher der Lauden des Ottaviano dei Petrucci," *ZfMW*, XII, 1929–30.
——— *The Style of Palestrina and the Dissonance*, London, 1927.
Joël, K. *Nietzsche und die Romantik*, Jena, 1905.
——— *Wandlungen der Weltanschauung*, Tübingen, 1928.
Jonas, O. *Das Wesen des Musikalischen Kunstwerks*, Vienna, 1934.
Julian, J. *A Dictionary of Hymnology*, rev. ed., London, 1925.

Kahl, W. "Zu Mendelssohns Lieder ohne Worte," *ZfMW*, III, 1920–21.
Kalischer, A. *Beethoven und Seine Zeitgenossen*, Leipzig, 1910.
——— ed. *Beethoven's Sämmtliche Briefe*, Berlin, 1906–08.
Kamienski, M. *Die Oratorien von Johann Adolf Hasse*, Leipzig, 1912.
Kantorowicz, E. *Frederick the Second*, New York, 1931.
Keiner, F. *Die Madrigale des Gesualdo von Venosa*, Leipzig, 1914.
Ker, W. P. *Essays in Medieval Literature*, London, 1931.
Kerts-Krehbiel. *Beethoven, the Man and the Artist as Revealed in His Own Words*, New York, 1905.
Kidson, F. *The Beggar's Opera: Its Predecessors and Successors*, Cambridge, 1922.
Kiesewetter, R. G. *Schicksale und Beschaffenheit des Weltlichen Gesanges*, Vienna, 1841.
Kinkeldey, O. "Music and Music Printing in Incunabula," in *Papers of the Bibliographical Society of America*, XXVI, 1932.
——— *Orgel und Klavier in der Musik des 16. Jahrhunderts*, Leipzig, 1910.
Kircher, A. *Musurgia Universalis sive Ars Magna Consoni et Dissoni*, Rome, 1650.
Kitchin, G. *A Survey of Burlesque and Parody in English*, Edinburgh, 1931.
Kiwi, E. *Studien zur Geschichte des Italienischen Liedmadrigals im XVI. Jahrhundert*, Würzburg, 1937.
Klein, J. W. "Nietzsche and Bizet," *MQ*, 11, 1925.
Klotz, H. *Über die Orgelkunst der Gotik, der Renaissance, und des Barock*, Kassel, 1931.
Klunger. C. *J. A. P. Schulz in Seinen Volkstümlichen Liedern*, Leipzig, 1909.

Kobald, K. *Joseph Haydn*, Vienna, 1932.
Koch, M. *Richard Wagner*, Berlin, 1907–08.
——— *Richard Wagners Geschichtliche Sendung*, Langensalza, 1927.
Köchel, L. von. *Chronologisch-Thematisches Verzeichmiss Sämtlicher Tonwerke W. A. Mozarts*, Leipzig, 1862; 3d ed. by A. Einstein, Leipzig, 1938.
——— *J. J. Fux*, Vienna, 1872.
Koechlin, C. *Fauré*, Paris, 1927.
Koeltzsch, H. *Franz Schubert in Seinen Klavier-Sonaten*, Leipzig, 1927.
Körte, O. *Laute und Lautenmusik bis zur Mitte des 16. Jahrhunderts*, Leipzig, 1901.
Körting, G. *Geschichte des Römischen und Griechischen Theaters*, Paderborn, 1897.
Korte, W. *Studie zur Geschichte der Musik in Italien im Ersten Viertel des 15. Jahrhunderts*, Kassel, 1933.
Krabbe, W. *J. Rist*, Bonn, 1910.
Kracauer, S. *Orpheus in Paris; Offenbach and the Paris of His Time*, New York, 1938.
Kraus, C. von. *Walther von der Vogelweide*, Berlin, 1935.
Kretzschmar, H. *Geschichte des Neuen Deutschen Liedes*, Leipzig, 1911.
——— *Geschichte der Oper*, Leipzig, 1919.
——— "Über die Bedeutung von Cherubini's Ouvertüren und Hauptopern für die Gegenwart," *PJ*, 13, 1906.
——— "Die Venezianische Oper und die Werke Cavallis und Cestis," *VfMW*, 1892.
Kroyer, T. "Das A-Cappella Ideal," *ActaM*, VI, 1934.
——— *Die Anfänge der Chromatik im Italienischen Madrigal*, Leipzig, 1902.
——— "Die Circumpolare Oper," *PJ*, 26, 1919.
——— "Zur A-Cappella Frage," *AfMW*, II, 1919–20.
Krüger, W. *Das Concerto Grosso*, Berlin, 1932.
Kurth, E. *Anton Bruckner*, Berlin, 1926.
——— *Grundlagen des Linearen Kontrapunkts*, Berlin, 1922.
——— *Die Romantische Harmonik und Ihre Krise in Wagners "Tristan,"* Berlin, 1920.

Lacan & Paulmier. *Traité de la Législation et de la Jurisprudence des Théâtres*, Paris, 1853.
Ladies' Library, Written by a Lady (The), 4th ed. (Steele), 1732.
Lafontaine, H. C. de. *The King's Musick, a Transcript of Records, 1460–1700*, London, 1909.
La Fontaine, J. de. *Œuvres*, ed. Regnier, 1883.
Laistner, M. L. W. *Thought and Letters in Western Europe, A.D. 500 to 900*, New York, 1931.
Lalo, C. *Eléments d'une Esthétique Musicale Scientifique*, Paris, 1939.
Laloy, L. *Rameau*, Paris, 1908.
Landormy, P. *Bizet*, Paris, 1924.
Landshoff, L. *J. R. Zumsteeg*, Berlin, 1902.
L'Art et Instruction de Bien Dancer, Paris, c. 1495. Facsim. ed. with bibliographical note by V. Scholderer, London, 1936.
Lasserre, P. *Le Romantisme Français*, Paris, 1919.
Laumonier, P. *Ronsard, Poète Lyrique*, Paris, 1910.
Laurencie, L. de la. *Les Bouffons*, Paris, 1912.
——— *Les Créateurs de l'Opéra Français*, Paris, 1921.
——— *L'Ecole Française de Violon de Lulli à Viotti*, Paris, 1922–24.
——— *Histoire du Goût Musical en France*, Paris, 1905.
——— *Lully*, Paris, 1911.
——— *Les Luthistes*, Paris, 1928.
Lavoix, H., fils. *Histoire de l'Instrumentation*, Paris, 1878.
Lawrence, W. J. "The Early Years of the First English Opera House," *MQ*, 7, 1921.
——— "Foreign Singers and Musicians at the Court of Charles II," *MQ*, 9, 1923.
——— "Music in the Elizabethan Theater," *MQ*, 6, 1920.
——— "Music and Song in the Eighteenth Century Theater," *MQ*, 2, 1916.
Lea, H. C. *A History of the Inquisition*, New York, 1908–11.
Lea, K. M. *Italian Popular Comedy*, London, 1934.
Leblond, Abbé. *Mémoires pour Servir à l'Histoire de la Révolution Opérée dans la Musique par M. le Chevalier Gluck*, Paris, 1781.
Lecky, W. E. H. *History of the Rise and Influence of the Spirit of Rationalism in Europe*, London, 1904.
Lehman, P. *Die Parodie im Mittelalter*, Munich, 1922.
Leichtentritt, H. *Geschichte der Motette*, Leipzig, 1908.
——— *Händel*, Leipzig, 1924.

Leichtentritt, H. *Reinhard Keiser in Seinen Opern*, Berlin, 1901.
———— "The Renaissance Attitude Toward Music," *MQ*, I, 1915.
———— "Was Lehren Uns die Bildwerke des 14.–17. Jahrhunderts," *SIMG*, VII, 1905–06.
Lenaerts, R. *Het Nederlands Polifonies Lied in de 16de Eeuw.*, Amsterdam, 1933.
Lengl, G. *Die Genesis der Oper*, Munich, 1936.
Lesage and d'Ornéval. *Théâtre de la Foire ou de l'Opéra Comique*, Paris, 1721.
Liliencron, R. von. "Die Horazischen Metren in Deutschen Kompositionen des 16. Jahrhunderts," *VfMW*, 1887.
Lintilhac, E. *Histoire Générale du Théâtre en France*, Paris, 1904–11.
Listenius, N. *Musica* (1533), ed. G. Schünemann, Berlin, 1927.
Liszt, F. *Briefe*, ed. La Mara, Leipzig, 1893–1904.
———— *Gesammelte Schriften*, Leipzig, 1881–1910.
Liuzzi, F. *La Lauda e i Primordi della Melodia Italiana*, Rome, 1935.
Locke, A. W. *Music and the Romantic Period in France*, London, 1920.
Lockspeiser, E. *Debussy*, London and New York, 1937.
Lodge, R. *The Close of the Middle Ages*, London, 1935.
Löhlein, G. S. *Anweisung zum Violinspielen*, 1781.
Lott, W. "Zur Geschichte der Passionskomposition, 1650–1800," *AfMW*, III, 1921.
Lucas, H. S. *The Renaissance and the Reformation*, New York, 1934.
Ludwig, F. "Die Entwicklung der Mehrstimmigen Musik im 14. Jahrhundert," *SIMG*, IV, 1902–03.
———— "Die Geistliche nicht Liturgische und Weltliche Einstimmige und Mehrstimmige Musik des Mittelalters," in Adler, *HdMG*.
———— "Die Mehrstimmige Messe des 14. Jahrhunderts," *AfMW*, VII, 1925.
———— "Perotinus Magnus," *AfMW*, III, 1921.
———— *Repertorium Organorum Recentioris et Motetorum Vetustissimi Stili*, Halle, 1910.
Lütgendorff, W. L. von. *Die Geigen- und Lautenmacher vom Mittelalter bis zur Gegenwart*, Frankfort, 1922.

McGiffert, A. C. *A History of Christian Thought*, New York, 1932–33.
Machabey, A. *Histoire et Evolution des Formules Musicales*, Paris, 1928.
———— "Philippe de Vitry," *RM*, 10, 1929.
Machaut, G. de. *Œuvres*, ed. Chichmaref, Paris, 1909.
McIlwain, C. H. *The Growth of Political Thought in the West, from the Greeks to the End of the Middle Ages*, New York, 1932.
Macran, H. S. *The Harmonics of Aristoxenus*, London, 1902.
Maeterlinck, M. *Théâtre*, Paris, 1921.
Mahrenholz, C. *Samuel Scheidt, Sein Leben und Sein Werk*, Leipzig, 1925.
Maine, B. *Elgar, His Life and Work*, London, 1933.
Mâle, E. *Religious Art in France in the Thirteenth Century*, New York, 1913.
Mangain, G. *Etude sur l'Evolution Intellectuelle de l'Italie de 1657 à 1750*, Paris, 1909.
Manitius, M. *Geschichte der Lateinischen Literatur im Mittelalter*, Munich, 1911–23.
Marcello, B. *Il Teatro alla Moda* (1722), ed. Lanciano, 1913.
Marix, J. *Histoire de la Musique et des Musiciens de la Cour de Bourgogne*, Strasbourg, 1939.
Marpurg, F. W. *Historisch-Kritische Beiträge zur Aufnahme der Musik*, 1754–62, 1778.
Marquand, A., and Frothingham, A. L. *A History of Sculpture*, New York, 1925.
Martelli, P. J. *Della Tragedia Antica e Moderna*, Rome, 1715.
Martin, J. *Die Kirchenkantaten Kuhnaus*, Leipzig, 1928.
Mason, D. G. *The Chamber Music of Brahms*, New York, 1933.
Mason, J. F. *The Melodrama in France from the Revolution to the Beginning of Romantic Drama*, Baltimore, 1912.
Masson, P. M. *Berlioz*, Paris, 1923.
———— *L'Opéra de Rameau*, Paris, 1930.
Mather, F. J. *History of Italian Painting*, New York, 1938.
Mattheson, J. *Grundlagen einer Ehrenpforte* (1740), reprint ed. M. Schneider, Berlin, 1910.
———— *Das Neu-Eröffnete Orchestre*, Hamburg, 1713.
———— *Der Volkommene Capellmeister*, Hamburg, 1739.
Mauclair, C. *La Religion et la Musique*, Paris, 1909.
Maurer, J. A. *Schweitzer als Dramatischer Komponist*, Leipzig, 1912.
Mead, G. H. *Movements of Thought in the Nineteenth Century*, Chicago, 1936.
Meilhac and Halévy, *Théâtre*, Paris, 1900.
Mendel, A. "Spengler's Quarrel with the Methods of Music History," *MQ*, 20, 1934.

Mendelssohn-Bartholdy, F. *Briefe*, Leipzig, 1863.
Mennicke, C. *Hasse und die Brüder Graun als Symphoniker*, Leipzig, 1906.
Merian, W. *Der Tanz in den Deutschen Tabulaturbüchern*, Leipzig, 1927.
Merriman, R. B. *The Rise of the Spanish Empire*, New York, 1918–34.
Mersenne, P. *Harmonie Universelle*, Paris, 1636.
Mersmann, H. "Beiträge zur Aufführungspraxis der Vorklassischen Kammermusik," *AfMW*, II, 1919–20.
Metastasio, P. *Opere*, Naples, 1816.
Meyer, K. *Der Chorische Gesang der Frauen*, Leipzig, 1917.
Mies, P. *Beethoven's Sketches*, transl. Mackinnon, London, 1929.
Miles, D. H. *The Influence of Molière on Restoration Comedy*, New York, 1910.
Miller, D. C. *The Science of Musical Sounds*, 2nd ed., New York, 1934.
Misset, E., and Aubry, P. *Les Proses d'Adam de Saint-Victor*, Paris, 1900.
Misson, M. *A New Voyage to Italy*, 4th ed., London, 1714.
Mitjana, R. *Cristobal Morales*, Madrid, 1918.
———— *Francisco Guerrero*, Madrid, 1922.
———— "La Musique d'Espagne," in Lavignac, *Encyclopédie*, part I, vol. I.
Mocquereau, A. *Le Nombre Musical Grégorien*, Tournay, 1927.
Molière. *Œuvres Complètes*, Paris, 1904.
Monod, B. *Le Moine Guibert et Son Temps*, Paris, 1905.
Montgomery, F. "Early Criticism of Italian Opera in England," *MQ*, 15, 1929.
Monumenta Musicae Byzantinae, ed. Hoeg, Tillyard, and Wellesz, Copenhagen, 1935.
Morphy, G. *Les Luthistes Espagnols du XVIe Siècle*, Leipzig, 1902.
Morris, R. O. *Contrapuntal Technique in the Sixteenth Century*, London, 1922.
Moser, H. J. *Geschichte der Deutschen Musik*, Stuttgart, 1928–30.
———— *Die Musikgenossenschaften im Deutschen Mittelalter*, Rostock, 1910.
———— *Paul Hofhaimer*, Stuttgart, 1929.
Mozart, W. A. *The Letters of Mozart and His Family*, ed. and transl. Emily Anderson, London, 1938.
Müller, E. H. *Heinrich Schütz*, Leipzig, 1925.
————, ed. *Schütz, Gesammelte Briefe und Schriften*, Regensburg, 1931.
Müller, G. *Geschichte des deutschen Liedes*, Munich, 1925.
Müller, H. "Zur Musikauffassung des 13. Jahrhunderts," *AfMW*, IV, 1922.
———— "Zur Urgeschichte des Deutschen Kirchenliedes," *Kirchenmusikalisches Jahrbuch*, XXIII.
Müller-Blattau, J. *Grundzüge einer Geschichte der Fuge*, Königsberg, 1923.
———— *Händel*, Berlin, 1924.
———— *Die Kompositionslehre Heinrich Schützens in der Fassung Seines Schülers Christoph Bernhard*, Leipzig, 1926.
Mumford, L. *Technics and Civilization*, New York, 1934.
Munzer, G. *Heinrich Marschner*, Berlin, 1901.
Murdoch, W. *Chopin*, New York, 1934.
Mursell, J. *Psychology of Music*, New York, 1937.
Musikalisch-Kritische Bibliothek, Gotha, 1778.
Musiol, J. *Cyprian de Rore*, Halle, 1932.
Myers, L. S. *Music, cantilenas, songs* . . . , London, 1906.

Nadler, J. *Literaturgeschichte der Deutschen Stämme und Landschaften*, Ratisbon, 1923.
Naylor, E. W. *Shakespeare and Music*, London, 1896.
Nef, K. *Die Neun Sinfonien Beethovens*, Leipzig, 1928.
———— *Geschichte der Sinfonie und Suite*, Leipzig, 1921.
Nejedly, Z. *Smetana*, London, 1924.
Nettl, P. "Freemasons' Music in the 18th Century," *MQ*, 16, 1930.
———— "Reproduzierende Kunst," in Adler, *HdMG*.
Nettleton, G. H. *English Drama of the Restoration and the Eighteenth Century (1642–1780)*, New York, 1914.
Newman, E. *Hugo Wolf*, London, 1907.
———— *The Life of Richard Wagner*, New York, vol. 1, 1933; vol. 2, 1937; vol. 3, 1941.
———— *Wagner as Man and Artist*, New York, 1924.
Newmarch, R. *The Russian Opera*, New York, 1914.
Nicolai, O. *Tagebücher*, ed. W. Altmann, Ratisbon, 1937.
Nicoll, A. *A History of Early Eighteenth Century Drama*, Cambridge, 1929.
———— *A History of Late Eighteenth Century Drama*, Cambridge, 1927.

Nicoll, A. *A History of Restoration Drama,* Cambridge, 1928.
Niecks, F. *Robert Schumann,* London, 1926.
Niedt, E. E. *Musicalische Handleitung,* Hamburg, 1700–1717.
Niemann, W. *Brahms,* New York, 1930.
Nohl, L. *Beethovens Leben,* new ed., Berlin, 1912–13.
Norlind, T. "Zur Geschichte der Suite," *SIMG,* VII, 1905–06.
North, R. *The Musicall Grammarian,* ed. Hilda Andrews, London, 1925.
Nottebohm, G. *Beethoveniana,* Leipzig, 1872.
———— *Neue Beethoveniana,* Leipzig, 1887.
———— *Ein Skizzenbuch von Beethoven,* ed. P. Mies, Leipzig, 1924.
Noverre, J. G. *Letters on Dancing and Ballets,* transl. C. W. Beaumont, London, 1930.
Nuitter and Thoinan. *Les Origines de l'Opéra Français,* Paris, 1886.

Oberst, G. *Englische Orchestersuiten um 1600,* Wolfenbüttel, 1929.
Oettingen, A. *The Harmonic System in Dual Development,* 1866; 2nd ed., *The Dual Harmonic System,* 1913.
Opienski, H. *La Musique Polonaise,* Paris, 1918.
Ortes, G. M. *Riflessioni sopra i Drammi per Musica,* Venice, n.d.
Ortiz, D. *Tratado de Glosas sobre Clausulas* (1553), ed. M. Schneider, Berlin, 1913.
Ortmann, O. "The Fallacy of Harmonic Dualism," *MQ,* 10, 1924.
Osthoff, H. *Die Niederländer und das Deutsche Lied (1400–1640),* Berlin, 1938.
Otto, O. *Deutsche Musikanschauung im 17. Jahrhundert,* Berlin, 1937.
Oxford History of Music, London, Introductory volume, 1929; vols. 1–2, 1929–32; vol. 3, 1938; vol. 4, 1902; vol. 5, 1904; vol. 6, 1931; vol. 7, 1934.
Oxyrhynchos Papyri, The, Part XV, ed. with translations and notes by B. P. Grenfell and A. Hunt, London, 1922.

Paldamus, F. C. *Das Deutsche Theater der Gegenwart,* Mainz, 1857.
Paléographie Musicale, 1889–1914.
Panoff, P. "Der Nationale Stil N. A. Rimsky-Korsakovs," *AfMW,* VIII, 1926–27.
Parfaict, Les Frères. *Mémoires pour Servir à l'Histoire des Spectacles de la Foire,* Paris, 1743.
Paribeni, G. C. *Muzio Clementi,* Milan, 1921.
Paris, G. *Chrestomathie du Moyen Age,* Paris, 1914.
———— *La Littérature Française au Moyen Age,* Paris, 1905.
Parsch, P. *The Liturgy of the Mass,* St. Louis, 1936.
Pasquetti, G. *L'Oratorio Musicale in Italia,* Florence, 1906.
Pastor, L. *History of the Popes,* London, 1940.
Pauli, W. J. *F. Reichardt; Sein Leben und Seine Stellung in der Geschichte des Deutschen Liedes,* Berlin, 1903.
Paumann, K. *Fundamentum Organisandi,* facsim. ed. by K. Ameln, Berlin, 1925.
Pedrell, F. *Hispaniae Schola Musica Sacra,* Barcelona, 1894–98.
———— "Jean I d'Aragon, Compositeur de Musique," in *Riemann Festschrift,* Leipzig, 1909.
———— "La Musique Indigène dans le Théâtre Espagnol du XVIIe Siècle," *SIMG,* V, 1903–04.
Pepys, S. *The Diary of Samuel Pepys, 1660–1669,* ed. O. F. Morshead, New York, 1926.
Perouse, G. "Georges Chastellain, Etude sur l'Histoire Politique et Littéraire du XVe Siècle," in Académie Royale de Belgique, *Mémoires (Lettres,* 2e Série, VII).
Piersig, F. *Die Einführung des Horns in die Kunstmusik und Seine Verwendung bis zum Tode J. S. Bachs,* Halle, 1927.
Pietzsch, G. *Die Klassifikation der Musik von Boetius bis Ugolino von Orvieto,* Freiburg, 1929.
Pincherle, M. "The Social Status of French Violinists Prior to the Eighteenth Century," *MQ,* 8, 1922.
———— "Antonio Vivaldi," *RMI,* 37, 1930.
———— *Les Violonistes,* Paris, 1922.
Pinson, K. S. *Pietism as a Factor in the Rise of German Nationalism,* New York, 1934.
Pirenne, H. *Histoire de Belgique,* Brussels, 1907–32.
———— *Medieval Cities,* Princeton, 1939.
Pirro, A. "L'Art des Organistes," in Lavignac, *Encyclopédie,* part 2, vol. II.
———— *Les Clavecinistes,* Paris, 1924.
———— "Les Couperins," *RM,* 1–2, 1920–21.
———— *Dietrich Buxtehude,* Paris, 1913.
———— "L'Enseignement de la Musique aux Universités Françaises," in *Bulletin de la Société Internationale de Musicologie,* 1930.

Pirro, A. L'Esthétique de Jean-Sébastien Bach, Paris, 1907.
——— H. Schütz, Paris, 1913.
——— J. S. Bach, 6th ed., Paris, 1924.
——— "Leo X and Music," MQ, 21, 1935.
——— La Musique à Paris sous le Règne de Charles VI, Strasbourg, 1930.
Plamenac, D. "Autour d'Ockeghem," RM, IX, 1929.
Playford, J. The English Dancing Master (1651), reprint ed. H. Mellor, London, 1933.
Pluche, Abbé. Spectacle de la Nature, Paris, 1732.
Pohl, C. F. Joseph Haydn, new ed., vols. 1–2, Berlin, 1928; vol. 3 by H. Botstiber, 1927.
——— Mozart und Haydn in London, Vienna, 1867.
Pollard, A. W. English Miracle Plays, Moralities and Interludes, London, 1904.
Ponnelle, L., and Bordet, L. St. Philip Neri and the Roman Society of His Times, London, 1932.
Ponte, L. da. Memoirs, transl. E. Abbott, New York, 1929.
Porte, J. F. Elgar and His Music, London, 1933.
Pougin, A. Auber, new ed., Paris, 1911.
——— Boïeldieu, Sa Vie et Ses Œuvres, Paris, 1875.
——— Monsigny, Paris, 1908.
——— Les Vrais Créateurs de l'Opéra Français, Paris, 1881.
Pratt, W. S. The Music of the French Psalter of 1562, New York, 1939.
——— The Music of the Pilgrims, Boston, 1921.
——— Musical Ministries in the Church, New York, 1902.
Prod'homme, J. G. "Austro-German Musicians in France in the 18th Century," MQ, 15, 1929.
——— Mozart Raconté par Ceux Qui l'ont Vu, Paris, 1928.
Prota-Giurleo, U. Alessandro Scarlatti, Naples, 1926.
Prunieres, H. Le Ballet de Cour en France avant Benserade et Lully, Paris, 1914.
——— Cavalli et l'Opéra Vénétien au XVIIe Siècle, Paris, 1931.
——— Claudio Monteverdi, Paris, 1924.
——— Lully, Paris, 1911.
——— Monteverdi, His Life and Works, London, 1926.
——— "Musical Symbolism," MQ, 18, 1932.
——— "Notes sur l'Origine de l'Ouverture Française," SIMG, XII, 1910–11.
——— L'Opéra Italien en France avant Lully, Paris, 1913.
——— La Vie Illustre et Libertine de J. B. Lully, Paris, 1929.
Pulver, J. Biographical Dictionary of Old English Music, New York, 1927.
——— Dictionary of Old English Music and Musical Instruments, New York, 1923.

Quadrio, S. Della Storia e della Ragione d'Ogni Poesia, Milan, 1742.
Quantz, J. J. Versuch einer Anweisung die Flöte Traversiere zu Spielen (1752), reprint ed. A. Schering, Leipzig, 1906.
Quinault, P. Théâtre Choisi, Paris, 1881.

Raabe, P. Franz Liszt, Berlin, 1931.
Radiciotti, G. Giovanni Battista Pergolesi, Milan, 1931.
——— Rossini, Tivoli, 1927–28.
Raguenet, Abbé. Parallèle des Italiens et des François en Ce Qui Concerne la Musique et les Opéra, Paris, 1702.
Rameau, J. P. Démonstration du Principe de l'Harmonie, Paris, 1750.
——— Nouvelles Réflections sur la Démonstration du Principe de l'Harmonie, Paris, 1752.
——— Traité de l'Harmonie Réduite à Ses Principes Naturels, Paris, 1722.
Ramsbotham, A., ed. The Old Hall Manuscript, Burnham, Buckinghamshire, 1933–38.
Rand, E. K. Founders of the Middle Ages, Cambridge, 1928.
Randall, J. H. The Making of the Modern Mind, New York, 1926.
Rashdall, H. The Universities of Europe in the Middle Ages, London, 1936.
Raugel, F. Les Organistes, Paris, 1923.
——— Palestrina, Paris, 1930.
Rebling, E. Die Soziologischen Grundlagen der Stilwandlung der Musik in Deutschland um die Mitte des 18. Jahrhunderts, Saalfeld, 1935.
Rebours, J. B. Traité de Psaltique, Paris, 1906.
Reese, G. "The First Printed Collection of Part-Music," MQ, 20, 1934.
——— Music in the Middle Ages, New York, 1940.
Reichardt, J. F. "Autobiography," in H. M. Schletterer, J. F. Reichardt, Augsburg, 1865.
——— Vertraute Briefe aus Paris, Berlin, 1804.

Reinach, T. *La Musique Grèque*, Paris, 1926.
Ribera, J. *Music in Ancient Arabia and Spain*, Stanford University Press, 1929.
Richard, E. *History of German Civilization*, New York, 1913.
Riedinger, L. "Carl von Dittersdorf als Opernkomponist," *StzMW*, 2, 1914.
Riegl, A. *Die Entstehung der Barockkunst in Rom*, Vienna, 1908.
Riemann, H. "Der Basso Ostinato und die Anfänge der Kantate," *SIMG*, XIII, 1911–12.
——— *Geschichte der Musiktheorie*, 2nd ed., Leipzig, 1920.
——— *Musiklexikon*, 11th ed., Leipzig, 1929.
Riemer, O. *Erhard Bodenschatz*, Leipzig, 1928.
Riesemann, O. von. *Monographien zur Russischen Musik*, Munich, 1923.
——— *Moussorgsky*, New York, 1929.
Riess, O. "J. A. P. Schulzs Leben," *SIMG*, XV, 1913–14.
Rietschel, G. *Lehrbuch der Liturgik*, 2nd ed., Tübingen, 1909.
Riezler, W. *Beethoven*, New York, 1938.
Riggenbach, C. J. *Der Kirchengesang in Basel seit der Reformation*, Basel, 1870.
Rimsky-Korsakov, N. *My Musical Life*, 2nd ed., New York, 1924.
Ritschl, A. *Geschichte des Pietismus*, Bonn, 1880–86.
Robbins, R. H. *Beiträge zur Geschichte des Kontrapunkts von Zarlino bis Schütz*, Berlin, 1938.
Rohloff, E. *Studien zum Musiktraktat des Johannes de Grocheo*, Leipzig, 1930.
Rokseth, Y. *La Musique d'Orgue au XVe Siècle et au Début du XVIe*, Paris, 1930.
Rolland, R. "Goethe's Interest in Music," *MQ*, 17, 1931.
——— *Histoire de l'Opera en Europe avant Lully et Scarlatti*, Paris, 1895.
——— *Musicians of Today*, 7th ed., London, 1928.
——— "L'Opéra au XVIIe Siècle en Italie," in Lavignac, *Encyclopédie*, part 1, vol. II.
Ronga, L. *Girolamo Frescobaldi*, Turin, 1930.
Ronsard, P. de. *Œuvres Complètes*, Paris, 1857.
Rosenmann, M. *Studie zum Gestaltungsproblem der Letzten Fünf Streichquartette L. v. Beethovens*, Vienna, 1930.
Rostovtzeff, M. *Social and Economic History of the Roman Empire*, London, 1926.
Rousseau, J. J. "Confessions," in *Œuvres Complètes*, VII, Paris, 1907.
——— "Dictionnaire de Musique," in *Œuvres Complètes*, VI, Paris, 1907.
——— *Lettre sur la Musique Française*, Paris, 1753.
Rousseau, N. *L'Ecole Grégorienne de Solesmes*, Tournay, 1910.
Rudhart, F. M. *Geschichte der Oper am Hofe zu München*, Freising, 1865.
Ruprecht, E. *Der Mythos bei Wagner und Nietzsche*, Berlin, 1937.

Sachs, C. "Barockmusik," *PJ*, 26, 1919.
——— *Geist und Werden der Musikinstrumente*, Berlin, 1929.
——— *Handbuch der Musikinstrumentenkunde*, 2nd ed., Leipzig, 1930.
——— *History of Musical Instruments*, New York, 1940.
——— *Musik des Altertums*, Leipzig, 1924.
——— "Musik der Antike," in Bücken, *HdMW*, 2.
——— *Musik und Oper am Kurbrandenburgischen Hofe*, Berlin, 1910.
——— *Musikgeschichte der Stadt Berlin*, Berlin, 1908.
——— *Reallexikon der Musikinstrumente*, Berlin, 1913.
——— "Die Streichbogenfrage," *AfMW*, I, 1918–19.
——— *World History of the Dance*, New York, 1937.
Saint-Evremond. *Œuvres Complètes*, Paris, 1739.
Saint-Foix, G. de. "Clementi, Forerunner of Beethoven," *MQ*, 17, 1931.
——— *Les Sinfonies de Mozart*, Paris, 1932.
Saint-Saëns, C. *Musical Memories*, London, 1921.
——— *Outspoken Essays on Music*, London, 1922.
Sainte-Beuve, C. A. *Causeries de Lundi*, Paris, 1857–62.
——— *Nouveaux Lundis*, Paris, 1868.
Saintsbury, G. *History of Criticism and Literary Taste in Europe*, London, 1900–04.
Sanctis, F. de. *History of Italian Literature*, New York, 1931.
Sandberger, A. *Ausgewählte Aufsätze zur Musikgeschichte*, Munich, 1921.
——— *Beiträge zur Geschichte der Hofkapelle in München unter Orlando di Lasso*, Munich, 1894–95.
——— "Zur Venetianischen Oper," *PJ*, XXXI, 1924.
Sandys, J. E. *History of Classical Scholarship*, Cambridge, 1903–08.
Sarcey, F. *Quarante Années de Théâtre*, Paris, 1900.

Saurat, D. *Literature and Occult Tradition*, London, 1930.
Scheel, O. *Luther, Vom Katholicismus zur Reformation*, Tübingen, 1916–17.
Schemann, L. L. *Cherubini*, Stuttgart, 1925.
Schering, A. *Aufführungspraxis alter Musik*, Leipzig, 1931.
——— *Geschichte des Instrumentalkonzerts*, Leipzig, 1927.
——— *Geschichte des Oratoriums*, Leipzig, 1911.
——— "Die Hochmeister des Musikalischen Barockstils," in *AHB*, II.
——— "Die Kantaten der Thomaskantoren vor Bach," *BJB*, 1912.
——— "Das Kolorierte Orgelmadrigal des Trecento," *SIMG*, XIII, 1911–12.
——— *Musikgeschichte Leipzigs*, Leipzig, 1926.
——— *Die Niederländische Orgelmesse in Zeitalter des Josquin*, Leipzig, 1912.
——— *Studien zur Musikgeschichte der Frührenaissance*, Leipzig, 1914.
Scheurleer, D. F. *Gedenkboek Aangeboden aan Dr. Scheurleer*, The Hague, 1925.
Schevill, F. *History of Florence*, New York, 1936.
Schiedermair, L. "Die Anfänge der Münchener Oper," *SIMG*, V, 1903–04.
——— *Beethoven; Beiträge zum Leben und Schaffen*, Leipzig, 1930.
——— *Die Deutsche Oper*, Berlin, 1901.
——— *Der Junge Beethoven*, Leipzig, 1925.
——— *Simon Mayr*, Leipzig, 1907.
——— "Zur Geschichte der Frühdeutschen Oper,' *PJ*, 17, 1910.
Schiller. *Letters*, ed. F. Jonas, 1892–96.
Schindler, A. *Biographie von Ludwig van Beethoven*, new ed., Münster, 1927.
Schmid, E. F. *Joseph Haydn, Ein Buch von Vorfahren und Heimat des Meisters*, Kassel, 1934.
——— *P. E. Bach und Seine Kammermusik*, Kassel, 1931.
Schmidt-Görg, J. *Nicolas Gombert*, Bonn, 1938.
Schmitz, A. "Die Aesthetischen Anschauungen Robert Schumanns in Ihren Beziehungen zur Romantischen Literatur," *ZfMW*, III, 1920–21.
——— *Beethoven*, Bonn, 1927.
——— *Beethovens "Zwei Prinzipe,"* Berlin, 1923.
——— *Das Romantische Beethovenbild*, Berlin, 1927.
Schmitz, E. *Beiträge zur Geschichte der Italienischen Kammerkantate im 17. Jahrhundert*, Leipzig, 1909.
——— *Geschichte der Kantate und des Geistlichen Konzertes*, Leipzig, 1914.
——— *Orlando di Lasso*, Leipzig, 1914.
——— *Palestrina*, Leipzig, 1914.
——— "Zur Geschichte des Italienischen Kammerduetts im 17. Jahrhundert," *PJ*, 23, 1916.
Schneider, Marius. *Die Ars Nova des 14. Jahrhunderts in Frankreich und Italien*, Berlin, 1930.
——— *Geschichte der Mehrstimmigkeit. I. Die Naturvökler*, Berlin, 1934.
——— "Der Hoquetus," *ZfMW*, XI, 1928–29.
Schneider, Max. *Die Anfänge des Basso Continuo*, Leipzig, 1918.
Schnerich, A. *Joseph Haydn und Seine Sendung*, Zurich, 1926.
——— *Der Messentypus von Haydn bis Schubert*, Vienna, 1892.
Schökel, H. P. *J. Christian Bach und die Instrumentalmusik Seiner Zeit*, Wolfenbüttel, 1926.
Scholes, P. A. *The Puritans and Music*, London, 1934.
Scholz, H. *Sigismund Kusser*, Leipzig, 1911.
Schrade, L. *Die Ältesten Denkmäler der Orgelkunst*, Leipzig, 1928.
Schreiber, O. *Orchester und Orchesterpraxis in Deutschland zwischen 1780–1850*, Berlin, 1938.
Schrems, T. *Über das Fortleben des Traditionellen Chorals in der Protestantischen Liturgie*, Freiburg (Sw.), 1930.
Schubart, C. F. D. *Schubarts Leben und Gesinnungen von Ihm Selbst im Kerker aufgesetzt*, 1791–93.
Schubiger, P. A. *Die Sängerschule St. Gallens vom 8. bis 12. Jahrhundert*, Einsiedeln, 1858.
Schünemann, G. *Carl Friedrich Zelter*, Berlin, 1937.
——— *Geschichte des Dirigierens*, Leipzig, 1913.
Schuh, W. *Formprobleme bei Heinrich Schütz*, Leipzig, 1928.
Schumann, R. A. *Letters*, transl. Bryant, New York, 1907.
——— *Music and Musicians*, 1st series, transl. F. R. Richter, 5th ed., London, 1877(?).
Schuré, E. *Le Drame Musical*, Paris, 1895.
Schurig, A. *W. A. Mozart, Sein Leben und Sein Werk*, Leipzig, 1923.
Schweitzer, A. *Jean Sébastien Bach, le Musicien Poète*, Paris, 1905; expanded German ed., Leipzig, 1908; English transl. of the latter, London, 1912.
Scott, H. A. "London's Earliest Public Concerts." *MQ*, 22, 1936.

Scribe, E. *Théâtre*, Paris, 1874.
Sedgwick, H. D. *Italy in the Thirteenth Century*, New York, 1912.
Seidler, K. *Untersuchungen über Biographie und Klavierstil Johann Jakob Frobergers*, Königsberg, 1930.
Seiffert, M. "Jan Pieters Sweelinck und Seine Direkten Schüler," *VfMW*, VII, 1891.
Séré, O. *Musiciens Français d'Aujourd'hui*, Paris, 1921.
Servien, P. *Lyrisme et Structures Sonores*, Paris, 1930.
—— *Les Rythmes comme Introduction Physique à l'Esthétique*, Paris, 1930.
Servières, G. *Fauré*, Paris, 1930.
—— *Saint-Saëns*, Paris, 1923.
Sharp, C. J., and Oppe, A. P. *The Dance—An Historical Survey of Dancing in Europe*, New York, 1924.
Shedlock, J. S. *Beethoven's Letters*, New York, 1909.
Shirlaw, M. *The Theory of Harmony*, London and New York, 1917.
Singebuch, rev. G. Munzer, Leipzig, 1906.
Sittard, J. *Zur Geschichte der Musik und des Theaters am Württembergischen Hofe*, Stuttgart, 1891.
Slonimsky, N. *Music Since 1900*, 2nd ed., New York, 1938.
Smith, A. L. *Church and State in the Middle Ages*, 2nd ed., London, 1913.
Smith, P. *The Age of the Reformation*, New York, 1920.
—— *Erasmus, A Study of His Life, Ideals and Place in History*, New York, 1923.
—— *A History of Modern Culture*, 2nd ed., New York, 1934.
—— *Life and Letters of Martin Luther*, New York, 1911.
Smith, W. *The Commedia dell' Arte*, New York, 1912.
Solerti, A. *Origini del Melodramma*, Turin, 1903.
Sondheimer, R. "Giovanni Battista Sammartini," *ZfMW*, III, 1920–21.
—— "Die Sinfonien Franz Becks," *ZfMW*, IV, 1921–22.
Sonneck, O. G. *Beethoven, Impressions of Contemporaries*, London, 1926.
—— "Dafne, the First Opera," *SIMG*, XV, 1913–14.
—— *Early Concert Life in America*, Leipzig, 1907.
—— *Early Opera in America*, New York, 1915.
—— "Italienische Opernlibretti des 17. Jahrhunderts," *SIMG*, XIII, 1911–12.
—— *Miscellaneous Studies in the History of Music*, New York, 1921.
—— *Suum Cuique, Essays in Music*, New York, 1916.
Soubies, A. *Histoire du Théâtre Lyrique de 1851 à 1870*, Paris, 1899.
—— *Le Théâtre Italien de 1801 à 1913*, Paris, 1913.
Souriau, M. *Histoire du Romantisme en France*, Paris, 1927.
Spanke. "Das Fortleben der Sequenzen in den Romanischen Literaturen," in *Zeitschrift für Romanische Philologie*, v. LI.
Spataro, G. *Dilucide et Probatissime Demonstratione* (1521), ed. Wolf, Berlin, 1925.
Specht, R. *Johannes Brahms*, New York, 1930.
Spectator, The, ed. Gregory Smith, New York, 1906.
Spitta, P. *J. S. Bach*, Leipzig, vol. 1, 1873; vol. 2, 1880; English transl. Bell and Fuller Maitland, London, 1884–85.
Spohr, L. *Autobiography*, London, 1878.
Stahl, W. *Franz Tunder und Dietrich Buxtehude*, Leipzig, 1926.
Stainer, J. *Dufay and His Contemporaries*, London, 1898.
—— *Early Bodleian Music*, London, 1901–03.
Stanford, C. *Interludes, Records, and Reflections*, London, 1922.
—— *Studies and Memories*, London, 1908.
Steele, R. *The Earliest English Music Printing*, London, 1903.
Steglich, R. *Die Questiones in Musica*, Leipzig, 1911.
Steinitzer, M. *Richard Strauss*, Stuttgart, 1927.
—— *Zur Entwicklungsgeschichte des Melodrams*, Leipzig, 1919.
Stendhal, *Vies de Haydn, Mozart, et Métastase*, new ed. D. Müller, Paris, 1914.
Stephan, W. *Die Niederländische Motette zur Zeit Ockeghems*, Heidelberg, 1934.
Stephens, W. R. W., and Hunt, W., eds. *History of the English Church*, 1899–1933.
Stravinsky, I. *An Autobiography*, New York, 1936.
Strich, F. *Deutsche Klassik und Romantik*, Munich, 1928.
Striffling, L. *Esquisse d'une Histoire du Goût Musical en France au 18e Siècle*, Paris, 1912.
Strobel, H. "Die Opern von Etienne Nicolas Mehul," *ZfMW*, VI, 1923–24.
Subirá, J. "Le Style dans la Musique Théâtrale Espagnole," *ActaM*, IV, 1932.

Subirá, J. *La Tonadilla Escenica*, Madrid, 1930.
Sullivan, H., and Flower, N. *Sir Arthur Sullivan*, London, 1927.
Sunyol, G. M. *Introducció a la Paleografia Musical Gregoriana*, Montserrat, 1925.
Symonds, J. A. *The Revival of Learning*, New York, 1881.
———— *Wine, Women, and Song*, New York, 1884.

Taille, J. de la. *La Manière de Faire des Vers en François comme en Grec et en Latin*, Paris, 1572.
Taine, H. *Nouveaux Essais de Critique*, Paris, 1901.
Taylor, A. *The Literary History of Meistergesang*, London, 1937.
Taylor, H. O. *The Medieval Mind*, London, 1914.
———— *Thought and Expression in the Sixteenth Century*, New York, 1920.
Teggart, F. J. *Theory of History*, New Haven, 1925.
Tenschert, R. *Haydn*, Berlin, 1932.
Terry, C. S. *Bach—A Biography*, London, 1928.
———— *Bach's Cantatas and Oratorios*, London, 1925.
———— *Bach's Cantata Texts*, London, 1926.
———— *Bach's Chorales*, Cambridge, 1915–21.
———— *Bach's Passions*, London, 1925.
———— *John Chr. Bach, A Biography*, London, 1929.
Terry, R. R., ed. *Calvin's First Psalter* (1539), London, 1932.
Tessier, A. *Les Couperins*, Paris, 1926.
Thayer, A. *The Life of Ludwig van Beethoven*, transl. and ed. H. Krehbiel, New York, 1921.
Thibaut, A. F. J. *On Purity in Musical Art*, transl. Gladstone, London, 1877.
Thoinan, E. *André Maugars, Célèbre Joueur de Viole*, Paris, 1865.
Thompson, H. *Wagner and Wagenseil*, London, 1927.
Thompson, O. *Debussy, Man and Artist*, New York, 1937.
Thorndike, A. *English Comedy*, New York, 1929.
Thorndike, L. *A History of Magic and Experimental Science*, New York, 1923–41.
———— *The History of Medieval Europe*, Boston, 1917.
———— *Science and Thought in the Fifteenth Century*, New York, 1929.
Thorp, W. *Songs from the Restoration Theater*, Princeton, 1934.
Thürlings, A. *J. Ronsard et la Musique de Son Temps*, Paris, 1903.
Tiersot, J. *Correspondance d'Hector Berlioz*, Paris, 1930.
———— *Les Couperins*, Paris, 1926.
———— *Un Demisiècle de Musique Française (1870–1917)*, Paris, 1924.
———— *Gluck*, Paris, 1910.
———— *Hector Berlioz et la Société de Son Temps*, Paris, 1904.
———— *Histoire de la Chanson Populaire en France*, Paris, 1889.
———— "Ronsard et la Musique de Son Temps," *SIMG*, IV, 1902–03.
———— *J. J. Rousseau*, Paris, 1920.
———— *Smetana*, Paris, 1926.
Tillet, T. du. *Le Parnasse François*, Paris, 1725.
Tilley, A. *Medieval France*, Cambridge, 1922.
Tillyard, H. J. W. "Byzantine Music," in Grove, G., *Dictionary of Music and Musicians*, vol. 2.
———— "Mediaeval Byzantine Music," *MQ*, 23, 1937.
Tintelot, H. *Barocktheater und Barocke Kunst*, Berlin, 1939.
Torrefranca, F. "La Creazione della Sonata Dramatica Moderna," *RMI*, XVII, 1910.
———— "Le Origini della Sinfonia," *RMI*, XX, XXII, 1913, 1915.
Tout, T. F. *The Empire and Papacy*, New York, 1898.
Tovey, D. F. *Beethoven's Ninth Symphony*, London, 1928.
———— *Essays in Musical Analysis*, London, 1935–39.
———— "Gluck," in *Encyclopædia Britannica*, 11th ed., vol. 12.
Toye, F. *Giuseppe Verdi: His Life and Works*, New York, 1931.
Trend, J. B. "Cristobal Morales," *MT*, 66, 1925.
———— *Luis Milan and the Vihuelistas*, London, 1925.
———— *The Music of Spanish History to 1600*, London, 1926.
Trésor de Musique Byzantin, ed. E. Wellesz, Paris, 1935 ff.
Turner, W. J. *Beethoven*, London, 1927.
————*Mozart: The Man and His Works*, New York, 1938.
Tutenberg, F. *Die Sinfonik Johann Christian Bachs*, Wolfenbüttel, 1928.

Unger, H. *Max Reger*, Munich, 1921.

Upton, W. T. *Anthony Philip Heinrich*, New York, 1939.
Ursprung, O. "Alte Griechische Einflüsse und Neuer Gräzistischer Einschlag in der Mittelalter-
  lichen Musik," *ZfMW*, XII, 1929–30.
——— *Jacobus de Kerle*, Munich, 1913.
——— "Die Katholische Kirchenmusik," in Bücken, *HdMW*, Ergänzungsheft, 3.
——— *Restauration und Palestrina-Renaissance in der Katholischen Kirchenmusik*, Augsburg,
  1924.

Valéry, P. *Pièces sur l'Art*, Paris, 1936.
Vallas, L. *Claude Debussy: His Life and Works*, London, 1933.
——— *Theories of Debussy*, London, 1929.
Vasari, G. *Lives of the Most Eminent Painters, Sculptors, and Architects*, London, 1900.
Vatielli, F. "Corelli e i Maestri Bolognesi del suo Tempo," *RMI*, 23, 1916.
Vetter, W. "Gluck und Seine Italienischen Zeitgenossen," *ZfMW*, VII, 1925.
——— "Gluck's Stellung zur Tragedie Lyrique und Opera Comique," *ZfMW*, VII, 1925.
Viénot, J. *Histoire de la Réforme Française des Origines à l'Edit de Nantes*, Paris, 1926.
Villari, P. *Life and Times of Savonarola*, London, 1923.
Villars, F. de. *La Serva Padrona. Son Apparition à Paris. Querelle des Bouffons*, Paris, 1863.
Villetard, H. *Office de Pierre de Corbeil*, Paris, 1907.
Virdung, S. *Musica Getutscht* (1511), ed. L. Schrade, Kassel, 1931.
Vogler, G. J. *Mannheimer Tonschule*, 1778–81.
Vogt. *Des Minnesangs Frühling*, Leipzig, 1920.
Volkmann, H. *Emmanuele d'Astorga*, Leipzig, 1911.
Voltaire. "Dissertation sur la Tragédie Ancienne et Moderne," in *Œuvres*, XXI.
——— *Lettres Philosophiques*, ed. Lanson, Paris, 1909.
——— "Siècle de Louis XIV," in *Œuvres*, XII.
Vossler, K. *Medieval Culture*, New York, 1929.

Wackenroder, W. H. *Werke und Briefe*, ed. Leyen, Jena, 1910.
Waddell, H. *Medieval Latin Lyrics*, 4th ed., London, 1933.
——— *The Wandering Scholars*, London, 1934.
Wagner, P. "Aus der Musikgeschichte des Deutschen Humanismus," *ZfMW*, III, 1920–21.
——— *Geschichte der Messe*, Leipzig, 1913.
——— "Der Gregorianische Gesang," in Adler, *HdMG*.
——— *Introduction to the Gregorian Melodies; A Handbook of Plainsong*, London, 1910.
——— "Das Madrigal und Palestrina," *VfMW*, VIII, 1892.
Wagner, R. *Beethoven*, transl. E. Dannreuther, London, 1893.
——— *Correspondence of Wagner and Liszt;* transl. F. Hueffer, new ed. W. A. Ellis, New
  York, 1897.
——— *Letters to His Dresden Friends*, transl. J. S. Shedlock, London, 1890.
——— *Prose Works*, transl. W. A. Ellis, London, 1892–99.
Walker, E. *A History of Music in England*, London, 1924.
Walter, F. *Geschichte des Theaters und der Musik am Kurpfälzischen Hofe*, Leipzig, 1898.
Warlock, P., and Wilson, P. *The English Ayre, 1598–1612*, London, 1932.
Wasielewski, J. W. *Geschichte der Instrumentalmusik im 16. Jahrhundert*, Berlin, 1878.
Waugh, W. T. *A History of Europe from 1837 to 1914*, London, 1932.
Weber, B. C. "Das Wohltemperierte Klavier," in *Publications of the New Bach Society*, XXXIV,
  Leipzig, 1933.
Weber, C. M. von. *Gesammelte Schriften*, Berlin, 1908.
Weber, M. *Gesammelte Aufsätze für Religions-Soziologie*, Tübingen, 1922–23.
——— *The Protestant Ethic and the Spirit of Capitalism*, London, 1930.
Weber, M. M. von. *Carl Maria von Weber*, new ed., Berlin, 1912.
Weinmann, K. *Johannes Tinctoris und Sein Unbekannter Traktat "De Inventione et Usu
  Musicae,"* Ratisbon, 1917.
Weitzmann, K. F. *Geschichte der Klaviermusik*, ed. Max Seiffert, Leipzig, 1899.
Wellesz, E. *Aufgaben und Probleme auf dem Gebiete der Byzantinischen und Orientalischen
  Kirchenmusik*, Münster, 1923.
——— *Byzantinische Musik*, Breslau, 1927.
——— "Die Oper in Italien im 17. Jahrhundert," in Adler, *HdMG*, I.
Welsford, E. *The Court Masque; A Study in the Relationship between Poetry and the Revels*,
  Cambridge, 1927.
Werner, A. *Geschichte der Musikpflege in Weissenfels*, Leipzig, 1912.

Westphal, K. "Der Romantische Klavierstil," *Die Musik*, XXII.
Westrup, J. A. *Purcell*, New York, 1937.
Wiessner, H. "Der Stabreim in Richard Wagners *Ring des Nibelungen*," in *Germanische Studien*, v. 30, Berlin, 1924.
Williams, C. F. Abdy. *The Aristoxenian Theory of Musical Rhythm*, Cambridge, 1911.
——— *Bach*, London, 1934.
Winterfeld, C. von. *Johannes Gabrieli und Sein Zeitalter*, Berlin, 1834.
Wittwer, M. *Die Musikpflege im Jesuitenorden*, Greifswald, 1936.
Wolf, F. *Über die Lais, Sequenzen, und Leiche*, Heidelberg, 1841.
Wolf, J. "Early English Musical Theorists," *MQ*, 25, 1939.
——— "Florenz in der Musikgeschichte des 14. Jahrhunderts," *SIMG*, III, 1901–02.
——— *Geschichte der Mensuralnotation*, Leipzig, 1904.
———, ed. *Musica Practica Bartolomaei Rami de Pareia*, Leipzig, 1901.
——— "Die Tänze des Mittelalters," *AfMW*, I, 1918–19.
Wolff, H. C. *Die Venezianische Oper in der Zweiten Hälfte des 17. Jahrhunderts*, Berlin, 1937.
Wooldridge, H. E. "The Treatment of Words in Polyphonic Music," *Musical Antiquary*, 1909.
Wright, E. H. *The Meaning of Rousseau*, London, 1929.
Wright, L. B. *Middle Class Culture in Elizabethan England*, Chapel Hill, N. C., 1935.
Wright, T. *The Political Songs of England*, London, 1839.
Wulf, M. de. *History of Medieval Philosophy*, New York, 1935–38.
Wyclif's English Works, ed. F. D. Matthews, London, 1880.
Wyzewa, T., and Saint-Foix, G. de. *W. A. Mozart, Sa Vie Musicale et Son Œuvre de l'Enfance à la Plein Maturité*, Paris, 1936–39.
——— "Un Maître Inconnu de Mozart," *ZIMG*, 10, 1908–09.

Young, G. F. *The Medici*, New York, 1933.
Young, K. *The Drama of the Medieval Church*, London, 1933.

Zahn, J. *Die Melodien der Deutschen Evangelischen Kirchenlieder*, Gütersloh, 1889–93.
Zarlino, G. *Tutte l'Opere del R. M. Gioseffo Zarlino da Chioggia*, Venice, 1589.
Zenck, H. *Sixtus Dietrich*, Leipzig, 1928.
——— "Zarlinos 'Istitutioni Harmoniche' als Quelle zur Musikanschauung der Italienischen Renaissance," *ZfMW*, XII, 1929–30.
Zielinski, T. *Histoire de la Civilisation Antique*, Paris, 1931.
Zimmer, H. *The Irish Element in Medieval Culture*, New York, 1891.
Zola, E. *Documents Littéraires*, Paris, 1881.
——— *Nos Auteurs Dramatiques*, Paris, 1881.
Zuth, J. *Handbuch der Laute und Gitarre*, Vienna, 1926–28.

INDEX

➤➤➤ ⫸⫸⫸

Compositions with generic titles (e. g., Symphony, Concerto, Sonata, etc.) are listed under their composers; compositions with distinctive titles (e. g., *Symphonie Fantastique, The Messiah, Die Forelle*) are listed under their titles and not under their composers.

a cappella style, 194, 197; "period" of, 196, 223 ff., 233; undermined by chromatic madrigal, 237; last stage of, 238; 306, 324; attempts to maintain, 369 f.; in German Passion, 398; 465 ff., 477; Handel's, 525; 704, 804; in 19th cent. historism, 1008

Abaco, Evaristo Felice dall', 482, 484, 594

Abbatini, Antonio Maria, 348, 455

Abduction from the Seraglio, The; see *Entführung*

Abel, Carl Friedrich, 638 f., 723, 761

Abel, Christian Ferdinand, 639

Abélard, 37

Abendmusiken, 400

Abert, Hermann, 155, 698

absolutism, 373 f.; repercussions of on art, 374-77; and the Enlightenment, 430 ff.; 447, 450, 524, 532; enlightened, 567-70; in Russia, 945

Abyngdon, Henry, 272

Académie Française, 304, 375

Académie Françoise de Poésie et de Musique, 254, 303 f., 378

Académie Royale de Musique, 407, 550, 721

Academy of Ancient Music, 683, 724

Acante et Céphise, opera, Rameau, 603

Acathistus Hymn, 28

acclamations (Byz. song), 26

accompagnato, operatic, in 17th cent., 369; in earlier 18th cent., 559; 711; Wagner's, 883; Verdi's, 914

accords fondamentaux, 546

acoustics, in antiquity, 17; in 14th cent., 163; 17th & 18th cents., 546; begin. of modern, 975; physiological, 976

Act of Supremacy, 275 f.

Act of Uniformity, 281

Actes and Monuments, 279

Actes of the Apostles, The, 282, 308

Actus Tragicus, cantata, Bach, 497

Adam de la Hale, 105, 108, 142

Adam de St. Victor, 73

Adam von Fulda, 60, 244

Adam, Adolphe, 832

Adam and Eve, lyric drama, J. Theile, 406, 476

Addison, 460, 515, 517, 521, 572, 580 f., 676

Adelung, Jacob, 401

Adieux, Les, sonata, Beethoven, 754, 860

Adlgasser, Anton Cajetan, 606, 637, 706

Aelred, Abbot of Rievaulx, 139 f.

Aeneid, 305

Aeschylus, 12, 328, 566

aesthetics of music, antiquity, 13 ff.; early M.A., 86 ff.; Gothic, 138 f.; Renaiss., 194 f.; system of establ. by *musica reservata,* 225; Renaiss. doctrines of, 292-96; baroque, the doctrine of temperaments and affections, 435 f.; appear. of term *goût* (taste) in mus. lit., 438; "imitation of nature," 439; preponder. of operatic in baroque, 444; change from baroque to rococo, 535; of *sensibilité,* 537; of church mus., transition from content to purpose, 540; of Rameau, 540; "back to nature," 549; of the era of the *Encyclopedia,* 552; operatic in first half of 18th cent., 553 f.; Gluck's dramaturgical, 555-58; the Enlightenment and the doctrine of temperaments and affections, 585 ff.; polarity of tonality and thematic material as new princ. of constr., 590; identity of form and content, 611; It. conceptions of lyric stage, 657 f.; 18th cent. vocal mus., 695 ff.; program as constr. princ. of mus. comp., 859-63; number opera *vs.* mus. drama, 890 f.; quest. of cons. and diss., theory of harmonic dualism, 974 f.; monistic syst. of harmony, 975; of romantic era, 976-79; new notions of tonality, 990 f.; atonality, 991; form in postromantic and impress. sch., 991 f.; program as formal and aesth. factor in Strauss, 997 f.; operatic, 1000 ff.; of song, 1011-14; of impressionism, 1014-20; impress. *vs.* express., 1024 f.; of Scriabin, 1025 f.; problem of modern mus., 1028 ff.

Aeterne Rerum Conditor (Ambrosian hymn), 48

affections; *see* doctrine of temperaments and affections

affects, 224, 334, 436

Affektenlehre, 440

Agamemnon (Aeschylus), 12

agape, 43

Agazzari, Agostino, 347, 360

Agincourt Song, 270 f.

agones, Greece, 15 f.; Rome, 33